For
reference

Not to be taken
from the room.

# LATIN AMERICAN WRITERS

## SUPPLEMENT I

# LATIN AMERICAN WRITERS

## Carlos A. Solé

*EDITOR IN CHIEF*

## Klaus Müller-Bergh

*ASSOCIATE EDITOR*

## SUPPLEMENT I

**CHARLES SCRIBNER'S SONS**

**GALE GROUP**

**THOMSON LEARNING**

*New York • Detroit • San Diego • San Francisco*
*Boston • New Haven, Conn. • Waterville, Maine*
*London • Munich*

1 3 5 7 9 11 13 15 17 19 20 18 16 14 12 10 8 6 4 2

*Library of Congress Cataloging-in-Publication Data*

Latin American writers. Supplement I / Carlos Solé, editor in chief; Klaus Müller Bergh,
associate editor
    p. cm.
    Includes bibliographical references and index.
    ISBN 0-684-80599-5 (hc.)
    1. Latin American literature—History and criticism. 2. Authors, Latin
American—Biography. I. Solé, Carlos A. II. Müller-Bergh, Klaus.

PQ7081.A1 L37 1989 Suppl.
860.9'98—dc21
[B]

2001040065

Acknowledgment is gratefully made to those publishers and individuals who have permitted the use of the following material in copyright.

**Oswald de Andrade**

Excerpts from Oswald de Andrade, "As Aves," "Meninas da Gare," in *Pau-brasil*. Au Sans Pareil, 1925. Reproduced by permission. Excerpts from "Brasil," "Cielo e mare," "Epitafio," "Pronominais," in *Primerio Caderno do Aluno de Poesia Oswald de Andrade*. Tipografia da Rua de Santo Antonio, 1927. Reproduced by permission.

**Mariano Brull**

Excerpts from Mariano Brull, "Poem #34," "Verdehalago," in *Poemas en Menguante*. Le Moil & Pascaly, 1928. Copyright © Ana Maria Vazquez. Reproduced by permission. Excerpts from "Isla de perfil," in *Canto Redondo*. Ediciones G. L. M., 1934. Copyright © Ana Maria Vazquez. Reproduced by permission. Excerpts from "A Toi-meme," "Poem #7," in *Rien que . . ./Nada mas que*. Translated by E. Noulet.

Pierre Seghers, 1954. Copyright © Ana Maria Vazquez. Reproduced by permission.

**João Cabral de Melo Neto**

Excerpts from João Cabral de Melo Neto, "A licao de poesia," "A palavra seda," "Alguns toureiros," "Antiode," "Fabula de um arquiteto," "Festa na casa grande," "Menino de engenho," "O cao sem plumas," "O engenheiro," "O vento no canavial," "Poesia," "Pregao turistico do Recife," "Rios sem discurso," in *Poesias completas*. Editora Sabia, 1968. Reproduced by permission. Excerpts from "Berceo's Catechism," "Tale of an Architect," "The Lesson of Poetry," "The Wind in the Cane Field," in *João Cabral de Melo Neto: Selected Poetry, 1937–1990*. Edited by Djelal Kadir. Reproduced by permission. Excerpts from "Catecismo de Berceo," in *Museu de tuto*. Jose Olympio, 1975. Reproduced by permission. Excerpts from "Duvidas apocrifas de Marianne Moore," in *Agrestes*. Nova Fronteira, 1985. Copyright © Les Ecrits des Forges. Reproduced by permission. Excerpts from *A escola das facas*. Jose Olympio, 1980. Reproduced by permission. Excerpts from "Viver Sevilha," in *Sevilha andando*. Nova Fronteira, 1989. Reproduced by permission.

# EDITORIAL AND PRODUCTION STAFF

# CONTENTS

# INTRODUCTION

It's really true, we've found a home!
How it happened?—no idea.
Never ask where we came from,
It's enough that we are here.

> (J. W. von Goethe, *Faust*, Part II, speech delivered by the Pygmies. Trans. by Martin Greenberg. Epigraph to Alejo Carpentier's "Problemática de la actual novela latinoamericana.")

Shortly after World War II, the French critic Roger Caillois referred to Latin American literature as the "literature of the future." The statement was no exaggeration considering the sophisticated artistic and aesthetic expression of that literature, its compassion for the drama of human existence and the dilemmas of life in our time, as well as the social milieu of literary production, especially in prose and poetry, in the Spanish, Portuguese, and French languages on the American continent. During the last half of the twentieth century, Latin American writers who found themselves in largely uncharted literary territory were particularly aware of the condition to which Caillois pointed and sought to give their literary creations a sharper, more modern image. Indeed, in 1964 the Cuban novelist Alejo Carpentier made some perceptive observations on his trade in "Problemática de la actual novela latinoamericana" (Problems of the present-day Latin American novel), an essay in *Tientos y diferencias* (Preliminary notes and modulations):

> *Montar el escenario de una novela en Brujas, Venecia, Roma, París, o Toledo, es cosa fácil y socorrida. Los decorados se venden hechos. El espectáculo puede manejarse a distancia, si se quiere, con tantos libros, fotografías, Baedeckers, visiones del Greco, de Guardi, de Monet, puestos a la disposición del escenógrafo. . . . Todas estas ciudades tienen un estilo fijado para siempre. Las nuestras, en cambio, están desde hace mucho tiempo, en proceso de simbiosis, de amalgamas, de transmutaciones—tanto en lo arquitectónico como en lo humano. . . . Y, sin embargo empezamos a descubrir ahora que tienen lo que podríamos llamar un tercer estilo: el estilo de las cosas que no tienen estilo.*

> To stage the setting of a novel in Bruges, Venice, Rome, Paris, or Toledo is an easy, common and useful thing. The scenery is sold ready made. The show can be put on long distance, if need be, with so many books, photos, Baedeckers or other guidebooks, views of El Greco, Guardi, or Monet readily available to the producer. . . . All these cities have a style that has been determined for as long as we can remember. Ours, on the other hand, have long undergone a symbiotic process, an amalgam, a transmutation of different organisms—in an eclectic mix of architectural and human dimensions. . . . And, nevertheless, we are just beginning to discover that they have what we might call a third style: the style of things with no style.

In other words, Latin American intellectuals were keenly aware that creating an adequate urban and human realm for the totality of Spanish American and Luso-Brazilian letters was still a formidable task similar to the accomplishments of the Russian writers—Pushkin, Lermontov, Turgenev, Dostoevsky, Tolstoy, Chekhov, Gorki—who founded, defined, and universalized the modern age of Russian literature in the nineteenth century.

The Brazilian novelist Machado de Assis (1839–1908) is widely seen as one of the finest Latin American authors of the nineteenth century. Indeed, the Brazilian Academy of Letters is known to this day as A Casa de Machado de Assis. As the Mexican novelist Carlos Fuentes has pointed out in "Las dos orillas de la modernidad" (The two shores of modernity), which appeared in Madrid in the *Suplemento Babelia* of *El País* on 25 August 2001, Machado's *Memorias póstumas de Brás Cubas* and *Dom Casmurro* were the only South American novels of the time to show an understanding of the profound lesson of Cervantes, whose *Don Quixote* and the tradition of La Mancha gave rise to the Western novel as we know it today. Those lessons were "Ficción como celebración y crítica de la ficción. Crítica de la lectura y crítica de la autoría. La realidad fundada en la imaginación. La burla y la mezcla de géneros. La poética de la digresión. La novela como repertorio de posibilidades" (Fiction as a celebration and criticism of fiction. Criticism of reading and criticism of authorship. Reality grounded in the imagination. Poking fun at and mixing up the genres. The poetics of digression. The novel as a repertory of possibilities). Semi-colonial Rio de Janeiro in Machado's time was more rural than urban and still subject to sporadic epidemics of yellow fever; yet it may well have been in his works, as well as in Graça Aranha's *Canaan* (1902), that the process of tapping into the urban wellspring of human life, of describing its particular style and raison d'être, had begun.

Jorge Luis Borges wrote in "Muertes de Buenos Aires":

*Porque la entraña del cementerio del sur*
*fue saciada por la fiebre amarilla hasta decir basta.*

Because the bowels of the cemetery of the South
were sated by yellow fever until it cried enough.

And what was true of La Chacarita, a small farm area of Buenos Aires, was even more so of the Cajú, a subtropical marshland burial ground on Cashew Beach, at the north end of Guanabara Bay, in the imperial capital of Brazil, or for that matter Havana or Panama where French attempts to build an interoceanic canal were thwarted by yellow fever. Thus it seems remarkable that only 100 years after the region was subject to debilitating waves of disease, Latin American letters had earned international recognition, particularly among the North American and the European reading public. This is evident in the large number of translations of Latin American writing, not only into French, English, and German—the languages that virtually determine the exchange of information at the Frankfurt Book Fair, the largest of such international events and a marketplace for ideas—but also, for instance, into Swedish and Rumanian, among others. By 1970 the works of Carpentier and Borges had been translated into more than fifteen languages. The process continues, a phenomenon reflecting quantity as well as quality. That quality is attested to by the wide recognition Latin American writers have won from the reading public in general.

Nobel prizes for literature have been awarded to several Latin American writers: the Chileans Gabriela Mistral (1945) and Pablo Neruda (1971); the Guatemalan Miguel Ángel Asturias (1967); the Colombian Gabriel García Márquez (1982); the Mexican

Octavio Paz (1990); and the Caribbean poet Alexis Saint-Léger Léger (1960). In 1998 the Portuguese novelist José Saramago was named a Nobel laureate, the first in the Portuguese-speaking world (whose population in Europe, Africa, and South America numbered over 200 million at the turn of the millennium). International awards for Brazilian authors should also materialize in the not-too-distant future.

In the last quarter of the twentieth century, the government of Spain has awarded twelve Latin American writers the Premio Cervantes de Literatura, the most prestigious award for Spanish-language authors: the Cubans Alejo Carpentier (1976), Dulce María Loynaz (1992), and Guillermo Cabrera Infante (1997); the Argentinians Jorge Luis Borges (1978), Ernesto Sábato (1984), and Adolfo Bioy Casares (1990); the Uruguayan Juan Carlos Onetti (1980); the Mexicans Octavio Paz (1981) and Carlos Fuentes (1987); the Paraguayan Augusto Roa Bastos (1989); the Peruvian Mario Vargas Llosa (1994); and the Chilean Jorge Edwards (1999). The Premio Príncipe de Asturias, Letras, another prestigious Spanish prize, was awarded to the Mexicans Juan Rulfo (1983) and Carlos Fuentes (1994); the Peruvian Mario Vargas Llosa (1986); the Venezuelan Arturo Uslar Pietri (1990); the Colombian Alvaro Mutis (1997) and the Guatemalan Augusto Monterroso (2000). Since the creation in 1992 of the Premio de Poesia Reina Sofia prize by the University of Salamanca and the Patrimonio Nacional de España, Spain continues to recognize the literary value of Spanish- and Portuguese-language writers as evidenced by five of the ten laureates of this prize: the Chilean authors Gonzalo Rojas (1992) and Nicanor Parra (2001), the Colombian Alvaro Mutis (1997), the Uruguayan Mario Benedetti (1999), and the Brazilian João Cabral de Melo Neto (1994). The Rómulo Gallegos Prize, awarded in Caracas, Venezuela, has been given to Mario Vargas Llosa (1967) of Peru; Gabriel García Márquez (1972) and Manuel Mejía Vallejo (1989) of Colombia; Carlos Fuentes (1977), Fernando del Paso (1982), and Angeles Mastretta (1997) of Mexico; Abel Posse (1987) and Mempo Giardinelli (1993) of Argentina; Arturo Uslar Pietri (1991) of Venezuela; and Roberto Bolaño (1999) of Chile. An appendix listing a selection of international literary prizes received by Latin American writers appears in the back of this volume. We have limited the listing to the subjects treated in *Latin American Writers*.

In the United States the Neustadt International Prize for Literature, a biennial award conferred by an international jury of twelve writers and critics convening at the University of Oklahoma in Norman, was awarded to Gabriel García Márquez (1972), Octavio Paz (1982), and the Brazilian João Cabral de Melo Neto (1992). Their company of illustrious Neustadt winners includes Czeslaw Milosz, Elizabeth Bishop, and Giuseppi Ungaretti. Latin American writers honored to date as Puterbaugh Fellows at the Puterbaugh Conferences on World Literature, a biennial series sponsored by *World Literature Today*, in collaboration with the University of Oklahoma's Department of Modern Languages, Literatures, and Linguistics and the Department of English, include Jorge Luis Borges (1969), Julio Cortázar (1975), Manuel Puig (1991), and Luisa Valenzuela (1995), all of Argentina; Octavio Paz (1971) and Carlos Fuentes (1983); Mario Vargas Llosa (1977); and Guillermo Cabrera Infante (1987). Other distinguished international recipients of the prize are Jorge Guillén, Yves Bonnefoy, and Ōe Kenzaburō, a Nobel laureate. Jorge Luis Borges, Octavio Paz, and Mario Vargas Llosa received the T. S. Eliot Award for Creative Writing from the Ingersoll Foundation, in Rockford, Illinois, in 1983, 1987, and 1991 respectively. The list of Ingersoll recipients also includes V. S. Naipaul, the 2001 Nobel laureate in literature, Zbigniew Herbert, and Richard Wilbur.

The international literary excitement generated by Latin American letters since the 1970s leads us to conclude that when a literature has not just a handful but rather a substantial critical mass of highly acclaimed writers that have become a subject worthy of serious study it already occupies a prominent place in world literature. In other words, as Goethe observed in the nineteenth century, and Carpentier foresaw, the pygmies have now occupied their rightful place in the realm of letters. At the same time it is worth noting that the Spanish language is still in a process of expansion, growing by leaps and bounds. With over 400 million native speakers at the turn of the millennium, it is the fourth-most commonly spoken language in the world and has become the second-most utilized language for international communication. Favored by a strategic geopolitical location in Europe, Africa, and South America, Portuguese is heading in the same direction.

The publication of *Latin American Writers* in 1989 was an early, comprehensive effort to acquaint the English-speaking world, and other countries where Spanish and Portuguese are not the mother tongue, with the rich and varied literature of Spanish America and Brazil. This three-volume reference work included 176 essays designed to introduce the reader to the life, work, and literary contribution of 149 Spanish American and 27 Brazilian representatives of Latin American letters over a period of almost five centuries, from the discovery and colonial times to the great boom in narrative prose of the 1960s and 1970s. However, it was up to the last two generations of twentieth-century authors to establish Spanish America's literary pan-Americanism and to bring Latin American literature to a universal plane, linking the unique promise of America to the problems and questions posed by our common human condition. Such a task was accomplished for Russian letters by Russian writers of the nineteenth century. The continuous intellectual and artistic vitality of Latin American letters, its increasing universal appeal, as well as the enthusiastic reception of *Latin American Writers* has demanded the publication of this supplement, which covers roughly the last quarter of the twentieth century in Latin American literary life.

The previous volumes and this new volume contain a number of essays on some of the most prominent and productive members of the *posvanguardistas* (post-avant-gardists) in Spanish America, the writers born approximately between 1909 and 1924. Among them are poets and essayists such as Octavio Paz, Alvaro Mutis, José Lezama Lima, Nicanor Parra, Gonzalo Rojas; essayists and novelists such as Ernesto Sábato, Juan Carlos Onetti, Julio Cortázar, José María Arguedas, Augusto Roa Bastos, María Luisa Bombal, Elena Garro; and novelists and authors of short fiction such as Juan José Arreola, Juan Rulfo, and Augusto Monterroso. With the exception of Lezama Lima and a few others, most of them were fortunate enough also to achieve long and prestigious international careers. Much the same holds true of those who followed the post-avant-gardists, writers born between 1924 and 1939, now at the height of their creativity and the most influential stage of their production. A definitive name for this group has yet to attach to them. The list comprises the novelists and essayists Sebastián Salazar Bondy, José Donoso, Gabriel García Márquez, Carlos Fuentes, Guillermo Cabrera Infante, Manuel Puig, Elena Poniatowska, Mario Vargas Llosa, Fernando del Paso, Jorge Edwards, Severo Sarduy, Luisa Valenzuela; the dramatists Emilio Carballido, José

Triana, Egon Wolf, Sergio Vodanovic; the poets Rosario Castellanos, Jaime Sabines, Roberto Juarroz, Carlos Germán Belli, Roberto Fernández Retamar, Enrique Lihn, and Ernesto Cardenal. It is true that the Chilean novelist José Donoso along with many others grew increasingly comfortable with calling themselves *la generación del boom,* a fashionable North American English label that seems to have stuck. *El boom* was followed by a "boomlet," *posboom,* or "the wave," better known in Mexico as *La onda.* From a globalized perspective, the Latin American boom generation may have points of contact with the Beat Generation in the United States in the 1950s and 1960s, England's Angry Young Men of the 1950s, and the French *La nouvelle vague* (New Wave) of the 1950s and 1960s.

A more plausible and precise explanation of the boom in the 1960s and 1970s might reasonably be offered. At that point in time, the finest writers of the *vanguardia,* the old avant-garde of the 1920s (Brull, Vallejo, Borges, Carpentier, Asturias, Yañez, Neruda, and others) had died or were approaching a highly successful and visible modern maturity after the long march of prominent international careers. The very best of the somewhat younger members of the post-avant-gardists (Cortázar, Paz, Lezama Lima, Garro, and many others) coincided with the drive and first successes of the men and women born between 1924 and 1939 (Donoso, Márquez, Fuentes, Cabrera Infante, Poniatowska, Triana, Vargas Llosa, and Valenzuela). If we look at the flux, or literary becoming, of Latin American letters from the broader perspective of almost five centuries, we may agree with Fuentes, one of the major players in this profound and auspicious confluence that produced the boom at a crucial moment of Spanish America. The Mexican novelist, an astute and knowledgeable observer of Latin America in our time, explains the correspondence as "una experiencia que venía gestándose desde hace mucho tiempo" (an experience that was a long time in coming). He argues that "el llamado 'boom', en realidad es el resultado de una literatura que tiene por lo menos cuatro siglos de existencia y que sintió una urgencia definitiva en un momento de nuestra historia de actualizar y darle orden a muchas lecciones del pasado" (the so-called "boom" is actually the result of a literature that has at least four hundred years of existence and that felt a definitive urgency at a moment in our history to update, modernize, and put in order many lessons of the past). Thus forces long in motion came together in the 1960s and 1970s to ignite a literary explosion. The promotion, diffusion, and consumption of the new Spanish American novel happened in bookstores, at book fairs, in cinema, television, and theater. The path was cleared as never before for the younger writers born after 1939: Rosario Ferré, Reinaldo Arenas, Ricardo Piglia, Olga Orozco, Tomás Eloy Martínez, Alfredo Bryce Echeñique, Ida Vitale, Antonio Skármeta, and many others. Authors born between 1937 and 1952 in Brazil—on the other side of the great linguistic divide of South America—experienced a related quickening of literary impulses.

During his exile in Petrópolis in 1941, the Austrian novelist and essayist Stefan Zweig wrote a fascinating essay called "Brasil" in which he envisioned that nation as "the country of the future." At the turn of the millennium, Brazil's population numbered 170 million. According to Stephen Graubard, writing in a special issue of *Daedalus* devoted to Brazil, Latin America's " 'Invisible Giant' is the world's fifth-largest country geographically, a landmass bigger than the continental United States, and boasts the seventh- or eighth-largest economy, in a league that includes such other giants as Japan,

France, Germany, Italy, Canada, and the United States." Brazil also belongs to an international literary tradition that goes back to the Iberian peninsula of the early medieval period and that over five centuries has taken root in three continents. A drawing by Hamilton J. Machado offers an image provocative to Portuguese, Brazilian, and some African intellectuals: A World Class soccer team of prominent authors stands on a level playing field before admiring fans in a World Cup playoff. The dream team consists of eleven Portuguese and Brazilian players, all proven champions: Antonio de Castro Alves, Gil Vicente, Camilo Castelo Branco, Eça de Queiroz, Luis de Camões, Graciliano Ramos, Fernando Pessoa, José de Alencar, João Guimarães Rosa, Jorge Amado, and "o insuperável, o eterno e moderno," the eternally modern goalie holding a typewriter, José Maria Machado de Assis. Nevertheless, the word is out in Portugal and Brazil that a new lineup is certain to include José Saramago and Clarice Lispector, both leading the pack with hot winning streaks, as forward and center forward. Local fans in Angola feel that their native son, Agostinho Neto, as well as Amilcar Cabral from Cape Verde, would have a fighting chance as soon as a few of the other more popular, prolific, but propagandistic authors who play to the gallery are relegated to warming the bench on the second string. As is usual in these family squabbles it is no holds barred, but time will tell.

What is incontestable is that Brazilian literature in the second half of the twentieth century (prose, poetry, drama, and essay) distinguished itself by its refinement, evaluation, analysis, and assimilation of the legacy of *modernismo*, or *modernismo brasileiro*, the Brazilian counterpart of the Spanish American *vanguardia*, or avant-garde on the one hand, and by the rupture with the old order on the other. The acceptance of the major tenets of the modernist credo—a peculiar mixture of populism, erudition, and revolutionary vanguard esthetic in search of the African, European, and Native American components of Brazilian culture in order to create an authentic national expression—has occurred in virtually all places in the Portuguese-speaking world and on all levels: in *ginásios*, university halls, newspapers, magazines, and reviews as well as on radio and television. The extent of Brazilian media promotion in the last quarter of the twentieth century can be fully appreciated by focusing briefly on some data on *TV-Globo* and *Veja* provided by Marcos Sá Corrêa in the Brazil issue of *Daedalus*: "The fourth-largest weekly newsmagazine on the planet is Brazilian—*Veja*, launched in 1968 by Editora Abril. Its readership is surpassed only by the three largest U.S. publications of its kind—*Time*, *Newsweek* and *U.S. News & World Report*. With 1.2 million copies sold each week, *Veja* exceeds the circulation of the principal European magazines, who claim to have a market that reaches a richer and more educated public than is possible in Brazil."

The first major break with the past since 1922 actually began well before the progressive Brazilian media penetration of the late twentieth century, which brought *Xica, La fuerza del deseo*, a pop tropicalist answer to *Desire under the Elms*, and even less-inhibited Brazilian soap operas to Spanish-language television in the United States. In the fabulous world of *Telemundo Internacional*, hidalgos speak with a Mexican accent, blacks and mulattos with a Cuban accent, and empowered women of leisure, who possess the fatal attraction of Silvina Ocampo or Eva Perón, speak in the refined *porteño* cadences of Buenos Aires. But in the urban centers of Rio and São Paulo in the early 1950s, when the magic world of television was new, a number of heterogeneous, often contradictory experimental schools bearing different labels—concretism, neoconcretism, praxis poems, semiotic poetry, process-poems, tropicalism—sought new idioms, systems, and signs as well as new communication in advertising and multimedia for the Latin American consumer and entertainment market.

The gradual assimilation of the modernist theories in Brazil and the translation of many works from Portuguese into English and other languages fostered greater refinement and introspection within Brazilian literature. This resulted in a more accurate assessment of Latin American reality, as well as a more precise definition of Brazil's identity, culture, and past. In addition, the introduction of new schools of thought, such as the New Criticism of the early 1950s and structuralism of the late 1950s and 1960s, brought about considerable changes in the concept of writing and criticism. Some of the novelists, poets, dramatists, thinkers, and essayists who had in one way or another participated in or been influenced by São Paulo's heroic, revolutionary Modern Art Week (1922), as well as by the modernist movement it spawned, were included in the previous volumes of *Latin American Writers*. Most of these authors were born approximately between 1892 and 1922. The exception is Manuel Bandeira (1886–1968), whose first book, *A cinza das horas* (1917; The ashes of the hours), has a Parnassian-symbolist title although he was one of the first to assimilate new ideas of modernity. The poet came into contact with new European thought when he spent some time at a sanatorium in Davos, Switzerland, in 1913—rather like a visit to Thomas Mann's magic mountain. Bandeira found a congenial companion in the young Eugène Grindel, who later became better known as Paul Eluard. Ultimately, Bandeira would become one of the finest lyric voices of *modernismo* with other poets such as Oswald de Andrade, Jorge de Lima, Ronald de Carvalho, Cecilia Meireles, Murilo Mendes, Carlos Drummond de Andrade, Augusto Meyer, Vinicius de Moraes, and João Cabral de Melo Neto. The major novelists to emerge at that time include Graciliano Ramos, José Lins do Rego, and Mario de Andrade, the last a man of many talents as well as a mover and a shaker who became the guiding influence of the movement. Other novelists who combine prose and short fiction are Enriqueta Lisboa, Erico Veríssimo, Mario Quintana, João Guimarães Rosa, Rachel de Queiroz, Dinah Silveira de Queiroz, Murilo Rubião, and the prolific, best-selling storyteller Jorge Amado. Other members of the Brazilian modernist generation include the essayist Gilberto Freyre, a sociologist, as well as essayists and literary critics such as Alceu Amoroso Lima, Afranio Coutinho, and Antonio Cândido. Some authors, such as Oswald de Andrade and João Cabral de Melo Neto, members of the modernist and postmodernist generations, have been given updated versions of entries from the original volume, whereas some are included here for the first time.

Since the 1970s the ranks of the major figures of the modernist generation have thinned, with the deaths of Erico Veríssimo and Carlos Drummond de Andrade. For some of the younger figures, the old avant-garde of modernism was just history. These include three poets, Vinicius de Moraes, João Cabral de Melo Neto, and Paulo Mendes Campos, and Clarice Lispector, possibly the best Brazilian prose writer of the second half of the twentieth century. This group is often labeled the Generation of 1945. The last quarter of the twentieth century also meant national success as well as international recognition for some of the best authors born between 1922 and 1937, whose work already represents a transition or a rupture from Brazilian modernism: novelists and writers of short fiction such as Antonio Callado, Lygia Fagundes Telles, Osman Lins, Clarice Lispector, Rubem Fonseca, Autran Dourado, Dalton Trevisan, Helena Parente

Cunha, Lêdo Ivo (a poet as well as a novelist), José Louzeiro, Eduardo Portela, Edilberto Coutinho, Ignacio Loyola Brandão, Ivan Angelo, and Ariano Suassuna (also a dramatist); poets and essayists such as Affonso Felix de Sousa, Decio Pignatari, Haroldo de Campos, Ferreira Gullar, Augusto de Campos, Gilberto Mendonça Teles, and Sonia Coutinho (also a writer of short fiction), to name a few. Some of them, such as Lêdo Ivo and Nelson Rodrigues, are included here for the first time. The latest writers staking out their territory and gaining ground fast are those born between 1937 and 1952: Nélida Piñón, Moacyr Scliar, Carlos Nejar, João Ubaldo Ribeiro, Luis Vilela, João Gilberto Noll, and Marcio Souza, among others. Some of them have already been elected to the Brazilian Academy of Letters.

The choice of representative subjects is as difficult and sensitive as it is personal. Three criteria have guided our selection for this volume: (1) the need to revise and update some essays from the earlier volume; (2) our wish to include earlier authors not featured in the previous volumes; and (3) our wish to include writers of the post-boom period. Since the publication of *Latin American Writers* in 1989 a number of literary figures of the so-called boom period have died—the Brazilians Jorge Amado and João Cabral de Melo Neto, the Chilean José Donoso, the Cuban Reinaldo Arenas, and the Mexican Octavio Paz—while others have continued to broaden and deepen their literary production—the Chilean Jorge Edwards, the Colombian Gabriel García Márquez, the Cuban Guillermo Cabrera Infante, the Mexican Carlos Fuentes, as well as the Peruvian Mario Vargas Llosa. Some of these authors' works have appeared simultaneously in English and Spanish editions on two continents, and it may be no exaggeration to say that the most prominent publish what they want, where and when they want, and are contenders for a Nobel Prize in the near future. Hence the need for updating and revising some essays from the earlier volume. While *Latin American Writers* originally intended to be as comprehensive as possible, the restrictions imposed on its length made it difficult to include several poets and novelists who now appear in this supplement. Since the boom period a new generation of writers has emerged. Their work, particularly in prose and poetry, continues to evolve and is already appearing in anthologies.

Finally, the quantity and quality of critical attention any given author has attracted, as well as the number of translations of that author's work, have also played an important role in the final selection of this group of contemporary voices. Again, restrictions on length have not allowed us to include as many writers as we might wish, and many deserve to be treated in future publications. In sum, the selection of Latin American writers for this volume is meant to offer a panoramic view of Latin American literature during the last quarter of the twentieth century.

In keeping with the objectives of the original collection, this reference work is intended for specialists and nonspecialists alike; we expect our readership to include high school and university students, teachers and professors, scholars, critics, editors and commentators, as well as the general public. The essays are presented in alphabetical order and vary in length from approximately eight thousand to twelve thousand words depending on the extent of each writer's oeuvre. We have tried to maintain a consistent format with a uniform tone and style while still allowing contributors to present their own unique perspective on each author. The essays begin with a brief biographical description, relating the individual to the sociohistorical and literary influences that have motivated that subject's work. The major portion of the text is dedicated to presenting each writer's production, evaluating it in its totality, and indicating its contribution to Latin American literature as a whole. Each essay ends with a selected bibliography, listing the author's works in chronological order and other works, grouped by genre, in alphabetical order. Each bibliography includes notable translations into English of the author's works. A section listing biographical and critical books and articles will guide the interested reader in continued research of the subject.

The volume follows a certain style when referring to titles. On first mention of a Spanish or Portuguese title, its publication date and the title and publication date of the English translation follow in parentheses. Subsequent references to that work use the English title. When a work has not been published in English translation, the English title in parentheses is set in roman type; the reader should note that this title is merely a literal translation of the original. Subsequent references to such works use the title in its original language. The reader should also be aware that occasionally a contributor has chosen to give a literal translation of the original title even though a published one already exists, with the understanding that the existing versions are either unavailable, out of print, or inadequate renditions of the original.

Regarding translations of quoted material, for works that have not appeared in English translation, authors have been asked to supply their own translations. English translations of titles of Spanish or Brazilian journals and newspapers are provided parenthetically in cases where the names are not obvious cognates, or when the title in its original language bears some special significance or would simply be of interest to those who do not read Spanish or Portuguese.

A distinguished group of contributors, including university professors, scholars, critics, intellectuals, and writers, have prepared the essays that appear in this supplement. They come not only from North American but also from Latin American and European intellectual and academic circles. In many cases the contributor is internationally recognized as the critic who speaks with greatest authority on his or her subject. (A complete list of these individuals and their professional affiliations appears in the back of this volume.) Their task has been to introduce an unfamiliar, often arcane subject matter to English-speaking readers, with the goal of explaining the nature of an individual literary contribution in the context of our time. Their concern is not to acclaim or censure, nor to argue the merits of a writer in comparison with others. In cases where essays were translated into English from the Spanish or Portuguese, this is noted at the conclusion of the entry.

We wish to reaffirm that the term "Latin America" is used here to refer exclusively to the Spanish- and Portuguese-speaking countries of the New World. That is, we do not use it in its broader meaning, which applies not only to the countries conquered and colonized by the Iberian powers but also the nations of the Western Hemisphere south of the Rio Grande whose languages are Spanish, Portuguese, and French. The term "Spanish America" includes only those countries conquered by Spain and that remained in its colonial sphere of influence until the nineteenth century; it is used here to refer to New World literature in the Spanish language, including Puerto Rico.

Ideally we would have liked to include in this supplement representative writers from every Spanish American country, as was the case with the original three-volume publication. However, owing to historical and cultural circumstances, literary production varies from country to country. At times the restrictions imposed by a single-volume publication have prevented us from including many authors from the various nationalities represented here but whose work should not be underestimated. It is important to point out that in considering literature, and many other endeavors of modern life, Latin Americans do not necessarily think in purely national terms; many writers have lived and prospered outside of their homeland, often in other Spanish-speaking countries which, in addition to the language, share a substantial part of their origin and culture. Hence the curious, illuminating title *Los nuestros* (Buenos Aires, 1966), by the Chilean writer Luis Harss—literally "Our writers" or "Our kind," but whose figurative, original English title aimed at the general reader is *Into the Mainstream.* Harss had read carefully Carpentier's *Tientos y diferencias* and offers a fascinating note of his own to introduce the volume: "Esta obra fue escrita originalmente en inglés. La versión española, sin embargo, es también, en cierta forma, un original. La traducción fue revisada y adaptada por el autor, con la ayuda providencial de Paco y Sara Porrúa" (This work was originally written in English. However, the Spanish version is also an original in its own right. The translation was revised and adapted by the author with the providential help of Paco and Sara Porrúa). In other words, Harss's work is a good example of the unity, originality, and adaptability, but also of the diversity, that reflects some of the main regional trends in seven of the major cultural areas of the Latin American continent. Harss was born in the seaport of Valaparaiso, Chile, spent his childhood and adolescence in Argentina, taught in the United States, and also lived in Guatemala, Paris, and London; perhaps this personal history predisposed him to being one of the first intellectuals during the boom period to write persuasively, and from the inside, about Spanish American and Brazilian writers.

Since independence, and particularly in the last quarter of the twentieth century, many regional literatures have taken shape—Mexican literature, Centro-American literature, Caribbean literature, Northern Andean, Southern Andean, and Southern Cone literature, River Plate literature, and other manifestations of special interests— seeking a place in the sun or a global forum for their ideas. Nonetheless, as Carlos Fuentes has eloquently stated and restated in essays, interviews, and the ambitious biography of his culture *El espejo enterrado* (*The Buried Mirror,* 1992), Spanish Americans continue to share a common language and cultural heritage as well as similar problems and concerns. In other words, "La literatura de la América Latina es una y es varias. Es la de 18 naciones distintas, pero sólo es comprensible como experiencia conjunta" (The literature of Latin America is one and varied. It is that of 18 different nations but as an experience it is only comprehensible as a whole). In his introductory essay on the work of Alejo Carpentier, Fuentes states that he would consider himself diminished as a writer, novelist, and Mexican intellectual had he not belonged to a tradition that includes the Nicaraguan Rubén Darío, the Argentinian Leopoldo Lugones, the Peruvian César Vallejo, or the Chilean Pablo Neruda; that goes back to the Iberian Peninsula and Spain's Golden Age, and ultimately to Seneca and the Stoics in the Roman Empire; that goes back to some of the earliest experiences of the human race in the Old World, as well as to the indigenous pre-Columbian civilizations and high cultures of the American continent; that in fact goes back to the inestimable contributions of the Africans brought to America by the Spanish and the Portuguese since the discovery, of the waves of non-Spanish and non-Portuguese European immigrants who began to arrive in the nineteenth century, and of the individuals of all nationalities, races, religions, and cultures from the four corners of the earth who came to the New World in the twentieth century. The names of Latin America's presidents (Juscelino Kubitchek, Arturo Frondizi, Alberto Fujimori, Vicente Fox) but also the names of its most gifted artists, writers, and musicians (Fayga Ostrower, Clarice Lispector, Elena Poniatowska, Daniel Barenboim, Astor Piazzola) reflect this reality.

The eclectic mix that has been one of the constants of Latin American culture from the very beginning might well have been formulated by José Martí for his time and circumstance. Above all, the man who was destined to become the first head of state of the Cuban Republic, and who died for his country in a rebel landing in Dos Rios in 1895, stresses the unity of Spanish American culture: "del Río Bravo a la Patagonia somos un solo pueblo" (from Rio Bravo to Patagonia we are one people). But in *Nuestra América* (1891; Our America) he also stresses the value of the local and universal components of Spanish American culture in a nationalistic metaphor of a nineteenth-century islander and emigré fighting for independence and trying to found a new nation: "Injértese en nuestras repúblicas el mundo; pero el tronco ha de ser de nuestras repúblicas" (let us graft the whole world into our republics, but let the trunk be from our republics). In *Discusión* (1932) Jorge Luis Borges saw this universality a bit differently, from his particular twentieth-century vantage point of the megalopois of Buenos Aires: "Creo que nuestra tradición es toda la cultura occidental, y creo que tenemos derecho a ello" ( I believe that our tradition is all of Western culture, and I believe we have every right to it). But what is also evident since colonial times is that some of the most enlightened Latin Americans of abiding importance from all cultural backgrounds have always seen their intellectuals as belonging to a single body of literature, often superseding present-day political and geographic boundaries, or religious and racial divisions. Garcilaso de la Vega, El Inca (1539–1616), a contemporary of Shakespeare and Cervantes, was the son of a Spanish conqueror and an Indian princess (*palla*), Isabel Chimpu Ocllo. In his *Comentarios Reales e Historia General del Perú* (1609; The royal commentaries of the Incas and general history of Peru), he was one of the first to exalt nature in its totality, in particular the universal dignity and equality of human nature.

As for the Portuguese-speaking Brazilians, they are regarded ambivalently by many Spanish-speaking neighbors as citizens of the Giant of the North, or of the South as the case may be, particularly in light of regional rivalries sparked by the World Soccer Cup. Thus does, for instance, Uruguay versus Brazil become David versus Goliath. However, increasingly there exists between Spanish Americans and Brazilians a spiritual bond, attesting to their geographical proximity under the constellations of the Southern hemisphere and their common Iberian and American roots that go back to the dawn of Native American civilizations. This bond might also include their own rhythm and tempo, the jazz and jive that govern their lives, evident in the complexity of musical expression, popular or classic, from the habanera, salsa, merengue, joropo, cumbia, huaino, tango, bolero, and pasodoble or for that matter the maxixe, samba, xaxado, baião, frevo, choro, morna, and fado, to Carlos Chavez's *Sinfonía india*, José Pablo Moncayo's brilliant *Huapango*, Ginastera's *Pampeanas*, or Héitor Villa-Lobos's *Concert for Guitar and Small Orchestra* and his nine Brazilian pieces in the manner of Bach, which comprise the majestic *Bachianas Brasileiras*. Their bond also bespeaks a similar concep-tion of (Roman) law and religion, the syncretic form of Catholicism that developed over the course of centuries and whose practice determines the daily lives of the vast majority of Latin Americans.

To this we might add some commonly shared economic alliances such as *Mercosur*, the shared hope for a better-positioned role in world affairs that might offer a global alternative on the American continent, as well as the mutual economic and social dependencies that unite Latin American nations in the twenty-first century. All of this is often reflected in a kind of pan-Americanism that encompasses the pursuit of an American destiny in a New World. More learned or introspective intellectuals might be aware that this bond ultimately comes from a deep sense of a common, providential past born from a unique and decisive transatlantic encounter, the voyage of the Spanish, Portuguese, and French languages. Octavio Paz, the last Spanish American Nobel Prize winner of the twentieth century, observed that language itself provides the continuity of the human word, which in turn shapes the continuity of new civilizations ripened with time, in a New World whose future is now and whose time has come. In "Las dos orillas de la modernidad," Carlos Fuentes, possibly the strongest contender for the first Latin American Nobel Prize for Literature in the new millennium, speaks of the literary past of his civilization as Aa veces rico, a veces pobre, siempre conflictivo. Hablo con optimismo de un presente y un porvenir diversificados como nuestras sociedades, cada vez menos clasificables y, por tanto, cada vez más novelables" (sometimes rich, sometimes poor, always conflictive. I speak with optimism of a diversified present and future like our own societies, less and less classifiable, and so, more and more worthy of being converted into novel form).

The essays presented here were conceived not as a literary encyclopedia but as a critical anthology as well as a useful and reliable reference work of representative Latin American writers. The volume thus possesses the virtues and limitations of such a collection. It does not offer the schematic organization of an encyclopedia nor the integrated perspective of a literary history. We believe that the present work continues our basic objective not to be limited by impersonality or by rigidity. We trust that these essays will continue to arouse the reader's enthusiasm for Latin American literature and stimulate interest in the authors presented here while at the same time providing the student of this literature with the basic materials for further discovery.

Finally, we wish to thank all our contributors for their excellent work, cooperation, and patience. We also wish to express our appreciation to Karen Day, former publisher at Scribners, for her interest in preparing this first supplement to *Latin American Writers*. We also extend our gratitude to José Juan Arrom, Professor Emeritus, Yale University; Francisco Moreno and Paz V. de Troya of the Instituto Cervantes; John A. Howard and Stacey Beck of the Howard Center for Family, Religion and Society; the Ingersoll Foundation and the Ingersoll Milling and Machine Company; Alexis Leonis of the Consulate General of Venezuela, Chicago; Graciela Bonit of the Casa Rómulo Gallegos and the Centro de Estudios Latinoamericanos Rómulo Gallegos; and José Miguel Sardiñas and Jorge Fornet of Casa de las Américas, Havana, Cuba, who helped us with our project. We thank also William Riggan and David Draper Clark, editor and managing editor respectively of *World Literature Today* of the University of Oklahoma, Norman, who provided valuable information and encouragement. To our colleagues Enrique Fierro and Pablo Brescia at the University of Texas at Austin; Orlando Menes at the University of Notre Dame; Reginald Gibbons at Northwestern

University; and Christopher Maurer and Juan Ignacio Calduch at the University of Illinois at Chicago go special thanks for their pertinent suggestions and sound advice. We thank the translators for their difficult labor. Thanks especially to Anna Sheets Nesbitt, who with the excellent editorial team at Scribners brought this work to completion.

Carlos A. Solé, The University of Texas at Austin
Klaus Müller-Bergh, University of Illinois at Chicago

# Isabel Allende

## (1942– )

## *Verónica Cortínez*

Of all Latin American writers, Isabel Allende is arguably the most popular, authoring novels, tales, and nonfictional works that regularly and instantly make it onto the best-seller lists in both the Spanish-speaking world and in translation all over the planet. Her fame is such that, in the United States, she has been featured on Oprah Winfrey's Book Club and television show and was one of the very few Latin American personalities included by ABC anchor Peter Jennings in his turn-of-the-millennium review of the twentieth century. In 1996 the city of Los Angeles named her "Author of the Year" and proclaimed January 16 of that year "Isabel Allende Day." Moreover, several of her stories have been made into Hollywood films—with a wide range of international stars—and turned into plays in the United States, England, and Puerto Rico. Her work has inspired a musical in Iceland, an opera in Germany, and a ballet in the United States. Indeed, for readers around the world, Allende has emerged as the archetypal Latin American author. This lofty, if contested, position is partially due to highly successful marketing strategies and the revolutionary symbolism of her family ties with Chile's deposed socialist president, Salvador Allende, but, most importantly, it is due to the very readable nature of her fiction: skillfully constructed yarns that engage readers in the sentimental lives and endless vicissitudes of a vast gallery of vividly developed characters, many of whom are strong, memorable women.

Despite—or perhaps because of—Allende's global stardom, the aesthetic value of her writings has often been questioned in certain academic and literary circles. In this, Allende's fortune is inextricably linked with the international rise of Spanish American fiction writers in the 1960s—the so-called Boom. The visibility of that earlier generation of authors, which includes such emblematic figures as Gabriel García Márquez, Carlos Fuentes, Julio Cortázar, and Mario Vargas Llosa, was at first attributed by some to the commercial acumen of the publishing establishment, especially the Barcelona literary agent Carmen Balcells.

After being rejected by several publishers, Allende's first novel, *La casa de los espíritus* (*The House of the Spirits*, 1985), finally came out in 1982, thanks to Balcells's visionary talent: not only did Allende have a politically resonant surname, she could also fill the boom's embarrassing gender gap. But if the older male authors were soon placed at the center of Latin America's literary canon, Allende is often dismissed as just a best-selling writer, a minor talent or, more specifically, a formulaic imitator of García Márquez's magical realism. However, one may view Allende's fiction, as some critics have, in the context of a more recent literary-historical category: the post-boom. This younger, larger generation of writers is often associated with a series of postmodern trends whereby popular culture and the referential capacity of narrative fiction acquire new worth even as the linguistic experimentation and intellectual elitism, which is arguably at the core of the Boom, are downplayed.

In a sense, Allende's works may be seen as a return to basics; half-jokingly, she herself has said that she should have been born in the nineteenth century. As in much traditional fiction, she spins heartfelt stories that are nothing if not page-turners, thrilling audiences that by 1998 had purchased about thirty million copies of her books in twenty-eight languages.

Isabel Allende was born in Lima, Peru, on 2 August 1942, to Chilean parents. Her father, Tomás Allende, held a position at the Chilean Embassy. Whereas Tomás's first cousin, Salvador Allende, later became president of Chile, Isabel's father was, in his daughter's eyes, an unreliable man. More of a bohemian and a dandy than anything else, he was the prototype for the unsympathetic character of Count Jean de Satigny in *The House of the Spirits*. He later vanished from his family's life, and Isabel would never see him again until, many years later, she was called to identify his body—a body whose face she did not remember—at the morgue in Santiago. Her mother, Francisca Llona Barros, known as Panchita, is clearly an indelible figure, not only Isabel's best friend but also the first hand—the *tinta roja*, or red ink—to edit all that her daughter writes. Traces of Panchita are apparent in *The House of the Spirits* in the character of Blanca, and she also contributed most of the sophisticated kitchen recipes that constitute a large section of *Afrodita: Cuentos, recetas y otros afrodisíacos* (1997; *Aphrodite: A Memoir of the Senses*, 1998), Isabel's playful, genre- (if not gender-) bending illustrated book.

In many ways, Panchita's biography is not unlike that of an Isabel Allende character. While in Lima, Panchita met and fell in love with Ramón Huidobro, also a Chilean and a career diplomat. He was married and had four children, and because his wife was opposed to having their marriage annulled (there is no divorce law in Chile), he was never able to marry Panchita, although they have lived together for over fifty years. In her nonfictional writings and in real life, Isabel refers to him as Tío (uncle) Ramón, but he never

made it into any of her fiction, at least those written before *Paula* (1994; *Paula*, 1995), where she describes him as too decent and commonsensical to share a novel with her very tormented characters.

Together with her two younger brothers, Francisco and Juan, Isabel was taken to Chile for the first time when she was three years old. They sailed into Valparaíso, the renowned port city on the Pacific that plays an almost mythical role in Allende's later fiction. Because Ramón Huidobro had stayed behind in Lima, Panchita and her three children settled at her parents' home in the well-heeled Providencia district of Santiago. The house, located on Calle Suecia 081, would later be transformed through Allende's imagination into the fictional "house of the spirits," her grandfather Agustín Llona and grandmother Isabel Barros becoming the novel's Esteban Trueba and his wife Clara del Valle. Allende has revealed that Clara is the most faithful representation of a living character in her first novel—though she is careful to point out that, unlike her tale's heroine, her grandmother never played the piano with the lid down—but she also regrets that her grandfather's memory may always be tainted because of her own corrosive fictional disfigurement of the real-world man. Another important person in Isabel's early childhood is Margara, the children's nanny; in Allende's works, as in many other Chilean works of fiction, nannies play a surprisingly commanding role within the otherwise rigidly patriarchal family structure.

Allende's formal education was somewhat erratic, for she attended several schools in various countries. In Santiago she was first enrolled at Las Ursulinas, a private school run by German nuns from which she was expelled, she says, after her mother's affair with Ramón Huidobro became known. There is, however, another story about the cause of her expulsion, one involving a panty-showing contest organized by little Isabel. She later attended Dunalastair, an upscale English school also for girls, before the family moved to La Paz, Bolivia. In Bolivia the family reunited with Ramón, who held a diplomatic post there. Not much information is available about Isabel's experience at the American coeducational school she attended in La Paz, except that it was her first exposure to Latin American nationalism. As a Chilean, she was blamed by her classmates for Bolivia's landlocked status, which had resulted from the nineteenth-century War of the Pacific, a subject of her latest novel. In addition, Allende had her first crush while she was a student there, on a boy that she now remembers only as having large ears.

The family next followed Ramón to a turbulent Middle East, where Allende continued her education at a British school in Beirut, Lebanon. She lived there for three years, imbibing an alien yet alluring culture that would leave its imprint in *Eva Luna* (1987; *Eva Luna*, 1988), *Cuentos de Eva Luna* (1989; *The Stories of Eva Luna*, 1991), and *Aphrodite*. Returning to Santiago in 1958, she next attended La Maisonette, yet another exclusive school for girls.

Throughout her childhood and adolescence, Isabel was a voracious reader, at first out of shyness and loneliness. She loved Emilio Salgari, Jules Verne, Mark Twain, and Jack London, as well as all of Shakespeare, whom she read (as she has confessed) for the pleasure of gossip and tragedy. Later she read in search of the forbidden worlds that adult books opened for her, as in the most erotic sections of *The Arabian Nights*. She especially identified with the villains in the stories, which may help to explain her own fictional insight into characters that society tends to shun. She has also written about her difficulty in keeping life and fiction apart.

Allende's first job, at the early age of seventeen, was as a secretary for the information department of the United Nations Food and Agriculture Organization (FAO) in Santiago. When asked to type a letter as an entrance requirement, she deployed her wild imagination and composed a tumultuous love epistle. She worked for FAO from 1959 to 1965, and this position, which included some work for television, allowed her to meet people connected to the media; broadcast and print journalism would later become her career and a platform to national fame.

During this period she met Miguel Frías, an engineering student, whom she married in 1962. Their first daughter, Paula, was born in 1963, before they moved to Belgium (she studied television there) and Switzerland for a year. Upon their return to Chile, they had a second child, Nicolás, who was born in 1966. One year later, as a young mother, she began to work as a journalist for *Paula*, a women's magazine that had just

been founded by Delia Vergara, a trailblazer in Chile's incipient feminist movement.

Allende's years at *Paula* were crucial in her development as an author and a public figure. Although Allende, as she tells it, had no formal training or experience of any kind as a writer, let alone as a journalist, Vergara had read the engaging, humorous letters that Allende wrote to her mother (who was still living in Beirut and happened to be Vergara's friend) and offered Allende a job. Unlike other members of the magazine staff, Allende was not called to write theoretical or combative essays on feminism, but rather to practice a lightweight kind of journalism that would attract and entertain readers. Despite the trivial nature of her articles, they ultimately emerge, when closely examined, as a liberating forum for Chilean women. In her humorous column, entitled "Los Impertinentes" (The impertinent ones), she resorts to the most egregious stereotypes of men and women in order to expose and dismantle them through the workings of irony and hyperbole. She advises her female readers, for instance, to overplay the cliche of women as dumb and weak in order to succeed in society, as one can read in one of the articles later collected and published in *Civilice a su troglodita* (1974; Civilize your troglodyte):

> *Hay que ponerse a gritar cuando ve una abeja, desmayarse si queda atrapada en el ascensor, ponerse histérica con los incendios, los temblores y las arañas. Finja que no entiende los chistes, parezca inútil, gastadora y chismosa. Eso es lo que los hombres entienden por "feminidad" y es completamente inútil tratar de hacerlos cambiar de opinión.*

> You should scream when you see a bee, faint if you're trapped in an elevator, become hysterical on account of fires, tremors, and spiders. Pretend you don't get any joke, and make sure to appear useless and gossipy and seem to be a big spender. That's what men understand by "femininity" and it's totally useless to try to change their minds.

Besides "Los Impertinentes," Allende also wrote an advice column entitled "Correo del Amor" (Love mail); her *nom de plume* for this particular endeavor was Francisca Rámon, a name that publicly yet cryptically acknowledged the romantic union and impossible marriage of her mother and stepfather.

At *Paula*, Allende was also responsible for the astrology section. Her forecasts for each sign were based not on any arcane knowledge or supernatural gift, but rather, quite imaginatively, on the adventures and misadventures of her own circle of friends. Her later confession that her practice of journalism did not always distinguish between fact and fiction, or her sense that she was not always taken seriously, then, should come as no surprise. One reader, however, who does seem to have valued her flair for writing was none other than Pablo Neruda, Chile's foremost poet and Nobel Laureate in literature as well as a personal friend of the Allende family. He suggested to Isabel that she compile her humorous pieces in one volume, and this is how Allende became the author of her first, if rather sui generis, book, *Civilice a su troglodita* (with illustrations by Ricardo Guiraldes). This may be seen as the beginning of a prolific career—not yet that of a novelist, but certainly an initial step toward defining a voice of her own. Also in 1974, she published two children's books, *Lauchas y lauchones, ratas y ratones* (Mice and rats, small and large) and *La abuela Panchita* (Grandmother Panchita), dedicated to her own children Paula and Nicolás, then eight and five years old respectively. The early 1970s also mark Allende's incursions into the theater; she wrote three plays that were staged in Santiago: *El embajador* (1971; The ambassador); *La balada del medio pelo* (1973; The poor man's ballad); and *Los siete espejos* (1974; The seven mirrors). During this time, she also wrote *La gorda de porcelana* (The porcelain fat woman), a short allegorical tale that would be published (by Madrid's Alfaguara) only in 1984, after the success of *The House of the Spirits*.

On the Chilean national scene, Allende was best known for her television shows, where she created a striking persona that challenged the conventional seriousness of the official media. Wearing the multicolor fashions of the 1960s and 1970s, and driving a very compact Citroën that she had personally decorated with daisies, the ultramodern Allende would interview everyone from politicians and entrepreneurs to prostitutes and drug addicts. Indeed, the female protagonist of *De amor y de sombra* (1984; *Of Love and Shadows*, 1987), written a decade later, closely resembles the Isabel of these years. But the world as she knew it would soon come to a shocking end because of political events

in Chile. The leftist coalition of Unidad Popular (Popular Unity) had resulted in the democratic election of President Salvador Allende in 1970, but his trouble-ridden administration collapsed, abruptly and violently, following the military coup of 11 September 1973 and the establishment of General Augusto Pinochet's dictatorial regime. For more than a year, at considerable personal risk, Isabel exerted an incredible effort to help those who were being persecuted by the military, but, after having been fired from her magazine and television jobs, she finally opted for exile and moved with her family to Caracas, Venezuela, in 1975. Only after thirteen years abroad, upon the announcement of a national referendum on the political fate of Pinochet, would she return to her country.

Seeking to continue her work as a journalist and playwright, Allende's initial years in Venezuela were defined by financial and professional hardship. These years were also a turning point in her career as a writer; she embraced fiction and began to write the novel that would catapult her to international fame. Many years later, in her book *Paula*, which is both a tale of her daughter's final year as well as an autobiographical essay of sorts, Allende recalls a conversation with Neruda during which he had playfully questioned her journalistic skills and counseled her to write fiction instead:

> *Usted debe ser la peor periodista del país, hija. Es incapaz de ser objetiva, se pone al centro de todo, y sospecho que miente bastante y cuando no tiene una noticia, la inventa. ¿Por qué no se dedica a escribir novelas mejor? En la literatura esos defectos son virtudes.*

> My dear child, you must be the worst journalist in the country. You are incapable of being objective, you place yourself at the center of everything you do, I suspect you're not beyond fibbing, and when you don't have news, you invent it. Why don't you write novels instead? In literature, those defects are virtues.

Despite Neruda's clearcut advice, it must be pointed out that Allende herself describes the textual origin of *The House of the Spirits* not as a novel but as a letter to her grandfather (who was dying in Chile), begun in

1981 and eventually mushrooming into an almost five-hundred page manuscript dealing with family and national lore.

Most of what Allende has written in the two decades that followed the publication of *The House of the Spirits* has been narrative fiction. Her second novel, *Of Love and Shadows*, also deals indirectly with Chile's twentieth-century history, with a focus on the brutal repercussions of the military coup. The next two books, *Eva Luna* and *The Stories of Eva Luna*, shift their setting to the tropical regions of Latin America, signaling what seems to be a constant in Allende's fiction: subjects and locales that correspond directly to phases in her own biography.

If Venezuela's physical and cultural makeup filter into the *Eva Luna* cycle, her next three novels follow her to California. Having divorced Miguel Frías in 1987, she married an American lawyer, William Gordon, in 1988 after a single meeting and moved to the San Francisco Bay area. Indeed, the first of the California novels, *El plan infinito* (1991; *The Infinite Plan*, 1993), retrieves numerous aspects of her second husband's life in the Golden State, from his childhood in East Los Angeles through their life together in San Rafael.

Allende's next two novels, *Hija de la fortuna* (1999; *Daughter of Fortune*, 1999) and *Retrato en sepia* (2000; *Portrait in Sepia*, 2001), go back to the period from the 1840s to 1910, uncovering the half-forgotten ties that bind the histories of California and Chile together. Her two nonfiction books of the 1990s are *Paula* (1994), published after her daughter's death from porphyria in 1992, and, after a long interval of silence, *Aphrodite* (1997), a joyful celebration of the present and life's sensual pleasures—an antidote to suffering, as it were. *Paula* is an unusual text, for it openly delves into a mother's pain even as it explores an author's salvation through storytelling. If Allende's novels had already afforded her a large readership, this long essay reached even more people, especially those who had gone through similar experiences in their own lives, and many wrote to the author with their own stories. Presently a resident of Sausalito, California, Allende lives with her husband not far from where her daughter's ashes were scattered, in a house with a sign that reads "the house of the spirits."

Although Allende has written both fiction and nonfiction, the truth of the matter is that both modes are more closely intertwined than they may first appear. Her first and still best-known work is *The House of the Spirits*, a work of fiction, but the text's origin in the letter that Allende wrote to her grandfather upon learning of his stroke cannot be underestimated. She started writing that letter on 8 January 1981. By the end of the following year, the novel had been translated into every major European language.

Much has been written about the seemingly fortuitous composition of *The House of the Spirits*, and some critics have taken this as proof that Allende is nothing more than an accidental author, yet there is much evidence also to suggest that she is a laborious artisan of her works. That she chooses to start every new book on 8 January suggests a certain degree of superstition, but it is at the same time the sign of a disciplined talent. Moreover, in more ways than one, it is possible to view Allende's craft as the destination of a long, if winding, road. Beyond her extensive and varied work as a journalist, one may also recall her first clerical job at the FAO in Santiago. There she at times amused herself by translating romances from English into Spanish, a task that contributed to the sense of genre that one clearly perceives in her works. Even when creating many of her characters, Allende has rendered them conscious of the different literary forms—poetry, romance, opera, erotic fiction, even aphrodisiac recipes—that men and women can appeal to when engaged in the act of creation. It is true that when Allende's letter to her grandfather became something much bigger, she was not yet able to wield absolute control over certain narrative matters; in fact, there is an anecdote that it was her engineer husband, Miguel Frías, who detected a number of chronological inconsistencies in Isabel's first manuscript and had to reconstruct, as it were, *The House of the Spirits* by sketching a blueprint of the final text on the walls of their own dining room. Given the numerous forking paths that pervade all of Allende's novels, her technical mastery over the art of fiction—her deft control over the numerous, and always interesting, twists and turns of characters and events—is nothing short of remarkable.

At a first reading, *The House of the Spirits* may be viewed as the chronicle of one family through several decades of the twentieth century in an unnamed Latin American country. The novel's setting is never explicitly acknowledged to be Chile, and there are no obviously Chilean words or phrases in the novel, yet there are several signs in the text that seem to hint at the author's homeland. This is not a regionalist text, like those written by previous generations, yet readers familiar with Chile's imagined community may, for instance, recognize Neruda in the figure of the Poet, Salvador Allende in that of the Candidate and later President, or singer Víctor Jara in the character of Pedro Tercero. Moreover, the story's social and political background fits well within a general history of Chile. (With the publication of *Daughter of Fortune* and *Portrait in Sepia,* the Chilean specificity of *The House of the Spirits* has become retroactively explicit.)

Similarly, the characters in the novel resemble those of Allende's extended family. One can trace, for example, clear parallels between Alba and the author herself; the del Valle brothers recall Allende's uncles; and Blanca, Clara, and Esteban Trueba seem to correspond to Allende's mother, grandmother, and grandfather respectively. Even the dog's name, Barrabás, which is the very first word in this vast saga, is the name of the Allende family dog in Chile. In many interviews, Allende has admitted to the autobiographical beginnings of all of her works, even saying that she does not need to "invent" anything, yet the relationship between historical truth and fictional representation is clearly more complex. When the novel first appeared, some of her relatives were aghast at the author's "indiscretions," on the one hand, and "falsifications," on the other; interestingly, the family has since adopted *The House of the Spirits* as their official story.

Critics of the novel have faulted Allende as a mere imitator of Gabriel García Márquez, whose status at the very pinnacle of Latin American literary culture is widely acknowledged. Like García Márquez's *One Hundred Years of Solitude,* which chronicles several generations of the Buendía family, *The House of the Spirits* is an ambitious saga of the del Valle family; and, like García Márquez's Macondo, a fictional place that is usually viewed as the archetypal Latin American town, the places in Allende's text also seek to have continental resonances. Indeed, certain aspects of Allende's work may be taken as conscious tokens of appreciation for

García Márquez's universe; the first chapter of *The House of the Spirits,* for instance, is named Rosa, la Bella (Rosa the Beautiful), an homage of sorts to the character Remedios la Bella in *One Hundred Years of Solitude.* Moreover, Allende's masterful use of such narrative devices as prolepsis (the allusion to an event that will take place in the future) recalls the essence of García Márquez's narrative art, as displayed in the memorable first line of *One Hundred Years of Solitude.*

The most controversial link between Allende and her predecessor concerns the issue of magical realism, the narration of strange or even supernatural events calmly through the codes of literary realism. Instances of magical realism appear throughout *The House of the Spirits,* from Clara's clairvoyance to Alba's naturally green hair (featured on the cover of some editions), all told without much ado. If many readers around the world relish the exotic undertones of magical realism, others, especially in Latin America, reject this narrative mode for its often formulaic deployment and its cliched simplification of the continent's cultures. The debate surrounding Allende's works and García Márquez's legacy is ongoing. Whereas Alberto Fuguet, a younger Chilean novelist, has proclaimed that he would like to write a novel like *The House of the Spirits,* but without the spirits, the critic Patricia Hart has provocatively explored "The Influence of Isabel Allende on Gabriel García Márquez" (*Narrative Magic in the Fiction of Isabel Allende,* 1989).

*The House of the Spirits* clearly belongs within the Latin American version of literature about exile, and its greatest value may well be its retrieval of the homeland not through dour or lachrymose nostalgia but by means of an obsessive search for the past. Whereas in Marcel Proust time is regained through metaphors and images, Allende's investigation relies on the seductive power of storytelling—an old-fashioned virtue—and a complex web of voices and documents that reminds one of Miguel de Cervantes's *Don Quixote.* Indeed, the novel's main subject may be not so much politics or the female condition but, rather, the intricacies of telling a story, especially as it concerns memory. How can one tell the whole story if one does not know, or remember, everything? The overwhelming nature of the storytelling process is suggested by the sporadic emergence of a first-person pronoun within the third-person omniscient narrative, an apparent inconsistency that is resolved only in the epilogue, when it is revealed that Alba is the novel's true narrator, including those passages where she is referred to in the third person as well as the intermittent sections told by Esteban Trueba in the first person. These narrative labyrinths are neither a self-reflexive game nor cerebral experimentation, but a device that underscores the novel's political moral: only by having access to a character's full story can one understand the feelings and actions of others.

The characters of *The House of the Spirits* and, for that matter, all of Allende's other novels as well, are prone to recount their life stories so that they can be truly known. In this regard a memorable episode in the novel is when Colonel García tells Alba about their childhood just before he rapes and mutilates her; for the reader, the Colonel's tale cannot justify his brutality, but it is nevertheless an essential part of a vast tableau in which he, too, must be understood. That a female consciousness should be the one in control over the narrative is significant, for it suggests an alternative to male-centered discourses that appear to be less capable of subtle discernment and reconciliation.

Begun on 8 January 1982, exactly a year after *The House of the Spirits* and before that novel's publication, *Of Love and Shadows* was Allende's response to Balcells's dictum that anyone can write a good first novel, but that only a good second one is proof of an author's talents. Like its predecessor, *Of Love and Shadows* deals with history and politics in a nameless Latin American country, but this time with a specific focus on a coup d'état and the ensuing repression and violence. That the action takes place in Chile is never made explicit, yet, as in *The House of the Spirits*, resemblances to real events and characters in that country are not a mere coincidence. The novel's General closely mimics Pinochet, while another character, Mario, makes Chilean readers think of Luigi, a flamboyant hairdresser in Santiago's fashionable circles.

According to Allende, each of her novels stems from a specific, concrete emotion. *The House of the Spirits* grew out of nostalgia; the impulse behind *Of Love and Shadows* is anger. This novel, then, emerges as a testimony of, and weapon against, tyranny, not just in Chile but across the continent and throughout the world. In this Allende adopts one of the consecrated stances of Latin American authorship: writers speak for those who do not have a voice, in order to record and preserve what would otherwise remain silenced. Like Neruda in "The Heights of Machu Picchu," the novelist behind *Of Love and Shadows* invokes and revives the memory of those who have unjustly suffered and died.

Specifically, the event that lies at the heart of this text is the 1978 discovery of a mass grave at Lonquén, in central Chile, that contained the bodies of fifteen peasants massacred by the military Right after the 1973 coup. Lonquén (called Los Riscos in the novel) became symbolically important because the Pinochet regime was not able to suppress the news that the mass grave had been discovered. The Catholic Church in Chile, contrary to what happened in other Latin American totalitarian regimes at the time, was instrumental in denouncing human rights violations and impeded official censorship. Indeed, one of the novel's characters is "the Cardinal," whose actions mirror those of Santiago's archbishop Raúl Silva Henríquez, founder of the Vicaría de la Solidaridad (Vicary of Solidarity). The novel's central heroes are two journalists, Irene Beltrán and Francisco Leal (played by Jennifer Connelly and Antonio Banderas in the film version), whose love story is intertwined with a political thriller that closely follows historical events. Likewise, the character of Irene is directly modeled on Isabel herself; she works for a magazine just like *Paula* (where a sense of normalcy must be maintained at all costs), helps the dictatorship's victims, and ends up by leaving the country. Curiously for a fictional work, it is journalism, not literature, that ultimately is praised for its detailed and truthful recording of reality by means of historical documents, personal notebooks, and even photography.

If the work of journalism is, to a large extent, the theme of *Of Love and Shadows*, storytelling emerges as the most powerful tool of survival in *Eva Luna*, Allende's third novel and the one during whose composition she first felt secure enough to start describing herself officially as a full-fledged writer. Whereas *The House of the Spirits* was written in a haphazard way, *Eva Luna* was carefully designed beforehand.

The tale of Eva Luna, the female character that Allende says she cherishes the most, is a story of empowerment. Eva, the illegitimate daughter of an indigenous gardener and a maid, becomes an orphan as a child, yet grows up to be a popular writer of *telenovelas* (television soap operas). Critics have underscored the parallels between *Eva Luna* and the picaresque romance, but, unlike Lázaro de Tormes, the original *pícaro* of Spanish literature, Eva is never corrupted by the class-conscious society into which she is born. In a sense, there are innumerable social and cultural differences between Allende and her new protagonist; Eva lives in a world that Alba and Irene, Isabel's previous literary alter egos, would find quite foreign, yet they all share the talent of forging their own unique destinies through the power of words.

Having already recovered and documented her own past in Chile, as well as the country's recent history, Allende seems liberated to invent a new fictional reality. Abandoning the landscapes of her two previous novels, the writer now sets the scene in the multiethnic tropics, peopled by mestizos, Europeans, Arabs, and indigenous people. This setting, however, is not a realistic copy of Venezuela but an exotic, more ardent version thereof, a region whose passionate exuberance somehow matches the melodramatic tenor of both the novel *Eva Luna* and the television scripts, such as "Bolero," that its protagonist creates. In this regard, this new text emerges as a kind of *ars poetica*, one in which women can improve, even save, their lives through the stories they know how to imagine and tell.

The novel's epigraph is taken from *The Arabian Nights* and retrieves the special magic of Scheherazade's art: "Hermana, por Alá sobre ti, cuéntanos una historia que nos haga pasar la noche" (Sister, for the sake of Allah, tell us a story that will help pass the night). In this ancient lineage of real-world and imaginary female storytellers, Allende makes sure that Eva Luna has stories she can call her own. With a fictional preface by Rolf Carlé, an Austrian photographer who is her true love in the novel, *The Stories of Eva Luna* are presented to the reader as the stories that the heroine composes to fulfill her lover's most intimate plea: "Cuéntame un cuento que no le hayas contado a nadie" (Tell me a story you have never told anyone before). Indeed, the twenty-three short stories that make up this collection, as varied as they are, are all tales of love. Some of these texts are highly erotic, and one of them, "Boca de sapo"

("Toad's Mouth"), has been blacklisted by some religious groups in the United States. Written when she went to live at William Gordon's rather chaotic household in San Rafael, Allende now claims that it was easier for her to write short fiction at the time, since writing an entire novel would have been virtually impossible in such an environment. Beyond these circumstances, however, Allende's first incursion into the short story denotes a new self-assurance regarding the forms of her craft: an author's mastery over each and every element of the text is a necessity imposed by the genre's brevity and, as Poe would have it, its demand for a "single effect."

*The Infinite Plan* introduces two noticeable changes in Allende's fiction. It is the first novel set outside of Latin America, and the only one, so far, to have a male protagonist. It is the story of Gregory Reeves, whose biography closely follows that of Isabel's second husband, from his early childhood traveling with an itinerant family (Gregory's father preaches "the infinite plan," his personal philosophy) to the couple's shared life together, the novel's narrative present, when Reeves speaks to his unnamed lover, who is a novelist. The text is framed by this oral confession—the female narrator asks Reeves to tell her the story of his life—but most of the novel is told in a conventional third-person form that, as always with Allende, easily captivates readers. At the text's beginning and end, not unlike the device used in *The House of the Spirits,* there is a first-person voice closely linked to Allende's own. Similarly, in a manner reminiscent of Esteban Trueba's memories, Reeves tells part of his own story in his own voice.

In this, her first novel about California, Allende begins to explore the United States as a multicultural society through the various episodes of Reeves's life: his childhood in the Hispanic neighborhood of East Los Angeles; his college years at Berkeley; the Vietnam War; and, finally, his work as a lawyer in San Francisco, helping members of different ethnic minorities. Although Reeves is a white Anglo-American male, his story may be read as a survivor's tale very much in the tradition of Allende's female protagonists.

As in *The House of the Spirits* and *Of Love and Shadows, The Infinite Plan* combines fact with fiction. The Vietnam episode did not actually happen to Allende's husband (it is inspired by a veteran's tale), but the rest of the novel is based on Allende's thorough research of her husband's life; rather than inventing, she describes her task as editing. Just as Isabel's Chilean relatives now view *The House of the Spirits* as a family album of sorts, Gordon has stated that not until reading *The Infinite Plan,* an experience he has called the happiest moment of his life, did he fully understand "the plan" underlying his own biography.

On 6 December 1991, while Allende was in Madrid to launch *The Infinite Plan,* she received the news that her only daughter, Paula, had been taken ill and was in a coma. Paula lived in Madrid, with her husband, Ernesto, so Isabel was able to rush immediately to the hospital. This was the beginning of a painful process that resulted in Paula's untimely death exactly a year later, at Isabel and William's home in California, a personal tragedy that Allende survived only through writing. It was Carmen Balcells, Allende's literary agent, who early on gave Isabel a yellow pad and urged her to record her feelings so that she could ease her nightmarish pain: "Toma, escribe y desahógate, si no lo haces morirás de angustia, pobrecita mía" (*Paula;* My poor Isabel. Here, take this and write. Unburden your heart; if you don't you are going to die of anguish).

In a gesture reminiscent of the origins of *The House of the Spirits,* Isabel began to write a letter to somebody who is dying—not her very old grandfather this time, but even more poignantly, a twenty-eight-year-old woman who was simply too young to die. The initial impulse behind the letter, besides assuaging her own suffering, is Isabel's need to recount Paula's experience, so that when she wakes from her coma she will have a record of this dark episode. But Paula never regained consciousness and, after her death, Isabel reshaped the original letter into a book based not only on Isabel's notes but also on the letters she had written to her mother, Panchita, during that year, and including as well the love letters that Paula and Ernesto had exchanged during their life together.

What surprised reviewers when *Paula* first came out was the extent to which the book does not deal with Isabel's child, but rather with the author's own biography—so much so that some suggested, rather critically, that the book ought to be entitled *Isabel.* Indeed, much of the text is Allende's recounting of her own life with utmost honesty, down to her most intimate secrets. Her florid loquacity stands out as a radical contrast to Paula's profound silence, and one wonders whether there is not a certain measure of exhibitionism in Isabel's torrent of words. A careful reading of *Paula,* however, reveals a deeper function for Allende's act.

As in the Eva Luna novel and stories, one key may be found in the figure of Scheherazade, whose desperate attempt to postpone her own execution by means of storytelling is invoked obliquely in the text: "Mi abuela escribía en sus cuadernos para salvar los fragmentos evasivos de los días y engañar a la mala memoria. Yo intento distraer a la muerte" (*Paula;* My grandmother wrote in her notebooks to safeguard the fleeting fragments of the days and outwit loss of memory. I am trying to distract death). In the original Spanish, the verb *distraer* means not only *to distract,* but also *to amuse,* thus recalling the delightful nature of Scheherazade's stories as well as Allende's own, in the sense that her grandmother's practice of writing may be equated with Clara's "cuadernos de anotar la vida" (notebooks for recording life) in *The House of the Spirits.* In fact, readers of *Paula* may have recognized in this autobiographical narrative many of the events that had been previously integrated into the fabric of the author's first novel, yet there is a fundamental difference between both tellings of the same story that explains and justifies the title *Paula.*

Allende's book is divided into three parts. The first covers the period from December 1991 to May 1992, the second runs from May 1992 to December 1992, and the third consists of an epilogue. The turning point in the story is Isabel's loss of hope that her daughter would ever wake up again. If the first part resorts to a second-person narrative directly addressed to Paula, the second part shifts to a third-person tale in which it is made clear that Paula will never read what has been composed for her: Paula is written about, not to. Death will no longer be distracted, so one wonders to what extent Paula's mortality can be reconciled with the second meaning of *distraer,* to amuse, a trait so much at the heart of Allende's imaginings and practice of writing.

There is no doubt that *Paula* is as engaging a text as any other written by the author, but here Allende opens up her bag of tricks and exposes its contents. In a sense, this work may be read as a kind of reflection on her previous fiction, especially the novel that consecrated her fame. If, in *The House of the Spirits*, Alba's green hair is presented to the reader as a token of reality's magic, in *Paula* one learns of a much more prosaic truth: "una vez que quise pintarme los pelos de amarillo y por un error del peluquero terminé con la cabeza verde" (once when I wanted to dye my hair yellow and the beautician bungled the job and it turned green). One could argue that Allende uncovers her magical realism and other aspects of her wild adornment of reality—her fiction's poetics—in order to make Paula's own view of the world stand out in contrast and, more important, be preserved.

Throughout the text, Allende underscores her daughter's maturity and simplicity, traits that she herself claims to lack. Seeking somehow to safeguard Paula's gaze and voice, Isabel tries to denude her account of anything that may be superfluous and lavish, what she calls "the beasts of imagination," which are therefore not entirely honest. Suspending disbelief, aiming at something higher than even memory, writing's illusion is to secure a scriptural reunion of mother and daughter: "No es recordarte lo que pretendo, sino vivir tu vida, ser tú, que ames, sientas y palpites en mí, que cada gesto mío sea un gesto tuyo, que mi voz sea tu voz" (I don't mean remember you, but live your life, be you, let you love and feel and breathe in me, let my gestures be yours, my voice your voice). In this regard, *Paula* is not only a fitting title for this book, but also, in a sense, a faithful signature.

After *Paula*, Allende's years of silence were followed not by a return to fiction but to a heterogeneous kind of writing that recalls her beginnings as a journalist in Chile. Indeed, the tone of *Aphrodite* is lighthearted, like "Los Impertinentes," the humorous column that she wrote for the women's magazine, *Paula*, before she became a famous author. The book was born half in jest when she and her friend Robert Shekter, an illustrator, came up with the idea of collaborating on a volume about aphrodisiacs that would include stories, images, and, last but not least, kitchen recipes, provided by Allende's mother (except one, a "soup for orgies," that was concocted by Carmen Balcells). To dismiss this book as a trivial pursuit would be unjust, because its apology for sensuality and the pleasures of life—sex, food, drink—is part and parcel of a long tradition in

literature that includes not only such recent phenomena as Laura Esquivel's novel, *Como agua para chocolate* (1989) and a number of international films, but goes back to such canonical works as Pablo Neruda's poetry, *The Arabian Nights*, and the *Kama Sutra*. Allende's research on the subject seems rather thorough, but, the book's objective being pleasure, she decided not to spend any time preparing a bibliography. What we find, instead, amidst the recipes, illustrations, and quotes from world literature and sex manuals, is a new collection of short stories that continues what the author had initiated in *The Stories of Eva Luna*. If Allende's manner here is lighter and more playfully sexual than in that earlier collection, what both sets of stories share is an unconditional defense of love, hailed in *Aphrodite* as the most powerful of aphrodisiacs. Pervading the entire book is the author's intimate dialogue with the reader, who, as in "Los Impertinentes," is addressed in the second person and given instructions to be acted upon or, very much in keeping with Allende's spirit, subverted or rebelled against.

The author's long-awaited return to fiction occurred in 1999, with the publication of *Daughter of Fortune*, followed a year later by that of *Portrait in Sepia*. These two novels should be read as a diptych, in the sense that the latter continues the threads left loose in the former. They are a patiently composed and carefully crafted tableau of numerous characters whom we follow through several decades and various places around the world. The story traces the multiethnic origins of Valparaíso and San Francisco, and takes the reader to the point where *The House of the Spirits* begins. Aurora, the narrator of *Portrait in Sepia*, happens to be Clara del Valle's cousin, a turn of events through which Allende's first novel reconstitutes itself. By means of the retroactive effect of these "prequels," one sees the del Valle clan living not in a mythical Latin American republic, but in a specific geographic and historical milieu: Chile is no longer hidden, and even regional words, such as *fundo* (country estate), are now confidently used. Moreover, the aristocratic del Valles acquire a new attribute: some characters are now more complex, as in the case of Severo del Valle, whose war mutilation is an added element, or Nívea, whose sexuality is graphically depicted. There is also a new transcultural filiation, in that the later novels embrace the racial and linguistic plurality of the Pacific Rim. Born in San Francisco of English, Chilean, and Chinese ancestors, Aurora boasts another name, Lai-Ming, also meaning sunrise. These two names reflect her mixed origin even as they continue the long lineage of del Valle women, Nívea, Clara, Blanca, and Alba, whose names suggest light and purity.

In their vertiginous spatial and temporal journeys across several cultures, traversing East and West as well as North and South, *Daughter of Fortune* and *Portrait in Sepia* reinscribe the supernatural theme not as a regional, or even Latin American, eccentricity, but as an ancient human condition that unites all peoples. In the novels, the most visible spirit is Lin, who died in Hong Kong and whose beneficent influence convinces her widowed husband, Tao Chi'en, a wise doctor who ends up in San Francisco, to marry Eliza Sommers, the Anglo-Chilean heroine of *Daughter of Fortune* and maternal grandmother of Aurora. In the end, love triumphs over all ethnic differences and prejudices. Indeed, the erotic in its multiple varieties emerges as a central concern in these works. Citing the principle, from *Aphrodite,* that love is the best aphrodisiac, Tao Chi'en discovers the virtues of sexuality in the spiritual meeting of souls. It is interesting that Tao Chi'en sails out of slavery on a ship named *Liberty,* for freedom and liberation are arguably the central themes in these novels. Eliza Sommers follows a similar path; arriving in California wearing men's clothes and calling herself Elías Andieta, she eventually stops viewing her gender as a burden, and realizes that she can also be truly free as a woman.

These novels may be read as historical fiction: *Daughter of Fortune* deals with the California Gold Rush, *Portrait in Sepia* with South America's War of the Pacific, among other topics. However, they are very different from other historical novels in the Latin American traditions, such as those by Alejo Carpentier and Carlos Fuentes. As in her previous works, Allende embraces melodrama, but this time with a newfound maturity and sense of freedom. Both novels abound in characters that practice one form or another of representation, such as journalism, diaries, letters, poetry, opera, photography, romances, erotic literature, and even sex manuals. Specifically, Rose Sommers ends up being the most successful author of formulaic love stories in the English language, while Aurora del Valle becomes the best photographer in Chile, taking pictures of peasants, indigenous peoples, and third-class passengers.

In a sense, the art of these two women may be interpreted as Allende's proud survey of her own practice of writing. That a writer of melodrama can be named by Queen Victoria as a Dame of the British Empire, and that a photographer can portray a reality in sepia that others ignore, may well be fictional signs that speak of the author's art. Perhaps as a composite of these two female characters, Allende confidently inhabits a room of her own, where a sentimental vision of reality does not need apologies. Her books are not just best-sellers, but "long-sellers," and the unconditional love of her readers around the world has allowed her to build an empire of her own.

It is still too early to tell what Isabel Allende's ultimate status in the canons of literature will be, but as one evaluates her writings, it may be wise to recall Pablo Neruda's words in a little-known manifesto, "Sobre una poesía sin pureza" (On an impure poetry):

> *Y no olvidemos nunca la melancolía, el gastado sentimentalismo, perfectos frutos impuros de maravillosa calidad olvidada, dejados atrás por el frenético libresco; la luz de la luna, el cisne en el anochecer, "corazón mío" son sin duda lo poético elemental e imprescindible. Quien huye del mal gusto cae en el hielo.*
>
> (*Caballo verde para la poesía*, October 1935)

> And let us never forget melancholy, worn-out sentimentality, perfect impure fruits of a fabulous but forgotten quality, left behind by bookish frenzy: moonlight, the swan at dusk, "my love": surely this is the elemental and essential poetry. For he who shuns bad taste falls into iciness.

From the start of her career as a journalist and through her various volumes of fiction and nonfiction, Allende continues to privilege a writer's intimate and heartfelt connection with her reader. Regardless of the strict and narrow guidelines of some official definitions of art, the legends of Isabel Allende have moved readers of Latin American literature in ways that few other authors have.

# SELECTED BIBLIOGRAPHY

## Primary Works

### Children's Literature and Humor Books

*Civilice a su troglodita: Los impertinentes de Isabel Allende.* Illustrations by Ricardo Guiraldes. Santiago: Editorial Lord Cochrane, 1974.

*Lauchas y lauchones, ratas y ratones.* Santiago: Editorial Lord Cochrane, 1974.

*La abuela Panchita.* Illustrations by Marta Carrasco. Santiago: Editorial Lord Cochrane, 1974.

*La gorda de porcelana.* Illustrations by Fernando Krahn. Madrid: Editorial Alfaguara, 1984. (Written in 1974.)

### Novels and Short Stories

*La casa de los espíritus.* Barcelona: Plaza & Janés Editores, 1982.

*De amor y de sombra.* Barcelona: Plaza & Janés Editores, 1984.

*Eva Luna.* Barcelona: Plaza & Janés Editores, 1987.

*Cuentos de Eva Luna.* Barcelona: Plaza & Janés Editores and Buenos Aires: Editorial Sudamericana, 1989.

*El plan infinito.* Barcelona: Plaza & Janés Editores and Buenos Aires: Editorial Sudamericana, 1991.

*Hija de la fortuna.* Barcelona: Plaza & Janés Editores and Buenos Aires: Editorial Sudamericana, 1999.

*Retrato en sepia.* Barcelona: Plaza & Janés Editores and Buenos Aires: Editorial Sudamericana, 2000.

### Short Essays

"Auto-entrevista a Isabel Allende." *Clan,* February 1982, pp. 12–14.

"La magia de las palabras." *Revista Iberoamericana* 51, nos. 132–133:447–452 (July 1985).

"Los libros tienen sus propios espíritus." In *Los libros tienen sus propios espíritus.* Edited by Marcelo Coddou. Jalapa, México: Universidad Veracruzana, 1986. Pp. 15–20.

"Writing as an Act of Hope." *Paths of Resistance: The Art and Craft of the Political Novel.* Edited by William Zinsser. New York: Houghton Mifflin, 1989. Pp. 39–63.

### Other Works

*Paula.* Barcelona: Plaza & Janés Editores and Buenos Aires: Editorial Sudamericana, 1994.

*Afrodita: Cuentos, recetas y otros afrodisíacos.* Illustrations by Robert Shekter. Barcelona: Plaza & Janés Editores, 1997.

### Translations

*The House of the Spirits.* Translated by Magda Bogin. New York: Knopf, 1985.

*Of Love and Shadows.* Translated by Margaret Sayers Peden. New York: Knopf, 1987.

*Eva Luna.* Translated by Margaret Sayers Peden. New York: Knopf, 1988.

*The Stories of Eva Luna.* Translated by Margaret Sayers Peden. New York: Atheneum, 1991.

*The Infinite Plan.* Translated by Margaret Sayers Peden. New York: HarperCollins, 1993.

*Paula.* Translated by Margaret Sayers Peden. New York: HarperCollins, 1995.

*Aphrodite: A Memoir of the Senses.* Translated by Margaret Sayers Peden. New York: HarperFlamingo, 1998.

*Daughter of Fortune.* Translated by Margaret Sayers Peden. New York: HarperCollins, 1999.

*Portrait in Sepia.* Translated by Margaret Sayers Peden. New York: HarperCollins, 2001.

## Secondary Works

### Critical and Biographical Studies

Agosín, Marjorie. "Isabel Allende: *La casa de los espíritus.*" *Revista Interamericana de Bibliografía* 35:448–458 (1985).

Antoni, Robert. "Parody or Piracy: The Relationship of *The House of the Spirits* to One Hundred Years of Solitude." *Latin American Literary Review* XVI, no. 32:16–25 (1988).

Berchenko, Adriana Castillo, and Pablo Berchenko, eds. *La narrativa de Isabel Allende: Claves de una marginalidad.* Perpignan, France: Université de Perpignan, 1990.

Carvalho, Susan de. "Narration and Distance in Isabel Allende's Novels and in *Cuentos de Eva Luna.*" *Antípodas: Journal of Hispanic Studies* 6–7:55–62 (1994–1995).

Coddou, Marcelo, ed. *Los libros tienen sus propios espíritus.* Jalapa, México: Universidad Veracruzana, 1986.

———. *Para leer a Isabel Allende.* Concepción: LAR, 1988.

Correas Zapata, Celia. *Isabel Allende: Vida y espíritus.* Barcelona: Plaza & Janés Editores, 1998.

Cortínez, Verónica. "La construcción del pasado en la *Historia verdadera de la conquista de la Nueva España* y *La casa de los espíritus.*" *Hispanic Review* 58, no. 3:317–327 (summer 1991).

———. "El pasado deshonroso de Isabel Allende." *Revista Iberoamericana* LX, nos. 168–169:1135–1141 (July–December 1994).

———. "*Paula*: Memorias en silencio." *Antípodas: Journal of Hispanic Studies* 6–7:63–75 (1994–1995).

Dulfano, Isabel. "Feminist Strategies in the Work of Isabel Allende." Ph.D. dissertation, Yale University, 1993.

Earl, Peter. "Literature as Survival: Allende's *The House of the Spirits.*" *Contemporary Literature* 28, no. 4:543–554 (winter 1987).

———. "De *Lazarillo* a *Eva Luna*: Metamorfosis de la picaresca." *Nueva Revista de Filología Hispánica* 36, no. 2:987–996 (1988).

Galarce, Carmen. *La novela chilena del exilio (1973–1987): El caso de Isabel Allende.* Santiago: Departamento de Estudios Humanísticos, Universidad de Chile, 1994.

Gordon, Ambrose. "Isabel Allende on *Of Love and Shadows.*" *Contemporary Literature* 28, no. 4:530–542 (winter 1987).

Guerra-Cunningham, Lucía, ed. *Splintering Darkness: Latin American Women Writers in Search of Themselves.* Pittsburgh: Latin American Literary Review Press, 1990.

Hart, Patricia. *Narrative Magic in the Fiction of Isabel Allende.* London and Toronto: Associated University Presses, 1989.

Invernizzi, Virginia. "The Novels of Isabel Allende." Ph.D. dissertation, University of Virginia, 1991.

Meyer, Doris. "Exile and the Female Condition in Isabel Allende's *De amor y de sombra.*" *International Fiction Review* 15, no. 2:151–157 (1988).

———. " 'Parenting the Text': Female Creativity and Dialogic Relationships in Isabel Allende's *La casa de los espíritus.*" *Hispania* 73, no. 2:360–365 (May 1990).

Moody, Michael. "Isabel Allende and the Testimonial Novel." *Confluencia* 2, no. 1:39–43 (1986).

Muñoz, Willy. "Las (re)escrituras en *La casa de los espíritus.*" *Discurso Literario* 5, no. 2:433–454 (spring 1988).

Reisz, Susana. "¿Una Scheherazada hispanoamericana? Sobre Isabel Allende y *Eva Luna.*" *Mester* 20, no. 2:107–126 (fall 1991).

Riquelme Rojas, Sonia, and Edna Aguirre Rehbein, eds. *Critical Approaches to Isabel Allende's Novels.* New York: Peter Lang, 1991.

Rojas, Mario. "*La casa de los espíritus* de Isabel Allende: un caleidoscopio de espejos desordenados." *Revista Iberoamericana* 132–133:917–925 (1985).

Salvador, Alvaro. "El otro boom de la narrativa hispanoamericana: los relatos escritos por mujeres en la década de los ochenta." *Revista de Crítica Literaria Latinoamericana* 41:165–175 (1995).

Shaw, Donald L. *The Post-Boom in Spanish American Fiction.* Albany: State University of New York Press, 1998.

Swanson, Philip. "Tyrants and Trash: Sex, Class and Culture in *La casa de los espíritus.*" *Bulletin of Hispanic Studies* 71, no. 2:217–237 (April 1994).

Teitelboim, Volodia. "Isabel Allende delinea su concepción de la novela." *Plural* 29, no. 210:29–33 (March 1989).

*Interviews*

Agosín, Marjorie. "Entrevista a Isabel Allende." *Imagine* 1, no. 2:42–56 (winter 1984).

Alvarez-Rubio, Pilar. "Una conversación con Isabel Allende." *Revista Iberoamericana* 60, no. 168–169:1063–1071 (July–December 1994).

Cortínez, Verónica. "Polifonía: Isabel Allende y Antonio Skármeta." *Revista Chilena de Literatura* 32:79–89 (November 1988).

Cruz, Jacqueline et al. "Entrevista a Isabel Allende." *Mester* 20, no. 2:127–143 (fall 1991).

García Pinto, Magdalena. *Entrevista.* Hanover: Ediciones del Norte, 1986. (Videocassette.)

Meyer, Doris. "The Spirits Were Willing." In her *Lives on the Line: The Testimony of Contemporary Latin American Authors.* Berkeley and Los Angeles: University of California Press, 1988. Pp. 237–242.

Moody, Michael. "Entrevista con Isabel Allende." *Discurso Literario* 4, no. 1:41–53 (1986).

———. "Una conversación con Isabel Allende." *Chasqui* 16, nos. 2–3:51–59 (November 1987).

Munro-Clark, Margaret. "An Interview with Isabel Allende: Love, Life and Art in a Time of Turmoil." *Antípodas: Journal of Hispanic Studies* 6–7:15–27 (1994–1995).

Piña, Juan Andrés. "Isabel Allende, la narradora de la aldea." In his *Conversaciones con la narrativa chilena.* Santiago: Editorial Los Andes, 1991. Pp. 185–221.

Rodden, John, ed. *Conversations with Isabel Allende.* Austin: University of Texas Press, 1999.

Zerán, Faride. "La pasión de Isabel Allende." In her *Al pie de la letra. Entrevistas de fin de siglo.* Santiago: Editorial Grijalbo, 1995. Pp. 83–89.

# Jorge Amado

## (1912–2001)

### Nelson H. Vieira

Recognized as a compelling, socially conscious, and humorous Brazilian satirist of international fame, Jorge Amado recreates the poignant saga and vibrant mindset of Brazil's masses. Amado's sweeping, best-selling novels also dramatize the national society's irrepressible vitality despite the dominance of an insensitive and powerful socioeconomic elite that adheres to socially rooted authoritarian codes stemming from colonial times. In addition, Amado recreates sociopolitical tensions, generated by the chronic influence of former military regimes of repressive authoritarianism, that have reinforced the rigid hierarchical tendencies which all too often foster the status quo. While Amado's writing presents a panoramic view of Brazilian society across class lines, his narratives primarily pit the lower-middle and lower classes (o povo), the victimized masses, against bourgeois and oligarchic oppressors, including religious and racial bigots who have denounced the nation's religious syncretism and racial mixture. Owing to his strong beliefs in social justice and socialism, especially in view of the presence of ongoing racial, religious, and class prejudices, Amado supports Brazil's racial and cultural admixture with verve and commitment. As his novels illustrate, this melange produces a rich hybrid culture of Afro-Brazilian folklore, music, art, and religion as well as dynamic values from other ethnic and subaltern cultures. Capturing the esprit of his mulatto and black characters, Amado also heralds Brazil's *mestiço* culture as singular, mediating, and inspiring. He celebrates its ubiquitous historical and creative hybridity, especially in the State of Bahia, the primary locus of his fiction, which in many of his novels becomes emblematic of Brazil's national gestalt. In short, his novels not only evoke a *mestiço* and black consciousness but also strive to provide the reader with a diversified and pluralistic perspective on racial and cultural identity.

Born in 1912 in southern Bahia, near the port city of Ilhéus, during the heyday of the cacao industry, Amado grew up amid the local battles between cacao planters and oligarchic bosses for possession of the fertile land. All of Amado's childhood was spent during this period of continuous disputes, which later became the inspiration for his early novels, particularly *Jubiabá* (1935; *Jubiabá*, 1984) and *Terras do sem fim* (1943; *The Violent Land*, 1965). He speaks reverently of how his father came to Ilhéus as a young man to buy land to plant sugar cane and later cacao. Amado also recalls the violence of the land and how on one occasion his father was shot and wounded in a local political quarrel. As a child and adolescent, he came into direct contact with the plantation workers and thus became acquainted with their existence, behavior, and dreams.

15

Amado received a Jesuit education in the state capital of Salvador. He first manifested his interest in and gift for literature after one of his teachers introduced him to the novels of Charles Dickens. Between 1927 and 1930 he worked as a reporter for a local newspaper, publishing stories and poems in small magazines and becoming a member of the Academia dos Rebeldes, a young, audacious literary group that led a bohemian life in the *bas-fonds*, or the seamier side of Salvador, the city that would come to serve as the sensual and lusty backdrop for most of his novels. In fact, part of his intimate knowledge of the city's culture and history stems from a period when he lived in a boardinghouse in the Pelourinho (Pillory Hill), known historically as the former site for buying, selling, and punishing slaves. In 1986 the United Nations declared the Pelourinho to be a Patrimony of Humanity site, and in 1987 Brazilian President José Sarney traveled to Bahia to inaugurate the Jorge Amado Cultural Foundation, located on Pillory Hill. With its many cultural and social programs, this foundation is dedicated to the study of Amado's work and to the betterment of society.

While preparing to study for a law degree and protesting the rapaciousness of the Brazilian oligarchy, Amado participated intensely in the ensuing stormy political activities related to the Revolution of 1930. He was motivated by this resistance's strong popular support. Amado repeatedly identified himself as a writer of the Generation of 1930 and as a product of those revolutionary times. Imbued with Marxist socialism and the political climate in his country, he wrote his first novel of social realism in 1931, *O país do carnaval* (The land of carnival). This novel and the next two, *Cacau* (1933; Cocoa), which was initially confiscated by the police, and *Suor* (1934; Sweat), were also inspired by Brazilian regionalism, a neorealist literary movement focusing upon the social injustices of the impoverished Brazilian northeast.

In 1933 Amado became acquainted with the primary regionalist writers from this area and was integrated into the literary life by contributing articles to newspapers, literary supplements, and magazines as well as by conversing with such famous authors as Graciliano Ramos, José Lins do Rego, Rachel de Queirós, and the sociologist Gilberto Freyre, who had organized the first Regionalist Congress in 1926. Amado and these figures became known as the major writers and thinkers of twentieth-century Brazilian regionalism.

Owing to the provocative political nature of his social realism, Amado began to gain notoriety and praise, while also becoming the object of political suspicion. The 1930s began a series of productive decades for Amado. He published six novels in this period, including his first notable title, *Jubiabá*, about class conflict and Afro-Brazilian culture in Bahia, considered then a subculture. *Jubiabá* is also notable for its real and fantasy portrayal of an invincible black hero. A year later came the lyrical and mythopoetic *Mar morto* (1936; *Sea of Death*, 1984) about Bahian fisherman and their orixá protectors (Afro-Brazilian deities). In 1937 *Capitães de Areia* (*Captains of the Sand*, 1988), a blatantly sentimental novel about a gang of homeless urchins, was seized and burned because of its "pornographic" depictions. Amado's use of detailed sexual scenarios can be found in his early as well as later fiction. Contemporary criticism has often failed to assess the presence of these features in his early writings; instead, critics have focused on his later works and charged him with depicting graphic sex in order to become a best-seller by catering to a broader market.

The 1930s was also a period of travel for Amado, taking him to the Pacific, the United States, and Mexico, where he became acquainted with the renowned muralists Diego Rivera, José Clemente Orozco, and David Alfaro Siqueiros. In the United States he met Michael Gold, who had written *Jews Without Money* (1930), a work that was to influence greatly Amado's future writing, as were the novels of John dos Passos. The international climate of socialism represented for Jorge Amado the essence of his social beliefs. The significance of his mounting reputation and leftist activity can be illustrated in his opposition to Getúlio Vargas's authoritarian, neofascist Estado Novo, or New State; the 1937 confiscation of his books, subsequently burned in a public square; the 1938 prohibition of his books in Brazil; a series of brief incarcerations; and again the book burning in 1943 of approximately 1,700 copies of his books. From 1937 through the early 1940s, Amado was recognized as politically subversive, and his work undeniably reflected his political commitment. For example, while he was in exile in Argentina in

1942, he published the biography of the leader and founder of the Brazilian Communist Party, Luiz Carlos Prestes. However, this book, *Vida de Luiz Carlos Prestes, o cavaleiro da esperança* (The life of Luiz Carlos Prestes, the knight of hope), was only published in Brazil and in Portuguese in 1945.

When Amado returned to Brazil in 1942 at the time of Brazil's entry into World War II, he settled in Bahia and began to write about the land he knew so intimately. With the publication of *The Violent Land*, Amado introduced a new aesthetic dimension into his work which overrode the politically charged social realism that dominated his early novels. Here, Amado wrote about the cacao wars as a type of tropical Western, infused with popular poetry and lyrical prose. This novel initiates his evolution as a socialist writer of literary narratives that reflect his Manichaean perspective in stories that are still politically inspired but reveal a literary style that would later bloom in *Gabriela, cravo e canela* (1958; *Gabriela, Clove and Cinnamon*, 1962). This latter book is recognized as the major turning point in Amado's development into one of Brazil's most influential literary voices.

Jorge Amado's life from the 1940s through the 1950s, until the publication of *Gabriela*, represents another of his productive literary periods as well as a time of intense political engagement. In 1944 *São Jorge dos Ilhéus* (Saint George of Ilheus) was published. It is set in the same locale as *The Violent Land* but during another time period, depicting the wars between the plantation owners and the exporters of cacao. This novel was followed by *Bahia de todos os santos* (1945; Bahia of all saints), a type of literary guide to the streets and mysteries of the city of Salvador. *Seara vermelha* (*The Golden Harvest*, 1992), published in 1946, denounces the socioeconomic problems caused by the unjust system of absentee landlords of large latifundia (estate farms) in the northeast of Brazil. This novel foreshadows the problems of agrarian reform and the reality of landless peasants, issues that dominated much political debate during the second half of the twentieth century and even up to the present. During this decade Amado's professional reputation was confirmed, evident in the editions and re-editions of twenty to thirty thousand copies of his books, a huge figure for publications in Brazil at that time.

In January of 1945 Amado traveled to São Paulo as president of the Bahian Delegation to the First Congress of Brazilian Writers (for which he served as vice-president). This event led to a democratic demonstration against the Vargas dictatorship, and he was imprisoned for a short time along with the iconoclastic modernist writer Oswald de Andrade. In 1933 Amado had married, but the union ended when he arranged for a legal separation in 1944 in order to marry Zélia Gattai from São Paulo in 1945; she became his lifelong companion and literary colleague. They wrote together and traveled all over the world.

With the fall of Getúlio Vargas in November of 1945, political parties were reinstated and Amado was elected to the Constitutional Assembly as Deputado Federal for São Paulo under the slate of the Communist Party. In this role he proposed several laws for artistic and cultural improvements. Most notable of all, he was the first to legislate against religious discrimination, motivated by the painful struggles of the followers of *candomblé* (Afro-Brazilian voodoo rites) in their quest for legal recognition as an established religious institution. As a result of the 1948 abolition of the Communist Party in Brazil, Amado lost his political post and embarked on a five-year period of self-exile in Europe, primarily in Paris, where he established residence. Forty years later, this residency became, along with his residency in Portugal, the primary locale for the writing of more manuscripts.

During his exile Amado became acquainted with internationally known artists such as Jean-Paul Sartre, Pablo Picasso, and Fernand Leger and traveled all over the Continent, going as far as Russia, where he stayed for several months. This period saw the launching of numerous translations (to date, in more than 48 languages) and the beginning of his life as a professional writer who earned his living from his publications, a rare phenomenon in Brazil where in 1980 less than 10 percent of the population managed to purchase books. His international status as a writer is attested to today by the publication of more than 30 books since 1931, in more than 850 editions, and recently in editions of 100,000 copies, uncommon for Brazilian publishers.

After his stay in Europe, his travel to Russia, and a brief residency in Czechoslovakia, Amado published

*O mundo da paz* (1951; The world of peace), about his travels to socialist countries. As soon as this book was published in Brazil, it was confiscated by Brazilian government authorities. However, Amado's most politically extensive work is the three-part, episodic *Os Subterrâneos da liberdade* (1954; The freedom underground) about the Vargas period and the communist revolutionary spirit. In 1951 Amado received the Stalin Peace Prize for the body of his work, and in 1952 he made an extensive trip to China and the Popular Republic of Mongolia.

With Stalin's death and the campaign of disparagement against the former dictator, led by Nikita Khrushchev, Amado and other members of the Brazilian Communist Party began to reexamine the rigid structure of the Party, which did not easily accommodate Brazil's social and political reality. This much debated realization led many to abandon the Party and, in the case of Amado, his Communist ideological verve began to wane, resulting in considerable changes in his public image and in his fiction. In a 1994 interview with Fritz Raddatz at the Frankfurt International Book Fair, Amado stated: "I am no longer a 'soldier of the party,' but I have neither left it nor been expelled from it." The novels that followed reveal a gradual transformation in their satirical attacks on the Left as well as the Right.

In retrospect, the major events of twentieth-century Brazilian social history can be gleaned from reading Amado's novels, for they provide numerous historical references to national political events and figures. In fact, his fiction has been frequently labeled a long roman à clef, owing to the presence of national figures, appearing as themselves or disguised. This is particularly evident in such novels as *Tenda dos milagres* (1969; *Tent of Miracles,* 1971), with its oblique allusion to scholarly critics of race such as Nina Rodrigues and the tropicalist musicians Caetano Veloso and Gilberto Gil; and in *O Sumiço da Santa* (1988; *The War of the Saints,* 1993) where hundreds of fictitious and real characters support the preservation of Afro-Brazilian culture. Among the real-life characters portrayed in the novel are the painter Carybé, the poet and singer Dorival Caymmi, and the high priestess, the *iyalorixá*, Mãe Menininha do Gantois, who presided over the vital force (*axé*) of *candomblé*.

*Gabriela* has been acclaimed as the watershed in distinguishing the earlier, more political and proletarian novels from the more literary and aesthetically sophisticated works of his mature phase. This novel, with its picaresque humor and evocative lyricism, clearly established Jorge Amado as a satirical rather than a polemical writer. Despite its innovation in the use of irony, parody, poetry, and word play, and especially with its focus on the love story between the free-spirited mulatto Gabriela and Nacib, the Syrian-born bar owner who hires her as a cook and eventually marries her, this novel is also the chronicle of a backwoods town, not unlike the dramas set in *The Violent Land* and *São Jorge,* in which money, power, and violence are dominant forces. However, in this novel the themes of development, progress, change, and civilization are interwoven in a beguiling manner, manifested in the city's growth as an important port and in Nacib's own growth as an individual, as reflected in his "civilized" treatment of the ingenuous Gabriela after she has committed adultery. This central drama is contrasted with a subplot representing traditional mores, in which murder is the only solution for punishing an adulterous wife. Therefore, the story of Gabriela is essentially one of change. Criticism has pointed to the elements of change in this novel as advocating openness and diversity. On a more allegorical level, these changes may refer to the Brazilian nation's shifting identity and signal Amado's critical challenge, already in the late 1950s, to the concept of the nation as a fixed entity with a single identity.

After the publication of this landmark work, Jorge Amado wrote more than a dozen major novels in addition to other titles. Until his last few years, Amado and his wife divided their time between Paris and their unpretentious house in Bahia, with occasional stays in Portugal. Considered to be a folk hero and a national institution in Brazil, Amado became a member of the Brazilian Academy of Letters in 1961. Consequently, Amado is considered to be the Brazilian model of the professional writer who commands respect and cultivates a relationship with his reading public, in spite of the charges of sexist and racist stereotyping hurled at him by much of the intelligentsia and literary scholars. Furthermore, his sentimental and apologetic populism is often misinterpreted by critics as the romanticizing of poverty. However, his ribald and epic novels might be read instead as recreations of a Brazilian world whose unique national cultural product is imagination and resilience. One could also consider these epic novels as variations of the story of Brazil's national tribulations and its irrepressible vigor, often emblematized by his abused yet enduring female protagonists. Furthermore, given the humane and humorous components in all of his works, it is easy to understand why Amado's fiction also generates universal appeal.

As a general observation on the novels since *Gabriela,* it is clear that all of them manifest comic overstatement and ironic understatement as well the double perspective, the use of the supernatural as a form of magical realism, humorous chapter titles, folk illustrations and woodcuts, iconoclastic pronouncements, and Bakhtinian and carnival literary features which dismantle canonical thinking via subtexts of double-voicedness. Included among these features are the use of metafiction, pastiche, and the staple of the roman à clef. Accused of producing works reminiscent of the parochial naturalist mode of the nineteenth century, Amado allows his literary innovations and narrative skills to speak for themselves. In terms of thematics, issues of race, class, sex, and politics permeate most of the novels of this second phase, but these subjects are usually placed in what the Brazilian anthropologist Roberto Da Matta calls a "triadic" structure which, via the mediation of opposing forces and contradictions, results in a third space, a kind of synthetic position in which ambiguity reigns supreme. This stance is based upon an ethics of the "relational," where cultural hybridity modulates situational behavior. Nevertheless, this structure does not always represent a peaceful or democratic solution because, as Amado dramatizes, there continues to exist a series of inflexible, strict, and unspoken hierarchies that often control the Brazilian social scene. One could say that Amado's novels are characterized by irresolvable contradictions and ambiguities which readers of other cultures may find unethical. On the other hand, one may wonder if his critics, frequently bourgeois, are not in fact "colonizing" Amado in order to impose their own cultural and moral codes of reference.

Downplaying his role as a sociopolitical activist, Jorge Amado has nonetheless taken, on numerous occasions, an overt stand on racial, social, and political issues of national scope. As a result he has become a Brazilian institution, representing via literature the voice of a people frequently marginalized by poverty, prejudice, and repression. Given his national recognition, his public statements are invariably scrutinized for their courageous and controversial stance, notably during times of political crises such as the military regime's formidable period of intense repression during the late 1960s and early 1970s, known as the *sufoco* (the suffocation). For example, in view of mounting state censorship in 1970, Amado proclaimed publicly that he would never again publish in Brazil if he were ever to be censored by the military regime. Since that date his fiction has never again been censored as it was, repeatedly, during the late 1930s and 1940s. Imprisoned several times and opting for self-exile during national periods of severe repression, Jorge Amado was often publicly attacked for being a communist. In response, he consistently stressed his belief in the tenets of socialism, even though today he denigrates party structures or theoretical and dogmatic concepts, such as communism, which he believes are too rigid and undemocratic. A former active member of the Communist Party, Amado was above all an undying socialist for he believed that humanity is drawn to socialism as a humanistic idea and as an evolutionary process which continually advances, albeit slowly and with many setbacks. In a 1994 interview, Amado voiced his dream of a "revolution without ideology." He recognized that political systems may perish while ideas such as socialism can remain and develop in a universal context.

Jorge Amado's literature has often been viewed critically as being merely social and political satire doused heavily with mordant humor, bawdy sex, and exotic characters. Although satire is indeed a staple of his work, it would be irresponsible to read his novels only as satirical, especially those that were written after *Gabriela,* with their sophisticated use of imagery, symbolism, historical allegory, narrative technique, humor, and a form of magical realism. These traits are masterfully exemplified in *Tent of Miracles and The War of the Saints.* His simultaneous handling of expansive plot lines and multiple stories in a given work point to one of Amado's outstanding features as a writer—his talent for storytelling, which he himself recognizes as his strongest trait. He stresses this feature of his writing to such an extent that he repeatedly downplays his craft as an artist per se, emphasizing his gift at narration, very much in tune with Brazil's oral tradition, manifested today, for example, in the *literatura de cordel* (chapbooks of dramatic verse composed for and recited at local fairs and markets) of northeastern Brazil.

While interested in characterization, highly developed in novels such as Gabriela as well as *Dona Flor e seus dois maridos* (1966; *Dona Flor and Her Two Husbands*, 1969) and *Tieta do Agreste, pastora de cabras* (1977; *Tieta the Goat Girl*, 1979), Amado primarily focuses upon the ethics of social justice and the dynamics of popular culture and behavior vis-à-vis an unjust world of inequality and bigotry. The Manichaean aspects of his literature, often graphically illustrated in his books since the 1950s with popular folkloric etchings or engravings, emerge vividly in most of Amado's fiction through the constant portrayal of the conflict between the forces of good and evil or in the troubadour (*cordel*) culture of the northeast—between *firmeza* (steadfastness) and *falsidade* (falsity). In this vein, Amado's narratives draw upon a populist mindset and popular culture that become the driving forces for the everyday dramas of his protagonists.

Despite the strong presence of social satire, his works are especially marked by a high degree of infectious and naughty humor that many critics have disparaged, failing to see its purposeful and structured role as the manifestation of the sociopolitical conflict of opposing forces between the *povo* and the bourgeoisie. In the 1994 Frankfurt interview, while referring to the influence of Mark Twain, Amado stated that "humor and laughter are much stronger weapons than violence against evil." Therefore, it is imperative to read Jorge Amado's oeuvre as essentially comic in order to understand its social commentary on race, women, class, patriarchy, economics, politics, and history. If the reader, amidst the humor and bawdy language, recognizes Amado's high regard for the Afro-Brazilian religion of *candomblé* as an inherent and significant cultural and revolutionary force against power elites, deftly portrayed in his *War of the Saints*, then he or she can begin to understand the writer's use of social, sexual, and at times shocking humor to contrast and ridicule opposing conventional and frequently unjust mores.

Amado has reiterated that his strongest social and literary commitment has been to the incisive depiction of racial prejudice and the concomitant social struggle to have Brazil's panoply of diverse cultures, including black culture, acknowledged alongside that of Brazil's elite. When Jorge Amado and his wife spent the fall semester at Pennsylvania State University in 1971, he stated during his first in a series of talks on Brazil and Brazilian literature that "Não somos latinos, senão em parte" (We are not Latins, only in part). This comment is an allusion to the spoken idiom of Brazil's hybrid culture, enriched by the mixture of languages and races and one that modernists and regionalist writers adopted as a violent act against a European academic style of Portuguese. Consequently, Amado's dedication to Afro-Brazilian culture is really an extension of his overall commitment to the diversity of Brazil's modern national culture.

The two novels that directly followed *Gabriela*, *Os velhos marinheiros* (1961; *Home is the Sailor*, 1964, which contains two narratives) and *Os pastores da noite* (1964; *Shepherds of the Night*, 1966, composed of three tales with the same characters), display a more novella-like structure. In the first title, the famous long story, *A morte e a morte de Quincas Berro D'Água* (The two deaths of Quincas Wateryell) represents another example of Amado's keen use of irony and humor. Here, via the use of a double perspective that relies upon ambiguity, Amado tells the story of the death of Quincas, a drunk and vagrant as well as a formerly respectable middle-class gentleman. By contrasting Quincas's double life and different versions of his physical state—was he or wasn't he dead?—Amado employs comic relief to illustrate how his vagabond buddies can take Quincas or his "corpse" out for one last fling on the town before he is buried at sea, according to his wishes. The ambiguous story about Quincas's supposed antics during the night of revelry is told by an unreliable narrator whose words actually question his own version of reality. Counterbalanced with views of Quincas's once respectable behavior, the story not only shows the hypocrisy of his former middle-class life of social taboos and restrictions, but also how the humor of the "fantastic" version contrasts with the inauthentic, serious aspects of the bourgeois version.

This amusing story also affords the reader a penetrating view of Brazil's personalized culture of death, thereby underscoring the power of spiritual forces vis-à-vis the materialistic and what actually constitutes a morally authentic existence. With *Shepherds of the Night*, Amado returns to the bohemian life of Salvador with the same jovial irreverence of "Quincas" except that here there are clear intimations of a utopian world based upon a male ego's vision. Criticism has commented on how this novel in fact creates a utopia of machismo, a type of bucolic ambience which even turns tragedy into a heartfelt experience. Amado's macho "shepherds" of the night (sexualized as female), adhere to the "relational" mode of dealing with contrasts, thereby mitigating the inequalities of life, in this case between men and women, elites and marginals.

*Dona Flor and Her Two Husbands* is an engaging and magical story about a sensuous cook, Dona Flor, and her love for a passionate and irresponsible husband, who dies at the beginning of the novel from the effects of a wild night of revelry during Carnival, and her love for a second, well-respected, responsible, and unromantic husband who provides her with the stability that was lacking in her first marriage. When her passionate husband returns from the grave, rekindling her sexual desire, Flor at first believes that she must make a choice. However, this novel, labeled by Roberto DaMatta as "relational" and allegorical, also manifests the "triadic" structure of conciliating binaries, leading to a third, synthetic space. In so doing, Amado demonstrates the triumph of ambiguity and defines the complexity of Brazilian society and its hierarchical and personalistic aspects which, surprisingly, function simultaneously. Consequently, Dona Flor chooses not to choose, and decides to keep both husbands as a form of alliance between the popular and the traditional which, on an allegorical level, represents Brazil's struggle for equity and balance among its disparate classes. Amado's heroine rejects binary choices, and, in true Brazilian fashion, reaffirms the pleasure of unsolvable situations. Here ambiguity and sexual pleasure represent positive cultural values that, in another culture, would be seen entirely differently. Flor also represents the flexibility of crossing the boundaries between "house" and "street" which DaMatta describes as Brazil's way of mediating between the realms of the personal and the public.

Seen as an allegory for national identity, *Dona Flor* also evokes the hybrid aspects of Brazilian society and the sense of compromise needed for Brazil to ally the popular with the elite.

*Tent of Miracles* is undoubtedly one of Amado's most incisive treatments of racism in Brazil. Accused of being a racist because of his use of the term "racial democracy" in the novel's reference to the racial hybridity rampant in Bahia and the rest of the nation, Amado counteracts this view via the story of Pedro Archanjo, a self-taught anthropologist and bon vivant who documents and champions Brazil's racial admixture, much to the anger of white supremacists who, in the early part of the twentieth century, still believed in superior and inferior races. He publishes his studies with his friend's printing press, housed in the Tent of Miracles, where the devout come to order miracle pictures as a manifestation of their gratitude for having their prayers answered. Archanjo, the embodiment of a divine messenger as indicated by his family name and his nickname, the "Eyes of God," spreads the word about the positive values of racial mixture across all classes. In this novel, Amado makes a distinction between biological racial mixture and class discrimination, the former being irrefutable and the latter reflecting culturally rooted prejudices. How else can the reader reconcile Amado's detailed description of racial bigotry and repression in this novel with his claim of "racial democracy"?

Criticisms of Amado for racial stereotyping are unfounded, for in this novel he clearly deconstructs racial discrimination and prejudice, providing a historical panorama of this theme from the mid-nineteenth century to the late 1960s. The work's sense of history, via its temporal structure, points to Amado's condemnation of a recurring paradigm of racial oppression and violent political and religious repression. Amado's allegorical treatment of these issues also reveals how he reports the historical truth during intense periods of censorship and repression. In fact, the novel ends with a contemporary (late 1960s) Carnival *afoxé* (ritual procession), paying homage to Archanjo as an affirmation of racial and cultural admixture as well as a statement on freedom and survival during one of Brazil's darkest moments of political repression. Amado's awareness of the volatility of the term "racial democracy" and his repeated use of it reflect his attempt to call attention to its subversive character in an authoritarian society. The novel also allegorically unmasks the state's dishonest use of this term to project a positive international image of Brazil, which in fact was a smoke screen for concealing the absence of racial and sociopolitical equality. In this case, Amado uncovers the hypocritical contradiction between image and reality while using Afro-Brazilian cultural myths to move his readers. This novel also confirms Amado as a master storyteller, because his deft use of an unreliable as well as an omniscient narrator reflects the author's sophisticated use of point of view and the subsequent double perspective inherent in the novel's allegorical implications.

*Tereza Batista, cansada de guerra* (1972; *Tereza Batista, Home from the Wars*, 1975) has generated considerable criticism and polemics about Amado's supposed sexism as well as his depiction of women and popular culture. Seemingly a romanticized tale about a prostitute abused by a series of brutal men, this novel dramatizes the double standard for men and women by giving voice and action to a subaltern woman within a patriarchy and in turn critically disclosing the patriarchal need to dominate women. The novel is structured into five humorously ironic episodes told by thirteen narrators, each with a different perspective on Tereza's survival. Tereza is seen first as an abused sexual "slave," then as a concubine, and finally as a prostitute and dancer whose reputation as a legendary heroine or warrior maiden is later reinforced by her heroic leadership in combating a smallpox epidemic and leading a prostitutes' strike.

Framed in the style of the *cordel folhetos* (chapbooks of verse) which create hyperbolic mythic figures, Tereza represents a modern-day legend whose exaggerated exploits symbolize the struggles of the poor, mulatto women, prostitutes, and other marginal figures in society. Harsh criticism of this novel stems from its graphic sexual scenes, evoking titillating pornography according to some readers, from its so-called romanticized poverty, and ultimately from Tereza's final and total submission to the love-of-her-life sailor who once saved her. In the view of some feminists, Tereza is not a symbol of female empowerment, especially since the use of the *cordel* romance suggests a mythic and not a

mimetic treatment, thereby diminishing her status as a model, modern-day heroine. Along these lines, the idea of empowerment is further undermined by the description of Tereza's conventional womanliness, which repeatedly overrides her image as a warrior heroine. Critics have also pointed to the authorial narrator's manipulation of point of view as an indication of an ambivalence toward the figure of the female warrior. Moreover, Amado's caricature treatment of female mulattos and good-hearted prostitutes has been interpreted as more of a projection of a white male ego than a depiction of the real world. In reaction to such critical statements, the reader may question to what extent the author's use of intentional irony has been effective in deconstructing the transgressions of patriarchy. Similarly, Amado's overt ironic treatment of the masses and populism goes a long way to dispel accusations of his naïve sentimentality and neo-Romantic perspective on poverty and underdevelopment. The reader may then wonder if the same ironic stance can also be applied to Amado's treatment of women under patriarchy.

*Tieta the Goat Girl* is a comic novel about another prostitute heroine who as a young girl is banished from her home because of her promiscuity; she then goes to São Paulo where she eventually becomes the owner of one of the city's best bordellos. As in *Tereza*, this novel is episodic, but here the reader is faced with just one narrator who recounts the tale of Tieta, a street-smart and country-shrewd heroine who returns from the big city to her hometown of Agreste after her lover has died. There she is welcomed back because her insensitive family believes she is now rich and respectable. She gains almost saintly status in the small town because she uses her connections to bring electricity to Agreste and to block the establishment of a titanium dioxide plant that a group of greedy entrepreneurs is planning to build. Amado juxtaposes the heroine's inherent rural skills with her urban savvy again to contrast Brazil's poor masses with its economic elites by having each group cultivate the wrong impressions about the other. This novel becomes another Amadian tour de force of humor and social commentary.

*Farda, fardão, camisola de dormir* (1979; *Pen, Sword and Camisole*, 1985) represents a different vehicle for Amado, because he stages this novel in Rio de Janeiro within a small community of intellectuals. They are strategizing to fill a vacancy in the Brazilian Academy of Letters in the face of pressure from a fascist candidate who represents the political and intellectual climate of the 1940s during World War II. Turning away from his previous settings, which have been primarily centered around Bahia and the Brazilian northeast, Amado presents a picture of European pro-fascism in Brazil that is historically valid. Another difference rests with the absence of the novel's hero, the poet Bruno, who dies at the beginning and thus creates an unexpected vacancy. Interestingly, the story revolves around a few old literary figures who wage a cultural and literary war against an avalanche of Nazi and Brazilian fascist authoritarianism and who are ultimately victorious. As an homage to the power and importance of culture and literature, the novel manifests this paean with the following moral refrain: "It is always possible to plant a seed, to kindle a hope." As a sensual love story with a political background, this novel becomes another version of Amado's condemnation of the abuses of the political bourgeoisie.

*Tocaia Grande: A face obscura* (1984; *Showdown*, 1988) is a frontier novel, very much in the vein of *The Violent Land* and *Gabriela* but taking place chronologically between the scenarios of the other two novels. With its epic structure, *Showdown* is narrated by an unidentified voice who tells the dark historical side of the transition of a settlement from a mule-train stop to a burgeoning city. As a type of revisionist history, the unofficial version that is not told in the press or in history books, this novel narrates the brutality, vengeance, and adventures of people living in a dangerous place at a dangerous time. The story begins with a violent ambush engineered by one of the protagonists, Capitão Natário, and concludes with his lying in wait to make another attack, which will be his last. As a haunting saga with a series of humorous, engaging, and unforgettable characters, *Showdown* is situated in the Bahian cacao region and becomes the site of the development of a community where honor and courage were the law, very much like the American Western frontier. Delving into the intimate thoughts of its many characters, this novel evokes Amado's childhood contact with figures such as murderers, adventurers, prostitutes, migrant workers, fugitives, and ethnics. One of the funny secondary stories involves a *turco* (Turk),

Fadul Abdala, actually a Christian Lebanese who finds himself to be an outsider attempting to read the many hidden codes of a new culture. In his pursuit of love and money, Fadul is seen as less assimilated than Nacib of *Gabriela* and very similar to some of the Arabs who populate his 1994 novel, *A Descoberta da América pelos Turcos* (The discovery of America by the Turks), in which he deals more directly with cross-cultural issues.

*The War of the Saints* is an exuberant story of overt racial and religious discrimination by authoritarians during the early period of the military dictatorship (1964–1985). It is Amado's most blatantly critical view of that period: "Recorde—se que os fatos narrados nesta crônica, pobre de brilbo, ríca de veracidade, se passaran nos piores anos da dictadura militar e da rígida censura à imprensa. Havia uma realidade oculta, um país secreto, não noticiados" (*Sumiço*; Let it be remembered that events narrated in this chronicle—full of veracity, albeit lacking in brilliance—took place during the worst years of the military dictatorship and the most rigid censorship of the press. There was a hidden reality, a secret country that didn't get into the news). Along the same lines, the metafictional narrator reveals how the repressed Afro-Brazilian population is eventually sensitized to racial consciousness and political mobilization, a reality that has evolved gradually since the mid 1970s. The authorial narrator's Afro-Brazilian ethics also address the injustices incurred by the political and economic authorities of the establishment and show how a minority culture, with its vibrancy and magic, can challenge powerful, institutionalized discourses. The story begins with a holy statue of St. Barbara of Thunder, also known as the Afro-Brazilian Iansã. The statue is being transported by boat from the parish of Santo Amaro in order to participate in the religious art exhibit at the Sacred Art Museum of Bahia, whose director is the German friar, Dom Maximiliano von Gruden. However, while the boat is docking, a miracle occurs: the Saint comes to life and blends in with the populace. The statue's significance lies not only in her African attributes, but also in the possibility that it is the creation of the famous eighteenth-century mulatto sculptor, Aleijadinho. Of course, this interpretation by the Director goes contrary to official opinion, which he hopes to dispel with the exhibit and his research book, thereby attesting to the richness of the too often neglected Afro-Brazilian heritage. The disappearance of the Saint, the reader learns, is due to the goddess's mission to make Adalgisa and her niece Manela, both mulattos, embrace their African culture. The former, a rigid, prudish, repressive, and intransigent Christian, wants nothing to do with Afro-Brazilian religious rituals and prevents her beautiful niece from associating with that culture. Adalgisa also tries to break up Manela's relationship with her mulatto boyfriend, Miro. When Adalgisa has Manela locked up in a convent to "cure" her, the Saint steps in, and, along with others from the community, fights for Manela's freedom. This is the war of the title, which also symbolizes the cultural wars between the intellectual elite and the Afro-Brazilian population.

While this story focuses primarily upon religious, racial, and cultural persecution, it also is in Amadian fashion a love story about sexual repression and macho brutality. Adalgisa's husband, Danilo, in his prime a renowned soccer player, is frustrated because, since his brutal behavior on their honeymoon, his wife rejects his sexual advances. Consequently he must frequent brothels in order to satisfy his desires. Although Danilo is drawn as a sympathetic figure in contrast to his shrewish wife, the narrator nonetheless points to Danilo's faults as a sexual glutton who is insensitive to his bride's virginity and inexperience. Here, the reader has another opportunity to witness Amado's critical depiction of the treatment of women in a patriarchal society: "Objetos de prazer, vítimas dos dogmas puritanos e da violência machista (*Sumiço*; Objects of pleasure, they are victims of puritanical dogmas and macho violence). Simultaneously, the self-deprecating authorial narrator incarnates machismo, using graphic, bawdy, and crude language in reference to sex. In so doing, Amado points to the endurance of the patriarchal, macho mindset, even though the narrator criticizes Danilo for being as rough and rash as a rapist on his honeymoon. Furthermore, the narrator shows how some female characters do possess sexual agency and equality in terms of physical pleasure. The paradoxical views of the narrator give another example of how ambiguity surfaces as a cultural paradigm. While the "enlightened" narrator criticizes the machismo in others, he may not possess sufficient insight to see it in himself.

If the behavior of Amado's characters appears irrational to some readers, it nevertheless reveals the predominance of a Dionysian stance, one that often transgresses the line of good taste in its desire to celebrate the joy of sex and living while at the same time disturbing the oppressive canonical social codes that often reign supreme. Here, Mikhail Bakhtin's concept of "carnivalization" can serve as a useful interpretative tool. As a celebration of racial admixture and "impurity" that advocates the hybrid advantages of cross-cultural practices, this novel honors mixture and ambiguity with a description that succinctly captures Amado's overall ethos and aesthetics: "esta terra da Bahia . . . Terra onde tudo se mistura e se confunde, ninguén é capaz de separar a vírtude do pecado, de destingúir entre o certo e o absurdo, traçar os limites entre a exatidão e o embuste, entre a realidade e o sonho" (*Sumiço*; the land of Bahia . . . where everything is intermixed and commingled, where no one can separate virtue from sin, or distinguish the certain from the absurd, or draw the line between truth and trickery, between reality and fantasy).

*Navegação de cabotagem* (1992; Coastal navigation), subtitled "Notes for Memoirs I'll Never Write" is a tour de force, a pseudo-autobiography of 600-plus pages in which Amado documents his literary, social, and political life of travel and writing. A significant work for understanding Amado as a writer and, above all, as a jovial, courageous, committed, and roguish character, this "memoir" is unusual because it is written in a non-chronological manner, not as an evolving recollection of the self. Consequently, the reader must reconstruct his or her image of Jorge Amado as a Brazilian and as a writer. The idea for this book came to Amado in 1986, when he and his wife were in New York to attend a PEN club event and both came down with pneumonia. Written in Paris between 1991 and 1992, the book is a series of vignettes or chronicles (*crônicas*) about travels, encounters and events that occurred during his trips and residencies in Brazil and abroad. On the surface these chronicles give the appearance of merely being a work of travel literature. However, while travel literature focuses upon places and experiences, as this work does, *Navegação* is very much an autobiography because, above all, it exposes the traveler himself. In revealing Amado's point of view as a writer, socialist, humanitarian, and *malandro* (rogue), this memoir projects an illuminating picture of the peripatetic Bahian writer as well as providing an opportunity for readers to glean another cultural context for understanding the universal and regional breadth and significance of his life and work.

Amado relates the events in the order he remembers each one, a structure which provides the reader with a simultaneous present/past temporal mode that enriches the memorialist's perspective. Interestingly, this construct shows Amado turning eighty years old while recording the major events of the twentieth century in Brazil and in the world, especially at the time of the collapse of Soviet communism. It is his ironic view of that historical happening which offers readers insights into Amado's glib disenchantment with Soviet communism and his enduring socialism. *Navegação* also provides an exciting account of Amado's relationship with the Soviet Union, where he made unforgettable friends such as Ilya Ehrenburg, who, along with Amado, had no illusions about the chauvinism of Soviet communism even before its collapse. For example, in a chronicle dated 1953 he refers to the Soviet prejudice against the Jews. In fact, Amado repeatedly takes to task party xenophobic attitudes by telling various anecdotes to ridicule the hyperbolic superlatives made by Russian communists.

The humor in this volume is rampant, and reveals Amado's playful proclivities, such as using the names of friends and real people for his fictional characters or mocking the international intelligentsia who presumably have no real contact with the "people" and who denigrate those who transgress the taboo of referring to television in the same context as high culture. Amado also relives his friendship in the 1930s, 1940s, and 1950s with such famous artists and writers as Pablo Neruda, Picasso, Sartre, Simone de Beauvoir, Lasar Sagall, and Ilya Ehrenburg. He also refers to his encounters with John Dos Passos in 1937 (*Cabotagem*) and the latter's unsentimental acknowledgment of his Portuguese heritage and his insistence that he is an American from Chicago, and with Aimé Césaire who, along with Leopoldo Senghors, Nicolás Guillén, the singers Dorival Caymmi and Gilberto Gil, and others, symbolize unquestionable "mulattery," be it in their creative works or in the originality of their cross-cultural selves.

Never losing an opportunity to speak of Brazilian hybridity, Amado repeatedly makes statements such as the following: "Brasil, país latino? Somos latinos, nós brasileiros? Uma espécie rara de latinos, a verdade é que somos mestiços, mulatos mais brancos ou mais negros, da cor de cobre dos índios" (Brazil, a Latin country? Are we Brazilians Latins? A rare species of Latins, for in truth we are mestizos, mulattos, more white or more black, like the copper tone of Indians). He also extols the originality of Brazil's humorists, who he believes translate via their comic routines and funny personages the unity and multiplicity of Brazil. One of the most touching aspects of the book is its depiction of the profound love relationship between Amado and his wife, thereby showing Amado to be more than an occasional romantic. Above all, *Navegação* enables the reader to confirm Amado's position on a number of issues such as censorship, political freedom, the power of literature, the paradoxes within the Brazilian character, and most importantly his condemnation of racism and his praise for the virtues of Afro-Brazilian culture.

*A Descoberta da América pelos Turcos* (1994, The discovery of America by the Turks), labeled a *romancinho*, a small novel, is perhaps Amado's most comic work. It begins with a "Rondó das bucetas" (The rondeau of pussies), setting the stage for a long joke about the discovery of America by the Turks, an absurd possibility but one that reminds the modern reader that as ethnics and immigrants, the *turcos* (translated as Turks, but in Brazil it is an erroneous name given to Arabs and Syrians) experienced the same sense of wonder and alienation as the first discoverers. Originally written for the quincentenary celebration (1492–1992) and commissioned in 1991 by an Italian state public relations firm for a volume (never published) of stories dramatizing the "encounter" between the Old and the New World, *A Descoberta* was completed before *Navegação* and interestingly only appeared in Brazil after having been published in French and Turkish translations. With its dirty joke frame and bawdy theme of sexual "conquest" taking place in the interior of Bahia during the early 1900s, Amado challenges the historical accounts of those who first "discovered" the New Land by telling his account of the Arabic "discovery/encounter" and conquest of the then virgin territory, symbolized by the Bahian backlands and "untouched" women. Inspired by characters from his novel *Showdown*, this novella stages a very sensual and telluric New World encounter, one that ridicules the "noble" accounts by European chroniclers. In sexual, sociohistorical, and geographic terms, Amado also evokes the polemics surrounding the 1992 commemoration of the Conquest as well as the true racial composition of the Brazilian people. Again, as a deft storyteller Amado challenges fixed notions of a single national identity while at the same time referring to the chronic authoritarian roots that have been implanted since 1500.

The anonymous narrator, a Brazilian mestizo who considers himself to be a product of the discovery since he embodies racial and cultural mixture, nevertheless criticizes early on the concept of conquest by mentioning the history of massacred Indians, enslaved blacks, and the many cultures that were abolished by mercenaries and by missionaries defending Christ. As a balance, the narrator ends the first chapter by praising the modern day amalgamation of Brazilians, Jews, Turks (really Arabs, Syrians, or Lebanese), and others. In so doing he depicts Brazil as an ethnic, cultural, and racial democracy, reaffirming Amado's defense of mestizo culture and hybridity. Told in nineteen short, fast-paced chapters, with black and white illustrations based upon classical paintings from the *Rubáiyat*, this narrative tells the tale of the betrothal of Adma, the ugly, elder daughter of Ibrahim Jafet. Adma is a morally righteous virgin who is driving her irresponsible father crazy. By marrying off Adma, Ibrahim expects to solve his problems. This is really a tropical *Taming of the Shrew* with a different cast of very funny and colorful characters. With emphasis upon sexual conquest, Amado makes a parody of patriarchy and machismo. Furthermore, the narrator's graphic description of Adma's surprising sexual gifts, seen as miraculous divine intervention by Jehovah *and* Allah, extends the joke with a detailed description that is sure to raise questions about Amado's sexist treatment of women. Ultimately the novel celebrates the mixture of Arab and Brazilian cultures within the New World context of syncretism and hybridity, as it is seen in customs, religion, language, food, and even literature, an example of which is the text itself.

During the 1990s Jorge Amado received many awards of recognition: honorary doctorates from such universities as Padua and Bari in Italy, as well as seminars dedicated to his work, such as at the Free University of Berlin, an exposition and seminar at the Georges Pompidou Center in France, and the Camões Prize from Portugal. In 1992 a series of events organized to celebrate his eightieth birthday, culminated in the book, *Jorge Amado: 80 Anos de Vida e Obra* (Jorge Amado: 80 years of life and work), published by the Fundação Casa de Jorge Amado. In 1996 the whole of Brazil paid close attention as Jorge Amado underwent a successful angioplasty operation. In 1997 his novel, *Tieta, the Goat Girl*, was selected as the theme for the Carnival celebrations in Bahia. On that Carnival Sunday, in homage to the writer, the *bloco* (carnival club) dance group "Friends of Jorge Amado" paraded in the streets, led by the famous singer and composer, Caetano Veloso. New editions of his novels, juvenile literature, biographies, plays, and travel guides continue to be published, along with new translations, documentaries, a CD-ROM, and film, theater, and television adaptations of his fiction.

Jorge Amado died in his Bahian home on 6 August 2001, four days prior to his eighty-ninth birthday. Weeks earlier he had been hospitalized for hyperglycemia, diabetes, and heart problems, which left him comatose for a brief period. Health problems had plagued the author since 1993, when he suffered a heart attack, which was followed by an angioplasty in 1996 and the insertion of a pacemaker in 1997. During his last years, Amado experienced bouts of depression due to his inability to read, caused by increasing failure of his eyesight. On the day that he died, Amado's body was taken to the sumptuous Bahian Palácio de Acalamação, where he lay in state until 7 August. During the wake, many artists and politicians arrived, paying words of homage to the famous writer. Included among them were former President José Sarney, the writer João Ubaldo Ribeiro, and Caetano Veloso. A large funeral cortege of thousands, along with his wife, Zélia Gattai, his two children, João Jorge and Paloma, then accompanied his body to the cemetery Jardin da

Saudade, where it was cremated. Amado's ashes were scattered under a mango tree planted in the backyard of his home. According to newspaper reports, Zélia Gattai, a writer in her own right, may eventually be elected to take her husband's seat in the Brazilian Academy of Letters. If this were to occur, it would be the perfect testament to Zélia and to the eternal love expressed by Jorge Amado in a 1993 interview: "My ideal happiness is my wife, Zélia."

In assessing Jorge Amado's impact upon Brazilian letters, recent studies by literary and anthropological scholars underscore the need to consider the author as an important postcolonial voice because of his early interest in dramatizing and problematizing the question of a single national identity in Brazil by calling attention to the cultural exclusion of subalterns and minorities. Amado's focus upon Afro-Braziliana points out not only its unique and rich culture, but also its roots in the colonial experience. It is therefore important to read his works within the postcolonial mindset and to avoid the impulse to critique his work according to the bourgeois values and expectations of other cultures. While some criticism has even interpreted his later work as postmodernist, due to Amado's use of pastiche in terms of multiple plots, structures, styles, and discourses, it is also important to recall that he had been applying these techniques since the 1950s and before. What remains clear is the significance of perceiving the multiple dimensions of his work and acknowledging his deft storytelling voice and techniques. As a final note on an evaluation of his work, Amado himself provided an oblique and ironic commentary, almost as an epilogue or postscript in *The War of the Saints,* using the voice of this novel's self-deprecating authorial narrator. The irony in the following statement rests with the fact that Amado has indeed manifested more literary sophistication than is acknowledged by critics: "É notória a incapacidade do Autor de renovar e de inovar" (*Sumiço*; The author's own inability to renovate or innovate is notorious). The narrator then confesses his main objectives, not unlike Amado's: "de levar a cabo o compromisao de contar para divertir e, divertindo, se ele próprio, mudar os termos do teorema e molhorar o mundo" (*Sumiço*; to fulfill his duties by telling a tale to amuse, and by amusing

himself, to change the terms of the theorem and better the world). Furthermore, the following roguish comment by this authorial narrator is reminiscent of Amado's own response to unenlightened critics: "Ineqaual audácia de um Autor, velho de idade e de batalhas perdidas, que ainda não conseguin levar a crítica a se esporrar de gozo com a lectura de seus cartapácios, de linguagen escassa, vazios de idéias, populacheiros" (*Sumiço*; It is the undeniable audacity of an author on in years, a veteran of lost battles, who has yet to bring literary critics to an orgasm of pleasure as they read his manuscripts, deficient in expression, devoid of ideas, plebeian). On the contrary, as a provocative, prolific, courageous, and insightful Brazilian author, Jorge Amado indeed stands as one of the most expressive and unique representatives of Brazilian and Latin American literature.

# SELECTED BIBLIOGRAPHY

## *Primary Works*

### Novels

*O país do carnaval.* Rio de Janeiro: Schmidt, 1931.

*Cacau.* Rio de Janeiro: Ariel, 1933.

*Suor.* Rio de Janeiro: Ariel, 1934.

*Jubiabá.* Rio de Janeiro: José Olympio, 1935.

*Mar Morto.* Rio de Janeiro: José Olympio, 1936.

*Capitães da areia.* Rio de Janeiro: José Olympio, 1937.

*Terras do sem fim.* São Paulo: Martins, 1943.

*São Jorge dos Ilhéus.* São Paulo: Martins, 1944.

*Seara vermelha.* São Paulo: Martins, 1946.

*Os subterrâneos da liberdade.* São Paulo: Martins, 1954.

*Gabriela, cravo e canela.* São Paulo: Martins, 1958.

*Os velhos marinheiros.* São Paulo: Martins, 1961.

*Os pastores da noite.* São Paulo: Martins, 1964.

*Dona Flor e seus dois maridos.* São Paulo: Martins, 1966.

*Tenda dos milagres.* São Paulo: Martins, 1969.

*Tereza Batista, cansada de guerra.* São Paulo: Martins, 1972.

*Tieta do Agreste, pastora de cabras.* Rio de Janeiro: Record, 1977.

*Farda, fardão, camisola de dormir.* Rio de Janeiro: Record, 1979.

*Tocaia Grande: A face obscura.* Rio de Janeiro: Record, 1984.

*O Sumiço da santa: Uma história de feitiçaria.* Rio de Janeiro: Record, 1988.

*A Descoberta da América pelos Turcos.* Rio de Janeiro: Record, 1994.

*O Compadre de Ogun: Um história de 'Os pastores da noite.'* Rio de Janeiro: Record, 1995.

### Other Works

*A Estrada do mar.* Estância, Brazil: Tipografia Popular, 1938. (Poetry.)

*ABC de Castro Alves.* São Paulo: Martins, 1941. (Biography.)

*O Cavaleiro da esperança.* São Paulo: Martins, 1945. (Biography.)

*Bahia de todos os santos.* São Paulo, 1942. (Travel guide.)

*Vida de Luiz Carlos Prestes: El caballero de la esperanza.* Trad. Pompeu de Accioly Borges. Buenos Aires: Claridad, 1942.

"História do Carnaval." In *Antologia do carnaval.* Rio de Janeiro: Cruzeiro, 1945. (Story.)

*O amor do soldado.* Rio de Janeiro: Editora do Povo, 1947. (Play.)

*O mundo da paz.* Rio de Janeiro: Editorial Vitória, 1951. (Travel memoir.)

"As mortes e o Triunfo de Rosalinda." In *Os dez mandamentos.* Rio de Janeiro: Civilizaçad Brazileira, 1965. (Story.)

*O gato malhado e a andorinha sinhá.* Rio de Janeiro: Record, 1976. (Children's literature.)

"O Milagre dos Pássaros." Salvador: Banco Econômico, 1979. (Story.)

*O menino grapiúna.* Rio de Janeiro: Record, 1981. (Memoir.)

"O episódio de Siroca." In *Playboy.* São Paulo, 1982. (Story.)

*A Bola e o Goleiro.* Rio de Janeiro: Record, 1984. (Children's literature.)

"De Como o Mulato Porciúnculo Descarregou o Seu Defunto." Rio de Janeiro: Civilizaçad Brasileira Dez, 1989. (Story.)

*Navegação de cabotagem: Apontamentos para um livro de memórias que jamais escreverei.* Rio de Janeiro: Record, 1992. (Memoir.)

*Rua Alagoinhas 33, Rio Vermelho: A casa de Zélia e Jorge Amado.* Salvador: Fundaçáo Casa de Jorge Amado, 1999. (Personal essay.)

### Translations

*Slums.* Trans. by Ann Martin. New York: New America, 1938.

*Gabriela, Clove and Cinnamon.* Trans. by William L. Grossman and James L. Taylor. New York: Alfred A. Knopf, 1962.

*Home Is the Sailor.* Trans. by Harriet de Onís. New York: Alfred A. Knopf, 1964.

*The Two Deaths of Quincas Wateryell.* Trans. by Barbara Shelby (Merello). New York: Alfred A. Knopf, 1965.

*The Violent Land.* Trans. by Samuel Putnam. New York: Alfred A. Knopf, 1945. Reprint, 1965.

*Shepherds of the Night.* Trans. by Harriet de Onís. New York: Alfred A. Knopf, 1966.

*Dona Flor and Her Two Husbands.* Trans. by Harriet de Onís. New York: Alfred A. Knopf, 1969.

*Tent of Miracles.* Trans. by Barbara Shelby (Merello). New York: Alfred A. Knopf, 1971.

*Tereza Batista, Home from the Wars.* Trans. by Barbara Shelby (Merello). New York: Alfred A. Knopf, 1975.

*Tieta, the Goat Girl.* Trans. by Barbara Shelby Merello. New York: Alfred A. Knopf, 1979.

*The Swallow and the Tomcat: A Love Story.* Trans. by Barbara Shelby Merello. New York: Delacorte Press, 1982.

*Jubiabá.* Trans. by Margaret A. Neves. New York: Avon Books, 1984.

*Sea of Death.* Trans. by Gregory Rabassa. New York: Avon Books, 1984.

*Pen, Sword, Camisole.* Trans. by Helen R. Lane. Boston: David R. Godine, 1985.

*Captains of the Sands.* Trans. by Gregory Rabassa. New York: Avon Books, 1988.

*Showdown.* Trans. by Gregory Rabassa. New York: Bantam Books, 1988.

*The Golden Harvest.* Trans. by Clifford E. Landers. New York: Avon Books, 1992

"Sailing the Shore: Notes for Memoirs I'll Never Write." Trans. by Alfred Mac Adam. *Review: Latin American Literature and Arts* 47:32–38 (fall 1993).

*The War of the Saints.* Trans. by Gregory Rabassa. New York: Bantam Books, 1993.

### Secondary Works

#### Critical and Biographical Studies

Almeida, Alfredo Wagner Berno de. *Jorge Amado: Política e Literatura.* Rio de Janeiro: Campus, 1979.

Baden, Nancy T. "Jorge Amado: Storyteller of Bahia." Ph.D. diss., University of California, Los Angeles, 1971.

———. "The Significance of Names in Jorge Amado's *Gabriela, cravo e canela.*" *Proceedings of the Pacific Coast Council on Latin American Studies.* 3:87–94 (1974).

———. "Popular Poetry in the Novels of Jorge Amado." *Journal of Latin American Lore* 2, no. 1:3–22 (1976).

Batista, Juarez da Gama. *Gabriela: Seu cravo e sua canela*. Rio de Janeiro: Ministério da Educaçad e Cultura, 1964.

Bernard, Judith. "Narrative Focus in Jorge Amado's Story of Vasco Moscoso de Aragão." *Romance Notes* 8, no. 1:14–17 (1966).

Brookshaw, David. "Jorge Amado: Populismo e Preconceito." In his *Raça e Cor na Literatura Brasileira*. Porto Alegre: Mercado Aberto, 1983. Pp. 131–136.

Brower, Keith H., Earl E. Fitz, and Enrique Martínez-Vidal, eds. *Jorge Amado: New Critical Essays*. New York: Routledge, 2001.

Bruno, Haroldo. "O Sentido da Terra na Obra de Jorge Amado." In his *Estudos de Literatura Brasileira*. Rio de Janeiro: O Cruzeiro, 1957. Pp. 121–134.

Cerqueira, Nelson. *A Política do Partido Comunista e a Questão do Realismo em Jorge Amado*. Salvador: Fundação Casa de Jorge Amado, 1988.

Chamberlain, Bobby J. "Humor: Vehicle for Social Commentary in the Novels of Jorge Amado." Ph.D. diss., University of California, Los Angeles, 1975.

———. *Jorge Amado*. Boston: Twayne Publishers/G. K. Hall, 1990.

———. "The *Malandro*, or Rogue Figure, in the Fiction of Jorge Amado." *Mester* 6:7–10 (1976).

———. "Double Perspective in Two Works of Jorge Amado." *Estudios Iberoamericanos* 4:81–88 (1978).

Coluccio, Félix. "Lo Folklórico en la Obra Literaria de Jorge Amado." *Folklore Americano* 49:19–40 (1990).

Curran, Mark J. *Jorge Amado e a Literatura de Cordel*. Salvador: Fundação Cultural do Estado da Bahia; Fundação Casa de Rui Barbosa, 1981.

Dimmick, Ralph Edward. "The Brazilian Literary Generation of 1930." *Hispania* 34, no. 2:181–187 (1951).

Duarte, Eduardo de Assis. *Jorge Amado: Romance em Tempo de Utopia*. Natal: UFRN, Editora Universitária, 1995.

Ellison, Fred P. *Brazil's New Novel*. Berkeley: University of California Press, 1954.

———. "Social Symbols in Some Recent Brazilian Literature. *Texas Quarterly* 3:112–125 (1960).

Fitz, Earl E. "The Problem of the Unreliable Narrator in Jorge Amado's *Tenda dos Milagres*." *Romance Quarterly* 30:3, 311–321 (1983).

Franceschi, Antonio Fernando de, ed. *Jorge Amado: Cadernos de Literatura Brasileira*. No. 3. São Paulo: Instituto Moreira Salles, 1997.

Galvão, Walnice Nogueira. "Amado: Respeitoso, respeitável." In *Saco de gatos: Ensaios críticos*. São Paulo: Duas Cidades, 1976. Pp. 13–22.

Gomes, Alvaro Cardos. *Jorge Amado: Seleção de Textos, Notas, Estudos Histórico e Crítico e Exercícios*. São Paulo: Abril Educação, 1981.

Hall, Linda B. "Jorge Amado: Women, Love, and Possession." *Southwest Review* 68:1, 67–77 (winter 1983).

Hamilton, Russell G. "Afro-Brazilian Cults in the Novels of Jorge Amado." *Hispania* 50, no. 2:242–252 (1967).

*Jorge Amado: Documentos*. Lisbon, 1964.

*Jorge Amado: Ensaios Sobre o Escritor*. Salvador: Universidade Federal da Bahia, 1982.

*Jorge Amado, Km 70*. Special issue of *Tempo Brasileiro* 74 (1983).

Lepecki, Maria Lúcia. "Morrer no Mar." In *Jorge Amado: Ricette Narrative*. Edited by Lanciani Giulia. Rome: Bulzoni, 1994. Pp. 49–75.

Lima, Joelma Varão. *A Mulher na Obra de Jorge Amado*. Master's thesis in history. São Paulo: Pontifícia Universidade Católica, 1994.

Lima, Luís Costa. "Jorge Amado." In *A Literatura no Brasil* 5. Edited by Afrânio Coutinho. 2d ed., Rio de Janeiro: Sul Americana, 1970. Pp. 304–326.

Losada, Basilio. "Jorge Amado Ya Tiene Premio." *Quimera* 129:18–21 (1995).

Manzatto, Antonio. *Teologia e Literatura: Uma reflexão Teológica a Partir da Antropologia Contida nos Romances de Jorge Amado*. São Paulo: Martins, 1994.

Martins, José de Barros et al. *Jorge Amado, Povo e Terra: Quarenta Anos de Literatura*. São Paulo: Martins, 1972.

———. *Jorge Amado: Trinta Anos de Literatura*. São Paulo: Martins, 1961.

Martins, Wilson. "Jorge Amado." In *The Modernist Idea: A Critical Survey of Brazilian Writing in the 20th Century*. Trans. by Jack E. Tomlins. New York: Greenwood Publishing, 1970. Pp. 289–293.

Mazzara, Richard A. "Poetry and Progress in Jorge Amado's *Gabriela, cravo e canela*." *Hispania* 46, no. 3:551–556 (1963).

Merquior, José Guilherme. "Nosso Dickens." In *Elixir do Apocalipse*. Rio de Janeiro: Nova Fronteira, 1983. Pp. 178–181.

Nunes, Maria L. "The Preservation of African Culture in Brazilian Literature: The Novels of Jorge Amado." *Luso-Brazilian Review* 10, no. 1:86–101 (1973).

Paes, José Paulo. *De 'Cacau' a 'Gabriela': Um Percurso Pastoral*. Salvador: Fundação Casa de Jorge Amado, 1991.

Patai, Daphne. "Jorge Amado's Heroines and the Ideological Double Standard." *New Scholar: An Americanist Review* 8, nos. 1–2:257–266 (1982).

Perez, Renard. *Escritores Brasileiros Contemporâneos*. Rio de Janeiro: Civilizaçad Brasileiro, 1960.

Picchio, Luciana Stegagno. "Cacau de Jorge Amado: Notes pour l'Histoire d'un Succes Litteraire." *Europe: Revue Litteraire Mensuelle* 67:724–731 (August–September 1989).

Portella, Eduardo. *Dimensões I*. Rio de Janeiro: Ediçóes Tempo Brasileiro, 1959.

———. *Dimensões II*. Rio de Janeiro: Ediçóes Tempo Brasileiro, 1959.

———. *Dimensões III*. Rio de Janeiro: Ediçóes Tempo Brasileiro, 1965.

Putnam, Samuel. "The Brazilian Social Novel, 1935–1940." *Inter-American Quarterly* 2:5–12 (1940).

Rabassa, Gregory. "The Five Faces of Love in Jorge Amado's Bahian Novels." *Revista de Letras* 4:94–103 (1963).

Raddatz, Fritz. "Ich träume von einer Revolution ohne Ideologie." Trans. by Len Cagle. *Die Zeit* 36:45–46 (2 September 1994). (Interview.)

Raillard, Alice. *Conversando con Jorge Amado*. Trans. by Annie Dymetman. Rio de Janeiro: Record, 1990.

Rocha, Carlos Eduardo da. *Comemoração: Jorge Amado 80 Anos*. Salvador, Conselho Estadual de Cultura, 1995.

Roche, Jean. *Jorge Bem/Mal Amado*. São Paulo: Cultrix, 1987.

Rubim, Rosane e Carneiro Maried. *Jorge Amado: 80 Anos de Vida e Obra—Subsídios para Pesquisa*. Salvador: Fundação Casa de Jorge Amado, 1992.

Russo, David T. "Bahia, Macumba and Afro-Brazilian Culture in Jorge Amado's *Jubiabá*." *Western Review* 6:53–58 (1969).

Sampaio, Aluysio Mendonça. *Jorge Amado, o Romancista*. São Paulo: Maltese, 1996.

Santos, Itazil Benício dos. *Jorge Amado: Retrato Incompleto*. Belo Horizonte, Brazil: Itatiaia, 1961.

Schade, George D. "Three Contemporary Brazilian Novels." *Hispania* 39, no. 4:391–396 (1956).

Silverman, Malcolm N. "An Examination of the Characters in Jorge Amado's *Ciclo da Comédia Baiana*." Ph.D. diss., University of Illinois, Champaign-Urbana, 1971.

———. "Allegory in Two Works of Jorge Amado." *Romance Notes* 13, no. 1:67–70 (1971).

———. "Moral Dilemma in Jorge Amado's *Dona Flor e seus dois maridos*." *Romance Notes* 13, no. 2: 243–249 (1971).

Táti, Miécio. *Estudos e Notas Críticas*. Rio de Janeiro: Ministério da Educaçad e Cultura/Instituto Nacimal do Livro, 1958.

———. *Jorge Amado: Vida e Obra*. Belo Horizonte, Brazil: Itatiaia, 1961.

Tavares, Paulo. *Criaturas de Jorge Amado*. São Paulo: Martins, 1969.

———. *O Baiano Jorge Amado e Sua Obra*. Rio de Janeiro: Record, 1980.

Turner, Doris Jean. "The Poor and 'Social Symbolism': An Examination of Three Novels of Jorge Amado." Ph.D. diss., Saint Louis University, 1967.

Vieira, Nelson H. "Testimonial Fiction and Historical Allegory: Racial and Political Repression in Jorge Amado's Brazil." *Latin American Literary Review* 17, no. 34:6–23 (1989).

———. "Myth and Identity in Short Stories by Jorge Amado." *Studies in Short Fiction*, spring 1986, pp. 25–34.

———. "Tent of Miracles by Jorge Amado." In *Masterplots II*. Edited by Frank N. Magill. Pasadena, Calif.: Salem Press, 1986. Pp. 1578–1582.

Vincent, Jon S. "Jorge Amado: Politics and the Novel." Ph.D. diss., University of New Mexico, 1970.

———. "The Brazilian Novel: Some Paradoxes of Popularity." *Journal of Inter-American Studies and World Affairs* 14, no. 2:183–199 (1972).

———. "Jorge Amado, Jorge Desprezado." *Luso-Brazilian Review* 15 (supplementary issue):11–17 (1978).

Wasserman, Renata R. Mautner. "E a Mágica? A Representação de Realidade Social em Jorge Amado e Gabriel García Márquez." *Revista Iberoamericana* 64:182–183, 171–92 (January–June 1998).

# Oswald de Andrade

## (1890–1954)

### Gilberto Mendonça Teles

In his "Auto Retrato" (Self portrait), published by Mário da Silva Brito in *As metamorfoses de Oswald de Andrade* (1972; The metamorphoses of Oswald de Andrade), José Oswald de Sousa Andrade disclosed what may be viewed as the stylistic mark of his entire oeuvre and the paradox of his life as a writer who seemed to be involved in everything. He rebelled against every type of order, but in his heart he held out a desire and hope—a utopian ideal—for a new, more just, and more humane order. At the end of his four-paragraph autobiography, the writer states:

> *Viajei, fiquei pobre, fiquei rico, casei, enviuvei, casei, divorciei, viajei, casei. . . . Já disse que sou conjugal, gremial e ordeiro. O que não me impediu de ter brigado diversas vezes à portuguesa e tomado parte em algumas batalhas campais. Nem de ter sido preso treze vezes. Tive também grandes fugas por motivos políticos. Tenho três filhos e três netos e sou casado, em últimas núpcias, com Maria Antonieta d'Alkimin. Sou livre-docente de literatura na Faculdade de Filosofia da Universidade de São Paulo.*

I've traveled, gone broke, gotten rich, gotten married, became a widower, gotten married, divorced, traveled, married. . . . I've already said I'm the marrying kind, sociable and orderly. But this did not prevent me from having my share of heated arguments and taking part in a few pitched battles, or from having been thrown in jail thirteen times. I also had to make great escapes for political reasons. I have three children and three grandchildren and I'm married, the last time to Maria Antonieta d'Alkimin. I'm a professor of literature in the School of Arts and Sciences at the University of São Paulo.

His was a life in upheaval, completely devoted to unsatisfactory romantic relationships, literary and political struggles, experimentation and avant-garde movements, and to producing works of poetry, novels, drama, criticism, and polemical writings that marked the cultural transformation of Brazil, which began in 1922, one hundred years after its independence.

The passage cited above is an example of how Oswald de Andrade's avant-garde literary tendencies had their point of departure in his restless personality. This restlessness affected his language—especially his syntax—which became abridged, enumerative, and reductive, as if between the thought and the phrase there was an initial hesitation, a moment of stuttering that caused him to repeat his ideas and concepts. This may explain his inability to assimilate metrical rules or manage any large-scale organization of thought; his delight in brief and consciously prosaic verses, primary phrases, short paragraphs, fragmented chapters; and his tendency to weave the thread of a story through a stream of consciousness that at times is hard to follow.

The writer's life, directly and indirectly, reflects this: he was inconstant in love, with friendships, at work, in his conception of literature, and in his literary production. The paradox lies in his desire to be "the marrying kind, sociable and orderly," and to construct and complete a literary project similar to what he saw Mario de Andrade create, which was the reason for his rivalry and, ultimately, his admiration for the man who wrote *Macunaíma*.

It is difficult, or at least implausible, to imagine a man like Oswald de Andrade (who would die, as he put it, a "sexappealgenarian") reaching the age of 100, just as it is difficult to conceive of an avant-garde literary history in any literature without encountering a contradiction. The early period of any avant-garde movement, such as futurism, cubism, dadaism, and surrealism, is rife with manifestos and contradictions. An avant-garde is always an uncomfortable presence, even though it is at times joyful and transforming. It can be said that there are two avant-gardes: one occurring outside of language, for example, futurism and dadaism; and another, occurring inside, that is silent, and expresses its originality by modifying or recreating traditional poetic structures, as happens with every great writer who breaks away from an old tradition and adds to it new topics and new ways of expression.

Oswald de Andrade, as a man and as a writer, was always a troublesome presence. He constantly opened himself up to new ideas and often burned himself up in his own renewal. His sense of dissatisfaction and inconstancy is apparent in his self-portrait, when he says, stressing the contrast, that he gave "a talk at the Sorbonne and another at the Union of Bakers, Pastry Makers and the like." It appears again in his joking confession: "I've traveled, gone broke, gotten rich, gotten married, became a widower, gotten married, divorced, traveled, married. . . . I've already said I'm the marrying kind, sociable and orderly." He even readily admits that he was thrown in jail thirteen times, but by then, who's counting?

Andrade's life and work are marked by an appreciation of the capriciousness and even the voluptuousness of the new, but a newness that he tried to render exotic in order to be authentically modern, a newness that he tried to make revolutionary in order to change the old aesthetic habits of Brazilian writers and readers of this

century. To achieve this, a boldly controversial challenge to tradition was not enough. He also had to discover an appropriate and effective language, one which would contain new response forces within its very structure. And this is where the work of Oswald de Andrade contributed—and continues to contribute—to the celebration of Brazilian modernity, from his poetry, novels, and drama, through his polemical writings, manifestos.

Seen as a whole, Andrade's work is somewhat protean and can be perceived as a sign of continuous metamorphosis, that is, an affirmation of a difference—of the new—with regard to the dominant cultural tradition. It was also an attempt to make this difference dynamic in a process that tried to be dialectic and Hegelian, but which was resolved in an accelerated reaction of entropy and the annihilation of difference. Through continuous repetition, the "new" in Oswald de Andrade eventually became "old," and was opposed by most of the writers of the generation of 1945. Nonetheless, it helped renew some aspects of Brazilian culture, beginning with the hundred-year anniversary of the country's independence, which was celebrated in 1922. Andrade's work continues to have an aesthetic influence on young writers, who have discovered him anew. Today he is sometimes designated by the fashionable term, "postmodern," which has little or nothing to do with the typically national forms and content that his work initially challenged.

In Oswald de Andrade's work, which is intimately linked to his romantic and literary life, there are three phases that complement each other and, to some extent, repeat themselves: a formative phase, from 1905 to 1920; a transformative phase, from 1920 to 1945; and a confirmational phase, from 1945 to 1954. Each literary genre that he cultivated relates to one or more of these phases, appearing in one and developing or being repeated in another in a way that makes it hard to determine the origin, the apex, or even the implementation of an avant-garde form or idea throughout his work.

The first, or formative phase, is somewhat biographical. It begins in 1905, when the author was fifteen years old and started to frequent literary circles, until 1920, by which time he had had some literary experiences in the fields of journalism, criticism, theater, poetry, and prose fiction. During this period he also traveled to Europe and strengthened his intellectual friendships in São Paulo, Rio de Janeiro, and Paris. He engaged in study and random reading and also began a series of literary projects that he would carry over into the next phase. In 1909 he started writing theater criticism in the newspaper *Diário Popular*. In 1910 he set up a painting studio with Oswaldo Pinheiro and traveled to Rio de Janeiro to visit his uncle, the writer Inglês de Sousa, with whom he maintained a correspondence. In 1911 he founded *O Pirralho* (The little squirt), which was published until 1917. During this period he also maintained a friendship with Emílio de Menezes and was involved in the civil rights campaign of Rui Barbosa. In 1912 he spent seven months in Europe, where he came into contact with the first manifestos of Marinetti, an Italian futurist. The revolutionary tenor of these manifestos so impressed Andrade's literary sensibility that, nine years later, it would constitute the leitmotif of his own "futurist" preaching, that is, of future Brazilian modernism. In 1913 Andrade met the painter Lasar Segall and wrote his first play, "A Recusa" (The refusal), which remains unpublished.

Beginning in 1915, Andrade's intellectual activities began to show a marked maturation. He became a member of the Brazilian Society of Men of Letters, founded in São Paulo by Olavo Bilac. In 1916, he wrote for *A cigarra* (The cicada) and *A vida moderna* (Modern life). Together with Guilherme de Almeida, he published two theatrical pieces, *Mon Coeur Balance* and *Leur Âme*, in a single volume, and in the same magazine he revealed parts of his novel, *Memórias sentimentais de João Miramar* (Sentimental memoirs of João Miramar). He also visited Emílio de Menezes and other intellectuals in Rio de Janeiro. By 1917 he had established his famous *garçonnière*, defending the painter Anita Malfatti from Monteiro Lobato's criticism. He had also met fellow author Mario de Andrade, about whom he would later say, in an interview with Mário da Silva Brito, that "Mario was my great stimulus and, in certain respects, I liked him for narcissistic reasons, since his writings ended up showing that my tendencies were right." In 1918 he participated in the first group of future modernists (Mario de Andrade, Guilherme de Almeida, Ribeiro Couto and Menotti del Picchia) and

began writing *O perfeito cozinheiro das almas deste mundo* (The perfect cook of the souls of this world) with Deisi (Maria de Lourdes Castro, also known as "Miss Cyclone") and other friends. In the following year he completed his law degree, married Deisi (who died later that same year), and published three more chapters of his *Memórias sentimentais de João Miramar* in the School of Law journal. In 1920 he discovered the work of the sculptor Brecheret and founded the short-lived journal *Papel e Tinta* (Paper and ink).

Until her death, Deisi had been the most important of Andrade's female companions, and he felt her loss keenly. He wrote of it in his later memoirs, *Um homem sem profissão* (1954; A man without a profession), in a poem entitled "Sob as ordens de Mamãe" (Under Mum's orders). Here is one of the final passages:

> *Sinto-me só, perdido numa imensa noite de orfandade. A amada que me deu a vida partiu sem me dizer adeus. / A francesa que trouxe de Paris veio buscar o dinheiro para outro homem. / Landa, que foi o primeiro sonho vivo que me ofuscou, tornou-se a estátua de sal da lenda bíblica. Olhou para o passado. / Isadora Duncan estrondou como um raio e passou. / A que encontrei, enfim, para ser toda minha, meu ciúme a matou . . . / Estou só e a vida vai custar a reflorir. Estou só.*

I feel alone, orphaned, lost in an immense night. My beloved who gave me my life left without saying goodbye. / The girl I brought from Paris loves another man's money. / Landa, the first live dream to blind me, turned into the pillar of salt of the biblical legend. She looked back. / Isadora Duncan rumbled like a clap of thunder and moved on. / The one I finally found to be all mine was killed by my jealousy . . . / I am alone and it will be hard for life to bloom again. I am alone.

Andrade's formative period ended with this personal loss, and over the next twenty-five years he consolidated the lessons of his early work in a series of productive activities and with objectives that were more broadly defined. His literary and aesthetic concepts, once narrow and fragmentary, acquired a consistency and boldness, forming an ideological body that manifested itself through language and metalanguage in the books and manifestos with which he began the next phase of his life.

This second, transformative, phase is the most important period of Andrade's literary career. It began in

1920, when his name became better-known during the preparations for the *Semana de Arte Moderna* (Week of modern art), scheduled to take place in 1922. His first novel was also published that year. This phase ended in 1945, when he completed the publication of two volumes of *Marco Zero* (Mark zero) and a new literary movement, known as the Generation of 1945, arose. This new movement favored a more aesthetic, serious use of language that Andrade was unable to comprehend. However, out of this new literary generation came a group of writers, "the concrete poetry group," whose members appropriated Oswald de Andrade's work and name. This is especially true of his poetry, which unfortunately ended up exerting a negative influence on most of the new poets from the interior of Brazil.

At the start of this new phase, however, in 1921, Oswald de Andrade placed all of the knowledge he accumulated during his formative period at the service of a revolutionary praxis. He began by seeing in the symbolist language of Alphonsus de Guimaraens some precursor elements of what later became modernism. He spoke in honor of the contemporary writer, painter, and sculptor Paulo Menotti del Picchia at a banquet given for politicians and poets and, in his article "My futurist poet," revealed the rich presence of Mario de Andrade, the writer who would influence all sectors of Brazilian culture in the twentieth century. In one of his last interviews, given to Marcos Rey in 1954, Oswald acknowledged that "deve-se a Mario de Andrade a eclosão do movimento modernista. A ele e a Di Cavalcanti. Minha ação foi apenas polêmica. De repente houve um clarão . . . e esse clarão era o Mario" (Mario de Andrade should be credited with the emergence of the modernist movement. He and Di Cavalcanti. What I did was merely polemical. All of a sudden there was a burst of light . . . and that light was Mario). In another interview that same year (this one with Heráclio Dias), he discussed the relationship between Mario de Andrade's *Paulicéia Desvairada* (Crazy São Paulo) and his own *Pau-brasil* (Brazilwood tree):

> *Quando Mario de Andrade publicou a* Paulicéia Desvairada, *aquilo me pareceu, apesar do nosso estado de espírito, uma novidade. Novidade absoluta. É que Mario escondia de nós, avaramente, os futuristas italianos que ele possuía. . . . Depois, quando conhecemos também os futuristas italianos, a impressão de novidade permaneceu, por que Mario nunca foi homem de macaquear. Os futuristas italianos deram-lhe o modelo formal, do qual ele se aproveitou para fazer a sua própria experiência estética. Além de tudo, eu que nunca soube fazer versos medidos vi ali a minha oportunidade de fazer poesia. Era a poesia libertada.*

When Mario de Andrade published *Paulicéia Desvairada*, despite our emotional state, it struck me as a novelty. An absolute novelty. You see, Mario would zealously hide his Italian futurists from us. . . . Later on, when we also knew the Italian futurists, the impression of novelty remained, because Mario was never one to copy others. The Italian futurists gave him the formal model, which he used to create his own aesthetic experience. Above all, I, who never learned how to make measured verses, saw my opportunity there to do poetry. It was unfettered poetry.

With the success of the *Semana de Arte Moderna*, which was celebrated on the 13th, 15th, and 17th of February in 1922, Oswald de Andrade made a definitive name for himself. As his intellectual boldness increased, the writer employed the audacious and corrosive language of his books and pamphlets to develop a variety of literary currents. This led him to cultivate a syncopated literary language, but one that was full of humor and rooted in anecdotal and humorous subjects as well as in puns and wordplay; he even drew upon the romantic and financial setbacks he suffered in life. In short, everything that was looked down upon in traditional literature began to appear in his work. Since he did not know how to use prosody or write long sentences, Oswald took the style of the Marinetti manifestos and the photographic language of Blaise Cendrars and Jean Cocteau as his models.

This is where Andrade's concept of cultural anthropophagy—cultural cannibalism—began, and it was then extended to include the idea of "autophagy" (devouring of the self): he began to make use of his own texts by modifying them, repeating them in other books, recycling them, and submitting them in new forms. Because of his temperament and restless spirit, he was unable to complete a number of his projects: the five volumes of *Marco Zero* and the four volumes of his memoirs are examples of this, as are the unfinished texts that appear in posthumous editions every so often. This is the case for the monumental 1990 edition of his *Obras completas* (Complete works) published by the University of Campinas in the state of São Paulo and projected to run to twenty-four volumes.

Andrade brought new features to literature, including collages of texts, as found in cubism; dismantling of syntax, as in dadaism; free words, as in futurism; and a disjointed stream of consciousness, as in surrealism. He was committed to what he believed was a new style which he ended up imposing, not on his contemporaries, but on the generations of writers that came of age after his death. His influence was first felt in São Paulo, and from there it spread to several cities in the interior of Minas Gerais and through the state of São Paulo itself. His work was a precursor of concrete poetry, and the new writers of the generation of 1956 considered him to be the most important writer in Brazilian literature. Since no one took the trouble to dispute this claim, it started to be taken as truth by many academics, who naively repeated it.

After playing an active role in the 1922 *Semana de Arte Moderna*, Andrade published his novel *Os condenados* (The damned). In 1924 he launched his *Manifesto da poesia pau-brasil* (Manifesto of brazilwood poetry) and, the following year, he published his first book of poems, *Pau-brasil*. Three years later, in 1928, he published his most famous manifesto, the *Manifesto antropófago* (Man-eater's manifesto). An expanded version of previous texts, in which he inserted a bit of philosophy and anthropology, this manifesto offers a series of theoretical prescriptions that are intended to function as cultural "panaceas" and to point toward new concepts of art, literature, and language that serve the most disjointed purposes.

In 1922, in the second issue of the magazine *Klaxon*, Andrade published a short but symptomatic article entitled "Escolas & Idéias (Notas para um possível prefácio)" (Schools and ideas [notes for a possible preface]). It is symptomatic because it is a draft, the first version of the *Manifesto da poesia pau-brasil*, which was published two years later. The discovery and launching of a new critical genre in Brazilian literature is the most important theoretical contribution that he ever produced, and is in large part the reason for his fame. This new type of text helped to introduce a new vision of literary language. It is inspired, in part, by the Marinettian models that impressed him on his first trip to Europe at the very time when the futurist manifestos were being unfurled.

In "Escolas & Idéias" Andrade attempted to create something new, to convey his perception of a new language that he had not yet mastered, as can be seen in passages such as the following:

*Benditos os que reagiram contra a Interpretação—Rimbaud, Lautréamont, Apollinaire e a Corja até Cendrars, Soffici, Ronald, Mario de Andrade, Manuel Bandeira, Luiz Aranha—"O Homem e a Morte", "Soror Dolorosa", Ribeiro Couto inédito e Serge [sic]. Antônio Ferro genial. . . . / Benditos, Brecheret, Malfatti, Di Cavalcanti, Avermaete, exato, descobrir. Pedro Álvares Cabral sem acaso.*

Blessed be those that reacted against the Interpretation—Rimbaud, Lautréamont, Apollinaire and Corja including Cendrars, Soffici, Ronald, Mario de Andrade, Manuel Bandeira, Luiz Aranha—"O Homem e a Morte," "Soror Dolorosa," Ribeiro Couto unpublished and Serge [sic]. Antônio Ferro fantastic. . . . / Blessed, Brecheret, Malfatti, Di Cavalcanti, Avermaete, exactly, discovery. Pedro Álvares Cabral not by chance.

In this text, nouns predominate, and syncopated ideas and sentence fragments are common. The author also uses mathematical symbols, such as "Metafísica + Realidade = Luz" (Metaphysics + Reality = Light), which is reminiscent of Mario de Andrade's "Prefácio Interessantíssimo" (Extremely interesting preface), published in his *Paulicéia Desvairada* (1922), and which is something that he, in turn, had taken from Paul Dermée. In fact, it is this combination of fragmented, classical, and very new ideas make this text a premanifesto, a draft of the *Manifesto da poesia pau-brasil*. It is easy to see in it the influence of the literary manifestos of Marinetti, Apollinaire, and Tristan Tzara. The supreme example of this genre is Mario de Andrade's preface.

Oswald de Andrade continued to work on his "notes to a preface" for two more years, and presented them to the public a second time on 18 March 1924 with the catchy title of *Manifesto da poesia pau-brasil*. The book was met with great acclaim among younger intellectuals, and great dismay among traditionalists who saw it all as a tasteless joke. Paulo Prado wrote the May 1924 preface to Andrade's first book of poems, *Pau-brasil*, in which he makes use of futurist elements such as "palavras em liberdade" (free words), but he also criticizes Andrade for following fashions that are "decrepit and reek of moth balls" and that show up here "twelve years after they were invented." With the creation of fascism in 1919 and Marinetti's becoming a member of that party, the younger Brazilian intellectuals, such Paulo Prado, began to look askance at him.

Oswald de Andrade continued to use Marinetti's manifestos and Blaise Cendrars's texts as a theoretical model while in Paris, however. He began to perceive the essence of Brazil, its most authentic cultural roots that were uncontaminated by European culture, and he chose to symbolize this with the *pau-brasil*, one of the most important commercial products of the colonial era. In a 1949 statement to Péricles Eugênio da Silva Ramos, he confirmed the influence of Blaise Cendrars on the development of *Pau-brasil*: "The primitive that in France appeared as exoticism was for us, in Brazil, just primitivism." In *O Mês Modernista que ia ser Futurista* (The modernist month that was going to be futurist), appearing in the 11 December 1925 issue of *A Noite*, Carlos Drummond de Andrade took issue with a claim by Paulo Prado that Oswald had discovered Brazil from "a fancy studio" in Paris. Referring to *Pau Brasil*, Carlos remarked that, rather than discovering Brazil, "what he [Oswald] did was discover himself." This manifesto ostensibly contributes toward changing the Brazilian intelligentsia's models in the 1920s.

The *Manifesto da poesia pau-brasil* (called "the boring manifesto" by Andrade's enemies) was based on the discontinuity of thought and language, that is, on Oswald de Andrade's aggressive and personal way of subverting most of the values that had up to that time been consecrated by cultural tradition. In this manifesto he criticizes our pretentiousness, our *lado doutor* (being highfalutin), and says: "We make everything sound erudite. We forget the *gavião de penacho* [harpy eagle]." In going against the grammar mania of the period, he asks for a "language without archaisms, without high-brow terms; natural and neological. The millionaire contribution of all errors. How we talk. How we are." This plea is echoed in Paulo Prado's preface to *Pau-brasil*, where he openly pleads for a "new Brazilian language," as did José de Alencar in the nineteenth century. In 1922 Mario de Andrade responded to this desire by preparing a *Gramatiquinha da*

*Fala Brasileira* (Little grammar of Brazilian speech). In lashing out against the repetition inherent in the poetic process, Oswald de Andrade has said that "the only reason a verse-making machine was not invented" was because "the Parnassian poet already existed." His *Manifesto* ends by calling for:

> *O contrapeso da originalidade nativa para inutilizar a adesão acadêmica./ A reação contra todas as indigestões de sabedoria. O melhor de nossa tradição lírica. O melhor de nossa demonstração moderna./ Apenas brasileiros de nossa época. . . . Tudo digerido. Sem meeting cultural. Práticos. Experimentais. Poetas. Sem reminiscências livrescas. Sem comparações de apoio. Sem pesquisa etimológica. Sem ontologia./ Bárbaros, crédulos, pitorescos e meigos. . . .*

The counterweight of native originality in order to thwart academic approval. The reaction against all of wisdom's indigestion. The best of our lyrical tradition. The best of our modern demonstration. / Only Brazilians from our era. . . . Everything digested. Without any cultural meeting. Practical. Experimental. Poets. Without bookish reminiscences. Without supporting comparisons. Without etymological research. Without ontology. / Barbaric, naive, picturesque and gentle. . . .

The following year, Oswald wrote a "Falação" (Speech), which appears as the preface of his book of poetry. In this preface he revisits the concepts, language structure, and style of "Escolas & Idéias" and the *Manifesto da poesia pau-brasil*, and offers another short "manifesto" that reconsiders the topic of Cabral, which appeared at the end of "Escolas & Idéias."

> *O Cabralismo. A civilização dos donatários. A Querência e a Exportação./ O Carnaval. O Sertão e a Favela. Pau-brasil. Bárbaro e nosso./ A formação étnica rica. A riqueza vegetal. O minério. A cozinha. O vatapá, o ouro e a dança./ Toda a história da Penetração e a história comercial da América. Pau-brasil./ Contra a fatalidade do primeiro branco aportado e dominando diplomaticamente as selvas selvagens. Citando Virgílio para os Tupiniquins. O bacharel.*

Cabralism. The civilization of overlords. The Homeland and Exportation. / Carnival. The backwoods and the slums. Pau-brasil. Barbaric and ours. / The rich ethnic make-up. The rich plant life. The ore. The cuisine. The *vatapá* [traditional dish from the Bahia region of Brazil], the gold and the dance. / The entire history of Penetration and the New World's trade history. Pau-brasil. / Against the fatality of the first white man who cast anchor and diplomatically tamed the savage jungles. Quoting Virgil to the Tupiniquins. The college educated.

The massive influence of the *Manifesto da poesia pau-brasil* is immediately apparent in this text. Entire sentences from that manifesto are reused here, such as in the last two lines cited above (in which Andrade seems to confuse Dante with Virgil). Employing this new concept and style, Andrade began taking over other texts, breaking them down in a process of autophagy, like a strange path in Brazilian culture.

But it is with the *Manifesto antropófago* of 1928 that Oswald de Andrade attains his highest level of aesthetic subversion, exclaiming that "Anthropophagy is the only thing that unites us." He creates a beautiful Shakespearean pun-parody in writing: "Tupy or not tupy, that is the question." He applies psychoanalysis and the modern meanings of totem and taboo, concepts that he had taken from cultural anthropology, and he asks intellectuals to "swallow" our myths, alluding to what the Caeté Indians did to D. Pêro de Fernandes Sardinha on the Alagoas coast in the Brazilian Northeast. Later on, in a 1942 interview (for a magazine tribute to *Dom Casmurro*, the classic novel by Machado de Assis) he stated that "the aesthetic roots of *Antropofagia* were in *Pau-brasil*" and indicated that from its beginnings "should come the social research that gave rise to the Brazilian novel from 1930 on. . . ." In his book of poetry, Andrade had already made use of intertextualizations from historical texts. Now, strongly influenced by psychoanalytic theory and becoming more culturally mature, the writer included in his new manifesto texts that have been taken from indigenous, Tupi-Guarani mythology, which he compares to "surrealist language" and to the "golden age." That is where phrases such as "Before the Portuguese discovered Brazil, Brazil had discovered happiness" come from. And, later on:

*A nossa independência ainda não foi proclamada. . . . Expulsamos a dinastia. É preciso expulsar o espírito bragantino, as ordenações e o rapé de Maria da Fonte. / Contra a realidade social, vestida e opressora, cadastrada por Freud—a realidade sem complexo, sem loucura, sem prostituições e sem penitenciárias do matriarcado de Pindorama. / Oswald de*
*Andrade / Em Piratininga / Ano 374 da Deglutição do Bispo Sardinha.*

Our independence has not yet been declared. . . . We expelled the dynasty. It is necessary to expel the spirit of the reigning Portuguese royalty, the ordinances and Maria da Fonte's snuff. / Against the costumed and oppressive social reality studied by Freud—a reality without a complex, without insanity, without prostitution, and without prisons from Pindorama's matriarchy. / Oswald de Andrade / In Piratininga / The year 374 of Bishop Sardinha is devoured.

This ritualistic anthropology was taken, in part, from the romantic poetry of Gonçalves Dias. It also shows the influence of a 1920 short story written by Marinetti and the magazine *Cannibale*, which was founded in 1921 and gave new meaning to the modernist nationalism that had already created *Macunaíma*.

In two other interviews in Belo Horizonte and in Rio de Janeiro, both in 1928, Andrade stated that his Anthropophagy seeks to "rehabilitate the nonconverted Indian and his extraordinary paradisiacal spirit." In addition, he explained the source of his term, "anthropophagy": "[it was] in Tarsila's [Amaral's] barbaric painting that I found that expression." Andrade eventually defined what he means by Anthropophagy in three successive phrases:

> *a. A Antropofagia é o culto à estética instintiva da Terra Nova.*
> *b. É a redução, a cacarecos, dos ídolos importados, para a ascensão dos totens raciais.*
> *c. É a própria terra da América, o próprio limo fecundo, filtrando e se expressando através dos temperamentos vassalos de seus artistas.*

> a. Anthropophagy is the cult of the instinctive aesthetics of the New World.
> b. It is the smashing into smithereens of imported idols, permitting the ascension of racial totems.
> c. It is the land of the New World itself; it is the fertile mud itself, filtered and expressed through the subjugated temperaments of its artists.

In an interview with Paulo Mendes Campos, in 1947, Oswald clearly acknowledged that his concept of Anthropophagy arose in the 1920s from his reading of a chapter from Montaigne's *Essais*, "De Canibale." He freely acknowledged, however, that he knew little or nothing about the subject and study of anthropophagy. In 1973 Heitor Martins clearly demonstrated Andrade's lack of formal understanding of the concept, in the first chapter of his *Oswald de Andrade e outros* (Oswald de Andrade and others), in which he cites the 1920 magazine *Cannibale,* the dadaist *Manifeste Cannibale* (1920) by Francis Picabia, and the short story "Il Negro" from Marinetti's 1922 collection of short stories, *Gli Amori Futurist.* It would be interesting to learn the source of and influences upon Oswald de Andrade's diachronic vision, wherein the subject of the Indian always seems to be viewed from a past perspective. In his work there is no synchronic vision of Brazil's indigenous peoples. Andrade does not view them anthropologically; he does not deal with their problems relating to land, illness, food, and preservation of their way of life under the onslaught of Brazilian culture.

The meaning of the manifestos appears in a very small and sententious way to be rooted in the conception of a nationalism that Andrade first revealed in the magazine *Klaxon.* He broadened this conception in the *Manifesto da poesia pau-brasil,* mixed it together with the *Klaxon* text, and reduced it into his prefatory "Falação" in the book *Pau-brasil.* Mario de Andrade's *Macunaíma* (1927) is what led Oswald de Andrade to develop his *Manifesto antropófago,* and to his work on the *Revista de Antropofagia* (Anthropophagy review) of which he became the editor in its second phase. He remained committed to this concept of cultural anthropophagy throughout his career, but writings such as his thesis "A crise da filosofia messiânica" (The crisis of messianic philosophy) and the essay "A marcha da utopias" (The march of utopias), both of which appear in the volume *Do pau-brasil à antropofagia e às utopias* (1972; From pau-brasil to anthropophagy and the utopias), suggest that he did not delve into it very deeply. The idea of anthropophagy surfaced in his work in 1922, grew with the public reaction to the *Semana de Arte Moderna,* gained momentum with the publication of *Pau-brasil,* and attained its apogee in the *Manifesto antropófago,* but after 1940 it lost its force and began to fall out of favor, until Andrade's followers revisited the subject and sought to better define and interpret it. It is interesting to note that although Oswald used this theme as the main topic of his discussions and did a little research on the subject, he never managed to develop a reliable concept that was scientifically appropriate to the Brazilian culture.

In "Um Documento" (A document), an essay that appears in *Telefonema* (1974; Telephone call), Oswald suggested that the plot of a narrative should have "the direct order of rivers." That is, it should be a narrative in its most traditional sense, with a beginning, middle, and end. Of course, this is the case in a story (diegesis), not a discourse, the structure of which depends on the technique, invention, and language of the novelist. The comparison between a narrative and a river is perhaps the oldest metaphor of the storyteller's art. In his 1943 article "Sobre o romance" (About the novel), which was published in *Ponta de lança* (Point of a lance), he introduces the idea of a novel-rider. He writes that "the novel is always a philosophical treatise, without cathedra, with no special terminology, and without the responsibility of a system. . . ." He immediately adds that "what makes a novel is the creative process" and that its purpose is "the restitution of the life suffered by the novelist. The role played by the unconscious is enormous. There is no difference between that restitution and poetry's."

There is no doubt that, in his novels, Oswald de Andrade tries to follow "the direct order of rivers," but it appears that the river he has chosen is one of those, typical of the Brazilian Northeast, that becomes a series of stagnant pools during the dry season. His fictional discourse is really a series of small, anecdotal chapters that sometimes manage to maintain the autonomy of their textual limit. They develop as fragments, each chapter containing just a part of the "thread" of the story that he is trying to tell. In a sense, the narrative comes in homeopathic doses, adapted to the writer's human condition and correlated to his manifestos, his poetry, and everything else he has written. Because they are so short, the chapters of his novels take the form of mosaics, small nuclei, autonomous narrative cells that the reader will always have difficulty in reassembling. In "Um documento" Andrade is brave enough to say, "if I work on my prose it is just to improve it." With Oswald de Andrade, a new language arises that becomes more and more polished with each book, at least during the last phase of his literary career.

This is one way to interpret most of the chapters in Andrade's *Trilogia do exílio* (1922–1934; Trilogy of exile): *Os condenados, A estrêla de absinto* (1927; The star of absinthe), and *A escada de Jacó* (1934; Jacob's ladder). Mário da Silva Brito has remarked that this trilogy is an "archive of personal experiences." It is loaded with the author's "personal, autobiographical experiences" but they constitute "the mournful prayer of a period." For instance, the character Alma in *Os condenados* has a lot in common with Andrade's beloved Deisi, who would frequent the young writer's *garçonnière*. *Os condenados* was retitled *Alma* (Soul) in 1941, when the trilogy was republished in a single volume. It is the almost cinematographic portrait of the romantic ups and downs of a sentimental and poetic man in São Paulo's social and political milieu during the revolution of 1932.

*A estrêla de absinto* takes the romantic dramas of the the previous novel's main character and expands them to include other characters. Andrade initially had some problems while writing this volume; he wanted it to be new, but he did not really know what it was that he wanted or how to achieve it. In *A escada*, however, he finally firms up the ideological problems he had been grappling with and, for the first time in Brazilian fiction, he creates a communist character, Jorge d'Alvelos. Alvelos is a precursor of the subversive character in Amando Fontes's *Os corumbas* (1967) and of characters appearing in some of Jorge Amado's novels. Here is one of the "mosaics" from *A escada* in which the author combines a parodic and ideological tone with poetic images to create enchanting shapes within his prose:

> *O camarada Deus num imenso macacão veio sentar-*
> *me à sua cabeceira e falou-lhe declamatoriamente:*
> —*Porque te nobilitei, dando-te a vontade livre, te*
> *rebelaste contra mim, renovaste, no pequeno*
> *cenário perdido de tua vida, a tragédia dos*
> *Arcanjos!*
> —*Senhor, foi a primeira luta de classes . . .*
> —*Os homens mesmos deliberam os seus infernos.*
> —*Que é necessário fazer então?*
> —*Sofrer.*
> —*E depois?*
> —*Serás conduzido entre sepulcros alados, verticais, até*
> *os primeiros degraus da eternidade conquistada!*
> *Jorge olhou e viu a manhã destacada da terra.*

> Comrade God wearing enormous overalls came and
> sat down at his bedboard and addressed him
> in a declamatory tone:
> —I made you noble and gave you free will and yet
> you rebelled against me. On the small-lost
> stage of your life you replayed the tragedy of
> the Archangels!
> —Lord, it was the first class struggle . . .
> —Men decide their own hells.
> —So what must be done?
> —Suffer.
> —And then?
> —You will be carried in winged upright tombs up
> to the first levels of conquered eternity!
> Jorge looked and saw the earth's clear morning.

Andrade's boldness in creating topics and in constructing new language is even more apparent in his novel entitled *Memórias sentimentais de João Miramar*, which, although published in 1924, was actually begun in about 1916. In a somewhat playful introductory note, the author claims that the book was largely improvised and has a language of it own, consisting of a "telegraphic style and the piercing metaphor," somewhat like the thought processes he attributed to Marinetti. Andrade goes on to talk about a historic moment in this book, a moment that deals with the treaty of Versailles, followed by the "organic boiling over of all social upheavals." The novel satirizes the sterile side of bourgeois society and its lack of human solidarity. *Memórias Sentimentais* is a memorialistic novel that is somewhat akin to Machado de Assis's *Memórias Postumas de Brás Cubas* (Posthumous memoirs of Brás Cubas). In the first chapter of Andrade's novel the child-narrator, speaking in the first person, recites one of the most common and well-known prayers in the Roman Catholic Church, the Hail Mary. Andrade uses the technique of simultaneous speech here in order to express two distinct sets of ideas that are running through the child's head while praying:

> *Senhor convosco, bendita sois entre as mulheres, as mulheres*
> *não têm pernas, são como o manequim de mamãe até em*
> *baixo. Para que pernas nas mulheres, amém.*

> Oh Lord, blessed art thou among women. Women don't
> have legs. They are like mother's mannequin, even down
> there. What do women have legs for, amen.

In 1934, by now having completed two novels, Oswald de Andrade published *Serafim Ponte Grande* (*Serafim Grosse Pointe*, 1979). In this book, Andrade fictionalizes one of the trips that he had made to Europe and the national political problems connected with the revolution of 1932 in São Paulo. The main character, a leftist intellectual, uses self-criticism to show that the person who calls himself the "iron jacket of the proletarian revolution" is, in fact, ineffective. In terms of form, this is the most well developed and most avantgarde of all of Andrade's novels. It was written after the publication of *Macunaíma*, and its preface acknowledges the author's simultaneous feelings of envy and respect for the writer of that earlier work, Mario de Andrade. *Serafim Grosse Pointe* is a novel in which several types of discourse are intertwined: letters, recitatives, memoirs, diary, jokes, notes, dialogues, poems, testament, playful essay, dictionary, in fact, every type of literary and nonliterary writing. It is a cubist narrative, consisting of several small texts that look at first to be randomly collected but which are tied together within a long humorous narrative. The sense and the direction of the narrative ultimately impose themselves on the reader. An example of the author's almost surrealist approach to description can be seen in this excerpt from part VI, "Cérebro, Coração e Pavio" (Mind, heart, and wick), in the chapter called "Musicól":

*A floresta brasílica e outras florestas.*

*Mulheres fertilizantes conduzem colunas, arquiteturas e hortaliças. Música, maestro! Matéria orgânica!*

*Corbeilles monumentais atiram do sétimo céu dos copos brancos ananases de negras nuas.*

*Periquitos, ursos, onças, avestruzes, a animal animalada. Rosáceas sobre aspargos da platéia. Condimentos. As partes pudendas nos refletores. Síncopes sapateiam cubismos, deslocações. Alterando as geometrias. Tudo se organiza, se junta coletivo, simultâneo e nuzinho, uma cobra, uma fita, uma guirlanda, uma equação, passos suecos, guinchos argentinos.*

*Serafim, a vida é essa.*

The brazilwood forest and other forests.

Fertilizing women conduct columns, architecture, and potherbs. Music, maestro! Organic matter!

Nude negresses' monumental Corbeilles cast ananases from the seventh heaven of white cups.

Parakeets, bears, jaguars, ostriches, beastly beasts. Roseates on the asparagus stalks of the crowd. Condiments. Genitals in the footlights. Steps syncopate cubisms, dislocations. Altered geometries. Everything is organized, is collectively linked, simultaneous and naked, a snake, a ribbon, a garland, an equation, Swedish steps, Argentine screeches.

Seraphim, all that is life.

In 1943 Andrade published his next novel, *A revolução melancólica* (The melancholy revolution). In 1974 this book was republished with the title *Marco zero I*. For this novel Andrade followed much the same approach to composition as he had followed previously. While it is true that the new novel features expanded chapters, the sense of the mosaic that characterized *Serafim Ponte Grande* remains. *A revolução melancólica* was intended as the first of a five-volume cyclical work, but only one other volume, *Chão* (1945; Ground), was actually published (it, too, was renamed upon republication, and was given the title *Marco zero II*). The author imagined himself publishing a "social fresco," believing that his novels were related to painting, cinema, and the public. This belief inspired him with the idea of a "mural novel," a really new approach in which he resorted to a wide range of techniques such as simultaneous presentation, cinematic effects, cubism, and image fragmentism. Once again, he employed short scenes that he filled with characters drawn from the most diverse social strata. The result was a vast panorama in which both the good and bad of Brazilian culture was reflected.

Written during a period of war and, later, of dictatorship, Andrade's novels truly reflected the situation of the common people, who were brushed aside by the events. Today they are once again extremely relevant because of the bold subjects that the author addressed. For example, his treatment of the wars of the landholders can be seen to presage the land-reform movement, and his depiction of swindlers, property owners, immigrant populations, bankers, and politicians remains relevant. In short, Andrade's "mural novels" addressed on a large scale the social, political, and economic problems of rural Brazil, issues that are still problematic today. *A revolução melancólica* and *Chão* are, in terms of critical nationalism, the best novels of Brazilian literature from that period and today continue to be valid in their aesthetic and ideological goals.

In addition to his prose fiction, Oswald de Andrade also wrote plays. He made it clear that he considered theater to be the best of the art forms, one which "requires a vocational passion, as is the case with Mr. Joraci Camargo, or a serious and specialized culture which faces and resolves its lofty problems" (*Ponta de lança*). He had previously written that Brazilian theater had not been developed because

> *caímos sempre na incapacidade de educar um certo número de espectadores para elevar o nível do nosso teatro às alturas que já alcançaram a poesia e o romance.*

> we were forever incapable of educating a critical mass of spectators so as to raise the standard of our theater to the standard that poetry and novels had already attained.

One of the problems of all periods and avant-gardes is precisely the issue of the relationship of art to the public: Should the playwright satisfy the spectator's taste, for example, or should he try to change that taste? Oswald de Andrade was a true man of the theater, and his plays and dramatic novels, especially *A revolução melancólica* and *Chão*, are his best literary creations. This is because they were free of the experimental furor that marked Andrade's earlier work and which he ultimately found that he had exhausted. Instead, for these later works the author was able to draw upon his personal experience and his social and political knowledge of Brazil to create an entire set of literary material that was organic and yet still relevant, and to give it a new treatment and a new language. By this point in his career, however, the days when he planned to convert the world to the avant-garde were long past. With regard to theater, however, his desire to "raise the standard" remained strong, and it made him ignore such practical considerations as the dimensions of the stage. He also ignored the impossibility of performing certain fantastical and surrealistic works. These circumstances make his three plays another type of novel; it is material to be read rather than to be performed.

It is worth remembering that Andrade's first book, written in partnership with Guilherme de Almeida, contained two plays, *Mon Coeur Balance* and *Leur Âme* from 1916. These two dramatic efforts had very little influence on his literary reputation, however. More important are his three later plays: *O homem e o cavalo* (The man and the horse), from 1934; *A morta* (The dead woman), from 1937; and *O rei da vela* (The candle king), also from 1937. Despite their unsuitability for the stage, some performances have in fact been attempted by theater groups hoping to revive Andrade's modernist period. These performances, however, have been unsuccessful, failing to engage an audience that tends to be more disposed toward the classics than toward incomprehensible existentialist ponderings from the World War II era.

Sábato Magaldi, a scholar who has specialized in Andrade's dramatic works, believes that "few authors make the literary critic regret that the theater has its specific requirements that make it impossible to perform as the texts of Oswald de Andrade." And he explains why:

> *A audácia da concepção, o ineditismo dos processos, o gênio criador conferem a essa dramaturgia um lugar à parte no teatro brasileiro—um lugar que, melancolicamente, é fora dele e talvez tenha a marca do desperdício.*

> The conceptual boldness, the novelty of the process, and the creative genius confer on these plays a separate place in Brazilian theater—a place that, unfortunately, is outside of it, and perhaps has a mark of wanton waste.

*O homem e o cavalo* is about the arrival, in a balloon, of characters from heaven to a place called the Red Planet, in other words, to the Earth after it has converted to communism. The characters include Madame Jesus Christ, Saint Peter, the Trojan Horse, Veronica, Eisenstein, and many others. Saint Peter says: "Let's start a revolution before the people do." The piece ends with a version of history in which Jesus is associated with the Romans, the apostles want to have a revolution, and Judas commits suicide. Andrade described his second play, *A morta*, as "the drama of the poet, the coordinator of all human action, which the hostility of a reactionary century gradually scared away from useful and ordinary language." As such, the play can be seen as the author's critique of his own work. Andrade's third play, *O rei da vela*, has been performed more often than his other two. Set in the city of São Paulo, it begins as a satire and ends as a tragedy. In the course of the play the author deals with all of the city's problems, which he sees as arising from the hypocrisy of the Marxist intellectuals who nonetheless serve the dictatorial regime of Getúlio Vargas.

Andrade's poetry rounds out the variety of literary genres in which he has made his mark. In the very beginning of his *Manifesto da poesia pau-brasil*, Andrade suggests that poetry should be for poets and adds that it constitutes "the joy of those who do not know and discover." There is much to speculate about in both statements: Why just for poets? Or are poets the only ones who "do not know" because they are innocents? Why is poetry only for poets and not for other writers, or for everyone, even the illiterate? All of these are metaphysical and demagogical guestions that Andrade never answers. The second statement is perhaps more interesting: is Andrade suggesting that happiness depends upon enthusiasm or innocence? These suppositions would be consistent with his later work in the *Manifesto antropófago*. Or is he locating happiness in the pleasure of random discovery or in the act of invention? We should remember that Andrade was a rather undisciplined man; perhaps he is suggesting that his own poetry was created through random discovery and through the joy of invention. For him, the intuitive and daring image, which commands attention because of its very strangeness, springs from a single theme.

In 1925, when *Pau-brasil* was published, Carlos Drummond de Andrade published an article entitled "O homem do pau-brasil" (The brazilwood man) in *O Mês Modernista que ia ser Futurista*, in which he pertinently states that *Pau-brasil* consists of a "babbling" poetry. He goes on to describe Oswald de Andrade as

> um dos nossos bons poetas, se bem que não entenda uma palavra de anatomia do verso. Não passou pelo serviço militar da métrica. Ora, eu acho isso quase indispensável. A gente só se liberta daquilo que não prende. Ninguém nasceu livre! . . . A poesia dele peca por nobreza de processos. É tecnicamente mal construída. . . . Agora é urgente que ele desbaste essa matéria tão densa, lhe infiltre lirismo, se comova mais. Menos caricatura e trabalho mais profundo da realidade. Arte.

one of our good poets, even though he doesn't understand a single word of verse anatomy. He never did prosodic military service. I believe this is almost indispensable. We only become free from that which we do not grasp. No one was born free! . . . His poetry's processes are quite poor and technically ill constructed. . . . Now he must clear out all that dense underbrush, and absorb lyricism. He needs to be moved more. Less caricature and a more profound crafting of reality. Art.

Andrade was angered when Graça Aranha of the Academy criticized his work by saying that "to be Brazilian is not to get caught up in idiotic babbling!" Oswald responded to this criticism by saying "It's up to me. . . ." and ironically adding: "Since I stopped using pretty phrases . . . I began stuttering."

*Pau-brasil* contains several very short poems and is divided into parts that are titled "História do Brasil" (History of Brazil), "Poemas da Colonização" (Poems of colonization), "São Martinho" (Saint Martin), "RP1," "Carnaval" (Carnival), "Secretário dos Amantes" (The secretary of lovers), "Postes da Light" (Lampposts), "Roteiro das Minas" (Route to the mine) and "Lóide Brasileiro" (Brazilian Lloyd). Throughout the volume, however, there is a semantic and thematic relationship that arises in his treatment of Brazil's history and its experiences of colonization, runs through his consideration of the city of São Paulo and the people of that city, and continues through his poems about other historic cities and a trip along Brazil's coasts on the ships of the now extinct company Lóide Brasileiro.

In this volume, Andrade contributed a series of new elements to modernist poetry. Perhaps the most important of these elements is his use of epigrammatical reduction, that is, his reappropriation of the texts of such colonial chroniclers such as Pero Vaz de Caminha, Gândavo, Claude D'Abbeville, Frei Vicente do Salvador, Frei Manoel Calado, and others. This reappropriation entails the use of the cubist technique of collage, which in contemporary poetry is called "intertextuality," and which includes strange discourses within the space of the poem, or using phrases from a previous text. An example of this is the well-known "Meninas da Gare" (Girls of the Gare):

> Eram três ou quatro moças bem moças e bem gentis
> Com cabelos mui pretos pelas espáduas
> E suas vergonhas tão altas e tão saradinhas

*Que de nós as muito bem fitarmos*
*Não tínhamos nenhuma vergonha.*

They were three or four girls very young and
    very gentle
With their jet-black hair hanging to their shoulders
And their private parts so high and tight
That even as we watched them closely
We did not feel ashamed.

However, Oswald inverts Caminha's notion, creating situations that are new and very successful in terms of being strange. His experimentation here is exceptional, and he creates truly beautiful images. An example of this is found in the poem "As aves" (The birds), which appropriates language from the chronicle of Frei Vicente do Salvador. In this poem the author creates a poem that is visually arresting and dynamic by overlaying a set of images that connote the relationship between the sea and the *sertão* (Brazilian backwoods interior):

*Há águias de sertão*
*E emas tão grandes como as de África*
*Umas brancas e outras malhadas de negro*
*Que com uma asa levantada ao alto*
*Ao modo de vela latina*
*Corre com o vento*

There are backwoods eagles
And ostriches as big as those from Africa
Some are white and some have black spots
With their wings raised high
Like storm sails
They run with the wind

In poems such as this, Andrade created parodies and carnivalesque language long before Bakhtin began his theorizing and before the fad of carnivalization had affected literary studies in Brazil. Andrade inaugurated a new sense of parody, as is evident in the poem "Canto de Regresso à Pátria" (Song for my return to my homeland) in which he glosses verses from Gonçalves Dias. He does the same thing in his second book of poetry, *Primeiro caderno do aluno de poesia Oswald de Andrade* (1927; The first notebook of Oswald de Andrade, student of poetry), which is actually a simple reworking of *Pau-brasil*. In the poem "Meus Oito Anos" (My eight years), Andrade plays with verses by

Casimiro de Abreu. In the poem "Brasil" (Brazil), he alludes to verses by Gonçalves Dias and Junqueira Freire, but he also achieves considerable comic effect by mixing Tupi and African words together into a language that is more Brazilian than Portuguese:

*O Zé Pereira chegou de caravela*
*E perguntou pro guarani da mata virgem*
*—Sois cristão?*
*—Não. Sou bravo, sou forte, sou filho da Morte*
*Tererê tetê Quizá Quizá Quecê.*
*Lá longe a onça resmunga Uu!-ua! Uu!*
*O negro zonzo saído da fornalha*
*Tomou a palavra e respondeu*
*—Sim pela graça de Deus*
*Canhém Babá Canhém Babá Cum Cum!*
*E fizeram o Carnaval.*

Zé Pereira arrived on a sailing vessel
And he asked the Guarani of the forest
—Are you Christian?
—No. I'm brave, I'm strong, I'm the son of Death'
Tererê tetê Quizá Quizá Quecê.
Far away a jaguar growls Uu!-ua! Uu
The dizzy negro came out of the furnace
Began to speak and answered
—Yes, thank God
Canhém Babá Canhém Babá Cum Cum!
And they created Carnival.

Thus the author arrived at a type of primary metalanguage, which he uses in poems such as "Vício na fala" (Speech defect), "O gramático" (The grammarian), "Pronominais" (Pronominals), and "Erro de Português" (Portuguese mistake), all of which were quite comical and sarcastic toward traditional criticism which, at the time (1925), was little more than a watchdog for proper grammar. Here we have "Pronominais":

*Dê-me um cigarro*
*Diz a gramática*
*Do professor e do aluno*
*E do mulato sabido*
*Mas o bom negro e o bom branco*
*Da Nação Brasileira*
*Dizem todos os dias*
*Deixa disso camarada*
*Me dá um cigarro.*

Give me a cigarette
Say the Grammars
Consulted by the teacher and the student
And the smart mulatto
But the true Brazilian Black and the true
    Brazilian White
Of the Brazilian Nation
Say everyday
Forget it, buddy
Gimme a cigarette.

Note that although Andrade eliminates punctuation and displaces his pronouns, he still manages to remain faithful to the tradition of beginning his verses with capital letters.

Andrade's poetry is quite abbreviated, and this has become one of the distinctive traits that characterize his work. In his brevity he achieves what Paulo Prado has called "minutes of poetry" and what Haroldo de Campos has termed "minute-poems." An original and daring example of this can be seen below:

AMOR
*Humor*

LOVE
Humor

Here the poem is practically reduced to a single word, since *amor* acts as a title, but it is also tightly integrated into the poem's tiny structure: it is the paronymous rhyme of the word *humor*. This poetic reduction is related to Ungaretti's minimalist poetry, a relationship that is especially evident in Andrade's poem "Cielo e mare," which takes its title directly from one of Ungaretti's own poems. Andrade is able to produce semi-concrete poems, as well. One example of this is the ironic verse entitled "A Europa curvou-se ante o Brasil" (Europe bowed before Brazil), a denotative poem which summarizes the match results of a soccer team on an international tour during the 1920s. In this poem the author makes semantic use of foreign words such as *Cette* (today, Sète), in the south of France:

*7 a 2*
*3 a 1*
*A injustiça de Cette*
*4 a 0*

*2 a 1*
*2 a 0*
*3 a 1*
*e meia dúzia na cabeça dos portugueses*

7 x 2
3 x 1
The injustice of Cette
4 x 0
2 x 1
2 x 0
3 x 1
and half a dozen against the Portuguese

Oswald's playful spirit led him to construct one of his few metrical poems. However, it is a seven syllable poem, a very popular genre and quite natural within Brazilian Portuguese's phonetic system, in which the normal spoken line is in fact seven metrical syllables long, just like a major *redondilha* (roundel). That is what one reads in "Epitáfio" (Epitaph), in which the author also takes advantage of the repetition of an expressive word like *redondo* (round, fat) to create a montage: *redondo* (round) + *ilha* (island) = *redondilha*. This poem, in addition to its plays on words and its critique of traditional forms, also shows us how a poet can take advantage of associations like *redondo* and *redondilha* to explore fanciful references like "my skull will laugh" in order to introduce the echo of a laugh outside of the metering, thereby breaking up the seven-syllable verse:

*Eu sou redondo, redondo*
*Redondo, redondo eu sei*
*Eu sou uma redond'ilha*
*Das mulheres que beijei*

*Por falecer de oh! amor*
*Das mulheres de minh'ilha*
*Minha caveira rirá ah! ah! ah!*
*Pensando na redondilha.*

I'm round, round
Round, round I know
I'm a round'island
Of all women I kissed

Since I will die for oh! love
At the women of my island

My skull will laugh há! há! há!
Thinking of the round island.

It is as if the poet himself, whether dead or alive, were laughing at people who compose *redondilhas*, and laughing at himself because he too had written these *redondilha* verses; or perhaps he is simply laughing at the English pronunciation of his name by Rio de Janeiro's academics.

In "Um Documento," a long critical text in mosaic form, Andrade makes the following statement of a literary principle for both poetry and fiction:

> Pau Brasil *contra o falso êxtase alemão*. Pau Brasil *contra o hermetismo malicioso dos negróides de Paris*. Pau Brasil *diferente da minha própria poesia desarticulada das "memórias sentimentais"—fase de desagradamento técnico. Necessária. Como no esporte, os movimentos preparatórios decompõem as performances*. Pau Brasil, *sobretudo, clareza, nitidez, simplicidade e estilo. A ordem direta dos nossos rios*.

> *Pau Brasil* against the false German ecstasy. *Pau Brasil* against the malicious hermeticism of the Negroids from Paris. *Pau Brasil*, different from my own disjointed poetry from the "sentimental memoirs"—a phase of technical disintegration. Necessary. Like in sports, the preparatory movements break down the performances. *Pau Brasil*, above all, clarity, purity, simplicity, and style. The direct order of our rivers.

Andrade admits that his poetry is "disjointed." He acknowledges that it has the same type of structure as *Memórias sentimentais de João Miramar*, which was written in a language that lies somewhere between poetry and prose, a narrative that is more vertical than horizontal with a heavy dose of poetry.

The 1940s were coincidentally the same period in which Jacques Prévert was having success with his somewhat surrealistic poems on everyday subjects. Many of them, such as "Mea Culpa," were also quite short. During this period, Oswald de Andrade published several small collections of poems: *Cântico dos cânticos para flauta e violão* (The song of songs for flute and guitar), which was written in 1942 in honor of his last wife, Maria Antonieta d'Alkmin; *Poemas menores* (Minor poems), which was written in 1944; and *O escaravelho de ouro* (The golden beetle), which was written in Rio de Janeiro and published in 1946. Also

during this period the author composed a dramatic poem entitled *O santeiro do mangue* (The Saint sculptor from the mangroves), which was never published.

Beginning in 1956, a new generation of critics and poets from São Paulo decided that the poetry of Oswald de Andrade was the most important literature ever written, not only in modernism, but also in all of Brazilian poetry. Unfortunately, his poetry does not stand up very well to any analysis that looks for both linguistic renewal and for continuity with tradition. Manuel Bandeira and, more corrosively, Mario de Andrade, Carlos Drummond de Andrade, João Cabral de Melo Neto, and Lêdo Ivo all fare better in such an analysis. Since Oswald did not adapt his poetry to the standards of traditional rhetoric, he had to create outside of the poetic tradition. This was the sphere in which he achieved his innovations, by showing writers and the public that there was something beyond established poetic forms. Instead he offered lightning-poetry made up of simple images and anti-metaphors, and dealing with common things that have been touched by something joyful, humorous, or by the puns that he used for the purpose of social criticism.

In 1945, during World War II and the Vargas dictatorship, poets needed to find new themes and techniques to create high poetry such as Carlos Drummond de Andrade's 1945 poem *A rosa do povo* (The people's rose); Lêdo Ivo's 1944 *As imaginações* (The imaginations); and João Cabral de Melo Neto's 1947 *Psicologia da composição* (Psychology of composition). The poetry that had been written in the 1920s and 1930s was now being taught in the schools, and the great poets of that era were now adopting more popularly accepted work. All, that is, except for Oswald, who continued to be viewed as the *enfant gaté* of modernism and whose work, primarily his poetry, was not viewed as serious. This neglect did not go unnoticed by Andrade; in a 1947 interview with Paulo Mendes Campos he complained of a "campaign of silence" against him because his name was not included in anthologies of Brazilian poetry.

In 1945 he collected all of his poems together and published them in *Poesias reunidas*. His last novel, *Chão*, was also published in that year, and he anthologized his most important articles in the 1945 work *Ponta de lança*. He still gave numerous talks, attended conferences, and wrote new essays, but in all of these he offered a theoretical repetition of an avant-garde attitude that was no longer avant-garde. He spent his time confirming the work that he had done during the golden years of his transformation phase, when everything was new and polemical. He wanted his work to be accorded the value and acclaim that he himself attributed to it. He did not really have any confidence that his work would be appreciated, nor did he believe any longer in the continuity of his own avant-garde tradition.

It cannot be said that Oswald de Andrade spent the last years of his life in an "acceptance" or "conformation" phase. At the end of his life he came to accept his fate, feeling resigned to the work he had done, which is quite ironic since he was always a nonconformist. The historical slant that wove through his literary discourse had the flavor of confirmation: he continued to preach his ideas to a new generation of poets, the generation of 1945. And at the first São Paulo Poetry Conference, held in 1948, members of this new generation argued with him about the future of poetic creation in Brazil, which was entering a new phase of modernism. Critics like Alceu Amoroso Lima and Péricles Eugênio da Silva Ramos were now touting neomodernism, whose aesthetic values went against those of Oswaldian aesthetics.

However, there was also another new generation in São Paulo, a group of poets who evolved from the aestheticism of the era to explore the structuralism of concrete poetry. This is the group of poets who "rediscovered" Oswald de Andrade. It also possible to believe that the writer may have reached an ambiguous phase at the end of his life. On the one hand, he adapted to the Latin *confirmatio*, seeking to have his ideas and works rationally confirmed. And yet he clung to the Portuguese goal of *conformação* (conformation), not in the sense of resignation, but in the sense of configuration, or rather, a con-formation (formation with or through others). This idea implies a collective continuity that, in 1954, he left to his newest disciples from São Paulo. In one of his last interviews (in September of 1954), he cited the names of Haroldo and Augusto de Campos, scholars and writers who made a specialty of Andrade's work and who had founded the poetic movement that came to be known as concretism.

When asked about the movement, Andrade responded with admirable correctness: "The concrete movement in Brazil is nothing more than a variant of true Modernism. In importing concretism, their adherents did not have the force that Modernism had in '22." With this, his anthropophagical prophecy was fulfilled: the new generations began to "swallow" his work while he, even after his death, continues autophagically to eat his own intellectual dissatisfaction.

## SELECTED BIBLIOGRAPHY

### Primary Works

#### Poetry

*Pau-brasil.* Preface by Paulo Prado, illustrations by Tarsila do Amaral. Paris: Au Sans Pareil, 1925.

*Primeiro caderno do aluno de poesia Oswald de Andrade.* São Paulo: Tipografia da Rua de Santo Antônio, 1927.

*Poesias reunidas.* São Paulo: Gaveta, 1945. (Contains *Pau-brasil, Primeiro caderno do aluno de poesia Oswald de Andrade, Cântico dos Cânticos para Flauta e Violão,* and *Alguns poemas menores.*)

*Poesias reunidas de Oswald de Andrade.* São Paulo: Difusão Européia do Livro, 1966. (In addition to the books contained in the 1945 edition, this volume also contains *O escaravelho de ouro* and an introduction by Haroldo de Campos.)

#### Novels

*Os condenados.* São Paulo: Monteiro Lobato, 1922. (This is the first volume of the *Trilogia do exílio,* which is completed by *A estrêla de absinto,* in 1927, and *A escada de jacó,* 1934. The three books were later published as *Os condenados.* Pôrto Alegre: Lluraná do Globo, 1941.)

*Memórias sentimentais de João Miramar.* São Paulo: Independência, 1924.

*A estrêla de absinto.* São Paulo: Hélios, 1927.

*Serafim Ponte Grande.* Rio de Janeiro: Ariel, 1934.

*Escada vermelha.* São Paulo: Companhia Editorial Nacional, 1934.

*A revolução melancólica.* Rio de Janeiro: José Olympio, 1943. Republished as *Marco zero I: A revolução melancólica.* Rio de Janeiro: Civilização Brasileira, 1974.

*Chão*. Rio de Janeiro: José Olympio, 1945. Republished as *Marco zero II: Chão*. Rio de Janeiro: Civilização Brasileira, 1974.

### Drama

*Mon coeur Balance/Leur Âme*. With Guilherme de Almeida. São Paulo: Tipografia Asbahr, 1916.
*O homem e o cavalo*. Rio de Janeiro: Civilização Brasileira, 1973. (Written in 1934.)
*A morta*. Rio de Janeiro: Civilização Brasileira, 1973. (Written in 1937.)
*O rei da vela*. Rio de Janeiro: Civilização Brasileira, 1973. (Written in 1937.)

### Collected Works

*Obras completas*. 12 vols. Rio de Janeiro: Civilização Brasileira, 1972–1975.
*Obras completas*. 24 vols. Campinas, São Paulo: Unicamp, 1990.

### Other Works

"Manifesto da poesia pau-brasil." *Correio da Manhã* (São Paulo), 18 March 1924.
"Manifesto antropófago." *Revista de Antropofagia* (São Paulo) 1, no. 1 (May 1928).
*Um homem sem profissão: Sob as ordens de mamãe*. Rio de Janeiro: José Olympio, 1954.
*Do pau-brasil à antropofagia e às utopias*. Vol. 6, *Obras completas*. Rio de Janeiro: Civilização Brasileira, 1972.
*Ponta de lança*, 3d ed. Rio De Janeiro: Civilização Brasileira, 1972.
*Telefonema*. Rio de Janeiro: Civilização Brasileira, 1974.
*O perfeito cozinheiro das almas deste mundo*. São Paulo: Ex Libris, 1987.

## Secondary Works

### Critical and Biographical Studies

"O ABC de Oswald de Andrade." *Correio da Manhã* (Rio de Janeiro), 29 June 1968.
Abreu, Brício de. "*Rei da vela*: Oswald 34 anos depois I." 11 January 1968.
Alencar, Audísio de. "Um homem sem profissão." *A Comarca* (Jundiaí) 28 October 1954.

Almeida, Guilherme de. "Revelação do Brasil pela poesia moderna." *O Estado de São Paulo,* 17 February 1962.
Almeida, Martins de. "Pau Brasil." In *Brasil: 1° Tempo Modernista: 1917–29 Documentação*. Edited by Marta Rossetti Batista, Telê Porto Ancona Lopez, and Yone Soares de Lima. São Paulo: Instituto de Estudos Brasileiros/Universidade de São Paulo, 1972.
Alphonsus, João. "Primeiro Caderno de Poesia." *Diário de Minas* (Belo Horizonte), 14 September 1927.
Alves, Henrique J. "Oswald e seus tabus." *Jornal de Letras* (Rio de Janeiro), May 1985.
Amado, Jorge. "Notícia do poeta, romancista e crítico." *O imparcial* (Salvador), 7 July 1944.
Amaral, Aracy. *Blaise Cendrars no Brasil e os modernistas*. São Paulo: Martins, 1970.
———. *Tarsila: Sua obra e seu tempo*. 2 vols. São Paulo: Perspectiva, Editora da Universidade de São Paulo, 1975.
Amaral, Tarsila do. "Galeria dos antropófagos." *Antropofagia* (Rio de Janeiro), 29 August 1929.
Andrade, Carlos Drummond de. "Os condenados de Oswald de Andrade." *Diário de Minas* (Belo Horizonte), 30 September 1922.
———. "Nacionalismo literário." *O Jornal* (Rio de Janeiro), 23 January 1925.
———. "Maiores de 50 anos." *Correio da Manhã* (Rio de Janeiro), 9 April 1950.
———. "O antropófago." *Correio Paulistano* (São Paulo), 24 October 1954.
———. "Ainda o 'Mês Modernista.'" *Correio da Manhã* (Rio de Janeiro), 7 March 1969.
———. "Lembrança do 'Mês Modernista.'" *Correio da Manhã* (Rio de Janeiro), 5 March 1969.
———. "O homem do *Pau Brasil*." In *Brasil: 1° Tempo Modernista: 1917–29 Documentação*. Edited by Marta Rossetti Batista, Telê Porto Ancona Lopez, and Yone Soares de Lima. São Paulo: Instituto de Estudos Brasileiros/Universidade de São Paulo, 1972.
———. *O observador no escritório*. Rio de Janeiro: Record, 1985.
———. "Entre Bandeira e Oswald de Andrade." In *Tempo vida poesia*. Rio de Janeiro: Record, 1986.
Andrade, Joaquim Pedro de. "O homem do *Pau Brasil*." In *Folha volante do filme*. Rio de Janeiro: Embrafilme, 1980.
Andrade, Mario de. "Oswald de Andrade." *Revista do Brasil* (São Paulo), September/December 1924.
———. "Oswald de Andrade: *Pau Brasil*. Sans Pareil, Paris, 1925." In *Brasil: 1° Tempo Modernista: 1917–29 Documentação*. Edited by Marta Rossetti Batista, Telê Porto Ancona Lopez, and Yone Soares de Lima. São

Paulo: Instituto de Estudos Brasileiros/Universidade de São Paulo, 1972.

———. *O movimento modernista*. Rio de Janeiro: Casa do Estudante do Brasil, 1942.

Andrade, Paulo Marcos de. "Redescoberto Oswald de Andrade: Statement by Professor Antônio Cândido." *Folha de São Paulo*, 28 August 1967.

Andrade, Rudá de. "Carta a Antônio Cândido." In *Vários escritos*, by Antônio Candido. São Paulo: Livraria Duas Cidades, 1970.

Andrade, Filho. "Oswald de Andrade: *Serafim Ponte Grande*, capitalista." *A Tribuna* (Santos), 19 August 1972.

Arinos Sobrinho, Affonso. "Oswald de Andrade. Poesia Pau Brasil." *Revista do Brasil* (Rio de Janeiro), 29 September 1926.

Arrabal, José. "Oswald: Processo." *Folha de São Paulo*, 1 November 1964.

———. "À Margem do *Rei da vela*." *O Jornal* (Rio de Janeiro), 21 February 1971.

Athayde, Tristão de. "Literatura suicida." *O Mundo Literário* (Rio de Janeiro), 5 September 1925.

———. "Queimada ou fogo de artifício?" *O Jornal* (Rio de Janeiro), 11 October 1925.

———. "Os Andrades I." *O Jornal* (Rio de Janeiro), 29 January 1928.

———. "*Os condenados.*" *O Globo* (Rio de Janeiro), 23 December 1941. (Review.)

———. "Os primeiros romances modernistas." *Folha de São Paulo*, 21 November 1960.

———. "Os Andrades." *Jornal do Brasil* (Rio de Janeiro), 29 July 1967.

———. "O deus perdido." *Folha de São Paulo*, 28 September 1967.

Ávila, Affonso. "Minas e poesia de Oswald de Andrade." *Minas Gerais* (Belo Horizonte), 10 December 1966.

Baciu, Stefan. "Algumas anotações sobre o poeta." *Tribuna da Imprensa* (Rio de Janeiro), 25–26 September 1954.

Bandeira, Manuel. "Poesia *Pau Brasil*." *O Mundo Literário* (Rio de Janeiro), 5 May 1924.

———. Oswald de Andrade Serafim Ponte Grande. *Literatura* (Rio de Janeiro), 5 August 1933.

———. *Apresentação da poesia brasileira*, 3rd ed. Rio de Janeiro: Casa do Estudante do Brasil, 1957.

Barata, Mário. "*Pau Brasil* de Tarsila a Oswald." *GAM* (Rio de Janeiro), 11, 1968.

Bárbara, Danusia. "O mito Oswald." *Jornal do Brasil* (Rio de Janeiro), 30 May 1982.

Barreto, Plínio. "Oswald de Andrade: *Marco zero.*" In *Antologia do ensaio literário paulista*. Edited by José Aderaldo Castelo. São Paulo: Conselho Estadual de Cultura, 1960.

Barros, A. Couto de. "*Os condenados*: Oswald de Andrade, Edição Monteiro Lobato." *Klaxon* (São Paulo), 15 October 1922.

Barroso, Antônio Girão. "Oswald de Andrade." *Correio do Ceará*, 8 January 1946.

Bastide, Roger. "*Os condenados* de Oswald de Andrade." *O Estado de São Paulo*, 7 June 1942.

———. "Notas de leitura: *Marco zero*." *O Estado de São Paulo*, 25 November 1943.

———. "Os poemas de Oswald de Andrade." *O Jornal* (Rio de Janeiro), 14 April 1945.

Bastos, Oliveira. "Oswald de Andrade." *Revista da Semana* (Rio de Janeiro), 1954.

———. "Oswald de Andrade e a antropofagia." *Jornal do Brasil* (Rio de Janeiro), 20 October 1957.

———. "Oswald de Andrade e a antropofagia." *Minas Gerais* (Belo Horizonte), 16 January 1971.

Bezerra, João Clímaco. "Oswald de Andrade." *O Jornal* (Rio de Janeiro), 5 December 1954.

Boaventura, Maria Eugenia. *Remate de males. Journal of the Literary Theory Department of Unicamp*, no. 6, 1986. (Issue devoted to Oswald de Andrade.)

———. *Os dentes do dragão: Entrevistas.* São Paulo: Secretaria de Estado de Cultura/Editora Glóbo, 1990. (Not all of the interviews are included and it has texts that were previously published in books from the *Obras completas*.)

———. *O salão e a selva.* Campinas: Unicamp, 1995.

Bonvincino, Régis. "Uma trajetória crítica." *Folha de São Paulo* (São Paulo), 27 November 1983.

Bopp, Raul. *Movimentos modernistas no Brasil.* Rio de Janeiro: Livraria São José, 1966.

———. *Vida e morte da antropofagia.* Rio de Janeiro: Civilização Brasileira, 1976.

———. "A antropofagia; um programa genuinamente nacionalista." *Correio do Povo* (Pôrto Alegre), 12 February 1982.

Bosi, Alfredo. "Oswald de Andrade." In his *História concisa da literatura brasileira.* São Paulo: Cultrix, 1970.

Braga, Edgard. "Máscara para Oswald." *Diário de São Paulo*, 21 November 1954.

———. "Máscara de Andrade Vivo." *Diário de São Paulo*, 20 December 1959.

———. "Da irreverência em Oswald de Andrade." *Leitura* (São Paulo), October 1960.

———. "Reinstauração do mito." *Diário de São Paulo*, 15 September 1963.

Braga, Rubem. "Oswald." *Correio da Manhã* (Rio de Janeiro), 24 October 1954.

Brito, Mário da Silva. "Os poemas de Oswald de Andrade." *O Jornal* (Rio de Janeiro), 14 April 1945.

———. *História do modernismo brasileiro*. Rio de Janeiro: Civilização Brasileira, 1964.

———. "A revolução modernista." In *A literatura no Brasil*. Edited by Afrânio Coutinho. Rio de Janeiro: Sul América, 1968.

———. *Ângulo e horizonte*. São Paulo: Martins, 1969.

———. *As metamorfoses de Oswald de Andrade*. São Paulo: Conselho Estadual de Cultura, 1972.

———. *Conversa vai conversa vem*. Rio de Janeiro: Civilização Brasileira, 1974.

———. *Cartola de mágico*. Rio de Janeiro: Civilização Brasileira, 1976.

———. "Oswald de Andrade." In his *O fantasma sem castelo*. Rio de Janeiro: Civilização Brasileira, 1980.

Broca, Brito. "A aventura modernista." *A Gazeta* (São Paulo), 22 February 1942.

———. "A Semana de Arte Moderna." *A Manhã: Letras e Artes*, no. 4. (Rio de Janeiro), 10 February 1950.

———. "O caso Oswald de Andrade: *Um homem sem profissão*." *A Gazeta* (São Paulo), 23 October 1954.

Bruno, Haroldo. "Confissões de Oswald de Andrade." *Diário de Notícias* (Rio de Janeiro), 30 January 1955.

Cámara, Jayme Adour de. "Antropofagia: Revolta da sinceridade recalcada." *Jornal do Brasil* (Rio de Janeiro), 12 August 1957.

Campos, Augusto de. "Revista re-vistas: Os antropófagos." *Revista de Antropofagia* (São Paulo), April 1975.

———. "Poesia, antipoesia, antropofagia." São Paulo: Cortez and Moraes, 1978. Pp. 107–126.

Campos, Haroldo de. "Oswald de Andrade." *Jornal do Brasil* (Rio de Janeiro), 1 September 1957.

———. "Lirismo e participação." *O Estado de São Paulo*, 6 July 1963.

———. "Estilística miramarina." *O Estado de São Paulo*, 24 October 1964.

———. "Miramar na mira." In *Memórias Sentimentais de João Miramar*, by Oswald de Andrade. Rio de Janeiro: Civilização Brasileira, 1971. Pp. xiii–xlviii.

———. "Uma poética da radicalidade." In *Poesias reunidas*, by Oswald de Andrade. 3rd ed. Rio de Janeiro: Civilização Brasileira, 1972.

———. "Oswald de Andrade." *Europe* 57, no. 599:27–37 (March 1979).

———. "Da razão antropofágica: A Europa sob o signo da devoração." *Colóquio* (Lisbon), July 1981.

———. "Serafim: Um grande não livro." In *Serafim Ponte Grande*, by Oswald de Andrade. São Paulo: Global, 1984.

Candido, Antônio. "Antes do *Marco zero*." *Folha da Manhã* (São Paulo), 15 August 1943.

———. "Estouro e libertação." In his *Brigada ligeira*. São Paulo: Martins, 1945.

———. "Prefácio inútil." In *Um homem sem profissão*, by Oswald de Andrade. Rio de Janeiro: Civilização Brasileira, 1954.

———. "Oswald viajante." *O Estado de São Paulo*, 27 October 1956.

———. "Osẃald, Oswaldo, Ôswald." *Folha de São Paulo*, 21 March 1982.

———. "Digressão sentimental sobre Oswald de Andrade." In *Serafim Ponte Grande*, by Oswald de Andrade. São Paulo: Global, 1984.

Carvalho, Flávio de. "O Antropófago Oswald de Andrade." *Manchete* (Rio de Janeiro), n.d.

———. "Oswald de Andrade." *Diário de São Paulo*, 21 November 1954.

Castelo, José Aderaldo. "Oswald de Andrade." *Anhembi* (São Paulo), December 1954.

———. "Oswald de Andrade." In his *Homens e intenções*. São Paulo: Conselho de Estado de Cultura, 1959.

Castro, Ruy. "A antropofagia cultural." *Correio da Manhã* (Rio de Janeiro), 21 January 1968.

———. "Os melhores desaforos de um mestre modernista." *Folha da Tarde* (São Paulo), 20 October 1984.

Cavalcanti, Gilberto. "Eles recordam os companheiros mortos." *Leitura* (Rio de Janeiro), August/September 1964. (Interview with Guilherme de Almeida.)

Cavalcanti, Sebastião. "Oswald, a flauta e o violão." *Correio da Manhã* (Rio de Janeiro), 22 August 1964.

Cavalcanti, Valdemar. "O avesso." *O Jornal* (Rio de Janeiro), 14 November 1954.

———. "Oswald de Andrade volta à tona." *O Jornal* (Rio de Janeiro), 18 October 1970.

Cavalheiro, Edgard. "A trilogia do exílio." *O Estado de São Paulo*, 8 February 1942.

Chalmers, Vera Maria. "Um texto jornalístico sem papas na língua." *Folha de São Paulo*, 20 October 1984.

Chamie, Mário. "Calidostópico e distaxia." In *Intertexto*. São Paulo: Praxis, 1971.

———. "O santeiro do mangue." *O Estado de São Paulo*, 20 October 1974.

———. *A linguagem virtual*. São Paulo: Quiron, 1976. Pp. 5–57.

Chaves, Flávio Loureiro. "Contribuições de Oswald e Mário de Andrade ao romance brasileiro." In *Aspectos do Modernismo Brasileiro*, by Flávio Loureiro Chaves et al. Porto Alegre: Comissão Central de Publicações, Universidade Federal do Rio Grande do Sul, 1970.

Chaves Neto, Elias. "Um romance." *Correio da Manhã* (Rio de Janeiro), 22 February 1942.

Coelho, João Marcos. "Concerto multimídia para Oswald." *Folha de São Paulo*, 27 October 1984.

Coelho, Ruy. "Oswald de Andrade: *Os condenados*." *Clima* (São Paulo), 8 January 1942.

Corção, Gustavo. "Encontros com Oswald de Andrade." *Jornal do Dia* (Pôrto Alegre), 16 January 1955.

Crespo, Angel. "Introducción breve a Oswald de Andrade." *Revista de Cultura Brasileña* (Madrid), 1968.

Cunha, Dulce Salles. "O movimento antropofágico." In *Autores Contemporâneos Brasileiros*. São Paulo: Cupolo, 1951.

Cunha, Fausto. "Tristão e Oswald: A volta ao campo de batalha." *Jornal do Brasil* (Rio de Janeiro), 29 February 1972.

Cutolo, Giovanni. "Oswald de Andrade do Giovanni Miramar." In *Memorie sentimentali di Giovanni Miramare*, by Oswald de Andrade. Milan: Feltrinelli, 1970.

Dantas, Pedro. "Os Andrades, da independência literária." *Jornal do Brasil* (Rio de Janeiro), 29 January 1972.

———. "Oswald, precursor e revolucionário." *Jornal do Brasil* (Rio de Janeiro), 30 June 1973.

Delamare, Germane. "O rei desce no Rio." *Jornal do Brasil* (Rio de Janeiro), 31 December 1967.

Del Picchia, Menotti. "Oswald d'Andrade." *Correio Paulistano* (São Paulo), 21 April 1921.

———. "*Memórias sentimentais de João Miramar*." *Correio Paulistano* (São Paulo), 10 October 1924.

———. "*Memórias sentimentais de João Miramar*." *Correio Paulistano* (São Paulo), 15 June 1925.

———. "Oswald, o destruidor." *A Gazeta* (São Paulo), 6 November 1954.

———. "Oswald e Corção." *A Gazeta* (São Paulo), 16 January 1957.

———. "Oswald." *A Gazeta* (São Paulo), 5 December 1958.

Di Cavalcanti, Emiliano. "Viagem de minha vida (memórias)." In *O testamento da alvorada*. Rio de Janeiro: Civilização Brasileira, 1955.

Diaféria, Lourenço C. "A vela e o dia depois do outro." *Folha de São Paulo*, 30 September 1967.

Doyle, Plínio. "História de revistas e jornais literários." *Revista do Livro* (Rio de Janeiro), 13 April 1970.

Eulalio, Alexandre. *Aventura brasileira de Blaise Cendrars*. São Paulo: Quiron, 1978.

———. "Caniboswáld." *Jornal da República* (São Paulo), 4 October 1979.

———. "O homem do *Pau Brasil* na cidade dele." *Vogue* (São Paulo), July 1980.

———. "O homem do *Pau Brasil*." In *Folha volante do filme*. Rio de Janeiro: Embrafilme, 1981.

Faria, Maria Alice. "Uma fonte de Oswald de Andrade." *O Estado de São Paulo* (São Paulo), 27 November 1954.

Ferraz, Geraldo. "Oswald de Andrade, uma apologia e um libelo." *Jornal de Notícias* (São Paulo), 19 February 1950.

———. "Os antropófagos no Diário de São Paulo." *Diário de São Paulo*, 21 November 1954.

Ferreira, Procópio. "Procópio fala de Andrade." *O Estado de São Paulo*, 23 September 1967.

Feres, Nites. "Mário de Andrade, leitor de Oswald." *Revista do Instituto de Estudos Brasileiros*. São Paulo: Instituto de Estudos Brasileiros/Universidade de São Paulo, 1962.

Fernandes, Almeida. "Totens e tabus na modernidade brasileira: Símbolo e alegoria em Oswald de Andrade." *O Estado de São Paulo*, 23 June 1985.

Fonseca, Maria Augusta. *Palhaço da burguesia*. São Paulo: Pólis, 1979.

———. Oswald de Andrade. São Paulo: Brasiliense, 1982.

Freitas, Maria Eurides Pitombeira de. "Oswald de Andrade e o modernismo." *Linguagem* (Rio de Janeiro), 1983.

Freyre, Gilberto. "Agitação beneficiou as letras e as artes." *O Estado de São Paulo*, 20 February 1972.

———. "Oswald de Andrade revisado." *O Estado de São Paulo*, 2 June 1985.

Gama, Mauro. "Oswald um antropófago de *Pau Brasil*." *Ele & Ela* (Rio de Janeiro), December 1982.

George, David. *Teatro e antropofagia*. São Paulo: Global, 1985.

Goes, Fernando. "As faces de Oswald de Andrade." *Jornal do Brasil* (Rio de Janeiro), 18 June 1974.

Gonçalves Filho, Antônio. "No palco, o épico antropofágico de Oswald." *Folha de São Paulo*, 17 December 1985.

Greenwald, José Lino. "Serafim e a prosa." *Correio da Manhã* (Rio de Janeiro), 8 January 1972.

Griecco, Agrippino. *Gente nova do Brasil*, 2nd ed. Rio de Janeiro: José Olympio, 1948.

Hecher Filho, Paulo. "Oswald: Uma correspondência." *O Estado de São Paulo*, 7 December 1968.

———. "Eu em compensação." *Correio do Povo* (Pôrto Alegre), 8 February 1969.

Helena, Lúcia. *Uma literatura antropofágica*. Rio de Janeiro: Cátedra, 1982.

———. *Totens e tabus da modernidade brasileira: Símbolo e alegoria na obra de Oswald de Andrade*. Rio de Janeiro: Tempo Brasileiro; Niterói: Universidade Federal Fluminense, 1985.

Inojosa, Joaquim. *Os Andrades e outros aspectos do modernismo*. Rio de Janeiro: Civilização Brasileira, 1975.

———. "O sempre lembrado modernista Oswald de Andrade." *Jornal do Comércio*, 26 October 1984.

Ivo, Ledo. *Modernismo e modernidade.* Rio de Janeiro: São José, 1972.

———. "De Oswald de Andrade a Oswald de Andrade." *Letras* (Suplemento Literário), 21 August 1977.

Jackson, Kenneth David. "A metamorfose dos textos em *Serafim Ponte Grande.*" *Travessia* (Florianópolis), January/June 1984.

Jacobbi, Ruggero. *O expectador apaixonado: Teatro de Oswald de Andrade.* Pôrto Alegre: Curso de Arte Dramática, Faculdade de Filosofia, Universidade Federal de Rio Grande do Sul, 1962.

Junqueira, Ivan. "As contradições de Oswald de Andrade se nenhuma compaixão." *Jornal do Brasil* (Rio de Janeiro), 27 April 1985.

Jurema, Aderbal. "Subindo a escada vermelha." *Boletim de Ariel* (Rio de Janeiro), 4 February 1935.

Kopke, Carlos Burlamaqui. *Faces descobertas.* São Paulo: Martins, 1944.

Lemos, Pinheiro de. "Um antropófago com fome." *O Globo* (Rio de Janeiro), 30 November 1954.

Lewin, W. "Oswald de Andrade, o polernista sem ressentimentos." *Jornal do Brasil* (Rio de Janeiro), 31 July 1971.

Linguanoto, Daniel. "Perdeu o apetite o terrível antropófago." *Manchete* (Rio de Janeiro), 17 April 1954.

Linhares, Temístocles. "Sobre o romance, o Sr. Oswald de Andrade e *Marco Zero.*" *Folha da Manhã* (São Paulo), 5 July 1945.

Lins, Álvaro. *Literatura e vida literária.* Rio de Janeiro: Civilização Brasileira, 1963.

Lins, Edison. *História e crítica da poesia brasileira.* Rio de Janeiro: Ariel, 1937.

Litrento, Cliveiros. "Oswald de Andrade." *Jornal do Comércio,* 7 November 1954.

Lucas, Fábio. "Oswaldianas. Diário Oficial." *Leitura* (São Paulo), 10 November 1984.

Machado, Lourival Gomes. "Testemunho reconfirmado." *O Estado de São Paulo,* 17 February 1962.

Machado Filho. "Aires da Mata. *Revista da Antropofagia* e novo livro de poemas." *O Estado de São Paulo,* 15 February 1976.

Magaldi, Sábato. *Panorama do teatro brasileiro.* São Paulo: Difusão Européia do Livro, 1962.

———. "É um rei da irreverência." *Jornal da Tarde* (São Paulo), 3 October 1967.

———. "Teatro: *Marco zero.*" In *O rei da vela,* by Oswald de Andrade. São Paulo: Difusão Européia do Livro, 1967.

———. "Defesa de Oswald." *Veja* (São Paulo), 27 December 1972.

Martins, Heitor. "A anatomia de *Serafim Ponte Grande.*" *O Estado de São Paulo,* 15 February 1969.

———. *Oswald de Andrade e outros.* São Paulo: Conselho Estadual de Cultura, Comissão de Literatura, 1973.

Martins, Luís. "Amicus Plato. . . ." *O Estado de São Paulo,* 3 October 1959.

Martins, Wilson. *O modernismo.* São Paulo: Cultrix, 1967.

———. "Fontes oswaldianas." *O Estado de São Paulo,* 19 May 1974.

Mendonça, Antônio Sérgio. *Poesia de vanguarda no Brasil: De Oswald de Andrade ao concretismo e o poema processo.* Petrópolis: Vozes, 1970.

———. "Re-leitura de Oswald." *Revista de Cultura* (Petrópolis), May 1972.

Michalski, Yan. "Considerações em torno do 'rei'—II." *Jornal do Brasil* (Rio de Janeiro), 16–17 January 1968.

Milliet, Sérgio. *Diário crítico.* São Paulo: Brasiliense, 1944.

———. *Diário crítico.* São Paulo: Martins, 1964.

Montello, Josué. "O poeta fidalgo." *Jornal do Comércio* (São Paulo), 19 September 1963.

Montenegro, Olívio. "As confissões de Oswald de Andrade." *O Jornal* (Rio de Janeiro), 28 November 1954.

———. "As confissões de Oswald de Andrade." *Diário de São Paulo,* 1 January 1955.

Moraes Neto, Prudente de, and Sérgio Buarque de Hollanda. "Oswald de Andrade: Memórias sentimentais de João Miramar." *Estética* (Rio de Janeiro), January/March 1925.

Morse, Richard M. "Triangulating Two Cubists: William Carlos Williams and Oswald." *Latin American Literary Review,* January/June 1986.

Mota Filho, Cândido. "A semana literária." *Correio Paulistano* (São Paulo), 20 August 1922.

———. "Ponta de lança." In his *Contagem regressiva.* Rio de Janeiro: José Olympio, 1972.

Mourão, Rui. "A instauração de uma vanguarda brasileira II." *O Estado de São Paulo* (São Paulo), 31 January 1970.

———. "Mário versus Oswald." *O Estado de São Paulo,* 18 July 1971.

Moutinho, José Geraldo Nogueira. "Oswald Miramar." *Folha de São Paulo,* 25 October 1954.

———. "Antropofagia, agora também em francês." *Folha de São Paulo,* 12 July 1982.

Novais, Frederico de. "Do *Pau Brasil* até a antropofagia: Duas fases de um movimento." *O Globo* (Rio de Janeiro), 13 February 1982.

Nunes, Benedito. *Oswald canibal.* São Paulo: Perspectiva, 1979.

Nunes, Cassiano. "A grandeza e a miséria de Oswald de Andrade." *A Gazeta* (Brasília), 28 October 1984.

Oliveira, Franklin de. "A emergência do novo." *Correio da Manhã* (Rio de Janeiro), 20–21 February 1972.

Oliveira, José Carlos. "A aventura paulista." *Jornal do Brasil* (Rio de Janeiro), 19 April 1963.

———. "Oswald de Andrade: Antropofagia libertadora." *Jornal do Brasil* (Rio de Janeiro), 5 December 1970.

Paes, José Paulo. "O menino inconsolável diante do mundo." *O Tempo* (São Paulo), 21 November 1954.

Peixoto, Silveira. "Oswald de Andrade é um saci-pererê." *A Gazeta* (São Paulo), 21 September 1941.

———. "Oswald de Andrade, o devorador de homens." *Jornal do Brasil* (Rio de Janeiro), 20 January 1968.

Peralva, Oswaldo. "Oswald e Picabia." *Folha de São Paulo,* 24 October 1984.

Pereira, Antônio Olavo. "Oswald, homem sem maldade." *Diário de São Paulo,* 21 November 1954.

Perrone-Moisés, Leyla. "Un grand écrivan joyeux." *La Quinzaine littéraire* (Paris), 13–31 July 1982.

Picchio, Luciana Stegano. *La letteratura brasiliana.* Florence: Sansoni; Milan: Accademia, 1972.

———. "Antropofagia: Cialla letteratura ai mito e dai mito alia letteratura." *Letteratura d'Americai* (Rome), 2 August 1981, pp. 5–43.

Pignatari, Décio. *Contracomunicação.* São Paulo: Perspectiva, 1971.

———. "Psicografando Oswald de Andrade." *Folha de São Paulo,* 27 June 1982.

———. "A mente e o ícone." *Folha de São Paulo,* 26 October 1984.

Pimentel, Cyro. "Imagens de Oswald." *Diário de São Paulo,* 21 November 1954.

Polvora, Hélio. "Tupy or not Tupy." *Jornal do Brasil* (Rio de Janeiro), 3 December 1969.

Pontes, Mário. "Oswald a exata medida de um iconoclasta." *Jornal do Brasil* (Rio de Janeiro), 27 March 1971.

Prado, Décio de Almeida. "A encenação de *O rei da vela.*" *O Estado de São Paulo,* 20 October 1967.

Prado, Paulo. "*Poesia Pau Brasil.*" *Revista do Brasil* (Rio de Janeiro), October 1924.

Queiroz, Rachel de. "Crônica partida em duas." *O Cruzeiro* (Rio de Janeiro), 13 November 1954.

Ramos, Graciliano. "Conversa de livraria." In his *Linhas tortas.* São Paulo: Martins, 1962.

Ramos, Péricles Eugênio da Silva. "O *Correio Paulistano* e o movimento modernista." *Correio Paulistano* (São Paulo), 26 June 1949.

———. *Poesia moderna.* São Paulo: Melhoramentos, 1967.

———. "O modernismo na poesia." In *A Literatura no Brasil.* Edited by Afrânio Coutinho. Rio de Janeiro: Editorial Sul América, 1968.

———. "Semana: Inventário e manifesto." *O Estado de São Paulo,* 27 February 1972.

Rawet, Samuel. "Teatro no modernismo: Oswald de Andrade." In *Modernismo: Estudos críticos.* Edited by Jose Saldanha Coelho. Rio de Janeiro: Revista Blanca, 1954. Pp. 101–111.

Rego, José Lins do. "As memórias de Oswald de Andrade." *O Jornal* (Rio de Janeiro), 21 July 1954.

———. "Oswald de Andrade." *O Globo* (Rio de Janeiro), 26 October 1954.

Rey, Marcos. "Um antropófago de cadillac." *O Tempo* (São Paulo), 23 October 1954.

Ribeiro, João. "Registro literário: O. de Andrade, *Serafim Ponte Grande.*" *Jornal do Brasil* (Rio de Janeiro), 13 September 1933.

———. "Oswald de Andrade." In *Crítica.* Rio de Janeiro: Academia Brasileira de Letras, 1952.

Ricardo, Cassiano. "O 'neo-indianismo' de Oswald de Andrade." *O Estado de São Paulo,* 21 October 1963.

———. *Algumas reflexões sôbre poética de vanguarda.* Rio de Janeiro: José Olympio, 1964.

———. "Oswald de Andrade, o descobridor do menestrel." *O Estado de São Paulo,* 22 October 1972.

Rodrigues, Nelson. "O venerando animal." *Última Hora* (São Paulo), 9 June 1952.

Rodriguez Monegal, Emir. "Carnaval/Antropofagia/Paródia." *Revista Iberoamericana* (Madrid) 108 (June/December 1979).

Roig, Adrien. "Une nouvelle 'recontre' Oswald de Andrade—Blaise Cendrars: Interprétation du poeme 'Morro Azul.'" *Caravelle* 33 (1979).

Salgado, Plínio. "Impressões de leitura." *Novíssima.* São Paulo, n.d.

Salles, Fritz Teixeira de. *Das razões do modernismo.* Rio de Janeiro: Brasília, 1974.

Santos, G. Ehrhardt. "Ainda os condenados." *A Manhã* (Rio de Janeiro), 10 October 1943.

Scalzo, Nilo. "A semana de 22: Antes e depois." *O Estado de São Paulo,* 20 February 1972.

Schmidt, Augusto Frederico. "Oswald." *Correio da Manhã* (Rio de Janeiro), 26 October 1954.

Schwartz, Jorge, ed. *Oswald de Andrade.* São Paulo, 1980.

Silva, Domingos C. da. "A poesia em 22." *O Estado de São Paulo,* 17 February 1962.

Silveira, Alcântara. "Nos bons tempos da antropofagia." *O Estado de São Paulo,* 16 June 1969.

Silveira, Homero. "Oswald, Joyce & companhia." *Convivium* (São Paulo) 280:265–267 (May/June 1985).

Silveira, Joel. "Um novo encontro com Oswald de Andrade." *Jornal do Brasil* (Rio de Janeiro), 18 December 1971.

Souza Filho. "*Marco zero.*" *A Gazeta.* São Paulo, 11 November 1943.

Teles, Gilberto Mendonça. *La poesia brasileña en la actualidad.* Montevideo: Editorial Letras, 1969.

———. *Vanguarda européia e modernismo brasileiro,* 16th ed. Petrópolis: Vozes, 1972.

———. *A retórica do silêncio.* São Paulo: Cultrix, 1979.

———. *Estudos de poesia brasileira.* Coimbra, Portugal: Almedina, 1985.

———. "O 'gremial e o ordeiro' Oswald de Andrade." In his *Oswald Plural.* Rio de Janeiro: Universidade do Estado de Rio de Janeiro, 1995.

———. *A Escrituração da escrita.* Petrópolis: Vozes, 1996.

———. *Camões e a Poesia Brasileira,* 4th ed. Lisbon: Imprensa Nacional-Casa da Moeda, 2001.

———. *Contramargem.* Rio de Janeiro: Pontifícia Universidade Católica, 2001.

Tenorio, Carlos Alberto. "Os Linguarudos." *Diário Carioca* (Rio de Janeiro), 13 March 1955.

Thiollier, Renê. "Oswald de Andrade." *O Estado de São Paulo,* 3 December 1954.

———. *Oswald de Andrade: Episódios da minha vida.* São Paulo: Anhembi, 1956.

Torres, João C. de Oliveira. "O paradoxo das revoluções brasileiras." *O Estado de São Paulo,* 20 June 1971.

Travassos, Nelson Palma. "As raízes intelectuais do nosso mal econômico." *Aula Maior,* November 1966.

Ungaretti, Giusseppe. *Il deserto e dopo.* Milan: Mondadori, 1961.

———. Preface to *Memorie Sentimentali di Giovanni Miramare,* by Oswald de Andrade Milan: Feltrinelli, 1970.

Vares, Luís Pilla. "Ausência de Oswald." *Zero Hora* (Pôrto Alegre), 14 March 1982.

Ventura, Aglaêde Facó. "João Miramar." *Correio Brasiliense* (Brasília), 1 June 1975.

———. "João Miramar e a prosa moderna brasileira." *Minas Gerais* (Belo Horizonte), 21 February 1981.

Vidal, Ademar. "Fascinação política." *O Jornal* (Rio de Janeiro), 23 January 1955.

Vita, Luís Washington. "Tentativa de compreensão do legado especulativo de Oswald de Andrade." *Revista Brasileira de Filosofia* 4, no. 4 (October/December 1956).

Xavier, Lívio. "Oswald de Andrade: A arte no horizonte do provável. Crítica, criação e informação (invenção)." *O Estado de São Paulo,* 13 February 1965.

Wernerck, Humberto. "Antropofagia. Os cinqüenta anos do maior festim da cultura brasileira." *Veja,* 17 May 1978.

Zuccolotto, Afrânio. "Três tempos de Oswald de Andrade." *O Estado de São Paulo,* 20 October 1974.

# Reinaldo Arenas

## (1943–1990)

## César A. Salgado

"Grito; luego existo" (I shout; therefore I am), Reinaldo Arenas often wrote. This proclamation of existential defiance, anger, and anguish helps explain the aesthetic, political, and erotic fury in Arenas's novels, poems, and essays. Arenas used literature as an irreverent vehicle of protest and self-expression against the marginalization he suffered as a homosexual and intellectual outsider under authoritarian regimes in his native Cuba and during his exile in the United States after 1980 until his death.

Each of Arenas's works can be regarded as a chapter in a vast, multiform, and compulsively revised fictional autobiography. In all of Arenas's fiction, a hounded protagonist rebels against familial dysfunction and abjection, state persecution and despotism, social intolerance and homophobia, unjust imprisonment, cultural uprootedness, and spiritual despair. The persistence of the social outcast to gain freedom and acknowledgment against all odds often is linked in Arenas's work to a fixation with writing as an act of self-legitimization and survival. The Cuban writer Severo Sarduy observed that in Arenas "everything says 'I' to vindicate its *access-to-being,* even what is most expendable, most mute." Ironically, this ferocious coming into being through literature culminated with Arenas's suicide in 1990, a conclusive signature that brought to completion both his life and his work.

Critical and popular appreciation of Arenas's writings grew after his death with the appearance in 1992 of his sensational, sexually frank autobiography *Antes que anochezca* (*Before Night Falls*, 1993). The 1990s were thus a boon for the publication of new translations, critical analyses, and queer theory studies of Arenas's works. This enthusiasm reached its peak in 2000 with the production of a major independent movie inspired by Arenas's memoirs. As a writer, Arenas was gifted with an exuberant imagination that could indulge in hyperbole and baroque excesses while maintaining a fundamental dreamy lyricism. He also showed a special talent for narrative experimentation, parody, and wordplay in the traditions of such modernist masters as the American novelist William Faulkner, the British writer Virginia Woolf, and the Argentine author Jorge Luis Borges. With these tools, he confronted the contradictions and vested interests of Latin American and Cuban official history through an iconoclastic and hallucinatory rewriting of some of its canonical documents.

Born on 16 July 1943, Reinaldo Arenas grew up in Perronales, a small and backward peasant community between the cities of Holguín and Gibara in the Cuban province of Oriente. Arenas's father abandoned his mother, Oneida Fuentes, three months after his conception; after that, Oneida avoided relationships with men. At five years of age, Arenas met his father briefly, when a stranger approached him with two pesos over Oneida's insults and aggressions. This memory of the yearned-for father haunted Arenas throughout his life. Young Reinaldo and Oneida were taken in by her parents, with whom they lived on a failing maize farm. Arenas continued to live there in destitute conditions with other disowned aunts and cousins, a bitter and reserved grandfather, and a charismatic and superstitious grandmother.

The wilderness in Oriente deeply influenced the child's poetic sensibility. Arenas later claimed that rapport with his tropical environment gave him a profound sense of freedom and that an animistic awareness of telluric spirits and forces initiated him into erotic life. In his memoir, Arenas described his childhood as "the most literary moment of my life"; it was then that he learned the distinctive idiom that Cuban country folk use for local fauna and flora, an emphatic diction full of tonalities and accents that he would later use to great effect in his novels. In 1954 his grandfather decided to sell the farm, and the extended family moved to Holguín. Still, the grocery store administered from their new home did not prosper. The Cuban revolutionary Fidel Castro's guerrilla rebellion against Fulgencio Batista's dictatorship spread from the Sierra Maestra into lower Oriente to the environs of Holguín in 1957, offering hopes of social change and deliverance from harsh poverty. When he was fifteen, Arenas tried to join the guerrillas in the mountains near Velasco. He was turned away when he was not able to stab one of Batista's soldiers and steal his gun. These events inspired several of his works, especially his novel *El palacio de las blanquísimas mofetas* (published first in French as *La palais de tres blanches moufettes*, 1975; *The Palace of the White Skunks*, 1990).

Like many other disenfranchised young men from the province, Arenas was swept up by the wave of change brought by Castro's revolution after Batista's fall. Between 1960 and 1962, Arenas trained as an agricultural accountant in the William Soler facility near Sierra Maestra; later in his life, he described it as a Soviet youth camp for communist indoctrination. In 1962, he moved to Havana with a scholarship to study public planning and worked at the Institute for Agrarian Reform. He chose to enroll in literature courses at the university, but never completed a degree. By this time, Arenas had a clear literary calling. In Holguín, inspired by Mexican B movies, he had completed three novels with such titles as "¡Qué dura es la vida!" (How harsh life is!) and "¡Adiós, mundo cruel!" (Goodbye, cruel world!) as well as three poetry books, all scribbled in school notebooks.

The next year was a turning point in his career. He entered a dramatic contest at the José Martí National Library in which he had to memorize and recite a famous children's story. Instead, he told one of his own, "Los zapatos vacíos" (The empty shoes), about a poor peasant boy who gets no presents during the traditional Three Kings Day (Epiphany, the festival celebrated on the twelfth day of Christmas and commemorating the visit of the Magi). Among the jurors were two poets from the noted 1940s and 1950s literary group Orígenes, Cintio Vitier and Eliseo Diego. Diego at that time headed the library's children's section. The two writers were so impressed with the story that they persuaded the library director, María Teresa Freyre de Andrade, to hire Arenas. There he worked as a researcher from 1963 to 1968. Under the tutelage and encouragement of the intellectuals affiliated with the library, Arenas voraciously read European and American classics. He also wrote poems, short stories, and a haunting novel about growing up in the province, *Celestino antes del alba* (1967; *Singing from the Well*, 1987). In 1964 Arenas submitted the manuscript of the novel to the Cirilo Villaverde contest sponsored by the Unión Nacional de Escritores y Artistas Cubanos (National Union of Cuban Writers and Artists, or UNEAC). He received honorable mention and an option for publication. The first edition was three thousand copies; it quickly sold out but was not reprinted.

The success of *Singing from the Well* brought Arenas's talent to the attention of the two deans of Cuban literature at the time, José Lezama Lima and Virgilio Piñera. They became Arenas's mentors and permanent points of reference in his work. Lezama Lima and Piñera represented conflicting cultural persuasions. The first was the author of esoteric, richly baroque poems, essays, and novels who professed Catholicism during the revolution. The second was an openly gay atheist who wrote terse, absurd plays and dark fables of alienation. Both were high modernists, Lezama Lima in the style of Stéphane Mallarmé, Marcel Proust, and James Joyce, Piñero in that of Ionesco and Franz Kafka. Their steadfast rejection of social realism as a valid formula for literature marked Arenas's literary temperament. In the 1960s their prestige as writers ensured them some official stature at the UNEAC despite their disaffection with Marxist ideology and the state's chauvinistic program to fashion an *hombre nuevo* (new man) under the revolution. They thus helped Arenas navigate the intrigues of Havana's literary circles in a period of increasing cultural closure. Lezama Lima broadened Arenas's readings through his *curso délfico* (route to Delphi), a tutorial on the best of world literature that Lezama offered to protégés in his private library. Piñera eventually became the stronger influence. He personally revised Arenas's writing methods and impressed upon the younger writer his creative, sardonic fascination with damnation and the grotesque.

While he was engaged in research at the library in preparation for a talk on the Mexican writer Juan Rulfo, Arenas was captivated by the memoirs of José Servando Teresa de Mier (1765–1827), a heretic Mexican friar and independence leader who spent most of life fleeing from the Spanish Inquisition and traveling through Europe. Inspired by Lezama Lima's discussion of Mier in his 1957 essay "La expresión americana" and drawing from other sources, Arenas fancifully rewrote the memoirs as *El mundo alucinante* (1969; *The Ill-Fated Peregrinations of Fray Servando*, 1987). Arenas submitted a jumbled draft of the novel to the 1966 UNEAC contest. The jurors José Antonio Portuondo and Alejo Carpentier refused to grant a first prize; *The Ill-Fated Peregrinations of Fray Servando* thus received the only honorable mention. Piñera, also a prize juror, helped Arenas revise the manuscript for publication; even then the authorities declined to print it. Although no clear reason was given, critics speculate that higher officials objected to the novel's homoerotic episodes and the profound skepticism toward linear historical progress manifest in its experimental narrative form.

In 1968 Arenas submitted a collection of stories under the title *Con los ojos cerrados* (1972; With eyes shut) to another UNEAC contest. Overall, the stories in this collection obliquely suggest that revolutionary reform could transform for the better a backward provincial life radically isolated and impoverished under Batista. The book won a prize, yet it also was refused publication. Piqued, Arenas sent both manuscripts out of the country—*The Ill-Fated Peregrinations of Fray Servando* to France and Mexico and *Con los ojos cerrados* to Uruguay—in search of a private publisher and without notifying the writers' union. *The Ill-Fated Peregrinations of Fray Servando*, quickly translated into French by Didier Coste, was first published by Editions du Seuil in 1969. A critical and popular success, it won that year's Médici Prize for best foreign novel published in France. In a 22 March 1969 article in *Le Monde*, Claude Couffon proposed that the novel could be read as a cloaked indictment of intellectual restrictions under the Castro regime. Arenas's reputation abroad as a *contestataire*, or political dissident, in Cuba thus was cemented. By the time the original version of the novel came out in Mexico in 1970, Arenas was already a writer of world renown while this fame was suppressed on the island.

In the late 1960s intellectual expression and literary production became more closely monitored and controlled in Cuba. Even books published after winning prizes at the UNEAC were censored publicly on the ground of ideological dissent. In 1968 an international jury that included Lezama Lima gave the UNEAC prize for poetry to Heberto Padilla's *Fuera del juego* (1969; Expelled from the game), a book that expressed critical disenchantment with collectivism and political militancy. The UNEAC board added in its edition a "declaration" that trenchantly denounced Padilla as a "diversionist" enemy of the revolution; it then rewrote its charter to exclude foreign jurors and antidogmatic submissions from its literary contests. The state also repressed homosexuals, *peludos* ("long-haired" Cuban hippies), and other groups with "extravagant" lifestyles through police raids and forced internment in military "rectification" camps known as UMAPS (an acronym for Unidades Militares de Ayuda a la Producción, or Military Units for Aids to Production). Even in this climate, after his gay awakening upon arriving in Havana, Arenas led an exceptionally active sexual life that flouted the state's moral rules. Embarrassed by the international success of *The Ill-Fated Peregrinations of Fray Servando*, the authorities plotted to ostracize Arenas as a writer. Arenas was invited to attend several conferences abroad, but the Cuban government did not allow him to leave the country, nor did it forward to him any foreign royalties earned for his work.

Even though his novels were not published or reprinted in Cuba, from 1967 to 1974 Arenas was able to work as an editor and writer at the Cuban Book Institute and at the two UNEAC journals, *Unión* and *La Gaceta de Cuba.* There he published highly idiosyncratic, vehement essays on Lezama Lima, José Martí, Gabriel García Márquez, and Antonio Benítez Rojo, among other topics. Secretly, however, he began work on what he considered would be his greatest work and "act of vengeance." Titled *Otra vez el mar* (1982; *Farewell to the Sea: A Novel of Cuba,* 1986), the text was to become a clandestine novel of frank homosexual character that unequivocally denounced the Castro regime. During this time, he also completed a bold, though not explicitly anti-Castro, experimental novel based on his adolescent years, *The Palace of the White Skunks.* Arenas envisioned these two works, together with *Singing from the Well* and two more he was still to write, as part of a five-novel cycle he called his *pentagonía* (a portmanteau word signifying "five agonies"). Conceived as a multidimensional autobiographical bildungsroman (coming-of-age saga) and a "secret history of Cuba," this *pentagonía* takes up the story of a young protagonist who dies in one novel and reincarnates under a different name in the next. Arenas's objective with the *pentagonía* was, as he notes in one of the novels, "cantar o contar el horror y la vida de la gente en medio de una época conmocionda y terrible con la misma airada rebeldía" (to sing or tell the horror and the life of people in the midst of a convulsive and terrible era with the same wrathful rebelliousness). Arenas thus put into practice Borges's aesthetic belief that, in a literary career, an author elaborated one unified and continuous book.

The year 1970 was onerous for Cuba and for Arenas. The failure to meet the ambitious ten-million-ton sugar harvest projected for that year threw the island into a deep economic crisis. Dependence on the Soviet Union increased enormously, communist dogmatism became absolute, and greater intellectual and social surveillance was institutionalized. Arenas and most of the writing staff at *La Gaceta de Cuba* were sent for six months to work and write journalistic reports on the great harvest at the Manuel Sanguily cane fields in Pinar del Río province. Arenas compared the exploitative and dehumanizing working conditions there to those of Indians and black slaves in Spanish *encomiendas* (estates) and sugar plantations; building on this analogy, Arenas secretly wrote during his breaks a furious condemnatory poem, *El central* (1981; *El Central: A Cuban Sugar Mill,* 1984). In the cultural sphere, the Stalinization of the regime climaxed with the notorious "Padilla affair" at the doctrinal 1971 Congress on Education and Culture. After the sudden gratuitous arrest of Padilla, state security coerced him into publicly retracting his "counterrevolutionary" writings while implicating other authors during a videotaped session held at the National Library. This forced confession, reminiscent of staged public trials under Joseph Stalin in the Soviet Union, drew international outrage. Intellectuals worldwide, many of whom had previously supported the revolution, signed letters demanding Padilla's immediate release, denounced Castro, and decried the revolution's new hard line with intellectual dissenters.

From 1970 to 1974, Arenas drew a salary from UNEAC but could not work or publish. Along with Padilla and other writers, he was turned into a "nonperson" and kept under constant state surveillance. Arenas trusted friends to hide his clandestine manuscripts. Back from the Sanguily harvest, he was led to believe that a zealous friend "outed" in *Farewell to the Sea* had destroyed the first version of the novel. In fact, the secret police had confiscated it. Undaunted, Arenas decided to rewrite it after smuggling out the manuscripts of *El central* and *The Palace* to Spain through foreign friends. To pretend normalcy and secure an apartment, Arenas married Ingrávida González, a famous Cuban film actress, but concerned about the potential publication abroad of *Farewell to the Sea,* state security opted to silence Arenas by prosecuting him for criminal homosexual acts. In this way they sought to circumvent the international uproar an "Arenas affair" could provoke.

In October of 1974, after being accused of molesting minors on the Guanabo beach, Arenas was detained, and criminal charges were filed against him. Thus began a desperate period of harrowing imprisonment and futile attempts to escape the island. Arenas broke parole, tried but failed to float to Florida in a rubber raft, attempted suicide, traveled under a false name to Oriente, and tried unsuccessfully to cross over to the U.S. naval base at Guantánamo. Still miraculously alive, he returned incognito to Havana and hid in subhuman conditions at the city's Lenin Park while a three-month island-wide police manhunt took place. In Havana wanted posters circulated portraying him as a murderer, a rapist, and an agent of the U.S. Central Intelligence Agency. In Paris, the UNESCO (United Nations Educational, Scientific, and Cultural Organization) and the press demanded proof of his whereabouts.

After his capture, he was sent to the dreaded Morro Prison, home to Cuba's most violent and hardened criminals. Meanwhile, Editions du Seuil published the French translation of *The Palace* in 1975. State security agents took Arenas out of his cell to interrogate him about his contacts abroad and about the manuscripts found after the police searched his home and those of his friends. He was coerced into signing a confession in which he acknowledged his "crimes," renounced his homosexuality and past writings, embraced the revolution, and declared his well-being and humane treatment. After serving a two-year sentence for *abusos lascivos* (lascivious acts), Arenas was set free. Arenas would later joke that during these years, he had been cursed to live out the life he fictionalized for Mier in his second novel.

After his release, Arenas disappeared into the limbo of those forsaken by the Cuban state, a picaresque underworld vividly described in his memoirs and his last novel, *El color del verano* (1991; *The Color of Summer,* 2000). Checking his old room, he discovered with regret that state security had removed the second version of *Farewell to the Sea* from its hiding place. He moved to a small room in a run-down Havana hotel; there he met the person who became his closest friend in his last years, Lázaro Gómez Carriles. Banned from state employment, Arenas survived by doing odd informal jobs, among them building apartment *barbacoas* (interior lofts), greatly in demand throughout housing-strapped Havana. Arenas resumed his writing and finished yet a third version of *Farewell to the Sea*; he participated discreetly in unofficial literary groups and reunions, but he had little hope of publishing. A 1979 interview with Cristina Guzmán, published in Caracas, finally brought him out of seclusion.

In 1980 the Peruvian embassy offered asylum to disaffected Cubans. Overnight, it was stormed by more than ten thousand people, Gómez Carriles among them; an international crisis ensued. Castro declared that anyone at the embassy who wanted to leave the island could do so. The Carter Administration responded by allowing U.S. boats to transport the refugees from Mariel, a harbor located east of Havana, to Florida. The Castro government took advantage of the Mariel boatlift to empty prisons and asylums, expelling all sorts of "undesirable" delinquents and misfits, including homosexuals. Using his criminal record, Arenas escaped from Mariel on 5 May, even though, as a censored writer, he was banned from leaving the island. Arenas later organized his only book of essays, *Necesidad de libertad* (1986, The need for freedom), as a collage of texts commemorating the Peruvian embassy takeover.

Arenas stayed three months in Miami after his arrival and gave his first U.S. talk at Florida International University. He found the city unremarkable and barren. After attending the Second Congress of Dissident Cuban Intellectuals at Columbia University in August of 1980, he moved to New York City. There he dedicated himself to recuperating, rewriting, and revising his books and salvaged manuscripts, including the 1971 novella *Arturo, la estrella más brillante* ("Arturo, the Shiniest Star," included in *Old Rose: A Novel in Two Stories,* 1989). He sorted out copyright issues so that he could publish these works in Miami, Caracas, and Barcelona presses. He also oversaw the translation of his works into English, German, Dutch, Polish, Japanese, and Portuguese. He was quickly awarded the Cintas Fellowship (1980, renewed in 1986) and the Guggenheim Fellowship (1981). With other boatlift exiles he founded and edited *Mariel,* a New York/Miami–based, vivacious literary magazine that lasted from 1983 to 1986. For the *Mariel* editorial board, he recruited the noted writer and Afro-Cuban folklorist Lydia Cabrera and the novelist Enrique Labrador Ruiz, rescuing them from obscurity.

In the mid-1980s Arenas found time to write and publish three new novels and novellas—*El portero* (1989; *The Doorman,* 1991), *La Loma del Angel* (1987; *Graveyard of the Angels,* 1987), and *Viaje a la Habana:*

*Novela en tres viajes* (1990; Voyage to Havana: A novella in three trips)—but left his pentagonía unfinished. Arenas became an energetic critic of Cuba's government. He founded or supported several anti-Castro organizations and human rights causes demanding a regime change in Cuba. He also was interviewed in several high-profile documentaries about oppression in Cuba: Jorge Ulla's *En sus propias palabras* (1980) and *L'altra Cuba* (1983), Nestor Almendros and Orlando Jiménez-Leal's *Mauvaise conduite* (1984), and Jana Bokova's *Havana* (1990). He was named writer-in-residence at the Center for Inter-American Relations (1982) and a fellow at the Woodrow Wilson Center in Washington, D.C. (1985). For several years he worked as a visiting professor at Florida International University (1980, 1983, and 1987) and at Cornell University (1985), and he lectured at Harvard, Yale, Vanderbilt, Tulane, Stockholm, the Sorbonne, and the University of Puerto Rico.

In 1987 Arenas discovered that he had contracted AIDS, and he felt the urge to conclude the last two novels of the *pentagonía* series. He first revised the fifth installment, nearly illegible, old rough draft of *El asalto* (1991; *The Assault*, 1994), with the help of friends. He then dedicated the last three years of his life to writing the fourth installment, the deliriously comic *The Color of Summer*. He also was able to finish the book of memoirs he had begun and lost while hiding in Havana's Lenin Park in 1974. Just a few days after concluding *The Color of Summer*, Arenas wrote a farewell letter announcing his suicide, which took place on 7 December 1990. The letter was published four days later in the Miami newspaper *Diario de las Américas* and appears as a postscript in editions of *The Color of Summer* and *Before Night Falls*. The letter ends with the sentence: "Cuba will be free; I am so now."

The first installment of the *pentagonía*, the prizewinning *Singing from the Well*, is an otherworldly novel of childhood situated in an impoverished, mythical Cuban countryside. Its bold formal originality prompted Lezama Lima's famous quip about Arenas recalled by Cuban writer Abilio Esteves: "The breath of genius knows no limits; it can even reach a shepherd in Holguín." Arenas's early years in the Oriente province inspired the story of Celestino, a boy whose compulsion to inscribe his poetry everywhere in nature—on tree trunks, shrubs, and leaves—is greatly resented by his ignorant and tyrannical family. Nevertheless, the novel's fragmentary mode of narration, oneiric unreality, and many temporal paradoxes make it more of a radical experiment in magic realism than a form of confessional fiction. *Singing from the Well* is better read as a grisly ghost story about purgatory told by a child. Alternating between first- and second-person narrative voices, the boy relates how all the characters in his barbaric family die or are murdered and yet remain alive in a hell-like nether world. Like many of Arenas's stories in *Con los ojos cerrados*, *Singing from the Well* is a bold departure into high fantasy and epistemological indeterminacy, traits that by the early sixties were systematically discouraged in Cuban fiction, when state publishers opted to promote *testimonios* (testimonial novels) and other documentary forms of socially committed literature.

The novel's most notable achievement is the candid tone of the narrator's voice, capable of telling horrific family incidents with great lyrical evocativeness and tenderness. It is a voice inspired by the surreal majesty of Oriente's landscape yet suffocated by the torpor and murderous oppression of the family household. Following a child's tendency to confuse reality and fantasy, outlandish events typical of fairy tales abound. Clouds fall and kill in avalanches; tropical rainfalls turn into snowstorms; humans change into birds, insects, or trees; a toy castle becomes a real-life palace; gnomes, witches, and the specters of dead cousins interact with "real" characters.

The novel's circular plot deals with the grotesque punishments Celestino suffers as he moves into his grandparents' maize farm after witnessing his mother's suicide. There he befriends the narrator, his cousin. Together, Celestino and the narrator take refuge in play and imagination from the relentless physical and emotional abuse inflicted by the adults. The grandfather uses his ax to fell the thousand trees Celestino inscribes or to terrorize and maim the children themselves. Although the narrator's mother is portrayed as nurturing and considerate, she blackmails her son psychologically during her depressive and suicidal spells.

In this perpetual cycle of humiliation and death, Celestino, the narrator, and the rest of the characters are impaled, covered in excrement, mutilated, burned, or drowned. The eternal recurrence implied in an epigraph by Jorge Luis Borges, "Amanecerá bajo mis párpados cerrados" (Dawn will break under my closed eyes), is reflected in the fact that the novel ends and restarts three times. Scenes of unspeakable hunger and cannibalism predominate in the second part; the starving characters eat their own limbs and hunt down the grandfather to devour him. In the third part, Celestino—now transformed into a bird (a *pájaro*, which is also Cuban slang for "homosexual")—is sacrificed by decapitation during a phantasmagoric Christmas Eve banquet when the narrator fails to assassinate his grandfather with a knife. Here it is revealed that, all along, Celestino has been a *primo mágico* (imaginary cousin), an alter ego that the narrator invents to project his creative faculties and find solace and companionship in the midst of loneliness and fear. While the children express benign feelings toward nature and family in dialogue, adults always speak in hostile admonitions in which homicide is an underlying threat. The gratuitous, yet matter-of-fact, eruptions of violence in the novel magically fulfill the death wish contained within these vulgar Cuban curses. The cruel, yet innocent world of *Singing from the Well* fictionalizes adult malediction as it is magnified phobically in the mind of a child.

Arenas's next novel, *The Ill-Fated Peregrinations of Fray Servando,* is his best-known and most successful work. Owing to its dazzling mixing of fantasy and history and its vertiginous narrative design, it is one of the novels of the so-called Boom (a period in the 1960s in which many Latin American masterpieces of fiction were published) that critics have studied most closely. The novel could be described as a fabled biography that whimsically recreates the life, imprisonments, and flights of Fray Servando Teresa de Mier. Mier was an outspoken Mexican Dominican friar, independence advocate, and professional fugitive who struggled and conspired against Spanish rule during the period of national emancipation in Latin America. A fiery preacher who criticized the backwardness of the waning Spanish Empire, Mier was singled out as a heretic by the Spanish Inquisition after a polemical public sermon he gave during the Virgin of Guadalupe festival on 12 December 1794.

Since the sixteenth century, the myth of the Virgin's bequest of her image to the Indian Juan Diego was used to legitimize Spanish Catholic hegemony over indigenous Mexico. Quoting studies of Aztec codices and hieroglyphs, Mier argued that her icon had been worshipped by Mesoamerican civilizations prior to the Spanish Conquest, since one of Christ's apostles—the apostle Thomas under the guise of the Toltec god Quetzalcoatl—had brought it to evangelize the heathen. Mier's claim that Mexicans had been converted to Christianity centuries before the arrival of the Spanish threatened the religious, political, and historical justifications of Spain's rule. Mier was sent to prisons in Mexico and then in Spain. In Spain he managed to escape prison twice and finally fled to France and traveled throughout Europe, leading a life of travails and adventures and writing endless self-apologies. He returned to Mexico in 1822 and was elected to Congress and hailed as a hero of independence for the rest of his life. All of these "biographical facts" are accounted for in *The Ill-Fated Peregrinations of Fray Servando.*

As a historical novel, Arenas's *Ill-Fated Peregrinations of Fray Servando* is as heretical as Mier's notorious sermon. The narration is split into three alternating voices—first-, second-, and third-person singular. These voices often give discrepant versions of events. Chapters are replayed and changed up to three times, creating contradictory episodic sequences. A definitive, linear account of the "facts" is impossible to make out in this novel. *The Ill-Fated Peregrinations of Fray Servando*'s convoluted narrative design recalls the splintered point of view in Carlos Fuentes's novel *La muerte de Artemio Cruz* (1962) and Borges's proposal of a chaotic novel encompassing multiplying parallel times in his story "El jardín de los senderos que se bifurcan" (1942). Arenas's use of primary documents is also highly unorthodox. In the novel's famous prologue, Arenas claims to rely on Mier's *Memorias* (Memoirs) as his principal source, but he eschews the causal logic that stipulates that event "a" generates event "b" in the interpretation of historical sources. Instead, he favors a hallucinatory treatment of Mier's memoir, as if it were a book of witchcraft rather than of facts. As in magic spells, what appears as a figural or metaphorical utterance in the document often becomes a fantastic literal entity in the novel. The memoir's occult-spouting savant "bachelor Borunda" literally appears as a grotesque witch in *The Ill-Fated Peregrinations of Fray Servando*. The hungry, expectant rats Mier regards as companions in his cell begin to speak and dance in a conga line in Arenas's imagination. A sheriff named León in the memoir appears as a "real" lion in the novel. Thus, Arenas transforms "fact" into sorcery in a delirious manipulation of historical sources.

Despite the epistemological uncertainties of the narrative, the fantastic intrusions, and the outlandish baroque excesses in the descriptions, events move forward, and Mier's international itinerary of imprisonments and flights is recounted. Rather than one character in history, Mier comes across as a quixotic archetype of the perennial rebel and idealist. Critics have been fascinated with the novel's prologue, a letter in which Arenas the author tells Mier that he has discovered that "they are the same person." This claim sets up a temporal and textual paradox. Arenas, the reader in the present, realizes that he is Mier, the writer in the past; this entitles him to rewrite the memoir as he reads it and to consider Mier both his double and his primary audience. This view of reading as a form of bi-authorial rewriting makes *The Ill-Fated Peregrinations of Fray Servando* a parody in the style of Borges's fictional plagiarist, Pierre Menard, "author" of *Don Quixote*. As a "re-authoring" of Mier's memoirs, Arenas's procedure could be described, following the terms of the French theorist Gérard Genette, as a palimpsest, a "doubled" or "layered" writing in which the echoes and phantasms of a previous document are heard and seen underneath a subsequent text.

There is a clever ruse in the construction of *The Ill-Fated Peregrinations of Fray Servando*. In the letter, Arenas claims that he only rewrites Mier's *Memorias*. The fact is that *The Ill-Fated Peregrinations of Fray Servando* is not just a palimpsest of Mier's memoirs but, in fact, is made up of many textual artifacts and traditions. Arenas transposes Mier's story but not Mier's style. Instead, Mier's story is refracted through styles Arenas takes from his many readings at the National Library. Arenas lifts passages from François Rabelais's lengthy sixteenth-century satire *Gargantua and Pantagruel*, from Spanish Golden Age verse dramas by Lope de Vega, and from canonical Spanish picaresque novels, such as the anonymous *Lazarillo de Tormes* (1554), Francisco de Quevedo's *El buscón* (1626), and Mateo Alemán's *Guzmán de Alfarache* (1599–1604). Other documents and secondary sources—such as Artemio Valle Arizpe's 1951 heroic biography on the friar, *Fray Servando*—weigh as much in the novel's composition as the *Memorias* themselves. Another important source is Lezama Lima's interpretation of Mier in his work *La expresión americana* as an American baroque thinker, romantic fugitive, and agent of freedom who wishes to break Old World bonds and create a new nation. At the Mexican National Palace, however, Mier discovers that under the new republic, he has escaped one form of captivity to end up in another. Like the character in Borges's story "Las ruinas circulares" (1944) who dreams up a utopian progeny only to realize that he is trapped in a dream himself, Arenas's Mier realizes that history itself is a "circular prison." Even so, even his corpse keeps trying to escape.

The second installment of the *pentagonía*, *The Palace of the White Skunks*, resurrects both the protagonist (now an adolescent named Fortunato) and the perturbing family feuds of *Singing from the Well*. Following Arenas's evolving exploration of novelistic form and technique in the pentagonía, *The Palace* evidences a more elaborate and plural narrative configuration. Arenas orchestrates a polyphonic novel, interlocking several independent points of view in the style of William Faulkner's *The Sound and the Fury* (1929) and Virginia Woolf's *Mrs. Dalloway* (1925). The points of view in *The Palace of the White Skunks* meld into a contradictory, cacophonic collage of several interior monologues, each expressing the deep frustrations of a destitute rural family moving to Holguín during the guerilla struggle against Batista. Thus, we learn of Fortunato's dead-end job at a guava paste factory, his feelings of social and sexual inadequacy, and his wish to flee his family and join the rebel forces.

Polo, the stubborn and uncommunicative grandfather, struggles to make ends meet by gouging prices in his home *venduta* (fruit stand). Jacinta, the superstitious grandmother, constantly scolds and curses her husband and daughters. Abandoned by her husband, the resentful Aunt Digna mistreats her two misbehaving children, Tico and Anisia. The compulsive Aunt

Adolfina, a spinster desperate to "find a man," spends hours sulking in the bathroom. After her daughter's suicide, Aunt Celia goes mad and sinks into dumb, incoherent reveries. Fortunato's mother, who has left to work as a housemaid in the United States, is present through the tedious letters she sends her family. Oddly, hardly any dialogue takes place between these self-absorbed and tormented characters. The reader is forced to extrapolate from each of their inner voices to reassemble fragmentary accounts of family crises that often cancel each other. Even so, Fortunato appears as a type of authorial figure for the whole text, since he is the only one capable of imagining, understanding, and expressing the others' terrible pain and isolation. This metafictional gesture—featuring an author inside the text—is repeated in all of the pentagonía novels.

In spite of its many points of view and fractured structure, stronger historical and geographical references distinguish the narrative in *The Palace* from the free-floating fabulations in *Singing from the Well*. There are many surreal episodes in *The Palace* that discourage a linear succession of events. Death itself, in the form of a monstrous housefly or personified as an old man spinning a bicycle wheel, often invades the narrative, stopping time. The novel opens with an "epilogue-prologue" that underscores the circular temporality typical of Arenas. Despite such disruptions, the second and last parts of the novel—divided into "agonies" instead of chapters—tend to move onward toward a climactic resolution in "real" time. *The Palace* concludes with a masterly interspliced narration of two simultaneous scenarios of departure, frustration, and death. Fortunato abandons the house but fails in his attempt to join the guerrillas; he is subsequently captured, tortured, and executed by the *casquitos* (Batista's forces). Adolfina leaves home at night and cruises Holguín's red light district seeking a man to sleep with; she ends up *prendiéndose en candela* (committing suicide by setting herself on fire).

Arenas's use of nonliterary documents at this juncture in *The Palace* reinforces a referential or "realist" dimension. As the novel approaches its double climax, clippings from guerrilla bulletins, Batista newspapers, and Cuban beauty manuals are inserted in blocks contained within the interlocking monologues. At times chronologically accurate and at others wildly anachronistic, these excerpts help date and situate the fictional happenings. Subjective "fantasy" thus is both mingled with and distinguished from historical fact. There are also interventions of a third-person "objective" narrator, a sort of academic voice that informs and comments on the social and economic life of Holguín and Cuba in the 1950s. In this way, *The Palace* demonstrates an uneasy historiographical intent absent in the unanchored circularity of *Singing from the Well*. *The Palace*'s pastiche-like play with archival sources also can be read to challenge the documentary realism prevailing in Cuban fiction at the time.

Arenas spent sixteen years writing and rewriting *Farewell to the Sea*, since state security in Cuba insisted on confiscating what they considered a politically threatening manuscript. The novel is his most polished work, a technical masterpiece. *Farewell to the Sea* is divided into two long sections exposing what a young married couple thinks while driving back to Havana after a six-day vacation at the state-run Guanabacoa beach resort. In the first half the reader is privy to the thoughts of an unnamed woman. "Ella" (She) is a frustrated wife and mother who longs for the affection of her husband (who is also her cousin). At a serene, seamless pace, Ella merges in her mind remote and recent memories, dreams, odd reveries, and perceptions of the present. An epigraph by the Mexican poet Octavio Paz, "La memoria es un presente que nunca pasa" (Memory is a now that never ends) signals that all of Ella's cognitions will be narrated in an absolute present tense. Chronology is thus up to the reader's critical conjecture.

Among these mental impressions and memories are Ella's sensory enjoyment of the seaboard during the drive, recollections of life in the province with her disagreeable mother, and flashbacks to events related to Cuba's developing revolutionary process. The reader learns that Ella and her husband, Hector, participate reluctantly in mass political demonstrations, rationing lines, and "voluntary" work campaigns. The systematic collectivization of all social activity under the revolution becomes an obsessive source of dissatisfaction for Ella and Hector. These long-term memories alternate with short-term remembrances of the vacation at the beach and the neighbors next door to their cabin: a middle-aged, pampering mother and her adolescent son. Overcoming a strong propensity for denial, Ella begins to suspect that her husband has become attracted to the boy and that some type of affair is going on. Ella's eccentric nightmares and hallucinations are especially well incorporated into this section. These visions include a Gargantuan phallic war waged by characters from Homer's *Iliad*; a divine procession in which God and the Virgin Mary walk on water dressed like fishermen; a rationing line that turns into a citywide, catastrophic riot; and the apparition of dinosaurs strolling on the beach or attending bizarre conferences. These fantastic episodes are not as exaggerated as those that populate other novels by Arenas. Psychological coherence and verisimilitude temper the characterization of Ella's free associations and fantasies.

Rather than an interior monologue divided into days, the second section consists of six long cantos combining free verse, rhyme, and narrative prose. Hector composes these cantos in his mind while driving. The text's dynamic spatial disposition on the page accentuates the pounding, crescendo rhythm of Hector's poetic monologue. The brazen shape and cadence of Hector's cantos recall both the verbal architecture of *poesía concreta* (concrete poetry) and the oceanic pulsations in the poetry of Walt Whitman. Defiant, blasphemous, cynical, vengeful, and desolate, Hector intones with these cantos a naked lamentation, following the section's epigraph by Lezama Lima, "El hombre desnudo canta su miseria" (The naked man sings of his miseries).

Hector begins by angrily addressing the sea, which he regards both as a force of freedom and as an accomplice in his confinement. After this invocation, Hector channels into his cantos several wrathful diatribes. He denounces the failure of socialism and the loss of freedom in Castro's Cuba. He bitterly complains about the miserable fate of homosexuals under persecution and prophesies, in a science fiction interlude, Castro's transformation into a despotic, galactic Mother God. He excoriates the phony social optimism in Whitman's poetry and fantasizes about a hysterical, orgiastic night of transvestite cruising in a sex-obsessed Havana. At the end, Hector devolves into meditations recalling those of the French philosopher Albert Camus about the dignity of suicide. The reader comes to discover that Hector has married to cover up his secret life as a homosexual. During his vacation, the sexual tryst he pursues with the adolescent next door ends in

tragedy. The boy throws himself off a cliff after Hector badgers him about the abuses and ostracism he will suffer as a gay man in Castro's Cuba. The theme of suicide as an inalienable human choice and act of freedom concludes the book. Hector veers the car to crash against the seaboard wall. In the last sentences the reader discovers that the other seats are empty. Hector, in fact, also has authored Ella's monologue, as if she were some type of imagined alter ego, like the narrator's Celestino or Fortunato's Adolfina.

*Farewell to the Sea* weaves together a devastating portrait of the Cuban revolution during the intense institutional Stalinization it endured in the late sixties. In rewriting, Arenas drew from the great animosity and disillusionment in Cuba after the Soviet repression of the Prague Spring experiment in decentralized socialism in 1968, the fiasco of the sugar harvest in 1970, and the Padilla affair in 1971. Both Ella and Hector review the suffering provoked by power shortages, food rationing, bureaucratic pettiness, moral pointlessness, and general dullness under built-up collectivism. The deft counterpoint between muteness and stridency, between Ella's quiet desperation and Hector's clamorous outrage, gives the novel great emotional and persuasive power. The choice of suicide over returning to socialism after a vacation's repose bitterly spoofs the revolution's famous slogan "Fatherland or Death." Hector's cantos are black anthems that rebuke the hymns to populism and a progressive Latin American social history sung by the Chilean poet Pablo Neruda in *Canto general* (1950). They also round out Virgilio Piñera's bleak vision of Cuba as an accursed island prison in his gnostic poem, *La isla en peso* (1943). In *Farewell to the Sea*, however, Arenas goes beyond contestatory politics into an existentialist realm of complaint against a sinister cosmos and the fate of the individual in a mechanized, meaningless universe.

*The Doorman* is a puzzling satirical fable. It is one of Arenas's few works dedicated to the predicaments of the Cuban exile community in North America. According to Arenas, the novel is based on Lázaro Gómez Carriles's adventures as a doorman in a luxurious Manhattan apartment complex. The story, however, is far from realistic; parody takes the plot into wild flights of fancy. Jean-Marie Saint-Lu's translation of the novel into French was a 1979 Médici Prize finalist for best foreign novel in France. Still, the novel's droning, flat style lacks the fierce rhythm and intensity of Arenas's best prose fiction. This lackluster quality is due in part to the satirical conceit of having the narrative voice be that of the Cuban exile community at large rather than that of an individual. This impersonal "million-person us" expresses itself in a trite, business-like, self-doubting Spanish full of anglicisms and circumlocutions. Throughout the novel, this collective narrator files an official report on Juan, a well-meaning, off-kilter doorman who turns into a personal crusade his wish to help the building's well-off tenants gain access to a mystical door of happiness.

The novel's best satirical moments are found in the hodgepodge of comic types that make up the building tenants (some acrimoniously based on real people). Among them are an absent-minded cybernetics inventor, a born-again Christian pastor who preaches "touching," a promiscuous yet impotent Columbia University professor, a pro-Castro political activist and academic who sleeps with a bear, a Forbes-type despotic magnate, and Juan's perennially suicidal Cuban-American girlfriend. At mid novel there is a sudden plot twist, as the pets kept by all these tenants confide in Juan their understanding of human language and plans to escape their confinement. In the second half of the book, Juan and the pets go east in a caravan-like procession during which many of the animals philosophize eloquently about the follies of humanity. *The Doorman* shows how much Arenas enjoyed giving voice to lowly and nonsentient creatures—plants, insects, reptiles, stones, and rats all talk loudly in his works. Such ventriloquism suggests that Arenas rebelled not just against tyranny in its historical forms but also against what he understood is an unjust cosmic order that overstates human authority over nature.

Arenas began writing an autobiography while he was hiding in Lenin Park as a fugitive. Its working title, *Before Night Falls,* referred to the fact that Arenas had only until dusk each day to write down his text. After being hospitalized in New York with AIDS in 1997, Arenas struggled to complete the book. He was too weak to hold a pen or type, and he recorded the chapters on audiotape and had friends transcribe them into a manuscript that he could revise. Composed just before what in the prologue Arenas calls "the imminent night of death," the memoir's account of Arenas's life is the most straightforward, linear narrative he ever produced. Organized as a sequence of vignettes with essay-like asides, this volume revisits many of the themes, characters, and events that inspired Arenas's fiction.

An air of scandal and sensationalism surrounded the publication of Arenas's memoirs. His detailing of a voracious, often reckless sex life (including childhood acts of bestialism and a fabulous claim of five thousand gay sexual encounters tallied by the age of twenty-five) startled many readers. Others were dismayed by the bitter, gossiping accusations against former friends and political enemies or appalled by Arenas's terrifying exposé of the prison system in Cuba. In Cuba, many accused Arenas of fabricating facts to vilify old foes. The Cuban writer Abilio Estevez recalls that, shortly before his death, the critic José Rodríguez Feo called the book "a masterpiece of slander." Still, the breathless rhythms and stormy excesses of his fiction are absent here. Even when the prose is punctuated with vindictive irony, as it often is, the tone of the memoir is generally introspective and contemplative. By its second reading, the text appears to be less a preposterous picaresque of sexual adventures or a settling of old grudges than a searching look into memory and imagination as a way of taking stock of a hazardous, intensely lived, bewildering existence.

When the American painter and filmmaker Julian Schnabel saw Arenas interviewed in Jana Bokova's documentary *Havana,* he was impressed with the candid, playful spirit Arenas showed in speaking of his inner child and his unreal situation as a Mariel refugee in New York. After reading some of Arenas's works, Schnabel bought the rights to make a film based on *Before Night Falls,* which came out in 2000. The film portrays Arenas as an innocent, childlike homosexual writer who yearns for liberty, beauty, and love while living under savage persecution in Castro's dictatorship. Visual and textual images of lonely, deprived children begin and close the film. Javier Bardem's star performance struck many of Arenas's friends as a "resurrection" and won an Oscar nomination. Bardem builds on Arenas's easy charm, ebullience, and shy, "bumpkin in the city" mannerisms and posture, but he neglects to convey the vengeful furor—what the writer

Carlos Victoria called the "cataract thunder"—in Arenas's mercurial personality.

The film is a lucid, well-documented interpretation of Arenas's basic life story. It relies on authoritative consultants who knew Arenas's character and work well. Arenas's closest friend, Lázaro Gómez Carriles, collaborated in writing the screenplay and appears as an important character. In a visceral concluding sequence that is a poignant homage to Arenas's own stark and polemical brand of honesty, Gómez Carriles is shown assisting in Arenas's suicide. The script gives deserved attention to Arenas's destitute yet enchanted childhood in rural Oriente, but it sanitizes Arenas's aggressive sexual cruising, spirited resentments, and famous "in your face" contentiousness. The movie inexplicably takes some unnecessary historical license regarding the Arenas-Lezama Lima-Piñera association. Piñera appears as Lezama's colleague and subordinate at a moment when they were disgruntled enemies and when Piñera held equal or higher official posts. It disregards Lezama Lima's famous and distinctive ultrapoetic manner of conversation, making him sputter an unlikely discourse on the perils of beauty under tyranny that is lifted verbatim from a passage authored by Arenas, not Lezama Lima. During their first meeting, Lezama gives Arenas a copy of Guillermo Cabrera Infante's *Tres tristes tigres* (1971), a novel published in Spain three years after Arenas's UNEAC prize. Moreover, Lezama appears as Arenas's principal mentor when, in the introduction to *Before Night Falls*, Arenas makes clear that Piñera was just as prized a teacher. The film quotes ingeniously from many of Arenas's novels but is disconcertingly oblivious to *Farewell to the Sea*, the work in which Arenas invested his greatest energy and genius.

Written while he was stricken with AIDS and finished barely before his death, *The Color of Summer* is Arenas at his most extravagant, profane, and transgressive. Hilarious, racy, and discomfiting, the novel blends literary parody, sexual farce, autobiographical fiction, vaudeville burlesque, and political satire with the speed of a mad carousel ride. Arenas described it as a "cyclonic novel." *The Color of Summer* retakes most of the events and themes covered in the previous pentagonía novels in a bold, ribald conceit. In the novel, everyone in the repressive state apparatus or the conspiring underground engages in some manner of homosexual behavior within a complicit, grotesquely libidinous, clandestine network. Arenas makes literal in this novel one of his most notorious witticisms: without exception, all Cuban males are *locas de atar* (profligate queens), closet gays, or macho *bugarrones* ("straights" for whom an active role in gay sex fortifies their masculine self-regard).

Divided into eighty-four sections and thirty "tongue twisters," the novel follows several fantastic story lines. In 1999 an egotistic Caribbean dictator named Fifo stages a lavish carnival to celebrate fifty years of rule (ten years before such a holiday is due) on an unnamed island. This carnival is a phantasmagoric extravaganza of learned conferences by Cuba's greatest writers, political demonstrations, and savage orgies with an outlandish list of world celebrities and dignitaries as participants. The list includes a rabbit-fancying U.S. president, Cuban literary personalities whom Fifo brings back from the dead to impress the audience, and a fornicating and vicious white shark that acts as Fifo's first security officer. Arenas thus spoofs Castro as an opportunistic and theatrical dictator who uses Cuba as a stage to play out local and world conflicts and fantasies for his personal advantage. Meanwhile, a ganglike sisterhood of salacious *locas de atar* (with such noms de guerre as Eachurbod, Pornopop, and Supersatanic) engage in a wild series of nonstop sexual exploits with military officials or undercover agents in buses, men's rooms, and aquarium tanks. The novel also replays Arenas's own story of persecution. Arenas the author appears as a sort of split personality divided among three roles: Gabriel, the bumpkin from Holguín who moves to Havana; the effeminate homosexual nicknamed Gloomy Skunk; and the reputed writer-in-exile Reinaldo. Gabriel/Gloomy Skunk/Reinaldo struggles to finish a novel titled *The Color of Summer* that the authorities constantly confiscate. At the end, the underground resistance, transformed into a gigantic school of fish, has gnawed the island loose from its foundations. The island floats adrift and sinks into oblivion.

*The Color of Summer* is also a farcical roman à clef about the literary establishment in Cuba. Arenas lampoons the main figures of pre- and post-1959 Cuban letters under twisted pseudonyms, recalling Cabrera Infante's famous caricatures of reputed writers in *Tres tristes tigres.* The novel mischievously recounts several literary myths, among them, Padilla's confession, Lezama Lima's esoteric lectures, Carpentier and the famous Afro-Cuban poet and UNEAC president Nicolás Guillén's servility under Castro, and Piñera's ostracism. The novel's explosive sarcasm has persuaded many readers that *The Color of Summer* is the crowning manifestation of Arenas's rebellious temperament. Its unbridled carnality, ludicrous excesses, and impudent irreverence have led critics to interpret Arenas's work in the light of the Russian critic Mikhail Bakhtin's theory of the carnival as exposed in his classic 1965 work *Rabelais and His World.*

In this study of the Renaissance writer François Rabelais, Bakhtin understood carnivalesque humor as the literary transposition of a medieval, popular spirit whose unfettered festiveness, earthy abundance, and life-affirming élan subverted social hierarchies and solemn official strictures. Despite its vibrant hilarity, *The Color of Summer* nevertheless remains as pessimistic a view of Cuba's past, present, and future as can be found in the rest of the *pentagonía.* The carnival staged in *The Color of Summer* does not liberate; it is orchestrated to satisfy the dictator's whims and to channel libidinal forces into reinforcing state power. Fifo's extravaganza might be better understood as a simulacrum, a screen on which the subconscious homoerotic desires of a militarized *machista* society are projected as a sort of obscene and demented Looney Tunes cartoon. Thus the society is kept in an entropic, self-destructive state of arousal and copulative stupor. Rather than leading to freedom, the carnival in *The Color of Summer* leads to cataclysm.

The carnival was, in fact, a phenomenon Arenas often viewed as malignant. He saw in it Castro's cleverest political tool. In many of his prose texts Arenas often remarked on how the Cuban state invested all remaining resources in exorbitant carnival-like marches to distract its citizens during the worst economic crises. "Almost all Cuban tragedies end in some sort of rumba," he wrote in his memoirs on this respect. Arenas also observed that homosexual activity in Cuba's military ranks secretly soared each time revolutionary discourse became more intolerant and puritanical. What *The Color of Summer* gloomily suggests is that there may be an escalating symbiosis between repression and licentiousness, despotism and eroticism, power and spectacle, prohibition and desire, machismo and homosexuality. In Arenas, summer's color could well be black. This interpretation of sexual abandon and carnivalesque license as part of a diabolical deception shows the extent to which, in spite of his libertarianism, Arenas was a gnostic skeptic in the line of Jorge Luis Borges. In Arenas's imagination, both Cuba and the world become a labyrinthine, abysmal prison within a prison that can be escaped only through fantasy, death, or orgasm. This close-to-cynical view is synthesized in the mid-novel prologue to *The Color of Summer*—in which Arenas calls "lo siniestro" (that which is sinister) Cuba's "implacable tradition"—and in the dismal, godless aphorisms of the section titled "Nuevos pensamientos de Pascal o pensamientos desde el infierno" (New thoughts on Pascal, or thoughts on hell).

Arenas intended *The Assault,* as the last installment of the *pentagonía,* to be a type of prophetic testament. The novel is an enigmatic and disturbing vision of future society as a series of dehumanized, violently mechanized collective camps and prisons. Here individualism has been thoroughly exterminated. *The Assault* prognosticates a dystopia more brutal and desolate than those imagined in the novels of George Orwell or Aldous Huxley. The inhabitants are grotesquely deformed creatures; instead of hands and faces, they have claws and snouts. They sleep corralled into "multifamilies"; deprived of memory and culture, they communicate in a stark, primitive form of Orwellian "newspeak." In penitentiary uniforms, they plow the fields in dangerous slave squadrons. When they are killed, their corpses are left behind as fertilizer. They live under the autocratic rule of one Represident, who greets them through loudspeakers each day with "Good morning, my sons and daughters." Among their holidays are a longer workday for the Represident's Grand Anniversary and a cockroach-stomping festival.

Although communist Cuba inspires Arenas's perturbing vision, he divests the novel of any references that might make the reader identify this world with any specific regime in history. The impression is that of a survivalist dictatorship in a dark science fiction underworld. The main plotline provocatively addresses the themes of matricide and magnicide. A member of the Represent's secret police narrates the novel. This nameless agent still has the capacity to hate and thus retains a faint glimmer of personhood and identity. He obsessively seeks out his fugitive mother to kill her, since, looking in his mirror, he is convinced that "he is slowly turning into her." In a political rally at the novel's conclusion, he realizes that the Represent is his mother. He kills her at the podium by assaulting him/her with his erected, spearlike phallus. This homicide appears to trigger a type of liberation. The crowd breaks out in a destructive frenzy, and the narrator flees "to lie down near the sand." The enigmatic chapter headings—a disjointed melange of stray titles and quotations patched together from selected works of literature, possibly those in Lezama Lima's *curso délfico*—suggest a state of cultural apocalypse, the conflagration of all civilized knowledge after humankind's return to a primal barbarism.

Often Arenas's early shorter fictions and novellas read as a preliminary rehearsal of the styles, character types, and plots that evolve fully in his novels. Many of the characters, situations, and experimental techniques in the short stories of *Con los ojos cerrados* resurface in *Singing from the Well*, *The Palace of the White Skunks*, and *Farewell to the Sea*. Arenas's briefer narratives thus demonstrate a tendency toward the open-ended multiplicity, perspective contrasts, and elaborateness associated with the novel as form. This inclination is reflected in Arenas's proclivity to cluster works first written as autonomous short stories into collections meant to be read as novels. For example, two novellas of subjective focalization, such as "Old Rose" and "Arturo, the Shiniest Star," appear as one "novel in two chapters" in the English edition. (The first tells the story of a despotic and frustrated rural matriarch who sets herself and her estate on fire when Castro's land reform is about to confiscate her land. The second is about an imprisoned writer who uses his imagination to evade the dreariness of a UMAP concentration camp.) Similarly, after the Mariel boatlift Arenas wrote a short story about the Peruvian embassy takeover titled "Termina el desfile" (The parade ends). First published

in *Termina el desfile* (1981), it was intended to serve as a "bookend" to his earlier tale "Empieza el desfile" (about the triumphal guerrilla entrance into Holguín when Batista fell, first published in *Con los ojos cerrados*, 1972). He thus completed a novel-like narrative series about revolutionary hope and disappointment.

The same procedure characterizes one of Arenas's best works, *Viaje a la Habana*. Here Arenas puts together as a "novel" three well-wrought yet discontinuous stories about homosexual awakening written at various moments of his life. "Que trine Eva" (Let Eva scream) is a camp fantasy about fanciful couture in a staid revolutionary culture. "Mona" is a gothic tale of comic horror, transsexuality, and paranoia set in Manhattan. "Viaje a la Habana" is a fascinating coda to Arenas's work, a tale about incest and an exile's return that ends with a disquieting yet hopeful vision of recovered peace. This trilogy about continuing yearning, even if unfulfilled—the only work evenly combining pre- and post-Mariel narrative projects—sets up a contrast to the stark despair of the *pentagonía* narratives. The collection, in fact, ends with the harmonious Christmas family dinner Arenas pined for as a child.

A less-studied but important part of Arenas's production is his poetry. Poets and poetry are central in Arenas's literary vision. In his lifetime Arenas published two poetry collections. *Leprosorio* (1990; The leper colony) reunites three long, historically informed poems of epic breadth that Arenas wrote from 1970 to 1976: *El central*, *Morir en junio y con la lengua fuera* (To die in June with one's tongue out), and *Leprosorio*. *Voluntad de vivir manifestándose* (1989; The will to live is manifest) puts together a selection of Arenas's shorter poems. Each reads like an entry in a diary that moves from the political to the lyrical, from the public to the personal, from outward to inward. The whole gamut of Arenas's talents and moods is present: from outrage and indignation to fancifulness and reflection. Formally, the poems range from free verse to meticulously polished rhyme schemes. "Sonetos desde el infierno" (Sonnets from hell) is an exceptional sequence of exquisitely macabre and despairing Golden Age–like sonnets showing Francisco de Quevedo's imprimatur. The baroque theme of *desengaño* (disillusionment) comes through powerfully in every line.

## SELECTED BIBLIOGRAPHY

### Primary Works

#### Novels

*Celestino antes del alba*. Havana: UNEAC, 1967. Rev. ed., published as *Cantando en el pozo*. Barcelona: Argos Vergara, 1982.

*El mundo alucinante*. Mexico City: Diógenes, 1969. Published first in French as *Le monde hallucinant*. Trans. by Didier Coste. Paris: Editions du Seuil, 1968.

*El palacio de las blanquísimas mofetas*. Caracas, Venezuela: Monte Avila, 1980. Published first in French as *La palais de tres blanches moufettes*. Trans. by Didier Coste. Paris: Editions du Seuil, 1975.

*La vieja Rosa*. Caracas, Venezuela: Librería Cruz del Sur, 1980.

*Otra vez el mar*. Barcelona: Argos Vergara, 1982.

*Arturo, la estrella más brillante*. Barcelona: Montesinos, 1984.

*La Loma del Angel*. Miami: Mariel Press, 1987.

*El portero*. Málaga, Spain: Dador, 1989. First published in French as *Le Portier*. Trans. by Jean-Marie Saint-Lu.

*Viaje a la Habana: Novela en tres viajes*. Miami: Universal, 1990.

*El color del verano*. Miami: Universal, 1991.

*El asalto*. Miami: Ediciones Universal, 1991.

#### Short Stories

*Con los ojos cerrados*. Montevideo, Uruguay: Arca, 1972.

*Termina el desfile*. Barcelona: Seix Barral, 1981.

*Final de un cuento*. Huelva, Spain: Diputación Provincial, 1991.

*Adiós a mamá: De la Habana a Nueva York*. Barcelona: Altera, 1995.

#### Other Works

*El central*. Barcelona: Seix Barral, 1981. (Poetry.)

*Persecución: Cinco piezas de teatro experimental*. Miami: Universal, 1986. (Plays.)

*Voluntad de vivir manifestándose*. Madrid: Betania, 1989. (Poetry.)

*Necesidad de libertad*. Mexico City: Kosmos-Editorial, 1986. (Essays.)

*Leprosorio*. Madrid: Betania, 1990. (Poetry.)

*Antes que anochezca*. Barcelona: Tusquets, 1992. (Autobiography.)

#### Translations

*Hallucinations: Being an Account of the Life and Adventures of Friar Servando Teresa de Mier*. Trans. by Gordon Brotherston. New York: Harper and Row, 1971.

*El Central: A Cuban Sugar Mill*. Trans. by Anthony Kerrigan. New York: Avon, 1984.

*Farewell to the Sea: A Novel of Cuba*. Trans. by Andrew Hurley. New York: Viking, 1986.

*Graveyard of the Angels*. Trans. by Alfred J. MacAdam. New York: Avon, 1987.

*The Ill-Fated Peregrinations of Fray Servando*. Trans. by Andrew Hurley. New York: Avon, 1987.

*Singing from the Well*. Trans. by Andrew Hurley. New York: Viking, 1987.

*Old Rose: A Novel in Two Stories*. Trans. by Ann Tashi Slater and Andrew Hurley. New York: Grove Press, 1989.

*The Palace of the White Skunks*. Trans. by Andrew Hurley. New York: Viking, 1990.

*The Doorman*. Trans. by Dolores M. Koch. New York: Grove Weidenfeld, 1991.

*Before Night Falls*. Trans. by Dolores M. Koch. New York: Viking, 1993.

*The Assault*. Trans. by Andrew Hurley. New York: Viking, 1994.

*The Color of Summer; or, The New Garden of Earthly Delights*. Trans. by Andrew Hurley. New York: Viking, 2000.

### Secondary Works

#### Critical and Biographical Studies

Abreu, Juan. *A la sombra del mar: Jornadas cubanas con Reinaldo Arenas*. Barcelona: Casiopea, 1998.

*Apuntes posmodernos/Postmodern Notes* 6, no. 1 (fall 1995). (Special issue on Arenas.)

Bakhtin, Mikhail. *Rabelais and His World*. Trans. by Hélene Iswolsky. Bloomington: Indiana University Press, 1984.

Barquet, Jesús J. "Conversando con Reinaldo Arenas sobre el suicidio." *Hispania* 74, no. 4:934–936 (1991).

———. "El socialismo en cuestión: Anti-utopía en *Otra vez el mar* y *El asalto* de Reinaldo Arenas." *La Palabra y el El Hombre* 85:119–134 (January–March 1993).

———. "La generación del Mariel." *Encuentro* 8–9:110–125 (spring–summer 1998).

Beaupied, Aida. "De lo anecdótico a lo conceptual en *El mundo alucinante* de Reinaldo Arenas." *Revista de Etudios Hispánicos* 11:133–142 (1984).

Béjar, Eduardo. *La textualidad de Reinaldo Arenas.* Madrid: Playor, 1987.

Bejel, Emilio. "*Antes que anochezca*: Autobiografía de un disidente cubano homosexual." *Hispamérica* 25, no. 74:29–45 (August 1996).

Borinski, Alicia. "Re-escribir y escribir: Arenas, Menard, Borges, Cervantes, Fray Servando." *Revista Iberoamericana* 41, nos. 92–93:605–616 (1975). Published in English as "Rewriting and Writings." *Diacritics* 4, no. 4:22–28 (1974).

Bush, Andrew. "The Riddled Text: Borges and Arenas." *MLN* 103, no. 2:374–397 (1988).

Cabrera Infante, Guillermo. "Reinaldo Arenas o la destrucción por el sexo." In his *Mea Cuba.* Barcelona: Plaza & Janés, 1992. Pp. 400–405.

Coffon, Claude. "Un contestaire cubain: Reinaldo Arenas." *Le monde des livres,* 22 March 1969. P. 6.

Diego, Eliseo. "Sobre *Celestino antes del alba.*" *Casa de las Américas* 7, no. 45:162–166 (1967).

Ellis, Robert Richmond. "The Queer Birds of Juan Goytisolo and Reinaldo Arenas." *Romance Quarterly* 42, no. 1:47–60 (winter 1995).

Epps, Brad. "Estados de deseo: Homosexualidad y nacionalidad (Juan Goytosilo y Reinaldo Arenas a vuelapluma)." *Revista Iberoamericana* 62, nos. 176–177:799–820 (July–December 1996).

———. "Proper Conduct: Reinaldo Arenas, Fidel Castro, and the Politics of Homosexuality." *Journal of the History of Sexuality* 6, no. 2:231–283 (1995).

Esterrich, Carmelo. "Locas, pájaros y demás mariconadas: El ciudadano sexual en Reinaldo Arenas." *Confluencia* 13, no. 1:178–193 (1997).

Esteves, Abilio. "Between Nightfall and Vengeance: Remembering Reinaldo Arenas." In *Bridges to Cuba/Puentes a Cuba.* Edited by Ruth Behar. Ann Arbor: University of Michigan Press, 1995. Pp. 305–313.

Ette, Ottmar, ed. *La escritura de la memoria. Reinaldo Arenas: Textos, estudios y documentación.* Frankfurt: Vervuert, 1992.

Foster, David William. "Consideraciones en torno a la sensibilidad gay en la narrativa de Reinaldo Arenas." *Revista Chilena de Literatura* 42:89–94 (1993).

Genette, Gérard. *Palimpsestes. La littérature au second degré.* Paris: Editions du Seuil, 1982.

González, Eduardo G. "A razón de santo: Últimos lances de *Fray Servando.*" *Revista Iberoamericana* 41, nos. 92–93:593–603 (1975).

González Echevarría, Roberto. "An Outcast of the Island." *New York Times Book Review,* 24 October 1983, pp. 1, 33.

Gordon, Ambrose. "Rippling Ribaldry and Pouncing Puns: The Two Lives of Friar Servando." *Review: Latin American Literature and Arts,* no. 8:40–44 (spring 1973).

Guzmán, Cristina. "Entrevista." *Diario de Caracas,* 4 August 1979, pp. 16–17.

Hernández-Miyares, Julio, and Perla Rozencvaig, eds. *Reinaldo Renas: Alucinaciones, fantasía y realidad.* Glenview, Ill.: Scott, Foresman/Montesinos, 1990.

Jara, René. "Aspectos de la intertextualidad en *El mundo alucinante.*" *Texto Crítico* 5, no. 13:219–235 (1979).

Kaebnick, Suzanne. "The Loca Freedom Fighter in *Antes que anochezca* and *El color del verano.*" *Chasqui* 26, no. 1:102–114 (1979).

Koch, Dolores M. "Reinaldo Arenas, con los ojos cerrados (July 16, 1943–December 7, 1990)." *Revista Iberoamericana* 57, nos. 155–156:685–688 (1991).

Mehuron, Kate. "Queer Territories in the Americas: Reinaldo Arenas' Prose." *Prose Studies: History, Theory, Criticism* 17, no. 1:39–63 (April 1994).

Méndez Rodena, Adriana. "*El palacio de las blanquísimas mofetas:* ¿Narración historiográfica o narración imaginaria?" *Revista de la Universidad de México* 39, no. 27:14–21 (1983).

Molinero, Rita. "Entrevista con Reinaldo Arenas: 'Donde no hay furia y desgarro, no hay literatura.' " *Quimera* 17:19–23 (March 1982).

*Nuez: Revista Internacional de ARTE y literatura* 4, no. 12 (1992). (Special issue on Arenas.)

Olivares, Jorge. "Carnival and the Novel: Reinaldo Arenas' *El palacio de las blanquísimas mofetas.*" *Hispanic Review* 53, no. 4:467–476 (1985).

———. "Otra vez 'Cecilia Valdés': Arenas con(tra) Villaverde." *Hispanic Review* 62, no. 2:169–184 (spring 1994).

———. "¿Por qué llora Reinaldo Arenas?" *MLN* 115, no. 2:268–270 (March 2000).

Pereira, Manuel. "Reinaldo antes del alba." *Quimera* 111:54–58 (1992).

Rodríguez Monegal, Emir. "The Labyrinthine World of Reinaldo Arenas." *Latin American Literary Review* 8, no. 16:126–131 (1980).

Rozencvaig, Perla. *Reinaldo Arenas: Narrativa de transgresión.* Mexico City: Oasis, 1986.

———. "Reinaldo Arenas's Last Interview." *Review: Latin American Literature and Arts* 44:78–83 (January–June 1991).

Sánchez, Reinaldo, and Humberto López Cruz, eds. *Ideología y subversión: Otra vez Arenas.* Salamanca, Spain: Centro de Estudios Ibéricos y Americanos, 1999.

Sanchez-Eppler, Benigno. "Call My Son Ishmael: Exiled Paternity and Father/Son Eroticism in Reinaldo Arenas and José Martí." *Differences* 6, no. 1:69–97 (1994).

Santí, Enrico Mario. "The Life and Times of Reinaldo Arenas." *Michigan Quarterly Review* 23, no. 2:227–236 (spring 1984).

Sarduy, Severo. "Textos inéditos de Severo Sarduy: Ciclón/diagonal—Armand/Arenas." *Revista Iberoamericana* 57, no. 154:327–335 (1991).

Schwartz, Kessel. "Homosexuality and the Fiction of Reinaldo Arenas." *Journal of Evolutionary Psychology* 5, nos. 1–2:2–20 (March 1984).

Smith, Paul Julian. "Néstor Almendros/Reinaldo Arenas: Documentary, Autobiography and Cinematography." *Vision Machines: Cinema, Literature and Sexuality in Spain and Cuba, 1983–93.* London and New York: Verso, 1996. Pp. 59–80.

Soto, Francisco. "Reinaldo Arenas's Literary Legacy." *Christopher Street Magazine* 13, no. 12:12–16 (April 1991).

———. "La transfiguración del poder en *La vieja Rosa y Arturo, la estrella más brillante.*" *Confluencia* 8, no. 1:71–78 (1992).

———. *Reinaldo Arenas: The Pentagonía.* Gainesville: University Press of Florida, 1994.

Valero, Roberto. *El desamparado humor de Reinaldo Arenas.* Miami: Hallmark Press, 1991.

———. "*Otra vez el mar,* de Reinaldo Arenas." *Revista Iberoamericana* 57, no. 154:355–363 (January–March 1991).

Victoria, Carlos. "La catarata." *Apuntes posmodernos/Postmodern Notes* 6, no. 1 (fall 1995): 36–38. (Special issue on Arenas.)

Volek, Emil. "La carnavalización y la alegoría en *El mundo alucinante* de Reinaldo Arenas." *Revista Iberoamericana* 51, nos. 130–131:125–148 (1985).

Willis, Angela. "*El mundo alucinante* vis-à-vis *Guzmán del Alfarache* and *El buscón*: The Living Traditions of the Baroque Picaresque." Ph.D. dissertation, University of Texas at Austin, 2001.

*Film Based on the Work of Reinaldo Arenas*

*Before Night Falls.* Screenplay by Julian Schnabel, Cunningham O'Keefe, and Lázaro Gómez Carriles. Directed by Julian Schnabel. Fine Line Features, 2000.

# Mariano Brull

## (1891–1956)

### Klaus Müller-Bergh

In the split night we already know
we are a reflection of ourselves
and that our truth lies beneath the waters.

(Trans. from Eugenio Florit's
*Epigramas de viaje*, 1955)

With Nicolás Guillén, Eugenio Florit, Emilio Ballagas, and José Lezama Lima, Mariano Brull may well be among the foremost creators of poetic language in his generation, as well as a distinctive poetic voice in the Latin American avant-garde. Born and educated in the last decade of the nineteenth and the first decade of the twentieth century, his talent, sensibility, and circumstance enabled him to participate fully in the literary life of two continents and to become a mediator in the marketplace of modernity in Spanish, Cuban, and French letters. Although Brull's distinguished diplomatic and literary career brought him considerable international recognition during the 1930s, 1940s, and 1950s, in the end his reception and literary fortune suffered from the turmoil of World War II, the dictatorship of Fulgencio Batista, and the ensuing chaos of the Cuban revolution, diaspora, and exile. This is particularly evident in the process of publication, dissemination, and dispersion of Brull's oeuvre, as well as in the quality of most of the literary criticism

regarding his work that has been written since his death in 1956.

Brull's poetic production is that of a miniaturist—sparse, refined, and profound—and largely unmatched in elegance and craftsmanship by his Cuban contemporaries. Brull was also a superb translator and innovator in the best sense of the word, an artist who witnessed some of the most controversial and groundbreaking ideas of his time in America and Europe. As a poet and intellectual he was keenly aware of the sound and the fury of the manifestos of futurism, cubism, dadaism, surrealism, *minorismo,* and the Afro-Cuban movement in music, literature, and painting. As a clear-headed diplomat he was also aware of the implications of communism and fascism from the very beginning. Although Brull managed to understand and profit from the ferment and innovation of an avant-garde in a new century, and to incorporate some of its best elements into his poetry, he also learned to distance himself from the most persistent and pernicious political illusions of his time.

Mariano Brull y Caballero was born in the city of Camagüey, capital of the same-named province, and cattle-raising center of the island, on 24 February 1891. One of the oldest settlements in Cuba, founded in 1515 by Diego Velázquez, the city went by the name of Santa María del Puerto Príncipe during the colonial period.

Mariano Brull was the son of Miguel Brull y Seoane and of Celia Caballero y Varela. His mother's birthplace was also Camagüey, the colonial Puerto Príncipe, where the first manifestation of a Spanish American, Cuban, creole consciousness occurred: the publication in 1608 of Silvestre de Balboa's *Espejo de paciencia* (Mirror of patience), the first creole work of literature written by a Spaniard born in urban Spain. As poet, essayist, and diplomat, Mariano Brull was honored with his country's Great Cross of the Order Carlos Manuel de Céspedes, as well as being named Commander of the Order of the Crown of Italy, Belgium's Knight of the Order of Leopold, and Official of the French Legion of Honor. These distinctions convey the definitive acclaim, both nationally and internationally, of an extraordinary literary and diplomatic career that took Brull to the United States of America, Peru, Spain, and France as a functionary of the Ministry of Foreign Relations; to Belgium, Switzerland, and Canada as minister; and, finally, to Uruguay as ambassador. Brull wrote more than a dozen essays that reflect both his day-to-day life as a diplomat and his literary art.

From the beginning of his career Brull translated poems from English, and later he translated French masterpieces such as Paul Valéry's monumental poems *Le cimetière marin* in 1930 and *La jeune parque* in 1949. In the Spanish- and French-speaking worlds, Brull's increasing reputation as one of the most brilliant writers of the Latin American *vanguardia* (the Spanish American avant-garde movement of the 1920s and 1930s) rests on his poetry and his translations. Among these are four collections of Spanish verse, entitled *La casa del silencio* (1916; The house of silence), *Poemas en menguante* (1928; Waning moon poems), *Canto redondo* (1934; Moonstone), and *Solo de rosa* (1941; Rose solo); a book of his poems translated into French, entitled *Quelques poèmes* (1925; Some poems); two books of translations; and three bilingual editions (French and Spanish) of verse, entitled *Poëmes* (1939; Poems), *Temps en peine/Tiempo en pena* (1950; Time in sorrow), and *Rien que.../Nada más que...* (1954; Nothing more than ...). In all these activities, Brull displayed the keen intelligence and sensibility of a cultivated humanist and intellectual in tune with the historic changes in which he participated.

Brull's creativity and sophistication were first recognized by the eminent Dominican scholar Pedro Henríquez Ureña (1884–1946), to whom the Cuban poet dedicated "Hace mucho tiempo fue la casa en fiesta" (Long, long ago there was a celebration in this house), the second poem from his book *La casa del silencio*. In this book one can also find two other introductory poems: the Mexican Enrique González Martínez's "Meditación bajo la luna" (Meditation under the moon) and the Nicaraguan Salomón de la Selva's "To a Young Poet." Later on, during his stays in Brussels and Madrid (1923–1926) and Paris (1926–1929), Brull also earned the friendship, trust, and appreciation of Spanish, French, and Spanish American writers. Among the Spaniards several authors figure prominently: Ramón del Valle Inclán, Pedro Salinas, Rafael Alberti, José Bergamín, Federico García Lorca, Jorge Guillén, and Juan Ramón Jiménez. Standing out among the French are such writers as Paul Valéry, Jules Supervielle, Francis Miomandre, and Mathilde Pomès. One should also include the Belgians Paul Werrie and Edmond Vandercammen. Finally, a number of Spanish American authors deserve mention: the post-*modernista* Colombian Porfirio Barba Jacob, the *vanguardista* Mexican Jaime Torres Bodet, and the Chilean Gabriela Mistral, awarded the Nobel prize for literature in 1945, with whom Brull maintained a long-standing correspondence, and, above all, the great Mexican humanist Alfonso Reyes (1889–1959).

Reyes and Brull, writers whose careers developed in the twentieth century, were universal Spanish Americans, indeed, as universal as some of the best statesmen and intellectuals of the nineteenth century from North and South America, such as Simón Bolívar, Thomas Jefferson, Andrés Bello, Henry Wadsworth Longfellow, Washington Irving, and José Martí. Reyes and Brull were joined by ties of friendship, a kindred sense of humor, a common interest in translation they shared with Longfellow, as well as the wish to make Spanish American literature less provincial, together with a humanistic desire to expand the frontiers of their art by widening the thematics and scope of Spanish letters. The multiple recognitions and friendships of Brull prompt these questions: What were the literary achievements of this poet and diplomat from Camagüey? Why were these achievements viewed with so much respect? Also, what drove him to go beyond the limits of traditional language, a characteristic desire of *vanguardista* writers? And in the final analysis, what makes him exceptional and unique among his Latin American contemporaries?

From a perspective that spans more than 110 years, one can clearly discern that Brull was an ecumenical Cuban who enriched the poetic discourse of the Castilian language in his time's principal current of thought. He was motivated by a desire to express in Spanish what before had only been said in English, French, and German. Brull shared this quality with the Argentine Oliverio Girondo, the Peruvian César Vallejo, and the Chilean Vicente Huidobro, writers who also sought to develop and modify the expressive possibilities of the language. Brull's poetry evolved gradually, from the delicate tone of a transitional post-*modernismo* in *La casa del silencio* (still under the influence of Romanticism and French Parnassian symbolism as well as Dante Gabriel Rossetti's *The House of Life*), followed by an eclectic *ultraísmo* that easily incorporated elements from futurism, cubism, and expressionism, and finally to his own *vanguardista* aesthetic in *Poemas en menguante*. Gloria Videla's *Direcciones del vanguardismo* (1990), to date one of the most serious and complete studies about the Spanish American *vanguardia*, summarizes some of the principal elements, those "semantic vectors" and "formal variants," related to the *vanguardista* aesthetics present in Brull's book of poetry:

> the *vanguardista* vector (with echoes of cubism and *ultraísmo*) . . . the vector that adopts and personalizes theories of Brémond and influences of Mallarmé, of Valéry, [and of] Guillén, integrating them in his own evolution . . . guided by "the lucid pleasures of thought and the secretive adventures of order" (Borges) . . . the vector influenced by popular Hispanic poetry . . . [and the one which] achieves the sonorous suggestion with little or no logical sense.

In "Inicial angélica," the prologue to Emilio Ballagas's *Júbilo y fuga* (1931), Juan Marinello had already understood the innovation and importance of Brull's work when he pointedly observed: "Desde los Poemas en menguante los ángeles nuevos fueron perdiéndose en esquivez. ¿Nos trajo Mariano Brull los ángeles de París,

nacidos de la cabeza de Juan Cocteau?" (Beginning with *Waning Moon Poems* the angels began to get lost in elusiveness. Did Mariano Brull bring us Parisian angels born in Jean Cocteau's head?). Therefore, one is not surprised that poem number 38 ("Esta palabra no del todo dicha" [This word not wholly uttered]), the poetic art or programmatic poem that closes *Poemas en menguante*, is where Videla observes that "pure poetry cohabits with the *vanguardista*, lucidity with literary creation and verbal play, and the elevated with the anti-solemn." Poem number 38 is also a good example of the new perspectives that Brull introduces in the May 1927 edition of *Revista de avance*, and something similar occurs in poem number 7, "I Am Going to the June Sea (1999)," which he dedicated to Alfonso Reyes:

> Yo me voy a la mar de junio,
> a la mar de junio, niña.
> Lunes. Hay sol. Novilunio.
> Yo me voy a la mar, niña.
> A la mar canto llano del viejo
> Palestrina.
>
> Portada añil y púrpura
> con caracoles de nubes blancas
> y olitas enlazadas en fuga.
> A la mar, ceñidor claro.
> A la mar, lección expresiva
> de geometría clásica.
> Carrera de lineas en fuga
> de la prisión de los poliedros
> a la libertad de las parábolas
> —como la vió Picasso el dorio—.
> Todavía en la pendiente del alma
> descendiendo por el plano inclinado.
> A la mar bárbara, ya sometida
> al imperio de Helenos y Galos;
> no en paz romana esclava,
> con todos los deseos, alerta:
> grito en la flauta apolínea.
> Yo me voy a la mar de junio,
> a la mar, niña,
> por sal, saladita . . .
>       —¡Qué dulce!

I shall go to the June sea,
to the June sea, my girl.
Monday. Sun is out. New moon.
I shall go to the sea, my girl.

Old Man Palestrina sings a plain
chant to the sea.

Indigo and purple portal
with white-cloud sea snails
and little waves laced in flight.
To the sea, bright band.
To the sea, vivid lesson
in classic geometry.
Lines race and flee
from the prison of polyhedrons
to the freedom of parabolas.
—As Picasso, the Dorian, saw it—
Still on the slope of the soul
it slips on the inclined plane.
To the barbaric sea already subject
to the empire of Hellenes and Gauls,
yet not enslaved in the pax romana,
to all desire an alert:
a cry of the Apollonian lyre.
I shall go to the June sea,
to the sea, my girl,
for a bit of salty salt . . .
            —So sweet!

The poem reflects Brull's life in Europe—those years spent in Brussels and Madrid and in Paris, when Paris was one of those avant-garde centers that, along with Zurich, Hanover, Berlin, and Milan, influenced the poetry of the *vanguardia*. This influence is particularly notable in the poem's references to geometric works of art, notably Pablo Picasso's cubism, and in the implied reference to the transformations of figurative painting in general. The impersonal constructions and plastic investigations of the cubists, Picasso as much as Braque and Gris, would end up taking the movement to its extreme limits. Other elements of the poem have been correctly commented upon by critics, among these the curious mixture of "apparently different codes: those closest to popular poetry in stanzas that open and close them, the predominance of the octosyllable, diminutives, musical rhythm, grace, lightness," as well as the link between the poem and pure poetry "by which lyrical and intellectual poetry name reality."

In addition, Brull's poem number 34 mentions another of Picasso's paintings, probably related to the artist's early, *modernismo* phase and to his blue and pink periods of 1901 to 1904: "Tras de este plano rosa Picasso / —playa coralina—el mar" (Behind this plane, Picasso pink / —coral beach—the sea). Poem number 7 possibly reflects the juxtaposition in cubist painting and collage of disparate elements chosen from the visible world; for instance, there is the collage and charcoal on paper of *Still Life with Violin and Fruit* (1913): "lección expresiva / de geometría clásica.— . . . Como la vio Picasso el dorio—" ( . . . vivid lesson / in classic geometry.— . . . As Picasso, the Dorian, saw it—). Among the painters who influenced Brull's work, one should also include the synthetic cubism of René Magritte, because in 1927 the Belgian painter was already exhibiting in the gallery Le Centaure paintings very similar to *Threatening Weather* (1928). In other words, specific thematic elements of Magritte's painting appear in Brull's poem number 7—a blue sky and a blue sea, choppy with small waves, framed by the violet hills of a coastline between indigo and purple—serve as a backdrop for ghostly white figures, a sculptured representation of a woman's trunk whose head and limbs are mutilated, a tuba and a chair that float over the horizon of a deserted, rocky beach: "Indigo and purple portal / with white-cloud sea snails / and little waves laced in flight."

Poem 34 adds to these references the exotic orientalism of the Japanese painter Foujita (Fujita Tsuguharu, named Léonard, 1886–1968): "El mar, —azul polvoso / y fugitivo de Foujita—vientre de loba / erizado de senos" (The sea, —dusty blue / and fugitive of Foujita —she-wolf's womb / bristled breasts). In reference to the paintings of Maurice Vlaminck and Giorgio de Chirico, one reads: "El cielo,— llamaradas de Vlaminck— / se pasma en gris" (The sky, sudden blazes of Vlaminck— / is stunned in grey); "De miel y de sol y de verde luna / dos potros encabritados de Chirico / pacen al unísono" (Of honey, of sun, and of green moon / two rearing colts of Chirico / graze in unison). "Green-moon" colts, like Antoñito el Camborio, are seen through the Lorcaesque lens of *Romancero gitano* (Gypsy ballads):

*Antonio Torres Heredia,*
*hijo y nieto de Camborios,*
*con una vara de mimbre*

*va a Sevilla a ver los toros.*
*Moreno de verde luna*
*anda despacio y garboso*

Antonio Torres Heredia,
son and grandson of Camborios
with his wicker wand
goes to Seville to see a bullfight.
Swarthy green moon
rising slowly and gracefully.

And it should not surprise us that after 1905/1906, especially beginning with the initial sketches for *Les Demoiselles d'Avignon* (the same year the first edition of Fernando Ortiz's *Los negros brujos* [The black sorcerers] was published), two of these artists, Vlaminck and Picasso, had already actively participated in the "hunt for black art." The purpose was to expand the aesthetic horizons of cubists and fauvists (André Derain, Vlaminck, Matisse) committed to the construction of autonomous spaces through the use of color, the handling of form, and the exclusion of any symbolically referential system, each one of these accomplished by virtue of the magical and totemic character of black African art.

For many years Brull was a benefactor of the plastic arts, offering generous moral and financial support to many young artists, including such outstanding ones as Pedro Figari, Wifredo Lam, Fidelio Ponce, and to Mariano Rodríguez and René Portocarrero, who illustrated *Solo de rosa*. In other words, at that time Brull lucidly took into account and incorporated into his poetry those painters representative of the European avant-garde (Picasso, Magritte, Vlaminck, de Chirico) who were associated with the two principal schools, cubism and surrealism, dedicated to transforming the representation of reality by way of figurative painting and the image. As the critic J. L. Daval stated in *Avant-Garde 1914–1939* (1980):

The Cubists after Cézanne, justified a new approach to figurative painting by using the image as a relay of perception; Chirico, and after him the Surrealists, used the image for its interrogative power. The question had been reversed: beneath the signs and marks lay a hidden sense which the artist still knew little about, but which his intuition enable him to bring to light . . .

From 1915 on, Chirico peopled his silent and deserted world with manikins (statues, rearing ponies, truncated torsos, etc., in a theatrical space) and pictures within the picture which raised for representational art the same questions, or similar ones, that had already been raised by Picasso: What does reality consist of and where is illusion to be found?

This whole environment, cubist, *ultraísta*, and surrealist, is reflected in Brull's poems, not just in number 7, the one dedicated to Alfonso Reyes, but also in the pictorial references found in two selections from *Poemas en menguante*, such as number 28, "La catedral engarzada en el ojo . . ." (The Cathedral set in the eye . . .), and number 34, "Tras de este plano rosa Picasso" (Behind the Picasso-rose plane).

Other poems document the games of sound, illogic, and onomatopoeia characteristic of futurism and of dadaism, or the metaphorical procedures of *ultraísmo* and *creacionismo*. Such compositions are "Poemas en menguante" (Poems of the waning moon), "La divina comedia" (The divine comedy), "La palma real" (The royal palm), "La catedral" (The cathedral), and "El polvo—ceniza etérea" (Dust—ethereal ash), all published for the first time with poem 7, "I Am Going to the June Sea," in the *Revista de avance*, dated May 1927, as well as with the other six selections from the collection published in the same journal in January 1929. "Verdehalago" ("Greenpraise"), number 16 from the *Poemas en menguante*, also appeared in the collection:

*Por el verde, verde*
*verdería de verde mar*
*Rr con Rr.*

*Viernes, vírgula, virgen*
*enano verde*
*verdularia cantárida*
*Rr con Rr.*

*Verdor y verdín*
*verdumbre y verdura*
*Verde, doble verde*
*de col y lechuga.*

*Rr con Rr*
*en mi verde limón*
*pájara verde.*

*Por el verde, verde*
*verdehalago húmedo*
*extendiéndome.—Extiéndete.*

*Vengo de Mundodolido*
*y en Verdehalago me estoy.*

Through the green, green
greenness of the green sea
Grr with Grr.

Venery, virgule, virgin
verdant dwarf
cantharis verdularia
Grr with Grr.

Greenery and verdigris
veggiegreen and vegetable
Green, double green
of cabbage and lettuce.

Grr with Grr
in my lime green
girlie green bird.

Through the green, green
damp greenpraise
I stretch out.— You stretch out.

I come from Worldweary
and in Greenpraise I hang about.

Alfonso Reyes was the first one to point out the intuitive, alliterative, and ludic character of poem 16 when he observed that "certainly ... it does not address reason, but rather sensation and fantasy. The words here do not search for a useful purpose. They play, alone almost." In addition, given Brull's poetical affinities, it is quite possible that "Greenpraise," as well as Federico García Lorca's "Romance sonámbulo" (1925)—"Verde que te quiero verde" (Green, I love you green)—and Gerardo Diego's "Romance del Júcar" (from the *Antología 1915–1931*)—"Agua verde, verde, verde" (Green, green, green water)—all stem from a reading of the work of Juan Ramón Jiménez, in particular his "Verde verderol," (Green greenfinch), included in *Baladas de primavera* (1907).

Even though in the case of "Greenpraise" one discerns a little reasoned and barely anecdotal composition, the last lines ("Vengo de Mundodolido / y en Verdehalago me estoy" [I come from Worldweary / and in Greenpraise I hang about]) provide the key to this dualist poem that effectively counterpoints two portmanteau words, "Worldweary" and "Greenpraise," metaphors that synthesize reality and desire (the basic principles of reality and pleasure) or what reality is and what one would like it to be. "Worldweary" represents the real world with all life's inadequacies, heartaches, contradictions, denials, afflictions, and sorrows, together with an awareness of all limitations that frustrate human aspirations. "Greenpraise" represents the world of sensations and affective feeling, and at the same time the imaginary, intuitive, and magical world of music, poetry, and fantasy, as well as the poet's vision of innocent childhood. This representation is achieved through a chaotic listing of nouns, neologisms, constant alliterations, and irrational metaphors that evoke "greenness," magical color par excellence, traditionally associated with hope, freedom, beauty, sweetness, and in Renaissance heraldry Venus, because the color green corresponds with the constant organic growth of vegetation and fertility, the vital force of nature. Throughout the poem these attributes would explain the obsessively sonorous and semantic insistence of "verde verdería de verde mar" (green, green / greenness of the green sea) or of "vírgula, virgen / enano verde" (virgule, virgin, / verdant dwarf). We also find "Venery" (from *veneris dies*, or *viernes* in Spanish, the fifth day of the week consecrated to the pleasures of Venus) and "cantharis verdularia" (neologism for verdure and *cantharis [Lytta] vesicatoria*, the golden green coleopteran insect used to prepare aphrodisiacs, better known as Spanish fly). In addition, without discussing at length matters of chronology and genetic background, one can conclude that these principles or variations on the theme constituted the zeitgeist, or the dominant spirit of Cuban letters, the Spanish American *vanguardia*, and contemporary Europe, as exemplified by Dylan Thomas, Pablo Neruda, Oliverio Girondo, and many others.

In short, Brull possessed the lyrical intuition to create his own literary language when writing a pure poetry remotely evocative of the verse of Juan Ramón

Jiménez and Paul Valéry, representatives of that intellectual lyricism created by Mallarmé, in addition to producing neo-popular ballads that evoke the balladry and ancient traditions of Spanish poetry in the manner of Federico García Lorca's *Romancero gitano*: "Por el ir del río" (River-run), "Las Marías, las María" (The Maria girls), "Romance de piedra y viento" (Ballad of stone and wind), "Duelo por Ignacio Sánchez Mejías" (Mourning for Ignacio Sánchez Mejías), and "Rosa de los vientos" (Windrose).

Indeed, by employing tongue twisters and experimental sounds, vigorous and unequaled in their inventiveness, the author cast a magical spell in poems like "Greenpraise" and "Pavo real" (Peacock) from *Poemas en menguante*, and "Verdejil" (Green[pars]ley) from *Temps en peine/Tiempo en pena*. This style ultimately results in those ludic compositions where semantic meaning is reduced to nonsense in the manner of Lewis Carroll's Jabberwocky from *Through the Looking Glass*:

> Twas brillig, and the slithy toves
> Did gyre and gimble in the wabe:
> All mimsy were the borogroves,
> And the mome raths outgrabe.
> "Beware the Jabberwock my son!
> The jaws that bite, the claws that catch!
> Beware the Jubjub bird, and shun
> The frumious Bandersnatch!"

Brull accomplishes his nonsense through a chaotic listing of metaphors, employing sound combinations and lexilogical permutations, wordplay that Alfonso Reyes calls *jitanjáforas*:

> *Filiflama alabe cundre*
> *ala olalúnea alífera*
> *alveolea jitanjáfora*
> *liris salumba salífera.*
>
> *Olivia oleo olorife*
> *alalai cánfora sandra*
> *milingítara girófora*
> *zumbra ulalindre calandra.*

While maintaining the assonant rhyme and the octosyllables, as well as the traditional rhythm of the ballad, the poem's linguistic and poetic emphasis nonetheless strips away any sense or logic, thus surpassing and overcoming the limits of the traditional lyric and in the process favoring purely sonorous elements, or the music of pure language. Or, as Brull himself explains in his first essay on the craft of poetry ("Poesía," 1931):

> *Solamente con la palabra así concebida podría intentarse el poema en que todo él fuera creación,—goce demiúrgico—, plástica total de trasluces y trasmundos íntimamente musicalizada que llegara a alcanzar, acaso, el mayor grado de aproximación al estado de poesía pura.*
>
> *Ese poema imposible tendría que ser fundido en palabras recién creadas reminiscentes de sentido y sentires eternos, y sometido a ritmo en función de sus asociaciones inmanentes.*

Only when the word is conceived in such a way can one attempt a poem that is pure creation, demiurgic joy, total plasticity of translucent lights and other worlds—an internal music—that will achieve, perhaps, the highest degree of proximity to a state of pure poetry.

That impossible poem would have to be forged in recently created words reminiscent of sense and eternal feelings, and subjected to rhythm in terms of its immanent associations.

These onomatopoeic games and nonce words created a literary style and diction different from the futurists' and dadaists' iconoclastic linguistic experiments with texture, form, rhyme, and sound. In addition Brull's poetry features other stylistic techniques characteristic of the *vanguardista* poetics of the time. These include (1) poetic prose, also practiced by Juan Ramón and Huidobro; (2) the deliberate cultivation of image and metaphor, though now frequently joined to the chaotic list; and (3) an eagerness to include the graphic visuality of the plastic arts in order to determine the nature of reality, incorporating into his poetic repertoire cubist and surrealist painting in particular.

Although metaphor is one of the bases of Darío's poetics, and Lugones, writing in the prologue of the first edition of *Lunario sentimental*, considers metaphor the very foundation of literary creation, those Spanish and Spanish American writers of the *vanguardia* had yet to consider verbal and mental imagery in any systematic way. In time, Gerardo Diego, Vicente Huidobro, Jorge Luis Borges, and many others would do this in reviews and other publications of this period. Although this cultivation of the image is indeed a constant feature of *Poemas en menguante* (1928), one that already encompasses Cuba's island geography (its coastal environment, its warm tropical nature, its humid, rainy, and sunny weather), it would perhaps be worthwhile to examine image and metaphor in greater depth in "Isla de perfil" (Profile of the island), poem 17 of *Canto redondo* (1934). The metaphorical density of the twenty-three lines of "Isla de perfil" create an almost absolute contrast with those of number 16 ("Sobre el lago del parque bajo cero" [Over the park's lake, subzero weather]) from the same book, which evokes a park scene set in wintry Europe, winter white, urban, full of aquatic birds. At the same time, poem 18 from *Canto redondo* contains luminous and colorful images ("Este claro silencio a luz entera, / —amarillo de todos los verdores—" [This clear silence in whole light, / —yellow of all greennesses—]) characteristic of Brull's poetics as illustrated in "Isla de perfil."

> Ilesa isla intacta
> bozal del mar nómada,
> cabezal de nardos
> ahogados en luz.
> Un ladrido en clave
> de nácares rudos
> y en ronda, soleados,
> estíos de agua.
> Clara y crespa aroma,
> alta en voz de gallo,
> la cresta levanta.
> Mordaza de azules
> con rizos de lumbre,
> la pulsa y la ciñe.
> No caimán artero,
> primavera ecuestre
> a hombros de hipocampo,
> abra de clamores,
> rubiales de mieles,
> espiral del gozo,
> zumo: ¡cima ilesa
> de la isla intacta!

> Island, unharmed and intact,
> bozal of the migrant sea,
> spikenard bolster
> drenched in sunlight.
> Coded bark
> roughed in mother of pearl
> and dancing in a circle,
> sunny, wet summers.

Clear, crisp scent
of a cock's high cry,
swollen comb rising.
Gag of many blues
with fiery curls
presses and encircles her.
Neither cunning caiman
nor equestrian spring
riding a seahorse.
Clamorous cove,
honeyed fields,
spiral of delight,
sweet juice: unharmed summit
of the intact island!

The title "Isla de perfil" indicates how this composition is a kind of tour de force, a miniaturist's feat of metaphor, a litany of images praising the homeland: twenty-two crafted lines of hexasyllables divided into two quatrains, two tercets, and an octave of loose hexasyllables with assonant rhyme. Because the allusive game of abstract images and local color makes it a rigorous and conceptually difficult poem, this synthetic and luminous miniature reveals like few others the poet's artistic sensibility. Some of Jorge Mañach's best-known essays—"Vanguardismo," "Indagación del choteo," and "El estilo de la revolución," this last one from *Historia y estilo* (1934)—also reveal him as a writer obsessed with fixing what he once defined as "the image of a harmonious Cuba" through the polarity of what was most cultured, noble, and new in the avant-garde, as well as what was most common, typical, and popular at the time: "un choteo, es decir, confusión, subversión, desorden; —en suma: 'relajo' " (mockery, in other words, confusion, subversion, disorder—in sum, mayhem). In addition, it is quite possible that this is one of the reasons why Brull dedicates the poem to Mañach, one of "The Five," founders of the *Revista de avance*, to whom Alejo Carpentier also dedicates one of his first short stories, "El Sacrificio" (The sacrifice), in May 1923.

The first quatrain of "Isla de perfil" opens with "Island, unharmed and intact," an image that highlights the insular geography of Cuba, surrounded by the Caribbean Sea and the Atlantic Ocean, through the use of adjectivals and sound. In other words, from the beginning the motherland is doubly admired because it is "unharmed" by virtue of not having been wounded or hurt despite all the political and natural disasters that have beset her, and also because it is "intact," that is, not having suffered any alteration, damage, or deterioration. These concepts are also underscored by the triple alliteration of the *i* and of the quadruple repetition of the *a*, three at the end of the word and finally as an internal rhyme. Following the image of "Island, unharmed and intact" in the first line are two complementary multifarious images.

The second image of "*bozal* of the migrant sea" (line 2) lends itself to three interpretations. Until the end of the nineteenth century a *bozal* was a black person who was recently brought from Africa in a slave ship and who spoke only the language of his homeland. During the colonial period the *bozal* was frequently contrasted with the native creole black population born and raised in America, who spoke Spanish. But in its second sense it is quite possible that "*bozal* of the migrant sea" could also be an evocation of the island as safe harbor, for the word signifies the muzzle that is placed on animals to prevent them from biting or doing damage. In this case it would be a marine *bozal*, one that tames a ship's rolling or the sea's pounding. And in its third sense *bozal* could well refer to the halter of bells worn by horses, or a precious, decorative object of an island whose traditional nickname is "Pearl of the Antilles."

"Spikenard pillow / drenched in sunlight" (ll. 3–4) is another multifarious image whose linked elements equal a "place of rest, flowery, perfumed, and luminous." The pillow, or *cabezal*, is the long bolster that lies against the entire headboard, once used in Spain and in many other places of the Hispanic world; spikenard is the herbaceous plant typical of Andalusia and of intertropical countries, which is cultivated for its beautiful and sweet-smelling flowers. In addition, the poetic voice intuits them as drowned flowers, suffocated by a luminosity that almost takes one's breath away, another essential characteristic of hot-weather countries, such as Cuba, found between the Tropic of Cancer and the twentieth parallel.

"Coded bark / roughed in mother-of-pearl / and dancing in a circle" (ll. 5–6) opens the second quartet with another ambivalent image whose components are "coded bark," "mother-of-pearl," and "dancing in a circle." Of course, a "bark" is the animal sound emitted

by the dog, though in a figurative sense it is also a cry or harsh expression played in *clave* (clef) or tapped in *clave* (code), a secret language. In other words, in this first sense "bark" recalls the symbol that is inserted at the beginning of a musical staff ("G clef," for example,) to indicate the pitch of the notes; however, in the second sense it might mean ciphered or secret language, such as *clave* Morse or Morse code. Nonetheless, in one of its local uses on the island, *clave* also refers to a Cuban and Caribbean percussive instrument: two polished, cylindrical hardwood (often ebony) sticks that are struck together to mark time, which reinforces the above sense of tapping code. Brull conceives this instrument as "roughed in mother-of-pearl," or nacreous shells in harmony, because the lyrical voice compares the shine of the sticks to this hard substance used in jewelry whose iridescence is produced by mollusks. "Dancing in a circle" signifies a circle of dancers holding hands that moves around an imaginary center. "Sunny, wet summers" closes the quartet in a luminous evocation of a warm, tropical, rainy season, nonetheless filled with flashes of sunlight.

The "clear, crisp scent" (l. 9) of the first tercet is a perfume, distinctive and unmistakable, at the same time also curly and coiled, that relates directly, through the use of synesthesia, to the lines "of a cock's high cry, / swollen comb rising" (10–11). In other words, an olfactory sensation ("clear, crisp scent") is described in terms of other sensations that affect the senses differently, in this case the aural "cock's high cry" and the visual "swollen comb rising."

The lines "Gag of many blues / with fiery curls / presses and encircles her" (12–14) open up the second tercet with a cerulean color that has been used in the Romantic literary traditions of both France and Spanish America to refer to the sky, the sea, and the ideal space of modernism, beginning with Victor Hugo's "L'art c'est l'Azure," Verlaine's "les yeux de l'Azur" from his "Art poétique" (1874), and Darío's *Azul* (1888). Although usually a gag is a cloth instrument placed on the mouth in order to silence someone, in this case it is associated with the intense blue colors of the island horizon, a tropical one with white clouds or luminous cumuli, whose rounded protuberances are perceived by the poet as curls, that is, locks of hair in the shape of waves or ringlets.

"Neither cunning caiman" (l. 15) is the first in a series of seven images from the final octave that closes the poem, and it defies the totemic image of Cuba, so frequently interpreted from maps, as the outline of a lizard swimming in Caribbean waters. Such is the case with Nicolás Guillén, who years later wrote in "Un largo lagarto verde" (A long, green alligator), from his collection *La paloma de vuelo popular* (1958; The dove of popular flight): "Por el Mar de las Antillas / (que también Caribe llaman) / . . . cantando a lágrima viva / navega Cuba en su mapa: / un largo lagarto verde, / con ojos de piedra y agua" (By the Antillean Sea / (which they also call Caribbean) / . . . Cuba navigates in its map / singing and shedding raw tears: / a long, green alligator / with eyes of stone and water). Brull substitutes the conventional and malicious caiman with another more playful and original image: " . . . equestrian spring / riding a seahorse" (ll. 16–17). For the poet, an experienced horseman from childhood when he stayed at his family's country home, Guaicanámar, spring was the best season for horseback riding. However, in accordance with the marine character of the island, the poetic voice intuits the spring season as if one were riding a seahorse.

The principal components of the other five images that close the circular structure of the poem are "cove," "fields," "spiral," "sweet juice," and "summit." "Clamorous cove" (l. 18) refers to the *abra*, inlet or bay, found in elevated coastlines, that allows the rough, clamorous waters to pass through, while in its second American meaning *abra* can also signify a large, open field, situated between forests, that allows the passing-through of loud noises. In the plural sense, *rubiales* of "honeyed fields" (l. 19) is also *blondie*, an informal or familiar reference to someone blond, though here the image is one of fields with ripe sugar cane waving in the wind. "Spiral of delight" (l. 20) is an abstract image that contains a noun belonging to science, geometry, and mathematics, a usage typical of the *vanguardista* period, which often employed such words as "eclipse," "irradiate," "voltaic arc," and "wireless telegraph." Here the spiral denotes the spiral of smoke emanating from a lit cigar, which rises ever higher. For Brull, an inveterate smoker, this "delight" indicates the pleasure produced by nicotine when tobacco is inhaled, one that intoxicates and stimulates as the pulse accelerates. "Sweet

juice: unharmed summit / of the intact island!" (ll. 21–22) is the liquid squeezed from vegetables and fruits; however, in this case *zumo*, or sweet juice, probably refers to *guarapo*, the liquid extracted from sugar cane that is a very popular fresh-squeezed drink in the Antilles as well as other tropical areas of Latin America. This juice is also distilled into spirits, and when concentrated and supersaturated, the purified essence gets processed into sugar crystals. Thus, the "honeyed fields" get reduced to a useful sweet essence. "Summit" equals zenith, superior grade, and the highest part, because it also relates to the sugar industry, the major source of income for the island.

In short, at the first level of reality, the poem condenses geographic, climatic, economic, and characteristic traits distinctive of Cuba, stylized and sublimated by art into an idealized vision consisting of fifteen brilliant, transcendent images that trace the profile of the island and the particular genius of the tropics that encircles her. Or, as G. Videla observes, "the creationist intent explains the cult of the 'created image' that is transformed into the most coveted fruit of the new lyric. The absolute image is pursued, with its own substance, for it does not have the function to compare, transpose, adorn, but rather to substantiate." And this seems to be Brull's purpose in finding richly semantic metaphors that reflect the language of his own baroque and Gongorist literary tradition, one revived by Spanish American poets of the *vanguardia*.

Through language and metaphorical play, the author incorporates and transforms into pure idea concrete elements derived from the reality of his native land—immediate, emotional, and paradisal—with a desire to synthesize, personify, and humanize what he had perceived, understood, and imagined as a young artist growing up in Camagüey. The poet focuses on Cuba's insular and marine character, her tropical brightness and humidity, her smells and sounds, the percussive rhythm and movement of her popular music, whose instruments also reflect the contributions of all the different ethnic elements (Indian, white, and black) that make up the Cuban man. Brull evokes the monoculture of sugar cane (sweet juice and summit), the Dance of the Millions, the ups and downs of the commodity exchange, as well as the abject dependence on the international market. Agustín Acosta had also done this earlier in his poem *La zafra* (1928) through a post-*modernista* aesthetic, as well as Alejo Carpentier, who had done the same through a nativist/*vanguardista* lens in his first novel *¡Ecue-Yamba-O!* (1933). Although the topic's complexity would exceed the limits of Brull's delicate miniatures, the final images of "Isla de perfil" already prefigure those found in Fernando Ortiz's *Contrapunteo cubano del tabaco y el azúcar* (1940).

The melancholic terseness and somber and reflexive mood of Brull's last books—*Temps en peine/Tiempo en pena* and *Rien que . . ./Nada más que . . .*—reveal a style that is fluid and more mature, one sharpened by personal tragedy, the black hole of existential emptiness. Writing "A Toi-même" ("To Yourself," 1999), his only poem in French, Brull adopted the persona or mask of another, the voice of a clairvoyant who speaks in an alien tongue, a poet who had swayed over the sands of nothingness or imaginatively explored the subconscious, the enigma of truth submerged beneath the waters of the eternal, or assimilating with ease some of the conceptual repercussions of surrealism.

> *Toi qui plonges dans l'éternel*
> *Et reviens les mains vides,*
> *Plein d'un oubli qui ne pèse*
> *Que sur les cils chargés de songes;*
> *Toi qui de rien combles ta vie*
> *Pour être plus léger à l'ange*
> *Qui suit tes pas, les yeux fermés,*
> *Et ne voit point que par tes yeux;*
> *As-tu trouvé le corps d'Icare*
> *A l'ombre de tes ailes perdues?*
> *Qu'est-ce qui t'a rendu muet*
> *Parmi les sables du néant,*
> *Toi qui plonges dans l'éternel*
> *Et reviens les mains vides?*

You who plunge into the eternal
and come up empty-handed,
full of a forgetfulness that weighs
your lashes down with dreams;
you who fill your life with nothing
to be lighter than the angel
that follows your footsteps, eyes shut,
seeing only through your eyes;
have you found the body of Icarus
in the shadow of your own lost wings?

What has struck you dumb
amid the sands of nothingness,
you who plunge into the eternal
and come up empty-handed?

And later on, in "Víspera" (The day before), the poetic voice acquires a tone of nihilism and desperation when it glimmers for the first time from the edge of chaos: "Al caos me asomo . . . / El caos y yo / por no ser uno / no somos dos. Vida de nadie, / de nada . . ." (I peek into chaos . . . / Chaos and me / not being one / we are not two. Life of no one, / from nothingness).

The same year *Temps en peine/Tiempo en pena* was published, and in a manner analogous to "Víspera," the author completed his translation of *La Jeune Parque et La joven parca*, based on Paul Valéry's last version of the poem: "Grita en todo mi cuerpo la palidez, la piedra . . . / ¡La muerte quiere oler a esta rosa sin precio / Cuyo dulzor conviene a su fin tenebroso!" (In my whole body cries paleness, the stone . . . / Death wants to smell this priceless rose / Whose sweetness suits its gloomy end!). In 1952 his wife, Adela Baralt y Zacharie, died, and in 1953 the poet was named Cuba's ambassador to Uruguay, though at year's end he was dismissed by Fulgencio Batista, whom the poet had disobeyed over a political controversy. Brull returned to Cuba and moved into a new house in Havana's Kohly neighborhood. He seems to have become more aware of his mortality, because on the cover of *Rien que . . . (NADA MAS QUE . . . )* the ellipsis of the title in French and the upper-case letters in Spanish could well signify "rendre l'âme" or "death." In addition, the cover of the 1954 bilingual edition contains a drawing in the shape of an hourglass, grains of sand falling. Repeated throughout the text as well, in poems like "Fuga" (Escape), "Si" (If), and "No," is the very consciousness of life's expiration, the theme of time's brevity, of hours and minutes counted in a life that is already escaping like water between one's fingers: "Se iba el agua de prisa entre los dedos / al querer sin querer . . ." (Time fled quickly between my fingers / wanting without wanting . . .); "Las arenas del tiempo sin retorno" (The sands of time without return); and "Cuando el tiempo gotea de maduro, en cada gota evaporada, tú—pez de los profundos abismos—callas" (When time drips ripe, in each evaporated drop, you—fish from the deep abyss—keep quiet).

Finally, as noted above, the preface to *Rien que . . ./ Nada más que . . .* is a reflection on poetic craft, in particular as a reflection at the intersection between history and memory. In the words of Jorge Mañach, a place "where [the author] defines himself not with concepts but with images only accessible to our intuition, to our prediction." Brull's preface, together with the poems "El encuentro" (The encounter) and "No," is among the best examples of poetic prose, an essential characteristic of his last book. But neither is it coincidental that this literary testament, this preface, is also an eloquent argument for the recovery and dissemination of the poet's own texts, subject to the vagaries of war, revolution, or the black hole of chaos.

*Nunca es ocioso para la curiosidad eternamente despierta del buscador, reconstruir al poeta por la ruina que dejó en los fragmentos esparcidos de una presencia que se eclipsa sin desaparecer del todo, por aquellos caminos a donde él va o lo lleva su predestinación. Porque el poeta es todo querer sin querer que, como agua despeinada, corre hacia su querencia momentánea con el temblor del alumbramiento. En su tránsito, la poesía lo elige como testigo, y no sabremos más de ella que cuanto ha quedado en el ámbito del recuerdo contorneado por la luz de otro momento. Asi encalla entre las islas del crepúsculo en menguante . . . Allí donde el lenguaje deja al poeta como náufrago, en la orilla de su propia resonancia perdido, le rescata el vuelo de la nube o del pájaro; o, en el ruido ahogado que devuelve al silencio su imperio merodeante, entonces es que empieza su singular nacimiento entre las cosas sin memoria.*

It is not unprofitable for the ever-vigilant truth-seeker to retrace the poet's journey along its predestined path out of the ruins evidenced by scattered fragments of a presence constantly eclipsed without ever being completely hidden. Because the poet is always full of determination without determining, what he rushes toward draws him with a bright shudder like ruffled water. Poetry elects the poet as witness to this journey, but we will never know more of it than what lingered in the locus of memory, grazed by the light of another moment. For poetry runs aground of islands of fading light . . . There, where language strands the poet like a castaway lost on the river of his own resonance, a drifting cloud or bird in flight rescues him. Unless even there, in the suffocating din that reverts to conquering silence, a singular birth delivers him into a world of things without memory.

What makes Brull unique among his Spanish American contemporaries is his rare combination of talent and circumstance, tradition and innovation. All the advantages of travel and of a prominent diplomatic career, which allowed him to take advantage of his own Hispanic heritage and that of the West (from those circle-dance children's songs from traditional popular poetry to the most erudite literary legacy from Latin America, the Spanish Golden Age, and the great classical French tradition) and in doing so assimilate and integrate all these elements into a synthesis of all the formal innovations that *vanguardismo* could offer, both in Spain and Spanish America. However, in the final analysis he not only had the opportunity of seeing and learning by personal experience, but he also possessed the intelligence and capacity to assimilate, adapt, and synthesize that life experience, which allowed him to transform the poetic language of his time, thus producing an original work of Cuban literature and creating poems and a poetic discourse characterized by individuality, an aesthetic achievement recognized by his contemporaries, Spanish, Latin American, and French. It is sufficient to cite two of them, his compatriot post-*vanguardistas* Cintio Vitier and Gastón Baquero, who accurately summarize the form and substance of Brull's formal and thematic merits.

Vitier highlights the most persistent thematic centers: "His work will be defined by the symbols it uses: the nude before the mirror, the enigmatic rose, the ghost of time that cannot be seized, the day-before of the self and the world; and because of his words' capacity for sensorial suggestion." In other words, Brull's merits might be summarized as follows: the reflexive self-contemplation, the self-knowledge, and the implacable analysis of the very psyche in the dynamic interaction of the combined human sensory, affective, and mental functions that also fascinated Freud. Brull's work is characterized by the constant examination of aesthetic experience and nature joined to "the desire of intellectual beauty"; and the exploration of the invisible fourth dimension of our three-dimensional globe: time, the bonfire in which we all burn. He also concerns himself with "the day-before of the self and the world" or the perpetual fascination with the individual and universal experience of *duermevela,* the twilight zone of fitful sleep that precedes the awakening to the reality that surrounds us. Finally, Brull persistently evokes sensory experience through the sonorous enchantment of words liberated from the chains of logic, whose creative sense is found in the phonic experimentation with language. Baquero summarizes some of Brull's formal merits, in addition to giving some lessons to all poets, whether post-*modernista, vanguardista,* or contemporary:

> the somber, calm tone . . . the shortening of oratory's flights, the rejection of ay! and of oh! . . . braking the emphasis, muffling the cries . . . Among his characteristics there is one that is very rare, virtually unknown in the poetry of the region: he is not abundant, he is not torrential, but rather labored, of slow production, as if resin were crystallizing drop by drop.

Mariano Brull, a distinguished man, restrained and sensible, died while in a coma from a malignant brain tumor on a Friday, 8 June 1956, as in his poem "I Am Going to the June Sea." For Brull, this boundless, migrant sea that encircles Cuba is a luminous, geometric vision of postclassical plenitude and order from chaos, a new beginning that often heralds the break of day in the Latin American avant-garde and lifts up the courage of the living.

# SELECTED BIBLIOGRAPHY

## Primary Works

### Poetry, Books, and Pamphlets

*La casa del silencio.* Introduction by Pedro Henríquez Ureña. Madrid: M. García y Galo Sáez, 1916. (Contains two introductory poems: "Meditación bajo la luna," by Enrique González Martínez and "To a Young Poet," by Salomón de la Selva.)

*Poemas en menguante.* Paris: Le Moil & Pascaly, 1928.

*Canto redondo.* Paris: Ediciones G.L.M., 1934.

"El poeta romántico cubano Juan Clemente Zenea y la influencia francesa." In *Cahiers de politique étrangère, études sur les pays étrangères et les questions diplomatiques et coloniales.* Edited by Gabriel Louis-Jaray. Paris: Congrès des Nations Américaines, 1937.

*Solo de rosa: Poemas con dos rosas de Mariano y Portocarrero.* Havana: La Verónica, 1941.

*Zenea: Poemas selectos.* Preface by Mariano Brull, with drawings by Amelia Peláez. Havana: Revista de La Habana, 1944.

"Réponse de Son Excellence Mariano Brull." In *Réception de Son Excellence Mariano Brull au Pen-Club Belge d'Expression Française.* Brussels: La Maison du Poète, 1952.

"José Martí." In *Sonetario Martiano: 100 sonetos dedicados a José Martí por poetas cubanos, latino-americanos y españoles.* Selection by Rafael G. Algilagos, with artwork by Carmelo González. Havana: Servi-Libros, 1960.

### Essays

"¿Cómo hace usted sus versos?" *El Fígaro* (Havana) 31, no. 48:769 (1915).

"Manuel Ponce." *El Fígaro* (Havana) 32, no. 24:693 (1916).

"El salón de 1917." *El Fígaro* (Havana) 33, no. 1:3 (1917).

"Poesía, 1931." *Revista Bimestre Cubana* (Havana) 28:13–23 (1931).

"L'Art et l'État." In *L'Art et la Realité, L'Art et l'État.* Paris: Institut International de Coopération Intellectuelle, 1935. Pp. 302–306.

"En torno a Racine." *Revista Cubana* (Havana) 14:161–170 (July–December 1940).

"La cooperación intelectual o los caminos de la inteligencia." *Revista de La Habana* 3:272–275 (November 1942).

"El arma secreta de Ulises." *Revista de La Habana* 1:69–72 (September 1942).

"Conmemoración del Aniversario de la Indepenencia de Checoeslovaquia el 28 de octubre de 1942." *Revista de La Habana* 4:374–377 (December 1942).

"El mercader y el libro." *Revista de La Habana* 1, no. 5:450–453 (January 1943).

"Eternidad de Simón Bolívar." *Revista de La Habana* 6:552–553 (February 1943).

"Walter Lipman y la política exterior de los Estados Unidos." *Revista de La Habana* 2, no. 20:144–152 (April 1994).

"Juan Clemente Zenea y Alfredo de Musset: Diálogo romántico entre Cuba y Francia." In *Zenea: Poemas selectos.* Havana: *Revista de La Habana,* 1944. Pp. 7–24.

"Una interpretación de la poesía de Paul Valéry." In *La joven parca,* by Paul Valéry. Havana: Ediciones Orígenes, 1949. Pp. 5–14.

"Frente y perfil del coronel Cosme de la Torriente y Peraza, el liberator infatigable." In *Libro homenaje al coronel Cosme de la Torriente en reconocimiento de sus grandes servicios a Cuba.* Havana: Úcar, García & Cía, 1951. Pp. 321–324.

### Translations by Mariano Brull

"Una versión poética de Mariano Brull: El regreso de Henry Vaughan," by Henry Vaughan. *Revista de avance* I, no. 1 (March 15, 1927).

"Variété: Une traduction inédite de Paul Valéry en espagnol/ fragment de *La Jeune Parque.*" *Revue de Littérature Comparée* 11, no. 1:74–75 (January–March 1931).

"La mañana del mundo," by Jules Supervielle. In *Bosque sin Horas.* Madrid: Editorial Plutarco, 1932. Pp. 37–38. (This volume also includes the poem "Romances," by Rafael Alberti, which is dedicated to Brull.)

*La poesía francesa del romanticismo al superrealismo.* Edited by Enrique Díez-Canedo. Buenos Aires: Losada, 1945. (Translations by Brull in this anthology include "Herodías," "Fragmento," and "El nenúfar blanco," by Stephane Mallarmé, and a fragment of *La joven parca,* by Paul Valéry.)

*La joven parca,* by Paul Valéry. Havana: Ediciones Orígenes, 1949. (Also includes Brull's "Una interpretación de poesía de Paul Valéry.")

*La jeune parque/La joven parca,* by Paul Valéry. Preface by Mathilde Pomès. Paris: Civilisations du Sud, S.A.E.P., 1950.

### Translations of Mariano Brull's Works

*Quelques poèmes.* Trans. by Francis de Miomandre and Paul Werrie, with an introduction by Paul Werrie. Brussels: Éditions L'Equerre, 1925.

"Quelques poèmes de Mariano Brull." Trans. by Paul Werrie. *Social* (Havana) XI, no. 3: 19, 22 (March 1926).

*Poëmes.* Trans. by Mathilde Pomès and Edmond Vandercammen, with a preface by Paul Valéry. Brussels: Serie Poetique Collection, 1939.

*Temps en peine/Tiempo en pena.* Trans. by Mathilde Pomès. Brussels: La Maison du Poète, 1950.

*Rien que . . ./Nada más que . . .* Trans. by E. Noulet. Paris: Pierre Seghers, 1954.

"Three Poems and One Essay by Mariano Brull." Trans. by Klaus Müller-Bergh, Michael Anania, and Brooke Bergan. *Caribe: Revista de Cultura y Literatura* 2, no. 1: 107–116 (June 1999). (Includes "I Am Going to the June Sea," "Greenpraise," "To Yourself," and the preface to *Nothing but . . .* ).

### Secondary Works

#### Critical and Biographical Studies

Arciniegas, Germán. "Alfonso Reyes por la gracia de América." *Cuadernos* (Paris), no. 41: 9–10 (March 1960).

Baquero, Gastón. *Mariano Brull: La casa del silencio (Antología de su obra: 1916–1954).* Madrid: Cultura Hispánica, 1976.

———. *Indios, blancos y negros en el caldero de América.* Madrid: Cultura Hispánica, 1991.

Carpentier, Alejo. *La consagración de la primavera.* Mexico City: Siglo XXI, 1978.

———. *Crónicas,* vol. I. Havana: Instituto Cubano del Libro, 1976.

Chacón y Calvo, José María. "Alfonso Reyes, profesor en La Habana." *Casa de las Américas,* no. 210: 122–124 (January–March 1998).

De Armas, Emilio. "Prólogo: La poesía de Mariano Brull." In *Mariano Brull: Poesía.* Edited by Emilio de Armas. Havana: Letras Cubanas, 1983. Pp. 5–41.

Dennery, Étienne, Gérard Willemetz, Florence De Lussy, Madeleine Barbin, and Claude Bouret, eds. *Paul Valéry: Exposition du Centenaire.* Paris: Bibliothèque Nationale, 1971.

Drot, Jean-Marie. *Les heures chaudes de Montparnasse.* Paris: Hazan, 1995.

Florit, Eugenio. *Obras completas,* 4 vols. Edited by L. González del Valle and Roberto Esquenazi. Lincoln, Neb.: The University of Nebraska Press, 1983.

García Elío, Diego. "Mariano Brull." In *Una antología de poesía cubana.* Mexico City: Oasis, 1984. Pp. 12–27.

Gutiérrez Vega, Zenaida. *Epistolario Alfonso Reyes–José María Chacón.* Madrid: Fundación Universitaria Española, 1976.

Hemingway, Ernest. *A Moveable Feast: Sketches of the Author's Life in Paris in the Twenties.* New York: Charles Scribner's Sons, 1964.

Jiménez, Juan Ramón. *Tiempo y espacio.* Prologue and notes by Arturo del Villar. Madrid: Edaf, 1986.

———, ed. *La poesía cubana en 1936 (colección).* Presentation by Fernando Ortiz, with a prologue and appendix by Juan Ramón Jiménez, and a conclusion by José María Chacón y Calvo. Havana: Institución Hispanocubana de Cultura, 1937.

———. *Juan Ramón Jiménez.* Presentation, selection, translations, and bibliography by René L. F. Durand. Paris: Pierre Seghers, 1963.

*Kurt Schwitters.* Paris: Centre Pompidou, 1994.

Larraga, Ricardo. *Mariano Brull y la poesía pura en Cuba.* Miami: Universal, 1994.

Lezama Lima, José. *Coloquio con Juan Ramón Jiménez.* Havana: Publicaciones de la Secretaría de Educación, Dirección de Cultura, 1938.

———. *Obras completas,* vols. I and II. Introduction by Cintio Vitier. Madrid: Aguilar, 1975.

———. *La expresión americana.* Edited by Irlemar Chiampi. Mexico City: Fondo de Cultura Económica, 1993.

Linares Pérez, Marta. "Mariano Brull, el iniciador." In *La poesía pura en Cuba.* Madrid: Playor/Nova Scholar, 1975. Pp. 55–82.

Lizaso, Félix, and José Antonio Fernández de Castro. *La poesía moderna en Cuba (1882–1925).* Madrid: Librería y Casa Editorial Hernando (S.A.), 1926. (Critical anthology.)

Müller-Bergh, Klaus. *Mariano Brull: Poesía reunida.* Madrid: Ediciones Cátedra, 2000. (The bibliography of this book is the best available for critical purposes.)

Patout, Paulette. *Alfonso Reyes et la France.* Paris: Klincksieck, 1978.

Peters, Hans Albert, ed. *Die Sammlung Kahnweiler: Von Gris, Braque, Léger und Klee bis Picasso.* Düsseldorf: Kunstmuseum Düsseldorf, Prestel, 1995.

Rela, Walter. *Diccionario de escritores uruguayos.* Montevideo: Ediciones de la Plaza, 1986.

Reyes, Alfonso. "De la traducción" and "Las jitanjáforas." In *La experiencia literaria (Coordenadas).* Buenos Aires: Losada, 1942. Pp. 141–155 and 193–235.

———. *Obras completas,* 19 vols. Mexico City: Fondo de Cultura Económica, 1968.

———. *Prosa y poesía.* Edited by Willis Robb. Madrid: Cátedra, 1975.

Rice, Argyll Pryor. *Emilio Ballagas: Poeta o poesía.* Mexico City: Ediciones de Andrea, 1966.

Sainz, Enrique. "La poesía pura en Cuba: Algunas reflexiones." In *Ensayos críticos.* Havana: Ediciones Unión de Escritores y Artistas de Cuba, 1989. Pp. 110–131.

Thomas, Hugh. *Cuba: The Pursuit of Freedom.* New York: Harper & Row, 1971.

Torres Bodet, Jaime. *Selected Poems of Jaime Torres Bodet.* Bloomington: Indiana University Press, 1964. (A bilingual edition with translations by Sonia Karsen.)

Vitier, Cintio. *Lo cubano en la poesía.* Santa Clara: Universidad Central de Las Villas, Departamento de Relaciones Culturales, 1958. Second edition, Havana: Instituto del Libro, 1970.

———. *Cincuenta años de poesía cubana 1902–1952.* Havana: Dirección de Cultura del Ministerio de Educación, 1952.

# Alfredo Bryce Echenique

## (1939–    )

## César Ferreira

Although he began writing in the 1960s, the work of Alfredo Bryce Echenique continues to enjoy a growing readership. For some time now, his great appeal in Latin America and Europe, especially in Spain and France, has made him a major protagonist in the development of the contemporary Latin American novel and, along with Mario Vargas Llosa, he is Peru's most widely read novelist internationally. As of the year 2001, Bryce had authored eight novels, four books of short stories, a collection of novellas, a volume of memoirs, and three volumes of journalism. More important, however, Bryce is the creator of a unique style of writing, characterized by orality and humor, along with a personal fictional universe with themes ranging from the sentimental education of members of the Peruvian bourgeoisie to the experience of exile in Europe.

Alfredo Marcelo Bryce Echenique was born in Lima, the capital of Peru, on 19 February 1939, to an upper-middle-class family of Scottish and Basque descent. His father, Francisco Bryce, was a banker, and his mother, Elena Echenique, was the granddaughter of a former president of Peru, José Rufino Echenique. The future writer was educated in exclusive schools attended by Peru's elite: Inmaculado Corazón and Colegio Santa María, both run by American nuns and priests. He later attended Colegio San Pablo, a British boarding school in the outskirts of Lima, from which he graduated in 1956.

Bryce has said that he grew up in a large family, where the art of storytelling was always practiced. His early vocation as a writer was nurtured by his mother's admiration for French literature, particularly the works of Marcel Proust. His father, however, strongly opposed a career in literature, and against his better judgment, Bryce entered the University of San Marcos in Lima in 1957, where he studied law. At the same time he earned a degree in literature, graduating in 1964 upon completing a thesis on Ernest Hemingway.

After graduating from San Marcos, Bryce was awarded a scholarship from the French government to study French literature at the Sorbonne. Departing for Paris in 1964, he did not return to live in Peru permanently until 1999, a circumstance that had a profound effect on his creativity. Bryce's arrival in the French capital coincided with the emergence of the Latin American Boom, arguably the most important group of novelists to come out of Latin America in the twentieth century. Led by such writers as Julio Cortázar, Guillermo Cabrera Infante, Mario Vargas Llosa, José Donoso, and Carlos Fuentes, this group of authors was known for the great aesthetic and verbal innovation in their novels, and they internationalized Latin American fiction to an unprecedented degree. In Paris, Bryce also befriended

Julio Ramón Ribeyro, a canonical author in contemporary Peruvian literature who had been living in the French capital since the 1950s and who became one of Bryce's mentors. After an intense first year in Paris, Bryce spent several months in Perugia, Italy, in 1965. There he wrote his first book, a collection of short stories entitled *Huerto cerrado* (Closed garden). After his return to Paris in 1967, he married his girlfriend from Lima, Maggie Revilla, whom he was later to divorce, and began to work as a lecturer in Spanish at the University of Nanterre, in suburban Paris.

In 1968 *Huerto cerrado* received an award in a prestigious literary contest sponsored by Casa de las Américas in Cuba, and the book was published in Havana. *Huerto cerrado* is an important starting point in Bryce's literary career, announcing a number of themes that he would later develop in his novels. The book is strongly influenced by the works of Hemingway. In fact, the collection of twelve stories is modeled after the Nick Adams tales of *In Our Time* (1925). In Hemingway's stories, one main character is the protagonist of a variety of experiences that serve as his initiation into adulthood. Such is also the case for Manolo, the young hero of *Huerto cerrado*. In stories set among the Peruvian bourgeoisie, such as "El camino es así" (The road is like this) and "Un amigo de cuarenta y cuatro años" (A forty-four-year-old friend), Manolo experiences various rites of passage in school and with his peers. He discovers love and undergoes sexual initiation in "Una mano en las cuerdas" (A hand on the strings), "El descubrimiento de América" (The discovery of America), and "Yo soy el rey" (I am the king), and he acquires an awareness of class differences in "Su mejor negocio" (His best deal). Stylistically, many of these texts pay tribute to Hemingway's concise use of dialogue, as shown in "El hombre, el cinema y el tranvía" (The man, the cinema, and the streetcar), "Las notas que duermen en las cuerdas" (Notes that sleep on strings), and "Dos indios" (Two Indians). This last story is also a first look into the experience of exile, a central theme in Bryce's later novels.

Of all the stories in *Huerto cerrado*, particularly important is "Con Jimmy, en Paracas" (With Jimmy, in Paracas), where the theme of initiation is treated with unique psychological depth and intensity. "Con Jimmy, en Paracas" tells the story of Manolo, a fourteen-year-old boy of the Peruvian middle class, who accompanies his father to Paracas, a beach resort south of Lima, on a weekend business trip. There he is confronted with his wealthy classmate, Jimmy, whose father is also Manolo's father's employer and who patronizes the lower classes. In the course of an afternoon with Jimmy, Manolo experiences the unexpected discovery of drinking, smoking, and sex, underscored by Jimmy's arrogant ways. Although Manolo initially sees his father as a figure of authority, in the course of the story the boy discovers, much to his shame, his father's servile attitude toward his boss. Bryce has always maintained that "Con Jimmy, en Paracas" represents the discovery of his narrative style, and the author links the writing of this story to his first novel, *Un mundo para Julius* (1970; *A World for Julius*, 1992). Indeed, in the short story, the narrator stands out for his confessional tone, which is emphasized by the conversational, friendly quality of his storytelling. Bryce also shows a preference in his fiction for misplaced and fragile protagonists who are destined to become losers. Emotionally incapable of asserting themselves in the world, these characters painfully endure their weaknesses and failures, but nevertheless demonstrate a true sense of humanity and compassion.

The publication of *A World for Julius* in 1970 made Bryce an important contemporary Latin American novelist. The book quickly received critical acclaim because of the author's distinctive ease in storytelling—the evident oral quality of the narrative and his ability to involve the readers in the novel in an intimate way, making them accomplices of the narrator's actions. Critics also noted Bryce's preference for sentimentally fragile characters with a strong sense of marginality. Peruvian critics in particular complimented Bryce on his ironic sense of humor, a trademark largely absent from Peruvian letters since the writings of Ricardo Palma in the late nineteenth century and José Diez-Canseco's little-known novel *Duque* (1930; Duke). *A World for Julius* shares with *Duque* another common denominator: an inside knowledge of Peru's upper class, a neglected theme in Peruvian literature.

A narrative of more than five hundred pages, *A World for Julius* is the story of a charming and sensitive boy of the privileged world of the Peruvian upper class, growing up between the ages of five and eleven. The youngest child among two brothers, Santiago and Bobby, and a sister, Cinthia, Julius is largely ignored by his rich and snobbish stepfather, Juan Lucas, and his beautiful but frivolous mother, Susan. As a result, he must turn to his many servants, particularly his Indian nanny, Vilma, for the attention and affection he needs. Set in Lima in the 1950s, the novel illustrates Peru's transition from a colonial agrarian society to a more modern precapitalist state. In fact, the marriage of Juan Lucas to Julius's widowed mother represents the merging of the traditional oligarchy with the new emerging technocrats who cater to the influence of American capitalism. The novel, however, is far from being so politically explicit. Instead, it chronicles the rich, happy life of an affluent social group that considers its privileged surroundings to be the natural order. In this environment Julius stands out as a child of enormous inquisitiveness and sensitivity, who grows up innocently questioning the status quo of which he is part. His innocence is finally lost when, at the end of the novel, he learns that Vilma, to whom he has grown very attached, has been raped by his older brother Santiago and dismissed from the family mansion, then reduced to making her living as a common prostitute.

Clearly, the novel's greatest achievement is Bryce's unique manipulation of language. He captures the reader's attention through his extraordinary use of humor and the rich orality of his style. *A World for Julius* reproduces the language of the various social groups of Peru, particularly upper-class residents of Lima, and elicits a narrative tone that moves progressively from the hilariously funny to the utterly grotesque. The narrative point of view switches subtly, allowing the narrator to mix whimsically omniscient narration, memories recounted in conversation, and passages of stream of consciousness. Language slowly emerges as the tool that unveils the sordid reality composing the frivolous world of the rich. In the course of the novel the narrator constantly appears and disappears from the story, slowly crafting his own personality and his presence. Although he never intends to condemn openly the unjust social order he portrays, his ambiguous voice, filled with poignant irony, allows him to look at the world of the Peruvian upper class with nostalgia and pity. Through the aural quality and the tone of the rich reproduced by the narrator, the reader learns of the insensitive and selfish nature of such a class, and in so doing must despise it.

*A World for Julius* had an immediate impact on the Peruvian cultural scene as soon as it was published. The book's publication coincided with the rule of a left-wing revolutionary government, led by Gen. Juan Velasco-Alvarado. In 1968 Velasco-Alvarado had seized power, nationalized the country's U.S.-owned industry, and imposed sweeping land reforms. Such measures destroyed Peru's old ruling oligarchy, changing the country's social structure forever. Bryce's novel was soon read by supporters of Velasco Alvarado's regime as the swan song of a disappearing Peruvian elite and, much to his surprise, it earned the young writer the National Literary Award of Peru in 1972. However, *A World for Julius* outlived this first political reading, and due to its unquestionable artistic value, the novel is regarded today as a classic of Peruvian letters. In fact, the enormous popularity of Bryce's novel was confirmed in 1995. In that year, *Debate,* one of Peru's leading publications, conducted a survey in which *A World for Julius* was chosen as the best Peruvian novel of the twentieth century, overshadowing the many important novels of writers such as José María Arguedas and Mario Vargas Llosa.

Bryce continued to explore the world of the Peruvian upper class in his second collection of short stories, entitled *La felicidad, ja, ja* (Happiness, ha, ha), published in 1974. This book insists that the happiness of the wealthy is frivolous and illusory. In most of the stories, the moral decadence of that social class prevails as a main trait. Along with these themes, reflections of Bryce's Parisian exile permeate his work. In "Florence y nos tres" (Florence and us), a young Latin American, a former student at the Sorbonne, is leading an unhappy, frugal life in Paris while earning a miserable living as a Spanish professor. In his solitude and misery, he falls in love with one of his students, who slowly destroys his hopes for affection. For the first time in Bryce's works, Paris is here portrayed as a city that does not live up to its reputation of charm and bohemian lifestyle. Rather, it is a city that leaves Latin Americans lonely and marginalized.

Solitude and marginality also characterize "Muerte de Sevilla en Madrid" (Death of Sevilla in Madrid), one of Bryce's short-story masterpieces. An orphan raised by two piously religious spinster aunts in Lima, Sevilla is a boy whose life is destined for tragedy. Ugly, shy, and incapable of coping, Sevilla leads a secluded existence as an office bureaucrat. Totally unassertive, he expects nothing from life, wanting only to be left alone. However, in a contest organized by a new airline that is headed by an arrogant Spanish manager named Conde de la Avenida, Sevilla unexpectedly wins a free trip from Lima to Madrid. Although Sevilla's trip is intended to be a great public-relations campaign for the airline, it turns into a complete disaster. Distraught by having to deal with what proves to be an overwhelming experience, from the moment he steps on the plane in Lima and throughout his stay in Spain, Sevilla suffers from a chronic case of dysentery. His state of anxiety and desperation is such that he finally jumps out of the window of his hotel room and dies. Ironically, when Sevilla's corpse is being shipped back to Peru, the formerly elegant and self-assured Conde de la Avenida is returning to Spain on another plane, now the victim of a nervous breakdown because of the failure of his public-relations campaign. While the story is narrated with an extraordinary display of humor, its tone ultimately turns grotesquely cruel. "Florence y nos tres" and "Muerte de Sevilla en Madrid" are also Bryce's first attempts to link in a single narrative two different geographical settings: the Latin American homeland and the foreign cultural space of Europe, where the protagonists of both stories suffer from a sense of abandonment and displacement.

In 1977 Bryce published *A vuelo de buen cubero y otras crónicas* (Wayward journeys and other chronicles). This collection of essays chronicles a trip by the author through various cities of the deep South in the United States during the late 1970s. Bryce describes his visits to places such as Richmond, Virginia; Memphis, Tennessee; Atlanta, Georgia; and New Orleans, Louisiana, with a personal slant. He is something of a voyeur of American life, in search of the myths that American culture exports, many of which owe their origins to film and literature. Reality, however, will ultimately remind the writer that those myths are only the product of fiction. In another section, the volume includes a number of reflections on Bryce's European experience, particularly of Paris and the riots of May 1968. He also pays tribute to the writers and film directors he admires,

such as Julio Cortázar, F. Scott Fitgerald, Ernest Hemingway, Tom Wolfe, and Orson Welles. In 1988 the book was reissued in an expanded edition entitled *Crónicas personales* (Personal chronicles).

In 1977 Bryce returned to Peru for six months, his longest visit since his first departure in 1964. During his stay, he earned a doctorate in literature from the University of San Marcos, after writing a thesis on the theater of the modern French writer Henri de Montherlant. He also published his second novel, *La pasión según Pedro Balbuena que fue tantas veces Pedro, y que nunca pudo negar a nadie* (The Passion according to Saint Pedro Balbuena, which became the many lives of Pedro, who could deny no one), which was later republished in 1981 as *Tantas veces Pedro* (The many lives of Pedro). By then it was obvious that Bryce's European experience had had a defining impact on his creative consciousness. *Tantas veces Pedro* is the story of a middle-aged Peruvian writer, Pedro Balbuena, who leads a vagabond life of amorous bohemian adventures in the United States and Europe. He is trying to overcome a tragic love affair, conducted entirely in his mind, with a French woman named Sophie, whose picture he had seen in his youth in a magazine. Pedro finally meets the real Sophie, who proves to be a selfish and frivolous person, and she eventually kills Balbuena.

*Tantas veces Pedro* is a novel about the writer as artist. Balbuena is a failed writer who claims to lack the necessary discipline because he instead prefers to enjoy life and reinvent it profusely through conversation. Ironically, it is his great skill as a conversationalist that in turn produces a story, which appears as a text embedded within the novel. Thus, the book also becomes a reflection of the artist's creative process in writing a novel. Perhaps the most experimental of Bryce's books, *Tantas veces Pedro* is, in retrospect, an important novel of transition for the Peruvian novelist. Bryce's abandonment of Peru as a setting represents the author's first attempt to narrate at length his own European exile, as told from the perspective of a Latin American. This topic would remain at the core of his fictional world throughout the 1980s and beyond.

Meanwhile, tired of living in Paris and distraught by a long love affair, Bryce abandoned the French capital for the southern city of Montpellier in 1980. There he taught Latin American literature at the Université Paul

Valéry while he finished writing his third novel, *La vida exagerada de Martín Romaña* (1981; The exaggerated life of Martín Romaña). One of Bryce's most ambitious and lengthy works, *La vida exagerada de Martín Romaña* is the first part of a diptych, entitled "Cuaderno de navegación en un sillón Voltaire" (Navigation log in a Voltaire chair), and it was followed by *El hombre que hablaba de Octavia de Cádiz* (1985; The man who spoke of Octavia de Cádiz). Martín Romaña, the protagonist, is the son of a wealthy Peruvian family who travels to Paris in the early 1960s to break away from his privileged background in hopes of becoming a writer. Martín is a kind of Peruvian Woody Allen who finds himself caught in numerous misadventures that underscore his personal insecurity and lack of assertiveness. Martín soon discovers that the French capital is far from the romantic and mythical city of Hemingway's fiction, in which he had so firmly believed while in Lima. Instead, he finds it to be an insular place, where Latin Americans are not particularly welcome.

In Paris, Martín encounters a group of Latin American student revolutionaries, known as "El Grupo," who pretend to be preparing for the grand revolution of the proletariat that will occur upon their return to their respective countries. They constantly criticize Martín for his lack of revolutionary conviction, the strongest critic being his sweetheart from Lima, Inés. Although Inés marries Martín in Paris, she constantly threatens to abandon him, having grown tired of his personal insecurity and of his ideological apathy. In an attempt to salvage his marriage, Martín tries to write a socially committed novel about a Peruvian fishermen's union, a reality about which he is totally ignorant, and so, of course, he fails. His failure leads to Inés's departure from Paris, which triggers his nervous breakdown. But while Inés, like others in "El Grupo," eventually grows out of her revolutionary phase and marries a wealthy Brazilian, Martín remains firm in his determination to become a writer. Years later he begins to write the story of his life in a blue notebook. As he recalls his misfortunes while sitting in his so-called Voltaire chair, he ultimately achieves the original ambition that had first brought him to Paris, becoming a writer.

A novel of literary apprenticeship, *La vida exagerada de Martín Romaña* defines Bryce's narrative voice and thematic interests. Set in the framework of a fictional autobiography, the story is mainly narrated in the first person and has close ties with the narrative tradition of the picaresque novel, as well as with Laurence Sterne's *Life and Opinions of Tristram Shandy, Gentleman* (1759–1767). As are the protagonists in the picaresque novel and *Tristram Shandy*, Martín is an egotistical character, one who exerts a wide variety of emotions ranging from self-deprecation to self-pity, constantly manipulating the events of the narrative and seeking the reader's attention and sympathy. Cervantes's *Don Quixote* (1605) and François Rabelais's *Gargantua* (1532) and *Pantagruel* (1532/1533), are two other important influences on the Peruvian novelist, and, like the authors of these books, Bryce seeks to expand the limits of reality. He intermixes other stories in the main course of the narration, and he uses multiple points of view that ultimately create a large canvas of multifaceted perspectives on reality. In addition, the novel includes a character named Bryce Echenique, a successful writer also living in Paris at the time. Martín envies and abhors Bryce Echenique, and during an encounter actually knocks him down. Martín Romaña is Bryce's typical antihero, marked by a sense of tragedy and absurdity and caught in a world of solitude and marginality. At the same time, he is a Peruvian cosmopolitan who constantly moves about in the hope of finding affection and a sense of belonging in the world.

Bryce arguably comes to terms with Paris as a personal experience in *La vida exagerada de Martín Romaña*, while he reinvents the French capital as a mythical city for Latin Americans of his generation. For many aspiring Latin American artists since the nineteenth century, Paris has been a literary mecca. The novel's depiction of Paris, however, seeks to destroy such a fiction. For Martín, one creator of that myth was Hemingway, by whom he feels repeatedly betrayed and who is cited with scorn and irony throughout the novel. Once the false image of the city is acknowledged and destroyed by Martín, Paris becomes a place that, instead, reinforces Latin American cultural identity. Thanks to the experience of exile, Bryce's characters undergo a reevaluation of their Latin American identity through a painful conflict with a differing cultural code. As in the works of Henry James and Julio Cortázar, two authors whose exploration of a similar theme influenced Bryce's fiction, the confrontation with the "other" serves as an experience of apprenticeship and personal reaffirmation in a foreign cultural space.

In 1984 Bryce abandoned French academia and moved to Barcelona. There he published the second volume of Martín Romaña's saga, *El hombre que hablaba de Octavia de Cádiz*. Written in what Martín calls his red notebook, the novel begins after Inés's departure from Paris and narrates his sentimental relationship with Octavia de Cádiz, an idealized woman who, in the protagonist's imagination, fluctuates between reality and fiction. Often the line between reality and fantasy is erased by the author's ingenious use of language and storytelling. The novel rehearses many of the themes of the first volume, particularly those of exile, displacement, and the search for a Latin American cultural identity. If in the novel's first volume Martín was criticized by his compatriots for his bourgeois spirit and lack of revolutionary convictions, this time he is rejected by Octavia's aristocratic family, who see him through European eyes as nothing but a subversive, Third World revolutionary. The novel is also a rejection of the frivolous world of money and modernity in which Martín suddenly finds himself immersed, yet he always remains true to his vocation as a writer.

Bryce's next book was a collection of short stories, *Magdalena peruana y otros cuentos* (1986; Peruvian Magdalena and other stories). A volume of twelve stories, it repeats many of the themes explored in previous books, such as solitude, exile, marginality, and social decadence. Many of Bryce's pieces in this volume are based on a technique in which the events narrated occur in the same time and space, thereby erasing the dubious borders between reality and fiction. One of the most singular traits of the collection is the reappearance of many characters from Bryce's previous books, including Manolo, Florence, and Martín Romaña. The art of storytelling itself is also a recurring theme, with several characters potrayed as writers or painters. The concept of author as artist is explored in some of the collection's stories, underscoring the importance of the craft of storytelling as an underlying topic in Bryce's writing.

By the late 1980s, Bryce's reputation as an author was well established in Latin America and Europe. In 1987 the Instituto de Cooperación Iberoamericana in Madrid sponsored a symposium to discuss his works.

He was also invited to the University of Texas at Austin as a Tinker Visiting Professor, and he lectured at several other universities in the United States. In Texas, he also finished writing his fifth novel, *La última mudanza de Felipe Carrillo* (1988; The last round of Felipe Carrillo). The shortest of the author's novels, it nevertheless once again explores the conflict of exile and deracination. Felipe Carrillo is a successful Peruvian architect who has lived in Paris for many years and who is married to a Frenchwoman, Liliane. Distraught by Liliane's unexpected death, he questions his sense of belonging in Paris. Shortly after, he meets Genoveva, a divorced Spanish journalist who is also the mother of Sebastián, an adolescent. Sebastián suffers from a profound Oedipus complex, making it hard for him to bear Felipe's relationship with Genoveva. In a last attempt to salvage the relationship, all three travel from Spain to Colán, a beach resort in northern Peru, but once there, the situation turns into an absurd ménage a trois. Equally absurd are the novel's later events. Disillusioned with his relationship with Genoveva, Felipe gets involved with Eusebia, a *mulata* who has been serving the guests during their visit to Colán and with whom he later elopes to the hacienda of a wealthy friend in the area in a helicopter. After the couple's amazing departure from Colán, Felipe is confronted by the fact that he is caught between two worlds. He yearns to return to his Peruvian roots, all the while pretending that he will take Eusebia back to France. However, the cultural and social gap separating the two make such a wish impossible. He finally returns to Paris alone, destroyed by his solitude and lack of belonging.

Perhaps one of Bryce's most experimental texts, *La última mudanza de Felipe Carrillo* is the result of meticulous intertextual crafting. Language and the art of storytelling, rather than plot, are the main focus of this novel. As in *La vida exagerada de Martín Romaña*, it is the protagonist's painful memory that directs the story's narrative. As he digressively reassesses his sentimental failure with Genoveva and Eusebia, the narrator directly addresses the reader, commenting repeatedly on the creative process he is conducting. Moreover, reaching out for the reader's empathy as a character by Laurence Sterne would do, Felipe explicitly confesses the names of the writers he is trying to emulate in his account, and even demands that the reader share the same hatred he feels for Genoveva and her son. Bryce devises a fast-paced text that is psychologically intense in tone, for Felipe Carrillo is a character who most dramatically illustrates the writer's concept of uprootedness and solitude.

While focusing on the fragile nature of the human condition and the strong display of emotions that is conveyed in the narrative, *La última mudanza de Felipe Carrillo* also parodies the scientific nature of psychoanalytic discourse and the rigidity of political ideology. Instead, a unifying factor in the narrative is Latin American popular music, Bryce's latest stylistic novelty. Well blended with his orality, the numerous references to tangos, boleros, Peruvian waltzes, and Mexican *rancheras* unify an otherwise seemingly chaotic story line. In fact, it is popular music which makes Felipe and Eusebia's extravagant love affair possible: thanks to its romantic nature, music proves the only source of real communication between the two lovers, allowing them to overcome the social and cultural barriers that separate them. Through the narrator's final reconstruction of events, the reader once again witnesses the creative process that has unfolded. As earlier with Octavia de Cádiz, the protagonist learns that Eusebia is nothing but the product of his own imagination. Similarly, the therapeutic nature of the act of writing is revealed in Felipe's new awareness of his existential condition.

Shortly after publishing *La última mudanza de Felipe Carrillo,* Bryce left Barcelona and moved to Madrid in 1989 to marry Pilar de Vega, whom he would later divorce. In Madrid he became a regular contributor to various Spanish and Latin American periodicals, as well as an active participant in Spain's cultural scene.

The 1990s proved to be Bryce's most prolific decade as a writer. He published a collection of novellas entitled *Dos señoras conversan* (1990; Two ladies converse), a format which evidenced a new dimension in his writing. This book is a return to a Peruvian setting for his fiction. Bryce uses recent historical events in Peru (the military government of the late 1960s and 1970s, the return of the country's democratic rule and the rise of terrorist activity in the 1980s) as the background for the three stories in the book.

In the first novella of the volume two elderly sisters, Carmela and Estela, reminisce about their aristocratic lifestyle in earlier twentieth-century Peru. Through their memories, Bryce is able to give the reader a quick view of Peru's contemporary history and hints at the conflicts that plague its society. A sharp exchange of dialogue between the two characters slowly unveils the two sisters' solitude since the death of their respective husbands. The closed nature of Peru's elite is suggested by the fact that the husbands, Juan Bautista and Luis Pedro, were also brothers. The sisters' insulation from the outside world, in particular from the radical social experiments of the 1960s, becomes evident when they comment on the difficulty of finding good servants. The violent nature of Peru's present-day social conflict is portrayed as the reader learns that Jesús Comunión, the son of the family's longtime chauffeur, instead of following in his father's footsteps as a servant, has entered the University of San Marcos, becoming a member of a guerrilla group. Bryce once again focuses on the decadence of the Peruvian ruling class, reproducing a reality that is sentimentalized by nostalgia for the past, while also addressing the dilemma presented by social conflict in Peru in the 1980s.

Nostalgia also permeates the book's second novella, "Un sapo en el desierto" (A frog in the desert). Its protagonist is a Peruvian literature professor in Austin, Texas, Mañuco Cisneros. While drinking beer with three friends in a local bar called La Cucaracha, he tells them of his rare friendship when he was fifteen with Don Pancho Malkovich, an important executive for an American mining company in Peru in the 1950s. With Don Pancho, Mañuco used to eat, drink, and play a Peruvian game called *sapo* (frog). As a youngster, he is invited by Don Pancho to spend time at his mining camp in the Peruvian Andes, and in spite of Don Pancho's apparent sympathy for the country's customs and its people, Mañuco also learns of the mining company's exploitation of the Indian workers. Later, when an Indian rebellion takes place, Don Pancho is injured and eventually leaves Peru, guilty of the social injustice of which he has been part. On retirement, Don Pancho moves to San Antonio, Texas, where, now many years later, Mañuco wants to visit him. When he does, he encounters a sickly and lonely man who remembers the good days in Peru. As Mañuco leaves the old man's home, he spots the broken *sapo* game that Don Pancho used while in his garden in

Peru, and this time the game serves as a symbol of Don Pancho's decadence. "Un sapo en el desierto" is a story of social apprenticeship and awareness, as well as of a disillusioning encounter with the past. Like many of Bryce's texts, it expresses the notion of a lost paradise that inhabits the psyches of many of his characters.

The third novella, "Los grandes hombres son así y también asá" (Great men are like this and also like that), presents an ironic view of the human contradictions of a left-wing Peruvian leader. Set in the wake of Peru's return to democratic rule in the late 1970s, it tells of the friendship of Raúl and Santiago, both members of the upper-class Peruvian bourgeoisie. As a boy, Santiago had idolized Raúl, who early in school proved to have leadership qualities. In adulthood, however, Raúl has become a clandestine leftist revolutionary in Peru, while Santiago, despite his fear of bugs, has become an entomologist in Paris. Upon the sudden death of Raúl's wife, Eugenia, Santiago returns to Peru to see his old friend. They plan a trip to the Peruvian jungle, to remember Eugenia together and to cure Santiago's fear of spiders, but once in Lima, Santiago is forced to meet with Raúl in a slum in the outskirts of Lima, where Raúl carries out his secret political activities. Santiago learns that Raúl has already suppressed his feelings for the loss of his wife and has taken a new girlfriend, the beautiful Nani Peters, a mutual friend from adolescence. All three travel to the Amazon region in the Peruvian jungle, where their visit is marked by a series of burlesque adventures that include Raúl's obsession to remain anonymous throughout the trip, while still carrying out his "heroic" revolutionary activities in a humorous, nonclandestine manner. These activities are counterbalanced by Santiago's neurotic fear of being bitten by insects, and especially by spiders. The lifelong friendship of Raúl and Santiago is frequently narrated through the use of Santiago's diary, which slowly accounts for the passing of time and the mutual respect for each man's particular way of dealing with reality, in spite of their differing concerns. Eventually the friends meet again in Paris, where Raúl is in exile and is finally confronted with Eugenia's loss. As in many of Bryce's stories, friendship and loyalty are presented as untouchable assets, always capable of bringing together opposite psychologies, despite differing political beliefs.

By the early 1990s, Bryce's place in Latin American literature and in the Spanish-speaking world was unquestionable. A prolific decade for the writer, his many contributions as a cultural ambassador for the Hispanic world were recognized by the king of Spain, who named him a "Comendador de la Orden de Isabel La Católica" in 1993. That same year Bryce also published his first volume of memoirs, *Permiso para vivir (Antimemorias)* (1993; License to live: Anti-memoirs), which enjoyed many editions in Spain and Latin America. The book, an amusing self-portrait of Bryce the storyteller and world adventurer, is divided into two long sections. In the first section, "Por orden de azar" (In random order), the author reflects on the illusory nature of autobiographical writing and freely engages in a lengthy, nostalgic voyage through many moments in his life. At center stage, however, is always Bryce, the Peruvian novelist, who by now has lived in Europe for over half of his life, committed to the one vocation that defines him: the vocation of writer. Memory functions in these anti-memoirs (a term borrowed from the French writer André Malraux) as a free-winded, loose element to expand the realm of Bryce's storytelling. The reader soon learns about the author's family in Peru and his exclusive childhood and adolescence in Lima; about his early decision to become a writer while still a student at the University of San Marcos and about his stubborn commitment to abandon Peru in the early 1960s to become a writer in Paris. A casual, conversational tone permeates Bryce's prose, and the reader is soon met by a more intimate persona who tells of his struggles as an author in Europe while writing his first books, his friendships with writers he admires (Juan Rulfo, Julio Cortázar, Julio Ramón Ribeyro, and Carlos Barral, among others), his adventurous love life, his attitudes toward fame and alcohol, and the ever-changing nature of his self-exile in Europe. Bryce also offers a very personal portrait of Cuba in the second half of the book, entitled "Cuba a mi manera" (Cuba, my way). This is a long chronicle prompted by five trips to the island, beginning in the 1980s, during which the novelist reflects on the place of the Cuban Revolution in Latin American history. He recalls the 1960s when, thanks to Casa de las Américas, the island was a haven for many young left-wing intellectuals, many of whom were members of the Boom generation. At the time,

Bryce was still an aspiring writer in Paris and remained a careful spectator of the events that took place in Cuba. Some twenty years later, Bryce is a privileged observer of the inner circles of power on the island as he describes his many visits, including his encounters with Fidel Castro himself. However, the author's look into the world of Cuba's Communist regime is often a background for the many stories of friendship and love which he also recalls in these pages. Such narrative strategy ultimately results in a lucid and honest portrait of Cuba's political reality in the 1990s. While he is critical of Castro's ideological stagnation, Bryce clearly makes a case for the personal friendships and sentimental loyalties he left behind on the island, all of which seem more rewarding than the political contradictions he may have encountered. *Permiso para vivir* is a sentimentally charged narrative that reviews many facets of Bryce's life. Memory often serves as an invisible bridge to an understanding of Bryce the man, who is also Bryce the novelist. Ultimately, the text itself is a reaffirmation of an individual fidelity to the art of storytelling, where the author's life and fiction are impossible to separate.

Bryce's next literary endeavor is yet another tour de force set largely in Peru, *No me esperen en abril* (1995; Don't wait for me in April). Critics were quick to claim that this novel begins where *A World for Julius* ends. While it is true that Bryce returns to many of the scenarios of *A World for Julius*, namely the world of the Peruvian upper class, such a rushed judgment does not do justice to this lengthy novel. In fact, *No me esperen en abril* is a vast fresco of Peru's historical and social development during the second half of the twentieth century, as seen by its rich elite. A novel of apprenticeship, it tells the story of Manongo Sterne, a member of Peru's upper class, who with Teresa Mancini discovers love at the age of fifteen. Manongo attends the Colegio San Pablo, an exclusive British boarding school built outside of Lima in the 1950s by Peru's influential and anachronistic finance minister, don Alvaro de Aliaga y Harriman. At Colegio San Pablo, the country's future leaders are educated in traditional British style, largely ignoring modern Peru's social and historical reality of severe class contradictions. There, Manongo will meet most of his lifelong friends, many of whom, as members

of Peru's white social elite, go on to inherit their families' privileged lifestyles. Manongo will as well, but in his own peculiar way. Like many of Bryce's protagonists, Manongo is an outcast who is never quite comfortable with himself or with his social surroundings. He will grow up to become a nostalgic and cynical millionaire, longing for his sentimental past with his friends from San Pablo and yearning to recover Teresa's youthful love, to no avail.

Through Manongo and Teresa's love story, Bryce constructs a mosaic of Peruvian society between the 1950s and the 1990s. As in *A World for Julius*, Peru's elite is shown to be a myopic and self-contained group, viewing its political and social power as a natural right. Moreover, its members stubbornly refuse to see the country as an evolving society, one struggling to redefine its national identity in a more democratic fashion. As the aristocracy's political power slowly dwindles, Lima becomes a microcosm of Peru in the 1990s, with Peruvians of all cultural identities sharing space that was once controlled by only a few. Bryce chronicles society through a polyphonic narrative voice. In fact, the author's torrential oral prose incorporates an ample variety of tones into its long-winded narration, underscoring humor and irony as powerful tools to explain an unjust social order. At the same time, a deep sense of nostalgia for the collective past of Bryce's youthful characters is evoked, thanks to repeated references to popular culture, particularly music and cinema. The result is the portrayal of a country of many social contradictions, a melting pot of many voices with new populist leaders (Velasco, Alan García, Fujimori), who have dethroned Peru's old rich. Much has changed in Peru since the 1950s, including Manongo's beloved Teresa. Still, he refuses to let go of the past until love, the guiding force of his youth, finally destroys him.

*No me esperen en abril* is the work of a storyteller at his best. Manongo Sterne is one of Bryce's most sentimentally charged characters, a true antihero who personifies solitude and cynicism, friendship, and genuine love. The novel's rich narrative leaves the reader sharing the same sense of melancholy as its protagonist, who remembers the lost paradise of his youth. Such virtues are enough to make *No me esperen en abril* one of the author's most ambitious fictional achievements.

Bryce's visit to Peru in 1995 was a turning point in his personal life. His immense popularity among readers was confirmed at the presentation of *No me esperen en abril* in Lima and during the many lectures he gave on his life and works. In addition, a survey conducted that year by the bimonthly *Debate* to determine the most important Peruvian novel of the century resulted in the selection of *A World for Julius.* Tired of his self-exile in Europe, Bryce made the decision to return to Peru permanently during that stay. In the meantime, he published a volume of *Cuentos completos* (1995; Collected short fiction), as well as two representative anthologies sampling his entire literary production, *Para que duela menos* (1995; So that it hurts less) and *Antología personal* (1995; Personal anthology). He was also a Visiting Professor of Latin American literature at Yale University during the latter part of that year.

In 1996 Bryce published a new volume of essays entitled *A trancas y barrancas* (Against many odds). In addition to an interesting foreword, in which the author shares his personal opinions about his own journalism and the roles of fact and fiction in his writing, the volume presents a variety of pieces written for Spanish and Latin American newspapers over the past ten years. Many articles cover a number of contemporary political topics pertaining to Peru, Europe, and Latin America. Also included is a travel memoir on Prague, in the former Czechoslavakia, in 1988, one year before the fall of the Berlin Wall. In another section, Bryce reflects on the many writers he admires from Latin America (Onetti, García Márquez), France (Victor Hugo, Voltaire, Stendhal), and the United States (Hemingway, Henry James, J. D. Salinger).

Bryce's plans to return to Peru were delayed by many personal and professional circumstances. In early 1997, he returned for a semester to Montpellier as a visiting professor at Paul Valéry University. In fact, the medieval university town in southern France is the setting for Bryce's next novel, *Reo de nocturnidad* (1997; Prisoner of night), which he finished shortly before his stay in France. The protagonist of *Reo de nocturnidad* is Max Gutiérrez, a Peruvian professor of literature who arrives in Montpellier after a painful love affair with the aging Italian model Ornelia Manuzio. Distraught by Ornelia's rejection and infidelities, Max enters a mental institution to undergo long and painful treatment for his depression and chronic insomnia. Incapable of writing in the hospital, he dictates his love affair, a long-winded oral monologue where reality and fantasy are intertwined, to Claire, an eighteen-year-old former student and old flame.

*Reo de nocturnidad* soon presents Max as the narrator of two stories, one within the other. In the first story, which serves as the scaffold for the other, the protagonist has conquered his insomnia, resides in Lima, and maintains a long-distance relationship with Claire. The second story is Max's detailed recollection of his tormented love affair with Ornelia. It is this second narrative, often interrupted by dialogues between the Peruvian professor and Claire, where Max bares his soul in a pathetic effort to recapture his impossible love with his former student. Max's obsession with Ornelia is further aggravated by his nightmarish portrayal of Montpellier, a somber place inhabited by grotesque, low-life characters who become his faithful companions in his painful descent to the abyss of night, in a torturous search for impossible love and sleep. As these two stories unfold, the counterpoint between the two plots finds an internal unity in which Bryce's digressive, overflowing narrative style shares center stage with humor and tragedy. Feeling like a true outcast, Max Gutiérrez yearns to return home to Peru and eventually does so. Before then, however, Montpellier proves to be a painful purgatory where he must overcome the demons of a long, sentimental journey and the inevitable scars that such a journey leaves. The tragic and lyrical qualities of this novel made *Reo de nocturnidad* a favorite among Bryce's readers. In 1997 the book was awarded the prestigious Premio Nacional de Narrativa (National Fiction Prize) in Spain.

Yet another love story is the topic of Bryce's next novel, *La amigdalitis de Tarzán* (1998; Tarzan's tonsilitis). Fernanda María de la Trinidad del Monte Montes (also known as Fernanda Mía) is a wealthy young woman from El Salvador who meets Juan Manuel Carpio, a starving Peruvian musician, while they are both living in Europe. From the beginning, theirs is an impossible love: other relationships, households in many cities, money, and fate will never allow them to live in the same place again. Nonetheless, as the two characters part, they begin a long-distance love affair, conducted through the writing of letters, that will last for several decades. This form of intimate discourse provides the framework on which to display Bryce's oral style. Soon, the epistolary mode proves to be an ample imaginary space in which the old love affair between the two characters grows, mainly through the voice of Fernanda Mía. In their many exchanges through the years, Fernanda Mía and Juan Manuel share not only true affection, but also witty, humorous dialogues, often accompanied by countless references to popular music, from Frank Sinatra to Violeta Parra. A well-crafted feminine psychology commands the narrative of the novel, while the exchange of letters also serves as a vast metaphor for the craft of writing. In fact, the written word is not only a therapeutic exercise for Fernanda Mía's sentimental longing, but also the tool through which the individual realities of the two loves multiply as their parallel lives follow their course. As they reach old age, the withering psychology of Fernanda María and Juan Manuel becomes obvious. Feeling the toll of time, the cheerful Fernanda Mía becomes an old, disenchanted woman, whose family's wealth disappears along with her many broken dreams. The novel's title then becomes clear to the reader, as the once vivacious Fernanda Mía, in her early years as strong and energetic as Tarzan, is in the end a vulnerable and fragile woman, no longer capable of fighting or voicing the frustration and pain of life's hardships. As nostalgia and senility invade Fernanda Mía's letters, she seeks solace in the kind memories and the lyrics of the ever-distant Juan Manuel, whose talent as a musician finally receives recognition.

Bryce's next book is a volume of short fiction, *Guía triste de París* (Sad guide to Paris), published in 1998. In fourteen pieces, Bryce evokes the misadventures of Latin Americans in the French capital during the 1960s and 1970s. Consistent with his previous portrayals of the city, Bryce insists on the idea of Paris as a somber and unwelcoming place for foreigners. Nevertheless, Paris is a place where starving Peruvian students, aspiring artists, political activists, and a variety of eccentric individuals gather in search of the city's old glamour and enchantment. As the old myth of Paris slowly crumbles, Bryce's many characters often find themselves leading marginal day-to-day lives in the Latin Quarter, far removed from mainstream French society. In spite of this somber atmosphere, however, Paris remains a place where it is possible to talk about left-wing solutions for Latin America and where one can still hope to live up to the image of a Latin lover, as in "Machos caducos y lamentables," (Pitiful and obsolete men); plan the impossible assassination of an Argentine dictator, as in "El carísimo asesinato de Juan Domingo Perón" (The very expensive assassination of Juan Domingo Perón); or experience the events of the revolution of May 1968 in the fictional world of cinema, as in "La muerte más bella del 68" (The most beautiful death of 1968). Many Peruvian characters see love escape them in many of these stories, only to find solitude and death as their inevitable destiny. Such is the case in "París canalla" (Cowardly Paris), "Lola Beltrán, *in concert*," and the lengthy "Debbie Lágrimas, Madame Salomon y la ingratitud del alemán" (Debbie Tears, Madame Salomon, and the ingratitude of the German). Disillusion and tragedy are common traits for the many protagonists of *Guía triste de París*. Aware of their identity as outsiders, they often try to curtail their vicissitudes with humor and a stubborn imagination, knowing full well that Paris will never live up to their intimate expectations.

Bryce's intention to return to Peru was finally realized in February of 1999, after thirty-four years in Europe and shortly before the author turned sixty. While rediscovering the new face of his native Lima, a city now ten times as large as when he left for Europe, Bryce began working on a second volume of memoirs and became an important participant in Peru's literary scene.

Through all the characters that make up his fictional world, Bryce has proven to be an outstanding chronicler of contemporary Peruvian society, his writing constantly exposing its numerous individual and social contradictions through his insightful portrayals. The act of writing becomes a survival tool for his many characters, who are marked by a deep sense of existential anguish reminiscent of the heroes of the picaresque, and more recently, of Jewish American writers, such as J. D. Salinger and Philip Roth. In the solitude of their displacement, Bryce's antiheroes are also acute explorers of their inner selves, with echoes of his admired Stendhal, as well as critical observers of the worlds that surround them, carrying their personal quests to their limits. A deep sense of authorship permeates Bryce's writing, with orality and humor proving to be useful elements in his fiction. Noted for its profound sense of vitalism, Bryce's literature evidences an urge to recapture a lost paradise through the profound exercise of nostalgic imagination and a keen awareness of the many contradictions of the human condition. Multifaceted alter egos of the author, these characters prove capable of reasserting themselves in the world, despite their weaknesses, and of remaining loyal to their individual beliefs.

Bryce's works bring a renewed sense of cosmopolitanism to contemporary Peruvian literature. Many of his characters embody the contradictions inherent in a Peruvian identity through the experiences of exile. By the same token, however, these characters reveal a critical reassessment of Latin American idiosyncrasies that transforms them, in the long run, into natural citizens of the world. It is perhaps this trait of cosmopolitanism, along with a confessional, ironic voice marked by a profound sentimentalism, that appeals most to Bryce's readers. If the novel of the "Boom" in the 1960s was praised for its great verbal and structural experimentation, it is these new individual traits that clearly distinguish the latest narrative production to come out of Latin America in the so-called post-Boom generation. Along with the writings of Isabel Allende, Angeles Mastretta, Luis Rafael Sánchez, José Emilio Pacheco, and Antonio Skármeta, the works of Alfredo Bryce Echenique undoubtedly point to a renewed aesthetic, as well as a healthy future for the contemporary Spanish American novel.

# SELECTED BIBLIOGRAPHY

## Primary Works

### Novels and Short Story Collections

*Huerto cerrado.* Havana, 1968.
*Un mundo para Julius.* Barcelona, 1970.
*Muerte de Sevilla en Madrid; Antes de la cita con los Linares.* Lima, 1972.
*La felicidad, ja, ja.* Barcelona, 1974.
*La pasión según Pedro Balbuena que fue tantas veces Pedro, y que nunca pudo negar a nadie.* Lima, 1977.

*La vida exagerada de Martín Romaña.* Barcelona, 1981.
*El hombre que hablaba de Octavia de Cádiz.* Barcelona, 1985.
*Magdalena peruana y otros cuentos.* Barcelona, 1986.
*Goig.* Madrid, 1987.
*La última mudanza de Felipe Carrillo.* Barcelona, 1988.
*Dos señoras conversan.* Barcelona, 1990.
*No me esperen en abril.* Barcelona, 1995.
*Reo de nocturnidad.* Barcelona, 1997.
*La amigdalitis de Tarzán.* Lima, 1998.
*Guía triste de París.* Lima, 1999.

### Nonfiction

*Permiso para vivir (Antimemorias).* Barcelona, 1993.
"Qué he hecho yo para merecer esto." *Debate* 81:35–39 (1995).
*Del humor quevedesco a la ironía cervantina.* Lima, 1998.
*La historia personal de mis libros.* Lima, 2000.

### Journalistic Works

*A vuelo de buen cubero y otras crónicas.* Barcelona, 1977.
*Crónicas personales.* Barcelona. 1988.
*A trancas y barrancas.* Madrid, 1996. Augmented edition, Lima, 1997.

### Collected Works

*Todos los cuentos.* Lima, 1979.
*Cuentos completos.* Madrid, 1981. Augmented edition, Madrid, 1995.
*Antología personal.* San Juan, Puerto Rico, 1995.
*Para que duela menos.* Edited by Juan Angel Juristo. Madrid, 1995.
*15 cuentos de amor y humor.* Edited by Carlos Garayar. Lima, 1996.

### Translation

*A World for Julius.* Translated by Dick Gerdes. Austin, Tex., 1992.

## Secondary Works

### Critical and Biographical Studies

Cabanas, Miguel A. " 'Con los ojos bien abiertos': La picaresca y *Tantas veces Pedro* de Alfredo Bryce Echenique." *Hispanófila* 125:91 (1999).

*La Casa de Cartón. Epoca* 2, no. 18 (1999). (Special issue on Bryce.)

Castañón, Adolfo. "Nueva muerte de Bryce Echenique." *La Gaceta del Fondo de Cultura Económica* 290:21–23 (1995).

*Con Eñe—Revista de Literatura Hispanoamericana* 8(1999). (Special issue on Bryce.)

Cornejo Polar, Antonio. "La vida exagerada de Martín Romaña." *Revista de Crítica Literaria Latinoamericana* 16:161–162 (1982).

*Co-textes.* 9 (1985). (Special issue on Bryce.)

*Co-textes.* 34 (1997). (Special issue on Bryce.)

Duncan, Jennifer Ann. "Language as Protagonist: Tradition and Innovation in Bryce Echenique's *Un mundo para Julius.*" *Forum for Modern Language Studies* 16:120–135 (1980).

Escajadillo, Tomás G. "Bryce: Elogios varios y una objeción." *Revista de Crítica Literaria Latinoamericana* 6:137–148 (1977).

Eyzaguirre, Luis. "*Tantas veces Pedro*: Culminación de ciclo en la narrativa de Alfredo Bryce Echenique." *Dactylus* 8:13–16 (1987).

———. "La última mudanza de Bryce Echenique." *Hispamérica* 18:195–202 (August–December 1989).

Ferreira, César. "Bryce Echenique y la novela del posboom: Lectura de *La última mudanza de Felipe Carrillo.*" *Chasqui* 22, no. 2:34–48 (November 1993).

———. "A Rare Portrait of Peru's Elite." *American Book Review* 15, no. 5:15–22 (December 1993–January 1994).

———. "Viaje al fondo del espacio de *Un mundo para Julius.*" *Revista Hispánica Moderna* 50, no. 1:144–157 (1997).

———. "Bryce Echenique y el género epistolar: Notas sobre *La amigdalitis de Tarzán.*" *Movimiento Actual*, nos. 48–51 (January 2001).

Ferreira, César, and Ismael P. Márquez, eds. *Los mundos de Alfredo Bryce Echenique (Textos críticos).* Lima, 1994.

Ferrero, Grazia Sanguineti de. "Axiología del humor y la ironía en *Un mundo para Julius.*" *Revista de la Universidad Católica* 11, no. 12:257–285 (1982).

Fuente, José Luis de la. *Cómo leer a Alfredo Bryce Echenique.* Madrid, 1995.

———. *Más allá de la modernidad: Los cuentos de Alfredo Bryce Echenique.* Valladolid, 1998.

Gallego, Isabel. "Alfredo Bryce Echenique en el fin de siglo." *Revista Iberoamericana* 64, nos. 184–185:611–626 (1998).

García-Montero, Luis. "Lectura de *Un mundo para Julius.*" In his *El realismo singular.* Bilbao, 1993. Pp. 209–236.

Gutiérrez-Mouat, Ricardo. "Travesía y regresos de Alfredo Bryce: *La última mudanza de Felipe Carrillo.*" *Hispamérica* 63:73–79 (1992).

Higgins, James. "*Un mundo para Julius*: The Swan-song of the Peruvian Oligarchy." *Journal of Iberian and Latin American Studies* 4, no. 1:35–45 (1998).

Houston, Robert. "What He Learned from the Servants." *The New York Times Book Review*, 24 January 1993.

Juristo, Juan Angel. "El retorno crepuscular de Julius." *Oiga*, 24 April 1995, pp. 38–40.

Kelly, Alita. "Translation as Cultural Translation: Working with Alfredo Bryce Echenique's First Novel." *Journal of Latin American Cultural Studies* 7, no. 2:249–259 (1998).

Krakusin, Margarita. *La novelística de Alfredo Bryce Echenique y la narrativa sentimental.* Madrid, 1996.

Lafuente, Fernando R., ed. *Semana de Autor: Alfredo Bryce Echenique.* Madrid, 1991.

Lander, María Fernanda. "*No me esperen en abril* o el relato de la nostalgia y el olvido." *Inti—Revista de Literatura Hispánica* 45:243–248 (1997).

Luchting, Wolfgang. *Alfredo Bryce: Humores y malhumores.* Lima, l975.

Mora, Gabriela. "*Huerto cerrado* de Alfredo Bryce Echenique, colección integrada y cíclica de cuentos." *Revista de estudios canadienses* 16, no. 2:319–328 (1992).

Ortega, Julio, ed. *Un mundo para Julius*, by Alfredo Bryce Echenique. Madrid, 1992.

———. *El hilo del habla: La narrativa de Alfredo Bryce Echenique.* Guadalajara, 1994.

———, ed. *La vida exagerada de Martín Romaña*, by Alfredo Bryce Echenique. Madrid, 2000.

Porras, María del Carmen. "Los mundos de *Un mundo para Julius.*" *ALPHA—Revista de Artes y Letras* 14:7–25 (1998).

Rama, Angel. "Bryce Echenique, triste de fiestas." *El Universal* (Caracas), 26 March 1978.

Rodríguez-Peralta, Phyllis. "Narrative Access to *Un mundo para Julius.*" *Revista de Estudios Hispánicos* 3:407–418 (1983).

———. "The Subjective Narration of Bryce Echenique's *La vida exagerada de Martín Romaña.*" *Hispanic Journal* 2:139–151 (1989).

Rose, Sonia V. "Peruanos en el extranjero: El exilio en *Permiso para vivir* de Alfredo Bryce Echenique." In *Literatura peruana hoy: Crisis y creación.* Edited by Karl Kohut, José Morales Saravia, and Sonia V. Rose. Frankfurt, 1998. Pp. 80–95.

Saavedra, Guillermo. "La condición luminosa de las palabras." *La Nación* (Buenos Aires), 12 September 1999.

Sánchez León, Abelardo. "Un cierto imaginario oligárquico en la narrativa de Alfredo Bryce Echenique." In *Tiempos de ira y amor.* Edited by Carlos Iván Degregori. Lima, 1990. Pp. 9–45.

Schwartz, Marcy E. "Cultural and Linguistic Trespassing in Alfredo Bryce Echenique's *La vida exagerada de Martín Romaña.*" In her *Writing Paris: Urban Topographies of Desire in Contemporary Latin American Fiction.* Albany: SUNY Press, 1999. Pp. 89–113.

Serna, Mercedes. "Del amor y otras (divertidas) tragedias: Bryce Echenique retrata de nuevo a la oligarquía peruana." *Quimera,* May 1995, pp. 60–63.

Snauwaert, Erin. *Crónica de una escritura inocente: La focalización implícita como base interpretativa de las novelas de Alfredo Bryce Echenique.* Louvain, Belgium: Louvain University Press, 1998

Stavans, Ilán. "Roll Over, Vargas Llosa." *The Nation* 256, no. 7:244–245 (22 February 1993).

Vargas, Germán. "Un hombre y una mujer." *Debate* 105:70–71 (1999).

Wood, David. "Bibliografía de Alfredo Bryce Echenique." *Revista Interamericana de Bibliografía* 44, no. 1:81–108 (1994).

———. *The Fictions of Alfredo Bryce Echenique.* London, 2000.

*Interviews*

Barnechea, Alfredo. "Entrevista a Alfredo Bryce Echenique." In his *Peregrinos de la lengua: Confesiones de los grandes autores latinoamericanos.* Madrid, 1997. Pp. 43–76.

Ferreira, César. "Entrevista con Alfredo Bryce." *Antípodas* 3:41–47 (1991).

García Huidobro, Cecilia. "Entrevista a Alfredo Bryce Echenique: A caballo entre dos culturas." *Revista Universitaria* 32:65–72 (1991).

Mora, Rosa. "Bryce Echenique: 'La amigdalitis de Tarzán' es un canto a la amistad." *El País* (Madrid), 16 January 1999, pp. 4–5.

Ortiz de Zevallos, Augusto, and Abelardo Sánchez León. "Entrevista a Alfredo Bryce." *Debate* 28:8–23 (1984).

Pollarolo, Giovanna, and Abelardo Sánchez León. "Alfredo Bryce: 'Me dio la volvedera.'" *Debate* 106:12–20 (1999).

# João Cabral de Melo Neto

## (1920–1999)

### *Richard Zenith*

Several poetic movements—most notably that of Brazilian concrete poetry—have claimed João Cabral de Melo Neto as one of their own, in spirit if not through any formal association. The fact is, he never belonged even passively to any literary group. This was not because he was coy or deliberately aloof; it was simply that his poetry did not quite fit any particular school. And yet Cabral seems very much like a "movement" poet. There is an implicit manifesto that runs throughout his poetry, lying just under the surface when it is not the outright subject of his verses, and we can summarize it in two major propositions. The first is "See life unpoetically, as it really is, in all its roughness, incompleteness, poverty and fragmentation." (Life, of course, also has great natural riches and beauties, but Cabral—both as a poetic corrective and as a social statement—preferred to document reality's bleaker side.) The second proposition is "Basing your poem in that reality, raise it up like an architecture, with the logic of geometry and the tools of engineering." This is poetry as construction rather than expression.

João Cabral's poetry is partly a practical demonstration of what he advocated, and partly an exposition of his principles. His poetry is very much about poetry: how it is made, what it stands for, what it can and cannot do. And some of his book titles—Psychology of composition, Education by stone, The school of knives (in English translation)—suggest the didactic, doctrinaire spirit of certain literary schools. But austere "teaching materials," which include stone for acquiring hardness, knives for precision, and wind and desert for arriving at what is essential, are hardly conducive to the gregarious and euphoric agitation that typically informs a literary or social movement. Given the ascetic nature of his poetics—which took its relentless pursuit of matter to the point of antimatter, "the reverse side of nothing"—Cabral could have no direct followers, only emulators.

"Poesia Povera" is how we could designate João Cabral's one-man school of poetry, and this allusion to the Italian Arte Povera movement is doubly appropriate, since he favored "poor," commonplace objects for his poetic raw material, and since he was greatly influenced by visual artists, including Piet Mondrian and Joan Miró. Cabral knew Miró when serving as Brazil's vice-consul in Barcelona from 1947 to 1950, and in a book-length essay on the artist published in 1950, he wrote: "Miró has painted what was heretofore only an object of representation in painting. . . . That moon or that star is never a metaphysical moon or a dreamed moon. They are painted moons and stars unadulterated by other representations of moons or stars." Written near the beginning of Cabral's career as a poet, this critical observation reflects his own artistic ambition: to remake the world with pen and ink, giving things a reality made of words that do not merely represent but that in a certain way constitute, or reconstitute, the things they name. By making things new, Cabral forced his readers to see them anew, to see them as if for the first time. Virtually every critic who has written about this poet notes the all-important place he gives to things; one of the best panoramic studies of his work is Marta Peixoto's *Poesia com coisas: Uma leitura de João Cabral de Melo Neto* (1983; Poetry with things: A reading of João Cabral de Melo Neto), with its apt and eloquent main title. But those things are not meant to replace humanity; it is, rather, as if each one were reaching out to us, saying, "Look at me!" Cabral's poetry is not about things qua things but about how we see things, the need to see them better, and the limits to our seeing.

Born in Recife, Brazil, on 9 January 1920, João Cabral spent his early childhood on the family's sugar plantations in the fertile coastal region of Pernambuco, and those formative years, besides providing his poetry with some of its richest source material, helped determine his way of seeing the world and relating to it. His own social and economic condition was radically different from that of the sugar-mill workers, whom the plantation owners and their politician friends view as subhuman creatures in "Festa na casa grande" (Party at the manor house) in *Dois parlamentos* (1961; Two parliaments); but as a child Cabral was in intimate contact with them. In the evenings the workers would gather around to hear him recite popular verse narratives known as cordel poems, which were published in pamphlet form and sold in the marketplace, where they hung from strings (hence the name cordel). This kind of versified storytelling—informed as well by the narrative verse traditions of medieval Iberia—became the major vehicle for what could be called Cabral's "socially engaged" poetry. If this term is used here with reservations, it is because the poet himself never employed any such epithet. The great originality of his poetry in this vein is its absolute objectivity, not only in its dispassion but also in the way it objectifies the poem's subject.

"Fiesta na casa grande" is a veritable morphology of the sugar-mill worker, who is hardly distinguishable from the sugar which is the beginning, middle, and end of her or his exploited life. The sugar-mill worker "in child form" is

> cana de soca,
> repetida e sem força:
> A cana fim de raça,
> de quarta ou quinta folha.

> cane that is weak
> from overharvesting,
> —A degenerate breed
> of the fourth or fifth cutting.

The female sugar-mill worker is

> como um saco:
> —De açúcar, mas sem ter
> açucar ensacado.

> like a sack
> —Of sugar without
> any sugar inside.

The sugar-mill worker, when on the job,

> tem o ritmo pesado:
> —O do gesto do mel
> deixando o último tacho.

> has a heavy rhythm:
> —Like the final molasses
> from the final vat.

There is no inner "spiritual man" that can remain untouched by the outer condition of "sugar-mill worker." After the worker dies and the worms and dry earth have disposed of his body, finally the wind of the cane field arrives, to sweep away "the gases of his soul." In fact, there is no "engagement" with the mill worker's condition. It is presented without comment or compassion. Let the reader react; the poet stands to one side. Cabral's compulsion to report and the journalistic detachment that made him a good reporter can both be traced back to his childhood on the sugar plantations. In "Menino de engenho" (Plantation boy), one of his few overtly autobiographical poems, published in *A escola das facas* (1980; The school of knives), João Cabral tells how a stalk of sugarcane once cut and almost blinded him, leaving no visible scar but lingering forever in memory. The final stanza reads:

> *A cicatriz não tenho mais;*
> *o inoculado, tenho ainda;*
> *nunca soube é se o inoculado*
> *(então) é vírus ou vacina.*

> Though I no longer have the scar,
> what was inoculated has remained;
> I have never discovered if
> it is a virus or vaccine.

In fact it was both. The impressions "inoculated" into Cabral the child periodically broke out in the poetry of his adulthood, as if of their own volition, but his early experience also gave him a lifelong immunity to facile emotional responses. His poetry displays no pity, and hence no condescension.

João Cabral received a similar, equally important "inoculation" later in his childhood. When he was ten years old, he moved with his family to Recife, where the Capibaribe River and the life that lined its shores stamped his poetry both thematically and technically. In "Pregão turístico do Recife" (Tourist pitch for Recife), from *Paisagens com figuras* (1956; Landscapes with figures), we can infer that the old majestic row houses that flanked the river in the city center taught him "um certo equilíbrio leve, / na escrita, da arquitetura" (a delicate equilibrium / in writing, as in their architecture), and that—outside the center—the desperate poor who stagnated

> *nas mucosas deste rio,*
> *morrendo de apodrecer*
> *vidas inteiras a fio*

> in the river's mucous membranes,
> entire lives rotting
> one by one to death

taught him "que o homem / é sempre a melhor medida" (that man / is always the best measure). The Capibaribe and all that it represents would keep cropping up, like the sugarcane world, throughout Cabral's poetic career. He even wrote a 960-verse tour de force, *O rio; ou, Relação da viagem que faz o Capibaribe de sua nascente à cidade do Recife* (1954; The river; or, Account of the Capibaribe's journey from its source to the city of Recife), narrated by the Capibaribe itself.

João Cabral was from a literary family—the poet Manuel Bandeira and the sociologist Gilberto Freyre were his cousins—and in his late teens he began to frequent the Café Lafayette, where Recife's intellectuals met. Cabral was always an avid reader, and French authors such as Stéphane Mallarmé, Guillaume Apollinaire, and Paul Valéry were among his earliest literary influences. Cabral was twenty years old when he met Murilo Mendes and Carlos Drummond de Andrade, probably the two Brazilian poets who most influenced his work, and they helped him publish his first book, *Pedra do sono* (1942; Stone of sleep). (The title is also the name of a small town in Pernambuco.) He moved that same year to Rio de Janeiro, where he associated with modernist poets such as Bandeira, Mendes, and especially Drummond. In 1945 he was admitted into the Brazilian foreign service, and in the following year married Stella Maria Barbosa de Oliveira, with whom he had five children.

Cabral would in later years speak disparagingly of his first book, in which he had indeed not yet found his poetic way, yet he was at least half on track. Although in his future books sleep would be replaced by full alertness, the stone remained. The images for the poems of *Pedra do sono* come directly from the world of dreams or else are wrapped in a dreamy, surrealist aura, but the poet handled them like hard objects, deliberately and carefully organizing them in the manner of a cubist, as the critic Antônio Cândido remarked in "Poesia ao norte," an astonishingly perceptive and even prophetic review published in the newspaper *Folha de manhã* in 1943. He called the book "the work of an extremely conscious poet" who "demands a kind of constructivist rigor." Noting the book's epigraph from Mallarmé, "Solitude, récif, étoile . . ." (Solitude, reef, star . . .), Cândido warned that the pursuit of a pure poetry implied a certain inhumanity, a failure to communicate, since "such autonomously constructed poetry becomes isolated in its hermeticism." The twenty-two-year-old poet was aware of the problem, having addressed it in a poem titled "Poesia," in *Pedro de sono*:

> *jardins de minha ausência*
> *imensa e vegetal;*

*ó jardins de um céu*
*viciosamente frequentado:*
*onde o mistério maior*
*do sol da luz da saúde?*

gardens of my vast
and vegetable absence;
O gardens of an enchanting,
addictive sky:
where is the greater mystery
of the sun, light, health?

The pure world of dreams that informs *Pedra do sono* threatened, on the immediate level, to obscure the daylight world. More generally, and more dangerously, the "addiction" to poetry—or to pure poetry—implied abstention from and ultimate loss of contact with the real world. Cabral's poetry would become, if anything, even more marked by absence, even more hermetic, but he countered these tendencies by firmly grounding it in reality. The reality he chose was itself marked by lack, by emptiness, by absence, and so the poet managed, in a certain way, to bring lofty abstraction down to earth.

Though a few lingering clouds and wispy dream figures still haunt the poems of *O engenheiro* (1945; The engineer), this book set in place Cabral's definitive program of poetry as lucid construction, achieved by hard work. The engineer of the title poem has a dream, but it is of "coisas claras: / superfícies, tênis, um copo de água" (clear things: / surfaces, tennis, a glass of water) and is surrounded by "A luz, o sol, o ar livre" (Light, sun, and the open air). The poet-engineer has found the "greater mystery" that was missing in "Poesia," and now calmly, rationally, unmysteriously proceeds to build his poem. "A lição de poesia" (The lesson of poetry) shows the poet agonizing all day and all night before a blank sheet of paper, but in the end generating only twenty words,

> . . . *de que se servirá o poeta*
> *em sua máquina útil.*

*Vinte palavras sempre as mesmas*
*de que conhece o funcionamento,*
*a evaporação, a densidade*
*menor que a do ar.*

to be used by the poet
in his efficient machine.

Always the same twenty words
he knows so well: how they work,
their evaporation, their density
less than the air's.

Those twenty words mark the limits of inspiration; even if the poet produces more words, they still weigh less than air. But Cabral will put them into his machine, which converts them into bricks useful for making poems. Eschewing verbal effusion and the piling on of images, Cabral focused on single words, single images—water, wind, knife, stone—exploiting them to exhaustion. From their being used so insistently and in so many ways, these words acquired functional weight and substance, independent of whatever weight their literal meaning suggested. The best instance of this obsessive concentration on a restricted lexicon occurs in his 1956 work, *Uma faca só lâmina (ou: serventia das idéias fixas)* (A knife all blade; or, The usefulness of fixed ideas), where three words, or images, or metaphors—a knife, a clock, and a bullet—weave in and around and in place of each other over the course of 332 verses.

"Antiode," one of the three works that make up *Psicologia da composição: Contra a poesia dita profunda* (Psychology of composition: Against so-called profound poetry), published in 1947, further elucidates the poem machine. The narrator tells how he rejected the word "flower" as an acceptable metaphor for poetry, preferring the unpoetical "feces." To rehabilitate the flower for use in poetry, he had to strip away all its preconceived lyricism, reducing it to nothing but "a palavra / flor" (the word / flower), which became

*uma explosão*
*posta a funcionar,*
*como uma máquina,*
*uma jarra de flores*

an explosion
made to work,
like a machine,
a vase of flowers.

In a process analogous to the Freudian sublimation of sexual energy into the creative forces of civilization, Cabral reined in direct emotion as well as aesthetic or intellectual exaltation, using their energy to power his poetry machine. For him poetry resided not in the words—or flowers, emotions, images, ideas—themselves, but in their careful arrangement. The machine functioned on its own, with no need for the reader to relate to the man who created it. This freeing of the poem from the poet has its price, of course. The relationship with the author created by a well-made poetry of personal confession or remembrance will more easily captivate and move the average reader. The resolute impersonality of Cabral's work—in which the word "I" rarely occurs—puts a heavy burden on technical accomplishment, and demands readers who appreciate that accomplishment. "Impersonal" does not mean "unfeeling," however. Cabral's rigorous configurations placed words in a state of high tension capable of provoking, at certain moments, emotions of a rare order, and this was an essential aspect of the poet's program. According to Cabral, his constructivist approach to poetry owed its greatest debt not to any of the writers and painters he admired but to Le Corbusier, whose theoretical works he had read already as a teenager. But if the Swiss architect's most famous proposal was to see a house as a "machine à vivre" (machine for living), Cabral chose another phrase of Le Corbusier for the epigraph to *O engenheiro*: "machine à émouvoir" (machine for stirring emotion).

With the publication of *O cão sem plumas* (The dog without feathers) in 1950 Cabral, who was allergic to pamphleteering and never publicly subscribed to any political cause, applied his quiet machine to his country's social problems. This long narrative poem, in which the mangy dog is the Capibaribe River, is actually less machinelike than most of Cabral's poetry. Its stanzas and verses vary in length, and there is no set pattern for the assonance employed. This formal relaxation is justified by the poet's concern that form reflect content. The poem's narrator is not a sociologist but a common, unsophisticated man whose apparently poor diction and poetic technique—some words are repeated without grammatical necessity, other words are missing, and the main figure of speech is the simile, introduced by the banal *como* (like)—mirror the river's

irregular, poverty-stricken banks that are his story. Cabral's poetry machine yields to the "máquina / paciente e útil" (patient and useful / machine) formed by the river's "mangues de água parada" (mangrove swamps of stagnant water). If the poem's form is infected by its content to the point where they unite as one, a similar sort of marriage occurs within the second section, where those who dwell along the shores of the river have "doloroso cabelo / de camarão e estopa" (painful hair / of shrimp and tow) and can hardly be distinguished from the river itself:

> Na paisagem do rio
> difícil é saber
> onde começa o rio;
> onde a lama
> começa do rio;
> onde a terra
> começa da lama;
> onde o homem,
> onde a pele
> começa da lama;
> onde começa o homem
> naquele homem.

> In the river landscape
> it is hard to know
> where the river begins;
> where the mud
> begins from the river;
> where the land
> begins from the mud;
> where man,
> where his skin
> begins from the mud;
> where man begins
> in that man.

This kind of physiological equivalence between the poorest Pernambucans and the environment they inhabit or the work they are bound to (in the case of the sugar-mill workers) is an obvious denunciation of the dehumanization that results from dire poverty, but it is also part of a more general poetic process that suggests that no one—rich or poor—can remain uncontaminated by his milieu. "Man is the best measure" ("Pregão turístico do Recife"), but he has no substance, no existence, apart from his surroundings. In *Paisagens com figuras* (Landscapes with figures), this human mingling with environment, implicitly expressed in the title, is vividly enacted by the poems. In "Alguns toureiros" (A few toreadors), Manuel Rodríguez is described as "o mais mineral" (the most mineral) of all toreadors,

> o de nervos de madeira,
> de punhos secos de fibra,
> o de figura de lenha,
> lenha seca de caatinga

> the one with wooden nerves,
> whose fists are dry and fibrous,
> with a figure like a stick,
> a piece of dried-out brush

And in "Encontro com um poeta" (Encounter with a poet), the Spanish poet Miguel Hernández (1910–1942)—posthumously present in a desert region of Castile—has a voice "de terra sofrida e batida" (of tortured and beaten earth), with "gumes de pedra" (blades of stone) like an "árvore amputada" (amputated tree). But even in life, before Francisco Franco's forces threw him into the jail where he died, Hernández's outspoken voice was materialized, "cristalizada," as a "voz métrica de pedra" (metric voice of stone).

João Cabral was not necessarily a materialist. His poetic attitude seems to have paralleled the philosophical attitude of Ludwig Wittgenstein, who concluded his 1921 work, *Tractatus logico-philosophicus*, with these words:

> The right method of philosophy would be . . . to say nothing except what can be said, i.e. the propositions of natural science, i.e. something that has nothing to do with philosophy: and then always, when someone else wished to say something metaphysical, to demonstrate to him that he had given no meaning to certain signs in his propositions.

Wittgenstein recognized that "there is indeed the inexpressible, . . . the mystical," but contended that—precisely because it is inexpressible—philosophy can have nothing worthwhile to say about it and should

therefore remain silent. This statement would probably be no less accurate if we substituted "Cabral" for "Wittgenstein" and "poetry" for "philosophy."

To compare Cabral with Wittgenstein might seem arbitrary were it not for the fact that the two men played similar roles in their respective fields. If the latter introduced linguistic analysis to purify philosophy of all that was vague and intuitive, the former brought objective rigor to a national poetry that had gone through various phases, marked now by technical indiscipline, now by ill-defined or ill-conceived ideas, and in any case relying on an uncritical subjectivity. The so-called Generation of '45, reacting against the parochial nationalism and formal carelessness into which some of their modernist predecessors had fallen, never really defined its goals. Nor could it point to any common denominator among its members except for the most narrow one that the word "generation" denotes, namely the time period in which they were born. Some, however, clearly wished to return to the poetic forms and even the "poetic" language of premodernist times. In 1952 Cabral published, in the *Diário carioca*, a series of four articles under the general title "A Geração de 45," in which he agreed that the preceding generation lacked direction and discipline, but faulted his own generation for propounding a superficially refined, ethereal poetry. In the last of the articles, he wrote: "It is a poetry made of super-realities, made with exclusive parts of man, and its ambition is to communicate extremely subtle details, for which the only useful writer's tool is the lightest and most abstract part of the dictionary." Cabral, for his part, preferred the "prosaic word . . . dirty with coarse realities."

In November 1952 João Cabral delivered a lecture to the São Paulo Poetry Club titled "Poesia e composição: A inspiração e o trabalho de arte" (Poetry and composition: Inspiration and the work of making art). Published four years later in the magazine *Revista Brasileira de poesia*, it was the clearest statement he would ever formulate on the problems of poetic creation and the function or use of poetry. The title announces the two camps into which Cabral divided poets: those for whom poetry depends on inspiration, on "the inexplicable moment of a discovery," and those for whom it is the fruit of a struggle, "the long hours of a search." Elsewhere in the lecture he divided the two kinds of poets according to "whether one thinks in terms of poetry or in terms of art." Those in the first camp, usually concerned to transmit a personal experience, want

> the reader to use their text to recompose that experience, the way a prehistoric animal is recomposed from a small bone. Their poetry . . . does not propose to the reader an object capable of prompting a definite emotion. The poem of these poets is the residue of their experience and requires that readers use that residue to try to put themselves in the original experience.

Cabral naturally included himself in the other camp—those for whom poetry is art, work, making—but he recognized the danger that "work can become exercise, an activity performed for its own sake, independently of its results." In that case the finished work of art would cease to be important, amounting to a mere pretext for the artist's labor, which would become increasingly subtle, painstaking, self-indulgent, leading ultimately to "the death of communication." At this point in his lecture Cabral indicted both camps for their communicative failure, for writing only for themselves and not for the reader, "the essential counterpart to the activity of creating literature." He complained that the "individualist poet" does not know how to receive and "doesn't understand that any richness he might have can only originate in reality." O cão sem plumas had been a first step toward a more "communicative" poetry, and Cabral would continue down that road, while at the same time pursuing the rather antithetical path of tight, uncompromising "machine" poems.

From 1952 to 1956 João Cabral lived in Brazil, having been called back there from London (his second diplomatic post, from 1950 to 1952) to answer sketchy charges of subversion that stemmed from his friendship with several Spanish leftists whom he had met during his tenure as vice-consul in Barcelona. Exonerated of the charges, he was sent back to the Catalonian capital, and shortly thereafter to Seville. Over his next thirty-four years as a diplomat, Cabral held posts in France, Switzerland, Paraguay, Senegal (where he rose to the rank of ambassador in 1972), Ecuador, Honduras, and Portugal. All left explicit traces in his poetry, but Spain—where he spent a total of fourteen years, in Barcelona, Madrid, and Seville—became the second

geographical pole around which his poetry flourished. This was not a pole of opposition but one that echoed, in a European register, Cabral's native Pernambuco. The relative socioeconomic backwardness of Franco-ruled Spain, the arid, harshly lit landscapes of Castile, and the stark essentiality of Andalusia's cante hondo, the singing style typical of flamenco, had their counterparts in Northeast Brazil, which—perhaps not by chance—was never a theme in Cabral's poetry until he went to Spain.

The reciprocal relationship of the two regions is demonstrated in Paisagens com figuras, where there is a pendular shift of geographical setting from one poem to the next. This alternation between Pernambuco and Spain would occur throughout the rest of the poet's career, sometimes within a single collection and sometimes on a larger scale, with entire books set in or evoking one or the other of the two places. Paisagens also set the technical parameters of Cabral's most typical machine mold: sixteen of the eighteen poems are built out of quatrains, and rhyme or assonance (more frequently the latter) is employed throughout in an "abcb" scheme. And the machine worked. Cabral put almost nothing into it and managed to pull out stunning poems. The landscapes are all bleak or empty—three cemeteries, the "anonymous, plain-faced" cane field, a "place in La Mancha / where the Castilian plain is hardest," the valley of the Capibaribe River where "nothing ever happened / no matter what century"—and the figures that inhabit them mostly dead or destitute; but Cabral was able to find or create life in these desolate scenarios.

To make their readers "see it new" (modifying Ezra Pound's dictum), poets often enough pursue a strategy of reversal, turning things on their heads or inside out, or walking around them to see them from the other side. Cabral followed this strategy but took it one step further, achieving reversal through transfusion. In "O vento no canavial" (The wind in the cane field), instead of offering a simple metaphor by calling a cane field a crowded public square, he gradually infuses the cane field with human and public-square characteristics. The process begins with the words "anonymous" and "plain-faced," followed by a comparison of the cane field to a large bedsheet resembling "penugem de moça ao sol" (a girl's downy skin in the sun). Then the poet detects, in the cane-field-turned-bedsheet, an "oculta fisionomia" (hidden physiognomy), a graceful pattern like the one made by the bricks of an empty public square. Next, when the wind blows, "seu tecido inanimado / faz-se sensível lençol" (its inanimate fabric / becomes a sensitive bedsheet), and what had been an empty square loses its even symmetry and becomes a waving green flag, then sea waves on sand, and finally "ondas da multidão / lutando na praça cheia" (waves of people / vying in the crowded square), so that the initially blank, undifferentiated cane field is ultimately seen as a teeming square with

> redemoinhos iguais,
> estrelas iguais àquelas
> que o povo na praça faz

> whirlpools like the ones
> crowds form, stars like those
> the people in the square compose

The use of such gradual and thorough metaphorical transformations is one of the features that give quasi-material weight to Cabral's poetry.

Though less bluntly than in Cabral's earlier works, the making of poetry continued to be a regular theme of his poems, and *Paisagens* contains what is probably his most famous *ars poetica*, "Alguns toureiros." The above-cited Manuel Rodríguez, who

> à tragédia deu número
> à vertigem, geometria,
> decimais à emoção
> e ao susto, peso e medida

> gave a number to tragedy
> geometry to vertigo,
> decimals to feelings
> and height and weight to fear

is singled out by Cabral to demonstrate to the poet, through his bullfighting prowess:

> como domar a explosão
> com mão serena e contida,

> sem deixar que se derrame
> a flor que traz escondida,

> e como, então, trabalhá-la
> com mão certa, pouca e extrema:
> sem perfumar sua flor,
> sem poetizar seu poema.

> how to tame the explosion
> with a quiet, restrained hand,
> being careful not to spill
> the flower he carries, hidden,

> and how, then, to fashion it
> with sure hand, soft and fierce,
> without perfuming his flower,
> without poetizing his poem.

This recalls the flower of "Antiode," whose explosion the poet had decided to harness into "a machine, / a vase of flowers." After that he perfected its functioning to a high degree, particularly in the technically precise *Uma faca só lâmina*, composed of eleven sections of eight stanzas with four lines containing seven syllables each. But in his concern to communicate, to avoid mere exercises of style, Cabral was capable of easing up to produce a lower-tension, higher-access poetry. In *Duas águas: Poesia de concentração reflexiva e poesia para auditórios mais largos* (1956; Two waters: Poetry of reflective concentration and poetry for wider audiences), the same book in which he first published *Paisagens com figuras* and *Uma faca só lâmina*, Cabral also presented what was to become his most popular work: *Morte e vida Severina: Auto de Natal Pernambuco* (1956; Death and life of a Severino: A Pernambuco Christmas play). A staged version of this dramatic poem, with music by singer and composer Chico Buarque de Holanda, won prizes in Brazil and France in 1966 and brought international stature to Cabral. "Somos muitos Severinos / iguais em tudo na vida" (There are many of us Severinos / all with the very same life), explains the protagonist, an archetype of the northeastern retiree who hopefully migrates to Recife from the drought-scourged interior.

João Cabral claimed this was one of his least favorite works, the one that was least carefully crafted. But its slackness was itself part of the overall plan he had delineated for his oeuvre and set forth in the book *Duas águas*, whose title, "Two waters," is actually the Portuguese term for a gable roof. (*Uma água* signifies a lean-to roof.) Cabral's three new works, along with all his previous titles, were collected under this one roof that sloped in two directions, as explained by the book's subtitle. The first, introspective "water" included works such as *O engenheiro*, *Paisagens com figuras*, and *Uma faca só lâmina*. The narrative poems—*O cão sem plumas*, *O rio*, and *Morte e vida Severina*—flowed in a less "concentrated," more "outgoing" direction, but they, too, were the fruit of careful reflection. The first of the three poems, though almost brashly unsophisticated in its prosody and lexicon, is by no means an easy one. Its tropes, as noted earlier, are introduced in the most commonplace fashion by the uneducated narrator, but they make strange leaps. Who ever spoke of a featherless dog, and who ever used a dog—with or without feathers—as a metaphor for a river? The language of the poem also leaps syntactically, through ellipses:

> Um cão sem plumas
> é quando uma árvore sem voz.
> É quando de um pássaro
> suas raízes no ar.

> A dog without feathers
> is when a tree without voice.
> It is when of a bird
> its roots in the air.

Cabral's two subsequent narrative poems, purged of linguistic obstacles, make a different kind of leap: back in time, to the narrative poetic tradition of Iberia in the Middle Ages. The epigraph to *O Rio*—"Quiero que compongamos io e tú una prosa" (I want you and me to make a prose together)—is from Gonzalo de Berceo, the thirteenth-century author of the poetry cycle *Milagros de Nuestra Señora* (Miracles of Our Lady) and the inspiration for Cabral's four-point "Catecismo de Berceo" (Berceo's catechism), published in *Museu de tudo* (1975; Museum of everything). The first point (and first stanza) of that catechism instructs "Fazer com que a palavra leve / pese como a coisa que diga" (Make the light word weigh / as much as the thing it tells), which Cabral accomplished in his narrative poetry by writing about the realities of his homeland's poor. The weight this conferred on his poetry derived not only from the gravity of the theme but from the down-to-earth perspective—that of the poor people themselves—used for exploring it. What Cabral seems to have appreciated in Berceo, the first poet known by name to have written in Spanish, was precisely his down-to-earthness, his concrete and colloquial, untranscendent style, which brought the Virgin down from heaven (as did popular medieval Catholicism in general) and made poetry into prose.

*Morte e vida Severina* harks back to the Middle Ages through its subtitle: *Auto de Natal Pernambucano* (A Pernambuco Christmas play). The *auto* was a short play of religious or profane character whose greatest exponent in Portugal was Gil Vicente, a dramatist of the late fifteenth and early sixteenth centuries. Drawing especially on the Spanish tradition of mystery and morality plays, as well as satires, farces, and court poetry, Vicente produced a diversified body of verse plays, written with colloquial zest in Spanish as well as in Portuguese. (Portugal's court at the time was bilingual.) The tradition was carried on by others, and various popular, religious *autos* traveled from Portugal to Brazil, where they were substantially adapted to fit the local cultural setting. Simple *autos pastoris* (pastoral plays), accompanied by music and dancing, form part of the folk heritage specific to Pernambuco. Thus Cabral, with his narrative poems, made a bridge to the formative period of Spanish and Portuguese poetry (and drama) as well as to the popular, largely oral verse tradition of his homeland.

The other side of Cabral's work, his "poetry of reflective concentration," reached its highest pitch in the 1960s, beginning with *Quaderna* (1960; Four spot), whose title seems to allude not only to a die but to the *cuaderna vía*, the monorhyming four-verse stanza typical of Berceo and other medieval Spanish *mester de clerecía* poets, who were mostly clerics and wrote their verses to be read, in contradistinction to the *mester de juglaría*, or minstrel, poets, who recited their verses from memory. Notwithstanding his recitative poetry "for wider audiences," Cabral claimed to hate music, said he imagined writing poems that could only be read silently, and reported that he was incapable of writing poetry without seeing the words on the page. (In fact, he quit writing it after he went blind in the 1990s.) Whatever poems he may have imagined writing, all the ones he actually did write are eminently suitable for reading out loud, but the intricate formal articulations of his poems from the 1960s can indeed only be appreciated by visually examining the collections that they constitute. Nineteen of the twenty poems in *Quaderna* are written in quatrains; the one exception is a poem composed of twenty-eight seven-verse stanzas, four operating as the multiplicand between the two figures.

*Serial* (1961), whose title evokes the series produced by constructivist artists and dodecaphonic composers, is even more driven by the number four. Its sixteen poems all have four parts consisting exclusively of quatrains. In the first poem each part has two quatrains; in the second poem, four quatrains; in the third poem, six quatrains; and in the fourth poem, eight quatrains. The series repeats, occurring four times in all. Four different indicators (numerals, lines, asterisks, and paragraph marks) are used to separate the parts, with each indicator being applied to four out of the sixteen poems, apparently at random. *A educação pela pedra* (1966; Education by stone) is built not on four but on its multiples, and on the number two. The forty-eight poems all contain either sixteen or twenty-four verses divided into two parts of varying length. The two narrative poems of *Dois parlamentos*, the second of which—"Fiesta na casa grande"—was discussed above, are structured on a partly serial, partly symmetrical plan; their sixteen and twenty sections (respectively) are numbered nonsequentially, according to a strict pattern.

This obsessive preoccupation with order and numbers may seem like an inconsequential game, and knowing all the details of the game is not likely to enhance most readers' appreciation of the poems. But the rules of the game were a challenge—like the rules of rhyme and meter for other poets—that no doubt stimulated Cabral's creativity. Cabral's most "mathematical" period was also the one in which his poetry reached its highest artistic level. Pernambuco and Andalusia, when they were not in the foreground as direct subjects, continued to be the inevitable backdrops of poems; but the thematic field widened to include women, suddenly and markedly present (in *Quaderna*), as well as lighthearted material (in *A educação pela pedra*) such as an encomium of aspirin (Cabral suffered greatly from headaches), a study on chewing gum, and a poem that singles out the toilet seat for being "ecumênico, / exemplo único de concepção universal" (ecumenical, / the only seat universally agreed upon). The subject matter was secondary, however. Cabral's passion was in the process, in the making of poetry, and his work seems to have become an activity pursued for its own sake, the very thing he had warned against in his 1952 São Paulo lecture discussed above. What saved his poetry from becoming precious or inaccessible was the artisan quality of its manufacture. Cabral's writing is not laden with literary references and presupposes no special knowledge on the part of the reader; his vocabulary is simple and his tone colloquial. There is nothing highbrow about his poetry. To understand and enjoy it, one need only have an appreciation of architecture and engineering as applied to words.

If his art was compositional, based on the piecing together of quatrains and other formal units that were his building blocks, Cabral was also concerned with the hard solidity of single words, as may be deduced from the second point of "Catecismo de Berceo":

> *Fazer com que a palavra frouxa*
> *ao corpo de sua coisa adira:*
> *fundi-la em coisa, espessa, sólida,*
> *capaz de chocar com a contígua.*

> Make the loose word adhere
> to the body of its referent:
> smelt it into a thick and solid thing,
> able to clash with the one next to it.

Our words and our ways of using words are worn out. Cabral's unusual poetic constructions attempted to renew words by placing them in new settings, but to unite words with their referents—to make them convey the full force of the things they signify—is an uphill if not doomed task. "A palavra seda" (The word "silk"), in *Quaderna*, directly confronts the difficulty. The poet wishes to use the word "silk" in reference to a woman, but to make it register, to make his meaning understood, he must first divest the word of the usual preconceived notions engendered by phrases such as "soft as silk." Once he has done this, however, the only way he can explain his meaning is by surrounding the word with other words. Fumbling, he asserts that there is something

> *muscular,*
> *de animal, carnal, pantera,*
> *de felino*

> muscular,
> animal, carnal, pantherish,
> catlike

something (and here he half repeats what he had just said):

> *de animal, de animalmente,*
> *de cru, de cruel, de crueza,*
> *que sob a palavra gasta*
> *persiste na coisa seda.*

> animal, animalistic,
> crude, cruel—a cruelty—which
> beneath the worn-out word
> persists in the thing silk.

It is important to note that João Cabral never subscribed to the notion espoused by certain concrete and language poets (at least in their purely theoretical texts) that words in themselves are things, independent of the objects they name. To his way of thinking, it was not innovative graphic treatment, aleatory placement, or revolutionary syntax that could enhance words in any more than fleeting way. Nor did his poetry invoke hidden meanings. He privileged the basic, or even the base, most physical meaning of words. By fusing word to object, as far as this was possible, he sought to get closer to the object and to objectify the word, to give it more color and weight.

As a poet Cabral naturally had a weakness for words, which he perhaps loved more than the things they named. In his acceptance speech for the 1992 Neustadt International Prize for Literature, he at one point described his poetic praxis as "the exploration of the materiality of words" and at another point as the "rigorous construction of lucid formal structures, lucid objects of language." The two comments should be understood in conjunction, since in Cabral's view words, when cut off from the structured ensemble known as language, become immaterial, impotent, like the water in a river whose flow has been interrupted:

> *Em situação de poço, a água equivale*
> *a uma palavra em situação dicionária:*
> *isolada, estanque no poço dela mesma,*
> *e porque assim estanque, estancada.*

> Situated in a pool, water resembles
> a word in its dictionary situation:
> isolated, standing in the pool of itself
> and, because it is standing, stagnant.

This ingenious face-off in "Rios sem discurso" (1966; Speechless rivers) between linguistic discourse and "o curso de um rio, seu discurso-rio" (the course of a river, its river-discourse) proceeds to show that the word, thus isolated, becomes mute: it says nothing. The metaphor becomes even more pregnant with meaning in the second part of the poem, which proposes a patient work of restoring the broken "river-discourse" in order to fight the chronic drought in Northeast Brazil.

"Rios sem discurso" and the other forty-seven poems of *A Educação pela pedra* are formulated like theorems whose truth is tested by antithesis. Counterpoint abounds, with frequent syntactic and semantic inversions, and the second part of each poem is usually a corollary, an analogue, or mirror version of the first part. The play of oppositions is most intense in "O mar e o canavial" (The sea and the cane field) and "O canavial e o mar" (The cane field and the sea). The first line of the first poem, "O que o mar sim aprende do canavial" (What the sea learns from the cane field), is negatively restated in the fifth line, "O que o mar não aprende do canavial" (What the sea doesn't learn from the cane field), and then inverted in the first line of the second part, "O que o canavial sim aprende do mar" (What the canefield learns from the sea), which is in turn negatively restated in the fifth line. The poem's sixteen verses are all repeated in the inversely titled poem ("O canavial e o mar"), but in different order, and with the verb "learn from" being replaced by its linguistic counterpart, "teach." The most famous poem in this collection, "Tecendo a manhã" (Weaving the morning), uses the interconnected cries of cocks crowing at dawn as a trope for the human solidarity that enables each day to take shape and proceed smoothly.

Cabral's *Educação*, a kind of poetic equivalent in verse to Bach's *48 Preludes and Fugues*, is his best demonstration of how words, things, and people are inextricably connected, and of how it is possible to highlight, reinforce, and augment those connections, thereby increasing meaning in language and in life itself. What Cabral ultimately wanted to offer his readers was not finished poetic products but their example, their lesson, an education in how to make words into stones suitable for building. His ideal for his verbal edifices is expressed in "Fábula de um arquiteto" (Tale of an architect), in *A educação pela pedra*. Here, architecture is conceived as the building of doors to open up, as the "building of openness," with houses consisting exclusively of doors and a roof. In this scheme the architect would be

> o que abre para o homem
>
> . . . . . . . . . .
>
> portas por-onde, jamais portas-contra;
> por onde, livres: ar luz razão certa.

> the one who opens to man
>
> . . . . . . . . . .
>
> doors-leading-to, never doors-against;
> doors to freedom: air light sure reason.

It is hard to imagine how Cabral's poetry could have developed any further as architecture or engineering, and the poet did not attempt a repeat performance of his achievement, but rather chose to explore other paths over the next several decades. The eighty poems of *Museu de tudo* were, as the title suggests, a diversified compendium, the themes ranging from Mauritania to Marcel Proust to soccer (Cabral was a champion player as an adolescent), but close to half of the compositions comment on writers and artists in epigrammatic fashion. In 1980 *A escola das facas*, all of whose poems have to do with Pernambuco, surprised everyone with its unprecedented autobiographical subject matter. The majority of the poems are set directly in Cabral's childhood or are based on reminiscences. We are still in school (*escola*), but now the subject is the lesson of his upbringing, not lessons on how to make stone-hard poetry, and the knives (*facas*) of the title also mean something different from what they once did. In *Uma faca só lâmina*, the knife represented linguistic trenchancy and sharpness of vision, and in "O sim contra o sim" (Yes against yes, from *Serial*) it took the place of a pencil for Marianne Moore and Francis Ponge, two of the poets Cabral admired most. In his 1980 work, however, the knife becomes the razor-sharp leaf of sugarcane (in the title poem) as well as the cutting stalk itself (in "Menino de engenho"). The engineer's principles are still at work in *Escola das facas* but have been internalized, and the new cutting edge made of memory and milieu confers a more intimate tone on the poems, even if the air they inhabit is as harsh as it ever was:

> A voz do canavial
>
> Voz sem saliva da cigarra,
> do papel seco que se amassa,
>
> de quando se dobra o jornal:
> assim canta o canavial,
>
> ao vento que por suas folhas,
> de navalha a navalha, soa,
>
> vento que o dia e a noite toda
> o folheia, e nele se esfola.

> The voice of the canefield
>
> Spitless voice of the cicada,
> of dry crumpling paper,
>
> of the newspaper when it folds:
> so is the singing of the cane field

in the wind which through its leaves
from razor to razor breathes,

wind which all night and day
leafs through and is left grazed.

True to his own program but again taking everyone by surprise, João Cabral returned to "poetry for wider audiences" in 1983 with the publication of *Auto do frade* (The friar), which tells the last day in the life of Frei Caneca, who was sent to his death by the Portuguese court in 1825 for his republican ideas and for his leadership in the Pernambuco revolutionary movement of the previous year. It had been almost thirty years since the publication of Cabral's first *auto, Morte e vida Severina,* and he had not lost his touch. The new verse play, consisting of seven dialogues between the condemned Carmelite friar and the people of Recife who make up the chorus, had the same dramatic force as the author's first effort in the genre and was poetically far superior.

The title *Agrestes* (1985) means "rough, wild, rustic" but also alludes to the semiarid, rocky region of Northeast Brazil that lies between the coastal zone known as the *mata* and the very dry hinterland called the *sertão.* The ninety poems of this collection constitute an unusual species of autobiography. It begins with poems about Pernambuco, particularly childhood remembrances of it, and ends with poems that comment on death in Cabral's customarily detached and sometimes wry voice. In between there are poems about places where he served as a diplomat—West Africa, Ecuador, and Spain—and about the writers and artists he admires, including Valéry, Paul Klee, W. H. Auden, Murilo Mendes, Elizabeth Bishop, and Marianne Moore, this last being the subject of three poems as well as the source of the book's epigraph: "Where there is personal liking we go. / Where the ground is sour . . ." Whereas a traditional autobiography cites historical details, places, and other people in order to convey the author's own story, Cabral tells about the people, places, and things he has known for their own sake. It is a an inside-out autobiography, the negative of a missing photo, but nonetheless revealing, for as Cabral muses through the persona of Moore in "Dúvidas apócrifas de Marianne Moore" (Apocryphal doubts of Marianne Moore):

*Sempre evitei falar de mim,*
*falar-me. Quis falar de coisas.*
*Mas na seleção dessas coisas*
*não haverá um falar de mim?*

I always avoided talking about myself,
telling myself. I preferred to talk
about things. But might not my choice
of those things speak for me?

In "Homenagem renovada a Marianne Moore" (Renewed homage to Marianne Moore), Cabral characterizes the American poet's view of poetry as a "muleta para a perna coxa" (crutch for a lame leg), as something that we create precisely because it does not exist inside us. This recalls a distinction Cabral made, in an interview with Selden Rodman published in 1974, between "crutch poets" and poets he called "bleeders." Writing, for the bleeders, is an overflow of their intense inner feeling, whereas crutch poets write to make up for what they do not feel.

In 1986, after his first wife died, Cabral married the Brazilian poet Marly de Oliveira, and in 1987 he moved to Rio de Janeiro from Oporto, Portugal, where he had served in his last foreign post as Brazil's consul general. That same year, with the publication of *Crime na Calle Relator* (1987; Crime on the Calle Relator), his poetry shifted in yet another direction, toward storytelling. The sixteen poems that make up the collection narrate tales and anecdotes culled from his own experience or from what others had told him. Fully half of the stories are set in Spain, and Cabral's last book would be entirely dedicated to Spain, or rather, to his favorite city there or anywhere: Seville. Cabral called himself a crutch poet, one who wrote verses to make up for an inner lack, but Seville brought out a bit of the "bleeder" in him. Not in the sense that his poetic style became a mere outpouring of heartfelt sentiment, for it was the very sparseness of expression and economy of gestures that Cabral admired in certain bullfighters, in the "cante a palo seco" (a severe, a cappella style of singing), and in the flamenco dancing that he celebrated in his renowned "Estudos para uma bailadora andaluza" (Studies for an Andalusian dancer, in *Quaderna*). But the world of Andalusia prompted an exuberance in Cabral that was otherwise rare. Flamenco music was the only kind he ever admitted to liking, and the women he loved were Sevillian, even if they had never lived there and had no Spanish blood. The leadoff poem of his last book, *Sevilha andando* (1989; Seville walking), titled "A sevilhana que não se sabia" (The woman from Seville who didn't know it), is an homage to his very Brazilian second wife. She is evoked in still other poems of the book, whose first part is mostly about women. Women and Seville were frequent poetic subjects as far back as *Quaderna*, though they tended to function as tropes. In *Sevilha andando*, Cabral delighted in them directly and sensually. That Seville was a key to Cabral's sensual side is clearly suggested by the fifth stanza of "Viver Sevilha" (Living Seville):

> Só em Sevilha o corpo está
> com todos os sentidos em riste,
> sentidos que nem se sabia,
> antes de andá-la, que existissem.

> Only in Seville are all
> of the body's senses at attention,
> senses you didn't even know
> existed until you went there.

Reading Cabral's last several books, we might suspect that he never really needed a crutch; that instead of making all those constructivist, thinglike poems to fill up an inner void, he could simply have spent more time in Seville, which brought out the hidden, perhaps repressed facets of his personality. But we may as readily suspect that the city that had such great power over Cabral was not the Seville that lies north of Cádiz and west of Córdoba but the Seville he invented, word-stone by word-stone, over several decades of his writing life. Whatever the case, the world he re-created in poetry—a kind of verbal reconstitution of what is—will endure for a long time, both as a highly original artistic monument and as an invaluable didactic example. Cabral has shown us a new way to see things and, what is more, a new way to see and make poetry.

Cabral, elected to the Brazilian Academy of Letters in 1968, received a number of awards over the next several decades, including the Camões Prize in 1991 and the Neustadt Prize the following year. The 1990s also saw the publication of various special and collected editions of his works. In 1993 he became too blind to read or write, and described himself to reporters as an "ex-writer." His last interview, given over the phone to a sports journalist a week before his death from heart failure in Rio de Janeiro on 9 October 1999, was limited to questions and answers about his involvement with soccer as a young man and the presence of the sport in his poetry (in about half a dozen poems).

## SELECTED BIBLIOGRAPHY

### Primary Works

#### Poetry

*Pedra do sono.* Recife, Brazil: privately published, 1942.

*Os três mal-amados.* Rio de Janeiro: supplement to *Revista do Brasil*, 1943.

*O engenheiro.* Rio de Janeiro: Amigos da Poesia, 1945.

*Psicologia da composição: Contra a poesia dita profunda.* Barcelona: O Livro Inconsútil, 1947.

*O cão sem plumas.* Barcelona: O Livro Inconsútil, 1950.

*O Rio; ou, Relação da viagem que faz o Capibaribe de sua nascente à cidade de Recife.* São Paulo: Comissão do IV Centenário da Cidade São Paulo, 1954.

*Duas águas.* Rio de Janeiro: José Olympio, 1956. (Includes all previous titles, plus *Morte e vida Severina: Auto de Natal Pernambuco; Paisagens com figuras;* and *Uma faca só lâmina [ou: serventia das idéias fixas].*)

*Quaderna.* Lisbon: Guimarães Editores, 1960.

*Dois parlamentos.* Rio de Janeiro: privately published, 1961.

*Terceira feira.* Rio de Janeiro: Editora do Autor, 1961. Includes *Quaderna, Dois parlamentos,* and the previously unpublished *Serial.*

*Antologia poética.* Rio de Janeiro: Editora do Autor, 1963.

*A educação pela pedra.* Rio de Janeiro: Editora do Autor, 1966.

*Poesias completas.* Rio de Janeiro: José Olympio, 1986. (Includes all previously published poetry.)

*Museu de tudo.* Rio de Janeiro: José Olympio, 1975.

*A escola das facas.* Rio de Janeiro: José Olympio, 1980.

*Poesia crítica.* Rio de Janeiro: José Olympio, 1982.

*Auto do frade.* Rio de Janeiro: José Olympio, 1983.

*Agrestes.* Rio de Janeiro: Nova Fronteira, 1985.

*Poesia completa, 1940–1980.* Lisbon: Imprensa Nacional-Casa da Moeda, 1986.

*Crime na Calle Relator.* Rio de Janeiro: Nova Fronteira, 1987.

*Poesia completa II: Museu de tudo de depois (1967–1987).* Rio de Janeiro: Nova Fronteira, 1988.

*Sevilha andando.* Rio de Janeiro: Nova Fronteira, 1989.

*Primeiros poemas.* Rio de Janeiro: Universidade Federal do Rio de Janeiro, 1990. (Early, previously unpublished poems.)

### Essays and Criticism

*Considerações sobre o poeta dormindo.* Recife, Brazil: supplement to *Renovação,* 1941.

*Joan Miró.* Barcelona: Edicions de l'Oc, 1950. (With original prints by Miró.)

"A Geração de 45." *Diário Carioca* (Rio de Janeiro), 23 November 1952, sec. 3, p. 3; 30 November 1952, sec. 3, p. 3; 7 December 1952, sec. 3., p. 1; 21 December 1952, sec. 3, p. 1.

"Poesia e composição—A inspiração e o trabalho de arte." *Revista Brasileira de Poesia* no. 7 (April 1956).

"Da função moderna poesia." In *Anais do Congresso Internacional de Escritores e Encontros Intelectuais.* Anhembi, Brazil, 1957.

"A América vista pela Europa." In *Anais do Congresso internacional de escritores e encontros intelectuais.* Anhembi, Brazil, 1957.

"A diversidade cultura no diálogo Norte-Sul." In his *Obra completa.* Rio de Janeiro: Nova Aguilar, 1994. A lecture presented in Barcelona, 1990.

### Collections

*Obra completa.* Rio de Janeiro: Nova Aguilar, 1994. (Includes poetry and prose.)

*Serial e antes.* Rio de Janeiro: Nova Fronteira, 1997.

*A educação pela pedra e depois.* Rio de Janeiro: Nova Fronteira, 1997.

*Prosa.* Rio de Janeiro: Nova Fronteira, 1997. (Collected essays and criticism.)

### Translations

*An Anthology of Twentieth-Century Brazilian Poetry.* Edited by Elizabeth Bishop and Emanuel Brasil. Middletown, Conn.: Wesleyan University Press, 1994. (The translations of poems by João Cabral were all incorporated in *Selected Poetry, 1937–1990* [1994].)

*Selected Poetry, 1937–1990.* Edited by Djelal Kadir. Hanover, N.H.: Wesleyan University Press, 1994.

*The Borzoi Anthology of Latin American Literature,* vol. 2. Edited by Emir Rodríguez Monegal. New York: Knopf, 1997. (Includes *O cão sem plumas,* translated by Thomas Colchie.)

## Secondary Works

### Critical and Biographical Studies

Barbosa, João Alexandre. *A metáfora crítica.* São Paulo: Editora Perspectiva, 1974.

———. *A imitação da forma.* São Paulo: Duas Cidades, 1975.

Campos, Haroldo de. "O geômetra engajado." In his *Metalinguagem.* Petrópolis, Brazil: Vozes, 1967. Pp. 67–78.

Cândido, Antônio. "Poesia ao norte." In *Folha da Manhã,* 13 June 1943, p. 5.

Carone, Modesto. *A poética do silêncio.* São Paulo: Editora Perspectiva, 1979.

Escorel, Lauro. *A pedra e o rio.* São Paulo: Duas Cidades, 1973.

*Folha de São Paulo,* 10 October 1999. (Special supplement with biographical and critical articles about Cabral, published the day after his death.)

Houaiss, Antônio. *Drummond mais seis poetas e um problema.* Rio de Janeiro: Imago, 1976.

Lima, Luís Costa. *Lira e antilira.* Rio de Janeiro: Civilização Brasileira, 1968.

———. *A metamorfose do silêncio.* Rio de Janeiro: Civilização Brasileira, 1974. Pp. 73–128.

Mamede, Zila. *Civil geometria: Bibliografia crítica, analítica e anotada de João Cabral de Melo Neto, 1942–1982.* São Paulo: Nobel, 1987.

Merquior, José Guilherme. *A astúcia da mimese.* Rio de Janeiro: José Olympia, 1972. Pp. 69–172.

———. "Nosso poeta exemplar." In his *As idéias e as formas,* 2d ed. Rio de Janeiro: Nova Fronteira, 1981.

———. "Nuvem civil sonhada." In his *Crítica.* Rio de Janeiro: Nova Fronteira, 1990.

Nunes, Benedito. *O dorso do tigre: Ensaios.* São Paulo: Editora Perspectiva, 1969.

———. *João Cabral de Melo Neto: Nota biográfica, introdução crítica, antologia, biografia.* Petrópolis, Brazil: Vozes, 1971.

Peixoto, Marta. *Poesia com coisas: Uma leitura de João Cabral de Melo Neto.* São Paulo: Perspectiva, 1983.

Secchin, Antônio Carlos. *João Cabral: A poesia do menos.* São Paulo: Duas Cidades/Instituto Nacional do Livro, 1985.

Senna, Marta de. *João Cabral: Tempo e memória.* Rio de Janeiro: Antares, 1980.

Sousa Tavares, Maria Andresen de. *Stevens, Ponge, João Cabral: Poesia e pensamento.* Lisbon: Caminho, 2001.

*World Literature Today* 66, no. 4 (autumn 1992). (Special issue dedicated to João Cabral upon his being awarded the 1992 Neustadt International Prize for Literature. Articles by João Alexandre Barbosa, Haroldo de Campos, J. Edilberto Coutinho, Paul B. Dixon, Aguinaldo José Gonçalves, Regina Igel, Curt Meyer-Clason, Wander Melo Miranda, John M. Parker, Flora Süssekind, and Richard Zenith.)

*Interviews*

"A arquitetura do verso." *Veja,* 28 June 1972, pp. 3–5.

"João Cabral, nu e cru." *Isto É,* 5 November 1980, pp. 53–55.

"João Cabral lança novo livro em janeiro." *Folha de São Paulo,* 28 August 1992.

Rodman, Selden. In his *Tongues of Fallen Angels.* New York: Norton, 1974. Pp. 219–231.

Secchin, Antônio Carlos. "Entrevista de João Cabral de Melo Neto." In his *João Cabral: A poesia do menos.* Saõ Paulo: Livraria Duas Cidades/ Instituto Nacional do Livro, 1985. Pp. 299–307.

# Lydia Cabrera

## (1899–1991)

### Nivia Montenegro

Lydia Cabrera liked to say that she was born 20 May 1900, at her family home on Galiano Street—at the time one of Havana's most fashionable venues. She affixed particular importance to this date, for it was on 20 May 1902 that U.S. intervention officially ceased on the island of her birth and the Cuban Republic was born. The first U.S. occupation (1898–1902) of the island came in the aftermath of what North American history calls the Spanish-American War, a title that leaves Cuba—on whose soil Cubans fought a protracted thirty-year-long battle—out of the historical archive. Cabrera apparently attached significance to the coincidence of births: her own, that of the Cuban nation, and the twentieth century's. The fact remains, though, that according to birth records she was actually born one year earlier, on 20 May 1899, a day that nevertheless linked the writer, both historically and imaginatively, to the beginnings of the Cuban nation. Indeed, Cabrera was linked as well to Cuba's national terrain by her father, Raimundo Cabrera Bosch, a lawyer and writer who was involved in the Cuban War of Independence in 1895 and who, while in exile, founded the separatist journal *Cuba y América* in 1897.

Like many other wealthy Cuban families of that period, the Cabreras spent half the year abroad, usually in Europe or the United States. According to the author, she was baptized in New York's Saint Patrick's Cathedral when she was three months old, though no records to support this claim have ever been found. Cabrera was the youngest of eight children born to Raimundo Cabrera and his second wife, Elisa Marcaida Casanova, a reserved Cuban woman of Basque and Canarian ancestry who married the widowed Cabrera. Probably because of the difference in age between Cabrera and her siblings, or because of her sickly physical constitution and strong will, young Lydia never went through a regular schooling system. Instead, she took lessons from different home tutors and studied informally with her older sister Emma, to whom she was particularly attached. Cabrera followed an informal, idiosyncratic course of learning, borrowing books from her father's library, accompanying him to daily *tertulias* (literary circle gatherings), interacting with the many servants and former slaves her well-to-do family employed in the home, and studying with several tutors. Her growing years were a compromise between her father's desires and her own. Originally, she had wanted to study painting at Havana's San Alejandro Academy, but her father forbade it and forced her to quit when he discovered she was secretly taking classes there. On the other hand, Cabrera grew up amidst an active social and intellectual milieu, since her home was visited by many Cuban intellectuals, some of whom, like Juan

Gualberto Gómez, had been veterans of the War of Independence.

One significant factor in Cabrera's intellectual formation was her keeping company with her father at the cafés where he attended daily *tertulias*. These frequent excursions placed her at an early age in the role of an observer in the adults' lively exchanges. This was, after all, a period when the young Cuban Republic was grappling with questions of national identity. It was also a period when the contribution of Afro-Cubans to the country's newly won independence was being ignored or, at least, not openly acknowledged. According to the historian Manuel Moreno Fraginals, rebel Cuban forces were at least 60 percent Afro-Cuban, including "negros de nación," that is, Cubans who had been born in Africa and brought to the island as slaves. This was also around the time of the infamous 1912 rebellion, when many war veterans, unsatisfied with the failed promises made to them during the war, attempted to form an Afro-Cuban political party. This party was quickly outlawed by the government, and, in response, some leaders and followers took to the countryside in protest. This uprising—known in Cuban history as *la guerrita de agosto* (the August war) or *la guerra de los negros* (the blacks' war)—was immediately suppressed, and several thousand Afro-Cubans, many of them war veterans, were quickly hunted down and killed by government forces, especially in Cuba's eastern region. Historical events like these deserve mention because, although Cabrera herself does not address them directly, they must have influenced her perception of the Afro-Cuban population and its role in Cuba's national configuration.

While these events were unfolding at the national level, the Cabrera household was structured around the work of Afro-Cuban servants. As a child who stayed at home most of the time, Cabrera was cared for by an army of Afro-Cuban nannies and maids, a daily, intimate contact that also must be viewed as a significant factor in her psychosocial upbringing. Afro-Cubans, most of them women, interacted with her at close range and must have introduced her to their particular vision of the world, whether through their language, their sayings, their reactions or conversations, or, just as important, through the stories and songs they would tell her at bedtime. Cabrera often remarked as much in

interviews, explaining, for example, how some of the African ritual songs she used in her short stories were those that had been sung to her by one of her nannies. She also related anecdotes about how, as a child, she would wander into the servants' daily world, occasionally playing tricks and incurring the wrath of the older women servants. This pseudo-colonial environment that nurtured her as a child no doubt helped shape her cultural views as an adult, facilitating—perhaps at an intuitive, subconscious level—the exchanges with Afro-Cuban informants she would go on to use in such works as *El monte: Igbó finda, ewe orisha, vititin finda (Notas sobre las religiones, la magia, las supersticiones y el folklore de los negros criollos y del pueblo de Cuba)* (1954; The woods: Igbó finda, ewe orisha, vititin finda [Notes about the religions, magic, superstitions, and folklore of Afro-Cubans and Cuban people in general]).

The intellectual world that marked Cuba's national birth, glimpsed through her father's conversations, coupled with the world of Afro-Cuban servants and former slaves, especially the latter world, allowed Cabrera to experience at close range the habits, rituals, and practices of the Afro-Cuban population. Armed with this broad intellectual framework, Cabrera was well prepared to undertake the study and inclusion of Afro-Cuban experiences within a national repertoire, and, at the same time, she was able to empathize with Afro-Cuban epistemological systems. In Cabrera's long conversations and personal exchanges with Afro-Cuban informants, for example, she always avoided using a tape recorder. In several interviews she stated that she followed her informants' wishes because they truly believed that the machine would "steal their voices."

Because of her class, her gender, and her colonial and postcolonial upbringing, Cabrera was well suited to participate in the recovery and documentation of key components of Afro-Cuban culture. Such qualities allowed her, back in the 1950s, to undertake what anthropologists in the 1980s and 1990s were attempting to do: establish dialogues with different cultures without silencing the Other's viewpoint, that is, portray a cultural Other without imposing one's own views. Thus, to the chorus of national voices Cabrera brought Afro-Cuban inflections, and she was careful to transmit them without altering or disturbing them. We know this, of course, to be a theoretical impossibility:

the ethnological process of recovery itself implies a certain violence. But Cabrera was aware of the dangers of drowning these voices within a scientific or detached discourse that would "whiten" the Afro-Cuban color she was attempting to recover. And herein lies part of this writer's mystique and appeal, not to mention her marginalization from canonical readings of the nation's intellectual and literary archives. Indeed, Cabrera remains something of a misfit. She refused to accept the title of scientist and claimed that she was only a novice, an amateur, or at best a tourist in the field of ethnology. What attracted her attention to the world she spent years getting to know, she claimed, was the richness of Afro-Cuban religious beliefs and the vast poetic qualities of their mythical worlds.

As a youngster, Cabrera lived at home and continued to study on her own, completing the equivalent of a bachelor's degree. Her father died in 1923, and two years later she and her sister Emma traveled first to Spain and then to France. Cabrera liked Paris and decided she would return to Cuba and earn enough money to settle one day in France and study painting. Back in Havana, she opened an exclusive antique furniture shop with two partners, only to sell her share of the business in 1927 and return to Paris accompanied by her mother. She then began taking painting lessons at L'Ecole du Louvre, from which she graduated in 1930. While there, Cabrera also met French, Spanish, and Latin American writers and artists, and she studied non-Western cultures under the influence of surrealism. She always claimed that she had discovered Cuba "a las orillas del Sena" (by the banks of the Seine). The claim was valid indeed, since her stay abroad by then had provided the necessary distanced outlook that allowed her to discover anew the rich cultural resources of her own native land. In this respect Cabrera resembled Alejo Carpentier, another Cuban writer who "discovered" Cuba through the distance afforded by life in Paris.

Contact in Spain and France with such figures as Federico García Lorca, who was exploring in his poetry Spain's gypsy lore, and the Cuban painter Wifredo Lam, who lived in Paris, contributed to the intellectual ferment that Cabrera brought back to Cuba in her sporadic visits to the island during the 1930s. In fact, Cabrera is said to have been influential in Lam's "rediscovery" of Cuba's African heritage at the point of his return to the island during World War II. Lam's most famous work, "The Jungle" (1944), shares some of Cabrera's interests in Afro-Cuban literature. A small portrait of Cabrera and a large painting of her friend and partner, María Teresa de Rojas, both painted by Lam, are housed in the University of Miami's Cuban Heritage Collection. Lorca, who visited Cuba and became fascinated by Afro-Cuban culture, dedicated a well-known poem, "La casada infiel," to Cabrera and an unnamed Afro-Cuban woman.

While living in Paris, Cabrera visited Cuba several times. During these trips, according to the author, her interest in the Afro-Cuban world began to grow. Cabrera's brother-in-law, the distinguished Cuban ethnologist Fernando Ortiz, was at the same time pursuing his own research into Afro-Cuban culture, beginning with the publication of Los negros brujos (Black witches) in 1906. Cabrera then began to develop relationships with the old Afro-Cubans who would become her informants at a later period, a labor facilitated by her close relationships with former nannies and maids. It was in Paris, however, that she began to write her first work, Cuentos negros de Cuba (originally published in French, 1936; first Spanish edition, 1940; Black tales from Cuba). Ostensibly this was a book of stories she wrote for her close friend, the Venezuelan writer Teresa de la Parra, who at the time was seriously ill in Switzerland. Some of the stories first appeared in French literary journals like Cahiers du Sud, Revue de Paris, and Les Nouvelles Littéraires, translated by the French critic Francis de Miomandre, and they were later collected and published by Gallimard as Contes nègres de Cuba. The book received immediate critical acclaim and was published in Spanish as Cuentos negros de Cuba. Both French and Cuban critics, including Jean Cassou and Alejo Carpentier, were quick to remark on the stories' marvelous images and metaphors. In a review of the collection, Carpentier himself said that the book gave Caribbean mythology "a universal dimension."

Cuentos negros gathers twenty-two stories that work a Dionysian, humorous view of life into African and Afro-Cuban tales and myths. The stories contain a mixture of African folklore, sometimes already transculturated by a Caribbean colonial context, together with the seeds of Cabrera's fertile imagination.

The author works with basic folklore material, although it might be difficult to ascertain how much of each—folklore or fictional material—has made its way into the stories. Cabrera relished the fact that even Ortiz was misled in his identification of certain elements of her stories as proceeding from African sources when, in fact, she had just invented them. Ortiz himself, who wrote the preface to the first Spanish edition of the collection, recognized the book's diversity, its valuable literary and folkloric elements, as well as its introduction to a world with different morals and values—one that was neither better nor worse than those cultivated by the white Cuban population, merely *different*. Cabrera liked to poke fun in her writing at any strict adherence to traditional mores and values, particularly bourgeois propriety and Cuban patriarchy. Her stories exhibit a liberating energy, a joie de vivre that evokes elements of the surrealist canon as they evince a critique of repressive cultural values.

The stories of *Cuentos negros* include animals and human protagonists, and they range from tales of origins that show clear African traits to creolized colonial episodes that stem from life in Cuba. The first story, "Bregantino, Bregantín," narrates a man-bull's unlimited patriarchal ambition. This macho prototype—a bully—not only kills all male creatures in his kingdom, including his own descendants, but even converts all masculine nouns into feminine ones so as to eliminate all potential forms of contest to his power. The story ends, predictably, with a son who challenges and kills the father and restores balance to the kingdom. Another story, "Walo-Wila," narrates lyrically the differences between the sun and the moon, here shown as two sisters, Ayere Kénde, the beautiful one with the "golden cup" whom everyone sees, and Walo-Wila, who is even more beautiful than her sister but who lives hiding behind windows in her room. "Walo-Wila" can be read as a poem because of its rhythmic patterns and poetic techniques.

Yet another characteristic of Cabrera's writing, even in this first book, is her use of African or African-like words and sounds to create a natural poetic setting to the themes she explores. Most of the time, the meaning of these words is made part of the story, or it can be derived from context. One such story is "Los compadres," in which the Supreme Being is referred to in Spanish by the narrator and in Lucumí by the character Yemayá, who calls him "Babamí." Another story "El limo del Almendares" (The slime of the Almendares River) touches on a very Cuban theme: the conflicted racial and sexual legacy from Cuba's colonial past. It tells of an amorous triangle that includes Soyán Dekín, a beautiful mulatto woman; the white city mayor whom she distinguishes with her preference at a dance function; and Bilillo, a black suitor who feels scorned and makes the woman drown in the river through the power of magic. The story concludes with the revelation that Soyán Dekín's beautiful long hair is the slime of the Almendares River.

After years spent caring for Teresa de la Parra in Switzerland and Madrid, both her friend's death and the imminence of World War II prompted Cabrera to return to Cuba in 1938. That year marked the beginning of her long and sustained effort to study and recover Afro-Cuban cultures and religions through the stories, myths, and beliefs confided to her by informants. In various interviews Cabrera admitted that her labors were an attempt to preserve for the nation's cultural archive a precious, but nevertheless undervalued, cultural legacy.

Once back in Cuba, Cabrera settled with her companion, the historian María Teresa de Rojas, in the Quinta San José. The Quinta was a beautiful colonial mansion that Rojas' family owned in the Marianao section of Havana, close to the Pogolotti neighborhood where some of Cabrera's informants lived. The building was badly in need of repair. Both Rojas and Cabrera began doing research and collecting historical documents, architectural odds and ends, and furniture to restore the Quinta San José. The two women wanted to document the historical evolution of the "Cuban Home," a project that would have resulted in the creation of a Museum of the Cuban Home at the Quinta. Thus, the friends took trips to various parts of the island, finding and collecting, for example, all the types of doorknobs that had been used in Cuba throughout several centuries. Judging by pictures left of the Quinta—the mansion burned soon after Cabrera left for exile in Miami—the two women had undertaken a tasteful restoration of a typical Cuban colonial mansion. The fact that Cabrera chose to live in this older house in an older neighborhood—away from more fashionable neighborhoods—and turned its restoration into a major life project speaks for itself. Friends and former employees have revealed that Cabrera was a rather private person who shunned the social limelight and instead enjoyed the peaceful atmosphere and solitude of the Quinta. She lived there according to her own rules, receiving her informants and chatting with them at a leisurely pace in a beautiful but understated setting that seemed to evoke, somewhat nostalgically, a bygone colonial era.

Cabrera's second volume of stories, *Por qué? . . .: Cuentos negros de Cuba* (Why? . . .: Black tales from Cuba), was published in 1948 as part of the Colección del Chicherekú (Ediciones Chicherekú, or C.R. for short), a venture that Cabrera and and Rojas created that year in Havana. In the stories from this collection Cabrera explores more extensively than before the myths of origin and creation. Though they were derived mainly from narratives of African origin, some of these myths show Cabrera's work on African themes, and some are her own fictional creations. The stories' titles all respond to the initial question "Why?"—each shaping a world in which questions of life and death, day and night, shapes and features of animals, *orisha's* (saint's) place and significance are all answered or narrated in mythical fashion. The tales portray a universe where good and evil, life and death, peace and war coexist in creatures and nature alike—a universe where questions of morality must be judged on the merits of each particular circumstance rather than according to some previously established, absolute moral standard.

The volume begins with "Hay hombres blancos, pardos y negros" (There are white, mulatto, and black men), a story on the creation of the races that is either an Afro-Cuban myth or a Cabrera fiction. It is the tale of three brothers who existed in primeval times, when Olofi, creator of all things, had made all men dark-skinned and was still close to the Earth and its creatures. One day, the youngest brother tells Olofi that he wishes to be "blanco como el día" (white as day), and Olofi, to grant this wish, tells him of a small, ice-cold lake whose waters will whiten his skin. The story proceeds with the youngest brother becoming white

and immediately deciding that he is better than his two siblings. The middle brother gets to bathe in the muddy waters, which lighten his skin, thereby making him a mulatto. This brother now envies his white brother and publicly despises and abuses the oldest brother, who remains black. Although this story's dynamic speaks directly to the origin of racial differences and prejudices within an abstract moral context, it also alludes to the complex process of racial mixture, the resultant hierarchy of power based on racism, and the economic exploitation of blacks that characterized Cuba's colonial past. The fact that Cabrera opens the volume with this story suggests her intention to ground the narrative upon the island's historical realities.

The volume's second story, "Se cerraron y volvieron a abrirse los caminos de la isla" (How the island's paths were closed and opened again), focuses on a pair of twins who ingeniously make use of their likeness to free the island of a monstrous being who has killed thousands of people and closed all roads and paths, keeping persons locked in their houses and isolated from each other. This story, which refers to a time when the island was unsafe for habitation, might well be an allegory for the death and destruction caused in Cuba by the two nineteenth-century wars for independence from Spain, the Ten Years' War (1868–1878) and the War of Independence (1895–1898). The figure of the twins who "free" the island has religious connotations, for in Santería, the Afro-Cuban religion derived from Yoruba (the West African region in southern Nigeria) and Catholic beliefs, the Ibeyes, or divine twins, are believed to be the children and messengers of Changó, the god of thunder and one of the most powerful deities in the Yoruba pantheon.

Taken together, these two initial stories suggest an interest in Cuba's more recent history. Both project the island onto a temporal frame—after its liberation from a monstrous past—and populate it with a racially mixed and conflictive society. The remaining stories in *Por qué?* include fables in which a conflict between forces proves that astuteness can overcome sheer power; stories about gods or goddesses that establish why each has a particular character, strength, or weakness; and stories that touch on the theme of racial and psychological difference.

In *Idapo: El sincretismo en los cuentos negros de Lydia Cabrera*, Hilda Perera argues that primitive magic used artistically to create magical realism is, in fact, a key element in Cabrera's descriptions as well as in her character presentation. In this respect, Perera joins other critics, Rosario Hiriart and Isabel and Jorge Castellanos among them, who claim that Cabrera's literary accomplishment has not been given all the recognition it deserves. They all concur that Cabrera was one of the first writers to use the modern, contemporary version of magical realism in literature that was made internationally popular by the Colombian writer Gabriel García Márquez in the 1960s. No doubt the worlds Cabrera recreates, or creates, in all her stories are permeated by an animistic view of nature, religious beliefs that confer a sacred, dangerous power to the environment, and a psychology that characterizes the oppressed group's viewpoint. All these traits set the tone for stories in which the "real" encompasses a much broader realm of experience, one that injects life, sense, and soul into all creatures, from the humblest stone to the most royal tree. Whether this approach to reality can be considered an example of magical realism or simply the "marvelous" is a subject for further research. But it is at least true that Cabrera was one of the initiators in Latin America of the fantastic treatment of reality used by writers like García Márquez.

Cabrera continued her work of preserving Afro-Cuban myths, beliefs, and rituals during the 1950s and in 1954 published her magnum opus, *El monte*. Dedicated to her brother-in-law, the Cuban ethnologist Fernando Ortiz, the book is a dazzling compilation, seven hundred pages in length, of mythical, religious, medicinal, and cultural narratives that offers readers an insider's look into the lives and beliefs of Afro-Cubans at the turn of the twentieth century. It also includes an alphabetical compilation of herbs and plants together with their medicinal properties and religious powers, the *orisha* (or saint) who rules over each, and their names in Congo and Lucumí (as the Bantu and Yoruba languages are referred to in Cuba).

*El monte* gives Cabrera a central place in Cuban letters and Afro-American culture, a fact that goes largely unrecognized both inside and outside the island. The preface is itself a unique document that helps us understand the author's concept of Cuban culture, particularly the place and value of Afro-Cuban rituals and beliefs in Cuba's cultural repertoire. Here, Cabrera begins by disclaiming any scientific pretension and explaining her "method," recounting in detail how she had to learn to listen patiently to different and often contradictory versions of a single myth or story told with infinite digressions. In other words, the author was forced to distinguish this digressive style from the linear, successive structure favored by Western narrative. From this comment we can gather that Cabrera was keenly aware of the difference between oral and written traditions and that she was interested in preserving the oral, digressive pattern of her informants' discourse as much as possible. And yet this fact, which shows how much of a pioneer of postmodern anthropology Cabrera was, earned the author the belated disparagement of Enrique Sosa, the Cuban anthropologist who prefaced the pirated 1989 Havana edition of *El monte*. In her own 1954 preface, Cabrera acknowledges the fact that she avoided reading anthropological and linguistic manuals that could interfere with the direct rapport she wished to achieve with her informants and their material. More important, she points out that she had to learn how to "think and perceive reality" in the same manner as her informants, whom she credits by saying that they are indeed the "true authors of this book."

Cabrera insists on a particular point:

*No omito repeticiones ni contradicciones, pues en los detalles, continuamente, se advierte una disparidad de criterios, entre las "autoridades" habaneras y las matanceras, éstas últimas más conservadoras; entre los viejos y los jóvenes, y los innumerables cabildos o casas de santo.*

I do not omit repetitions or contradictions, for in the details, continuously, one notices a disparity of criteria between the Havana and the Matanzas "experts," the latter more conservative; between the old and the young; and among the innumerable Afro-Cuban religious and social meeting places.

This passage is important because in it Cabrera illustrates what one could call her "unmethodical method" and stresses how important this flexible approach is to preserving the integrity—or complexity—of the cultural narratives related by her informants.

One can gauge that the author was not simply interested in pursuing a set of facts but rather appeared determined to preserve the formal complexities that make her topic rich and varied. She was careful, in other words, to maintain the dialogic nature of her material, its diversity. She makes a similar point further on:

> *He querido que, sin cambiar sus graciosos y peculiares modos de expresión, estos viejos que he conocido, hijos de africanos muchos de ellos; los más enterados y respetuosos, continuadores de su tradición, y cuya confianza pude conquistar, sean oídos sin intermediario, exactamente como me hablaron.*

> I wish that, without changing their neat and peculiar modes of expression, these old men and women I have gotten to know—born of African parents many of them, most of them knowledgeable and respectful, willful carriers of their traditions and whose trust I was able to win—are heard without intermediaries, exactly as they spoke to me.

Here another important point is added to her chosen methodology: not only does she wish to preserve narratives in their original dialogic wealth, but she also wants to record the informants' particular manner of speech, aware all along that oral patterns differ from written ones and that they are a window to a particular world vision—precisely what the author wished to convey. Indeed, one can deduce from her manner of gathering information and her professed need to "learn to speak their language" that she considered all this a prerequisite for guaranteeing the reliability of that linguistic substance. Clearly, process was, for Cabrera, part of the product itself.

What was Cabrera's goal in following this so-called unmethodical method? Why did she accommodate her informants' wishes not to use tape recorders? Why engage in these long and—to our modern eyes—circuitous conversations? The author is clear in this respect: she attempted to avoid what she termed the "dangerous filter of interpretation." One knows, of course, that

Cabrera could only strive for a transparent transmission yet could not avoid imposing on her material—by the very ordering and writing process—an interpretive angle. Her care to keep her conversations with informants within an oral framework, her decision not to use dictionaries or anthropological works but instead to record the different African languages and their variants as they were being spoken, indicate how keenly aware she was of the ethnological violence and consequent distortion inherent in any anthropological project. In fact, Cabrera tries to shape her project as a collaborative enterprise: "El único valor de este libro, aceptadas de antemano todas las críticas que puedan hacérsele, consiste, exclusivamente, en la parte tan directa que han tomado en él los mismos negros. Son ellos los verdaderos autores" (The only value of this book, despite all the criticism that one could level against it and that I accept beforehand, resides, exclusively, in the very direct part that blacks themselves have had in the process of making it. They are the real authors).

*El monte* was financed by Cabrera and her partner, Rojas. Commenting on the reception of this work at the time of its publication, Cabrera declared in an interview with Rosario Hiriart (1978) that one Cuban intellectual told her the book "desprestigiaba a Cuba" (devalued Cuba's image). We know that *El monte* became immensely popular among practitioners of Santería for its wealth of materials and the presumed accuracy of its content. It is no exaggeration to claim, then, that beginning with this book and continuing with her other major works—*La sociedad secreta Abakuá: Narrada por viejos adeptos* (1958; The Abakuá secret society: Narrated by old adepts/supporters), *Yemayá y Ochún, Kariocha, Iyalorichas y Olorichas* (1974; Yemayá and Ochún, Kariocha, Iyalorichas, and Olorichas), and *Reglas de Congo: Palo Monte Mayombe* (1979; Congo religions: Palo Monte Mayombe)—Cabrera's ethnological books have been read as much, if not more, by believers and practitioners as by traditional academic readers.

In 1955 Cabrera published *Refranes de negros viejos* (Old Afro-Cuban proverbs), a brief but telling compilation of proverbs that illustrates, perhaps more accurately and poignantly than any academic treatise, the difficult historical journey of blacks in Cuba and the psychological effects of the process of racial mixing. Two years later the author published *Anagó: Vocabulario lucumí* (Anagó: The Lucumí vocabulary) and in 1958 came her second major ethnological work: *La sociedad secreta Abakuá*. In the prologue to *La sociedad secreta Abakuá,* Cabrera again details the difficulty of garnering support for studying the island's African legacy. She attributes this resistance to the psychological inferiority complex that colors the process of "mestizaje" (racial mixing) in Cuba, a complex she claims even intellectuals of the time used to share.

*La sociedad secreta Abakuá,* like *El monte,* is a complex book that recounts, in the voices and modes of several informants, the origins, rituals, and beliefs of this all-male religious society. According to Cabrera, Abakuá society, created in Cuba around the end of the eighteenth century, is a Creole transposition of the type of socioreligious societies that existed in southern Nigeria, like the Egbó and the Ekkpé. Abakuá society, located in Havana and in the cities of Matanzas and Cárdenas, also attracted white and mestizo followers since at least the beginning of the nineteenth century. The sect is popularly known in Cuba as *ñáñigos,* and its followers adhere to strict rules of mutual help (*hermandad*) and conduct and are sworn to secrecy regarding initiation ceremonies and group rituals. That Cabrera was able to gather information on the history and rituals of this secret and secretive society is due largely to her gaining the confidence of some of the old Afro-Cuban practitioners who knew of her long-term interest and respect for Afro-Cuban culture. In her desire to remain faithful to the narratives told to her by informants, Cabrera includes in the book long phrases in Abakuá, which then are rendered in Spanish. According to Jorge and Isabel Castellanos, Abakuá is an Afro-Cuban dialect with original elements from Efik—an African language—and numerous borrowings and adaptations from Spanish and from other African languages.

In June of 1960, a year and a half after the Cuban dictator Fidel Castro came to power, Cabrera and Rojas left Cuba for good. They settled first in Miami and later resided briefly in New York and Madrid. Ten long and difficult years passed before Cabrera began publishing

again. She had kept most of the notebooks in which she had recorded cultural material for about a quarter of a century, but the loss of her homeland, the lack of daily contact with informants, and the realization that she would never again return to the island took an emotional toll on the writer. In 1970, again as part of the Chicherekú series that she had created in Cuba and continued in exile, Cabrera published *Otán Iyebiyé: Las piedras preciosas* (Otán Iyebiyé: Precious stones), a short volume on the qualities and powers associated with specific precious and semiprecious stones in different traditions, including the Afro-Cuban.

Cabrera's third short story collection, *Ayapá: Cuentos de Jicotea* (Ayapá: Turtle's stories) was published in Miami in 1971. *Ayapá,* the Yoruba word for turtle, and *jicotea,* the Cuban word for a small indigenous land turtle, point to the syncretism of these short stories, arguably Cabrera's best. As the title suggests, all of the stories center on Jicotea, a small (and to many unattractive) animal who nevertheless wins countless battles for survival based mainly, but not only, on her astuteness. As Cabrera's preface indicates, a Yoruba tradition of storytelling with this animal, or its African counterpart, as the main character had existed previously. In the author's opinion, the *jicotea* figure enjoyed particular favor in the island's storytelling tradition because of the affinities African slaves perceived between the turtle's persistent battle for survival and their own plight in colonial society. Thus, in these stories Jicotea represents the possibility of the weak or the less powerful to succeed by outsmarting the more powerful creatures. It matters little whether Jicotea wins out by sheer intelligence, tricks, lies, or betrayal. What the stories seem to celebrate is the small animal's uncanny ability to have its own way despite being in a sometimes threatening environment. Jicotea is also significant from a strictly religious perspective for this "trickster" animal is the vehicle and ritual food of Changó, the powerful god of thunder, drums, and fire, all of which explains why Jicotea can reside on land so long as it is in or near water.

The Ayapá volume has a circular structure: it begins and ends with the presence of death. The first story, "Vida o muerte . . ." (Life or death . . .), tells of the arrival of death into the newly created world through the will or knowledge of Jicotea, who asserts that "everything that begins has an end." The second tale recounts Earth's initial flooding and the origin of day and night, again through Jicotea's agency. The last two stories tell of Jicotea's punishment and death of old age in Havana's poor barrio of Jesús María. In the first of these two final stories, Jicotea shows her astuteness once again when she is captured and sentenced to be thrown into water, an element much to her liking. The last story, "La herencia de Jicotea" (Jicotea's inheritance), suggests that even after death, Jicotea continues to outsmart others, this time the Spanish merchant who pays for Jicotea's funeral. The crux of the story, the inheritance, turns on a linguistic twist, for the Spanish merchant who pays for the funeral believes that Jicotea has left a sizable inheritance (*do chiento*) of two hundred (*doscientos*) gold coins, when, in fact, Jicotea has left only two old and shabby chairs (*dos asientos*). Because of its temporal frame, from primeval times to contemporary urban settings, the Jicotea volume offers readers an oblique history of survival that rivals that of Afro-Cubans on the island.

Cabrera published *La laguna sagrada de San Joaquín* (The sacred San Joaquín lagoon), a detailed description of a ritual-offerings ceremony in the Matanzas countryside, in 1973. The ceremony, which the author was able to observe and photograph, was held on the banks of the San Joaquín lagoon in the 1950s. Cabrera then published *Yemayá y Ochún, Kariocha, Iyalorichas y Olorichas*, an introduction to and study of the origins, powers, characteristics, and rituals that accompany the worship of the two female deities Yemayá and Ochún, two of the most popular in Cuban Santería, derived from Yoruba tradition. Yemayá, ruler of salt waters, is associated in Cuba with the Virgin of Regla, the black virgin patron saint of the port of Havana. Her younger sister, Ochún (named after a river in Nigeria), rules over rivers and lakes and is the owner of gold and amber. Ochún is associated with the Virgin of Charity of el Cobre, patron saint of Cuba. Both deities have their feast day each year on 8 September, and each possesses attributes that are associated with certain colors, numbers, foods, and qualities. To Yemayá, for example, belongs the color blue in its different shades according to the "path," or personality, that the deity takes, while Ochún wears gold.

Cabrera explains in detail the stories that surround the appearance and retinue of these two most popular saints/*orishas*. She delves into their special traits, their relationship to other *orishas*, ceremonies and rituals that sons and daughters of Yemayá and Ochún must follow, appropriate offerings and necessary preparations for the granting of certain wishes or special favors by the goddesses, and the proper ceremonies to celebrate the earthly departure of any of the two deities' followers. This book, one of Cabrera's most popular according to Hiriart, is narrated more in lay terms than either *El monte* or *La sociedad secreta Abakuá*. In *Yemayá y Ochún*, Cabrera narrates mainly in her own voice and addresses a general public about these particular *orishas* because of general cultural interest.

In 1979 Cabrera published *Reglas de congo*, her third major ethnological effort. Here Cabrera sets out to explain and document the Congo (the generic name in Cuba for different Bantu groups) presence on the island and their culture, religious beliefs, and practices. Less well known than the Lucumís and less numerous in present-day Cuba than the Yoruba descendants, Congos as a group were reputed, according to Cabrera, to be less docile as slaves and more prone to rebellion. This was considered all the more reason for not transporting them to the island in the same numbers as the Lucumís. This book is probably Cabrera's most personal piece of writing. Her narratives about the slave trade, the treatment of slaves, and the slower pace of life in bygone eras reveal a desire to achieve a balanced account of life in colonial Cuba. Writing in exile and no longer having access to informants, Cabrera uses numerous quotations from nineteenth-century authors who traveled to the island, among them Fredrika Bremer, Arthur Morelet, and Richard Madden. This narrative is more direct than in her two previous ethnological studies, and she makes clear her wish to discuss the nature of slavery in Cuba and the specific rights afforded slaves on the island. She does this from a broad perspective that includes frequent comparisons with the English and French colonial systems, discussing, for example, how travelers to Cuba were surprised—and sometimes annoyed and offended—by a more relaxed code of racial and class difference. *Reglas de congo* details the differences that the plantation system adopted in the Caribbean following cultural and economic variants. As has been documented, these differences account for Hispanic, French, English, and Dutch models of racial relations, racial mixing, and racism in the Caribbean. According to H. Hoetink in his study of " 'Race' and Color in the Caribbean," the Hispanic model, owing to specific historical and cultural factors, has a greater "socioracial continuum" than any of the other models.

In *Reglas de congo,* Cabrera's lengthy narratives and protracted asides or recollections about her own childhood alternate with those from Afro-Cuban informants of different ethnic origins whom she had interviewed in Cuba decades earlier. The informants comment on popular perceptions about the Congos and the noticeable cultural differences among the various groups included in this general category. In addition, Cabrera explains in detail the practices and philosophy of Palo Monte, a religion that is less open than Santería: the beliefs in the powers of the *nganga* or *prenda* (the magic container inhabited by the spirit, or *nfumbi,* that will work for the *palero,* or the practitioner who now owns and controls the dead person's spirit). Cabrera notes that, according to her informants, the Congo religious societies, like those of the Lucumís, have a broader social function, not unlike that of the *cabildos* of colonial times. These religious organizations not only unite a specific group of people under the directions of a *palero* and a *casa* (an association) but also bind the group in a contract of mutual help. Prospective members, for example, contribute money to join the group; those funds then are distributed equitably among its members. As in her other major ethnological works, Cabrera quotes at length from informants on different parts of the island who discuss a number of topics: from the proper manner to make a powerful *nganga* to ritual prayers—called *mambos*—which are supposed to be sung in a whisper.

Cabrera's book on the Congos mirrors, at least in part, her own life at the time of its writing. She becomes at once more distanced and more personal in her outlook. Outside her native country and away from informants, the author still was able to utilize in this book the valuable material she had collected in Cuba years earlier. Here, however, she possesses a detached and achingly distant viewpoint, an emotional outlook Cintio Vitier defines as "lejanía," which for Vitier constitutes one of the foundational qualities of Cubanness in the emergence of Cuban poetry (*Lo cubano en la poesía*). Cabrera's book conveys the sense of an author who is looking not only for outside sources of information but also, and particularly, deep within herself, aware that her own life experiences constitute at this point a valuable archive that is destined to disappear.

Cabrera's last volume of short stories, *Cuentos para adultos, niños y retrasados mentales* (Stories for adults, children, and mentally retarded people) appeared in Miami in 1983. It was written in a rather short period of time, during a brief residence in Spain, and contains thirty-seven stories on different subjects that reflect a greater Spanish storytelling influence than does all of her previous fiction. Whether this change of style is related to the author's prolonged estrangement from informants or whether it was a conscious choice, the fact remains that this collection does not match her earlier prose fiction. Perhaps because it deals with a variety of themes, *Cuentos para adultos, niños y retrasados mentales* lacks a clear focus, though most of the stories are located in Cuba during the colonial period.

One of the most interesting and developed stories, "Por falta de espacio" (Because of lack of space), tells of a passionate and free, yet restricted and ultimately ironic, relationship between an older woman and her younger lover, whom she had raised as a child. Although Cabrera structures her stories within a conventional societal frame—that of colonial Cuba—she explores themes that expose and transgress racial, economic, and even sexual mores. Cabrera continues her interest in exploring and pushing the limits of traditional values, and in that sense at least she continues to work within the parameters of the surreal. These stories, as well as most of her fictional writing, incorporate a mixture of poetic description and transgressive freedom that are Cabrera's hallmark. They can be said to derive as much from her contact with Afro-Cuban cultures as from surrealism, both of which fueled her own irreverent attitude toward conventions.

Cabrera continued to write and publish in Miami into the mid-1980s, when she was in her mid-eighties.

After the death in 1987 of her companion, María Teresa de Rojas, she continued to work as much as possible despite her progressive blindness. During her last years she lived with a friend, the Cuban linguist Isabel Castellanos, and died of pneumonia on 19 September 1991, at home in Miami at the age of ninety-two. All of her papers and manuscripts, the result of more than fifty years of research and writing about Afro-Cuban cultures, are housed at the University of Miami's Cuban Heritage Collection. In Cuba there appeared to be some interest, after Cabrera's death, in more fully recognizing her role in the recovery and preservation of the Afro-Cuban legacy.

Among Cabrera's other publications are three bilingual compilations of Yoruba, Bantu, and Abakuá words used in Cuba. Although her writings are sometimes classified as either fictional or ethnological, all of her work is infused with the mythopoetic quality that, according to the author, was one of the principal qualities she admired in Afro-Cuban cultures. What distinguishes Cabrera from other ethnologists of her time and makes her more of a contemporary cultural writer is her willingness to travel the distance to other cultures, her complete lack of reverence toward her own work, and the vital empathy she maintained toward the human beings whose cultures she respected and recovered on behalf of the national archive.

An author who wrote more than twenty books, who crisscrossed a variety of disciplines in her writings, who refused to be considered "scientific" in her approach, Cabrera defies narrow categorization, as do her works. According to Cristina Guzmán in a *Zona Franca* interview, she entered folklore "through the door of phantasy and poetry." It is vital to recognize, however, that Lydia Cabrera was, very early on, a person, a woman, and a writer who was well ahead of her time. Her attitude, decades ago, to the resistance she encountered by those who criticized and opposed her desire to include the African legacy in the Cuban national canon is exemplary. In her preface to *La sociedad secreta Abakuá*, she openly criticizes the racism pervading Cuban society and its negative impact on the urgent task of fashioning an all-inclusive narrative of Cuban cultures. She refers, with characteristic irony, to the fact that in Cuba it is far safer to be an indianist

(because no indigenous people were left after the conquest) than to study the rich African cultural heritage brought to the island. Cabrera muses:

> *En algunos de nuestros intelectuales, en muchos de nuestros de arios, a veces con abuelas olvidadas por muy tostadas al sol indiscreto del Caribe, se observa que ese malestar acaso es solo comparable al de los ángeles cuando se les mojan las alas; a la del Pavo Real cuando se mira los pies.*

> In some of our intellectuals, in many of our whites, sometimes with forgotten grandmothers because of the color they picked up from our indiscreet Caribbean sun, one can observe that uneasiness, perhaps comparable only to that of angels when their wings get wet, or that of the peacock when he looks down at his own feet.

From these comments and the fact that she financed the publication of most of her books, in Cuba as well as in exile, one can gather that Cabrera's trajectory was marked more by persistence and dedication to her ongoing work than by academic recognition or canonical readings. Her extensive work, although studied by Cuban academics—mostly women—and read by religious practitioners, still awaits the wider recognition it deserves. Even *El Monte,* arguably her most valuable work, has not been translated into English. Her name is not well known outside Cuban circles and is practically ignored by North American and European academics and cultural critics who study the African diaspora or the current concept of "hybridity."

First in Cuba and then in exile, Cabrera carved out new cultural spaces, to draw an inclusive, transnational concept of the many cultures that make up the Cuban subject. She began studying what Ortiz described as "cubanidad," the part and parcel of being born, raised, and nourished by the island's cultures. By preserving and studying the contributions of different African groups and their descendants, she helped enlighten contemporary notions of the nation. By devoting many years to help stretch the limits of "the national," she drew a different map that guided readers to an understanding of some of the complex historical and cultural factors that make up the spiritual consciousness and will to belong that Ortiz once described as "cubanía"—or perhaps, in a more inclusive vein, the rich and fragmented cultural experience of the Caribbean that Antonio Benítez Rojo has termed "the repeating island."

# SELECTED BIBLIOGRAPHY

## Primary Works

### Fiction

*Contes nègres de Cuba*. Translated from Spanish to French by Francis de Miomandre. Paris: Gallimard, 1936. Published as *Cuentos negros de Cuba*. Preface by Fernando Ortiz. Havana: Imprenta la Verónica, 1940.

*Por qué? . . .: Cuentos negros de Cuba*. Havana: Ediciones C.R., 1948.

*Ayapá: Cuentos de Jicotea*. Miami: Universal, 1971.

*Cuentos para adultos, niños y retrasados mentales*. Preface by Esperanza Figueroa. Miami: Ediciones C.R., 1983.

*Cuentos (1936–1983)*. Madrid: Ediciones Cocodrilo Verde, 2000.

### Nonfiction

*El monte: Notas sobre las religiones, la magia, las supersticiones y el folklore de los negros criollos y del pueblo de Cuba*. Havana: Ediciones C.R., 1954.

*Refranes de negros viejos*. Havana: Ediciones C.R., 1955.

*Anagó: Vocabulario lucumí (el Yoruba que se habla en Cuba)*. Havana: Ediciones C.R., 1957.

*La sociedad secreta Abakuá: Narrada por viejos adeptos*. Havana: Ediciones C.R., 1958.

*Otán Iyebiyé: Las piedras preciosas*. Miami: Ediciones C.R., 1970.

*La laguna sagrada de San Joaquín*. Madrid: Ediciones R, 1973.

*Yemayá y Ochún, Kariocha, Iyalorichas y Olorichas*. Madrid: Ediciones C.R., 1974.

*Anaforuana: Ritual y símbolos de la iniciación en la sociedad secreta Abakuá*. Madrid: Ediciones R, 1975.

*Francisco y Francisca: Chascarrillos de negros viejos*. Miami: Peninsular Printing, 1976.

*La Regla Kimbisa del Santo Cristo del Buen Viaje*. Miami: Peninsular Printing, 1977.

*Itinerarios del insomnio: Trinidad de Cuba*. Miami: Peninsular Printing, 1977.

*Reglas de Congo: Palo Monte Mayombe*. Miami: Peninsular Printing, 1979.

*Koeko iyawó: Aprende novicia—Pequeño tratado de regla lucumí*. Miami: Ultra Graphics Corp., 1980.

*Vocabulario congo: El bantú que se habla en Cuba*. Miami: Ediciones C.R., 1984.

*Supersticiones y buenos consejos*. Miami: Universal, 1987.

*Los animales en el folklore y la magia de Cuba*. Miami: Universal, 1988.

*La lengua sagrada de los ñáñigos*. Miami: Universal, 1988.

*Consejos, pensamientos y notas de Lydia E. Pinbán*. Miami: Universal, 1993.

*Páginas sueltas*. Edited by Isabel Castellanos. Miami: Universal, 1994.

## Secondary Works

### Critical and Biographical Studies

Anhalt, Nedda G. de. "Lydia Cabrera: La Sikuanekua." *Vuelta* 125:35–44 (April 1987).

Beasley, Kecia Helena. "Magic Realism in *Yemayá y Ochún*." Master's thesis, Arizona State University, 1995.

Benítez Rojo, Antonio. *The Repeating Island: The Caribbean and the Post Modern Perspective*. Trans. by James E. Maraniss. 2nd ed. Durham, N.C.: Duke University Press, 1995.

Carpentier, Alejo. "Los cuentos cubanos de Lydia Cabrera." *Carteles* 28, no. 42:40 (11 October 1936).

Cassou, Jean. "Poésie, Mithologie Américaine." *Les Nouvelles Littéraires*. Paris, 2 May 1936.

Castellanos, Isabel, and Josefina Inclán, eds. *En torno a Lydia Cabrera*. Miami: Universal, 1987.

Castellanos, Jorge, and Isabel Castellanos. *Cultura Afrocubana*, vol 4. Miami: Universal, 1988–1994. Pp. 101–112.

Figueroa, Esperanza. "Lydia Cabrera: Cuentos negros de Cuba." *Sur* 349:89–97 (July–December 1981).

González, Manuel Pedro. "Cuentos y recuentos de Lydia Cabrera." *Nueva Revista Cubana* 2:153–161 (1959).

Gutiérrez, Mariela. *El cosmos de Lydia Cabrera: Dioses, animales y hombres*. Miami: Universal, 1986.

———. *Los cuentos negros de Lydia Cabrera: Un estudio morfológico*. Miami: Universal, 1986.

———. "La armonía cósmica africana en los cuentos de Lydia Cabrera." *Encuentro de la cultura cubana* 4–5:202–209 (1997).

———. *Lydia Cabrera: Aproximaciones mítico-simbólicas a su cuentística*. Madrid: Verbum, 1997.

Hiriart, Rosario. *Lydia Cabrera: Vida hecha arte*. New York: Eliseo Torres & Sons, 1978.

———. *Cartas a Lydia Cabrera: Correspondencia inédita de Gabriela Mistral y Teresa de la Parra.* Madrid: Torremozas, 1988.

Hoetink, H. *Race and Color in the Caribbean.* Washington, D.C.: The Woodrow Wilson International Center for Scholars, 1985.

Inclán, Josefina. *Ayapá y otras Otán Iyebiyé de Lydia Cabrera: Notas y comentarios.* Miami: Universal, 1976.

Lezama Lima, José. "El nombre de Lydia Cabrera." *Tratados en la Habana.* Buenos Aires: Ediciones de la Flor, 1969. Pp. 144–148.

Moreno Fraginals, Manuel. *Cuba/España España/Cuba: Historia común.* Barcelona: Grijalbo Mondadori, 1995.

Novás Calvo Lino. "El monte." *Papeles de Son Armadans* 50, no. 150:298–304 (September 1968).

Perera, Hilda. *Idapo: El sincretismo en los cuentos negros de Lydia Cabrera.* Miami: Universal, 1971.

Sanchez, Reinaldo, and José Antonio Madrigal, eds. *Homenaje a Lydia Cabrera.* Miami: Universal, 1977. (A collection of articles on African American literature, part of which are devoted to Cabrera's works.)

Soto, Sara. "Magia e historia en los *Cuentos negros, Por qué* y *Ayapá* de Lydia Cabrera." Ph.D. dissertation, New York University, 1985.

Valdés-Cruz, Rosa. *Lo ancestral africano en la narrativa de Lydia Cabrera.* Barcelona: Vosgos, 1974.

Vitier, Cintio. *Lo cubano en la poesía.* Santa Clara: Universidad Central de las Villas, 1958.

Zambrano, María. "Lydia Cabrera, poeta de la metamorfosis." *Orígenes,* no. 25:11–15 (1950).

*Interviews and Exhibit*

Guzmán, Cristina. "Angular: Diálogo con Lydia Cabrera." *Zona Franca* 3, no. 24:34–38 (May–June 1981).

Levine, Suzanne Jill. "A Conversation with Lydia Cabrera." Translated by S. J. Levine. *Review (Center for Inter-American Relations)* 31:13–15 (January–April 1982).

Simo, Ana María, curator, and Inverna Lockpez, gallery director. *Lydia Cabrera: An Intimate Portrait, May 14–July 13, 1984.* New York: Intar Latin American Gallery. (Includes a biographical text by Simo, photos, a chronology, and the short story "Obbara Lies but Doesn't Lie," translated by S. J. Levine. Exhibit of Lydia Cabrera's ritual stones, photographs, manuscripts, correspondence, and other ritual and autobiographical material.)

Zaldívar, Gladys. *Lydia Cabrera: De mitos y contemporáneos.* Miami: Asociación de Hispanistas de las Américas, 1986.

# Guillermo Cabrera Infante

## (1929–    )

## *Alfred Mac Adam*

The life and writing of Guillermo Cabrera Infante are inextricably bound to Cuban history. Three Cuban political leaders intervened directly in his life: Gerardo Machado, who in 1932 ordered the aerial bombing of Gibara, Cabrera Infante's hometown; Fulgencio Batista, whose court in 1952 forbade him to publish under his own name; and Fidel Castro, whose repressive policies obliged him to go into permanent exile in 1965.

Cabrera Infante was born on 29 April 1929, to Guillermo Cabrera and Zoila Infante, founders of the local cell of the Communist Party in Gibara, on Cuba's northern coast, in the province of Oriente (now Santiago de Cuba), where both Fulgencio Batista and Fidel Castro were born. In 1932 General Gerardo Machado had Gibara bombed (the first aerial bombardment of a New World city) to crush an uprising, in which both the author's father and uncle participated on the rebel side.

In 1936, when Cabrera Infante was seven years old, his parents were arrested by Fulgencio Batista, who was then persecuting Communists. Batista continued his harassment after their release from jail. Blacklisted, Guillermo Cabrera moved his family to Havana in 1941 to find work. Because of his parents' political commitment, Cabrera Infante lived in grinding poverty.

Being the child of political dissidents might have transformed Cabrera Infante into a revolutionary, but it actually made him a skeptic. Early in life he began to wonder how his fervent parents could execrate Fulgencio Batista at one moment (1936) and then work actively in Batista's presidential campaign at another (1939). He was also puzzled by his mother's sorrow when Madrid fell to General Francisco Franco in 1939 and her enthusiasm for the treaty between Joseph Stalin and Adolf Hitler in the same year.

The family's 1941 migration to Havana was more than a change of setting: the poor but happy country boy metamorphosed into a poor, unhappy urban adolescent. Coming of age in Havana is the point of departure for his autobiographical novel, *La Habana para un infante difunto* (1979; *Infante's Inferno*, 1984), a text that shows how all of the author's fiction should be read. Life and art are inseparable for Cabrera Infante, because any reflection he makes on life (his own or others') entails transforming it into words. Verbal expression always requires the stylization necessary to produce effects, which renders the final product artificial. Life becomes art because it can be understood only through interpretation, an act of fiction making.

This sense of life as writing seems to locate Cabrera Infante at a distance from everyday affairs, aesthetically detached in the manner of Stéphane Mallarmé (a poet he frequently quotes). But this is not the case, because whereas Mallarmé sought to purify the "words of the tribe," Cabrera Infante uses them to represent experience. Thus, as he turns experience into words, he strives to bring words and experience into closer proximity by using all the kinds of spoken and written language that are available to him.

Cabrera Infante frequently alludes to the gap between the silent permanence of writing and the noisy but ephemeral spoken word. This tension pushed him toward his second love, cinema, where the mute work of art is rendered both visible and audible at the same time. Both language and nonverbal communication are available to the invisible director, the role Cabrera Infante seeks to bring into literature. So while he pursues the spoken word in his writing, he also maintains directorial control over the text, either by delegating narrative authority to a character, as he does with Silvestre Isla in his first novel, *Tres tristes tigres* (1967; *Three Trapped Tigers*, 1971), or by inserting himself into the fiction, as he does in *Infante's Inferno*.

Being a film critic complicates this game of verbal alter egos. In 1952 he was jailed for publishing a short story containing English obscenities in the large-circulation Cuban weekly magazine *Bohemia*. The judge banished him from journalism school, ending his higher education. The judge also forbade him to publish under his own name. He invented an ironic pseudonym, G. Caín—from *Cabrera Infante*—which he used in 1954 to sign film reviews in another large-circulation Cuban magazine, *Carteles*. In 1962, already in disfavor with the Castro regime for editing the maverick Monday literary supplement (*Lunes*) of the non-Communist but semiofficial newspaper *Revolución*, and for being an independent intellectual, he was banished to Brussels as cultural attaché. There he compiled *Un oficio del siglo veinte* (1963; *A Twentieth Century Job*, 1991), a volume of Caín's film reviews published between 1954 and 1960 in *Carteles* and *Revolución*. Caín's texts were edited and introduced by Guillermo Cabrera Infante. In a 1983 *Paris Review* interview, he tells how the book should be read:

> As a novel. The Prologue, the Intermission, and the Epilogue are biographical comments on G. Caín, the critic. The reviews, his criticism, are the corpus—that is,

his body. The whole book is a rite of passage conducted over his dead body. That's what a novel is, don't you think?

*A Twentieth Century Job* may or may not be a novel, but Cabrera Infante thinks of himself in the same way that he thinks of life and language: he, too, is literary raw material, so by writing about himself as Caín, he creates a character.

This puts him on existentially shaky ground. Like Jean-Paul Sartre's actor-character, Kean, he seems "nothing in himself." But to reduce his blend of masks to bad faith is to misinterpret Cabrera Infante because to do so transforms him into a character in an existentialist allegory, much in the way Sartre turns Jean Genet into a character in *Saint Genet* (1952). Cabrera Infante is an ironic version of two writers—T. S. Eliot and Jorge Luis Borges—who discovered they can best deal with the writer's identity by viewing the production of art as the progressive loss of personality.

Eliot's antiromantic 1917 essay, "Tradition and the Original Talent," separates poetry from self-expression. Eliot liberates poetry from the romantic cult of personality and restores primary importance to the text itself, as if the text existed independently of its creator. For Eliot, "Poetry is not a turning loose of emotion, but an escape from emotion, it is not the expression of personality, but an escape from personality. But, of course, only those who have personality and emotions know what it means to want to escape from these things." To comprehend Cabrera Infante, we must side with Eliot and betray him at the same time by asserting that while the literary work of art is an escape from personality, it inevitably contains the artist's self-portrait.

In 1951 Borges delivered his lecture "El escritor argentino y la tradición" (The Argentine writer and tradition). Borges's title mockingly alludes to Eliot's by focusing exclusively on Argentine writers. Borges asks: How can the Argentine writer participate in the Western tradition and still be a "genuine" Argentine? Does having a national identity require authors to use exclusively national themes, speech patterns, and political or social situations? Borges answers, "I think our tradition is all of Western culture, and I think, as well, that we have a right to that tradition, which is stronger than that of this or that Western nation." He concludes: "We can use all European themes, use them without superstition, with an irreverence that can have, and already has had, fortunate consequences." Borges defines the ironic relationship between Latin American writers and the Western tradition: Latin Americans are part of Western culture, but they are not determined by it; rather, they manipulate it. The form of this manipulation, for Cabrera Infante and for many Spanish American writers of his generation, is parody, achieved through the aggressive inversion of received literary models.

Cabrera Infante's first discovery of literature was an unexpurgated Spanish translation of Petronius Arbiter's *Satyricon*, which he found among his father's books during a trip to Gibara in 1942. The thirteen-year-old reader stumbled simultaneously on the erotic, the literary, and an ancient world that he could readily translate into Cuban reality. That the *Satyricon* is also a parody written in the debased Latin of the provinces is something Cabrera Infante would learn only later, but there can be no doubt about Petronius's presence in both *Three Trapped Tigers* and *Infante's Inferno*.

Like Petronius, Cabrera Infante parodies romance (the Greek novels about separated, wandering lovers) to the point that Silvestre Isla and Arsenio Cué of *Three Trapped Tigers* discuss the adventures of the mutually betraying protagonists of the *Satyricon*, who are clearly analogous to them. The erotic element in Petronius, the pornographic delight of the adolescent, became a model for the author of *Infante's Inferno*, who was also fascinated by the sheer exuberance of the spoken language. If we add to this that Petronius fell afoul of politics—he was a victim of Nero—we see that Cabrera Infante may justifiably see his own life writ large in Petronius's.

Cabrera Infante published his first short story at age eighteen. Unlike earlier Latin American writers, he did not begin as a poet but as a kind of scriptwriter. Fascinated with mass culture as a child—he claimed to have learned to read by deciphering the words in the balloons above comic strip characters—he became involved with radio. He dramatized saints' lives for a Catholic association and wrote a radio play based on an American comic strip, "The Spirit," that was popular in Cuba. When his radio adaptation of the Sherlock Holmes tale "The Speckled Band" was rejected, he focused exclusively on written prose.

In 1947, as Raymond D. Souza recounts in his eponymously titled literary biography of Cabrera Infante, the latter got into an argument with Carlos Franqui (the future editor of *Revolución*) about Miguel Angel Asturias, whose *El señor presidente* (1946; Mr. President) was being reviewed extensively in Havana. Cabrera Infante declared that if Asturias's play with language was literature, then he could certainly play just as well; accepting Franqui's challenge that he prove it, he wrote "Aguas de recuerdo" (1948; Waters of memory). Franqui read the manuscript and urged Cabrera Infante to show it to Antonio Ortega, editor of *Bohemia*, the most widely read magazine in Cuba. Ortega published the story in the 13 June1948 issue.

"Aguas de recuerdo," despite the adolescent author's disdain for Asturias, has more in common with his brand of literature as social protest than it does with the philosophic or fantastic short stories that Jorge Luis Borges published during the 1940s. In fact, most Latin American prose fiction of the period refused to separate itself from a Zolaesque attitude toward writing that treats art as a means to change society.

It is in this line of social protest literature that Cabrera Infante wrote "Aguas de recuerdo," a story that is set in a small coastal town reminiscent of Gibara. The protagonist is a solitary old woman half-crazed with hunger. Her only possessions are her memories of her husband and sons, fishermen lost at sea in mysterious circumstances. The story demonstrates how hunger and poverty reduce people to the level of animals, and provides the pretext for pompous sermonizing: "A rational being (an animal with the ability to think, after all), having lost the notion of good and evil because of hunger and calamity, can, in moments of despair, reveal in broad daylight the savage atavism that sleeps, locked up behind the bars of the subconscious."

When a hurricane strikes the town and a nearby house catches fire, the protagonist, Doña Agustina, tries to save the man sleeping inside it. Having roused him, she interrogates him about what happened to her husband and sons. He confesses that they were murdered. Doña Agustina, impelled by revenge and animal fury, rows out to sea, finds her husband's murderer, kills him, and then commits suicide. This stilted, artificial melodrama shows Cabrera Infante writing in imitation of older Cuban and Spanish American writers, not ready to create his own literary space by means of parody.

The themes and style of Cabrera Infante's early writings derive from the milieu in which he grew up. While he may have been too skeptical to follow his parents and become a member of the Communist Party, he could hardly escape their influence. His father wrote and set type for the party newspaper *Hoy*, and Carlos Franqui, a close family friend who had been expelled from the Communist Party but who was nevertheless an important figure in Fidel Castro's 26 July Movement, actually shared their tiny apartment at Zulueta 408 for a time. Cabrera Infante describes the flat, a meeting place for many writers and artists on the left, in *Infante's Inferno*.

The aesthetic norms of such a political community included realism, social criticism, and "street" Spanish to make the writing accessible to the masses. Cabrera Infante might not have adhered to any particular political or literary orthodoxy during the 1940s and 1950s, but he would certainly have been imbued with the concerns of the Cuban left during the Cold War. A symptom of this would be his adoption of Jean-Paul Sartre as his philosophic and aesthetic mentor. In Sartre he would find both a quest for personal identity and the need to commit himself to sociopolitical ideals.

The most significant literary result of the combined influences of Sartre and socially critical literature is the short story collection *Así en la paz como en la guerra* (1960; As in peace, so in war), which includes material from the late 1940s that had not been published previously. Asked about that book in 1983, the author commented to Mac Adam:

> There's juvenilia in that book but also some senilia. . . . I have nothing against the stories. In fact, half a dozen or so may be salvageable. But it's the book itself I object to. . . . Because it's a book not written but collected under the perverse influence of Sartre and his idea that a writer must not only write about a moment in History (like Marx he always capitalized the word), but also comment on his writing as well. . . . It's aesthetically hideous, a kind of social realism with a human face or a species of naturalism with a socialist conscience.
>
> (*Paris Review*)

Cabrera Infante's repudiation was both political and aesthetic. He "rehabilitated" the book in 1993, when he published it in English translation (by himself, John Brookesmith, and Peggy Boyars) under the title *Writes of Passage*. The differences between the Spanish and English-language editions are significant: Cabrera Infante replaced the original prologue with a "Prologue for English Readers," deleted fifteen scenes of Cuba under Batista that were interspersed with the stories, and included "English Profanities," a recounting of the legal difficulties that arose when he published one of the tales.

During the 1940s and 1950s life in Cuba was conditioned by two factors: the constant U.S. intrusion in Cuban politics and business, and Fulgencio Batista's control over Cuban life. Batista seized power in 1933 and retained control for twenty-five years, allowing the election of two incompetent presidents, Ramón Grau San Martín (1944–1948) and Carlos Prío Socarrás (1948–1952). Batista's power base was the army, adept at bullying unarmed civilians but impotent against dedicated guerrilla fighters.

The United States wanted tranquillity in Cuba so business could be conducted smoothly. After the 1934 abrogation of the Platt Amendment, which sanctioned United States intervention in Cuban affairs, American governments were content to come to terms with Fulgencio Batista instead of invading. Disillusion polluted the political atmosphere of the 1944–1952 period because of the obvious failure of both Grau and Prío Socarrás. Then, the period between 1952 and 1959 was marked by steadily escalating outrage as Batista first effected a classic military coup in March 1952 and then openly declared himself dictator. That meant government censorship, the closing of the University of Havana, political repression, and police terrorism. At the same time, these seven years saw an upsurge in the Cuban economy, a building boom in Havana, and a proliferation of public works projects. Batista's critics fell silent because they found themselves economically well-off.

Batista's control over the press was not absolute, and on 5 October 1952, Cabrera Infante published yet another socially committed short story in *Bohemia*, "Resaca" (Undertow). The editors noted that the story received "First Honorable Mention in the Hernández Catá National Literary Competition," showing that recognition of its merits extended beyond *Bohemia*. The author himself regarded the tale as a satisfactory performance, as he included it in *Writes of Passage*. Like his first story, this one is filled with pathos and action, following the flight of two men who have just set fire to a sugarcane field. Recalling John Steinbeck's 1937 novel *Of Mice and Men*, "Resaca" deploys two protagonists, Cheo, a large man, wounded and dying, and García, a small man who distracts Cheo from his pain with his description of an "attainable Paradise," which will come into being when

> we are the ones who govern. You and I, and Yeyo and Sánchez and Graulio Pérez and all the workers from the sugar plantation, the ones from Sao, and from all the rest of Cuba; when all of us workers of the world seize power and govern and make just laws, there will be jobs for everyone and money. We'll go to the best hospitals. . . . They'll fix up your leg there, and no one will ever be able to tell you were hurt. We'll live in nice houses, clean, pretty little houses with electric light and radio and everything. . . .
>
> (*Bohemia*, 5 October 1952)

While alleviating Cheo's anguish, García gives the reader a lesson in politics:

> We'll all be equal. The Haitians will be equal to the owners. And we will be equal to the Chinese. There will be no unemployment or dead time when there's no work on the sugar plantations. . . . There will be justice for all. Social justice. Yes, it will be a Paradise a real Paradise. . . .

Cabrera Infante evokes the central issue in the Cuban economy: sugar. Harvesting sugarcane (the *safra*) requires many hands, but most of the workers find themselves virtually unemployed for the rest of the year. This is the "dead time" García mentions.

Like "Aguas de recuerdo," "Resaca" reflects the realist-naturalist literary tradition and is highly determinist in its worldview. Cheo and García set fire to the cane field on orders from a corrupt union leader who uses the protagonists to extort money from the plantation owners. Burning the field does not bring García's "attainable Paradise" any nearer, but it does enrich the union leader (who is meant to represent Emilio Surí Castillo, the secretary of the National Federation of Sugar Workers, according to Cabrera Infante in his preface to *Así en la paz como en la guerra*).

Two weeks after "Resaca," *Bohemia* published yet another story signed by Guillermo C. Infante and titled "Balada de plomo y yerro" (Ballad of lead and error), which Cabrera Infante included in *Así en la paz como en la guerra* and in *Writes of Passage* (where it bears the title "Ballad of Bullets and Bull's Eyes"). The Spanish title contains a pun: the word "yerro," or error, sounds like "hierro," or iron. The combination of lead (bullets) and iron has all the makings of a "hard-boiled" yarn and reflects Cuba's gangster world during the 1950s, where political assassinations and gangland murders were carried out by the same people. The "error" in the title refers to the fact that the assassins kill the wrong man, that they are working, as one puts it, "just for the fun of it."

The story is an exercise in black humor, but Batista's censors did not laugh. In the tale a drunken American sings an obscene song in English, and because this foul language is an "affront to common decency," as the author recounts in his prologue to *Así en la paz como en la guerra*, he is arrested. The author's pseudonym, G. Caín, was prophetically appropriate for the future outcast. (Cabrera Infante recounted the entire episode in the vignette "Obsceno," included in his 1975 book, *O.*)

The appearance in 1960 of *Así en la paz como en la guerra*, including both "Resaca" and "Balada de plomo y yerro," marked the end of the first phase of Cabrera Infante's career. He signed it with his complete name, Guillermo Cabrera Infante, using for the first time the last names of both his parents. (He had signed the three *Bohemia* stories Guillermo C. Infante.) The change is significant: Zoila Infante's influence on her son far outweighed that of Guillermo Cabrera. A handsome woman, she was also something of a maverick within the Communist Party, remaining a friend of Carlos Franqui after his expulsion from the party. She introduced her son to cinema, carrying him, according to family legend, to the movies when he was twenty-nine days old. Thereafter, like the Argentine novelist Manuel Puig and his mother, they attended films regularly together. The title of Cabrera Infante's third collection of film essays, *Cine o sardina* (1997; Movies or sardines), derived from one of Zoila's quips: since the family was so poor, it would be up to Guillermo to decide between film or food.

*Así en la paz como en la guerra,* which the author would repudiate (only to rehabilitate it much later), is a Janus: it looks back to his youth as a socially committed, realist-naturalist writer and forward to his explorations of literature as an end in itself. The book is caught between those two literary modalities and is divided into two independent sections. There are fifteen numbered vignettes (brief scenes of revolt and oppression in Batista's Cuba) and fourteen short stories that begin as politically oriented tales in the line of "Resaca" and end as short stories about specific characters. Cabrera Infante's model was Ernest Hemingway's early *In Our Time* (1925), which has the same blend of numbered miniature chapters depicting the violence of contemporary reality (World War I, bullfighting, urban life) and short stories about individuals.

Hemingway's most striking character is Nick Adams, his self-portrait, simultaneously an actor and a witness to the action. His parallel in *Writes of Passage* is Silvestre, who will reappear in *Three Trapped Tigers* as the novel's controlling authority. In "Un nido de gorriones en un toldo" ("A nest of sparrows in an awning," published as "Nest, Door, Neighbors" in *Writes of Passage*) Silvestre meets an American girl who pronounces his name as if it were "silver tray," while in *Three Trapped Tigers,* Silvestre's friend Arsenio Cué puns on his name, calling him Silver Star. Silvestre is an alter ego for Cabrera Infante, since the former writes down what all the other characters say; this fusion of character and author continues in the three vignettes included in *Delito por bailar el chachachá* (1995; Crime to dance the cha-cha-cha), where the unnamed narrator could be either Silvestre or his creator.

The anti-Batista vignettes interspersed in *Writes of Passage* strongly resemble those in *Vista del amanecer en el trópico* (1974; *View of Dawn in the Tropics,* 1988). From the late 1940s until the early 1980s, then, Cabrera Infante was writing in two distinct styles. *Writes of Passage* is more a work in progress than a definitive text, because it shows the author writing objective, reporter-like prose about the violence of the Batista era as well as subjective, psychological prose about his personal experiences—if, that is, we take Silvestre to be Cabrera Infante's literary double.

*Writes of Passage* is a prototype of what the original *Three Trapped Tigers* would have been had not politics intervened in the author's life: a book where vignettes from Cuban history about repression and revolt would be mixed with scenes from the lives of characters living in 1958 Havana. As the author says in his preface to *Writes of Passage:*

> The title of the book [*Así en la paz como en la guerra*] would seem to be a parody of the "Our Father." Actually I would have preferred to avoid any and all explanation. I haven't succeeded, but I feel obliged to say that the vignettes predate and contradict the stories to the same degree that the Revolution measured and eliminated the reality that appears in the stories. It's for this reason that the book ends with a triumphal vignette: their [anti-Batista graffiti on a cell wall] authors have been defeated, but their invincible literature remains on the walls.

*Writes of Passage* is, therefore, "occasional" literature derived from a reality the author was later happy to forget. The "view of dawn" in the title of the later *View of Dawn in the Tropics* also alludes to the Cuban Revolution. Originally, the dawn may have been exactly that, the dawn of a new age, but as the Revolution turned dark for Cabrera Infante, the title became ironic. It is especially so when we realize that he began to rewrite the book in 1965, while—having returned from a diplomatic post for his mother's funeral—he was forced to stay in Cuba for a time. *Three Trapped Tigers,* the rewritten version of the "Vista del amanecer" manuscript, tries to be the exact opposite of *Writes of Passage:* it preserves the memory of a lost time rather than trying to efface it. The triumphal song becomes an elegy.

Cabrera Infante's life is inseparable from his writing, as we see in *A Twentieth Century Job,* where the author treats himself, through his pseudonym, as a fiction. This self-fictionalization has a precedent in Spanish American literature. In his 1935 tale, "El acceso a Almotasim," Jorge Luis Borges showed that he could write reviews of imaginary books as well as of real ones, thus transforming the critic into the creator of the fiction. The inversion leads to the creation of a literary personality, Borges, who appears as narrator, actor, or both.

Caín is Cabrera Infante's pen name, but *A Twentieth Century Job* demonstrated that Cabrera Infante is as much a pen name as Caín. Cabrera Infante discovered by writing film reviews what Borges discovered by writing book reviews: when a person writes, he or she becomes an author, that is, a fiction. A writer is known by his writing; in a sense, the writer becomes the writing. Caín dies in this book because he ceases to write; thus, writing and living are identical.

But the last words in the book are not Caín's "last words." They belong to Cabrera Infante. Despite the play between alter ego and author, there is a conflict between author and language. Caín is the chronicler of films who objectifies himself—at least in his *Carteles* reviews—in the third person. Cabrera Infante notes that Caín develops his own double when he begins to write in the first person in *Revolución*, but he does not point out that in either case Caín is always subordinated to another voice. Caín is a persona, or mask, just as all the characters in *Three Trapped Tigers* are masks for Silvestre, because he composes the text by transcribing what they say. Behind Silvestre stands the author, the "authority" who controls language while remaining invisible: Cabrera Infante himself. The disintegration of the first-person, autobiographical narrator in *Infante's Inferno* marks the start of a new phase in Cabrera Infante's writing.

The behind-the-scenes struggle between author and surrogate in no way diminishes the importance of Caín's film reviews. Those articles, along with the lectures Cabrera Infante gave in Havana in 1962 on Orson Welles, Alfred Hitchcock, Howard Hawks, John Huston, and Vincente Minnelli (published in 1978 as *Arcadia todas las noches* [Arcadia every night]) established him as a major film critic, which the author reconfirmed in 1997 with another volume of film essays, *Cine o sardina*. Caín's reviews usually run to two thousand words (with some much shorter, some much longer), so he has more space than the average newspaper reviewer. Accordingly, he goes into greater detail and discusses technical matters such as camera work, color processes, and editing as well as direction and secondary characters, all in addition to evaluating the film. The extra information makes the articles more like essays in a specialized journal than ordinary reviews. Like Borges, who published extremely erudite book reviews in a Buenos Aires ladies' magazine, *El hogar,* during the late 1930s, Cabrera Infante introduced intellectual and professional concerns into a mass-market milieu and provided a crucial link between high and mass culture.

At the same time, Caín was not merely an aesthete; he salted his reviews with veiled attacks on Fulgencio Batista, which the dictator's police duly noted. For example, in his article on the film *Mau Mau* (21 April 1957), Caín spent more time discussing the political situation in Kenya than he did discussing the film. He vindicated the guerrilla war being carried out by the Mau Mau, a war his Cuban readers would have inevitably associated with the guerrilla war being fought by Fidel Castro's 26 July Movement and other armed groups. Caín's final, ironic statement about the fact that the Mau Maus fought English tanks and planes with machetes (the weapon of Cuban rebels since the nineteenth century) and that they had no weapons to fight propaganda films like *Mau Mau,* could only have been understood as an attack on Batista's U.S.-supplied army fighting poorly armed insurgents. The same sentiment appears in his 16 June 1957 review of a Spanish film, *Death of a Cyclist,* where Caín described the disenchantment of a former supporter of General Franco:

> Now, nevertheless, he is disgusted with everything: Spain is not the right-wing paradise, the Eden of the Church, the promised land of *falangismo.* It is, simply, that counterpart of the modern police-state which is also suffered in more tropical latitudes: the gangster-state, where what matters is theft, where the most important thing is theft, and where, if it is necessary to eliminate annoying witnesses, spying eyes, or denouncing lips, they are suppressed at dawn, "taken for a ride," the classic underworld style.
>
> (*A Twentieth Century Job*)

Cabrera Infante took even greater risks than his alter ego. With friends, he founded the Cinemateca de Cuba in 1951, which he turned into a serious institution by establishing links with the Museum of Modern Art in New York. In 1956 he tried to turn it into an anti-Batista organization, but the idea failed. The Batista regime took control of the Cinemateca, which quickly died. Cabrera Infante went on fighting Batista by writing for the underground newspaper *Revolución* and serving in 1958 as a liaison between the Communist Party and the non-Communist urban guerrillas in the

Directorio Revolucionario, for whom he procured weapons.

Batista's departure elevated Cabrera Infante to a position of prominence. In addition to his editorship of *Lunes*, he became chairman of both the National Cultural Council and the new Film Institute. He accompanied Fidel Castro on a tour of the New World, visiting the United States, Canada, and several Latin American republics. This was during the Revolution's "open" phase, from January 1959 until the Bay of Pigs in April 1961, a time when all Cuban intellectuals made propaganda for the Cuban Revolution.

After the Bay of Pigs, the Communist Party took control of the Revolution. *Lunes* tried to use television as a means of communicating with the Cuban people, as had Castro in 1959, and in 1960 Cabrera Infante's younger brother, Sabá, made a short film, *P.M.*, for *Lunes* about Havana nightlife. It was aired, but in 1961 the film was confiscated by the Film Institute and condemned as decadent. *Lunes* was closed and Cabrera Infante was fired from each of his positions.

Unemployed except for being vice president of the Writers Union, an honorary position and something of a joke, he began to write "Ella cantaba boleros" (She sang boleros), which eventually became the manuscript "Vista del amanecer en el trópico," and then *Three Trapped Tigers*. At the same time he pieced together *A Twentieth Century Job,* which was as subversive under Castro as it had been under Batista. To banish him without scandal, the Castro government named him cultural attaché in Belgium in 1962. *Así en la paz como en la guerra* was translated into French, Italian, and Polish in 1963, gaining the author some European fame. When the manuscript "Vista del amanecer" won the Biblioteca Breve Prize in 1964, Castro banished him further by naming him Cuban chargé d'affaires for Belgium and Luxembourg.

Upon his return to Havana in June 1965 for his mother's funeral, Cabrera Infante, already embittered, became totally disillusioned. During his three years abroad, the city had been transformed into a tropical version of the grim eastern European capitals he had visited in 1960, and his former friends had become political automatons. Suspicious that he might defect, the Castro regime would not allow him to return to

Brussels with his daughters (eleven and seven, respectively) by his first marriage until almost the end of 1965. (He had divorced in 1960 and married the actress Miriam Gómez the following year.)

Unlike his brother Sabá, who sought political asylum in the United States, Cabrera Infante thought he could sever his ties with Cuba by moving to Spain. Instead, he found himself politically and economically isolated because relations between Franco and Castro were cordial. First, the Spanish censor rejected the manuscript of *View of Dawn in the Tropics*; then, in 1966, he himself was expelled by the Spanish government for having published anti-Franco articles in *Lunes* and elsewhere.

Impoverished, Cabrera Infante moved his family in late 1966 to London, where he tried to make a living writing screenplays. At first, he was denied permission to work in England. However, to the author's delight a lawyer demonstrated to Her Majesty's government that writing was not work. The Cuban writer Calvert Casey gave Cabrera Infante money, and the Uruguayan critic Emir Rodríguez Monegal appointed him London correspondent for his literary magazine, *Mundo nuevo*, which was published in Paris. Cabrera Infante was just barely able to survive, but early in 1967, purged of its political content and completely rewritten in self-exile, *Three Trapped Tigers* appeared.

In 1968 Cabrera Infante publicly denounced the Castro regime in the Argentine weekly magazine *Primera plana*. He repeated his criticism in a long interview he granted to the Argentine journalist Rita Guibert in October 1970, which appears in her book *Seven Voices* (1973). The reaction from the pro-Castro camp was violent: within Cuba he was declared a traitor, and the regime's foreign supporters, among them Carlos Barral, publisher of *Three Trapped Tigers*, echoed the condemnation. Cabrera Infante became a man without a country twice over: he was persona non grata in Cuba and anathema to the Latin American intelligentsia still loyal to Castro.

These pressures took their toll. Despite his success in 1969 with the screenplay for the cult classic film *Vanishing Point* (1971), a Guggenheim Fellowship in 1970, and an invitation from Joseph Losey to write a script based on Malcolm Lowry's 1947 novel *Under the Volcano* (he finished the screenplay, but the film was not made with his script), his mental health deteriorated. In the summer of 1972 he suffered a mental collapse, was hospitalized, and was given shock therapy. He published nothing until the vignettes of *View of Dawn in the Tropics* appeared in 1974. With this volume, history repeated itself, but in reverse. Hemingway first published his vignettes in *In Our Time* as an independent volume, but never again published them alone. Cabrera Infante, conversely, excised vignettes from the first version of *View of Dawn in the Tropics* and published them alone, the only way they have ever been printed.

Living in London, slowly rebuilding his life and career, Cabrera Infante managed to publish two collections of literary essays, *O* in 1975 and *Exorcismos de esti(l)o* (Exorcisms of style) in 1976. *O*—the letter "o," even if "zero" better describes the author's situation while compiling the book—seems to be a miscellany. It covers, inter alia, the 1968 demise of "swinging London," Cabrera Infante's Siamese cat Offenbach, the Spanish popular novelist Corín Tellado (treated ironically), Lewis Carroll, and Cuban popular songs.

*O* seems to be the work of an author biding time between major projects, bringing together old material just to publish a book. However, just the opposite is true. Electrotherapy had, as he says, "practically eradicated what I use most to write (except for my typewriter)—I mean my memory" (*Paris Review*). *O*, adding yet another layer to the autobiographical quality of the author's writing, was an exercise in personal phenomenology. Cabrera Infante used it to reconstruct his world (his cat, his apartment, London), his immediate past (the late 1960s), his remote past (his 1952 incarceration), his cultural obsessions (Cuba, Cuban popular culture), and literature, that of the past (Lewis Carroll) and that of the present (Julio Cortázar, Manuel Puig).

Especially interesting is a digression included in the book's end piece, "Desde el Swinging London" (From swinging London): "Sobre por qué no ver a Martha Graham (ni oír a Stravinksy)" (On why one shouldn't see Martha Graham [or hear Stravinsky]). Cabrera Infante's most important publication at this point in his career was *Three Trapped Tigers*, which was heavily charged with nostalgia for a lost Havana; in this digression the author comes to grips with the nostalgia engendered by exile. He attempts to prove to himself that while the past—the raw material of his major fictions, as *Infante's Inferno* would later confirm—was of vital importance to his art, it must not dominate his thinking to the point of depriving him of a present:

> I remember how shocked a friend of mine (like almost all my friends, a movie fanatic) was when I told him I preferred the most mediocre new film to seeing a masterpiece from the past: Griffith, Eisenstein, Murnau, but also Ford, Howard Hawks or Welles. He couldn't and wouldn't understand. For me, that's what movies are: openings. It doesn't matter much to me that next week the film has aged more than yesterday's newspaper.
>
> (*O*)

How seriously should we take this statement, made by a man whose film reviews reveal his encyclopedic and historical appreciation of film? Here we see the artist urging himself not to get lost in the labyrinth of the past and to push on into the future.

That future came into sharper focus in *Exorcismos de esti(l)o* (the title plays on the word for style, *estilo*, and the word for summer, *estío*). In his *Paris Review* interview, Cabrera Infante described the book:

> The title is obviously an homage to Raymond Queneau and, at the same time, an advertisement for itself because of its complicated asymmetry. It means many things: the exorcizing of style, exercises in summertime, even the lure of the pen—all in a send-up of *Exercises de Style*. This is one of my favorites among my own books, and it closes the cycle begun in my collected movie reviews, *Un oficio del siglo veinte* (1963). In *Exorcismos*, I expanded my experience (not experiment, a word I loathe when I see it applied to art instead of science) with Havanese, the idiom of *habaneros*, who might perhaps be called *hablaneros* or total talkers. Most of it was written while I was a cultural attaché at the Cuban embassy in Brussels (1962)—and it shows.

The book is an overt homage to Raymond Queneau's playful, surrealist humor, but it is a covert homage to Jorge Luis Borges, who influenced all of Cabrera Infante's writings. *Exorcismos* is a parody of Borges's miscellaneous volume *El hacedor* (1960). That book's title, "the maker," comes from one of its vignettes, about an old soldier who gradually goes blind and becomes a bard, Homer. The story, which reminds us that poet means "maker" in Greek, is also an autobiographical statement: Borges slowly became blind and had to console himself with the image of Homer, the sightless bard who immortalized himself and others through his poems.

*El hacedor* ends with a metaphor. A man spends years drawing a picture of the world. Just as he is about to die, he realizes that the entire enterprise is a self-portrait. Cabrera Infante ends *Exorcismos* not with an "epílogo" but with an "epilogolipo," a word that combines epilogue with "logos," or speech and wisdom. In this, he restates and deforms Borges's epilogue, almost word for word. Where Borges has his artist "draw the world," Cabrera Infante has his "write the world." But the final sentence is identical in both: Art is autobiographical.

*Exorcismos* inverts Borges to find consolation in writing, the only way he can exorcise his demons. He summarizes his attitude in three sentences in "Las viejas páginas" (Old pages): "Old pages are like old snapshots. If they're of you, you feel a curious estrangement when you see them again. In some way, that's you, but you are not exactly yourself" (*Exorcismos*). Not surprisingly, the book is shot through with references to Narcissus, traditional icon of the self-contemplative artist, and to the Minotaur, the beast of two natures imprisoned in the labyrinth, itself a simulacrum of the universe. Cabrera Infante's Minotaur views Theseus, his murderer, as a liberator who will free his intellect from his bestial body. Read autobiographically, the Minotaur is Cabrera Infante liberated from exile and illness, and now able to write again.

Cabrera Infante's literary reputation is not based either on *O* or *Exorcismos*, and they remain relatively unknown, very personal books. His fame derives from his two major novels, *Three Trapped Tigers* and *Infante's Inferno*. In the first phase of his career (the early stories included in *Writes of Passage* and the vignettes included in the manuscript of *Three Trapped Tigers*), he viewed literature as a vehicle for social criticism, while in the second he used autobiography to reconstruct a rapidly disappearing past and its spoken language. The second phase includes the later stories in *Writes of Passage*, *A Twentieth Century Job*, *Three Trapped Tigers*, and *Infante's Inferno*.

Despite this shift away from social criticism to literature as disinterested aesthetic activity, there is a unifying presence in all his works: the controlling voice or directorial presence that first appears in *Writes of Passage* with the character of Silvestre, the author's surrogate. He reappears as the compiler-transcriber of *Three Trapped Tigers*, in which he himself is a character. He is to Cabrera Infante what Cabrera Infante is to Caín in *A Twentieth Century Job*, but there is a moral difference: Silvestre deforms the spoken word by writing it down, just as he betrays his friends by rewriting their words.

Written—actually rewritten, since the published version differs so radically from the original manuscript, itself altered by the Spanish censor—by a man who feels betrayed by the Cuban Revolution, *Three Trapped Tigers* is about betrayal, as Cabrera Infante remarked in the *Paris Review*: "But after all, betrayal is the name of the game in *TTT*: betrayal of life through language and literature. The ultimate betrayal is in translation, of literature, and of language, of life." Systematic and ubiquitous, betrayal is *Three Trapped Tiger*'s organizing principle.

Silvestre, the duplicitous first-person narrator, establishes the framework of betrayal, and the other characters reenact that idea on a personal level. The most important betrayal in the text is the collapsing friendship of the author surrogate and the actor Arsenio Cué. Their mutual betrayal is inevitable because they love the same woman, Laura Díaz. Silvestre and Cué, so different yet turned into doubles because they desire the same woman, is an homage to yet another of Cabrera Infante's favorite authors, Raymond Chandler, whose *The Long Goodbye* (1953) is also about one friend's betrayal of another. Silvestre wins the battle; he must, if only because this is his book.

Professional relationships also entail betrayal; to rise in the entertainment world in which most of them work, the characters must use one another as stepping-stones. Cuba Vanegas, a beautiful woman who is a mediocre singer, uses the bongo player Silvio Sergio Eribó to get her start. Once her career is launched, she drops him in favor of another man who can further her career. The physically grotesque but vocally spectacular Estrella Rodríguez uses the photographer nicknamed Códac to begin her career and forgets she knows him as soon as she is famous.

Betrayal also appears on a purely aesthetic level. The characters work in particular genres, so, for example, they may be seen or heard. Cuba Vanegas is meant to be seen even though she sings, but her story is told by Eribó, whose genre is sound, the bongo drums. Estrella should only be heard even if she appears on stage, but her story is told by Códac, whose medium is the camera. Arsenio Cué is a radio actor, meant to be heard, but his spoken words become visible when Silvestre transcribes them.

Both Silvestre and Cué are saddened when their friend Bustrófedon (a nickname) dies. The latter's art is oral improvisation, so the characters fail miserably when they try to record, with Cué standing in for Bustrófedon, a series of his literary parodies. Silvestre has written them down, and they make up the section of *Three Trapped Tigers* entitled "The Death of Trotsky Told by Several Cuban Writers, Years Later—or Before." That it is Trotsky is doubly significant; his story fascinated Cabrera Infante, who found Trotsky's betrayal by Stalin to be prophetic of his own relationship to the Cuban Revolution. Cabrera Infante contends, in *Mea Cuba* (1992; *Mea Cuba*, 1994), that Ramón Mercader, Trotsky's murderer, was Cuban.

The only stability in the book is the printed word. To transform the spoken word into the written word means killing it; translating the written word into another language entails violence. Only sameness, Narcissus staring at his image in the pool, is safe, but that security is sterile. This explains why there are so many metaphorical allusions to homosexuality in *Three Trapped Tigers*: same combined with same constitutes a static relationship, which is a kind of death.

Unlike the evanescent spoken word that dies in time, the written word endures. So the only possible way to preserve a relationship is to transform it into writing, that is, by killing it. This applies as well to memory, so *Three Trapped Tigers* may be taken as Silvestre's attempt to keep his memory of Havana alive on the eve of the Revolution by, paradoxically, turning it into dead, written words. The novel's epigraph is a slightly modified, translated quotation from *Alice's Adventures in Wonderland*: "Y trató de imaginar cómo se vería la luz de una vela cuando está apagada," which in its original form is "And she tried to fancy what the flame of a candle looks like after the candle is blown out." "Flame" becomes "light," and the violent "blown out" becomes "put out," but the quotation reflects Cabrera Infante's meditation on the lost Havana he loved, which his brother Sabá tried to record in his short film *P.M.* At the same time, it is Silvestre's attempt to avoid Marcel's mystical reexperience of the past in Proust's *À la recherche du temps perdu* and to capture it instead through writing.

*Three Trapped Tigers* is a melancholy novel, but it is by no means sad. It is shot through with comic action and verbal fun, though, paradoxically, the play with language has serious overtones. The fact that all of Cabrera Infante's writing, fiction and nonfiction, is saturated with puns makes unwary readers wonder if he suffers from a rare linguistic disorder. His explanation of why he puns so often is convincing:

> Writing for me, even what you call serious writing, is play. Puns, you see, are words whose meaning depends on play; it's the player who calls the shots. A great player, Lewis Carroll, saw that, but being a reverend he put the words in Humpty Dumpty's mouth. The question about language is not who is right or wrong but, in the old Hegelian scheme, who is the master and who the slave? Puns are my freedom and my control.
>
> (*Paris Review*)

The irony in this statement derives from the fact that so much of Cabrera Infante's verbal humor is the result of his exile, which locates him on the interface between Cuban Spanish and British English. Every moment is a translation, with the translator's place constituting a desert island in a linguistic sea.

This multilingual self-awareness lies at the heart of *Infante's Inferno*. Here the author does to himself what he has already done to Caín. His dead self, the "infante difunto" who punningly replaces the dead infanta, or princess, in Maurice Ravel's "Pavane pour une Infante défunte" ("Pavane for a Dead Infanta"), appears on the dust jacket of the novel. The photograph on the original dust jacket was taken by Cabrera Infante's friend Jesse Fernández in 1948; it shows a street photographer sitting in Havana's Parque Central, the purveyor of souvenirs (memories) transformed into a souvenir. This is yet another metaphor for Cabrera Infante's autobiographical writing, his use of a character within the fiction (Caín, Silvestre) to represent himself. But this self-representation is also self-objectification, because the writer can now deal with the externalized self as another being.

The narrator of *Infante's Inferno* differs from the earlier models because he remains anonymous. That is, he is a traditional first-person, autobiographical narrator in the tradition that runs from Proust back to Sterne, Jean-Jacques Rousseau, and Saint Augustine, though Casanova is clearly a model. The most important factor here is the illusory presence of the speaker and the real presence of the printed page; the human being must die so the text may come into existence.

All first-person narratives derive from a primordial question: Who am I? That is the first sentence of André Breton's *Nadja* (1928), a book usually read as an autobiography rather than a fiction. Like *Infante's Inferno*, it traces the narrator's search for himself through the double pursuit of art and love, but, unlike Cabrera Infante's novel, *Nadja* resolves the narrator's dilemma within a literary tradition. Breton's author-surrogate retains his identity while Cabrera Infante's loses his.

*Infante's Inferno* follows a subspecies of the confessional mode, the consolation, of which Boethius's sixth-century *Consolation of Philosophy* is the paradigm. Such texts develop in a standard fashion. At first, the narrator is spiritually confused, in an identity crisis. He wants help but has no idea about how to find it. Then, either through outside intervention (divine grace, for instance) or through a plunge into his inner self, he begins to organize his personal possibilities. He finds out both who he is not and who he might become. Then he succeeds in discovering or recovering his identity, and the narrative ends. Cabrera Infante parodies that structure, turning it upside down. At the outset, his narrator knows exactly who he is. The divided self of first-person narratives, the "I" who narrates as opposed to the "I" who existed in the past, analyzes himself objectively in the novel's first words:

I, we, went up what was for me then a sumptuous staircase. It was the first time I'd ever walked up a staircase: in my hometown, there were very few houses more than one story high, and those were inaccessible to me. This is my inaugural memory of Havana: going up a staircase whose steps were made of marble.

There is no ambiguity here; the reader enters a retrospective account about a twelve-year-old boy's move from a small town to Havana, from rural poverty to urban poverty. No detail is missing.

Over the course of some seven hundred pages, we follow the narrator's fascination with literature, film, and women. It is one of the longest prose fictions in the Latin American canon. Asked how such a long book could be popular, the author answers:

It is the first truly erotic book written in Spanish—a language and a literature that recoils in horror at living filth. That's what made it a best seller. My first big book, *TTT*, is about friendship, and *La Habana* is about love. . . . But in both books disillusion outlasts love. In *TTT*, friendship breeds betrayal, and in *La Habana* [*Infante's Inferno*], before the flowers of sex fade, sex fades.

(*Paris Review*)

Cabrera Infante's narrator is a Casanova doomed to erotic failure. He makes conquests, but is always flirting with three kinds of disaster: rebuff, sexual catastrophe, and falling in love. Rejection is a minor setback that the narrator can rationalize. Sexual failure is more serious because it entails loss of identity—he cannot be a Don Juan if he cannot fornicate. Falling in love means stopping the cycle of sexual conquests to which Don Juan is chained; this, too, involves loss of identity.

The narrator breaks with a woman, Margarita, who dares him to leave Havana and live with her in another country. To go with her would mean sacrificing himself, a species of suicide. He suggests that she become a lesbian, and she leaves. At that point the narrative breaks off with the narrator embittered but no closer to a metamorphosis. The transformation occurs years later, in the Epilogue, when the narrator follows Margarita into a movie theater. He sits next to her and (as he has done with so many women in theaters) begins to fondle her. The scene begins as a variation on his earlier seductions, until suddenly the narrator loses his wedding ring; it is inside Margarita's sex. Perplexed, he asks her about it, and she calmly tells him to remove it.

He tries, but this time loses his wristwatch. Then he loses his cufflinks. Finally, the exasperated Margarita hands him a flashlight and tells him to crawl inside to retrieve his lost possessions. Astounded but obedient, he does exactly that.

Here realism yields to fantasy. No longer in the superior position of being the narrator in the present describing himself in the past, he describes the impossible: his loss of identity. Inside Margarita, he finds a book, Jules Verne's *Voyage to the Center of the Earth*, whose final pages he begins to read. He never reaches the end, where Verne's characters are expelled from the center of the earth through a volcano—literally reborn from Mother Earth. Instead, the narrator is caught in a whirlpool, loses the book, and is sucked into an abyss: "I began to spin in a whirlwind with no center. Stop! Then there occurred something like a crash into a fault, a death rattle in the cavern, and I fell freely in a horizontal abyss. This is where we came in" (*Infante's Inferno*).

He loses the book because now he is the book. He is nothing but his own words becoming type; the narrator is the text. Margarita is experience, and through her, art is born, but this entails a metamorphosis: the man becomes an artist, who in turn becomes his text. As in Borges's vignette, "Borges and I," the artist's name on the title page of the book is all that remains of him.

In 1979 Cabrera Infante became a British subject. While Cuban Spanish remained his first language, he increasingly wrote directly in English. Examples are radically different texts, *Holy Smoke* (1985), a long, humorous essay on the relationship between cigars and movies (two of the author's personal vices), and "Bites from the Bearded Crocodile," an article that appeared in the *London Review of Books* (June 1981).

"Bites from the Bearded Crocodile," whose title playfully alludes to the Cuban version of the Soviet humor magazine *Krokodil*, called *El caimán barbudo* (The bearded crocodile), denounces the literacy program that the Castro regime proudly declared to be one of its major accomplishments. No enemy of literacy, Cabrera Infante pointed out that knowing how to read is superfluous if readers are not allowed to read whatever they please, that unless literacy is accompanied by intellectual freedom, it is a hoax. The essay goes on to debunk the idea that Castro nurtured art by pointing out how many writers and artists were persecuted during the antihomosexual campaign of 1961. The essay, republished in Spanish in a collection of political articles entitled *Mea Cuba*, sought to balance the idealized picture of revolutionary Cuba painted by its supporters.

As significant as these texts are, they do not suggest the author was abandoning Spanish in favor of English. He continued to produce myriad articles for Spanish and Spanish American newspapers and magazines (*El País* in Spain and *Vuelta* in Mexico, for example) and was a prominent commentator on music (particularly Cuban popular music), movies, and politics (especially Cuban politics). In this he was very much like other novelists who became prominent during the "Boom" of the Spanish American novel in the 1960s, in which Mario Vargas Llosa, Gabriel García Márquez, and Carlos Fuentes figured prominently.

Cabrera Infante's fiction writing after *Infante's Inferno* was dominated by an interminable work in progress, "Cuerpos divinos" (Divine bodies). This unfinished novel is set, like *Three Trapped Tigers* and *Infante's Inferno*, in Havana and takes place between 13 March 1957 and October 1962. The temporal framework commemorates momentous events in Cuban history: the first marks a failed commando raid on Fulgencio Batista's presidential palace by non-Communist guerrillas; the second refers to the Cuban missile crisis that took place during the presidency of John F. Kennedy. For Cabrera Infante, the first event showed the possibility that Batista could have been removed by forces other than those of Fidel Castro, while the second reinforced the author's despair because it confirmed Castro as the absolute leader of the Cuban Revolution.

Cabrera Infante has insisted that "Cuerpos divinos" is neither a political nor a historical novel, that its subject is language, the Spanish spoken in a still free Havana. The novel expands the process set into motion at the end of *Infante's Inferno*, the dispersion of the novelistic authority figure, the author surrogate previously dominant in Cabrera Infante's fiction. Here literary discourse is, literally, free speech, language unfettered from authorial control. This explains, at least in part, why the manuscript has grown so huge that the author despairs of publishing it. If political discourse coupled with power becomes the exclusive prerogative of a single person, the dictator (which derives from the Latin verb *dicere*, to speak), it could be represented by a funnel, through which liquid flows through an increasingly narrow tube: The top half points downward, its power ever narrowing. Literary discourse, as Cabrera Infante envisions it here, inverts that idea: the liquid flows from a source (the author) and spreads everywhere.

The open-endedness of "Cuerpos divinos" has not kept Cabrera Infante from publishing other fiction. *Delito por bailar el chachachá* is simultaneously an anomaly and a throwback in the author's production—an anomaly because it is barely eighty-five large-type pages long and a throwback because it consists of an introduction, three very concise tales (perhaps an echo of Gustave Flaubert's *Trois contes* in their being a digression from novel writing), and an epilogue. It is as if the author were returning to his early short-story career or to the brevity of his film reviews, an inevitable association here because the first two tales seem like directorial "takes" or variations on the same scene—a tense dialogue in a restaurant between a man and a woman at the end of an affair—while in the third a political apparatchik replaces the woman and cultural politics displaces love.

The introduction identifies the central character of each tale as an avatar of the author himself at the time the Castro regime came to power. Nevertheless, the prevailing tone is one of objectivity; that other self belongs to another era:

> The three stories in this book are made up from memories. Two take place at the apogee of the bolero, the third after the fall into the historic abyss. The times are, of course, different, but the space, the geography (or, if you prefer, the topography: all roads lead to love) is the same. The characters are interchangeable, but in the third story the man is more decisive than the woman in the only narrative written in—though it doesn't seem so—the first person.
>
> (*Delito*)

Cabrera Infante's personal notion of history bifurcates: he dates two stories by saying they take place when the bolero is popular, while locating the third in 1961, when the Castro government was tightening control over Cuban culture. Reflecting the author's heightened critical interest in Cuban music, it is music that hovers over the entire book:

> It would have been easy, really, to transpose the last narrative from the first to the third person (both, to be sure, singular persons), and the overall tone would have had more narrative coherence. But I wanted you to read it as a modulation. That is, as "digressions from the principal key," as one musical theory puts it. Cuban music is full of modulations that want to be contradictions of or contrasts to the key, visible or invisible, that sets the rhythm. The movement (and weight) from the *santería* ritual in the first story, which pulls the narrative and the characters along with it, sounds or should sound in the second story like a bolero, a song whose rhythm is barely perceptible because of the literary weight of its lyrics. The third story is brought to its culmination by "dat rhythm wit' no equal." That is, the chachachá.
>
> (*Delito*)

Cuban music and Cuban history are one, but the book, unlike the author, is optimistic. The first two stories concern a failed adulterous relationship, but the last ends with the beginning of a love affair that promises to be eternal.

Cabrera Infante's love affair with Cuban music has engendered myriad journalistic pieces but as yet no book. The Spanish critic and journalist Rosa Pereda and the Cuban critics-in-exile Enrico Santí and Nivia Montenegro have in effect taken the first step for the author. Pereda is the editor of the anthology *Mi música extremada*, containing fragments of Cabrera Infante's works up to 1996—with the exceptions of *Mea Cuba*, whose theme is politics, and *Holy Smoke*, which is in English—and editorial notes that explain the musical references contained in the fragments. The anthology's title is a complex reference to the sixteenth-century Spanish poet Fray Luis de León, whose "Ode to Salinas" (a music professor at the University of Salamanca) referred to the "exalted music" Salinas produced. "Exalted" is a poor translation of "extremada," which means "brought to an extreme point." In Cabrera Infante's revision, the music becomes "mi música extremada," my exalted and, by extension, distanced (by exile) music.

If *Mi música extremada* confirms the absolute intertwining of music, history, autobiography, and fiction in Cabrera Infante's literary output, his essays constitute the battlefield he has staked out for himself with Castro's Cuba. In 1993 Cabrera Infante published "Guantanamerías (sobre un emblema musical de los años sesenta)" (Guantaneramas [on a musical emblem of the sixties]), an article Santí and Montenegro included in their *Infantería* (1999). This essay is a superb example of using historical investigation to debunk political mythology.

The issue was the song, "La Guantanamera," whose lyrics derive from a poem by José Martí, hero and martyr in Cuba's struggle for independence from Spain. The song had been appropriated by the Left to rally support for the Cuban Revolution; it was even sung in London in 1968 by the actress Vanessa Redgrave, who announced it as a song written by a Cuban patriot named "Joseph Marty, a friend of Fidel Castro." The fact that José Martí had died in 1895 was symptomatic not only of Redgrave's ignorance but also of the fact that politics transforms art into propaganda.

Cabrera Infante delightedly pointed out that the creator of "La Guantanamera" was Julián Orbón, a Spaniard whose mother was Cuban. In 1962 a Cuban named Héctor Angulo, who had heard Orbón sing the song, sang it for the American folk singer and political activist Pete Seeger. Seeger recorded it in 1963, attributing it to himself and Angulo. Orbón won a two-and-a-half-year lawsuit for theft of intellectual property but received nothing but posthumous recognition and Cabrera Infante's wistful vindication of his talent.

As the twenty-first century begins, Guillermo Cabrera Infante might justifiably be bitter. With the collapse of the Soviet Union and the end of the cold war, a new era in European politics began. Cuba, however, remains under the tutelage of Fidel Castro, so the exile remains in exile. The fact is, however, that Cabrera Infante is neither a bitter man nor a bitter author; he realizes that exile turned a Cuban magazine editor into a world-class novelist. Personal happiness and professional success do not necessarily go hand in hand. The consolation, for both the author and his readers, is that from the crucible of hideous experience has emerged a magnificent body of writing.

## SELECTED BIBLIOGRAPHY

### Primary Works

#### Fiction and Nonfiction

"Aguas de recuerdo." *Bohemia*, 13 June 1948, pp. 20–21, 64–66.

"Resaca." *Bohemia*, 5 October 1952, pp. 23–24, 114.

"Balada de plomo y yerro." *Bohemia*, 19 October 1952, pp. 23–24, 127–129.

*Así en la paz como en la guerra.* Havana: Editiones R, 1960. (All quotations from this work are taken from the 1971 edition published in Spain.)

*Un oficio del siglo veinte.* Havana: Editiones R., 1963.

*Tres tristes tigres.* Barcelona: Editorial Seix Barral, 1967.

*Vista del amanecer en el trópico.* Barcelona: Editorial Seix Barral, 1974.

*O.* Barcelona: Editorial Seix Barral, 1975.

*Exorcismos de esti(l)o.* Barcelona: Seix Barral, 1976.

*Arcadia todas las noches.* Barcelona: Editorial Seix Barral, 1978.

*La Habana para un infante difunto.* Barcelona: Editorial Seix Barral, 1979.

"Bites from the Bearded Crocodile." *London Review of Books* 3, no.10:3–8 (June 1981).

*Holy Smoke.* London: Faber, 1985.

*Mea Cuba.* Barcelona: Plaza and Janés, 1992.

*Delito por bailar el chachachá.* Madrid: Santillana, 1995.

*Cine o sardina.* Madrid: Alfaguara, 1997.

#### Collected Works

*Mi música extremada.* Edited by Rosa M. Pereda. Madrid: Espace Calpe, 1996. (A selection of texts by Cabrera Infante related to music.)

*Infantería.* Edited by Nivia Montenegro and Mario Enrico Santí. Mexico City: Fondo de Cultura Económica, 1999. (A massive anthology of Cabrera Infante's fiction and nonfiction, including a chronology by Cabrera Infante listing significant moments in his life from his birth in 1929 to 1998.)

#### Translations

*Three Trapped Tigers.* Translated from the Spanish by Donald Gardner and Suzanne Jill Levine in collaboration with the author. New York: Harper & Row, 1971. (The English translation of *Tres tristes tigres*.)

*Infante's Inferno.* Translated by Suzanne Jill Levine. New York: Harper & Row, 1984. (The English translation of *La Habana para un infante difunto.*)

*View of Dawn in the Tropics.* Translated by Suzanne Jill Levine. London: Faber, 1988. (The English translation of *Vista del amanecer en el trópico.*)

*A Twentieth Century Job.* Translated by Kenneth Hall and the author. London: Faber, 1991. (The English translation of *Un oficio de siglo veinte.*)

*Writes of Passage.* Translated by John Brookesmith, Peggy Boyars, and the author. London: Faber and Faber, 1993. (The English translation of *Así en la paz como en la guerra.*)

*Mea Cuba.* Translated by Kenneth Hall and the author. London: Faber and Faber, 1994. (The English translation of the Spanish work of the same name.)

*Puro humo.* Translated by the author and Iñigo García Ureta. Madrid: Santillana des Ediciones, 2000. (The Spanish translation of *Holy Smoke.*)

*Unpublished Screenplays*

"Vanishing Point," 1969. (Film released in 1971.)
"Under the Volcano," 1972. (Unproduced.)

*Secondary Works*

*Critical and Biographical Studies*

González Echevarría, Roberto. *The Voice of the Masters: Writing and Authority in Modern Latin American Literature.* Austin: University of Texas Press, 1985.

Goytisolo, Juan. "Lectura cervantina de *Tres tristes tigres.*" In his *Disidencias.* Barcelona: Seix Barral, 1978.

*Ideas '92: A Journal to Honor 500 Years of Relations among Spain, Latin America, and the United States,* no. 10 (spring 1992). (Contains a lecture by Cabrera Infante titled "El ave fénix en el paraíso" and studies by Raymond D. Souza, Alfred Mac Adam, Kenneth Hall, and Ardis Nelson.)

Levine, Suzanne Jill. "Three Trapped Tigers and a Cobra." *Modern Language Notes* (Hispanic issue) 90, no. 2:265–277 (March 1975).

———.*The Subversive Scribe: Translating Latin American Fiction.* Saint Paul, Minn.: Graywolf Press, 1991.

Ludmer, Josefina. "*Tres tristes tigres:* Órdenes literarios y jerarquías sociales." *Revista Iberoamericana* 108–109: 493–512 (July–December 1979).

Mac Adam, Alfred. "Guillermo Cabrera Infante: The Vast Fragment." In his *Modern Latin American Narratives:*

*The Dreams of Reason.* Chicago: University of Chicago Press, 1977.

Merrim, Stephanie. *Logos and the Word: The Novel of Language and Linguistic Motivation in "Grande Sertão: Veredas" and "Tres tristes tigres."* Utah Studies in Literature and Linguistics, vol. 23. New York: P. Lang, 1983.

Nelson, Ardis. *Tres tristes tigres y el cine.* J. M. Hill Monograph Series, no. 3. Bloomington: Department of Spanish and Portugese, Indiana University, 1976.

———. *Cabrera Infante in the Menippean Tradition.* Newark, Del.: Juan de la Cuesta, 1983.

———, ed. *Guillermo Cabrera Infante: Assays, Essays, and Other Arts.* New York: Twayne, 1999. (A compendium of critical essays showing late-twentieth-century developments in Cabrera Infante studies.)

Oviedo, José Miguel. "Nabokov/Cabrera Infante: True Imaginary Lives." *World Literature Today* 61, 559–567 (autumn 1987).

Ríos, Julián. *Guillermo Cabrera Infante.* Madrid: Editorial Fundamentos, 1974. (Includes essays by Julio Ortega, Julio Matas, Luis Gregorich, Emir Rodríguez Monegal, and David Gallagher.)

Santí, Enrico Mario. *Por una politeratura: Literatura hispanoamericana e imaginación política.* Mexico City: Consejo Nacional para la Cultura y las Artes, Ediciones del Equilibrista, 1997.

Siemens, William L. "*Heilsgeschichte* and the Structure of *Tres tristes tigres.*" *Kentucky Romance Quarterly* 1, 77–90 (1975).

Souza, Raymond D. *Guillermo Cabrera Infante: Two Islands, Many Worlds.* Austin: University of Texas Press, 1996. (An extremely valuable work because of its biographical information and its extensive bibliography of works by and about Cabrera Infante.)

*Interviews*

Guibert, Rita. *Seven Voices: Seven Latin American Writers Talk to Rita Guibert.* Translated by Frances Partridge. New York: Vintage, 1973. (Includes an introduction by Emir Rodríguez Monegal.)

Mac Adam, Alfred. "The Art of Fiction LXXV." *Paris Review,* no. 87:154–195 (spring 1983).

Siemens, William L., comp. "Guillermo Cabrera Infante: Man of Three Islands." *Review* 8–11 (January–April 1981).

# Ernesto Cardenal

## (1925–    )

## *Alan West-Durán*

A writer of rich, fruitful, even visionary contradictions, Ernesto Cardenal might seem puzzling to some: a priest whose most famous poem is about Marilyn Monroe; a Marxist and a Catholic who is heretical to both of those traditions. Furthermore, Cardenal is an anti-imperialist Sandinista poet profoundly influenced by U.S. literature; a Christian who has written works exalting the virtues of pre-Columbian culture and mythology; a deeply spiritual, inward being with mystical inclinations whose aesthetic focuses on the world in all its myriad concrete details, which he labels "exteriorist." He even embodies these contradictions literally: he looks more like a beatnik (beret, long hair) than a priest (he never wore a cassock). As far as Cardenal is concerned, he is merely embracing the layered and complex realities of life, a life and work that mirror the convulsive history of Nicaragua and Central America since the 1950s. He is one of Latin America's most widely read poets.

Cardenal's work is an amalgam of political commentary, spiritual fervor, and mystical utopianism, written in a vivid montage/cinematic style that is both learned and accessible. Some of his less favorable critics have claimed that his verses border on propaganda, that the spirituality seems half-baked, and that his utopian yearnings are well-intentioned but naive. But none can deny his pervasive influence on Latin America's cultural scene since the 1960s.

Cardenal's life seemed destined for poetry by geography, tradition, and family. In an interview he claimed to have begun writing poetry at the age of four. Two of his cousins were major poets: Pablo Antonio Cuadra and José Coronel Urtecho. His grandmother, Doña Agustina, was extremely cultured and an avid reader. Cardenal was born in Granada, Nicaragua, on 20 January 1925, and spent several years of his childhood in León, where Rubén Darío spent several years. Rubén Darío was Nicaragua's most cherished poet and a leader of the modernismo movement in Latin America, which lasted from about 1880 to 1920. If that were not sufficient, he also witnessed the haunting presence of another Nicaraguan poet, Alfonso Cortés (1893–1969), who "inherited" Darío's house, lost his mind by 1927, and remained insane for the rest of his life. Cardenal, who later edited and anthologized Cortes's work (1970), remembers him being chained to a roof beam of the house. Cardenal quotes Cortés often in his monumental *Cántico cósmico* (1989; *Cosmic Canticle*, 1993).

At age seventeen, Cardenal was sharing his lyrical and surrealist love poems in literary *tertulias* (informal literary gatherings), and during that period, according to Pablo Antonio Cuadra, wrote the long poem "La ciudad deshabitada" (1946; The uninhabited city). It centered on a love betrayal, and the poet's reaction (in the poem) was to set Granada in flames. Although it made him a known poet, he has refused to publish the poem.

In 1943 Cardenal studied at the National Autonomous University in Mexico City and obtained a licentiate in letters with a thesis on Nicaraguan poetry in 1947. In the period 1943–1945 he wrote more love poetry ("Carmen y otros poemas"; Carmen and other poems) that is still unpublished. In Mexico he worked with anti-Somoza groups in exile. He returned to Nicaragua, then studied at Columbia University in New York City (1947–1949), where he was exposed to poets such as Ezra Pound, William Carlos Williams, and Charles Olson, who had a decisive influence on his work. By 1949, Cardenal's social commitment was overtly expressed in poems such as "Raleigh."

"Raleigh" reveals many features of Cardenal's later work: a Poundian penchant for mixing genres, a use of documentary (archival, historical, archaeological) material, a supple and often humorous use of nonpoetic language (statistics, newspaper headlines, advertising slogans), a complex nonindividualistic poetic voice. Drawing on Raleigh's accounts of the exploration of what is now Guyana, Cardenal crafts a poem that captures the sense of adventure and wonder in "discovering" unknown lands, as well as some of the hardships and disappointments, all narrated with a highly musical and often alliterative flair. In another poem from that period, "With Walker in Nicaragua," Cardenal assumes the voice of a colleague of William Walker, the nineteenth-century filibuster who wanted to conquer Nicaragua and annex it to the South as a slave state. Walker was captured and executed in 1857.

Cardenal's most important work from the 1950s is *Hora 0* (1960; *Zero Hour and Other Documentary Poems*, 1980), written from 1954 to 1956. A poem in four parts, it begins with an almost hallucinatory recollection of Central America under the military dictatorships of Jorge Ubico (Guatemala), Tiburcio Carías (Honduras), and, of course, Anastasio Somoza in Nicaragua. It is a landscape of curfews, spies, troops in the streets, and the cries of prisoners being tortured in police stations laid out in a spare, descriptive tone. The second part focuses on the United Fruit Company and its far-reaching control of the region, arm-twisting local producers to lower their price for bananas. Its corrupt influence even infects the language, a claim that Cardenal makes after quoting the bureaucratese of a company document. The third section tells the story of Augusto César Sandino, his seven-year guerrilla war against U.S. forces (1926–1933) and his subsequent ambush and assassination by Somoza. The fourth part is autobiographical, retelling the failed "April Conspiracy" of 1954, in which Cardenal participated. Many of its leaders were captured and tortured and Cardenal had to go into hiding.

In 1956 Cardenal suffered two crises with both political and personal dimensions: a woman he loved decided to marry a Somoza ambassador, and Somoza was the godfather of the wedding. Less than four months later, Somoza was assassinated by Rigoberto López Pérez. Shaken, Cardenal experienced a spiritual transformation, which he described as God revealing himself as a lover to him, and himself as surrendering. In 1957 he joined the Trappist monastery in Gethsemane, Kentucky, where he met Thomas Merton. He resonated to Merton spiritually, aesthetically, and politically. Although Cardenal strongly denounced all forms of injustice, he was committed to nonviolence. In 1959, without being ordained, he left the monastery for health reasons. With the Trappists he was not allowed to write poetry, but he did make sculptures.

A year later, however, he wrote and published *Gethsemani, Kentucky* (1960), a book of some thirty haiku-like poems and sketches. His *Epigramas* (1961; *Epigrams*, 1978) were mostly written from 1952 to 1957; some were written in the 1940s. Both books were published while he was at a Benedictine monastery in Cuernavaca, Mexico.

The epigrams were well received, and are an intriguing and original blend of love and politics, although the portrayal of women now seems antiquated. The book encompasses some fifty poems ranging from one to fourteen lines, and draws on the epigrammatic tradition in being brief, witty, and/or sardonic. No doubt Catullus's Clodia is echoed by Cardenal's Claudia. Passion for a loved one (Claudia, Myriam) and passion for politics (specifically anti-Somoza politics) form a suggestive echoing. As in *Zero Hour*, Cardenal continues to refer to how tyranny distorts language and how important it is for poets to safeguard the vitality and communicative promise of the word, to ensure that it builds a community of justice.

The 1960s was a productive decade for Cardenal. Aside from the Gethsemane poems and *Epigrams,* he published four more books of poems and a meditative essay, *Vida en el amor* (1970; *To Live Is to Love,* 1972). *Salmos* (1964; *Psalms,* 1981), published in Colombia, was a key work in establishing Cardenal's reputation throughout Latin America. Using the biblical tradition, Cardenal refashions twenty-six hymns from the Old Testament, songs of lamentation, praise, supplication, entreaty, and collective deliverance. For example, Psalm 43 states:

> Vindicate me, O God, and
> defend my cause
> against an ungodly people;
> from deceitful and unjust men
> deliver me!
> For thou art the God in whom I take refuge;
> why hast thou cast me off?
> Why go I mourning
> because of the oppression of the enemy?

Cardenal's "Salmo 43" deals with the Jewish people, but recontextualizes it within the Holocaust experience in wrenching and apocalyptic terms. He ends by asking God why he has hidden his face, imploring the Lord to wake up and help, in order to restore his former prestige. It is a typical strategy of this book, a wry, sardonic way of stating that the biblical traditions are still relevant to the present, and also still carry within them a profound prophetic thrust.

In a more jocular tone, Cardenal ends with "Salmo 150," actually a "close" paraphrase of the original, which sings praises to the Lord and his creations, and asks us to do so to the accompaniment of music.

> *Alabadle con el violín y la flauta*
> *y con el saxofón . . . alabadle con blues y jazz*
> *y con orquestas sinfónicas*
> *con los espirituales de los negros*
> *y la 5ta. de Beethoven*
> *con guitarras y marimbas*
> *alabadle con tocadiscos*
> *y cintas magnetofónicas.*

> Praise him with violins and flutes
> and with the saxophone . . . Praise him with
>     blues and jazz
> and with symphony orchestras
> with Negro spirituals
> and Beethoven's 5th
> with guitars and marimbas
> Praise him with record players
> with tapes.

While the original uses the word "firmament," Cardenal mentions interstellar space, atoms, galaxies, and light-years. An analogous expression occurs with the music: instead of lutes, harps, cymbals, and trumpets, Cardenal has violins and saxophones, pianos, guitars and marimbas. He invokes the blues, jazz, spirituals, Beethoven's Fifth Symphony, and cassettes. He ends exactly as the original but replaces "everything that breathes" with "every living cell." Cardenal's juxtaposition of two different times is a recurrent strategy in his poetry, as it also throws into sharp relief changes in language (specifically, religious and scientific in Psalm 150) and worldviews. The superimposition, or ideogrammatic effect, as Pound would say, makes the modern reader look at what is taken for granted nowadays (technology, transportation, production, and science) in a refreshing or new way.

In the *Psalms,* Cardenal expounds a reading of the Bible that addresses issues of poverty, oppression, social injustice, and political tyranny, anticipating liberation theology texts by Gustavo Gutiérrez and Leonardo Boff. As Tamara Williams states: "Besides revealing Himself in history, the God of the Bible is a God who not only governs history, but who orients it in the direction of the establishment of justice and right. He is more than a provident God, He is a God who actively sides with the poor and the afflicted in their struggle for liberation from misery, poverty, slavery, and oppression" ("Ernesto Cardenal," 1994). God provides the spiritual and ethical underpinning for social change. For Cardenal, as well as others, liberation theology was not merely another way of reading the Bible, but a call to action. And that action must be initiated, nourished, and carried out by the poor and the oppressed themselves, not by the paternalism of the liberal state, nor by a well-intentioned but authoritarian revolutionary vanguard.

With these goals in mind, Cardenal returned to Nicaragua in 1965 to preach and spread these authentic Christian values. On 15 August he was ordained, and soon after he began searching for a place in which to establish a community of believers. Our Lady of Solentiname was founded on 16 February 1966, on the island of Mancarrón in Lake Nicaragua. The inhabitants, including Cardenal, lived modestly, prayed, planted, and painted. Since the community was small and relatively isolated, the Somoza regime did not initially find its presence threatening.

Cardenal published *Oración por Marilyn Monroe y otros poemas* (1965; *Marilyn Monroe and Other Poems*, 1975) and *El estrecho dudoso* (1966; *The Doubtful Strait*, 1995). The Monroe poem, probably his most famous and most often anthologized, is a trenchant criticism of consumerism, advertising, and the Hollywood star system. Cardenal feels sorrow (and rage) for Monroe, and, in the vein of the *Psalms* (he is praying, conversing with God), says we are at fault for Monroe's suicide. He claims Marilyn acted out the script we gave her, and it was an absurd script, to be sure. Drawing on the clichés of the movie industry, linked to the image of her corpse with her hand on the telephone, he ends forcefully imploring God to answer the telephone. Another poem from the collection, "Apocalipsis" (Apocalypse), has the poet hearing an angel prophesying nuclear destruction and doom, illustrating what critic Ronald Christ has called "the poetry of useful prophecy."

In *The Doubtful Strait*, Cardenal turns to the painful history of the Spanish conquest. Though the focus is Mexico and Central America, specifically Nicaragua, its relevance to the rest of Latin America is unquestionable. In twenty-five cantos, Cardenal draws on the histories or chronicles of the period: Columbus's diary and letters, Bernal Díaz del Castillo's *Historia verdadera de la conquista de Nueva España*, Bartolomé de las Casas's *Historia de las Indias*, Francisco Fuentes y Guzman's *Recordación florida*, Francisco López de Gómara's *Historia general de las Indias*, Pedro Mártir de Anglería's *Décadas del orbe novo*, Antonio de Remesal's *Historia general de las Indias*, and other less well-known documents. Cardenal also uses the Mayan book of prophecies, *Los libros del Chilam Balam*. The book spans from 1492 to 1609, and many incidents are written or commented on to draw parallels to more recent historical events.

Cardenal often quotes whole passages from the original texts, retaining archaic usages and spelling, as well as the erratic punctuation of the times, mixed in with modern Spanish usage. The work has an epic dimension, even if it is presented like a vast "cinematic mural." There are scenes from the conquest of Guatemala; we witness Cortés's (and La Malinche's) role in the subjugation of Mexico and Central America; in canto XVIII we see Las Casas plead his case and the plight of the indigenous peoples before the king of Spain. We also hear of different indigenous leaders: Panquiaco (canto IV), Nicaragua (canto VI), Cuauhtémoc (canto VIII), and Lempira (canto XVII).

Perhaps one of the most dramatic segments is canto XXIV, which narrates the events pertaining to Rodrigo de Contreras (and his sons Hernando and Pedro). Rodrigo had been appointed governor of Nicaragua by Charles I (Emperor Charles V) in 1534. However, his rule was so arbitrary, cruel, and abusive that the citizens of Granada, Las Casas, and the bishop of Nicaragua, Antonio Valdivieso, petitioned the king for his removal ten years later. Rodrigo was stripped of his title and possessions in 1548; his son Hernando sought revenge, murdered Valdivieso not long after, and, with his brother, Pedro, attempted to make himself ruler of all the region from Mexico to Chile. In Panama he was killed by royalists and decapitated, and his head was exhibited in a cage. Cardenal's matter-of-fact tone makes the story even more chilling; but, being more than just a tale of perfidy and greed, canto XXIV foreshadows more recent events in Nicaraguan history, such as William Walker in the nineteenth century and the Somoza dynasty of the twentieth. The following segment paraphrases the period documents:

> *"Los agravios de los indios son cotidianos"*
>               *(en julio de 45)*
> *Escribe en duplicado, en la misma nao,*
>   *por la censura. . . . Porque hay censura en Nicaragua.*
> *Interceptan las cartas. . . . Espionaje, etc.*
> *La provincia es pobre, no por falta de riquezas*
>   *(dice) sino de buen gobierno.*
> *Por los que han gobernado desasosegando la tierra*
>   *(pobladores i conquistadores por igual).*

"Affronts to the Indians occur daily"
(in July of 45)
He writes in duplicate, aboard the ship itself,
because of censorship. . . . Because there is
    censorship in Nicaragua.
They intercept the letters. . . . Spying, etc.
The province is poor, not for want of riches
(he says) but of good government.
Because of those who have governed creating
    unrest in the land
(settlers and conquistadors alike).

Cardenal's use of historical documents allows him to delve into a church that defended the human rights of indigenous peoples, as well as a prophetic tradition of redemption and hope, buttressed in the text by references to the Mayan prophecies of the *Chilam Balam.* The book ends with an eerie description of Cardenal's native Granada, an accursed and excommunicated city (because of Archbishop Valdivieso's murder) being "punished" by the eruption of the Momotombo volcano. Women become infertile, there is a plague, and, because of the eruption, the waters of the lake are rising as the city sinks into sulfurous oblivion. As always, for Cardenal there is a glimmer of hope as he describes one of the walls of the city with Valdivieso's bloodied handprint.

In *The Doubtful Strait* Cardenal achieved a double purpose. His socially committed Catholicism allowed him to portray the indigenous peoples as the Christs of Latin America, those who have been crucified by history, subjected to cultural genocide and colonial oppression. Second, since God reveals himself and acts in and through history, it became important for Cardenal to reexamine Latin American history because it was written by the victors. Analogous to revisiting the biblical tradition of the Psalms, Cardenal revisits and rewrites history from the perspective of those silenced, vanquished, or unable to have their accounts written down, whether in Spanish or in their own languages. A next step in that rewriting and revisiting was his *Homenaje a los indios americanos* (1969; *Homage to the American Indians,* 1973), in which Cardenal, after both personal and scholarly research, attempts to celebrate the ethos of pre-Columbian societies of North, Central, and South America: the Kunas (or Cunas) in Panama and Colombia; the Maya in Mexico, Guatemala,

Honduras, and Belize; the Aztecs in Mexico; the Incas in Peru; the Pawnees in Texas and the Great Plains; and the Iroquois in the northeastern United States.

The book begins with "Nele of Kantule" (1870–1944), a leader and medicine man of the Kuna. Cardenal's interest in the Kuna is manifold. First, he has visited them on several occasions. Second, they are one of the few indigenous peoples to have risen up against an established Latin American government and acquired a large degree of autonomy to run their own affairs. In 1925, led by Nele, they carried out the revolution of Tule and, using the United States as a mediator, they were granted schools, medical aid, trade with Colombia, and a "hands off" policy in their internal affairs. Third, the Kuna have maintained their traditions, but have also embraced modernity. For example, Kuna women weave *molas* (ancestral cloth weavings), known the world over for their bright, colorful, and imaginative designs. Usually the designs are abstract or represent the flora and fauna of the region, but in the last decades *molas* have depicted spaceships, President John Kennedy, Tony the Tiger, Teenage Mutant Ninja Turtles, and even bras. This unabashed transculturation seems consistent with Cardenal's poetic-ideogrammatic strategy of superimposing ancient or traditional texts and worldviews on those of modern technology and society, as was the case with *Psalms* and *The Doubtful Strait.*

In a more lyrical vein, "Los cantares mexicanos" ("Mexican songs I & II") are written from the point of view of Nezahuacóyotl (1402–1472), a ruler of Texcoco, poet, and philosopher. Cardenal glosses Nezahuacóyotl's poems, with their rich imagery of flowers, the plumage of the quetzal, and sacred drums that is often mixed with rueful meditations on the brevity of life. It is followed by the poem "Nezahuacóyotl," which is more biographical, although it also draws on some of the poet's writings.

In the poems on North American indigenous peoples, Cardenal focuses on their abilities to live in peace and fashion systems of governance, as well as on their struggles against loss of land, culture, and lives. Though the poems in *Homage to the American Indians* idealize their societies and beliefs, and in some instances make false claims (that the Maya did not use forced labor),

Cardenal never gives in to sentimentality or condescension, and the non-Eurocentric view they convey is both challenging and engaging.

Cardenal's ideogrammatic techniques in both *The Doubtful Strait* and *Homage to the American Indians,* in their radically eclectic views and representations of history, exemplify what Fernando Ortiz might have called a transculturated view of Latin American history. Cardenal's fluid historical epistemology incorporates European, indigenous, and African viewpoints within a modern perspective that questions fixed and essentialist notions of truth and objectivity.

In 1970 Cardenal published *To Live Is to Love,* with an introduction by Thomas Merton (which dates from 1966). It is a crucial book that enables us to understand the religious and mystical side of the author, and certainly merits more study. A series of poetically written meditations, each from one to eight pages long, that dwell on different aspects of love, usually with its divine connotations, it can be read as a series of love letters to God. Many of its images or metaphors turn up later in Cardenal's poetry. For example, in *To Live Is to Love,* references to cosmic rhythms being rhythms of love prefigure *cantiga* 20 ("Music of the Spheres") in *Cosmic Canticle* (1989). In the latter poem Cardenal writes:

> *La música de las esferas.*
> *Un universo armonioso como un arpa.*
> *El ritmo son tiempos iguales repetidos.*
> *El latir del corazón.*
> *Día/noche.*
> *. . . La materia es música.*
> *Materia en movimiento en espacio y tiempo*
> *Rítmico los corazones y astros.*
> *El universo canta y lo oyó Pitágoras.*
> *. . . más que música clásica música de jazz*
> *La danza alborotada de cosas.*
> *. . . El calor es movimiento. Unicamente*
> *la energía del movimiento de las moléculas,*
> *únicamente el movimiento de las moléculas individuales.*
> *Y el amor, que es calor, es movimiento.*

> The music of the spheres.
> A harmonious universe like a harp.
> Rhythm is equal beats repeated.
> The beating of the heart.
> Day/night.

> . . . Matter is music.
> Matter in perpetual motion in space and time.
> Rhythmic hearts and stars.
> The universe sings and Pythagoras heard it.
> . . . a music closer to jazz than to classical music.
> The disorderly dance of things.
> . . . Heat is movement. Merely
> the energy of molecules in motion,
> merely the movement of individual molecules.
> And love, which is heat, is movement.

Similarly, references to novas and the laws of thermodynamics in section 23 of *To Live Is to Love* remind us of the scientific bent of the later poem, *Cosmic Canticle.* In another segment, his descriptions of the sounds, the voices of nature (birds, volcanoes, clouds, trees) remind one of the onomatopoeic descriptions of birds in *Canto nacional* (1972). In another section (113) he quotes the passage from the Bible (Luke 9:24) that inspired the title of his memoirs, *Vida perdida* (1999).

By 1970, Cardenal's work had matured, and exhibited the traits that would be predominant in his later writings. Cardenal has referred to his aesthetic as "exteriorist," which he contrasts to a type of poetry that is oneiric, surrealist, laden with metaphor, and somewhat hermetic. The translator and critic Robert Pring-Mill sums it up admirably in "The Redemption of Reality through Documentary Poetry":

> All Cardenal's poetry "debunks," "corroborates," and "mediates" reality. His esthetic principles are clearly ethical, and most of his poems are more than just "vaguely" religious. . . .
>
> But all eight texts of *Zero Hour* . . . set out to "document" reality (and so redeem it) in a more dialectically visual way: picturing things, peoples, and events in the light of a clear-cut sociopolitical commitment; selecting, shaping and imposing interpretative patterns on the world, with liberal use of such filmic "editing" techniques as crosscutting, accelerated montage, or flash frames; and pursuing the "redemption of physical reality" by bringing us "back into communication" with its harshness and its beauty. . . . Cardenal's recording of the present or the past is aimed at helping to shape the future—involving the reader in the poetic process in order to provoke him into full political commitment, thus fostering the translation of the poet's more prophetic visions into sociopolitical fact.

As stated before, this montage or superimposition (temporal, historical, linguistic) of details, realities, or images gives the reader an epistemological jolt. Redemption (of the past) is intertwined with revolution (changing the present, building a future); a poet must help this revolution come about. Perhaps this is what Merton had in mind when he said, "There is no revolution without poets who are also seers. There is no revolution without prophetic song" (Strout, "Nuevos cantos de vida y esperanza"). In a poem from the mid-1970s, Cardenal said, "Revolucíon / que para mí es lo mismo que reino de Dios." (Revolution / which for me is the same thing as the kingdom of God; *Zero Hour*).

Other critics, such as Isabel Fraire (1976) and Paul Borgeson (1995), have pointed out other stylistic traits in Cardenal's poetry: focusing on the concrete and suggestive detail (going from the specific to the general); the importance of the visual aspect of the poem (extending lines; the use of pictograms, as in VVVVVVV for birds in flight or asterisks to symbolize stars); the use of unadorned language or even prosaic language (headlines, scientific jargon, obscenities, statistics, words in other languages). Cardenal almost always abandons the personal lyric voice of poets; his "documentary" voice is almost detached, unsentimental in a Brechtian sense. In terms of the construction of lines, rhythms, and so on, Cardenal uses free verse, often fragments the lines in unusual ways, and often achieves interesting rhythms through repetition and alliteration. Rhetorically speaking, he does not often use metaphor or hyperbaton (where the normal order of words is changed), but he often uses similes and synechdoche with great effect (besides anaphora and alliteration).

Much has been made of Pound's influence on Cardenal (to which he readily admits), and though he borrowed many of Pound's techniques and shared his anticapitalist views, Cardenal's poetry is quite different: not only his "redemption of reality" (or the past) and his prophetic voice in combating injustice, but also his respect and compassion for the reader. To read and understand Cardenal, you don't need to be an expert in Chinese ideograms, Italian poetry, Confucian philosophy, Japanese Noh theater, and Egyptian and Provençal love poetry. Clearly, knowing something about pre-Columbian cultures and the history of Latin America will help the reader of *The Doubtful Strait* or *Los

ovnis de oro: Poemas indios* (1988; *Golden UFOs: The Indian Poems*, 1992), but they are not indispensable. Most of his oeuvre is quite understandable and engaging, given the right amounts of curiosity, empathy, and sense of outrage.

Cardenal's poem "Coplas a la muerte de Merton" ("Verses on the Death of Merton") reveals many of these attributes. He begins with "Nuestras vidas son los ríos / que van a dar a la muerte / que es la vida" (*Nueva antología poética de Ernesto Cardenal*, 1992; Our lives are rivers / that empty into the sea / which is life), a reworking of the famous poem by the Spanish poet Jorge Manrique titled "Coplas a la muerte de mi padre." Yet Cardenal adds the following in the next two lines: "Tu muerte más bien divertida Merton / (o absurda como un koan?)" (Your more or less diversion(ary) death Merton / [or is it absurd like a koan?]). The word *divertida* can mean both a diversion or a distraction, but also something amusing. Only the reference to Zen koans in this poem keeps it from being flippant. Merton was Cardenal's mentor, and the poem is certainly a heartfelt homage to him. Cardenal could also be referring to Merton's *Mystics and Zen Masters* (1961), which has a chapter on Zen koans.

Further on, Cardenal tries to understand death from a Christian and Zen perspective, saying that we often sleepwalk through life transfixed by desire:

> *Hemos deseado siempre más allá de lo deseado*
> *Somos Somozas deseando más y más haciendas*
> *More More More*
> *y no sólo más, también algo "diferente"*
> *Las bodas del deseo*
> *el coito de la volición perfecta es el acto*
> *de la muerte.*

> We have always desired beyond what is desired
> We are Somozas desiring more and more haciendas
> More More More
> and not only more, but also something "different"
> The nuptials of desire
> the coitus of a perfect will is the act
> of death.

Similar to the mystical beginning of his poem "La noche" ("The Night"), Cardenal evokes St. John of the Cross and his dark night of the soul torn asunder by desire. But he also mentions the desire beyond what is desired, which would be the love of God.

Cardenal gives full reign to these thoughts, equating love (desire beyond desire), death, and contemplation later in the poem:

> Sólo en los momentos en que no somos prácticos
> concentrados en lo Inútil, Idos
> se nos abre el mundo.
> La muerte es el acto de la distracción total
> también: Contemplación.
> El amor, el amor sobre todo, un anticipo
> de la muerte
> Había en los besos un sabor a muerte
> ser
> es ser
> en otro ser
> sólo somos al amar
> Pero en esta vida sólo amamos unos ratos
> y débilmente
> Sólo amamos o somos al dejar de ser
> al morir.

> Only in the moments we are not practical
> concentrating on the Useless, Gone
> is the world opened to us.
> Death is the act of total distraction
> also: Contemplation.
> Love, above all love,
> an advance
> on death
> A taste of death in the kisses
> being
> is to be
> for other beings
> we can only be by loving
> But in this life we only love a few moments
> and weakly
> We only love or can be by ceasing to be
> by dying.

Cardenal is being both literal and metaphorical about this death, and this tension gives this segment and the poem as a whole its verve. As a counterpoint, he refers to consumerist culture as being necrophiliac ("[cadáveres, máquinas, dinero, heces] / y si sueñan con una mujer es en la imagen / de un automóvil"; [corpses, machines, money, feces] / and if they dream of a woman it's in the image / of an automobile).

In these quoted segments (and in other works) Cardenal exhibits the standard traits of mysticism: an active and practical yearning for the absolute, the attainment of a transcendental and spiritual state of consciousness, the ultimate reality of love, the remaking of one's self in order to obtain a unitive state with God, the abolition of ego and ambition. If a mystic becomes self-seeking, according to St. John of the Cross, then he becomes a "spiritual glutton," a Somoza of desire, sentiments also echoed in Merton's insightful essay "False Mysticism." Yet Cardenal departs from traditional mysticism by leaving the world as it is; he wants to change the world, believing that revolution and spiritual transcendence cosmically join in Teilhard de Chardin's omega point.

But not all is mystical in "Coplas a la muerte de Merton." Cardenal's use of capitalization (NO EXIT, MAKE IT NEW, THE AMERICAN WAY OF DEATH, SIGN OF JONAS, YANKI GO HOME, GONE WITH THE WIND, *C-I-T-R-O-E-N*, WE REGRET TO INFORM YOU) at crucial junctures in the poem not only accentuate a point, but also show his rather promiscuous borrowings from high and low culture and everything in between, from the Bible, Sartre, Pound, political slogans, movie titles, and advertising, to the telegram that informs him of Merton's death.

Cardenal's borrowings are done with a breathtaking velocity, in what critics have called his collages, cinematic montages, and flash frames.

> la ciudad bajada del cielo que no es Atlantic City—
> Y el más allá no es un American Way of Life
> Jubilación en Florida
> o como un Week-end sin fin.
> La muerte es una puerta abierta
> al universo
> No hay letrero NO EXIT
> y a nosotros mismos
> (viajar
> a nosotros mismos
> no a Tokio, Bangkok
> es el appeal
> stewardess en kimono, la cuisinev
> Continental
> es el appeal de esos anuncios de Japan Air Lines)
> Una Noche Nupcial, decía Novalis
> No es una película de horror de Boris Karloff

*Y natural, como la caída de las manzanas*
*por la ley que atrae a los astros y a los amantes*
*—No hay accidentes*
        *una caída del gran Arbol*
*sos una manzana más*
*Tom.*


the city descended from the heavens is not
        Atlantic City—
                And the Hereafter is not the American
        Way of Life
                        Retirement in Florida
or like an endless Week-end.
Death is an open door
to the universe
                No sign saying NO EXIT
and to ourselves
                        (traveling
        to our selves
                not to Tokyo, Bangkok
                        that's the appeal
                stewardess in a kimono, the cuisine
Continental
is the appeal of those Japan Air Lines ads)
        · A Nuptial Night, said Novalis
Is not a horror film starring Boris Karloff
And natural, like apples falling
because of the same law that attracts stars
        and lovers
—There are no accidents
                        another fall from the
        great Tree
you are just one more apple
Thud.


Here Cardenal mixes philosophical statements with prosaic language and constructs his collages by spatially ordering the lines to throw the reader off balance, as well as skillfully cutting in with parentheses to interrupt the natural flow of the verses. The beginning ("the city descended from the heavens") is also a reference to Merton's remarkable poem "The Heavenly City." Cardenal also uses English, onomatopeia, and repetitions effectively, all filtered through his objective and documentary voice. A truly complex meditation on death (and life) that draws not only on Christian mystical thought, Zen, indigenous religions (Comanches, Koguis), the poem also situates itself within modern times by addressing World War II, Vietnam,

and credit-card capitalism. All of this is done poignantly, with humor, even irreverence, and yet at the same time the poem radiates with spirituality.

Cardenal's second conversion, as he claims, came during a three-month trip to Cuba in the summer of 1970. Invited to be a juror for the prestigious Casa de las Américas poetry contest, Cardenal published his observations as *En Cuba* (1972; *In Cuba*, 1974). Here is what he said of this new transformation: "It was like another conversion. I had discovered that nowadays in Latin America to practice religion meant to make revolution. There can be no genuine Eucharist without a classless society.... Also, I had seen that in Cuba socialism allowed one to live according to Scripture in society." Although Cardenal was pleased with the general course of the Cuban Revolution (health, education, culture), he did notice certain things that disturbed him. Catholics were not admitted to the university or to the Communist Party; there was a stifling bureaucracy, abuses of power, censorship, and many shortages of goods. (Not to mention Cardenal's mistaking unity of purpose for a crippling kind of conformity or a Franciscan disdain of wealth for economic ineptitude or mismanagement.) Most important for Cardenal, his Cuban experience convinced him that genuine social change in Latin America could be accomplished only by violent means. Increasingly he spoke of a convergence of Marxism and Catholicism as belief systems committed to transforming unjust structures and creating societies where human solidarity and spirituality reigned.

Cardenal's *Canto nacional* (1972; "Nicaraguan Canto" in *Zero Hour and Other Documentary Poems*, 1980) is an extraordinary confluence of the poet's love of nature, religious beliefs, fascination with history, deep admiration for indigenous cultures, and increasingly revolutionary political commitment. The poem is dedicated to the FSLN (Sandinista National Liberation Front). Stylistically, the poem is more lyrical than most of his work, but it is strongly characterized by Poundian collages and "nonpoetic language," as well as by a strong Nerudian influence (mostly, but not exclusively, from his *Canto general*). Clearly Cardenal's bucolic years at Solentiname inspired the exhaustive depictions of birds and birdsong that suffuse the poem. Running over 800 lines, *Canto nacional*, after an initial evocation of the fauna and flora of the country, quickly shifts into the area of political economy with a telling line: "But another country found it needed all these riches" (*Zero Hour*).

Cardenal then concentrates on how the banks, and then the U. S. Marines, took over Nicaragua. While some of the images of the U.S. imperial designs are not original (vultures, sharks), Cardenal's overall strategy successfully shows how one country can control another without overt military occupation. But Cardenal is not interested in showing Nicaragua just as a victim, but as actively and successfully resisting U.S. domination in the figure of Augusto César Sandino. In a passage of the "Nicaraguan Canto" that foreshadows his *Cosmic Canticle*, Cardenal says:

> La Revolución empezó en las estrellas, a millones
> de años luz. El huevo de la vida
> es uno. Desde
> el primer huevo de gas, al huevo de iguana, al
>     hombre nuevo.
> Sandino se gloriaba de haber nacido del "vientre de los
>     oprimidos"
> (el de una indita de Niquinohomo).
> Del vientre de los oprimidos nacerá la Revolución
> Es el proceso.

> The Revolution started in the stars, millions
> of light-years away. The egg of life
> is one. From
> the first bubble of gas, to the iguana's egg, to
>     the New Man.
> Sandino was proud he had been born from the
>     "womb of the oppressed"
> (that of an Indian girl from Niquinohomo).
> From the womb of the oppressed the Revolution
>     will be born.
> It is the process.

Cardenal returns to one of the etymological roots of the word "revolution," but more important is his vision that revolution is a cosmic process, one that will sometimes take a long time to gestate, but then quickly burst into history, propelling monumental changes (a new society, a new human being).

In typical fashion, Cardenal quotes the Bible, Ruben Darío, Sandino, Wall Street brokers, newspaper headlines, the *Popol Vuh*, the Tupamaros' political program,

the Nicaraguan poet-revolutionary Leonel Rugama, the Nicaraguan "Vanguardist" poet Joaquín Pasos, the sixteenth-century Spanish chronicler of the Indies Gonzalo Fernández de Oviedo, and other historical documents or chronicles. One key concept, *kupiakumi*, the Miskito Indian word for "love," which means "all-one-heart," is woven into the poem beautifully, not only to speak about love (which Cardenal also equates with revolution) but also as an overarching metaphor for Nicaragua's spirit of resistance and the efforts of its artists and activists to build a national culture and psychic wholeness. Although unjustly neglected and little studied compared with some of his major works, *Canto nacional* reveals a remarkable synthesis of all the dimensions of Cardenal's work.

A year later, Cardenal's *Oráculo sobre Managua* ("Oracle over Managua," also in *Zero Hour and Other Documentary Poems*) appeared, and, as in *The Doubtful Strait*, Cardenal establishes parallels between natural and historical events. On 23 December 1972, Managua was hit by a devastating earthquake that killed thousands and left tens of thousands homeless. The corruption of the Somoza regime was manifested by its clumsy and greedy handling of the aid efforts. It was to be one of the events that catalyzed the decline and eventual downfall of the Somoza family dynasty, which lasted forty-five years (1934–1979). Although Cardenal does not dwell on the details of the earthquake, its devastation and aftermath form the backdrop of the poem. Initially, the poem focuses on Acahualinca, a slum area of Managua that is also the site of prehistoric footprints of men and animals fleeing a volcanic eruption.

> Allí empieza Acahualinca, las casas de cartón y lata
> donde desembocan las cloacas . . .
> Calles oliendo a cárcel
> ese olor característicos de las cárceles, a
> mierda y orines rancios
> casas de bolsas de cemento, latas de gasolina, ripios
> trapos viejos.

> Acahualinca begins there, the houses of
>     cardboard and cans
> where the sewers empty . . .
> Streets that smell of jails,
> that characteristic jail smell
> of shit and urine

houses of cement bags gasoline cans rubble
  old rags.

Cardenal then begins to work in quotes from the poet Leonel Rugama (1949–1969) until he explicitly mentions Rugama, who said "Revolution is communion with the species." Midway through the poem Cardenal narrates the story of Rugama, an ex-seminary student turned FSLN guerrilla who held off over 200 National Guardsmen for several hours before he was killed in a shootout. Rugama's well-known poem "The Earth Is a Satellite of the Moon" is quoted by Cardenal in the poem. Rugama's poem also refers to generations of the poor who have lived in Acahualinca. Even in a country with such an extraordinary poetic tradition as Nicaragua's, Rugama became a kind of poetic-political saint within the Sandinista pantheon.

"Oracle over Managua" is one of Cardenal's most militant poems, peppered with quotes from or references to Che Guevara, Mao Tse-tung, and Fidel Castro. Despite the devastation (Cardenal describes Managua as one big Acahualinca after the quake), the poem ends on a positive note:

> Sólo los muertos resucitan
> Otra vez hay otras huellas: no ha terminado la
>   peregrinación
> A medianoche una pobre dio a luz un niño sin techo
> y ésa es la esperanza
> Dios ha dicho: "He aquí que hago nuevas todas
>   las cosas"
> y ésa es la reconstrucción.

> Only the dead are reborn.
> Once more there are more footprints: the
>   pilgrimage has not ended.
> At midnight a poor woman gave birth to a baby in
>   an open field
> and that is hope.
> God has said: "Behold I make all things anew"
> and that is reconstruction.

Cardenal published no poetry between 1973 and 1981 (two years after the Sandinistas took power). However, there are two letter-poems from that period, printed in *Zero Hour,* that merit mention, one to Pedro Casáldiga, and another to José Coronel Urtecho. Both poems are unusual in that they are among the few instances where Cardenal's poetry takes on a first-person voice. The first, "Epistle to Monsignor Casáldiga" (1974), written to the Brazilian liberation theology priest, begins in a very personal tone (rarely does Cardenal refer to himself in the first person). It also confronts a serious political situation, one in which the author had unwittingly been implicated.

> Monseñor:
> Leí que en un saqueo de la Policía Militar
> en la Prelatura de São Félix, se llevaron, entre
> otras cosas, la traducción portuguesa (no sabía
> que hubiera) de Salmos de Ernesto Cardenal. Y
> que a todos los detenidos han dado electrodos
> por Salmos que muchos tal vez no habían leído.
> He sufrido por ellos, y por tantos otros, en
>   "las redes de la muerte . . . los lazos del Abismo"
>     Hermanos míos y hermanas
> con la picana en los senos, con la picana en el pene.
> Le diré: esos Salmos aquí también han sido prohibidos
> y Somoza dijo hace poco en un discurso
> que erradicaría el "oscurantismo" en Solentiname.

> Monsignor:
> I read that in the sacking by the Military Police
> In the Prelature of São Félix, they carried
>   off, among
> other things, the Portuguese translation (I didn't
> know there was one) of *Psalms* by Ernesto
>   Cardenal. And
> that all those arrested were given electric schocks
> for Psalms that many had perhaps not read.
> I have suffered for them, and for so many others, in
>   "the nets of death . . . the snares of
>   the Abyss"
>     My brothers and sisters
> with the goad at your breasts, with the goad at
>   your penis.
> I will tell you: those Psalms have been
>   banned here too
> and Somoza said a short while ago in a speech
> that he would eradicate the "obscurantism" of
>   Solentiname.

The mention of his work is not mere authorial vanity: Cardenal admits responsibility for the fact that people who had the *Psalms* were tortured. It is a heartfelt admission that literature, least of all his own, is not innocent. It is a poem-letter of encouragement to Casáldiga and the Brazilians in the hope that ultimately they will rid themselves of their military dictatorship, and it also contains one of the most succinct and devastating definitions of capitalism: "Sube el precio de las cosas / y baja el precio de los hombres" (The price of things goes up / and the price of people goes down).

The second letter-poem, "Epistle to José Coronel Urtecho" (1975), is not quite as effective, but it has some verses which help define Cardenal's oeuvre and aesthetic. The poem's optimism may sound quaint today—for example, when Cardenal claims that private enterprise will soon be a thing of the past. However, a third of the way into the poem there is a segment that brings Cardenal's religious and political commitments into sharp focus:

> Le han dicho que yo ya sólo hablo de política
> No es de política sino de Revolución
> que para mí es lo mismo que reino de Dios.

> They've told me I talk only about politics now.
> It's not about politics but about Revolution
> which for me is the same thing as the
> kingdom of God.

For Cardenal, the liberating and transformative dimensions of revolution go far beyond politics, a theme that is present later in his *Cosmic Canticle.* Speaking about poetry and prose in *Zero Hour,* he prefers the former:

> I prefer verse, you know, because it's easier
> and briefer
> and the people understand it better, like posters.

Cardenal had met Carlos Fonseca Amador, one of the founding members of the Sandinistas (the FSLN was founded in 1961) in the late 1960s, and although he sympathized with the FSLN's aims, he personally could not commit to violence. In 1975 he published the first of four volumes titled *El evangelio en Solentiname* (1975–1977; *The Gospel in Solentiname,* 1978–1982), containing poetry, commentary on scripture, and paintings. By 1976 Cardenal was a member of the FSLN, but not carrying arms. A planned Sandinista insurrection in 1977 brought the retaliation of the Somoza government, which bombed and subsequently destroyed

Cardenal's community in Solentiname. Cardenal went into exile in Costa Rica.

Cardenal's return to Nicaragua was part of the Sandinista revolutionary triumph of 19 July 1979. Quickly, he became Nicaragua's minister of culture, a position he held until 1988. As minister he oversaw massive campaigns to involve Nicaraguans from all walks of life in the cultural life of the country, most notably the National Poetry Workshops and the Galleries of People's Art. Cardenal saw these and other efforts as a democratization of culture, and drew a sharp contrast to the United States: "The U. S. has made business its culture, and culture its business. In Nicaragua, on the other hand, we've made Revolution our culture, and our culture a Revolution" (White, *Culture & Politics in Nicaragua*). Many (including himself) thought his revolutionary duties would leave little time for writing, but Cardenal published *Tocar el cielo* in 1981, then later reworked it into the longer *Vuelos de Victoria* in 1984 (*Flights of Victory,* 1988); *Golden UFOs: The Indian Poems* in 1988; and his lengthy magnum opus *Cosmic Canticle* in 1989, only a year after he left office.

*Flights of Victory,* though not his best book, nevertheless has remarkable poems in it. Many of them deal with the Sandinista revolution before and after its triumph, yet even the most political poems are suffused with wit, lyrical passages of great beauty, and rueful parables on everything from love to revolutionary martyrdom. In "Reflexiones de un ministro" ("Reflections of a Minister") Cardenal is on the way to an embassy reception when the car headlights illuminate the eyes of a cat along the road, eliciting feelings of wanting to be with the cat. The jolt of this image makes him think of Marianne Moore's cat poem, but almost immediately afterward the moment vanishes and Cardenal is greeting the ambassador. Cardenal's playful, skillfully crafted intertextual musing is both a brief primer on poetry and a deft commentary on his conflicting loyalties: service to art and to revolution.

Even a political parable like "Las loras" ("The Parrots"), which recounts the tale of the birds being smuggled illegally to the United States, where they would learn English, is done with a light touch.

> Mi amigo Michel es responsable militar en Somoto,
> allá por la frontera con Honduras,

*y me contó que descubrió un contrabando de loras*
*que iban a ser exportadas a EE.UU.*
> *para que allí aprendieran inglés.*
*Eran 186 loras, y ya habían muerto 47 en sus jaulas.*
*. . . Los compas verdes como loras*
> *dieron a las loras sus*
*montañas verdes.*
> *Pero hubo 47 que murieron.*


My friend Michel is the military leader in Somoto,
> there near the border with Honduras,
and he told me he discovered a contraband
> shipment of parrots
set for export to the U.S.
> so that there they would learn to speak
English.
There were 186 parrots, and 47 had already died in
> their cages.
. . . Our brother soldiers green like parrots
> gave the parrots their green
mountains.
> But there were 47 who died.


Cardenal uses both the inherent comic nature of parrots and their imitative traits to draw a political parallel between the parrots and Nicaraguans, and finishes with the sad fact that 47 of the 186 birds had died. The survivors flew off into the green mountains, which returns to the central metaphor of the book: the flights of victory, freedom, and the imagination.

The Sandinista revolution had many Catholic militants in its ranks. The increased polarization between certain sectors of the church and adherents of liberation theology came to a head with the pope's visit to Nicaragua in 1983. There is an unforgettable photo of Cardenal at the Managua airport, kneeling in reverence to Pope John Paul II, with a beatific smile on his face. The pope has a lifted finger, as if scolding him, while President Daniel Ortega, in his Sandinista fatigues, looks anxiously on, behind and to the right of the pope. The pope requested that Cardenal resign from his post as minister of culture, which he refused to do, and in 1985 the Vatican suspended him (and others) from being able to administer the sacraments. The prohibition still stands.

In 1988, financially pressed, the Nicaraguan government downgraded the Ministry of Culture to an institute. Cardenal resigned, and devoted himself more to his writing. He had been a cultural and political ambassador for Nicaragua all over the world, trying to build solidarity with the Sandinista revolution. His work was translated into German (since 1967), Russian, French, Czech, Italian, English, Portuguese, and at least five other languages.

*Golden UFOs: The Indian Poems* is an expansion of Cardenal's earlier *Homage to the American Indians*. It includes the original sixteen poems, plus fourteen new ones. The newer poems include the title poem; a long poem, "Quetzalcóatl"; and "The Secret of Machu Picchu." "Golden UFOs" derives from conversations Cardenal had with the Kunas. Their mythologies speak of a hero or demigod coming down from the sky on a golden cloud. However, in more recent times they claim the same hero descended in a golden flying saucer or UFO. Cardenal loved the image and decided, true to the Kunas' "postmodern traditionalism," to use it as the title of the new version.

"Quetzalcóatl" was originally published separately in 1985, in a handsomely illustrated volume honoring the author's sixtieth birthday. By far the longest poem in the collection, it radically historicizes Quetzalcóatl, whose name means Plumed Serpent in Náhuatl. Quetzalcóatl was a major divinity, the most important religious, cultural, and historical figure of the pre-Columbian area that today stretches from Mexico to Nicaragua. He was a key figure for the Olmecs (1100 B.C.–200 B.C.), the natives of Teotihuacán (200 A.D.–850 A.D.), the Zapotecs in Monte Alban (100 B.C.–900 A.D.), the Toltecs in Tula (950–1250 A.D.), the Mixtecs and Aztecs, and for all the Mayan peoples in Yucatán, southern Mexico, Guatemala, Belize, and Honduras. Initially he was portrayed as a deity in the form of an animal (a serpent with feathers), but by the Late Classic period (600–900 A.D.), he began to assume human form, with a conical cap, wind jewelry (a conch), and other shell jewelry. Quetzalcóatl's powers were manifold; he is linked to major creation myths closely associated with maize, water, wind, being both an earth and sky god (in Mayan "serpent" and "sky" carry the same meaning). Also a scribe and a sage, he is linked to writing, the arts, and philosophy.

From the beginning of the poem, Cardenal asks which form of the divinity we are going to talk about.

The deity of wind, creation, and the arts? The one who set himself on fire and reappeared as the morning star? The one who vanished but vowed to return during the epoch of the Fifth Sun? The priest-ruler of Cholula who taught metallurgy and social ethics? The one who was rejected by the sorcerers because he rejected human sacrifice?

In the final part of the poem Cardenal addresses Quetzalcóatl's displacement by Huitzilopochtli, a warrior god, under the Aztec empire (1325–1519 A.D.). He describes how Quetzalcóatl became a useful, manipulative tool by the Aztec ruling classes, as part of their sacrificial ideology. It is interesting to note that Cardenal sees Quetzalcóatl as someone who believes in self-sacrifice, not the sacrifice of others, and that earlier in the poem he links Quetzalcóatl to Christ. Montezuma pays for this abandonment of the Quetzalcóatl legacy, and his regret becomes interwoven with the crushing blow of Cortés's imperial conquest. Mexico and Mesoamerica are still recovering from that oversight, which Cardenal calls "the historicity of myth." The poem ends: "Carrasco calls him subversive." Not only is Cardenal revealing his sources (David Carrasco's *Quetzalcóatl and the Irony of Empire*, 1982), but the term "subversive," with obvious positive connotations for the revolutionary Cardenal, also points to the fact that the figure of Quetzalcóatl changed over time and place. Cardenal suggests that myth is not atemporal or ahistorical and that it is risky to see it as such, whether from an anthropological, a cultural, or a political perspective.

Cardenal's *Cosmic Canticle* was published in 1989. Probably the longest poem written in twentieth-century Latin American letters (David Huerta's *Incurable* comes close), it weighs in at over nineteen thousand lines, almost twice as long as Goethe's *Faust* but less than Alonso de Ercilla's sixteenth-century epic *La Araucana* (1569–1589). Dividing it into forty-three *cantigas*, Cardenal constructs a vast canvas that begins with the Big Bang theory of the universe (*cantiga* 1), moves on to the Word in *cantiga* 2, and finishes with a cosmic convergence reminiscent of Teilhard de Chardin's omega point some 570 pages later. *Cosmic Canticle* is a philosophical poem that attempts to unite religion, science, and poetry, and understandably has been compared to Lucretius's *De Rerum Natura* as well

as Dante's *Divine Comedy*. One could add Goethe's *Faust* in the spirit of George Santayana's *Three Philosophical Poets*. Despite the similarities with Lucretius (his interest in the material world), Cardenal is not a materialist, philosophically speaking. Lucretius was loath to credit any godly or divine presence in the universe; Cardenal finds God in neutrons, sees a Pythagorean miracle in the cosmic dance of the music of the spheres, and feels the divine breath in all living creatures.

But critics have perhaps overlooked Latin American precedents: Sor Juana Inés de la Cruz's *Primero sueño*, a baroque masterpiece that combines both theology and the science of her times, and Nezahuacóyotl (ca. 1402–1472), ruler, poet, and philosopher of Texcoco to whom Cardenal had dedicated a poem in his *Homage to the American Indians* twenty years before. Despite the modern scientific terminology (quasars, subatomic particles, asteroids, supernovas), the feel of Cardenal's poem is more of a pre-Socratic philosopher like Anaxagoras or Heraclitus, or of God-intoxicated mathematician-philosophers like Leibniz and Spinoza. Furthermore, Cardenal draws on the cosmologies and myths of the indigenous populations of the Americas, from the Kuna in Panama to the Hopi in the United States.

Cardenal's largest debt is to Pierre Teilhard de Chardin (1881–1955), the French paleoanthropologist, priest, and philosopher. Like his predecessor, Cardenal aims to show that evolution and Christianity are not antithetical. Also similar is their belief in a spiritual energy that all elements in the cosmos possess, from subatomic particles to human beings. Within his evolutionary framework, Teilhard de Chardin also spoke of a new thinking layer ("noosphere"), distinct from but superimposed on the biosphere. This noosphere would eventually become a planetary Hyperpersonal Consciousness, an omega point of convergent integration, an integration made possible by love, or the spirit of Christ in nature. All of this is evident throughout *The Cosmic Canticle*, and in the last *cantiga* (43, also called "Omega") Cardenal refers to Chardin and his ideas.

But not all is cosmic wonder in the poem. *Cantiga* 24 ("A Latin American Documentary") is a litany of imperial chicanery, military oppression, torture, and squalor. *Cantiga* 21, "Robber Barons," details the economic despoiling of Nicaragua. "Flights of Victory," *cantiga* 18, narrates the difficult struggle by the FSLN to overthrow the Somoza dictatorship, ending with the names of the martyred who died in combat. *Cantiga 32*, "In the Heavens There Are Dens of Thieves," focuses on consumerism, capitalist wastefulness, and ecological devastation of the planet. But ultimately, as in most of his work, Cardenal believes in resurrection, redemption, and revolution. In *The Cosmic Canticle*, animal, human, religious, and scientific spirits unite in a cosmic dance of celebration and insurrection.

The critic Steven F. White has suggested that *The Cosmic Canticle* is "amorphous, poorly edited and shares none of the precision and refinement of Dante's poem [*The Divine Comedy*]"; and should be compared to "Pound's botched magnum opus, the *Cantos*" ("Ernesto Cardenal"). Clearly the poem could have benefitted from editing (so would many of Cardenal's longer poems published over his career), but the comparison with Pound is only superficially correct. Cardenal's *Cosmic Canticle*, despite its operatic sprawl, is much more coherent thematically, structurally tighter, ideologically more focused and philosophically more cogent than Pound's work, not to say much more accessible and easier to comprehend, even if it requires considerable physical and intellectual stamina of the reader. White also suggests that incorporating many of the poems (all but three) from *Flights of Victory* marred the longer and more ambitious text. There is some truth to this observation, but overall they make up less than 10 percent of *Cosmic Canticle*. Cardenal ardently defends their inclusion in the volume, arguing that they support his views on the convergence of revolution and mysticism.

After the Sandinistas were voted out of power in 1990, interest in Nicaragua and in Cardenal seemed to vanish, although translations of his work continued to appear. In 1993 *Telescopio en la noche oscura*, a book of poems, was published in Spain. Cardenal was still politically active, but internal divisions within the FSLN prompted him to resign (1994), as well as to revoke the rights and royalties to his works which he had given to the FSLN. In his resignation letter Cardenal stated that the FSLN was being run in a despotic, "verticalist," and authoritarian manner, and he denounced a lack of ethical standards, corruption, and the theft of public funds. He still considers himself a

revolutionary and a Sandinista, but is not a member of the Frente Sandinista. In a radio interview, when asked about the Sandinistas' chances of success in the next elections (2002), he replied:

*No puedo predecir, creo que van a la derrota con el candidato con el que van [Daniel Ortega], y es una derrota merecida, se la han buscado. Ellos se están suicidando, traicionando al pueblo con el secuestro de la Revolución y la venta de los ideales y la traición a los muertos.*
(Interview with Milvian Jerez, Radio La Primerísima, Managua, 17 March 2001)

I can't predict, but I think they are headed for defeat with the candidate they are running [Daniel Ortega], and it's a defeat they deserve; they've brought it on themselves. They are committing suicide, betraying the people by hijacking the Revolution, selling their ideals and betraying the dead.

Cardenal has devoted more and more time to his sculptures, which have a charming, Brancusian touch, and is writing a three-volume memoir. In 1996 new anthologies of his poetry were released, and in 1998 his correspondence with Thomas Merton was published in Chile as *Del monasterio al mundo: Correspondencia entre Ernesto Cardenal y Thomas Merton (1959–1968)*.

The first volume of his memoirs, *Vida perdida*, which runs to over 450 pages, was published in 1999, first in Nicaragua, then in Spain. Written with an almost disarming simplicity, it covers the first half of his life (1925–ca. 1961) unsparingly, without any trace of nostalgia and with considerable humor, often directed at himself. The English title would be "A Lost Life," which has intrigued many, but Cardenal explains by quoting Luke (9:23–24): "If any man will come after me, let him deny himself and take up his cross daily, and follow me. For whosoever will save his life will lose it; but whosoever will lose his life for my sake, he will save it." Undoubtedly, Cardenal's autobiography is concerned with the choices and sacrifices he made to become a priest. This first volume begins with his first conversion, in 1956, to become a Trappist monk. An early section talks about his youthful loves and gives useful information on some of the romantic circumstances that inspired his *Epigrams* and, much later, segments of his *Cosmic Canticle*. Cardenal then moves on to his years in Mexico and New York; the personal, political, and spiritual crisis that took him to Gethsemane; and his friendship with the poet Ernesto Mejía Sánchez.

Cardenal spends almost a quarter of the book narrating with immense detail his daily life at Gethsemane, as well as his growing relationship with Thomas Merton. It is followed by a section of his thoughts and writings during that period, many almost aphoristic in their brevity. His period in Cuernavaca, Mexico, with the Benedictines is remembered, including undergoing psychoanalysis. Jumping back in time, Cardenal returns to his childhood and early adolescence in Granada and León. *Vida perdida* ends thus: "Espero en vos, Amor, que esta vida, en más de un sentido perdida, sea después de todo una vida ganada" (I place my hope in you, Love, that my life, in so many ways lost, will be, after all, a life gained). The book's popularity prompted a second printing of the Nicaraguan edition in 2000.

No longer a political militant in the strict sense, Cardenal still closely follows and comments on national and international affairs. Though aware of the shortcomings of one-party socialist regimes, he is still deeply committed to a mystical utopianism and Marxism, and is harshly critical of neoliberal economic policies in Latin America. He stated his position thus:

> El artista ha estado siempre perfectamente integrado en la sociedad. Pero no en la de su tiempo, sino en la del futuro. El artista, el poeta, el sabio y el santo son miembros de la sociedad del futuro que existe ya en el planeta como una semilla, aunque dispersa—con independencia de las particiones de la geografía política—aquí y allá en individuos y pequeños grupos. Como poeta—en la medida que lo soy—, como el sacerdote que trato de ser, y en lo político como pacifista, anarquista cristiano y seguidor de Gandhi, me siento bien integrado en esa sociedad que acerca el futuro y quiere llevar a su plenitud el proceso de progreso tan rápidamente como sea posible . . . contra los poderes caducos.
>
> (quoted in Solle, *Salmos*, 1998)

The artist has always been perfectly integrated into society. But not that of his times, but of the future. The artist, the poet, the sage, and the saint are members of a future society that exists on the planet as a seed, though scattered here and there in individuals or in groups, and independent of geopolitical divisions. As a poet—to the degree that I am one—, as the priest I try to be, and in the political realm as a pacifist, anarchist Christian and follower of Gandhi, I feel quite part of a society that brings the future nearer and that wants to fully bring to fruition this progress as quickly as possible . . . against the senility of established powers.

Even though most Latin American countries have rid themselves of military dictatorships that were all too numerous in the 1970s and 1980s, Cardenal's critiques of poverty, social injustice, racism, illiteracy, and inadequate health care still resonate among many Latin Americans. Perhaps chastened by political disillusionment, Cardenal now draws more and more on the social and ethical dimensions of the Bible and other religious sources. Whether expressed in cosmic-philosophical works of epic length, or in shorter, collage-like satirical sketches, Cardenal's poetry elicits an intensity of feeling, a need for reflection, and a call to action that is refreshing, insightful, and compassionate.

## SELECTED BIBLIOGRAPHY

### Primary Works

#### Poetry

*Gethsemani, Kentucky.* Mexico City: Revista de Poesía Universal, 1960.

*Hora O.* Mexico City: Revista Mexicana de Literatura, 1960.

*Epigramas.* Mexico City: UNAM, 1961.

*Salmos.* Medellín, Colombia: Universidad de Antioquía, 1964.

*Oración por Marilyn Monroe y otros poemas.* Medellín, Colombia: La Tertulia, 1965.

*El estrecho dudoso.* Madrid: Ediciones Cultura Hispánica, 1966.

*Mayapán.* Managua: Editorial Alemana, 1968.

*Homenaje a los indios americanos.* León: Universidad Autonóma de Nicaragua, 1969.

*Canto nacional.* Managua: Colección COUN, 1972. (Clandestine.)

*Oráculo sobre Managua.* Buenos Aires: Ediciones C. Lohlé, 1973.

*Tocar el cielo.* Managua: Lóguez, 1981.

*Nostalgia del futuro.* Managua: Editorial Nueva Nicaragua, 1982.

*Vuelos de victoria.* Madrid: Editorial Visor, 1984.

*Quetzalcóatl.* Managua: Editorial Nueva Nicaragua, 1985.

*Los ovnis de oro: poemas indios.* Mexico City: Siglo XXI, 1988.

*Cántico cósmico.* Managua: Editorial Nueva Nicaragua, 1989.

*Telescopio en la noche oscura.* Madrid: Editorial Trotta, 1993.

*Antología Nueva.* Madrid: Editorial Trotta, 1996.

## Prose

*Vida en el amor.* Buenos Aires: Ediciones C. Lohlé, 1970.

*En Cuba.* Buenos Aires: Ediciones C. Lohlé, 1972.

*El evangelio en Solentiname.* 2 vols. Salamanca: Ediciones Sígueme, 1975–1977.

*La paz mundial y la revolución de Nicaragua.* Managua: Ministerio de Cultura, 1981.

*La democratización de la cultura.* Managua: Ministerio de Cultura, 1982.

*Del monasterio al mundo: Correspondencia entre Ernesto Cardenal y Thomas Merton (1959–1968).* Edited by Santiago Daydí-Tolson. Santiago, Chile: Editorial Cuarto Propio, 1998. (Letters.)

*Vida perdida.* Barcelona: Seix Barral, 1999. Reprint, Managua: Editorial Nueva Nicaragua, 1999; 2nd edition, 2000.

## Translations

*To Live Is to Love.* Trans. by Kurt Reinhardt. New York: Herder and Herder, 1972. Also trans. by Dinah Livingstone as *Love. Vida en el amor.* London: Search Press, 1974.

*Homage to the American Indians.* Trans. by Carlos Altschul and Monique Altschul. Baltimore: Johns Hopkins University Press, 1973.

*In Cuba.* Trans. by Donald Walsh. New York: New Directions, 1974.

*Marilyn Monroe, and Other Poems.* Trans. by Robert Pring-Mill. London: Search Press, 1975.

*The Gospel in Solentiname.* 4 vols. Trans. by Donald Walsh. Maryknoll, N.Y.: Orbis Books, 1976–1982.

*Apocalypse and Other Poems.* Trans. by Robert Pring-Mill, Donald Walsh, Thomas Merton, Kenneth Rexroth, and Mireya Jaimes-Freyre. Edited by Robert Pring-Mill and Donald Walsh. New York: New Directions, 1977.

*Epigrams.* Trans. by K. H. Anton. New York: Lodestar Press, 1978.

*Zero Hour and Other Documentary Poems.* Trans. by Paul W. Borgeson, Jr., Donald Walsh, Jonathan Cohen, and Robert Pring-Mill. Edited by Donald Walsh. New York: New Directions, 1980.

*Psalms.* Trans. by Thomas Blackburn et al. New York: Crossroads, 1981.

*With Walker in Nicaragua and Other Early Poems* (1949–1954). Trans. by Jonathan Cohen. Middletown, Conn.: Wesleyan University Press, 1984.

*Flights of Victory.* Edited and trans. by Marc Zimmerman with Ellen Bamburger, Mirta Urroz et al. Willimantic, Conn.: Curbstone Press, 1988.

*Golden UFOs: The Indian Poems.* Trans. by Carlos Altschul and Monique Altschul. Edited by Russell O. Salmon. Bloomington: Indiana University Press, 1992.

*Cosmic Canticle.* Trans. by John Lyons. Willimantic, Conn.: Curbstone Press, 1993.

*The Doubtful Strait.* Trans. by John Lyons. Bloomington: Indiana University Press, 1995.

## Secondary Works

### Critical and Biographical Studies

Borgeson, Paul W., Jr. "Bibliografía de y sobre Ernesto Cardenal." *Revista Iberoamericana* no. 108–109:641–650 (July-December 1979).

———. *Hacia el hombre nuevo: Poesía y pensamiento de Ernesto Cardenal.* London: Tamesis, 1984.

———. "Ernesto Cardenal." In *Diccionario enciclopédico de las letras de América Latina,* vol. 1. Caracas: Monte Avila, 1995. Pp. 875–882.

Cohen, Jonathan. "From Nicaragua with Love." Introduction to *With Walker in Nicaragua and Other Early Poems, 1949–1954.* By Ernesto Cardenal. Middletown, Conn.: Wesleyan University Press, 1984. Pp. 3–17.

Coronel Urtecho, José. "Carta a propósito del *Estrecho dudoso.*" In *El estrecho dudoso.* By Ernesto Cardenal. Managua: Editorial Nueva Nicaragua, 1985. Pp. 9–38.

Cuadra, Pablo Antonio. "Sobre Ernesto Cardenal." *Papeles de Sons Armadans* no. 187:5–33 (1971).

Daydí-Tolson, Santiago. "Ernesto Cardenal: Resonancias e ideología en el discurso lírico hispanoamericano." *Revista Canadiense de Estudios Hispánicos* 9, no. 1:17–30 (1984).

Dorfman, Ariel. "Ernesto Cardenal: ¡Todo el poder a Dios-proletario!" In his *Ensayos quemados en Chile.* Buenos Aires: Ediciones de la Flor, 1974. Pp. 193–223.

———. "Tiempo de amor, tiempo de lucha: La unidad en los *Epigramas* de Ernesto Cardenal." In *Texto Crítico* 5, no. 13:3–44 (1979).

Elías, Eduardo. "El estrecho dudoso: Del discurso histórico a la épica contemporánea." *Revista Iberoamericana,* no. 157:923–931 (1991).

Fraire, Isabel. "Pound and Cardenal." *Review,* no. 18:36–42 (fall 1976).

Gibbons, Reginald. "Political Poetry and the Example of Ernesto Cardenal." *Critical Inquiry* 13, no. 3:648–671 (spring 1987).

Merton, Thomas. Prologue to *Vida en el amor*. Buenos Aires: Ediciones C. Lohlé, 1970. Pp. 9–22. (Trans. by Kurt Reinhardt as "Introduction." In *To Live Is to Love*. New York: Herder and Herder, 1972. Pp. 7–18.)

Oviedo, José Miguel. "Ernesto Cardenal: Un místico comprometido." *Casa de las Américas* 53:29–48 (1969).

Pastor Alonso, María Angeles. *La poesía cósmica de Ernesto Cardenal*. Huelva, Spain: Diputación Provincial de Huelva, 1998.

Pring-Mill, Robert. "The Redemption of Reality through Documentary Poetry." In *Zero Hour and Other Documentary Poems*. By Ernesto Cardenal. New York: New Directions, 1980. Pp. ix–xxi.

———. "Acciones paralelas y montaje acelerado en el segundo episodio de Hora O." *Revista Iberoamericana*, no. 118–119:217–240 (January-June 1982).

Promis Ojeda, Jose, et al. *Ernesto Cardenal: Poeta de la liberación latinoamericana*. Buenos Aires: Fernando García Cambeiro, 1975.

Salmon, Russell. Introduction to *Golden UFOs: The Indian Poems*. By Ernesto Cardenal. Bloomington: Indiana University Press, 1995. Pp. ix–xli.

Smith, Janet L. *An Annotated Bibliography of and About Ernesto Cardenal*. Tempe: Center for Latin American Studies, Arizona State University, 1979.

Solle, Dorothee. "Prólogo." In *Salmos*. By Ernesto Cardenal. Madrid: Editorial Trotta, 1998. Pp. 9–13.

Strout, Lilia Dapaz. "Nuevos cantos de vida y esperanza: *Los salmos* de Cardenal y la nueva ética." In *Ernesto Cardenal: Poeta de la liberación latinoamericana*. Edited by José Promis Ojeda et al. Buenos Aires: Fernando Garcia cambeiro, 1995.

Valdés, Jorge H. "Cardenal's 'Exteriorismo': The Ideology Underlying the Esthetic." *Mid-Hudson Language Studies* 10:63–70 (1980).

———. "Cardenal's Poetic Style: Cinematic Parallels." *Revista Canadiense de Estudios Hispánicos* 11, no. 1:119–129 (autumn 1986).

White, Steven F. *Culture & Politics in Nicaragua: Testimonies of Poets and Writers*. New York: Lumen Books, 1986. Pp. 59–74.

———. "Ernesto Cardenal." In *Encyclopedia of Latin American Literature*. Edited by Verity Smith. Chicago: Fitzroy Dearborn, 1997. Pp. 164–166.

Williams, Tamara R. Introduction to *The Doubtful Strait/ El estrecho dudoso*. By Ernesto Cardenal. Bloomington: Indiana University Press, 1992. Pp. vii–xxxi.

———. "Ernesto Cardenal's *El estrecho dudoso*: Reading/Rewriting History." In *Hispanic Literary Criticism*. Detroit: Gale Research, 1994. Pp. 357–361. (An excerpt first published in *Revista Canadiense de Estudios Hispánicos* 15, no. 1:111–121 [fall 1990].)

Zimmerman, Marc. "Ernesto Cardenal after the Revolution." Introduction to *Flights of Victory*. By Ernesto Cardenal. Willimantic, Conn.: Curbstone Press, 1988. Pp. vii–xxxii.

# Jorge Carrera Andrade

## (1902–1978)

### J. Enrique Ojeda

Jorge Carrera Andrade's poetry evolved throughout the sixty years of the author's literary life, from 1917, when his first verses appeared, up to 1976, the year in which he published his *Obra poética completa* (Complete poetry). During the course of those years, Carrera Andrade's work as a journalist, diplomat, traveler and, above all, as poet not only reflected the American landscape from which he originated but also the universal concerns of his time. His poetry emerged and developed under the inspiration of the intensely bucolic setting of his childhood in Ecuador as well as his early readings. During his first travels in Europe between 1928 and 1933, however, he began to focus on man's being and destiny, subjects he explored with growing absorption. With the sharp sensibility of an American abroad, he perceived in European society the gradual decadence of humanism and its ideal of individual perfection, while at the same time he was to witness the rise of existentialism and the uncertainty, disillusion, and anguish that followed from it.

The poetry written during his mature years expresses a theme that twentieth-century European literature repeated in various contexts: the isolation and helplessness of contemporary man. However, the originality of his attitude resides in the integrity with which he faced man's destiny, in the pathos of his ceaseless efforts to guard against the shipwreck of the anguish that arises from existentialism. His work is further distinguished by a lyrical fullness and by the originality and brilliance of the metaphoric language he uses to configure his experience of human existence. The wide variety of Carrera Andrade's literary production, enriched by his indefatigable readings and continuous travels, finds unity in the autobiographical character of his poetry. The poet himself called attention to this in three autocritical essays, published as *Mi vida en poemas* (1962; My life in poems), in which he asserted that his poetry must be interpreted in close relation to the interior and exterior circumstances of his personal life. "Mis poemas son visuales como una colección de estampas o pinturas que integran una autobiografía apasionada y nostálgica" (My poems are just as visual as a collection of prints or paintings that integrate a passionate and nostalgic autobiography), he declared in a lecture given at Columbia University.

Jorge Carrera Andrade's date of birth and the chronology of his publications place him in the group of poets who, after the last reverberations of *modernismo*, gave new splendor to Spanish American lyric poetry: César Vallejo, Jorge Luis Borges, Pablo Neruda, and Octavio Paz, among others. He was born in Quito on 13 September 1902. His father, a distinguished lawyer, was for many years Minister of the Supreme Court of

Justice. His mother, possessed of a fine artistic temperament, played guitar and painted. She taught Jorge the French language, encouraging him to read the authors who later came to have considerable influence on his early poetic production.

Carrera Andrade's childhood and youth coincided with a time of profound transformations in Ecuador. In the political arena, the dictator Elroy Alfaro's rise to power completed the consolidation of liberalism. The poet's father, an ardent liberal, had recruited Jorge, then in his early twenties, into Alfaro's political party, but this was a time when Marxist doctrines were spreading among the young Spanish American intellectuals. Jorge, disillusioned by corrupt politicians and their general disinterest in solving social ills, collaborated in founding the Ecuadorian Socialist Party. Liberalism and Marxism, as practiced in Ecuador and the other Andean countries, carried with it the disavowal of religious faith, a fact that will have a deep and lasting impact on Carrera Andrade's literary work. His poetry, like that of many writers of his time, arose "from the darkness left by the absence of God," as poet and philosopher Paul Claudel said of modern French literature (quoted by Marcel Raymond, in *De Baudelaire au surréalisme*, 1963).

Carrera Andrade's earliest writings correspond in time and spirit to a period in which a late *modernismo* had fleetingly crystallized in Ecuador. Friend and almost contemporary of his *modernista* compatriots, particularly of Humberto Fierro whose book *El laúd en el valle* (1919) Carrera Andrade helped get published when he was seventeen years old, it was only to be expected that his first poetry would be composed under the influence of the French masters who had inspired his countrymen: Paul Verlaine, Charles Baudelaire, Arthur Rimbaud, and Albert Samain. The intense elegiac tone of Ecuadorian *modernismo* owed its origin to Samain, that delicate poet who composed his work in a minor key, on the frontier that separated symbolism from vanguardism. Samain died in 1900. His poetry was a nostalgic farewell to the close of a century. The brief efflorescence of Ecuadorian *modernismo* bid farewell to a period of tedium and melancholy, followed by a new era—affirmative and hopeful—which was that of Carrera Andrade and his literary companions. A happy intuition revealed to them that *modernismo* had wasted

away in the fire of its own stylistic excesses and that all efforts to prolong it would be fruitless.

Carrera Andrade's early writings show that the poet responded to a variety of influences. During his childhood he spent his summers on the family farm on the outskirts of Quito, in intimacy with a lush and gentle natural setting. He lived there among Indians who worked on the farm and who inspired in him a lifelong empathy for their conquered race. He was further influenced by a change in the literary spirit of the times. In 1917 the journal *Letras*, the organ of Ecuadorian *modernismo*, published an interview with Guillaume Apollinaire by Gaston Picard in which Apollinaire declared: "It is necessary to react against the pessimism that has plagued writers from the beginning of the nineteenth Century. It is necessary to exalt man and not diminish and demoralize him. . . . In this sense I am anti-Baudelaire." Similarly, Maurice LeBlonde declared at the end of the century (1896): "We have admired Baudelaire and Mallarmé for too long. We want to rejuvenate our individualism in a universal embrace. We return to nature. We look for the pure and divine emotion" (quoted by Raymond, *De Baudelaire au surréalisme*).

These recommendations had an extraordinary impact at the outset of the young poet's literary career. He read André Gide's novel *Nourritines Terrestras* (1887), the most eloquent expression of this new, vital ardor, and he prefaced his first book of poems with quotes taken from Gide. But even more influential in his formative years was the neonaturalist poetry of Francis Jammes. During the twilight of symbolism, Jammes predicated a new alliance between the spirit and material world. Eschewing symbols and allegories, Jammes insisted that objects be treated as having a life of their own. In Jammes's view, all things, even the most humble and ordinary, could be described and sung.

Everything he read and experienced predisposed Carrera Andrade to be impressed by the personality and poetry of Jammes: his long experience in the countryside, the patriarchal character of his family, the quiet, uneventful city where he dwelled. Referring to that time he wrote: "The rural sense of the country where I was born permeated me. . . . Ecuador itself was like a great countryside whose life of stagnant water was not stirred by anything" ("Edades de mi poesía," in *Edades poéticas*, 1958).

Carrera Andrade's first volume of verses, published in Quito in 1922, was *El estanque inefable* (The ineffable pond). It includes twenty-seven poems, written between 1920 and 1922, that respond to diverse spirits: Verlaine, Rubén Darío and, above all, Francis Jammes. This latter influence is expressed in poems like "El éxtasis familiar" (A familiar ecstasy), later entitled "Vida de la alacena" (Life of the cupboard), in which the poet sings with quiet affection of domestic objects, echoing the Jammes poem "El comedor" (The dining room).

Four years elapsed between *El estanque inefable* and his second book of verses, *La guirnalda del silencio* (1926, Garland of silence). It was a period in which the poet was consumed by political action and by a journalism so critical of the government that he was imprisoned. In May of 1925 Carrera Andrade took a leading role in the creation of the Ecuadorian Socialist Party and became its secretary general. His enthusiasm for the cause inspired poems with strong Marxist content, including "Canto a Rusia" (Song to Russia), and "Lenín ha muerto" (Lenin has died). These poems were highly popular in those days, but never included in his books. At this time he also composed *Cuaderno de poemas indios* (Notebook of Indian poems), which was published in 1930.

In *La guirnalda del silencio* the poet who began by singing to the earth has turned his attention to the crystalline forms of the universe. The poem "Regreso a la transparencia" (Return to transparency), dated 1924, affirms: "Vuelvo al aire y al agua elementales / después de haber amado tierra y fuego / y el color y la forma de las cosas" (I return to elemental air and water / having loved earth and fire / and the color and form of things). He who contemplates "the recondite signs" finds that poetry is a "high science written in letters of pure water." In this invitation to diaphaneity, the poet who will come to sing to windows, mirrors, and stars early on appears to be attracted to light and to conceive of poetry as a decantation of clarity.

> *Vidriera: libro de agua, donde los ojos leen*
> *la unción maravillosa de los árboles,*
> *las parvas de rodillas, el portillo de siempre*
> *con arbustos más quietos que bancos de corales.*

> Windowpane, liquid book where the eyes read
> the marvelous balm of trees,
> grain kneeling unwinnowed heaps
> the same gate as always, with bushes quieter than
>   coral reefs.

The spirit of Francis Jammes lives in the tender simplicity of these lines from "El libro de la bondad." The young poet directs his attention to the humble beings and things that populated typical Jammes verses: "the patient ass," "the glass of clean water," "the sky with cranes and slow swallows." Referring to this moment of his lyrical creation Carrera Andrade affirmed: "My world revolved around an axis: the love of things for themselves, not for their reflections or echoes that they awake in our intellect" (*Mi vida en poemas*). At this stage of his poetic development, his themes are limited to small creatures: "Vida del grillo" (Life of the cricket), "La vida perfecta [del conejo]" (The perfect life of the rabbit), "Los gorriones beben la perla del buen tiempo" (The sparrows that drink the pearl of good weather). He also deals with humble objects: "La escalera" (The staircase), "Los caramillos" (The reed), "Los naipes" (Playing cards), and he tries to capture the charm of a fleeting moment: "Después de llover" (After the rain), "Tiempo ventoso" (A windy time), "La hora de las ventanas iluminadas" (The hour of illuminated windows). In this creative period, which Carrera Andrade synthesized with the term "provincia" (countryside), his inspiration derives from the bucolic world that surrounds him. Years later he recalled his concerns of that period: "There is a colored and ever-changing immediate universe made up of small beings [that] our hand can move to our will by placing them in a more or less harmonious order. In this brief and lively universe that surrounded me from childhood I could signal my favorite friendships and surrender to a kind of cosmic and yet nontranscendental game" ("Ordenando un universo" [Ordering a universe], *Microgramas*, 1940). In *La guirnalda del silencio*, the poet's inclination to define objects by means of metaphors and to forge epigrammatic formulas that are lyrical miniatures in which tenderness takes the form of humor and a subtle inventiveness stands out: "El pájaro es un periódico / de la mañana en el campo" (The bird is the morning newspaper / in the fields), "Luciérnaga / linterna diminuta que se enciende en el campo" (Firefly / tiny lantern that lights in the field), "Reloj: / picapedrero del tiempo" (Clock: / stonecutter of time). It is in this second book of verses where his essentially visual character and extraordinary metaphoric capacity are first manifested. From then on these stylistic devices would be a defining element of his work.

*La guirnalda del silencio* contains several poems that were written in 1928 and dedicated to the exaltation of the monuments of his native city. This was the eve of his departure to the outside world, and, as in "Campana de San Blas," he erected lyrical altarpieces in which the playful air of short lines in the minstrel style (*versos de arte menor*) hardly shrouds the poet's pensive mien:

> *Más, siempre más, mi vida*
> *hasta el fondo, hasta el cielo,*
> *más allá de las islas.*
>
> *Hasta la Tierra Firme*
> *Más allá de la tierra:*
> *a las Islas Felices.*
> . . . . . . .
> *¡La vida me dio todo,*
> *pero yo ansiaba más!*

> More, always more, my life
> to the depths, to the sky,
> beyond the islands.
>
> To Terra Firma.
> And beyond the earth:
> to the Isles of Bliss.
> . . . . . . .
> Life gave me everything,
> but I longed for more!

The aspirations embodied in these lines point to the poet's later work, which he defined as utopian because in poems like "Aurosia" (published in *Moneda del forastero*, 1958) and "Comarcas lejanas" (Distant regions; published in *Floresta de los guacamayos*, 1964) he daydreams of the lands of paradise where happiness is plentiful and everlasting.

Until May of 1928 Carrera Andrade had been dedicated to journalism and political activism, and had lived such an intense bohemian life that he put his health and literary work in danger. He gives testimony to this psychic exhaustion in the poem "Crucifixion":

> *Desde la eternidad, aleteó por los aires*
> *un mensaje de pájaros.*
> *Hasta mi sed altísima tiende su esponja de oro*
> *y vinagre el ocaso.*
>
> *En el madero del Silencio*
> *mi cuerpo está clavado.*
>
> *Turba el aire oloroso de la zarza quemada*
> *la madre que me extiende su escalera de llanto.*
> *Y en la noche que llega, los recuerdos*
> *mi amor como una túnica se juegan a los dados.*

> From eternity, there flitted through the air
> an epistle of birds.
> The setting sun holds out its sponge of gold.
> and vinegar to my utmost thirst
>
> And to the wood of Silence
> my body is nailed.
>
> The air, heady with burning brambles, is stirred
> by the mother who extends me the ladder of
>     her tears.
> And as the night comes on my memories
> cast lots for my love, as if it were a tunic.

A departure to the outside world was now called for and, in May 1928, at twenty-six years of age, he left for Europe. His first two published books had exalted the "countryside," exhausting the topic and the influence of Francis Jammes. Did the young poet surmise that his first departure from his native land was to be the beginning of a pilgrimage that would last until three years before his death? Carrera Andrade felt the urge to travel early, and the desire endured. In "Milagro," in *La guirnalda del silencio*, he announced: "itinerario de los mares altos / hacia donde le empuja / al barco de mi carne la vela del espíritu" (Itinerary of the high seas / towards which the sail of the spirit / propels the ship of my flesh). And in his autobiography, *El volcan y el colibri* (1970; The volcano and the hummingbird), he declared: "I traveled first to educate myself . . . later, traveling became the very reason of my existence."

One has to conclude that his most moving poetry was written in lands which were not his own, and yet his work was nurtured in the living waters of his native landscape and sentiment. As Rilke intimated, the work of the writer's maturity must be explained by the experiences of the author's early years.

The purpose of Carrera Andrade's first trip to Europe was to represent the Ecuadorian Socialist Party at the Fifth International Socialist congress that was to take place in Moscow. The meager funds assigned to him delayed his arrival, however, and bureaucratic problems eventually prevented him from attending the congress. Instead, Carrera Andrade embarked on a pilgrimage through several countries in Europe, saying "Yo he visto la Europa tatuada de luces desde a la ventanilla de un furgón proletario" (I have contemplated Europe tattooed by lights from the window of my proletarian carriage). He traveled from Holland to Germany and then to France, and was blissful finally at arriving in Paris, which he saw as the "first port of men, city multiple and singular," the "desideratum" of every young South American intellectual (*Latitudes*, 1934).

In Paris he met the Peruvian poet César Vallejo and the Chilean poet Gabriela Mistral, future winner of a Nobel Prize in literature, who invited the Ecuadorian to her villa of Bedarrides in the Vaucluse valley of Provence. Those summer days were dedicated to intense readings in the villa's excellent library and to participating in lively discussions. In December of 1929 Carrera Andrade settled in Barcelona, beginning a period of external serenity and economic leisure that allowed him to read and write for three years while he observed the stormy events that shook the Spanish republic between 1930 and 1933. In 1930 his third book of poems, *Boletines de mar y tierra* (Bulletins from the earth and sea), which gathered compositions inspired by his travels, appeared in Barcelona. This slender volume initiated a new era in the works of Carrera Andrade, a period of discovery or "registry of the world." "Then the poetry of travel was revealed to me," he wrote years later, "and I was initiated into the green magic of geography. New forms, new symbols came to me during these encounters. The transparent and infantile creature of my poetry had to swallow a lot of salt water and climb into the riggings and travel in to every port" (1972; *The Selected Poems of Jorge Carrera*

*Andrade*, 1973). Far from the "calm pond" of his native Quito, he contemplates the world at a rapid traveler's pace:

> *Estoy en la línea de trenes del Oeste*
> *empleado en el Registro del Mundo,*
> *anotando en mi ventanilla*
> *nacimientos y defunciones de horizontes,*
> *encendiendo en mi pipa las fronteras*
> *ante la biblioteca de tejados de los pueblos*
> *y amaestrando el circo de mi sangre*
> *con el pulso cordial del Universo.*

> I am on the railway of the West
> employed in the Registry of the World,
> noting the births and deaths
> of horizons from my window,
> lighting the borders in my pipe
> with a library of village rooftops before me
> and using the cordial pulse of the Universe
> to train the circus of my blood.

*Boletines de mar y tierra* brings twelve lyrical miniatures—*microgramas*—dedicated to Gabriela Mistral and the *Cuaderno de poemas indios*, that he had written in 1928, when his work was still inspired by Marxist themes. These *Cuaderno* poems are the only political works he included in his books, perhaps because he found them to be less ideological and more poetic than others written during that period. In *Boletines de mar y tierra* the author's themes coalesce around the light. It is "matutinal poetry," according to the author, which sings of the effulgence that makes visible forms and colors, giving them a metaphysical entity: the light is the existence of things. Of the nineteen poems of *Boletines de mar y tierra*, seven are dedicated to the light and to beings and things associated with it: the dawn, the day, the window, the mirror. In one such poem, "Biography," the window appears as a living and beneficent reality whose "history" the poet synthesizes this way:

> *La ventana nació de un deseo de cielo*
> *y en la muralla negra se posó como un ángel.*
> *Es amiga del hombre*
> *y portera del cielo.*

> The window born from a desire for sky
> and alighted on the black wall like an angel.

It is friend to man,
and gatekeeper of the sky.

For the poet who professes the cult of the light, there is no higher destiny than that of the window. In the same poem, he states: "With diaphanous harangues it leads the multitudes. / The window distributes to everyone a quart of light, a bucket of air." It is the radiance of his native landscape that becomes present in his work. In an unpublished autobiographical essay he affirmed: "My vision of the world became realistic. There is nothing phantasmagoric in my work, which is totally constructed from matter and clarity. Meridian, equatorial clarity made out of solar light that descends vertically upon objects."

If an air of melancholic stillness pervaded Carrera Andrade's two previous books, the feeling that prevails in *Boletines de mar y tierra* is of an essential felicity, a jubilant vision of the world. The word "happiness" abounds in these lines, revealing their author's "vital euphoria," his youth, his delight in being the "joyful traveler," for whom the "harbors, like children, whirled gaily on the carrousel of the horizon." "It was a time of human love," he wrote years later, "a station of sun and vital sweetness that rendered light and appealing the image of foreign cities" (*The Selected Poems of Jorge Carrera Andrade*). This third volume of poetry, prefaced by Gabriela Mistral's cordial foreword, was well received by critics and gained for the author international recognition. Alfonso Reyes commented from Mexico: "*Boletines de mar y tierra* kept me 'listening' with delight and rapture"; and Jorge Guillén wrote from Spain: "The *Boletines de mar y tierra*: precious, exquisite, very 'felicitous,' happily poetic."

In July 1933 Carrera Andrade returned to Ecuador. He wanted to put the experiences he acquired during his three years in Republican Spain to use in service of his homeland. His concern for his country, which was afflicted by chaotic and at times violent political events, inspired him to write six long articles while in Spain, all of which first appeared in a local newspaper and then in the form of a pamphlet entitled *Cartas de un emigrado* (Letters from an émigré). What stands out from those pages is his deep concern for his country and his faith, certainly naive, in the changes being attempted in Republican Spain, such as the policy of agrarian reform that, in his opinion, could also solve the Indian problems in Ecuador and the other Andean countries. However, Carrera Andrade's aspiration was to enter into the foreign service, and in February 1934 he was appointed Consul in Paita, Peru, a small town on the Ecuadorian border. Thus begun his diplomatic career which, intermittently, extended to 1968.

The tranquil existence in Paita allowed him to prepare the edition of his first book of essays. *Latitudes* (1934) is partially a journal that details the stages of his itinerary across the Atlantic and in Europe. It is therefore a prose version of *Boletines de mar y tierra*, and much of the lyrical enchantment of this book is reflected in its brief and densely poetic travelogues. To these geographical reports Carrera Andrade added critical essays inspired by the readings that constituted his intellectual journey of that time: Georges Duhamel, Juan Montalvo, Emile Zola, Jaime Torres Bodet, Jorge Guillén, and Paul Eluard. *Latitudes* also contains political commentaries, in which the author displays extraordinary clairvoyance. In "Pieles, solados y vodka" (Furs, soldiers and vodka), for instance, he points out the positive aspects of international communism, while yet affirming its enormous errors: "There is a lack of theoreticians who know the process of world economic development and they send mistaken directives to parties affiliated to the International, promoting an anti-intellectual reaction among the labor classes and thus sacrificing the best militants to their absurd attempts."

In November of 1934 Carrera Andrade returned to France as Ecuador's consul in Le Havre. The enthusiasm and novelty of his first year in the Breton port was followed by a period of loneliness and discouragement, expressed in his personal correspondence as well as in poems written at the time. He refers to Normandy as "a desert without sun and books." He kept himself busy preparing an anthology of contemporary French poets, facilitated by regular visits to bookstores and by his friendship with some of the writers whose works he was translating. In 1935 a new volume of his own verses, *Rol de la manzana* (Role of the apple) appeared in Madrid. This is partially an anthology that gathered the best from his previous books. Among the new poems included in the volume are twenty *microgramas* in which the poet tries to apprehend the intimate reality of objects, their "secret attitude," in intensely lyrical notes. Examples of these new pieces include "Golondrina" ("Swallow"): "Ancla de plumas / por los mares del cielo / la tierra busca" (Anchor of feathers / through the sea of the sky / it seeks the earth); and "Manzana" (Apple): "Celda de todo el aroma / y la frescura del mundo / es tu pintada redorna" (A chamber of fragrance / and the freshness of the world / is your colorful sphere). In the brief foreword to the book he notes: "For me it was a time of discovery of things, and the small globe loaded with vegetable essences summarized all that life can offer of secret delight. . . . Apple: canteen of the sky in this life of noise and coal. Promise of virginal enjoyment without duplicity. Emblem of a simple life."

Another book of verse also appeared in Madrid during this year, *Tiempo manual* (Manual time). This volume responded to a spirit radically different from his works to date. The period of the "discovery of things" was followed now by one that can be defined as a "discovery of man": "Las ciudades se hablaban a lo largo del aire. / Descubrí al hombre. Entonces / comprendí mi mensaje" ("Boletín de viaje," *Obra poética completa*; Cities were conversing through the air. / I discovered man. Then / I understood my message). If the stanzas of *Boletines de mar y tierra* were penetrated by vital joy and left a poetic record of his geographical and sentimental itinerary, the poet perceives now that "the only common profile of the cities he visited was the gesture of old age and history endured like a family illness" (*Edades poéticas*). In "Soledad de las ciudades" (Loneliness of cities), the opening poem sets the tone to this new volume of verses as the poet questions:

> ¿Dónde estuviste, soledad,
> que no te conocí hasta los veinte años?
> En los trenes, los espejos y las fotografías
> siempre estás a mi lado.
>
> . . . . . . . .
>
> Todo se ha inventado,
> mas no hay nada que pueda librarnos de la soledad.

> Where were you, loneliness?
> Why did I not know you until I was twenty?
> In trains, mirrors and photographs
> you are always beside me
>
> . . . . . . . .

> Everything has been invented
> but there is nothing that can free us from
>     loneliness.

In the essay "Edades de mi poesía," published in *Edades poéticas*, Carrera Andrade asserts: "Loneliness is certainly the final exit from our planet. It is also the prime matter of which all things are made. It is mother of the elements and ephemeral forms. The river is a loneliness of water. The wind, a loneliness roving in space. Everything is an affirmation of the vast loneliness of the earth." Referring to this period of his lyrical output he affirmed: "That was the time of the workers' movement and political turmoil, which I called 'Manual Time.' " Loneliness revives in the poet a sentiment of solidarity: "Among images of social struggle . . . I intended to contain in my series of poems from *Tiempo manual* a feeling of human solidarity and universal unity."

The social connotations of this book are to be found in "Poemas de pasado mañana" (Poems of the day after tomorrow), published in *El tiempo manual*. Its five compositions relate to the functioning of a factory, a lockout due to overproduction, an ensuing strike, and the repressive military response to the strike, and it ends with the massacre of the workers. Carrera Andrade's metaphoric language adapts itself well to these new themes, as when he refers to "los motines del viento," "la huelga de los vegetales," "el atentado terrorista del crepúsculo" (winds' mutinies, the strike of vegetables, the terrorist plot of the sunset), and other such poetic lines. There is also a radical change in the structure of the poems. Whereas in previous books the alexandrine and hendecasyllable prevailed, in *Tiempo manual* free verse stands out, and the poet's interest in assonance disappears.

During Carrera Andrade's four years on the coast of Normandy he had married Paulette Colin Lebas and had a son, Juan Cristóbal. The poems composed there were published in 1937 with the title *Biografía para uso de los pájaros* (Biography for the use of birds). The first two lines of the opening poem ominously attest to the victory of the industrial order upon the natural world: "I was born in the century of the death of the rose / when the motor had already frightened away the angels." The insecurity and anguish felt in Europe on the eve of the Second World War echo in the desolate lines of "Morada terrestre" (Earthy dwelling):

> *Habito un edificio de naipes,*
> *una casa de arena, un castillo en el aire*
> *y paso los minutos esperando*
> *el derrumbe del muro, la llegada del rayo,*
> *el correo celeste con la final noticia,*
> *la orden como un látigo de sangre*
> *dispersando en el viento una ceniza de ángeles.*

> I live in a house of cards,
> a house of sand, a castle in the air
> and spend the minutes awaiting
> the collapse of the wall, the thunderbolt's arrival,
> the celestial mail with its final news,
> the order like a lash of blood
> that scatters to the wind the ashes of angels.

Referring to those years he later wrote: "Dispossessed, a foreigner, ignorant of the commercial languages of men, locked in my 'terrestrial dwelling,' the certainty of the inevitable collapse of the highest human constructions overcame me" (*The Selected Poems of Jorge Carrera Andrade*). The euphoria of his first trip abroad has given way to a new experience: one of exile that, with time, becomes more intense and philosophical. Thus the lines of "El extranjero" (The foreigner) are pervaded by loneliness and nostalgia:

> *Un territorio helado me rodea,*
> *una zona impermeable y silenciosa*
> *donde se apagan los ardientes signos*
> *y su sentido pierden los terrestres idiomas.*

> A frigid territory surrounds me,
> a silent, impenetrable zone
> where the blazing signs are put out
> and the earthly languages lose their meaning.

Frightened, he expresses in "La alquimia vital" (Vital alchemy) his experience of his own slow but inescapable annihilation: "Un viejo vive en mí fabricando mi muerte / A su soplo se tornan en ceniza los años" (An old man lives in me fabricating my death. / At his breath years turn to ashes). And yet he still sings to the objects of his predilection: "Ventanas, puertas, claravoyas: íntimas amigas, / cómplices de un mundo claro y ágil" (Windows, doors, skylights: intimate friends, / accomplices of a clear and agile world). But more and more his lyrical work becomes melancholy, pensive, philosophical. It is an extraordinary accomplishment that a South American poet, precariously settled in a port of France, was able to capture and give voice to the pervading anguish felt in Europe in those years, in a language that deeply affected the readers of his poems. Both *Tiempo manual* and *Biografía para uso de los pájaros* appeared in French translations, in 1936 and 1938 respectively, and these translations gained Carrera Andrade a reputation that grew and deepened over time.

Carrera Andrade remained in Le Havre until February 1938, when a new consular appointment took him to Japan. When he settled in Yokohama as Ecuador's Consul General in Japan, the city of Tokyo was still marred by the ruins caused by recent earthquakes. By then the Japanese government had declared a general mobilization, and the proliferation of soldiers attested to the expansionistic policy of Japan and its imminent war with the United States.

Carrera Andrade remained in Japan for two years, and his experiences are reflected in two books published in Tokyo in 1940: *Microgramas* and *País secreto* (*Secret Country*, 1946). The first volume gathers thirty-one lyrical miniature poems, which are preceded by a lengthy study of this minor genre. The second is a slender tome that includes ten poems written in the midst of a desolate Japanese landscape. In "Viento nordeste" ("Northeast Wind") the violence of the typhoon, "architect of ruins" is represented with epic force in the shape of an armed assault:

> *Alarmando a los árboles,*
> *a las velas y peces,*
> *inician secundados por sus brigadas de agua*
> *Norte y Este sus planes de desorden terrestre;*

> *e irrumpen las confusas caballadas del viento,*
> *los salvajes del viento con unánime grito . . .*

> Alarming trees,
> sails and fish,
> North and East, backed by their brigades of water
> set their plans for earthly disorder in motion;

> and the confused horses of the wind break out,
> all the wind's savages in a unanimous war cry . . .

While in Japan, news of his mother's death engulfed him in a period of deep and lasting depression which, in turn, inspired his "Segunda vida de mi madre" ("Second Life of My Mother," *Secret Country*), which, due to its pathos and metaphorical plasticity, is one of his most beautiful poems:

*Brújula de mi larga travesía terrestre,*
*Origen de mi sangre, fuente de mi destino.*
*Cuando el polvo sin faz te escondió en su guarida,*
*me desperté asombrado de encontrarme aún vivo.*

*Y quise echar abajo las invisibles puertas*
*y di vueltas en vano, prisionero.*
*Con cuerda de sollozos me ahorqué sin ventura,*
*y atravesé, llamándote, los pantanos del sueño.*

*Mas te encuentras viviendo en torno mío.*
*Te siento mansamente respirando*
*en esas dulces cosas que me miran*
*en un orden celeste dispuestas por tu mano.*

Compass of my long earthly crossing.
Origin of my blood, source of my destiny.
When faceless dust hid you in its lair
I awoke, astonished to find myself yet alive.

And I wanted to tear down the invisible doors
and vainly I traveled in circles, a prisoner.
I hung myself with a rope of sobs, to no avail,
and crossed the swampland of dreams, calling
          out to you.

But here you are, alive, around me.
I can feel you gently breathing
in the sweet things that look down upon me,
their heavenly order arranged by your hand.

The poems of *Secret Country* reveal Carrera Andrade's state of mind during his stay in Japan. "Corpses," "dust," "ruins," "death," and "silence" are words he uses repeatedly throughout the poems. The dominant color of the desolate landscapes he describes is gray: "Gray of age, gray of the common and final dust, gray of ash." His return to Ecuador in August 1940 was a soothing interlude spent among relatives and the familiar things of his native country. During this brief, three-month period he published *Registro del mundo* (Registry of the world), with a prologue by Pedro Salinas. The

Spanish poet praises the Ecuadorian for his interest in the things of the universe that compose "its envelope of wonder," for the visionary character of his poetry, and for his will to avoid abstractions and his exceptional metaphoric capacity ("the power and metaphoric success of this poet are truly exceptional"). According to Salinas, this volume constitutes the first poetic period of Carrera Andrade; the second is inhabited by shadows and omens.

In December 1940 Carrera Andrade arrived in San Francisco as Ecuador's Consul General to that city. After his experiences in Japan and the sorrow of seeing his mother country invaded by Peru and his beloved France invaded by Germany, he considered his new destiny in California as a period of "reconstruction of happiness," as he wrote to a friend. When the United States joined the war against the Axis powers, Carrera Andrade was inspired to write two poems with epic resonances: "Canto a las fortalezas volantes" (Song to the flying fortresses) and "Cuaderno del paracaidista" (Notebook of the parachutist). Of the two, the most accomplished is the second:

*Sólo encontré dos pájaros y el viento,*
*las nubes con sus mapas enrollados*
*y unas flores de humo que se abrían buscándome*
*durante el vertical viaje celeste.*

I only found two birds, and the wind,
the clouds with their rolled up maps
and some flowers of smoke that bloomed,
          seeking me
during my vertical journey through the sky.

Two other poems were inspired by his stay in California: "Canto al puente de Oakland" ("To the Bay Bridge"), published in a bilingual edition in 1942, and "Señas del parque Sutro" (Signs of Sutro park), which appeared in Venezuela in 1945. The presence of Carrera Andrade in the United States generated a remarkable interest in his work among North American poets, translators, and critics of that period. English versions of his poems as well as critical essays were published in literary journals. Muna Lee provided the translation for a bilingual volume of *Secret Country*, which deeply impressed the poets of this country, as evidenced in letters to the translator. Carl Sandburg declared:

"Carrera Andrade is my brother in the poetic endeavor more than any other [poet] in this hemisphere." Archibald MacLeish defined Carrera Andrade's poetry as "a fountain of living water amid the barrenness of our time," and William Carlos Williams wrote: "I don't know when I had so clear a picture, so unaffected by the problems of the mind which are our daily bread. The images are so extraordinarily clear, so close to the primitive that I am seeing as a native and I am participating in a vision already lost to the world. It is a sad picture but a great one." In 1943 Carrera Andrade took a retrospective glance at his life and denoted the stages of his spiritual and poetic itinerary. The result, the essay entitled "Edades de mi poesia," details with amiable simplicity his literary autobiography and reveals the lyrical heights to which his works in prose could rise.

Political events in Ecuador brought Carrera Andrade back to his country. By then his international reputation had inspired a group of young Ecuadorian writers, and they invited him to elucidate his work. In the periodical *Letras del Ecuador*, he obliged: "My poetry has evolved in three stages. Discovery of my own country; exit to the outside world and discovery of the universe and human solidarity; and return from the vast world into the interior country, to the spiritual zone where lie the darkest keys of man's existence and drama." At the end of 1947 Carrera Andrade sailed to England to represent his country in the Court of St. James. London with its perpetual fog and monumental architecture, its landscape pocked with ruins caused by German bombs, and its never-ending lines of people waiting for food rations, deeply affected this poet from the tropics who was accustomed to the precision of lines and joy of light. In "To the Bay Bridge," he had stated:

> nada se oculta a mis abiertos ojos
> de hombre de una tierra sin vocación de nube,
> donde la luz exacta
> ninguna forma olvida,
> y enseña el peso justo y el sitio de las cosas
> la línea ecuatorial

> Nothing hides from the open eyes
> of a man born in a land with no aptitude
>     for clouds,
> where the precise light

forgets no form
and the line of the Equator
points out the proper weight and place of things.

Now, however, was the time for elegies. Carrera Andrade's desolate meditations dictated a brief book, *El visitante de niebla y otros poemas* (1947; *Visitor of Mist and Other Poems*, 1950). In "Torre de Londres" ("Tower of London") the poet intimates that the whole world has become a prison, an invisible prison whose material symbols arise everywhere: "Las nubes nos vigilan, condenados / prisonero y guardián a igual sentencia / en la terrestre cárcel encerrados" (The clouds watch over us, / prisoner and guard condemned to the same sentence / incarcerated in the terrestrial jail). "Juan sin cielo" ("John without Heaven"), one of Carrera Andrade's best known poems, presents modern man as one who has exchanged his treasures for glass beads and trinkets. He spoke of the inspiration behind this poem in *Interpretaciones hispanoamericanas*:

> From amidst the ruins, "John without Heaven" came to meet me: the wounded universal being, the image of contemporary man who has lost all his possessions, his "treasure of centuries"—that is, his principles, his beliefs, his hopes—because he has trusted in the force and has let himself be seduced by the new materialism as preached by the merchants of mirrors and executioners of swans.

"Formas de la delicia pasajera" ("Forms of Fleeting Delight"), the second of four sonnets, because of its perfection of form and depth of disillusion, brings the reader back to the best of the disconsolate sonnets of the Spanish baroque:

> El pájaro y el fruto: forma pura,
> cárcel uno de miel y flor del vuelo
> el otro, en una altísima aventura
> como un cáliz de plumas por el cielo.

> Prisioneros los dos de la hermosura
> que acaba nada más en sombra y hielo
> ya gastado el tesoro de dulzura,
> ya el puñado de plumas en el suelo

> Bird and fruit: pure form,
> one the prison of honey and flower of flight

the other, in an adventure high aloft
like a chalice of feathers across the sky.

Both are the prisoners of beauty
that ends in ice and darkness, nothing more,
the treasure of sweetness used up,
a handful of feathers on the ground.

Carrera Andrade, at this stage of his poetic maturity, returns to the classic metric form of the sonnet and consonance, after his prolonged use of free verse. Perhaps this was due to his devotion as a reader and translator of Paul Valéry, whose "verbal alchemy" he admired. His presence in London provided English intellectuals with an opportunity to celebrate the works of the Ecuadorian poet. G. S. Fraser organized a recital of his poetry, and in presenting Carrera Andrade he affirmed that "the characteristic of the poetry of Carrera Andrade is its rich atmosphere and a style more controlled than that of Neruda's." In 1950 *Visitor of Mist* appeared in English, translated by G. R. Coulthard and Kathleen Knott, bringing the number of English translations of the poet's work to forty-four. Fraser compared Carrera Andrade's work with the poetry of Archibald MacLeish, whose *Act Five and Other Poems* had just been published: "The similarity between these two poets is in their sense of the mutability of things, in the afflictive limitation of the days that follow," and Fraser went on to declare that "while in MacLeish the force resides clearly in his verbal music, Carrera Andrade achieves his poetic power by force of imaginative evocation." In 1949 the *Adam International Review* of London dedicated an issue to his work: "We chose Jorge Carrera Andrade when we discovered in his work those elements of cosmic sensitivity and universal amplitude that, in our opinion, allow poets of today to have freedom from their increasing contradictions and dilemmas." If the English translators and critics manifested an uncommon interest in his work, the French did not lag far behind. Between 1948 and 1949, six books of French translations of his poetry appeared, as well as several important critical essays.

In March 1951 Carrera Andrade was back in Ecuador. "The trees and births of the equinoctial America visited me in my dreams. My native land was calling me," he wrote at the time. The fifteen months spent in his country allowed him to publish two important books: *Poesia francesa contemporánea* (Contemporary French poetry) and *Lugar de origen* (1951; Place of origin). The first is a work of vast scope, encompassing fifty-two French and Belgian poets represented in three hundred poems, some of them lengthy, chosen and translated by Carrera Andrade. One has to admire the knowledge of contemporary French poetry displayed by the anthologist and translator. "These pages have taken many days of my life," wrote the poet in the introduction to this work, "and are intended as a tribute to France. Of the French culture, poetry is the highest flower, its more delicate and original expression. French poetry is not only an aggregate of forms and music but also, and above all, a direction of the spirit." France rewarded Carrera Andrade with the decoration L'Ile St. Louis, and French critics exalted this book as the best anthology of contemporary French poetry in any language. *Lugar de origen* was a 1941 anthology of Carrera Andrade's work. The updated version also presented six new sonnets of rare perfection.

Carrera Andrade left the foreign service in 1946 for political reasons, but he remained in Paris as a writer for UNESCO's Spanish publications and latter became the director of the journal *El Correo de la Unesco*. For six years, far removed from the glittering life of a diplomat, a virtual prisoner in his office or in the National Library where daily he searched for materials for his studies on Ecuadorian history, he lived a life of solitude and total dedication to his intellectual work. His deep sense of futility and isolation finds expression in the melancholy lines of "Transformations."

> *Mi trabajo se trueca en dos ventanas*
> *a la calle, en diez metros de terreno,*
> *en un plato de luna cada noche*
> *y un bostezo de cántaros vacíos.*
>
> *Todos los días para mí son lunes:*
> *siempre recomenzar, pasos en círculo*
> *en torno de mí mismo, en los diez metros*
> *de mi alquilada tumba con ventanas.*

> My work turns into two windows
> overlooking the street, ten meters of space,
> a plate of moonlight every night
> and the yawn of empty pitchers.

Every day is Monday for me:
forever starting anew, walking in circles
around myself, in the ten meters
of my rented tomb with windows.

The gray monotony of those years was interrupted by invitations and homages. In September 1952 he spoke at the inaugural session of the First Biennial of International Poetry in Knokke-le-Zoute, Belgium. His speech was entitled "A Half Century of Spanish American Poetry." In November Paul Valéry's literary circle organized an event in his honor at the Sorbonne. In 1953 a new book of poetry was published in Paris, entitled *Familia de noche* (Family of night) which is, for all its brevity, perhaps the work in which the poet achieved the fullest expression of his lyrical powers. He departs from his usual brief meters and compositions to write long poems in which he interprets human destiny and sings to the most diaphanous beings of creation: water and light. The poem that gives its name to the book brings us back to his last return to Quito (1950–1951), which was for him an experience of extraordinary impact: his father had died and his childhood home "of resonant corridors" had been sold. The twenty-one stanzas of *Familia de noche* not only modulate an elegy to his lost youth but enter into the realm of history by exploring the living roots of his personal existence. Through the effect of the lyrical process, the poet becomes the representative of Eternal Man:

> Si entro por esa puerta veré un rostro
> ya desaparecido, en un clima de pájaros.
> Avanzará a mi encuentro
> hablándome con sílabas de niebla,
> en un país de tierra transparente
> donde medita sin moverse el tiempo
> y ocupan su lugar los seres y las cosas
> en un orden eterno . . . .

> If I go through that door I will see a face
> now vanished, in an atmosphere of birds.
> It will come to meet me
> speaking in syllables of mist,
> in a country of transparent earth
> where time meditates unmoving
> and things and beings take their places
> in an eternal order . . . .

The great figures of history—Moses, Heraclitus, Columbus, Magellan, and others—move through these stanzas, followed by the images of his parents as he saw them in his childhood:

> Aquí desciendes, padre, cada tarde
> del caballo luciente como el agua
> con espuma de marcha y de fatiga.
> Nos traes la ciudad bien ordenada
> en números y rostros: el mejor de los cuentos.

> Here you dismount every evening, Father,
> from the horse that glistens like water
> with the foam of walking and weariness.
> You bring us the city in its good order
> of numbers and faces: the best of tales.

And even more movingly, the memory of his mother returns:

> En esa puerta, madre, tu estatura
> medías, hombro a hombro, con la tarde
> y tus manos enviaban golondrinas
> a tus hijos ausentes
> preguntando noticias a las nubes,
> oyendo las pisadas del ocaso
> y haciendo enmudecer con tus suspiros
> los gritos agoreros de los pájaros.

> In that door, mother, you measured
> your stature, shoulder to shoulder with the evening
> and your hands sent swallows
> to your absent children
> asking the clouds for news
> listening to the footsteps of the sunset
> and with your sighs quieting
> the sinister cries of the birds.

Pedro Salinas had died by then, and in his memory Carrera Andrade offered an elegy of remarkably affecting intensity. But from the point of view of pure lyrical beauty "Dictado por el agua" (Dictated by the water) and "Las armas de la luz" (Weapons of light) are perhaps Carrera Andrade's best poems. "The water dictated to me a few transparent images," wrote the author of those six "cantos," which are variations on the theme of water and objects related to it by their kinship of clarity and innocence. Thus the magnolia:

*Sueñas, magnolia casta, en ser paloma*
*o nubecilla enana, suspendida*
*sobre las hojas, luna fragmentada.*
*Solitaria inocencia recogida*
*en un nimbo de aroma.*
*Santa de blancura inmaculada.*
*Soledad congelada*
*hasta ser alabastro*
*tumbal, lámpara o astro.*

You dream, chaste magnolia, of being a dove,
a tiny elfin cloud, suspended
over the leaves, a shattered moon.
Solitary innocence collected
into a halo of fragrance.
Saint immaculately white.
Solitude frozen
until it is sepulchral alabaster,
lamp or star.

The poet knows that those winged and luminous beings "En la alquimia fugaz de los olores / preparan su fragante acabamiento" (In the fleeting alchemy of scents / prepare their fragrant annihilation). In the background of this universe of splendors, death awaits:

*Soy a la vez cautivo y carcelero*
*de esta celda de cal que anda conmigo,*
*de la cual ¡oh muerte! guardas el llavera.*

I am both, captive and jailer
of this prison of lime that walks with me
of which, oh death, you keep the key.

The stylistic perfection of these compositions and their consonant rhyme connects them to the best poems of the Spanish baroque and, perhaps more closely, to the most accomplished lyrical creations of Paul Valéry. Carrera Andrade had proclaimed, throughout his poetic endeavors, his cult of the light but never before had he expressed it with such fullness, depth, and lyrical intensity as he did in the seven stanzas that form "Las armas de la luz":

*Me entrego al sitiador esplendoroso,*
*prisionero de sombra sin combate,*
*rendido a la evidencia meridiana*
*omnipresente en árbol, roca, insecto . . .*

I give myself up to the resplendent besieger,
prisoner of darkness without a fight,
surrendering to the evidence of broad daylight
that is there on every tree, rock, insect . . .

The poet discovers, in the empire of light, the fundamental principle of universal unity and the antidote against death:

*Amistad de las cosas y los seres*
*en apariencia solos y distintos,*
*pero en su vida cósmica enlazados*
*en oscura, esencial correspondencia*
*más allá de sus muertes, otras formas*
*del existir terrestre a grandes pasos*
*hacia el gris mineral inexorable.*

Friendship of things and beings
alone and separate in appearance,
but in their cosmic life entwined
in obscure, essential correspondence
beyond their deaths, other forms
of earthly existence in great strides
towards inexorable mineral gray.

In 1958 a bilingual (Spanish and French) edition of a brief volume of poems, *La moneda del forastero* (The stranger's coin), was published. The four compositions contained therein are of a high lyrical temperature, particularly "Invectiva contra la luna" (Invective against the moon) and "La visita del amor" (Love's visit), which is perhaps Carrera Andrade's best love poem. With "Aurosia," about a mythical planet where joyful inhabitants experience happiness without end, the author embarks upon the period of his work that he has defined as "utopian." Disillusioned by the limitations of life, he dreams of places of paradise, among which "Aurosia" is the first.

Carrera Andrade returned to Ecuador in 1958. He wrote three historical volumes in which he reconstructed the past of his fatherland from the pre-Columbian period to the present: *El camino del sol* (1959; The highway of the sun), *El fabuloso reino de Quito* (1963; The fabulous kingdom of Quito), and *Galeria de místicos y de insurgentes* (1959; Gallery of mystics and insurgents). This last title is a cultural and literary history of the country from colonial to republican times. The author's extensive research at the National Library in Paris renders these volumes a valuable contribution to an understanding of Ecuadorian history, and the clear and harmonious style makes them immensely readable.

In 1961 Carrera Andrade was appointed Ambassador to Venezuela, where he remained until 1963. During these years, he published two editions of *Hombre planetario* (Planetary man), one in Bogotá in 1959, the other in Quito in 1963. This long and complex work, with its twenty poems, deals with the theme of contemporary man and his destiny. In the title poem, the poet at first tries to identify himself:

> *¿Soy ese hombre que mira desde el puente*
> *los relumbres del río,*
> *vitrina de las nubes?*
> *Fui Ulises, Pársifal,*
> *Hamlet y Segismundo, y muchos otros*
> *antes de ser el personaje adusto*
> *con un gabán de viento que atraviesa*
> *el teatro de la calle.*

> Am I that man on the bridge who watches
> the light flashing on the river,
> a cabinet where clouds are displayed?
> I was Ulysses, Parsifal,
> Hamlet and Segismundo, and many others
> before I became the taciturn figure
> who, in an overcoat of wind, crosses
> the theater of the street.

His convictions and his yearning for social justice inspire him to offer harsh accusations against the "potentates of this world" who "weigh on their fraudulent scales friendship, love, even the sky." Full of irony, he intones a hymn to the manufacturers of automobiles and inventors of the "Great Universal Vitamin." He asks:

> *¿Qué haré yo sin mi angustia metafísica,*
> *sin mi dolencia azul? ¿Qué harán los hombres*
> *cuando ya nada sientan, mecanismos*
> *perfectos, uniformes?*

> What will I do without my metaphysical anguish,
> without my blue malady? What will men do,
> perfect, uniform mechanisms,
> when they no longer feel a thing?

Facing this artificial world the poet turns once more to the symbols of the natural realm and asks the rose, emblem of life, for its vital secret:

> *¿Dónde se encuentra, rosa,*
> *la máquina secreta*
> *que te forma y enciende, brasa viva*
> *del carbón de la sombra*
> *y te impulsa a lo alto*
> *a expresar en carmín y terciopelo*
> *el gozo de vivir sobre la tierra?*

> . . . . . . . . . . .

> *¿Qué vienes a decir con tantos labios?*
> *¿Eres sólo una boca del misterio*
> *que intenta pronunciar una palabra*
> *nunca oída hasta ahora*
> *para cambiar el curso de este mundo?*

> Where, rose, is
> the secret mechanism
> that shapes and sets fire to you, glowing ember,
> out of darkness's charcoal,
> and drives you upwards
> to express in crimson and velvet
> the joy of living on the earth?

> . . . . . . . . . . .

> What have you come to say with all those lips?
> Are you only the mouth of mystery
> which is trying to pronounce a word
> never heard before
> to change the course of this world?

The early stanzas, in which the poet attempts to define his identity, find an answer in the following lines: "Soy hombre, mineral y planta a un tiempo, / relieve del planeta, pez del aire, / un ser terrestre en suma" (I am man, mineral and plant at the same time, / raised work of the planet, fish of the air, / a terrestrial being in short). To this certainty he joyfully adds his conviction that he is identified with human beings from all times and latitudes:

> *Yo soy el habitante de las piedras*

> . . . . . . . . . . .

> *yo soy el ciudadano de cien pueblos*

> . . . . . . . . . . .

> *el Hombre Planetario,*
> *tripulante de todas las ventanas*
> *de la tierra aturdida de motores.*

I am the inhabitant of the stones

. . . . . . . . . . . . . . .

I am the citizen of a hundred towns

. . . . . . . . . . . . . . .

the Planetary Man,
Upon my heart the nations sign
a treaty of peace until death.

The hesitations, the uncertainties regarding his own identity, the ironies of contemporary life, the enigma of the universe, all yield at the end to the sureness that the destiny of the human being is to be a "Planetary Man." It is the only defense against individual death and the singular hope for immortality.

At the end of 1963 Carrera Andrade was appointed ambassador to Nicaragua, Rubén Darío's country. His brief presence there inspired poems collected under the title *Floresta de los guacamayos* (1964; Verdant grove of the macaws) in which he exalted the radiant beauty of the tropics, represented by the bird of fiery plumage. It is not a descriptive poetry. The promise of this regional paradise awakens in him a visceral yearning for an everlasting bliss:

> *Ave de la Utopía:*
> *Tu ojo soñoliento*
> *y voz fingida*
> *me muestran las señales en las plantas y rocas*
> *que guían a las islas del Eterno Domingo.*

> Bird of Utopia:
> Your somnolent eye
> and hypocrite voice
> show me the signs in plants and rocks
> that point the way to the Isles of Eternal Sunday.

In "Comarcas ignotas" (Unknown regions), to entertain his hunger for immortality, he reconstructs the utopian realms dreamed of by poets of past ages:

> *Acroceraunia, Aurosia, Acuarimántima*
> *fantásticas regiones del eterno verdor*
> *en donde no hay vestigios de la muerte*
> *¡oh patrias suspiradas de mi ser verdadero!*

> . . . . . . . . . . . . . .

> *¡Oh nombres que repite*
> *mi corazón en el exilio!*

> . . . . . . . . . . . . . .

> *¿Os hallaré algún día*
> *guiado por la luz de mi deseo?*

> Acroceraunia, Aurosia, Acuarimántima
> fantastic regions forever green
> where there is no trace of death
> oh longed-for homelands of my true being!

> . . . . . . . . . . . . . . .

> Oh names that my heart
> repeats in its exile!

> . . . . . . . . . . . .

> Will I find you some day
> guided by the light of my desire?

With this poetry, written upon reaching his sixtieth birthday, Carrera Andrade links in a most intimate way his old passion for the material world with his more recent longings for a transcendent life.

After a four-year absence, in the summer of 1964 Carrera Andrade returned to Paris. To the joy of once again being "the man from Ecuador under the Eiffel tower," he adds the prestige of his appointment as Ecuadorian ambassador to France. The French intellectuals welcomed him with joy, and events in his honor were celebrated in Paris. In September of 1965 he attended the Second International Biennial of Poetry at Knokke-le-Zoute, where he gave the inaugural lecture "The Poet and the Material World" (printed in *Interpretaciones hispanoamericanas*). In that lecture he analyzed the relationship that poets have long had with the material world, from Greek and Roman times to the poets of contemporary Spanish America, whose original posture in this regard he sums up this way:

> *Es en América Hispana en donde la poesía se abreva en la fuente primera de las cosas sin reflejos lógicos ni metafísicos. El hombre del Nuevo Mundo no sintió en su espíritu los carbones ardientes de la Edad Media y pudo contemplar libremente el fenómeno del mundo material desplegado con una riqueza sinfónica ante sus ojos. . . . El fracaso del Surrealismo como imitación en nuestra América y los estertores de toda una poesía desmesurada, hidrópica, retorcida, inexpresiva, deprovista de conceptos y de lenguaje y, en suma antipoética, anuncian la próxima restauración lírica del Nuevo Mundo, con su contribución propia: la actitud del hombre que interpreta los mensajes de las cosas y establece un pacto de alianza con el universo.*

> (*Interpretaciones hispanoamericanas*)

In Spanish America poetry feeds on the primeval fountain of things, without logical or metaphysical considerations. The man of the New World did not feel in his spirit the burning coals of the Middle Ages and could freely contemplate the phenomena of the material world unfolding before his eyes with symphonic richness. . . . Surrealism's failure as imitation in our America, and the death rattles of a whole body of misshapen, dropsical, convoluted, inexpressive poetry, devoid of concepts and language and, in sum, antipoetic, announce the approaching lyric restoration of the New World with its own contribution: the attitude of the man who interprets the messages of things and establishes an alliance with the universe.

In December 1965 the epic poem *Crónica de las Indias* (Chronicle of the Indies), was published in Paris. The poem is based on historical facts related to the despot Gonzalo Pizarro, discoverer of Peru and founder of Lima, who was assassinated as a result of internal political struggles. Carrera Andrade wanted to lecture modern dictators by arguing the futility of their exorbitant ambitions and spilled blood, using this poem to illustrate the unavoidable final fall represented by the emptiness and vanity of all human destiny.

Once more, political transformations in his country had a decisive impact on the life of Carrera Andrade. In November 1966 the new president of Ecuador appointed him Secretary of State. Among the farewell homages held in Paris to mark his departure, the most important was the book *Jorge Carrera Andrade* by René L. F. Durand. This French professor analyzed the life and poetry of the Ecuadorian by dividing it into three stages: "The World's Inventory," "Country Without a Map," and "Ecuador of the Heart." He concluded his remarks by noting that, "In his evolution we can appreciate the singularly passionate accents that make Carrera Andrade the poet of our anguish, but also the poet of our hope, more human and fraternal as he is profoundly rooted in his America and his country, Ecuador." Six months later, again due to political pressure, Carrera Andrade resigned from his post as Secretary of State and in September he traveled to Holland in his new capacity as Ambassador to the Low Countries. Prior to leaving Quito he published the volume of essays, *Interpretaciones hispanoamericanas*, in which he displays his broad understanding of South American culture and the constantly deepening reality

and destiny of the continent. As ever, this work displayed his dazzling lucidity in poetic matters, his ever-present drive to illuminate those mysterious regions of the self where poems are conceived. Among his books of essays this is perhaps the most indispensable for those who may want to better understand the author's human and literary personality.

In 1968 Carrera Andrade represented Spanish America at a festival organized by New York's Poetry Center and Lincoln Center, as well as at the International Poetry Festival sponsored by the State University of New York at Stony Brook, Long Island. At the same time *Poesía última* (Recent poetry) was published in New York. This volume also included his most recent unpublished compositions, under the title "Dawn Knocks at the Door." In one of the poems of this book, "El reino efímero" (The ephemeral kingdom), he places his identification with nature in opposition to the feeling of the essential vacuity of things: "Soy el hombre del bosque y soy el bosque mismo" (I am the man of the forest and I am the forest itself), he writes, "El dolor de los árboles sin hojas / entraba en la penumbra de mis huesos" (The sorrow of the trees without leaves / enters the penumbra of my bones). This identification extends to the human family of all times and latitudes: "Yo soy un hombre-pueblo, un hombre sucesivo / que viene desde el ser original / hasta formar la suma: un hombre solo" (I am a man-people, a successive man / who comes from the original being / to form the sum: a single man). It is only then, after a silence that has lasted his whole life, that a religious feeling arises in him:

> El alba llama a la puerta
> y cada día despierta
> mi sed de cielo y de sol
> y mi apetito de Dios.

> Dawn knocks at the door
> and each day awakens
> my thirst for sky and sun
> and my appetite for God.

After retiring from the foreign service in 1969 Carrera Andrade was named Distinguished Visiting Professor at the State University of New York at Stony Brook. What followed was twenty-two months dedicated to reading and reflection in the midst of the lovely vistas of Long Island Sound. Lectures given at Stony Brook, Vassar College, and Harvard University appeared in an English edition with the title *Reflections on Spanish American Poetry* (1973). In these pages he returns to the themes that have concerned him throughout his career as a writer: his interest in defining the essence of his continent's culture, particularly in regard to its lyric poetry; and his desire to elucidate his own literary production of the last ten years. Upon completing his contract at Stony Brook, Carrera Andrade returned to Paris.

At age sixty-nine he began a period beset by sickness, financial problems, and estrangement from his wife that forced him to return to Ecuador in 1975. There was of course consolation brought on by the international recognition of his poetry: in 1970 a bilingual Spanish-Italian edition of *Hombre planetario*, entitled *Uomo planetario*, with an introduction and translations by professor Giuseppe Bellini, appeared in Milan. In 1972 the critical study *Jorge Carrera Andrade: Introducción al estudio de su vida y de su obra* by J. Enrique Ojeda, was published in Madrid. In 1973 a bilingual anthology, *Selected Poems of Jorge Carrera Andrade* with an introduction and translations by H. R. Hays appeared; in the same year *Reflections on Spanish American Poetry*, translated by Don C. Bliss and Gabriela de C. Bliss, was published in New York.

Living now in Ecuador, Carrera Andrade became Director of the National Library, which afforded him a modest stipend. He resisted with fortitude an incapacitating illness and the loneliness and unconcern that marked his last three years. The publication in 1976 of his *Obra poética completa*, prepared with utmost care by the author himself, was enthusiastically celebrated in Ecuador. Its government rewarded him with the Eugenio Espejo prize, the highest accolade accorded to a literary figure in Ecuador. He died unexpectedly in Quito on 7 November 1978. He was seventy-six years old.

Carrera Andrade, besides being a poet, was a gifted prose writer, and he left behind a large body of work of high artistic value. In fact, the content of many of his pages in prose reappears, quintessentially molded, in his poems. According to him there is a moment in the poet's life when verse stops flowing to make way for prose. "First youth seems to mysteriously prepare the poetic gift. . . . Once youth's Cape Horn has been rounded, the song's liquid vein flows into the wide gulf of prose" (*Latitudes*). Of all his abundant prose work the most interesting is perhaps his autobiography, *El volcan y colibri,* published in 1970. Its pages reflect an attentive and concerned observer of Ecuadorian and international events. By virtue of his diplomatic assignments Carrera Andrade was eyewitness to the horrors of World War II and to the reconstruction period and the prolonged Cold War era that followed. Perhaps no Spanish American writer has had such a rare opportunity to live through all the vicissitudes of our century and to recreate those experiences in the crystal-clear mirror of a prose that, with the maturity of its author, had reached a transparency, harmony, and expressiveness not to be found outside his most accomplished poems. But, above and beyond his power of observation, his exquisite sensitivity, his prodigious memory that evoked details and events from many years before, and his lyrical style, it is the love for his country and for America that gives this autobiography its fascination and enchantment and, finally, its highest significance.

*Portions of the poetry have been translated*
*from the Spanish by Esther Allen.*

## SELECTED BIBLIOGRAPHY

### *Primary Works*

#### Poetry

*El estanque inefable.* Quito, 1922.
*La guirnalda del silencio.* Quito, 1926.
*Boletines de mar y tierra.* With a prologue by Gabriela Mistral. Barcelona, 1930.
*Rol de la manzana.* Madrid, 1935.
*El tiempo manual.* Madrid, 1935.
*Biografía para uso de los pájaros.* Paris, 1937.
*La hora de las ventanas iluminadas.* Santiago de Chile, 1937.
*Microgramas.* Tokyo, 1940.
*País secreto.* Tokyo, 1940.
*Registro del mundo: Antología poética.* Quito, 1940.
*Canto al puente de Oakland/To the Bay Bridge.* Trans. by Eleanor I. Turnbull. Stanford, 1941.
*Poesías escogidas.* With a prologue by Pedro Salinas. Caracas, 1945.

*Lugar de origen.* Caracas, 1945. Exp. ed, Quito, 1951

*Canto a las fortalezas volantes: Cuaderno del paracaidista.* Caracas, 1945.

*El visitante de niebla y otros poemas.* Quito, 1947.

*Aquí yace la espuma.* Paris, 1950.

*Familia de la noche.* Paris, 1953.

*Edades poéticas.* With "Edades de mi poesía." Quito, 1958. (An anthology and an essay by the author discussing his poetry.)

*Moneda del forastero: Monnaie de l'étranger.* Dijon, 1958.

*Hombre planetario.* Bogotá, 1959. 2d ed., Quito, 1963.

*Mi vida en poemas.* Caracas, 1962. (Autocritical essay followed by a selection of poems.)

*Los primeros poemas de Jorge Carrera Andrade.* Caracas, 1962. With a study by Giuseppe Bellini.

*Floresta de los Guacamayos.* Managua, 1964.

*Crónica de las Indias.* Paris, 1965.

*Poesía última.* New York, 1968. Edited and with an introduction by J. Enrique Ojeda.

*Libro del destierro: Livre de l'exile.* With a message to Africa and an introduction to the author by René L.-F. Durand. Dakar, 1970.

"Vocación terrena." *Arbol de fuego* (Caracas), no. 51, 1972.

*Misterios naturales.* Paris, 1972.

*Obra poética completa.* Quito, 1976. Reissued as *Obra poética.* Edited by Raúl Pacheco and Javier Vásconez, with a prologue by Alejandro Quejereta. Quito, 2000.

*Los caminos de un poeta: Obra poética completa.* Edited by Jorge Aravena. Quito, 1980.

*Jorge Carrera Andrade, Antología poética.* Selections and prologue by Vladimiro Rivas Iturralde. Mexico City, 2000.

### Prose

*Cartas de un emigrado.* Quito, 1933.

*Latitudes.* Quito, 1934.

*Rostros y climas.* Paris, 1948.

*La tierra siempre verde.* Paris, 1955. 2d ed., Quito, 1977.

*El camino del sol.* Quito, 1959.

*Galería de místicos y de insurgentes.* Quito, 1959.

*Viaje por países y libros.* Quito, 1961.

*El fabuloso reino de Quito.* Quito, 1963.

*Interpretaciones hispanoamericanas.* Quito, 1967.

*El volcán y el colibrí (Autobiografía).* Puebla, Mexico City, 1970. 2d ed., Quito, 1989. (The second edition contains a prologue by J. Enrique Ojeda.)

"Reflexiones sobre la poesía hispanoamericana." *Cultura.* Quito: Banco Central del Ecuador, 1983. Reissued in Quito in 1987 with an introduction by J. Enrique Ojeda.

*Relatos de un gozoso tragaleguas.* Selections and prologue by J. Enrique Ojeda. Quito, 1994.

### Translations by Carrera Andrade

*El séptimo camarada.* Barcelona, 1930. (A novel by Boris Lavrenef.)

*Antología poética de Pierre Reverdy.* Tokyo, 1940.

*Cementerio marino, Cántico de las columnas. Otros poemas de Paul Valéry.* Caracas, 1945.

*Poesía francesa contemporánea.* Quito, 1951. (Includes translations of the works of fifty-five French poets, annotated and with bibliographies.)

### Translations

*Canto al puente de Oakland/To the Bay Bridge.* Trans. by Eleanor L. Turnbull. Stanford, 1941.

*Secret Country.* Trans. by Muna Lee, with an introduction by John Peale Bishop. New York, 1946. (Translation of *País secreto.*)

*Visitor of Mist.* Introduction and trans. by G. R. Coulthard. London, 1950. (Translation of *El visitante de niebla y otros poemas.*)

*Emblems of the Season of Fury.* Trans. by Thomas Merton. Norfolk, Conn., 1961.

*Skin Diving in the Virgins.* Trans. by John Malcolm Brinnin. New York, 1960.

*Selected Poems of Jorge Carrera Andrade.* Introduction and trans. by H. R. Hays. Albany, 1973.

*Reflexions on Spanish American Poetry.* Trans. by Don C. Bliss and Gabrielle de C. Bliss. Albany, 1973.

### Secondary Works

#### Critical and Biographical Studies

Beardsell, Peter R. *Winds of Exile: The Poetry of Jorge Carrera Andrade.* Oxford, 1977.

Bellini, Giuseppe. "Etapa actual de la poesía de Jorge Carrera Andrade." *Lírica hispana* XX:234 (1962).

———. "Jorge Carrera Andrade." In his *Quevedo nella poesia ispano-americana del 900.* Milan, 1967. Trans. by J. Enrique Ojeda. In *Quevedo en la poesía hispanoamericana del siglo XX.* New York and Madrid, 1976. Pp. 21–35.

Cassou, Jean. "Jorge Carrera Andrade." In *Les ecrivain celebres.* Paris, 1965.

Córdova, José Hernán. *Itinerario poético de Jorge Carrera Andrade.* Quito, 1986.

Darío Lara, A. *Jorge Carrera Andrade. Memorias de un testigo,* 2 vols. Quito, 1998.

Durand, René L.-F. *Jorge Carrera Andrade.* Paris, 1966.

Mistral, Gabriela. "Explicación de Jorge Carrera Andrade." Barcelona, 1930. (Prologue to Carrera Andrade's *Boletines de mar y tierra.*)

Ojeda, J. Enrique. *Jorge Carrera Andrade: Introducción al estudio de su vida y de su obra.* New York and Madrid, 1972.

————. "Resonancia universal de la poesía de Jorge Carrera Andrade." *Cuadernos del Guayas,* 44:15–37 (March 1977).

————. "El americanismo literario de Jorge Carrera Andrade." Quito, 1987. (Introduction to Carrera Andrade's *Reflexiones sobre la poesía hispanoamericana.*)

————. "Jorge Carrera Andrade y la vanguardia." *Revista Iberoamericana,* July-December 1988, pp. 144–145.

Salinas, Pedro. "Registro de Jorge Carrera Andrade." *Ensayos de literatura española.* Edited and with a prologue by Juan Marichal. Madrid, 1961. Pp. 9–21.

Vandercammen, Edmond. "Lyric Profile of Jorge Carrera Andrade." *Adam International Magazine* XVI, no. 33:27–29 (April 1948). (Special issue dedicated to Carrera Andrade.)

# Fernando del Paso

## (1935–    )

## Vittoria Borsó

Fernando del Paso was born in Mexico City on 1 April 1935. He spent his adolescent years living on Mexico City's Justo Sierra Street, which he later chose as a setting for his second novel, *Palinuro de México* (1977; *Palinuro of Mexico*, 1996). Since he attended a state school, he did not receive a bi- or multilingual education. This is hard to believe in view of the fact that later he was so deeply rooted in English and French culture. His multilingualism is mainly a consequence of his passion for reading. By reading, first of all, Spanish translations of works by Alexander Dumas, Sir Walter Scott, Jules Verne, Eugène Sue, Emilio Salgari, William Faulkner, and Erskine Caldwell, and later the original English and French texts, he became well acquainted with European and North American literature.

After finishing high school, Del Paso attended medical school. He left, however, in order to study biology and economics at the Universidad Nacional Autónoma de México, earning bachelor's degrees in both fields. He then pursued graduate studies in economics for two years. At the same time he participated in a seminar on comparative literature at the Faculty of Philosophy and Letters. However, it was his extensive reading that played a role in his choice of writing as a career. In 1970, when he left Mexico for the United States, his personal library included more than two thousand volumes. His passion for books also led him to become the head of a major library (as were Jorge Luis Borges, Leopoldo Lugones, Alfonso Reyes, and many other Latin American authors).

Del Paso's first book, a poetry collection titled *Sonetos de lo diario* (Everyday sonnets), was published by the Mexican short story writer Juan José Arreola in his literary periodical *Cuadernos del unicornio* (1958). Arreola and other Mexican writers who appreciated the quality of Del Paso's writings supported his application for a fellowship of the Mexican Center for Writers (1964–1965). This fellowship enabled him to finish his first novel, *José Trigo*, which appeared in 1966. The success of that novel is evident from the fifteen editions published in Mexico alone.

Del Paso worked for an advertising agency in Mexico City until, on the recommendation of Juan Rulfo, Miguel Ángel Asturias, and Octavio Paz, he obtained a fellowship from the John Simon Ford Foundation that enabled him to attend the International Writing Program at the University of Iowa (1970–1971). In Iowa he worked on *Palinuro of Mexico*, his second novel, which was published in Spain in 1977 and in Mexico in 1980.

In 1974 Del Paso went to London, where he was hired as a newscaster for the BBC and as a producer of programs for its Latin American section. He also worked as a journalist. He later stated that the work in journalism forced him to become acquainted with an encyclopedic range of subjects, which in turn influenced his writing and the creation of his third novel, *Noticias del imperio* (1987; News from the empire). For the writing of this novel, Del Paso was awarded another fellowship by the John Simon Ford Foundation (1981–1982). In 1985 Del Paso moved to France, where he was a journalist for Radio France Internationale. A year later he entered Mexico's diplomatic service as cultural attaché at the Mexican embassy in Paris. He resigned in 1992 and returned to Mexico, where he accepted the directorship of the Biblioteca Iberoamericana Octavio Paz at the University of Guadalajara. Despite Del Paso's dissident position toward the Mexican government in his younger days, as a diplomat and as director of the Biblioteca Octavio Paz (established by the Mexican government), he was following in the Mexican tradition of critical intellectuals, writers, and artists (including José Vasconcelos, Jaime Torres Bodet, and Octavio Paz) by working for the government. Del Paso maintained a strict distinction between state politics and the cultural perspective of the country. Even as a representative of the Mexican state, he refused to consider the country's politics from a political point of view. This attitude is particularly obvious in the main theme of *Palinuro of Mexico,* which criticizes the student massacre by the Mexican government at Tlatelolco Square on 2 October 1968.

Del Paso is also a highly esteemed artist. Since 1973 he has had exhibitions in Mexico (Museo de Arte Moderno), the United States, England (Institute of Contemporary Art London), and Spain (Galería Juana Mordo, Spain). A 1997 exhibition was titled *Destrucción del orden* (Destruction of order). Kathleen Hjerter included Del Paso's art in her *Doubly Gifted* (1986), in which his work is shown with that of other famous writers who were also accomplished painters, among them William Blake, Edgar Allan Poe, Paul Verlaine, Charles Baudelaire, Victor Hugo, and Jean Cocteau. The "doubly gifted" writers find expression in painting, drawing, and graphic design when words are inadequate. For example, in his *Tres tristes tigres* (1967) Guillermo Cabrera Infante includes a full page printed in black ink to describe darkness. Julio Cortázar, Georges Perec, Umberto Eco, John Barth, and Carlo Emilio Gadda also have made use of pictorial language.

Despite his artistic talent, Del Paso's writings are less pictorial than they are highly poetic texts whose dynamic structures are based on carnivalesque strategies and on a network of different voices and discourses. Del Paso's texts are hence dialogical in the sense of Mikhail Bakhtin's reading of Dostoevsky, and they correspond also to the carnivalesque aesthetics related by Bakhtin to the work of Rabelais. In Del Paso's novels each character's voice is linked to a different discourse and a different consciousness, eventually leading to different perspectives, which are independent from the narrator's point of view. Such a polyphonic architecture is based on carnivalesque strategies, that is, grotesque processes developing ambivalent meanings and alternative visions of reality. The so-called *carnivalesque comique* eventually destabilizes oppositions, such as life and death, body and soul, fiction and reality, as well as ideologic and politic hierarchies. In fact, in Del Paso's characters, his description of the world, and his historical references, reality and fiction are intertwined, yet Del Paso stresses that the world described in his novels is very much part of reality. The combination of heterogeneous fragments of reality, as absurd as in René Magritte's paintings, shows the relativity of the systems of order we see as natural and take for granted. Because of his relativism and plurality of views, Del Paso has been considered a postmodern writer. He states that there are close fundamental connections between his work and Magritte's paintings. In a 1986 interview with Julio Olaciregui, Del Paso says, "Magritte travaille avec le réel; la locomotive telle qu'elle est, la pierre, le château, la pomme, le peigne, tout cela existe, c'est le contexte dans lequel il les met qui crée l'absurde, et c'est ce qui fait la grandeur de Magritte" (Magritte works with the real; the locomotive as it is, the stone, the castle, the apple, the comb, all those things exist, it is the context in which he puts them that creates the absurd, and that constitutes the greatness of Magritte). Del Paso expresses the absurdity of the ideological structures of the world and the plurality of the experience of reality through his writings as well as his painting.

Del Paso's works are mainly prose. After his first book of sonnets, a poetic form he continued to cultivate throughout his life, he did not publish poetry again until the early 1990s, when he started writing poetry for children: *De la A a la Z* (1990) and *Paleta de diez colores* (1992). He published essays in such periodicals as *Excélsior, Ovaciones, Proceso, Vuelta, La Jornada,* and *Tierra Adentro.* Some of his essays were collected in *El coloquio de invierno* (1992), along with works by Carlos Fuentes and Gabriel García Márquez.

Del Paso received the Premio Internacional España de Radiodifusión in 1986 for his radioplay *Carta a Juan Rulfo* (Letter to Juan Rulfo), which had been broadcast by Radio France Internationale as part of its Latin American programming. Del Paso's familiarity with the mass media influenced his writings. In fact, in his novels the world of publicity and other modern mass media is as real as the physical world. Del Paso demonstrates the permeability of fiction and reality in a world dominated by the media. Concrete and imaginary details—such as dreams, tales, myths, and literary characters—are intertwined. In this respect Del Paso shows his literary debt to Alfred Döblin and Günter Grass, a relationship studied by Susanne Lange (1995), who translated *Palinuro of Mexico* into German.

Del Paso has been awarded a number of prizes, including the National Prize for Linguistics and Literature (1991) and the Creador Emérico Prize, awarded by Sistema Nacional de Creadores de Arte (1993). Since 1995 he has been a member of the Colegio Nacional (Humanidades).

Having spent fifteen years (1970–1985) in Iowa City and in London, Del Paso acquired a familiarity with the English language that changed his attitude to his mother tongue. In *Palinuro of Mexico,* which mirrors the globetrotting of its author, the Spanish language experiences syntactical interferences from English. This is a creative device resulting from Del Paso's cosmopolitanism and his own ideology. In fact, when he left Mexico, Del Paso, like Octavio Paz and others, became aware of the fact that besides the Indian traditions, Mexican identity consists of hybrid cosmopolitan traditions, such as the Western Judeo-Christian, which are present and obvious in all cultural strata of the Mexican population. The cosmopolitan view of Mexican culture, which is in contrast to the nativism and the indigenous view of it reinforced by the Mexican Revolution (1910–1914), had been familiar to Mexicans since the cultural theories expounded by the Ateneo de la Juventud, and Del Paso himself recognized the influence of Alfonso Reyes, one of the leading members of the Ateneo, on his own work.

By the time Del Paso started writing his novels, the literature of the economic boom had abandoned the *novela de la revolución,* and had begun to favor a cosmopolitan type of literature which explores new linguistic structures. Juan Rulfo's *Pedro Páramo* (1955) had already led to the destruction of the myth of the revolution. The writers who became known as the Generation of the 1960s constructed expansive and synthesizing visions in which history and philosophy, religion and myth, linguistics and the visual arts are fused. The urban setting became more and more interesting. Carlos Fuentes's *La region más transparente* (1958; *Where the Air Is Clear*), the first novel to focus on Mexico City, is one of the major examples. Del Paso started writing his first novel, *José Trigo,* in 1959, a year after *Where the Air Is Clear* was published. In *José Trigo,* however, which was published in 1966 and awarded the Xavier Villaurrutia Prize in the same year, history plays a major role. The protagonist is Demetrio Vallejo, one of the leaders of the trade union that organized the strikes by railway workers in 1958–1959, which were suppressed by military force on the orders of President Adolfo López Mateos.

By contrast, *José Trigo,* in spite of its historical subject, represents a highly literary, linguistic, and sociological experiment. The historical material is used only for linguistic and textual purposes. Instead of being straightforwardly chronological, the text combines different periods as well as both historical and fictional settings. The principal setting is Nonalco-Tlatelolco during five centuries of national life, from the pre-Columbian period to contemporary times. Myths and history are combined, and historical and archetypal characters are fused. History is both a pretext and the point of departure for a symbolic interpretation of Mexican society by means of a linguistic experiment. Language is the real protagonist of this novel, in which the author, having written sonnets, creates rigorous poetic structures in a prose text. Del Paso is attracted by the rhythm, musicality, and plasticity of language.

Influenced by James Joyce as much as by classical Spanish authors, he discovers the appeal of embellishing language with both archaisms and neologisms. Aztec, Latin, and everyday Mexican words are intermingled. The linking of high and low styles is reminiscent of the experiments of the "Estridentistas," a nineteenth-century avant-garde group of Mexican writers.

*José Trigo* represents a verbal setting where the origin of language, as well as of the world, is lost in a primordial chaos. Objects are products of an imagination which is both absolute and independent of the referential world. Imagination thus is not escapism. It is, rather, a form of hyperrealism, a real world which is closer to experience. This kind of writing induces the submission of the author and the reader to the exuberance of language, for the imagined world upsets the normal structures of reality. As in the pictures of Magritte, reality and imagination are intertwined, yet the difference between them does not disappear. On the contrary, the difference between them underlines the historical relativity of reality as well as of the imagination.

In *José Trigo*, Del Paso's intention is to create a story which expresses the history and the myth of Mexico City. This is achieved by a superimposition of different periods: the characters belong both to contemporary life and to the pre-Columbian Aztec culture, a device already employed by Elena Garro in her short stories as well as in her novels, such as *Los recuerdos del porvenir* (1963). In relation to *José Trigo*, Nora Dottori, the Argentine scholar who has focused on Del Paso's writing, speaks of a rich language which combines dialectical, poetic, realistic, and allegoric discourse and such contrasting styles and types of words as antirhetoricism and solemnity, irony and elegy, archaisms and neologisms. Narrative techniques range from the realism of chapter 7 to the epic smoothness of chapter 5 (of both parts of the text), where the Cristíada, the Cristeros' revolt of the late 1920s, is the main topic; and from the chronological rigidity of historical sections to the free verse of chapter 4: "Porqué todo será mentira, / andar tragando miedo y llorar calando fríos, / se tiene sed a botellones huecos, / se sabe hambre a zopilotes lentos, se llueve y se mojan / pedazos / de piedras, / de ríos, / de pollos, / de moscas . . ." (Because everything

will be a lie, / wandering and swallowing the fear, and crying dripping wet cold, / one is thirsty for huge empty bottles, / one knows hunger for slow roosters, one rains and one gets wet / [rains and gets wet by] chunks of stones, / of rivers, / of chickens / of flies . . .).

Echoes of Agustín Yáñez's *Al filo de agua* (1947); of Juan Rulfo's *Pedro Páramo*, which Del Paso considers the most important book ever written in Mexico; and of Carlos Fuentes's *Where the Air Is Clear* are apparent. The prose poem, which Del Paso developed differently than Yáñez or Fuentes did, plays an important role, in particular in the section ("El puente"); in the two chapter 8's: "Una oda," which is dedicated to the Mexican railways, and "Una elegía," which portrays the history of the temple of Santiago Tlatelolco. Corresponding to Julio Cortázar's self-irony demonstrated in the character Oliveira in *Rayuela*, in *José Trigo* the function of irony is to correct the abuse of linguistic excess. Nevertheless, irony and the linguistic agility of *José Trigo* are in danger of becoming an exercise in baroque artificiality, except in the chapters on the Cristíada, where the rhetoric, irony, and imagination produce unexpected views of history expressed in extremely heterogeneous creative metaphors and images. An example is the Indian who brings news of the outbreak of the Cristeros' revolt. He carries both a letter and a dead pigeon, possibly the Holy Ghost or the emblem of the destiny of the Mexican Church if it is not saved by the Cristeros.

Del Paso constructs a plot which corresponds to the "non-Euclidean" expression that Valle Inclán required for modernity. In fact, the manipulation of the temporal dimension, such as the overlapping of different times or the combination of heterogeneous spaces unfolded from the link between reality and dream builds a dynamic network of parallel spaces. Another technique of such a narrative is the desegregation of grammar, since the rules of grammar are based on the logics of the Euclidean space. The heterogeneity of language of *José Trigo* unfolds from several genres and styles developed from the national traditions, including Nauhatl poetry, the colonial chronicles, the "novel of the revolution," and the antirhetorical style of Juan Rulfo.

Having abandoned the exotic view of Latin American magical realism, Del Paso stresses the characteristics attributed by Carlos Fuentes to the *nueva novela latinoamericana,* such as the reflection, on a metaliterary level, of the implications of language and historicity within the process of writing. This becomes even more evident in his second novel, *Palinuro of Mexico,* which Del Paso wrote in Iowa City and London. The twenty-five chapters took almost eight years to write, and the editorial revision of the book several months more; the author's spelling errors, resulting from linguistic interference from English, had to be corrected. The novel received several literary prizes: the Premio Novela México (1979); the Premio Internacional de Novela Rómulo Gallegos for the best Spanish-language novel (1982); the Casa de las Américas (Cuba, 1985); the Diana Prize (1987); and the Prix Médicis for the best foreign novel published in France (1985–1986). However, this novel was received less enthusiastically in Mexico than it was in Spain. For instance, the manuscript was awarded the Novela Mexico Prize, sponsored by Editorial Novaro, a firm that published mainly comic books and second- and third-rate titles. However, the owner of Editorial Novaro refused to publish the prize-winning manuscript because it was too long. Therefore, the book was first published in Spain.

Del Paso considers himself an excessive writer in style and references, "a baroque writer, extravagant and immoderate" (Stavans interview, 1996). Baroque exuberance is not typical of the Mexican novel. Rather, during the twentieth century, the baroque style is identified with the works of Cuban writers such as Alejo Carpentier, José Lezama Lima, Guillermo Cabrera Infante, Severo Sarduy, and Reinaldo Arenas. Baroque style—which has a number of (often contradictory) definitions—is sometimes defined as a self-referential, parodic, and carnivalesque style which ambiguously links a variety of levels of meaning and interpretation. Because of their hybrid exuberance and despite the concrete references to Mexican history, the novels of Del Paso, especially *Palinuro of Mexico,* must be seen in relation to the baroque. Del Paso's baroque style developed not only from his reading of Cuban literature but also from the important colonial Spanish-American traditions (*barroco de Indias*) in Mexico. During the colonial period, when Indian and Christian cultures came together in the valley of Anáhuac, an enormous number of texts were produced in New Spain which testify to the blending of cultures as well as to the

negotiations between the Spanish and the pre-Columbian traditions. After the Conquest, Mexico became the site of "transferences" and "translations" that created the Mexican colonial baroque style. More recent studies have dismissed the conception of colonial baroque and the idea of a lack of identity resulting from the lack of authentic cultural traditions after the Conquest. The magnificence of the Latin American baroque appears to be its parodistic reflection of the repressive climate in New Spain. The mixture of European genres and Indian traditions, as well as the combination of lofty forms and the proliferation of marvelous details, have been likened to precolonial churches. According to the subversive reading carried out within the framework of the more recent studies, colonial poets such as Sor Juana Inés de la Cruz adapted the Continental baroque to Mexican literature, transforming it in a parodistic way. In keeping with these studies, Del Paso considers Indian art and mythology (for instance, the Aztec goddess Coatlicue) to be "baroque" in the sense of "a style that tries to saturate space by abusing curves to the point of hyperbole."

The generation of Del Paso belongs to a period when Mexican literature opened itself to the crossing of cultures and texts resulting from the intertextual networks of world literature. The intertwining of voices and the emphasis on oral discourse in written literature is also a characteristic of this time. In addition, during the 1970s, when Del Paso started writing *Palinuro of Mexico,* the mass media began to transform Mexican literature. The boundary between the real and the virtual became permeable.

An example of the metaliterary principles which characterize the *nueva novela* is the metaliterary reflection about the genesis of the book at the end of *Palinuro of Mexico.* Del Paso evokes several literary figures as witnesses to the birth of his protagonist, Palinuro. The fictional characters that appear in *Palinuro of Mexico* stem from novels by Rómulo Gallegos, Carlos Fuentes, Mario Vargas Llosa, Julio Cortázar, Alejo Carpentier, José Lezama Lima, Juan Rulfo, and Gabriel García Márquez, as well as by European writers ranging from the authors of the picaresque genre in the Spanish Golden Age and Cervantes, to Rabelais, Swift, Goethe, Jules Verne, Kafka, Robert von Musil, Thomas Mann,

James Joyce, Italo Calvino and Günter Grass. Moreover, the mass media are as omnipresent as the Bible.

Palinuro is born into a polyethnic family: Uncle Esteban, who fled from Hungary during the Great War and traveled across the world to Mexico, clinging to his dream of becoming a doctor; Grandpa Francisco, a Freemason and companion of Pancho Villa, and the literary representative of Del Paso's own grandfather, Francisco del Paso y Troncoso; Uncle Austin, a former British marine; and grandmothers, aunts, and cousins. The protagonists of this novel, Palinuro and Cousin Walter, are the two sides of the same person. The novel has features of Del Paso's life, yet at the same time it is linked to fictional characters. Whereas the protagonists are variations on the same individual, the secondary characters (Grandfather Francisco, Mama Clementina, Papa Eduardo, Aunt Luisa, Jean Paul, the French botanist) are more clearly defined.

Palinuro and Walter, a globetrotter who travels to Europe, are antithetic personalities. They also represent the most important characteristics of Del Paso's prose: the encounter of opposing logics, opposing realms of reality, without any possibility of synthesis. The opposition between different principles serves to prove the relativity of each. Cousin Walter is a student of medicine; Palinuro wants to study medicine. The topic of their disputes is the realm of medical science: the human body becomes the means of questioning the anthropological foundation of humanity. Walter represents encyclopedic scientific knowledge; Palinuro, the imagination. Whereas Walter defines reality through the scientific logic of verification, Palinuro is not satisfied with this. The operation which is their topic of discussion is the dissection. For Walter the human body is a series of organs, an abstract fragmented object, which can be defined medically. Nevertheless, Walter cannot perform a dissection because he sees beyond the organic body and considers the dreams, wishes, and imagination of each human being, of each individual existence.

The imagination, represented by Palinuro, is a means of criticizing the logical and scientific view of the world. The imaginary world is deeply rooted in reality. The imagination of Palinuro, even his imaginary journey to the islands of advertising agencies, is a reference to concrete reality. Palinuro reflects the problematic aspects of Mexican society as well as the universal problems of civilization. The first is a reference to the crisis of Tlatelolco; the second is a criticism of scientific abstractions from human existence through technological and scientific progress, which is represented through the science of medicine. With respect to Tlatelolco, the novel can be approached as a political novel. One of its leitmotifs is the student massacre on 2 October 1968, at Tlatelolco Square (the Square of the Three Cultures). Just as the Olympic Games were about to begin, the Mexican government was facing strong pressures for democratic reform. Refusing to institute reforms, the ruling Partido Revolucionario Institucionalizado, under the leadership of President Gustavo Díaz Ordaz, ordered the army to suppress the student uprising with tanks and bullets. More than a thousand died, and many more were injured. The massacre marked the end of the illusion of Mexico as a democracy; it also substantially changed the course of the Mexican narrative, impelling it away from the experiments with time and space and point of view, and toward a direct and penetrating examination of the political structures and the nature of political power in Mexico. The complex, extensive literature of Tlatelolco is the direct testimony written by the Generación de la Onda ("Generation of the Wave," José Agustín, Gustavo Sáinz, Parménides García Saldaña), and presented in novels such as Elena Poniatowska's *La noche de Tlatelolco* (1979) or in critical essays by Carlos Monsiváis in his *Días de guardar* (1971) and *Entrada libre: Crónicas de la sociedad que se organiza* (1987).

However, *Palinuro of Mexico* differs from other works of Mexican literature directly linked to the Tlatelolco crisis. It is written from a distance, and it is an example of the critical power of the imagination to fight politics (Palinuro does not die during the massacre but later, when in a vain endeavor he tries to fight a tank, just as Don Quixote had tried to fight the windmills). It was the protagonist in *José Trigo*, which appeared two years before Tlatelolco, who died at the hands of army squads at Tlatelolco. The political message of *Palinuro of Mexico* is delivered through the imagination. Throughout the novel, the dreams of Palinuro are as real as the reality of advertising or the reality of violence. The same is true of the leitmotif of illness and medicine. In chapter 18 Palinuro imagines the model of an enormous hospital which contains the complete world and in which the obsessions of sick people become reality.

Cousin Walter represents an encyclopedic scientific knowledge. He is interested in psychology, philosophy, the history of art, and botany, as well as in modern forms of knowledge such as advertising. Walter's use of this knowledge shows the metaphysical power of the mass media in contemporary culture. Contrasting this knowledge with the imagination of Palinuro, Del Paso criticizes the natural sciences in a modern technological framework (a criticism presented as early as Gustave Flaubert's *Bouvard et Pécuchet* [1881]). The realm of medicine is particularly interesting, because it eventually leads to the crucial question of how to understand, define, and experience the body. Del Paso is familiar with the phenomenological discovery of the differentness and the oddity of his own body by the cognitive subject. The body as a function belonging to the subject as well as to the object (the body of the physician is, for instance, a part of his own subjectivity as well as of the object the physician wants to investigate) has been the crucial question of phenomenology from Edmund Husserl to Maurice Merleau-Ponty. Del Paso's conception of Cousin Walter and his observations corresponds to the idea of the differentness of the body developed by phenomenology: "cuándo . . . físicamente hablando, uno comenzaba a dejar de ser uno mismo" (when . . . in a physical sense, one began to stop to be oneself). In keeping with Merleau-Ponty's thesis of the schism between the body as a subject and as an object, Walter recognizes the inability of the eye, the primary organ of scientific knowledge, to see itself. Del Paso considers medicine to be a science which fails. Although it succeeds at times, it is truly powerless in that it cannot give a final explanation of the enigmas of the human body. Medical science reflects the progress of civilization as well as the fascination of the body.

Eroticism is another leitmotif of *Palinuro of Mexico*. Since childhood, Palinuro has loved his first cousin, Estefania, with an overwhelming and consuming passion. They fulfill their incestuous desires and bizarre fantasies in a room on the Plaza Santo Domingo. The erotic body is, hence, the other aspect of the medical abstraction of the body. In spite of criticism of the pornographic dimensions of this novel, pornography is only parodied, and eroticism is more a way of rebelling against bourgeois society and civilization. In this respect, the function of eroticism corresponds to the more recent interpretation of the Marquis de Sade's work, as well as of the work of modern writers who have been influenced by the subverting power of eroticism, such as James Joyce, William Faulkner, and John Dos Passos. In fact, according to recent interpretations of de Sade related to the works of Georges Bataille and of Michel Foucault, erotic discourse reverses the Western opposition between body and spirit by revealing the apories of Western traditions and by deconstructing the logics of philosophical and political discourses based on them. In addition, the heterogeneity of sensual perceptions and erotic desires eventually attacks the ideological hierarchies of politics.

In *Palinuro of Mexico* the characters are facets of the world and represent a multiplicity of attitudes toward reality. This multiplicity, together with the oscillation between the third person and first person, gives the text a dialogic structure which fragments the vision of the world rather than unifying it. Palinuro is, like Gulliver, on a "voyage of self-discovery" (Fiddian, 1982). *Palinuro of Mexico* is a good example of what Gustavo Sáinz called "the encyclopedic novel," which is characterized by different kinds of knowledge viewed from a critical perspective; overstepping the conventional narrative limits through an epic style; detailed description of a technology or a science; and a multiplicity of styles and rhetorical devices (see Fiddian, 1990). Influenced by works such as Thomas Pynchon's *Gravity's Rainbow*, *Palinuro of Mexico* also shows the fragmentation of the self. Palinuro is motivated to write by witnessing reality from a perspective composed of myriad different selves. The intertextuality of the work and the pastiche destabilize the "natural" relationship between fiction and reality; fiction eventually becomes the means of criticizing reality and history. The emphasis on historicity underlying Del Paso's first two novels eventually led to the *nueva novela histórica*, the outstanding genre of Latin American literature since the 1970s.

Historicity is also the crucial topic of *Noticias del imperio*, Del Paso's third monumental novel. In it history and metahistory (the question of how to write history) are the main concerns. This novel was awarded the Mazatlán de Literatura Prize for 1987. Like *Palinuro of Mexico, Noticias del imperio* has been translated into several languages (including Chinese). It was adapted as a drama by Susana Alexander and Roberto D'Amico (*Requiem para un imperio*; published in 1988). Del Paso had worked on *Noticias del imperio* for ten years, collecting historical material and searching for sources on the lives of Juárez, Maximilian, and Carlota. He also wrote a dramatic adaptation of the first monologue of Carlota, *La loca de Miramar* (1988; The madwoman of Miramar).

In *Noticias del imperio* the imagination again establishes a counterpower to politics and reality. Reality is linked to the past and to the rigorous documentation of historical facts. Del Paso demonstrates his command of historiographical sources and historical records. Twelve of the twenty-five chapters are devoted to the monologue of Empress Carlota, virtually imprisoned in her castle of Bouchout, where her demented mind constructs a theater of memory inspired by Rodolfo Usigli's *Corona de sombra* (1943). Her mind alternates between the evocation of the tragic course of Maximilian's venture as the emperor of Mexico (1865–1867), who was sent by Napoleon III, and the contemplation of the disintegration of the Habsburg and other European empires as the result of World War I. Carlota's madness is, in addition, the continuation of Palinuro's imagination and dream. Its role is to dissolve the power of history and historiography. Carlota is also the character who allegorically represents the passages, translations, and transferences between the European and Latin America cultures. She is therefore the mediator who constructs a particular type of "new historical novel."

Latin American new historical novels, which focus on nineteenth-century history, concern the interpretive model of representing the nation as well as of legitimating national historiography within the cultural memory of Latin America. (This was also the focal point of eighteenth-century novels about the founding heroes of independence, such as Bolívar.) Such historical novels concentrate on the early national history and isolate the identifying features of each country. The new historical novels also question the national identity and reflect a crisis in the definition of the Latin American nation. They both respond to questions about the truth of the past or the needs of the present, and question the cognitive means of historical knowledge. They show

the relative value of historiographical discourse. By invalidating the cognitive mechanisms of historiography through an imagination which admits multiple views of the past, the new historical novel responds to the claims of postmodernism. Del Paso's novels are representative of this type of new historical novel based on the rejection of monological rules and of a homogeneous, authoritarian concept of the past.

*Noticias del imperio* subverts the concept of history in the sense of a privileged vehicle for reconstructing the past. It also destroys Western beliefs in the superiority of written texts. The authority of religious and political power is subverted through parody as well as the use of many voices. The latter first of all concerns the narrator. The "editor" choosing fragments and historical documents is the first narrative voice. In addition, the implicit author is the fictional one who, as a historian, is in dialogue with other historians. Furthermore, there is an involved narrator speaking in the first person; his most impressive speeches are in the fragments of the last chapter, which functions as an epilogue: "el problema *no* es que en México hayamos matado a Maximiliano . . . hayamos vuelto loca a Carlota" (the problem is not that we have killed Maximilian in Mexico . . . that we probably have provoked the insanity of Carlota). In addition, there are chapters organized as dialogues between characters and other chapters containing letters, such as the incomplete correspondence of two brothers, Jean Pierre, a historian living in Mexico, and Alphonse, a soldier in the French army accompanying Maximilian in Paris. The historian ironically criticizes the purpose of civilizing Mexico and rejects the excuse used by Napoleon III for starting the invasion. In the end we have a traumatized narrator (Carlota) and several voices without any identifiable origin.

Oral traditions are included as an emblem of pre-Columbian cultures, but also as a sign of the power underlying everyday Mexican urban culture. Both are used as means of subversion. In contemporary Mexican literature, everyday culture has become a subversive principle which was developed by the chronicles, an important genre developed from the elaboration of chronicles about Tlatelolco, but also applied in several essays by Carlos Monsiváis. The parody of various kinds of written sources, from the fictional "Ceremonial para el fusilamiento de un Emperador" ("Ceremoniales de la Corte, escrito por Maximiliano," or ceremonials as at a king's court) to the historiographic sources, reverses the methodology of history without the reintroduction of other authorities. Even oral history is parodied—for instance, in the chapter entitled "Camarón, camarón . . . ," where historical events are related by a charlatan trying to augment his salary.

In addition to this criticism of historiographical discourses, Del Paso uses Carlota's insanity as a special approach to history. In *Palinuro of Mexico* he anticipated the topic of Carlota's insanity: Luisa, Palinuro's aunt, who had lost her mind following the death of her fiancé, Jean Paul. Palinuro's grandfather, Francisco, compares Luisa and Carlota, as well as Jean Paul and Maximilian, because of the implied liberal tendencies of Maximilian. Whereas the madness of Luisa in Palinuro was an ironical means of showing the limitations of rationality, in *Noticias del imperio* Carlota's insanity serves to demonstrate the limits of a historiography which is unfolded from the concept of nation. In contrast to the national historiography, Carlota constructs a double perspective toward the historical crisis through her memory, which links European and Mexican history. Her memory is a model of cultural transferences, displaying the long history of misreading between cultures, of reciprocal expectations, of reciprocal stereotypes of self and of others. Her hybrid memory rewrites the trauma of the double origin of the Mexican nation. However, it also shows the subsequent history of Mexico and of Europe as an answer to the trauma of the origin of the nation. National identities, hence, are the reaction against a preexisting "other" founding the national origin: the other which is excluded, is dominated, or is the active hegemonic power destroying the self.

The crucial point of Carlota's narration is her madness and her longevity. Because of her long life, the memory she builds has an archaeological topography where epochs and times are intertwined, going from the middle of the nineteenth century (the utopia of ideological modernization) to the beginning of twentieth century (the utopia of technical modernization as an offspring of World War I). Through her double view, Carlota is a mirror of two continents and several nations included in the chronological and geographical spaces of her memory. Carlota, a traveler between the Old World and the New World, experiences rites of passage; she is initiated into a world which is both transparent and opaque, and, in the last analysis, inaccessible. Del Paso's Carlota is a nomadic subject. He stresses the "initiation" of the Belgian princess—her transformation from Charlotte to Carlota—showing all the paradoxes of cultural contact with the inaccessible "otherness" of other cultures. Carlota thus feels she plays a double role much like that of Malinche, the Indian woman, who became the mistress of and translator for Cortez, the mythical mother of Mexicans, who was considered to be both the translator and the traitor of her people.

The heterogeneous memory displacing times and spaces is also a "memory of the end of century." Here the "text" of the history becomes a web in which the processing of historical data occurs without centering or decentering frames. There is an important difference between the demythification of history in this novel and in the novels developed since the 1970s. By means of the imagination, the latter deconstruct history, rejecting the truth of official historiography or complementing it with the tangential historical facts, personal histories. These texts eventually create new "possible histories." However, Carlota's heterogeneous memory goes beyond this. The plurality of perspectives which are intertwined in these texts not only provide a historical relativism, which eventually leads to a historical pluralism, but also attack the idea of history itself corresponding to the questioning of the rule of the historian, as Linda Hutcheon (1989) has pointed out.

Moreover, in *Noticias del imperio* the crisis of Mexican history also implicates Europe, not only because of Carlota's nomadic life but also because of the allusion to the emergence of the crisis of modernity during her long life in the castle of Bouchout. In addition, by relating the development of Benito Juárez from Indian adolescent to enlightened hero, the narrator reminds us of the myth of Rousseau's noble savage. By means of Carlota, the narrator intertwines perspectives from both sides of the ocean. History therefore unravels, which rules out the possibility of returning to a definitive origin.

In *Noticias del imperio,* the resolution of contradictions and antinomies is not through an open commitment to an idea. This principle of Mikhail Bakhtin's dialogism, cited by Seymour Menton (1993) as an important structure of the new historical novel, becomes the most important means of linking dialectically different historical discourses and points of view. Del Paso responds to the question formulated by Jorge Luis Borges in *Historia universal de la infamia* about the relationship between history and literature. If the focal point of the historical novel had been the narration of the past verified by reality, then in the new historical novel the debate between the "historically verifiable" and the "symbolically true" is the point of departure. In spite of Borges's argument favoring the "symbolically true," and his lack of interest in the "historically verifiable," the dialectical contradiction between the two is not resolved. Neither of them can be rejected or accepted as a reliable method for interpreting history. The use of multiple voices as a means of pluralism leads not only to the continuous opposition of different voices and visions, of high and low discourses, but also of history and imagination. In *Noticias del imperio* popular culture and its oral communication question the authority of the written historical accounts as parts of the "official" version of history. Carlota is, again, a good example. On the one hand, she represents the European political system; on the other hand, she Mexicanizes herself, adopting fantastic titles such as "Regente de Anáhuac, Reina de Nicaragua, Baronesa del Mato Grosso, Princesa de Chichén Itzá," a parodistic invalidation of European monarchies.

One passage is particularly important in *Noticias del imperio.* According to Del Paso, the culpability of Mexicans lies in the misunderstanding of the history of Maximilian as a part of their own history. Historical criticism of both national history and the occupation of Mexico by the troops of Napoleon III is necessary in order to bury the ghosts of history. The reintegration into Mexican history of the European emperor and the empress who wanted to become Mexican is an urgent necessity that only literature is able to achieve: "El problema *no* es que en México hayamos matado a Maximiliano, que en México, tal vez, hayamos vuelto loca Carlota: el problema es que a ninguno de los dos los enterramos en México. . . . ninguno de los dos, ni él ni ella, quedaron integrados a esta tierra fertilizada al parejo con los restos de todos nuestros héroes y todos nuestros traidores" (The problem is not that we have killed Maximilian in Mexico, that we probably have provoked the insanity of Carlota in Mexico: the problem is that we did not bury either one of them in Mexico. . . . neither he nor she has remained part of this soil which has been fertilized equally by the remains of all our heroes as well as of all our traitors).

The title *News from the Empire* is a paratextual allusion to what Del Paso proposes to accomplish in this novel: he wants to offer new knowledge about a period of Mexican history neglected by Mexican historians. In addition, the concept "news" emphasizes that, despite the strong and attentive documentation by the author, the "news" given in this novel does not claim to be the ultimate version of history. Rather, this "news" seeks to destabilize and to question an official historical discourse claiming to give an authentic, true, and complete record of what happened in the past.

Del Paso's last novel, *Linda 67. Historia de un crimen* (1995; Linda 67. History of a crime), has as its protagonist David (Dave) Sorensen, a Mexican living in San Francisco with his wife, Linda Lagrange, the daughter of a Texas millionaire. Dave, who is working for a small advertising company but leading an expensive life, is financially dependent on his wife and his father-in-law. When Linda starts planning to divorce him, Dave kills her. Despite his very elaborate alibi, Dave is arrested and eventually condemned to death.

*Linda 67* did not receive the same enthusiastic reception as Del Paso's other novels, probably because it did not meet readers' expectations. In his earlier novels, in fact, Del Paso explored novelistic possibilities, archetypal topics, language theories, artistic movements, and the history of medicine, as well as Mexican history, in order to represent the fragility of life, its relationship to death, and the limitation of sciences to ultimately understand human existence. At the same time the novels offered the power of imagination, eroticism, and love as a means of overcoming human limitations. In *Linda,* Dave is a perfect representative of both the power of imagination, love, and eroticism and the limits of humanity. His power to dream reawakens after meeting Olivia, a Mexican woman who is the opposite of the gringa Linda. Olivia represents the freedom she and Dave experience during a short weekend in Cuernavaca, just before he is imprisoned and condemned to death. Linda, who has lost the "natural" relationship to her own body and to eroticism, is a perfect representation of the rational and bourgeois modern life. The opposition between the sterile rationality of the American culture and the creativeness of mythical communion between bodyness and nature in Mexico, earlier pointed out by Octavio Paz (*El laberinto de la soledad*, 1950) and by Carlos Fuentes in several writings, is also a crucial aspect of this novel. Nevertheless, like in the other novels of del Paso, the reader does not find a definite solution.

Imagination and eroticism remain, in *Linda*, an unreal moment existing only in a heavenly *locus amoenus*. There is no longer a real chance for imagination to cope with the power of rationality and everyday life. What remains in this pessimistic novel is the memory of the lost right to dream. In fact, although Dave commits the crime, and he will pay for it, the novel shows that the real crime lies in the pathological communicative structures of modern bourgeois society. Del Paso uses the genre of the detective novel to demonstrate the impossibility of overcoming the limitations of human beings. Every character, even the detective, is imprisoned in a labyrinth of neurotic passions; and the passion of Linda's father for his daughter, as well as his disgust with Dave, inspire him to set the lethal trap that discloses Dave's murder. The mediocrity of the characters and the indifference of the narrator with respect to moral judgments remind the reader of Albert Camus's *L'Etranger* (1942; *The Stranger*). As in *The Stranger*, in *Linda 67* there is no escape from the absurdity of existence—here the absurdity is the offspring of bourgeois capitalism and a global economy. In addition, in contrast to the earlier novels, imagination no longer offers an escape from the limitation of existence, except for the duration of one chapter of the text.

However, because the discursive means of the novel is Dave's memory, the melancholy toward the lost paradise of imagination, eroticism, and love prevails. Confronted with the knowledge of the unavoidable end of life, Dave's memory, combining times and spaces, continues to claim the right of dreaming and the freedom of imagination.

## SELECTED BIBLIOGRAPHY

### Primary Works

#### Novels

*José Trigo*. Mexico City: Siglo XXI,1966.
*Palinuro de México*. Madrid: Alfaguara, 1977. Reprint, Mexico City: Joaquín Mortiz, 1980.
*Noticias del imperio*. Madrid: Mondadori, 1987.
*Linda 67. Historia de un crimen*. Mexico City: Plaza y Janés, 1995. Reprint, Barcelona: Plaza y Janés, 1996.

#### Short Stories

"Fragmento muy breve de una novela larga." *Revista de la Universidad de México* 2, no. 8:19–20 (April 1968).
"Camarón, Camarón." In *Novísimos narradores hispano-americanos en marcha, 1964–1980*. Edited by Ángel Rama. Mexico City: Marcha Editores, 1981.

#### Poetry

*Sonetos de lo diario. Cuadernos del unicornio* 21 (1958).
*De la A a la Z*. Mexico City: Origen, 1990.
*Paleta de diez colores*. Mexico: CIDCLI, 1992.

#### Essays

"La imaginación al poder. El intelectual y los medios." *Revista de la Universidad de México* 34, no. 2:15 (October 1979).
"Mi patria chica, mi patria grande." *Casa de las Américas* 146:154–160 (January–February 1983).
"With an Arrow Through his Heart." *Review: Latin American Literature and Arts* 33:24 (1984).
*El coloquio de invierno*, vol. 3. Mexico City: FCE/UNAM/ CNCA, 1992. (Essays by Del Paso, Carlos Fuentes, and Gabriel García Márquez.)

#### Translation

*Palinuro of Mexico*. Trans. by Elisabeth Plaister. Normal, Ill.: Dalkey Archive Press, 1996.

### Secondary Works

#### Critical and Biographical Studies

Barrientos, Juan José. "La locura de Carlota: Novela e historia." *Vuelta* (Mexico City) 10, no. 113:30–34 (April 1986).

———. "Del Paso y la historia como readymade." *Biblioteca de México* 32:51–56 (March–April 1996).

Borgman, Patricia Dawn. *Función del espacio en "José Trigo" de Fernando del Paso*. Santa Barbara, Calif.: University of California Press, 1992.

Bruce-Novoa, Juan. "*Noticias del Imperio*: La historia apasionada." *Literatura mexicana* 1, no. 2:421–438 (1990).

Clark, Stella, and Alfonso Gonzales. "*Noticias del imperio*: La 'verdad histórica' y la novela finisecular en México." *Hispania* 77, no. 4:731–737 (December 1994).

Chávez, Daniel. "Propuestas para un análisis del discursos en Noticias del imperio de Fernando del Paso." *Revista de Literatura Mexicana Comtemporánea* 1, no. 3:29–34 (May–August 1996).

Cortés, Eladio. *Dictionary of Mexican Literature*. London: Greenwood, 1992.

Dottori, Nora. "*Jose Trigo*: El terror a la historia." In *Nueva novela latinoamericana*. Edited by Jorge Lafforgue. Buenos Aires: Editorial Paidós, 1969. Pp. 262–299.

Fell, Claude. "Sexo y lenguaje en *Palinuro de México* de Fernando del Paso." In *Coloquio internacional: Escritura y sexualidad en la literatura hispanoamericana*. Madrid: Centre de Recherches Latino-Américaines/Fundamentos, 1990.

———. "Historia y ficción en *Noticias del imperio* de Fernando del Paso." *Cuadernos Americanos* (Mexico City) 28:77–89 (July–August 1991).

Fiddian, Robin W. "*Palinuro de México*, a World of Words." *Bulletin of Hispanic Studies* 58:121–133 (1981).

———. "Beyond the Unquiet Grave and the Cemetery of Words: Myth and Archetype in *Palinuro de México*," *Ibero-Amerikanisches Archiv* 8:243–255 (1982).

———. "A Case of Literary Infection: *Palinuro de México and Ulysses*." *Comparative Literature Studies* 19, no. 2:220–235 (summer 1982).

———. "James Joyce y Fernando del Paso." *Insula* 455 (Madrid) 39:10 (October 1984).

———. "James Joyce and Spanish-American Fiction: A Study of the Origins and Transmission of Literary Influence." *Bulletin of Hispanic Studies* 66:23–39 (1989).

———. "Fernando del Paso y el arte de la renovación." *Revista Iberoamericana* (Pittsburgh) 56, no. 150:143–158 (January–March 1990).

Foster, David William. *Mexican Literature: A Bibliography of Secondary Sources*. Metuchen, N.J.: Scarecrow Press, 1981. Pp. 265–266.

Gonzales, Alfonso. "Literatura y revolución en *Palinuro de México*." *Romance-Languages Annual* (West Lafayette, Ind.) 2:431–433 (1990).

———. "Neobarroco y carnaval medieval en *Palinuro de México*." *Hispania* 74, no. 1:45–49 (March 1991).

———. "*Noticias del imperio* y la historiografía postmodernista." In *Actas Irvine 92, Asociación Internacional de Hispanistas*, I–IV. Irvine; Calif: Juan Villegas, 1994. Pp. 251–267.

Hancock, Joel. "New Directions in Historical Fiction: *Noticias del imperio*, Fernando del Paso and the Self-Conscious Novel." *Hispanic Journal* (Purdue University) 12, no. 1:109–121 (spring 1991).

Hjerter, Kathleen G. *Doubly Gifted: The Author as Visual Artist*. New York: Abrams, 1986.

Hölz, Karl. "Fiesta der Worte: Sprachmagie und politische Vision in Fernando del Paso, *Palinuro de México*." In *Sprachspiele und Sprachkomik/Jeux des mots et comique verbal*. Edited by Michael Herrmann and Karl Hölz. Frankfurt: Peter Lang, 1996. Pp. 165–195.

Hutcheon, Linda. *The Politics of Postmodernism*. London: Routledge, 1989.

Hwang, Byong-Ha. *Narratological-Effectist Analysis of Fernando del Paso's Noticias del imperio*. Los Angeles: University of California Press, 1991.

Lange, Susanne. "El traductor en la galaxia de palabras: *Palinuro de México* de Fernando del Paso y los laberintos de la traducción." *Texto y contexto* (Bogota) 28:209–219 (September–December 1995).

Menton, Seymour. "La nueva novela histórica mexicana." In *Literatura Mexicana/Mexican Literature*. Edited by José Oviedo. Philadelphia: University of Pennsylvania Press, 1993. Pp. 104–113.

Pons, Maria Cristina. "*Noticias del imperio*: Entre la imaginación delirante y los desvarios de la historia." *Hispamérica* 23, no. 69:97–108 (December 1994).

Quirarte, Vicente. "*Noticias del imperio* de Fernando del Paso: La visión omnipotente de la historia." In *Perfiles: Ensayos sobre la literatura mexicana reciente*. Edited by Frederico Patán. Boulder, Colo.: Society of Spanish and Spanish-American Studies, 1992. Pp. 141–146.

Rodríguez-Lozano, Miguel. "*José Trigo* y la crítica literaria." *Literatura Mexicana* 5 no. 2:479–495 (1994).

———. *José Trigo: El nacimiento discursivo de Fernando del Paso*. Mexico City: Universidad Nacional Autónoma de México, 1997.

Ruiz-Rivas, Héctor. "Francia en México: La expresión de lo local y lo foreano en *Noticias del imperio* de Fernando del Paso." *Cahiers du Monde Hispanique et Luso Brésilien Caravelle* (Toulouse) 58:49–64 (1992).

Sáenz, Inés. *Hacia la novela total: Fernando del Paso*. Philadelphia: University of Pennsylvania Press, 1992. Madrid: Pliegos, 1994.

Sáinz, Gustavo. "Fernando del Paso o el arte de imitar." *El Día* 12 (October 1966).

———. "Carlos Fuentes: A Permanent Bedazzlement." *World Literature Today* 57:568–572 (1983).

Seligson, Esther. "*José Trigo*: Una memoria que se inventa." Twentieth Century 5:162–169 (1976).

Thomas, Peter N. "Historiographic Metafiction and the Neobaroque in Fernando del Paso's *Noticias del imperio*." *Indiana Journal of Hispanic Literatures* 6–7:169–184 (spring–fall 1995).

Xirau, Ramón. "Lecturas: José Agustín, Navarrete, Del Paso." *Diálogos* 14:24–26 (1967).

*Interviews*

Cabrery, Enriqueta. *El Día*, 23–25 March 1988.

Cañedo, Patricia. "La novela europea está en decadencia." El Buho (Mexico City), 28 June 1987.

Ochoas, Gerardo. *Sábado* (supplement of *Unomásuno*), 23 July 1988.

Olaciregui, Julio. "Palinuro ou le nuage encyclopédique de Fernando del Paso." *Américas* (April 1986).

Stavans, Ilan. "A Conversation with Fernando del Paso." *Review of Contemporary Fiction* 16, no. 1:122–132 (spring 1996).

*Radioplay*

*Carta a Juan Rulfo.* Produced by Radio France Internationale (Latin American programming), 1986.

# José Donoso

## (1924–1996)

## Cedomil Goic

José Donoso was born in Santiago, Chile, at 292 Avenida Holanda, in the borough of Providencia, on 5 October 1924, the son of Dr. José Donoso and Alicia Yáñez. His father was a prestigious physician who belonged to a family of professionals connected socially to landowners of central Chile. His mother was the niece of Don Eliodoro Yáñez, the founder of the newspaper *La Nación* and an outstanding figure in Chilean politics. She was related to the novelist and storyteller María Flora Yáñez and to Alvaro Yáñez, the author of *Miltín* (1935), *Diez* (1937), *Umbral* (1977), and other narratives of the avant-garde.

From 1932 to 1942, Donoso studied at the Grange School in Santiago. He attended the school along with Luis Alberto Heiremans and Carlos Fuentes, whose father was the Mexican ambassador to Chile. He then attended the Patrocinio de San José school and the Liceo José Victorino Lastarria. In 1943 he quit school and went to work. During 1945 and 1946, he traveled to Magallanes and Patagonia, in the far south of Chile, where he worked on the sheep farms for eight months, and then he went to Buenos Aires, Argentina, where he worked at the docks as a bookkeeper and then as a waiter in a restaurant. With a friend he visited Jorge Luis Borges at the National Library.

In 1947 he returned to Chile to finish high school, and then he began his studies at the College of Philosophy and Educational Sciences at the University of Chile, in the old Pedagogical Institute, concentrating on English literature. In 1949 he was awarded a scholarship by the Doherty Foundation. From that year until 1951, he studied English literature at Princeton University. At that time he wrote his first short stories in English, "The Blue Woman" (1950) and "The Poisoned Pastries" (1951), both of which were published in *MSS*, a student literary magazine. In 1952, after traveling around the United States, Mexico, and Central America, he returned to Chile.

Donoso then began a period of increasingly creative activity, producing short stories, novelettes, and novels. During this stage, the reading public and the critics gradually recognized the originality and value of his work, although he made his living by teaching and through an increasing dedication to journalism. He taught at the Kent School in Santiago and lectured on English literature at Catholic University in Santiago. He participated in the Primeras Jornadas del Cuento (First Sessions of the Chilean Short Story), organized by the writer Enrique Lafourcade in 1953. Lafourcade selected Donoso's story "China" for inclusion in his *Antología del nuevo cuento chileno* (1954; Anthology of the new short story in Chile).

A year later Donoso published his first book, *Veraneo y otros cuentos* (1955; Summer vacation and other stories), which won that year's Municipal Literary Prize. In 1956 he published *Dos cuentos* (Two short stories), and in 1957 he published his first novel, *Coronación* (*Coronation*, 1965). From 1958 to 1960 he lived in Buenos Aires, Argentina. After returning to Chile, he began writing as a journalist for *Ercilla*, an important national weekly magazine where he soon became a staff reporter. He was awarded the Chile-Italia Prize for excellence in journalism in 1960. That year he published his book of short stories *El charleston* (*Charleston and Other Stories*, 1977). On 13 October 1961, in Santiago, he married María Pilar Serrano, a Bolivian painter he had met in Buenos Aires, and in the same year he began teaching at the University of Chile School of Journalism. At the 1962 Writer's Workshop at the University of Concepción he began writing *El obsceno pájaro de la noche* (1970; *The Obscene Bird of Night*, 1973). He then participated in the 1962 Writer's Congress in Concepción. During this period, he renewed his friendship with the Mexican novelist Carlos Fuentes. In 1964 Donoso traveled to Chichén Itzá, Mexico, after an invitation from the Third Symposium of the Interamerican Foundation for the Arts, and in 1965 he traveled to New York, to be present at the publication of the English translation of *Coronation*. He returned to Mexico to write for the literary magazines *Siempre* and *Diálogos*. As a guest in Carlos Fuentes's home, he wrote the novels *El lugar sin límites* (1966; *Hell Has No Limits*, 1972) and *Este Domingo* (1966; *This Sunday*, 1967).

After 1965 Donoso matured as a writer, and his work was increasingly recognized. In 1962 he had won the William Faulkner Foundation Prize for the Latin American Novel, for *Coronation*. From 1965 to 1967, he was writer-in-residence at the University of Iowa's Writers' Workshop. He received a Guggenheim Fellowship in 1968 (and again in 1973), and during the late 1960s he lectured at numerous universities in the United States. In 1965 he completed five years of reporting for *Ercilla*; his collected short stories, *Los mejores cuentos de José Donoso* (The best stories of Jose Donoso) were also published that year. In 1967 he traveled to Portugal and Spain; while staying in Mallorca, he suffered a depression. In 1968, while teaching at Colorado State University, Fort Collins, during the winter semester, he underwent emergency surgery to cure him of his ulcer attacks. Because of the surgery he was subjected to morphine injections, which caused hallucinatory side effects. He also acquired hepatitis C as a result of contaminated blood transfusions, and this caused him to suffer recurrent attacks of encephalitis throughout the remainder of his life. He returned to Mallorca and afterward settled in Barcelona. There, after eight years of strenuous work, he finished *The Obscene Bird of Night*. Under pressure by his literary agent, Carmen Balcells, Donoso eliminated several chapters and wrote the final pages in a single night. The novel, published in 1970, gave him a distinguished place among contemporary novelists. This book was to be awarded the 1970 Premio Biblioteca Breve, but that year the award was permanently suspended due to an internal crisis at the Spanish publishing company Seix Barral. Donoso settled down in the small village of Calaceite, in Teruel, where he lived in a seventeenth-century house and where he remained until 1974.

In 1971 he published in Spain a compilation of his *Cuentos* (Short stories), and the following year, his *Historia Personal del Boom* (1972; *The Boom in Spanish American Literature: A Personal History*, 1977). In this book, Donoso scrutinizes with humor and grace Emir Rodríguez Monegal's discussion of the editorial boom of the new novel, as presented in *El boom de la novela hispanoamericana* (1972; The Boom of the Latin American novel). With *Tres novelitas burguesas* (1973; *Sacred Families: Three Novellas*, 1973), Donoso defined a new genre, the *novelita* (novelette), ironically representing a world that breaks with the practical, materialistic bourgeois way of life and its characteristic common sense. This meant a radical innovation in the way the world had been represented. In 1974 he moved to Sitges and then to Madrid. In 1975 he taught at Princeton University. Later in the year he taught at Dartmouth College and attended a colloquium on his work at the Congress of the International Institute of Iberoamerican Literature in Philadelphia. During that same year, he wrote *Casa de campo* (1978; *A House in the Country*, 1984) while staying in Calaceite, adding for the first time a political note to his narrative production. In 1976 he returned for a few months to Chile, after a ten-year absence. His mother, who had been ill for some time, died in Santiago. Carlos Flores, a Chilean filmmaker, made a short documentary film entitled *José Donoso*, which was later distributed as a videocassette. Interesting biographical information accompanies the images and dialogues with fellow writers of his generation.

In 1978 *A House in the Country*, Donoso's second great novel, was published. The novel won the Premio de Crítica (Critics' Prize) in Madrid. He later published two new novels, first *La misteriosa desaparición de la marquesita de Loria* (1980; The mysterious disappearance of the marquise of Loria), in which several erotic narrative genres popular at of the beginning of the twentieth century converge, and then *El jardín de al lado* (1981; *The Garden Next Door*, 1992), a novel about exile. He also published his only book of poems, *Poemas de un novelista* (1981; Poems of a novelist).

In 1981 the Winthrop College Symposium on Major Writers met to study his work. The following year Donoso returned to live in Santiago. This year and through the next fifteen years, he wrote journalistic articles for Agencia EFE, and these were published in newspapers like *El Universal*, of Mexico; *Prensa Libre*, of San José, Costa Rica; *El Tiempo*, of Bogotá; *El Nacional*, of Caracas; *La Nación*, of Buenos Aires; *El Comercio*, of Quito; *El Expreso*, of Lima; *O Globo*, of Rio de Janeiro; and *El Mercurio*, of Santiago. This stage in Donoso's life was characterized by his increased interest in Chile's social and cultural realities. He started offering a writers' workshop at his home in Galvarino Gallardo Street. He published his second collection of novellas, *Cuatro para Delfina* (1982; Four stories for Delfina), continuing with the genre he had originated with *Sacred Families*. In 1983 a dramatic version of *Sueños de mala muerte* (Miserable dreams), one of his novelitas, was staged by the Ictus Theatre Company in Santiago, and later in Buenos Aires, Caracas, and Cádiz, Spain. The dramatic text was published as a book in 1985.

In 1984 he traveled through the United States, lecturing at the University of Michigan, Ann Arbor, and other universities. He then traveled to Montevideo and Buenos Aires. He finished his ninth novel, *Donde van a morir los elefantes* (Where the elephants go to die), and started writing his memoirs, which would be completed and published in the year of his death. During 1986, Donoso and his wife went to Castro on the island of Chiloe in southern Chile, where he rented a house. Both were detained for sixteen hours by the Castro city police during a public demonstration in support of schoolteachers who had been fired from their jobs. Hours later the news of their detention was known all over the world, and both were freed without explanation. Through this experience he was inspired, and he immediately began writing the novel *La desesperanza* (1986; *Curfew*, 1988). Later that year he attended the International Book Fair at Frankfurt, West Germany, to launch the novel; afterward, he traveled to Madrid for the same purpose. This novel was very well received by the reading public. Donoso, for the first time, makes direct reference to the political and social situation in Chile. He was then invited by the Woodrow Wilson Foundation to come to Washington, D.C., where he was given the opportunity to do research on a subject of his interest. In 1987 he traveled to Spain, where he received the Encomienda de la Orden de Alfonso X, el Sabio (Knight-Commander of the Order of King Alphonse, the Sage) from the hands of King Juan Carlos I.

In Rome a theatrical adaptation of *The Obscene Bird of Night* was staged by Caterina Merlino and Antonio Arevalo and the Aleph Teatro company at the theater L'Orologio, under the title "L'osceno uccello della notte." The same work was also staged in Montreal, adapted by Pierre Larroque and performed by the Théatre L'Eskabel. During the same year he began a new writers' workshop at his home. In 1988, during the month of October, an Italian translation of *Curfew* was published in both Italy and in France. That same year, in which Pinochet was defeated in the national plebiscite, he joined the PPD Party (Party for Democracy) in an effort to encourage the return to democracy in Chile. He started writing a novel he entitled *El pez en la ventana*, but the book was never finished.

In 1990 he won the Premio Nacional de Literatura (National Literary Award), the most important literary award in Chile. He was the first writer to receive this award under democracy after seventeen years of dictatorship. He published *Taratuta: Naturaleza muerta con cachimba* (1990; *Taratuta: Still Life with Pipe. Novellas*, 1993). That year he also won Italy's Mondello Award, and in 1991 he received France's Roger Caillois Award, as well. In 1992 he was invited for the second time by the Woodrow Wilson Foundation. He spent the time in Washington, D.C., doing research. In 1994 the

Ministry of Education celebrated the author's seventieth birthday with an international colloquium of scholars and writers and issued a publication of the papers that were presented at the colloquium (*Donoso 70 años*, 1997). He received from the Chilean government the medal of Gran Oficial de la Orden del Mérito Docente y Cultural (Grand Officer of the Order of Teaching and Cultural Merit), and the Medal of the City of Santiago was awarded to him by the mayor of the city. In the same year, the city of Madrid honored him during Semana de Autor (Author's Week), from 28 November to 2 December. He was unable to attend, however, because he was experiencing another of his health crises and had to remain in Barcelona. Soon afterward, however, he recovered enough to visit Geneva, Milan, and Rome before returning to Chile.

In 1995 Donoso traveled to Buenos Aires to attend the International Book Fair in order to launch his most recently published novel, *Donde van a morir los elefantes* (1995; Where the elephants go to die). He traveled then to Madrid, where the Council of Ministers of Spain awarded him the Gran Cruz del Mérito Civil. (Great Cross of Civil Merit). In Vigo, Spain, on 16–17 October he delivered a lecture and participated in a dialogue about his book with the Spanish writer Carlos Casares. Once back in Chile he conducted a new writer's workshop at his home, which was attended by the younger generation of writers.

In 1996 Donoso received a honorary doctorate from the Universidad Nacional de Cuyo, Mendoza, Argentina, and was awarded an Honorific Citizenship of the City as well. He attended the XVI Feria Internacional del Libro de Santiago (XVI International Book Fair of Santiago), where he launched his book *Nueve novelas breves* (1996; Nine short novellas). He looked weak and walked slowly through the book fair, accompanied by his secretary. The last year of his life he spent writing a script for the Mexican TV series. He published his memoirs under the title of *Conjeturas sobre la memoria de mi tribu* (1996; Conjectures on the memoirs of my tribe).

José Donoso died of cancer in Santiago on 7 December 1996. Two months later, on 13 February 1997, his wife María Pilar Serrano, died of a stroke. From 11 February to 14 February 1997 the University of Murcia,

Spain, sponsored a colloquium in honor of the writer and his work. He was buried in Zapallar, a summer resort on the central coast of Chile, next to his wife, his parents, and his old nanny. His tenth and last novel, *El Mocho* (1997; The novice), and a collection of his journalistic articles, entitled *Artículos de incierta necesidad* (1998; Articles of dubious need), were published after his death.

Donoso began to write at the age of twenty-five. His literary beginnings coincided with the first stirrings of the Generation of '50, whose writers began to publish between 1950 and 1965. These were the writers who participated in the Jornadas del Cuento, organized by Enrique Lafourcade, who collected their stories in two anthologies, *Antología del nuevo cuento en Chile* (1954; Anthology of the new short story in Chile) and *Cuentos de la generación del cincuenta* (1959; Stories of the Generation of '50). The so-called Generation of '50 was, as a matter of fact, only a small group of writers—those participating in Lafourcade's Jornadas—and did not include all the writers of the generation. The group even lacked internal cohesiveness. There were dissidents within the group who broke with Lafourcade and did not want their stories collected in the anthologies, and there were others whose stories were rejected by him. The most important factor explaining their coming together was their age, their generational proximity, and that in the years between 1950 and 1965 they all began to publish their works. Members of this generation, besides Donoso, were Jorge Edwards, who in 1999 would become the first Chilean writer to be awarded the Premio Cervantes de Literatura (Cervantes Literary Award), Guillermo Blanco, Jorge Guzmán, Enrique Lafourcade, Enrique Lihn, Luis Alberto Heiremans, Jorge Díaz, and Egon Wolff. Over the years, they all were awarded literary prizes and received the recognition of the reading public. Donoso, undoubtedly the most outstanding figure of the group, was the first to attain international recognition. His stature is comparable to that of his contemporaries Carlos Fuentes and Gabriel García Márquez, a Nobel Prize winner. Translation of his books into numerous languages, his prolonged visits to many Latin American countries, and his protracted stay in Spain have all contributed to the international scope of his literary reputation. In addition to being identified as a representative figure of Latin American literature, he is considered part of the Latin American literary "boom."

Donoso has contributed significantly to the discussion and clarification of this term in *The Boom in Spanish American Literature: A Personal History.* Following Emir Rodríguez Monegal's coinage of the concept, Donoso presents the different layers or age groups that were part of the publishing phenomenon of Latin American writers in the 1960s. He begins with the boom's *gratin* (kernel), composed of Donoso's own generational peers, the Mexican novelist Carlos Fuentes (1928), the Colombian Nobel Prize winner Gabriel García Márquez (1927), the older Julio Cortázar (1914–1984), and the comparatively young and very successful Peruvian novelist Mario Vargas Llosa (1936). During the 1960s all of them were favored by a widening of the European and North American markets to include the Latin American novel. After describing this fundamental layer of the boom's geology, Donoso further distinguishes the "proto-boom," or predecessors, Alejo Carpentier (1904–1980), Juan Carlos Onetti (1909–1995), Juan Rulfo (1918–1986), Jorge Luis Borges (1899–1986), and José Lezama Lima (1910–1976); and the younger generation, or "junior boom," composed of Alfredo Bryce-Echenique (1939), José Emilio Pacheco (1939), Gustavo Sáinz (1940), Severo Sarduy (1937–1993), Antonio Skármeta (1940), and other young writers.

Donoso tells the story of the boom with humor and ingenuity, describing both its central and marginal components. His book is a clever reflection on the external aspects of literature in general and the novel in particular from 1962, the year of the first Seix Barral Biblioteca Breve Prize, to 1971, when the dissident Cuban poet Heberto Padilla was arrested by Fidel Castro's government, an event that seriously affected the political stance of Latin American writers and changed many of their views regarding the significance of the Cuban Revolution.

Donoso's book, which grounds its discussion of the boom on facts and on shared literary beliefs, is nonetheless written from an intuitive point of view. Structured as a literary memoir, it is enriched with irony and skepticism. The expanded second edition, published in 1983, adds two appendices, one written by María Pilar Serrano, that turn the book into a minor chronicle of the lives of contemporary Latin American writers. Serious scholars have used Donoso's classification as their own when studying the "new" Latin American novel.

The dominant trait of Donoso's narrative style is disregard for the conventions of realism he has systematically practiced, which gives him a place of his own among the great contemporary Latin American novelists. Representations from the dark side of the imagination (forms of confinement, transformations, a descent into Hell) produce in Donoso's narrative a network of rich and complex connections. On the one hand, his narrative draws on classical and modern European works, popular and learned; on the other, it harks back to fundamental works of Latin American literary tradition and folklore. Charles Dickens, Henry James, James Joyce, Virginia Woolf, D. H. Lawrence, and William Faulkner are his closest affinities within English-language literature. The French writers Jean-Paul Sartre and Albert Camus have been of decisive importance for Donoso, as well as for other Latin-American writers of his generation. Anthropologist Claude Lévi-Strauss's *Tristes tropiques* (1955) also had a revelatory effect on Donoso.

Donoso's narrative style is characterized by the disintegration of the narrator, which he accomplishes through the creation of multiple narrative voices; the cancellation of the narrator's interpretive capacity and authority coincides with the assumption of a skeptical cognitive position or a dialogic intertwining of different narrative voices that share the same cognitive capacity. He has also practiced, like Borges, the deception of the narrator, canceling in an unexpected ending the momentum gained up to that point. In this regard, Donoso has made use of several possibilities, such as the deception of the basic narrator, in *The Garden Next Door,* who is replaced unexpectedly in the final chapter by a female narrator; the romantic irony of the nineteenth-century narrator in *A House in the Country,* and in a parodic mood, the successful mixing of several narrative genres, especially the erotic novel, the mystery novel, and the novel of humor and satire.

An English critic considered Donoso's first work, *Coronation,* a "vastly overfurnished novel. We have not seen anything like it since 1890." Local critics, similarly on the wrong track, thought that it was a response to the *neorrealismo* (neorealism) or social realism that was on the decline during the 1950s. The novel was, in fact, something quite different. *Coronation* portrays three types of existence: inauthentic, as contrasted with authentic, existence; the existence of madness; and innocent existence. The middle-aged protagonist, Andres, lives an inauthentic existence, conducting his life according to a methodical and disciplined daily routine, symbolized by his collection of walking sticks, which he maintains at ten pieces, selling one when he acquires a new stick and buying new ones only to improve the quality of the collection. The security and stability with which he has planned his life become problematic when Andres's alienated and impersonal existence is invaded by a presence that bursts into his world and gradually begins to undermine its security.

Andres has long fantasized and idealized the world of inauthentic existence in a place he calls Omsk, a city in which everyone leads a life of routine. He was first motivated to create this dreamworld when a glimpse of authentic consciousness filled him with anguish. All the insecurity of his existence finds its refuge in his harmless and recurrent dream. Omskians live the gregarious, undifferentiated forms of existence adopted by society, in which individuality and personality remain alienated. Omsk reflects the existence Andres has always led and now hesitates to abandon, because leaving it would entail the sacrifice of placidity and security.

Andres's gradual descent into madness at first takes on an ominous and dark form that does not make its way into his consciousness; we are introduced to it through the novel's objective narration. The arrival of the maid Estela establishes the motif that allows us to trace the process of change in Andres's psyche. The girl's modest aspect is presented, along with the first occurrence of the image that will dominate the narration: the vision of her pink palms. The sight of Estela's palms at first fills Andres with disgust, which later turns into a feeling of ominous and brutal torment. While for Andres this feeling is still dark and intangible, his mad grandmother speaks out, with exact lucidity, on the significance of what is happening. The violence of the old woman unsettles her grandson, who considers her

reasoning absurd and intolerable. The situation is intensified when the old woman orders Estela to wear a pink shawl, an image that repeats the motif of the palms. These images reappear as Andres's disturbed consciousness suffers a crisis and the full import of his overwhelming anguish becomes clear to him.

Andres has been contacted by a seller of antiques, who wants to show him a walking stick. At the seller's house, Andres is confronted with the deformed and perverse sensuality of the antique dealer's wife, who is draped in her own pink shawl. The full epiphany in Andres's consciousness occurs when he leaves the antique dealer's house and the presence of the abominable woman. Only then does he realize that he desires Estela and accepts the existence of his desire. When he comes across Estela and her boyfriend, he discovers what has attracted him to the girl has been true passion, more than just desire. Eventually, Estela will falsely yield to Andres for a moment. Then, when she uses his passion as part of her own self-interested scheme, she pushes him headlong into self-annihilation.

Andres is thus propelled into the second form of existence: that of madness, which has been emblematized in the novel by his grandmother. Andres had noticed, first of all, her clairvoyance and, through her, the cognitive virtues of madness, which render one capable of understanding reality with perfect lucidity. He has also observed that she frequently speaks about death, without anguish. He has had a conversation with his doctor about the disorder of the universe and its congruence with the insanity and thoughtlessness that are part of anarchy, injustice, and the world's turmoil. When Andres finds that he has been deceived by Estela, he recognizes the absurdity and meaninglessness of everything and, at that point, enters the existence of madness: he will consciously and deliberately alienate himself in order to avoid the harrowing anguish of a fall he cannot endure. In this manner, inauthentic existence, briefly transformed into anguished authenticity, leads to another mode, in which he can escape the fear and trembling of authentic existence.

The third form of existence characterized in the novel is the lack of conscientiousness that antecedes good and evil, and that may be called innocent existence. Full of precariousness and of extreme helplessness, this miserable condition is the manifestation of the merely vital, of the purely instinctive, the blind, and the spontaneous. At the same time, it is a form of existence capable of recognizing the deformation of personal dignity and even of experiencing evil as an ominous presence, although not clearly or distinctly. In *Coronation*, this form of existence essentially represents life, and the interplay of life and death shapes the represented world. This interrelationship is felt in every significant moment of the story, engendering the interdependence between the different modes of existence. From a slightly different perspective, members of the social classes are presented as projections of either decaying or life-giving realities. In Donoso's later novels, characters who belong to the higher class absorb life anxiously from the lower-class characters, who generously share with them their vitality.

*Hell Has no Limits* and *This Sunday* were written at Carlos Fuentes's home in Mexico. Both novels destroy binary oppositions, emphasize ambiguity, and construct narrative worlds that are close to and at the same time remote from the representation of a common world. Allusions to social and political strata and power, dominance, and dependency, are allegorically built. The accent is on that which is disturbing or strange, or which violates common experience of behavior, accepted norms, and social restrictions, and also on that which is artistic, as in children's games and in masked or disguised impersonations.

Donoso began *The Obscene Bird of Night* in Chile and finished it in Spain. A writer's diary on the novel's composition, its planning stages, and the author's reflections is available in Donoso's "Note Books," numbers 37 to 47, which are on file at Princeton University's Firestone Library, and in "A Small Biography of *The Obscene Bird of Night*," published in *The Review of Contemporary Fiction* 12, no. 2 (1992), and added to the most recent Spanish edition of the novel (1997). The title, presented in its context in the novel's epigraph, is taken from a letter to William and Henry James from their father; it is an image that points to the dark side of the imagination. The world represented in the novel lends an animated existence to a grotesque reality: the persistent, indeterminate existence of a plurality of worlds that constantly affirm and deny their identities, giving rise to impersonation, transformation, masks, and disguises. Multiplying the number of worlds and

tensions, and adding to them the blurred conscience of an elaborately structured narrator, the novelist unfolds his labyrinthine novel with his unequaled genius for the monstrous, for all that does violence to the common norm.

Donoso goes beyond the disintegrated narrators who exist in the novels of Onetti and Fuentes, offering us something markedly different. His narrator embodies the greatest complexity that a novel can propose, in that he is narrator as well as a character and a witness, presented through an extraordinary structure. Within the apparent unity of the narrator, each dimension takes on a totally novel character and a strangeness that subjectively conditions the objectivity of the narrated world. The disintegration of the narrator consists in the shapeless fluctuation of multiple identities—his substitution and participation in different personalities—and, at the same time, in a reductive movement, accompanied by a physical dwarfing, down to the level of the minuscule and contemptible. Upon the ambiguity of this double movement, the narrator bases both his will to live and his will to self-annihilate. Two myths polarize this double tension: one, that of Oedipus; the other, that of the *imbunche*, a myth of the Indians of southern Chile, in which a sacrificial victim is monstrously transformed by closing all the openings of the body.

The ambiguity of the narrator is presented, in one aspect, in the character of Humberto Peñaloza, author of the biography of the wealthy Don Jerónimo de Azcoitía and the intended chronicler of La Rinconada, an estate inhabited by a society—created by Don Jerónimo as a way to hide his deformed son, Boy—that shields abnormal beings from the ordinary context of life. The ambiguity of the narrator is also presented in Mudito, who narrates and hides manuscripts under his bed, as do his fellow inhabitants at the Casa de Ejercicios Espirituales de la Encarnación de la Chimba (House of Spiritual Exercises of the Incarnation at La Chimba), a retreat house dating from the eighteenth century that now offers asylum to elderly female servants and orphan girls, and which serves as a storehouse for their personal junk and useless possessions. On two planes—that of the narrator as such and that of the narrator as a character—the tensions are overlapped. It is on this novel within a novel that part of the identity of the narrator is founded. On the one hand, Humberto Peñaloza's name is repeated 9,300 times in the one hundred volumes of the biography that is kept in the library of Don Jerónimo; on the other, the chronicle of La Rinconada is imagined but not written and, in a similarly unsatisfactory way, not perfected. Mudito's narration to Mother Benita and the entire narration in the second person, whose degree of immediacy, ensured by the constant use of *usted* or *tu* (the formal and familiar forms of "you" in Spanish), fails to certify its reality because no voice is proffered by the narrator, who is mute. This expressive impotence characterizes the narrator in all his dimensions.

The ambiguous nature of the narrator is achieved in singular manner, beginning with his perspective, that is, his interpretation of reality, his peculiar point of view. This is the most characteristic aspect of any narrator in fiction, and as used by Donoso it is the one that appeals most vividly to the active and credulous participation of the reader, because it concerns a magical view of the world. This viewpoint establishes a cause-and-effect relationship between distant but synchronic situations with unusual traits, presented with surprising efficacy in a series of repetitions, participations, and substitutions of demonological resonance. These devices describe a world in which reality is partly at a standstill (time has been suspended) and partly blurred, fluctuating, and indeterminate (the dislocation of time is absolute). Through this magical view, the novel expresses the strangeness of the world: there is instability in every narrative sequence. With the transfiguration of the narrator, the narration controls and then loses its point of view, only to redefine it in a new context of discourse, exploiting at the same time the indicative possibilities of the personal pronouns of the first and second person.

The reader must constantly readjust to the narrator's fluctuating perspective, in order to harmonize it with the new "point of speech" (*punto de hablada*, in the Spanish philosopher José Ortega y Gasset's terminology). The disintegration of the narrator is thus governed by a pervading lack of determination. The identity, the personality of the narrator, his point of speech, his spatial-temporal positioning, are in constant fluctuation and contradiction. The narrator's own degree of knowledge is affected by his lack of determination, to the extent that he represents himself as impotent to grasp the real condition of what he observes or experiences, or the consistency of his own sphere of reality. To him, the real seems ambiguous, an uncertainty that lies somewhere between hallucination, dream, nightmare, magic, ritual, invention, and practical reality. Yet, at the same time, some constants are established in the tortuous conscience of the narrator: the suspicion and even the conviction he has developed concerning the virtues of magic; the dark and unconscious impulses of the characters; the duplicity and disguises of the world; the compulsion for order and the determination of the self by the "Other"; the intolerance of the world for the foreign and the transformation of the latter into the monstrous and the obscene; the unendurable anguish of being a stranger in the world.

In his function as witness, the narrator defines his condition as that of voyeur. This voyeurism is used to interpret the power of the servants and the dispossessed. The narrator interprets his own power in terms of voyeurism and represents it magically. The narrator-as-witness projects the characteristics of the world in a sexual sense, with an explicit phallic symbolism, especially with the attribution of that sense to the eyes, which, magically, transmit their power to those who do not have it and who need a witness in order to perform adequately. The expression coincides with resentment and aggressiveness that are expressed in a sexually ambiguous way. This sense forms part of the magical situation in which the son of Don Jerónimo is conceived, that is, in the synchronism of a magical coupling that renders the impotent fertile from the dark side of the real. The magical participation is negatively experienced, in accordance with the loss of the narrator's identity.

Humberto's feeling of divestment, that is, the theft of his identity by his father, who reveals to Humberto the insignificance of his name and of his social extraction, motivates his identity crisis and the search for a face of his own. This search is represented in the fluctuating aspect of the transformations of the character, in whom the longing for a face of his own is confused with the longing or the demand for love, which takes on attributes of the Oedipus complex. When, toward the end, circumstances throw the witness into total annihilation, in a parallel to the myth of the *imbunche,* Humberto still senses another presence. He then forgets his purpose of self-abandonment and desperately opens himself up to the presence he has perceived, "because there is someone out there waiting to tell me my name and I want to hear it." But this possibility is denied, and his being is annihilated, perfectly, by a blind, terrible, and grotesque power.

As a character, the narrator-as-witness embodies different identities of miserable beings who are either dispossessed or servants. These—the narrator included—are regarded not merely as inhabitants of a low and contemptible sector of the universe, but as a complementary part, intimately and dialectically linked to the owners. The two classes, servants and owners, support one another, each possessing its own order, governed by a legality that tolerates transgressions. The narrator-as-character is in charge of relating the different orders of the universe to each other. On his shoulders falls the demonic and unsatisfactory possibility of not belonging to any order, and therefore the desire to belong to one of them: his condition is that of an ambiguity full of longing and anguish. His ubiquity is the expression of the loss of his face, of the insignificance of his name, and of the search for the mask that may be identified with his true face.

The story of Humberto Peñaloza unfolds in crucial stages. The first is the one in which the motherless child receives from his father the revelation of the insignificance of his name. This first deprivation has a profound influence on his subsequent existence. The second deprivation has to do with the wound inflicted on Humberto when he and Don Jerónimo escape from a violent protest over a fraudulent election. Don Jerónimo appropriates that wound, staining his bandaged hand with Peñaloza's blood and showing himself as a wounded man in order to take political advantage of the situation. Humberto feels involved in Don Jerónimo's deceit, involved in his being, but at the same time, he is deprived of his own wound and of the meaning of its blood. The third deprivation entails his nightmarish sexual encounter with Inés. Under the direction of the witch Peta Ponce, the ritual of fertilization takes place, synchronized in the actions of two couples: one dark and the other luminous. In that act, only power, only sexual potency, is accepted by Inés, who rejects and ignores the body and the identity of

Humberto. His muteness originates in this denial, in Inés's rejection of his kiss.

Another series of deprivations takes place in the monstrous world of La Rinconada. There the monsters who have gathered to build an isolated world, in which they have no experience except of themselves, nullify Humberto Peñaloza, whom they see as a stranger and as a monstrous being. Following the frenzied experience of a pierced ulcer and under the vague impression that he has undergone an operation that reduced his stomach by eighty percent, Humberto imagines that his entire body has been reduced by that proportion (a sensation in fact experienced by Donoso). The exchange of his organs for those of the monsters creates a confusion between his normality and the monstrous condition.

In the final series of deprivations, the papier mâché mask of a giant carnival figure (symbolizing the acquisition of power) is wrested away from him by neighborhood children, who destroy it, signifying the end of his power. The phallic symbolism is evident, clear, and explicit in the text. In this series, Mudito is presented. A servant in the Casa de Ejercicios, he assists the three nuns who care for the elderly women and the orphan girls. His identification with the elderly women derives from this final deprivation. He identifies himself as one of the seven old ladies who await the miraculous agent of their salvation, the son of the orphan Iris Mateluna. Humberto is then identified with the miraculous child and finally emasculated by Inés in a frustrated repetition of the magical possession. Once the symbol of power and the longing to be and to love are obliterated in this character, the reduction, the self-annihilation, and the myth of the *imbunche* are realized, making up a new order of existence, which, like every other order presented in the novel, finally breaks apart, giving way to the experience of anguish and mystery.

*A House in the Country* differs from Donoso's previous work in that this novel is a political allegory, a rich system of allusions to Chile's political life during the administration of Salvador Allende and the military coup of 1973. Nonetheless, the world represented in the novel is, as in the author's other works, essentially unreal, uncertain, and indeterminate—another remarkable narration in which Donoso fills the rooms of the house with the products of his spectacular ability for the grotesque. With the configuration of space—upstairs/downstairs and inside/outside—as a backdrop, the central adventure of the allegory is the exploration and occupation of the house by the children, whose parents have left for the weekend (for the children, this is the equivalent of a year). The absence of their repressive parents allows the children to invade forbidden and secret rooms and to explore them in ways that are both childlike and imitative of the adults' games. The children transgress prohibitions and dare to enter strange spaces, making contact with human sectors from which they are normally kept away and constantly violating the rules of the adult world. When the adults return, so do limitations and repressions imposed in the past. Allegorical allusions to Chilean political events of the 1970s are easily identifiable, including verbatim excerpts from Salvador Allende's political speeches, attributed by the narrator to the character Adriano.

The narrative proposes a vision of the social order similar to that of Chilean historian Alberto Edwards in his book *La fronda aristocrática en Chile* (1928; The aristocratic frond in Chile), which conceives all national political manifestations as the expression of one of two forces that dominate the Chilean aristocracy. The character Adriano, a dissident within a social group that contemptuously isolates him, is represented in the novel as a member of the aristocratic class, a trait shared by Allende. All in all, the representation of the world offers a view of reality that affirms the aristocratic bent of its perspective. The two antagonistic forces that have alternately governed and characterized Chilean politic life—the one conservative, with the accent on traditional, intellectual, and historical values, and the other liberal, rebellious, adventurous, and innovative—are in this way confirmed in the narration. In spite of this, the novel constructs a world of prevailing unreality, of duplications, the use of trompe l'oeil regarding the painted figures on the ballroom fresco, and real figures that propose the grotesque ambiguity of real and pictorial representation. Doors and fences systematically point to what is shut away and forbidden. Upward and downward movement through the spaces of the house evokes the symbolism of the celestial and the infernal. The ambiguity of time—one weekend for the parents amounts to a year for the children—is a major factor in the deformation of the

experience of reality. Its allegorical value sets clear bounds on the blend of seriousness and humor that affects the world view of this novel.

The narrator is at all times engaged in commentary on the events he narrates and on the text itself. A narrator's extensive, intrusive presence, under the guise of romantic irony, was a dominant trait of the nineteenth-century novel, constituting a control by the narrator-author over the narration that generally lessened the autonomy of the characters. Yet in this novel, rather than exhibiting control or romantic irony in the nineteenth-century sense, the intrusive narrator is part of a grotesque parody, a sustained act of humor. More important still, such a narrator does not make for an ostentatious, superior interpretive capacity or an exceptional conscience, as in the nineteenth-century novel. On the contrary, *A House in the Country* draws the image of a narrator-author who works in favor of uncertainty and self-irony; when he speaks directly to the reader, it is with the intention of undermining his confidence in an ordinary reading of the novel, of denying him the apparent advantages of an exact, unequivocal interpretation of the narration. A cognitive skepticism deprives the narrator's interpretive faculty of authority, making him a manifest parody of the nineteenth-century narrator.

*La misteriosa desaparición de la marquesita de Loria* is an erotic divertimento that follows the steps of a Spanish literary tradition, mixed with terror and the fantastic and the added tortuosity of Donosian grotesque. *The Garden Next Door*, on the other hand, represents the world of exiled Chileans in Spain: Julio Méndez, a frustrated writer; Gloria, his wife; his son Pato or Patrick; and the writer's agent, Nuria Monclus. When living in Madrid they see a garden next door that is similar to the garden they had at home in Chile (this is an allusion to the garden at Holanda Street, Santiago, called Roma Street in the novel). At one point Julio sees—a voyeuristic perception—the social and erotic playing of young couples engaged in erotic activity in the garden next door during the night. The agent Nuria tells Julio that not one of three publishers is interested in publishing his novel, which is a refurbished version of a previous manuscript that had also been rejected. The publishers criticize its lack of originality, calling it an imitation of Vargas Llosa or Julio Cortázar. In the world of *The Garden Next Door,* the successful Latin American writers at that time are García Márquez, Carlos Fuentes, and, the most famous, Marcelo Chiriboga. Chiriboga is a fictional writer who will reappear later as a character in the novel *Donde van a morir los elefantes,* and he also appears in Carlos Fuentes's novel *La frontera de cristal.* The end of Julio's novel deceptively changes the direction of the story and deprives Julio of his dream to publish it. The last chapter is narrated in Gloria's voice. Gloria and Nuria Monclus talk, and as they talk, the reader can see the conclusion of the last chapter of what, up to now, we have understood to be Julio's novel. The novel's narrator changes and its authorship is attributed to Gloria.

The novel *La desesperanza* was written as a result of Donoso's immersion in the political life of his country after his return there in 1982 following a protracted absence. The novel marks a clear change in the author's narrative, with a marked interest in the life of present-day Chile. The context of the dictatorship, the repression and pauperization of society, the political indifference to daily outrage, the sclerosis of society, and the frustrated longing for social change—all these motifs shape the background of the novel. The action takes place in Santiago, over the course of twenty-four hours. Within this period, two central events converge: the return to Chile of Mañungo Vera, an internationally renowned popular singer, and the funeral of Matilde Urrutia, the widow of Pablo Neruda. The experience of one day and one night in Santiago is sufficient to introduce the singer to the extremes of life under the dictatorship: the curfew hours, the fear, the machinery of repression, torture, and death, and, above all, the sense of hopelessness in the lives of the people, who find no other alternative to their condition than the occasional protest or the impotent act of violence. The funeral of Matilde Urrutia gives rise to negotiations over the establishment of the Pablo Neruda Foundation for the study of poetry, exposing the ways in which the ruling power and its beneficiaries take personal advantage of the situation. The funeral itself reveals the impossibility of engaging in any social act of importance without the ominous presence of repressive force. Mañungo Vera, moved by constant dreams and illusions about his native land, gives life to the profound

urge for social transformation by means of his evocation of the story of El Caleuche, a traditional Chilean myth allegedly inspired in the Dutch legend of the Ghost Ship.

In the short time that has elapsed since his arrival, affected by his personal experience and that of his foreign-born son, he makes the decision to settle down in his country and to confront its harsh and desolate reality. Mañungo Vera's decision stands out against the unbearable hopelessness as a positive sign, a universal call to change and transformation that reaches those who hold power, as well as those who remain indifferent to the cause of dissidents and the persecuted. This strange chronicle of a day in Santiago is thus exposed to partisan consideration and to an exacting analysis of the conduct of its characters, whose motives, in several instances, are weak and unconvincing. In the context of Donoso's works, this novel reveals a gradual displacement of the mythic dimension by that of everyday life, allusion and fictive representation giving way to the context of present-day reality. Myth is nevertheless still present as the most constantly reiterated aspect of the narrative discourse, the most important recurrent theme, and the bearer of the dominant meaning of the narrative.

*Donde van a morir los elefantes* is a humorous and grotesque novel that ironizes the encounter of Spanish American writers and scholars with the American world and with U.S. universities in particular. The protagonist, Gustavo Zuleta, is a Chilean specialist on the work of a fictitious Latin American novelist, called Marcelo Chiriboga, who received the Cervantes Prize. For the first time, Zuleta has the opportunity to meet Chiriboga at a midwestern university campus, located in the corn belt of the United States. At the university, Zuleta meets an old and prominent scholar, Jeremy Butler, and his sister, Maud. In addition, he meets another couple of Chileans, the mediocre Rolando Viveros and his wife, Josefina, the beautifully obese concierge of the university hotel, Ruby MacNamara, and a couple of Chinese foreign students.

The novel's story is narrated from the end—*in extremas res*—when the Chinese students kill their teacher and themselves after failing their exams. During the two months spent at the university, Gustavo Zuleta has a love affair with Ruby, the concierge. In one scene he, unexplainably hidden under the bed, saw her making love and fighting with Chiriboga, and defending her virginity. She later confesses to Gustavo that she uses the argument of her virginity as a way to protect herself from unwanted advances. The nude scene is repeated when Zuleta and Ruby plan to meet in his room in the hotel. She undresses as she comes up the stairs but, surprisingly, when she opens the door nude, she discovers that there is a woman in Zuleta's room. She gets away in time to avoid being recognized.

Zuleta later goes to his room and finds that his wife, Nina, has arrived, with her newborn child, Nat. She wanted to surprise her husband after having been separated from him for two months. She soon finds that she cannot stand the American way of life and suddenly decides to return to Chile. Soon Gustavo follows her. Six years later he returns to the United States to attend a meeting in Washington, D.C. There he finds Félix, a Spanish friend who does not recognize him, and a rejuvenated, slim Ruby, who is accompanied by two small girls. With the help of Josefina Vivero, a Chilean teacher he met at the university, who has also moved to Washington, he learns that Ruby suffered an accident and then married Félix, and that the rejuvenated Ruby is in fact Ruby's sister, who takes care of the children as their baby-sitter. The world has changed: Chiriboga is dead, the writer's wife assumes a new way of life. Gustavo has returned to an entirely different world.

Donoso's novel ironizes American abundance symbolized in Ruby's obesity, which can be compared to Rubens's and Botero's figures or to the Venus of Willendorf. He also ironizes the American scholars' attraction for the Latin American literary boom and its writers. He describes the carnivalesque celebrations of American students, and the Latin American's suffocating experience of the American way of life. As an extension of his previous novels, Donoso's narrator speculates on possibilities of subjective knowledge and experience, and of liberation from the political engagement and contemporary ideology characteristic of the times of the Latin American literary boom. The novel is a satire of the American university of the kind illustrated by Vladimir Nabokov's *Pnin* (1957) or the Chilean author Carlos Morand's *Ohtumba* (1979).

*El Mocho* is Donoso's tenth and last, posthumously published, novel, about coal mining in southern Chile,

its history, decadence, and myths. At the same time, it deals with the confused genealogy of a coal miner's family, whose mixed roots link them to both the coal-mine owners and to indigenous origins. One of the prominent characters is Elba, a woman who dares to disguise herself as a coal miner in order to enter the mine galleries, hoping to find her husband. By doing this she has committed a transgression, because no woman is admitted into the mine and she is seen as guilty of causing the catastrophe. She is forced to leave the village, and appears later as a *chinchorrera*, a hand-picker of coal residues by the seashore. Two other important figures are El Mocho, the novice, and his counterpart, the young Mocho, who is called Mocho chico. These two figures represent alternative paths in life that eventually converge in similar ways: as workers or owners of a miserable circus, a bar, or a cheap restaurant. Tragedy, misery, and the adventurous life of the mine workers is contrasted with the mine owner, who lives in Europe and has built a beautiful park and a pavilion as part of a palace that is never finished, and in which he has never lived. Instead, it is El Mocho who for quite some time has been the keeper of the park and the inhabitant of the pavilion. As in Donoso's other novels, strangeness, the horror of bat attacks, myths, and sexual life complement ordinary spaces, times, and events.

The short story was the narrative genre Donoso cultivated in his first books: *Veraneo, Dos cuentos*, and *Charleston and Other Stories*, all of which are collected in the volume *Cuentos* (1971) and some of which are masterfully written tales. In them, everyday life and the magical or mysterious come together in an ambiguous convergence that is one of the main characteristics of the grotesque in Donoso's writings. A further step, in which the author's greater maturity and ambition become evident, is taken with *Sacred Families, Four for Delfina*, and *Taratuta: Still Life with Pipe*, all three of which have been collected in *Nueve novelas breves*. Donoso's original *novelitas* maintain the characteristics of his earlier works, but these are enhanced and perfected by his imaginative genius and his extraordinary narrative ability. Urban themes and complicated artistry alternate with simpler subjects and a persistent mixture of common experience and the feeling for the strange, the mysterious, and the marvelous. Donoso's narrative artistry looks with one eye to Borges, although he is more verbose than that great Argentinean innovator, while with the other he looks to Cortázar. However, Donoso's style rejects the self-reflective commentary or the theoretical stance characteristic of both Borges and Cortázar, who thereby provide interpretive help to the reader. More sensitive than intellectual, Donoso creates a unique and unmistakable personal narrative style. His work enjoys worldwide acclaim, and his renown exceeds that of any other Chilean author of his time.

Experimenting with new ways of expression and of rapport and communication with the public, the novelist Donoso has tried his hand at other literary genres: poetry and theater, memoirs, and journalistic chronicles. He added a new dimension to his works with his memoirs, *Conjeturas sobre la memoria de mi tribu*, where interesting information can be found about his novels and possible narrative plots.

A collection of his journalistic chronicles was posthumously published with the title *Artículos de incierta necesidad*. This volume was prepared by the author with the help of the editor during the last two years of his life. It collects chronicles written for *Ercilla* magazine (1960–1965), as well as pieces written for the EFE news agency that were published all over the Spanish-speaking world during the 1980s and 1990s. The large volume collects in seven sections more than seventy chronicles written between 1960 and 1991. The articles illustrate autobiographical, memorialistic, and personal knowledge of varied Spanish and Spanish American writers and artists (Gabriela Mistral, Juan Ramón Jiménez, Pablo Neruda, José Saramago), North Americans (Ezra Pound, Thomas Wolfe), and Europeans (Giorgio de Chirico, Vladimir Nabokov, Elias Canetti), and discuss Donoso's favorite readings, travels, and his concepts and literary preferences, especially as they pertain to the English and the North American novel. Several articles address particular moments of his own literary work and present his perception of the novel of his time.

Some of Donoso's stories and novels have been staged, among them an adaptation of *Coronación*, by José Pineda. In 1982 the story *Sueños de mala muerte* (Miserable dreams), from Donoso's *Four for Delfina*, was performed at the Ictus theater. This dramatization makes evident the inherent dramatic tension that is a component of central importance in Donoso's narratives. *Sueños de mala muerte* presents Donoso's usual grotesque style, mixing humor and death, and ordinary and extraordinary people, such as a fortune-teller, a woman who is also a beggar, who plays a role that is somehow anticipatory and ominous. This character establishes the actual self-reflecting interpretation of the entire comedy: "hay que inventarse cada día para sobrevivir" (to survive you must reinvent yourself every day; act I, scene 8). The beggar's sporadic appearances in the play, though incidental, are the certain indicator that the fortune of one of the characters is about to change. The beggar acts as the helper of the main character who, though propertyless, is in love with a woman who dreams of marrying a property owner. The beggar reveals to the hero the existence of his family mausoleum, to which he is entitled and which qualifies him as a property owner. The woman he loves marries him, fulfilling her dream. Then, when happiness has apparently prevailed, the bride suffers an accident, caused inadvertently by the presence of the beggar, and she suddenly dies. She is buried in one of the two remaining niches in the family mausoleum, which the couple had both expected to use when they died. However, the burial of a recently deceased aunt deprives the husband of the right to be buried in the remaining niche, frustrating his dream of being laid to rest next to his wife. People's thwarted illusions and frustrated dreams are the main theme of the comedy. The protagonist is supposed to reinvent his life, but it is clear that he will never be free of cruel frustrations. A realistic description of Chilean life is provided by the scenes of the picturesque, common life of a boarding-house, but the atmosphere is altered by grotesque black humor.

In 1990 a version of *This Sunday*, written in collaboration with Carlos Cerda, was staged and published. Donoso also wrote several scripts, beginning with the script for *La luna en el espejo*, a film directed by Silvio Caiozzi in 1990. Cinematographical versions of his work include *El lugar sin límites*, by the Argentine director Arturo Ripstein, filmed in Mexico; *Sueños de mala muerte*, filmed by Silvio Caiozzi in 1983; and *Coronación*, which had a very successful film version by the same Chilean director (2000).

Donoso's fictional narratives stand out as the most important part of his creative work. His novels, particularly *The Obscene Bird of Night* and *A House in the Country*, constitute the most valuable narratives of the contemporary period in Chile. They are also significant manifestations of the contemporary Spanish-American novel, standing alongside García Márquez's *Cien años de soledad* (1967) and Carlos Fuentes's *Terra nostra* (1975). Donoso's literary expression is distinctive and represents the dark side of the imagination, a grotesque re-creation of myth, folklore, psychology, and the fantastic. The mixed, peculiar voices of his narrative constitute the unmistakable feature of his style.

# SELECTED BIBLIOGRAPHY

## Primary Works

### Novels and Short Stories

*Veraneo y otros cuentos.* Santiago, Chile, 1955.
*Dos cuentos.* Santiago, Chile, 1956.
*Coronación.* Santiago, Chile, 1957.
*El charleston.* Santiago, Chile, 1960.
*Este domingo.* Santiago, Chile, 1966.
*El lugar sin límites.* Mexico City, 1966.
*El obsceno pájaro de la noche.* Barcelona, 1970.
*Tres novelitas burguesas.* Barcelona, 1973.
*Casa de campo.* Barcelona, 1978.
*La misteriosa desaparición de la marquesina de Loria.* Barcelona, 1980.
*El jardín de al lado.* Barcelona, 1981.
*Cuatro para Delfina.* Barcelona, 1982.
*La desesperanza.* Barcelona, 1986.
*Taratuta: Naturaleza muerta con cachimba.* Barcelona: Mondadori, 1990.
*Donde van a morir los elefantes.* Madrid: Alfaguara, 1995.
*El Mocho.* Madrid: Alfaguara, 1997.

### Essays, Poetry, and Theater

*Historia personal del boom.* Barcelona, 1972.
*Poemas de un novelista.* Santiago, 1981.
*Sueños de mala muerte.* Santiago, 1985.
*Este domingo.* Santiago: Editorial Andrés Bello, 1990.

*Casas, voces y lenguas de América Latina: Diálogo con el escritor chileno.* Washington, D.C.: Centro Cultural del BID, 1993.
*Conjeturas sobre la memoria de mi tribu.* Madrid: Alfaguara, 1996.
*Artículos de incierta necesidad.* Santiago: Alfaguara, 1998.

### Collected Works

*Los mejores cuentos de José Donoso.* Santiago, 1965.
*Cuentos.* Barcelona, 1971.
*Cuentos.* Madrid, 1997.
*Nueve novelas breves.* Madrid: Alfaguara, 1997.

### Translations

*Coronation.* Translated by Jocasta Goodwin. New York, 1965.
*This Sunday.* Translated by Lorraine O'Grady Freeman. New York, 1967.
*Hell Has No Limits.* Translated by Hallie D. Taylor and Suzanne Jill Levine. In *Triple Cross. Carlos Fuentes: Holy Place, Jose Donoso: Hell Has No Limits, Severo Sarduy: From Cuba with a Song.* New York, 1972. Pp. 145–229.
*The Obscene Bird of Night.* Translated by Hardie St. Martin and Leonard Mades. New York, 1973.
*Sacred Families: Three Novellas.* Translated by Andrée Conrad. New York, 1973.
*The Boom in Spanish American Literature: A Personal History.* Translated by Gregory Kolovakos, with a foreword by Ronald Christ. New York, 1977.
*Charleston and Other Stories.* Translated by Andrée Conrad. Boston, 1977.
*A House in the Country.* Translated by David Pritchard with Suzanne Jill Levine. New York, 1984.
*Curfew: A Novel.* Translated by Alfred MacAdam. New York: Weidenfeld and Nicolson, 1988.
*The Garden Next Door.* Translated by Hardie St. Martin. New York: Grove Press, 1992.
*Taratuta: Still Life with Pipe. Novellas.* Translated by Gregory Rabassa. New York: W.W. Norton, 1993.

## Secondary Works

### Critical and Biographical Studies

Achúgar, Hugo. *Ideología y estructuras narrativas en José Donoso, 1950–1970.* Caracas, 1979.

Adelstein, Miriam, ed. *Studies on the Works of José Donoso: An Anthology of Critical Essays*. Lewiston, 1990.

Boorman, Joan Rea. *La estructura del narrador en la novela hispanoamericana*. Madrid, 1976. Pp. 111–123.

Borinsky, Alicia. "Repeticiones y máscaras: *El obsceno pájaro de la noche*." *Modern Language Notes* 88, no. 2:281–294 (1973).

Cánovas, Rodrigo. "Una relectura de *El lugar sin límites*, de José Donoso." *Anales de Literatura Chilena* 1:87–99 (2000).

Castillo-Feliú, G. I., ed. *The Creative Process in the Works of José Donoso*. Rock Hill, S.C., 1982.

Caviglia, John. "Tradition and Monstrosity in *El obsceno pájaro de la noche*." *PMLA* 93, no. 1:33–45 (1978).

Cerda, Carlos. *José Donoso. Originales y metáforas*. Santiago, 1988.

———. *Donoso sin límites*. Santiago, 1997.

Cornejo Polar, Antonio, ed. *José Donoso: La destrucción de un mundo*. Buenos Aires, 1975.

Donoso, Pilar. *Los de entonces*. Barcelona, 1987.

Edwards, Esther. *José Donoso: Voces de la memoria*. Santiago, 1997.

Finnegan, Pamela-Mary. *The Tension of Paradox: José Donoso's "The Obscene Bird Of Night" as Spiritual Exercises*. Athens, Ohio, 1992.

Gertel, Zunilda. "Metamorphosis as Metaphor of the World." *Review* 9:20–23 (1973).

Goic, Cedomil. *La novela chilena: Los mitos degradados*. Santiago, 1968. Pp. 163–176, 211–214.

———. *Historia de la novela hispanoamericana*. Valparaíso, Chile, 1972. Pp. 260–270, 274.

———. *Historia y crítica de la literatura hispanoamericana*, vol. III. Barcelona, 1988. Pp. 445–447, 450–458.

González Mandri, Flora María. *Jose Donoso's House of Fiction: A Dramatic Construction of Time and Place*. Detroit, 1995.

Guntsche, Marina. "Lenguaje de la teatralidad y de la diáspora en *Casa de campo*." *Anales de Literatura Chilena* 1:101–116 (2000).

Gutiérrez Mouat, Ricardo. *José Donoso: Impostura e impostación. La modelización lúdica y carnavalesca de una producción literaria*. Gaithersburg, Md., 1983.

Hasset, John J., Charles M. Tatum, and Kirsten Nigro. "Bio-bibliografía: José Donoso." *Chasqui* 2, no. 1:15–30 (1972).

Iñigo-Madrigal, Luis. "Alegoría, historia, novela a propósito de *Casa de Campo*." *Hispamérica* 9, nos. 25–26:5–31 (1980).

———. "Santelices, capas medias, fascismo." *Texto Crítico* 7 (1981).

Joset, Jacques. *Historias cruzadas de novelas hispanoamericanas: Juan Rulfo, Alejo Carpentier, Mario Vargas Llosa, Carlos Fuentes, Gabriel García Márquez, José Donoso*. Frankfurt am Main: Vervuert Verlag, 1995.

Lipski, John M. "Donoso's Obscene Bird: Novel and Anti-Novel." *Latin American Literary Review* 5, no. 9:39–47 (1976).

Luengo, Enrique. *José Donoso: Desde el texto al metatexto*. Concepción, Chile, 1992.

MacAdam, Alfred J. *Modern Latin American Narratives: The Dreams of Reason*. Chicago, 1977. Pp. 110–118.

———. "José Donoso y la novela académica." In *Crisis, apocalipsis y utopías: Fines de siglo en la literatura latinoamericana. XXXII Congreso del Instituto internacional de literatura iberoamericana*. Edited by Rodrigo Cánovas and Roberto Hozven. Santiago: Instituto de Letras, Pontificia Universidad Católica de Chile, 2000. Pp. 96–98.

Magnarelli, Sharon. *Understanding José Donoso*. Columbia, S.C., 1993.

Marco, Joaquín. *Literatura hispanoamericana: Del modernismo a nuestros días*. Madrid, 1987.

———. "El Mocho." *ABC Literario* (Madrid) (18 July 1997).

———, ed. *José Donoso. La semana de autor*. Madrid, 1997.

Martínez Z., Nelly. "El carnaval, el diálogo y la novela polifónica." *Hispamérica* 6, no. 17:3–21 (1977).

———. "Lo neobarroco en *El obsceno pájaro de la noche*." In her *El barroco en América*. Madrid, 1978. Pp. 635–642.

———. "*El obsceno pájaro de la noche*: La productividad del texto." *Revista Iberoamericana* 46, nos. 110–111: 51–65 (1980).

———. "*Casa de campo* de José Donoso: Afán de descentralización y nostalgia del centro." *Hispanic Review* 50, no. 4:439–448 (1982).

———. "*Casa de campo*, de José Donoso: Entre antropófagos, marquesas y dictadores." *Hispamérica* 27, nos. 80–81:5–16 (1999).

McMurray, George R. "La temática en los cuentos de José Donoso." *Nueva Narrativa Hispanoamericana* 1, no. 2:133–138 (1971).

———. "José Donoso: Bibliography-Addendum." *Chasqui* 3, no. 2:23–44 (1974).

———. *José Donoso*. Boston, 1979.

Medina Vidal, Jorge, et al. *Estudio sobre la novela "Este Domingo," de José Donoso*. Montevideo, 1978.

Montero, Oscar. "*El jardín de al lado*: La escritura y el fracaso del éxito." *Revista Iberoamericana* 49, nos. 123–124:449–467 (1983).

———. "Writing on the Margin: José Donoso's Notebooks." *Dispositio* nos. 24–26:237–243 (1984).

Moreno Turner, Fernando. "La inversión como norma. A propósito de *El lugar sin límites.*" *Cuadernos Hispanoamericanos* 295 (1975).

Morrel, Hortensia, R. *Composición expresionista en "El lugar sin límites," de José Donoso.* Río Piedras, P.R., 1986.

———. *José Donoso y el surrealismo: "Tres novelitas burguesas."* Madrid, 1990.

Murphy, Marie. *Authorizing Fictions: Jose Donoso, Casa de Campo.* London, 1992.

Nigro, Kirsten F. "From Criollismo to the Grotesque: Approaches to José Donoso." In *Tradition and Renewal: Essays on Twentieth-Century Latin American Literature and Culture.* Edited by Merlin H. Foster. Urbana, Ill., 1975. Pp. 208–232.

Ocanto, Nancy. "Bio-bibliografía de José Donoso." *Actualidades* 2, no. 2:191–215 (1977).

Ostrov, Andrea. "Espacio y sexualidad en *El lugar sin límites* de José Donoso." *Revista Iberoamericana* 187:341–348 (1999).

Picado, Isabel. "Bibliografía anotada seleccionada: La crítica de José Donoso." *Hispania* 73, no. 2:371–391 (1990).

Pollard, Scott. "Artists, Aesthetics, and Family Politics in Donoso's *El obsceno pájaro de la noche* and James' *The Golden Bowl.*" *Comparatist: Journal of the Southern Comparative Literature Association* 23:40–62 (May 1999).

Promis, José. "El mundo infernal del novelista José Donoso." *Anales de la Universidad del Norte* 7:201–223 (1969).

———. "La desintegración del orden en la novela de José Donoso." In *La novela hispanoamericana: Descubrimiento e invención de América.* Edited by Cedomil Goic. Valparaíso, Chile, 1972. Pp. 209–238.

———. *La novela chilena actual: Orígenes y desarrollo.* Buenos Aires, 1977.

Pujals, Josefina A. *El bosque indomado, donde chilla "El obsceno pájaro de la noche": Un estudio sobre la novela de Donoso.* Miami, Fla., 1981.

Quain, Estelle E. "The Image of the House in the Works of José Donoso." In *Essays in Honor of Jorge Guillén on the Occasion of his 85th Year.* Cambridge, Mass., 1977.

Quintero, Isis. "Artículos publicados por José Donoso en la revista *Ercilla.*" *Chasqui* 3, no. 2:45–52 (1974).

———. *José Donoso: Una insurrección contra la realidad.* Madrid, 1978.

Rodríguez Monegal, Emir. "La novela como 'happening.' Una entrevista sobre *El obsceno pájaro de la noche.*" *Revista Iberoamericana* 37:517–536 (1971).

Sarduy, Severo. "Writing/Trasvestism." *Review* 9:31–33 (1973).

Sarrochi, Augusto. *El simbolismo en la obra de José Donoso.* Santiago, Chile, 1992.

Solotorewsky, Mirna. *José Donoso. Incursiones en su producción novelesca.* Valparaíso, Chile, 1983.

Swanson, Philip. "Concerning the Criticism of the Work of José Donoso." *Revista Interamericana de Bibliografía* 33, no. 3:355–365 (1983).

———. *Jose Donoso. The "Boom" and Beyond.* Liverpool, 1984.

Tatum, Charles M. "*El obsceno pájaro de la noche*: The Demise of a Feudal Society." *Latin American Literary Review* 1, no. 2:99–105 (1973).

Ulibarri Lorenzini, Luisa, ed. *Donoso 70 años. Coloquio internacional de escritores y académicos.* Santiago, Chile, 1997.

Valdés, Adriana. "El 'imbunche': Estudio de un motivo en *El obsceno pájaro de la noche.*" In *José Donoso: La destrucción de un mundo.* Edited by Antonio Cornejo Polar. Buenos Aires, 1975. Pp. 125–160.

Valenzuela, Luisa. "De la Manuela a la Marquesita avanza el escritor custodiado (o no) por los perros del deseo." *Revista Iberoamericana* 60:1005–1008 (1994).

Vidal, Hernán. *José Donoso: Surrealismo y rebelión de los instintos.* Barcelona, 1971.

Weber, Frances Wyers. "La dinámica de la alegoría: *El obsceno pájaro de la noche.*" *Hispamérica* 4, no. 11–12:23–31 (1975).

Zamora, Félix. *Jose Donoso. A Bibliography.* Liverpool, 1984.

# Rosario Ferré

## (1938–    )

---

## *Mercedes López-Baralt*

Rosario Ferré was born in Ponce, Puerto Rico, on 28 September 1938, into a distinguished and powerful familywho played an important role in the industrialization of the island by establishing two successful companies, the Porto Rico Iron Works (1918) and Ponce Cement (1942), later known as the Puerto Rican Cement Company. Don Luis Antonio Ferré, Rosario's father, is an engineer educated at MIT who embraced politics as a young man. In 1967 he founded the New Progressive Party, which aims to attain statehood for Puerto Rico. As a member of this party he became the third elected governor of the island (1968–1972). He is also an accomplished pianist who studied at the New England Conservatory of Music in Boston. His sister, Sor Isolina Ferré, known locally as the Puerto Rican version of Mother Teresa, devoted her life to social work in the slums. Ferré's mother, Lorencita Ramírez de Arellano, also from a prominent family, was the aunt of the Puerto Rican poet Olga Nolla. Doña Lorencita wrote, as did her seven sisters, and Ferré's grandmother wrote short prose and kept a diary, but none of these literary efforts were published.

Ferré is the younger of two children: her brother, Antonio Luis, has distinguished himself in journalism, transforming the family's newspaper *El Día* into the modern and progressive *El Nuevo Día*, of which he is president and editor in chief. Ferré sees her family as an icon of the Puerto Rican transition from feudalism to capitalism, from agriculture to industrialization. Her mother was heiress to an agricultural fortune, and her father's middle-class family benefited from the U.S. presence on the island through being involved in the process of industrialization.

As a child, Ferré wanted to become a ballerina. She studied ballet formally for eight years, but her parents opposed a career in dance, believing that it was not a decent way for a young lady of good family to make a living. Though she had to choose another path, she later paid homage to her lost dream in her writings. The most recent example is two chapters in *The House on the Lagoon* (1995), "The Kerenski Ballet School" and "The Firebird." The first instance in which she publicly mourns (with a feminist twist) this important loss in her life is in the poem "La bailarina" (The ballerina; *Papeles de Pandora*, 1976):

> *tú bailas la ira cantando*
> *una ira larga y roja como tu corazón*
> . . . . . . . . . .
> *te envolvías en la ira bailando*
> *y el baile era espléndido*
> . . . . . . . . . .
> *entonces alguien dijo: una señora bien educada no baila*
> *te clavaron gemelos en los ojos y tacos en los pies*

*te colgaron los brazos de carteras y las manos
    de guantes
te sentaron en palco rojo para que vieses mejor
te sirvieron un banquete de cubierto de plata
y te dieron a almorzar tu propio corazón*

you dance away your anger, singing
an anger long and red like your heart
. . . . . . . . . . . . . .
you shrouded yourself in anger, dancing,
and the dance was splendid
. . . . . . . . . .
then someone said: a well-brought-up lady
    doesn't dance
they nailed opera glasses to your eyes and high
    heels to your feet
they hung purses from your arms and covered your
    hands with gloves
they sat you in a red theater box so that you could
    have a better view
they served you a banquet with fine silver
and they gave you your own heart for lunch

Deprived of dance, her first love, as a young woman Ferré studied English literature, first at Wellesley College and then at Manhattanville College, where she received her B.A. in 1960. But "dancing shoes and poetry books" would remain equated in her mind. Years later Ferré stated that she writes instead of dancing—or, rather, that she makes the words dance. Before completing her graduate work—which focused on Spanish and Latin American literature—Ferré began her writing career in San Juan, Puerto Rico, in 1970, as the editor and coauthor of the journal *Zona carga y descarga.* The short-lived journal, of which only nine issues appeared, would become a milestone in the literary history of contemporary Puerto Rico. It provided a venue for young, unpublished writers, including Ivonne Ochart, Manuel Ramos Otero, Vanessa Droz, and Edgardo Sanabria Santaliz, who had no access to the mainstream journal *Sin Nombre.* It also gained international recognition by including previously unpublished works by Mario Vargas Llosa, Severo Sarduy, and José Lezama Lima. With its iconoclastic stance, critical of both paternalism and traditional realism in Puerto Rican fiction, *Zona* drew a declaration of war from the island's literary establishment when one of its foremost writers, René Marqués, published a furious

open letter to Ferré in its pages in 1975. Accusing Ferré's journal of publishing pornographic material with vulgar language and of treating the United States with crude derision, the letter further insinuated, by sending fond regards to her father, Don Luis, that Ferré had become famous simply because of her family's prominence. In the closing paragraph of his letter Marqués also scorned Ferré's feminism. Fortunately, the letter had no impact on the young writer's work. But, more important, in *Zona* Ferré published her first short story, "La muñeca menor" (The youngest doll).

With an M.A. from the University of Puerto Rico (1976), where she met one of the writers and two of the scholars who would become her first literary mentors—Vargas Llosa, Angel Rama, and Margot Arce—and a Ph.D. from the University of Maryland (1987), Ferré entered the academic world and became a full-fledged writer. She published her first three books in Mexico: *Papeles de Pandora* (1976; Pandora's papers), *Sitio a Eros* (1980; The site of Eros) and *Fábulas de la garza desangrada* (1982; Stories of the heron bled white). Her first novel, *Maldito amor* (Damned love), published in 1986, was translated into English as *Sweet Diamond Dust* in 1988. The German translation, *Kristalzucker,* received the Literatur Preis in 1992.

Ferré has published several books of literary criticism besides *Sitio a Eros: El acomodador: Una lectura fantástica de Felisberto Hernández* (1986; The usher: A fantastic reading of Felisberto Hernández), *El árbol y su sombra* (1989; The tree and its shadow), *Cortázar: El romántico en su observatorio* (1990; Cortázar: The romantic in his observatory), and *El coloquio de las perras* (1990; Roundtable of the bitches). Entranced by the centuries-old wisdom of fairy tales, to which she owes both her interest in literature and her compassion for the weak, Ferré has also written short stories for children, collected in *Sonatinas* (1989). Since *Fábulas de la garza desangrada* and *Papeles de Pandora,* as a poet she has authored *Las dos Venecias* (1992; The two Venices), *Antología poética* (1994; Poetic anthology), and *Antología personal* (1994; Personal anthology). Yet, it is her work in fiction that has won Ferré literary acclaim. After her first novel she published *La batalla de las vírgenes* (1993; The battle of the virgins), and stirred a controversy in Puerto Rico with her decision to write her next two novels, *The House on the Lagoon* and

*Eccentric Neighborhoods* (1998), in English. Both were translated into Spanish by the author as *La casa de la laguna* (1997) and *Vecindarios eccéntricos* (1998).

Ferré has taught at Rutgers University, at Johns Hopkins, and at the University of Puerto Rico, and lectures frequently at home as well as in the United States. She has published essays in literary journals around the world, and in Puerto Rico she is also known as a contributor to the newspapers *El Mundo, San Juan Star* and *El Nuevo Día*. A member of the board of directors of the Ponce Museum of Art, founded by her father, Ferré has also served on the governing board of the Institute of Culture in Puerto Rico. She is married to the Puerto Rican architect Agustín Costa, and devotes most of her time to writing.

"La hija rebelde de un gobernador de Puerto Rico" (the rebel daughter of a Puerto Rican governor), as she was called by Mexican novelist Elena Poniatowska, Ferré has worked hard to carve a niche for herself, fighting the constraints of a traditional family and the expectations that both class and gender have imposed upon her. When her father was governor, she caused a scandal by publishing an angry letter denouncing capitalism, becoming a member of the Socialist Party, and contributing to its newspaper, *Claridad*. At that time she staunchly opposed statehood, believing that as part of the United States, the island would slowly lose its Spanish language, just as the native language had been lost in Hawaii; she also denied the possibility of bilingualism in Puerto Rico. She told Poniatowska in a 1977 interview, "Yo también me desclasé" (I also forsook my class). By publicly opposing her father's views on statehood and relinquishing her role as a housewife, carefully nurtured by her Catholic education, during the 1960s and 1970s Ferré became an outcast, at least within her own family. An ardent advocate of independence, she was not allowed to publish in her brother's newspaper, *El Nuevo Día*.

Interestingly, Ferré's social and political conscience was first awakened in the United States, when she attended Dana Hall, a Protestant prep school in Massachusetts, where she began to question her traditional views on religion and society. For a few years she became an atheist; since then she has been aware of the complexities of a world until then alien to her. It was also at Dana Hall that she decided to become a writer.

However, years would pass before her new consciousness left a mark in her life. Upon graduating from Manhattanville, Ferré married and swiftly assumed the role she would later dismiss: that of a dutiful wife and mother. She married Benigno Trigo, a Puerto Rican businessman, in 1960. They had three children, and in 1970 were divorced. Ferré then enrolled in graduate school at the University of Puerto Rico.

Soon she felt a strong pressure to leave Puerto Rico. The conflict with her family, her divorce, her political affiliation, and even *Zona carga y descarga*, which was unfairly criticized, bred a dense atmosphere in which the young writer gasped for air. As luck would have it, at that moment she received an invitation to study for her Ph.D. at the Colegio de México. In Mexico City she had a close friend, the novelist Jorge Aguilar Mora, whom she had dated during her visits to Mexico and his to Puerto Rico. She had decided to marry him, but when she was about to leave the island, the court in Puerto Rico denied her permission to take her three children with her, claiming that because she did not have a job, she would not be able to support them. Ferré experienced the humiliation of her picture being on "wanted" posters in the San Juan airport that stated Rosario Ferré was not allowed to leave the island. Only after she married Aguilar Mora (the marriage was short-lived) did the court yield, granting her permission to depart because, as a married woman, "she had to follow her husband wherever he went."

Ferré's feminist consciousness was aroused by this episode, which made her reflect that until a woman is married, she is part of the Third World: like children, like blacks, like all of the oppressed. Thus, her literature is full of bourgeois women, for they, too, are victims. Her first book, *Papeles de Pandora*, was conceived as feminist testimonial fiction. As Ferré asserted in an interview with Julio Ortega, it was written, like Mariano Azuela's *Los de abajo* (The downtrodden), in the context of war—not the Mexican Revolution, but a war of liberation in its own right: that of women.

"Every woman should be a republic unto herself!" Rebecca proudly states in *The House on the Lagoon*. As her protagonist did, Ferré found in writing a way of legitimizing herself. In the process of becoming a writer, she was moved by a strong desire for authority, but authority of a feminine kind, over her own life, not masculine authority over the life of others. She views writing as a key to knowledge, and as a way to penetrate and overcome her own shadows. And for this story-teller who always wanted to be Virginia Woolf, the other motivation was poetic intuition, "the central axis of my work." Sometimes poetry takes over and she writes verse; on other occasions poetry becomes the lens through which she views the characters of her fiction. That is the case in many of the hauntingly beautiful short stories of *Papeles de Pandora*, such as "La muñeca menor" and "El collar de camándulas," in which language is probably the main character.

With *Papeles de Pandora*, empowered by a rich, baroque literary voice and backed by a prestigious publishing house (Joaquín Mortiz), Ferré made her grand entrance into the new narrative of the Latin American "boom." In "Cuando las mujeres quieren a los hombres" (When women love men), a story that, according to Juan Gelpí (1993), completes Luis Palés Matos's literary project of validating the island's mixed racial heritage, the points of view of the white wife (Isabel Luberza) and the black whore (Isabel la Negra), united by their love for Ambrosio, become intertwined in an admirable accelerando with an erotic pulse that reads like a blasphemous litany. "Maquinolandera," based on a popular salsa tune made famous by Puerto Rico's *sonero mayor* (greatest salsa singer), Ismael (Maelo) Rivera, constitutes a tour de force in which prose imitates the song's contagious rhythm. The song, inspired by the unintelligible words uttered by the author's mother in a spiritual trance, celebrates fun and dance as a vehicle (*máquina*) which takes the downtrodden on their road to liberation. The "gospel of the Black Christ Maelo"—Ferré's words—also extols nonsense (*maquinolandera, chumalacatera*) and African ritual invocations (*ecuahey*) as freedom from the constraints of Anglo logic. Because of the alternation of Maelo's lyrics with those of the *cocolo* (black lower class) narrator, an apocalyptic preacher who dignifies his slang by inventing words (*lucimbrarlos, lunizarlos, cucaracheados*) with which to impress the faithful, some passages of the story are almost as untranslatable as the song:

Nostros, los maquinolanderos, somos los que somos, señores, venimos, los maquinolanderos, en nuestra máquina. Nosotros, los chumalacateros del señor, ecuahey, venimos hoy aquí,

señores, a vaticinarlos, a profetizarlos el día de San Juan. Nosotros, los vates de San Clemente, los profetas del mondongo encocorado de los cueros de los congos, nosotros los gozaderos, los bendecidos, los perseguidos por los agentes de la ley, venimos a divinizarlos, llegamos a lucimbrarlos, venimos a lunizarlos hasta hacerlos dar a luz. Maquinitamelleva, gritamos, mellevelagozadera, soneamos, seformólachoricera, bombeamos, bajo el mando de Ismael. Nosotros los condenados, los jusmeados por los hocicos jediondos, los jedidos por las jetas joseadoras de los agentes de la ley. Nosotros, los cucaracheados de los escondrijos, los evacuados por los canales de los arrabales donde nos solemos estar? . . . Maquinitamelleva, gritamos, maquinitolandera, tumbeamos, chumalacatera, bombeamos, bajo el mando de Ismael.

We, the *maquinolanderos*, we are the ones in command, folks; we are coming, the *maquinolanderos*, in our *maquiná*. We, the Lord's *chumalacateros, ecuahey*, we come here today, folks, to foretell, to prophesy for the feast of Saint John. We, the prophets of Saint Clement, the prophets of the tripe simmering with the leather of our congas, we the fun seekers, the blessed, the persecuted by the fuzz, we come to shed divine light on you, we have arrived to enlighten you, to fill you with the moon's luminescence till you are reborn. Mylittlemachinewilltakeme, we shout; takemetofunland, we sing; formingahullabaloo, we dance, under the spell of Ismael. We, the damned, the chased by smelly snouts, the fucked by the sniffing snouts of the fuzz. We, driven like cockroaches from our hiding places, evacuated from the slum canals where we live? . . . Mylittlemachine takes me, we shout; *maquinolandera*, we swirl; *chumalacatera*, we dance, under the spell of Ismael.

In her short stories, Ferré often combines poetry and prose in a single text. And in two books written simultaneously, *Fábulas de la garza desangrada* (poems and a short story) and *Sitio a Eros* (essays), she approaches feminism from two angles, that of poetry and that of prose. As Ferré sees it, at that moment she was several women: by day, she was Penelope, weaving—guided by reason—the lives of her characters; by night she became Ariadne or even Nictimane, Sor Juana Inés de la Cruz's allegorical owl of knowledge, searching through the dark of her own self for the hidden thread that could bring her to understand the conflicts of her contemporary sisters. But as a modern Sor Juana, she has not lost touch with reality and the humble toil of daily life. "Yo mantengo una sensatez y una serenidad muy grandes al estar pegando botones, vigilando un cocido" (I maintain my common sense and my serenity by sewing buttons or watching a stew cook), she told Poniatowska. And like the Uruguayan poet Juana de Ibarbouru, she strives for joy. In a poem from *Fábulas de la garza desangrada*, she claims that her social consciousness goes hand in hand with sensuality:

> porque río y cumplo y plancho entre nosotras
> los mínimos dobleces de mi caos,
> me declaro a favor del gozo y de la gloria.

> for I laugh and fulfill my duties and iron, as so
>     many of us do,
> even the small creases of my chaos,
> I declare my quest for joy and glory.

A confessed heir to the Brontës, Julia de Burgos, Sylvia Plath, Erica Jong, and Virginia Woolf, and identified with George Sand, Ferré sees virtue in wrath. In the feminist essays of *Sitio a Eros*, dedicated "A mi hija, por la ferocidad de su esperanza" (To my daughter, for the ferocity of her hope), she sees herself as immersed, like her predecessors, in the most cruel civil war in the history of humankind: the battle of the sexes. Yet, Ferré is an independent feminist who shies away from the dogma of "feminine writing": "Es necesario reconocer que el escritor femenino no existe: la voz femenina, el estilo femenino, tradicionalmente identificado a lo intuitivo, a lo sensible, a lo delicado, a lo sutil, no es sino un mito más creado por los hombres" (We need to admit that the feminine writer does not exist: the feminine voice, the feminine style, traditionally linked to intuition, to sensitivity, to frailty, to gentleness, is no more than a myth created by men). Refusing to yield to simplification and Manichaeism, Ferré embraces Virginia Woolf's acceptance of ambiguity in a novel long forsaken by critics, *The Waves* (1931). In that work she recognizes the mark of her own writing, that of conflict. For *The Waves* is at the same time an elegy for a society about to disappear and an affirmation of the need to establish a new order; in it Woolf struggles to recapture the lost world of her forebears, to make it immortal, while denouncing the injustice of its very foundations.

Feminism is strongly linked with autobiography in Ferré's work. Though she does not believe that there is such a thing as feminine writing, she recognizes that some literary genres, such as letters and diaries, have been long preferred by women. Modern female writers like Colette, Simone de Beauvoir, and Woolf have produced important diaries; Anaïs Nin went so far as to keep hers in a bank vault, not because she was convinced of its literary value, but because she saw in it a habeas corpus for her existence, the indisputable proof of her identity. For Ferré, the diary is a strong tool for self-knowledge, and thus for controlling one's destiny. She has not kept diaries, however. Instead, she has woven her life history, her family saga, her inner conflicts, and her struggles into her fiction.

That is true of her most recent novels, *The House on the Lagoon* and *Eccentric Neighborhoods*. Referring to the latter, Ferré admitted to Julio Ortega the strong link between life and art in her fiction: "*Vecindarios eccéntricos* es, como toda autobiografía, una historia de provincia; en este caso, de esa provincia que era el Puerto Rico de mi niñez" (*Eccentric Neigborhoods* is, like all autobiographies, the story of a province; in this case, the Puerto Rico of my childhood). Like *Maldito amor* and *The House on the Lagoon*, the novel is a showcase of Puerto Rican twentieth-century history, and dwells on the transition from a backward agrarian society to one of modernity and progress. Unabashedly autobiographical, it tells the story of Ferré's maternal family, landowners, and of her paternal forebears, bent on industrializing the island (the name of her father's relatives in the novel—Vernet—is a phonetic transformation of Ferré). The story is told through the eyes of Elvira, an alter ego for Ferré. Almost no family detail has been ommitted: Elvira's father, Aurelio, who had decided in his early years to become "moderno, agnóstico y norteamericano" (modern, an agnostic and North American), plays the piano, is a die-hard statehooder, and becomes governor of Puerto Rico in 1968. Like Luis A. Ferré, he establishes a powerful cement company. Never losing social consciousness, he creates a health plan and a retirement fund for his employees, and insists on paying them the federal minimum wage. Aurelio's sister, akin to Sor Isolina, becomes a nun. Ponce, the birthplace of the Ferrés, is present in the depiction of La Concordia, with its splendid architecture and its unabashed aim to become Puerto Rico's cultural capital. Antonio Luis Ferré, Rosario's brother, emerges as Alvaro, who takes care of his father's cement corporation while the father devotes his time to political campaigns.

One of Ferré's personal conflicts is worked out in the novel, she told Ortega: "El texto es en gran parte la historia de mi madre. Tuve de pequeña una relación conflictiva con ella" (The text is, to a great degree, the story of my mother. I had, since I was a little girl, a tormented relationship with her). A sickly child, Ferré escaped from feeling ignored in favor of her brother and being overprotected by listening to her nanny's fairy tales and, later on, through writing. In the autobiographical short story "Las dos Venecias," which later became *Eccentric Neighborhoods*, the protagonist also learns to escape, this time in the lap of her mother, who sings an old song about Venice, where she spent her honeymoon. The song is so nostalgic that the child suspects that for her mother the idyllic Venice is a symbol for her parents' house, which she desperately missed as a married woman. But Venice was also a faraway and dangerous place which the mother warned her daughter to avoid. Nevertheless, the child falls in love with the mythical Venice of the song, and in *Las dos Venecias* cherishes it in the poem "Cristales venecianos" (Venetian glass), as "un vitral que se desangra en el Adriático" (a stained glass window that bleeds to death into the Adriatic). From this ambivalence Ferré learned that writing is a voyage that can free the spirit from the constraints and the fears of the past (a variation of this obsessive autobiographical theme appears in *The House on the Lagoon*, where Isabel breaks away from an abusive marriage through writing a novel about the family history).

*Eccentric Neighborhoods* presents the strained relationship of Elvira with her mother, Clarissa, as the result of her "falling in love" with her father when she was a small child, thus becoming her mother's rival. Yet, in spite of Elvira's adoration of Aurelio, which began with the spell that his piano music cast on her, ideology was not a common ground: "La estadidad es el paraíso terrenal para Aurelio. Yo no estoy de acuerdo con él, me siento más puertorriqueña que norteamericana, pero prefiero no llevarle la contraria" (Statehood is earthly paradise for Aurelio. I do not agree with him, I feel more Puerto Rican than North American, but I prefer not to contradict him). Later on,

we learn that Elvira's rage toward Clarissa probably came from the realization that she was slowly becoming her mother: a frustrated woman who was prevented from pursuing a professional career by Aurelio. Read as autobiography, the story portrays the generation gap that separated the young Ferré from her parents; she felt trapped in a conventional marriage to a violent man and longed to flee her home. She felt that she first belonged to her father (her resentment toward the father figure can be easily detected in "Isolda en el espejo," one of *Maldito amor*'s short stories, in which she makes fun of his second marriage to a young woman) and then to her husband, and that her social jail was much like that of colonized nations. Ironically, the mother's death gives both Ferré and Elvira the key to a much longed-for freedom. With her inheritance, the writer and her character are able to get a divorce, and to achieve both economic independence and a career in letters.

In her interview with Poniatowska, Ferré confesses both her admiration for Gabriel García Márquez and her fear of "contagion" from reading his novels. His influence on her writing is evident, and probably comes through the mediation of Isabel Allende. For in García Márquez's *Cien años de soledad*, Allende's *La casa de los espíritus*, and Ferré's last two novels, *The House on the Lagoon* and *Eccentric Neighborhoods*, we have the history of Latin America seen through the saga of a colorful dynasty: each starts with a family tree, followed by a narrative full of passion, sex, violence, and politics. Nothing postmodern about these novels; each aims to totalize history. Suzanne Ruta notes in her review of *The House on the Lagoon*, "Ms. Ferré, in effect, declares Puerto Rican literary independence by giving the island the same mini-epic treatment accorded sovereign nations like Chile and Colombia in the work of their leading novelists."

In Ferré's case, politics has always been of foremost importance. Since her first novel, *Maldito amor*, she has tried to capture its ill effects on Puerto Rico. In her own words, quoted in an interview with Javier Molina in the Mexican journal *Jornada* in 1986, the title—the name of a traditional Puerto Rican *danza*—is ironic, for love is not the ultimate issue in the novel. Instead, it deals with the silent civil war that exists on the island between those who defend independence and those who want assimilation to the United States. The notion of love referred to in the title is not romantic love, but love of country, as well as the frustrated love within the Puerto Rican family, divided by political conflict. One of the island's most vocal political analysts, Juan Manuel García Passalacqua, was among the first readers to recognize the historical importance of the novel, comparing *Maldito amor* with Magali García Ramis's *Felices días, tío Sergio*. In both works he admires the courage with which the novelist presents a critical view of the Muñoz Marín era. In contrast, for Rubén Ríos Avila the novel, framed tightly within the constraints of nineteenth-century realism, lacks distance between the author and its subject matter: "It seems that Ferré is the victim of her damned love for her country." In much the way García Passalacqua praises *Maldito amor* for being a witness to history, the historian Fernando Picó, a Jesuit, admires Ferré's *La batalla de las vírgenes* (The battle of the virgins), a parody of the island's religious fanaticism. "Ferré's Dose of Criticism May Be Cure for Social Ills" is the title of his review in the *San Juan Star*.

"Puerto Rico es una nación de 'Hamlets' . . . , todos nos estamos siempre preguntando quiénes somos" (Puerto Rico is a nation full of 'Hamlets' . . . , all of us are always asking who we are), Ferré stated to Ana María Echeverría in 1999. A decade earlier, in "Memorias de *Maldito amor*" (1988), she had pinpointed the island's national obsession: "No creo que exista otro país latinoamericano donde la definición de la nacionalidad constituya un problema tan agudo como lo es hoy todavía en Puerto Rico" (I do not believe that there is another Latin American country where the definition of nationality is such an acute problem as in Puerto Rico); "los puertorriqueños no están nunca seguros de si su isla de veras existe" (Puerto Ricans are never sure that their island truly exists). And in *El coloquio de las perras* (1990) she stresses that "Durante los últimos cien años la literatura puertorriqueña ha estado íntimamente relacionada a la política" (During the last hundred years Puerto Rican literature has been closely linked to politics).

The strong political dimension of Ferré's narratives is unavoidable in twentieth-century Puerto Rican literature. Since the North American invasion of the island brought about by the Spanish-American War in 1898, nationhood and identity have been either the explicit or the underlying preoccupation of the literary production of the country. As Puerto Rico changed hands as war booty, from one empire to another, just after having been granted autonomy by Spain in 1897, intellectuals and writers were moved to reflect on the island's situation, its origins, its history, and its destiny as a nation. In Spain the Generation of 1898 reacted to defeat in war and the end of the empire; in Puerto Rico many voices were raised in despair, such as that of the patriot Ramón Betances, who demanded immediate independence for the island, claiming that if it was not granted that same year, Puerto Rico would always be a colony of the United States. Julio Henna, whose initial optimism about the invasion promptly turned into bitter disillusionment, protested before the Congress of the United States: "the occupation has been a perfect failure. We have suffered everything. No liberty, no rights, absolutely no protection, not even the right to travel. . . . We are Mr. Nobody from Nowhere. We have no political status, no civil rights" (*Committee Reports and Hearings*, 1902).

Through the pen of Manrique Cabrera, the Generation of the Thirties named the invasion "the trauma of 1898" or "the violent historical wound inflicted on us without our intervention." Antonio S. Pedreira reflected on "our tragedy" in his 1934 essay "Insularismo," the canonical text of the century, portraying the island as a "nave al garete" (a ship adrift); in his *Prontuario histórico de Puerto Rico* (1935), Tomás Blanco saw the nation as "una isla encallada" (an island stranded in the sands of imperialism); Emilio Belaval depicted it as "la barca de los sueños fallidos" (the ship of empty dreams); the poet Luis Palés Matos, the main exponent of Puerto Rican negritude, in a bitter poem named it "barca de ron" (ship of rum), deploring its immobilization in the dark molasses sea of colonialism. Decades later, Luis Rafael Sánchez called the island "colonia sucesiva de dos imperios" (the successive colony of two empires) in *La guaracha del Macho Camacho* (1976), and in *La guagua aérea* (1994) he would transform the icon of the island as an adrift or stranded ship into that of a floating nation determined to smuggle hope between two ports, San Juan and New York ("una nación flotante entre dos puertos de contrabandear esperanzas").

Ferré, like many of her peers—Ana Lydia Vega in *Encancaranublado* (1983), Magali García Ramis in *Felices días, tío Sergio* (1986), Edgardo Rodríguez Juliá in *Puertorriqueños* (1988), Esmeralda Santiago in *When I Was Puerto Rican* (1994)—is engaged in the same endeavor as their predecessors: trying to shed light on Puerto Rican history and identity. Within this context, the opening image of *Eccentric Neighborhoods*, that of an old Pontiac stranded in the muddied waters of the Río Loco, becomes a clear signal that Ferré—who had portrayed San Juan as a vessel in the poem "La ciudad navío" (*Las dos Venecias*)—is a conscious heir to the kaleidoscope of icons of the island studied by Hugo Rodríguez Vecchini, Juan Gelpí, and Luce and Mercedes López-Baralt.

Ferré's immediate source here seems to be Sánchez's *La guaracha*, which opens with a terrible traffic jam in which thousands of cars are stranded (a more remote but unavoidable source would be Julio Cortázar's "Autopista del sur"). But his motionless car, a transformation of the island-ship and the nation-plane, turns into a killer car as the alienated teenager Benny runs over the retarded child of la China Hereje. Suggesting the displaced aggressiveness of the colonized, the killer car reappears in later narratives. Such is the case with Ferré's Mercedes in her short story "Mercedes Benz 220 SL" (*Papeles de Pandora*) and of Manuel Martínez Maldonado's blue Chevy in his novel *Isla verde* (1999). Interestingly, Benny's episode and the better part of Ferré's story about the Mercedes display the same syntactical freedom (both reduce punctuation to a minimum) and the same accelerated rhythm, a loud metaphor for the wild race toward disaster. Yet there is no filiation here, for *Papeles de Pandora* and *La guaracha del Macho Camacho* were both published in 1976.

Puerto Rico's troubled identity dramatically comes into the limelight in Ferré's work with the publication in 1995 of what she considers her main work, *The House on the Lagoon*. The novel, which tells of the events of Isabel Monfort's literary vocation against the background of twentieth-century Puerto Rican history, caused a literary scandal on the island because of the language chosen to tell the story. Three years later Ferré justified her use of English in literary, psychological, and political terms. Insisting that she was not interested in making money, only in being read, and

that she wanted to break the provincial barriers that limit the circulation of Puerto Rican books abroad, she explained that she could deal with the death of her mother only through the necessary distance provided by another language. According to Mireya Navarro, though Ferré had been an ardent defender of independence for the island for more than two decades, she argued that conditions have changed: as Hispanics have become the fastest-growing minority in the United States, bilingualism and multiculturalism are now vital aspects of American society, and statehood is no longer a threat for Puerto Rican culture. Yet, for Gerald Guinness, the literary critic of the *San Juan Star*, the choice of a language other than the vernacular was a mistake: "Rosario Ferré's English is more than competent, but she doesn't, in my opinion, write English *con amore*; by the highest standards, her use of the language is colorless, at times even flat."

On the other hand, Carmen Dolores Hernández, literary critic of *El Nuevo Día*, was very pleased with the rich textuality of the novel, whose underlying theme—the ambivalence between history and fiction—poses Isabel Monfort's literary version of the island and the family history against that of her amateur historian husband, Quintín. Yet, Hernández ends her review with a question: Will writing in English become a new trend for Ferré, or is it only an experiment to try to get the attention of the powerful North American editorial world? What for the reviewer was just a question became an issue that engendered strong disapproval from many of the island's writers and intellectuals, who felt that the vernacular language, as the foremost expression of an endangered culture, should never be relinquished in order to pursue new markets. The matter was further entangled when on 19 March 1998, Ferré published in the *New York Times* an article titled "Puerto Rico, USA," which almost immediately was published in Spanish in *El Nuevo Día* (21 March). In it she revealed her passionate adherence to an ideal she had strongly attacked for many years, that of statehood. But her change of perspective did not trouble many of her readers as much as her way of defending her new position. Claiming that Puerto Ricans have been North Americans since 1898, she stated: "Como escritora puertorriqueña, constantemente me enfrento al problema de identidad. Cuando viajo a

Estados Unidos me siento como una latina, como Chita Rivera. Pero en América Latina, me siento más norteamericana que John Wayne" (As a Puerto Rican writer, I continually confront the problem of identity. When I travel to the United States, I feel Latina, like Chita Rivera. But in Latin America, I feel more North American than John Wayne).

Reactions were immediate. Ana Lydia Vega, one of Puerto Rico's most important contemporary writers and Ferré's longtime friend, answered in *El Nuevo Día* through "Carta abierta a Pandora" (Open letter to Pandora; 31 March 1998), confronting Ferré with her abandoned ideals and deploring her discovery of two opposite Rosarios:

> *Como las dos Isabeles de tu célebre cuento, se enfrentan hoy tal vez, en ese campo de batalla que es la página, dos escritoras. Ojalá, querida Pandora, que aquella que una vez abofeteara la cara hipócrita de la sociedad con la explosiva verdad de sus papeles, no se haya rendido ante la que hoy derrama estereotipos y clisés en apoyo a una postura desmentida por sus libros.*

> Like the two Isabels of your famous story, today, on the battlefield of the page, two writers confront one another. I wish, dear Pandora, that she who once slapped the hypocritical face of society with the explosive truth of her writings has not surrendered to the one who today publishes stereotypes and clichés to sustain a position that her own books contradict.

A few days later (8 April), Lilliana Cotto, a sociologist at the University of Puerto Rico, published an open letter to Ferré in the same newspaper, contesting her statements on Puerto Rico's having conquered poverty and entering the "First World" by quoting figures from the U.S. census, which show 59 percent of Puerto Ricans as living below the poverty level. Cotto also denied the island's purported bilingualism and repudiated Ferré's identification with someone as notorious for his ultrarightist inclinations as John Wayne, a comparison that, according to her, signals a profound identity crisis in the writer.

Ferré's initial response was silence. After four months and without addressing her critics, she published in *El Nuevo Día* an article titled "Al filo del XXI" (Toward the twenty-first century; 26 July 1998), in which she reflected on the North American invasion of the island. Many readers felt that, duly embarrassed, she was making an implicit apology for her published "outburst." After pointing to two different reactions to the invasion—that of Esteban López Giménez, who, fearing the loss of his language and culture, shed tears of shame, and that of her paternal grandfather, who welcomed the American troops in Ponce—Ferré seemed to side with the former: she adamantly declared that, being a woman who has always rejected injustice and arbitrary authority, she still looks at these historical events with resentment. Furthermore, Ferré quoted as "an undeniable truth" the bitter words of Bernardo Vega, who in his memoirs deplores the fact that as a result of the invasion, Puerto Rico was passed from one owner to another as if it were a farm, including its people, its houses, its animals, and its trappings. Not until publishing "Un diálogo necesario" (A necessary dialogue; 6 September) that same year and in the same newspaper, did Ferré explicitly address the controversy stirred by her decision to write in two languages and her recent statements. Taking offense at the accusations pointing to her denial of Puerto Ricanhood, she defended her rights as a writer living in a democracy and concluded that as the frontiers of the modern world become blurred, Puerto Rican identity has been enriched and can claim a multiple legacy: that of Spain, Africa, the native Tainos, Latin America, the Caribbean, Corsica, and even North America.

Before these two articles, Ferré had restated her motives for writing in English in her acceptance speech upon receiving an honorary doctorate from Brown University on 28 April 1997, going so far as to defend Spanglish as a language. Yet, referring to the ceremony, and in words that strongly resemble those of the militant Ferré of the 1970s, she told Leonor Mulero: "Me dieron ganas de llorar, sobre todo cuando Carlos Fuentes dijo que escribir desde Puerto Rico es mantener nuestro sentido de nación, de ser puertorriqueños, de que no vamos a desaparecer de la memoria colectiva" (I felt like crying, especially when Carlos Fuentes said that writing from Puerto Rico amounts to preserving our sense of nationhood, of being Puerto Ricans, so that we will not disappear from the collective memory).

In an interview granted to Carmen Dolores Hernández and published on 6 August 2000 in *El Nuevo Día,* Ferré declares herself a "Puerto Rican and

Latin American writer," and sheds new light on her controversial decision to write in English:

> *Antes que nada quiero aclarar que yo me considero a mí misma como una escritora puertorriqueña y latinoamericana. No soy una escritora norteamericana aunque no me molesta que me identifiquen con los escritores Latinos que viven en los Estados Unidos. Ellos comparten unas vertientes de nuestra cultura aunque hayan perdido desgraciadamente el idioma, y llevan a cabo una importante labor relacionada con la lucha por los derechos civiles. La diferencia es que yo no me veo a mí misma como una escritora de minorías sino como representante de una mayoría o de un pueblo homogéneo. . . .*
>
> *No me quería quedar en el ámbito hispánico: quería llegar a Europa, Francia, la idea era pasar a Francia. . . . Soñaba con publicar una novela en Europa: no creía que lo pudiera hacer. Eso para mí fue lo máximo. Cuando* La casa de la laguna *se publicó en francés, Papi la cogió y dijo "está en el lenguaje de los abuelos." . . .*
>
> *Aquí en Puerto Rico, cuando publiqué* Papeles de Pandora, Sitio a Eros *y* Maldito amor, *se planteaba siempre la cuestión de si tenía éxito porque era buena escritora o porque era hija de Ferré. . . . Entonces yo quería validarme, tener éxito donde no fuera hija de nadie; donde nadie me conociera.*

First of all, I would like to declare that I consider myself a Puerto Rican and a Latin American writer. I am not a North American writer though it doesn't bother me to be identified with Latino writers who live in the United States. They share with us some aspects of our culture, though unfortunately they have lost the language, and they are part of an important struggle for civil rights. The difference is that I do not see myself as a writer from the minorities, but as the representative of a majority, a homogeneous nation. . . .

I did not want to be limited to the Hispanic world: I wanted to reach Europe, France, I wanted to reach France. . . . I dreamed of publishing a novel in Europe, I didn't believe I could do that. That for me was the most. When *The House on the Lagoon* was published in French, Daddy took it in his hands and said, "It is written in the language of our ancestors." . . .

Here in Puerto Rico, when I published *Papeles de Pandora, Sitio a Eros* and *Maldito amor,* there was always the question of whether I was successful because I was a good writer, or because I was the daughter of Ferré. . . . Then I needed to prove myself, I wanted to be successful where I was not anyone's daughter, where no one would know me.

Tongue in cheek, in *The House on the Lagoon* Ferré creates an ironic icon for the political indecision of her alter ego Isabel Monfort. While reminiscing about the innocence of her childhood, the young girl reflects:

> During the forties and fifties, Sears had no stores on our island. Sears wasn't a place, it was a state of mind; ordering from the Sears catalogue was like ordering from heaven, . . . I like to think of myself as apolitical, and when election time comes around, I don't like to take a stand. Maybe my indecision is rooted in the Sears catalogue; it goes back to the times I sat as a child in the living room of our house in Ponce with the catalogue on my lap, wishing for independence and at the same time dreaming about our island being a part of the modern world.

Consciously accepting her ideological contradictions as ambivalence, with *The House on the Lagoon* Ferré distances herself from the fiery militant writer who produced *Papeles de Pandora.* She continues to defend her right to be read in both Spanish and English, and is writing a new novel in English, *The Flight of the Swan.* At the same time she has just published a book of essays in Spanish, *A la sombra de tu nombre* (Under the shadow cast by your name), and is writing a bilingual book of poems, *La batalla de la lengua/Language Duel.* Inspired by the life of Anna Pavlova, *The Flight of the Swan* tells the story of a Russian ballerina who arrives in Puerto Rico in 1917, loses her passport, and is unable to leave the island. *A la sombra de tu nombre* is an intimate collection wrapped—in the words of Mario Alegre—in the shadows of literature and in the author's own name, Ferré. *La batalla de la lengua/Language Duel* does not contain translations; each poem is written either in Spanish or in English.

All things considered, Ferré's about-face, which takes her, through the reconciliation with her father, back to the beginning, is emblematic of the conflicts of twentieth-century Puerto Rican history. Conflicts that are allegorically expressed in her own recent writing, particularly in *The House on the Lagoon,* where the tension between the vehicle—English—and the message—the affirmation of Puerto Rican history and identity—makes the novel intriguing. In a recent interview wih Alegre, Ferré takes yet another stance regarding the political status of the island. Insisting that she has always been true to herself, she says:

*Si bien en una época pensé sinceramente que la independencia era lo más conveniente para Puerto Rico, después he llegado a la conclusión de que como estamos es lo mejor. Yo no intentaría ser un estado . . . en ese aspecto no soy como mi papá. Prefiero estar como estoy y, si no podemos seguir como estamos, como último recurso buscaría la estadidad.*

If I once believed that independence was the best solution for Puerto Rico, I later arrived at the conclusion that we should stay as we are [meaning the present status of commonwealth or Estado Libre Asociado.] I would not strive for statehood . . . in that respect, I am not like my father. I prefer to stay the way we are, and only as a last option would I consider statehood.

This ideological ambivalence is not the exclusive domain of a Puerto Rican writer; it is readily recognizable in the works of great writers such as Honoré de Balzac, Benito Pérez Galdós, and Fyodor Dostoyevsky. Closer to home, José María Arguedas goes from socialism to magic and has been harshly criticized for not adhering to a clear ideological stance in his novels; Domingo Faustino Sarmiento displays a love-hate relationship toward the gauchos he seeks to denounce in his 1845 *Facundo*; and in *Lituma en los Andes,* Vargas Llosa strives to diminish the Quechua culture of Peru, at the same time paying lyrical homage to the power of the Andean mountain gods in pages of exquisite prose.

Yet, though *The House on the Lagoon* may appear as a boulder that divides Ferré's work into two eras, there is an inescapable continuity in her writing. She has not lost her sense of outrage in the face of injustice, nor her compassion for the downtrodden. *The House on the Lagoon,* a novel which in Quintín's words may be read as an "Independentista manifesto," harshly denounces the police repression of the Left, commanded by former governor Carlos Romero Barceló, a strong statehooder, who is barely disguised in the story. Though his fictitious name is Rodrigo Escalante, his white mane and the confrontational stance of the bully that has long characterized his speeches and public appearances are recognizable. The novel's heroes are the oppressed and the weak: the black, the poor, *independentistas,* and women, who at the end begin to take their destiny into their own hands. And these heroes utter the undeniable and hurtful truths about the island; Carol, a young independence advocate, says: "Just think, we're a country

that in its five hundred years of existence has never been its own self. Don't you think that's tragic?" Furthermore, the house—a longtime symbol of hierarchy in Puerto Rican canonical literature, as Gelpí has observed (1993)—is invaded by marginal people, a fact that turns the novel into a Caribbean sequel to Cortázar's allegory "La casa tomada" (The invaded house).

Other dimensions help us to discover a sense of the coherence of Ferré's work. First of all, the underlying theme of her essays, her stories, her poems, and her novels is that of a woman striving for freedom through the written word. For this independent feminist who, following in the steps of the poets Julia de Burgos and Clara Lair, became the model for Puerto Rican female writers of the 1970s, there is a persistent pattern in her literary production that takes her from "La muñeca menor" through "La bailarina" and *The House on the Lagoon* to her forthcoming novel *The Flight of the Swan.* She told Carmen Dolores Hernández that the metaphoric thread here is that of a dancer who expresses, through the silent language of her body, the haunting, dying world from which she comes and that she is eager to leave behind. On the other hand, Ferré's love for metaphors and allegories—the invaded house, the killer/stranded car, the ballet slippers, the manuscript—speaks of the poet always present behind her prose.

Another role that Rosario Ferré has never abandoned is that of the storyteller. Even though she forsook the baroque style of *Papeles de Pandora* for the terse prose of *The House on the Lagoon* and *Eccentric Neighborhoods,* she has always been, first and foremost, a wonderful teller of short stories. Even in her novels, each story about her fictitious ancestors is self-contained, rich, and complete. Ferré is well aware of it; she makes Quintín say of Isabel in *The House on the Lagoon:* "The Kerenski chapters were especially well written and could probably be published alone as a short story." Quintín is probably right: for many readers—among them Ana Lydia Vega—these two chapters bear the imprint of the most powerful Ferré, that of *Papeles de Pandora.*

But perhaps the most authentic mark of the work of this poet, essayist, novelist, short story writer, and pioneer feminist may be found in her pride in being Puerto Rican, which surfaces regardless of the language she chooses to convey it. "Escribir en ambas lenguas es una decisión personal mía, que me permite afirmar la puertorriqueñidad tanto en inglés como en español" (Writing in both languages is my personal decision, a decision that allows me to assert Puerto Ricanhood in English as well as in Spanish), she stated in "Un diálogo necesario." Ferré told Carmen Dolores Hernández in an interview, "Yo creo que mis libros dan a conocer a Puerto Rico; ése es el propósito. Quiero que la gente nos respete como puertorriqueños y como pueblo que hemos mantenido la dignidad a pesar de todas las barbaridades que se han cometido contra nosotros" (I believe that my books tell what Puerto Rico is all about; that is my purpose. I want people to respect us as Puerto Ricans and as a nation that has preserved dignity, in spite of all of the barbarities that have been inflicted upon us).

# SELECTED BIBLIOGRAPHY

## Primary Works

### Poetry and Short Stories

*El medio pollito.* Río Piedras, P.R: Ediciones Huracán, 1976. (Children's stories.)

*Papeles de Pandora.* Mexico City: Joaquín Mortiz, 1976. Revised 2nd edition, Mexico City: Joaquín Mortiz, 1979. (Poems and short stories.)

*La caja de cristal.* Mexico City: Máquina de Escribir, 1978. (The story is included in the 2nd edition of *Papeles de Pandora.*)

*La muñeca menor/The Youngest Doll.* Translated by Antonio Martorell. Río Piedras, P.R: Ediciones Huracán, 1979. (A bilingual edition of one of the short stories in *Papeles de Pandora.*)

*La mona que le pisaron la cola.* Río Piedras, P.R: Ediciones Huracán, 1981. (Children's stories.)

*Los cuentos de Juan Bobo.* Río Piedras, P.R: Ediciones Huracán, 1981. (Children's stories.)

*Fábulas de la garza desangrada.* Mexico City: Joaquín Mortiz, 1982. (Poems and a short story.)

*Sonatinas.* Río Piedras, P.R: Ediciones Huracán, 1989. (Contains revised versions of *Medio pollito, Los cuentos de Juan Bobo,* and *La mona que le pisaron la cola.*)

*La cucarachita Martina.* Río Piedras, P.R: Ediciones Huracán, 1990. (Children's stories.)

*Las dos Venecias.* Mexico City: Joaquín Mortiz, 1992. (Poems and short stories.)

*Antología poética.* San Juan, P.R.: Cultural, 1994.

*Antología personal.* San Juan, P.R.: Cultural, 1995. (Poems from 1976 to 1994.)

### Novels

*Maldito amor.* Mexico City: Joaquín Mortiz, 1986. (A short novel and three short stories: "El regalo," "Isolda en el espejo," and "La extraña muerte del capitancito Candelario.") Second ed., Río Piedras, P.R: Ediciones Huracán, 1988. (Includes a prologue by the author, "Memorias de *Maldito amor.*")

*La batalla de las vírgenes.* San Juan: Editorial de la Universidad de Puerto Rico, 1993.

*The House on the Lagoon.* New York: Farrar, Straus & Giroux, 1995.

*Eccentric Neighborhoods.* New York: Farrar, Straus & Giroux, 1998.

### Literary Criticism

"Editorial." *Zona carga y descarga,* May–June 1973, pp. 2–3. (Essay on feminism.)

*Sitio a Eros.* Mexico City: Joaquín Mortiz, 1980. Revised and enlarged, Mexico City: Joaquín Mortiz, 1986. (Essays on feminist literary criticism.)

"La cocina de la escritura." In *Literature in Transition: The Many Voices of the Caribbean Area.* Edited by Rose S. Minc. Gaithersburg, Md.: Hispamérica, 1982. Pp. 37–51. Reprinted in *La sartén por el mango: Encuentro de escritoras latioamericanas.* Edited by Patricia Elena González and Eliana Ortega. Río Piedras, P.R.: Ediciones Huracán, 1984. Pp. 137–154.

*El acomodador: Una lectura fantástica de Felisberto Hernández.* Mexico City: Fondo de Cultura Económica. 1986.

*El árbol y su sombra.* Mexico City: Fondo de Cultura Económica, 1989.

*Cortázar: El romántico en su observatorio.* San Juan, P.R.: Editorial Cultural, 1990. (Originally Ferré's doctoral dissertation.)

*El coloquio de las perras.* San Juan, P.R.: Editorial Cultural, 1990.

*A la sombra de tu nombre.* Mexico City: Alfaguara, 2001.

### Biography

*Memorias de Ponce: Biografía de Don Luis A. Ferré.* Barcelona: Grupo Editorial Norma, 1992.

*Newspaper Articles*

"El poder del idioma." *El Nuevo Día,* 8 June 1997, pp. 14–15. (Speech accepting honorary doctorate from Brown University.)

"Puerto Rico, USA." *New York Times,* 19 March 1998, p. A21. (Translated by the author into Spanish and published in *El Nuevo Día,* 21 March 1998, p. 91.)

"Al filo del XXI." *El Nuevo Día,* 26 July 1998, p. 10.

"Un diálogo necesario." *El Nuevo Día,* 6 September 1998, p. 69.

*Translations*

*The Youngest Doll.* Translated by the author and Diana Vélez. Lincoln: University of Nebraska Press, 1991.

*La muñeca menor/The Youngest Doll.* Translated by Antonio Martorell. Río Piedras, P.R: Ediciones Huracán, 1979. (A bilingual edition of one of the short stories in *Papeles de Pandora.*)

*Sweet Diamond Dust.* Translated by the author. New York: Ballantine Books, 1988.

*La casa de la laguna.* Translated by the author. Barcelona: Emecé Editores, 1997; New York: Vintage, 1998.

*Vecindarios excéntricos.* Translated by the author. Mexico City: Editorial Planeta Mexicana, 1998; Barcelona: Ediciones Destino, 1999; New York: Vintage, 1999.

*Secondary Works*

*Critical and Biographical Studies*

Albino, Ramón. "Presentan lo nuevo de Ferré." *El Nuevo Día,* 25 September 1995, p. 58. (On *The House on the Lagoon.*)

Ballantyne, Lucinda. "*Sweet Diamond Dust,* by Rosario Ferré." *Boston Phoenix Literary Section,* February 1989, p. 4.

Barradas, Efraín. "Reseña sobre *Papeles de Pandora.*" *Sin Nombre* 1:97 (1978).

———. "(C)er(C)os a Eros." *Claridad,* 27 February–7 March 1981, pp. 6–7.

———. "Por los ojos de un niño: Nuevos cuentos de Rosario Ferré." *Claridad,* 25 February 1982, pp. 4–5.

Candelario, Andrés. "Literatura infantil para los adultos." *El Nuevo Día, Suplemento en grande,* 27 December 1981, p. 11.

Cotto, Lilliana. "Carta abierta a Rosario Ferré." *El Nuevo Día,* 8 April 1998, p. 71.

Chaves, María José. "La alegoría como método en los cuentos y ensayos de Rosario Ferré." *Third Woman* 2:64–76 (1984).

Cheuse, Alan. "A Mature Talent Debuts in English." *Chicago Tribune,* 13 January 1989, p. 5.

Davis, Lisa E. "La puertorriqueña dócil y rebelde en los cuentos de Rosario Ferré." *Sin Nombre* 9:82–88 (1980).

Díaz Quiñones, Arcadio. "Prólogo." *Sin Nombre* 5:5–8 (1975).

Escalera Ortiz, Juan. "Perspectiva del cuento 'Mercedes Benz 220SL.' " *Revista Interamericana* 12:407–417 (1982).

Fernández Olmos, Margarite. "Sex, Color and Class in Contemporary Puerto Rican Women Authors." *Heresies* 4:46–47 (1982).

———. "From a Woman's Perspective: The Short Stories of Rosario Ferré and Ana Lydia Vega." *Contemporary Women Authors of America: Introductory Essays.* Edited by Doris Meyer and Margarite Fernández Olmos. Brooklyn, N.Y.: Brooklyn College Press, 1983. Pp. 78–90.

———. "Constructing Heroines: Rosario Ferré's *Cuentos infantiles* and Feminine Instruments of Change." *The Lion and the Unicorn: A Critical Journal of Children's Literature* 10:83–94 (1986).

———. "Luis Rafael Sánchez and Rosario Ferré: Sexual Politics and Contemporary Puerto Rican Narrative." *Hispania* 70:40–46 (1987).

———. "Los cuentos infantiles de Rosario Ferré, o la fantasía emancipadora." *Revista de Crítica Literaria* 14:151–163 (1988).

Franco, Jean. "Self-Destructing Heroines." *The Minnesota Review* 22:105–115 (1984).

García Passalacqua, Juan Manuel. "Visiones de clase y política." *El Nuevo Día,* 24 June 1986, p. 43.

Gelpí, Juan. "Apuntes al margen de un texto de Rosario Ferré." In *La sartén por el mango: Encuentro de escritoras latioamericanas.* Edited by Patricia Elena González and Eliana Ortega. Río Piedras, P.R.: Ediciones Huracán, 1984. Pp. 133–135.

———. "Especulación, especularidad y remotivación en *Fábulas de la garza desangrada* de Rosario Ferré." In *La Chispa '85: Selected Proceedings.* Edited by Gilbert Paolini. New Orleans: Tulane Uiversity Press, 1985. Pp. 125–132.

———. "Rosario Ferré: La trasposición del canon." In his *Literatura y paternalismo en Puerto Rico.* San Juan: Editorial de la Universidad de Puerto Rico, 1993. Pp.154–171.

Guerra-Cunningham, Lucía. "Tensiones paradójicas de la femineidad en la narrativa de Rosario Ferré." *Chasqui: Revista de Literatura Latinoamericana* 13:13–25 (1984).

Guinness, Gerald. "Beyond History, Imagination." *San Juan Star,* 22 October 1995, p. 12.

Hernández, Carmen Dolores. *"La mona que le pisaron la cola."* *San Juan Star Magazine,* 3 January 1982, p. 11.

———. "Nuevas ficciones de Rosario Ferré." *El Nuevo Día,* 29 July 1986, p. 12B. (On *Maldito amor.*)

———. "Las Venecias evocadas." *El Nuevo Día,* 24 May 1992, p. 26.

———. "La poesía de Rosario Ferré." *El Nuevo Día,* 27 November 1994, p. 14. (On *Antología personal.*)

———. "La saga de una 'gran' familia puertorriqueña." *El Nuevo Día,* 8 October 1995, p. 14. (On *The House on the Lagoon.*)

———. "Scheherezada boricua." *El Nuevo Día,* 8 March 1998, p. 14. (On *Eccentric Neighborhoods.*)

———. "Valiente escritora nuestra." *El Nuevo Día,* 11 March 2001, pp. 14–15.

Lagos-Pope, María Inés. "Sumisión y rebeldía: El doble o la representación de la alienación femenina en narraciones de Marta Brunet y Rosario Ferré." *Revista Iberoamericana* 51:731–749 (1985).

López Jiménez, Ivette. "*Papeles de Pandora*: Devastación y ruptura." *Sin Nombre* 14:41–58 (1983).

Maldonado Denis, Manuel. "La disección de una clase." *¡Ahora!,* 7 March 1977, p. 24.

Méndez-Clark, Ronald. "La pasión y la marginalidad en la escritura: Rosario Ferré." In *La sartén por el mango: Encuentro de escritoras latioamericanas.* Edited by Patricia Elena González and Eliana Ortega. Río Piedras, P.R.: Ediciones Huracán, 1984. Pp. 119–130.

Mulero, Leonor. "Honores a Rosario Ferré." *El Nuevo Día,* 29 April 1997, p. 39.

Navarro, Mireya. "Bilingual Author Finds Something Gained in Translation." *New York Times,* 8 September 1998, p. B2.

Ortega, Julio. *Reapropiaciones: Cultura y nueva escritura en Puerto Rico.* San Juan: Editorial de la Universidad de Puerto Rico, 1991.

Pérez Marín, Carmen Ivette. "Estrategias emancipadoras en 'Pico pico mandorico' de Rosario Ferré y 'Goblin Market' de Christina Rossetti." Unpublished, 1989.

Picó, Fernando. "Ferré's Dose of Criticism May Be Cure for Social Ills." *San Juan Star,* 13 March 1994, p. 8.

Poniatowska, Elena. "Rosario Ferré: *Maldito amor.*" *El Semanario* (Mexico City), 18 May 1986, p. 5.

Rama, Angel. *Novísimos narradores hispanoamericanos en Marcha (1964–1980).* Mexico City: Marcha Editores, 1981.

Ríos Avila, Rubén. "Nueva visita al país de *Maldito amor.*" *Suplemento del Puerto Rico ilustrado,* 14 August 1988, p. 14.

Ruta, Suzanne. "Blood of the Conquistadores: A Novel About the Rise and Fall of a Puerto Rican Dynasty." *New York Times Book Review,* 17 September 1995, p. 28.

Santaliz, Coqui. "Elogian *Sitio a Eros* en México." *El Nuevo Día,* 21 April 1981, pp. 32–33.

Sotomayor, Aurea María. "Rosario Ferré: El revés del bordado." In *Lengua, razón y cuerpo.* Edited by Aurea María Sotomayor. San Juan, P.R.: Instituto de Cultura, 1987. Pp. 64–69.

Umpierre, Luz María. "Los cuentos ¿infantiles? de Rosario Ferré: Estrategias subversivas." In *Nuevas aproximaciones críticas a la literatura puertorriqueña contemporánea.* Edited by Luz María Umpierre. San Juan, P.R.: Ediciones Culturales, 1983. Pp. 89–101.

———. "De la protesta a la creación: Una nueva visión de la mujer puertorriqueña en la poesía." *Imagine: International Chicano Poetry Journal* 2:134–142 (1985).

———. "Reseña de *Sitio a Eros.*" *Revista Iberoamericana* 123–124:678–680 (1985).

Vega, Ana Lydia. "Carta abierta a Pandora." *El Nuevo Día,* 31 March 1998, p. 57.

Vega, José Luis. "Rosario Ferré: A la sombra de las obras." *El Nuevo Día,* 21 January 1990, p. 11.

Vega Carney, Carmen. " 'Cuando las mujeres quieren a los hombres': Manifiesto textual de una generación." In *Continental, Latin American and Francophone Women Writers,* vol. 1. Edited by Eunice Myers and Ginette Adamson. Lanham, Md.: University Press of America, 1987. Pp. 183–193.

———. "Sexo y texto en Rosario Ferré." *Confluencia: Revista Hispánica de Cultura y Literatura* 4:119–127 (1988).

Zapata, Miguel Angel. "Rosario Ferré: La poesía de narrar." *Inti: Revista de Literatura Hispánica* 26–27:133–140 (1987–1988).

*Interviews*

Alegre, Mario. "Sombras que iluminan." *El Nuevo Día,* 11 March 2001, pp. 6–7.

Echeverría, Ana María. "Moderna Scheherezade." *El Nuevo Día,* 2 January 1999, p. 81.

Gazarian Gautier, Marie-Lise. "Rosario Ferré." In *Interviews with Latin American Writers.* Elmwood Park, Ill.: Dalkey Archive Press, 1989. Pp. 81–92.

Heinrich, María Elena. "Entrevista a Rosario Ferré." *Prismal/Cabral* 7–8:98–103 (1982).

Hernández, Carmen Dolores: " 'Escribo para conocerme y para reconocer lo que hay de mí en el prójimo.' Entrevista a Rosario Ferré." *El Nuevo Día,* 6 August 2000.

Herrera, Bernal, and Leo Cabranes Grant. "Entrevista a Rosario Ferré." *Plaza* 16:7–11 (1989).

Levine, Linda Gould, and Gloria Feiman Waldman. "No más máscaras: Un diálogo entre tres escritoras del Caribe: Belkis Cuza Malé—Cuba, Matilde Daviu—Venezuela, Rosario Ferré—Puerto Rico." In *Literatures in Transition: The Many Voices of the Caribbean Area.* Edited by Rose S. Minc. Gaithersburg, Md.: Hispamérica, 1982. Pp. 189–197.

Molina, Javier. "Mi novela refiere la guerra civil sorda, de Puerto Rico." *Jornada,* 14 May 1986, p. 24.

Ortega, Julio. "Una entrevista inédita con Rosario Ferré." *Diálogo,* January–February 1991, pp. 24–25.

Poniatowska, Elena. "La literatura de Puerto Rico no ha trascendido todavía a Latinoamérica." *Novedades,* 11 July 1977.

———. "Rosario Ferré habla de su vida familiar." *Novedades,* 12 July 1977, n.p.

———. "Rosario Ferré dice que es una feminista independiente." *Novedades,* 13 July 1977, n.p.

———. "Rosario Ferré, la hija rebelde de un gobernador de Puerto Rico." *Novedades,* 10 July 1977, pp. 1, 12.

*Bibliographies*

Hintz, Suzanne Steiner. "An Annotated Bibliograhy of Works by and About Rosario Ferré: The First Twenty Years, 1970–1990." *Revista Interamericana de Bibliografía,* n.vol.:n.p. (1991).

Schon, Isabel. "Recent Hispanic Children's Literature: A Selected Annotated Bibliography." *Monographic Review* 1:97–100 (1985).

# Carlos Fuentes

## (1928–     )

## Lanin A. Gyurko

This essay, which is intended as a companion piece to the article on Fuentes in volume III of *Latin American Writers*, examines new trends in Fuentes's writing, such as postmodernism, as he creates works that are metafictional, antimimetic, self-reflective, and suffused with irony and parodic elements. Yet Fuentes's paradoxical art is both innovative and traditional. His postmodern works fuse such characteristics as indeterminacy, character fragmentation and openness in time and space with compelling plots, precise and elaborate settings, and exploration of Mexico's extraordinarily complex sociopolitical and mythical identity.

Born in Panama City on 11 November 1928, under the sign of Scorpio, as he is fond of mentioning, Carlos Fuentes—novelist, short story writer, essayist, playwright, and filmscript writer, and one of the preeminent writers of Latin America—is the son of Rafael Fuentes Boettiger, a career diplomat and at the time attaché to the Mexican legation in Panama, and Berta Macías Rivas. Carlos spent much of his childhood in the capital cities of Latin America, including Montevideo and Rio de Janeiro, where his father was Secretary to the Mexican ambassador to Brazil, the distinguished poet and essayist Alfonso Reyes, who later became Carlos's mentor. From 1934 to 1940, Fuentes attended the Henry D. Cooke public school in Washington, D.C., where his father was Counselor to the Mexican Embassy, and where his sister Berta was born. While still a student at the Cooke school, Carlos experienced a decisive event that led him to recognize his Mexican nationality for the first time. Mexican President Lázaro Cárdenas declared the nationalization of all the oil wells in Mexico, and news of this action appeared in the headlines of the Washington newspapers. Up to that time, Fuentes had been very popular with his North American classmates, but he suddenly found himself snubbed and then shunned. For the first time he became aware of the ambivalent relationship between the United States and Mexico, at times cordial and at other times antagonistic. He would later develop this theme in several of his works, culminating in two of his most significant novels: *Gringo viejo* (1985; *The Old Gringo*, 1985) and *La frontera de cristal* (1996; *The Crystal Frontier*, 1997). *The Old Gringo*, which rapidly became a best-seller in the United States, depicts the experiences of two North Americans in the turbulent Mexico of the Revolution of 1910, which many historians have seen as the most decisive event in the entire history of Mexico.

Fuentes has become friends with American presidents such as Bill Clinton and with leading U.S. writers such as Arthur Miller, Norman Mailer, and William Styron. In fact, Fuentes dedicated his major play *Todos los gatos son pardos* (1970; All cats are gray in the night) to Miller, and he dedicated *The Old Gringo* to William Styron's father. Fuentes's cosmopolitanism is exemplified by the character of Harriet Winslow in *The Old Gringo*, the inspiration for which came to him while he was conversing with Jane Fonda. She later produced the Hollywood film version of the novel, which starred Gregory Peck as the curmudgeon Ambrose Bierce, supposedly put to death by Pancho Villa, Jimmy Smits as the fictional Villista general Tomás Arroyo. Fonda herself played the strong-willed and uncompromising Gibson girl, Harriet Winslow. *The Old Gringo* is as much the story of the Harriet's adventures as it is of the North American journalist and short story writer Ambrose Bierce, who sought a glorious death in battle in Mexico. It marks a major shift in emphasis for Fuentes, whose many subsequent works focused on women characters, as opposed to Fuentes's early, male dominated novels, like *La región más transparente* (1958; *Where the Air Is Clear*, 1960), *La muerte de Artemio Cruz* (1962; *The Death of Artemio Cruz*, 1964), and *Cambio de piel* (1967; *A Change of Skin*, 1968). Indeed, the overwhelming importance of female characters is evident in the very titles of Fuentes's later works: *Constancia y otras novelas para vírgenes* (1990; *Constancia and Other Stories for Virgins*, 1991); *Diana, o, la cazadora solitaria* (1994; *Diana, the Goddess Who Hunts Alone*, 1995); *Los años con Laura Díaz* (1999; *The Years with Laura Díaz*, 2000), an epic novel of twentieth-century Mexico that complements *The Death of Artemio Cruz*; and *Instinto de Inez* (2001).

When Rafael Fuentes was named chargé d'affaires in Santiago, Chile (1941), Carlos attended the Grange School, where one of his classmates was José Donoso, who would also become an important Latin American writer. Donoso credits Fuentes with being the founder of the Latin American Novel of the Boom, which began in 1958, achieved its most brilliant realization in the 1960s and the 1970s, and a half century later is still the most significant movement in Latin American fiction. A constellation of novelists, including Argentina's Julio Cortázar, Colombia's Gabriel García Márquez, Peru's Mario Vargas Llosa, and Donoso himself, along with Fuentes, developed the all-encompassing *novela totalizante*, an exuberant fusion of social, psychological, and metaphysical concerns, of history and myth, and elaborate experiments in language, time, space, and

point of view. Donoso's extensive essay *Historia personal del Boom* (1972) provides a glowing tribute to Fuentes, to both his artistic inspiration and his efforts to open the publishing houses of the United States to contemporary Latin American authors. Gustavo Sainz, the pre-eminent member of La Onda (the Wave), the narrative movement in Mexico that began in 1966, has acknowledged his great debt to Fuentes's narrative *Where the Air Is Clear*, a mammoth and dazzling work that changed the course of Mexican and Latin American literature.

In the 1940s Fuentes lived in Buenos Aires, where his father was in charge of Mexican business affairs, a Buenos Aires that Fuentes would later evoke nostalgically in another of his seminal *novelas totalizantes*, *A Change of Skin*. In 1946 Fuentes attended the Colegio de Mexico, later studying at the Institut des Hautes Études in Geneva before returning to Mexico to become a student in the School of Law at the National University of Mexico. During the early 1950s, he was press secretary for the United Nations Information Center in Mexico City and Secretary in the Bureau of Cultural Diffusion at the National University of Mexico. In 1956 Fuentes and the literary critic Emmanuel Carballo founded the *Revista mexicana de literatura*, one of Mexico's most prestigious journals. Following in the diplomatic footsteps of his father, Fuentes served from 1956 until 1959 as director of international and cultural relations for Mexico's Ministry of Foreign Affairs, and from 1974 to 1977 he served as Mexico's ambassador to France, having been appointed by President Luis Echeverría. In 1959 Fuentes married Rita Macedo, a screen actress, and in 1962 his daughter Cecilia was born. He was elected to the Colegio Nacional in 1972, and his welcoming address was delivered by the Mexican essayist, poet, and Nobel Prize winner Octavio Paz, whose elaborate investigation of *la mexicanidad* in major essays such as *El laberinto de la soledad* (1950) and *Posdata* (1970) have exerted a marked influence on Fuentes's narrative vision.

Fuentes's brilliant achievements in the novel have been recognized through his being awarded many distinguished prizes. *A Change of Skin* is one of his most intricate and problematic novels, with several endings that contradict and undercut one another, throwing everything into doubt. It features an extremely protean and unreliable narrator, Freddy Lambert, who is both human and godlike, an emanation of Xipe Totec, the ancient Aztec god of spring, when the Earth changes its skin. The book was awarded the Biblioteca Breve Prize by the Barcelona publishing house of Seix Barral. In 1975 Fuentes received the Xavier Villaurrutia Prize in Mexico City and in 1977 was awarded the Rómulo Gallegos prize in Venezuela, both honors having been awarded to his magnum opus, the *novela totalizante* *Terra nostra* (1975; *Terra Nostra*, 1976), which he wrote in 1974 while a Fellow at the Woodrow Wilson International Center for Scholars in Washington, D.C. In 1984 Fuentes was awarded Mexico's National Prize for Literature by President Miguel de la Madrid; in 1987 he received the Cervantes Prize in Madrid, awarded by King Juan Carlos; in 1988 he received the Rubín Darío Prize; and in 1994 he was awarded the prestigious Príncipe de Asturias de las Letras prize.

Divorced from Rita Macedo in 1969, Fuentes married Sylvia Lemus, a journalist, in 1972. His son Carlos Rafael was born in 1973, and his daughter Natascha in 1974. Father and son collaborated on a book of photographs of personages such as Styron and Mailer, Robert Mitchum, Audrey Hepburn, and Gregory Peck, as well as Mexican figures, such as Lola Beltrán and José Luis Cuevas. In 1999 Carlos Rafael, after an extended illness, passed away.

Throughout his many articles in leading newspapers and journals in Mexico and the United States, and his myriad speeches at major universities in both countries, Fuentes has acted as "ambassador without portfolio," seeking to define the complex and ever-changing relationship between the United States and Latin America and to promote international peace and understanding. He has taught at the University of Cambridge and at Princeton and Harvard universities. At Harvard, Fuentes was Robert F. Kennedy Professor in Latin American Studies and offered very well received courses in comparative literature.

Fuentes's postmodernist writing began with his short novel *Cumpleaños* (1969; Birthday) but achieves its most striking and complete expression in *Cristóbal nonato* (1987; *Christopher Unborn*, 1991), which in recent years has received substantial critical attention. Indeed, *Christopher Unborn* holds the key to many of Fuentes's most important works in the 1980s and 1990s

and even into the second millennium. In several works, Fuentes experiments with the dead, dying, or spectral narrator. Artemio Cruz lies on his deathbed; *Aura* (1962; *Aura,* 1965) is narrated by Felipe Montero, a person who is spiritually dead, who is no longer an "I" but a disembodied "you." Montero finds the center of his existence in two ghosts: Llorente and Consuelo.

The dead narrator is a device that characterizes several Latin American novels, foremost of which is Juan Rulfo's *Pedro Páramo* (1955), in which Juan Preciado narrates from the tomb. In the lead story from Fuentes's *El naranjo, o, Los círculos del tiempo* (1993; *The Orange Tree,* 1994), Jerónimo de Aguilar also narrates from the grave, as his ghost returns to challenge the official, historical versions of the Conquest given to us by the conquistadores Bernal Díaz and Hernán Cortés. In contrast to these cadaverous works, which reach a macabre pinnacle in Elena Garro's bizarre drama *Un hogar sólido* (1958), in which all of the characters speak from the grave, *Christopher Unborn* is the first work in Mexican and perhaps Latin American literature as well to present a fetal narrator, as it pays homage to the masterful eighteenth-century work by the English novelist Laurence Sterne, *Tristram Shandy* (1760), which also evokes its protagonist/narrator from the moment of his conception, when he is an homunculus. Tristram's father's statement, "My Tristram's misfortunes began nine months before ever he came into the world," could apply just as well to the traumatic experiences recounted by the fetal Christopher.

In the fatalistic work that is *Where the Air Is Clear,* the lower classes are portrayed as constantly victimized, as preying on one another in their desperation, but as politically passive, resigned to their adverse fate. In *Christopher Unborn* their plight has markedly worsened. Here Fuentes focuses on the anger of those who have been repeatedly pushed back from their homesites in beautiful Acapulco into the distant mountains, out of sight of the tourists. The callous treatment that the peasants receive sparks their revolt, and an immense tide of offal rapidly covers the hotels, suffocating the tourists in their rooms. Others are poisoned by the beverages that they consume, an event modeled upon the horrifying way in which the black inhabitants of Haiti exact vengeance on their French exploiters in

Alejo Carpentier's novel *El reino de este mundo* (1949). This powerful work demonstrates the ultimate futility of rebellion, as the overthrow of one repressive regime is followed by the institution of a new one that is equally tyrannical or worse. It has had a significant influence on Fuentes.

Throughout *Christopher Unborn*, Fuentes puns incessantly on the names of the two principal cities in the novel, Mexico City, which is referred to as Mugsicko City and Makesicko City, and Acapulco, which is satirized as Kafkapulco, Sacapulco, Akapulque, and Acapulcalipsis. This novel unsparingly presents modern Mexico as a grim world where a black acid rain falls incessantly, and an old woman cackles hideously as she smashes flower pots on the heads of persons passing underneath her window, where a predominant emotion of the people is one of self-loathing because they realize that despite the relentless media blitz they will never enjoy the glamorous worlds with which the government tantalizes them, a government ever anxious to placate without resolving problems. Yet, despite its reiterated emphasis on violence, this novel ends optimistically. The authorities plan the construction of a huge dome over the whole of Mexico City that will purify the air and ration it out to all the inhabitants. They convert the metropolis into a Potemkin Village, an allusion to the model villages constructed by the eighteenth-century Russian general Potemkin in order to deceive the German-born empress of Russia, Catherine, into thinking that the peasants were living a life of prosperity and happiness.

Much of *Christopher Unborn* is dominated by a cyclical, fatalistic time, as is true for so many of Fuentes's narratives. At the close of the twentieth century, Mexico is portrayed as losing vast portions of its territories, just as it had in the nineteenth century. The border region between Mexico and the United States has become an entirely new country, Mexamerica; the territory of the Yucatan is ceded for the exclusive use of an international Tourist Club until the interest on the national debt is paid off; and the regions of Chiapas, Tabasco, and Campeche are ceded to an oil consortium as collateral until the principal of the enormous and ever-mounting national debt is paid. Yet, despite its surface pessimism, *Christopher Unborn* is a novel of exuberant life, and as such it foreshadows *The Years*

*with Laura Díaz*, which also celebrates the family throughout several generations. This is in stark opposition to three of Fuentes's major works from his early period: *Where the Air Is Clear*, *The Death of Artemio Cruz*, and *Aura*, novels of death. In these early narratives, and to a lesser degree in *Change of Skin* and *Terra Nostra* as well, Fuentes emphasizes the constrictive weight of the historical and mythic, particularly Aztec, past on the present.

Although *Christopher Unborn*, like Fuentes's earlier epic novels, unflinchingly depicts the grave problems faced by Mexico, it posits a new, apocalyptic time for the nation. Christopher, as narrator and eloquent fetal consciousness, provides a moral center to the work, which is divided into nine major units to emphasize the nine months of Cristobal's traumatic existence in the womb. Yet despite the many shocks that he experiences, Christopher, like Mexico itself, is a survivor, and the narrative ends happily and indeed triumphantly with the birth of twins: Christopher and his sister, *la nina* Ba, who throughout the narrative has been treated as an invisible presence.

Again foreshadowing *The Years with Laura Díaz*, *Christopher Unborn* is a counter-narrative to Fuentes's greatest work, *The Death of Artemio Cruz*. Cruz's anguished narrative is self-contained; all of his efforts to reach out to family are rebuffed. Indeed, Cruz is depicted as a person who for many years prior to his death has been enduring a kind of living death, a spiritually hollow existence. Cruz's ponderous narrative rolls over the reader, who is often swirled along in its torrential and chaotic flux. In contrast, the reader in the highly humorous *Christopher Unborn*, is referred to as the Elector, which like so many aspects of this paradoxical novel has a dual significance. It signifies that the reader is able to choose, to elect to continue reading or not, and it also refers to the reader's ability to decide how certain scenes in the narrative are to be completed. In addition, it converts the reader into a voter who can influence the outcome of a contest that has been sponsored by the federal government in commemoration of the five-hundredth anniversary of the discovery of the New World, to be celebrated on 12 October 1992. The primary reason for Christopher's conception is so that his parents, Angel and Angeles, might win this contest, in which the first child born on the anniversary date and given the name Christopher or any variant thereof will be designated as heir-apparent to the presidency of Mexico and on his twenty-first birthday will become president with hereditary rights. Throughout Christopher's open narrative, in which many of the scenes are deliberately left incomplete for the reader's collaboration, the protagonist exhorts the reader not to put down the novel, to work along with him, to help him to imaginatively re-create his world and to bolster him until the climactic moment of his birth arrives.

At many junctures in *Christopher Unborn*, the Elector is invited to become a co-creator of the novel. One of the pages of the novel is even left blank, as the narrator exhorts the reader to imitate the farrago of the rapacious revolutionary leader Matamoros. The entire novel is open, in the sense that the ending is but the beginning of Christopher's life, and the Elector is called upon to imagine Christopher's destiny. That destiny can be positive, with Christopher emerging as a new force for Mexico, or he may succumb to the immensely powerful and seemingly ineradicable forces symbolized by Robles Chacón and Homero Fagoaga, suffering a fate similar to what occurs with Jaime Ceballos in *Las buenas conciencias* (1959; *The Good Conscience,* 1961) and the weak, vacillating Félix Maldonado in *La cabeza de la hidra* (1978; *The Hydra Head,* 1978) or the obsequious Padilla in *The Death of Artemio Cruz.* Coinciding with the major theme of the protagonist in gestation, symbolic of a new, redemptive Mexico, many of the episodes of *Christopher Unborn* are presented in embryonic form, in order to give the active, creative reader the opportunity to develop them. Or, as at the end of *A Change of Skin,* another of Fuentes's *obras abiertas* (open works), several scenes, such as the encounters between Angel and Angeles and the malefic Fagoaga, end with multiple suggestions, and the reader can choose the one he prefers. Many times the fate of Christopher is left in suspension, and the reader is called upon to come to the rescue. The reader is important not only as Christopher's "midwife" but also as his complement. Christopher implores the reader to become his memory and conscience after he is born, when he is suddenly and forever deprived of his omniscience.

In several of his most recent works, Fuentes has focused on the return of the Virgin to Mexico. Most of the stories included in the collection *Constancia and Other Novels for Virgins* evoke, most often ironically, the fascination that the Mexican people have for the Virgin Mother. In "La desdichada" ("The Unfortunate One") the Virgin of Sorrows assumes the form of a mannequin in a store window on historic Tacuba Street. Two college students, Bernardo and Toño, purchase this sorrowful mannequin, who rapidly seems to come to life once the roommates have brought her back to their apartment. This, in a sense, is a Christian parallel to what occurs in one of Fuentes's first short stories, "Chac Mool," in which the hapless Filiberto purchases a stone idol in the flea market of Lagunilla and places it in his basement, where it achieves a fleshlike texture, then comes to life. The idol ultimately demands the blood sacrifice of Filiberto, who mysteriously drowns in Acapulco. In "La desdichada," at first Bernardo, then Toño, then a communal Bernardo-Toño perspective focuses on the strange and mesmerizing mannequin. The two roommates vie with one another in their devotion to her and are jealous when she seems to be favoring one over the other. At the end, the Virgin seems to desire that her devotees emulate the martyrdom of her Son.

Two manifestations of the Virgin Mother compete in *Christopher Unborn.* In contrast with the self-sacrificing, serene, long-suffering mother Angeles, there is the false Virgin, the goddess Mamadoc, created by Robles Chacón. As in so many of Fuentes's character creations, Mamadoc fuses fiction and reality; she is the female equivalent of the Haitian dictators, Papa Doc Duvalier and his successor, Baby Doc. Like so many of Fuentes's characters, Robles Chacón—the son of Frederico Robles and Hortensia Chacón conceived at the end of *Where the Air Is Clear* as a symbol of hope on the familial and on the national level, and hence a precursor of Christopher—betrays revolutionary ideals. He becomes the shrewd politician who seeks to sublimate the great frustration and pent-up urge for violence in the downtrodden populace by giving them a new symbol through which their negative emotions can be transcended, as they venerate this "Mother and Doctor of all Mexicans." It is ironic that Mamadoc should be exalted as a national mother—a surrogate of the Virgin of Guadalupe—because her womb is sewn shut; she is prohibited from bearing children. Her sole function is to utter the famous Grito de Dolores (the cry of Dolores) once every year, on 16 September, the day that celebrates the independence of Mexico from Spain, repeating the desperate cry uttered at the town of Dolores by the impassioned followers of an insurgent priest named Hidalgo. Her cry is not a theatrical one, but rather a genuine expression of her own victimization.

Even though he is the son of a revolutionary and an Indian woman who has spent most of her life in poverty, Robles Chacón—a parody of the revolutionary leaders like Venustiano Carranza, Álvaro Obregón and Plutarco Elías Calles—views with horror the leadership of the popular heroes Pancho Villa and Emiliano Zapata, idealistic leaders of the people who were eliminated by fellow revolutionary forces, and posits instead an eternal oligarchy for Mexico. He links the popular leaders with anarchy and mindless destruction. He creates Mamadoc as a fusion of all the mother symbols in Mexico, from the ancient Aztec goddesses Coatlicue and Tonantzín to the Virgin Mary and the revolutionary Adelita. Adelita's humility and self-abnegation are underscored by the fact that she is never to wear shoes. On the other hand, Robles, one of whose favorite Hollywood personages is Mae West, converts Mamadoc into a provocative sex symbol on the Hollywood model. Although she symbolizes chastity, she is attired in a lavish gown embroidered with rhinestones and is taught to swing her hips lubriciously in order to pander to the erotic desires of the pueblo. This combination of purity and sensuality, of abject poverty and ostentatious wealth, is Fuentes's way of parodying the distorted manner in which the Mexican *macho* perceives woman, as either spiritualized, immaculate Mother symbol, or as prostitute; she is worshipped for her purity as *la santa madre*, an emanation of the Virgin, or defiled for her provocativeness.

*La campaña* (1990, *The Campaign*, 1991) represents another new direction in the artistic trajectory of Fuentes. At the same time, it testifies to the remarkable versatility of this highly protean author, who on the one hand has created vast baroque narratives, such as *Christopher Unborn*, and has continued with the *novela totalizante* even in one of his later works, *The Years with*

*Laura Díaz*, and yet also creates taut, compact metaphysical works—such as *Instinto de Inez*, which is, in many respects, a continuation of the metaphysical vision of *Aura* and *Cumpleaños*—and his historical novels, with a linear time sequence and a single line plot development. *The Campaign* is a dense and fascinating novel. As a prime example of the "new historical novel" in Mexico and Latin America, it ranks alongside García Márquez's novel of Simón Bolívar, *El general en su laberinto* (1989), and Homero Aridjis's novel of the Spanish Inquisition, *1492: Vida y tiempos de Juan Cabezón de Castilla* (1985).

*The Campaign*, an adventure novel, focuses on one of the most turbulent epochs in Latin American history, the decade from 1810 to 1820—the Latin American struggle for independence from Spain, after three centuries of authoritarian colonial rule. Evoking the dramatic birth of new nations, *The Campaign* follows the course of rebellion across the continent, from Argentina to Peru to Chile and Venezuela and finally to Mexico. This dramatic novel provides the intricate development of one of Fuentes's favorite themes, that of the double, a phenomenon that functions on multiple levels: psychological and metaphysical, social and historical, literary and mythic. Baltasar is the protagonist, a young, bold, and enthusiastic advocate of Latin American independence who makes a ten-year journey across the vast Latin American continent as an insurgent. Along the way he encounters many persons—military leaders like Miguel Lanza and San Martín, Jesuit priests like Julian Ríos and Father Ildefonso de las Muñecas, whom he perceives as emanations or mirror reflections of his ideal self. On the textual level, *The Campaign* is explicitly doubled in novels such as Cervantes' *Don Quixote*. Fuentes, who has written the prologue to an English translation of Cervantes' masterpiece, presents the fiercely idealistic but hopelessly naive Baltasar as setting out to reform Latin American society single handedly, modeling the character after the self-deluded sixteenth-century hidalgo, Alonso Quijano (Quixote). (Fuentes had done this before, modeling Ambrose Bierce, in *The Old Gringo*, after the fantasy-crazed Knight of La Mancha, as Bierce crosses the frontier from the United States into Mexico on a white horse and carries in his saddle bag a copy of the *Quixote*.) For Baltasar, the writings of the French philosophers of the Enlightenment, in particular the works of Jean Jacques Rosseau, have a parallel effect to that which Quijano was subject after his extensive readings of the novels of chivalry. Just as Don Quixote sallies forth to right the wrongs of the world, tilts at windmills that for him are giants, and in his misguided idealism liberates a group of galley slaves who immediately return to their criminal activities, so too is the idealism of Baltasar sincere and impassioned but misguided. In his fervent desire immediately to effect social justice and equality, he kidnaps the privileged child of the Marqués de Cabra and his beautiful wife Ofelia, and substitutes a black child, the offspring of a prostitute. Baltasar thus believes that the black child will enjoy a life of comfort, power, and privilege, while the white child will be forced to endure the sufferings of the unfortunate black. Reality provides a different fate for the two children. As a result of a mysterious fire, the black child is burned to death, and the blond child whom Baltasar kidnaps is mysteriously reunited with Ofelia.

On one level, *The Campaign* is a realistic work, evoking glorious battles for independence, court intrigue, and unfulfilled passion. But paralleling *The Old Gringo*, on another, deeper level, *The Campaign*, like *Cumpleaños*, is heavily influenced by the metaphysical world of Borges; it is a novel of dreams and visions. The real cities, the colonial centers of Buenos Aires, Lima, and Santiago de Chile, are complemented by fantasy cities: the vision of the magnificent City of Light that Simón Rodríguez allows Baltasar to glimpse, and the nightmarish city of ashes that Baltasar enters in Venezuela and that symbolizes the despair that he has experienced in the endless and seemingly futile struggle for national self-determination.

The theme of the double appears most strikingly in the character of Ofelia Salamanca, the woman about whom Baltasar incessantly fantasizes. Indeed, Baltasar's social and political "campaign" for freedom is, on the personal level, an attempt to win the love of the alluring Ofelia, the most paradoxical character in the work. The wife of royalty, she has accompanied her fustian husband from Chile to Buenos Aires, where she maintains an affair with Baltasar's close friend, Manuel Varela. The product of this affair is the enigmatic blond-haired youth whom Baltasar never suspects is not his beloved Ofelia's legitimate son. Although by marriage and social position an adherent of the royalist cause, Ofelia apparently is a secret ally of the insurgents, but Baltasar never frees himself of his suspicions that Ofelia is a traitor who has sent countless insurgent officers to their deaths.

In Cervantes' *Don Quixote,* the protagonist can relate to women only as fantasy beings. In the febrile imagination of Don Quixote, the foul-smelling village girl, Aldonza Lorenzo, metamorphoses into the princess-like Dulcinea del Toboso. Similarly, Baltasar can never relate to Ofelia as a human being. She is always a vision of Tantalus—mesmerizing, erotic, obsessive—and Baltasar never realizes that while he is so lovingly fantasizing, his duplicitous friend Varela is possessing his beloved. Even the manner in which Baltasar dreams about Ofelia's beauty, as a fusion of Romantic and Classical ideals, emphasizes her complex, ambivalent function within the narrative, similar to the enigmatic and treacherous Teódula in *Where the Air Is Clear* and the wily and destructive Consuelo/Aura in *Aura.* Ironically, like Felipe Montero with the seductive Aura and like the neurotic Javier in *A Change of Skin* with Isabel, Baltasar Bustos is not in love with the real Ofelia Salamanca, but rather with a romantic illusion to which he tenaciously clings. Indeed, so strong is his fantasy that when Baltasar is finally reunited with his "beloved" Ofelia, whom he has pursued across the Latin American continent, he has no way whatsoever of relating to the cancer-wracked, disheveled woman that he finally meets.

The theme of *cainismo* (betrayal) also occurs in many of Fuentes's novels, including *Where the Air Is Clear, The Death of Artemio Cruz, Terra Nostra,* and *Christopher Unborn.* On both the personal and the national or continental levels, *The Campaign* time and again also exemplifies this negative theme. On the personal level, Baltasar is betrayed by his closest friend, Varela, who sends his ingenuous companion off to war and possible death, and who never confesses his affair with Baltasar's beloved. On the national level, the struggle for independence is continually betrayed by the insurgents themselves. San Martín, one of the insurgency's greatest leaders, is evoked as a forthright and self-sacrificing idealist on whom Baltasar models his own career. Yet he is extremely pessimistic regarding the outcome of the struggle. He gloomily predicts that the struggle will end in internecine strife, no longer between Spanish oppressor and insurgents but among the *criollos* themselves, this time fighting not for liberty but for sheer power. This is exactly how Fuentes sees the pessimistic course of the Mexican Revolution, which ended with the disintegration of revolutionary ideals into a monstrous series of battles by revolutionaries against fellow revolutionaries.

Artemio Cruz is just the opposite of Baltasar, an opportunistic and self-aggrandizing revolutionary fighter. He incarnates Fuentes's pessimism about the triumph of the Revolution. So too are the two armchair insurgents, Varela and Dorrego, who stay comfortably in Buenos Aires and exhort Baltasar to press on. Baltasar himself constantly risks his life for his beliefs, as do Echague and Arias, his two valorous companions in battle. Both of them lose their lives, and Baltasar, who has been spared, must now live for them as well as for himself. He has a sense of responsibility for the fallen that the cynical and mercenary Cruz, even on his deathbed, is incapable of experiencing. Indeed, because he is a multiple identity, because he lives for self and for others, Baltasar gains the respect of the formidable independence leader in Mexico, the priest Quintana, who serves as the literary double of the noble Padre Hidalgo and Padre Morelos, historical figures who gave their lives for the cause of Mexican independence.

*The Campaign* traces the emergence of new identities in the three Argentine friends—Baltasar, Echague, and Arias. They start off as colonial subjects and end up as citizens of the new Argentine republic, under the government of the liberal Rivadavia. Even time is multiple in this highly intriguing novel. At the outset, the dominant time is an apocalyptic one, similar to the beginning of *Terra Nostra* and paralleling the exhilarating sense of the impending birth of a new society, of a new Mexico, linked with the apocalyptic figure of Pancho Villa in *The Old Gringo*. The three comrades have a mania for time because suddenly they feel the exalting sensation of owning time, of controlling their own destinies. Symbolic of this newfound freedom is the throwing away of the elaborate wigs and courtly attire that were so much a part of stifling colonial rule

and which are suddenly out of fashion. Soon, too, the stately minuet, the dance par excellence of the colonial courts, will disappear forever and be replaced by the vibrant assertion of new rhythms of independence and national identity—the popular rhythms like the *cumbia* and the *vidalita*, which celebrate throughout the continent the ardent romance between Baltasar and Ofelia. Yet casting a shadow over this new time of national exuberance and joy is another, far more fatalistic time, alluded to by Varela when he mentions his Calvary watch. This is the time that marks the passion and death of Christ, and constitutes an allusion to independence as a period of sanguinary martyrdom. It is significant that the positive time, that of the resurrection of Christ, is omitted in Varela's evocation of his fatalistic timepiece.

Throughout his fiction, Fuentes has been preoccupied with the theme of birth and rebirth. The beginning of *Terra Nostra*, which evokes the imminent destruction of the world in the second millennium, focuses on a frantic communal birthing rite, in response to the specter of annihilation. *A Change of Skin*, which evokes the horrendous torture and death in the Nazi concentration camps, ends with an emphasis not only on the death in retribution of the German architect, Franz, who collaborated with the Nazis, but also on the birth of a mysterious child, whom Elizabeth and Javier discover in the trunk of the car where the body of Franz has been placed. Angel Fagoaga in *Christopher Unborn* is the offspring of two scientists, Diego and Isabel, who had initially resolved never to have children, presumably in response to the overpopulation crisis in Mexico. Despite their resolution, they conceive their only child on the fateful night of 2 October 1968, the night of the massacre of the student protestors peacefully assembled in the Plaza of Nonoalco–Tlatelolco. As a response to this night of horrendous violence, to the destruction of their scientific experiments by the soldiers, and to the death all around them, they determine to affirm new life. By this choice, these inveterate idealists symbolize the purpose of this narrative as a whole, in which death is constantly juxtaposed with new life. This juxtaposition is stunningly manifested after the cataclysmic earthquake that struck Mexico City in 1985, when tons of rubble covering hundreds of dead bodies nonetheless yielded the bodies of infants, still alive, who had in some miraculous way survived their sudden burial. It is equally revealed in *The Years with Laura Díaz*, in which Fuentes once more returns to the theme of the massacre in 1968, which haunts him. Here, the violent death of Laura's idealistic grandson, Santiago, is followed by the birth of her great-grandson, whose introduction and conclusion frames the novel, and whose career as filmmaker, recording the restoration of magnificent works by the Mexican muralists Diego Rivera and David Alfaro Siqueiros in the United States, renders homage to the brilliant photographic career of his indefatigable great-grandmother.

The most frightening example of Fuentes's use of the double phenomenon in *The Campaign* is the complex way in which Baltasar becomes initiated into the life of a soldier, when he kills his first antagonist. The irony here is that, although he fights against royalist Spain, his actual enemy is an Indian, the peoples most exploited by the *conquistadores* and their successors, the *encomenderos* and *hacendados*. The Indian has been pressed into service by the Crown. The battle is presided over by supernatural forces: the angel of peace and the angel of death, who are, so characteristic of Fuentes, initially depicted as opposites but who rapidly merge to become doubles. This fusion of opposites establishes the pattern for the hand to hand combat, in which Baltasar finally recognizes that his Indian opponent is not an enemy but rather a spiritual double. For this reason, after he has slain the Indian, Baltasar strips off his own clothing and dresses his victim with it, then dresses himself in the clothing of the dead man. Paradoxically, after nullifying his adversary, Baltasar seeks to commemorate his death, to supply him with an identity, with a face. At this point, a metaphysical process occurs by which the face of Baltasar and that of his enemy-double seem to merge. Here is perhaps Fuentes's most profound use of the double theme, as Baltasar's conflicting emotions—his guilt, fear, triumph, and horror—are exteriorized. The act of donning the dead man's clothes marks the dramatic interchange of identities—the painful merging of self and double, of Indian and *criollo*. Baltasar, who has delivered eloquent speeches promising equality to the Indian populace, which ironically does not even comprehend the Spanish language, now must live his victim's life.

Baltasar is paralleled in the character of his commander in Upper Peru, the despotic chieftain Miguel Lanza. Lanza's career, his existence, is dedicated to his two brothers, both of whom have become martyrs to the cause of independence, and he attempts to compel Baltasar into assuming the role of one of his dead brothers. Life is not individual but collective in *The Campaign*. One of Lanza's closest friends, the Indian Baltasar Cárdenas, becomes another double of the protagonist, Baltasar Bustos, by virtue of his very name. After the dark-eyed Indian is slain, the clear blue eyes of Miguel Lanza suddenly turn dark, an act of magical realism that symbolizes how Lanza too has assumed the valiant identity of his former friend.

Why is the double so important a phenomenon in *The Campaign*? Perhaps because the initial self, Baltasar, who appears both as an individual and as a symbol of the weakened identity of Latin America on the verge of independence, is so inchoate, so nebulous. Indeed, Latin America's great socio-economic and political dependency on Spain, on the *madre patria*, to which it is indebted for its language, its Catholicism, its educational system, and many of its customs and traditions, is paralleled by the impact that the elder Bustos exerts on Baltasar. At one point Baltasar almost worships patriarchal authority, which is, on the national level, the only form of authority that Latin America has known for almost three centuries. Yet even though this novel examines many facets of the fight for Latin American independence, Fuentes is careful to avoid setting up any Manichean dichotomy between unjust and oppressive royalist forces and the shining knights of a new world order, the insurgents. While in upper Peru, Baltasar naively believes that by addressing the subjected peoples from astride his horse he can instantaneously reverse centuries of oppression. He finds, instead, that he is regarded as the representative of centralist Buenos Aires, an aloof and impersonal authority that reflects the imperiousness of Spain.

Between the insurgents and the royalists is another group—characters such as Miguel Lanza, who are the leaders of the *republiquetas* and whom Fuentes sees as arbitrary and despotic powers, perhaps forerunners of the myriad *caciques* and *caudillos* who emerged in Latin America after independence had been attained. This group is necessary to tip the balance in favor of the insurgent forces, after the initial exuberance of victory gives way to a virtual stalemate between insurgent Buenos Aires and royalist Lima, with the increasing possibility that the royalist forces would gradually wear down the insurrectionists. Power centers multiply in this decades-long war that becomes hydra-headed, spawning many local warlords who are not at all interested in continental independence but only in asserting their authority over the limited area in which they rule supreme. The irony is that the glorious ideas of liberty, equality, and fraternity that Baltasar cherishes must immediately be compromised; by becoming one of Miguel Lanza's followers he places himself at the service of rapacious and despotic forces. Here Fuentes depicts a war for independence within a war for independence, by showing groups of fanatic rebels loyal only to their commanders and extremely suspicious of both royalists and insurgents. The way in which Fuentes evokes these chieftains makes them appear as precursors of the implacable Mexican *caudillos* of the Revolution and its aftermath, figures such as Pancho Villa, who are supreme in their authority, arbitrary and despotic in their judgments, and demand from their troops absolute loyalty to the death.

Fuentes's most engaging novel from his second period is *The Crystal Frontier*. Like Fuentes himself, this novel incessantly crosses boundaries, even on the structural level, as is suggested in its subtitle: *una novela en nueve cuentos* (*A Novel in Nine Stories*). In *The Old Gringo* Fuentes evokes Mexico's northern border with the United States as a wound, as a scar that will not heal. He returns to this fascinating geographic area in *The Crystal Frontier*, depicting it as a borderland whose socioeconomic importance has vastly increased in the last twenty years. As Leonardo Barroso, the exploitative owner of a *maquiladora* (factory) in Ciudad Juárez, exuberantly exclaims, Mexico in 1965 had zero *maquiladoras* on the border and in 1994 had one hundred thirty-five thousand, and even this immense number is ceaselessly expanding. This growth is transforming Mexico, severely altering its population patterns as economically impoverished Mexicans from the southern region migrate to the borderlands in quest of an ever-elusive paradise, a phenomenon depicted by screenwriter Gregory Nava through the characters of Enrique and Rosa in his border film, *El norte*.

*The Crystal Frontier* is a highly readable work because of both its compelling theme and its deft and convincing creation of a host of characters on both sides of the border—Mexicans and gringos; chicanos and owners of *maquiladoras*; Mexicans like Juan Zamora, who crosses the border to study medicine at Cornell University, and the *Malintzín de las maquiladoras*'s Marina, who crosses the border from Ciudad Juárez to El Paso to rendezvous with her lover; and fictional characters and historical ones like Benito Juárez, Sam Houston, and Stephen Austin. *The Crystal Frontier*, like almost all of Fuentes's writings, but in this case much more directly, is addressed to a North American audience; the author constantly contrasts national character and customs, political ideologies, and even the great difference between Mexican and U.S. cuisine (he lambastes the United States for the sterility of its cuisine, with its emphasis on fast food, as opposed to the immense variety of Mexican dishes).

Fuentes offers a critique of the gringo for the prevalence of racial prejudice, seen in extremely supercilious and racist characters like the widowed Miss Amy, who treats her servants with contempt and incessantly seeks to find defects in her loyal Mexican maid Josefina. Nonetheless, Fuentes does not present a facile dichotomy between the wealthy and prejudiced gringos and aggressive North American business interests (symbolized by the shadowy gringo Murchison) who exploit Mexico for financial gain, and the ever downtrodden, submissive Mexicans. Indeed, Fuentes's criticism is much more harshly directed toward his fellow countrymen. The character Leonardo Barroso, like Artemio Cruz, wants desperately to be accepted by his North American financiers, wants them to call him "Len," but on the other hand has little but contempt for his workers and for the city, Ciudad Juárez, that has made him a multimillionaire. Instead, he characterizes the city sardonically as "el desmadre montado sobre el caos" (a defiled mother seated atop chaos). As in *The Death of Artemio Cruz*, the gringos in *The Crystal Frontier* most often appear as background figures—the Wingate family who board Juan Zamora in Ithaca but who are uneasy because of his homosexuality; the "silent partner," Murchison, whom Leonardo Barroso slavishly courts, sanctimoniously presenting himself as the benefactor of the new Mexican women to whom he is providing employment and the professional opportunity to liberate themselves from domestic oppression. In the story "Las amigas" ("The Friends"), the house servant Josefina works to pay the legal expenses of her husband, incarcerated because members of the Mexican community have falsely accused him of murdering a fellow Mexican. Josefina sees her husband's accusers as highly resentful of their own countrymen who have but recently arrived in the United States. In this narrative, although the aged, reclusive, and imperious Miss Amy is depicted as filled with racial prejudice and constantly finding fault with her domestic servants, the North American is nonetheless evoked positively. For example, Miss Amy's nephew, the lawyer Archibaldo, not only defends Josefina's husband but teaches him about the law so that he can defend himself, and at the end Miss Amy crosses the harsh border of social class and racial prejudice, which has led her to her seeing Josefina as an indolent thief, and achieves reconciliation and even friendship with her Mexican servant.

The story "La pena" ("Pain") is a complex narrative. Even though it is written in a clear, direct, persuasive style, it crosses the frontier between reality and dream. Here Fuentes develops his most enigmatic characters, Juan Zamora, who falls in love with an upper-class North American, Jim Rowlands. Rowlands is referred to as "Lord Jim" not only to indicate the class superiority of the gringo but also to show that he is dominant in the relationship. When Lord Jim finally breaks off with Juan, the sensitive Mexican is devastated. Juan Zamora takes refuge in a recurrent dream in which he and Lord Jim commit suicide together, jumping from the Triphammer Bridge in Ithaca into Fall Creek Gorge. This is a dream of purely ironic unity, unity achieved only through self-obliteration. In *The Crystal Frontier*, as throughout Fuentes's work, from *Where the Air Is Clear* and *The Death of Artemio Cruz* to *A Change of Skin* and *Diana*, one of the most difficult of all the boundaries for Fuentes's fated characters to cross is that of the self; interpersonal relationships are seldom, if ever, successful. The same is true of the affair depicted in *Malintzín de las maquiladoras*. Marina is betrayed by Rolando, whom she visits in El Paso only to find him in bed with his gringa lover. Like Juan Zamora, like Félix Maldonado in *The Hydra Head* and Felipe Montero in *Aura*, like Elizabeth and Isabel in *A Change*

*of Skin*—Marina finds not love but permanent disillusionment. It is not love but death that predominates, both in this chapter and at the end of *The Crystal Frontier*.

Dinorah, one of Barroso's many female employees, laments the lack of adequate day-care facilities and leaves her young son alone at home, tied up. The son dies accidentally, hanging himself; but Barroso's only concern is to raze the slums where she lives, purchasing the land for a pittance and then developing it with the assistance of North American capital and expanding his empire, on the model of Federico Robles and Artemio Cruz. The narrative ends tragically; Barroso crosses the final border, the one between life and death, when he is gunned down on the international bridge between Juarez and El Paso. Most of the time, however, boundaries are never crossed; although Juan Zamora attempts to save the life of Barroso, it is too late, and Zamora never recognizes the person whom he is attending as his benefactor, the one who paid his tuition at Cornell. Violence engulfs the exploiters and the exploited; more than thirty illegal border-crossers are slain by a group of crazed white supremacist skinheads.

The image of the crystal (glass) frontier is repeated, in various manners, throughout the work. It first appears in the opening story. "La capitalina" ("A Capital Girl"). Michelina, who has nothing but disdain for the Mexican side of the border, and regards the border town Campazas as culturally vacuous. She views contemptuously the town's unique baroque architecture, lovingly fixing her gaze on the glass skyscrapers on the United States side of the border. Here Fuentes's attitude toward the borderlands is a continuation of that seen in Mexican authors like Martín Luis Guzmán at the beginning of the twentieth century. In *El águila y la serpiente* (1928; *The Eagle and the Serpent*, 1930), Guzmán draws a marked contrast between the prosperous and dynamic town of Nogales, Arizona, and the lethargic and impoverished Nogales, Sonora. The contrast is even more pronounced in Guzmán's evocation of Ciudad Juárez, as Guzmán, like Michelina a *capitalino*, journeys from Mexico City to Ciudad Juárez for a personal encounter with Pancho Villa. Ciudad Juárez is viewed as a primitive region where sidewalks rapidly disappear and the houses loom as replicas of those in ancient

Mesopotamia. Guzmán, both the narrator and a character in *The Eagle and the Serpent,* presents Pancho Villa as more animal than human, as a jaguar in his lair, recumbent but deadly.

The crystal frontier again appears in the one-way mirrors, the walls of plate glass that separate Barroso from his workers, on whom he can spy at will, as he looks out for the slightest signs of union organizing. It is evoked again, in dramatic close-up, in the story by the same name, which treats the abortive romantic interlude between the gringa office worker, Audrey, and the Mexican worker, Lisandro Chávez. The ever-opportunistic, wily Barroso, who maintains that Mexico's greatest export is not oil or agricultural products but human labor, devises a scheme whereby he flies Mexican workers into New York City just for the weekend to clean the windows of the skyscrapers. Audrey, divorced from her husband and longing for romance, remains separated from her exotic new acquaintance by "la frontera de cristal," which for reasons left ambiguous cannot he crossed. She writes her name on the glass but Chavez, out of shame, or a sense of inferiority, or the deep-seated realization of the impossibility of their relationship, writes only his nationality on the other side of the glass before disappearing.

Fuentes has always been fond of inversions, as he is in *The Orange Tree,* in which the lead story "Las dos orillas" tells of the counter invasion of Spain by a force of two thousand Mayan Indians who invade Cadiz. In *The Crystal Frontier* he emphasizes that the first "wetbacks," the first persons to cross the northern frontier illegally and to occupy the territory of another nation, were North Americans: Sam Houston and Stephen Austin and the *tejanos* who eventually took possession of what was originally part of Mexico. Fuentes sees this North Americanization of Mexico as being countered by the Mexicanization of the United States. Indeed, he is an advocate of open boundaries between the two nations. In *Nuevo tiempo mexicano* (1995; *A New Time for Mexico,* 1996) he has indicated his support for NAFTA (North American Free Trade Agreement), and the ending of *The Crystal Frontier* seeks reconciliation between the two countries, again indicative of Fuentes's great diplomatic abilities. Here he takes a bitter, cynical proverb from the nineteenth century, "pobre México, tan lejos de Dios, tan cerca el Estados

Unidos" (poor Mexico, so far from God and so close to the United States), and transforms it to link the two countries in a common plight, in a common destiny: "pobre México, pobre Estados Unidos, tan lejos de Dios, tan cerca el uno del otro" (poor Mexico, poor United States, so far from God, so close to one another).

A key figure in *The Crystal Frontier,* the spokesperson for Fuentes himself, is the iconoclastic José Francisco, who as a border person defines himself as neither Mexican nor gringo but chicano. Riding his motorcycle back and forth across the border, he delivers chicano writings to Mexico and Mexican writings back to Texas. In his advocacy of international understanding, in his dynamic quest for the form that is absent from the solipsistic narrative of *Aura* and the equally alienated narrative of *Artemio Cruz,* José uses the *we* form, signifying brotherhood. His mission parallels that of Fuentes, who on several occasions has referred to himself as a chicano writer. Underscoring the concluding optimism of *The Crystal Frontier* and dramatically conveying the exuberance of the highly mobile José Francisco, Fuentes develops concluding segments that repeatedly cross the frontiers between prose and poetry; in a series of italicized monologues he plunges into the remote past of Mexico to provide a lengthy ode to this fascinating region of the Rio Bravo and the Rio Grande.

The one genre that Fuentes has not cultivated is poetry, yet he is a poet nonetheless. Herman Melville, the great North American novelist of the nineteenth century and author of the epic novel *Moby Dick,* was a master of poetic prose, and in his sweeping, intensely lyrical prose monologues, Fuentes's poetry can also be found. An example of this is the tumultuous, all-encompassing concluding monologue in *Where the Air Is Clear,* delivered by Ixca Cienfuegos. This marvelous technique is repeated at the end of *The Crystal Frontier,* as Fuentes's exhilarating multitemporal and multispatial monologue flashes back thirty thousand years, focuses on the first, anonymous indigenous inhabitants of the region, then moves rapidly forward in time to trace the invasion of this territory by the Spanish. In the course of this monologue Fuentes evokes Francisco Vázquez de Coronado and his futile search in Coahuila and Chihuahua for the Cities of Gold, focuses on Cortés and Pizarro and De Soto as frontier personages even in their native Spain, comes down to the nineteenth century to evoke Santa Anna and Benito Juárez, and repeatedly crosses the magic frontier between fantasy and history, expertly and compactly and dynamically fusing all epochs of border history just as he does all epochs of Mexican history as a whole at the end of *Where the Air Is Clear*. In so doing, Fuentes produces the literary equivalent to Borges' wondrous object, the Aleph—the one point from which all points of the universe can be descried.

*The Years with Laura Díaz* demonstrates, as Fuentes himself has stated, that his work is all of one piece. An elaborate narrative, both epic and lyric in tone, it is an eloquent evocation of female consciousness. It both responds to and complements Fuentes's masterpiece, *The Death of Artemio Cruz,* and ideally should be read in conjunction with this earlier text. Indeed, Artemio Cruz makes a brief appearance in *The Years with Laura Díaz,* along with another Laura, Cruz's lover Laura Rivière, who he forfeits when she demands that he divorce his wife, Catalina. The character of Artemio Cruz represents Mexico's history, not only the history of the Mexican Revolution, but also, symbolically, Mexico's early history. Cruz is a twentieth-century *conquistador,* much like Cortés; he is also depicted as the decadent Aztec emperor Montezuma II. The character of Laura Díaz, however, is significantly more modest. Laura is a witness to twentieth-century Mexican history and a sensitive recorder and interpreter of that history, as well as a national conscience figure. Moreover, while Cruz is alienated from his family (his daughter, Teresa, hates him and his wife, Catalina, is preoccupied with finding where he has hidden his will), Laura celebrates her family, both her ancestors and her descendents. Cruz's anguished narrative moves between self-exaltation and self-loathing; Laura's life is lovingly evoked by her great-grandson, Santiago IV.

In *The Years with Laura Díaz* Fuentes once again returns to the city that has fascinated him throughout his work, toward which he continues to maintain an ambivalent, love-hate relationship: Mexico City. A sampling of the chapter headings reveals Fuentes's role as the unofficial chronicler of the city: "Paseo de la Reforma: 1930"; "Parque de Lama: 1938"; "Café de París: 1939"; "Colonia Roma: 1941"; and "Chapultepec-Polanco: 1947." Like Cruz, who loses the people he

most loves—Regina, during the Mexican Revolution, and his only son, Lorenzo, a martyr in the Spanish Civil War—Laura loses the people she most cherishes, all named Santiago, an allusion to the patron saint of Spain: her brother, Santiago I, assassinated by a federal firing squad because of his revolutionary activities; Santiago II, Laura's beloved son, who dies prematurely, at age twenty-six; and Santiago III, Laura's only grandson, who is killed the night of the student massacre in the Plaza of Nonoalco–Tlatelolco. Although the geographical and spiritual center of both *The Death of Artemio Cruz* and *The Years with Laura Díaz* is Mexico City, both novels keep returning to Veracruz, the origin of their respective protagonists, and, significantly, the origin of Fuentes himself.

Fuentes's paternal grandmother, Emilia Boettiger de Fuentes, was born in Catemaco, Veracruz, the same place where Laura Díaz is born, and married Rafael Fuentes Vélez, manager of the Banco Nacional de México in Veracruz. Just as Cruz returns to Cocuya, Veracruz, and restores his ancestral home, the mansion of the Menchaca family, so too does Laura return to Catemaco. Time in both novels is cyclical. For example, the moment of Cruz's death in Mexico City is imaginatively juxtaposed with the moment of his birth in Veracruz, and Laura dies in 1972 in the place of her birth. Yet Cruz and Laura are contrasting personalities. Cruz is depicted as an ancient Aztec god, as a parasitic deity, one who incessantly demands the blood sacrifice of the idealists, like Regina and Lorenzo, in order to fulfill or prolong his own existence. Indeed, even on his deathbed, the arrogant Cruz demands that they die again so that he may continue to live. The supremely egotistical Cruz lives only for himself. Laura, on the other hand, lives only for others. The death of Cruz, which constitutes the central theme of the work, is depicted in naturalistic and clinical detail; in contrast, the death of Laura is veiled in ambiguity. It is evoked in terms of a disappearance, as a fusion of Laura with the natural world, as she loses herself in the forest. The forest is a magical realm, infused with the spirits of the ancient, beneficent Aztec goddesses of nature. Cruz dies stubbornly affirming the material. Laura, in contrast, succumbs while affirming the spiritual. She dies embracing the ceiba tree, an allusion to the death of the valorous Aztec emperor Cuauhtémoc, who was hanged by Cortés from a ceiba tree. Throughout Fuentes's works, Aztec and Christian imagery are fused in literary *sincretismo*. The ceiba tree is therefore representative of Christ, and Laura is depicted as a Christian martyr. Cruz fears death and even attempts to bargain with God for inmortality; Laura welcomes death, believing that she will be made immortal through her descendants: "la ceiba, la reina de la selva virgen, cuya corona son las espinas desparramadas como puñales hirientes a largo y ancho de su gran cuerpo pardo" (the ceiba, the queen of the virgin forest, whose crown are the spines scattered like wounding daggers all over its great brown body).

*The Years with Laura Díaz* is Fuentes's most personal, and in many respects, his most poignant novel. Inspiration for the young artist, the painter Santiago II, comes from Carlos Fuentes Lemus, Fuentes's beloved son, who also died tragically, at age twenty-six. In an 11 May 1999 article in *El País*, Fuentes writes a moving elegy to his son, in which he traces the link between Carlos Lemus and Santiago, and regards his creation of the latter as an exorcism.

The dominant symbol in *The Death of Artemio Cruz* is the mirror. All of the novel's myriad characters reflect Cruz's existence in some sense. Physical mirrors, at times cracked or shattered, abound, and mirror imagery underscores the entrapment of Cruz in his physical self, his putrefying body, and his ossified idealism. In contrast, the dominant image in *The Years with Laura Díaz* is the photograph or painting. The narrative is framed by paintings—at the outset the murals of Rivera in Detroit and Siqueiros in Los Angeles, about which Laura's great-grandson is making a film documentary, and, later, the wondrous painting by Santiago II, which exemplifies magical realism, as it evokes two human beings who ascend to heaven.

The majority of Fuentes's works concern expulsion—at an early age Cruz is expelled from the paradisiacal world of Veracruz and later from the private paradise of his relationship with Regina, and he spends the rest of his life attempting to regain these lost paradises. Similarly, in *A Change of Skin* the central characters, Elizabeth and Javier, enter a chapel where the dominant iconography is again of the expulsion—the expulsion of Adam and Eve from paradise, an allusion to the impossibility of Elizabeth and Javier finding the change of skin, the physical and emotional and spiritual renewal that they are so desperately seeking. But in *The Years with Laura Díaz,* the protagonist, at age sixty, does achieve this "change of skin" as she launches a new career as a photographer and quickly achieves overwhelming success. The positive, uplifting, transcendental nature of *The Years with Laura Díaz* is symbolized by the theme of Santiago's most important painting, which Laura saves from destruction. In this work, whose theme is the expulsion of Adam and Eve from Paradise, the two mortals do not fall but rise. Fuentes depicts an Adam and Eve who are not ashamed, stricken, banished, and defeated, but rather a first couple who are triumphant. The painting is of an ascension.

The muralists have always been present in Fuentes's vast, epic novels, which fuse all epochs of Mexican history. In *The Years with Laura Díaz* they appear explicitly; Rivera and Frida Kahlo, who is now regarded as the foremost Latin American woman painter, are close friends of Laura. Laura becomes an assistant to Frida and in many senses her double. Laura's career is launched by her most valuable photograph, one taken of the dead body of Frida. Laura repeatedly photographs the other Mexico, the one kept hidden by official representatives and tourist propaganda. She photographs the poverty and crime, in particular the horrendous violence in the ubiquitous slums. Moreover, the intrepid Laura photographs the massacre in Nonoalco–Tlatelolco and smuggles out the film. Like Frida Kahlo, Laura achieves international renown for her professional achievements and symbolizes the great contribution of women artists to twentieth-century Mexican culture.

Characteristic of Fuentes's fiction is the intermingling of fantasy and history. Laura's husband, Juan Francisco, strongly supports the Revolution and adapts to the ever-changing, ever-shifting course of power and finally regards himself as "un guardián del orden, un administrador de la estabilidad" (a guardian of order, an administrator of stability). The major presidents of the post-Revolutionary period are brought to life, from Obregón and Calles to Cárdenas and Miguel Alemán Valdés and Gustavo Díaz Ordaz. The epicenter of *The Death of Artemio Cruz* is the Revolution of 1910, which brings Cruz to life, which imbues him with a new identity, and whose ideals he betrays. The epicenter of *The Years with Laura Díaz* is the Spanish Civil War, during which Laura's greatest love is the Spanish republican, Jorge Maura. Laura pays tribute to the great Spanish writers in exile, who were welcomed to Mexico by Cárdenas: Emilio Prados, Luis Cernuda, Max Aub, and the filmmaker Luis Buñuel. Finally, the moving words of Laura, "our existence has no other meaning but to complete unfinished destinies," contrast so markedly with the imperiousness of the solipsistic Cruz and seem once more to reflect Fuentes's own life and brilliant career.

Fuentes has stated that contemporary civilization is founded on amnesia. One of the primary purposes of his art is to record the past, specifically to recapture what life was like in Mexico City during the 1940s, 1950s, and 1960s, so that his readers will not forget these formative decades. One of Fuentes's most complex and vibrant character creations is Claudia Nervo, who is much like the ancient Greek and Roman god Proteus, for she constantly changes, playing new cinematic roles and adopting new lifestyles, in an effort to defy and transcend chronological time and to defeat its ruinous course. Fuentes, too, is like Proteus, as he relentlessly expands the boundaries of his art. Yet, at the same time, Fuentes continues to be an eloquent, incisive, and profound interpreter of Mexico and Latin America.

# SELECTED BIBLIOGRAPHY

## Primary Works Since 1986

### Novels

*Cristóbal nonato.* Mexico City: Fondo de Cultura Económica, 1987.

*La campaña.* Mexico City: Fondo de Cultura Económica, 1990.

*Diana, o, la cazadora solitaria.* Madrid: Alfaguara, 1994.

*La frontera de cristal: Una novela en nueve cuentos.* Mexico City: Alfaguara, 1996.

*Los años con Laura Díaz.* Madrid: Alfaguara, 1999.

*Instinto de Inez.* Madrid: Alfaquara, 2001.

### Novellas and Short Stories

*Constancia y otras novelas para vírgenes.* Mexico City: Fondo de Cultura Económica, 1990.

*El naranjo, o, Los círculos del tiempo.* Mexico City: Alfaguara, 1993.

### Essays

*Valiente mundo nuevo nuevo: Épica, utopía y mito en la novela hispanoamericana* Mexico City: Fondo de Cultura Económica, 1990.

*El espejo enterrado.* Mexico City: Fondo de Cultura Económica, 1992.

*Geografía de la novela.* Mexico City: Fondo de Cultura Económica, 1993.

*Tres discursos para dos aldeas.* Mexico City: Fondo de Cultura Económica, 1993.

*Nuevo tiempo mexicano.* Mexico City: Aguilar, 1995.

### Other Works

*Ceremonias del alba.* Mexico City: Siglo Veintiuno Editores, 1991. (This play is an expanded version of *Todos los gatos son pardos*.)

*Retratos en el tiempo.* With photographs by Carlos Fuentes Lemus. Mexico City: Alfaguara, 1998.

*Los cinco soles de México: Memoria de un milenio.* Mexico City: Editorial Seix Barral, 2000.

### Translations

*Buried Mirror: Reflections on Spain and the New World.* Boston: Houghton Mifflin, 1992.

*The Campaign.* Trans. by Alfred J. Mac Adam. New York: Farrar, Straus & Giroux, 1991.

*Christopher Unborn.* Trans. by Alfred J. Mac Adam and Carlos Fuentes. New York: Farrar, Straus & Giroux, 1991.

*Constancia and Other Stories for Virgins.* Trans. by Thomas Christensen. New York: Farrar, Straus & Giroux, 1991.

*The Crystal Frontier: A Novel in Nine Stories.* Trans. by Alfred J. Mac Adam. New York: Farrar, Straus & Giroux, 1997.

*Diana, the Goddess Who Hunts Alone.* Trans. by Alfred J. Mac Adam. New York: Farrar, Straus & Giroux, 1995.

*A New Time for Mexico.* Trans. by Marina Gutman Castaneda. New York: Farrar, Straus & Giroux, 1996.

*The Orange Tree.* Trans. by Alfred J. Mac Adam. New York: Farrar, Straus & Giroux, 1994.

*The Years with Laura Díaz.* Trans. by Alfred J. Mac Adam. New York: Farrar, Straus & Giroux, 2000.

## Secondary Works Since 1986

### Critical and Biographical Studies

Conde Ortega, José Francisco, and Arturo Trejo Villafuerte. *Carlos Fuentes: Cuarenta años de escritor.* Mexico City: Universidad Autónoma Metropolitana, Azcapotzalco, 1993.

D'Lugo, Carol Clark. *The Fragmented Novel in Mexico: The Politics of Form.* Austin: University of Texas Press, 1997.

Egan, Lirida. "Sor Juana and Carlos Fuentes between Times and Lines." *Revista Canadiense de Estudios Hispánicos* 23, no. 2:239–245 (winter 1999).

Gyurko, Lanin A. "Role Playing and the Double in Fuentes' *Orquídeas a la luz de la luna.*" *Horizontes* 30:57–92 (October–April 1987).

———. "The Quest for and Terror of Identity in Fuentes' *Gringo vijo.*" In *Estudios en Homenaje a Enrique Ruiz-Fornells.* Edited by Juan Fernández Timénez, José J. Labrador Herraiz, and L. Teresa Valdivieso. Erie, Penn.: ALDEU, 1990. Pp. 295–303.

———. "Fuentes, Guzmán, and the Mexican Political Novel." *Ibero-Amerikanisches Archiv* 16, no. 4:545–610 (1990).

———. "Self and Double in Fuentes's *Gringo viejo.*" *Ibero-Amerikanisches Archiv* 17, no. 2–3:175–244 (1991).

———. "Borges' Impact on the Postmodern: Fuentes's *Cumpleaños.*" *La Chispa '99: Selected Proceedings.* Edited by Gilbert Paolini and Claire Paolini. New Orleans: Tulane University, 1999. Pp. 177–186.

Helmuth, Chalene. *The Postmodern Fuentes.* Lewisburg: Penn.: Bucknell University Press, 1997.

Martínez, Z. Nelly. "*La campaña* de Carlos Fuentes y otros textos en los albores del nuevo siglo." *Revista de estudios hispánicos* 35, no. 2:309–332 (May 2001).

Menton, Seymour. *Latin America's New Historical Novel.* Austin: University of Texas Press, 1993.

Payne, Judith. "Laura's Artemio: Failed Sexual Politics in *La muerte de Artemio Cruz.*" *Hispanófila* 38, no. 1:65–76 (September 1994).

Rivero-Potter, Alicia. "Columbus' Legacy in *Cristóbal nonato* by Carlos Fuentes." *Revista Canadiense de Estudios Hispánicos* 35, no. 2:309–332 (May 2001).

Wilford, Lynn M. "Mess as the Natural State: Echoes of Baktin and Heisenberg in Carlos Fuentes' *Cristóbal nonato.*" *Hispanic Journal* 13, no. 2:245–256 (fall 1994).

Williams, Raymond L. *The Writings of Carlos Fuentes.* Austin: University of Texas Press, 1999.

# Gabriel García Márquez

## (1927–      )

## *Michael Palencia-Roth*

M ost biographical works about Gabriel García Márquez state that he was born on 6 March 1928. Baptismal records, however, indicate that the year was actually 1927. He is the eldest of the eleven children of Gabriel Eligio García and Luisa Santiaga Márquez. Raised mostly by his maternal grandparents in the village of Aracataca in banana country in northern Colombia, he remembers their house as large and full of ghosts, with dead people living in the corners of the rooms and terrifying him as soon as darkness fell. In comparison with such terrors, García Márquez has said, nothing much has happened to him since he left Aracataca after his grandfather's death in 1937. That statement does contain a grain of truth. Much of his work up through *Cien años de soledad* (1967; *One Hundred Years of Solitude*, 1970) was inspired by his experiences during those early years, and by the stories that both his grandfather and grandmother told him. From his grandfather he heard of the period during and after the civil wars of Colombia, including the famous *la guerra de los mil días* (the thousand-day war) at the turn of the twentieth century, in which his grandfather had fought. He also listened to his grandmother's incredible tales, which she told with calm conviction. Years later, while a first-year law student in Bogotá, García Márquez read Franz Kafka's *The Metamorphosis* (1915) and discovered in its objective and detached prose the

literary equivalent of his grandmother's storytelling. It was then, he has said, that he made the irrevocable decision to become a writer.

Following the death of his grandfather, García Márquez moved with his family to Sucre, a small town in the department of the same name, and from there he was sent to the Colegio San José in the coastal city of Barranquilla. In 1943 he won a national scholarship to attend the Liceo Nacional de Varones (National High School for Boys), a Jesuit school in Zipaquirá, a colonial town near Bogotá. He traveled most of the way to and from Bogotá by paddleboat on the Magdalena River, which would later figure prominently in *El amor en los tiempos del cólera* (1985; *Love in the Time of Cholera,* 1988) and *El general en su laberinto* (1989; *The General in His Labyrinth,* 1990). Often homesick and depressed by the damp climate in Zipaquirá and by the excessive formalism he encountered in Bogotá, García Márquez generally spent his weekends in the school library reading novels and poetry, most of them popular and mediocre, but some of them excellent in quality and formative in effect. It was there that he read texts such as *A Thousand and One Nights* (which he had stumbled upon earlier, at the age of nine), *Amadis of Gaul,* and many works of Colombian, Latin American, and Spanish literature as well, especially the poetry of the

Spanish Golden Age (sixteenth and seventeenth centuries) and of a Colombian literary movement called Piedra y Cielo (Stone and Sky). In his literature classes he was exposed to the works of Homer, Sophocles, Virgil, Dante, Shakespeare, Tolstoy, Dostoyevsky, Cervantes, Garcilaso de la Vega, and Francisco de Quevedo, and to such Latin American poets as Rubén Darío and Pablo Neruda, as well as to the major texts of Colombian literature.

Upon graduation from the Liceo Nacional de Varones in 1947, García Márquez entered law school at the National University in Bogotá. In August of that year, he read in Eduardo Zalamea Borda's column in *El Espectador*, a prominent national newspaper, that there was a dearth of talented young writers in the country. Immediately, he completed a Kafkaesque short story, "La tercera resignación" (The third resignation), and sent it to Zalamea Borda, who published it on 13 September 1947. García Márquez was so poor in those days that he did not even have the five *centavos* needed to buy the newspaper in which his story appeared; a friend had to lend him the money. A few weeks later the newspaper published his second story, "Eva está dentro de su gato" (Eve is inside her cat), and Zalamea Borda praised García Márquez as a new writer of noteworthy talent and originality. It was an auspicious beginning. Between 1947 and 1952, *El Espectador* published almost a dozen of his stories. These self-consciously literary stories are clearly derived from, among others, Edgar Allan Poe, Franz Kafka, William Faulkner, Ernest Hemingway, and Jorge Luis Borges.

García Márquez had begun to study law with the encouragement of his father, a practical man who worked as a telegraph operator in Aracataca and later as a pharmacist in Sucre. He was, however, an indifferent law student and chose to spend much of his time sitting in cafés and riding the trolleys of Bogotá, reading all the while. Perhaps it was providential that on 9 April 1948, the popular Liberal Party candidate for president, Jorge Eliécer Gaitán, was assassinated just a few blocks from where García Márquez lived, triggering a series of riots known as the *bogotazo*, which effectively shut down the National University and other institutions. The building where García Márquez lived was destroyed in the riots, and he lost his few possessions. He decided to return to the coast and devote himself to writing. His father's reaction was swift and negative: "comerás papel" (you'll eat paper). García Márquez soon found a job on the main newspaper of Cartagena, *El Universal*. On 20 May 1948, he published his first newspaper column, thus beginning a career in journalism that has lasted into the twenty-first century. He has called journalism "the best job in the world," and regularly reserves his best interviews for journalists. Moreover, he often uses newspaper columns to test his ideas for fictional works.

During his time at *El Universal*, García Márquez came under the influence of a master teacher, the editor in chief, Clemente Manuel Zabala, who had read García Márquez's early stories in *El Espectador* and who was also a friend of Eduardo Zalamea Borda. Most of García Márquez's early journalistic pieces were thoroughly line-edited in red pencil by Zabala and returned to him for revision. As Jorge García Usta has documented in his book on García Márquez's early years, Zabala drummed into his pupil the importance of good writing. Under his tutelage García Márquez first experimented with some of the narrative techniques and modes of expression that have come to be identified as quintessentially his. He worked on *El Universal* until the end of 1949, when he moved to Barranquilla and began to write a column for the newspaper *El Heraldo*, which he signed with the nom de plume Septimus, an allusion to Virginia Woolf's novel *Mrs. Dalloway* (1925).

In Barranquilla, García Márquez found another master teacher, a Catalan named Ramón Vinyes, who ran a bookstore in town and often recommended authors for him to read. In the company of a group of literary friends later to be known as El Grupo de Barranquilla, García Márquez read and studied—for the first or second time—major American, English, French, German, and Latin American novelists. His two master teachers and two groups of literary friends (the first in Cartagena, the second in Barranquilla) became in effect his graduate seminar on literature. García Márquez would pay homage to El Grupo de Barranquilla by including the first names of Alvaro Cepeda Samudio, Germán Vargas, and Alfonso Fuenmayor in one of the last chapters of *One Hundred Years of Solitude* and identifying them as "the friends of Gabriel."

In March 1952 García Márquez returned to Aracataca with his mother, after an absence of many years. The purpose of the trip was to sell the ancestral home where he had been born and had lived with his maternal grandparents. The experience of that return to a dusty village of barely remembered people helped García Márquez to understand that his literary material could best be found not in his European and American models or in surrealistic dreamscapes, but in his hometown of Aracataca and in the Caribbean culture of northern Colombia. He learned the lesson that Faulkner and many before him had learned: a universal and universalizing art can be achieved if one mines one's own local culture deeply. After that trip, he revised *La hojarasca* (1955; *Leaf Storm and Other Stories*, 1972), set in fictional Macondo, which he had begun to write in 1949. A version of *Leaf Storm* was rejected in early 1952 by the publisher Losada in Argentina. Its director, Guillermo de Torre, dispatched the novel with the now famous judgment that García Márquez had no talent for writing, and should dedicate himself to another line of work.

*Leaf Storm* takes place in Macondo between 1903 and 1928, and is narrated through the eyes of three central characters: an old colonel, his daughter Isabel, and his grandson. All three think about their lives while attending the wake of a family friend, a mysterious and reclusive French doctor who came to Macondo in 1903 and has just committed suicide. The colonel is intent on burying the doctor in hallowed ground in the town cemetery, but there is opposition because of the suicide. This theme of an individual's obsession with the proper burial of a friend or relative has much in common with Sophocles' *Antigone*, a work pressed on García Márquez in 1949 by Gustavo Ibarra Merlano after the latter had read the first draft of the novel. García Márquez perused *Antigone*, revised the manuscript with Sophocles in mind, and included as an epigraph a passage from *Antigone* on the treatment of the corpse of Polynices.

If *Antigone* may be said to have deepened the subject matter of *Leaf Storm*, it is Faulkner's *As I Lay Dying* (1930) that is probably closest to *Leaf Storm* in theme and technique. In both works, the main situation is the fact of a death and the question of how the corpse is to be treated. In both, the story is narrated from several points of view, presented in a contrapuntal or dialogical manner. In both, stream of consciousness alternates with third-person omniscient narrative. And also in both, the reader obtains a general picture of a way of life through reactions to a death.

The earliest instance of the kind of narrative magic that García Márquez would weave in *One Hundred Years of Solitude* is a short story, "Monólogo de Isabel viendo llover en Macondo" (1955; "Monologue of Isabel Watching It Rain in Macondo," 1984). In this three-thousand-word vignette, it begins to rain in Macondo after mass on a Sunday morning. At first, everyone welcomes the respite from the suffocating heat. But the steady rain penetrates people's bones and sensibilities. Their initial pleasure turns into tedium, then into annoyance. "Paralyzed," they come to feel "drugged." They lose their sense of time and of the order of things, to the point of wondering whether they are alive or dead. This short story was published in the country's most prestigious literary magazine, *Mito*. While the rain in the story lasts just five days, it prefigures the rain of more biblical proportions in *One Hundred Years of Solitude* that lasts four years, eleven months, and two days.

After returning to Bogotá in January 1954, García Márquez earned a living as a journalist for *El Espectador*, the newspaper that had published his first short story. In 1954 and 1955 he began to experience success at the national level. In July 1954 he won a prize for his story "Un día después del sábado" ("One Day After Saturday," 1984). In 1955, the same year that he published "Monologue of Isabel . . . ," *Leaf Storm* was published by Sipa, Ltda. (which also publishes under the name Ediciones S.L.B.). Meanwhile, in February 1955 something happened that would make him a household name in Colombia. That month, eight members of the crew of the Colombian destroyer *Caldas*, on a voyage from Mobile, Alabama, to Cartagena, Colombia, were swept overboard into the Caribbean Sea during what was described as a storm. Despite the best efforts of search-and-rescue teams from Colombia and from American armed forces stationed in Panama, after four days the men were declared lost at sea. A week after that, crewman Luis Alejandro Velasco, who had survived on a raft, drifted ashore on a northern Colombian beach. He became a national hero. A couple of months later, García Márquez accepted the assignment of telling his story in installments. *El Espectador*'s circulation doubled, and fifteen years later García Márquez became famous as the author of *Relato de un náufrago* (1970; *The Story of a Shipwrecked Sailor*, 1986).

In July 1955 García Márquez went to Europe as a foreign correspondent for *El Espectador*. His first assignment was the Four Powers Summit in Geneva, Switzerland. From there he went to Rome, where in addition to sending dispatches back to *El Espectador,* he studied cinematography. From Rome he journeyed to Paris, where he spent Christmas. There he learned that because his story of the shipwrecked sailor had brought to light a government secret (that illegal cargo was being transported on the destroyer), Gustavo Rojas Pinilla, then the dictator of Colombia, instituted repressive measures against *El Espectador* that led to its closing in early 1956. The closure of the newspaper impoverished García Márquez.

During the bleak winter and spring of 1956 he worked in Paris on what would become *La mala hora* (1962; *In Evil Hour,* 1979). As he wrote, one of the characters acquired a life of his own, and García Márquez detached his story from *In Evil Hour.* That person became the central figure of *El coronel no tiene quién le escriba* (1961; *No One Writes to the Colonel, and Other Stories,* 1968), which he finished in January 1957 and published in the Colombian literary magazine *Mito* in 1958 (and three years later as a book). Many critics consider *No One Writes to the Colonel* an almost perfect novella, and certainly one of García Márquez's best works. Its controlled intensity probably owes something to the parallels between the situation of the colonel and that of García Márquez himself. He, like his colonel, was waiting in vain for the arrival of a letter bringing good news.

If *Leaf Storm* was inspired by Faulkner, *No One Writes to the Colonel* was inspired by Hemingway. In prose that was both lean and supple, with an economy of language he would match only years later in *Crónica de una muerte anunciada* (1981; *Chronicle of a Death Foretold,* 1982), *The General in His Labyrinth,* and *Del amor y otros demonios* (1994; *Of Love and Other Demons,* 1995), García Márquez drew the portrait of a man whose difficult circumstances do not destroy a quiet, if naive, optimism. A veteran of the thousand-day war of 1899–1902, the colonel believes, along with many fellow combatants, that he is entitled to a pension. When the novella begins, fifty-six years have passed since the end of the war and the colonel still has not received the expected pension notice. Virtually destitute, living in a small, dirt-floored house with his asthmatic wife and the memory of a dead son, the colonel waits for his letter from the federal government. His wife, being more realistic, wants him to sell his fighting cock in order to get money for food and other necessities. The colonel at first refuses, but finally gives in and sells the fighting cock to his friend Don Sabas. Shortly afterward, seeing the bird in a training bout, he takes it back and resolves to return the money to Don Sabas, and to take his own chances at the cockfight, which is scheduled to take place in a few weeks. His wife, alarmed at her husband's quixotic stubbornness, asks him how they are going to live in the meantime and what they are going to eat. With the dignity and resolve acquired through seventy-five years of penury and pain, the colonel answers with the final word of the novella: "shit."

*No One Writes to the Colonel* has been characterized often as a work of *la violencia,* the period of civil unrest following the *bogotazo* of 1948. Though the potential violence in the story concerns preparations for a cockfight, the threat of actual violence hangs over the lives of these forgotten, insignificant people in a forgotten, insignificant Colombian town. The curfew siren sounds nightly. The press is censored. An underground newspaper circulates secretly among several of the townspeople, including the doctor and the colonel. In this way, with a few deft brush strokes, García Márquez paints a picture of life in Colombia under the dictatorship of General Gustavo Rojas Pinilla.

Some critics have seen *No One Writes to the Colonel* as an allegorical work. For example, one of them regards the fighting cock as a symbol of Jesus Christ, bringing salvation to the village. García Márquez is well aware of the allegorical interpretations, and he likes to poke fun at such critics with the following anecdote. While his son Gonzalo, born in 1962, was taking a course in Latin American literature at the English High School in Mexico City, he took an exam that, as was customary, had been drawn up by the central office in London and sent to Mexico City. The essay question which confronted Gonzalo that day was "Discuss the symbol of the fighting cock in *No One Writes to the Colonel* by Gabriel García Márquez." Gonzalo's essay presented the view that "after long conversations with the author himself," he had come to understand that the rooster was just a rooster and not a symbol at all in the conventional sense. The London office gave the exam a failing grade. In response, Gonzalo's teacher wrote an explanation: Gonzalo García was actually the son of the story's author, who did in fact interpret the significance of the fighting cock in that manner. London replied that while Mr. García Márquez might be entitled to his opinion, the correct answer was that the fighting cock symbolized the political and social oppression of the Colombian people.

García Márquez remained in Europe for more than two years, and by the time of his departure for Caracas in December 1957, he had acquired a cosmopolitan outlook and had experienced life beyond the borders of Colombia. He had lived in Rome and Paris. He had traveled throughout both Western and Eastern Europe, writing journalism and fiction as he went. In Caracas he worked on the magazine *Momento* and other journals. In March 1958 García Márquez married his longtime sweetheart, Mercedes Barcha Pardo, in Barranquilla. In August 1959 his first son, Rodrigo, was born in Bogotá. Three years later, in Mexico City, his second son, Gonzalo, was born. Those first five years of marriage were years of travel and intense literary and journalistic activity. In 1958 he covered the fall of the dictator Marcos Pérez Jiménez in Venezuela, an experience that he would use in writing *El otoño del patriarca* (1975; *The Autumn of the Patriarch*, 1976). In 1959, back in Colombia, García Márquez became a bureau chief for Prensa Latina, the news agency of the Cuban government. In 1960 he spent several months in Cuba, attending the trials of the collaborators in the Batista regime. In December 1960 he moved to New York City, where he continued his work for Prensa Latina, and in 1961 he moved to Mexico City. The short stories written during these years appeared in book form in 1962 under the title *Los funerales de la Mamá Grande* (*Big Mama's Funeral*, 1968). The novel that he worked on during these years also was published in 1962 as *La mala hora* (*In Evil Hour*, 1979). The previous year its manuscript had won the ESSO prize for fiction in

Bogotá. It was submitted as "Sin título" (Untitled) and was later called "Este pueblo de mierda" (This shitty town), which accurately reflects García Márquez's bleak view of his subject, before acquiring its definitive title.

*In Evil Hour* is more explicitly about *la violencia* than *No One Writes to the Colonel*, although it begins in the same understated manner and depicts a similar scene: an early morning in October, probably in the 1950s. *No One Writes to the Colonel* opens with the colonel preparing his meager breakfast. *In Evil Hour* opens with a parish priest awakening and musing on life and death as he prepares to begin the day. However, whereas that mood continues throughout *No One Writes to the Colonel*, a different atmosphere pervades *In Evil Hour*. The ordinariness of the priest's morning vanishes when his servant tells him that during the night more *pasquines* (lampoons) have appeared. These lampoons are broadsheets that appear on the doors of houses, accusing the residents of misbehavior of one kind or another. Scandal hovers over the entire town, drawing everyone into the grip of gossip and mutual recrimination. Entire families leave town. Fights erupt. Feuds are rekindled. The lampoon most central to *In Evil Hour* appears one morning on the door of César Montero's house, accusing his wife of having an affair with a young man named Pastor. Without questioning whether the accusation is true, César Montero takes his shotgun, goes to Pastor's house, and shoots him. For more than two weeks the lampoons continue, and although everyone in town is affected, the rich and powerful are the principal targets. That detail has led some critics to identify class warfare as the major theme of the novel. Other critics, perhaps more mindful of the novel's conclusion, consider social revolution to be the novel's principal theme. In its final pages, a number of prisoners have escaped from the city jail and gone to the mountains to join the guerrillas. The problem of the lampoons remains unresolved.

The characters in this novel are more types than individuals: the priest, the judge, the mayor, the dentist. All are obsessed by the social chaos in town and all want order restored. Some, like the priest, are willing to see the police crack down, however arbitrarily. Others, such as the mayor, are more careful in advocating solutions. The mayor prefigures, in his solitude and political power, Colonel Aureliano Buendía of *One*

*Hundred Years of Solitude* and the title character of *The Autumn of the Patriarch*. Other references to the world of Macondo include the name of the judge, Arcadio, and the priest's story about the rain of dead birds that fell on Macondo. The latter detail links the novel to the short story "Un día después del sábado" (1962; "One Day After Saturday," 1984), as well as to the apocalyptic plagues besieging Macondo in *One Hundred Years of Solitude*.

Both *No One Writes to the Colonel* and *In Evil Hour* are set in Sucre in northern Colombia. In both there is considerable social realism. Real people and real events are utilized. Lampoons were in fact circulated in Sucre in the late 1940s, in much the same manner as they are in the novel. Lampoons were also the initial catalyst for the assassination of one of García Márquez's very good friends, Cayetano Gentile Chimento, on 22 January 1951. So poisonous did the atmosphere of Sucre become that García Márquez's family moved to Cartagena barely a month after the assassination. For almost thirty years, thoughts on the death of Cayetano Gentile smoldered in García Márquez's mind, until the tragedy became an obsession. As a consequence, the whole experience and its complicating factors became the basis of *Crónica de una muerte anunciada* (*Chronicle of a Death Foretold*), published in Spanish in 1981 and in English in 1982, shortly before he won the Nobel Prize for literature in the latter year.

The apprentice stories of García Márquez, most of them written and published between 1947 and 1953, appeared in book form as *Ojos de perro azul* (Eyes of a blue dog) only in 1972, after García Márquez had gained international prominence. *Los funerales de la Mamá Grande* is a collection of eight stories that were written later (between 1954 and 1961) but published in book form in 1962. All but the title story in the 1962 collection belong primarily to the school of literary realism. They are modeled after the works of Gustave Flaubert, who searched always for "the right word" to describe an object; Anton Chekhov, whose dispassionate prose endows ordinary objects, events, and lives with significance; James Joyce, whose notion of epiphany is probably behind a similar technique in some of these stories; and Ernest Hemingway, whose terse and rhythmic sentences describe behavior and actions rather than inner thoughts and feelings.

García Márquez relied on both Hemingway and Chekhov in writing "La siesta del martes" (Tuesday's siesta), a story that for years he considered to be his best. In it he turned to an incident from his childhood in which a woman and her daughter came to Aracataca in order to place flowers on her son's tomb. Throughout the town the rumor ran that she was the mother of the thief. In the story, a woman and her daughter arrive by train in an unnamed sleepy banana town at siesta time, when all the stores and public offices are closed and the streets are empty. Mother and daughter proceed to the rectory of the Catholic church and the mother requests, with the "scrupulous serenity of the impoverished," the keys to the cemetery in order to visit the grave of her son. When the priest asks her why, she says that her son was killed the week before in an attempted robbery. Surprised by her dignity, the priest gives her the keys. As mother and daughter prepare to leave the rectory, the priest notices children's faces pressed against the metal grate of the door. He sees more children out in the street, and adults as well. First he advises the woman to leave by another door, then to wait until sunset. Refusing, the mother takes her daughter by the hand and goes out to the street. There the story ends.

The dialogue is as spare as Hemingway's, the sentences similarly brief and rhythmic. As in a Chekhov work, nothing much seems to happen. And yet a family and a society have been delineated: a son turns to petty theft and is killed; his mother is dignified in her poverty and stoic in her grieving; his sister is learning to be the same; a priest seems to be more dutiful than compassionate. Everyone in the village seems to know immediately, through a sort of magical osmosis, the purpose of the woman's visit. And as Chekhov so often does, García Márquez ends the story just before we know the outcome.

In the title story of the collection, we see García Márquez's first extensive use of "magical realism" (a term generally used to describe *One Hundred Years of Solitude* and thus glossed in that section of this essay). In addition, using what would become one of his most common narrative strategies, García Márquez begins the story of Big Mama by announcing her death and then winds back through the circumstances leading to it, finally coming full circle, on the last page, to her death and its consequences. Such narrative circularity is common among writers who elevate the ordinary into the extraordinary, the historical into the mythical, and whose main concern is reiterative consciousness, that is, the conservation of the past by locating it within the present.

In addition to experimenting with narrative circularity in this story, García Márquez tries out the rhetorical exaggeration that became his hallmark. Big Mama has for ninety-two years been the absolute sovereign of the kingdom of Macondo: she owns all the water, even the rain that has not yet fallen; she owns all the telegraph poles, all the ranches in the territory; she even owns the heat. Now that she has died, the pipers of San Jacinto, the contrabandists of the Guajira, the witch doctors of the Sierpe, the rice farmers of Sinú, the prostitutes of Guacamayal, and the banana growers of Aracataca—all towns or regions in northeastern Colombia, where García Márquez was reared—can resume their normal lives. At the end of the story, after her funeral, a funeral that the pope himself attended, all that is left to do is to clear Macondo's streets of the debris from the century's grandest funeral celebration and to tell the story behind all the commotion. Such exaggeration satirizes the self-importance of Colombia's ruling class and especially of the country's institutions.

On 2 July 1961 García Márquez and his family arrived in Mexico City after a bus trip from New York City via the American South. (He wanted to see Faulkner country.) He remembers the exact date of his arrival because it coincided with the suicide of one of his most important literary masters, Ernest Hemingway. There to greet him was Álvaro Mutis, a close friend since their first meeting at Cartagena in 1949, who had lived in Mexico City since 1956. Mutis introduced García Márquez to his own literary and artistic friends, easing the new arrival's transition into life in Mexico, where he has maintained a pied à terre ever since. Almost immediately, Mutis gave him *Pedro Páramo* (1955) and *El llano en llamas* (1953) by Juan Rulfo, telling him, "Read these books and learn how to write." The story goes that García Márquez spent the entire night perusing these two slim masterpieces, became obsessed by the spare beauty of Rulfo's prose, and for months quoted passages, at the drop of a hat, to anyone who would listen. Rulfo is one of the major influences, still not fully explored, on *One Hundred Years of Solitude*.

During his early years as a journalist, García Márquez worked on "La casa," the novel that eventually became *One Hundred Years of Solitude*. As he has said, however, the project was too much for him, and so he turned to a slim novel eventually entitled *La hojarasca* (*Leaf Storm*). Meanwhile, in newspaper articles he explored characters and situations for "La casa." These articles were entitled "La casa de los Buendía" (The house of the Buendías), "La hija del coronel" (The colonel's daughter), "El hijo del coronel" (The colonel's son), "El regreso de Meme" (The return of Meme) and "Soledad" (Solitude). Try as he might, García Márquez could not find the key to the novel. Then, one day in 1965, he has told several interviewers, as he was driving down the highway to Acapulco from Mexico City, he suddenly saw the novel whole, "all at once." García Márquez says that he could have dictated the first chapter to a secretary, line by line, right then and there. He returned home, consulted with his wife, Mercedes, shut himself up in his study, and began to write. García Márquez has said that the inspired first pages, up to "Macondo is surrounded by water on all sides," streamed out virtually in one sitting. Things became more difficult after that, but eighteen months after shutting himself away, he had finished a thirteen-hundred-page manuscript.

"Muchos años después, frente al pelotón de fusilamiento, el coronel Aureliano Buendía había de recordar aquella tarde remota en que su padre le llevó a conocer el hielo" (Many years later, as he faced the firing squad, Colonel Aureliano Buendía was to remember that distant afternoon when his father took him to discover ice; *One Hundred Years of Solitude*). This famous initial sentence of *One Hundred Years of Solitude* provides one of the best examples of García Márquez's use of time and memory. At a distant future moment (which is already in the past!), narrated from a present moment so vague as to be unidentifiable, we are told that a colonel, anticipating his last seconds of life, would remember a moment in his personal past as remote from that future as prehistory is from history, or as the inarticulate innocence of childhood is from the wisdom of old age. Readers cannot count on being oriented by the usual signposts of time in fiction: a specific action, narrated in past tense, set in a specific time and place. Thus disoriented, the reader must depend on a character's memory (*había de recordar* / was to remember) to place him in a past time that is narrated in the traditional manner. (*su padre lo llevó* / his father took him). This past is remote, however, and the concrete action narrated is of the elemental discovery of ice, a miracle in the heat of the tropics before refrigeration. The next sentence descends more deeply into the remote past: "Macondo era entonces una aldea de veinte casas de barro y cañabrava construidas a la orilla de un río de aguas diáfanas que se precipitaban por un lecho de piedras pulidas, blancas y enormes como huevos prehistóricos" (At that time Macondo was a village of twenty adobe houses, built on the bank of a river of clear water that ran along a bed of polished stones, which were white and enormous, like prehistoric eggs; *One Hundred Years of Solitude*). This is the "once upon a time" of fairy tale and myth, the *illud tempus* of the fabled golden age, and it links *One Hundred Years of Solitude* to the Edenic, Arcadian, and pastoral traditions of Western literature.

From the biblical beginnings of this idyllic village to its apocalyptic end, the history of Macondo is narrated primarily through the experiences of a single extended family, the Buendías, across five generations. The first generation of that family consists of José Arcadio Buendía and his wife, Úrsula, who feel guilty about their consanguinity (they are cousins), for it is believed in the family that incest will be punished by the birth of a child with the tail of a pig. Because José Arcadio has killed a man (as had García Márquez's maternal grandfather), he and his wife flee their hometown and, after wandering in the wilderness, come upon "la tierra que nadie les había prometido" (the land that no one had promised them), and found Macondo. At first, life is harmonious and orderly in the tiny village: José Arcadio is the young patriarch; Úrsula, the young matriarch.

However, Gypsies, among them a man named Melquíades, soon arrive in Macondo, bringing with them news of the outside world, and nothing is the same afterward. A series of changes transforms Macondo in ways that echo the history of Colombia. A time of rural peace and prosperity is succeeded by civil wars between Conservatives and Liberals. These civil wars are followed by years of relative peace. Foreign entities like the United Fruit Company come into the region, exploit its agricultural resources, create a short-lived economic boom, and then withdraw, abandoning luxurious houses and gated communities, leaving a populace demoralized and impoverished by the loss of foreign capital. Throughout these times of war and peace, boom and bust, parents grow old and die; children grow up, leave home, and return, eventually to die; new generations are born and shape a world utterly different from the one of their grandparents. *One Hundred Years of Solitude* is thus a family saga in the manner of *The Forsyte Saga* (1922) by John Galsworthy or *Buddenbrooks* (1901) by Thomas Mann.

Enhancing such ordinary and universal life patterns are events and descriptions so startling that readers have henceforth associated them with García Márquez's distinctive narrative strategies and with the term "magical realism." A rain may last four years, eleven months, and two days. Another rain may consist entirely of yellow flowers. The people of Macondo may suffer a plague of insomnia that turns into a plague of amnesia in which they forget the names and functions of even the most ordinary things. A priest may succeed in levitating by drinking a cup of hot chocolate. When the aging patriarch José Arcadio Buendía loses his sense of time and then his mind, his family decides to tie him to a tree in the patio. There, exposed to the wind and the rain, the insane old man babbles away in an unfamiliar language that turns out to be Latin, a discovery made by a priest who visits him. The matriarch Úrsula eventually becomes so wizened and tiny that her grandchildren carry her around and play with her as though she were a doll. Colonel Aureliano Buendía instigates thirty-two uprisings and loses them all, fathers seventeen sons with seventeen different women, survives fourteen assassination attempts, and is so powerful that the central government fears him above all other people. In old age, making "a pact with solitude," he gains serenity through goldsmithing, endlessly fashioning miniature gold fishes, melting them down, and fashioning them anew.

A daughter in the third generation, Remedios the Beauty, ascends to heaven one day, lifted by the wind and wrapped in freshly laundered sheets that have been taken out to the garden to be folded; a son in the third generation, also named José Arcadio, is sent to Rome to study for the priesthood but instead becomes a sybarite who, on returning to Macondo, organizes orgies with young boys who one morning drown him in his own pool; a son in the fifth generation, Aureliano Babilonia, falls in love with his aunt (Amaranta Úrsula, a daughter in the fourth generation), and together they produce the very last Aureliano and the creature most feared by generations of Buendías: the child born with the tail of pig. It is at this point, just as Aureliano Babilonia is deciphering the Sanskrit manuscripts of the Gypsy Melquíades that foretell, down to the most trivial details, the entire history of the Buendía family one hundred years ahead of time, that the novel ends.

*One Hundred Years of Solitude* is the work most often cited by critics when they characterize García Márquez as a writer of magical realism. The meaning of the term is often contested, but the following may be said of it. Magical realism represents an attitude toward reality in which both the magical and the real appear to be equally true. If presented in the proper manner, everything and anything can be believed. García Márquez has called this the "principle of verisimilitude," which he regards as the writer's most important challenge. He makes the real and surreal coexist successfully, in part by adopting an attitude of authorial equanimity toward whatever happens, presenting events without judging their truth or falsehood, and generally linking something unbelievable with something utterly ordinary. For instance, an event as unbelievable as the levitation of a priest is made credible by his drinking a cup of hot chocolate at the same time. Or the utterly ordinary sight of drying sheets being whipped up by the wind is, in the context of the novel, what makes Remedios the Beauty's ascension to heaven believable.

Magical realism is not something that García Márquez came upon suddenly during his writing years and then employed. In fact, his own grandmother, without being aware of the term or the concept, exemplified the magical realist attitude in the stories she told him when he was a child. He learned the attitude as much from her as from reading Kafka or Borges, whose relationship to the "reality" behind the fiction remains problematic.

But after all, the issue of the fictionality (or truth) of fiction or literature is an old problem in the Western tradition. Authors from Homer to Cervantes have wrestled with it, and Aristotle discussed the problem in his *Poetics* when he compared the truth of poetry with the truth of history. Although magical realism may be only the Latin American angle on the same issue, in García Márquez's hands, as in the hands of several other Latin American writers (most notably Juan Rulfo, Alejo Carpentier, and, sometimes, Jorge Luis Borges), the term "magical realism" suggests a uniquely Latin American vision of reality.

García Márquez finished *One Hundred Years of Solitude* in September 1966. Editorial Sudamericana in Argentina accepted it immediately, and it became an instant best-seller. In August 1967, while in Buenos Aires to promote the book, he and his wife attended a premiere at a theater. As they moved toward their seats, caught by a spotlight, a man in the audience shouted, "Bravo, por su novela" (Bravo for your novel), and the entire theater gave him a standing ovation. Ever since, García Márquez has lived as a public figure and celebrity. According to the author himself, there is nothing so like the solitude of fame as the solitude of power, an insight that he would exploit fully in at least two of his subsequent novels, *The Autumn of the Patriarch* and *The General in His Labyrinth*. The publication of *One Hundred Years of Solitude* was the high point of the so-called boom in Latin American literature during the 1960s. Influenced by such earlier Latin American writers as Rulfo, Carpentier, and Borges, as well as by the major writers of European and American modernism from Joyce to Faulkner, the boom writers burst onto the scene with a string of commercial and critical successes that, in the aggregate, may never before have been surpassed. Writers of the boom, besides García Márquez, include Julio Cortázar, Carlos Fuentes, José Donoso, and Mario Vargas Llosa. They are as important to Latin American culture as, say, Dante and Petrarch were to Renaissance Italy, and as Cervantes and Pedro Calderón de la Barca were to Spain in the sixteenth and seventeenth centuries. The boom writers were friends, colleagues, and competitors. Sometimes they fought. They influenced and cited each other. They wrote reviews about each other's works. For instance, Carlos Fuentes enthusiastically previewed the first three chapters of *One Hundred Years of Solitude* in the Mexican magazine *Siempre!* (29 June 1966), calling them "magisterial." And Mario Vargas Llosa published the first major critical work on García Márquez, *García Márquez: Historia de un deicidio* (1971).

In the fall of 1967 the García Márquez family moved to Barcelona. García Márquez chose the Catalan city because, having begun years earlier a novel about a dictator who was larger than life, he wanted to write in a totalitarian society in the grip of an aged dictator. Believing that General Francisco Franco, then seventy-five years old and in uncertain health, would soon die, García Márquez chose to go to Spain rather than, say, to Castro's Cuba or to another Latin American country.

When García Márquez began *The Autumn of the Patriarch,* he found himself repeating the sentence rhythms of *One Hundred Years of Solitude.* He therefore tore up what he had written and turned instead to creating stories that he hoped would purge him of his Macondo style. Some of the stories of *La increíble y triste historia de la cándida Eréndira y de su abuela desalmada* (1972; *Innocent Eréndira and Other Stories,* 1984) were stylistically and thematically familiar, including the title story, "El mar del tiempo perdido" ("The Sea of Lost Time"), and "Un señor muy viejo con unas alas enormes" ("A Very Old Man of Enormous Wings"). Others were experiments that he considered essential for the writing of *The Autumn of the Patriarch.* These include "Muerte constante más allá del amor" ("Death Constant Beyond Love"), which treats the final illness and death of a powerful political figure, Senator Onésimo Sánchez; "El último viaje del buque fantasma" ("The Last Voyage of the Ghost Ship"), which in a single seven-page sentence presents the thoughts of a vengeful and somewhat mad narrator about an ocean liner running aground and destroying a village; and "Blacamán el bueno vendedor de milagros" ("Blacamán the Good, Seller of Miracles"), which in long, run-on sentences tells the surrealistic tale of a charlatan and embalmer who can so transform the faces of dead viceroys that they govern better dead than alive. The themes and techniques practiced in these three stories later enriched *The Autumn of the Patriarch.*

That novel was not well received when it was published in 1975 because it was so different in subject and tone from *One Hundred Years of Solitude.* Some reviewers were offended by the absence of paragraphs, very long sentences, and minimal punctuation, all reminiscent of the best (or the worst, depending on the critic) Proustian, Joycean, or Woolfian stream of consciousness. The main reason for the difference between *One Hundred Years of Solitude* and *The Autumn of the Patriarch* is stated easily enough: García Márquez, like all great writers, wanted to go beyond what he had already accomplished.

At the time of its publication, *The Autumn of the Patriarch* was only the latest literary depiction of a traditional figure in Latin American history: the dictator. The first major literary portrait of the Latin American tyrant was *Facundo,* published in Argentina in 1845. The most important twentieth-century works of this kind prior to 1973 are (in English) *Nostromo* (1904), written by Joseph Conrad and depicting dictatorship in an imagined Central American country, and (in Spanish) *Tirano Banderas* (1927), by the Spanish writer Ramón del Valle-Inclán; *El señor presidente* (1946), by the Guatemalan Miguel Angel Asturias; *La muerte de Artemio Cruz* (1962), by the Mexican Carlos Fuentes; and *El recurso del método* (1974) by the Cuban Alejo Carpentier.

Each of the six unnumbered chapters of *The Autumn of the Patriarch* consists of one long paragraph. Written from points of view that shift fluidly from first to second to third person, both singular and plural, as much in obedience to the demands of poetic rhythm as to any narrative necessity, the novel portrays the life and times of a dictator who has just died. Each chapter begins with a description of matters regarding the Patriarch's death, then circles back through episodes of his exaggeratedly long life (estimates range between 107 and 232 years), and ultimately winds its digressive way forward to focus on a few important events.

Although García Márquez based *The Autumn of the Patriarch* on a historical type and alludes to specific dictators, and although he includes particular events from Latin American history as intertextual moments in the narrative, he did not intend to write a historical novel. Far from it. One such moment may be adduced as a case in point. Toward the end of the first chapter, García Márquez adapts language from Columbus's diary of 1492 that describes the first encounter between European and Native American in the New World. The Patriarch awakens one morning and "relives" a historic October morning. He finds his subjects wearing odd little red hats (*bonetes colorados*) and chattering excitedly about the foreigners who have just arrived. These strangers speak in strange tongues and are dressed like the Jack of Clubs despite the heat ("la sota de bastos a pesar del calor"). Curious, the Patriarch looks out of his palace window and sees the three caravels of Columbus (*las tres caravelas*) at anchor in the quiet bay, not far from the ever-present twentieth-century American destroyer. By so collapsing almost five hundred years of Spanish and American imperialism into one jarring and historically impossible image, García Márquez at once criticizes imperialism per se, does away with the ordinary requirements of mimesis in historically resonant novels, and suggests not only that Latin American history repeats itself but also that the best way to understand it might be through poetry. Perhaps this is why García Márquez maintains that his main stylistic model for writing the novel was the Nicaraguan poet Rubén Darío, and that the book was written in the poet's style and in homage to him.

While García Márquez sometimes achieves his aesthetic effect by the juxtaposition of images or events or characters, at other times he does so through a single, startling, surrealistic image. An example of this technique is the incident regarding General Rodrigo de Aguilar, the Patriarch's once-trusted friend whom the Patriarch suspects of planning a coup. The Patriarch decides to invite a number of distinguished guests to a state banquet at which De Aguilar will be the guest of honor. At midnight, after the guests have assembled at the banquet table, they are shocked to see the general's body, roasted to perfection like a suckling pig, brought in on a silver platter. When each guest has been served a portion of the general, garnished with pine nuts and aromatic herbs, the Patriarch gives the order to begin to eat: "bon appétit." Such barbarism may not be original in literature (after all, the ancient Greeks described cannibal banquets), but it is startling to see that motif brought into twentieth-century literature

and converted into an image representative of a dictator's absolute power and cruelty.

In 1974, before his novel on the Patriarch was published, he founded the journal *Alternativa* in Bogotá and again devoted himself to journalism. However, the memory of the murder of his friend Cayetano Gentile in Sucre so many years earlier began to occupy his mind. After the publication of *The Autumn of the Patriarch*, García Márquez returned to fiction, publishing a novel based on that murder: *Crónica de una muerte anunciada* (1981; *Chronicle of a Death Foretold*, 1983). Appropriately, he created in it a marriage between literature and investigative journalism. Here, as in much of his subsequent work, journalism and fiction become complementary ways of telling stories.

The novel immediately addresses the expectations raised by its title. The first sentence reads: "El día en que lo iban a matar, Santiago Nasar se levantó a las 5:30 de la mañana para esperar el buque en que llegaba el obispo" (*Crónica de una muerte anunciada*; On the day they were going to kill him, Santiago Nasar got up at five-thirty in the morning to wait for the boat the bishop was coming on; *Chronicle of a Death Foretold*, 1982). From these first words to the last words of the novel ("se derrumbó . . . de bruces en la cocina" [he fell . . . on his face in the kitchen]), only ninety minutes elapse. A complex web is woven between the novel's beginning and end, a web of honor, betrayal, and revenge in which the truth itself becomes suspect and the search for the truth becomes as interesting as the high drama of an assassination. The situation that gives rise to the death of the main character is tragically simple. Bayardo San Román (based on a man named Miguel Reyes) marries Angela Vicario (in reality Margarita Chica) and discovers on their wedding night that she is not a virgin. Outraged, he returns her to her family. Her two brothers learn from her that the "author" of her condition is Santiago Nasar (who is based on Cayetano Gentile), and they decide to kill him. Soon almost everyone in town seems to know of the decision, but no one stops the brothers or warns Santiago Nasar. Apparently everyone assents to setting in motion the wheels of fate and accepts as unavoidable the death of a young man who, it turns out, might not be guilty of the offense for which he is to be killed.

(Angela Vicario, the reader learns, might have lied about Santiago Nasar.)

"Reasonable doubt" concerning Santiago Nasar's supposed crime thus enters into the story and is heightened by García Márquez's narrative strategies. He adds several layers of hermeneutical complexity by inserting himself into his own story as the narrator in whose presence people recall the past as he tries to ascertain, years after the event, the true circumstances that led to the killing of his friend Cayetano Gentile. Also appearing in the novel are García Márquez's mother, Luisa Santiaga; his sister Margot; and his wife, Mercedes, each in a minor role. Autobiography thus mingles with fiction, and truth with illusion, as the act of interpretation itself becomes a central part of the story. The brevity and engaging simplicity of the book mask for many readers the complexity of the hermeneutical and narrative issues that are probed. In this book, creating fiction becomes for García Márquez an intensely self-conscious enterprise. *Chronicle of a Death Foretold* is as close to a theory of writing and interpretation as García Márquez ever comes, for like many fiction writers he is generally skeptical of abstract thought and critical theory.

In October 1982 García Márquez won the Nobel Prize for literature. Few doubted that he would one day win it; the main question was when. In his acceptance speech that December in Sweden, he placed his own work in the context of Latin American history and literature, finding in Latin American reality the source of the magical realism so often attributed to him. According to García Márquez, Latin American reality is sometimes so fantastic that the main problem is not so much to depict it as to make that representation believable. After receiving the Nobel Prize, García Márquez took what he termed a "sabbatical" of one year in order, he said, to "administrar la fama" (to manage his fame). When during the early 1980s he was neither writing fiction nor managing his fame, he dedicated himself to journalism. Journalistic exercises, he has said, keep him from losing touch with storytelling.

When he won the Nobel Prize, García Márquez was already deeply into the writing of *Love in the Time of Cholera*. After his sabbatical year, he returned to the novel and completed it while living in Cartagena, where the novel is set. He had returned to Cartagena in order to continually experience its atmosphere as he wrote. The wild popularity of the novel did little to prevent Colombian critics from fulminating at what they considered its pornographic excesses or at the decadence implicit in describing the sensual exuberance of a couple in their seventies, so unlike the model of romantic love in the nineteenth-century Colombian classic, Jorge Isaac's *María* (1867). García Márquez again attempted something that was, for him, new and different: his version of a nineteenth-century romance that unfolds at a leisurely pace and tells a grand story of passion long deferred and finally fulfilled, spanning more than five decades of the characters' lives.

The novel begins, as so many of García Márquez's novels do, with a death. Jeremiah de Saint-Amour, a refugee from the Antilles and a disabled war veteran, has just committed suicide. Dr. Juvenal Urbino, one of the three main characters of the novel and the best friend of the deceased, has been called to the house to determine the cause of death. It immediately becomes clear that Jeremiah de Saint-Amour has committed suicide because he was terribly afraid of getting old; after a few pages, he disappears from the novel, not to be heard of again. Some early reviewers of the novel considered such an opening to be a mistake, but in fact it is brilliantly conceived. In his famous essay on Sisyphus, Albert Camus maintains that the most fundamental question that one can answer about life, and hence the most profound question in all philosophy, is why one does not commit suicide. Put positively, why should one continue to live? García Márquez's answer to that question is love. His entire novel thus becomes a response to Camus's question.

The "cholera" of the title refers to the plague, one of García Márquez's more enduring fictional obsessions, present in his early short stories and in *One Hundred Years of Solitude*. It is therefore fitting that Camus's *The Plague* (1947) frames the novel. But there are other plagues behind it as well: the plague which threatened Thebes in Sophocles' *Oedipus Rex*; the Black Death that devastated Europe in the fourteenth century and became the background against which Boccaccio's *Decameron* (1353) takes place; the plague that destroyed London in Daniel Defoe's *Journal of the Plague Year* (1722); and, of course, the historical plagues that afflicted Cartagena and other Colombian cities in past centuries.

The plot of *Love in the Time of Cholera* can be told in a deceptively straightforward manner. In their youth, Florentino Ariza and Fermina Daza fall in love. However, Fermina later discovers that she does not really love Florentino, and therefore terminates the relationship. She is subsequently wooed by Juvenal Urbino, scion of an oligarchic family. They marry, spend a long honeymoon in Europe, return to Colombia, and live out their lives. Their mostly serene and mostly uneventful marriage lasts about fifty years, until the day on which Dr. Urbino climbs a ladder in the patio to capture an escaped parrot; he slips, falls, and dies. A few days later Florentino, who has carried a torch for Fermina all these years, declares his endless love for her and, with a cunning enhanced by fifty years of patient longing, begins to woo her again. Eventually he induces her to travel with him up the Magdalena River on one of the paddleboats that he, as the president of a river transportation company, possesses. There, on the boat, they finally make love. Yearning for privacy, they raise the flag of cholera on the boat so as to be able to travel unmolested by other passengers or inspectors. Finally arriving back at their home port, they are reluctant to disembark and resume their former lives. Florentino orders the captain to turn the boat around and go back upriver. "How long do you think that we can keep up this goddamn coming and going?" the captain asks Florentino. The answer had been "ready for fifty-three years, seven months and eleven days and nights: 'for the rest of our lives.' "

Such a summary conceals the leisured complexity and digressiveness of this novel, and it conceals as well its thematic depth. *Love in the Time of Cholera* is an extended meditation on old age, marriage, love, obsession, perseverance, and personal character. That meditation is intensified by the nearness of death in the characters' lives, as well as by the knowledge that death, even in the best of circumstances, is just around the corner. Yet despite the novel's reflective and meditative qualities, it is not a psychological exploration of the interior life of characters, as one might expect from a major novelist in the late twentieth century. Rather, García Márquez portrays his characters' interior lives

through exteriorized descriptions of their actions and their behavior. This is an ancient and venerable mode of narration, as old as Homer in the West, and as familiar to García Márquez as the *Thousand and One Nights* he read as a child or as the great nineteenth-century European realists, Balzac, Dickens, Flaubert, and Tolstoy, who influenced, at least implicitly, the pace and style of *Love in the Time of Cholera*.

In an interview with María Elvira Samper for the Colombian weekly newsmagazine *Semana* (14 March 1989), García Márquez compared *The General in His Labyrinth* to *No One Writes to the Colonel*. He said that there were great similarities between them, the major difference being that the former, a novel about Simón Bolívar, was more historically grounded. His comment suggests a number of connections. Both works portray an emotionally strong man who, though he lives surrounded by people, is reclusive. Both portray a man who spends virtually all of his time anticipating something: a government pension in the case of the colonel, death in the case of Simón Bolívar. Both novels are written in an objective tone and with a compressed style reminiscent of the best of Hemingway. In addition, *The General in His Labyrinth* represents in some ways a renewal of the social realism found in *No One Writes to the Colonel*.

The opening sentence of the novel sets the mood precisely, and the first two pages establish beyond question the desperation of Simón Bolívar's condition: "José Palacios, su servidor más antiguo, lo encontró flotando en las aguas depurativas de la bañera, desnudo y con los ojos abiertos, y creyó que se había ahogado" (José Palacios, his oldest servant, found him floating in the purifying waters of his bath, naked and with his eyes wide open, and thought he had drowned). Bolívar is here seen through the eyes of an Afro-Venezuelan man who was once a slave of Bolívar's family and who has been his servant since both were young. The reference to drowning prefigures Bolívar's actual death, and the passivity of his body reinforces the view of him as submissive in the face of his final illness. And yet, grabbing the handrail, he emerges from his bath with the apparent ease of a dolphin rising through the waters (*con un ímpetu de delfín*), an ease surprising in a body so wasted by disease. Such contrasts—between strength and weakness, health and illness, affluence and destitution, persistence and surrender—will be the basis for many of the descriptions of Bolívar throughout the novel.

The tale of Simón Bolívar's journey toward death is told from the Olympian perspective of a third-person omniscient narrator. That perspective serves several functions: first, it controls the pathos inherent in the task of describing the physical decline and death of a powerful and beloved historical figure; second, it reinforces the conventions of the genre of historical fiction that García Márquez has chosen for the first time in his career; and third, it obliges the reader to follow a story told in a nineteenth-century manner. Not once in this novel does García Márquez break aesthetic distance and tell the story from within Bolívar's mind. Whatever knowledge we have of Bolívar's mental state is gained only through dialogue that has been documented as historically accurate and through other documented commentary or descriptions.

The novel begins on the evening before 8 May 1830, the day of Bolívar's definitive departure from the capital of Bogotá, en route to the coast and to an intended exile in Europe, and it ends on the afternoon of 17 December 1830. On that day Bolívar dies surrounded by a handful of friends and aides, in a borrowed bed in a bare room in the ranch house of the Hacienda San Pedro Alejandrino, not far from the coastal city of Santa Marta. The story of those seven months and nine days is told in eight chapters, each about thirty pages long.

Bolívar and his retinue travel by horse from Bogotá to Honda, on the Magdalena River. There he embarks on a boat for the journey to the coast. This trek of two weeks' duration is the least documented part of Bolívar's torrentially documented life (which is how García Márquez describes it in his afterword to the book). That lack of documentation gives García Márquez the authorial freedom to imagine how the days might have passed. Simón Bolívar leaves behind in Bogotá a divided government, a number of enemies, and the love of his life, Manuela Sáenz. The novel thus becomes in part the story of loss.

In 1992 García Márquez published *Doce cuentos peregrinos*, translated as *Strange Pilgrims: Twelve Stories* (1993). Each of his three prior short-story collections—*Ojos de perro azul*, *Los funerales de la Mamá Grande*, and *Innocent Eréndira*—is an assortment of stories not designed as parts of a whole. In contrast, as García Márquez explains in his prologue to the collection, each of the twelve stories in *Strange Pilgrims* was conceived in accordance with a plan to write about the "strange things that happen to Latin Americans in Europe." He began working on them in 1976, just after publishing *The Autumn of the Patriarch*. Although at one point he had ideas for sixty-four stories, he used only twelve of those ideas in *Strange Pilgrims*, each concerning an outsider or pilgrim in one way or another. In virtually every story García Márquez appears as a character, generally as the narrator to whom the story is told, but sometimes as an active participant (as in, for instance, "El avión de la bella durmiente" ["Sleeping Beauty and the Airplane"] and "Espantos de Agosto" ["The Ghosts of August"]).

The themes of the stories are varied. In "Buen viaje, señor presidente" ("Bon Voyage, Mr. President"), a former president of a Caribbean country is spending his declining years in exile in Geneva. Diagnosed with a potentially fatal illness, he is befriended by two poor countrymen who, though they initially plan to rob him, eventually help him return to his island. In "La Santa" ("The Saint"), a seven-year-old girl who dies in Colombia is venerated because her body does not decompose in her coffin. Aided by funds from the community, her father, Margarito Duarte, journeys to Rome to ask the Vatican to ratify the miracle and declare his daughter a saint. García Márquez tells us that he himself was a student in Rome at the time that Margarito Duarte was first making his rounds. Twenty-two years later, returning to the Eternal City, García Márquez happens upon Margarito Duarte, who tells him that the tiny would-be saint is still in her coffin, unchanged, waiting for canonization. In "Me alquilo para soñar" ("I Sell My Dreams"), an expatriate Colombian woman makes a good living in Europe by interpreting dreams for a family and thus guiding them in their activities. In "Sólo vine a hablar por teléfono" ("I Only Came to Use the Phone"), a woman's car breaks down on a highway in Spain and the woman is rescued by a bus driver who is transporting a group of women to an insane asylum. By mistake she is processed along with the others. Her claims that she only came to use the telephone and that she is perfectly sane are viewed as symptoms of her insanity. In "María dos Prazeres" an aged and retired Brazilian prostitute selects her cemetery plot in Barcelona, where she worked for many years, teaches her dog to weep over her gravestone (so that she will be mourned after she dies), and at the end of the story assents to sex requested by a young and virile chauffeur. The reader expects the story to end in death; instead, it ends with a life-affirming act. In virtually each of the stories, the main character finds a way to triumph in exile or otherwise to be a successful pilgrim.

All of García Márquez's fiction derives from disparate experiences that he fuses into an aesthetically coherent work. The "true" prologue of *Del amor y otros demonios* (1994; *Of Love and Other Demons,* 1995) purports to describe such a series of events. One late October afternoon in 1949, Clemente Zabala, the editor in chief of *El Universal,* sent García Márquez to the convent of Santa Clara to cover the moving of the bodies from some crypts that were to be destroyed, "just in case anything interesting" should present itself. Among the last crypts to be excavated was that of a young girl named Sierva María de Todos los Ángeles, who had died two hundred years earlier. Workers discovered that her copper-colored hair had continued to grow after her death and was now more than seventy feet long. That image brought to García Márquez's memory one of the stories his grandmother used to tell him about a twelve-year-old marchioness who had beautiful long hair, and one day was bitten by a rabid dog and died. Later, she would be venerated as a miracle worker throughout the region. The mere possibility that the legendary marchioness and this young girl might be one and the same person inspired García Márquez to write *Of Love and Other Demons.*

It is a riveting prologue, but little of it is true. There was no disinterment in October 1949 of the crypts in the convent of Santa Clara. There was no twelve-year-old corpse with more than seventy feet of hair. In fact, the story has several more likely origins. First, about eight years after García Márquez's father died in 1984, it became necessary to remove his casket from the original place of burial. García Márquez accompanied the workmen and saw that the hair on his father's head had continued to grow after death and was down

around his shoulders. Second, in a series of newspaper articles in 1954, García Márquez described a local marchioness of great beauty, Spanish descent, and fabulous wealth who lived for two hundred years, performed many miracles or cures, and had made a pact with the devil. The detail of the pact with the devil is directly relevant to García Márquez's novel. Third, on 25 October 1949 García Márquez published in *El Universal* an unsigned article entitled "Un infanticidio en el barrio de La Esperanza" (An infanticide in Hope neighborhood), in which he described how a stray dog with the grisly name of Calavera (Skull) dug up the perfectly formed body of an infant girl from loose dirt in the street. A picture of her in a tiny open coffin was published on page 6 of the newspaper. These apparently unrelated experiences and previous works of García Márquez are behind *Of Love and Other Demons.*

The opening scene of the novel establishes the original cause of everything that is to follow and places the work in the only historical context that can explain and justify those actions: eighteenth-century Cartagena, a society of colonial privilege and prejudice, of caste and class, of slavery and religious persecution, of witchcraft and superstition, of Jews and Christians, of paganism and of a transplanted European Enlightenment. On 7 December, the twelfth birthday of Sierva María de Todos los Ángeles, an ash-colored dog, crazed by rabies, runs through the marketplace, upsetting carts and tables along the way, and bites four people. Three of them are slaves and the fourth is Sierva María, the only daughter of the second Marquis of Casalduero, Don Ygnacio de Alfaro y Dueñas.

The story ends on 29 May of the following year. Each of the five, thirty-page chapters of the book narrates about a month of the main plot but also winds back through memory to earlier experiences of the main characters: the father and mother of Sierva María, the Portuguese-Jewish doctor, the bishop, the exorcist. Gradually, a picture of colonial Colombian society is painted. Gradually, García Márquez reveals how Sierva María's wound is considered rabid (though there are no symptoms of rabies at any time), how in the mind of her father and in the eyes of the church the bite becomes a sign of demonic possession, how she is then sequestered in a convent and subjected to painful and frightening rituals of exorcism. Condemned by a process medieval in its justification and relentless in its thoroughness, Sierva María de Todos los Ángeles is transformed from a healthy and vibrant twelve-year-old child, at ease and happy in the Africanized culture of colonial Cartagena, into a persecuted creature. Yet during the last month or so of her life, while incarcerated in the convent of Santa Clara and accused of demonic possession, she experiences great passion. Her exorcist, a priest named Cayetano Delaura, falls desperately and irrevocably in love with her and, though knowing that he will be tried and punished for his actions, introduces her to the pleasures of desire without, however, actually deflowering her. It is passion rather than the devil that possesses her. Passion so transforms her in mind, heart, and body that one morning her guardian, entering her cell to prepare her for a sixth session of exorcism, finds her "dead of love."

In some respects, *Of Love and Other Demons* is one of García Márquez's most accomplished works, as well as one of the most typical. It is relatively brief and written with the stylistic restraint of *No One Writes to the Colonel* and *Chronicle of a Death Foretold*. As was the case with those works, *Of Love and Other Demons* combines an understated, detached style with conceptual and thematic profundity. It would have been easy—and it must have been tempting, given the intensity of feeling inherent in subjects like torture, exorcism, demonic possession, and desperate love—for García Márquez to have indulged in stylistic exaggeration and emotionalism, as he did in parts of *One Hundred Years of Solitude*, *The Autumn of the Patriarch*, and *Love in the Time of Cholera*. In *Of Love and Other Demons*, the restrained prose serves to heighten the horror that any reader must feel at witnessing the relentless destruction of a young and innocent life.

García Márquez began to work as a journalist in May 1948. Although he no longer needs either the money or the exposure, he continues to write for newspapers in Colombia, Mexico, and Spain. This "best job in the world," as he puts it, schooled him in the art of writing stories in clear prose that holds the reader's attention. It also gave him the opportunity to travel throughout much of Europe and in the Soviet Union during the 1950s. After he returned to Latin American in late 1957, journalistic assignments enabled him to witness history as a correspondent in Venezuela, Cuba, the United States, Mexico, Spain, and elsewhere. His articles fill several thick volumes and are a useful complement to his fiction. Some of the journalistic pieces are monograph length, such as *The Story of a Shipwrecked Sailor* and *La aventura de Miguel Littín: Clandestino en Chile*. The last work, published in 1986, narrates the return to Chile of a famous film director after many years of exile.

García Márquez's most substantial and sustained piece of journalistic writing is *Noticia de un secuestro* (*News of a Kidnapping*, 1997), on which he began to work in October 1993 and which was published in 1996. In its acknowledgments he calls the book "the most difficult and sad . . . autumnal assignment" of his life, as well as a "heartrending and unforgettable" experience. The book narrates in detail the actual kidnapping and ransom of ten people, two of whom die in captivity, at different times and in different parts of Colombia. The kidnappings were masterminded by the drug lord Pablo Escobar and his associates, in an attempt to influence the president of Colombia, César Gaviria, to abrogate an extradition treaty between Colombia and the United States. Seeking to influence public opinion and government policy, the drug lords embarked on a campaign of terrorism. Eventually the campaign worked, for Escobar and others were allowed to serve time in Colombian jails rather than in American ones.

The picture of Colombia that García Márquez paints in *News of a Kidnapping* is bleak indeed. Ordinary citizens live as if in a state of siege. No one can be completely safe, and everyone in the country is affected. Some of the ten kidnapping victims in *News of a Kidnapping* are prominent; for instance, one of the two who die in captivity is the daughter of former president Julio César Turbay Ayala. But most are ordinary Colombians who just happen to be present during someone else's kidnapping. The distance—historically, morally, and emotionally—between the Colombia of *One Hundred Years of Solitude* and that of *News of a Kidnapping* is immense. In traversing that distance, in documenting and transforming so much of Colombian reality into fiction through more than fifty years of writing, García Márquez has succeeded in creating a body of work that treats virtually every period of Colombian history, several of its cultural heroes, and many of its most central issues.

For years García Márquez has been working on his memoirs, titled "Vivir para contarlo" (literally, Living to tell the story). According to an interview in the Colombian newspaper *El Tiempo* (10 December 2000), his serious bout with cancer in the summer of 1999 moved him to focus intensely on his work and on his friends. By shutting himself away from 8 a.m. to 2 p.m. every day and dedicating each workday to the three volumes of his memoirs and two planned collections of short stories, he has been able to recapture, he said, a feeling of productivity and a sense of serenity and happiness. The first of these three volumes is complete (at approximately twelve hundred manuscript pages) and is scheduled for publication in 2001. It begins with the lives of his maternal grandparents, narrates the courtship of his mother and father, and ends with the Spanish-language publication of *Leaf Storm* in 1955. The second volume will cover the years up to the publication of *One Hundred Years of Solitude* in Spanish in 1967, and the third will describe his personal experiences with the presidents of several countries.

With the publication of *One Hundred Years of Solitude*, García Márquez became one of the most important figures in Latin American literary history. Had he stopped there, however, that book might have become merely an interesting footnote in literary history, its author remembered as the creator of a single luminous and brilliant work. According to Arthur Lundkvist, a member of the Nobel Prize Committee, it was *The Autumn of the Patriarch*, appearing in 1975, that moved the committee to conclude that he had produced a body of work distinguished and excellent enough to justify the Nobel Prize for literature. The books written by García Márquez since 1982, when combined with those that won him the Nobel Prize, place him in the pantheon of world literature, alongside writers like Homer, Dante, Shakespeare, and Cervantes, writers who will be read and studied as long as there are readers. And yet those writers are not the only or even the principal ones with whom García Márquez can be compared. In fact, the authors whom he has carefully

read, and who are identified in this essay, may be said to be his closest precursors. They make up, in effect, his literary genealogy. The extraordinary quality of his literary dialogues with them and their own precursors has secured his place in the great conversation that is the history of Western literature.

## SELECTED BIBLIOGRAPHY

### Primary Works

#### Fiction

*La hojarasca.* Bogotá: Ediciones S.L.B., 1955.

*El coronel no tiene quien le escriba.* Medellín, Colombia: Aguirre, 1961.

*Los funerales de la Mamá Grande.* Jalapa, Mexico: Editorial de la Universidad Veracruzana, 1962.

*La mala hora.* Madrid: Pérez, 1962.

*Cien años de soledad.* Buenos Aires: Sudamericana, 1967.

*La increíble y triste historia de la cándida Eréndira y de su abuela desalmada.* Barcelona: Barral, 1972.

*Ojos de perro azul.* Rosario, Argentina: Equiseditorial, 1972.

*El otoño del patriarca.* Barcelona: Plaza y Janés, 1975.

*Todos los cuentos por Gabriel García Márquez, 1947–1972.* Barcelona: Plaza y Janés, 1975. (Contains "La tercera resignación," 1947; "La otra costilla de la muerte," 1948; "Eva está dentro de su gato," 1948; "Amargura para tres sonámbulos," 1949; "Diálogo del espejo," 1949; "Ojos de perro azul," 1950; "La mujer que llegaba a las seis," 1950; "Nabo: El negro que hizo esperar a los ángeles," 1951; "Alguien desordena estas rosas," 1952; "La noche de los alcaravanes," 1953; "Monólogo de Isabel viendo llover en Macondo," 1955. Also contains "La siesta del martes," "Un día de estos," "En este pueblo no hay ladrones," "La prodigiosa tarde de Baltazar," "La viuda de Montiel," "Un día después del sábado," "Rosas artificiales," "Los funerales de la Mamá Grande," all dated 1962 but written between 1957 and 1962; and "Un señor muy viejo con unas alas enormes," 1968; "El mar del tiempo perdido," 1961; "El ahogado más hermoso del mundo," 1968; "Muerte constante más allá del amor," 1970; "El último viaje del buque fantasma," 1968; "Blacamán el bueno vendedor de milagros," 1968; "La increíble y triste historia de la cándida Eréndira y de su abuela desalmada," 1972.)

*Crónica de una muerte anunciada.* Bogotá: Oveja Negra, 1981.

*El amor en los tiempos del cólera.* Barcelona: Oveja Negra, 1985.

*El general en su laberinto.* Bogotá: Oveja Negra, 1989.

*Doce cuentos peregrinos.* Buenos Aires: Editorial Sudamaericana, 1992.

*Del amor y otros demonios.* Bogotá: Norma, 1994.

## Journalism

*Relato de un náufrago.* Barcelona: Tusquets Editor, 1970.

*Cuando era feliz e indocumentado.* Caracas: El Ojo del Camello, 1973.

*Chile, el golpe y los gringos.* Bogotá: Editorial Latina, 1974.

*Crónicas y reportajes.* Bogotá: Instituto Colombiano de Cultura, 1976.

*Periodismo militante.* Bogotá: Son de Máquina Editores, 1978.

*Obra periodística.* Vols. 1–2, *Textos costeños.* Barcelona: Bruguera, 1981. Vols. 3–4, *Entre cachacos.* Barcelona: Bruguera, 1982. Vols. 5–6, *De Europa y América, 1955–1960.* Barcelona: Bruguera, 1984.

*La aventura de Miguel Littín: Clandestino en Chile.* Madrid: Ediciones El País, 1986.

*Notas de prensa 1980–1984.* Madrid: Mondadori, 1991.

"Gabo y el alma colombiana." *Semana* (Santa Fe de Bogotá) no. 638:44–48 (26 July–2 August 1994).

*Noticia de un secuestro.* Santa Fe de Bogotá: Mondadori, 1996.

## Translations

*No One Writes to the Colonel, and Other Stories.* Translated by J. S. Bernstein. New York: Harper & Row, 1968.

*One Hundred Years of Solitude.* Translated by Gregory Rabassa. New York: Harper & Row, 1970.

*Leaf Storm and Other Stories.* Translated by Gregory Rabassa. New York: Harper & Row, 1972.

*The Autumn of the Patriarch.* Translated by Gregory Rabassa. New York: Harper & Row, 1976.

*Innocent Eréndira and Other Stories.* Translated by Gregory Rabassa. New York: Harper & Row, 1978.

*In Evil Hour.* Translated by Gregory Rabassa. New York: Harper & Row, 1979.

*Chronicle of a Death Foretold.* Translated by Gregory Rabassa. New York: Harper & Row, 1982.

*Collected Stories.* Translated by Gregory Rabassa and J. S. Bernstein. New York: Harper & Row, 1984.

*The Story of a Shipwrecked Sailor.* Translated by Randolph Hogan. New York: Knopf, 1986.

*Love in the Time of Cholera.* Translated by Edith Grossman. New York: Knopf, 1988.

*The General in His Labyrinth.* Translated by Edith Grossman. New York: Knopf, 1990.

*Strange Pilgrims: Twelve Stories.* Translated by Edith Grossman, New York: Knopf, 1993.

*Of Love and Other Demons.* Translated by Edith Grossman. New York: Knopf, 1995.

*News of a Kidnapping.* Translated by Edith Grossman. New York: Knopf, 1997.

## Secondary Works

### Bibliographies

Fau, Margaret Eustalia, comp. *Gabriel García Márquez: An Annotated Bibliography, 1947–1979.* Westport, Conn.: Greenwood Press, 1980.

Fau, Margaret Eustalia, and Nelly Sfeir de González, comps. *Bibliographic Guide to Gabriel García Márquez, 1979–1985.* Westport, Conn.: Greenwood Press, 1986.

González, Nelly Sfeir de, comp. *Bibliographic Guide to Gabriel García Márquez, 1986–1992.* Westport, Conn.: Greenwood Press, 1994.

### Critical and Biographical Studies

Arango, Gustavo. *Un ramo de Nomeolvides: Gabriel García Márquez en "El Universal."* Cartagena, Colombia: El Universal, 1995.

Arnau, Carmen. *El mundo mítico de Gabriel García Márquez.* Barcelona: Ediciones Península, 1971.

Bell, Michael. *Gabriel García Márquez: Solitude and Solidarity.* New York: St. Martin's Press, 1993.

Bell-Villada, Gene H. *García Márquez: The Man and His Work.* Chapel Hill: University of North Carolina Press, 1990.

Booker, M. Keith. "The Dangers of Gullible Reading: Narrative as Seduction in García Márquez' *Love in the Time of Cholera.*" *Studies in Twentieth-Century Literature* 17, no. 2:181–195 (summer 1993).

Carrillo, Germán Darío. *La narrativa de Gabriel García Márquez: Ensayos de interpretación.* Madrid: Editorial Castalia, 1975.

Cobo Borda, Juan Gustavo, ed. *Para que mis amigos me quieran más: Homenaje a Gabriel García Márquez.* Bogotá: Siglo del Hombre Editores, 1992.

Collazos, Oscar. *García Márquez, La soledad y la gloria: Su vida y su obra.* Barcelona: Plaza y Janés, 1983.

Danow, David K. "The Figural Labyrinth in *The General in His Labyrinth* (García Márquez)." In his *Models of Narrative: Theory and Practice.* New York: St. Martin's Press, 1997. Pp. 101–111.

———. "Memory as Duration: *Love in the Time of Cholera* (García Márquez)." In his *Models of Narrative: Theory and Practice.* New York: St. Martin's Press, 1997. Pp. 57–67.

Davis, Mary E. "The Town That Was an Open Wound." *Comparative Literature Studies* 23, no. 1:24–43 (spring 1986).

Esteban, Carmen. "El amor cortés en los tiempos del cólera." In *Quinientos años de soledad: Actas del Congreso Gabriel García Márquez.* Edited by Túa Blesa. Saragossa, Spain: Banco Zaragozano, 1997. Pp. 465–475.

García Usta, Jorge. *Cómo aprendió a escribir García Márquez.* Medellin, Colombia: Editorial Lealon, 1995.

Gómez Buendía, Blanca Inés. *La intertextualidad en "Del amor y otros demonios."* Bogotá: Universidad Pedagógica Nacional, 1999.

González Echevarría, Roberto. "*Cien años de soledad*: The Novel as Myth and Archive." *Modern Language Notes* 99, no. 2:358–380 (March 1984).

———. "García Márquez y la voz de Bolívar." *Cuadernos Americanos*, nueva época 4, no. 28:63–76 (July–August 1991).

Gullón, Ricardo. *García Márquez o el olvidado arte de contar.* Madrid: Taurus, 1970.

Janes, Regina. *Gabriel García Márquez: Revolutions in Wonderland.* Columbia: University of Missouri Press, 1981.

———. "*One Hundred Years of Solitude*": Modes of Reading. New York: Twayne, 1991.

Kline, Carmenza. *Los orígenes del relato: Los lazos entre ficción y realidad en la obra de Gabriel García Márquez.* Bogotá: Ceiba Editores, 1992.

Levine, Suzanne Jill. *El espejo hablado: Un estudio de "Cien años de soledad."* Caracas: Monte Avila, 1975.

McGuirk, Bernard, and Richard A. Cardwell. *Gabriel García Márquez: New Readings.* Cambridge: Cambridge University Press, 1987.

McMurray, George R. *Gabriel García Márquez.* New York: Frederick Ungar, 1977.

Maturo, Graciela. *Claves simbólicas de Gabriel García Márquez,* 2d ed. Buenos Aires: Fernando García Cambeiro, 1977.

Mejía Duque, Jaime. *Mito y realidad en Gabriel García Márquez.* Bogotá: Editorial Oveja Negra, 1970.

Menton, Seymour. "The Bolívar Quartette, or Varieties of Historical Fiction." In his *Latin America's New Historical Novel.* Austin: University of Texas Press, 1993. Pp. 95–124.

Minta, Stephen. *García Márquez: Writer of Colombia.* New York: Harper & Row, 1987.

Müller-Bergh, Klaus. "*Relato de un náufrago*: Gabriel Garciá Márquez's Tale of Shipwreck and Survival at Sea." *Books Abroad* 47, no. 3:460–466 (summer 1973).

Ortega, Julio, ed. *Gabriel García Márquez and the Power of Fiction.* Austin: University of Texas Press, 1988.

———. "Del amor y otras lecturas." In *Repertorio crítico sobre Gabriel García Márquez,* vol. 2. Edited by Juan Gustavo Cobo Borda. Bogotá: Instituto Caro y Cuervo, 1995. Pp. 405–423.

Palencia-Roth, Michael. *Gabriel García Márquez: La línea, el círculo, y las metamórfosis del mito.* Madrid: Editorial Gredos, 1983.

———. "Prisms of Consciousness: The 'New Worlds' of Columbus and García Márquez." In *Critical Perspectives on Gabriel García Márquez.* Edited by Bradley A. Shaw and Nora Vera-Goodwin. Lincoln, Neb.: Society of Spanish and Spanish-American Studies, 1986. Pp. 15–32.

———. "Gabriel García Márquez: "Labyrinths of Love and the Love of History." *World Literature Today* 65, no. 1:54–58 (winter 1991).

———. "*Del amor y otros demonios*: Tragedia inquisitorial, beatificación africana." In *Apuntes sobre literatura colombiana.* Edited by Juan Gustavo Cobo Borda et al. Bogotá: Ceiba Editores, 1997. Pp. 109–121.

———. "Los peregrinajes de Gabriel García Márquez o la vocación religiosa de la literatura." In *Quinientos años de soledad: Actas del Congreso Gabriel García Márquez.* Edited by Túa Blesa. Saragossa, Spain: Banco Zaragozano, 1997. Pp. 81–90.

Rodríguez-Monegal, Emir. "*One Hundred Years of Solitude*: The Last Three Pages." *Books Abroad* 47, no. 3:485–489 (summer 1973).

Saldívar, Dasso. *García Márquez, el viaje a la semilla: La biografía.* Madrid: Alfaguara, 1997.

Shaw, Donald Leslie. "*Chronicle of a Death Foretold*: Narrative Function and Interpretation." In *Critical Perspectives on Gabriel García Márquez.* Edited by Bradley A. Shaw and Nora Vera-Goodwin. Lincoln, Neb.: Society of Spanish and Spanish-American Studies, 1986. Pp. 91–104.

Vargas Llosa, Mario. *García Márquez: Historia de un deicidio.* Caracas: Monte Avila Editores, 1971.

Vergara, Isabel. *El mundo satírico de Gabriel García Márquez.* Madrid: Pliegos, 1991.

———. "Escritura, creación y destrucción en *Doce cuentos peregrinos* de Gabriel García Márquez." In *Repertorio* crítico sobre Gabriel García Márquez, vol. 2. Edited by Juan Gustavo Cobo Borda. Bogotá: Instituto Caro y Cuervo, 1995. Pp. 359–379.

———. "Del amor y otros demonios: Incinerando la colonia." In Apuntes sobre literatura colombiana. Edited by Juan Gustavo Cobo Borda et al. Bogotá: Ceiba Editores, 1997. Pp. 123–136.

Williams, Raymond. Gabriel García Márquez. Boston: Twayne, 1984.

Zamora, Lois Parkinson. "The Myth of Apocalypse and Human Temporality in García Márquez' Cien años de soledad and El otoño del patriarca." Symposium 32, no. 4:341–355 (winter 1978).

———. "Ends and Endings in García Márquez' Crónica de una muerte anunciada." Latin American Literary Review 13, no. 25:104–116 (January–June 1985).

Interviews

Borda, Juan Gustavo Cobo. " 'Piedra y cielo' me hizo escritor." Cromos (Bogotá), 28 April 1981, pp. 26–30.

———. "Entrevista a Gabriel García Márquez." In Repertorio crítico sobre Gabriel García Márquez, vol. 1. Edited by Juan Gustavo Cobo Borda. Bogotá: Instituto Caro y Cuervo, 1995. Pp. 113–144.

Castro, Rosa. "Con Gabriel García Márquez." In Recopilación de textos sobre Gabriel García Márquez. Havana: Casa de las Américas, 1969. Pp. 29–33.

Couffon, Claude. "Gabriel García Márquez habla de Cien años de soledad." In Recopilación de textos sobre Gabriel García Márquez. Havana: Casa de las Américas, 1969. Pp. 45–47.

Domingo, José. "Entrevista a García Márquez." Insula (Madrid) no. 259:6, 11 (June 1968).

Dreifus, Claudia. "Playboy Interview: Gabriel García Márquez." Playboy, February 1983, pp. 65–77, 172–178.

Fernández-Braso, Miguel. La soledad de Gabriel García Márquez: Una conversación infinita. Barcelona: Planeta, 1972.

Guibert, Rita, ed. "Gabriel García Márquez." In Seven Voices: Seven Latin American Writers Talk to Rita Guibert. Translated by Frances Partridge. New York: Vintage, 1973.

Kennedy, William. "The Yellow Trolley Car in Barcelona and Other Visions: A Profile of Gabriel García Márquez." Atlantic Monthly, January 1973, pp. 50–59.

El olor de la guayaba: Conversaciones con Plineo Apuleyo Mendoza. Barcelona: Brugera, 1982.

Pombo, Roberto. "En Colombia no hay secretos: García Márquez habla de su nuevo libro Noticia de un secuestro." In Repertorio crítico sobre Gabriel García Márquez, vol. 2. Edited by Juan Gustavo Cobo Borda. Bogotá: Instituto Caro y Cuervo, 1995. Pp. 453–460.

Rentería Mantilla, Alfonso, ed. García Márquez habla de García Márquez: 33 reportajes. Bogotá: Rentería, 1979.

Simons, Marlise. "García Márquez on Love, Plagues, and Politics." New York Times Book Review, 21 February 1988, pp. 1, 23–25.

———. "The Best Years of His Life: An Interview with Gabriel García Márquez." New York Times Book Review, 10 April 1988, pp. 48–49.

Stone, Peter H. "Gabriel García Márquez." Paris Review 23:45–73 (winter 1981).

Vargas Llosa, Mario. La novela en América Latina: Diálogo. Lima: C. Milla Batres, 1968.

# Elena Garro

## (1920–1998)

### Adriana Méndez Rodenas

Mexico offers one of the most vibrant literary cultures in twentieth-century Latin America. Within that culture, Elena Garro stands out as one of the most controversial and innovative of contemporary Mexican writers. The life of this precocious woman writer reflected both the tensions of Mexican political life and her own internal contradictions. Born in Puebla, Mexico, on 11 December 1920, Elena Garro spent her early childhood in Mexico City. Her father, José Antonio Garro, a native of Asturias, Spain, opened her eyes to the Spanish classics, while her mother, Esperanza Navarro, a teacher from northern Mexico, inspired the dreamy quality that pervades her writing. Garro claimed that "Mi madre entra en otro orden: fuera de la realidad" (Rosas Lopátegui, *Yo sólo soy memoria*; My mother belonged to another world: out of the real). In 1926 the family moved to Iguala, in the state of Guerrero, following her Uncle Roni, who had set up a lucrative textile business in the state. Along with her sisters, Deva and Estrella, and her brother, Albano (another sister, Sofía, died in infancy), Garro enjoyed an idyllic childhood in Iguala, a town without electricity where the lack of formal schooling was compensated for by the rich tradition of folklore and legend whispered in children's ears by the Indian nannies who rocked them to sleep. This legendary setting surfaces in much of Garro's fiction, notably in *La semana de colores*

(1964; The week of colors), a collection of short stories whose child protagonists echo Garro and her sisters, and in her first novel, *Los recuerdos del porvenir* (1963; *Recollections of Things to Come*, 1969). Within this magical setting lurks the shadow of history, namely, the Cristero rebellion during the presidency of Plutarco Elías Calles, begun in 1926 and drawn out into a bitter three-year struggle between church and state. This turbulent period of Mexican history, particularly the townspeople's resistance to military siege, is imaginatively documented.

In 1934 Garro and her family moved back to Mexico City, where she attended the Universidad Nacional Autónoma de México (National Autonomous University of Mexico). There Garro's artistic temperament was nurtured by ballet classes taught by a Russian émigré and by her love of theater. Despite her later prominence as a writer, Garro never abandoned dance as artistic form. That influence, combined with her compelling attraction to Russian expatriates as living symbols of a people displaced from history, explains why the elusive protagonist Mariana and her daughter fleetingly appear as ballerinas in a Russian ballet in Garro's most haunting novel, *Testimonios sobre Mariana* (1981; Testimonies on Mariana). Her career as an aspiring actress and choreographer in Julio Bracho's university-sponsored troupe was cut short by her marriage in 1937 to Octavio Paz, the silent young poet who courted her against her parents' wishes. That same year the married couple traveled to Spain to attend a congress of antifascist writers in defense of the Republic. Garro narrates the details of this memorable journey in *Memorias de España* (1992; A Spanish memoir), an inside look into the radical intelligentsia, many of whom are satirized with scathing portraits or off-color anecdotes.

After returning to Mexico, Garro did not resume her college education, perhaps because of the birth of her daughter, Helena Paz, in 1939, or because, as she claims, "[Octavio] never let me go back to the university" (Rosas Lopátegui). Instead, Garro assumed the traditional domestic role, following Paz to the United States, and then to Paris as a diplomat's wife after Paz was appointed cultural attaché at the Mexican embassy there. This early Parisian period, from 1946 to 1951, was merely a prelude to the prolonged, painful, and poverty-stricken exile that Garro and her daughter Helena endured in the City of Light during the 1980s. In the stimulating intellectual atmosphere of surrealism and the avant-garde, Garro had an affair with the Argentine writer Adolfo Bioy Casares, a sign that her marriage to Paz was likely on the rocks. When Paz was transferred to a diplomatic post in Japan in 1952, Garro committed the daring act of writing a letter to the Mexican president, Miguel Alemán, that resulted the following year in his transfer to what Paz and Garro regarded as a more favorable post in Bern, Switzerland. While recovering from illness amid the snowy Alps, Garro wrote her most famous and most critically acclaimed novel, *Recollections of Things to Come*, a belated homage to her childhood in Iguala. The fate of this novel emblematizes the lapse between creation and publication characteristic of Garro's mature fiction: tucked away in a trunk for nearly a decade, the novel finally came to light in 1963, when it was awarded the coveted Xavier Villaurrutia Prize in Mexico.

In 1953 Garro returned to Mexico with Paz, launching her literary career and participating actively in political groups advancing the rights of indigenous peoples and peasants. During this period she wrote a historical play, *Felipe Ángeles*, in homage to one of the few true heroes of the Mexican Revolution who did not betray the cry for social justice. Despite its social and political relevance, the play was not published until 1967, when it appeared in the journal *Coátl*. During the 1950s, Garro entered one of her most vital periods, acting in the Poesía en Voz Alta (Poetry recited out loud) drama group and writing the luminous plays collected in *Un hogar sólido y otras piezas en un acto* (1958; A solid house and other plays in one act). Her growing involvement in the struggle for Indian land rights threatened the ruling Partido Revolucionario Institucional (PRI; Institutional Revolutionary Party). That is why in 1959, the year of the Cuban Revolution's triumph, an event hailed by many progressive Latin American intellectuals, Mexican President Adolfo López Mateos pressured her into leaving the country. From New York City she flew to Paris to join Paz. Three years later Paz was named ambassador to India, and Garro returned to Mexico with her daughter, an act that was later to be repeated at the crossroads of her life.

The separation from Paz spurred Garro's literary production during the 1960s, when she wrote the novels *Testimonios sobre Mariana* and *Reencuentro de personajes* (1982; A gathering of characters), postmodern works that were not published until the early 1980s. The 1960s were a watershed for Garro in political as well as literary terms, for her alleged involvement in the events leading up to the massacre at Tlatelolco clouded her role in the Mexican literary scene, at least until near the end of the twentieth century.

During the summer months of 1968, a student movement grew in opposition to the measures taken by the government of President Gustavo Díaz Ordaz. They had numerous complaints, but many of them focused on the costly construction of sites for the upcoming Olympic Games. Tensions grew, leading to large demonstrations during August and September of that same year, and culminating in a convocation at the Plaza de las Tres Culturas (The Three Cultures Plaza), also known as Tlatelolco Square. On 2 October 1968, thousands of people gathered in the square in silent protest, only to be shot arbitrarily by rapid gunfire from an unknown source, while the police and military, which had surrounded the square, blocked any escape. Estimates of the number of casualties vary. The government claimed that only 30 had died, but many who were there believe 300 or even 500 perished (Kathy Taylor, *The New Narrative of Mexico: Sub-versions of History in Mexican Fiction*, 1994).

Most student protestors blamed the government for the attack, while the government claimed that they had not fired and instead blamed radical agents among the protestors themselves. Many student leaders and intellectuals were arrested or otherwise harassed by the government following the massacre. This repression of the student movement under the presidency of Gustavo Díaz Ordaz generated an intense reaction among Mexican intellectuals. Garro's husband, Octavio Paz, renounced his post as ambassador to India. In the midst of this turmoil, Sócrates Campos Lemus, one of the captured student leaders, publicly denounced Garro "as one of the instigators of the student movement," presumably due to her cloesness to Carlos Madrazo, former governor of the province of Tabasco and president of the PRI. A few days after the massacre, on 7 October, Madrazo rejected the charges of political subversion, claiming he was not directly involved with the student movement, and criticizing as well the government's repressive strategy.

Garro, who had been implicated in these charges, reacted in a way that some critics consider irrational or inconsistent, but which becomes somewhat more understandable once one grasps the pattern of her involvement in public matters. Instead of simply dismissing the accusations against her, Garro launched a public attack against other Mexican intellectuals, exposing their presumed complicity with the PRI regime: "Those guilty of this subversive movement, because it is subversive, are the so-called intellectuals, many of which have political aspirations and receive high salaries from the government" (as quoted by Lucía Melgar in "Writing Dark Times," 2000). Garro then went on to declare her own innocence in the events. Her mistake was that she actually named specific people who she believed were connected to the student movement, turning these powerful people against her. Lopátegui says that Garro categorically denied giving names to the press and suggests that the *machista* (male-dominated) Mexican establishment might have been responsible, setting up Garro in order to get revenge on Madrazo, a close associate of Garro. Melgar also points out that Garro was under great pressure,

having been arrested by the secret police, and may have acted out of panic. In any event, as a result of her statements, Garro became an object of scorn for both the government and her peers.

Much of Garro's participation in this turbulent period is open to discussion and controversy; what is undeniable is that the government mounted an intimidation campaign that forced Garro and her daughter Helena to flee the country in 1972. Though Garro's intentions were at first to fly to Houston, to get treatment for her daughter's cancer, the two of them ended up in New York City in a precarious financial situation, only to be expelled from the United States for political reasons, like a fugitive character in her short story collection *Andamos huyendo Lola* (1980; In perpetual flight, Lola). After seeking refuge in Madrid, Garro wandered "from hotel to hotel," to echo Rosas Lopátegui's apt phrase, much like the persecuted women in her chilling *Reencuentro de personajes*. Transcending economic uncertainty, during her residence in Spain, Garro wrote a number of works that remained unpublished until the 1990s. They consist of the novellas *Un traje rojo para un duelo* (1996; A red dress for a wake), *Busca mi esquela y Primer amor* (1996; *First Love and Look for My Obituary: Two Novellas*, 1997), and *Un corazón en un bote de basura* (1996; A valentine thrown in the garbage bin), and three collections of tales: *La vida empieza a las tres* (1997; Life begins at three p.m.), *Hoy es jueves* (1997; Today is Thursday), and *La feria, o, De noche vienes* (1997; Festival time, or, You come only at night).

Madrid never really agreed with Garro, and in 1981 she moved to Paris, where she was to remain for a dozen years in a productive if solitary exile, accompanied only by Helena and her cats. Perhaps remembering the plot hatched after the massacre at Tlatelolco, Garro wrote a police novel that also reads as a tale of political intrigue, *Y Matarazo no llamó . . .* (1989; Matarazo never showed); *Memorias de España*, the memoir devoted to the Spanish Civil War; and *Mi hermanita Magdalena* (1998; My little sister Magdalena), a posthumously published novel.

The last chapter of Garro's life was written upon her return to Mexico, first for a brief celebratory visit in November 1991, then to stay in July 1993. High-ranking members of the Mexican cultural establishment had wooed Garro back with offers of a home and a stable income, but these promises never materialized. Perhaps lured by the lushness of *tierra caliente* (the semitropical regions of Mexico), Garro and Helena rented a modest apartment in the town of Cuernavaca. Only after her death on 22 August 1998 in Cuernavaca, of a heart attack related to emphysema, did the critics hail one of Mexico's most notorious contemporary writers, who voiced the silence of the oppressed—whether women, children, or Indians—in a highly crafted and symbolic novelistic art.

Despite the systematic exclusion of women writers in Latin America, Elena Garro is considered a pioneer of the magical realism school that dominated the literary scene there during the 1960s. Yet magical realism in Garro's fiction fulfills a very different narrative purpose than it does in the work of Gabriel García Márquez, Alejo Carpentier, and Jorge Luis Borges, those epigones of the marvel of the real and of the fantastic.

Elena Garro has been hailed as a pioneer of magical realism, a literary trend that dominated the Latin American literary scene during the 1960s. Magical realism (a term originally coined by German art critic Frank Roh to refer to post-expressionist painting) gained currency primarily as a critical term to categorize the "boom" in the Latin American novel during the 1950s and 1960s, characterized by writers as diverse as Alejo Carpentier, Gabriel García Márquez, Juan Rulfo, and Jorge Luis Borges. Their novels and short stories explored an alternative view of reality that would absorb the heterogeneous social fabric of a multiracial continent, as well as meditate upon the ontological question of Latin American identity. Despite often conflicting definitions of the term, magical realism served as a critical formula for a new type of fiction in Latin American letters, which recognized, in general terms, the dreamy, otherworldly quality of reality, often expressed by means of a cyclical or recurrent conception of time, or by the presence of surprising or supernatural elements. Based on the theory of "lo real maravilloso" or "real marvelous" coined by Cuban novelist Alejo Carpentier, magical realism could also imply a broad narrative canvas geared to depict a historical epoch or epochs, with the objective of illuminating the "magical" or surreal quality believed to be inherent in Latin American history. Critics agree that,

above all, the magical realist novel enacted a renovation in literary language and narrative form that influenced subsequent generations of writers.

In this context, magical realism in Garro's fiction fulfills a very different purpose than in the works of the other major Latin American writers considered principal exponents of the form. It is perhaps Garro's innovative use of magical realist techniques that have led to her exclusion, for the most part, from literary histories of the movement, or her relegation to the margins along with more contemporary women writers under the uncomfortable rubric of "magic feminism." For Garro's magical realism is an alternative magic that conveys an ephemeral and evanescent female universe, a fragile Imaginary susceptible to fracture at the onslaught of the rigid, authoritarian rule of the male Symbolic (to use Jacques Lacan's categories for the structure of the psyche). Garro's imaginative world depicts the spirit of the feminine associated with a magical realm beyond the confines of the Real. Whereas the male domain is governed by a strict chronology of time and the imposition of a masterful will, the female realm opens up to desire, imagination, and dreams that, for the most part, remain unfulfilled within a prosaic universe. In Garro's theater, collected in *Un hogar sólido y otras piezas en un acto*, the male and female worlds either appear in opposition, as in the fanciful play *Andarse por las ramas* (Daydreaming), or are transfused by means of a symbolic exchange between life and death.

In *Andarse por las ramas*, the main character, Titina, manages to escape the absolute control exercised by her husband, aptly named Don Fernando de las Siete y Cinco (Mister Fernando 7:05), who dictates their lives by the monotonous ticking of the clock. Defying the rigid chronology imposed by the patriarchal order, Titina believes in the magical substance of time, a recurrent theme in Garro's early fiction:

TITINA: *¿Ha pensado usted don Fernando . . . en dónde se meten los lunes? En siete días no sabemos nada de ellos.*

DON FERNANDO: *Los lunes son una medida cualquiera de tiempo . . . una convención. Se les llama lunes como se les podría llamar. . .pompónico.*

TITINA: *(Riéndose). ¡Ay, don Fernando, me hace usted reir! . . . Pompónico no sería nunca lunes. ¡Pompónico sería algo con borlas!*

TITINA: Have you thought, Don Fernando 7:05, where the Mondays hide? For seven days we don't hear anything about them.

DON FERNANDO: Mondays are just a measure of time . . . a convention. They are called Mondays . . . one could call them . . . pomponic.

TITINA: (Laughing). Oh, Don Fernando, you make me laugh! . . . Pomponic would never be Monday. Pomponic would be something with tassels!

(Unruh, "(Free)/Plays of Difference: Language and Eccentricity in Elena Garro's Theater")

In a literal performance of the play's title, the denouement finds Titina amid the treetops, seeking refuge with the fanciful Lagartito. Because "like the tree, Titina is connected to both the earth and the upper spheres" (Messinger Cypess, "Visual and Verbal Distances in Mexican Theater"), this ending brings both man and woman closer to the Imaginary realm, according to Frank Dauster. Whether the title of the play means "to beat around the bush," as Sandra Messinger Cypess believes, or "to digress," according to Vicky Unruh, or "daydreaming," according to Adriana Méndez Rodenas, this ending suggests that only by setting herself apart from the world can the woman subject find her lost unity. In the play *La señora en su balcón* (1969; "The Lady on Her Balcony," 1990), the celestial realm of the biblical Nínive, with its infinite perfection and harmony, lies ever beyond the reach of the protagonist, who can attain it only by leaping to her death.

Echoing the technique of Juan Rulfo's classic *Pedro Páramo* (1953), Garro's *Un hogar sólido* (1958) portrays a similar exchange between life and death. In her play the characters are living corpses who find fulfillment after they descend to the inner chamber of the crypt. For many of them, the cold slab of the tomb is the only "solid home" they have ever known, described by Vicky Unruh in her "(Free)/Plays of Difference" (1990) as "an ambivalent space, associated both with the positive childhood recollections of . . . the characters and the tomb that incarnates the monotony of life and the finality of death." The newlywed Lidia arrives inside the ghostly space longing for a room filled with love, in contrast to "the strange house" she knew as a married woman. Her cousin Muni, in contrast, sighs for "una ciudad alegre, llena de soles y de lunas . . . como la casa que tuvimos de niños, con un sol en cada puerta, una luna para cada ventana y estrellas errantes en los cuartos" (Garro, *Un hogar sólido*; a happy city, full of sunlight and moonlight . . . like the house we had as children, with sunshine in every door, a moon for every window and wandering stars in the rooms; Unruh, "(Free)/Plays of Difference"). This yearning for an ethereal world beyond the Real remains a constant in Garro's narrative universe, contrasting with the imperfect patriarchal order that frustrates woman's desire by infinite deferment.

Yet it is in the play *El Encanto, tendajón mixto* (1958; Illusion, a mixed-goods store) that Garro makes her strongest statement by postulating the existence of an autonomous female sphere, broken off from the world of commerce and governed by its own internal laws, the elusive values of "el eterno femenino" (the feminine mystique), to echo Rosario Castellanos and Betty Friedan. One night, three tired muleteers see a mysterious apparition while traveling along *el camino real* on their way back to town. Vicky Unruh interprets *el camino real* literally, as either "a royal road or a real road—that is, a path firmly anchored in reality" ("(Free)/Plays of Difference"). However, the symbolic charge of the play suggests that the men walk "the difficult road toward psychic maturity," as Richard J. Callan aptly describes it in "Elena Garro's 'El Encanto, Tendajón mixto': The Magical Woman and Maturity" (1992). *El camino real* is, indeed, the "royal road to the unconscious" postulated by Sigmund Freud as the nocturnal dreamworld.

During the muleteers' nighttime journey a lovely brunette, dubbed La Mujer del Hermoso Pelo Negro (the woman with the beautiful black hair), appears as the archetype of the feminine, enticing the men to enter her store of magic tricks with a cup of wine. According to Callan, she not only embodies the archetypal feminine but also its avatar, the Aztec goddess Mayauel: "The Woman is also the soothing darkness attested to by the shade of her hair which she offers the men as shelter and pleasure from the heat of the day." Similarly, Gloria Feman Orenstein classifies the dark seductress as "the prototype of the new female surrealist protagonist": a seer ("Surrealism and Women: The Occultation of the Goddess: Elena Garro, Joyce Mansour, Leonora Carrington," 1975). In accordance with the poetics of magical realism, El Encanto appears and disappears by chance, as its owner seemingly offers respite and shelter while enticing the men with magic liquor. As Callan observes, "The four cups on the counter of El Encanto presumably mean one for the Woman and the three men." Yet only one of the men, the youthful Anselmo, lets himself be seduced by the dark goddess, walking into her magical tent in disregard of his peers' warnings. When he drinks from the cup offered him by the phantasmagorical woman, Anselmo embraces the other side of his psyche, what Jungian psychology terms the *anima,* or feminine, described by Callan as "the fervor of living" or "the spark of life," identified with the regenerative life force, Eros. Forever lost to the world of men, Anselmo—having experienced the mysteries of the feminine, as in classical Greek ritual—vanishes with the mysterious woman in an ecstatic trance. Emphasizing again the contrast between male chronology and the magical present, the play ends when, on the anniversary of Anselmo's 3 May disappearance, the two remaining muleteers visit the site at exactly the same time he vanished, hoping to see their companion's return from the paradisiacal region beyond. The symbolism of the triad supports the process "of Anselmo's psychic transformation" enacted in the play.

*El Encanto, tendajón mixto* underscores a recurrent and dominant theme in Garro's oeuvre: the contrast among different temporalities, marked by the sharp divergence between the male-dominated, violent time of history and the female-centered, nearly infinite time of erotic desire and the imagination. Through this struggle against time, Garro filters her obsession with the paradox of femininity, exploring both the possible and the impossible existence of women subjects who appear lost in a world not of their making. Garro's first collection of short stores, *La semana de colores,* combines her relentless inquiry of time with her equally recurrent obsession with women's destiny, subjectivity, and repressed potential in a hostile world. Because the language of the stories re-creates the magic of words, the Mexican poet Esther Seligson has dubbed this collection *In illo tempore* ("*In illo tempore*—Aproximaciones a la obra de Elena Garro," 1975).

The title story, "La semana de colores," evokes the lost paradise of childhood in a household dominated by a distracted father and the menacing portrait of Philip II of Spain. Set in a provincial town similar to Garro's native Iguala, "La semana de colores" depicts two little girls, Eva and Leli, still in their innocence but soon to awaken to sexuality. Their initiation to the mysteries of the flesh takes place through their interaction with don Flor, a *brujo* (sorcerer) whose strange practices in a forbidden house on the hill stand in marked contrast to their father's adherence to Catholic liturgy. Wielding occult powers, don Flor holds captive the days of the week, incarnated in a sequence of women, each of whom represents one of the seven vices and virtues. Don Flor shows the girls how he picks a woman on her respective day, then enjoys her in a sadomasochistic ritual. Each day of the week is tinted a particular color, representing a particular perversion of the sexual drive. In this way "la semana de colores" acquires a double symbolic purpose. First, it suggests both the girls' alternative calendar, where the days do not proceed in consecutive order but rather happen by simultaneity and repetition: "Era mucho más probable que del lunes saltáramos bruscamente al viernes y del viernes regresáramos al martes" (It was much more likely that from Monday we would suddenly jump to Friday, and from Friday, come promptly back to Tuesday). Second, it evokes don Flor's jaded week of perverse sexuality, the exact opposite of their father's holy calendar. In Garro's tale the two temporalities are interchangeable, since both don Flor's black magic and the father's white-robed liturgy sustain the same Symbolic order: a patriarchy erected on women's submission and sacrifice.

Defying this hidden decree of subordination, one day the days of the week fly away to the festivities at Teloloapan. At the end of the story, a surprised reader learns that don Flor was found dead on the very day that the week took flight: "Dicen que fueron las mujeres las que lo mataron, porque la Semana desapareció . . ." (They say it was the women who murdered him, because the Week suddenly vanished). As witnesses to these events, Eva and Leli not only lose their childish innocence but also enter the open door of the imagination. Contrasting with Jorge Luis Borges's dictum in "El arte narrativo y la magia" that magic is the crowning achievement of causality, Garro's short story collection rewrites magical realism as the festive time of a feminine (and feminist) escape.

The most anthologized story of *La semana de colores* is "La culpa es de los tlaxcaltecas" (1964; "It's the Fault of the Tlaxcaltecas," 1986), an exploration of Mexican history through the lens of magical realism. Contrasting two different time frames as well as two marginal characters, a modern Mexico City woman and a pre-Hispanic Indian, Garro conjures past and present time in order to suggest how their fates converge, since they are both equally marginalized, the first as a woman and the latter as an Indian. This love story of a contemporary upper-class woman named Laura and her indigenous "cousin-husband," a courageous Aztec warrior at the time of the Spanish conquest, is emblematic of Garro's use of magical realism. Trapped, like many of Garro's characters, in an unhappy marriage (in this story, to a boorish government official named Pablo), Laura falls in love with the silent Aztec noble after a car accident following a day trip to Guanajuato magically thrusts her into a legendary past. Echoing the Borgesian theme of *azar*, or arbitrary fate, but with an original twist, Garro enables Laura to shift from present to past for furtive meetings with her lover in the thick of the Aztecs' defense of their fabled city, Tenochtitlán, in 1521. The temporal split thus duplicates a spatial contrast in which the Café Tacuba, at the heart of Mexico City, is strangely transported into the Calzada de Tacuba, where the Spaniards launched their last attack against the Aztec kingdom. As Cynthia Duncan has noted in her essay "La culpa es de los tlaxcaltecas: A Reevaluation of Mexico's Past Through Myth" (1985), the spatial/temporal dissonance underlines the contrast between mythic and historical time: "In mythic time, unlike historical time, an event is not limited to one particular chronological period, and the past, present, and future can co-exist in harmony." Duncan claims that by juxtaposing myth and history, Garro's story collapses the three temporal categories into one.

Duncan identifies Laura as an indigenous woman who has "betrayed" her native culture by marrying an upwardly mobile mestizo, thus transforming herself "into a white woman in the twentieth century." Yet the theme of betrayal has further consequences, for Laura is explicitly identified in the story as a white Mexican woman, which suggests a reverse of the Conquest that stages the founding family romance in Mexican history. In "The Figure of the Malinche in the Texts of Elena Garro" (1990), Sandra Messinger Cypess sees Laura as a present-day rendering of Malinche, the princess whose mother sold her into slavery to the Tabascan Indians. At the time of the Conquest, Malinche—also known as doña Marina—was handed over to Hernán Cortés, serving him as both mistress and translator or, in the picturesque metonym of the Spanish chronicles of conquest, as his "tongue." Legend has it that Malinche facilitated the conquest of Mexico, for she enabled Cortés to "talk" at the throne of Montezuma, the last living Aztec emperor. Thus, Malinche has been cast in Mexican history as a traitor for opening herself up sexually to the conquistador, a view stated in Octavio Paz's influential *El laberinto de la soledad* (1959). As Messinger Cypess explains, "To generations of Mexicans, in popular parlance her name is associated with betrayal, of selling out to the enemy; *malinchismo* has entered the lexicon as a disparaging term that means to exalt anything foreign and to undervalue anything that is native to Mexico." Traditional Mexican history and popular belief blame the Tlaxcaltecan tribe for the defeat of the Aztec Empire because it sided with Cortés in revenge for the Aztec domination of their territory.

Contrary to both interpretations, Garro presents Laura as being responsible for double treason. If at first Laura betrays her legitimate husband, who remains unaware of her escapades, she is also capable of systematically betraying her long-lost, illegitimate "cousin-husband" (her indigenous lover):

> Each time Laura finds herself within the time of the Conquest, she disobeys her *primo marido* [cousin-husband] and returns to the twentieth century instead of remaining with him in that early period. Yet Laura finds herself more critical of Pablo and his world, and each time she stays longer with the Indian; after the third encounter she finally leaves Pablo to remain with the Indian at the beginning point of Mexican civilization.
> (Messinger Cypess, "The Figure of the Malinche in the Texts of Elena Garro")

Laura's awareness of her high treason makes her confess unabashedly: "Yo soy traidora. . . ." (I am like them: traitors). At the end of the story, the protagonist abandons her arrogant, emotionally abusive husband with the silent complicity of her indigenous servant, Nacha. Messinger Cypess interprets this as an active choice on Laura's part, one that reflects a nascent feminist consciousness as well as a deeper awareness of the cultural values represented by each male representative of *lo mexicano* (Mexican national identity).

Messinger Cypess's reading emphasizes Garro's symbolic reversal of "a Malinche figure who refuses to accept the burden of guilt that Mexican society has placed on her," thus reversing the negative equivalence between this legendary figure and all Mexican women. "It's the Fault of the Tlaxcaltecas" thus rewrites Octavio Paz's questionable interpretation of the Malinche in *El laberinto de la soledad* as vulnerable and open to the conqueror's attack, as well as his rendering of all Mexicans as sons of Malinche whose collective psyche is clouded by both an ambivalent relationship to their Spanish father and an instinctive rejection of their native mother. Instead, the pointed allusion of Garro's title to the Malinche legend is subverted by the story's ironic twist, which—against Paz's interpretation—puts the blame squarely onto the Spaniards for their systematic rape of Indian women and their destruction of pre-Hispanic civilizations.

At another level, the story also suggests *mestizaje* (miscegenation) and the blending of cultures as the only real alternative to the dilemmas of Mexican national identity. It is not by chance, then, that the *primo-marido* forgives Laura her treason, showing the Indians' capacity to endure and suggesting a way for the Mexicans to erase the trauma of the Conquest by embracing their dual heritage. This new romance, to endure the test of time, is forged by a true spiritual and carnal union between white and indigenous, male and female; it suggests, too, that these races and cultures were already bonded by a secret kinship, since Laura and her Aztec lover are first cousins. In line with the other tales collected in *La semana de colores*, "It's the Fault of the Tlaxcaltecas" suggests a reshuffling of historical time as well as a new magical realist paradigm emphasizing woman's psychic liberation from male abuse of power.

When the mythical defeat of Montezuma draws to a close, Laura escapes with her phantom lover to the end of time, much as Titina in *Andarse por las ramas* and the elusive Julia in *Recollections of Things to Come* do. In Garro's play with time, if these three works emphasize the magical potential of each moment, "¿Qué hora es?" (What time is it?), in *La semana de colores*, presents the underside or shadow latent in the ticking of the clock. Lucía Mitre, the unhappy protagonist of the story, waits eternally in a Paris hotel for the magical instant her lover is expected to appear: 9:45 P.M., the time his flight is supposed to arrive. After a long and fruitless wait, in which the anxious moment is repeated for all eternity, Lucía dies at the precise instant of her lover's anticipated arrival. Like Anselmo in *El Encanto, tendajón mixto*, the French hotelier Brunier and his agent Gilbert fall prey to the seductive qualities of the mysterious foreigner, who gives away her jewels in order to pay for her room. For a moment, they come to believe that Lucía's heightened desire had brought her lover back from the high sierras of Mexico. This belief is almost corroborated by the appearance of a tennis racket at the foot of Lucía's bed the same day as her departure from life. How did it get there? This puerile detail proves that Gabriel Cortina, the longed-for lover, actually did fly in from Mexico, with his sporty look and light-hearted virility, but too late for the unfortunate Lucía. Like her double, Clara, in "The Lady on Her Balcony," she disappears from view without fulfilling her deepest wish; worse, she is destined to defer it forever in an infinite game of self-delusion. Anticipating the image of the married woman drawn in Garro's most celebrated novel, *Recollections of Things to Come*, Lucía's classic features, enveloped in a soft peach scarf, leave no trace of her being ("en su rostro no quedaba nada de ella, nada"; her face showed not a trace of her, nothing).

The many magical endings, reversals, and foreshadowings in *La semana de colores* resurface in Garro's *Recollections of Things to Come*, most notably in the famous scene describing the flight of the clandestine lovers Julia and the "foreigner" Felipe Hurtado, a scene which, according to Frank Dauster in "Elena Garro y sus *Recuerdos del porvenir*" (1980), neatly divides the novel into two mirror images. In turn, each narrative half comes under the spell of a woman character who functions as a double of the other. Whereas the first half of the novel is dominated by the beautiful Julia Andrade—metaphorically associated with a softly feminine, rose-colored gown—the second tells the tragic ending of Isabel Moncada, a village girl turned "bad" by her insistent passion for the caudillo Francisco Rosas. While Julia's and Isabel's final destinies resemble one another because they loved the same man, their object of desire is split in two, duplicating the division of the narrative structure into two separate parts. As Marta Gallo points out in her essay "Entre el poder y la gloria: Disyuntiva de la identidad femenina en *Los recuerdos del porvenir*" (1995), "while in the first half Rosas loves Julia but is not reciprocated, in the second he is converted into Isabel's object of desire, although [he remains] as elusive and impossible as Julia was for Rosas." Besides these two protagonists, a female presence is forged in two separate and antagonistic spheres: the lovers of Rosas's troops, huddled inside the euphemistically named Hotel Jardín, and the "decent" townswomen, the most notable of whom is a widow, doña Elvira Montúfar, who, like the sad Lucía Mitre, "forgot" what she looked like after her marriage.

Tormented by his inability to elicit Julia's erotic surrender, Rosas channels his psychic frustration onto the townspeople of Ixtepec, whom he holds under military siege. Set during the period of the Cristero rebellion (1926–1929), a civil war sparked by President Plutarco Elías Calles's campaign against the Catholic Church, *Recollections of Things to Come* has been read as a historical novel, yet its deployment of events follows not a progressive temporal frame, but an alternative order in which the past conditions the future. In line with the juxtaposition of myth and history in "It's the Fault of the Tlaxcaltecas," the historical plot is structured as a struggle against time. At the beginning of the novel, Isabel's brothers leave to join the Cristero uprising, while she and her father remain trapped in a home where the clock stops every night, echoing Laura and Titina's domestic enclosure. Later, the townspeople try to trap Rosas by holding a party for him, a false truce whose real motive is to gain time to put their parish priest out of danger. Yet in typical Garro fashion, the trick turns back on them, as Rosas captures not only the priest but also a local buffoon who speaks directly out of the dictionary, as well as Isabel's two brothers. At the end of the night, Isabel Moncada betrays her family's honor as well as her community by giving herself to Rosas in her crumpled red party dress—a symbol of her transformation into an indecent woman or harlot—along with the other illicit lovers guarded inside the Hotel Jardín.

As Adriana Méndez Rodenas has shown in her "Tiempo femenino, tiempo ficticio: *Los recuerdos del porvenir* de Elena Garro" (1985), the innovative strategy of converting the town of Ixtepec into an omniscient narrator accounts both for the historical frame of the novel and for its tale of unrequited love. In a manner reminiscent of Gabriel García Márquez's *Cien años de soledad* (1967) but in a more subtle way, Garro connects the surprise ending, in which Isabel Moncada turns into stone, with its beginning, as the town's authorial voice is intimately tied to, if not enabled by, "esta piedra aparente" (this seeming stone) that is Isabel's petrified silence. According to Robert K. Anderson in "La realidad temporal en *Los recuerdos del porvenir*" (1980–1981), "Ixtepec" means "a hill made out of obsidian" in Náhuatl. Just as Aztec soothsayers used obsidian mirrors as a means of divination, so Garro's Ixtepec meditates on its place in history by projecting the past onto the future. Ixtepec's recollections order time in a manner similar to the Aztecs' divining stone, swirling like crystal lights around the mystery of Julia's face (and fate): "yo me veía como joya" (I saw myself as a jewel). In *The Usable Past: The Imagination of History in Recent Fiction of the Americas* (1997), Lois Parkinson Zamora states that this opulent imagery suggests "intermingling, conjoining" rather than separation and abstraction, a mirror of memory hearkening back to "the cosmology of the Nahuatl-speaking peoples"; hence affirming "the agrarian, communitarian, mythic underpinnings of Mexico's indigenous heritage."

By far the most intriguing aspect of the novel is the magical-realist scene in which the elusive Julia escapes with her lover, Felipe Hurtado, who came from Mexico City to rescue her. While hiding in the Moncada home, Hurtado challenges the military might of his rival, Francisco Rosas. Just as Rosas, escorted by men on horseback, is about to retaliate, time is halted at a pregnant moment (like the instant in which Laura flees with her Aztec warrior), allowing the lovers to flee in the night. In a manner reminiscent of Jorge Luis Borges's "El milagro secreto," the rest of the world progresses in chronological time while Ixtepec is detained in a time capsule. Since the collective narrator is unsure how long "the miracle" lasted, the reader also remains uncertain, and it is he or she who must determine what happened: "El tiempo se detuvo en seco. No sé si se detuvo o si se fue y sólo cayó el sueño: un sueño que no me había visitado nunca. . . . No sé cuánto tiempo anduvimos perdidos en ese espacio inmóvil." (Time stood still. I don't know if it stopped altogether or if it slipped away and sleep fell upon us: a dream which had never haunted me before. . . . I don't know how long we were lost in that motionless space.)

This magical-realist scene is tainted by ambiguity, in Ixtepec's terms: "En verdad no sé lo que pasó. Quedé fuera del tiempo, suspendido en un lugar sin viento, sin murmullos, sin ruido de hojas ni suspiros" (I really don't know what happened. I remained outside of time, suspended in a windless place, where no whispers were heard, with no sound of leaves falling nor of sighs). The ambiguity is partly resolved by the sole witness to Julia and Felipe's escape. At the break of dawn, a muleteer (an echo of the muleteer who discovers the dead don Flor in the short story "La semana de colores"), noticing "la noche cerrada" (the sealed-off night) that fell on Ixtepec, claims he saw "un jinete llevando en sus brazos a una mujer vestida de color de rosa. El iba de oscuro. . . . La mujer se iba riendo" (a jockey who carried in his arms a woman in a rose-tinted dress. He was in black. . . . She was laughing). Upon this minor character falls, then, the weight of the reader's expectations because, as with Gilbert and Brunier in "¿Qué hora es?," we want to believe in the triumph of love and in a happy ending.

Whereas the first part of *Recollections of Things to Come* closes with Ixtepec's dictum "Nunca más volvimos a oír de los amantes" (We never heard from the lovers again), the second unravels the love triangle left by Julia's absence—felt in the trace of her vanilla perfume—Isabel's usurpation of her role, and Rosas's own divided feelings. After the town's public humiliation by Rosas, Isabel demands that he free her brother Nicolás. Although at first a tormented Rosas agrees to replace him with another condemned prisoner, in the thick of the shooting Nicolás cries: "Falto yo!" (I'm the only one missing!), forcing Rosas's men to fire and hence inadvertently transforming Rosas into a traitor. Though at first Isabel leaves Rosas, she is suddenly struck by the memory of her lover and cries out that, despite his high treason, she wishes to see him again, which cloaks her unspoken wish to make love to him again. In the most commented-upon scene of the novel, Isabel at the end is turned to stone in what many critics interpret as a punishment for a desire that transgressed the social and moral order. Because Rosas was responsible for ruining Isabel's family and for killing her brothers, Messinger Cypess sees Isabel as a Malinche figure who betrayed her community, noting that "her refusal to change is symbolized by her transformation into a stone statue."

Critics have speculated as to the possible meanings of this enigmatic ending. The most suggestive readings interpret the scene in psychoanalytic terms, viewing it as the end process of Isabel's maturation, as in Marta Gallo's interpretation in "Entre el poder y la gloria" that Isabel's final transformation signals the last stage of an inconclusive process toward psychic integration. In this reading, Isabel is caught, on the one hand, between a strong oedipal bonding with her brother Nicolás—the first psychic stage on which to construct a female identity—and, on the other hand, the equally pressing need to redefine her femininity in terms of the masculine ideal represented by Rosas. Gallo concludes that the rigidity of Isabel in stone marks the impossibility of finding an authentic female identity in a specular world ruled by the power of the phallus.

In "Relectura desde la piedra: Ambigüedad, violencia, y género en *Los recuerdos del porvenir* de Elena Garro" (2000), Lucía Melgar offers an opposite point of view, gleaning a strong feminist message from the final scene. Pointing out the strict gender roles assigned to women in the town of Ixtepec, Melgar argues that Isabel does not conform to the acceptable norms for female behavior. After a period of passive rebellion against these codes, Isabel's sole act in defiance of them, daring to become Rosas's mistress, "[la] ha convertido en paria" (transforms her into a pariah), with no place to go and, more important, without a place in the Symbolic order. This is why, in her final days, "Isabel es un escándalo: la mujer que no puede clasificarse de ningún modo" (Isabel is a total scandal: the woman who cannot be pigeonholed). Downplaying the erotic charge of the scene, Melgar interprets Isabel's conversion to stone as a metaphor for psychological disintegration, concluding that

*La petrificación corresponde tanto a un proceso psicológico real como a un castigo en términos del código literario en que se*

*inscribe. Por otra parte, en cuanto hecho fantástico, la metamórfosis de Isabel no supone, como la huida milagrosa de Julia, un salto en el tiempo, sino una expulsión fuera del tiempo. Se trata de una metamórfosis integrada a la lógica de la violencia del mundo . . . , no de una transgresión fantástica de ésta.*

Petrification is the result of a psychological process and it also functions as a punishment within the novel's literary code. Moreover, as a fantastic event, Isabel's metamorphosis does not imply, like Julia's miraculous escape, a leap [forward] in time, but rather being banished out of time. [We have here] a type of metamorphosis woven into the logic of violence [that regulatees] the [social] world, instead of a fantastic transgression of this world.

Lucía Melgar reads Isabel's transformation into stone as a sign of her radical marginality and expulsion from the social body. In *Reading the Body Politic: Feminist Criticism and Latin American Women Writers* (1993), in contrast, Amy Kaminsky concludes that the scene never happened, questioning its validity and attributing it solely to the town's soothsayer Gregoria's fantasizing. That is not borne out, however, by the book's ending, since the circularity marked by Ixtepec's narrative function is predicated precisely on Isabel's metamorphosis. Lastly, Méndez Rodenas situates the petrification scene within a baroque as well as a biblical tradition, linking it to the repression of women's desire under patriarchy. In this reading, Gregoria's final inscription on the body of Isabel—the stone as petrified writing—rekindles for all time the flame of erotic longing. While for Jean Franco, in *Plotting Women: Gender and Representation in Mexico* (1989), "Garro's novel . . . represents an impasse" because the two main characters lie "outside history," Méndez Rodenas affirms its radically female-centered view, based on an alternative Symbolic—what the feminist theorist Julia Kristeva has termed "women's time"—operating within the parameters of historical time.

The shadow of Malinche lurking behind Isabel Moncada surfaces in another Garro character who is equally enigmatic: the absent protagonist of *Testimonios sobre Mariana*, who, like the fabled Malinche, is constituted by the accounts of others, which are layered over her lived, historical experience. As Kathy Taylor claims in *The New Narrative of Mexico: Sub-versions of History*

*in Mexican Fiction* (1994), "*Testimonios sobre Mariana* is situated in the realm of pure fiction," yet at the same time reflects on the truth-value of narrative, alluding as it does to Latin American testimonial narrative and its claim to historical authenticity. Mariana is a purely fictional persona; her existence is real only insofar as the other characters remember her, which forces the reader to reconstruct her life from the shattered fragments of words. The play between the real and the nonreal is exemplified in the narrative structure, composed of three parts, each of which corresponds to the testimonies of three character-narrators who knew Mariana well and were touched by her presence in Paris. They are Vicente, her South American lover; Gabrielle, an impoverished Frenchwoman who fought in the Resistance; and André, an idealistic young Frenchman who falls in love with her at first sight. All three comment on Mariana's troubled relationship to her husband, Augusto, a Latin American archaeologist who appears as a parody of the Roman Emperor Augustus, and whose sadomasochistic games of control ultimately cause Mariana's demise and tragic disappearance from the text. With the exception of André, no one does anything to save her, and the sole female narrator, Gabrielle, betrays Mariana by remaining in Augusto's service.

As a detective novel, *Testimonios sobre Mariana* tells "the story of a woman who is persecuted and eventually killed"; however, "the 'case' to be solved" is not only the life and death of Mariana but also the answer to the question, "Who is Mariana?" (Taylor, *The New Narrative of Mexico*). Though ostensibly the text revolves around the mystery of Mariana's identity, the three narrators project themselves onto Mariana as if she were a mirror of their own subjectivity, providing dissonant versions of her life in Paris after World War II. Ultimately, their testimonies control her life, over and beyond the nearly absolute control exercised by the despotic Augusto and his coterie of displaced Latin American intellectuals, parodied in the novel as a cadre of opportunistic parasites playing the role of the engagé left.

With its sole protagonist and her literal absence from the text, the novel is a direct inversion of Elena Poniatowska's *La noche de Tlatelolco: Testimonios de historia oral* (1971), whose collective narrator gives testimony to a concrete historical event, the violent repression of the 1968 student movement in Mexico. In contrast, Garro's *Testimonios sobre Mariana* concerns the repression of the female psyche in a Parisian setting, thus marking its distance from Mexican history. Contrary to the tenets of the *novela testimonio*, or testimonial novel, which purports to be historical truth, here the testimonies are neither real nor false. They consist of three separate accounts narrated by characters who verbally reconstruct their relationship with Mariana, an enigmatic woman without a past and without a future, much like the mythical Julia Andrade in *Recollections of Things to Come*. Mariana is a historical figure only insofar as she represents the antithesis of history, an antiheroine whose silence signifies the modern subject's—and specifically the female's—alienation from history. As if to deny the possibility of female agency, Mariana's association with Russian émigrés makes her an outcast from history as well, provoking Gabrielle's description of her as "un grave error histórico" (A grave historical error).

From a feminist perspective, Mariana's fictional biography marks the limit of the representation of woman. As Rebecca Biron has shown in her essay "*Testimonios sobre Mariana*: Representación y la otra mujer" (1995), the text depicts Mariana as both affirming and denying the possibility of representing her/self, moving in between the barrier separating absence and presence, silence and voicing. In constant tension, "el control que las dispersas narrativas ejercen sobre el texto hacen resaltar el silencio de Mariana" (the control exercised by the text's dispersed narratives serve to highlight Mariana's silence). By the same token, the narrators' fictional status as characters undercuts the validity of their accounts, resulting in a self-reflexive text that resists yet paradoxically complements Augusto's sadistic control over his blonde and frightened spouse. As an object of ridicule in Augusto's pompous salon, where intellectual theories are played out with her as a case study, Mariana is portrayed as a victim, scorned as a puppet in a ritualistic circle devoted to the Marquis de Sade. Yet, in Biron's opinion, Garro also shows us how, through Mariana's silence and abject submission, "she controls her oppressors" (Taylor, *The New Narrative of Mexico*), thus resisting the narrators' efforts to contain and restrict her within their own symbolic orbits. According to Gabrielle, who serves as Augusto's secretary and at times as Mariana's confidante, the dangerous game of control and domination hinges on the manipulation of Mariana's image:

> "*Voy a domar a Mariana!*," *repetía Augusto mirando con fijeza un punto en el vacío. Me pregunto si la domó o si la chica murió en la doma. No lo sabré jamás. Aunque lo que sí puedo asegurar es que de aquella Mariana en rebeldía perpetua, no quedó inada! . . . "Para destruir a alguien primero hay que destruir su imagen," me repito.*
>
> (Garro, *Testimonios sobre Mariana*)

"I'm going to tame Mariana!" Augusto repeated, looking fixedly at a point in space. I ask myself whether he succeeded in taming her or whether the young girl died in the taming. I will never know. All I can say for sure is that, of Mariana the perpetual rebel, there is nothing left—nothing! . . . "In order to destroy someone, it is first necessary to destroy their image," I told myself over and over.

Mariana's image disappears from the photos taken of her by her lover Vicente, which results in a specular game of broken images as the narrators try to piece together the puzzle of Mariana's life. As object of the gaze, "Mariana's existence is composed by the look of others," but the multiple gazes also serve to control and contain her (Taylor, *The New Narrative of Mexico*). In contrast to the lovers' flight in *Recollections of Things to Come*, *Testimonios sobre Mariana* offers no easy escape. Gabrielle documents a frightening scene in which Mariana is pushed to the brink either of suicide or of madness because of Augusto's efforts to have her committed to an insane asylum. Structured around Mariana's fragmented image in a mirror, the episode corroborates what Gabrielle had stated at the beginning of her testimony: that Augusto had succeeded in erasing Mariana's image and, consequently, in destroying her:

> *La mano que borró la imagen de Mariana guardada en la memoria de sus amigos como una imagen reflejada en el agua, fue la mano de Augusto su marido, que implacable revolvió el agua, desfiguró su rostro, su figura, hasta volverla grotesca y distorsionada. Al final, cuando las aguas se aquietaron, de Mariana no quedó inada! Cambiar la memoria para destruir una imagen es tarea más ardua que destruir a una persona.*

*Temo que no descubriré nunca el secreto de la pareja Mariana-Augusto, que nunca fue pareja.*

(Garro, *Testimonios sobre Mariana*)

The hand that erased the image of Mariana in her friends' memories, like an image reflected in the water, was the hand of Augusto, her husband, who inexorably stirred up the water, disfiguring her face, her figure, until he had made her grotesque and distorted. In the end, when the waters had quieted, there was nothing left of Mariana! To change memory in order to destroy an image is a more arduous task than to destroy a person. I am afraid I will never discover the secret of the couple Mariana-Augusto, who never were a couple.

(augmented from Taylor, *The New Narrative of Mexico*)

As a blank page or screen upon which the narrators project their own fears and obsessions, Mariana eventually vanishes from view, transforming herself into "the memory of a memory" (Taylor, *The New Narrative of Mexico*). The obsidian mirror exhibiting the play of temporalities of *Recollections of Things to Come* in a shimmering array of lights is here inverted into an opaque mirror of doubles.

In parallel fashion, if in "La semana de colores" and *Recollections of Things to Come* the magical realist scene cancels the abuse of male power, in *Testimonios sobre Mariana* it is radical ambiguity that channels the resistance against male violence. Gabrielle's testimony, by far the most intimate about Mariana's life, ends with two discrepant versions regarding her final destiny: either Mariana was seen "pidiendo limosna a las puertas de la Ópera de Viena" (Garro, *Testimonios sobre Mariana*; begging alms at the gate of the Vienna Opera), or else she appeared almost simultaneously as a ballerina in the Bolshoi Ballet, dancing with her daughter among the "dance chorus" of *Giselle*. It is the magical-realist version of reality: "La verdad y única verdad es que casi todas las noches las veíamos en escena, confundidas entre las figuras blancas de los coros de baile. A veces nos hacían alguna seña desde el escenario" (The truth and only truth is that almost every night we would see them on stage, hidden among the white figures of the dance chorus. At times they would send us signals from the stage; Taylor, *The New Narrative of Mexico*).

Of the three *testimoniantes*, the only one who refuses to believe that Mariana's life has ended is André, her devoted, platonic lover. In a state of psychological denial, he reverses the fact of Mariana's suicide, committed in faraway Liverpool in a frustrated attempt to escape Augusto's demonic chase. By proclaiming himself Mariana's savior, André prevents her from falling to her death: "Mi amor ha salvado a Mariana de caer todas las noches con su hija desde un cuarto piso" (Garro, *Testimonios sobre Mariana*; My love has saved Mariana from falling each and every night with her daughter from a fourth floor). In contrast to the final leap of "The Lady on Her Balcony," here the power of love is strong enough to prevail against violence and death. Yet in the end, the "testimonies on Mariana" eventually kill her, since each witness is transformed into a type of serial killer by becoming an accomplice, if not in the crime itself, then in Mariana's eventual disappearance—from the text, from the world, and from history. Much like the white Russians or other Eastern European émigrés who populate Garro's later fiction, seeking refuge but with no place to go, or like the wandering Isabel Moncada, whose pariah status petrifies her into nonbeing, Mariana is expelled, like a postmodern Eve, from Paradise: Paris, her native country, her real self.

By its depiction of radical exile, *Testimonios sobre Mariana* marks a watershed in Garro's literary production. *Reencuentro de personajes* is emblematic of the second phase, which coincides with Garro's exile in France. In a 1991 interview with Patricia Rosas Lopátegui and Rhina Toruño, Garro describes exile as "un error porque es como estar en el vacío, no hay eco para nada, es un poco desdichado, el exilio" (a big mistake because it is like being lost in a vacuum, without any echo, an unhappy experience, exile is). This reflects the negative cast of her Parisian period. After *Testimonios sobre Mariana*, Garro's fiction follows the fate of her characters, caught as they are in a repetitive cycle of destructive acts and flights from reality. As María Silvina Persino aptly claims in her "Elena Garro: La mirada vigilante" (1999), Garro's obsession with the fate of the persecuted, and the recurrent appearance of a woman character tormented by criminal rings, spies, or vindictive ex-lovers, haunt her later fiction, from *Reencuentro de personajes* in 1982 to *Inés* in 1995, the latter being perhaps the most chillingly sinister of all her tales.

In her "Text and Authority in Elena Garro's *Reencuentro de personajes*" (1991), Julie Jones underscores the novel's autobiographical import as well as its intertextual overtones:

> *Reencuentro de personajes* involves a cast of Mexican expatriates whose sense of self is based on their having met Scott Fitzgerald years ago and their conviction that he has described them in *Tender Is the Night* and that they also served as models for characters in Evelyn Waugh's *Brideshead Revisited*. The protagonist of *Reencuentro*, a young Mexican woman modeled on Garro herself, has left her husband for one of this group . . . , who uses her as a cover for his homosexual liaisons and as an object of humiliation. The plot turns on Verónica's attempt to decipher who, or what, Frank is, and through him, who or what she is herself.

Echoing Mariana's elusive aura, but reversing the question of identity onto the male character, *Reencuentro de personajes* repeats the pattern of submission-domination already traced in *Testimonios sobre Mariana*. Like Mariana, the main character is in perpetual flight:

> Verónica, la protagonista de Reencuentro de personajes, *se encuentra desde el comienzo inmersa en una situación de dominación, casi secuestrada por su amante Frank. Como otras protagonistas de Garro, Verónica es una desposeída, y en su vida itinerante cuenta, por toda ropa, con un solo vestido. Su dependencia de Frank es absoluta y este único vestido amarillo, ajándose progresivamente a lo largo de su viaje, constituye el síntoma visible de un deterioro interior.*
>
> (Persino, "Elena Garro")

Verónica, the protagonist of *Reencuentro de personajes*, finds herself from the beginning immersed in a relationship of domination, practically abducted by her lover Frank. Like other Garro protagonists, Verónica is dispossessed, and her wandering life hangs on one dress as her only protection. Her dependence on Frank is absolute and her single yellow dress, torn to shreds as her journey progresses, is the only visible sign of her internal collapse.

While Jones, among others, has read this novel as a roman à clef exorcising Garro's troubled marriage to Octavio Paz, at another level it underlines the theme already exploited in *Testimonios sobre Mariana* regarding the inevitability of women's fate. Like Mariana, Verónica appears to have no control over her own life,

which forces a reinterpretation of the title: "Viewed as reenactment, the characters' lives seem to be already written, therefore predestined, and their identities subsumed in the role" ("Text and Authority in Elena Garro's *Reencuentro de personajes*").

The no-exit quality of these characters in perpetual motion reverts, ultimately, to the question of narrative authority explored in *Testimonios sobre Mariana*. Despite her usurpation of Fitzgerald and Waugh, Jones concludes that "in *Reencuentro*, only Garro is the final source of authority. . . . Garro claims the authority of the victim, of one who has suffered and learned from real experience." Yet in her interview with Patricia Rosas Lopátegui and Rhina Toruño, Garro clarifies her relationship with these two model authors as well as her semiautobiographical heroines:

> *No, yo no me identifico con Mariana. Mira, a Scott Fitzgerald le dijeron: "¿En cuál personaje se reconoce usted?" Y dijo: "Soy todos mis personajes." Y yo creo que eso le pasa a todos los autores. Cada personaje tiene parte del autor. Si, hay partes de Mariana en que me reconozco . . . pero hay partes de Mariana en que no . . . las he sacado de una amiga. . . . Mariana está sacada . . . de una mujer española que murió y que tuvo un amante argentino, que ya murió también. . . . Y ella me decía: "Cuando se cae en el círculo de los homosexuales ya no se escapa nunca."*
>
> ("Entrevista a Elena Garro")

No, I do not identify myself with Mariana. Look, somebody asked Scott Fitzgerald once: "Do you identify with any one of your characters?" He replied: "I am each and every one of my characters." And I think the same thing happens to all authors. Each character has something of their author. Yes, I recognize myself in parts of Mariana . . . but in other parts of her I don't . . . I took them from a friend of mine. . . . Mariana is drawn after . . . a Spanish woman who died and who had an Argentine lover, who also died. . . . And she used to tell me: "When you fall inside a homosexual ring, there is no escape."

However, although Jones affirms that Garro projects the shadow of Paz onto Frank, she is mistaken in her contention that the purpose of the novel was "to defame Paz in such a way that he would be unable to defend himself." Rather, Garro's irony is meant to subvert accepted notions of Latin American identity, including, but not limited to, Paz's interpretation of Mexican identity in *El laberinto de la soledad*. Echoing the author's own appraisal of the novel, Jones claims that here "the archetypal Mexican [is presented] as a homosexual thug with a veneer of culture and a history of crime, and his consort as a victim who is terrified that her lover will murder her." Like *Testimonios sobre Mariana*, *Reencuentro de personajes* exposes the Sartrean bad faith of the Latin American leftist intelligentsia, of which Paz was a part early in his career, in order to minimize its aggrandized self-image. The appropriation of canonical novels in *Reencuentro* ultimately belies Garro's efforts to exorcise the function of authorship, as if to clear a new stage in her literary work.

The transition between the radical alienation of *Reencuentro de personajes* and the destructive orgy narrated in *Inés* is the short tale *La casa junto al río* (1983; The house by the river). Whereas the settings of *Testimonios sobre Mariana* and Reencuentro are in Paris and in postmodern Europe, both *La casa junto al río* and *Inés* hearken back to the nostalgic role of Spain in Garro's Imaginary, although in reverse direction. Both novellas follow the pattern of Garro's late fiction portraying displaced women: "mujeres [que] viven un lugar que no es el propio ni es permanente" (Persino, "Elena Garro"; women who live in a place that is neither their own nor permanent). Consuelo, the protagonist of *La casa junto al río*, returns to her native Spain after many years in exile, hoping to find a home and the solace of origins. More than any other work by Garro, *La casa junto al río* dramatizes the dilemmas of exile, for Consuelo is treated more like a stranger than as a prodigal daughter. Instead of finding loving relatives, she is soon trapped in a labyrinth set by intriguing townspeople who pretend to be related to her but seek only to rob her of her inheritance. In a heightened climate that evokes the chilling anxiety of *Reencuentro de personajes*, Consuelo is mercilessly persecuted and eventually killed while walking on the bridge leading to a legendary "house by the water." Resembling the tragic protagonist of "The Lady on Her Balcony," who reaches her beloved Nínive only after death, or Mariana, who makes a tragic leap to escape the abandonment of exile, Consuelo reenters the mythic dimension of her past at the moment of death.

The cycle of female destruction initiated in "¿Qué hora es?" in *La semana de colores* culminates in *Inés*, the destiny of whose eponymous character is determined by a phone call from a distant cousin. He tells her of an opportunity to work as a servant for don Javier, the rich patron by whom he is employed in Paris. Orphaned since childhood and living peacefully as a ward in a nunnery, Inés abandons her beloved Spain and the flowered patio of the convent for the fearsome walls of a Parisian mansion. Like Consuelo, Inés is soon ensnared in a trap not of her own making, and is unable to free herself because of her uncertain status in France. As a pariah and a female subject, she cannot escape the vigilant control of Ivette, the sadistic secretary of don Javier, who keeps tight control over her money and immigration papers. Inés soon realizes that the nocturnal activities of Javier and his flamboyant lover, Gina, are only a facade for a darker, more sinister reality. Rituals of demonic possession are presented only indirectly in the novel, narrated through Inés's radiant innocence, a focal point that serves to highlight the evil that chokes the protagonist. Her innate goodness also blocks the possibility of escape, as she cannot figure out a ruse that might allow her to break free of her confinement. While locating the dangerous passageways inside the house, Inés gains the help of Enríquez, an exiled Spanish Republican who reveals to her the duplicity of her master. From the outside, he appears as a high-class gentleman; yet, inside, he is truly evil. In this gothic tale of horror and intrigue, the memory of the Spanish convent's garden is the only solace Inés finds in an increasingly hostile environment:

*¡Estaba perdida! Recordaba su vida en España como un paraíso perdido para siempre. ¿Por qué no podía ver los muros sosegados de su convento ni la huerta verde en la que amaba trabajar? El olor a la tierra le llegó como una bocanada de santidad, perfumada de tomillo. ¿Por qué debía estar en aquel patio inhóspito y extraño?*

She was lost! She remembered her life in Spain like a paradise lost forever. Why could she not see the quiet walls of her convent or the green garden patch in which she loved to work? The smell of earth overpowered her like a breath of holiness, touched by a hint of thyme. Why did she have to stay in that hostile and strange courtyard?

Trapped in a repetitive chain of events, Inés befriends Irene, the unfortunate daughter of don Javier, who is violently thrown out of the house by her father and later abducted by his underlings. But though Inés shows solidarity with Irene, no one ever returns the gesture to her. In an effort to protect Irene from her father's wrath, Inés is abducted by don Javier's ring of thugs, taken to Gina's house, and severely beaten. These scenes of cruelty and horror are among the most gripping in Garro's writing, dramatizing the power of the abject and its hold on the human psyche. Converted into a sacrificial victim, Inés is subjected to ritual humiliations and forced to consume drugs, finding respite only during a brief interlude when Javier reconciles with his ex-wife, Paula. Though she holds the key to Inés's salvation, Paula herself is trapped, like many Garro heroines, within a closed circle of immobility and fear engendered by economic dependence and woman's traditionally subordinate role. Paula justifies her cowardly failure to save Inés because "El menor reparo, la menor rebeldía, le costaría un castigo grave. Lo sabía. Lo había experimentado muchos años y en tanto que Irene fuera menor de edad, su sujeción era completa" (The least hesitancy, the least rebellion, would put her in grave danger. She knew it. She had experienced it for many years and insofar as Irene was a minor, she was completely submissive). After a brutal experience of total dejection and despondency, Inés is found dead in a morgue; no one, not even her cousin, claims her body. A threshold in Garro's experimental fiction, *Inés* closes a narrative cycle—launched in *Andamos huyendo Lola* and followed by *Testimonios sobre Mariana* and *Reencuentro de personajes*—of persecuted women haunted by fear and flight.

Though the scene is Mexico, *Y Matarazo no llamó...* (1989; And Matarazo never showed) replicates the frightful climate of *Inés* while adding political overtones. The novella revolves around the eccentric Eugenio Yáñez, a solitary man minding his own business who inadvertently gets involved in a workers' strike. *Y Matarazo no llamó...* conveys the climate of terror surrounding the 1968 repression in Tlatelolco. A pair of strikers deposits a wounded man in Yáñez's Mexico City apartment; Yáñez is visited nightly by a somber character named Matarazo, who gives him cryptic instructions about what to do with the intruder. One night Matarazo fails to call, evoking the uncertainty of the title, and Yáñez flees to northern Mexico. After a police chase, he is taken back to Mexico City; there, in a dark cell, he encounters Matarazo, who like him is a victim of a political plot. Evoking the way Garro herself was framed after Tlatelolco, at the end both Matarazo and Yáñez are scapegoated by the two strikers, seemingly innocent idealists who have accused and betrayed them in order to save themselves.

The works that compose Garro's final literary output repeat the themes of her earlier period of fragmentation and exile, with the difference that they either substitute allegory for magical realism or close off the possibility of escape. The tale *Busca mi esquela*, collected in *Busca mi esquela y Primer amor* (1996; *First Love and Looking for My Obituary: Two Novellas*, 1997), opens with the possibility of love as an unhappily married man, Enrique, and a young girl in flight, Irene, find each other. At the end, however, Irene is forced to marry the boorish entrepreneur chosen by her family. Much like the elusive Mariana, Irene evades Enrique's efforts to locate her in Mexico City's urban maze. A coincidence of dates—Irene's birthday coincides with the death of Enrique's father—seals their union, according to the romantic creed which dictates that such a coincidence signifies they were destined for each other. The outcome of the story, however, subverts this expectation by showing that their love was doomed; in the final scene Enrique reads Irene's "obituary" in the society column: the announcement of her wedding to another man. Like Julia Andrade, Irene is "un ser irreal, un habitante de la lluvia, una criatura escapada del mar" (an unreal being, a resident of the rain, a sea creature escaped from the waters). Echoing the destruction of the female subject traced in *Testimonios sobre Mariana*, *Busca mi esquela* sensitively draws a picture of a man who is "víctima de un destino fatal" (victim of a fatal destiny).

In "Invitación al campo" (An invitation to a day in the country), a short story included in *El accidente y otros cuentos inéditos* (1997; The accident and other unpublished stories), the fatality of personal destiny is thrust upon the entire nation, forging an allegory for the frustration of Mexican political life after sixty years under the ruling party. In this hauntingly beautiful story, a wise, middle-aged woman is invited to tour the countryside with a high-ranking government official, a tour that illustrates the omnipotence of the state even in remote corners of the Mexican countryside. Cruising in "el ministro's" luxurious limousine, the woman is amazed at the repetitive occurrence of the same events. Every time the car draws near a town, it is stopped by three of the official's henchmen. In each case the Indian community comes out to greet the minister, carrying a long list of claims, demands, and recriminations. Every time, their ancient rage is subdued by empty promises of reform emitted by government officials resembling an impersonal and invisible power. In a final twist typical of Garro's implacable irony, we realize at the conclusion that the silent chauffeur who has led the fateful tour is a *campesino* (rural) leader whose death has already been determined by the wrathful minister. This surprise ending not only negates the attempts of the oppressed natives to redress their history, but also effectively silences the female historical witness, for she is either unwilling or unable to speak out against this outrage. By seemingly denying both the Indians' and the woman's historical agency, their ability to affect change, Garro reclaims these hidden voices in the magical texture of the tale, which evokes the lyrical quality of "It's the Fault of the Tlaxcaltecas."

Unrequited love, or the fate of star-crossed lovers, was a constant in Garro's literary production. With its magical setting at a village festival, "La feria, o, De noche vienes" (Festival time, or, You come only at night)—the third story in the collection *La vida empieza a las tres*—captures a bit of the mystery of "La semana de colores." Set in northern Mexico, the story follows Andrés as he rejects his real-life girlfriend, Carmen, in order to pursue a mysterious woman in white who appears to him at the festival. Claiming to be the real Carmen, this ideal woman—who by her beauty evokes the brunette seductress of *El Encanto, tendajón mixto*—remains forever beyond his grasp: "*¿Había sufrido una alucinación? . . .* [italics added] Caminó por la feria abigarrada en busca de aquella mujer apenas entrevista como un cometa*" (*Did he have a hallucination? . . .* He walked through the crowded fair in search of that

nearly imperceptible woman, as if she were a comet). Toward the end of the story, he thinks he finds her in the wife of Marcial Pastrana—a relative of the first Carmen who is also the governor of the province, and she seduces him in a manner reminiscent of his first encounter with the mysterious woman. Their furtive meetings occur only at night and Andrés—unaware of her identity as the wife of the governor—reproaches her. Even after the surprise ending, when the governor eliminates Andrés at an official ball, we do not know the true identity of the woman in white. Whether or not she was always the governor's wife, or if Andrés only believed her to be, is unclear, reflecting Garro's belief in a feminine ideal that cannot be fully incarnated in flesh.

The title story of *Un corazón en un bote de basura* (1996) reads as a swan song to romantic love while also conveying a sense of disillusionment at the political fate of post–World War II Europe. The novella is set in Paris, where the beautiful Ursula is pursued by a trio of hapless lovers: the penniless Hungarian, Dimitri, associated with a group of exiled Slavs; Alfonso, her rich ex-husband who still propositions her; and André, a dandy with no other occupation than allowing Ursula to luxuriate in his bath. In a faux tale of intrigue, Ursula debates her fate as she goes off first with one lover and then another, only to discover a mysterious man wearing an astrakhan hat stalking her. Thinking that she is threatened by a trap, Ursula runs off with Dimitri. Meanwhile, the reader is informed that the mystery man was a ploy in her ex-husband's scheme to get her to return to him. Whereas the fanciful ending contrasts with the heavy, somber tone of *Inés*, the coupling of amorous intrigue with the power of evil links both works to Garro's posthumous novel, *My hermanita Magdalena* (1998), a fitting end to the author's narrative enterprise.

Set in Paris and Switzerland, *Mi hermanita Magdalena* narrates the itinerant destinies of two sisters, one of whom—Magdalena—has married the dashing Enrique merely to challenge parental authority. Fearing that Magdalena was abducted, their father sends young Estefanía to follow her lost sister's steps in Paris. In the meantime Enrique's mother, doña Justa, insinuates herself at Magdalena's family's dinner table. Her daily visits seem to provoke a chain of events that forces the family to leave Mexico. While in Paris, Estefanía meets members of Parisian high society and then moves with her sister to Ascona, Switzerland, where they are soon enmeshed in a series of plots and subterfuges involving such eccentric characters as a Bolivian homosexual guru and a Hungarian professor. Ever the master stylist, Garro makes this novel of intrigue a fascinating puzzle, for the reader must unravel the secret identity of Enrique, who is at the service of a gang of Algerian terrorists. At the end the two sisters outsmart Enrique and doña Justa, managing to arrange Magdalena's divorce just in time for her to marry her dashing German sweetheart, Helmut, in a Gothic cathedral. This happy ending counters the haunting downfall of *Inés,* where neoromance triumphs over melodrama in depicting women's destinies.

Though on the surface Garro's fiction offers no solution to woman's agency—her capacity to act, either as an individual or as a member of a national enclave—her work nevertheless revolves around the theme of female identity and archetypes. From the elusive Mariana to the precocious Magdalena, woman's psyche remains resilient and defiant, though subject to persecution, violence, and control. Unable to fit into patriarchal categories, woman's subjectivity, Garro seems to say, must be defined in her own terms, her own time, and her own language.

The story of Elena Garro's role in Mexican literary history is beginning to be told by critics like Lucía Melgar, who discovered in the archive of Garro's correspondence the extent of her involvement in the peasant movement as well as her marginalization in the aftermath of Tlatelolco. An intriguing chapter in this larger tale is the ambivalent relationship that other contemporary Mexican women novelists have forged with Garro's legacy. Elena Poniatowska, for one, reads Garro's later fiction as a literal staging of her life with Paz, while casting Garro herself in unflattering terms. Her "wandering" fictions, from *Reencuentro de personajes* to *Mi hermanita Magdalena,* speak, rather, to woman's fate as a nomad from her private world of dreams, desires, and longings. Ultimately, the key to Garro's position in Mexican literary history may resemble the fate of the white Russians who populate her fictions like

phantoms of the past. The images of Slavic characters haunt her later fiction as living witnesses both to the ravages of history and to its hope. From exile to prodigal daughter, Elena Garro emerges as a paradox in Mexican letters, but her rich store of magic books will surely enthrall generations of readers.

## SELECTED BIBLIOGRAPHY

### Primary Works

#### Novels and Short Stories

*Los recuerdos del porvenir.* Mexico City: Joaquín Mortiz, 1963. 2d ed., 1977.

*La semana de colores.* Xalapa, Mexico: Universidad Veracruzana, 1964.

*Andamos huyendo Lola.* Mexico City: Joaquín Mortiz, 1980.

*Testimonios sobre Mariana.* Mexico City: Grijalbo, 1981.

*Reencuentro de personajes.* Mexico City: Grijalbo, 1982.

*La casa junto al río.* Barcelona: Grijalbo, 1983.

*Y Matarazo no llamó . . . .* Mexico City: Grijalbo, 1989.

*Inés.* Mexico City: Grijalbo, 1995.

*Busca mi esquela y Primer amor.* Monterrey, Mexico: Ediciones Castillo, 1996.

*Un corazón en un bote de basura.* Mexico City: Joaquín Mortiz, 1996.

*Un traje rojo para un duelo.* Monterrey, Mexico: Ediciones Castillo, 1996.

*El accidente y otros cuentos inéditos.* Mexico City: Seix Barral, 1997.

*La vida empieza a las tres: Hoy es jueves; La feria, o, De noche vienes.* Monterrey, Mexico: Ediciones Castillo, 1997.

*Mi hermanita Magdalena.* Monterrey, Mexico: Ediciones Castillo, 1998.

#### Theater

*Un hogar sólido y otras piezas en un acto.* Xalapa, Mexico: Universidad Veracruzana, 1958.

"La dama boba." *Revista de la Escuela de Arte Teatral* 6:77–126 (1963).

*El árbol.* Mexico City: Raphael Peregrina, 1967.

"Los perros." In *Doce obras en un acto.* Edited by Wilberto Cantón. Mexico City: Ecuador, 1967.

*Felipe Ángeles.* Mexico City: Difusión Cultural, Universidad Nacional Autónoma de México, 1979.

"Perfecto Luna." In *Puerta abierta: La nueva escritora latinoamericana.* Edited by Caridad L. Silva-Velázquez and Nora Erro-Orthman. Mexico City: Joaquín Mortiz, 1986. Pp. 131–139.

*La señora en su balcón.* Mexico City: Consejo Nacional para la Cultura y las Artes, 1994.

## Nonfiction

"A mí me ha ocurrido todo al revés." *Cuadernos Hispanoamericanos* 346:38–51 (April 1979).

*Memorias de España.* Mexico City: Siglo Veintiuno, 1992.

*Revolucionarios mexicanos.* Mexico City: Seix Barral, 1997.

## Translations

*Recollections of Things to Come.* Trans. by Ruth L. C. Simms. Austin: University of Texas Press, 1969.

"It's the Fault of the Tlaxcaltecas." In *Other Fires: Short Fiction by Latin American Women.* Edited and trans. by Alberto Manguel. New York: Clarkson N. Potter, 1986. Pp. 159–178.

"The Dogs." Trans. by Beth Miller. In *A Different Reality: Studies on the Work of Elena Garro.* Edited by Anita K. Stoll. Lewisburg, Pa.: Bucknell University Press, 1990. Pp. 68–79.

"The Lady on Her Balcony." Trans. by Beth Miller. In *A Different Reality: Studies on the Work of Elena Garro.* Edited by Anita K. Stoll. Lewisburg, Pa: Bucknell University Press, 1990. Pp. 59–68.

"Perfecto Luna." Trans. by Cynthia Steele. In *Beyond the Border: A New Age in Latin American Women's Fiction.* Edited by Nora Erro-Peralta and Caridad Silva-Núñez. San Francisco: Cleis Press, 1991. Pp. 80–87.

*First Love and Look for My Obituary.* Trans. by David Unger. Willimantic, Conn.: Curbstone Press, 1997.

## Secondary Works

### Bibliographies

Mora, Gabriela. "Elena Garro." In *Women Writers of Spanish America: An Annotated Bio-Bibliographical Guide.* Edited by Diane Marting. Westport, Conn.: Greenwood Press, 1987. Pp. 151–153.

Stoll, Anita. "Elena Garro." In *Spanish American Women Writers: A Bio-Bibliographical Source Book.* Edited by Diana Marting. Westport, Conn.: Greenwood Press, 1990. Pp. 199–209.

### Critical and Biographical Studies

Anderson, Robert K. "La realidad temporal en *Los recuerdos del porvenir.*" *Explicación de Textos Literarios* 9:25–29 (1980–1981).

Biron, Rebecca. "*Testimonios sobre Mariana*: Representación y la otra mujer." In *Sin imágenes falsas, sin falsos espejos: Narradoras mexicanas del siglo XX.* Edited by Aralia López González. Mexico City: Colegio de México, 1995. Pp. 161–183.

———. "The Eccentric Elena Garro: Critical Confrontations in the 1960s." *Torre de Papel* 10, no. 2:102–117 (summer 2000).

Callan, Richard J. "Elena Garro's 'El Encanto, Tendajón Mixto': The Magical Woman and Maturity." *Crítica Hispánica* 14, nos. 1–2:49–57 (1992).

Dauster, Frank. "Elena Garro y sus *Recuerdos del porvenir.*" *Journal of Spanish Studies: Twentieth Century* 8:57–65 (spring–fall 1980).

Duncan, Cynthia. " 'La culpa es de los tlaxcaltecas': A Reevaluation of Mexico's Past Through Myth." *Crítica Hispánica* 7, no. 2:121–127 (1985).

Feman Orenstein, Gloria. "Surrealism and Women: The Occultation of the Goddess: Elena Garro, Joyce Mansour, Leonora Carrington." In her *The Theater of the Marvelous: Surrealism and the Contemporary Stage.* New York: New York University Press, 1975. Pp. 99–147.

Franco, Jean. *Plotting Women: Gender and Representation in Mexico.* New York: Columbia University Press, 1989.

Gallo, Marta. "Entre el poder y la gloria: Disyuntiva de la identidad femenina en *Los recuerdos del porvenir.*" In *Sin imágenes falsas, sin falsos espejos: Narradoras mexicanas del siglo XX.* Edited by Aralia López González. Mexico City: Colegio de México, 1995. Pp. 149–160.

Jones, Julie. "Text and Authority in Elena Garro's *Reencuentro de personajes.*" *Canadian Review of Comparative Literature* 18, no. 1: 41–50 (March 1991).

Kaminsky, Amy. *Reading the Body Politic: Feminist Criticism and Latin American Women Writers.* Minneapolis: University of Minnesota Press, 1993. Pp. 77–95.

Melgar Palacios, Lucía. "Relectura desde la piedra: Ambigüedad, violencia y género en *Los recuerdos del porvenir* de Elena Garro." In *Pensamiento y crítica: Los discursos de la cultura hoy.* Edited by Javier Durán, Rosaura Hernández Monroy, and Manuel Medina. Mexico City: Michigan State University Press, Louisville University Press, and Casa Lamm, 2000. Pp. 58–73.

————, ed. "Elena Garro: Testigo y recreadora de su tiempo." *Torre de Papel* 10, no. 2 (summer 2000).

————. "Writing Dark Times: Elena Garro, Writing and Politics." Working Paper no. 5. Princeton, N.J.: Program in Latin American Studies, Princeton University, November 2000.

Méndez Rodenas, Adriana. "Tiempo femenino, tiempo ficticio: *Los recuerdos del porvenir* de Elena Garro." *Revista Iberoamericana* 51: 843–851 (July–December 1985).

Messinger Cypess, Sandra. "Visual and Verbal Distances in Mexican Theater: The Plays of Elena Garro." In *Woman as Myth and Metaphor in Latin American Literature.* Edited by Carmelo Virgillo and Naomi Lindstrom. Columbia: University of Missouri Press, 1985. Pp. 44–62.

————. "The Figure of La Malinche in the Texts of Elena Garro." In *A Different Reality: Studies on the Work of Elena Garro.* Edited by Anita K. Stoll. Lewisburg, Pa.: Bucknell University Press, 1990. Pp. 117–135.

Parkinson Zamora, Lois. *The Usable Past: The Imagination of History in Recent Fiction of the Americas.* Cambridge: Cambridge University Press, 1997.

Paz, Octavio. *El laberinto de la soledad.* Mexico City: Fondo de Cultura Económica, 1959.

Persino, María Silvina. "Elena Garro: La mirada vigilante." In *Hacia una poética de la mirada: Mario Vargas Llosa, Juan Marsé, Elena Garro, Juan Goytisolo.* Buenos Aires: Ediciones Corregidor, 1999. Pp. 101–129.

Poniatowska, Elena. "Elena Garro y sus tormentas." In *Baúl de recuerdos: Homenaje a Elena Garro.* Edited by Mara L. García and Robert K. Anderson. Mexico City: Universidad Autónoma de Tlaxcala, 1999. Pp. 5–15.

Rosas Lopátegui, Patricia, and Rhina Toruño. "Entrevista a Elena Garro." *Hispamérica: Revista de Literatura* 60:51–67 (1991).

————. *Yo sólo soy memoria: Biografía visual de Elena Garro.* Monterrey, Mexico: Ediciones Castillo, 2000.

Seligson, Esther. "*In Illo Tempore* (Aproximaciones a la obra de Elena Garro)." *Revista de la Universidad de México* 29:9–10 (August 1975).

Taylor, Kathy. *The New Narrative of Mexico: Sub-versions of History in Mexican Fiction.* Lewisburg, Pa.: Bucknell University Press, 1994.

Unruh, Vicky. "(Free)/Plays of Difference: Language and Eccentricity in Elena Garro's Theater." In *A Different Reality: Studies on the Work of Elena Garro.* Edited by Anita K. Stoll. Lewisburg, Pa.: Bucknell University Press, 1990. Pp. 38–58.

*Films Based on the Works of Elena Garro*

*Juego de mentiras o La venganza de la criada.* Screenplay by Archibaldo Burns. Directed by Archibaldo Burns. Cinematográfica Astro, 1967.

*Los recuerdos del porvenir.* Screenplay by Julio Alejandro and Arturo Ripstein, Jr. Directed by Arturo Ripstein, Jr. Imperial Films Internacional, César Santos Galindo, and Alfredo Ripstein, Jr., 1968.

# Alberto Girri

## (1919–1991)

## *Saul Yurkievich*

Alberto Girri created an austere poetry, rigorously clean-edged. He stripped his verb of flesh, divested it of sensuous seductions, melodious sentimentality, fantastic flights. He created a lean, dry poetry. Endowed with strict conceptual pacing, his poems cogitate, argue, are inclined more to reflection than to representation, to "the sense, more than the beauty of the apples." His poetic act, a speculative investigation in pursuit of the clear statement and an exact representation of the signified thing, usually ends in a value judgment, and often in diagnosis or dictum. The seductiveness of his work arises from that discourse which imprints itself on memory, from a precise and pondered coursing through time. Gnomic (aphoristic) poetry such as Girri wrote fosters an analytical approach to each thing it judges. This requires a syntax of strict articulation, the lucid eloquence of baroque casuistry (more that of John Donne and the English metaphysical poets than that of Francisco de Quevedo or Baltasar Gracián). Forgoing the task of individuating, of personalizing his writing, the lyric locutor here preserves an objective distance, rarely announcing himself in the first person. His aphoristic verses preserve, without flattery or euphony or meter, a vigorous contention. His pace is not rhythmic—melodious but ideographic; his verses form separate units of sense and are linked together in meditative sequences.

Girri's poetry presents, describes, defines, and evaluates a referent that is half literal and half literary, half real and half textual. That is, a world where literature is an indispensable mediator for apprehending and making sense of the world, a world where books constitute a component of equal or greater importance than phenomenological occurrences. Literature and art, for Girri, are unavoidable filters or screens that condition and shape our relationship with ourselves, with others, and with the other; they are the redemption or the dregs of what is experienced. Girri discourses within a palpable and permanent intertextuality: he evokes and invokes writers of every language and every epoch. His bond with the world, with and through the literati and the citation of authorities, is often a work of endorsement and examination.

In Argentina, Alberto Girri is generally considered to be a renowned exponent or paradigm of the Generation of 1940, often referred to as "the 40," a broad term including poets born between 1903 and 1930, united by an epochal manner and certain esthetic affinities. Among the best known members of this group are Enrique Molina, Olga Orozco, Silvina Ocampo, and Juan Rodolfo Wilcock, the polyglot poet par excellence, the masterful translator into Spanish of T. S. Eliot's *Four Quartets*. The post avant-garde Eliot was to have a fundamental influence, as both a writer and ecumenic figure, on

Girri's work. Under the aegis of the "ultra," transplanted from Madrid by Jorge Luis Borges, the avant-garde revolt exploded in Buenos Aires in the 1920s. At that time, the avant-garde acquired a vernacular aspect, and its adepts adopted the paradoxical group name Martín Fierro.

After a time lapse of two decades, the virulence of the avant-garde moderated and gave way to a return to the traditional order by that anomalous and numerous Generation of 1940. This generation reacted against the compulsive innovation proclaimed by the avant-garde, against its rigorous militancy, against its transgressions, aggressions, and derision, against its excessive exercise of liberties in writing. The poets of the 40 were to eschew the esthetics of the dissimilar, the discontinuous, the fragmentary, rejecting permanent change and constant experimentation. Their nay-sayings and rejections allows them to be characterized as much in a national context as in an international one.

The poets of the 40, neither heterodox nor apocalyptic, sought to have poetry recover its specific pride, its power of exaltation and catharsis, its excellence and its transcendence. The poets returned to traditional patterns and to canonical models. Invention was displaced by tradition and by widespread and eclectic translation. In accordance with his literary group and in the spirit of the magazine *Sur (South)*, on which he collaborated, Girri was an active and frequent translator. He translated English poetry with William Shand and Italian poetry with Carlos Viola Soto. He published poems of Wallace Stevens and Robert Lowell in the book *Quince poetas norteamericanos* (1966; Fifteen North American poets), John Donne's *Devotions* (1970), and Edgar Lee Masters' *Spoon River Anthology* (1974). From *El ojo* (1963; The eye) onward, and under the title "Versiones" (Versions), Girri usually ended his books with a section of poems that he had translated, thereby assimilating them, by means of this pouring of others' wine into his own bottles, into his own writing. Girri believed translation is a poetic act of a character and rank similar to the act of creation. To him, creation and translation are complementary transfers and transformations of a single circulatory system, of a single *organon* of signs.

Refined and cosmopolitan, circumspect and prudent, following international literary fashions, the learned poets of the 40 adopted models of assured worth and, contrary to the boldness of the avant-garde, promoted rhetorical, prosodic, and lexical retro-action. What predominated in them, as in Girri, was a euphuistic extraterritorial reinvigoration. Like the modernist poets, those of the 40 reunited muse and museum. Devoted to citation and mentioning sources, they exhibited an ostentatious bibliophilia in their texts. Girri invoked, evoked, and paraphrased his most beloved authors: Homer, Dante, Blake, Byron, Shelley, Keats, Mallarmé, Eliot, Auden, Michaux. In his poem "Literati" from *El ojo* he declares his supreme literary aspiration, his gamble on all or nothing:

> *Ser Proust, Henry James, Valéry,*
> *o no ser nadie,*
> *ser Baudelaire*
> *o no escribir ninguna línea. . . .*

> To be Proust, Henry James, Valéry,
> or to be no one,
> to be Baudelaire
> or not to write a line. . . .

According to Girri, attainment of the splendor of a masterwork requires assumption of the voracity and tenacity of Balzac's effort or Flaubert's arduous struggles, or, failing that, to submit to sinking without bitterness into an amiable struggle with the average and to settle down to a paltry fecundity.

The list of references to poets that Girri included in his poems is extensive. To it must be added the list of translated poets clustered at the end of each poetry collection, in the final "Versiones" section. This list includes Auden and Eliot, as well as Wallace Stevens (a trio with a prosy tendency that has exercised a well-known influence on Girri's mature style), and Gerard Manley Hopkins, Robert Graves, and Eugenio Montale. Girri directly shows us his library, his biographical nursery, the nutrient source that nourished his own work, the authors who incited his writings, the paragons he emulated. This bibliophilia explains why his poetry exhibits a reverent dependence on the vast collection of culture that humanity has amassed during historical millennia. Girri wanted to deprive of authority the romantic myth of miraculous creativity ex nihilo, of inspired autogenesis, and so stated his own genesis clearly: the factors of insemination and the forms of contamination, the heritages and transfers, the tree of his literary genealogy. He declared his indebtedness to the universal library, which knowingly borrows, paraphrases, emulates, imitates, which writes starting from what is already written and in conformity with what is "writable." Girri recognized himself as a manipulator of an ancient art that is combinatorial, rhetorical, and sophistic, and in his craft he recognized his position as disciple, as tributary.

In *Notas sobre la experiencia poética* (1983; Notes on the poetic experience), in order to justify the abundance of overarchingly literary and artistic cultural references in his poetry, Girri evoked T. S. Eliot and Ezra Pound as the authenticators of this course. For Girri, this characteristic of contemporary poetry was not mere rhetoric or vain erudition, but a redeemer of values that can underpin the poem in an epoch of crisis and chaos, a reparatory procedure to avoid general disorganization and especially disorganization in the arts, sunk into self-destruction. Girri believed the most real of our reality is art, the privileged access road to the real per se:

> El mundo de los valores culturales y artísticos, posee una realidad infinitamente más verdadera que la de la vida corriente . . . un texto de Catulo, una pintura de Ñnet, están más presentes y vivos en nuestros gestos diarios, que en ciertosentido son espectrales, pues estamos presos del fantaseo negativo de n uestra mente, condicionada por hábitos de todo tipo.
> ("El poeta en su crítico" [The poet through his criticism], *Notas sobre la experiencia poética*)

> The world of cultural and artistic values possesses a reality infinitely more true than that of ordinary life . . . a text of Catullus, a painting of Ñnet, is more present and alive in our daily gestures than the certainly felt specters which are prisoners of the negative phantasy of our minds, conditioned by customs of every kind.

Not only did Girri indicate his poetic sources, not only did he engage in dialogue or start a polemic with his poetic rhetorical masters, but he also commented and argued with philosophers, with Plotinus, Berkeley, Pascal, and Wittgenstein, who framed his intellectual reference points, who limned the transit of Girri across the history of ideas, who located that transit in positions defined with respect to a certain horizon of consciousness. Girri, a thoughtful, speculative, disquisitive poet, manifested an expressed philosophical inquietude that always resounded in his poems. In the manner of Nietzsche, Bergson, or Heidegger, his poetic enunciation approached philosophy, and problematic matters were not distinguished if, in Girri's view, they are alike: being and time, word and world, soul and body, thought and existence, humanity and animality. In the same way, Girri did not establish any basic difference between prose and verse; he did not believe he could have a language proper to just one or the other form. Girri did separate the appropriate word from the inappropriate, the relevant from the irrelevant, and, in order to blur the prosodic boundary, he wrote a prose poetry that bore the title "Prosas" (Prose pieces), the second versified section of *En la letra, ambigua selva* (1972; In literature, ambiguous jungle), which included the poem called "Prosa textual" (Prose text).

Nature, incarnate in our own bodies, which weigh and attract, in the animal that precedes and constitutes us, revealing to us the immediacy of elemental perceptions, is an ever-present mystery, applying its force but nonetheless inscrutable. We are definitively separated from it because we cannot comprehend it; we remain imprisoned in the house of the mind; ineluctable mental mediation separates us from our nature and from the world. As in the vision of Borges, for whom reality and reason were definitively divorced, Girri thought that the mirror of literature confines us, that it interferes with and constricts all experience, which is beyond words. Girri, simultaneously both stubbornly cultured and contemptuous of the cultural, felt himself vocationally and fatally a man of letters, his work prodigal with connections and bookish linkages in an overample intertextuality that at once expands and encloses it.

The cultural scope and, more specifically, the esthetic in which Girri operated is inhabited by both writers and painters. Girri always brought verbal art into close proximity with the plastic arts ("*ut pictora poesis*"), finding that formal iconic stimulation is transferable from one to the other, finding the corporeal configuration of visible and tangible matter transferable to the fantastic order of symbolic figurations projected by language. And the pictorial delight of Hieronymus Bosch, Miguel Angel, Breughel, Hokusai, Monet, Picasso, Modigliani, the delight that Fresnaye or Klee had in such prodigiality, at times incited a verbal version of the visible, at times incited a moral, a deductive commentary:

Contrapunto
entre lo que muestran las figuras
y una pasión moral
a la que jamás se le ocurriría
condenar un acto por sí,
 sea el del mendigo tras su limosna

. . . . . . . . . . . . . .

sea el ciego guiado por ciegos,
sea el triunfo de la muerte
en el famélico perro que la canta
junto a la sequedad de las bocas,
las temblorosas manos, la densa
e intensa música del postrer segundo
con los que sin hablar
palpan en el que agoniza
su personal, idéntica sentencia.

("Ejercicios con Breughel" [Exercises
with Breughel], El ojo)

Counterpoint
between what the figures show
and a moral passion
to which would never occur
condemnation of an act per se,
be it of the beggar following his alms

. . . . . . . . . . . . . .

be it the blind leading the blind,
be it the triumph of death
in the starving dog who sings it
together with dry mouths,
trembling hands, the dense
and intense music of the last second
of those who without speaking
throb in agony
over its personal, identical sentence.

Girri's progress from *Playa sola* (1946; Lonely beach) to *El ojo* is clear. By means of step-by-step demolition, by retention, by concentration, by weighing himself down, Girri succeeded in settling himself into the word that was most appropriate to his strict decorum, into the proverbial word corresponding to his inquisitive

rigor. Let us retrace the phases of his growth, follow it in the soaring flight that results in that art of figurative conception or of conceptual figuring which will later be converted into his personal matrix, into that aphoristic elocution which is his mark of literary identity.

Girri started from overabundance, from fervent grandiloquence, from lexical diversification, from iconic heaps, from tonal highs and lows, from flowing prosody, from resounding effusiveness, long verses, expansive developments, verbosity. Poetry that is eruptive or high-flown is compelled by a pathetic "I" that craves to monopolize the voice, to refer to itself, to express itself, to extend itself, that struggles to overflow. Centripetal ego seeks to manifest itself to the utmost by means of a turbulent monologue that registers like a seismograph the disturbances of an afflicted consciousness. The poem is absorbed by the crowded vision of the rhapsodist:

No te quiero como una mancha inerme entre
 dos fechas
con los habituales testigos que componen toda historia
disueltos en la cruz de la ventana—transida vena.
No es el amor ni es negocio del alma,
es un agradecimiento dispar y sin rigor,
redención parapetada en los atardeceres
que demora el aire muerto de los espejos,
mi orgullo esquivo
y tu aliento mojando la ciudad dormida y admirable.
No es el amor ni es negocio del alma,
es la acción particular del tiempo,
y debes saberlo,
porque las horas que declaro ciertas
estaban gobernadas por el único metal que escucha:
el fuego.

("El amor" [Love], Playa sola)

I do not love you like a disarmed patch between
 two dates
with the usual witnesses that comprise all history
dissolved in the cross of the window—a
 pinched vein.
This is not Love nor is it the business of the soul,
it is a thankfulness unlike and without rigor,
a protected redemption in the late afternoons
which holds off the dead air of mirrors,
my pride scornful
and your breath drenching the dormant
 admirable city.
This is not Love nor is it the business of the soul,

it is the particular action of time and weather,
and you should know,
because the hours that I declare certain
are governed by the only metal that listens:
fire.

This poem expands upon the confession of an eloquent ego that demonstrates its confusion, its exaltation. The troubled "I" inscribes its psychic disturbances, registers the record of its heart, its deceit, and its affliction of love. It enlarges on and expands its passion, tumultuously putting into play phantasmagoric metaphors, the capricious casuistry of the reasoning (or lack of it) of love. A torrid torrential surrealism here makes an alliance with the cult of the lady that derives from troubadour lyrics.

In *Coronación de la espera* (1947; Coronation of hope), the elegiac canto variously exalts and execrates the adventures, ventures, and misadventures of the erotic relationship. The poem acts like a seismograph or stethoscope, marking the oscillations of devotion: agreements, disagreements, occurrences, and incidents of emotional anxiety. The clamor or the lament (*pianto,* or "cry") aims not only to move the woman addressed; by romantic amplification it overflows into a universal disturbance.

This early poetry by Girri, bombastic and abundantly extroverted, affects overemphasis, rapture, and fantastic magnificence, it charges the scene of the poem with the prodigality of an imagination freed to follow its own impetus; it conceives metaphors from extraordinary connections and summons the supernatural:

> *Allá donde las vocaciones infantiles que sirven*
> *la soledad*
> *miran irritadas como en lugar de sortijas*
> *el azar, el ocio, la intangible venda del amor,*
> *les coloca sombras lánguidas de niñas*
> *para recibir dignamente la sed que se inaugura,*
> *el ángel (se adivina su gracia de ciego),*
> *rendida sólo a la blanca codicia de perderse*
> *o devastarse contra un hombro.*
> *Lo demás, collar vergonzoso de palabras,*
> *flechas lanzadas hacia prostituciones*
> *y engaños,*
> *y uniones criminales,*

> *y bien dotados hechizos para tranquilizar a los poetas,*
> *conservémoslo también.*
>
> ("El agradecido" [The grateful],
> *Coronación de la espera*)

> There, where the childish vocations that serve
> solitude
> are watching irritated as instead of ringlets
> the accident, the idling, the intangible
> blindfold of love
> locates the languid graces of girls so that they
> may receive with dignity the thirst being unveiled,
> is the angel (its grace of blindness divined),
> attentive only to the white cupidity of self-loss
> or self-destruction against a man.
> The rest, a shameful chain of words,
> arrows launched at prostitutions
> and deceits,
> and criminal unions,
> and well-spelled charms to tranquilize poets,
> let us also preserve.

Thus Girri abandoned himself to the conjunctive energy of an imagination which, freed to its maximum willfulness, disrespectful of the distinctions and separations of the empirical real, imposed its prolific impulse, its zeal for coupling.

In his early books Girri chose (or incurred) lexical disparity, shifting within a single poem among very diverse zones and language levels, introducing in more linguistically elegant contexts cultist idioms of the region of the Río de la Plata (the region encompassing Buenos Aires and La Plata, Argentina, and Montevideo, Uruguay) or obvious neologisms of extreme resonance. These works display many stylistic reminiscences of Girri's immediate mentors, the poets of the Martín Fierro group, and above all of Borges. He soon drew back, however, circumscribing his idiomatic agents to the area traditionally considered proper to literature. He reduced his vocabulary to the prestigious domain of the elevated style, planted his poems in the area traditionally allowed to the lyrical genre. He revered the assured, protective authority of illustrious models, and these are omnipresent in his writings and frequently invoked in his recognition of them as his literary ancestors.

Soon Girri showed that he had become a literary poet who accepted the condition inherent in a poem, that it is a verbal stratagem, a specific type of linguistic intervention that presupposes a certain technical competency and that proposes to model, to configure, a perceptive order subject to its own requirements. He accepted not only what a poem implies of artifice and fiction, but also that which gives a special ardor to the literary temper of the text.

In Girri, literariness is doubly manifest, both as a game of reflections, as calls and echoes rendered through resources of stylization which denaturalize the poem in order to accentuate its condition as an esthetic entity, and through reiterated references to the literary sources that act as sponsor to his work. Girri reverently and fiercely took up his memorable heritage, which he indicated by expressly pointing out his situation as a persistent tributary, a memorialist of the history of art and literature. Under the advocacy of his patrons, he wrote a poetry that is not only furnished from them, that emulates them formally and thematically, that transcribes them, but that also makes them reappear as principal personnel on the page, in poems that carry in their titles the names of their motivators. Examples of such poems include "A Thomas de Quincey" (To Thomas de Quincey), "Baudelaire," "San Agustín hubiera visto en mi" (Saint Augustine may have seen into me), "Byron revisited," "G. S." (Gertrude Stein), and "Auden, 1934," in *Coronación de la espera*.

Girri wrote a literature devoted to borrowing, to the explicit citation of authorities, as in "A unas líneas de San Juan de la Cruz recordadas en la mañana del 20 de mayo de 1964" (On some lines of Saint John of the Cross remembered on the morning of 20 May 1964), or implicit citation, as in "Pro Michaux" (For Michaux). His work was presented as the agent of an intertextual relationship, as one of the possible crossroads of texts drawn from all provenances, including sources as disparate as the Bible, Catullus, Paracelsus, Lao Tse, and Yeats.

After the always-starting-from-zero and tabula rasa approach that had been proclaimed by the avant-garde in its desire to recover a vital immediacy, after the "latest" word, after the explosion of language that the avant-garde provoked in order to adapt it to the transforming insanity of our era, Girri, in a manner similar to what was also generally happening in European literature, re-established a creative connection with Hispano-American poets Octavio Paz and José Lezama Lima. Like Rubén Darío, Leopoldo Lugones, and then Borges, Girri practiced a trans-historic, trans-geographic, and trans-linguistic poetry, representing in his poetry a kind of polyglot universal memory of the cultural legacy of humanity.

From that ideal reservoir, Girri extracted with euphuistic fruition the bulk of his symbolic material. From that warehouse of paradigms came the mythic and the magic-religious, those archetypical seducers that literature, by imaginatively bringing them forth, expropriates and reanimates. In *Propiedades de la magia* (1959; Properties of magic), Girri parodies the hermetic books, arcane manipulations, talismans, cabalistic formulas, magic circle, and lodestone in order to elaborate his own magical book:

> *Trazado con carbones*
> *y encerrando un cuadrado,*
> *un triángulo,*
> *una piedra imán*
> *un sello*
> *donde se lee un nombre,*
> *dos talismanes*
> *y un castillo ruinoso,*
> *es la ruta cabalística*
> *de la eternidad,*
> *el infinito, el espacio,*
> *lo desconocido,*
> *del tiempo, de lo oculto,*
> *de las apelaciones*
> *y despedidas de los genios.*
>     ("Círculo" [Circle], *Propiedades de la magia*)

> Traced with coal
> and encircling a square,
> a triangle,
> a lodestone
> a seal
> whereon is read a name,
> two talismans
> and a falling-down castle,
> is the cabalistic route
> of eternity,
> infinity, space,
> the unknown,
> of time, of the occult,
> of the appeals
> and farewells of the daemon.

Girri availed himself of the aura, of the power of wonder found in mysticism and myth, of occult bewitchment, of resonators of the profound and remote. He used them for the mytho-poetic power of demonology and angiology (the study of blood circulation), transferring these thaumaturgies (workings of miracles) to the esthetic Eden. Although these transports, transformed into literary ritual and eventually reduced to a simulacrum of the sacred and esoteric, do not presuppose belief, do not credit a more intimate adherence, they nonetheless imply Girri's personal propensity toward the religious, a metaphysical inquietude that is projected toward the transcendental. Girri's moral preoccupation colluded with the divine. His moral reasoning approached theology:

*No sé el fondo, la naturaleza de mi ministerio, pero me basta con servir, y florar la tentación de los desobedientex que quisieron bastarse con la inteligencia. Feliz en la fuente de la verdad, sin la persunción, sin la excusa que busca lo ilusoriamente amoroso para engañar y engañarme; gozando de Aquel que no tiene comienzo porque está y estuvo en mi piedra, en mi color, en el origen de mi forma, en el que concociéndose a sí mismo y neqándose talló mi imagen en la piedra.*

("No sé el fondo" [I do not know the basis], *Examen de nuestra causa* [1956; Examination of our cause])

I do not know the basis, the nature of my ministry, but it is enough for me to serve, and to mourn the temptation of those disobedient ones who wish intelligence to suffice. Happy in the source of the truth, without presumption, without looking for the excuse that it is mildly illusory in order to deceive others and deceive myself; enjoying the One who has no beginning because He is and was in the rock on which I stand, in my color, in the origin of my form, in what likewise recognizes itself and, denying itself, engraved my image in the rock.

Girri rejected any neat separations among hallucinogenic poetry, orgiastic oneirism (belief in dreams), and the ideology of unconsciousness which propitiates the oracular trance, which abolishes the conscious censorship that impedes the flow of deep-felt intensities. Girri refused all rapture. His poetry, growing evermore controlled, discards any turn toward the inquisitive, the intellectual. The poem is displayed as a disquisition that operates simultaneously with both the directly felt and the figurative. It is turned towards the

explicative; it is an investigation that occurs at times conceptually and at times figuratively, an exercise of skill and wit in art. His poetry is above all the art of reflection, in the double sense of reflecting (showing an image) and reflection (considering). This reflection is subject to a perception that guides not only an esthetic conduct but also a fundamentally moral conduct. Subject as far as possible to the proverbial, to the precepts of the Ten Commandments, Girri cultivated the aphoristic condensation, the imprecatory verse in search of the difficult reconciliation of beauty with truth. Girri abandoned spiraling fluency and florid style for the word that is definitive, lapidary.

If at times he employed sensual enticements in his poetry, Girri repressed the voluptuous. He was not a somatic poet—although he registered the conditions, attractions, and weaknesses of the body; he avoided the throbbing flow, the disorder of the senses; he fundamentally wanted to domesticate the animal within him, to prevent it from invading and destroying his vigils. In "La sombra" (The shade) he confessed the ardent, imperious, bloody, oppressive attraction of the body for the beloved lady, promoter of passion and of its representations:

*De algún modo soy tu cuerpo,*
*Cuando la rica, inexplicable sangre,*
*Transcurre en medio de representaciones.*
*Y lo seré hasta que cenizas*
*Acaricien tu prestada, última parcela*
*Pero no me lo permitas,*
*No me dejes ser sólo tu cuerpo.*

("La sombra," *El tiempo que destruye* [1951; The time that destroys])

In some way I am your body
When the rich, inexplicable blood
Courses among representations.
And I will be so until ashes
Caress your last, lent particle.
But you did not permit me,
Did not allow me to be only your body.

At the same time that he recognizes carnal primacy, which propels the poem, the poet claims to liberate himself from that lascivious yoke, from the absolutism of that ardent overflow, from sexual subjugation. In order to configure his image, he needs to objectivize it, to abstract himself in order to think, to detach himself from visceral corporeality, to operate with intrepid symbols and not with confused and imperious substances. Alternatively, as in "Llamiento" (Divine call), which appears in *La condición necesaria* (1960; The necessary condition), Girri glimpses the animal as an alterity, as a regressive force against which the bothersome personality of vigil is constructed by differentiation, and as a fundamental constituent that keeps us subject to bestial impulses, appetites, and fears "cons sus tropismos, sus ritos de seducción, sus acoplamientos lúbricos, las palomas" ("Palomas" [Easy virtues], *Examen de nuestra causa*; with their tropisms, rites of seduction, lubricious couplings, easy virtues). This bestiality withholds by force, in the aridity of urban life, that pristine power which men have lost. Thus, in the poem "El tigre" (The tiger), the caged tiger conserves "la majestad / como la más implacable de las fuerzas (majesty / like the most implacable of forces), and reminds his onlookers of the precarious peace man imposes on the jungle in order to civilize our wild and cruelly carnivorous nature (*La penitencia y el mérito* [1957; Penitence and value]). Also, in "Los monos" (The monkeys), the monkeys serve as intercessors between man and the savage world, and await the erect industrious animal (man) before its extinction; the presumed speaker recognizes his own image in them. Girri expresses attraction and distrust for other bodies, distrust of the repressed appetites of his own body, fascination and wonder for the creatures of that nature from which we cannot release ourselves and into which we cannot reintegrate ourselves. His cats tame their ferocity, concede to us a momentary attention, and then immediately return to their own universe of perceptions without interposition:

> A media tarde
> dejamos de interesarles,
> enmudecen,
> y con envidiable solidaridad
> corren hacia sus iguales,
> la abeja que revolotea en el jardín,
> la hoja cayendo en espiral
> sin sentido aparente:
> velos rojizos
> y dorados lustres vegetales
> cuelgan de las zarpas.
>
> ("Gatos" [Cats], *La condición necesaria*)

In midafternoon
we cease to interest them,
they are silent,
and with enviable solidarity
run to their equals,
the bee that flutters in the garden,
the leaf falling in a spiral
without apparent feeling:
reddish veils
and golden vegetable lusters
dangle from their claws.

Cats enjoy contact with things per se, in their particular materiality, something of which we are deprived and for which we long. Girri sensed that atavistic nostalgia for the lost instinctive capacity of interacting directly with material reality. He felt that we could recover the power to free ourselves of the cerebral constructions that interfere with such interactions if we could return to a simple way of acting, guided by spontaneous impulses, by primordial inklings:

> ojalá
> que los manoseados símbolos del arte
> terminen por parecer errores,
> efectos vacíos, menos legítimos
> para lograr entenderse con el universo
> que un simple intercambio de amor y de odio.
>
> ("Historia del arte" [History of art],
> *La condición necesaria*)

God grant
that manipulated symbols of art
end by seeming to be errors,
hollow effects, less legitimate
for success in understanding the universe
than a simple exchange of love and hate.

Girri knew that the way literature interacts with the natural cannot but be symbolic, that all naturalism in art is only symbolic figuration, ghostly transposition, artificial copying. Girri believed it is better to set aside all arrogance that pretends to confer upon art a transcendental faculty, a supposed perpetuity, a demiurgic power. It is better to resign oneself to its phantasmal entity, to its condition of mirage, to its ways of figurative representation (not of something *in itself* but of something *as if*), to its unreality versus nature. It is better to observe the impotence of literature, which does not create, but rather re-creates, the world. It is better to know that literature operates with logograms (symbols representing words) in order to set up logomachies (disputes about words only). It is better, as Girri accepted in "Comentario" (Commentary), from *La penitencia y el mérito*, to be resigned to repeating the fables of the tribe, to realize those fables with adequate ornamentation, and to pour them into the grooves of the most skillful hexameters.

Girri did not subscribe to the Semitic belief in the power of the word; he deemed it impossible to nullify the distance between signs and the things signified. In his view, either we take the side of things or the side of words; once the passage from the natural to the symbolic is made, the reverse proves impracticable. Girri execrated barbaric rituals; his poetry wants neither throbbing flux nor visceral probing, no prying into the closer or farther recesses of consciousness. Neither elixir nor philter nor magic carpet restores his not very libidinal, peculiar universe of the felt to the fringes of possible consciousness. Without hard work it is neither redeemer nor transfigurer; the poetry of Alberto Girri pursues clairvoyance.

His images are notional, an art of clarification by means of figurative discourse; they incite discernment. Girri restricted the liberties of the poetic text (the liberties of association, of direction, of extension, of composition) in favor of a careful (dis)course, one of strict concatenation. He practiced the art of expert vigilance in order to disentangle "nuestra selva de inquietudes" (our jungle of inquietudes), an art not of strangeness but of perspicacity, operating more by stylization than by sublimation; he can distort a word, carving and measuring it in search of the concise and forceful form. Not permitted is humor, which is a factor of irreverent dislocation, of the confusion of categories and hierarchical reversal, an ambiguous liberator from empirical restrictions.

Girri almost never had recourse to irony, that elucidating irony arising from a skepticism that rejects frank optimism. He cast aside the daydream, was not diverted by roads of fantasy. Each item is played out with full and implacable lucidity. A poetry knowing but disquieted: it demonstrates hard work, making evident

the conflict of a consciousness that is desperate, conceding, hopeless, simultaneously a consciousness passing judgment and admonishing and a consciousness afflicted and atoning. When consciousness appears, the poem is turned to examine it:

> *Dueles, soliloquio*
> *buscas*
> *la desquiciada conciencia*
> *que colmó sus límites,*
> *y paralizas*
> *mi ramada antigua, nostálgica,*
> *mitad huesos,*
> *mitad presiones,*
> *y ahora queja.*
> *Por ti, para ti,*
> *me duele*
> *la meta que confiaba ser,*
> *la ruinosa dialéctica*
> *de la experiencia,*
> *intransigente, entera memoria,*
> *actualizando*
> *tornadizos niveles de culpa*
> *donde por caridad malentendida*
> *paso sin reconocerme*
> *sombra imbécil*
> *desgranando arisca*
> *tu justicia.*
>
> ("Del remordimiento" [From remorse],
> *Examen de nuestra causa*)

> You hurt, soliloquy,
> you seek
> the unsettled consciousness
> that overflowed its limits,
> and you paralyze
> my ancient covering, nostalgia,
> half mortal remains,
> half pressures,
> and now lament.
> Through you, for you,
> the goal that was relied on to exist,
> the dialectic ruins
> of intransigent experience
> hurts me
> informs memory,
> bringing up to date
> changeable levels of guilt
> through which by ill-learnt charity
> I pass without recognizing myself,

a moronic, wicked shadow
falling away from
your justice.

An expurgatory consciousness, condemned to mental purgatory (see "Purgatio" [Purgation] in *La condición necesaria*) by the irreducible absurdity always hanging over us; consciousness of guilt, of the damned; consciousness cast into an abyss, abysmal.

Deprived, according to Girri, of grace and the ability to receive it, fatally subject to misery without the power of transcending it, innocence, unity, permanence all lost, identity falsified, without the excuse that mitigates helplessness, yet with consolation for "la endeble significación de nuestro tránsito" (the worthless significance of our passing), Girri's poetry is converted in *Examen de nuestra causa*, as required in *La condición necesaria*, and in *La penitencia y el mérito*.

Girri's poetry is argumentative, explanatory, but full of personal implication, of existential throbbing. His poetry is demonstrative, enunciative, but the assuring thought that would be able to confer certainty upon it is undermined by the poet's own belief in the precariousness of the word, by his poetry's fundamental impertinence, by its indecisive sense, by its intrinsic insignificance that enfeebles all cognitive anchorage. As he asserts in *En la letra ambigua selva*, literature simultaneously figures and disfigures—when it would be, it simulates. Words are entities that create distance, "fallidas incursiones" (unsuccessful incursions) into a world that remains outside their purview, or at most speechless, in suspense:

> Señales desalentadoras,
> las que anuncian
> que únicamente cabe acuerdos
> por símbolos, condicionales,
> y que nuestro lenguaje usual
> adolece de precario en todas sus instancias,
> literal, figurada, sugerida,
> y de falsedad
> los pensamientos hablados.
> ("En la palabra, a tientas" [In the word, in the dark],
> *En la letra, ambigua selva*)

> Discouraging signs,
> those that announce
> memories are possible only
> through conditional symbols
> and that our daily language
> is precarious in every instance,
> literal, figurative, suggestive,
> and spoken thoughts
> are false.

Words, symbols of a referent that, to be significant, needs to absent itself, are phantasms. The poem that craves to transcend the inanity of signs turns out to be an examination, a memory conditioned by the prescriptive (the pre-written), and finally an impediment to expressing the ultimate knowledge that Girri boldly pursued ("apoderarse / de la totalidad atreviéndose / a lo banal absoluto de escribir" [to seize hold / of the totality daring / the absolute banality of writing]). In order to take risks in pursuit of the real, however, we possess nothing but words: "nuestra única identitad son palabras" (our only identity is words) or "Nuestra identidad no es real sino verbal" (Our identity is not real but verbal). Subject to the exigencies of truth, of whose allure art can be considered an extension, Girri postulated an "arte objetivo" (objective art), without emphasis or affectation. This would be the only art capable of opening itself to the real. It opens itself to the relative real, because according to Girri's conclusion in *Diario de un libro* (1972; Diary of a book), there is no contradiction between a real object and an image. All is names, language.

*Diario de un libro* is the compass stand for *En la letra, ambigua selva,* to which Girri consigned all that was related to his elaborations ("Los múltiples avatares de los poemas: génesis, correcciones, variantes, características de los temas, influencias, lenguaje, técnicas, juicio" [The multiple incarnations of the poems: genesis, corrections, variants, characteristics of the themes, influences, language, techniques, decisions]). Girri's poetry claims and demands the utmost poetic discernment, requiring investigation for knowledge of what the poem is, what it says, and how it says it. Girri's poetry presupposes a lucid poet who employs the poem as a messenger of multiple kinds knowledge, and at the same time as an examination, as an elucidation of its own nature, purpose, and operative modes. Because there are no pre-existing permanent rules, no unanimously accepted canons that can give a work of supreme art a reason for its being, as is right for a modernity which has re-established the division between the lyrical and the critical, Girri dissociates, alternating between the poem which establishes itself by directly exercising its powers and the poem which is relativized, disintegrating and de-authorizing itself, questioning its own epistemological condition and its esthetic entity. In addition, such an intellectual, clairvoyant poet needs to complement his poetic experience by means of complementary texts, reflective in nature, in which he meditates on the poem and the poet—on his function, on his poetics, on poetics in general, in which he further analyzes the relationship that further disquiets him, that of poetry in the face of the reality in which it operates.

In 1983 Girri compiled, in one volume, *Notas sobre la experiencia poética* (Notes on the poetic experience), all his "approximations," all his meta-literary reflections: *Diario de un libro, El motivo es el poema* (1976; The motive is the poem), *Lo propio, lo de todos* (1980; The suitable, the totality). To these books of brief thoughts, formally inclined to aphorism, he added, as an expression of his "puntas de vista privativos" (private points of view), two interviews, "El poeta en su crítico (1979; The poet in his role as critic) and "De carmina scribendo" (1979; On writing lyric poetry), where, according to Girri, he developed more organically several of the dispersed and fragmented propositions enunciated in the book. Also remember that the second volume of his *Obra poética* (1978; Poetic works) incorporates, as an introduction, an interview with Danubio Torres Fierro that bears the emblematic title of "Poesía y conocimiento" (Poetry and understanding). Thus, in addition to the poetic experience, here the personal experience of the poetic is referred to that of its own author; the poetics on view is directly or implicitly exemplified by his work. Girri's forewords pretend to confine the gnomic substance of both his poems and his commentaries to a particular realm, his own, which rejects any insistence on theoretical generalization. Girri's claim is that he does not enunciate general truths but personal truths.

For Girri, poetry is a "mecanismo verbal" (verbal mechanism), set up and exactly arranged. It is an alliance of elocutionary adjustment and an alignment of thought; it is a system of correspondences that claims a scaffolding of reasoning. Poetry is something serious; it is not playing or joking. Girri did not allow himself to go slowly or to ramble, nor to get off-center, nor to dislocate the poem, nor to dissociate or subvert the sense. His are the polyhedric, apodictic (incontrovertible) words of an epitomized, concentrated poetry. He was concerned with character, implying a way of conduct. More than eros, he aimed at ethos. Girri insisted on the moral responsibility of the poet, aspired to endow language with the utmost sense: "a la unversalidad por la impersonalidad" (to the universal through the impersonal). Expressive neutrality is used to speak even more aphoristically, more incisively. Girri seems impassive, never either exclamatory or interjective, avoiding all emphasis. He never seeks suggestion by incongruence (scarcity alone can provide conceptual density); he tends to be univocal (the enigmas are not in the background, in the connotation; they are up front, in the poem's teeth). The compact word is stripped of "escolares / retóricas inmóvil" (scholastics / idolatrous rhetorics) so that all enunciation is inexorable, acquiring the "validez de lo immóvil" (validity of the immovable), the persuasive permanence that preserves the living from corrosion, deformation, and violence because:

> lo duradero es estático, sólo
> el arte consigue el punto de equilibrio
> entre una masa y su punto de apoyo.
> ("Validez de lo inmóvil," in *En la letra, ambigua selva*)

> the durable is static, only
> art attains the equilibrium
> between a mass and its center of gravity.

Girri, by emulating the Elizabethan metaphysical poets, appeared to belong to a time other than his own, as much in his expression as in his problematics. In spite of alluding to the demoiselles d'Avignon, in spite of his "Pro Wittgenstein" (For Wittgenstein), both appearing in *Quien habla no está muerta* (1975; Whoever speaks is not dead) and his "Gertrude Stein sugeriría" (Gertrude Stein would suggest), from *El motivo es el poema* (1976; The motive is the poem), he seemed to write at the margin of his epoch, almost without relation to circumstances and surroundings. All that is immediate, incidental, or anecdotal is filtered and distanced by that logopoiesis that projects it toward the plane of supra-personal speculation. Predominating in his vision and his focus was an objectivity which often rejected the enunciation of a poem in the first person. With the "I" absent or reticent, impersonal and abstract, he created poetry in which the notion of the lyrical locutor wavers. Set against the sentimental, against giving rein to subjectivity, against self-confession, Girri does not establish an intimate nexus with the reader. Thus he contravenes the refined romantic predilection towards poetry as a suspension of judgment, as a rapture that anesthetizes the reflective consciousness. The message is sent out by an enunciating, autonomous "It," attributable to an author, but which is not presented as an incarnation close to the author's own persona. The marks of identity are scarce, and these are more concerned with moral character than with a singular individual's psychology.

Girri gave no indication of autobiography. The poem is the "epítome del yo" (the epitome of "I"), but that "I" renounces all egocentrism, all lyrical privilege of monopolizing the voice, of being the singing voice. The speaking "I" conceives and configures the poem and infuses it with its own cadence: "El ritmo de lo escrito / es el ritmo del que escribe" (The rhythm of the written / is the rhythm of what writes). However, the "I" does not possess substance because, according to Girri, what counts, what weighs heavily, what is decisive, is produced far from the sphere of the personal ("Doppelleben" [Double life], *En la letra, ambigua selva*).

In this poetry the signifiers do not distract from the signified, never act for their own sake, never are liberated from the tightly defined role of messenger; their narrow mission is to communicate and illustrate consciousnesses. Girri polishes and unifies in order to eliminate unevenness, deviations, bumps in the rigorous and harmonious unfolding of the poem (with no exemption for times of loquacity). A concerted act, the poem restrains all tendency toward dispersion, toward instability, toward diversification; it avoids all fracture and places limits on polysemy (multiple meanings). The poems of Girri are monothematic and monodic—"Monodia" [Monody] is the title of one of the *Lírica de percepciones*—but not univocal (no poetry

is that), because it operates with the figurative senses, because it employs figurative language as much as concrete language, because Girri, in spite of his objectivist tendency, of his propensity to the prosaic and proverbial, could not confine his poetry to the literal and denotative.

Girri created poetry by means of maxim or concept, but also by image, by allegory, and by metaphor. Just as he had recourse to figures, to symbolic substitutions or metaphorical transpositions, he provoked transferences from one order to another; sense was bifurcated, trifurcated, commenced to operate figuratively by the unstable unfolding of the figurative signifiers. Metaphor opens the fan of connotations, compels removal of the plane of literal signifiers in order to seek in the adventitious those possible other meanings which are not lexical. The poem is opened, reverberates, plays with plurals, and simultaneously with disparate senses that do not tolerate reductive interpretations. Teeming with latencies, the connotative potentiality is the most reactive, significant weight in the poem. Metaphor provokes unusual intersections between contiguous or distant semantic fields. It is an imaginative operator which presents a fusion between sense and sense, between the word sense and the sensorial sense; metaphor represents the sense of the sensible; it is a verbal icon. Metaphor removes from language its didactic function in order to open it to access to reality under the mode of fiction. When Girri has recourse to images, above all with symbolic-allegoric intention, the poem destroys the literal world in order to substitute for it another world, a world of metaphor that is ruled by the philosophy that all matter has life. Where metaphor unfolds its fabulous capacity or mythopoetic admissibility, the poem postulates an imaginary order not subject to proof of existence:

> y no cavilar, cavilar,
> sobre que si también alojara dragones,
> blancos, de hielo, tierra
> sería lo que le pedimos:
> talismán que por el piso
> nos mueva a seguir el curso, regirlo,
> de las nubes, ríos,
> neutralizar
> del acre sabor nocturno esa

aprensión de que los cielos
pudieran derrumbarse.

("Alfombra como lírica" [Carpet as lyrics],
*Lírica de percepciones*)

and not to cavil, to cavil,
about what may also have been dragons,
white, of ice, land
would be what we demand of them:
talisman that for the treading
may stir us to follow the course, steer it,
from the clouds, rivers,
to neutralize
from the biting taste of night that
apprehension from which the skies
may have crumbled.

The solidity of the poem is illusory, illusory also is any presupposition that the poem is closed and concluded. Subject to constant variation, the weakening and even inversion of sense, the poem cannot be settled into any definite state of completion. Times change, the readers change, the readings change:

*Al realizarse,*
*paralelamente asisten a un mudar*
*de sus bríos, sutilezas,*
*irónicos contrastes,*

*y a negruras, olor*
*marchito de sus variaciones del ánimo,*
*exuberancias, variedades, ternuras,*
*gracias, ornamentos,*

*un resquebrajarse*
*de la adecuación del sentido al sonido, . . .*

("La incertidumbre como poema" [Uncertainty
as poem], *El motivo es el poema*)

Parallel to their fulfillment,
they are undergoing a molting
of their spirits, subtleties,
ironic resistances and contrasts,
and are present at darkenings, the
withered
promise of their variations of intention,
exuberances, variety, tendernesses,
graces, ornaments,
beginning to fracture
the suitability of sense to sound, . . .

*Translated from the Spanish by Mark Herman*

## SELECTED BIBLIOGRAPHY

*Primary Sources*

*Poetry*

*Playa sola*. Buenos Aires: Nova, 1946.

*Coronación de la espera*. Buenos Aires: Ediciones Botella al Mar, 1947.

*Trece poemas*. Buenos Aires: Ediciones Botella al Mar, 1949.

*El tiempo que destruye*. Buenos Aires: Ediciones Botella al Mar, 1951.

*Escándalo y soledades*. Buenos Aires: Ediciones Botella al Mar, 1952.

*Línea de la vida*. Buenos Aires: Editorial Sur, 1955.

*Examen de nuestra causa*. Buenos Aires: Editorial Sur, 1956.

*La penintencia y el mérito*. Buenos Aires: Editorial Sur, 1957.

*Propiedades de la magia*. Buenos Aires: Editorial Sur, 1959.

*La condición necesaria*. Buenos Aires: Editorial Sur, 1960.

*Elegías Italianas*. Buenos Aires: Editorial Sur, 1963.

*Poemas elegidos*. Buenos Aires: Editorial Losada, 1965.

*Envíos*. Buenos Aires: Editorial Sudamericana, 1967.

*Casa de la mente*. Buenos Aires: Editorial Sudamericana, 1968.

*Antología temática*. Buenos Aires: Editorial Sudamericana, 1970.

*Valores diarios*. Buenos Aires: Editorial Sudamericana, 1970.

*En la letra, ambigua selva*. Buenos Aires: Editorial Sudamericana, 1972.

*Poesía de observación*. Buenos Aires: Editorial Sudamericana, 1973.

*Galería personal*. Buenos Aires: Editorial Sudamericana, 1975. With 22 drawings by Hermenegildo Sábat.

*Quien habla no está muerto*. Buenos Aires: Editorial Sudamericana, 1975.

*El motivo es el poema*. Buenos Aires: Editorial Sudamericana, 1976.

*Bestiario*. Buenos Aires: Ediciones La Garza, 1976. (Contains 13 wood engravings by Luis Seoane.)

*Obra poética I*. Buenos Aires: Editorial Corregidor, 1977.

*Arbol de la estirpe humana*. Buenos Aires: Editorial Sudamericana, 1978.

*Obra poética II*. Buenos Aires: Editorial Corregidor, 1978.

*Obra poética III*. Buenos Aires: Editorial Corregidor, 1980.

*Lo propio, lo de todos*. Buenos Aires: Editorial Sudamericana, 1980.

*Lírica de percepciones*. Buenos Aires: Editorial Sudamericana, 1983.

*Obra poética IV*. Buenos Aires: Editorial Corregidor, 1984.

*Monodias*. Buenos Aires: Editorial Sudamericana, 1985.

*Existenciales*. Buenos Aires: Editorial Sudamericana, 1986.

*Tramas de conflictos*. Buenos Aires: Editorial Sudamericana, 1988.

*99 Poemas*. Madrid: Alianza III, 1988.

## Prose

*Crónica del héroe*. Buenos Aires: Editorial Nova, 1946.

*Un brazo de Dios*. Buenos Aires: Americalee, 1966.

*Diario de un libro*. Buenos Aires: Editorial Sudamericana, 1972.

*Prosas*. Caracas: Monte Avila, 1977.

*Notas sobre la experiencia poética*. Buenos Aires: Editorial Losada, 1983.

*Cuestiones y razones*. Buenos Aires: Editorial Fraterna, 1987.

## Translations by Girri

*Canto del sol poniente* (Rabindranath Tagore). Buenos Aires: Argentine Commission to Pay Homage to Tagore, 1961.

*Quince poetas Norteamericanos*. First Series. Buenos Aires: Bibliográfica Omeba, 1966.

*Poemas de Wallace Stevens*. Buenos Aires: Bibliográfica Omeba, 1967.

*Quince poetas Norteamericanos*. Second Series. Buenos Aires: Bibliográfica Omeba, 1969.

*Poemas de Robert Lowell*. Buenos Aires: Editorial Sudamericana, 1969.

*Devociones* (John Donne). Buenos Aires: Ediciones Brújula, 1970.

*Versiones*. Buenos Aires: Editorial Corregidor, 1974.

*Antología de Spoon River* (Edgar Lee Masters). Barcelona: Barral Editores, 1974.

## Translations in Collaboration

*Poesía Inglesa de la guerra Española*. With William Shand. Buenos Aires: Editorial El Ateneo, 1947.

*Poesía Inglesa contemporánea*. With William Shand. Buenos Aires: Editorial Nova, 1948.

*Poesía Italiana contemporánea*. With C. Viola Soto. Buenos Aires: Editorial Raigal, 1956.

*Poesía Norteamericana contemporánea*. With William Shand. Buenos Aires: Editorial Raigal, 1956.

*Poemas de John Donne*. With William Shand. Buenos Aires: Ediciones Culturales Argentinas, 1963.

*Stephen Spender: Poemas*. With William Shand. Buenos Aires: Editorial Losada, 1968.

## Secondary Sources

### Critical Studies and Interviews

Borinsky, Alicia. "Interlocución y aporía: notas a propósito de Alberto Girri y Juan Gelman." *Revista Iberoamericana*, no. 125: 879–87 (1983).

Capello, Jorge A. "Alberto Girri: 'La penintencia y el mérito.'" *Sur*, no. 253: 77–80 (1958).

Cueto, Sergio. *Seis estudios girrianos*. Rosario, Argentina: B. Viterbo Editora, 1993.

Murena, H. A. "La dialéctica del espíritu ante la soledad." *Sur*, no. 168: 58–67 (1948).

Pizarnik, Alejandra. "El Ojo." *Sur*, no. 291: 84–87 (1964).

Slade Pascoe, Muriel. *La poesía de Alberto Girri*. Buenos Aires: Sudamericana, 1986.

Suárez, María Victoria. *Existencia y lógica poética*. Buenos Aires: Corregidor, 1987.

Torres Fierro, Danubio. "Poesía y conocimiento." *Plural*, México, (July 1976). Reprinted as a Prologue in *Alberto Girri: Obra Poética II*.

Vittor, Luis Alberto. *Simbolismo e iniciación en la poesía de Alberto Girri*. Buenos Aires: 1990.

Zárate, Armando. "Alberto Girri: 'El motivo es el poema.'" *Revista Iberoamericana*, nos. 102–103: 304–305 (1978).

# Felisberto Hernández

## (1902–1964)

## *Pablo Rocca*

Felisberto Hernández's narrative work developed over the course of two decades, between 1942 and 1962, although he started writing and publishing a number of private texts sometime in the mid-1920s. In the context of Spanish literature, and especially of Latin American literature, Hernández's works clearly belong within that group of texts which questioned the traditional realism of the nineteenth century, which had dominated Latin American literature up until the middle of that century. His most frequent subjects can be divided into two general types. First, he employed a form of poetical remembrance, similar to that of Marcel Proust, in which the narration unfolds with a special attention paid to the small events of childhood and adolescence. In these works, the author himself stands at the structural center of the story. Examples of this can be seen in such works as *Por los tiempos de Clemente Colling* (1942; In Clemente Colling's time), *El caballo perdido* (1943; *The Stray Horse*, 1993), and the posthumously published *Tierras de la memoria* (1965; Lands of memory), although it was written around 1945. And second, Hernández produced a group of short stories in which he breaks away from the rhetoric of realism. In these stories he does not set aside the subjects of childhood and remembrance, but his primary focus is on the vicissitudes of adult life. These stories are exemplified in the collection of tales *Nadie encendía las lámparas* (1947; No one lighted the lamps) and, particularly, in "El cocodrilo" ("The Crocodile"). The use of humble settings and equally humble characters, who survive with difficulty in a hostile environment, predominates. This latter element of his work has distinguished Hernández in Latin American literature and has made him a forerunner of later writers, such as Julio Cortázar of Argentina and Juan José Arreola of Mexico.

Felisberto Hernández was born in Montevideo on 20 October 1902, to a lower-middle-class family in Atahualpa, a popular suburban neighborhood of the Uruguayan capital, which is recalled in a text entitled "Primera casa" (First home). His father, Prudencio Hernández González (1878–1940), was an islander, a native Spaniard from the Canary Islands, a plumber by trade who owned a small construction firm. His mother, born Juana Silva (1884–1971), was given the surname Martínez after her aunt, Deolinda Arecha de Martínez, "to whom she was given when she was eight months old" (Giraldi, 1975). The couple got married in the year 1900, and had four children: Felisberto, Deolinda (1905), Ismael (1906), and Mirta (1911). The eldest was called Feliciano Felisberto, but his name was wrongly recorded as Feliciano Felix Verti, an administrative mistake which caused considerable bureaucratic complications throughout his life.

In the year 1907 the family moved to Cerro, a village situated within Montevideo district though far away from the capital's center. Two years later the family moved to an old house in Joaquín Suárez Avenue, in a residential zone surrounded by country houses and near the Prado, a neighborhood of large mansions. In the places where he spent his childhood there were small houses with large gardens and backyards, horses moved freely along in the open air, and streetcars regularly passed by. All of these scenes would be recreated by Hernández in much of his fiction, especially in the "memory novels": *Por los tiempos de Clemente Colling*, *The Stray Horse*, and *Tierras de la memoria*.

The first decisive event in his life occurred when he was nine years old: he started studying piano with the French teacher Celina Moulié, a longtime acquaintance of his mother. Frequently, his mother or his maternal grandmother, who used to punish him severely, accompanied young Hernández to his piano lessons. These scenes are recalled in *The Stray Horse*, in a passage that shows how piano lessons at Celina's house could become an oasis of peace and safety for the boy:

En casa de Celina—y aunque ella no estuviera presente—los arrebatos de mi abuela no eran peligrosos. Algo había en aquella sala que se los enfriaba a tiempo. Además, aquel era un lugar en que no sólo yo debía mostrar educación, sino también ella. Tenía un corazón fácil a la bondad y muchas actitudes mías le hacían gracia. Aunque el estilo de mis actitudes fuera el mismo, a ella le parecían nuevas si yo las producía en situaciones distintas y en distintas formas: le gustaba reconocer en mí algo ya sabido y algo diferente al mismo tiempo. Todavía la veo reírse saltándole la barriga debajo de un delantal. . . . En casa de Celina, apenas si se le escapaba la insinuación de una amenza. Y mucho menos un manotón: yo podía sentarme tranquilamente al lado de ella. Aún más: cuando Celina era muy severa o se olvidaba que yo no había podido estudiar por alguna causa ajena a mi voluntud, yo buscaba a mi abuela con los ojos; y si no me atrevía a mirarla, la llamaba con la atención, pensando fuertemente en ella y endureciendo mi silencio.

(*Obras completas*, vol. II)

At Celina's house—even when she was absent—my grandmother's sudden bursts of rage were not dangerous. There was something about that room that cooled them in time. Besides, it was not just my behavior and upbringing that was on public display there, but hers as well. She was kind at heart, and much of what I did amused her. And even familiar behaviors seemed new to her in these new surroundings: she enjoyed the opportunity to see me in a new and different light. I still see her belly quivering under her apron as she laughed. . . . At Celina's house, there was little threat of her rages, let alone of physical blows: I could sit by her without fear. What is more, when Celina was very severe or when she forgot that something beyond my control had prevented me from study, I sought my grandmother with my eyes, and if I did not dare to look at her, I would concentrate, trying to attract my grandmother's attention by making my silence more noticeable.

In 1914 Hernandez was twelve years old and, though still studying piano, he was also a student at the "Artigas" School. There he was the pupil of the important writer José Pedro Bellan (1889–1930), who was then working on two important projects, a novel (*Doñarramona*, 1918) and a play (*¡Dios te salve!* 1920; God save you!). Bellan was the first to urge Hernandez to write. The two shared a friendship and mutual admiration that lasted until Bellan's early death. The influence of Bellan's work on the young Hernandez is evident; one of Bellan's tales, "Los amores de Juan Rivault" (1922; Juan Rivault's loves) even prefigures an idea that Hernández carefully develops in his novel *Las hortensias* (1949; The hydrangeas): the use of animated sex dolls.

In 1917 Felisberto traveled abroad for the first time. Three years before, together with his brother Ismael, he had joined the Vanguardias de la Patria, a youth group that sponsored participation in cultural and sporting events. As a member of the Vanguardias, Hernandez travelled to Mendoza (in Argentina) and crossed the Andes on his way to Chile. Also on that trip was a young man named José Rodríguez Riet, who would later play a role in Hernandez's early career. As an adult, he became the owner of the publishing company that brought out Hernandez's first book. The author's experience of this first trip beyond the borders of Uruguay was thoroughly recalled in *Tierras de la memoria*:

I was fourteen years old and this was the first time I had ever been separated from my familiy so far and for such a long time: the journey lasted for a little over a month. We walked about five hundred kilometers and climbed mountains more than four thousand meters high.

Even before starting that journey, Hernández had already met another person who would become important later in life: Clemente Colling. Colling's role in Hernández's life was essential in two senses. First, he encouraged the young writer to continue his musical studies, and second because he provided the model for one of Hernández's characters. Colling had been born in France and had settled in Montevideo when he was very young. He had lost his sight when he was seven years old, and by 1914 he was in dire financial straits. In those days Hernández had begun giving small concerts under the patronage of a group of ladies who helped the National Institute for the Blind, which had just been founded. At one of these concerts, in 1915, Hernández first made Collings's acquaintance:

> Clemente Colling was known as "The Basque's Church organist" or "The blind man that plays in the Basques," . . . Some time before this meeting, I had been taken to hear a piano concert he gave at the Verdi Institute. It was one of the first concerts I ever heard. . . . The lights went out; leaving us to wait for a while in the dark. Two men came on stage, instead of just one: I did not realize that, being blind, Colling quite naturally needed to be led to the piano.

Colling soon began Hernández's new piano teacher, and the two grew to be close friends. In time, between 1924 and 1925, Hernández convinced his parents to take Colling into the family home, where he was given a place to sleep in a hallway. This made it possible for Hernández to intensify his musical studies, while at the same time providing Colling with food and shelter. Colling was an extraordinarily slovenly man, and the Hernández family hoped that this new living arrangement would make it possible to clean him up. In this, however, they failed completely; According to Norah Giraldi, the family eventually had to separate from the piano teacher because their friends "stopped visiting their house owing to [Colling's] presence and slovenliness, which irritated them" (*Felisberto Hernández: Del creador al hombre*, 1975). Almost three decades later, Colling would make an important contribution to Hernández's career as a writer: he became the model for one of the author's most endearing characters.

In 1917 the Hernández family's financial situation was not good at all, and fifteen-year-old Felisberto had to start earning some money. At first he got a job playing piano accompaniment to silent films at a cinema in Montevideo. This job was to the writer both personally and professionally. From his days at the theater he became addicted to the cinema, a fact that is incorporated in such stories as "El acomodador" (The usher). In addition, the films he saw provided him with narrative resources that he would make use of in his work: flashbacks, narrative shifts, ruptures of the temporal line, and the like. He makes direct reference to this in a story written sometime around 1942: "Juan Méndez o Almacén de ideas o Diario de pocos días" (Juan Méndez, or the ideas' grocery, or diary of a few days):

> *Pero en este momento he caído en una sensación superficial: es el placer del cuaderno en que escribo; quisiera llenarlo enseguida y después leerlo ligero como cuando apuran una cinta cinematográfica; y para llenar el cuaderno y hacer el juego del cine me servirán muchas prevenciones contra mí, contra los vicios y contra muchas ideas filosóficas.*
>
> (*Obras completas*, vol. I)

> But at this moment I have fallen into a superficial sensation: it is the pleasure of the notebook on which I write; I would like to fill it immediately and then quickly read it back, as when cinematographic film is fast-forwarded; and I can play this cinema game by filling my notebook with the many dispositions against me, against vices and against many philosophical ideas.

In 1927 Alan Crosland's *The Jazz Singer* ushered in the age of the "talking pictures." Hernández, as a frequent moviegoer, always sat in the front row of the theater, a habit he had acquired during his years as a piano accompanist:

> The Usher's flashlight illuminated my steps and my shoes gleamed in the light. I was constantly in danger of treading on his feet. He stopped suddenly to offer me a seat and he found it strange that I liked sitting so near the screen. I thought: "He doesn't know that I used to play the piano in cinemas when I was young and I got used to watching movies from really close up."
>
> (*Tierras de la memoria*)

In 1918 Hernández settled in a house on Minas Street, near the heart of Montevideo. There, on the top floor, he opened the "Hernández Conservatoire," where he gave piano lessons to a few young pupils. At that time, according to Giraldi, "he applied himself between twelve and fourteen hours a day to the study of piano" (1975). In the summer of 1919 he went on a trip to Maldonado, a town in eastern Uruguay, where he met Venus González Olasa. This most unusual fellow, originally a schoolteacher, became Felisberto's manager, organizing modest concert performances throughout Uruguay and Argentina. In gratitude to him, Hernández dedicated one of his first works, entitled "La barba metafísica" (The metaphysical beard), in which he recalls one of Olasa's most prominent features:

There were things that attracted one's attention from a distance: his beard, his whistle, his wide-brimmed hat, his walking stick, and his yellow shoes. But what attracted one's attention most was the beard.

During this same trip Hernández met María Isabel Guerra, also a schoolteacher, with whom he became romantically involved. María Isabel began taking piano lessons from Hernández, who in turn began to make frequent visits to Maldonado, as a teacher, concert player and suitor. The romance lasted six years, but there is little information available about the affair. As José Pedro Díaz notes in his biography of the author, *Felisberto Hernández: su vida y su obra* (2000; Felisberto Hernández: His life and work), "we only have the information that one of his letters can give us." This letter refers to the opposition he faced from María Isabel's parents and to the deep affection he felt for his beloved. In 1925 the couple finally overcame objections of the Guerra family and were wed.

The newlywed couple moved in with Hernández's parents, who were now living in the same general neighborhood as the philosopher Carlos Vaz Ferreira (1872–1958), who surrounded himself with a select group of intellectuals that included Hernández's former mentor, Bellan. Hernández started frequenting those meetings, where he read his texts aloud. Vaz Ferreira showed a great interest in these early works, and encouraged the young writer to persevere. However, María Isabel was already pregnant with the couple's first child, and Hernández needed to earn some money. He began touring the country, performing in a series of concerts. On one of these tours, in 1926, he stopped off in Mercedes, the capital of the department of Soriano, three hundred kilometers from home. He remained there for several months, making new friends and writing articles for the local press. When he was still in that city his daughter Mabel was born, in June 1926. He did not see his firstborn child until she was about four months old. This early estrangement from his daughter foreshadowed a longer separation to come. Giraldi (1975) notes that Hernández and his wife were at this time quarreling frequently, and ultimately the couple separated. Hernández did not see Mabel again until her wedding day. When he learned that she was getting married, he went to the church where the ceremony was to be held. He had not seen her for quite some time, and he was concerned that he would not be able to recognize her among the many other brides being married that day. They rarely met again after that.

Between 1925 and 1931 Hernández published four books: *Fulano de tal* (1925; Such a one), *Libro sin tapas* (1929; The uncovered book), *La cara de Ana* (1930; Ana's face) and *La envenenada* (1931; The poisoned woman). These were cheaply produced by small publishing houses in Montevideo and the rest of the country. Although they were deemed valuable by Hernández's own small, close circle (which included Vaz Ferreira, Esther de Cáceres, Juan Carlos Welker, and Carlos Benvenuto), they were ignored by contemporary literary critics. In the 1960s, however, inspired in part by the production of writers such as Julio Cortázar and by a new rereading of other Latin American avant-garde literature, these books came to be viewed as the writer's "prehistoric" books by critics such as Mario Benedetti, José P. Díaz, Carlos Martínez Moreno, Ángel Rama, and Arturo S. Visca, who nonetheless rated them as the purely experimental works of a beginner. An important group of Latin American academic critics, including Hugo Achugar, Nelson Osorio, Jorge Schwartz, and Hugo Verani, have argued that these books should be read not as mere autobiographical documents or as an introduction to a major work, but as having their own intrinsic value as "first inventions."

Nevertheless, the author's next three books, *Por los tiempos de Clemente Colling, The Stray Horse,* and *Tierras de la memoria*, show clear autobiographical tendencies. In these works, which share an elliptical approach to facing and constructing reality, the author's own memories and experiences are the main topics. In his earlier works, by contrast, the most interesting feature is not the direct narration of an event, but rather lies in the author's precise observation of objects, his concern with their "behavior," as if they were autonomous entities, and his focus on the successive stages or moments through which matter passes. A prime example of this can be seen in "Historia de un cigarrillo" (The story of a cigarrette), from *Libro sin tapas*. All of his first four works are extremely abstract, as in "Genealogía" (Genealogy), also from *Libro sin tapas*, which is an unclassifiable story of an endless horizontal line and of a circumference; there is also a tendency to free-ranging, sometimes epigramatic philosophizing, similar in style to work by Vaz Ferreira. This can be seen in "Cosas para leer en el tranvía" (Things to read on the streetcar) and "Diario" (Diary), from *Fulano de tal*. At the same time, Hernández uses his prose to evoke emotions, sometimes associated with memory, and the narrator's perspective alternates between immersion in the text and commenting about it in a self-referential exercise designed to engage the reader and make him take an active part in the fiction:

> Dear colleague: yes, yes, I am referring to you, reader, whom I see through the eyes, holes, bodies, and from the angles of these letters. You will try to do the same and we will pretend to play an innocent game of "hide-and-seek," except that, when we move between letters, we hide weapons.
>
> ("El taxi" [The taxi])

This playful, humorous spirit, this willingness to break the conventions of literary genres, was a truly bold move in contemporary Uruguayan literature. For decades, critics have attributed Hernández's aesthetic to the influence of dadaism, ultraism, or even of the budding surrealism of that era, although these influences could not be verified. Few recognized that the author was embarking upon a personal search, one that attempted to establish a dialogue with Latin American avant-garde literature but which was, at the same time, autonomous, since it was being conducted by a writer who had not read much, and had remained apart from the few local groups that were interested in any innovation.

These curious works were eventually published in a handful of provincial newspapers, and therefore the little books circulated only among a chosen few. Some features of these early fictions appear again in the tales written between the years 1943 and 1961, when Hernández was grappling with concerns that were only hinted in these first works. One such concern is the idea of the "mystery" that surrounds all beings and things and that can be penetrated only by the artist (as in the eponymous narration from *La envenenada*). Other recurrent themes include the author's boyish way of writing, expressing a kind of naiveté when recalling and referring to things, and his natural use of urban and even suburban colloquialisms. Above all, Hernández's fiction breaks free of the traditional forms of realism which still dominated in the Latin American literature of his time. This places him within the ranks of a few other groundbreaking Latin American writers, such as the Argentinians Macedonio Fernández and Santiago Davobe, the Venezuelans Julio Garmendia and José Antonio Ramos Sucre, the Ecuadorean Pablo Palacio, and the Peruvian Martín Adán, all of whom were initially unappreciated and who were virtually unknown to Hernández.

During this period, Hernández continued to support himself by giving concert performances throughout Uruguay, often playing in small towns where his art was not properly appreciated. However embittering this experience might have been, it provided him with valuable material for his literary work. The sordidness of his concert venues, the indifference of the people he encountered, and the funny or even grotesque incidents that occurred during his concerts would appear frequently in his tales and would be expressed through the anguished voice of his first-person narrators. Examples of this can be found in the stories included in *Por los tiempos de Clemente Colling*: "Mi primer concierto" (My first concert), "El cocodrilo" ("The Crocodile"), "El balcón" (The balcony), "El comedor oscuro" (The dark dining room), and "En gira con Yamandú Rodríguez" (A tour with Yamandú Rodríguez). One important tale written during this time is entitled "Buenos días (Viaje a Farmi)" (Good morning [A trip to Farmi]), which provides a clarifying, self-referential sketch:

> *Daré algunas noticias autobiográficas. Jamás se dan todas. Color de pelo negro y 38 años. . . . Mi primer cartel lo tuve en música. Pero los juicios que más me enorgullecen los he tenido por lo que he escrito. No sé si lo que he escrito es la actitud de un filósofo valiéndose de medios artísticos para dar su conocimiento, o es la de un artista que toma para su arte tema filosóficos. Creo que mi especialidad está en escribir lo que no sé, pues no creo que solamente se debe escribir lo que se sabe. . . . Pero me seduce cierto desorden que encuentro en la realidad y en los aspectos de su misterio. Y aquí se encuentran mi filosofía y mi arte.*
>
> (*Obras completas*, vol. I)

I will give some autobiographical information, since I've never given it all before. Black hair, 38 years old. . . . My first success was in music. Nevertheless, the reviews of which I am most proud refer to my written work. I am not sure if what I write is philosophy expressed in artistic terms, or if it is art that concerns itself with philosophical matters. Since I do not believe that people should write only about what they know, I have specialized in writing about what I do not know. . . . I am seduced by a kind of disorder that I perceive in reality, and by the different aspects of its mystery. And it is here where my philosphy and art are situated.

However, in *La envenenada*, the author states: "if I want to have a subject matter I have to plunge into life," presenting this almost as if it were a program that he charged himself to follow. He succeeds in doing so in his "memory" novels, which were published during a highly productive and, at the same time, critical period of his life. In 1937 he married the painter Amalia Nieto, with whom he would have a second daughter, Ana María, who was born in Montevideo in 1938. Once again Hernández faced financial problems, and once again music became the only way for him to make a living. He was booked on long tours throughout Argentina, and continued to tour until the beginning of the year 1942. He made several efforts to stop touring and settle down in Montevideo, as in 1940, when he and his wife opened up a bookshop called The Little White Donkey in Pocitos, a neighboorhood located near the River Plate. He also tried working as a shorthand typist, during which job he created his own shorthand system.

Neither enterprise permitted him to quit touring, but his invented system of shorthand must have been very useful on tour, helping him to write more quickly during the nights he spent in small provincial hotels. Ultimately, however, he decided to give up music and concentrate exclusively on literature. He wrote of this decision in a letter adressed to his wife:

> And now in this room, in this town that is sunk into a donkey's sleep, I have been walking about desperately, like a crazy man, wondering what I should do about this vague, recurring idea, and this [desperation] may have one good result: a strong decision. For the time being I have decided to write, no matter what happens. If I can, I will dilute, hasten, or adapt myself as much as possible. But if not, whatever: writing, reading and thinking about such things.
>
> (Díaz, 2000)

*Por los tiempos de Clemente Colling* narrates, with mild irony, the life of Hernández's much admired piano teacher, showing how he became part of the author's childhood and adolescence. This theme of remembrance is continued in *The Stray Horse*, but with a difference. In the later work, thinking about his own memories becomes an essential part of the author's writing process. Remembrance is symbolized in the metaphor of the horse that wanders from one place to another in complete freedom. This powerful metaphor reappears in later texts, such as "La mujer parecida a mí" (The woman who looked like me), from *Nadie encendía las lámparas* (No one lighted the lamps), and even the last of his ambitious texts, "Diario del sinvergüenza" (A rogue's diary), which first appeared in *Tierras de la memoria* again employs reminiscence, with the author concentrating on his experiences during his fourteenth year and on the process of remembrance itself. In this work, Hernández expresses himself in a poetical prose that is similar to that used by Marcel Proust in his *À la recherche du temps perdu* (Remembrance of Things Past):

> There are some memories that live in lighted pieces of space; they come again to my mind, making me feel we are approaching each other and entering into the dark stripe of night; the two days of that jouney were separated by that stripe.

In these narrations, some features of his style, already evident in his initial works (1925–1931), become more pronounced: the animation of objects; the use of an almost colloquial language or, at least, of one that avoids exaggerated forms of expression; the use of unusual metaphors; the taking advantage of what seems to be irrelevant or unimportant; the sinking into the character's inmost world; the use of a subtle, sometimes melancholic humor. A brief example, taken from *The Stray Horse*, exemplifies this trend:

*Fue una de esas noches en que yo estaba triste, y ya me había acostado y las cosas que pensaba se iban acercando al sueño, cuando empecé a sentir la presencia de las personas como muebles que cambiaran de posición. Eso lo pensé muchas noches. Eran muebles que además de poder estar quietos se movían; y se movían por voluntad propia. A los muebles que estaban quietos yo los quería y ellos no me exigían nada; pero los muebles que se movían no sólo exigían que se les quisiera y se les diera un beso sino que tenían exigencias peores; y además, de pronto, abrían sus puertas y le echaban a uno todo encima. Pero no siempre las sorpresas eran violentas y desagradables; había algunas que sorprendían con lentitud y silencio como si por debajo se les fuera abriendo un cajón y empezaran a mostrar objetos desconocidos. (Celina tenía sus cajones cerrados con llave.) Había otras personas que también eran muebles cerrados, pero tan agradables, que si uno hacía silencio sentía que adentro tenían música, como instrumentos que tocaran solos.*

(*Obras completas*, vol. II)

It was during one of those nights when I was sad, and was already in bed, and the things of which I thought were getting close to dreams, when I began to feel people's presence as if they were pieces of furniture that changed place. I thought many nights about that. They were pieces of furniture that, in spite of being still, could move; and they moved of their own will. I loved the ones that remained still, because they did not ask anything from me. However, the ones which moved not only demanded to be loved and kissed, but their demands were even worse. What is more, they opened their doors suddenly and threw everything all over me. Surprises, though, were not always violent and disgusting; some of them were slow and silent, as if beneath them a drawer was being opened and beginning to show unknown objects. (Celina had her drawers locked.) Some other people were also locked drawers, but they were so nice that if you remained silent you felt they had music inside them, as if they were self-played musical instruments.

In 1943 Hernández broke off with Amalia Nieto and started a new relationship with the writer María Paulina Medeiros (1905–1992). His long correspondence with her was published in 1974. By that time Hernández was concentrating obsesively on his literary work, writing at his lover's place or in cafés, where he spent quite a lot of his time.

Also in 1943 the author met the Franco-Uruguayan writer Jules Supervielle (1884–1960), who would become an important personal—and, in some way, literary—influence. On the one hand, in Montevideo, Supervielle carefully read his tales and made several suggestions; on the other hand, he supported him and even got him a scholarship to Paris, where Hernández remained from October 1946 to May 1948. In the French capital, Supervielle introduced him at the Sorbonne. Felisberto soon contacted the refined Uruguayan poet Susana Soca (1907–1959), who took him to London and, as directoress of *La Licorne*, a Parisian magazine, included a translation of his short story "El balcón." This greatly raised Hernández's expectations, but he remained insecure.

However, in those hard postwar times, Hernández could not establish a solid relationship with any important European intellectual, and his main worry seems to have been the difficulty he faced in getting coffee and cigarrettes, which were rationed. He had to wait his turn in long lines to buy them, and would often get confused, due to his problems in speaking French.

Hernández carried on with his creative work and adopted a new style, replacing his "memory narrations" with fantastic or near-fantastic tales. These are the texts included in *Nadie encendía las lámparas*, which was published in Buenos Aires by Sudamericana. This achievement was due to Supervielle, who put him in touch with the publishing house. Another example of these fantastic tales is "The Crocodile," published in Montevideo's weekly *Marcha* (30 December 1949), and *Las hortensias*, which was published in the December 1949 issue of the magazine *Escritura* upon the author's return to Uruguay.

Many of these stories were censured by Uruguayan critics. In the 9 April 1948 issue of *Marcha*, Carlos Ramela stated that *Nadie encendía las lámparas* could not be called literature; about the same book, relentless Emir Rodríguez Monegal—who had already judged

*The Stray Horse* severely—pointed out in the magazine *Clinamen* that the author did not know Spanish and had a morbid and excessive curiosity about sexual matters. Nevertheless, some exceptions can be mentioned. When Ángel Rama and Manuel Flores Mora were the directors of *Marcha*'s literary section, an unsigned review about *Las hortensias* stated:

> His books, and especially the great collection *Nadie encendía las lámparas,* have meant—and it is necessary to repeat it since prejudices have prevented silly critics from noticing it—a substantial improvement in our narrative. After having repeated for years the narrative molds imposed on our literature by [Eduardo] Acevedo Díaz and others, Felisberto Hernández suddenly presents an entirely new and original form and subject matter.
>
> (*Marcha*, no. 524, 28 April 1950)

Many years later some of these works, such as "El balcón," "El acomodador," and "La mujer parecida a mí," were included in the most serious Uruguayan and Latin American anthologies. Recognition of the value of Felisberto Hernández's work was slow in coming. In the later 1960s, however, thanks to Ángel Rama, José Pedro Díaz, and Ida Vitale's critical work, and the support of Arca Publishers (which belonged to Rama and Díaz), his writings were read beyond the Uruguayan border. Hernández's complete works (1965–1974) were issued in several volumes. During the 1960s, Julio Cortázar translated many of these third-period tales into French, and in Italy, through the influential publisher, Einaudi, Italo Calvino did the same.

Almost simultaneously, academic attention and even acclaim for Hernández's work was added to the support it was receiving from critics and publishers. In 1973, at a symposium held at Poitiers University in France, the writers and critics Juan José Saer, Rubén Barreiro Saguier, and Saúl Yurkievich joined specialists such as Alain Sicard and Claude Fell in honoring Hernández's work. By the end of the 1970s it became generally understood that Felsiberto Hernández was a powerful innovator in the development of the midcentury Spanish narrative. His literature became the focus of academic conferences held in New York and Lille, for example, and was the subject of a great number of university theses and articles in specialized and cultural journals in Europe and North America, not just in Latin America.

All the tales included in *Nadie encendía las lámparas* have a first-person narrator, and in the short story that gives its the book its name, the writer himself, who reads a text before an audience, is present. Discourse and story are mingled, and reality is seen from a subjective point of view. The rest of the characters tend to be drawn from the River Plate's lower middle class, although there are some bourgeois and, above all, an important group of "irregulars," people who deviate from the norm: fat ladies, a female dwarf, people who behave oddly. The author intentionally avoids locating his tale in a specific place and time. For example, in "El balcón" he describes the scene thus:

> There was a town which I liked to visit during the summer. At that time almost one entire neighborhood went to a nearby seaside resort. One of the abandoned houses was very old.

The same sort of vagueness is evident in "El acomodador":

> *Apenas había dejado la adolescencia me fui a vivir a una ciudad grande. Su centro—donde todo el mundo se movía apurado entre casas muy altas—quedaba cerca de un río.*
>
> *Yo era acomodador de un teatro; pero fuera de allí lo mismo corría de un lado para otro; parecía un ratón debajo de muebles viejos.*
>
> (*Obras completas,* vol. II)

> As soon as my adolescence ended I moved to a big city. In the center, which was close to a river, everybody moved in a hurry among tall buildings.
>
> I was an usher at a theater. However, in my spare time I ran from one place to the other; I was like a mouse moving under old furniture.

These typical features of Hernández's writing are immediately apparent. In this volume they are intensified by a complete lack of any concrete references, relying instead on such devices as metonymy, "the bold foreheaded young man," or through references to gender or sex ("the woman in the wall") or, finally, by invoking "some oddity which makes [others] feel uncomfortable." Such "oddities," which he would also call "to write the other," introduce a dreamlike and fantastic atmosphere to his tales.

The double appears as subject matter in "La mujer parecida a mí" and "Las dos historias," in which the narrator remarks that "as soon as my human body lay down, my horse memories started to wander." The symbolic space related to spectacle as subject matter is displayed in the light that comes from the eyes of the protagonist in "El acomodador" and, above all, in the tunnel of "Menos Julia" ("Except for Julia"), a highly erotic tale, in which the first-person narrator takes part in a strange ceremony. This takes place in the house of an old friend, who explains in some detail what is going to occur:

> Everything will take place in a tunnel . . . in my country house, and we will go into it on foot. That will happen at night fall. The girls will be inside, waiting for us, in couches along the left wall. Their faces will be covered by dark veils. On the right, some objects will be displayed over an old, long counter. I will touch the objects and try to guess what they are. I will also touch the faces of the girls, thinking I do not know them.

The abrupt irruption of the absurd—the unusual presence of humor—is noticeable in "Muebles 'El Canario'" (El Canario furniture): an injection is given to the passengers of a streetcar, who then become able to hear a radio program. Mystery, which was a very important element in the author's "memory novels," is polished and renewed by the angst suffered by many of his characters. Most of the time, this angst is caused by the indifference of others, as in "Mi primer concierto," or by the lack of communication among people, who are destroyed by a materialistic and cold-hearted world or displaced by greed. This motif of angst is made even clearer in his later work "The Crocodile," which was published in book form for the first time in 1960, with "La casa inundada" ("The Flooded House"). It is the story of a stocking salesman who bears the burden of his loneliness and his financial problems while traveling through the small towns of some unnamed country. He is also a pianist, and had traveled through these places to give piano concerts. The alienation of artists and workingmen is clear in this tale, even though the narrator conceals the explanation of the problem behind a smoke screen of self-deprecating humor:

> *Yo había sacado el segundo premio en las leyendas de propaganda para esas medias. . . . Pero vender medias también me resultaba muy difícil y esperaba que de un momento a otro me llamaran de la casa central y me suprimieran el viático. Al principio yo había hecho un gran esfuerzo. (La venta de medias no tenía nada que ver con mis conciertos: y yo tenía que entendérmelas nada más que con los comerciantes.) Cuando encontraba antiguos conocidos les decía que la representación de una gran casa comercial me permitía viajar con independencia y no obligar a mis amigos a patrocinar mis conciertos. En esta misma ciudad me habían puesto pretextos poco comunes: el presidente del Club estaba de mal humor porque yo lo había hecho levantar de la mesa de juego y me dijo que habiendo muerto una persona que tenía muchos parientes, media ciudad estaba enlutada. Ahora yo les decía: estaré unos días para ver si surge naturalmente el deseo de un concierto; pero les producía mala impresión el hecho de que un concertista vendiera medias.*
>
> (Obras completas, vol. III)

I had won the second prize for the written advertising for those stockings. . . . However, it was very difficult to sell socks and I expected to be summoned to the main branch at any moment and told that my traveling expenses had been denied. In the beginning I made a great effort. (Selling socks had nothing to do with my concerts: and I only had to deal with tradesmen.) When I met old aquaintances I told them that working for a big commercial house allowed me to travel independently, so I didn't have to force my friends to patronize my concerts. In one town I was given unusual excuses: the president of the Club was in a bad mood because I interrupted him at the gaming table, and he told me half the town was in mourning because someone who had lots of relatives had died. So I told them: I will be around for a few days to see if a natural desire for a concert arises; nevertheless, the fact that a concert player would sell stockings made a bad impression on them.

In Paris, Felisberto not only achieved some success with a public which had ignored him up to that moment; he also fell in love. In that city he met someone whose name was, for decades, believed to be María Luisa de las Heras, a "prestigious Spanish dressmaker who was in Paris as a refugee, having left Spain during the war [1936–1939]" (Giraldi). Actually, as José P. Díaz discovered, her name was not María Luisa but África María, and she was a KGB agent operating under the pseudonym of Patria. She had been an active soldier during the Spanish Civil War, and after the Republican defeat she escaped to Moscow, and was later sent to Paris (Díaz, 2000). Felisberto married her in 1949, but they lived together for only two years. Hernández was a professed anticomunist, but he provided his wife with the opportunity to go to Uruguay, a country open to exiles, where she could remain without her identification papers. From there, she organized Soviet spying activities throughout Latin America. Hernández was never aware of this. He would have been horrified by the mere suspicion of his wife's activities. His opposition to Marxism and Leninism was so strong that by about 1956 he began speaking out against them at the "Radio Carve" in Montevideo, and he published two articles on the same subject in the 27 December 1957 and 2 January 1958 issues of the newspaper *El Día*. (Neither of these has ever been collected in book form.)

Settling again in Montevideo in mid-1948, Hernández returned to the modest job at the Uruguayan Authors General Association (AGADU) that he had held five years earlier. Actually, he loathed that job, which required him to keep a daily record of the tangos that were broadcast by different radio stations. Felisberto, who had loved classical music since he was a boy, and who had composed some short pieces for the piano ("Negros," "Bordoneos" [Bass sounds], and others) hated tango, a very popular music from the River Plate. The job eventually overwhelmed him, and some of his friends, very important intellectuals, asked the Uruguayan Parliament to provide him with a "suitable job" that would allow him to continue his literary activities without discomfort. However, this request was ignored.

In 1954 he began an affair with the teacher Reina Reyes, who used her official contacts to get him a job in the offices of the National Press. During this period, as well, Hernández returned to music after having spent several years away from the piano. He took part in a dramatic piece called *Caracol col col . . . o largando el coturno* (1959), directed by José Estruch, a Spanish exile in Montevideo, and by Antonio Larreta of Uruguay. He also published "The Flooded House." In a letter to Supervielle, dated 28 December 1952, he had said that he was about to finish it and that "I had never worked harder at the same thing; actually, I have

remade it thousands of times" (Sicard, 1977). At this time he also wrote the fragmentary and experimental "Diario del sinvergüenza," which was published after his death, as well as some theoretical works, such as "Algunas maneras de pensar la realidad" (Some ways of thinking about reality). In these texts, especially in "The Flooded House," Hernández achieves a high degree of literary elaboration and poetic and philosophical thinking. As in *Las hortensias*, "Menos Julia," and "El acomodador," this story evokes a strongly mysterious atmosphere and a single symbol (in this case, water) pervades everything. In this tale a writer is invited by a fat woman to her home, a big house that she has flooded in order to conduct a strange ceremony within it.

*El frente de la casa estaba cubierto de enredaderas. Llegamos a un zaguán ancho de luz amarillenta y desde allí se veía un poco del gran patio de agua y la isla. El agua entraba en la habitación de la izquierda por debajo de una puerta cerrada. El botero ató la soga del bote a un gran sapo de bronce afirmado en la vereda de la derecha y por allí fuimos con las valijas hasta una escalera de cemento armado.*

(*Obras completas*, vol. III)

The front of the building was covered with creepers. We reached a wide hall with a yellowish light from where we could see a little of the great waterlogged garden and the island. Water seeped into the room on the left under a closed door. The boatman tied the boat's rope to a bronze frog affixed to the pavement on the right, and we walked that way with our suitcases up to a cement staircase.

The most interesting thing in this tale may not be the plot, full of "strange situations," but the fact that the text itself can be read as a theory of narration, in which, as the story unfolds, "all the possible forms of the origin are thought: the origin of the subject, of language, of writing, of narration, of the tale itself," as Jorge Piranesi says (Rama, 1982). In spite of his limited academic background and the fact that he was not widely read (he knew Proust, but he came across Kafka and Whitehead quite late, and near the end of his life he read lots of detective novels), Felisberto Hernández was always conscious of the narrative process. He wrote several brief texts that could be considered his poetics. The first one, the very short "Explicación falsa de mis cuentos" (A false explanation of my tales), came out in 1947, during the period when the magazine *Entregas de la licorne* was published in Montevideo. It was written at the request of Roger Caillois, an important French critic, and it develops, through the metaphor of botany, into a theory of literary creation:

> *Obligado o traicionado por mí mismo a decir cómo hago mis cuentos, recurriré a explicaciones exteriores a ellos. No son completamente naturales, en el sentido de no intervenir la conciencia. . . . Mis cuentos no tienen estructuras lógicas. . . . En un momento dado pienso que en un rincón de mí nacerá una planta. La empiezo a acechar creyendo que en ese rincón se ha producido algo raro, pero que podría tener porvenir artístico. . . . sólo presiento o deseo que tenga hojas de poesías; o algo que se transforme en poesía si la miran ciertos ojos. Debo cuidar que no ocupe mucho espacio, que no pretenda ser bella o intensa, sino que sea la planta que ella misma esté destinada a ser, y ayudarla a que lo sea.*
>
> (*Obras completas*, vol. III)

Forced or betrayed by myself to tell how my stories are made, I will use explanations which are outside them. They [the stories] are not entirely natural, since consciousness takes no part in their construction. . . . My tales do not have any logical structure. . . . At a given moment I think a plant will be born in a corner inside me. I begin to sense it, feeling that something strange has taken place in that corner, something that might have an artistic destiny. . . . I only sense that it has leaves of poetry; or something that could become poetry if properly perceived. I must prevent it from filling to much space, from intending to be beautiful or intense, and help it to be the plant it is destined to be.

Roberto Echavarren explains that "if the plant refers to the product—the narration itself—its origin refers to the writing process" (1991). In other texts, which are almost sketches, such as those which were entitled by the editors "He decidido leer un cuento mío . . ." (I have decided to read a tale by myself . . .) and "Hoy quisiera mostrar . . ." (Today I would like to show . . .), Hernández insists upon the distinction between consciousness and "the natural," which are not necessarily opposed. He also expresses the idea that his tales require an oral reading, and so he would seek a sort of musical rhythm in his prose that would take him back to his origins. This dissociation becomes extreme in

"Diario del sinvergüenza," in which identity is fragmented and there is a search for its reconstruction through the act of writing:

> *Una noche el autor de este trabajo descubre que su cuerpo, al cual llama "el sinvergüenza," no es de él; que su cabeza, a quien llama "ella," lleva, además, una vida aparte: casi siempre está llena de pensamientos ajenos y suele entenderse con el sirvergüenza y con cualquiera.*
>
> *Desde entonces el autor busca su verdadero yo y escribe sus aventuras.*
>
> (*Obras completas*, vol. III)

One night the author of this work finds out that his body, which he calls "the rogue," is not his; that his head, which he calls "she," has a life of her own; she is almost always full of foreign thoughts and deals with the rogue and with everybody else.

From then on, the author looks for his true self and writes of his adventures.

After breaking off with Reina Reyes, Hernández, as in similar circumstances in the past, moved in with his mother. He did not write much, and yet his publishing situation improved, for one of his books, which contains "The Flooded House" and "The Crocodile," was included by Ángel Rama in the select collection *Letras de hoy* (Letters of today), which he edited for the Alfa Press in 1960. Some of his tales were included in anthologies, both in Uruguay and elsewhere, and he experienced the moderate pleasure of a final public tribute, which took place in the Amigos del Arte (Friends of Art), attended by a group of important young critics, including Rama and Díaz, as well as Guido Castillo. However, by this time his health had become impaired.

In 1963 he was admitted to the Hospital de Clínicas in Montevideo, where he was diagnosed with acute leukemia. Shortly before his death in 1964, *The Stray Horse* was released in a new edition, published by Ediciones del Río de la Plata. The young editor, Gustavo Rodríguez Villalba, asked Hernández for some information about his life and works, in order to write an introduction to the book. These pages, written in a laconic prose but full of illustrative and obsessive details (such as every favorable opinion he had received), were reprinted in the *Revista de la Biblioteca*

*Nacional* (*National Library Review*) in 1987. Felisberto Hernández died on 13 January 1964.

Hernández's work, which was ignored until 1960, has since become an essential part of Latin American literature. It is unusual to find an anthology of Latin American short stories of his period that does not include his texts, with "El balcón" and "The Crocodile" being the stories most frequently included in such collections. Every book about the history of Latin American literature reserves a place of privilege for him, at least since the mid-1970s, primarily because of his contributions to antirrealistic narrative, which began to prosper in Latin America only after his death. In university courses in Latin American literature his texts are increasingly studied. The number of Spanish editions of his books has multiplied, although he has had one edition of his complete works translated into French (published by Seuil in 1997, translated by Gabriel Saad), and his books have not yet been translated into other languages, such as Portuguese and English, while only a handful of his short stories have been translated into English. Thus, it remains difficult for non-Spanish readers to gain access to his work.

# SELECTED BIBLIOGRAPHY

## *Primary Works*

### *Books*

*Fulano de tal.* Montevideo: José Rodríguez Riet, 1925.
*Libro sin tapas.* Rocha: La Palabra, 1929.
*La cara de Ana.* Mercedes, 1930.
*La envenenada.* Florida, 1931.
*Por los tiempos de Clemente Colling.* Montevideo: González Panizza Hermanos, 1942.
*El caballo perdido.* Montevideo: González Panizza Hermanos, 1943.
*Nadie encendía las lámparas.* Buenos Aires: Sudamericana, 1947. (Contains "Nadie encendía las lámparas," "El balcón," "El acomodador," "Menos Julia," "La mujer parecida a mí," "Mi primer concierto," "El comedor oscuro," "El corazón verde," "Muebles 'El Canario,'" and "Las dos historias.")

"Autobiografía." *Revista de la Biblioteca Nacional* (Montevideo), 30 December 1949. Reprinted in *El espectáculo imaginario, I.* Edited by José Pedro Díaz. Montevideo: Arca, 1991.
*El cocodrilo.* With drawings by Glauco Capozzoli. Montevideo: Marcha, 30 December 1949. Reprint, Punta del Este: El Puerto, 1961.
*Las hortensias.* Montevideo: Talleres Gráficos Gaceta Comercial, 1949. *Separata* of *Escritura*, no. 8 (December).
*La casa inundada.* Montevideo: Alfa, 1960. (Contains "La casa inundada" and the short story "El cocodrilo.")
*Tierras de la memoria.* Epilogue by José Pedro Díaz. Montevideo: Arca, 1965.

### *Correspondence*

"Selección de cartas a la familia." In *Felisberto Hernández: Del creador al hombre.* Montevideo: Banda Oriental, 1975. (Contains 17 letters from the author to his mother and brothers, written between 30 January 1922 and 12 January 1948.)
"Selección de cartas a Lorenzo Destoc." In *Felisberto Hernández: Del creador al hombre.* Montevideo: Banda Oriental, 1975. (Contains 10 letters dated between 26 December 1939 and 8 June 1943.)
"Carta a Lorenzo Destoc." In *Felisberto Hernández ante la crítica actual.* Edited by Alain Sicard. Caracas: Monte Ávila, 1977. (Written in Paris on 9 October 1947.)
"Dos cartas a Jules Supervielle." In *Felisberto Hernández ante la crítica actual.* Edited by Alain Sicard. Caracas: Monte Ávila, 1977. (Includes correspondence dated between 28 December 1952 and 10 March 1955.)
"Correspondencia entre Felisberto Hernández y Paulina Medeiros." In *Felisberto Hernández y yo.* Montevideo: Biblioteca de Marcha, 1974. (Includes about 100 letters dating from January 1943 to 7 April 1948. A second edition of *Felisberto Hernández y yo* was published by Libros del Astillero in 1982.)
"Las cartas de Felisberto Hernández a Reina Reyes." In *¿Otro Felisberto?* by Ricardo Pallares and Reina Reyes. Montevideo: Casa del Autor Nacional, 1983. (Contains eight letters written between 8 August 1954 and 1 October 1954.)
"Carta a Washington Lockhart." In *Felisberto Hernández, una biografía literaria,* by Washington Lockhart. Montevideo: Arca, 1991.
"Carta-relato de viaje de Felisberto Hernández [a Alfredo y Esther de Cáceres]." In *Deslindes. Revista de la Biblioteca Nacional* (Montevideo), 2–3 (May 1993).

## Collected Works

*Primeras invenciones.* Montevideo: Arca, 1965. Introduction by Norah Giraldi de Dei Cas. (It corresponds to volume I of the first edition of the *Obras completas* and contains the books published between 1925 and 1931, and some works that had not been published, specifically some poems and a brief drama).

*Diario del sinvergüenza y últimas invenciones.* Montevideo: Arca, 1974. (It is volume IV of the *Obras completas,* first edition).

*Obras completas.* 3 vols. Edited by José Pedro Díaz. Montevideo: Arca, 1981–1983. Second edition, edited by David Huerta. Mexico City: Siglo XXI, 1983.

## Translations

"The Crocodile." In *Fiction* 5, no. 1:5–8 (1976). (This special issue of *Fiction* is subtitled *A Tribute to Marcha,* and was edited by Emir Rodríguez Monegal.)

*Piano Stories.* Translated by Luis Harss. New York: Marsilio, 1993. (This collection includes stories previously published in *Nadie encendía las lámparas,* such as "The Daisy Dolls" ["Las Hortensias"], and "The Flooded House" ["La casa inundada"], along with *The Stray Horse* [*El caballo perdido*].)

## Secondary Works

### Bibliographies

Rela, Walter. "Bibliografía, 1926–1982." In *Felisberto Hernández: Valoración crítica.* Montevideo: Ciencias, 1982.

Rivera, Jorge B., with Pablo Rocca. "Bibliografía del autor." In *Felisberto Hernández, una escritura de vanguardia: Historia de la literatura uruguaya contemporánea,* vol. 2. Montevideo: Banda Oriental, 1997. Pp. 63–67.

### Critical and Biographical Studies

Antúnez, Rocío. *Felisberto Hernández: El discurso inundado.* Mexico City: Katún, 1985.

Barrenechea, Ana María. "Ex-centricidades, di-vergencias y con-vergencias en Felisberto Hernández." In *Textos Hispanoamericanos, de Sarmiento a Sarduy.* Caracas: Monte Ávila, 1978. Pp. 159–194.

Benedetti, Mario. "Felisberto Hernández o la credibilidad de lo fantástico." In *Literatura Uruguaya siglo XX.* Montevideo: Seix Barral, 1997. Pp. 154–157.

Benítez Pezzolano, Hebert. "Felisberto Hernández y Vaz Ferreira: Las trazas del origen" and "Clemente Colling o el otro itinerario del 42." In *Interpretación y eclipse. Ensayos sobre literatura uruguaya.* Montevideo: Fundación Bank Boston/Linardi y Risso, 2000.

Calvino, Italo. Introduction to *Nessuno accendeva le lampade,* by Felisberto Hernández. Turin: Einaudi, 1974. Pp. v–viii.

Córtazar, Julio. Prologue to *La casa inundada y otros cuentos,* by Felisberto Hernández. Barcelona: Lumen, 1975. Pp. 5–9.

Díaz, José Pedro. "Felisberto Hernández." In *El espectáculo imaginario. I.* Montevideo: Arca, 1991.

———. Introduction to *Novelas y cuentos,* by Felisberto Hernández. Caracas: Biblioteca Ayacucho, 1995.

———. *Felisberto Hernández, su vida y su obra.* Montevideo: Planeta, 2000.

Echavarren, Roberto. *El espacio de la verdad: Práctica del texto en Felisberto Hernández.* Buenos Aires: Sudamericana, 1991.

Ferré, Rosario. *"El acomodador": Una lectura fantástica de Felisberto Hernández.* Mexico City: Fondo de Cultura Económica, 1986.

Giraldi de Dei Cas, Norah. *Felisberto Hernández: Del creador al hombre.* Montevideo: Banda Oriental, 1975.

———. *Felisberto Hernández: Musique et littérature.* Paris: Indigo and Côté-Femmes Éditions, 1998.

———, et al. *Actas del coloquio: Homenaje internacional a Felisberto Hernández. Nadie encendía las lámparas, 1947–1997, Nuevas variaciones críticas.* Lille: Ediciones del Río de la Plata, 1998.

Gómez Mango, Lídice, ed. *Felisberto Hernández. Notas críticas.* Montevideo: Fundación de Cultura Universitaria, 1970.

Lasarte, Francisco. *Felisberto Hernández y la escritura de "lo otro."* Madrid: Ínsula, 1981.

Lockhart, Washington. *Felisberto Hernández, una biografía literaria.* Montevideo: Arca, 1991.

Panesi, Jorge. *Felisberto Hernández.* Rosario: Beatriz Viterbo, 1993.

Rama, Ángel. *Felisberto Hernández.* Capítulo Oriental, 29. Montevideo: CEDAL, 1968.

———, ed. "Felisberto Hernández." *Escritura* (Caracas), (January–February 1982).

Sicard, Alain, ed. *Felisberto Hernández ante la crítica actual.* Caracas: Monte Ávila, 1977.

Vitale, Ida. "Tierra de la memoria, cielo de tiempo." *Crisis* (Buenos Aires), October 1974, pp. 4–11.

Xaubert, Horacio. *Desde el fondo de un espejo: Autobiografía y (meta)ficción en tres relatos de Felisberto Hernández*. Montevideo: Fundación Bank Boston/Linardi y Risso, 1995.

Zum Felde, Alberto. *Proceso intelectual del Uruguay*, vol. 3, third edition. Montevideo: Nuevo Mundo, 1967. Pp. 195–205.

# Lêdo Ivo

## (1924– )

### Gilberto Mendonça Teles

Brazilian writer Lêdo Ivo was born in Maceió, Alagoas, Brazil, on 18 February 1924. In *O aluno relapso* (1991; The lapsed schoolboy), a hybrid book that blends poetry, the short story, essay, and testimonial, the author tells a story in the first person, beginning thus: "I was the first in the class; he was the last. . . . But I envied him: for me he represented the adventure of transgression." That schoolboy ends up being expelled from the Marist School, and it is not until forty years later, on a trip to Maceió, that the narrator meets up with him again, by this time "a professor of law and a high court judge, rich and respected, with rigid conservative or even authoritarian political beliefs. He considered religion an indispensable restraint for human excesses." At the end of *O aluno relapso* is a particularly revealing comment, with a great touch of modesty and autobiography: "The formidable desertion made me the heir of the lapsed schoolboy. The sense of adventure and transgression that he shed in his spiritual metamorphosis went on to become mine." The narrator continues:

> Eu desmentira os vaticínios que rodeavam a minha austera reputação de primeiro da aula, tornando-me um poeta, e era agora, na idade madura, o aluno relapso que secretamente desejara ser na adolescência.

I put the lie to the predictions that surrounded my stark reputation as the first in the class, becoming a poet and now, in middle age, the lapsed schoolboy that I secretly wished to be as an adolescent.

There is no doubt that this figure resembles Professor Serafim Gonçalves in Ivo's later novel, *Ninho de cobras: Uma história mal contada* (1973; *Snakes' Nest: A Tale Badly Told*, 1981), but what is of interest here is the discussion of the "lapsed schoolboy," the desire of an adolescent "I" who was well-behaved and who silently admired the "unruly classmate"—who smoked during recess, broke the rules, proclaimed the nonexistence of God, and bragged about his sexual exploits. The future writer unconsciously took him as a model during his formative years. And, throughout his long literary career, though he may not have taken up smoking or proclaimed himself an atheist, he seems to have assimilated the feeling of unruliness, the sense of adventure and of the transgression of literary rules, all the while retaining deep inside his creative spirit the memory of the well-behaved schoolboy, illuminated from time to time by the flashes of lapses. Ivo preserves in his work traditional forms that are constantly renewed, along with a dissatisfied sense of aesthetic restlessness that makes him move ahead and, at the same time, turn back, improving upon himself, following the oldest meaning of relapse. (In Portuguese, the term also refers to someone who is obstinate, tenacious, who goes beyond the limits of the ordinary. The Latin *lapsus* derives from the Indo-European root *lab-* or *leb-*, which conveys the idea of viscosity and slipperiness. Figuratively, the Latin term also denotes that which flows back, turns back, or changes. Thus the term incorporates both its ordinary meaning and a psychological one as well, and Ivo uses it metaphorically and rhetorically to indicate a person who knows how to cleverly weasel out of his adversary's traps.)

This same tenacity, insistence, and sense of continuity characterizes Ivo himself, placing him among the most important poets in contemporary Brazilian literature. In the 1974 essay "A indecisão semiológica de Lêdo Ivo" (The semiologic indecision of Lêdo Ivo), we had already perceived this *glissante*, slippery feeling in his poetry, where the poet's "I" is located at the same time in a "place" and in an "in-between place," simultaneously "in this one" and "in that one," in Europe, in the United States, in Mexico, or in Brazil, like an alibi, searching always for new aesthetic adventures, but always within the *Ethic of Adventure,* as the title of one of his books from the early 1980s puts it.

In Ivo's creative output—poetry, the short story, novel, or essay—the traditional is in an ongoing dialogue with the new, regardless of the genre in which it manifests itself. His creative process merges the two extremes of literary time, whether the poet is at the heart of his works, in the almost arid plain of Academia, or in the heights of the constellations at his place on the outskirts of Teresópolis.

It is undeniable that poetry holds a fundamental place in Ivo's works taken as a whole. It is the seminal point of his creative output, for which reason we will deal with it first, then go on to examine his works of fiction, and finally his essays, which reflect, directly or indirectly, all of his literary production, intellectually fleshing out his poetry and fiction.

As with any great poet, Ivo has from time to time throughout his more than fifty years of literary activity thought to collect his books of poetry in editions emblematic of the time, as he did in 1962, bringing together his first five books under the title *Uma lira dos vinte anos* (A lyre of the twenties). In 1974, at age fifty,

he put together another volume, again gathering together nearly all of his poems to date, and giving it the suggestive title *O sinal semafórico* (The semaphoric signal). That collection did not include the award-winning *Finisterra* (1972), which would appear in the large anthology *Estaçaõ central* (1976; Central station). There are other anthologies, such as *Os melhores poemas de Lêdo Ivo* (The best poems of Lêdo Ivo), published by Global in 1983, that gather some previously unpublished poems. In addition, anthologies of the poet's works have been published in various countries such as Mexico, the United States, Peru, Ecuador, Venezuela, Spain, and Holland. But it is Ivo's first two collected editions—*Uma lira dos vinte anos* and *O sinal semafórico*—that constitute the high points, the *suma,* of his poetic process. They form two series that oppose and complement each other, giving his poetry greater meaning.

A comparison of the two series helps illustrate the aesthetic contours of the generation of '45, and the author's success in moving beyond those contours. In *O sinal semafórico,* the poet likens himself to a transmitter of signals, to a semaphore—better yet, to the signal emitted by the semaphore; he sees himself as a beacon on the seashore, a telegraph pole on the street, or a lighted signal in the center of the city, emitting messages for the aesthetic satisfaction of man. But with Ivo, the the signal itself is of less consequence than the adventure of its transmission, or the adventure of transgressing it. When we recognize this, we arrive at a better reading of the writer's work, seen first in its role in ordering the historical and literary process of its time, and then in ordering itself, and we recognize the writer as the producer of a discourse whose aesthetic unity constitutes a model of one of the many possibilities of modern Brazilian poetry.

For Alceu Amoroso Lima (Tristão de Athayde), modernism renews itself not through opposition, but through indefinite transition, through a difference in nature and not in time, for the modernist poets endeavored to adhere to discipline, not to creative freedom, attempting to restore ties with the public and establishing the primacy of verse in poetry. In the chapter on neo-modernism from *Quadro sintético da literatura brasileira* (1959), Lima also calls attention to the sense of universality that characterizes the new generation. As was the case in Europe following World War I and the first avant-garde movements, the purely destructive impetus no longer made sense in Brazil in 1945. It was a time of democratic reconstruction and of full freedom of speech, a freedom that called for new inquiries and approaches.

The greater part of the aesthetic feats around 1945 were germinating in the works of the first modernist poets, many of whom had begun their production within the Parnassian and symbolist canons, so that they did not always manage to free themselves of rhyme and metrics. Without the experiments of the modernists of 1922 and the discipline of the modernists of the 1930s, there would not be that literary convention, that predominant poetic and rhetorical thought that allowed the poetry of the new generation of '45 to be accepted. The new generation had the intention of combating the poetry of the modernists, already felt to be "old"; in reality, what it did (as with João Cabral and Lêdo Ivo) was to perfect certain elements that were abandoned or least explored by the earlier generation, always attempting to go further in the creation of new forms of diction that would affirm and perfect the differences and oppositions.

Ivo is, without doubt, the most active and the most polyvalent of his contemporaries. As a result of his temperament, his literary culture, his multifaceted capacity as a creator, and his natural competence as a craftsman, he assumed a position of leadership early on among a group of poets who, under the influence of foreign literatures that brought them up to date, ended up transforming the poetic and rhetorical concepts that some (not all) of the modernists had initially abandoned. In his preface to the *Antologia da moderna poesia brasileira* (1967; Anthology of modern Brazilian poetry), edited by Fernando Ferreira de Loanda, Ivo wrote a forcible manifest in favor of the "new poetry," clearly setting forth his critical viewpoint of modernism and of the contexts in which the generation of '45 appeared.

Ivo's poetry began to appear at a time when almost all of the Brazilian poets, fulfilling a natural cycle of evolution, were focusing on language—not only on meter or on rhyme, for it is the conditioning of language that motivates or requires those figures. It is undeniable

that his work contributed greatly to the diffusion of new ideas and to some rhetorical elements being revitalized and prepared for the effectiveness of a new language. Meanwhile, motivated perhaps by his "didactic instrument," by his use of poetry to make proselytism and attract new readers to the 1945 generation's aesthetics, the critics began to see the poet as the guide of his generation, with time silencing the excellence of his poetry and transferring to it all the weaknesses and dilutions of his colleagues and followers.

"O laboratório da noite" (The nighttime laboratory) is the second poem in *As imaginações* (1944; The imaginings), a book with surrealist tendencies which already presaged a new poetic diction in the sense of aesthetically breaking off with modernism. This poem already bears some of the characteristic elements of Ivo's various poetic and theoretical compositions. The poem reveals that its inspiration arises from Arthur Rimbaud in the "alchemy of dreams"; it represents the beginning of the author's concern with the opposition of the sky and the earth, which will constitute the backbone, the paradigm, of the majority of the poet's images. In addition, it focuses on literary language, manifesting a theory and a practice that accord with the conscious line of literary creation:

> Ó livro de poesia
> meu didático instrumento
> de solidão e de dor
> és mecânico à noite
> e náufrago voltado à praia
> ou clima sem intuição.

> The poetry book
> my didactic instrument
> of loneliness and of pain
> is a mechanic at night
> and a shipwreck returning to shore
> or climate without intuition.

An apt observation, this reflection on his own poetry is to be found in various poems in his opus, such as those "flowers of rhetoric" in his "Pequena elegia" (Small elegy) from *Cântico* (1949). It is the result of an inner necessity, in which the poet sees literary language from the inside, intransitively. Apparently, this type of metalanguage is of an external nature—that is, the poet appears to choose the elements of artistic language like objects and speaks of them as participating in a transitive relationship, from A to B, attempting to reduce them to an expression, an "ex-pression" or pressure that moves from the inside outward, as did Rimbaud (whose *Une saison en enfer* and *Illuminations* Ivo translated in 1957) and as some expressionist poets did at the beginning of the twentieth century. Ivo's expression is thus a presentation and at times a representation of an idea or of an aesthetic and literary concept, the communication of some knowledge, having much in common with Romantic realist expression.

Hailed as the young prodigy of the new generation, Ivo mixed the "alchemy of dreaming" with the "didactic instrument" in his nighttime laboratory, in this manner delineating the guidelines of a lyricist's craft. Ambiguity runs through all of his poetry. There is an undeniable concern with didactics, with rhetoric, and above all with the lesson, with the word "lesson," as if behind each poem there were a calculated and silent attitude of proselytism, of example, of a vague Platonic ideal that his "didactic instrument" was analyzing.

Ivo's concern with the word "lesson" is documented abundantly in his work, appearing at the level of expression and sometimes disrobing itself at the level of content. This is the case with some of the poems in *Estação central*, where the realism of didactic representation is achieved. Take, for example, "Primeira lição" (First lesson):

> *Na escola primária*
> *Ivo viu a uva*
> *e aprendeu a ler.*

> *Ao ficar rapaz*
> *Ivo viu a Eva*
> *e aprendeu a amar.*

> *E sendo homem feito*
> *Ivo viu o mundo*
> *com seus comes e bebes.*

> *Um dia num muro*
> *Ivo soletrou*
> *a lição da plebe.*

> *E aprendeu a ver.*
> *Ivo viu a ave?*
> *Ivo viu o ovo?*

> *Na nova cartilha*
> *Ivo viu a greve*
> *Ivo viu o povo.*

> At elementary school
> Ivo saw a grape
> and learned to read.

> On becoming a young man
> Ivo saw Eva
> and learned to love.

> And being a mature man
> Ivo saw the world
> with its food and drink.

> One day on a wall
> Ivo slowly read
> the common people's lesson.

> And he learned to see.
> Did Ivo see the bird?
> Did Ivo see the egg?

> On the new primer
> Ivo saw the strike
> Ivo saw the people.

*Estação central* establishes an idea of irradiation and confluence and, moreover, of the irradiation of poetic energy, but in its first part it also expresses a clear political and social involvement. For this reason it was hailed as a "new era in Lêdo Ivo's poetic career," as can be seen on the flap for the first edition. This also makes *Estação central* a book that is truly central to his work, as the title suggests: it constitutes an experiment that is essentially extraneous to the two collections of his poetry. First, this book marks the end of the "didactic instrument" in the consolidation of the generation of '45, so much so that the poet makes apologies for its presence: "Forgive me if I am didactic. I do not come to discourse nor do I nourish educational intentions." In addition this book marks the birth of another concern (social alienation) in a period in which the majority of Brazilian poets were pressured, on the one hand, by leftist critics and, on the other, by the aesthetic dictatorship, the avant-garde experiment of concrete poetry, which led many poets to experiments that were not always adequate or convincing.

Leaving aside the contextual relationships and considering it now as a whole, Ivo's work can be analyzed on the basis of two collections that oppose and complement each other: *Uma lira dos vinte anos*, with texts from the writer's formative period, which are very representative of the generation of '45; and what is referred to here as *Linguagem* (1951; Language), containing the books from his transformation phase, which represent the poet's attempt to better himself and to improve upon the subject matter of his poetry, revisiting his preferred subjects and elaborating upon the possibilities of their literary conception. These two collections together form *O sinal semafórico*, the general title for the bulk of his poetry up to 1974. The books that came afterward did not rigorously alter the "semaphoric signal" and of transgressing and running it. Perhaps they can be read as a confirmation phase (in the sense of *confirmatio*, that is, of maturing, of confirmation in the religious sense), as a synthesis or a *suma*, as the vertex of these two collections, the time of the poet's greatest and freest expressiveness.

The author of *O sinal semafórico* knows how to seek balance, combining long, free-form verses with the fluent decasyllables of his innumerable sonnets; he knows how to energize his verses and poems, not leaving among them the porosity and the slackness that weaken style and poetry; in addition, he knows how to combine lessons from the classics and lessons from daily life in the text itself.

The title of the first anthology of his poems, *Uma lira dos vinte anos*, must be read as possessing a double reference: it points simultaneously to the intuition of Rimbaud and to the lucidity of Álvares de Azevedo. Ivo virtually and ironically compares himself to the two poets, given that the title, in addition to entailing an implicit comparison in that both Lêdo Ivo and Álvares de Azevedo "are" in their twenties, also expresses a snide quality and indirectly suggests that, as the German poet Johann Goethe noted, there is a perfection that is to be had only in one's twenties.

Ivo's poetry is a constant dialectic between a chaos that wishes to be poetic and a cosmos that wishes to be poetry. Hence the struggle between order and disorder, between poetics and rhetoric, between day and night, between enlightenment and blindness, for the poet "aspires to an unknown and lucid discipline," and, with regard to Poetry, he sees himself as a "blind man who waits for the restoration of the great enlightenment" and is always "undecided between inventing it or discovering it." It is through this avowed indecision that Ivo becomes strong, constructing a poetry that has withstood the experiments of the Brazilian avant-garde movements gallantly and advantageously.

Ivo's poetry also reflects an alliance between formalism and emotion. With his in-depth knowledge of the poetic rhetoric, from medieval poetry and the balladeers on up to contemporary poetry, Ivo is among those who have revalidated the sonnet (a genre abhorred by modernism), as in the book *Acontecimento do soneto* (1948; The sonnet event), through experimentation and the exploration of possible ruptures within that set form of literary tradition. But in addition to such formal and aesthetic rigor, there is in his work the presence of geographical elements which, at first glance, seem prosaic, an ancestral and native earthiness which celebrates the daily things of Maceió, such as the semaphore of his childhood, the rusty and rotted ships, the dunes, the mangroves, the blue crabs, the bats, and so many other items that serve as a counterpoint to the astronomical and cosmological images that run through his books. With that in mind, one can perceive the difference between Ivo's poetic work and that of João Cabral, for example. The poet's semiologic indecision, his apparent contradictions, constitute the base, the platform for his learning and for his certainty—for it is in the vertex of that contradiction that we find his departure from the commonplace, from life, and from language. These prosaic elements accentuate the contrast between Ivo's work and the aseptic poetry of his own generation. Too much emphasis has been given to the poet's status within his generation, when its guide, its leader, and some might say its "father" was João

Cabral de Melo Neto, and Ivo himself was in fact considered something of a transgressor, a *mauvais sujet*. For example, Ivo's work departs from the rhetoric of '45 in its use of unusual, surreal images, which some American critics equate with the imagist poetry of William Carlos Williams, despite its musicality or fluidity. *Estação central,* written after a sojourn in the United States in 1963, marks a stylistic turning point for the author. Previously, his work showed traces of European poetry (Charles Pierre Baudelaire, Giuseppe Ungaretti, Rimbaud, Rainer Maria Rilke, Stéphane Mallarmé, Paul Valéry, T. S. Eliot, Ezra Pound, and Jorge Guillén), deriving from both his stay in Paris and from his own humanist education.

The books *Acontecimento do soneto* and *Ode ao crepúsculo* (1948; Ode to twilight) characterize well the duality present in Ivo's canon. They are opposite to one another, yet alike. The opposition arises at the level of the poem, and comes from the use of different rhetorical elements, but they share similar elements at the level of language. The technical elements are easily perceived in their commutations—the fixed form of the sonnet (often dismantled, which corresponds to an evident transgression) and the free form of the modernist ode; metrics and free verse; rhyme and no rhyme; regular and irregular stanzas—which, as a general observation, can be taken as a defining feature of the semantic level: opposition and contrast. Note the profession of faith in the first sonnet, when the poet states, "and immersed in the past, I would be / ever more modern and more ancient."

With the precise free verse of *Ode e elegia* (1945; Ode and elegy) and *Ode ao crepúsculo,* the poet introduced the aesthetic phrase into Brazilian poetry. Regarding *Ode e elegia,* Álvaro Lins wrote that its verses are "unfurled like waves"; at the same he proclaimed that Ivo is "the most powerful and complete representative of the new generation." Sérgio Buarque de Holanda, in conversation with the poet, emphasized the difference between the poet and his contemporaries by drawing attention to his incantatory and metaphorical language and to the multiplicity of his rhythms and meters. Ivo is, then, a true transgressor in terms of his generation, of which João Cabral de Melo Neto is a typical and representative poet: the iconic figure par excellence. In

the poem "Balada à bruma" (Ballad to the mist), from *Ode e elegia,* there is a long verse in which the contrast and the consequent visual emphasis placed on the word "constellation," one of the poet's favorite terms, become evident: "Have I gone crazy or are the constellations going to be reborn in these misty skies?"

At times the contrast expresses admirable sensual nuances, as in this verse from the second piece in *Ode ao crepúsculo*: "Your breasts swell in the shadows, expelling the rotations of adolescence." The meaning of the word "rotations," of astronomical significance, creates corporal and temporary associations, resolving itself in a visual and dynamic expression, as if the moon's rotation each month, expressed menstrually, were expelling the image of the adolescent and were amplifying the secret vibrations of love blossoming. The comma divides the verse into two segments, which are also opposed to each other; and each segment is constructed on the figure of a contrast: breasts swelling, shadows, expulsion, adolescence. The dynamism of "breasts swelling" is identified with the dynamism of "expelling." It is the basis of the similarity of the images. And the darkness of the "shadows" is opposed to the brightness of "adolescence." Underneath it all, meanwhile, total brightness is subjacent: the breasts swell, destroying the shadow, expelling the "shadows" of adolescence, which harks back to the "lyre" of the twenties.

Ivo's *Linguagem* represents virtually the last segment of the poetic discourse that is *O sinal semafórico.* If there exists an avowed "didactic" intention in the first segment, a creative struggle between inspiration and conscience from which the equilibrium between contrasting images (day and night) issues, what predominates in the second segment, under the sway of the emphasis on language, is the concern with the claim to be lucid in the creative act, gradually becoming content with the brevity of the writing. Take, for example, this excerpt from the poem "Fronteira" (Frontier) in *Um brasileiro em Paris e o rei da Europa* (1955; A Brazilian in Paris and the king of Europe):

> *Do ofício e do artifício conjugados*
> *como o faro e os cães no dia de caça,*
> *resta a fronteira sonora que atravesso*
> *transformado em sintaxe.*

From craft and artifice conjoined
like scent and dogs on hunting day,
the sonic barrier that I cross remains
transformed into syntax.

One of Ivo's major concerns is with the ideal of a "separate kingdom," and indeed he composed a poem with that title. In it, there is a reference to "abstract beauty"; a statement: "In profile, I am words"; and a philosophical postulation of poetic language: "From the sea that I think up I make the sea that exists. What am I if not language?" This ontological vision of language is an important feature of this collection, though in it the balance between consciousness and intuition is maintained, in the sense of ever more rational content and ever more conscious formulation.

*Linguagem* furnishes excellent material for understanding this new conception of the poet's. It affirms that "life can be summarized in a few symbols" and that "at a sign from its spirit, the rocks dance." At the level of the signifier, balanced expression continues: long verses and decasyllables, free-form poems and sonnets, verbal effusiveness and contained expression. At the level of meaning, balance is achieved at a higher degree: along with the oppositions of day and night, and sunlight and shadow, fusions of these contrasts begin to appear. The poet now speaks of "light of darkness," "blind lamp," "blind knowledge," and even of "nighttime sun," as in the tradition of Cruz e Sousa, a theme studied in *A escrituração da escrita* (1996). But an attempt at repudiating the "heroic acts" of '45 can already be noted here. That is why the poet says that his "mouth no longer knows how to say the old words" and that he is "always on the street talking with men / distilling the bare afternoon out from among the dust and the rhetoric." Another great contradiction is set up here, and it is quite characteristic of this collection: the containment of language in the face of political and social concerns. The poet wishes to think up his discourse, wishes to feel it "disconnected" from the '45 group, but he finds himself "pressured" by his surroundings to also think about the ideological spectacle. Hence his attitude—wishing to take part, although he finds it better to hide himself in language:

*Na beira de tudo, acima da zona onde a linguagem,*
*isenta da visão dos objetos, só se lembra a si mesma,*

*escondo-me, puxando as cortinas dos símbolos,*
*para fitar um mundo sem intérpretes.*

Up on the eaves of it all, above the zone where
      language,
free of the vision of objects, remembers only itself,
I hide, drawing aside the curtains of symbols,
to gaze at a world without interpreters.

From here—or, rather, from the contradiction of "Goodbye, secrecy, land of feigned death"—Ivo's poetry engenders a new contradiction: that of placing itself on a middle road between the beacon and the semaphore, according to an expression that is repeated in his work. It is already the road of *O sinal semafórico:* hesitating between the significant ambiguity of beacon and the metalinguistic meaning of semaphore. It is as if the poet were also hesitating between the signal and the symbol, as if his poetic message wished to reach the receiver and were held back by the net of images that makes it murky, that is to say, specifically literary. In this manner, the message involved becomes expressed, for example, in a sonnet on the atomic bomb; the reflection on language itself becomes illuminated only by the "bonfire of images" which contents itself with keeping a "sun in equilibrium." Even so, Ivo's poetry becomes more and more magical, continually more full of luminosity, of constellations, galaxies, suns, planets, heavenly phenomena, beacons and semaphores, in such a manner that it is only by "drawing aside the curtains of symbols" that the reader catches a glimpse of that signal of "light within light" into which the poetry of his later books slips.

In the second part of *Estação central,* there is a prose poem, "Além do passaporte" (Beyond passports), which also can be read both as a creative act and as a look at that creative act, as Roland Barthes might say. There are propositions in it that reiterate the opposition that dissolves, through a special series of images, into material of the language code. They are oppositions that go on from book to book and, as is inevitable, appear in the greatest unit of his poetic discourse. They are expressed through a graded network of synonyms which, selected and ordered, offer an optimum view of the transition, of the passage from the ideological universe (the real world) to a purely literary universe, as in the examples that can be taken as models, given the frequency of these words in all of the poet's books: on the one hand, the graded series "constellation" to "sun" to "day" to "beacon" to "signal"; on the other hand, in opposition word-for-word with the previous series, the gradation "twilight" to "eclipse" to "night" to "blindness" to "blind sun"; finally, as a convergence of the two series, the words "semaphore" and "symbol." But it is necessary to remember that another series exists as well, which at the same time celebrates the mangroves and crabs of Maceió and the skyscrapers of New York, which sings of Paris, San Francisco, Washington, Rome, Amsterdam, and Copenhagen, revealing a vision of the world and a planetary awareness of mankind at the end of the twentieth century.

The poet continually avails himself of a baroque game, which is processed through antithesis, through opposition, contrast, and paradox, going from light to shadow and frenetically seeking the ideal synthesis in the fabrication of hybrid images, such as "blind sun," "the other side of dawn," "day with its blind eye," or, as in the poem, "O Homem e a chuva" (Man and the rain) from *Magias* (1960): "You are in between the light and the shade, / in the place of sorcery." But a greater example of these contrasts lies in the spatial opposition between the constellations in the sky and "the occasional earthly constellations" in the poem "Além do passaporte," mentioned above:

> A noite dá a sua lição de universo: as estrelas
>   caem. . . .
> De súbito, surgem debaixo das estrelas as ocasio-
>   nais constelações terrestres: ilhas, criolas, paraísos
>     explosivos que se espraiam, no mar
> espumoso, como frag-
> mentos de um continente esfarelado.

> The night offers up its lesson on the universe: the
>   stars fall. . . .
> All of a sudden, arising underneath the stars
>   are the occa-
> sional earthly constellations: islands, natives,
>   explosive paradises that splay themselves, in
> the foamy sea, like frag-
> ments of a crumbled continent.

There are not two universes, but one, with its two hemispheres or with its zenith and its nadir, since for the poet heavenly accidents (falling stars), seen from

the airplane on a trip to New York in 1963, "are inscribed in the rhetoric of the cosmos where everything is order and precision." And earthly accidents (including the political allusion to explosive paradises) "reiterate to the pallid sun the tiring vigor of symbols." The idea of the order and precision of the "rhetoric of the cosmos," representative of the lucid side of poetic creation, questions the chaos of the explosive paradises (Cuba) and the tiring vigor of symbols (the Statue of Liberty, for example), representative of that political and social impetus of the era in which the book was written.

That order and that precision may have had an indirect relationship with the new avant-garde movements that were at their height in the early 1960s. But what was order and precision at the level of equilibrium between similarities and differences, as in the poetry of the generation of '45, became order and precision merely at the level of differences, as in the radical nature of concrete poetry. Having taken on the adventure of form, Ivo did not entirely risk the new adventures in language, preferring to remain, for the good of Brazilian poetry, "between inspiration and the dictionary," fabricating its "day of rhetoric," saying that he was inventing some form ("I am the form that I invent and I invent the form / that invents me and launches me among the stars"), but, as he puts it, "torn between inventing it and discovering it."

It is through this ambiguity—better said, this polysemic dimension transformed into rhetorical material—that Ivo achieved the individual style which has made him the exponent of a generation, which affiliates him with the best Brazilian modernism and gives him, ultimately, that aura of a great poet which he has been confirming book by book, as is the case with those published since 1980. Among these: *A noite misteriosa: Poesia* (1982; Mysterious night: Poems), a species of bucolic poem in which the subject is linked to the mythical space of its site, with poems of all types of forms, from metered to free verse, long and short, as in "O Lugar" (The place): "Where is God? / Hidden in the swamp / between the rubber trees. // God is nowhere. / God is everywhere." In *Mar oceano* (1987; Ocean sea), the same subject matter continues, including a touch of the erotic, of original sin, as in "A mancha irreparável" (The irreparable stain): "You pubis—the black sheep / in the white flock of your body." And such books as *Crepúsculo civil* (1990; Civil twilight), *O aluno relapso,* and *Curral de peixe* (1995; Fish pen) extend and deepen the subject of the quotidian, treating it in the freest manner possible—free in the sense that the poet really appears spontaneous, recording like a chronicler the *fait-divers* of poetry. A beautiful example can be taken from *Crepúsculo civil,* in the poem "Na cadeira do engraxate" (The shoe shine chair):

> *Amanheci Deus.*
> *E curvado aos meus pés*
> *um pálido engraxate*
> *entoa a sua prece.*
>
> *Do alto do meu trono*
> *contemplo ao meu redor*
> *a poeira do universo*
> *e os pecados dos homens.*
>
> *Do couro avariado*
> *uma flanela extrai*
> *espelhos e lampejos.*
>
> *Uma boa gorjeta!*
> *Os meus sapatos brilham*
> *E ofuscam as estrelas.*

> I awoke having become God.
> And hunched over at my feet
> a pale shoe shiner
> intones his prayer.
>
> On high from my throne
> I survey my surroundings
> the dust of the universe
> and the sins of men.
>
> A flannel cloth extracts
> mirrors and lights
> from damaged leather.
>
> A beautiful tip!
> My shoes shine
> and outshine the stars.

A reading of Ivo's work, aimed at perceiving that "simultaneous unity" of which Northrop Frye speaks (in *The Critical Path,* 1973), immediately reveals a quality of semantic opposition. A binary structure is inscribed in its poetic discourse that becomes articulated in the direction of an ideal synthesis, corroborated by the more recent books and finding its reason for being in language.

Antithetical images truly are a constant in Ivo's poetry. The poet has, on the one hand, the blindness of creative intuition; on the other, the almost mathematical lucidity of expression. Hence, we have the two poles of images, of "light that shines hidden in the bluish white night," that are common in his poetry, counterpoised baroquely and coming together in the contrast and paradox of common phrases in his work, such as "blind sun" and "sun seen backwards," where both the signifier and the meaning appear affected by the magical clash between predominantly visual images. Although initially a concern with balance exists, the poet knows that he goes "through life aimlessly / almost lucid from drunkenness!" Afterward, we witness the poet digging into "the inexorable / treasure of language," lifting up "the skirt of syllables" and curiously contemplating "consonants." In his later books, Ivo approaches language as a human product, with its "gestures, voices, signs," its "idiom of tears," its "eternal recurrence," its "sand that refracts writings," its "luminous myth," and its "excess cum parsimony," as in the poem "Fronteira seca" (Dry frontier) from *Finisterra.*

What draws the readers' attention most in the work of this poet is an almost exaggerated concern with the beacon, the signal, the sign, and the semaphore, above all with this latter, as a symbol of departure and evasion, visible in the numerous references to ports and wharves. It is clear that these words already appear in the earlier books, as well as in the prose texts, but it is only here that they acquire a poetic function which is no longer that of simple reference to a reality recalled. The transition seems to take place in *Magias,* where there are such verses as "And what was content deception is today a beacon," in which the Camões phrase, "ledo engano" (content deception), blends with the poet's name, and both blend together in the light of that beacon, which can be read in many directions. In *Estação central*, the poet says that beacons and semaphoric signs are the world, and in *Finisterra* there is an "Homenagem a um semáforo" (Homage to a semaphore):

> *Aquele semáforo junto ao mar, na minha infância.*
> *Sempre amei as coisas que indicam ou significam algo*
> *—tudo o que, em silêncio, é linguagem.*

> That semaphore by the sea, during my childhood,
> I always loved things that indicate or signify
>     something
> —all that, in silence, is language.

The line of antithetical images finds, on the syntactical plane, a type of expression that serves it as a complement. The poet, who states that he is torn between inventing and discovering poetry, who speaks of his duel between inspiration and the dictionary, also has an ostensible preference for the midpoint. He is always in between something: "between booing and cheering," "between the beacon and the sea," "between the sea and the beacon," "between the ship and the sea," "between mystery and fluff," "between the morning light and my lamp," "between the bright and the shady," "between the earth and the telstar," "between the green and the red," and "between the beacon and the semaphore," a phrase which is repeated three times in his work. This midpoint assumes at times the character of a manifest: "and I would be, immersed in the past, / ever more modern and more ancient," writing, like Bergson, that "the poet is not merely his verses. It is outside of these, / in what is inexpressible and in what is unarticulated, that his richness / is made and remade." Thus Ivo, knowing of the pleasure of adventure and transgression, seeks balance in his poetry, preferring to transgress from within, without fanfare, constructing the best with his intuition, with his artistic lucidity, and making his own ambiguity, his semiologic indecision, the main impetus for his poetic creation.

The narratives of Lêdo Ivo—his novels, stories, and tales—form a less exuberant picture than his poetry, but they maintain a dialogic relationship of complementariness with it: what cannot be said in poetic language, surrealistically, earns its place of realism in a work of fiction. His narratives can be seen as paraphrases, that is to say, as an exposition of subjects which, given their nature, are not suitable to the more circumscribed form of the poem.

Ivo's debut novel, *As alianças* (1947; The alliances), is set in southeastern Rio de Janeiro (Maceió, the poet's hometown, is in the northeastern part of Brazil) in the 1940s. In addition to that geographical "transgression," this novel, then considered immature by some critics, is noteworthy because of another technical current: that of the English Romantics, especially James Joyce, Virginia Woolf, and Rosamond Lehman. A story of unfulfilled ambitions, frustrated destinies, loneliness, and abandonment in a big city, *As alianças* won the Graça Aranha Prize previously bestowed upon Clarice Lispector.

Sixteen years after his prose debut with the novels *As alianças* and *O caminho sem aventura* (1948; The unadventurous road), Ivo wrote his third novel, *O sobrinho do general* (The general's nephew), published in 1964, the year of the military coup against the administration of João Goulart. Aside from the title (which points to militarism and thereby to the nepotism common in periods of dictatorship), the novel—better said, the novella—has nothing to do with that period of Brazilian politics. It does, however, deal with the preceding period, against which the military staged its revolution. In this sense, the relationship it bears with future events is one of contiguousness, metonymy, and prophecy. As a narrative, it is technically traditional, with a drama of estrangement and arbitrariness. Set in Rio de Janeiro, the story stars, on the one hand, a general who is "the pillar of the system" and, on the other, the troubled figure of Arthur, tied up with the absurdity of a crime he did not commit.

But the novel that garnered the most attention from critics both in Brazil and abroad was *Ninho de cobras* (*Snakes' Nest*, 1981), first published in 1973, which earned the honor of winning the fourth Walmap Prize, the most prestigious prize for fiction then awarded in Brazil. "Ninho de cobras" is a Brazilian slang expression. It is equivalent to the "ninho de rato" of the Portuguese, for it means "confusion," "messy business," "difficulty," "a group or place of perverse, ill-behaved people." As the title of the novel, it refers symbolically to Maceió, in northeastern Brazil, which it compares to a "ninho de cobras." In reality, the novel underscores the writer's objective of portraying the Alagoans who did not emigrate—those who love their native land the way cobras love their rocky nests.

The action of the narrative takes place in the capital of Alagoas, a place of sugar barons, gunmen, and many poor people. The novel, which takes place in twenty-four hours, begins with a vixen traversing the city's streets at dawn, a strategy to create the verisimilitude necessary for the novel's context. The vixen will be beaten to death early in the morning, causing great commotion in the city, described from the vixen's point of view. Along with the city, its inhabitants appear, and along with them, the history of the region, where the Caetes Indians (the subject of a novel by Graciliano Ramos, another Alagoan) "swallowed up" the Portuguese bishop Pero Fernandes Sardinha in the fifteenth century. It is actually a great satire, in which the characters appear with their spurious desires and their petty miseries caricaturized. Among these are the famous attorney associated with the Death Syndicate, who waits for the fall of the New State to grab political power; the poor prostitute whose dream is to become part of the city's most important brothel; the man who writes anonymous letters to tell the city's secret stories and who, after various frightening experiences, ends up being murdered; and the nun who spends nights at the window. In the midst of it all, the region's historical past emerges: the Caetes' anthropophagy, the betrayal of Calabar (joining up with the Dutch, "with honey-colored eyes and blonde hair," as in the offspring of Professor Serafim Gonçalves), the visit of Pedro II and the taking up again of an absurd process, and, exemplifying the novel, the critical and satirical description of the portrait of Getúlio Vargas that appears everywhere, sometimes alongside the Sacred Heart of Jesus. It is a novel that it is a pleasure to read, with language that is constantly interspersed with poetic images, a book which, according to Josué Montello in an article for *Jornal do Brasil*, renews the modernism of northeastern Brazil and, in the words of Antônio Olinto, is "without any doubt a masterpiece of the modern novel in any language."

There is yet another novel, *A morte do Brasil* (1984; The death of Brazil), but equally important are Ivo's books of stories, among them *Use a passagem subterrânea* (1961; Use the underground passageway) and *O flautim* (1966; The piccolo), both set in Rio de Janeiro. The dialogue between fiction and poetry resolves itself in favor of the latter, which predominates, invading the narratives as if these expanded upon subjects that it is difficult to reduce to poetic language. That is more or less also the case with his literary essays.

Like any great poet, Ivo creates and, at the same time, thinks poetry. While his theoretical musings may well lack the coherence and the degree of rigorousness of the philosophers of Poetics, they have a clarity and a feeling of personal sincerity that attracts the reader and illuminates him or her with the force of their limpid language, as in the studies he gathered together under the title *Poesia observada* (1967; Poetry observed), or in such books as *Modernismo e modernidade* (1972; Modernism and modernity), *Teoria e celebração* (1976; Theory and celebration), *Confissões de um poeta* (1979; Confessions of a poet), *A ética da aventura* (1982; The ethics of adventure), *O aluno relapso*, and *A república da desilusão* (1995; The republic of disillusionment), in which art, literature, and primarily poetry are contemplated theoretically in the sense of the root of theory, which is the same as Ó, God and, more remotely, the Indo-European root dei-, with the original meaning "to shine," a passive, almost mystical, poetic, and not totally active contemplation, as in the science of literature.

Ivo's essays constitute a great polyphonic dialogue, in the sense of Mikhail Bahktin: they are voices surrounding the poet's great voice, which are closely related to his poetry and to his narratives, voices which confirm them, which establish the authorial context, in which the writer's intelligence flares and flares again on the most varied literary subjects, in a language with great emotional attraction, as in one of the final texts of *Confissões de um poeta*:

> *Aos cinqüenta nos, presumo já ter vivido o bastante para assistir a um acontecimento que, apesar de minha formação artística, não deixa de surpreender-me. Quero referir-me à mudança de gostos nos jovens. Eles adoram outros ídolos, e desconhecem ou desprezam aqueles que iluminaram a minha adolescência e juventude. . . . Consolo-me imaginando os jovens de hoje reunidos numa melancólica festa de sobreviventes,*

*cada um deles agarrado ao osso de uma nostalgia ou ao fiapo de um desilusão. . . .*

*Esta idéia de que Deus mata os homens como se eles fossem moscas—visão poética, que encontro em Shakespeare—é mais completa do que muitas teologias e filosofias acumuladas. A teoria de um Deus indiferente, que ignora o nome de suas almas, ou mesmo de um Deus lúdico (que vê no homem um brinquedo ou divertimento) não me parece carente de sedução.*

*Por que Deus haveria de ter respeito pelos homens? Pergunto-me. E, em torno de mim, zunem moscas importunas.*

At the age of fifty, I presume that I have lived enough to be able to attend an event, which, despite my artistic background, does not fail to surprise me. I am referring to the changing tastes among young people. They worship other idols and are unaware of or look down upon those that lit up my adolescence and young adulthood. . . . I console myself imagining the young people of today gathered together in a melancholy celebration of survivors, each one of them holding on to the bone of a nostalgia or to the thread of a disillusionment. . . .

This idea that God kills men as if they were flies—a poetic vision I find in Shakespeare—is more complete than many theologies and philosophies put together. The theory of an indifferent God who has no idea of the name of their souls, or even of a playful God (who sees man as a toy or diversion) does not seem to me to be lacking in seductiveness.

Why should God have respect for man? I ask myself. And all around me buzz annoying flies.

*O aluno relapso*, discussed earlier, has precious information for understanding the poetry itself as well as the process of its creation. The following statement is truly critical and absolutely faithful to Ivo's literary project:

*A minha predisposição para escrever poesia surgiu na adolescência, na época das primeiras leituras e descobertas. Eu me via diante de um universo que reclamava uma celebração. A ele confiei a minha singularidade, a minha expressão. Assim, desde o início a Poesia se impôs a mim como uma linguagem especial dentro da linguagem geral—uma linguagem tornada arte, e dotada ao mesmo tempo de som e signo, música e significação.*

*Eu aspirava a criar uma magia que me permitisse ser e existir no mundo dos homens.*

*Poderei chamá-lo de poeta? O apressado e ambicioso figurante da cena literária ignora a significação das cesuras na cadência de um verso, a diferença entre vogais longas e breves e os segredos das assonâncias e dissonâncias que produzem a sedução verbal do poema. Não sabe ainda que a poesia, sendo uma expressão, só expressa o que a retórica lhe permite exprimir.*

*Assim como um pintor deve saber pintar, e conhecer os segredos das combinações das tintas, e o músico deve conhecer as notas que se organizam para a composição, o poeta deve conhecer a sua arte—a arte de fazer poemas. . . .*

*A última vanguarda no Ocidente foi o surrealismo. Depois, todos os poetas e escritores se tornaram herdeiros e usuários de tudo. Aqui no Brasil, que é um país cosmético e epidérmico, muitos pensam que a imitação da vanguarda é também vanguarda, quando não passa de uma paráfrase suburbana.*

My predisposition to write poetry surfaced in adolescence, during the period of my earliest readings and discoveries. I saw myself before a universe that demanded celebration. To it I entrusted my singularity, my expression. Thus, from the start, Poetry imposed itself on me as a special language within language in general—a language become art and, at the same time, endowed with sound and signs, music and meaning.

I aspired to create a magic that would allow me to be and to exist in the world of man.

Should I call him a poet? The hurried and ambitious figurant of the literary scene not to know the meaning of caesuras in the cadence of a verse, the difference between long and short vowels and the secrets of the assonances and dissonances that produce the verbal seductiveness of a poem. He does not yet know that poetry, being a form of expression, only expresses, and that rhetoric allows him to express.

Just as a painter must know how to paint and know the secrets of the combinations of hues, and the musician must know the notes that are organized into a composition, the poet must know his art—the art of making poems. . . .

The last avant-garde movement in the West was surrealism. Thereafter, all poets and writers became the heirs and users of it all. Here in Brazil, a country that is cosmetic and skin-deep, many think that imitating the avant-garde is itself avant-garde, when it is nothing other than suburban paraphrase.

There, in more or less summary form, is the key to understanding Ivo's work as a poet, fiction writer, essayist, and translator who—in a career spanning more than five decades—continued to dignify his art and Brazilian literature at the dawn of the new millennium.

*Translated from the Portuguese by*
*Elizabeth Welborn Cardinale*

## SELECTED BIBLIOGRAPHY

### Primary Works

#### Poetry and Poetry Anthologies

*As imaginações*. Rio de Janeiro: Pongetti, 1944.

*Ode e elegia*. Rio de Janeiro: Pongetti, 1945.

*Acontecimento do soneto*. Barcelona: O Livro Inconsútil, 1948.

*Ode ao crepúsculo*. Rio de Janeiro: Pongetti, 1948. (Contains *A jaula*.)

*Cântico*. Illustrations by Emeric Marcier. Rio de Janeiro: José Olympio, 1949.

*Acontecimento do soneto e Ode à noite*. Introduction by Campos de Figueiredo. Rio de Janeiro: Orfeu, 1951.

*Linguagem*. Rio de Janeiro: José Olympio, 1951.

*Ode equatorial*. Wood engravings by Anísio Medeiros. Niterói: Hipocampo, 1951.

*Um brasileiro em Paris e o rei da Europa*. Rio de Janeiro: José Olympio, 1955.

*Magias*. Rio de Janeiro: AGIR, 1960. (Contains *Os amantes sonoros*.)

*Uma lira dos vinte anos*. Rio de Janeiro: Livraria São José, 1962. (Contains *As imaginações, Ode e elegia, Acontecimento do soneto, Ode ao crepúsculo, A jaula*, and *Ode à noite*.)

*Antologia poética*. Rio de Janeiro: Leitura, 1965.

*50 poemas escolhidos pelo autor*. Rio de Janeiro: MEC, 1966.

*Antologia da moderna poesia brasileira*. Edited by Fernando Ferreira de Loanda. Preface by Ivo. Rio de Janeiro: Orfeu, 1967.

*Finisterra*. Rio de Janeiro: José Olympio, 1972.

*O sinal semafórico*. Rio de Janeiro/Brasília: José Olympio/INL, 1974. (Contains the bulk of the author's poetry through *Estação central*.)

*Central poética*. Rio de Janeiro: Nova Aguilar, 1976.

*Estação central*. Rio de Janeiro: Tempo Brasileiro, 1976.

*O soldado raso*. Recife: Edições Pirata, 1980. Exp. ed., São Paulo: Massao Ohno, 1988.

*A noite misteriosa: Poesia*. With an essay by Carlos Montemayor. Rio de Janeiro: Record, 1982.

*Os melhores poemas de Lêdo Ivo*. São Paulo: Global, 1983.

*Calabar*. Rio de Janeiro: Record, 1985.

*Cem sonetos de amor*. Rio de Janeiro: José Olympio, 1987.

*Mar oceano*. Rio de Janeiro: Record, 1987.

*Crepúsculo civil*. Rio de Janeiro: Record, 1990.

*Antologia poética*. Selection by Walmir Ayala, with an introduction by Antônio Carlos Villaça. Rio de Janeiro: Ediouro, 1991.

*Curral de peixe*. Rio de Janeiro: Topbooks, 1995.

*Noturno romano*. Teresópolis, Brazil: Impressões do Brasil Editora, 1997.

*O rumor da noite*. Rio de Janeiro: Nova Fronteira, 2000.

#### Novels

*As alianças*. Rio de Janeiro: AGIR, 1947. 3d ed., São Paulo: Parma, 1991.

*O caminho sem aventura*. São Paulo: Instituto Progresso Editorial, 1948. 2d ed., wood engravings by Newton Cavalcanti. Rio de Janeiro: O Cruzeiro, 1958.

*O sobrinho do general*. Rio de Janeiro: Civilização Brasileira, 1964.

*Ninho de cobras: Uma história mal contada*. Rio de Janeiro: José Olympio, 1973.

*A morte do Brasil*. Rio de Janeiro: Record, 1984.

#### Short Stories and Tales

*A cidade e os dias*. Rio de Janeiro, 1957. 2d expanded edition, published as *Rio, a cidade e os dias*. Rio de Janeiro: Tempo Brasileiro, 1965. Republished with the essay *Ladrão de flor* as *O navio adormecido no bosque*. São Paulo: Duas Cidades, 1971.

*Use a passagem subterrânea*. Introduction by Adonias Filho. São Paulo: Difusão Européia do Livro, 1961.

*O flautim*. Rio de Janeiro: Bloch, 1966.

*80 crônicas exemplares*. Compiled by Herberto Sales. Rio de Janeiro: Ed. De Ouro, 1968.

*O menino da noite*. São Paulo: Companhia Editora Nacional, 1984. (Children's tale.)

*10 contos escolhidos*. Brasília: Horizonte, 1986.

*O canário azul*. São Paulo: Scipione, 1990. (Children's tale.)

*Os melhores contos de Lêdo Ivo*. São Paulo: Global, 1995.

*Um domingo perdido*. São Paulo: Global, 1998.

*O rato na sacristia*. São Paulo: Global, 2000. (Children's tale.)

#### Essays

*Lição de Mário de Andrade*. Rio de Janeiro: Ministry of Education and Health, 1951.

*O preto no branco.* Rio de Janeiro: Livraria São José, 1955.

*Raimundo Corrêa. Poesia.* Introduction, selection, and notes by Ivo. Rio de Janeiro: AGIR, 1958.

*O girassol às avessas.* Rio de Janeiro: Assoc. Bras. do Congresso pela Liberdade da Cultura, 1960.

*Paraísos de papel.* São Paulo: Conselho Estadual de Cultura, 1961.

*Ladrão de flor.* Rio de Janeiro: Elos, 1963.

*O universo poético de Raul Pompéia.* Rio de Janeiro: Livraria São José, 1963.

*Poesia observada.* Rio de Janeiro: Orfeu, 1967. (Essays on the creation of poetry; includes *Lição de Mário de Andrade, O preto no branco, Paraísos de papel,* and previously unpublished sections titled *Emblemas* and *Conveniências.*)

*Modernismo e modernidade.* Commentary by Franklin de Oliveira. Rio de Janeiro: São José, 1972.

*Teoria e celebração.* São Paulo: Duas Cidades, 1976.

*Alagoas.* Rio de Janeiro: Editora Bloch, 1976.

*A ética da aventura.* Rio de Janeiro: Francisco Alves, 1982.

*A república da desilusão.* Rio de Janeiro: Topbooks, 1995.

### Translations by Ivo

*A abadia de Northanger,* by Jane Austen. Rio de Janeiro: Editora Pan-Americana, 1944.

*Nosso coração,* by Guy de Maupassant. São Paulo: Livraria Martins, 1953.

*Uma temporada no inferno e Iluminações,* by Arthur Rimbaud. Rio de Janeiro: Civilização Brasileira, 1957.

*O adolescente,* by Fyodor Dostoyevsky. Rio de Janeiro: José Olympio, 1960.

*O holocausto,* by Albrecht Goes. Rio de Janeiro: AGIR, 1960.

### Other Works

*Confissões de um poeta.* São Paulo: Difel, 1979. (Autobiography.)

*O aluno relapso.* São Paulo: Massao Ohno, 1991. (Autobiography.)

Sant'Ana, Moacir Medeiros de. *Lêdo Ivo de corpo inteiro: Exposição biobibliográfica comemorativa de seus 70 anos.* Maceió, Brazil: Department of Culture, 1995. (Biobibliography.)

### Translation

*Snakes' Nest: A Tale Badly Told.* Trans. by Kern Krapohl, with an introduction by Jon M. Tolman. New York: New Directions, 1981. (Translation of *Ninho de cobras: Uma história mal contada.*)

### Secondary Works

### Critical and Biographical Studies

Albuquerque, S. J. "Lost in Maceió: Alienation in Ramos and Ivo." *Chasqui: Revista de Literatura Latinoamericana* 16, no. 2–3:11–21 (1987).

Araújo, Cleber Neves de. "Antologia poética de Lêdo Ivo." *Leitura* 109 (December 1967).

Azevedo Filho, Leodegário A. de. "Lêdo Ivo e a imagem poética contundente." *Jornal do Commercio,* 15 October 2000.

Baciu, Stefan. "Lêdo Ivo." In *Antologia de la poesia latinoamericana.* Albany: State University of New York Press, 1974.

Baden, Nancy T. *The Muffled Cries.* Boston: University Press of America, 1984.

Brait, Beth. "Lêdo Ivo, geografando nossa literatura." *Jornal da tarde* (São Paulo), 14 January 1983.

Bustamante, Alejandro Rodríguez. "Lêdo Ivo. El sembrador de incertidumbre." *Primera Plana* 43 (17–23 February 1984).

Campos, Marco Antonio. "Lêdo Ivo" and "Com Lêdo Ivo." In *Literatura em voz alta.* Mexico City: Universidad Autónoma de México, 1996.

Carvalho, José Cândido de. "Verão veio com romance de Lêdo Ivo." *O Cruzeiro,* 30 January 1974.

Castillo, Ignacio Carvallo. "Antologia poética de Lêdo Ivo." *El Universo,* 8 May 1966.

Corrêa, Wilson. "Lêdo Ivo e suas poesias." *Tribuna da Imprensa,* 14 June 1974.

Evans, Stuart. "From a View to a Death." *Times* (London), 23 March 1989.

Figueira, Gastón. *Nuevas expresiones de la poesia del Brasil.* Montevideo: ICUB, 1957.

Fischer, Almeida. "A luta pela expressão num romance primoroso." *O Estado de São Paulo,* 3 February 1974.

———. *O áspero ofício.* Brasília: Cátedra, 1983.

———. "*A morte do Brasil.* A nossa realidade vista por Lêdo Ivo." *O Estado de São Paulo,* 10 March 1985.

Guerra, José Augusto. "Ficção, memória e catarse." *O Estado de São Paulo,* 30 June 1974. Reprinted in *Correio do Povo,* 27 July 1974.

Helena, Lúcia. "Os melhores poemas de Lêdo Ivo." *Colóquio/ Letras* 84 (March 1985).

Junqueira, Ivan. "*Ninho de cobras.*" In his *O signo e a sibila.* Rio de Janeiro: Topbooks, 1993.

Keys, Kerry Shawn. "Lêdo Ivo e sua poesia." Trans. by Antônio Olinto. *O Jornal* (Maceió, Brazil), 5 December 1999.

Lima, Alceu Amoroso. *Quadro sintético da literatura brasileira.* Rio de Janeiro: AGIR, 1959.

Linhares, Temístocles. "Estado atual da poesia brasileira." *Gazeta do Povo,* 11 February 1973. Reprinted in his *Diálogo sobre a poesia brasileira.* São Paulo: Melhoramentos, 1976.

Lins, Álvaro. *Jornal de crítica.* Rio de Janeiro: O Cruzeiro, 1947.

Lisboa, Eugênio. *"Confissões de um poeta."* In *As vinte e cinco notas do texto.* Lisbon: Imprensa Nacional, Casa da Moeda, 1987.

———. *"A noite misteriosa."* *Colóquio/Letras* 74 (July 1983). Reprinted in *As vinte e cinco notas do texto.* Lisbon: Imprensa Nacional, Casa da Moeda, 1987.

McDowell, Edwin. "U.S. Is Discovering Latin America's Literature." *New York Times,* 16 February 1982.

Menezes, Carlos. "Calabar, de Lêdo Ivo. Um poema com vozes ancestrais do Nordeste." *O Globo* (Rio de Janeiro), 7 October 1985.

Montello, Josué. "Um romance de maturidade." *Jornal do Brasil,* 11 February 1975.

Montemayor, Carlos. "A poesia de Lêdo Ivo." In *A noite misteriosa: Poesia,* by Lêdo Ivo. Rio de Janeiro: Record, 1982.

Moutinho, Nogueira. "Lêdo Ivo: *Ninho de cobras.*" *Folha de São Paulo,* 17 February 1974.

Mutis, Álvaro. "Testimonio de un poeta." *De lecturas y algo del mundo.* Barcelona: Seix Barral, 2000.

Nunes, Cassiano. "Multiplicidade de Lêdo Ivo." *O Diário,* Part I, 9 December 1995; Part II, 16 December 1995; Part III, 23 December 1995. Reprinted together as *Multiplicidade de Lêdo Ivo.* Penedo: Fundação Casa de Penedo, 1995.

Olinto, Antônio. "Do romance que busca as origens do país." *O Globo,* 15 October 1973.

———. "Uma obra prima do romance moderno." *O Globo,* 5 December 1973.

———. "Lêdo Ivo na ficção de agora." *O Globo,* 27 December 1973.

Oviedo, José Miguel. "El romanticismo de Lêdo Ivo." *Quimera* 9–10 (July–August 1981).

Peixoto, Sérgio Alves. "Uma poesia de Lêdo Ivo ou uma teoria de pássaros." In *Os melhores poemas de Lêdo Ivo,* 3d ed. São Paulo: Global, 1998.

Pereira, Armindo. *De Drummond a Lêdo Ivo, e outros estudos.* Rio de Janeiro: Companhia Brasileira de Artes Gráficas, 1991.

Pinto, J. "Peircean Semiotic and Narrative Time: Ledo Ivo, *Ninho de Cobras.*" *Romance Notes* 27, no. 1: 4–12 (1986).

Pontes, José Couto. "A criação poética de Lêdo Ivo." *Correio do Estado,* 15–16 (December 1973).

Rebelo, Gilson. "Lêdo Ivo: Interrogação como seu fio condutor." *O Estado de São Paulo,* 30 September 1984.

Rennó, Elizabeth. *A aventura poética de Lêdo Ivo.* Rio de Janeiro: ABL, 1989.

Secchin, Antônio Carlos. "Perdas e danos." In his *Poesia e desordem.* Rio de Janeiro: Topbooks, 1996.

Silva, Mário Ferreira da. "Um olhar cultural sobre o espaço em *Ninho de cobras* de Lêdo Ivo." In his *Culturas, contextos e contemporaneidade.* Salvador, Brazil: Abralic, 1999.

Studart, Heloneida. "O diabólico Ivo." *Manchete,* 15 June 1974.

Teles, Gilberto Mendonça. "Estudo da poesia de Lêdo Ivo." *O Popular,* 14 July 1974.

———. "A indecisão semiológica de Lêdo Ivo." In his *A retórica do silêncio.* São Paulo: Cultrix, 1979.

———. *A escrituração da escrita.* Rio de Janeiro: Vozes, 1996.

Villaça, Antônio Carlos. "A geração de 45." *Jornal do Brasil,* 1 March 1975.

———. "Lêdo e Orlando." *Jornal de Letras,* November 1984.

*Interviews*

Antônio, João. "O nome curto é de um senhor poeta." *Tribuna da Imprensa* (Rio de Janeiro), 26–27 August 1995.

Ary, Antônio. "Um *Ninho de cobras* e amor." *Última Hora* (Rio de Janeiro), 9 January 1974.

"La creación poética en Lêdo Ivo." *Poesía* (Venezuela) 73 (1989).

Gomes, Osmar. "Poesia é aventura sem fim." *Anexo,* 12 March 1995.

"Lêdo Ivo, a poesia viva." *O Globo* (Rio de Janeiro), 23 June 1974.

Menezes, Carlos. "Lêdo Ivo: Uma seleção de poemas é chamariz para a obra completa." *O Globo* (Rio de Janeiro), 22 August 1983.

Name, Daniela. "Lêdo Ivo faz um mapa das desilusões na literatura." *O Globo* (Rio de Janeiro), 16 April 1995.

Penido, Samuel "Lêdo Ivo: Maldito ou subversivo, o poeta é um dos porta-vozes da sociedade." *Diário Popular* (Rio de Janeiro), 29 August 1980.

Yáñez, Ricardo. "La literatura mexicana es la mejor de la lengua española, dice el poeta Lêdo Ivo." *Unomásuno* (Mexico City), 24 May 1979.

# Tomás Eloy Martínez

## (1934–    )

### Nicolas Shumway

Although he has been a major force in the intellectual life of Argentina and Latin America since the early 1960s, Tomás Eloy Martínez did not attract widespread international attention until 1988, when the English translation of his 1985 *La novela de Perón* (*The Perón Novel*) was published in the United States. His reputation became truly global ten years later with the publication of his best-selling novel *Santa Evita* (1995; *Santa Evita*, 1996), which, by the end of the twentieth century, had been published in thirty-seven languages in fifty-four countries. While this article pays particular attention to these two novels, it also offers an overview of Martínez's remarkable and varied writings in many fields and genres. First is an overview of his intellectual biography, followed by analyses of his most important work.

Martínez was born on 16 July 1934 in the northwestern Argentine province of Tucumán. Like Argentina itself, Tucumán was once prosperous and promising. With income from large sugar plantations, the province developed a sophisticated aristocracy and produced some of the country's chief intellectuals, including the legendary Juan Bautista Alberdi. But for Martínez, Tucumán was a place of memories and spent mythologies, of families with high-sounding last names and exhausted fortunes. Martínez's own family history was one of loss and decay. Once large, the family fortune had been squandered by the time Martínez was born. Although his father was an architect, Martínez never knew wealth or even comfortable prosperity. With decline everywhere, idealization of the past became a provincial (and national) pastime. During his crucial formative years, Martínez witnessed the triumph of Peronism, that peculiar Argentine phenomenon that transfixed a nation and gave the budding author his richest narrative subject.

Juan Domingo Perón came on the national stage in the coup of 1943, was elected president of Argentina in 1946, and was ousted from office in a military coup in 1955. In 1973, at the age of eighty-three, he was re-elected president, only to die ten months later. Although he lived in exile from 1955 to 1973, Perón never ceased influencing Argentine politics, and even after his death Peronism as a political force and intellectual problem continued to haunt Argentina. Always at his side, in some sense even after her death, was the charismatic Eva Duarte, his second wife, whose tragic death from cervical cancer in 1952 at the age of thirty-three was only the beginning of her mythical life. To suggest the impact of Peronism on Martínez, note that he was twelve years old when Perón became president, eighteen when Evita died, and twenty-three when Perón was forced into exile in yet another coup. The author participated in the debates about Peronism during Juan

Domingo's exile and, in 1970 in Madrid, was allowed extensive interviews with the caudillo-in-waiting. In sum, Martínez's life, like that of most of his fellow Argentines, inevitably included an unending dialogue with Perón and Peronism. Many critics would agree that no one has succeeded in explicating the Peronist phenomenon better than Martínez.

Coincidental with the rise and fall of *peronismo*, in 1957 Martínez completed his *licenciatura* (roughly the equivalent of a combined bachelor's and master's degree) in literature at the Universidad Nacional de Tucumán. His thesis on the fiction of the avant-garde helped him become conversant with the best writers of the early twentieth century, and as a teenager he was already writing literary essays and reviews for *La Gaceta*, Tucumán's leading newspaper. Like many ambitious and talented provincials, Martínez eventually moved to Buenos Aires (in 1957) and soon after landed a job as film critic for *La Nación*, Argentina's most self-consciously cosmopolitan newspaper. In 1961, while still at *La Nación*, he wrote his first book, *La obra de Ayala y Torre Nilsson en las estructuras del cine argentino* (The work of Ayala and Torre Nilsson in the structures of Argentine cinema), a superb study on the work of one of Buenos Aires' best filmmakers. Although it is in part a history and critical study, this book reveals a fascination with the representation of reality and the Borgesian notion that our understanding of the world is shaped by the forms of representation we choose.

In 1962 Martínez joined the staff of the new weekly magazine *Primera Plana*, founded and directed in its early years by Jacobo Timmerman, an exceptional journalist who would later write *Prisoner without a Name, Cell without a Number*, a highly significant exposé of the human rights abuses of the military regime that governed (and brutalized) Argentina from 1976 to 1983. Since articles in *Primera Plana* are mostly unsigned, one can only suppose that much of the superb film criticism in the magazine was penned by Martínez. By 1965 he had become editor-in-chief of *Primera Plana*, a position he held until 1969. It was also in 1969 that he published his first novel, *Sagrado* (The sacred).

During the period 1969–1971, Martínez lived in France, where in 1971 he received a second master's degree, the Maétrisse de Littérature, from the University of Paris. His thesis, "Borges et la littérature fantastique" (Borges and the literature of the fantastic), reveals not only a profound comprehension of Jorge Luis Borges' thought but also a theoretical understanding of the fantastic as a literary genre. It was also during this time in Europe that Martínez made contact with Juan Domingo Perón, who was living in exile in Madrid. Much to Martínez's surprise, Perón took him into his confidence and in 1970 allowed him to record interviews over several days. These interviews were not published in their entirety until 1996, as part of the book titled *Las memorias del general* (Memories of the general).

In 1971 Martínez returned to Buenos Aires, where he first held a position with the weekly magazine *Panorama* and later became head of the cultural supplement of Jacobo Timmerman's newest daily newspaper, *La Opinión*, which quickly became Argentina's most stylish paper, both in format (derivative of *Le Monde*) and ideas (fashionably on the Left). The *suplemento cultural* (cultural supplement) brought to Argentine readers texts by some of the world's best writers and put Martínez in contact with key figures in Latin American letters, including Carlos Fuentes and Mario Vargas Llosa. Under Martínez's direction, the *suplemento* also provided informed and sophisticated commentary on literary and cultural tendencies of the time; some of the best were written by Martínez himself.

In 1974, however, the author's writing took a new turn that would set the course for much of his later work. In Trelew, a tiny city near a naval base in southern Argentina, twenty-two people associated with Argentina's leftist guerrilla movement were arrested and held in a local jail. Six managed to escape to Chile and eventually to Cuba. Their embarrassed military jailers tortured the remaining prisoners for information on further subversive movements and they groundlessly accused and jailed many civilians for sympathizing with the subversives. These detentions without evidence or due process anticipated the abduction, during the so-called Dirty War, of thousands of innocent Argentines, who would form the bulk of that country's "disappeared."

Things at Trelew spun rapidly out of control, ending in the massacre of the sixteen remaining prisoners. At that point, the civilian population joined in a mass protest against the military; in response, the military quickly backed down—at least for the time being. In Buenos Aires, Martínez got wind of the affair and immediately booked passage to Trelew, where, by sifting through news reports and interviewing hundreds of witnesses, he reconstructed the violent story and published it in a moving book titled *La pasión según Trelew* (1973; The passion according to Trelew).

The book is remarkable for several reasons. First, in great detail Martínez prophetically describes the paradigm of military oppression that would brutalize Argentina between 1976 and 1983. Second, having realized that traditional narrative strategies alone simply could not represent the events, he included news reports, verbatim interviews, military decrees, popular poetry, drama, political pamphlets, and essayistic passages of his own composition. The resulting prose collage forces the reader to become a co-narrator rather than a passive spectator viewing whatever the author has decided to offer. And, finally, the book suggests that Argentine reality defies any neat narrative line, that symbols, suggestions, open questioning of cherished national myths, and a prose style that asks more questions than it answers are the only possible approaches to describing this country's stormy history. Consequently, *La pasión según Trelew* is the real precursor of the narrative strategies of both *The Perón Novel* and *Santa Evita* and signals Martínez's growing conviction that the ever-elusive reality of Argentina can best be portrayed by blending history with fiction.

*La pasión según Trelew* also got Martínez into a lot of trouble. The original edition was quickly suppressed by the tottering new government of Isabel Perón, her husband having died only weeks earlier. Undoubtedly, however, the real force behind the campaign against the book was José López Rega, a Rasputin-like figure who had been present during Martínez's interviews with Perón in Madrid and was now Isabel Perón's principal adviser, depending by many accounts on spiritual consultations with the deceased Perón and Evita for guidance. Whatever his contacts with the spirit world, López Rega quickly recognized that a writer of Martínez's talents was an enemy in the here and now and thus, in May of 1975, forced him into exile under the threat of death.

Exile is, lamentably, an experience shared by many Argentines. As Martínez's fictionalized Perón in *The Perón Novel* notes, "En la Argentina no hay más hogar que el exilio" (In Argentina there is no home but exile). While not discounting the personal dangers and tragedies exile entails, Argentina's losses often proved to be gains for the countries that received the expatriates. Indeed, Hispanic studies outside Hispanic countries would be considerably impoverished were it not for intellectuals exiled by Francisco Franco's Spain, Perón's Argentina, and Fidel Castro's Cuba. And, in some sense, Argentina itself benefited from the perspective gained by the exiles as they reconsidered their country from afar.

All of this could be said of Martínez in exile. After a rocky beginning in Caracas, Venezuela, where he lived from 1975 to 1983, he was appointed editor of the *Papel Literario*, the literary supplement of a leading Venezuelan newspaper, *El Nacional*. In this task he was assisted by his wide experience as a journalist and editor in Buenos Aires as well as by the extensive contacts he had developed with Latin American intellectuals as cultural editor of *La Opinión*. Few Argentines entered exile supported by as wide a network of writers, editors, and publishers. Later, Martínez founded and directed a daily newspaper, *El Diario de Caracas*, in which he showed that no aspect of the newspaper business was alien to him. In Venezuela he also published three books. The first two were collections of his best essays: *Los testigos de afuera* (Witness from the outside) in 1978 and *Retrato de un artista enmascarado* (Portrait of a masked artist) in 1979. The third, also published in 1979, was a collection of short stories titled *Lugar común de la muerte* (The commonplace of death). After the return to democracy in Argentina in 1983, these three volumes were republished in Buenos Aires. All of them are enormously helpful in reproducing some of Martínez's best shorter pieces, but it is highly unlikely that a complete works will ever be published. The author began contributing on a weekly, if not daily basis to different newspapers in his late teens. Moreover, many of his reviews and commentaries in *Primera Plana* are unsigned. Indeed, one wonders if he would even recognize some of them as his own work.

In 1983, after compiling an appalling record of human rights abuses, economic mismanagement, and strategic ineptness in the war with the United Kingdom over the Falkland/Malvinas Islands, Argentina's thuggish and thoroughly discredited military leaders finally allowed the country to return to democracy. Many exiled Argentines returned, thus contributing to a long overdue cultural renaissance. Between 1984 and 1987 Martínez lived for six months in Argentina and six months in the United States, where he had an appointment at the University of Maryland. Martínez's columns again appeared in Buenos Aires' leading newspapers and magazines. Later, the author became director of the *suplemento cultural* of the daily newspaper *Página 12,* heir in style and readership to Timmerman's *La Opinión.* But in some sense Martínez had become accustomed to a bigger stage, for also in 1983, he received a fellowship from the Woodrow Wilson International Center for Scholars, where he began working on *The Perón Novel.*

Published in Spanish in 1985 and then in English in 1988, this work was an instant literary success and no doubt contributed to Martínez's winning a John Simon Guggenheim Fellowship to write a third novel, *La mano del amo* (The hand of the master), which was published in Buenos Aires in 1991. While *La mano del amo* was a critical success, it never gained a wide readership. Also in 1991, Martínez was contacted by a Mexican entrepreneur who wanted him to start up a newspaper in Guadalajara, Mexico, that country's second most populous city. The result was a classy and successful daily titled *Siglo 21,* on whose board of advisers Martínez still served a decade later.

In 1995 Argentina's Editorial Planeta published *Santa Evita,* which became a longtime best-seller in Latin America and Spain. While it is thematically similar to *The Perón Novel, Santa Evita* is a much more evocative book, less concerned with Evita's life than with her symbolic importance in Argentina's collective imagination. Within three years *Santa Evita* was translated into thirty-seven languages and published in fifty-four countries.

In May 1996 Editorial Planeta published Martínez's *Las memorias del general,* which includes transcriptions of the now-famous recorded sessions he held with Juan Domingo Perón in Madrid in 1970. The book also includes several essays on Peronism and Argentine culture that had appeared previously in other venues.

Two years later Planeta published a second edition of Martínez's collection of short stories, *Lugar común de la muerte,* which until then had been available only in its Venezuelan edition of 1978. The new edition includes three new short works. Then, in April of 1999, Martínez published *El sueño argentino* (The Argentine dream), a collection of previously published essays on the Argentine identity. Two new novels by Martínez, tentatively titled "El vuelo de la reina," (The flight of the queen) and "El cantor de tango" (The tango singer), are set to be published in 2002.

Martínez's new visibility as a world-class writer led to several academic appointments. From 1984 to 1987 he taught Latin American literature and history at the University of Maryland, lecturing on topics ranging from the Spanish conquest to the contemporary period. He has delivered lectures and seminars at the leading universities of North America and Europe, including Yale, Harvard, Texas, the Free University of Berlin, and the University of London, as well as at universities in virtually all of Latin America. The recipient of honorary doctoral degrees from the John F. Kennedy University of Buenos Aires and his alma mater, the Universidad Nacional de Tucumán, in 1995 Martínez became distinguished professor and director of the Latin American Program at Rutgers University in New Jersey. While living in Highland Park, New Jersey, he has attained worldwide visibility and continues to be a major intellectual force in Argentine and Latin American letters.

Since Martínez's international fame rests almost entirely on his novels, the remainder of this article is devoted primarily to his prose fiction with some final notes on his essays. Martínez's first novel, *Sagrado,* garnered little attention at the time of its publication and probably would have been forgotten altogether if Martínez's later work had not attracted so much interest. *Sagrado* reflects three hallmarks of Martínez's art: his interest in fantastic literature, his stylistic virtuosity, and the bond that brings him back repeatedly to the Tucumán of his childhood. Fantastic literature is a subgenre of Argentine and Uruguayan literature, which in some sense anticipated the much better known magical realism of Gabriel García Márquez. Fantastic literature is not science fiction, nor does it reflect the values of Alejo Carpentier's marvelous realism.

Carpentier could marvel at the complexities, oddities, and multiple time frames of Latin American reality without seeing these phenomena as anything magical or unworldly. In *Sagrado*, as in much fantastic literature, things happen with no reference to reality. A cousin brings *criaditas* ("little maids") from Buenos Aires, "para que la estirpe de las criaditas no se extinguiera en Tucumán" (so that the lineage of little maids would not become extinct in Tucumán). The same cousin opens her house to bats, so that no room would remain unoccupied. A character named Gosi becomes entrapped in spider webs but is rescued by a woman assisted by vixens and hens. Included in the book are twenty strategies virgins can use to defend themselves against men who would deflower them. Both Gretel (Hansel's sister in the fairy tale) and Snow White show up at a wedding in time to toast the newlyweds. And so it goes.

Attempts to read literature of this sort as allegory, as though every book has to have another book behind it, will probably fail, although we must not underestimate the ability of some readers to find meaning in odd places. What *Sagrado* does offer in spades, however, is a raucous good time, with a great deal of humor and a sense of the vibrancy and abundance of life. Moreover, however fantastic the details, the characters show humanity in their passions, and Martínez reveals a fondness for a Tucumán, which in his childhood probably did seem magical. The novel also shows his staggering talents as a stylist whose control of Spanish syntax and vocabulary has few equals.

Martínez's best-known novels are the very successful *The Perón Novel* and the blockbuster *Santa Evita*. Although easily able to stand on their own merits, these novels constantly invite comparison with history. Indeed, history is in some sense their primary subject, for Martínez repeatedly points out the similarities between historical and fictional narratives. Of course, historians strive to base their narratives on evidence. Ultimately, however, generating any narrative involves a selection process that eliminates the vast majority of the details, favoring some over others. In making these selections, historians decide what is important, choosing to focus on economic factors, personalities, natural phenomena, or some other aspect. Such selections inevitably reflect the historian's time and personal bias.

How else can we explain the exclusion of minorities and women in much historical writing? Nor can historians avoid interpretation. The evidence does not always speak for itself. Historians inevitably try to tell what the evidence means and how it leads to certain results—just as the novelist strives to create a plausible, believable plot. Perhaps no single phenomenon illustrates the difficulties of historical writing better than that sprawling, complex, and contradictory phenomenon known as Peronism. Given the centrality of Peronism to Martínez's work, a short description is in order.

Peronism does not begin with Perón. Indeed, some would say that the roots of Peronism and the resentments on which it thrived began with the country itself. From the earliest days of its national history, Argentina has faced tumultuous periods of internal division, opposition, and exclusionary practices. In an interview with Caleb Bach for *Americas*, Martínez himself referred to his native land as "a complicated country." Despite these divisions, in the early 1900s Argentina was one of the great success stories of the New World. With widespread prosperity resulting from the agricultural bounty of the country's generous and seemingly inexhaustible pampas, Argentina had a wealthy upper class with aristocratic pretensions, a large professional and commercial middle class, a world-class city in Buenos Aires, and an educational level that rivaled that of the world's most advanced countries. Moreover, its population had grown enormously, partly by natural increase but mostly from the hordes of impoverished European immigrants (primarily Italian and Spanish) who swarmed to Argentina's shores between 1860 and 1920, attracted by the promise of better living conditions. And for many those hopes became a reality; even Argentine working classes attained a standard of living often equivalent to that of their counterparts in developed countries.

But there were fissures under this seemingly tranquil social landscape. Argentina's prosperity had been attained under the rule of a smallish oligarchy dominated by a landed gentry and foreign traders. Tensions and disagreements occurred among the ruling classes, giving the country the appearance of a genuine democracy. Such disputes, however, were treated largely as family matters to be resolved by the gentry, the *gente decente*, and were not the sort of thing with which the lower classes should concern themselves. Elections were rigged to keep the already powerful in power, and leaders in every walk of life were often from old families—families "with a lot of last name" (*de mucho apellido*), as the phrase goes. Moreover, not everyone benefited from the country's bounty, particularly the working poor in the countryside and in the burgeoning slums of Buenos Aires. Within this economic framework, the wealthy, like their European counterparts, developed a sense of entitlement, although in Argentina the pretensions of the upper classes often seemed more theatrical, perhaps because the roots were less deep. Predictably, with entitlement for the few came resentment among the many.

Perón burst onto the national stage in 1943 as a participant in a military coup. A brilliant speaker who was both folksy and eloquent, he soon overshadowed his comrades-in-arms. Among his many talents, none seemed more remarkable than his ability to meld diverse, sometimes contradictory, forces into a single political movement. Left-leaning anti-imperialists, nationalists, traditionalist Catholics, fascists, workers, poor people, and provincials—all seemed to think that he was one of theirs. Perón fed—and fed on—resentment, gathering much of his support from people who felt left out. As one union man put it, Perón made workers feel good about themselves. Perón also galvanized a remarkably diverse group of detractors, including some who hated him for his fascist and authoritarian tendencies and others who merely found him vulgar. Given this huge range of attitudes, what may be the most remarkable and baffling aspect of Peronism is its ability to symbolize so many different things to so many different people. This is a story that Tomás Eloy Martínez tells better than anyone.

While no one knows exactly when the idea of a novel based on Perón began to germinate, the project received a big push when Perón allowed Martínez nearly twenty-four hours of interviews in 1970. Martínez quickly observed that Perón showed a peculiar indifference to the few facts that were known about him prior to 1943; rather, Perón embellished, added, suppressed, and invented, indicating that he mostly wanted to portray himself in the best possible light, to tell a compelling story. Perón, in a very real sense, was dictating his own novel, his own version of the past,

mingling fact with fiction in ways that perhaps even he did not perceive. While Perón was certainly capable of conscious falsification, Martínez suggests that he quite probably believed much of his own "novel." Adding to Martínez's growing sense of unreality were the interventions of his personal secretary, José López Rega, who indicated familiarity with details not even Perón could have known, including some that occurred before he was born. As it turned out, López Rega often indulged in visionary trances in which he claimed to have "seen" events where he was not physically present.

In these discussions, it readily became apparent that no one knew a great deal about Perón before the coup of 1943, when Perón was already fifty-three years old. Nor, for that matter, is it easy to do research on Perón after the coup, since the Argentine government has yet to give researchers full access to Peronist archives. Of course, the material written about Perón is as vast as it is contradictory. We know the basic facts—that he was raised in the country in southern Argentina, that he entered military school when he was fifteen, that he was an admired instructor of weaponry who attained the rank of colonel, and that throughout it all he was both likeable and distant. We know little, however, about what made the man and almost nothing about his highly significant formative years of childhood, adolescence, and early adulthood. It is in these areas that Martínez noticed the silences—that Perón hardly mentioned his mother, his first wife, or his aunts in Buenos Aires. Martínez later noticed how assiduously Perón hid other elements of his life, including his uncle's suicide and his own illegitimate birth. History—the facts and the hard evidence—cannot fill in these blanks, but Martínez, the informed and imaginative novelist, fills them in with probabilities (often more than one) that end up creating a much more plausible character than the one left by reliable evidence. In short, just as Perón "writes" his own novel, Martínez writes a novel based on the novel "written" by Perón.

Martínez pushes this idea even further by suggesting that all Argentines in some sense create their own novel of Perón, their own way of understanding how their lives interact with this figure of mythological dimensions. Indeed, the novel is a virtual catalog of different perceptions regarding Juan Domingo. One character is Héctor Cámpora, a Peronist true believer who became president solely to prepare the way for Perón's return. Cámpora sees Perón as the country's savior, a messianic figure who was expelled by unrighteous forces in the coup of 1955 and must reclaim his rightful place in Argentine history. Similarly, Martínez does a splendid job of reconstructing the confused enthusiasm of the so-called Peronism of the Left, which needed to create its own version of Perón. Argentine leftists often felt isolated from the popular classes in whose name they spoke. It was therefore only logical that they would seek to claim the idolized Perón as one of their own, a co-religionist seeking a Cuban-style revolution in Argentina, albeit with a different vocabulary, or to claim that Evita, had she lived, would be a leftist militant. In short, both Perón and Evita were signifiers waiting for others to invest them with whatever meaning their supporters and detractors wanted or needed.

Martínez argues that Perón consented to these many roles, perhaps because he could never decide on a single role for himself. Like a character in a novel, and despite his charismatic sway over many Argentines, he, too, was condemned to play the role others gave him. As the second paragraph of the novel affirms, "Nada le había pertenecido, y él mismo se pertenecía menos que nadie" (Nothing belonged to him; even his own self belonged to him less than any other self). Alternately resenting and glorying in the roles imposed on him, Martínez's Perón declares to López Rega:

*Si he vuelto a ser protagonista de la historia una y otra vez, fue porque me contradije. . . . ¿La patria socialista? Yo la he inventado. ¿La patria conservadora? Yo la mantengo viva. Tengo que soplar para todos lados, como el gallo de la veleta. Y nunca retractarme, sino ir sumando frases. La que hoy nos parece impropia puede servirnos mañana. . . . La historia es una puta, López. Siempre se va con el que paga mejor. Y cuántas más leyendas le añadan a mi vida, tanto más rico soy y con más armas cuento para defenderme.*

If I have become the protagonist of history over and over again, it is because I contradicted myself. . . . The socialist fatherland? I invented it. The conservative fatherland? I keep it alive. I have to blow in all directions, like the rooster on a weather vane. Rather than retract, I keep accumulating phrases. The one that today seems inappropriate can be useful to us tomorrow. . . . History is a whore, López. It always goes with the person who pays the most. And the more legends people add to my life, the richer I am and the more arms I have to defend myself.

What ultimately emerges from the novel, then, is a plethora of voices, some allegedly from Perón's public and private diaries, others from people who wanted to make him over in their own image, others from fabricated news reports and interviews, and still others that could well be Perón's inner dialogues with himself—in which, by the way, Martínez captures the tone and cadence of the historical Perón with uncanny accuracy. Consider, for example, the lengthy passages from his memoirs as dictated to López Rega, interspersed with passages affirming alternate versions of the same history. Martínez achieves not so much a complete portrait of a man as a series of colossal, but vague sketches to which others add their own brush strokes. Furthermore, readers emerge from the novel knowing that the real "Novel of Perón"—the one to which we all add as we seek to understand the man and the mythology he left behind—will never end; that, ultimately, the last symbol of the book is a question mark.

Lurking behind all this, of course, are questions like, What is history? Can history ever really represent something as complex and contradictory as the past? The past consists of absolutely everything that happened, from each frog's croak to every falling leaf. Obviously, no historian can possibly grasp the past in all its detail, much less reconstruct it in coherent, understandable narrative. Consequently, the first task of the historian is to reduce the past to a few essential details by selecting what appears to be important. In this process, much is deliberately left out, which explains why history for years could disregard the contributions of women or other marginalized groups. The historian's task is further constrained by the available evidence that is in virtually all cases incomplete, fragmentary, and subject to interpretation. Given the limitations of historical evidence—particularly in the case of someone like Perón, where so much was suppressed or fabricated by him, his followers, and his detractors—can a historian ever offer as true a picture of the past as the novelist? The novelist, like a painter, adds whatever details are necessary to give a painting a sense of completion. We do not lack for professionally competent biographies of Perón, one of the best in English being that of Joseph Page (*Peron: A Biography*, 1983). The problem with such studies is that the existing evidence simply cannot tell us who Perón was, nor can it explain his ongoing presence in the Argentine imagination. Page, for example, tells a complete and well-documented story. The problem is that his Perón—the Perón supported by documentation and sober research—simply could not have done all that Perón did. Martínez's Perón, in contrast, like Shakespeare's Richard III, is a highly believable character who, in spite of and perhaps because of the contradictions in the person and in the movement he created, renders the Peronist phenomenon more knowable if not always understandable.

With *Santa Evita*, written nearly ten years after *The Perón Novel*, Martínez published his first international best-seller. While it is certainly not a better novel than *The Perón Novel*, *Santa Evita* has the advantage of addressing the life of a more sympathetic character. Eva Duarte's obscure and illegitimate birth; her successful struggle to get ahead; her rise to political prominence; her child's sense of justice, which made her a ferocious enemy of privilege and a genuine defender of the poor; her untimely death—these are already themes of epic dimensions. Add to these themes the saga of her repeatedly embalmed body, which was hidden in Argentina, shipped secretly to Italy, present in Perón's Madrid house, and finally interred permanently in Buenos Aires more than twenty years after her death, and one has ample material for a great story—despite Borges' mordant comment that had Peronism been a novel, it would have been rejected as too bizarre. To make a great novel, however, great material is not enough. It is here that we are again awed by Martínez's imagination and virtuosity.

*Santa Evita* begins with Evita's death scene. Ravaged by cancer, she recalls key moments of her life. She dies but does not vanish. Throughout the novel she reappears, sometimes as herself but often as someone's memory of her. As in *The Perón Novel*, Martínez creates numerous other narrators, including one called Tomás Eloy Martínez, who interviews and interacts with other characters in the novel. In much of the novel Tomás Eloy (as I will call the fictional character) tries to understand who Evita was and what she represents in Argentina's collective imagination. Early in the novel,

Tomás Eloy recognizes the futility of this task, noting: "Todo relato es, por definición, infiel. La realidad, como ya dije, no se puede contar ni repetir. Lo único que se puede hacer con la realidad es inventarla de nuevo" (All reporting is, by definition, unfaithful. Reality, as I already said, cannot be told or repeated. The only thing one can do with reality is to invent it again). And such is the purpose of this novel: to narrate and reinvent again and again.

Of the secondary narrators in the novel, the most important is a dedicated military man, Colonel Carlos Eugenio de Moor Koenig, who, as an army intelligence officer, was assigned by Perón to monitor Evita's medical decline. After her death, Koenig continues monitoring her body, observing how the Catalonian master embalmer Pedro Ara fills the body with chemicals, rendering her both incorrupt, like a medieval saint, and forever alluring. Initially, Perón has the body stored, waiting for an appropriate monument to be constructed to mark her grave. When Perón is ousted from power, the new provisional government instructs Koenig to make the body disappear. This turns out to be an impossible task. Koenig moves the body from one hiding place to another, but her followers always find it, leaving flowers and lighted candles in their wake. Koenig himself begins to dream of the body, fantasizing it in ways that eventually define his descent into insanity.

Evita's cadaver eventually is shipped to Italy and interred under a false name, but she is not gone. As Tomás Eloy discovers, people from all walks of life, from her hairdresser to her priest, want to tell their story of her. Even he himself seeks to explain Evita in a screenplay that is never produced and in this novel that, as we will see, somehow never ends. Other Argentines, particularly of the lettered classes, want to explain their hatred of her, refusing to pronounce her name and merely calling her "esa mujer" (that woman). In a later chapter, Tomás Eloy tries to evaluate the myths she left as "Benefactora de los Humildes y Jefa Espiritual de la Nación" (Benefactrice of the Poor and Spiritual Leader of the Nation), her work as a kind of female Robin Hood, and her emerging sacramental nature, by which touching her meant touching heaven.

The final chapter narrates how Tomás Eloy receives a mysterious late-night phone call from two alleged former intelligence officers who offer to tell him the real story of Evita, the one that he failed to tell in *The Perón Novel*. Tomás Eloy initially refuses, until the mysterious caller states, "Ese cadáver somos todos nosotros. Es el país" (That body is all of us. It is the country). Thus, Tomás Eloy is drawn into the unending narration of Evita. It is a duty thrust on him by his own desire for truth. As he writes:

*Me he pasado la vida sublevándome contra los poderes que prohíben o mutilan historias y contra los cómplices que las deforman o dejan que se pierdan. Permitir que una historia como ésa me pasara de largo era un acto de alta traición contra mi conciencia.*

I have spent my life rebelling against the powers that prohibit or mutilate stories and against the accomplices who deform them or allow them to be lost. Allowing a history like this one to escape me would be an act of high treason against my conscience.

And so he begins the interviews, the research of forgotten radio broadcasts and newspaper stories, the obsessive search for films in which Evita appears. In the end, on the last page of the novel, he writes the words "Al despertar de un desmayo que duró más de tres días, Evita tuvo al fin la certeza de que iba a morir" (Upon waking from a fainting spell that lasted more than three days, Evita finally was certain that she was going to die). These, of course, are also the opening lines of the novel. This repetition suggests a circular narration from which Tomás Eloy, his readers, and Argentina will never escape. He makes this explicit at the very end:

*Desde entonces, he remado con las palabras, llevando a Santa Evita en mi barco, de una playa a otra del ciego mundo. No sé en qué punto de mi relato estoy. Creo que en el medio. Sigo, desde hace mucho, en el medio. Ahora tengo que escribir otra vez.*

From that moment [since beginning the novel], I have rowed with words, carrying Santa Evita in my boat from one shore to another in this blind world. I don't know where I am in the story. I believe I'm in the middle. I continue, as I have for a long time, in the middle. Now I have to write again.

Thus, Evita, like her husband, is a signifier whose meaning will never be fully determined. She stands as an eternal question: What is Argentina?

The success of *The Perón Novel* no doubt helped Martínez win the Guggenheim Fellowship that allowed him to write his third novel, *La mano del amo*, another Peronist tale. Like his first novel, *Sagrado, La mano del amo* attracted a polite critical response but never remotely attained the success of *The Perón Novel* and *Santa Evita*. Nonetheless, *La mano del amo* is, in fact, a superbly conceived, albeit not immediately accessible, work that deserves more attention.

While at times recalling the otherworldly exuberance of *Sagrado, La mano del amo* quickly strikes a much more somber note that ultimately leads to the total disintegration of its main character, the doomed Carmona. The novel opens with a dreamlike chapter that is simultaneously nightmare, memory, and prophecy. Carmona's mother, surrounded by seven cats—the only creatures she loves—says to his father, "¿Por qué no matás a Carmona de una vez, Padre, qué estás esperando?" (Why don't you kill Carmona, once and for all, Father? What are you waiting for?). Carmona dreams of escaping, perhaps by river into the Yellow Mountains that might be paradise. We are told that "Carmona sabía que el cielo estaba allí porque aun en lo más tenebroso del sueño las montañas lucían siempre iluminadas, y no había insecto, árbol o persona que tuviera padre o madre. La dicha del paraíso consistía en ser huérfano" (Carmona knew that heaven was there because, even in the darkest moment of his dream, the mountains were always luminous, and in them there was no insect, tree, or person who had a father or a mother. The joy of paradise consisted in being an orphan). Yet visitors to the mountains do not see paradise; instead, they see a film (literally) that simply retells their own past, suggesting that one never escapes from the past, that memory is our most lasting burden.

This bleak opening presages the novel's essential theme: Carmona's attempt to survive as his own person. In the second chapter Mother dies, but for Carmona her physical absence is more than filled by the memories of her affective distance, her disapproval, and her repeated attempts to use her son for her own benefit. And if the memories are not enough, her cats—with highly suggestive names like Sacrament, Altar, and Rosary—inhabit his life, keep him from socializing, and tighten the bands of misery first forged by Mother. Whether the cats are literal animals, evil messengers sent by Mother from the grave, or neuroses that Carmona will never escape matters little to their narrative function, which is to frustrate Carmona's every attempt at individuation. As Mother tells him just before her death, "En cuánto te descuidés, Carmona, los gatos te matarán" (In the moment that you fail to be careful, Carmona, the cats will kill you). In a reverse oedipal relationship, Mother also fears her son: "Madre quería que Carmona estuviera siempre a su alcance, pendiente de sus órdenes, pero a la vez tenía miedo de que él la matara" (Mother always wanted Carmona to be close at hand, waiting for his orders, but, at the same time, she feared that he would kill her).

Carmona, however, is not without resources. Blessed with an extraordinary voice, in early childhood he sings arias from George Frideric Handel and Henry Purcell, often with poignant names like "What Shall I Do to Show How Much I Love Her?" or "Mother, I Will Have a Husband." Even his voice becomes something for Mother to exploit, first by forcing him to sing for her friends and later by suggesting to Father that Carmona be castrated lest his voice lose its beauty as it deepens in puberty. Although Father is known for his ability to castrate farm animals, he objects, since he does not want a son of his to sing like a soprano all his life. In some sense, however, Carmona voluntarily castrates himself by telling Mother that he will sing in falsetto, taking on the tessitura of a woman and dedicating himself to roles formerly sung by the *castrati* of baroque times. Mother is no kinder to her twin daughters, but they have less to exploit. Nor does she give much quarter to Father, forcing him to pass a sexless honeymoon and consenting to sex only to meet the social norms of having children. Beyond the social norms, however, she does nothing for her children, even to the point of almost letting Carmona die rather than nurse him.

Throughout the novel Mother's ability to chain her son to herself is shown repeatedly. When he has the opportunity to sing a recital in the capital city, Mother fakes a heart attack. When he shows sexual interest in another woman, it is Mother's memory that drives him away. Indeed, the only episode of shared sex for Carmona pairs him with one of the cats. Shortly after this scene Carmona dresses in his dead mother's clothing and is shocked to look in the mirror and see her reflection rather than his. Eventually, he sinks into alcoholism, thus losing whatever contact he had with reality and, at the same time, losing his ability to sing. In the final scenes of the story he exists merely to take care of the seven cats that entered the house the day Mother died. In short, Carmona never comes to exist as himself, nor does he escape the roles Mother imposes on him.

While the oppressive mother is certainly the most visible burden Carmona carries, allusions of other sorts suggest that she is not the only source of trouble. The novel is replete with geographical oddities: the regions beyond the Yellow Mountains that suggest a possible paradise; the river that leads to the mountains but is filled with blocks of sulfur; and the massive man-made trench that divides the country in two, with salvation perhaps lying on the other side (although in its construction, hundreds die). What oppresses Carmona is not just the memory of Mother but memory itself—the memory that forces one to live according to learned and inherited roles. As Carmona notes, "Me gustaría no tener ya patria. . . . Me gustaría no haber tenido Madre nunca y saber elegir libremente" (I would have liked to have never had a fatherland. . . . I would have liked to have never had Mother and to have known how to choose freely).

In the end Carmona knows that salvation is not to be his. In the final episode he drowns in the river, but even in death, as he floats toward the Yellow Mountains, he cannot escape Mother, who calls from the "tribe of the dead," first saying, "No te alejes tanto, hijo. Ya se está haciendo tarde" (Don't get too far away, son. It's getting late). She then repeats the demand that opened the novel, saying to Father, "¿Por qué no matás a Caromona de una vez? ¿Qué estás esperando?" (Why don't you kill Carmona once and for all? What are you waiting for?). In response, Carmona begs, "No quiero que me peguen. . . . No me maten" (I don't want you to hit me. . . . Don't kill me). Then Mother again enjoins Father, "¡Acabalo de una vez, Padre! No tardés más. ¿Siempre vas a seguir siendo el mismo cobarde?" (Finish him off once and for all! Don't wait any longer. Are you always going to be the coward you always were?). At this point Carmona begins to float away toward the Yellow Mountains. Just as he is about to escape Mother, however, she grabs him by the hair and pulls him to shore, saying, "¿Quién te dio permiso para alejarte tanto? . . . ¿Ya no te importa nada de tus padres? Quedate acá y no seas un desconsiderado" (Who gave you permission to go so far away? . . . Don't your parents mean anything to you anymore? Stay here and don't be so inconsiderate). And with that she places a golden cord around his neck and ties him to a tree.

Clearly, the title of the novel, which translates into English as "the hand of the master," in no sense refers to the divine hand that fashioned the universe or guides the destiny of human beings. Rather, it is the hand of the devouring, castrating mother and the hand of the indifferent father that frustrate every attempt of the doomed son to be his own person. It is also the hand of memory, the hand of a conformist society, the hand of an inadequate language and everything else that binds the human spirit. This is suggested by a series of puns on the title, which, like virtually all puns, do not translate well but which suggest that "the hand of the master" is the burden of life. Significantly, the Spanish word for "master," *amo,* is identical to the first person singular "I love." The word thus embodies polar opposites: one being love, the other being control. In Carmona's world, there is no love—only a stifling, stunting domination. Indeed, the geography of the novel, with its yellow mountains and river, blocks of sulfur, and relentless heat, almost suggests that the entire novel takes place in Hell.

As for his nonfiction prose works, Martínez started a career in journalism very early in life. For this reason, his complete works in prose probably will never be collected. Yet he has given us several superb collections of essays that reveal the remarkable range of his interests. In *Los testigos de afuera* he develops ideas about the perspective exile bequeaths. *Retrato de un artista enmascarado* develops similar ideas but also ponders the role of the writer in societies without strong institutions and suggests that in such societies the artist feels obligated to assume the role of social conscience and critic. *Las memorias del general* contains one essay, "Perón y los Nazis" (Peron and the Nazis), that shows

Martínez to be a capable historian whose every assertion must be based on documentary evidence. In the same volume his essays on José López Rega expose the raw, irrational side of Argentine society, quite distant from the Europeanized façade carefully sculpted by Argentina's upper classes.

After his country embarked on its nightmare journey through the military regime of the late seventies, Martínez's thought deepened, as reflected in his superb 1999 collection of essays, *El sueño argentino.* In several pieces from this volume, including "Una civilización de la barbarie" (A civilization of barbarousness), he claims that after decades of lying to itself about being the France of Latin America and thus better than its neighbors, Argentina must now face its destiny as an underdeveloped, badly governed country. It is certainly no better than its neighbors and every bit as Latin American and third-world. In the same collection the author vigorously denounces the lies Argentines tell themselves, particularly those who claim that the evil of the military years and the stupidity of the Falklands/Malvinas War somehow can be set apart from the country itself. Indeed, Martínez almost seems a man with a mission who must not allow Argentina to forget the horrors of its recent history. All this he says in a style that is forceful yet controlled, eloquent yet lean. His ability to find exactly the right word and turn exactly the right phrase has earned him comparisons to Octavio Paz as well as Carlos Fuentes and Mario Vargas Llosa.

Martínez's only volume of short stories, *Lugar común de la muerte,* first appeared in Venezuela in 1979 and was later published with three new stories in Buenos Aires (1998). Most of these tales show Martínez trying to imagine real people using a mixture of history and his own imagination. The objects of these musings include the nineteenth-century Argentine dictator Juan Manuel de Rosas, as well as Argentina's dyspeptic essayist Ezequiel Martínez Estrada, the German Jewish philosopher Martin Buber, and Uruguay's eccentric writer Felisberto Hernández, along with meditations on what the survivors of Hiroshima might have thought. Martínez's short stories—in many ways, his literary musings—anticipate what has become the author's hallmark, namely, his ability to see the world more clearly by enriching fact with fiction.

Tomás Eloy Martínez's relatively recent international prominence is well deserved. His extensive examination of Argentina and her myths has led an array of reviewers to refer to his best-known writings as nothing short of "brilliant." As a novelist he has few peers in Latin American letters, and as an interpreter of his country he may have none.

# SELECTED BIBLIOGRAPHY

## Primary Works

### Novels

*Sagrado.* Buenos Aires: Sudamericana, 1969.
*La pasión según Trelew.* Buenos Aires: Granica, 1973.
*La novela de Perón.* Buenos Aires: Legasa Literaria, 1985.
*La mano del amo.* Buenos Aires: Editorial Planeta, 1991.
*Santa Evita.* Buenos Aires: Editorial Planeta, 1995.

### Other Works

*La obra de Ayala y Torre Nilsson en las estructuras del cine argentino.* Buenos Aires: Ediciones Culturales Argentinas, Ministerio de Educacion y Justicia, 1961. (Critical study.)
*Los testigos de afuera.* Caracas: M. Neumann, 1978. (Collected essays.)
*Retrato de un artista enmascarado.* Caracas: Orinoco Editores, 1979. (Collected essays.)
*Lugar común la muerte.* Caracas: Monte Avila, 1979. (Short stories.)
*Las memorias del general.* Buenos Aires: Editorial Planeta, 1996. (Interviews and essays.)
*El sueño argentino.* Buenos Aires: Editorial Planeta, 1999. (A collection of previously published essays on the Argentine identity.)

### Translations

*The Perón Novel.* Translated by Asa Zatz. New York: Pantheon Books, 1988.
*The Perón Novel.* Translated by Helen Lane. New York: Vintage International, 1999.
*Santa Evita.* Translated by Helen Lane. New York: Knopf, 1996.

## Secondary Works

### Critical and Biographical Studies

Bach, Caleb. "Tomás Eloy Martínez: Imagining the Truth." *Americas* (English Edition), June 1998, p. 14. (Interview and profile.)
Brzezinski, Steve. *Antioch Review* 55, no. 2:241 (spring 1997). (Review of *Santa Evita.*)
Foster, David William. *World Literature Today* 70, no. 2:368 (spring 1996). (Review of *Santa Evita.*)
Fraser, Nicholas, and Marysa Navarro. *Eva Peron.* New York: Norton, 1981.
Howard, Matthew. *Nation* 263, no. 13:50 (28 October 1996). (Review of *Santa Evita.*)
Kakutani, Michiko. *New York Times,* 20 September 1996. (Review of *Santa Evita.*)
Mujica, Barbara. *Americas* (English Edition), November 1999, p. 62. (Review of *The Perón Novel.*)
Page, Joseph A. *Peron: A Biography.* New York: Random House, 1983.
Rama, Angel. "Angel Rama o el placer de la crítica." In his *La crítica de la cultura en América Latina.* Caracas: Biblioteca Ayacucho, 1985. Pp. xxv–xli. (Contains extracts from works published between 1972 and 1984.)
Rock, David. *Argentina: 1516–1987: From Spanish Colonization to Alfonsin.* Berkeley: University of California Press, 1987.

# Augusto Monterroso

## (1921–    )

## Jorge Ruffinelli

Augusto Monterroso was born into a middle-class family in Tegucigalpa, Honduras, on 21 December 1921. Because of various circumstances, among them the fact that school bored him, he did not complete primary schooling. Later, to make up for his lack of formal schooling, Monterroso decided to study on his own and began reading Greek and Roman classics, as well as European literatures of different periods. He eventually became one of the most cultured writers of Latin America, capable of reciting long poems in Latin without making the slightest error. Monterroso began working in a butcher shop at the age of fifteen, and in an interview, he recalled a peculiar image of reading classical authors in his leisure time while the quartered cows passed by him, hanging from hooks. Even though he may have added an element of fantasy to that memory, it represents his role as a writer fairly well, as can be inferred from his short stories, fables, essays, and interviews. All of Monterroso's work, as well as his very presence in Mexican culture, in which he has been immersed for most of his life, is—like that image from his adolescence—untypical, paradoxical, contradictory, and, to a point, grotesque. For example, he devoted most of one of his best books to flies.

A very brief short story, made up of one line ("When he awoke, the dinosaur was still there") and titled "El dinosaurio" ("The Dinosaur"), gave Monterroso a celebrity status (and praise from Italo Calvino, Carlos Fuentes, Mario Vargas Llosa, and Gabriel García Márquez) that he eventually resented. He has been identified for decades with the term "brief texts." Because one of the great virtues of his writing style is conciseness, the perception one has of him is that of a writer condemned to writing only short texts and perhaps incapable of writing extensive ones. While other Latin American writers of his generation, or younger, aspire to write the total novel or roman-fleuve under the influence of James Joyce, Jacques Roumain, or Thomas Mann, Monterroso belongs to the Franz Kafka and Jorge Luis Borges lineage of writers who work on concise and synthetic texts that are at times fragmentary, sometimes under the guise of rewriting or translating other fundamental texts.

Monterroso has contributed to his own legend, voluntarily or unwillingly, when trying to explain the characteristics of his literature or his dedication to it as stemming from biographical or existential circumstances. Thus, the extraordinary rigor and exigency of his work, the epigrammatic and satirical style he prefers to a realist and serious one, and the extremely high literary quality achieved could all hypothetically result from a desire to compensate for personal deficiencies. He once interpreted his literary vocation as deriving from his short stature and various other physical impediments that made him inept at sports activities. Monterroso says that because of these, he concentrated on reading instead of devoting himself, like other young men, to sports and pursuing girls. Besides the always doubtful psychological interpretations about what makes someone a writer, especially a writer of valuable and important works, it is appealing to consider such "genetic" hypotheses, which can be as humorous and the fruit of as much satire about himself as about his literature.

Unlike most of his contemporaries, Monterroso does not seem to have come to literature with a preconceived project. Also, he has tried to avoid repeating each niche of originality that his critics and readers celebrate. After "The Dinosaur," he avoided writing such brief texts. Yet hundreds of writers, to this day, have been inspired by him to write "minimal short stories," although in the final analysis they are mere parodic exercises. Although it would be attractive to dwell on the same parody by quoting the memoirs of his adolescence and saying, "When he looked up from the book, the beef was still there," the apparent opposition in that image provides a good conceptual base to understand his literature. In fact, throughout Monterroso's more than sixty years of literary production, a tension has incited and helped to produce that literature. It is the tension between reality (here in the form of raw meat) and literature (the elaboration, or what is cooked). For example, throughout his life Monterroso has been loyal to his progressive and leftist commitments, and at the same time faithful to literature. Although literature and politics coexisted in some of his early stories, he found a way—artistic elaboration—to avoid making the literary a mere "vehicle" of political goals. The solutions were not easy, but in finding them Monterroso demonstrated that he was capable of being demanding in both worlds.

In any case, the tension between two equally important concerns—life within social reality and life in literature—are perceived dynamically in all his books, but they also change from one book to another. That tension disappears or is diluted up to a point in two of Monterroso's later books, *Los buscadores de oro* (1993) and *La vaca* (1998). In them literature "wins," and paradoxically, in them Monterroso begins to write about life, his life, in autobiographical terms and even

as a testimony of the aesthetic, ethical, literary, and political itinerary that culminated in those two books.

Monterroso's aesthetic decisions began early, and they probably have some relation to his family tree, in which there are lawyers, military men, intellectuals, and politicians involved in their country's affairs. Because Monterroso was born in Tegucigalpa, we could consider him a Honduran writer, but as we will see later, he has always considered himself Guatemalan (and literary histories grant him that nationality). His paternal grandfather was a Guatemalan general, Antonio Monterroso; his grandmother was Rosalía Lobos. His grandfather protected many writers and poets, such as the Colombian Porfirio Barba Jacob, because he himself was a learned man. On his mother's side, his grandparents were the Honduran lawyer César Bonilla and his wife, Trinidad Valdés. Bonilla was the cousin of two Honduran presidents, Policarpo and Manuel Bonilla. Monterroso's father was Vicente Monterroso; his mother, Amelia Bonilla. In 1936 his immediate family settled in Guatemala, whose culture the young man absorbed. His father founded newspapers and magazines, investing (and losing) his own money and his wife's. Because of work commitments, he split his life between Tegucigalpa and Guatemala, dragging his family along in both directions.

Because of these frequent changes in location—and also, according to Monterroso, because of his laziness and fear of formal education—he did not complete grammar school. When the family stopped traveling and settled in Guatemala for good, Monterroso was already a writer with a foot in two countries. In 1937, still very young, he started to work as a cashier in a butcher shop, where he had only one day off a year and naturally felt exploited by the owners. Yet while the butcher shop consumed almost all of his time and attention, one of his bosses noticed his natural talent and encouraged him to read the classic authors. He gave works by them to his young employee, thereby starting the future writer down a path of decision making.

> As a child I was not good at running or swimming, or at any exercise. I always remember someone, above all my brother [César] pulling me out of the river time and time again, half drowned. Suddenly, as an adolescent I found I lacked not only an education but also very basic things like shoes good enough to meet the girls with whom you

fall in love, and, as a consequence, other necessary things, like the ease and daring to hold their hands.

It is then that you find refuge in books, or billiard dives. On the other hand, I supposed that by extension anyone who had a career knew everything. With time I've realized that it is not always so. But at that time I felt the need to know something and of starting with universally known authors.

Studying Latin on his own must have been difficult for someone who had not finished grammar school. Yet the obstacles to be overcome served as stimuli. In those years of learning, Monterroso read Shakespeare, Horace, Plato, Lord Chesterfield, Victor Hugo, Madame de Sévigné. In the hours stolen from natural recess or the nights he went to Guatemala's National Library, where he was fascinated by the works of Arcipreste de Hita, Don Juan Manuel, Pedro Calderón de la Barca, Baltasar Gracián, and, above all, Miguel de Cervantes. Since the library was almost entirely devoted to accumulating Spanish classics, at home he read the aforesaid authors as well as Montaigne, Samuel Johnson, and Joseph Addison.

His immersion in the classics as opposed to popular and mass culture created in Monterroso the notion that literature was legitimate in proportion to its quality and depth. Writing was an arduous and difficult endeavor because it was not a matter of generating words and putting out commonplace ideas, but rather of getting to that magical, incandescent moment that, defying easy explanations, produces the greatest writers. The demand of maximum quality for the written word, and with a minimal or nonexistent ambition to publish and be known, were guiding principles for Monterroso's literary activity, and they indirectly explain why his work is so scant in pages and so excellent in literary achievement.

While he lived in Guatemala, Monterroso's political activism overshadowed his cultural interests. On this point it should be remembered that in Latin America, cultural associations are often formed with objectives that are as much political as cultural, and that sometimes a clear distinction is not made between them. By 1940 Monterroso had established some literary connections and at that time he joined together with some of the writers of his generation to found the Asociación de Artistas y Escritores Jóvenes de Guatemala (Association of Young Artists and Writers of Guatemala) and the literary journal Acento. The following year he published his first stories in the newspaper El imparcial and in Acento. The association dropped its literary dimension almost immediately as the young writers assumed a political stand by denouncing President Jorge Ubico's dictatorship and by organizing clandestine activities. If censorship had been the only risk (indeed, his first short story was banned), the struggle would have had only minor consequences. In 1944, however, Monterroso was one of the signers of the Manifiesto de los 311, which demanded the dictator's resignation. When Ubico fell from power (not because of the political manifesto) in 1946, the police, under the command of General Federico Ponce Váides, Ubico's successor, detained Monterroso. He managed to escape and find refuge in the Mexican embassy. In September 1944, after obtaining safe-conduct, Monterroso journeyed to Mexico. It was his first Mexican exile. The second one, which would be definitive, came a few years later.

The movement known later as the Revolución de Octubre and headed by left-leaning Jacobo Arbenz Guzmán took power in Guatemala in 1944, the year Monterroso left the country. Monterroso stayed in Mexico, and the Guatemalan Revolutionary Junta assigned him to a minor post in the Guatemalan consulate in Mexico. In 1953 the government of Arbenz, who had become president in 1951, appointed Monterroso to the positions of first secretary and consul in the Guatemalan Embassy in La Paz, Bolivia. He held these posts for barely a year, at the end of which he watched in pain as the United States occupied Guatemala militarily, ending the democratically elected Arbenz regime. Monterroso left for exile in Chile. During his two years there he met writers including Pablo Neruda, José Santos González Vera, and Manuel Rojas, who befriended him. The newspaper El Siglo published his story "Mr. Taylor," in which the writer offers a literary challenge to U.S. political power. It was his first attempt to reconcile his two vocations, to mix the raw and the cooked.

Monterroso returned to Mexico in 1956. In Mexico City he joined the Universidad Nacional Autónoma de México (UNAM) as an editor for Revista de la Universidad *de México,* and at the same time was an employee in the university's publishing department. The fact that he was self-taught made him stand out among the university professors, who nevertheless considered him an equal. Thanks to his wide reading in the classics, and to his ability to quote them frequently in their original languages, Monterroso was able to demonstrate a well-guided intelligence. In addition to his UNAM posts, he established links with the Fondo de Cultura Económica, a publishing house, where he was a proofreader and occasionally a translator. He also obtained a fellowship to study philology at the graduate center of the Colegio de México, taught Cervantes and *Quixote* courses at the UNAM extension, was a researcher at the Instituto de Investigaciones Filológicas, and was a literature professor at that university's School of Philosophy and Letters. Monterroso was also codirector of the Nuestros Clásicos series published by the university, coordinator of the Narrative Workshop at the Instituto Nacional de Bellas Artes, professor of language and literature at the Colegio de México, and publications coordinator for the National Council of Science and Technology.

By now the tense relationship between crude reality and literary elaboration was at the center of Monterroso's literary production. Unamenable to formulas, it was not an easy relationship. His work seems to sway among three directions: making a fable of the real through short-story writing, which represents the greatest distance possible from any concrete historical reference, and a return to reality in the form of imaginative and literary autobiography. These three approaches have marked Monterroso's work from his first short stories to those written almost sixty years later. His reading of the classics as a youth taught him early on that the closer literature was to historical fact, the less time it took to age. A path had to be found that would allow writing to go beyond being just a civic duty, yet at the same time would not lose literature among philosophical abstractions. After all, Dante's *Divine Comedy* is not valuable because of its numerous allusions to characters and circumstances of its time, many of them soon forgotten, but rather because of a power that reaches the purest poetic expression.

Regarding literature's role in politics—what Jean-Paul Sartre and his contemporaries called committed literature—Monterroso was well aware that events in society which motivate a legitimate artistic and intellectual reaction may have faded into oblivion by the time the reader obtains the committed literature based on those events. Almost always out of synchrony, committed literature has the shortcoming of giving answers to questions that have probably disappeared. Thus, for his first texts Monterroso had to find a stylistic option and a literary genre that would save his work from premature aging and a dwindling of validity.

The stories in Monterroso's first published book, *Obras completas y otros cuentos* (1959; *Complete Works and Other Stories,* 1995), provide an accurate rendering of his concern. One of the characteristics that has given Monterroso's literature its special nature is its amazing diversity. Just as we can attribute fear of the void to baroque writers, so we can recognize in Monterroso the fear of repetition. Another fundamental characteristic of his writing is its immersion in the literary. With the passing of time, that immersion would become a more and more important and decisive option in various aspects of his life and writing. Whereas some writers get their inspiration from social or psychological reality, Monterroso's main source of inspiration was literature, and it became increasingly so as time went on. An important model for that choice was Jorge Luis Borges, about whom Monterroso was already writing in the 1940s. Other sources can be traced back to Cervantes and the Spanish baroque poets Monterroso read. All of them help account for his abundant exercises in intertextuality, that is, oblique references to other writers, books, poems, and verses, or to characters such as Don Quixote. Together, the eagerness to not repeat himself and the immersion in literature itself produced a diverse body of writing based on familiar characteristics. Reader competence is essential to understanding Monterroso's work, as Wilfrido H. Corral, one of his first major critics, has demonstrated.

Early on, Monterroso generally used the short story as the vehicle for his literary worldview without overtly questioning the short story's traditional form. Thus, he produced enjoyable, magisterial pieces characterized by an outstanding sense of humor, and, frequently, by sarcasm. These stories were collected in *Complete Works and Other Stories,* in which the title itself signals the short-story genre, as well as a taste for paradox. Ten years later Monterroso published *La oveja negra y demás fábulas* (1969; *The Black Sheep, and Other Fables,* 1971), a collection in which he explores a "new" genre derived from an ancient literary tradition: the fable. This volume is not a simple adoption of a form canonized by Aesop, La Fontaine, and writers closer to Monterroso, such as James Thurber. Instead, it is a parodic recycling of that genre. When Monterroso published *Movimiento perpetuo* (1972), later included as *Perpetual Motion* in the English version of *Complete Works and Other Stories,* neither the classic short story nor the fable was the chosen literary form. Once again, the "horror of reiteration" guided his hand and, without abandoning the literary terrain, he elaborated a series of brief texts that are difficult to define. It is prose that is midway between narrative and essay, but always far from poetic prose.

Six years later *Lo demás es silencio: La vida y la obra de Eduardo Torres* (1978) allowed Monterroso to explore the novel; the work is a unique, fragmented novel whose only unity is provided by a character who had grown up as a historical mistake but was once taken as a real person. *Lo demás es silencio,* a title that alludes to the famous phrase "the rest is literature," explores a phenomenon as well as a genre. The genre, as already stated, is the novel. The phenomenon is the ambiguous and mistaken frontiers between reality and fiction, the everyday in literature, the raw and the cooked.

Not happy with these explorations in diversity, in *La palabra mágica* (1983) Monterroso brought together a palimpsest of miscellany, including essays and brief prose, notes and more elaborate texts. Then, in *Los buscadores de oro* (1993) and *La vaca* (1998), he surprised his readers once again. Under the guise of a miscellany, Monterroso presented a series of confessional texts (criticism included), many humorous in nature yet marked by the melancholy of an autobiography written at the end of a life.

Returning to the author's origins, it is worth repeating that he began publishing in a recognized genre, the short story. "Mr. Taylor," "Primera dama" ("First Lady"), "El concierto" ("The Concert"), and "The Eclipse" are good examples of his stories, and above all are representative of the link between literature and politics in his early writing. The stories contain specific historical references and are wrought with careful literary elaboration. Yet "First Lady" and "The Concert" are also good examples of Monterroso's mocking intention and

satirical bent, which he employs in observing the customs and "dramas" of a social and political class with which he did not identify, but which he acknowledged as influential in Latin America. "First Lady" finds the victim of that mocking gaze in the institutionalized figure of a country's first lady. For "The Concert," Monterroso found inspiration in real persons and in a situation existing throughout history. About this story, he commented:

> One of President Truman's daughters was a singer. She gave concerts during her father's presidency and the press commented on them with benevolence and even praise, except on two or three occasions. The fact is that she gave those concerts by taking advantage of her father's power. I saw a theme in that, but in order to not make the political side obvious I made her a pianist and her father a great financier, who could pay for her public shows, attract a public and manage to get good reviews in the papers. Yet in the story this poor woman became her father's protégée, little by little, something that I did not want. The theme became the artist's doubt of praise and success.

Of Monterroso's earlier stories, "Mr. Taylor" is the most political. Monterroso has often pointed out that he wrote that story in Bolivia around 1954, when the United States and the United Fruit Company brutally toppled Arbenz's government. This story, with its politically charged theme, posed aesthetic problems of finding a balance "between indignation and what I understand to be literature." The effort to disassociate himself from historical circumstances forced Monterroso to find an oblique way to put them in a story but at the same time to overcome and transcend them. "Mr. Taylor" became a sort of symbolic "treatise on economic politics" valid for the situation represented or for any like it, while at the same time being a fable about real situations and persons.

At the beginning of the story, an American named Percy Taylor, described as a "poor gringo" because of his "famished" look and the rings under his eyes, appears in South America's Amazon region. Almost accidentally, Mr. Taylor buys a shrunken head from an Indian who offers it to him. When he sends it as a gift to a Mr. Rolston, his uncle in New York City, he unleashes a growing export flow of little shrunken heads that in no time alters the native country's economy, penal system, and social customs, as well as the exchange relations with the metropolis.

By constructing a story about a "poor" American passing through South America more as an adventurer than as a tourist, Monterroso appeals to the grand American "rags to riches" narrative. That is, he draws on the myth that in the United States everyone has the opportunity to become rich, given the supposed absence of social classes or the rapid ascension in the social scale. That myth, rooted in the era of the pioneers and the Wild West, lives on in the imagination of Americans as the best selling point of their democracy.

In describing that export's impact on the unnamed Latin American country, Monterroso has the opportunity to comment on the speciousness of the economic development that occurs in the context of dependence upon the United States. His story illustrates how, no matter what the "native" export product is, the country apparently benefited by it goes from "riches to rags" when the capitalist cycle of exploitation and depletion ends. Initially, the country prospers tremendously, although the improvements that result are portrayed with sarcasm by the narrator. A "small path around the Legislative Palace" is constructed, one on which the smug congressmen ride "the bicycles that the company had given them." At the conclusion of the tale, in the midst of a grave economic crisis caused by the lack of shrunken heads for exportation—a typical depletion of raw materials by indiscriminate exploitation—Mr. Rolston jumps out of a window. He does so after receiving a package with Mr. Taylor's head, a head that smiles at him "with the false smile of a child who seemed to say: 'Sorry, sorry, I won't do it again.' "

A student of political economy would find in "Mr. Taylor" a perfect allegory of the dependence of a country that exports its riches on commercial relations with a country that has the money to consume them. The fact that the product is shrunken heads alludes, on the one hand, to the persistent prejudice of seeing Latin America as underdeveloped and barbarous. On the other hand, those heads also allude to the attitudes of politicians, social classes, and governments that take part in the politics of giving up.

How did Monterroso manage to build a story that is timeless—given that the same situation could be applied to countries in Africa or Asia—and at the same time Latin American, anchored in a historical moment? His main technique is allusion, which allows one to employ a fairly transparent symbolism, as when the Instituto Danfeller is mentioned. Given that organization's millions in contributions geared toward "promoting the development of that exciting cultural manifestation [shrunken heads] of Spanish American peoples," one can read an allusion to the Rockefeller Foundation. There are also allusions to real treaties that benefit the United States (relating to the Panama Canal and Guantánamo naval base in Cuba, for example), when territorial concessions of ninety-nine years are mentioned. There is also a humorous allusion to Coca-Cola when a "very cold refreshment (with a magic formula)" is mentioned, and the thirsty natives are said to drink it as a "pause" during their hard work ("formula" and "pause" being terms taken from commercials for that refreshment). But the story also feeds on literature because it is inspired by Jonathan Swift's *A Modest Proposal* (1729), another economic and commercial allegory, and "Mr. Taylor" shares with the Irish bishop the pose of logically and sensibly proposing the greatest absurdity, death, as a purported national benefit.

"Mr. Taylor" alludes to a topic that Latin American and North American sociologists have examined in essays and articles: the brain drain. This expression has a humorous equivalent in Spanish—*la exportación de cerebros*—if it is interpreted literally as "brain exportation," or the "fleeing of brains." For a long time that expression was equated with the dependent economy's typical export of raw materials. In an essay in *Perpetual Motion*, Monterroso would return to this topic, which is additionally a private joke addressed to intellectuals who think they have market value. In the essay, "La exportación de cerebros" (1972; "The Brain Drain," 1995), he says:

It is only reasonable that we have grown weary of more developed countries making off with our copper or bananas under constantly deteriorating trade conditions; but, as anyone can see, the fear that they will also take away our brains is vaguely paranoic, for the truth is we don't possess many that are very good. We take pleasure in our illusions, but as the saying goes, the man who lives on illusions dies of hunger.

If it is possible to read this essay as a reformulation of the theme in "Mr. Taylor," there are some changes in the expository strategies, which may be linked to the difference in genres. In the essay "The Brain Drain," Monterroso employs the first-person plural, a sweeping and compromising "we" that involves the reader in the problem being treated, a "we" that brings Latin America generally into the situation being considered. (The essay does not need to mention Latin America because that is the place from which the author writes.) On the other hand, "Mr. Taylor" narrates in a distant third-person singular, establishing a rhetorical separation between text and reader. Yet the story encourages the readers' complicity so that they may decipher the allusions and know what is being said between the lines (or in the background) in the fable. Thus, there are different demands for different genres, as calculated by Monterroso.

The stories of *Complete Works and Other Stories* initiated Monterroso's reputation as a demanding writer of clear and careful prose. But it was *The Black Sheep, and Other Fables* that, with its rapid and successful change of literary genres, attracted the greatest praise from his fellow writers. They were so precise in their laudatory phrasing that they seemed to be writing promotional blurbs. It was as if the textual precision that Monterroso achieved was inspiring his fellow writers when they wrote about him. Gabriel García Márquez wrote, "This book has to be read with your hands up. Its danger is based on its sly wisdom and the deadly beauty of its lack of seriousness." This and other plaudits constituted more than literary praise: they expressed the enthusiasm of readers who find a jewel in the motley literary jungle.

Isaac Asimov wrote of the English version of the fables:

> The brief texts of *The Black Sheep and Other Fables* . . . apparently inoffensive, bite if you come close to them without the proper care and leave scars, and that is precisely why they are worthwhile. After reading "The Monkey That Wanted to Be a Satirical Writer" I will never be the same.

Carlos Fuentes provided Monterroso with a letter of literary introduction by inviting to read him *from* literature: "Imagine Borges's fantastic bestiary having tea with Alice. Imagine Jonathan Swift and James Thurber exchanging notes. Imagine a frog from Calaveras County that had really read Mark Twain. Meet Monterroso."

The publication in 1969 of *La oveja negra y demás fábulas,* the original Spanish-language edition of *The Black Sheep, and Other Fables,* marked the high point of critical appreciation for Monterroso's literature. What is it about this book that has triggered so much admiration on the part of both average readers and reader-writers? One possible answer is that with this book, which subtly tries to revive a worn genre belonging to the past, Monterroso found the perfect literary boiling point. Through the renewed fable, he refers to the world that surrounds him without descending from literature to essay writing or social commentary. If one of the major requirements of Monterroso's literature is imaginative richness, then by that standard this work is impeccable throughout its forty texts. And if another and no less important requirement is high literary quality, that is also present in these texts. The raw and the cooked become neutralized and enrich one another in a work that achieves the perfect elaboration point. Thanks to that, the fables "bite" the readers instead of leaving them indifferent.

Monterroso's fables brought him closer in reputation to Jorge Luis Borges, the most admired writer of his time. Borges had also managed, in his own way, to write works different from those of any other writer, weaving a difficult composite of fiction, reality, erudition, and careful writing. In Monterroso's case it was not a matter of imitating Borges but rather of opening his own parallel path. Monterroso did so, and with his fables distinguished himself from Borges.

From its title, whose intent is to call attention to the genre, *The Black Sheep, and Other Fables* is deceptive. The fable as it is known has its own rhetorical system and its own ethical and aesthetic objectives. Nevertheless, it would be erroneous to state that Monterroso tried to do with the fable what Cervantes wanted to do with novels of chivalry. Instead of taking an active form, as Cervantes did, Monterroso exhumed one that apparently had achieved closure, and then redefined it.

He did away with its original purpose of teaching through example, and imposed on it a dose of modern satire. Thereby Monterroso, a reader of Aesop, Phaedrus, La Fontaine, Félix María Samaniego, and Tomás de Iriarte, distanced himself from all of them.

The rhetoric of the fable was incorporated into Latin American culture beginning in the eighteenth century, with authors such as Irrisari and José Joaquin Fernández de Lizardi, but Monterroso's fables are different from theirs as well. In his innovative use of the genre, Monterroso manages to displace its characteristics from the inside. On the one hand he fills the genre with boorish humor. On the other, he introduces parody through speech that feigns other speech, and it is in that feigning that these fables are different from the originals. Thus, while the fable was originally addressed to the reader as a teaching device, in Monterroso's modern version the fable makes the reader participate, incorporating him or her into his game, a game that is marked by the absurd.

His fables' rebellious and solvent attitude is the basis for a new narrative strategy. It is a proposal for a game shared with the reader—as Corral has proved is the case for all of Monterroso's works—a game of intelligence and nonsense that acquires sense only when the presence of a new structured code is accepted. The expectations of a reader of fables are flouted because in Monterroso's fables the usual rules for the genre are not followed, nor do his fables adopt the attitude of moral usefulness and didacticism. Monterroso does, however, employ those of that form's characteristics which he can put to good use. One example is the almost epigrammatic concision of discourse, which was already characteristic of his writing. Another is the very apt handling of the absurd, which is a defining characteristic of his fables. It is as if Jonathan Swift suddenly had beenreplaced by Lewis Carroll.

The bestiary introduced by these fables is very different from Borges's bestiary of the fantastic. Monterros's has a strategic reason for being, a reason of which the author is aware, as he has devised a set of procedures aiming for specific effects. Monterroso has theorized about this, expressing an insistence on discursive strategies:

In a modern short story no one tries to say lofty things, because it is considered in bad taste, and it probably is; on the other hand, if you attribute profound ideas to an animal, let us say to a flea, readers accept it because they then think it is a joke, and they laugh and the lofty notion doesn't harm them, or they don't even notice it.

Fearful that employing an outdated genre would make him anachronistic, Monterroso establishes a tacit contract with the reader. He proposes the fable as a Trojan horse that mocks the reader's sense of prevention against certain topics (the "lofty notions") that modern aesthetics has discarded. The reader immediately notices that the fable has another meaning, different from the original, and becomes its accomplice.

The great triumph of Spanish American realism subsequent to *modernismo* presupposed a positive sanction of *humilitas* and a corresponding negative sanction of *sublimitas*. To dwell on the sublime became a haughty gesture. On the other hand, *humilitas* was in tune with popular culture, one of whose major defining traits was humor. By using the fable for its satirical potential rather than its didactic possibilities, Monterroso can put himself in tune with the modern reader's sensibility. His triumph, then, consists once again in achieving balance: using close, everyday facts and circumstances, and at the same time employing selected forms of a literary genre with a long lineage. It is not a matter of finding a "cooking point" but rather of making the raw pass through the renewed filter of the cooked. As a consequence, the Trojan horse is able to speak about lofty things (the human condition and its weaknesses) with humble humor.

All of the above is transparent in Monterroso's fables, as are the playful manipulating of images and the intelligent recycling of ancient fables (Achilles and the turtle, the cicada and the ant, and the hen and the golden eggs). In each of those cases it is useless and inadvisable to look for the usual moral. The reader, rather, is invited to exercise his or her cognitive faculties—assisted by the cultural markers included in the fables' allusions—at a fairly cultured level of competence, although never excessively sophisticated or specialized. In this game of *agnorisis* (the possibility of "recognizing" a genre in its parodic projection), Monterroso does not go beyond the level of *doxa* nourished by basic cultural knowledge. He goes a bit beyond the elementary level of children's fables deposited in a cultured commonplace, as do texts such as *Don Quixote* and Kafka's *Metamorphosis* (1915).

The fables' conciseness leaves no room for distraction, and their effect is immediate. In many of them Monterroso uses paradox as a springboard for thought, and irony to make received notions appear relative. Thus, "El paraíso imperfecto" refers to the relativity of dreams, and even of perfection: "It is true—said the man with melancholy, without taking his eyes off the flames that burned in the chimney that winter night—that in Paradise there are friends, music, some books; the only bad thing about going to Heaven is that no one can see Heaven from there."

"Caballo imaginado a Dios" refers to the human practice of anthropomorphizing everything and at the same time subjecting human beings to purported divine forces:

Despite what they say, the idea of a heaven inhabited by Horses and presided over by a God with an equine figure is repulsive to good taste and the most elementary logic, reasoned the horse the other day. Everybody knows—he continued with his reasoning—that if we Horses were capable of imagining a God we would imagine him in the shape of a horse.

As an alarm against the slavery imposed by rationalism, Monterroso wrote "El burro y la flauta," a brief fable about an unusual meeting:

A flute that nobody played lay in the countryside for a long time, until one day a Donkey that was passing by there blew hard on it, making it produce the sweetest sound of its life, that is, of the Donkey and the Flute. Unable to comprehend what had happened, for although both believed in rationality, they separated in a hurry, embarrassed about the best thing that both of them had done during their sad existence.

Political thought, with Latin American dictatorships as background, appears in the fable that gives the book its title. "La oveja negra" ("The Black Sheep") is also a warning about fear of diversity:

In a faraway country there was many years ago a black Sheep. It was shot. A century later, the repentant flock put up an equestrian statue of it, which looked very nice in the park. Thus, from then on, every time that black sheep appeared they were rapidly shot, so that future generations of plain and common sheep could also practice sculpture.

In "El conejo y el león," using paradox as his operative center, as he so often does, Monterroso surprises us, for he seems to be undermining common sense and reflecting about the relativity of judgments. The fable tells of a Psychoanalyst who observes animal conduct in the jungle. Upon returning to the city he publishes a treatise

showing that the Lion is the most infantile and cowardly animal in the jungle, and the Rabbit is the bravest and most mature. The Lion roars and gestures, threatening a universe moved by fear. The Rabbit is aware of this, knows its strength, and withdraws before losing patience and finishing off that extravagant being beside itself, which he understands and that after all has not done anything to him.

The closest thing to a fable with an implicit moral is "El mono que quiso ser escritor satírico," which deep down is a mordant comment about the cronyism of literary groups whose members' judgments are shaped by their opportunistic agendas. The Monkey in this fable studies customs and becomes "the greatest expert in human nature." But when he decides to apply that knowledge, he discovers that he is compromised by social considerations. He wants to write against thieves (the Magpies), but some magpie friends could feel insulted. He wants to write against opportunists (the Snakes), but faces the same problem. He wants to satirize "compulsive workers," but fears offending the Bees, and to criticize sexual promiscuity, but has friends among the adulterous hens. The effect of social compromise is paralysis: "At that moment he stopped being a satirical writer and became interested in Mysticism, Love and things like that; but after that, you know how people are, everybody said he was crazy and did not receive him well or with so much pleasure."

These examples alone prove the existence in Monterroso's writing of basic strategies for satirizing his readers' occasional or essential human frailties, such as stupidity, cruelty, cowardice, aesthetic insensitivity, and compulsive behavior. But he employs them delicately, so that the readers will not be offended (Monterroso shares the fear of the Monkey in the fable) and can acquire the ability to use satire as a weapon within their own mental horizons. Monterroso's use of fables as a double-edged sword is what finally justifies characteristics like the ones Asimov (texts that "bite") and García Márquez (a book to be read with your "hands up") attributed to them.

Monterroso starts from the axiom that readers recognize others, but not themselves, in satire. Within this axiom the text's satire consists in getting rid of signs that particularize places and people. This decontextualizing sets up a mythic space (the jungle), although there are some markers that bring us back to social reality. (Mexico City's Bosque de Chapultepec is one.) In some cases, the readers of these fables have tried to discover identities within a purported allusion. For example, they have sought to find in "El Zorro es más sabio" an allusion to Juan Rulfo, or have identified Ernesto Che Guevara or Thomas Moore in "The Black Sheep." (And why not Christ?)

No matter how much readers may venerate the book they have in hand, they have the advantage of being able to dominate it. Ultimately, readers are free to love or abhor a book, to read it or leave it, to feel in consonance or dissonance with it. Aware that any contract with the readers is a result of the delicate management of strategies, Monterroso has rationalized his own attitude, which is valid for all his books, and perhaps especially so in *The Black Sheep, and Other Fables*. *Lo demás es silencio* offers advice that is virtually axiomatic, and a paradoxical exercise as well: "Try to say things in such a way that the reader feels that deep down he is as or more intelligent than you. Once in a while try to make it so; but to achieve that you will have to be more intelligent than him."

Although Monterroso usually writes his books slowly, over a period of years, frequently working on several simultaneously, the publication of the Spanish-language edition of *Perpetual Motion* in 1972 and of *Lo demás es silencio* in 1978 was to some degree the consequence of the great literary success of *The Black Sheep, and Other Fables*. Above all, the writer had found a voice and a style, and although he continued to explore different literary genres in order to avoid repeating himself, that voice and style were already unmistakable. In *Perpetual Motion* Monterroso intends to remove all specificity from the text, to blur the boundaries between short story and essay. *Perpetual Motion*'s epigraph could be interpreted as a sort of *ars poetica* in which life and text are reconciled within the notion of perpetual motion. It reads: "Life is not an essay, although we attempt many things; it is not a story, although we invent many things; it is not a poem, although we dream many things. The essay about the story about the poem about life is perpetual motion; that's it exactly, perpetual motion."

This apparently tautological definition also functions as an expression of Monterroso's original concern with finding the place of literature and reality without abandoning either. And since he is a writer, not a philosopher, and his texts do not tend toward metaphysical abstraction, but rather toward poetic and narrative concretion, Monterroso fills his book, symbolically and figuratively, with that perfect representative of perpetual motion: the fly.

After *The Black Sheep, and Other Fables* Monterroso's books tended to be actual objects, not just continents of writing. Drawings, peculiar typography, and a whole artistic arsenal, clean and woven into the writing, suggest another consideration: the notion that each book is not only writing but also, or even mainly, an object, and therefore a palpable part of reality. It should not be surprising, then, that *Perpetual Motion* is filled with drawings of flies and many literary references to them. Never before or since has the fly received such a great tribute in literature.

*Lo demás es silencio* carries denaturalization and the reinvention of genres to extremes, and because of that it is one of Monterroso's more complex and interesting books. It is subtitled *The Life and Work of Éduardo Torres*, and according to Monterroso it is a novel, the only one he has published in his first eighty years. The book has some of the conventional requirements of a novel: a central character around whom various situations are created within a fragmentary structure. There is also character development up to a point, in the guise of a fictitious biography. To accomplish the development of character, Monterroso returned to the Latin American tradition of mixing real and fictitious characters. This tradition's most outstanding practitioner was Jorge Luis Borges, as when he devoted an entire book, *Historia universal de la infamia* (1935), to synthetic biographies that fuse the real with the invented. Monterroso also went back to Borges's predecessor, Marcel Schwab, a French writer who expressly created such biographies in his book *Les vies imaginaires* (1896).

Monterroso's character Eduardo Torres appeared long before *Lo demás es silencio* was published, in 1959, in *Revista de la Universidad de México*. Subsequently, Torres accompanied Monterroso for twenty years of his life and work, until Torres found his "natural" place in a book. Before finding that place, Eduardo Torres's signature was known in Mexican cultural circles, and his ambiguous nature had some people believing him to be a real person rather than an imaginary character. *Lo demás es silencio* centers on him, collecting the texts Monterroso wrote concerning Torres over the years. It is constructed like a mosaic, with testimonials from characters as fictitious as Torres: his brother, his former personal secretary, his wife, and his valet. The volume also includes a section of *selecta* (essays, aphorisms, sayings, and so on). The game of shifting mirrors goes so far as to have Torres review Monterroso's *The Black Sheep, and Other Fables*, the first known case since Luigi Pirandello of a character who comments in writing on its author.

The importance of *Lo demás es silencio* within the body of Monterroso's work lies above all in the fact that the book allows the author to find his own, stronger place. Fiction and reality belong to literature together. Seldom has a book been so efficient in dissolving the apparent frontiers between these aspects usually considered at odds. Monterroso creates a character, Torres, with whom other writers dispute, believing him to be real (to the point of reviewing a book by this "author"). In doing so, Monterroso is not merely playing, but rather is exploring the problematic differences between the real and the literary, the object and the text, what is true and what is false, the concrete world and the idea. Where one places oneself among these opposites, with one's own relative autonomy, and what mutual relations those autonomies maintain, are problems that philosophy only pretends to resolve, Monterroso exposes them with literary wisdom, without claiming to elucidate them.

The fact that we are dealing with literature, and not philosophy, is what clearly marks the cartography of Monterroso's efforts. It explains the literary nature of his literature once again, that is, its constant feeding off literature. It would be easy to speak of intertextuality as merely a means of citation, but in fact each work rigorously calls upon others because it is together that they make up their universe. Roland Barthes used to say that literary writing is a dialogue by other writings inside of writing, and Monterroso states: "Any art first feeds on itself. Literature is made with literature."

None of Monterroso's other books is as rich in intertextuality as *Lo demás es silencio,* where it becomes the basis of an equivocal and malicious attitude. It is an invitation to an intelligent game that begins with the planting of a false quote as an epigraph: "The rest is silence. Shakespeare, *The Tempest.*" Another game involves the use of the biography genre. In the texts attributed to Eduardo Torres and the testimonials about his work and person, the figure of Torres, the wise man of San Blas, is introduced ambiguously. Is he astute or mediocre? Are we dealing with a writer of intelligent texts or of texts that slide into unintelligibility and absurdity? The effect of this ambiguity turns out to be grotesque.

Eduardo Torres's autobiography could have been presented as another triumph of *humilitas* because instead of dealing with a great man—as is traditional in the biographical genre, since it does not generally admit stories of insubstantial persons—it presents Torres, who is mediocrity itself and who embodies the characteristics of cultured pedantry that are widely ridiculed. The irony and paradox of the matter is that, as a character and a scholarly authority, Torres has accompanied Monterroso for so many years that at times he has been perceived as Monterroso's alter ego, embodying the real author's greatest fears: being ridiculed, being guilty of solemnity, and making the wrong step. Instead of satirizing writers with a ridiculous figure that may embody these characteristics, Monterroso is telling us that we are all Eduardo Torres to the degree that we have not overcome what he is. Torres is the negation of the literary vocation and a warning against any writer who assumes literature to be a race toward social success, fame, and money.

While Gustave Flaubert said "Madame Bovary, c'est moi" (I am Madame Bovary), Monterroso could say "I am not Eduardo Torres," "I don't want him to be me, nor I, he," or "Eduardo Torres is everything that I would be afraid of being." Significantly, one of the reviews of his book was titled "We Are All Eduardo Torres," which is reminiscent of an old saying: "No one is free of guilt."

In *Perpetual Motion* Eduardo Torres is identified as the author of a brief text, "Humorismo" ("Humor"), but it could easily have been signed Augusto Monterroso. It states, " 'Man is not content with being the stupidest animal in Creation; he also permits himself the luxury of being the only one that is ridiculous.' " Monterroso has more than once rejected the label of humorist, defining his work and attitude as realist. He achieves a humorous result by taking realism to its utmost consequences. Although the judgment that the human being is "the stupidest animal in Creation" may be debatable, it would be hard to deny that the human being is the only animal with a sense of the ridiculous, a sense that surely inspired Monterroso to create Eduardo Torres. Nevertheless, the quote is Torres's, not Monterroso's or both of theirs. In other texts, as we shall see, the author seeks to illustrate the sense of being both himself and the other at the same time.

When Monterroso refers to Torres in *La palabra mágica* (1983), he alludes to a text that he later included in *Lo demás es silencio,* saying: "Some years ago Eduardo Torres made a mistake, or made like he was making a mistake, and explained line by line the wrong stanza (from [Luis de] Góngora's *Polifemo*), calling it 'a forgotten stanza.' " Monterroso's maliciousness in saying that Torres "made a mistake, or made like he was making a mistake" creates a doubt about Torres's intelligence that is applied to practically all of the character's attitudes and actions. The author is thus placing him on a border where he could be an example either of the highest and most astute intelligence or of extreme foolishness. As Luciano Zamora, Torres's valet and secretary, says, his master was at the same time a "coarse spirit, a humorist, a wise man [and] a fool."

In interviews, Monterroso has brought Torres into his own life. In 1969 the writer informed Margarita García Flores that he was preparing a biography (which we might surmise became *Lo demás es silencio*), that forced him to make numerous trips to interview the subject of his biography:

I am busy with Eduardo Torres's biography, which has been excessively delayed. The research has been slower and more difficult than I expected. The trips to San Blas are expensive and tiresome (because of my unfounded fear of planes I have to go by bus, jeep, or mule). But that would not matter. The bad thing is that the result depends on the master's mood. When he is in a bad mood he simply speaks to me about things that have nothing to do with his life, and I know then that it is impossible to get a fact, a precise date.

In 1980, after *Lo demás es silencio* had reached his readers' hands, Monterroso told Graciela Carminatti about the origin of Eduardo Torres, and although recognizing his fictive status, he continued to refer to him as a real person:

What was the original idea? That of rescuing a series of articles by a small town writer, specifically Dr. Eduardo Torres, from San Blas, S.B. It was hard for me to find him, to familiarize myself with him (I try to stay away from familiarity), and to decide to do it. This gave me time to reject a lot of material that . . . found an appropriate place: the darkest place in my desk.

A selection of material about a negative alter ego rather than a novel, Eduardo Torres's fictitious biography is certainly a text that fits the biographical genre. Biography's principles fail to the degree that Monterroso never really planned to construct a biography per se. As Corral, one of Monterroso's most incisive critics, has pointed out, Torres "is a pretext, his absence is his presence; the only thing that the reader perceives are what Roland Barthes, in his *Roland Barthes,* calls 'biographemes,' that is a few details, preferences, inflections, destined to disperse, [and] to not inform the reader."

In the fables and in Torres's life, Monterroso finds his place in literature. But also, and more important, he finds that his place *is* literature, which somehow becomes the world of "the magic word," different from the common word. His work has mainly spoken about the worlds of others, and has fought vigorously to maintain the relative autonomy of reality and literature and to avoid making one subservient to the other. In his subsequent books, Monterroso finds and emphasizes the tone to insert his identity into the world (and into literature). It is an untransferable identity, which has always been under discussion but not mentioned as such. In other words, Monterroso's subsequent books are more transparently his to the degree that they assume an autobiographical discourse. That discourse appears in his interviews over the years that he brought together under the title *Viaje al centro de la fábula* (1981). It also appears in the essays of *La palabra mágica,* in which he "essays" his ideas about books, friends, reality, and fiction; in *Los buscadores de oro* (1993), a direct and candid autobiography that ends before Monterroso reaches sixteen; and in *La vaca* (1998), a book of miscellaneous texts that he justified as being sparked by "friends" (all of whom come from literature).

These books, and especially the last two, belong to a new stage in Monterroso's work where he is much more open in terms of revealing himself, and much more defining of himself as a writer and of his literature. In this stage he provides the narrative of how his trip in search of identity began, and of how the journey took him to the station called literature.

Two notable aspects of *Los buscadores de oro* are its stark style, which simulates the directness of oral expression, and his search for identity as leitmotif. Monterroso's writing here tends toward the pristineness associated with language of high literary quality, and—as in his earliest books—one does not find tensions within his writing. It is as if the struggle between the real and the literary, the raw and the cooked, has finally ended in favor of the latter of each pair. That explains the characteristics of Monterroso's "autobiography": instead of narrating circumstances for their affective value, in *Los buscadores de oro* he chooses those that have a direct connection to literary vocation. Everything else is left out. He strips his memory of insubstantial anecdotes, and deals with the everyday only because of the meaningful values in his writing that overlay the everyday. The book is an allegory of a personal quest; Monterroso turns out to be the "gold seeker" of the title, and the gold, literary vocation.

Since Monterroso's search is subjective, much of it deals with identity, which here has two dimensions: civic and literary. Regarding its author's birth, *Los buscadores de oro* asks a rich variety of questions. Monterroso was born in Honduras. Does that make him Honduran? Is he Guatemalan because he spent his formative years in Guatemala and because his father was from there? Or is he Mexican because he has lived most of his adult life, and especially his years of literary production, in Mexico? For a man so profoundly and unequivocally Mexican as Juan Rulfo, that problem could not be insignificant. That is why, Monterroso relates, Rulfo, who was his friend, was amazed and amused when seeing Monterroso attempt to use an old Guatemalan passport on his trips: " 'Why do you travel with that?' he said, accentuating the 'that.' I can get you a Mexican one." "Is it not the same thing?" Monterroso asks. Actually, it was not the same thing for someone who stills struggles internally to establish his identity in the world.

*Los buscadores de oro* begins with a narrative of the feelings of discomfort and perplexity Monterroso felt while he gave a talk at the University of Siena in Italy. After introducing himself to the audience as an "unknown," or rather "ignored," writer, he asked himself:

What was I doing there, then? To begin with, I stuck to the idea that, precisely, if those who heard me ignored who was speaking to them, it was good that I let them know who I was, and I started to do it. But upon listening to my own words linking each other . . . the suspicion that I also did not know very well who I was started to incubate within me.

In fact, all of *Los buscadores de oro* is written as a voyage of self-knowledge whose objective is to respond to the apparently easy but devilishly complex question: Who am I?

The book touches on various aspects of this question, and various attempts are made to respond. The most important thing is that Monterroso has asked the question, and through it has managed to express a singular feeling of not belonging. The identity dilemmas go hand in hand with that sort of guilt which impedes him from feeling deserving: "Throughout my life I have lived things as if what happens to me was happening to someone else, who is and is not me." Freud would have liked Monterroso's answer, which expresses a feeling the latter relates to one of his earliest memories: the feeling of guilt when he was found examining the genitals of a little girl his own age. Monterroso suspects that the drama of being "expelled from that innocent childish paradise [could have stamped] on me an indelible feeling of guilt and condemnation, of plainly not deserving what is good and pleasant, things that at any future time should be forever and by right only for others."

Tracing his origins and feeling of not belonging, of not being or being someone else and himself at the same time, Monterroso follows various paths, some of which fail to add any certainty to his anguished identity. One path was that of seeking his ancestors. After narrating a beautiful story of an epistolary and then personal relationship with a Catalan scholar regarding some writers, Monterroso concludes that "One can chose one's most remote ancestors." And after that story, which creates the possibility that one of his ancestors was the forgotten poet Janus Vitalis de Monterroso, Monterroso tells us that he was never really interested in genealogical trees, and ends with a humorous conclusion that is typical of him: "My interest in genealogies is nil. By direct English lineage we all descend from Darwin."

Nevertheless, his personal search is serious, since his identity depends on it. That is why he tries to support himself on more than one pillar. "I am, I feel and have always been Guatemalan; but my birth happened in Tegucigalpa, the capital of Honduras," he says at the start of one of the chapters. Yet a bit later he asserts the insignificance of birthplace for a writer: "I am convinced that for someone who at a given moment, suddenly or gradually, decides to become a writer, there is no difference at all between being born someplace in Central America, Paris, Florence or Buenos Aires." Here Monterroso speaks succinctly of two worlds and two corresponding citizenships: civic and literary.

In another chapter Monterroso alludes again to his two parallel commitments and passions. He refers to a child's dream about the condition of some "real peasants" and, at the same time to Cervantes's *Don Quixote.* That conjunction of the real and the fictitious, Monterroso points out, is what "is deciding the path, which is really long and tortuous but not necessarily dramatic, through which the child will arrive, already arrived without suspecting it, to two things that will be

basic in his life: literature and taking the side of the weak against the powerful." This text refers, once again, to double citizenship: a progressive inclination in relation to political and social causes and, alongside it, an irrevocable vocation for literature.

Monterroso is far from defining these two dimensions as easy and universal solutions to problems of identity or of the relationship between reality and literature, but they are at least his personal definitions. The whole book breathes the need to find answers or clues. He refers to the "feeling of uprootedness, of not belonging, that has accompanied me" from the first moment he traveled with his family from Tegucigalpa to Guatemala. The fact of not having voted in national elections (the basic right of the political citizen) makes him feel that "I am not a citizen of the world but of nowhere," and that "I live with the uncertainty of my right to even step on the thirty-five square centimeters of the planet on which I stand every morning."

That same uncertainty leads him to relate the anecdote mentioned above about his dialogue with Juan Rulfo and to think about the symbolic meaning of country. Is one's country the place where the umbilical cord is buried? Is it the country printed on a passport obtained by a friend or the country inscribed on the passport given by a nation in which one was not born? Or is it an affective territory determined by will? Monterroso answers these questions only in personal terms. He is not interested in creating dogmas or certainties valid for everyone. Not all have lived Monterroso's personal circumstances, his political exile (starting in Mexico in the 1940s), or his existential exile (the absence of roots in any one place).

Given that *Los buscadores de oro* is a narrative of searches, it incorporates stages and journeys in Monterroso's life. In one chapter he remembers childhood games connected with the presses in his father's publishing establishment. To what extent did his games with movable type determine his path toward literature? In another chapter he cites his mother as the one who introduced him to reading. Then there is the chapter in which he relates how he began to "be conscious of my individuality, the clear and precise feeling of my person." A subsequent chapter starts at the beginning of a stage: "Owning my name already."

In a chapter near the end, Monterroso speaks extensively about his father and questions what he recognizes as his paternal inheritance. In the remainder of the book, the paternal figure is emotionally displaced by the maternal one, and sometimes appears to be responsible (in the imagination of the son) for squandering the maternal fortune. That is why we are moved by the son's imaginary reconciliation with his father through the son's acknowledgment of his paternal legacy.

> My father always lived submerged in dreams and most assuredly died wrapped in them. Going from a world of fiction without objective to a more defined one, as literature's would be, is perhaps the little I saved from his inheritance, transmitted who knows how: it could be that his poet friends were already influencing the course of my life when they came to our house to recite their poems.

*Los buscadores de oro* is a rich introspection by a mature man into the child he was. Traditionally one abandons that child when he reaches adolescence, when innocence ends and gives way to knowledge, to the individual's construction of a series of strategies for survival. In Monterroso's case, however, the childhood phase—pristine and pure because there was no need to compete, to seduce, to employ the various social masks of the adult world—is progressively replaced by culture. That is why ultimately this book is not a conventional autobiography. It is actually a description of Monterroso's ultimate literary goal, which he reached, and the tale of his path toward it. In this sense it is also an implicit delivery of clues for reading his previous work.

Five years later Monterroso published *La vaca*, another of his slim volumes. He prefaced it with two warnings. One is an epigraph by the French poet Stéphane Mallarmé, "Toda abundancia es estéril" (All abundance is sterile). That is followed by a very brief prologue in which he holds that the book's existence is due to the affectionate insistence of his friends. We do not find in this book the gold seekers of the previous book, but we do find the autobiographical character who compiles a series of texts as if they were part of his literary persona.

The volume closes with the strictly autobiographical part of the text, "Vivir en México" (To live in Mexico).

Written in 1990, that text is obviously the contemporary of *Los buscadores de oro*, having the same tone of personal rescue. It also contains some of the most melancholy pages written by Monterroso, pages that seem to say good-bye. Given the emotional importance that friendship has in Monterroso's life and work, it is interesting that when discussing his "life in Mexico" from 1944 to 1990, the author refers to the thousands of displaced people and exiles such as he, produced by world wars.

Monterroso then proposes to praise Mexico. Not wanting it to appear that he is writing out of personal gratitude, he employs an allegory which identifies that country with magic and the marvelous (something that the French literary figure André Breton had done sixty years before, when he said that Mexico was "surrealist" by nature). In *La vaca* Monterroso says:

> *Hace poco me pidieron en España que hablara de la literatura fantástica mexicana. Y la he buscado y perseguido: privadas, y esa literatura casi no aparece, porque lo más fantástico a que pueda llegar aquí la imaginación se desvanece en el trasfundo de una vida real y de todos los días que es, no obstante, como un sueño dentro de otro sueño. Lo mágico, lo fantástico y lo maravilloso está siempre a punto de suceder en México, y sucede, y uno sólo dice: pues sí.*

A little while ago I was asked to speak in Spain about Mexican literature of the fantastic. I have looked for it and pursued it: in my own and in public and private libraries that literature almost does not exist, because the most fantastic level the imagination can reach here vanishes in the background of a real everyday life that is, nevertheless, like a dream within a dream. The magic, the fantastic, and the marvelous are always about to happen in Mexico, and they happen, and one can only say: well, yes.

Monterroso concludes *La vaca* with this farewell:

> *En medio del riudo de la ciudad inmensa hay un gran silencio en el que pueden oírse voces, voces atlas y voces apagadas como los murmillos, que emitía mi amigo Juan, Juan Rulfo, ante de desaparecer en su proprio silencio. Y entre esas voces vivo y persisto, y con una adecuada dosis diaria, bueno, tal vez sólo semanal, de Séneca, estoy contento aquí, voy y vengo, me alejo y regreso, como desde el primer día. Aquí tengo familia, tengo mujer y tengo hijos: y tengo amigos, cada vez menos, porque las amistades se degestan, desaparecen o se van concentrando en*

*unos pocos que, a su vez, empiezan a ver las cosas del mismo modo, es decir, con nostalgia, porque la vida ésta acabando y es mejor irse despidiendo en vida, sin decirlo, simplemente dejándose de ver, de llamar, de amar.*

In the midst of the immense city's noise there is a great silence in which one can hear voices, loud voices and hushed voices similar to the murmurs my friend Juan, Juan Rulfo, emitted before disappearing in his own silence. I live and persist among those voices, and with an adequate daily, well, perhaps weekly, dose of Seneca, I am happy here, I come and go, move away and return, as from the first day. I have family here, a wife and children; and I have friends, fewer each time, because friendships dwindle, disappear or concentrate in a few who, at the same time, start seeing things the same way. That is, with nostalgia, because life is ending and it is better to say farewell while living, without saying it, simply by not seeing, calling or loving one another.

Although the text's emotion is legitimate and certain, it also allows for an important correction. During the 1990s, when *La vaca* was written, Monterroso received many important tributes: in 1993, the Semana de Autor in Madrid; in 1996, the Premio Juan Rulfo in Mexico. The proceedings of both tributes were subsequently published. In 2000 he received Spain's Premio Príncipe de Asturias and the Homenaje a Monterroso in Jalapa, Veracruz state. There have also been many editions and reprints of his books in Spain, Mexico, and other Spanish-speaking countries, as well as translations in other languages.

In Latin American literature Monterroso represents the kind of writer who is very demanding of himself and his readers, and who has written in many genres, always maintaining his high literary standards. He has written in genres that had been institutionalized in literary traditions, and has managed to renew them, creating unexpected variations. Belonging to the very select lineage of Jorge Luis Borges, Julio Torri, Macedonio Fernández, Felisberto Hernández, Julio Cortázar, and Juan José Arreola, he has written short stories, fables, essays, and miscellaneous short forms in which a high level of imagination goes hand in hand with a heightened sense of language and style. His place in literature is beyond national contexts such as Central American or Mexican literature. His knowledge of the cultures of ancient Greece and Rome and of Europe, as well as his uninterrupted immersion in Latin American classics, have helped him produce a body of literature that does not belong to a single tradition or move in a single direction.

## SELECTED BIBLIOGRAPHY

### Primary Works

#### Books

*El concierto y el eclipse.* Mexico City: Los Epígrafes, 1947.
*Uno de cada tres y el centenario.* Mexico City: Los Presentes, 1952.
*Obras completas y otros cuentos.* Mexico City: Imprenta Universitaria, 1959.
*La oveja negra y demás fábulas.* Mexico City: Joaquín Mortiz, 1969.
*Movimiento perpetuo.* Mexico City: Joaquín Mortiz, 1972.
*Lo demás es silencio: La vida y la obra de Eduardo Torres.* Mexico City: Joaquín Mortiz, 1978.
*La palabra mágica.* Mexico City: Era, 1983.
*Los buscadores de oro.* Barcelona: Anagrama, 1993.
*La vaca.* Mexico City: Alfaguara, 1998.

#### Translations

*The Black Sheep, and Other Fables.* Trans. by Walter I. Bradbury. Garden City, N.Y.: Doubleday, 1971. (Translation of *Oveja negra y demás fábulas.*)
*Complete Works and Other Stories.* Trans. by Edith Grossman, with an introduction by Will H. Corral. Austin: University of Texas Press, 1995.

### Secondary Works

#### Critical and Biographical Studies

Abad Faciolince, Hector, et al. *A propósito de Augusto Monterroso y su obra.* Bogotá: Norma, 1994.
Campos, Julieta. "No todos los gatos son pardos." *Revista de la Universidad de Mexico* (Mexico City) 37, no. 5:48–50 (September 1981).
Campos, Marco Antonio, et al. "Alrededor de Augusto Monterroso." *Casa del Tiempo* (Mexico City), 23 July 1982, pp. 23–27.
———. *La literatura de Augusto Monterroso.* Mexico City: Universidad Autonoma Metropolitana, 1988.

Corral, Wilfrido H. *Lector, sociedad y genero en Monterroso.* Xalapa, Mexico: Universidad Veracruzana, 1985.

———, ed. *Refracción: Monterroso ante la crítica.* Mexico City: Universidad Nacional Autonoma de México/ Ediciones Era, 1994.

———, ed. *Augusto Monterroso: Semana de Autor Augusto Monterroso.* Madrid: Cultura Hispánica, 1997.

Liano, Dante. "Itinerario de Augusto Monterroso." In his *Ensayos de literatura guatemalteca.* Rome: Bulzoni, 1992. Pp. 55–68.

Noguerol, Francisca. *La trampa en la sonrisa: Sátira en la narrativa de Augusto Monterroso.* Seville: Universidad de Sevilla, 1995.

Rama, Angel. "Augusto Monterroso: Fabulista para nuestro tiempo." *Eco* 28, no. 3:315–319 (July 1974).

Ruffinelli, Jorge, ed. "Monterroso: Disparen sobre la solemnidad." *Crisis* (Buenos Aires) no. 32:14–16 (November 1975).

———. *Monterroso.* Xalapa, Mexico: Universidad Veracruzana, 1976.

———. "Monterroso: Fobias y literatura." *Sabado* (*Unomasuno*) (Mexico City), 30 June 1984, p. 8.

———. "Homenaje a Monterroso en España, incluido perro cantor." *Nuevo Texto Crítico* (Stanford, Calif.) 4, no. 8:211–216 (1991).

Schneider, Luis Mario. "Monterroso: Humor y verdad." *Revista de la Universidad de Mexico* 15, no. 5:29–30 (May 1960).

Sosnowski, Saul. "Augusto Monterroso: La satira del poder." *Zona Franca* (Caracas) 111, no. 19:53–57 (July–August 1980).

*Viaje al centro de la fábula.* Mexico City: Universidad Nacional Autónoma de Mexico, 1981. (Interview collection.)

Zaid, Gabriel. "Preguntas fabulosas." *Vuelta* (Mexico City) 5, no. 55:46 (August 1981).

# Alvaro Mutis

## (1923–      )

## *Michael Palencia-Roth*

A ny panoramic consideration of the career of Alvaro Mutis must take into account the fluidity of the boundaries between his poetry and prose; the central position that Maqroll el Gaviero, his main character, has occupied for some fifty years in both his poetry and his fiction; and his international and antiquarian tastes in literature and history. In addition, one must recognize that the fifteen months he spent in a Mexican prison were equally significant for his development. Critics have identified a number of themes as central to Mutis's work—the concept of *fortuna* (or the interrelationship between chance and fate), misery, despair, decay or deterioration, nostalgia, travel, friendship, love, death, and the striving toward the unattainable. All of these themes find expression in the adventures of Maqroll. Maqroll himself may be viewed as Mutis's deliberately constructed alter ego or, as the author himself has put it, "esta especie de otro yo que escribe mis cosas" (this kind of other 'I' who writes my stuff; Bradu, *Vuelta*).

Mutis was born on 25 August 1923 in Bogotá, Colombia. His parents were Santiago Mutis Dávila and Carolina Jaramillo Angel. The author, in an interview with Jacobo Sefami (in *Tras las rutas de Magroll el Gaviero, 1988–1993*) has testified that he is descended from "conversos," Spanish Jews who had been forcibly converted to Christianity. The surnames of his parents also indicate ties to some of Colombia's oldest families. On his father's side, for instance, he is a descendant of Manuel Mutis, who arrived in Colombia in the eighteenth century and was the brother of José Celestino Mutis, one of Colombia's earliest and most famous scientists, head of the Royal Botanical Expedition of New Granada and friend of Alexander von Humboldt. His mother's side includes several generations of prosperous landowners who cultivated of coffee and sugar cane primarily. Mutis's mother inherited one of these holdings, a plantation named Coello, in the department of Tolima, and this became the main inspiration for Mutis's portrayal of rural life and of nature in the high valleys and foothills of the Andes mountains.

When Santiago Mutis Dávila was 18, he became the private secretary of the Colombian president Jorge Holguín, and served President Pedro Nel Ospina as well. In 1925 Mutis Dávila, who read, spoke and wrote French fluently, was named a member of the Colombian diplomatic legation to Brussels. The infant Alvaro Mutis thus moved to Belgium at age two. There he began his schooling, at the Jesuit School of Saint Michel. He spent nine years in Belgium, and became so immersed in the culture that today he considers French to be his first language.

Summer vacations were sometimes spent at Coello, and the ocean voyages to and from Colombia inspired

Mutis's love for the sea and his fascination with ships and their ports of call. In 1934 the family returned permanently to Colombia, after the unexpected death of Santiago Mutis Dávila at age 33. Eventually, the family settled in Bogotá, alternating, as Colombian families often did in those days, between periods in the countryside (at Coello) and in the capital city.

As a schoolboy in Bogotá, Mutis attended the Colegio Mayor de Nuestra Señora del Rosario. He was an indifferent student—billiards was his passion, he has said—but he was also a voracious reader. He devoured the works of Jules Verne, Joseph Conrad, and Charles Dickens, among others. At school he came under the influence of one of Colombia's most prominent poets, Eduardo Carranza, who taught him poetry and encouraged him to use the school library to read further. Scolded by the head of the school for indulging in too much outside reading and not paying enough attention to his assigned work, Mutis replied, "Pero Monseñor, tengo muchas cosas serias que hacer y no puedo perder el tiempo estudiando" (But monsignor, I have too many serious things to do and can't waste time studying; Cobo Borda, *Alvaro Mutis*). Before finishing high school, he dropped out.

Mutis first married at eighteen. With his wife Mireya Durán, he had three children: María Cristina, Santiago, and Jorge Manuel. Immediately after the wedding, ordered by his mother to seek gainful employment rather than live on family wealth, he began a career of sorts in radio, working first for six months as the host of a cultural program, then as an actor and announcer for Radio Nacional, and finally as a classical music announcer under the tutelage of Otto de Greiff, brother of the Colombian poet, León de Greiff, another of Mutis's earliest mentors. From 1947 to 1956, in addition to publishing his first poems, he worked in various capacities for the Compañía Colombiana de Seguros (Colombian National Insurance Company), where he edited the journal *Vida*. He also worked for Bavaria (a brewing company), for Lansa (an aviation company), and finally for Esso (a subsidiary of Standard Oil).

An excess of generosity and an admitted carelessness with corporate funds landed him in trouble. The details remain unclear, even though Mutis has commented on the matter a number of times. Apparently, he used company funds in an unauthorized manner to host lavish dinners as well as to help his friends in the arts and in politics, some of whom were opponents of the dictatorship of Gustavo Rojas Pinilla, who was then in power. In a 1959 interview with Elena Poniatowska he provided this explanation:

> *En Bogotá fui jefe de Relaciones Públicas de la Standard Oil, la Esso. Se me acusó de aplicar indebidamente ciertos fondos de esa compañía destinados a servicios de beneficiencia. En esto hubo mucho de verdad. Pero es que yo consideraba una actividad benéfica, entre otras, el ayudar a desterrados políticos y a otros perseguidos por el dictador de mi país. En todo caso hubo un indiscutible desorden por lo que a mí respecta. . . . Empecé a manejar el dinero como si fuera mío, la selección de mis beneficiados fue caprichosa, caí el en desorden.*
>
> (Poniatowska, *Cartas*)

In Bogotá I was head of public relations for Standard Oil, Esso. I was accused of having mismanaged certain company funds which had been targeted for charities. There was a lot of truth [in this accusation]. But in fact I considered it a charitable act, among other charitable acts, to help political exiles and other people who were being persecuted by the dictator of my country. In any case, there was an undeniable disorder in what I was responsible for. . . . I began to use the money as if it were mine, my selection of the beneficiaries was capricious, and I got into trouble.

In 1956, about to be arrested for fiscal mismanagement, Mutis fled to Mexico, arriving on 24 October. For over a year he had a busy cultural life among the Mexican intelligentsia, but it was not carefree, as he continually feared the long reach of the Colombian authorities. In time he noticed that he was being shadowed by a Colombian agent. Ultimately he was arrested and threatened with deportation. However, rather than being forcibly returned to Colombia, he was allowed to be detained in Mexico, in Lecumberri Prison (also known as El Palacio Negro: the Black Palace) while lawyers argued about his case. Mutis was an inmate there for 15 months. On 22 December 1959, upon being declared innocent by the then President of Colombia, Alberto Lleras, Mutis was released.

Before entering Lecumberri, Mutis had been working in Mexico City for the Barbachanos Public Relations Agency. During his months in prison, his employer continued to send the Mutis family the monthly paychecks he would otherwise have earned. Upon leaving Lecumberri in late 1959, Mutis, deeply grateful, went to thank the head of the agency for his generosity; the agency head responded by simply putting Mutis back to work as if nothing had happened.

After some time, Mutis moved to the Latin American offices of Twentieth-Century Fox and Columbia Pictures in Mexico City, where he was put in charge of Latin American distribution. This position required him to travel throughout Latin America and beyond, giving him the kind of wide experience that is reflected in Mutis's novels. He retired from Columbia Pictures in 1983, at the age of 60, and since then has devoted himself to writing. Indeed, the bulk of his work has been written in retirement.

After his marriage with Mireya Durán ended, Mutis married María Luz Montané Zañartu, with whom he had a daughter, María Teresa. This second marriage did not survive the Lecumberri experience, however. Mutis lived alone for several years before marrying again in 1966. His third wife was Carmen Miracle Feliú, a widow with a young daughter, Francine. It is Francine who gave him his grandson Nicolás, the inspiration for the character Jamil in the third novella of Mutis's last book of narratives to date, *Tríptico de mar y tierra* (1993; *Triptych on Sea and Land*, 1995).

Prior to the early 1980s, relatively few scholars and critics paid attention to Alvaro Mutis. Of those, most were Colombians, with the notable exception of Octavio Paz. In 1959, Paz praised Mutis's poetry chapbook, *Los elementos del desastre* (1953; The elements of the disaster) as well as some poems that had been published in the Colombian journal, *Mito*, in 1955 under the title "Reseña de Hospitales de Ultramar" (Review of the overseas hospitals). By 1980 only sixty or so critical articles, notices, and reviews of his work had appeared, and yet he had been writing for more than 30 years. It cannot be denied, however, that the writing published before 1980 adds up to a relatively slim body of work.

After publishing *La balanza* (1948; The scales), *Los elementos del desastre*, and the poems of the "Reseña de Hospitales de Ultramar," Mutis brought out, in 1960, *Diario de Lecumberri*, his prison memoir, in an edition that also contained three short stories: "La muerte del Estratega" (The death of the strategist), "Sharaya," and "Antes de que cante el gallo" (Before the cock

crows). These works were followed by *Los trabajos perdidos* (1965; The lost works), a collection of twenty poems, and *Summa de Maqroll el Gaviero: Poesía 1947–1970* (1973; The *Summa* of Maqroll el Gaviero: Poetry 1947–1970), which gathered all of the poetry published up to that time. Also in 1973, he published his first extended prose narrative, *La mansión de Araucaíma* (The house of Araucaima), in an edition that also included "Sharaya" and "La muerte del Estratega."

Mutis had the great good fortune of seeing one of his oldest and best literary friends, Gabriel García Márquez, win the Nobel Prize for literature in 1982. Mutis and García Márquez first met in 1949, and it was Mutis who obtained for García Márquez his first major position as a journalist on the *El Espectador* staff in 1954. Perhaps in order to reciprocate, in March of 1954 García Márquez published a laudatory notice of *Los elementos del desastre* and an interview with Mutis in *El Espectador*. These articles are among the earliest pieces on Mutis to appear in a national publication. This would be the first of many times that these two major Colombian authors would be personally and professionally linked in print.

It was Mutis who met García Márquez at the train station when the latter arrived in Mexico City in 1961, and it was Mutis who introduced him to the literary elite of Mexico. Mutis also urged Garcia Márquez to read and to study Juan Rulfo's *Pedro Páramo*, a book that would influence him greatly in the writing of *One Hundred Years of Solitude*. And it was Mutis who, in his words, would "visit the patient" on those afternoons in 1966 after he had finished his daily stint of writing *One Hundred Years of Solitude*. Mutis accompanied García Márquez to Sweden on the occasion of his Nobel Prize for Literature in 1982 and García Márquez spoke at the ceremony in honor of Mutis's 70th birthday in 1993 (the speech was subsequently published with two different titles, "Una amistad en tiempos ruines" and "Mi amigo Mutis") when Mutis received Colombia's highest order of merit, the Gran Cruz de la Orden de Boyacá. García Márquez appears as a character in Mutis's poetry, for example, in "Tríptico de la Alhambra" (Triptych of the Alhambra), and in his prose, as in "Razón verídica de los encuentros y complicidades de Maqroll el Gaviero con el pintor Alejandro Obregón" in (True account of the meetings and schemes of

Maqroll el Gaviero and the painter Alejandro Obregón) in *Tríptico de mar y tierra*.

When Garcia Márquez won the 1982 Nobel Prize, a welcome spotlight was cast upon a number of his friends and associates. The flame from that fifteen minutes of worldwide fame would soon have flickered out for Mutis, however, had it not been for the fact that, beginning about 1981, his literary productivity increased exponentially. Several collections of poetry appeared in the early and mid-1980s: *Caravansary* (1981), *Los emisarios* (1984; The emissaries), *Crónica Regia y alabanza del reino* (1985; Royal account and praise of the realm), and *Un homenaje y siete nocturnos* (1986; An homage and seven nocturnes). In 1982 Mutis's son, Santiago Mutis Durán, a poet and critic in his own right, edited a collection, *Poesía y Prosa: Alvaro Mutis*, which was published by the Ministry of Culture of Colombia. In 1985 Santiago Mutis Durán again edited his father's work, producing a two-volume set, *Poesía* and *Prosa*, which was once again published by the Ministry of Culture of Colombia.

These two collections presented, in widely available editions, virtually all of Mutis's writings up to that point, together with some of the more salient critical opinions on his work. The result was a revelation to many readers and critics, as the thematic coherence and aesthetic evolution of a substantial body of work now became evident. By the mid-1980s, Mutis had clearly become a writer to be reckoned with. His reputation was further enhanced when, beginning in 1986, he began publishing a series of novels about Maqroll and his world. Long accustomed to thinking of Mutis as a poet, critics now began to recognize him as a novelist as well. Between 1986 and 1993, the Maqroll cycle of seven novels appeared: *La Nieve del Almirante* (1986), *Ilona llega con la lluvia* (1987), *La última escala del Tramp Steamer* (1989; *The Tramp Steamer's Last Port of Call,* 1995), *Un bel morir* (1989; A good death), *Amirbar* (1990; *Amirbar,* 1995), *Abdul Bashur, soñador de navíos* (1990; *Abdul Bashur, Dreamer of Ships,* 1995), and *Tríptico de mar y tierra*. These novels were collected in a single large volume entitled *Siete novelas, Mutis. Empresas y tribulaciones de Maqroll el Gaviero* (1995; Seven novels by Mutis: the trials and tribulations of Maqroll el Gaviero).

In 1983 Mutis received the National Prize for Poetry in Colombia. That was followed in 1988 by the Mexican order of merit, the Aguila Azteca, which accorded him the rank of comendador. Mutis was honored with a host of other prizes, awards, and commendations from Mexico, Italy, France, Colombia, and Spain. In 1997 alone he received four major awards: the Grinzane-Cavour Prize and the Rossone d'Oro Prize from Italy and the Prince of Asturias Prize in Literature and the Reina Sofía Prize in Poetry, both from Spain, for his work as a whole.

When he left Colombia in 1956, Mutis enjoyed a reputation as an up-and-coming poet. His first book of poems, *La balanza*, was a collaborative effort: half of it consisted of poems by Mutis, the other half was poetry written by his friend Carlos Patiño Roselli. *La balanza* went up in flames the day after its publication, victim of the *bogotazo*, riots that erupted in Bogotá on 9 April 1948, after the assassination of the Liberal Party candidate for president, Jorge Eliécer Gaitán. Mutis's first solo effort, the chapbook of poetry entitled *Los elementos del desastre* was a slender booklet of just twelve poems, published in 1953. It is generally thought that the next chapbook to appear was *Reseña de los Hospitales de Ultramar*, in a special issue of *Mito* in 1959, but this view is difficult to support (Ruiz Barrionuevo; Rodríguez Amaya, *De MUTIS a Mutis*). What is certain is that Mutis did publish, in *Mito*'s second issue, four poems and an introductory prose fragment that identified the poems to be works by "Maqroll" in his old age (*Mito,* no. 2:72–76, 1955).

This small collection is given the title "Reseña de los Hospitales de Ultramar" and includes the poems "El hospital de la bahía" (The hospital by the bay), "El hospital de los soberbios" (The hospital of the prideful), "Fragmento" (Fragment), and "Las plagas de Maqroll" (The plagues of Maqroll). Also included is an announcement that other poems will appear in future issues of *Mito*. In *Mito*'s fourth issue, in late 1955, Mutis published "Moirologhia"; the term refers to a threnody or lament generally sung by Peloponnesian women at a coffin or tomb. In 1959, in *Mito* no. 26, Mutis published several more Maqroll poems under the title "Memoria de los Hospitales de Ultramar." In prison, Mutis continued to write poetry, including "Poema de lástimas a la muerte de Marcel Proust" (Poem of regret on the death of Marcel Proust), and penned some of his first fictional works, as well as his *Diario de Lecumberri.*

Prison was a transformational experience for Mutis, as he told Elena Poniatowska when she visited him in jail:

*El carcelazo es todo un terrible estado de ánimo, una total desesperanza. Es cuando se le cae a uno encima la cárcel, con todos sus muros, rejas, presos y miserias. . . . Todos los sentidos se concentran en eso tan ilusorio y que se hace cada día más imposible y extraño: ¡salir!*

(Cartas)

Imprisonment is a state of total despair. Everything weighs heavily: the walls, the railings, the other prisoners, the miseries. . . . All of one's senses are concentrated on one illusory thing only, made every day more impossible and strange: to leave!

The experience taught him about limitations. He saw human beings in degradation and despair. He befriended, and was befriended by, the most desperate of criminals, and he saw that they, too, were capable of acts of deep kindness and generosity. In jail, he adopted an attitude that not only would serve him well for the rest of his life but would also be central to the character of Maqroll el Gaviero: we cannot judge other people; we must cultivate tolerance (Poniatowska, *Cartas*).

Prison deepened Mutis, both as person and as a writer. Themes that previously had been mostly aesthetic explorations came to have profoundly existential dimensions. Nowhere is this more evident than in his comments on the relevance of the Lecumberri prison experience to his portrayal of Maqroll el Gaviero. His experience, he wrote Elena Poniatowska on 18 June 1959, was very much like Maqroll's in any poem of the "Review of the Overseas Hospitals" (*Cartas*). Some critics have seen in the closeness between Mutis and Maqroll the influence of the Portuguese poet Fernando Pessõa, whose creation of literary alter egos or masks was admired by Spanish-American writers of Mutis's generation and after. But for Mutis that closeness is not a matter of literary influence strategy. It is the result of a visceral understanding, acquired through incarceration and its attendant sufferings, of the trials of Maqroll.

In 1997, looking back at his life during an interview with Poniatowska, Mutis states that, ultimately, his writing has the character of testimony. He returns to his time in prison and muses on its meaning for his work:

*Sin Lecumberri no hubiera escrito mis siete novelas, ni nada de lo que ves. Realmente fue una experiencia muy enriquecedora. Lo he repetido muchas veces pero vale la pena volverlo a decir, en la cárcel tú llegas al final de la cuerda. En la cárcel lo que sucede es verdad absoluta. Pierdes todos tus privilegios, nada te sirve para nada salvo la situación desnuda y brutal del encierro y eso es muy sano. . . . No quisiera volver a tener esa experiencia pero el hecho de que haya podido escribir un libro de relatos y siete novelas me parece significativo. Yo sólo había escrito poesía. Sin Lecumberri la Summa de Maqroll el Gaviero no existiría. Lo que te quiero decir es esto: mi primera novela, La Nieve del Almirante, data de 1986. Cuando la terminé, empezó a destilarse una cantidad de material que se convirtió en las otras seis novelas. Me di cuenta de que estas novelas, que son ficción pura, provenían de mi vida en la cárcel. De esto no me queda ninguna duda. Tampoco hubieran sido posibles mis cuatro libros de poesía sin la visión interior que me dio permanecer solo, conmigo mismo, en una celda.*

(Cartas)

Without Lecumberri I would not have written my seven novels, indeed nothing that you see. It was really quite an enriching experience. I have said this many times, but it bears repeating: in jail, you get to the end of your rope. What happens there is the absolute truth. You lose all your privileges, nothing is worth anything to you except the bare and brutal fact of imprisonment, and that is a healthy thing. . . . I would not like to relive that experience, but I think it significant that I have been able to write a book of stories and seven novels. Up to that point I had only written poetry. Without Lecumberri the *Summa de Maqroll el Gaviero* would not exist. What I want to tell you is this: my first novel, *La Nieve del Almirante*, is dated 1986. After I finished it, a mass of material began to distill itself into the other six novels. I became aware that these novels, which are completely fictional, came from my life in prison. Of that I have no doubt. Neither would my four books of poetry [after Lecumberri] have been possible without that inner vision that was produced by my solitude, by being alone with myself in my cell.

Gabriel García Márquez once commented that "en general, un escritor no escribe sino un solo libro, aunque ese libro aparezca en muchos tomos con títulos diversos. Es el caso de Balzac, de Conrad, de Melville, de Kafka, y desde luego de Faulkner" (a writer writes, at bottom, only one book, though that book might appear in many volumes and with different titles. This is the case with Balzac, Conrad, Melville, Kafka and of course Faulkner; *El olor de la guayaba: Conversaciones con Plineo Apuleyo Mendoza*). For Alvaro Mutis, that "one book" is not based on a particular theme or themes, or centered upon a single place, but focuses instead on a character, Maqroll. The name is an invented one, chosen by Mutis to sound exotic in Spanish and indeterminable as to country of origin. Mutis never gives Maqroll's place of birth; neither does he describe him physically. He is known in his world as "Maqroll el Gaviero." A *gaviero* is a lookout, usually a boy, who scans the horizon from the crow's nest of a sailing ship for approaching ships, whales, storms, and the like.

From one perspective, Maqroll himself remains ever a boy in his enthusiasm for adventure and in his gullibility. But at the same time, symbolically, the vantage point of the crow's nest enables him to see farther and more accurately than other men. The variety and depth of Maqroll's experiences endow his character with a jaded weariness that belies his boyishness. Moreover, the figure of the *gaviero*, being someone whose life is characterized by movement from one port to another and across the seas, embodies Mutis's ever-present theme of *errancia* or wandering, a theme established as paradigmatic for Western literature by Homer's *Odyssey*.

Mutis is fully conscious of Maqroll as his alter ego. As he told Eduardo García Aguilar in a 1993 interview:

> [El renombre, el poder, la acción, todo termina en nada.] Por esto existe Maqroll el Gaviero, el pobre carga con todo lo que yo hubiera querido ser, con todo lo que yo hubiera tenido que ser y que no fui capaz de ser y comparte lo que yo he sido para que pueda dar una mezcla más o menos balanceada.
>
> (*Celebraciones*)

> [Fame, power, action, everything ends in nothing.] That is the raison d'être of Maqroll, that poor man has the burden of being everything that I wanted to be, everything that I would have had to be but was not capable of being, and he shares what I have been so that the result is a more or less equitable mixture of the two of us.

Maqroll thus embodies the attitudes central to Mutis's most deeply held convictions: that decadence and decline are inevitable but, at the same time, that there

is no teleology to history; that all is vanity; that "the day before yesterday"—especially when represented by epochs as remote from us as the Byzantine Empire in the seventh century, the fall of Constantinople, the Napoleonic era, and a few days in the last months of Simón Bolívar's life—is as interesting as contemporary events, if not more so. Maqroll, like his creator Mutis, believes that, in the face of present conditions and the lure of the past, the best that one can do is to resign oneself to changes in fortune and, wearily perhaps, to adapt to them. Beyond this, there is in Mutis the conviction that the aesthetic stance toward life is more important than the moral stance.

Given this conviction, and given his background and his literary tastes, it is clear that Mutis's sensibility aligns him less with twentieth-century Colombian writers than with French writers such as Montaigne, Chateaubriand, Baudelaire, Rimbaud, J. K. Huysmans, Proust, Céline, St. John Perse, Valéry Larbaud, and Apollinaire. He was exposed to a few of these writers as a child, while still living in Belgium; the majority, however, he read during his adolescence and as a young man, after his return to Colombia. In a sense he has never stopped reading them. His literary alter-ego, Maqroll, also never stops reading. Whether in a dilapidated port of call in the Mediterranean, the Indian Ocean, the Caribbean, or the Pacific; whether living in Panama or California; in the Andean highlands or the jungle; Maqroll reads. He may be reading engineering and geological texts (which he consults in order to explore a potential "gold mine" in *Amirbar*), or we may find him immersed in *Mémoires du Cardinal de Retz,* in Chateaubriand's *Mémoires d'Outre-Tombe,* in the memoirs of the Belgian Prince of Ligny, or in Joergenson's *Life of St. Francis of Assisi.* Maqoll is a writer, as well, entrusting an unfinished manuscript on the secret life of Cesare Borgia to his biographer, Mutis (*Obra poética*).

For Mutis, the boundaries between poetry and fiction are fluid, and many of his poems are really prose-poems. Some are not even that: they are prose fragments or prose lists. As early as 1948, Eduardo Zalamea Borda, recognizing this quality in Mutis's early works, urged him to cultivate prose-poetry (Cobo Borda, *Alvaro Mutis*). In most of his poetry chapbooks, intensely lyrical texts exist side by side with prose pieces shaped by an entirely different sense of language. His second poetry chapbook, *Los elementos del desastre,* was perceptively characterized by Gabriel García Márquez in a 1954 review as being written "neither in prose nor in verse" and as "not resembling, in its originality, any books in prose or in verse written by Colombians."

The dissolution of boundaries between poetry and prose is further complicated by Mutis's use of repetition and intertextuality across genres. For example, the prose fragment "Cocora," which is the name of a mine where Maqroll is the caretaker, first appears in the poetry collection, *Caravansary.* Mutis then repeats it, verbatim, in the coda to *La Nieve del Almirante,* along with three other prose poems (or fragments) that had been published earlier in poetry collections. Some of his novels, for instance *Amirbar,* include footnotes that point to sources and parallels in other works. This intertextual strategy encourages readers to consider each novel, even each poem, as part of a continuous dialogue conducted between the author and himself as well as with his readers.

Mutis the poet has an eye for narrative, for the story behind the image; Mutis the novelist has a sense of the image and of the portrait. The result is sometimes narrative poetry that is vaguely epic in its echoes, and sometimes fiction that is static and imagistic.

From his earliest publications on, Mutis displays a substantial consistency of vision, as well as repeated treatments of favorite issues. Before he left Colombia in 1955, that vision and those issues included the use of his family farm, Coello, as a setting of his poetry (a setting he adapted to fit differing aesthetic intentions); reference to exotic locales and peoples; and a Borgesian inclination for the startling short narrative told in an objective and detached manner. He often explored themes of decadence, despair, frustration, illness, solitude and failure; presented a view of history as more arbitrary than progressive; and commented on poetics and the significance of poetry. In addition, he established Maqroll el Gaviero as his most important literary persona long before he wrote the Maqroll novels.

The process of writing and the nature of poetry obsessed Mutis from the beginning of his career. In an early prose poem, "Programa para una poesía" (1952), he urged writers:

> *Busquemos las palabras más antiguas, las más frescas y pulidas formas del lenguaje, con ellas debe decirse el último*

*acto. Con ellas diremos el adiós a un mundo que se unde en el caos definitivo y extraño del futuro.*

(Obra poética)

Seek the oldest words, the freshest and purest forms of language, for it is with them that the "final act" should be expressed. With them we shall bid farewell to a world that is being submerged in the definitive and strange chaos of the future.

Despite issuing this clarion call to versify and to create, however, he is pessimistic about any poet's chances of success. For Mutis, as T. S. Eliot might put it, poetry represents a raid on the inarticulate. "Todo poema es la constatación de un absoluto fracaso" (Every poem is proof of an absolute failure; Sefamí, 1993). Words cannot possibly capture reality, they can be only an imitation or substitute, and yet the poet has no alternative: he must try to express the inexpressible. One of Mutis's earliest pronouncements on this aspect of poetic creativity occurs in a poem published in *Los elementos del desastre:*

> *La poesía substituye,*
> *la palabra substituye,*
> *el hombre substituye,*
> *los vientos y las aguas substituyen . . .*
> *la derrota se repite a través de los tiempos*
> *¡ay, sin remedio!*

> Poetry substitutes,
> words substitute,
> man substitutes,
> the winds and the waters substitute . . .
> The defeat repeats itself from time inmemorial,
> oh, without remedy!

The sentiments of these six lines from the poem "Los trabajos perdidos," which became the title of a 1965 collection of poetry, recur with variations throughout Mutis's career.

Although "La creciente" (The swollen stream) is not actually Mutis's first published poem ("Miedo" [Fear] is, according to Mutis's comments to Sefamí), Mutis does consider this poem first in significance among his early works, and it generally heads any collection or anthology. In a conversation with Fernando

Quiroz, Mutis explained that he tried to express all his emotions concerning the River Coello and its rushing, swollen waters (*El reino que estaba para mí*, 1993). He told Eduardo García Aguilar that the poem contains a large dose of despair while at the same time portraying the acceptance of fate (*Celebraciones*, 1993). In its narrative strategy, its emphasis on exotic and sometimes sordid locales, its sense of decay and view of nature as a raw and indifferent power, "La creciente" resembles Rimbaud's "Le bateau ivre" ("The Drunken Boat").

The poem begins with dawn and a view of swollen waters rushing down the mountain carrying ripe oranges, tree trunks, dead calves, and the wreckage of straw roofs. The narrator, a boy or young man, awakens and goes to the bridge over the river. As he looks at the onrushing waters and vainly waits for a miracle, his inspired memory visits the places frequented by the lovers of cedars, as well as by other people. Just as the drunken boat remembers its journeys, its ports of call, and its crews, the narrator of "La creciente" remembers perfumes, abandoned houses, hotels, dirty railroad stations, and waiting rooms. Just as the drunken boat returns to its European puddle, the narrator realizes that everything eventually ends up in this hot tropical land: the song of the high mountains, the steam rising from overheated oxen, the fog shrouding the foot trails, the full and promising udders of cows, the frozen anguish in the sightless eyes of carrion, old saddles. At the end of Rimbaud's poem, the drunken boat becomes once again what it always was: a child's plaything. In Mutis's poem, childhood returns, heavy as a blanket ("pesada como un manto"). The river rolls on through the afternoon and into the evening, moaning as it carries its defeated cargo. In the last image of the poem, the narrator resumes his journey toward the unexpected, accompanied in his imagination by the swollen waters of the Coello River.

Maqroll's first appearance in print is in "Oración de Maqroll" (Maqroll's prayer), a poem in Mutis's second chapbook of poetry, *Los elementos del desastre*. In this prayer, Maqroll demonstrates an attitude of defiance. It is a stance that functions as "un antídoto eficaz contra la incredulidad y la dicha inmotivada" (an antidote to skepticism and unmotivated delight). Toward the end of the poem, Maqroll asks for "la gracia de morir envuelto en el polvo de las ciudades, recostado en las graderías de una casa infame e iluminado por todas las estrellas del firmamento" (to be allowed to die wrapped in the dust of cities, leaning against the steps of a brothel, his face lighted only by the stars). He reminds God that he has patiently studied the laws of the herd and cannot be duped. The poem may be a prayer, but it is not a plea. At this point, the motivation behind the creation of Maqroll seems to be as much to *épater les bourgeois* as to reflect on issues of life and death. Deep reflection comes later.

Maqroll next appears in the poems published in *Mito* in 1955 and 1959 and gathered under the title *Reseña de los Hospitales de Ultramar*, published while Mutis was in prison. It is in this work that Maqroll's character acquires its definitive shape. These nine prose poems and two verse poems, characterized by Mutis as "fragments," are introduced by three epigraphs attributed to obscure eighteenth-century medical texts and by a prefatory statement concerning Maqroll el Gaviero. The epigraphs and their sources are invented, Mutis told Sefamí in an interview. They lend an oddly antiquarian air to the entire collection, as if suffering, bleeding, disease, and death could be assuaged by captions from ancient and rare books. Such a conjunction of bookishness and the raw stuff of life is a principal characteristic of Mutis as a writer. The prefatory statement identifies the fragments as belonging to "un ciclo de relatos y alusiones tejidos por Maqroll el Gaviero en la vejez de sus años, cuando el tema de la enfermedad y de la muerte rondaba sus días y ocupaba buena parte de sus noches, largas de insomnio y visitadas de recuerdos" (a cycle of stories and allusions woven together by Maqroll el Gaviero, in the autumn of his life when the subject of illness and death haunted his days and occupied his nights, long nights of insomnia visited by memories). In these fragments, the preface continues, there is "una amplia teoría de males, angustias, días en blanco en espera de nada" (a whole theory of wrongs, of anxieties, of empty days spent waiting for nothing).

The bulk of the collection is given over to descriptions of Maqroll in this or that "overseas hospital," convalescing from multiple illnesses and injuries acquired on numberless journeys by land and sea. Each illness is marked by its own special despair, and each hospital is different, sharing with the others only the reality of pain and suffering. There is the Hospital by the Bay, a place of heat, dirt, sweat, and blinding sun, where starved patients copulate at noon, moaning, in the middle of the wards. There is the Hospital by the River, where Maqroll has gone to be cured of wounds suffered in fights in the brothel quarter of an unnamed city, and where the forced immobility and the long convalescence teach him to value solitude and reverie. There is the waterfall where Maqroll washes his wounds and learns to face the truth of his miserable condition. Another hospital is an abandoned railroad car where Maqroll, this time exhausted by malaria and by hunger, is visited by two women who occasionally satisfy themselves sexually on his wasted body. There are the Hospital of the Salt Mines and the Hospital of the Proud, among others. So distinct are the hospitals that Maqroll has resorted to a kind of navigational chart (the poem is called "El mapa" [The map]) to orient his friends; and he has accompanied the map (which we never see) with nine cryptic vignettes on the illustrations or cartouches of the map itself.

The poems of the *Reseña de los Hospitales de Ultramar* recall the decay and corruption of the flesh found in Baudelaire's "Les Fleurs du Mal" ("Flowers of Evil") and Rimbaud's "Une Saison en enfer" ("A Season in Hell"). In their form, they recall Rimbaud's prose poems and León de Greiff's experiments with narrative verse and with prose poems (the "relatos" or "tales" and the *Prosas de Gaspar*) in the 1920s and 1930s. Maqroll's condition first anticipated (in 1955) Mutis's prison experience and then (in 1959) echoed it. Incarceration was Mutis's season in hell, his days and nights filled mostly by boredom and emptiness, as well as by painful memories of past delights and of freedom.

In other collections of poetry, Maqroll muses on the collapse of his body during long nights of insomnia in the jungle ("Soledad"); pushes a cart, much in the manner of Sisyphus, up a mountain toward a mine ("La carreta"); bathes in the rushing waters of a delta as he recites a litany of suffering ("Letanía"); manages a small roadside cafe and inn called "La Nieve del Almirante" in a high mountain pass in the Andes; dies in the estuary of a South American river ("En los esteros"); and reviews his life for the benefit of the

listener, Mutis himself, who someday will tell his tale ("La visita del Gaviero").

Maqroll is not the sole subject of the poetry, however. Moreover, Maqroll's presence in the poetry begins to fade as, apparently, Mutis exorcizes the demon of his persona through verse. As he does so, Mutis tends to drop his poetic masks and to speak directly to the reader. The poetry explores a number of themes, characters, and settings that will later be utilized in some form in the fiction. For instance, early in his career, Mutis becomes fascinated by Middle Eastern cultures. He quotes extensively from the *Encyclopaedia Britannica* to explain the term "caravansary" in the poetry collection of that name (it refers to a public shelter for caravans and wayfarers). It is a fascination that has deepened with the years. "A Cordoba Street" ("Una calle de Córdoba") celebrates that city's architectural resonance with Cartagena and other Caribbean cities, as well as the confluence of the Arabic and the Jewish in its architecture and history. A poem on the Alhambra does the same, while awakening in him a deep nostalgia for his personal past. Alongside his interest in the Middle East, in simple pleasures, in his family and friends, Mutis also celebrates European literature (Proust and Rimbaud, for instance) and European history, in particular that of Spain (Philip II is a favorite subject).

Over much of Mutis's poetry there hovers the specter of death as our ultimate and inescapable fate, one of the most constant themes in Spanish and Latin American verse since Jorge Manrique's *Coplas por la muerte de su padre*. Mutis has acknowledged a keen awareness of death ever since experiencing his father's death (Quiroz, *El reino que estaba para mí*). The central theme of the poem "Cita en Samburán" is that however much we may try to flee from our appointment with death, it will find us. Throughout Mutis's writing, one finds related themes of fate, fortune, and chance, all within the context of characters attempting the impossible; of seeing dreams deferred and illusions destroyed; of experiencing the disappearance of friends and lovers; of learning that, in the end, nothing is permanent. Friendship serves as a kind of antidote to death as well as to the pain that is much of life. As Mutis matures as a writer, that theme gains importance. It culminates in the friendship between Maqroll and Abdul Bashur, one of the deepest and most enduring in all literature.

The prose poem, "El sueño del Príncipe-Elector" (The dream of the elector prince), published in *Caravansary*, presents a theme that will become pervasive in the fiction: striving toward an unattainable goal. The poem tells the story of a prince who takes shelter one night along the roadside and dreams that he is first on horseback in a narrow valley surrounded by high mountains and then suddenly in a deep mountain pool, delighting in the freshness of the water. He senses that he is being watched. There, facing him in water that rises only up to her knees, is a beautiful naked woman who smiles invitingly. He swims toward her and begins to caress her thighs, feeling a passionate intensity that he has never before felt. A hoarse laugh from the bank interrupts him. A bearded man in rags calls out: "No, Alteza Serenísima, no es para ti la dicha de esa carne que te pareció tener ya entre tus brazos. Vuelve, señor, a tu camino y trata, si puedes, de olvidar este instante que no te estaba destinado" (No, your serene highness, this delight of the flesh, which you thought that you held in your arms, is not for you. Go back to your dominions and try to forget, if you can, this moment, for it was not destined for you). The Elector Prince resumes his journey, altered forever by the experience of this unattainable pleasure and conscious that he is driven by a different destiny.

Mutis utilizes a similar dream of a beautiful woman to characterize the final days of Simón Bolívar in "El último rostro" (*Obra literaria: Prosas*) and to symbolize as well the impossibility of Bolívar's dream of a Greater Colombia. The theme of the unattainable dream will come to characterize both Maqroll el Gaviero and his friend Abdul Bashur. Mutis himself remarks that in *La Nieve del Almirante* and *Ilona llega con la lluvia*, Maqroll has exactly the same attitude toward his experiences as does the Elector Prince (García Aguilar, *Celebraciones*).

Space mitigates against a detailed examination of Mutis's prison memoir, *Diario de Lecumberri*, or the fiction that he first published with the *Diario* in 1960. Suffice it to say, that while the *Diario* directly engages his prison experiences in a manner as haunting as a Dostoevsky or a Solzhenitsyn, the stories published with it are clearly escapist. Each has an exotic setting or context: "Sharaya" takes place in India; "Antes de que cante el gallo" derives its symbolism from Peter's betrayal of Christ; "La muerte del Estratega" is set in the Byzantine Empire after the death of Constantine IV in 685.

Of greater relevance to Mutis's principal concerns in the later fiction is *La mansión de Araucaíma*, subtitled "Relato gótico de tierra caliente" (Gothic tale of the tropics), the subtitle pointing to Mutis's characteristic commingling of the European with the Latin American. Constructed as a series of prose vignettes, the novella tells the story of six people living in a large and isolated mansion situated, as was the actual Mutis family house and farm, at the confluence of two rivers. The atmosphere is decadent, sensuous, and broadly suggestive, as so much of Mutis's work is, of the corruption of the flesh and of moral decay. Each vignette is narrated from the third-person omniscient perspective and focuses generally on a single character: thus the watchman (el guardián), who introduces the novella, is an erstwhile multi-lingual soldier of fortune who lost his arm in an unnamed incident; the owner of the mansion, named Graciliano, or Don Graci for short, is an obese former pederast and graffiti artist; there is also a former airline pilot who, after working as a crop duster for Don Graci, has stayed on in the mansion; "La Machiche," a mature and Rubenesque woman, is sexually attracted to every man in the house except the owner. A middle-aged and handsome friar, occasional spiritual advisor to some of the house's inhabitants, possesses the only weapons—a diver's knife and a pistol which he polishes incessantly; Cristóbal, a gigantic black servant from Haiti, is the principal lover of "La Machiche" and a good friend to the friar and to the pilot.

Into this menagerie bicycles "the girl" (la muchacha), a blonde, seventeen-year-old actress named Angela. Long of limb and beautifully proportioned, she has been exploring the countryside after completing work on a film. Her arrival initiates a string of events which soon end in tragedy: first she commits suicide after she has made love to, one after the other, the pilot, the friar, the Haitian, and La Machiche. Then, as she is being buried near the river by three of the men, two shots ring out at the mansion, followed by the sound of blows. Hurrying back, the three discover that the pilot has shot La Machiche with the friar's pistol and that the Haitian has bludgeoned the pilot to death. La Machiche is buried with the girl, the pilot is incinerated in the ovens of the sugar mill, and a few days later everyone abandons the mansion.

The strategy of identifying the main characters less by their names—even when names are used, they are also clearly symbolic—than by their types or roles points to Mutis's mythmaking intention. This novella demands an allegorical reading: of the voracity of nature; of the dangers of temptation and the corruptibility of the flesh; of the explosive and tragic potential present whenever beauty, heat, and desire meet and mingle. In *Mansión de Araucaíma*, Mutis elevates the family coffee-and-sugarcane plantation Coello into the realm of myth and allegory. Coello, thus poetically transposed, is set beyond a particular time or space and represents eternal truths about the human condition.

Through repeated distillations in the poetry, Maqroll el Gaviero comes to acquire for readers the condensed symbolic feel of personal allegory. By the 1970s, his is a rounded and complex poetic persona. That persona, a kind of demon which has been exorcized through poetry, returns in all its obsessive attractiveness in Mutis's fiction, where it is developed further. There, Maqroll evolves from being mostly a personal allegory, the representation of Mutis's alter ego, to being a larger allegory of everyman.

*La Nieve del Almirante*, Mutis's first novel about Maqroll, was not intended as a novel. It was inspired by Mutis's reaction to a French translation of his poem of the same name. In a videotaped interview with Alberto Ruy Sánchez (*Escala íntima*, 1999) the poet explained what happened: "yo me dije, 'esto es una sección de una novela.' Traté de desenredar el nudo que estaba allí. Pero no intenté escribir una novela" (I said to myself 'this is part of a novel.' I tried to untangle the knot that was there. But I did not intend to write a novel). He sent the work to his agent in Barcelona, Carmen Barcells (who was also García Márquez's agent), seeking only her opinion of the piece, and shortly thereafter was shocked to learn that she had sold it to Alianza Editorial. Despite his protest that the book was not even a novel, it was published in 1986. Thus was launched Mutis's career as novelist.

Most of the text of *La Nieve del Almirante* consists of a diary kept by Maqroll, which is preceded by a prologue narrating its discovery, one of the oldest tricks of the literary trade. It is followed by four prose poems that

had been published previously. The prologue recounts how, in a second-hand bookstore in Barcelona, the narrator (Mutis) stumbles upon a book that he has long sought: *Enquête du Prévôt de Paris sur l'assassinat de Louis Duc D'Orleans* (Inquiry by the provost of Paris on the assassination of Louis, Duke of Orleans), published in 1865. Buying it, he moves outside to sit on a park bench and begins to peruse it. Out of a sleeve on the inside back cover fall sheets of paper covered with words written in a tremulous hand. It is the diary of Maqroll el Gaviero, which the narrator Mutis then presents as *La Nieve del Almirante*.

Such a coincidence of circumstances and events tests even the most tolerant reader's willing suspension of disbelief, but that is part of Mutis's point. *El azar* (chance, fortune) plays an enormous role in Mutis's work: in every novel characters continually run into each other, apparently by accident, in widely scattered ports of call, in different cities on different continents, on different mountain ranges, rivers, and seashores, as if such astonishing coincidences and chance encounters were the most ordinary of events. Such a tactic in effect transforms the world into a village, where such chance encounters are an everyday occurrence. In Mutis, the macrocosm is treated microcosmically, the reverse of what happens in writers like Faulkner and García Márquez.

Maqroll's diary begins on water. He has travelled up the Amazon river to Manaos, and from there up the Xurandó (one of the tributaries of the Amazon) until he gets to the *cordilleras*—the Andes mountains. His scheme, which is financed by his lover, Flor Estévez, is to buy lumber from some enigmatic Finns who own a sawmill high in the mountains and to bring it downriver, where he can resell it for a much higher price. With the money gained from the transaction, he intends to live out the rest of his days in leisure. In almost every Maqroll novel there is a business scheme that goes awry. This one is so impractical that it boggles the mind. At some level, Maqroll knows this, although the knowledge does not alter his behavior. As he writes in his diary, "siempre me ha sucedido lo mismo; las empresas en las que me lanzo tienen el estigma de lo indeterminado, la maldición de una artera mudanza. Y aquí voy, río arriba, como un necio, sabiendo de antemano en lo que irá a parar todo" (the same thing has always happened to me. The enterprises which I throw myself into have the stigma of being inconclusive, the curse of a crafty moodiness. And here I am, going upriver like a naughty boy, knowing beforehand how everything is going to turn out; *Empresas y tribulaciones*).

*La Nieve del Almirante* resembles nothing so much as a cross between a Conrad novel and the myth of Sisyphus, with a soupçon of Kafka. It is an adventure story, recounting a journey deep into the forbidding vastness of nature and into a world of unsavory characters, in pursuit of goal that is as exhausting as it is impossible. *Heart of Darkness, Almayer's Folly, Lord Jim,* and *Nostromo* are behind more than one of Mutis's novels, less as direct influences than as a kind of resonating chamber to which Mutis listens as he places his own characters in analogous situations and observes their reaction to forces beyond their control. For instance, while traveling upriver with several men, who try in vain to dissuade him from his unlikely scheme, Maqroll barely survives the journey. A tropical fever almost kills him and the guerrillas in the area are a threat to his life. An army mayor, whom he had met early in his journey, is there toward the end to pluck him from danger and fly him out of the jungle in his seaplane. When Maqroll finally does reach the sawmill, he is turned away at the gate by a shadowy figure of a man who says only, "we are not allowed to receive strangers here" and "our instructions are to speak to no one. It's no use insisting." The utter failure of Maqroll's quest to obtain lumber makes it a parable of futility worthy of Kafka's *The Trial* or *The Castle.* At the end of the novel proper the reader comes upon a fragment of text, written by Maqroll on stationery from a Flemish hotel, in which he describes how he had tried to return to Flor Estévez, the love of his life, and to the cafe-and-inn called La Nieve del Almirante, where both of them had lived and made love while he was recovering his health. Maqroll had thought about her often while on the Xurandó River and in the high mountains. Now, as he writes in that Flemish hotel, he describes his return to La Nieve del Almirante only to find it in ruins, and confesses that he does not know how he will bear his lover's absence.

The pattern is set with this novel: the unlikely business scheme or impossible dream, the quest to achieve it, and the failure of that quest. Along the way Mutis presents musings on the meaning of life, love, friendship, and other universal themes. There is danger in each novel. In each, too, there is a wonderful woman, always sensuous and usually beautiful, who makes the nights of the central character much more bearable and is for him a source of wisdom and comfort. Thus Flor Estévez in *La Nieve del Almirante*, Ilona in *Ilona llega con la lluvia*, Warda in *La última escala del Tramp Steamer*. Sometimes there are two principal women in a novel; in *Un bel morir,* for instance, one of the women (the old blind landlady) is wise and the other (Amparo María) is beautiful and young. Sometimes the pairing is of a good woman and a dangerous one: Ilona and Larissa in *Ilona llega con la lluvia*; Dora Estela and Antonia in *Amirbar.*

In *Ilona llega con la lluvia*, Maqroll, down and out in Panama City, turns into a small and not inelegant hotel in order to escape a sudden downpour. There, in another one of the astonishing coincidences that characterize the fictional world of Alvaro Mutis, he comes upon Ilona feeding coins into a slot machine in the lobby. Ilona Grabowska, born in Trieste, is Maqroll's former lover as well as the lover of Maqroll's best friend, Abdul Bashur. At some point, all three of them had been romantically intertwined at the same time. The encounter with Ilona leads inevitably to lovemaking. After that, the two of them cook up a scheme intended to make them rich, to allow them to retire, and to give Abdul Bashur sufficient money to buy the ship of his dreams (Ilona, Mutis has commented in interviews, is in some senses a female version of Maqroll).

Their plan is to staff a brothel with beautiful and exotic women, all dressed in airline stewardess uniforms and purporting to be flight attendants of international airlines who want to earn cash discretely by selling their bodies during stopovers in Panama. The business is more lucrative than a prior scheme of theirs to smuggle gold in Flanders, though less successful than another enterprise, smuggling oriental carpets. After a while, however, they tire of the brothel business and decide to leave Panama City. Before they are able to get away, Ilona is killed by one of her prostitutes, Larissa, in an explosion just before Abdul Bashur docks his ship, 'The Fairy of Trieste,' in Panama.

In *Un bel morir* Mutis returns to the rivers and mountains of Colombia and sets Maqroll down in a river town (La Plata) at the foot of a towering mountain range. Hired by a mysterious Belgian named Van Branden, Maqroll, improbably incurious, ferries some boxes of unknown materials to a mountain railroad camp accessible only by mule. The journey, which he makes several times, takes him from the river's edge to a coffee plantation at a higher elevation, where he meets and makes love to the sensuous Amparo María, then up a steep and dangerous path to a wayfarer's hut and from there on up to the railroad camp. Upon delivery of his cargo, he does not see railroad machinery and becomes suspicious. He learns that he has been running guns to the guerrillas in the area. After various plot twists, in which Amparo María loses her life and the army arrives to flush out the guerrillas, Maqroll is arrested and threatened with execution for gun running. His ignorance of his cargo and his evident lack of involvement in the insurgency gain him his liberation. He is then allowed to leave the area, traveling downriver in an old boat whose outboard motor eventually gives out.

At the end of the novel, in a scene reminiscent of *The African Queen*, Maqroll and an injured prostitute whom he picked up along the way are found dead in their boat, which had been floating about for some time in the labyrinthine channels of the estuary. Back in La Plata, the army captain who arrested Maqroll had said "estas tierras no son para gente como usted" (this land is not for people like you). That may be, but Maqroll (and Mutis) keeps coming back to these territories, lured by the lushness of nature, the sensuality of people, the variety of climates, and the limitless opportunities for love, adventure, danger, and wealth that the culture seems ever to offer.

In two of Mutis's next four works of fiction, *The Tramp Steamer's Last Port of Call* and *Abdul Bashur, Dreamer of Ships*, Maqroll does not figure as a central character. Mutis gets around the difficulty of having killed off his main character in the previous novel by recounting episodes from the time before his death.

Both novels are set up in a similar manner: a narrative frame describes how the story has come about. In *Tramp Steamer*, the narrator Mutis keeps coming upon the same tramp steamer: off the Pacific coast of Central America, near Jamaica, at the harbor of Helsinki, even in the waters of the Orinoco River. As if running across the ship in such separated waters were not enough of a coincidence, he encounters the boat's captain, Jon Iturri, travelling on another boat on the Orinoco. To while away the long, hot evenings, the two new friends talk, and Iturri tells the narrator his story. Maqroll is part of the story's background, as is Abdul Bashur, but the protagonist is Warda, Abdul Bashur's sister, who has bought the tramp steamer (named *Alcion*). She eventually seduces her captain, Iturri, or he seduces her. For the remainder of the *Alcion*'s working life, Warda and Iturri arrange to meet in whatever port of call the ship will next dock. They have a passionate, if intermittent, affair. Abdul Bashur, Wanda's brother, characterizes it precisely: "It will last as long as the *Alcion* lasts." The affair breaks apart as naturally as the *Alcion* itself breaks apart and sinks on a mud bank in the Orinoco River. The plot is banal, but its banality is not the lasting impression of this or any other Mutis narrative. Rather, the plot seems to function primarily as a frame for musings on the nature of love, life, coincidence, friendship, and fate.

One's death, Mutis maintains, has been scripted long before the event, and one is blessed if one meets that death and no other. This theme, in essence, shapes *Abdul Bashur, Dreamer of Ships*. This book, probably the most structurally accomplished of the Maqroll cycle, begins with another coincidence: the narrator Mutis meeting by chance, in a train station in Brittany, another of Abdul Bashur's sisters, Fatima. Abdul has died and Fatima wants Mutis to take a look at some papers that her brother has left behind. As he peruses them, Mutis decides to tell of his relationship to Abdul Bashur and the story of the friendship between Abdul and Maqroll.

This latter tale is about Abdul Bashur's dream of owning the perfect cargo ship. Pursuing that dream leads him (and Maqroll and Ilona) into all sorts of tight corners and adventures. The tale of the oriental rug smuggling is told here, as it is the profit from that episode that allows Abdul Bashur finally to buy the ship of his dreams. First, however, he must experience an adventure of extreme danger: in the room of twin exotic dancers in Southhampton (England), Bashur spied a photograph of what he believes to be a perfect ship. He writes the owner and requests a visit. The ship, named the *Thorn*, is docked in the headwaters of the Mira River, on the Pacific coast of Colombia, near the border with Ecuador. He arrives there only to find the *Thorn* moored in shallow waters and stripped of all her machinery. The owner, Jaime Tirado, nicknamed "Rompe Espejos" (Mirror Breaker), is a drug smuggler, vastly wealthy, and of course unhappy that he has been sought out, whatever the motive. He makes plans to kill Abdul Bashur, who then escapes.

After other adventures in other seas, Abdul Bashur does locate the ship of his dreams in the Madeira islands and flies there in order to buy it. As the airplane approaches the airport of Funchal, a storm makes the pilot lose control and the plane goes down. Abdul Bashur dies. Traveling to Funchal to pick up the remains of his friend, Maqroll asks to see the crash. There, silhouetted against the twisted and molten metal, at anchor in the bay, is the ship that Abdul Bashur had traveled to Funchal to buy. In effect, Abdul Bashur has died the death destined for him alone: in sight of his goal, reaching for it but not attaining it. Maqroll speaks what in effect could be his own as well as his friend's epitaph: "Esta sí era tu propia muerte, Jabdul, alimentada durante todos y cada uno de los días de tu vida" (this indeed was your proper death, Jabdul, nourished through each and every one of all the days of your life; *Empresas y tribulaciones*).

In *Amirbar* Mutis returns to the setting of Coello, but he does so in a characteristically round-about way. The frame of the story has Maqroll recuperating in Northridge, California, from yet another of his devastating tropical illnesses. In the evenings, to while away the time and as a kind of therapy, he tells the assembled company (which includes the narrator Mutis) the story of Amirbar, a gold mine (there actually was one in the Mutis family in his grandfather's generation) in the mountains of Colombia which he explored and tried to mine in yet another vain attempt at great wealth and, thus, a life of leisure. At the end, Maqroll, having accumulated a great deal of money, loses it, and also leaves in his wake the detritus of so many grand schemes come to naught in Colombia: dead friends, destroyed families, and a society whose civic fabric is torn by strife and violence.

The last of the Maqroll books to date is made up of three unrelated tales, thus *Triptych on Sea and Land*.

The first, "Cita in Bergen," expands into story length the theme and plot of the poem, "Cita en Samburán." It is the story of a suicide, long deferred but finally achieved. The second tale, "Razón verídica de los encuentros y complicidades de Maqroll el Gaviero con el pintor Alejandro Obregón," puts a fictional character together with a real one (Obregón is a Colombian painter who died in April 1992, and whom Mutis memorializes in this story). By casting him as Maqroll's friend, and by giving him a series of adventures worthy of Maqroll himself, Mutis transforms Obregón's life into literature. Obregón was a friend of both Mutis and García Márquez, who also figures in the story, at the end. The third story, "Jamil," is the most sentimental of Mutis's works. Basing it on his relationship with his grandson, Nicolás, Mutis recounts how Maqroll is changed, perhaps forever, by taking care of Abdul Bashur's son Jamil while his mother tries to earn money in Germany. It is the tale of a jaded man experiencing life anew through the solemn innocence of an alert, curious, and lovable boy. The Alvaro Mutis of the 1980s and before could not have written "Jamil," and the Maqroll of the poetry and the first several novels could not have had the experience; or, having it, could not have understood it. Of all the Maqroll narratives, this one, short as it is, comes the closest to wisdom.

As a Colombian writer, Mutis is nonetheless a profound internationalist. His models are mostly European: the authors he cites most often are French, and Paris remains a favorite city; his preferred novelists include Charles Dickens, Robert Louis Stevenson, and Joseph Conrad; his most intimate precursors in poetry are from Spain (Antonio Machado) and Chile (Pablo Neruda). If one adds up the years he spent in Colombia itself (1923–1925; 1934–1956), they are few in a long life. And yet he is deeply Colombian. His deep sense of identification is not without its difficulties and ironies, however, for Mutis has been criticized by some of his countrymen as being anti-Colombian. He responds:

*Colombia es esencial para mí: todo lo que yo tengo de perdurable, todo elemento gracias al cual yo sostengo mi vida está en Colombia y es colombiano. El que uno tome una actitud crítica e irritada ante Colombia sólo prueba, obviamente, la preocupación por algo que le es tan importante. Yo soy esencialmente colombiano y no hay testimonio más auténtico que mi poesía.*

(Cobo Borda, *Para leer a Alvaro Mutis*)

Colombia is essential to me: everything that I have of a lasting nature, everything that sustains me in life is in Colombia and is Colombian. If one's attitude is critical and of annoyance toward Colombia, that proves, of course, that it is important to one. I am essentially Colombian, and there is no better proof of that than my poetry.

Colombia, Alvaro Mutis has also said, rests on a series of falsehoods: among them, that Colombia is one of the most ancient democracies of the Americas, when in truth that democracy barely conceals an ongoing savagery and violence; that Colombia is a land of poets, which might have been once true but no longer is; and that the best Spanish in the world is spoken in Colombia, when in truth the language is safeguarded by pedantic grammarians who have made Colombian Spanish the most formalistic and least vital of all the versions of the language in the continent (Cobo Borda, *Historia portátil*). There is bitterness in this characterization, the bitterness of exile, of suffering at the hands of one's countrymen, of seeing the vast potential of one's own culture and country diminished by greed, corruption, scandal, pettiness, and violence. Maqroll is both the product of such a culture and an answer to it. His message is: survive.

The drive to survive has an odd analog in the fate of Maqroll himself as a literary creation. Mutis has tried to kill him more than once, and even has described his death in *Un bel morir,* but, like King Charles's head, Maqroll keeps turning up. Four of the seven Maqroll novels were written after Maqroll had supposedly died. To continue writing on Maqroll has required some imaginative adjustments on Mutis's part. He includes him in *Tramp Steamer* by having the narrator (Mutis) run into a character who has also crossed Maqroll's path and whose story concerns Maqroll's friends. In *Amirbar* the narrator (again Mutis) returns in memory to a time in California when he nursed Maqroll back to health after one of his tropical illnesses. Hints are dropped here and there in the novels that perhaps Maqroll's death, as narrated in the appendix to *Un bel morir* and commented upon elsewhere, is apocryphal after all. In the second story in *Triptych on Sea and Land,*

Mutis writes the following: "De Maqroll el Gaviero hace años que nada sé; muchas versiones corren sobre su muerte. Como no es la primera vez que esto sucede, aún solemos sus amigos indagar sobre noticias suyas" (It has been many years since I've had news of Maqroll el Gaviero; there are many stories about his death, none of them confirmed. Since this is not the first time this has happened, we friends of his still inquire after him). Even Gabriel García Márquez, writes Mutis, has contributed to the confusion by recounting how Alejandro Obregón, Colombian painter and good friend of both García Márquez and Mutis, found Maqroll's body in Ciénaga Grande. In the end, the truth about Maqroll always eludes us. Such hints about his immortality—his nine lives—are playfully supported by Mutis's dedication of this story in *Triptych* to his cats.

The inextinguishable nature of Maqroll the character testifies as well to a certain stubbornness and strength on the part of the author. Maqroll survives corruption, greed, assassination attempts by other characters as well as by the author, natural disasters, imprisonment, and scandal. He endures. Mutis, too, endures. Out of the difficult soil that has been his life and the Colombian experience, he has nurtured and honed his talent for more than fifty years. It has grown into a substantial and enduring body of literary work, an oeuvre in the fullest sense of the term. Along the way, he has created a character of mythic proportions. García Márquez himself perhaps said it best: "Maqroll is not only [Alvaro Mutis], as is so cavalierly said. Maqroll is all of us" (García Márquez, "Mi amigo Mutis," *El País*, 30 October 1993).

# SELECTED BIBLIOGRAPHY

*Primary Works*

### Poetry

*La balanza.* With Carlos Patiño. Bogotá: Talleres Prag, 1948.
*Los elementos del desastre.* Buenos Aires: Editorial Losada, 1953.
"Reseña de los Hospitales de Ultramar." *Mito* 1, no. 2:72–76 (June–July 1955).
"Moirologhia." *Mito* 1, no. 4:219–220 (October–November 1955).

"Memoria de los hospitales de ultramar." *Mito* 5, no. 26:103–110 (August–September 1959).

*Los trabajos perdidos*. Mexico City: Ediciones ERA, 1965.

*Summa de Maqroll el Gaviero. Poesía (1947–1970)*. Inroduction by Juan Gustavo Cobo Borda. Barcelona: Barral Editores, 1973.

*Maqroll el Gaviero*. Edited by Fernando Charry Lara and Juan Gustavo Cobo Borda. Bogotá: Instituto Colombiano de Cultura, 1975.

*Caravansary*. Mexico City: Fondo de Cultura Económica, 1981.

*Poesía y Prosa*. Edited by Santiago Mutis Durán. Bogotá: Instituto Colombiano de Cultura, 1981.

*Poemas*. Serie Poesía Moderna, 24. Mexico City: UNAM, 1982.

*Los emisarios*. Mexico City: Fondo de Cultura Económica, 1984.

*Crónica regia y Alabanza del reino*. Madrid: Cátedra, 1985.

*Obra literaria: Poesía 1947–1985*. Vol. 1. Edited by Santiago Mutis Durán. Bogotá: Procultura, 1985.

*Un homenaje y siete nocturnos*. Mexico City: Ediciones El Equilibrista, 1986.

*Antología de la poesía de Alvaro Mutis*. Edited by José Balza. Caracas: Monte Avila Editores, 1992.

*Obra poética*. Bogotá: Arango Editores, 1993. (Contains "Primeros poemas," "Los elementos del desastre," "Reseña de los hospitales de Ultramar," "Los trabajos perdidos," "Caravansary," "Los emisarios," "Diez Lieder," "Crónica Regia," "Poemas dispersos," and "Un homenaje y siete nocturnos.")

## Prose

*Diario de Lecumberri*. Xalapa: Universidad Veracruzana, 1960. (Contains also "La muerte del Estratega," "Sharaya," and "Antes de que cante el gallo.")

*La mansión de Araucaíma: Relato gótico de tierra caliente*. Buenos Aires: Sudamericana, 1973. (Contains "La muerte del Estratega," "Sharaya." The second edition also contains "El último rostro.")

*La verdadera historia del flautista de Hammelin*. México: Ediciones Penélope, 1982.

*Obra literaria: Prosas*. Vol. 2. Edited by Santiago Mutis Durán. Bogotá: Procultura, 1985.

*La Nieve del Almirante*. Madrid: Alianza Editorial, 1986.

*Ilona llega con la lluvia*. Bogotá: Oveja Negra, 1987.

*La muerte del Estratega: Narraciones, prosas y ensayos*. Mexico City: Fondo de Cultura Económica, 1988. (Contains *Diario de Lecumberri, La mansión de Araucaíma*, "La muerte del Estratega," "El último rostro," "Antes de que cante el gallo," and "Sharaya," along with the newspaper columns, "Intermedio en Querétaro," "Intermedio de Constantinopla," "Intermedio en Schoenbrunn," "Intermedio en Niza," "Intermedio en el Atlántico sur," "Intermedio en el Strand;" and including the newspaper columns published under the pseudonym "Alvar de Mattos;" two lectures, "La desesperanza" and "¿Quién es Barbabooth?")

*Un bel morir*. Bogotá: Oveja Negra, 1989.

*La última escala del Tramp Steamer*. Bogotá: Arango Editores, 1989.

*Amirbar*. Bogotá: Editorial Norma, 1990.

*El último rostro*. Madrid: Siruela, 1990. (Contains "El último rostro," "La muerte del Estratega," "Sharaya," and "Antes de que cante el gallo.")

*Abdul Bashur, soñador de navíos*. Santafé de Bogotá: Editorial Norma, 1991.

*La mansión de Araucaíma y Cuadernos del Palacio Negro*. Madrid: Siruela, 1992. (*Cuadernos del Palacio Negro* is an alternate title of *Diario de Lecumberri*.)

*Tríptico de mar y tierra*. Santafé de Bogotá: Editorial Norma, 1993.

*Siete novelas, Mutis: Empresas y tribulaciones de Maqroll el Gaviero*. Santafé de Bogotá: Alfaguara, 1995. (Contains *La nieve del Almirante, Ilona llega con la lluvia, Un bel morir, La última escala del Tramp Steamer, Amirbar, Abdul Bashur, soñador de navíos*, and *Tríptico de mar y tierra*.)

*Contextos para Maqroll*. Edited by Ricardo Cano Gaviria. Montblanc (Tarragona): Ediciones Igitur, 1997.

*De lecturas y algo del mundo. (1943–1998)*. Edited by Santiago Mutis Durán. Santafé de Bogotá: Planeta Colombiana Editorial, 1999. ("De lecturas" contains 40 reviews of single authors or books, written from 1943 on; "Algo del mundo" contains 54 occasional columns, most of them published in *Novedades* in Mexico, beginning in 1978.)

## Translation

*The Adventures of Maqroll: Four Novellas*. Trans. by Edith Grossman. New York: Harper Collins, 1995. (Contains *Amirbar; The Tramp Steamer's Last Port of Call; Abdul Bashur, Dreamer of Ships*; and *Triptych on Sea and Land*.)

## Secondary Works

### Bibliographies

Hernández, Consuelo. *Alvaro Mutis: Una estética del deterioro*. Caracas: Monte Avila Editores, 1995. Pp. 277–289.

Ruiz Barrionuevo, Carmen, ed. *Summa de Maqroll el Gaviero. Poesía, 1948–1997*. Salamanca: Ediciones Universidad de Salamanca, 1997. Pp. 49–57.

*Critical and Biographical Studies*

Alstrum, James. "Metapoesía e intertextualidad: Las demandas sobre el lector en la obra de Alvaro Mutis." *Revista de Estudios Colombianos* 12–13:43–46 (1994).

Balza, José. "Mutis: Disoluciones y mudanzas." *Inti* 34–35:193–198 (fall/spring 1991–1992).

Benedetti, Mario. "El Gaviero Alvaro Mutis." *Nexos* 15, no. 169:20–22 (January 1992). Reprinted in Benedetti, *El ejercicio del criterio*. Madrid: Alfaguara, 1995. Pp. 340–344.

Bradu, Fabienne. "Vida y biografía." *Vuelta* 17, no. 200:54–55 (July 1993).

Canfield, Martha. "Alvaro Mutis: Soñador de navíos." *Hispamérica* 23, no. 67:101–107 (April 1994).

Castañón, Adolfo. "¿Quién es El Gaviero?" *Vuelta* 21, no. 249:46–50 (1997).

Castro-García, Oscar. "La muerte, espejo de la vida, en los cuentos de Mutis." *Lingüística y Literatura* (Medellín, Colombia) 15, no. 26:67–82 (July–December 1994).

Cobo Borda, Juan Gustavo. *Historia portátil de la poesía colombiana (1880–1995)*. Bogotá: Tercer Mundo Editores, 1995.

———. *Para leer a Alvaro Mutis*. Santa Fe de Bogotá: Planeta Colombiana Editorial, 1998.

Eyzaguirre, Luis. "Transformaciones del personaje en la poesía de Alvaro Mutis." *Revista de Crítica Literaria Latinoamericana* 18, no. 35:41–48 (1992).

García Márquez, Gabriel. "Alvaro Mutis." *El Espectador*, 13 September 1954, p. 4. Published also in *Gabriel García Márquez. Obra periodística, vol. 3. Entre cachacos II*. Edited by Jacques Gilard. Barcelona: Editorial Bruguera, 1982. Pp. 920–921.

———. "Una amistad en tiempos ruines," *El Espectador* (Bogotá), 29 August 1993; "Mi amigo Mutis," *El País* (Madrid), 30 October 1993.

Hernández, Consuelo. "Razón del extraviado: Mutis entre dos mundos." *Cuadernos Hispanoamericanos* 523:69–78 (January 1994).

Lefort, Michel, ed. *Alvaro Mutis. Transversales. No. 1*. Paris: Editions Folle Avoine, 1999.

Levy, Kurt L. "Un sesquicentenario y un cumpleaños, trayectoria de una leyenda: el *Tramp Steamer*." *Revista de Estudios Colombianos* 12–13:7–12 (1994).

Martin, Gerald. "Alvaro Mutis and the Ends of History." *Studies in Twentieth-Century Literature* 19, no. 1:117–131 (winter 1995).

Menton, Seymour. " 'El último rostro': Nada de fragmento." *Revista de Estudios Colombianos* 12–13:39–42 (1994).

Motato C., Hernando. *Voces de la desesperanza*. Bucaramanga: Universidad Industrial de Santander, 1999. Pp. 1–62.

Moreno, Belén del Rocío. *Las cifras del azar: Una lectura psicoanalítica de la obra de Alvaro Mutis*. Santa Fe de Bogotá: Planeta Colombiana Editorial, 1998.

O'Hara González, Edgar. " 'Los emisarios': Respuestas que son preguntas." *Revista de Crítica Literaria Latinoamericana* 11, no. 24:263–268 (1986).

Ordóñez, Montserrat. "Alvaro Mutis: *La última escala del Tramp Steamer*." *Revista Iberoamericana* 151:644–649 (June 1990).

Paz, Octavio. "Los Hospitales de Ultramar (1959)." In his *Puertas al campo*. Mexico City: UNAM, 1966. Pp. 131–136.

Rodríguez Amaya, Fabio. *De MUTIS a Mutis. Para una ilícita lectura crítica de Maqroll el Gaviero*. Imola: University Press of Bologna, 1995.

———. "Los puertos en la poesía de Alvaro Mutis." *Caravelle* 69:173–191 (1997).

Romero, Armando. "Los poetas de *Mito*." *Revista Iberoamericana* 50, nos. 128–129:689–755 (July–December 1984).

Saldívar, Dasso. *García Márquez. Viaje a la semilla. La biografía*. Madrid: Alfaguara, 1997. (Contains useful information on the relationship between Mutis and García Márquez.)

Sarduy, Severo. "Prólogo para leer como un epílogo." *Hispamérica* 21, no. 63:69–71 (December 1992).

Stackelberg, Jürgen von. "El que sirve una revolución ara en el mar: Simón Bolívar bei Alvaro Mutis und Gabriel García Márquez." *Iberomania* 36:38–51 (1992).

Volkening, Ernesto. "El mundo ancho y ajeno de Alvaro Mutis." *El Espectador*, 20 September 1981, pp. 4, 10. Reprinted in *Obra literaria*. Vol. 1, *Poesía 1947–1985*. Edited by Santiago Mutis Durán. Bogotá: Procultura, 1985. Pp. 230–235.

*Interviews*

Alstrum, James. "Alvaro Mutis habla de Rulfo, García Márquez y Maqroll." *Revista de Estudios Colombianos* 16:34–39 (1996).

Balboa, Rosina. "Entrevista con Alvaro Mutis: Perseguidor de nostalgias." *Quimera: Revista de Literatura* (Barcelona) 108:26–30 (1991).

Barnechea, Alfredo, and José Miguel Oviedo. "La historia como estética" In *Poesía y Prosa*. Edited by Santiago Mutis Durán. Bogotá: Instituto Colombiano de Cultura, 1981. Pp. 576–597.

*Escala íntima. Alvaro Mutis.* Mexico City: Conaculta, 1999. (Videotape directed by Rodrigo Castaño.)

García Aguilar, Eduardo. *Celebraciones y otros fantasmas: Una biografía intelectual de Alvaro Mutis.* Bogotá: Tercer Mundo Editores, 1993.

García Márquez, Gabriel. "Los elementos del desastre." *El Espectador,* 21 March 1954, p. 8. (Brief review of the chapbook followed by a more extensive interview with Alvaro Mutis. Published also in *Gabriel García Márquez. Obra periodística, vol. 2. Entre cachacos I.* Edited by Jacques Gilard. Barcelona: Editorial Bruguera, 1982. Pp. 131–135.)

———. *El olor de la guayaba: Conversaciones con Plineo Apuleyo Mendoza.* Barcelona: Editorial Bruguera, 1982.

Gillard, Jacques. "Entretien avec Alvaro Mutis." *Caravelle* 64:179–192 (1995).

Poniatowska, Elena. *Cartas de Alvaro Mutis a Elena Poniatowska.* Mexico City: Alfaguara, 1998.

Quiroz, Fernando. *El reino que estaba para mí: Conversaciones con Alvaro Mutis.* Santafé de Bogotá: Editorial Norma, 1993.

Sefamí, Jacobo. "Maqroll, La vigilancia del orden." In *Tras las rutas de Maqroll el Gaviero, 1988–1993.* Edited by Santiago Mutis Durán. Bogotá: Instituto Colombiano de Cultura, 1993. Pp. 117–160.

Sheridan, Guillermo. "La vida, la vida verdaderamente vivida." In *Poesía y Prosa,* by Alvaro Mutis. Edited by Santiago Mutis Durán. Bogotá: Instituto Colombiano de Cultura, 1981. Pp. 616–651.

# Olga Orozco

## (1920–1999)

### Melanie Nicholson

Olga Orozco, who has come to be considered one of Argentina's most respected twentieth-century poets, was born on 17 March 1920 in the remote, dusty town of Toay in the province of La Pampa. Toay and its surroundings are later re-created with striking surrealist imagery in her collection of autobiographical short stories, *La oscuridad es otro sol* (1967; Darkness is another sun). Her mother was a descendant of Basque and Irish immigrants who had come to Argentina in the eighteenth and nineteenth centuries; her father, Carmelo Gugliotta, was a Sicilian who, the poet discovered later in life, fled to Argentina to avoid a situation of unwanted paternity. Orozco spent the first eight years of her life in Toay, in a spacious criollo house near the center of the town, with her parents, an older brother, and two older sisters, as well as their maternal grandmother. Her father was for many years the *intendente* (mayor) of the town, as well as a landowner, and the family prospered. The death of her brother, Emilio, when she was six years old was a profound emotional event for Orozco; as a writer, she re-created this first experience with death, loss, and alienation in the story "Y todavía la rueda" (And still the wheel). The incessant attempt to reach into the realm inhabited by the dead, prefigured in the child's consciousness portrayed in this story, became one of Orozco's most prevalent poetic motifs.

Orozco cites the significance of her maternal grandmother (who was Irish) in the formation of her worldview. In a 1990 interview with Jacobo Sefamí, Orozco explains that this grandmother "tenía una concepción bastante mágica, bastante animista del mundo, que sin duda venía de sus antepasados celtas. De modo que todo el mundo era algo en movimiento. Los objetos siempre estaban en acecho para ayudarte o para condenarte, para protegerte o para llevarte al abismo. Todo era un peligro y un asilo" (she had a rather magical, animistic view of the world, which undoubtedly was inherited from her Celtic ancestors. For her, the entire world was made up of things in motion. Objects were always lying in ambush, ready to help you or to condemn you, to protect you or to carry you into the abyss. Everything was a danger and a refuge). The perception of a world inhabited by magical or otherworldly forces that Orozco describes here became the basis for her poetics.

The other significant factor in the early formation of Orozco's worldview, according to the poet herself, is the geography of her native province of La Pampa, an extremely arid land of "fantastic" proportions, with winds so powerful that entire sand dunes shift places from one day to the next. "Además," adds Orozco in the Sefamí interview, "como hay grandes zonas desérticas, sin vegetación, cada pequeño objeto—un hueso, una piedra—toma un relieve importantísimo, desmesurado, como podría suceder dentro de un cuadro surrealista. Cualquier presencia aislada adquiere las características de una revelación, de una aparición" (Moreover, since there are wide reaches of desert, with no vegetation, each little object—a bone, a rock—takes on a striking relief, it appears enormous, as it might in a surrealist painting. Any isolated presence takes on the characteristics of a revelation, an apparition). Among other important factors, the formation of Orozco's poetic voice is grounded in the spectacle of this geography. Although the family moved to the coastal city of Bahía Blanca when Orozco was eight, and to the capital, Buenos Aires, when she was sixteen, it was her early years in Toay that gave her the unique poetic vision that remained with her throughout her life.

Frequenting the family library from an early age (she remembers having read novels by Fyodor Dostoyevsky at age eleven or twelve), and following the lead of both parents, who read to her from the Greek and Roman classics, from Dante, and from the Italian romantic poet Giacomo Leopardi, Orozco developed a passion for literature. During her adolescence she attended a Catholic school, but she became so imbued with the religious spirit of the institution that her mother resolved to place her in public school, to see if the fervor would attenuate. At the age of eighteen (in 1938) Orozco graduated from normal school, formally prepared to be a teacher, and soon thereafter entered the University of Buenos Aires, where she completed a degree in the Facultad de Filosofía y Letras (Humanities). It was also at the age of eighteen that she published her first poem and began to frequent the informal gatherings of poets whom critics later called the Argentine "Generation of 1940."

From age eighteen onward, Orozco participated in the literary life of Buenos Aires. She worked as a journalist and literary critic, publishing essays and reviews in such prestigious periodicals as Sur, La Nación, Vuelta, and Clarín, as well as in more popular magazines such as Claudia. In addition, Orozco published translations of French and Italian works. Although she traveled often and widely (mainly to Mexico, Brazil, and Europe), she never resided for any significant period of time outside of Argentina. Unlike many of her contemporaries in the literary and artistic communities of Buenos Aires, Orozco never gave serious consideration to the question of exile. Although exile is indeed a leitmotif in her work, it is the spiritual sense of human alienation from God or the absolute, and not the sense of political exile from a temporal order, that characterizes this recurrent theme. It is worth noting, in this respect, that Orozco's orientation was never toward politically oriented poetry or poésie engagée. For her, the distinction between the aesthetic realm and the sociopolitical realm must be kept intact.

One of Orozco's journeys deserves particular mention. In 1961, having received a grant from Argentina's Fondo Nacional de las Artes, she traveled to several European countries to complete a research project titled "The Occult and the Sacred in Modern Poetry." This research deepened her knowledge of poets such as Charles Baudelaire, William Butler Yeats, and the French surrealists, and led her to further explore the work of scholars such as the historian of religions Mircea Eliade, the philosopher of science Gaston Bachelard, and the psychoanalyst Carl Gustav Jung. The formal study of topics such as occultism, myth, magic, the irrational, the sacred, shamanism, and archetypal symbols undoubtedly furthered the process by which Orozco integrated into her own poetic voice an interest that she had experienced since childhood.

With the exception of occasional journeys abroad and to her home province of La Pampa, Orozco remained in Buenos Aires until her death. At age seventy-nine, her career as a writer was at its apogee: she had published nine volumes of poetry, all highly acclaimed both in Argentina and abroad, as well as two volumes of short stories. In 1988 she was awarded the Premio Nacional de Poesía in Argentina; in 1998 she was chosen among writers from all over Latin America to receive the prestigious Juan Rulfo Prize for Literature (Mexico). Olga Orozco died of heart failure in Buenos Aires on 15 August 1999.

Orozco is generally considered one of the most representative members of the Argentine Generation of 1940. This group of lyric poets, which also included Enrique Molina, César Fernández Moreno, León Benarós, Daniel Devoto, Juan Rodolfo Wilcock, and Alberto Girri, demonstrates a clear aesthetic kinship with the German modernist poet Rainer Maria Rilke.

Like Rilke, these neoromantics demonstrate a preoccupation with the themes of love, death, and human anguish; there is, accordingly, a rather constant elegiac note in their poetry. Without a doubt, the other immediate literary influence on this generation of writers—and on similar groups throughout Spanish America—was the Chilean poet Pablo Neruda. Neruda's *Residencia en la tierra* (1933) exercised a clear and direct influence on Orozco and her contemporaries. Often described as introspective, hermetic, and surrealistic, Neruda's early poetry not only captured the spirit of surrealism's incursions into the realm of the irrational, it also spoke directly to a generation of young Argentines who had come of age in an era of confusion and pessimism.

Argentina's political and economic instability in the 1930s and early 1940s was compounded by both the Spanish Civil War (1936–1939) and the outbreak of World War II, and thus intensified their anguish and disillusion. As the poet León Benarós observes in his characterization of his contemporaries, "Nosotros somos graves, porque nacimos a la literatura bajo el signo de un mundo en que nadie podía reír. De ahí, pues, que casi toda nuestra poesía sea elegíaca" (We are grave because we were born into literature under the sign of a world in which no one could laugh. That's why almost all our poetry is elegiac). The bitter experience of the Spanish *exiliados* who took up residence in Argentina (including such influential poets as Rafael Alberti and Juan Larrea) was shared by the Generation of 1940. A more immediate impact was felt, however, when the populist leader Juan Domingo Perón rose to power in 1946. The first Peronist period (1945–1955) saw a tightening of government control over the media, the implementation of policies favoring popular culture over "high" culture, and a marked restriction of the role intellectuals played in the life of the nation. César Fernández Moreno, another of Orozco's contemporaries who chronicled the movements of this generation, comments that "La mayoría de la generación aguantó los años del peronismo en la soledad y el silencio" (Most of the generation withstood the Peronist years in solitude and silence).

Although Orozco repeatedly denied any affiliation with a literary generation or movement, many qualities characteristic of the Generation of 1940 are apparent in her early work, and bear further examination. The decade of the 1940s in European poetry generally signaled a return to individual, existential concerns after the primarily social orientation of the 1930s. Spanish modernist poets such as Luis Cernuda and Vicente Aleixandre, who wrote in both metaphysical and neoromantic veins, were widely read and highly regarded by young poets throughout the Hispanic world. In addition to these more or less contemporary models, there were also inherited poetic styles and philosophies to be grappled with. The poets who published their first books in Argentina in the 1940s found themselves in quiet rebellion against the self-consciously inventive approach to language that had characterized the previous generation of avant-garde writers. The *vanguardia* poets—of whom the Chilean Vicente Huidobro is perhaps the most striking example on Latin American soil—strove to liberate poetic language from its communicative function. They featured the unusual visual image and the unexpected metaphor, discarded any notion of classical beauty or form, and raised the poet to the status of inventor supreme. It fell to Orozco's generation, then, to restore to poetry what they conceived of as lyric beauty and a humanistic orientation. Their indebtedness to the avant-garde movements, however, was patent. Above all, the poets of the Generation of 1940 retained the primacy that the *vanguardia* had given to the poetic image. Of the various European avant-garde movements, it was surrealism that undoubtedly left the most significant mark on later generations of Latin American writers; for Orozco and her contemporaries, this is apparent in their widespread use of dream-related imagery and in their insistence on looking beyond quotidian reality toward a more authentic "elsewhere."

Many critics have commented on the remarkable internal coherence of Orozco's oeuvre, which spans five decades. Although certain concerns or rhetorical approaches shifted gradually over time, there remains an overall unity that is formal, tonal, and thematic. Critics have generally observed that while Orozco's voice increased in complexity, her vision remained unified and forceful. The following chronological overview of her major publications will, of necessity, emphasize the qualities that distinguish one book from another, but the reader should keep in mind the overall coherence of the work as a whole.

Orozco's first published book of poetry, *Desde lejos* (1946; From afar), laid the formal foundations for her entire subsequent body of work. The tone is elegiac, reflecting the neoromantic bent of her generation. An obsession with the past, with lost childhood, and with presence and absence plays itself out in long-breathed lines that reveal an alienated, questioning speaker. These qualities are apparent in the following passage from "Lejos, desde mi colina" (Far, from my hill):

> *¿Quién eras tú, perdida entre el follaje como las*
> *anteriores primaveras,*
> *como alguien que retorna desde el tiempo a repetir los*
> *llantos,*
> *los deseos, los ademanes lentos con que antaño*
> *entreabría sus días?*

> Who were you, lost among the foliage like previous
> springs,
> like someone who returns from time to repeat the
> weeping,
> the desires, the slow gestures with which, long ago,
> she set her days ajar?

Unlike her *vanguardista* predecessors, Orozco was not concerned with linguistic inventiveness or formal experimentation. The balanced syntax, the extended, rhythmic line, and the measured tone encompassing a mourned-for past and an enigmatic present are the formal elements from which her poetry virtually never strays. *Desde lejos* establishes the fundamental rhetorical characteristic of Orozco's poetry as a liturgical, ceremonious discourse with prophetic overtones. These qualities are reinforced by the length of the poems, which often extend over two or three pages. Reminiscent perhaps of the biblical Psalms, or of the longer poems of Rilke or the modernist Antillean poet St.-John Perse, Orozco's poems function as extended meditations whose flow is counterbalanced by the intense, almost hallucinatory quality of the images.

Her second volume, *Las muertes* (1951; The deaths), takes as its subject a number of literary characters—from Faulkner's Gail Hightower to Rilke's Christoph Detlev Brigge to Dickens's Miss Havisham—all of whom are conceived of as "the dead." The poems are constructed as lyric meditations in the voices of the characters themselves, apostrophes to them by an external speaker, or poetic epitaphs. In the last lines of "Miss Havisham," the speaker invites unnamed onlookers (who, by extension, include the reader) to observe the scene of the old bride's death:

> *Ahora ya está muerta.*
> *Pasad.*
> *Ésa es la escena que los años guardaron en orgulloso*
> *polvo de paciencia,*
> *es la suntuosa urdimbre donde cayó como una*
> *colgadura envuelta por las llamas de su muerte.*
> *Fue una espléndida hoguera.*
> *Sí. Nada hace mejor fuego que la vana aridez,*
> *que ese lóbrego infierno en que está ardiendo por una*
> *eternidad,*
> *hasta que llegue Pip y escriba debajo de su nombre: "la*
> *perdono."*

> Now she is dead.
> Enter, please.
> Behold the scene the years have held in the proud
> dust of patience,
> the sumptuous warp where she fell like a tapestry
> wrapped in the flames of her death.
> It was a splendid blaze.
> Yes. Nothing makes a better fire than vain aridity,
> than that gloomy hell in which she burns for an
> eternity,
> until Pip arrives and writes beneath her name: "I
> forgive her."

*Las muertes* is undoubtedly the most self-consciously literary of Orozco's books; perhaps for this reason it seems to lack the metaphysical complexity of the other volumes. In an ironic twist, the book ends with a poem titled "Olga Orozco," in which the lyric voice, placing herself in the company of fictional characters, certifies her own death: "Yo, Olga Orozco, desde tu corazón digo a todos que muero" (I, Olga Orozco, from your heart say to everyone that I die).

*Los juegos peligrosos* (The dangerous games), published in 1962, employs a system of tropes based directly on the esoteric traditions. What had been a partial approach in the previous books, a shamanistic tone or an occasional reference to "las magias y los ritos" (magic and rites), now becomes the organizing principle of the book. What, exactly, is meant by "the dangerous games"? This structural metaphor can be interpreted on at least two discernible levels. First, it is evident that the practices involved in the occult sciences—magic, witchcraft, alchemy, and divination, among others—have the potential for disastrous personal and social consequences. Indeed, Orozco obtains the material for much of her poetry from the consideration of this potential. Drawing upon a long-established mythico-religious tradition that was given literary shape by the Romantics, Orozco considers the transgression inherent in perceiving too clearly or in knowing too much. A passage from the poem "La cartomancia" (The tarot reading) illustrates this perceived danger: "Las Estrellas alumbran el cielo del enigma. / Mas lo que quieres ver no puede ser mirado cara a cara / porque su luz es de otro reino" (The Stars illuminate the sky of the enigma. / But what you want to see cannot be looked upon face to face / because its light belongs to another realm).

Second, as the critic Naomi Lindstrom points out, there is a purely literary danger involved in the utilization of an occult-oriented lexicon: the writer runs the risk of producing a sensationalist text, one whose deepest concerns will not be taken seriously. The rhetorical risk taken by Orozco in this book is compensated for by several factors, most notably the metaphysical depth from which this rhetoric springs. In brief, Orozco's use of a suprarational system of metaphor is solidly grounded in a worldview that gives precedence to the hidden, the unknown, the unreachable. In this poetry, magic is not a facile trick, rhetorically or existentially. It is, rather, one of several plausible means by which an attempt is made to cross the threshold into the desired *otro reino* (other realm). Ultimately, Orozco leads the reader to conclude that poetry itself is the most dangerous game.

In *Museo salvaje* (1974; Wild museum), as in subsequent volumes, the rhetoric of the occult becomes less evident, although an esoteric worldview continues to inform the poems on many levels. This volume, like the previous three, is organized around a central theme or organizing principle, in this case the metaphor of the speaker's body as a savage museum. The speaker's stance in relation to this museum is one of microscopic intimacy coupled with extreme alienation. In this volume Orozco experiments for the first time with the long prose poem, although many poems follow the free-verse form of previous books. The poetic method is to investigate the physical minutiae of the various organs or limbs of the body from a metaphysical, though intensely subjective, perspective. The initial poem, "Génesis," constitutes an ironic re-creation of the body of the speaker, ending with her enigmatic appearance "en el alba primera del olvido" (in the first dawn of oblivion). Other poems in *Museo salvaje* reinforce the recognition of the body's double character as the only means of comprehending the absolute and, simultaneously, as the very substance that blocks that comprehension: "Este cuerpo tan denso con que clausuro todas las salidas, este saco de sombras cosido a mis dos alas . . ." (This dense body with which I close off every exit, this sack of shadows sewn to my two wings . . . ).

Orozco's next book, *Cantos a Berenice* (1977; Songs for Berenice), is a cycle of seventeen poems that serve as an extended epitaph for a cat. Orozco again enters dangerous literary territory by offering an ordinary house cat (an adopted stray, as Orozco tells it) as the subject of a panegyric. As in previous volumes, it is the dignity of tone and the rhythmic solemnity of the verses that effectively lyricize and problematize the quotidian subject matter. Orozco's approach is to link the domestic cat Berenice with legends and myths surrounding the feline species from Babylonia onward:

> Tú reinaste en Bubastis
> con los pies en la tierra, como el Nilo,
> y una constelación por cabellera en tu doble del cielo.

> You reigned in Bubastis
> with your feet on the ground, like the Nile,
> and a constellation for your hair in your celestial
>     double.

The poetic speaker in this book does not address an ordinary cat, but rather a magical, mythical animal, perhaps a witch's familiar. This approach constitutes a return to the realm of the occult, but with a new focus: in *Cantos a Bernice*, Orozco begins the cultivation of a distinctively feminine orientation. The speaker as witch, with the black cat as her familiar, is only one of several means by which Orozco explores the world of the occult arts through female archetypal figures.

With her next volume, *Mutaciones de la realidad* (1979; Mutations of reality), Orozco effectively abandons the practice of grouping poems within a clearly identifiable thematic unit. In true postmodern fashion, the organizing metaphor here is a lack of metaphor, or a metaphor in constant disintegration. Though the subject of the book is "reality," both the poetic speaker and the reader are constantly thwarted in the attempt to grasp that reality as any sort of meaningful whole. The title poem, "Mutaciones de la realidad," attempts various metaphorical approaches to this mutable reality:

> No niego la realidad sin más alcances y con
>     menos fisuras
> que una coraza férrea ciñendo las evaporaciones del
>     sueño y de la noche
> o una gota de lacre sellando la visión de abismos y
>     paraísos que se entreabren
> como un panel secreto
> por obra de un error o de un conjuro.

> I don't deny reality with no greater scope and with
>     fewer fissures
> than an iron armor encircling the evaporations of
>     dream and the night
> or a drop of wax sealing the vision of abysses and
>     paradises that barely open
> like a secret panel
> by an act of error or incantation.

This passage clearly demonstrates Orozco's preoccupation with a hidden realm forbidden to the uninitiated, which is one of the basic tenets of esoteric thought. The vision of this realm is obtained fleetingly through a secret door, accessible only through "error" (the opposite of discursive reason) or through *conjuro*, incantatory magic.

The same poem locates the allegorized "reality" within the sphere of the occult:

> Guardiana, como yo, de una máscara indecifrable del
>     destino,
> se viste de hechicera y transforma de un soplo las aves
>     centellantes en legiones de ratas,
> o pone a evaporar en sus marmitas todo el vino de ayer
>     y el de mañana. . . .

> A guardian, like me, of an undecipherable mask of
>     destiny,
> she dresses like an enchantress and with a single
>     breath transforms the sparkling birds into
>     legions of rats,
> or distills in her cauldrons all the wine of yesterday
>     and tomorrow. . . .

It is interesting to note that reality, linguistically marked as feminine in Spanish, assumes the role of sorceress in this passage. Her black magic involves turning the positive into the negative (sparkling birds into legions of rats) and distilling time, both past and future. The assumption underlying *Mutaciones de la realidad,* in sum, is that reality is unknowable. Echoing *Museo salvaje,* the speaker ties the abstract and all-encompassing *realidad* to the concrete, finite human body. Both entities, she concludes, are unreliable sources of meaning: "Sé que de todos modos la realidad es errante, / tan sospechosa y tan ambigua como mi propia anatomía" (I know that reality is, after all, nomadic, / as suspicious and as ambiguous as my own anatomy).

In *La noche a la deriva* (1983; Night adrift), Orozco continues to pursue motifs associated with gaining knowledge, with escaping the bounds of visible reality, and with employing magic or other nonrational means for crossing the threshold into the absolute. The night, allegorized as a godlike personage, is seen as the keeper of the mysteries that fascinate the speaker: "descubro en medio de tus altas malezas el esplendor de una ciudad perdida" (I discover in your high underbrush the splendor of a lost city). Night is traditionally associated with dreaming, and several poems of this volume build upon the allegory of human existence as the dream of a superior dreamer that was popularized by Orozco's well-known compatriot Jorge Luis Borges. The above-cited line also reiterates Orozco's concern with crossing—or eliminating—physical or temporal boundaries. The dream state evoked in much surrealist imagery is an artistic or literary version of the shaman's leap into other realms of consciousness, and *La noche a la deriva* can be seen as a poetic testimonial to this sort of extramundane experience.

Orozco's next volume of poetry, *En el revés del cielo* (1987; The other side of the sky) takes up the same transcendental themes as the previous books, but the tone darkens and the motifs of silence, abandonment, and frustration prevail. The image reflected in the book's title—the other side or the reverse of the sky—recalls the lost paradise that the speaker finds increasingly remote and unattainable. This book, perhaps more than any other of Orozco's, conveys a fundamental pessimism regarding earthly existence. She employs gnostic imagery in lines such as "Somos duros fragmentos arrancados del reverso del cielo" (We are hard fragments torn away from the other side of the sky), in which the basic human condition is envisioned as one of fragmentation and alienation. All attempts to transcend it are nullified by the limitations of life itself: "Nunca con esta vida que no alcanza para ir y volver" (Never with this life that is not sufficient for going and returning).

This book is framed by two key poems whose subject is discourse itself, or the logos of the poetic word. In both poems (as in "La Sibila de Cumas" [The Cumaean Sibyl], another in this collection), the possibility of oracular discourse as a means to knowledge is examined and ultimately rejected. The speaker of the first poem, "El resto era silencio" (The rest was silence) ironically awaits "the dictate of silence," making silence itself into her muse. The final dictate of the poem, however, appears to negate the very vocation of writing: "Y haz que sólo el silencio sea su palabra" (And make silence alone be your word). Likewise, the book's concluding poem, "En el final era el verbo" (In the end was the word), metaphorically establishes the speaker's disillusionment with the power of words:

> Como si fueran sombras de sombras que se alejan las
>     palabras,
> humaredas errantes exhaladas por la boca del viento,
> así se me dispersan, se me pierden de vista contra las
>     puertas del silencio.

> As if they were shadows of shadows that grow
>     distant, words,
> wandering clouds of smoke exhaled by the mouth
>     of the wind,
> so they scatter from me, so they disappear from my
>     sight against the doors of silence.

In Orozco's last volume of poetry, *Con esta boca, en este mundo* (1994; With this mouth, in this world), silence and the imminence of death seem to overwhelm the lyric voice. There is a deepening sense of the impossibility of contact with the realm of the invisible, and of the failure of poetry to effect that desired contact. The first line of the book, in fact, reads "No te pronunciaré jamás, verbo sagrado" (Never will I pronounce you, sacred word). Some of these poems have a more subjective or purely personal tone than poems in previous collections, often conveying emotions connected with loss and despair. One poem ends with a triple negative that underscores the sense of irreparable loss: "porque nunca, jamás, ninguna recompensa desandará la pérdida" (because never, not ever, will a single recompense retrace the steps of loss). Significantly, the word *adiós* appears several times in this volume. The lyric voice reflects a mature poet in stoic opposition to death: "Ahora estamos cerca del final, de cara contra un muro que no cede" (Now we are close to the end, facing a wall that will not yield).

As the preceding overview has shown, Orozco's sequence of nine volumes of poetry, spanning the period from 1946 to 1994, displays a remarkable internal coherence in its principal concerns as well as in its rhetorical modes and formal presentation. Beginning with the first volume, there is a tendency toward oracular discourse and rhythmic organization that echoes liturgy, ritual, or even magical incantation. Certain techniques mark Orozco's style, with little change over time. Chief among these are parallelism (particularly anaphora), the use of the rhetorical question, and the building of complex figures that play themselves out in extended periods. There are significant developments, however. The tendency in her earlier work to construct each volume around a single organizing trope (such as the body/museum or the dangerous games) gives way, in the last four volumes, to a more subtle internal organization. The later books are also characterized by a darkened tone and a more pessimistic approach to the existential problems presented. Broadly speaking, the later poetry acquires a more metaphysical character, although the subjective and emotive qualities of the lyric voice never dissolve into heady intellectualism.

Although Orozco's two collections of stories have not elicited the same critical attention as her poetry, an overview of her work would be incomplete without a brief examination of these books. Critics have generally noted that the prose of these stories is highly poetic in nature, and that their treatment of the themes of childhood, irrationality, magic, and loss sheds light on the thematics of her poetry. Like her volumes of poetry, *La oscuridad es otro sol* (1967; Darkness is another sun) and *La luz también es un abismo* (1995; Light is also an abyss) are densely textured works, utilizing unusual imagery to explore the depths of human experience. In her interview with Sefamí, Orozco characterizes the language of her prose narratives in terms associated with lyric poetry: "No es un lenguaje desnudo, ¿no? No es la acción urgente, no están hechos simplemente para contar; están hechos para sugerir también, para suscitar, para hacer señales" (The language isn't bare, is it? There's no urgent action, they aren't made simply to narrate; they're also made to suggest, to excite, to make signs). *La oscuridad es otro sol* is a collection of fifteen largely autobiographical stories that re-create Orozco's early childhood in Toay, an isolated town on the pampa where electricity is a recent arrival and where medieval superstitions still hold sway.

Although the stories stand well on their own, the collection has the internal coherence of a novel; indeed, some critics have referred to it as a novel. The first-person narrator, Lía, is a re-creation of Orozco's childhood self, a sensitive, highly imaginative girl of five or six who observes a world that is moved by mysterious, often incomprehensible forces. The other characters who occur with frequency are children (her older sisters play particularly significant roles) and eccentric, even mad, adults. Orozco explained in interviews that both her father and her grandmother welcomed into their home the misfits of the town, or the hapless wanderers who needed a meal and a bath—figures who take shape in the stories as the local fortuneteller and *curandera* María Teo, the failed opera singer Nanni Fittipaldi, and "la Lora" (Miss Parrot), who wears a big yellow hat and lives in a cave with her son, whom she believes to be Jesus Christ. Although the town and its characters are created with vivid and memorable images, the prose of these stories tends to be highly metaphorical and suggestive, as the following passage from the initial story of the collection illustrates: "Llegué. Frente al umbral hay un médano que debe pasar por el ojo de una aguja, y detrás un jardín donde comienzan las raíces de la muerte. Todavía no sé hablar; cuando aprenda, habré olvidado el camino por

donde vine" (I arrived. On the other side of the threshold is a sand dune that must pass through the eye of a needle, and behind that a garden where the roots of death begin. I still don't know how to speak; when I learn, I will have forgotten the road that brought me here).

Orozco's only other collection of stories, *La luz también es un abismo,* was published in 1995, almost thirty years after *La oscuridad es otro sol.* It also includes fifteen stories and is structured along the same lines as the previous collection. Here again the experiences of small-town life on the pampa are seen through the eyes of Lía. The cast of characters again includes Lía's sisters Laura and María de las Nieves, other children of the town, and the eccentric or mad adults. The time frame has shifted only slightly: Lía is now seven or eight years old. The last story, in fact, chronicles the child's bewilderment and grief as the family leaves Toay to resettle in the city of Bahía Blanca. Orozco's characteristic meshing of experiential event with metaphysical contemplation is apparent in the child-narrator's internal monologue in this story: "Adiós, casa de las luciérnagas, casa de los rincones abrigados y cómplices, de las misteriosas y enmarañadas selvas. Desde el centro de ti, que eres el centro del mundo, con una escalera hacia lo alto hubiéramos podido llegar al centro del cielo" (Good-bye, house of fireflies, house of sheltered and accessory corners, of mysterious and tangled jungles. From the center of you, who are the center of the world, with a ladder raised toward the heights we could have arrived at the center of the sky). Although the subject matter of Orozco's two collections is similar, with *La luz también es un abismo* her narrative style has evolved toward greater simplicity and clarity. Whereas the stories of the first collection are characterized by an often hermetic interior monologue that involves a baroque profusion of images and perceptions, the narrative voice of *La luz también es un abismo* is more straightforward, descriptive, and calmly contemplative.

With regard to Orozco's work as a whole, critical debates have tended to revolve around two main issues: the question of Orozco's placement within the Generation of 1940, and the degree to which her work can be considered surrealist. With regard to the first issue, it is important to point out that the Generation of

1940 is a category invented a posteriori by critics and anthologists; apart from some rather limited group activities focused on the publication of short-lived magazines, such as *Canto* and *Verde memoria*, there were no manifestos or public demonstrations of common purpose, and little consciousness on the part of the poets of writing in similar styles. Although the nostalgic, neoromantic vein and the tone of pessimism or angst are recognized as common factors by virtually all critics, others point out, quite accurately, that Orozco does not participate in other typical manifestations of this generation, such as an exaltation of the land or a nationalistic bent. Similarly, critics have arrived at different conclusions regarding Orozco's surrealist tendencies. Whereas some argue in favor of her surrealist orientation, observing that Orozco privileges the irrational, cultivates oneiric imagery, and generally strives for a poetic leap into a dimension that may well be called "marvelous," others point out that her poetry is extremely well crafted—a product of the rational imagination—and that her technique bears little resemblance to the surrealist automatic writing or psychic automatism. To these two critical debates may be added a third, which weighs Orozco's lyric subjectivity against her more metaphysical approach. As often happens with such debates, all sides have a degree of truth. The genius of Orozco's poetry, one might conclude, is that it deftly negotiates the line between the personal and the universal, between subjective anguish and detached contemplation.

Beyond these debates, critical approaches to Orozco's work have generally concentrated on explicating her philosophical grounding and on unraveling her complex symbolic systems. Although not all writers are reliable interpreters of their own work, Orozco has elucidated much of her approach to poetry through commentary in essays and in interviews. An attempt to delineate the major thematic concerns of her writing might begin with her own encapsulated mythology, articulated in a 1981 interview with Danubio Torres Fierro: "Al haber sido arrojado del paraíso, el hombre recorre un camino, hacia arriba y hacia abajo, que lo conduce al encuentro de un verbo primordial. ¿Quién es capaz de negar que la poesía es la búsqueda de ese verbo primordial?" (Having been cast out of paradise, man follows a road, toward the heights and the depths, that leads him to the encounter with the primordial word. Who can deny that poetry is the search for that primordial word?). Orozco's work, both poetry and prose, reflects a worldview predicated upon alienation and loss, the condition of having been cast out of the Garden of Eden, to which one nevertheless continually strives to return. At the heart of this work lies the conviction that truth and reality reside elsewhere, and that the human endeavor to regain this lost paradise, or to cross the threshold into absolute being, is doomed to failure.

Although elements of this worldview are drawn from the biblical account of creation, Orozco's modern reshaping of this material is grounded in other sources, both religious and literary. Several critics have called attention to the particularly gnostic and hermetic flavor of her mythopoetic stance. Gnosticism and hermeticism, like the Neoplatonic doctrines with which they share several fundamental tenets, spring from revisions of the archetypal myth of the fall of man. Both belief systems posit a redemptive scheme based on rituals leading toward gnosis, true knowledge of the absolute. Orozco's work is permeated with symbolism drawn from these two traditions.

Gnostic cosmogonies (like those of the cabala) are based upon the idea of an original unity that was shattered by the forces of error or evil, an event that is often portrayed with the symbol of the infinitely fragmented vessel. Thus, the gnostic worldview (developed in the early centuries of the Christian era) posited a radical dualism of good and evil, locating the human subject at an unbridgeable distance from the divine world. This dualism lies at the heart of Orozco's symbolic system; it is, in fact, the primary assumption behind the term *revés* (reverse, other side), which becomes one of the leitmotifs of her work. A passage from *En el revés del cielo* (whose title directly reflects a gnostic longing for the unreachable absolute) illustrates the implications of a dualistic view of the cosmos:

> Ésta es la tierra esquiva,
> la tierra de no llegar jamás, la tierra del fantasma en
>    la pared.
> Otro es sin duda el sitio del encuentro, del combate
>    invisible,
> de la línea de fuego donde se cierra el foso entre la piel
>    y el alma.

This is the elusive land,
the land where one never arrives, the land of the
    ghost on the wall.
Surely the site of encounter is elsewhere, that of
    the invisible fight,
of the line of fire where the chasm between skin
    and soul closes up.

The fundamental frustration with existence that arose from this inherently pessimistic doctrine is reflected in numerous passages in Orozco's work. The speaker of "Remo contra la noche" in *Mutaciones de la realidad,* for example, despairs that "ningún fulgor del cielo hemos logrado con tantas migraciones arrancadas al alma" (not a single gleam from heaven have we achieved with so many migrations torn out of the soul). Light and darkness symbolized for the gnostics the divine "first principle" and the created cosmos, respectively. The material world was said to have sprung from the mixing of pure light with impure darkness; hence, Orozco's speaker in *La noche a la deriva* echoes a gnostic lament: "Ah, si pudiera separar otra vez la luz y las tinieblas" (Oh, if only I could separate once again the light from the darkness). Other gnostic motifs appearing in Orozco's poetry include the "call from without" (a sign or voice from the other world that attempts communication with this world), the sacred garment, and the celestial twin.

The hermetic tradition, more inherently optimistic than the gnostic, holds that the universe is a direct and visible unfolding of God. All that makes up the world is therefore a manifestation of divinity, a symbolic representation of the divine mind. Although Orozco clearly positions herself more upon gnostic than hermetic lines, certain aspects of hermetic thought do contribute to the wealth of her imagery. The hermetic recognition of magic, alchemy, and astrology as means of divine revelation links the philosophical underpinnings of Orozco's work with the occult arts as a praxis for attaining transmundane knowledge—a practice that informs the poetry of *Los juegos peligrosos.* The positive, symbolic value of the universe—the analogous relationship of the terrestrial to the divine—appears in Orozco's frequent use of lexical terms related to *reflejo* (reflection) and *espejo* (mirror). The speaker of *La noche a la deriva* adopts a clearly hermetic posture when she observes that "el alma que te habita es también la mirada del cielo que te incluye" (the soul that inhabits you is also the gaze of the heaven that includes you).

The hermetic notion that the human intellect is a reflection of the divine Nous or Mind leads to the conception of the world as a text to be deciphered, an idea that Orozco recalls metaphorically in several passages. A final, somewhat curious manifestation of hermetic mythology in Orozco's work occurs in the motif of the human statue. The soul of a god, say some hermetic texts, may be induced to enter a statue, whereby the statue becomes an oracle. This repeated motif in Orozco is perhaps best illustrated with the following passage from *Mutaciones de la realidad*: "Me embalsaman en estatua de sal a las puertas del tiempo. / Soy la momia traslúcida de ayer convertida en oráculo" (They embalm me into a statue of salt at the doors of time. / I am yesterday's translucent mummy turned into an oracle). In this passage, the oracular stance that many critics have attributed to Orozco's poetic speaker is given direct metaphorical value.

Gnosticism and hermeticism, as heterodox traditions within Judeo-Christian culture, were maintained in many cases through underground sects in which knowledge was shared only by adepts. In literature, it was the German Romantics who took up the esoteric notion of secret practices known only to the initiated, and applied it to the act of writing poetry. Orozco consciously situates herself within the line of literary predecessors that begins with the late-eighteenth-century German writer Novalis, who claimed that the poet was also a priest and a magician. In a poem from *Mutaciones de la realidad,* Orozco's speaker states that "en el fondo de todo hay un jardín / donde se abre la flor azul del sueño de Novalis" (at the bottom of everything there is a garden / where the blue flower of Novalis's dream opens). The blue flower, for Novalis, is a symbol of poetry. For many Romantics and their successors, the recuperation of primordial powers held a particularly linguistic significance, for they believed in the existence of a primitive and universal language as the divine expression of being in the material world. To retrieve that language is to act in a reverent but irrational manner, one which depends on faith in verbal magic.

In the nineteenth century, the French writers Gérard de Nerval, Charles Baudelaire, and Arthur Rimbaud each reinterpreted in his own way Novalis's notion of poetry as a transcendental act, "the raising of mankind above itself." Baudelaire's well-known sonnet "Correspondances," which suggests that the universe is "a forest of symbols," is in fact an example of the hermetic doctrine of analogy, which characterized the visible world as a reflection of the divine. From this it was inferred that human—particularly poetic—language was a reflection of divine language. The poetic word, or *logos*, proposed Rimbaud, could actually change life. Its power lay in the hands of the poet who was a *voyant* (seer), one destined to penetrate the mysteries of the universe and interpret them for the uninitiated. It is in this spirit that Orozco's speaker, in "Para ser otra," from *Los juegos peligrosos*, pronounces the prophetic lines "Voy a poder mirar. / Voy a desenterrar la palabra perdida entre las ruinas de cada nacimiento" (I am going to be able to see. / I am going to unearth the word lost among the ruins of each birth). In the twentieth century, André Breton and the French surrealists refashioned many of the esoteric notions delineated above, marking the human unconscious as realm of the sacred, the unknown, or the marvelous.

With all of these thinkers and writers—Novalis, Nerval, Baudelaire, Rimbaud, and the surrealists—Orozco shares the vision of a primordial unity and of the fallen state of humankind, an analogical view of the universe, and a sense of poetry as revelation, as a means of gaining access to the realm of the absolute. In "Surgen de las paredes," from *La noche a la deriva*, the speaker alludes to the momentary glimpse that may be achieved in such revelatory moments: "Se abre por un instante la trama entretejida por el humo y el brillo del abismo" (For a brief instant it opens, the weft interwoven by smoke and the gleam of the abyss). Although she refers to it as "my only talisman in the darkness," the poetic word for Orozco is not an easy consolation for the anguish of existence; rather, it is a watchword allowing an Orphic rite of passage: "Palabra inaudible, palabra empecinada, palabra terrible—mi mantra del ascenso y del retorno—palabra como un ángel suspendido entre la aniquilación y la caída" (Inaudible word, obstinate word, terrible word—my mantra of ascent and return—word like an angel suspended between annihilation and the fall).

The above-quoted passage points to the inherently contradictory nature of poetic language for Orozco. On the one hand, it is evident that the crucial movement of her work as a whole is toward a virtually unreachable sacred space, and that a magical, incantatory rhetoric is employed, like the primitive rhetoric of charm, to bridge that chasm. It is equally evident, however, that the occult energy of language is repeatedly dissipated, even as it is evoked. The sense of fragmentation or loss is almost palpable, as is evident in these lines from *Mutaciones de la realidad*: "esas sílabas rotas en la boca / fueron por un instante la palabra" (Those broken syllables in the mouth / were, for an instant, the word). In each of her volumes of poetry, particularly from *Los juegos peligrosos* on, Orozco subjects the poetic word to intense scrutiny, and the faith that remains after such scrutiny is not a facile one.

As critics such as Naomi Lindstrom and Thorpe Running have noted, the last three volumes in particular reveal a profound anxiety or frustration on the part of the speaker with regard to poetry's power to communicate or to realize an existential leap into the invisible realm. Like a shaman, Orozco believes in the power of the word; like a modern skeptic, however, she continually calls that power into question. It could be argued that the often-cited internal coherence of Orozco's work rests largely upon the creative tension between primitive faith in, and modern denial of, the authority of poetic language. As the Mexican writer Octavio Paz observes, the work of Arthur Rimbaud marked a turning point: since the publication of Rimbaud's *A Season in Hell*, the highest function of poetry has been the negation of poetry. Orozco's work—like that of other twentieth-century Latin American poets such as Alejandra Pizarnik and Roberto Juarroz (Argentina), David Huerta (Mexico), and Paz himself—undoubtedly falls under the rubric of Paz's "critical poetry."

The dramatization of the poet's impasse regarding language, in sum, is Orozco's fullest expression of a worldview that places human life at an impossible distance from the absolute. Although in some passages she declares her defeat unreservedly, Orozco's vocation as a poet returns her unremittingly to the act of writing. Poet and poem are locked in combat, not against each other but against silence. The title poem of Orozco's last published volume, *Con esta boca, en este mundo*, concludes with these words:

> Hemos ganado. Hemos perdido,
> porque ¿cómo nombrar con esta boca,
> cómo nombrar en este mundo con esta sola boca en
>   este mundo con esta sola boca?

> We have won. We have lost,
> because how can we name with this mouth,
> how can we name in this world with this mouth in
>   this world with this mouth?

The stammering, maddening question will require another poem as answer.

## SELECTED BIBLIOGRAPHY

### Primary Works

#### Short Stories

*La oscuridad es otro sol.* Buenos Aires: Editorial Losada, 1967.
*La luz también es un abismo.* Buenos Aires: Emecé Editores, 1995.

#### Poetry

*Desde lejos.* Buenos Aires: Editorial Losada, 1946.
*Las muertes.* Buenos Aires: Editorial Losada, 1952.
*Los juegos peligrosos.* Buenos Aires: Editorial Losada, 1962.
*Museo salvaje.* Buenos Aires: Editorial Losada, 1974.
*Cantos a Berenice.* Buenos Aires: Editorial Sudamericana, 1977.
*Mutaciones de la realidad.* Buenos Aires: Editorial Sudamericana, 1979; Madrid: Ediciones Rialp, 1992.
*La noche a la deriva.* Mexico City: Fondo de Cultura Económica, 1983.
*En el revés del cielo.* Buenos Aires: Editorial Sudamericana, 1987.
*Con esta boca, en este mundo.* Selection and introductory note by Jacobo Sefamí. Mexico City: Casa Abierta al Tiempo (Universidad Autónoma Metropolitana), 1992.
*Con esta boca, en este mundo.* Buenos Aires: Editorial Sudamericana, 1994.

#### Other Works

*Páginas de Olga Orozco, seleccionadas por la autora.* Edited and introduced by Cristina Piña. Buenos Aires: Celtia, 1984. (Includes two essays on poetry by Orozco, a selection of her poetry and prose, the text of a previously unpublished play, a selection of her journalistic pieces, two interviews with Orozco, a chronology of the poet's life, and a selection of critical commentary on her work.)
*Travesías.* Buenos Aires: Editorial Sudamericana, 1997. (Interviews with Olga Orozco and Gloria Alcorta, coordinated by Antonio Requeni.)

#### Collected Works

*Las muertes. Los juegos peligrosos.* Buenos Aires: Losada, 1972.
*Veintinueve poemas.* Prologue by Juan Liscano. Caracas: Monte Ávila, 1975.
*Obra poética.* Buenos Aires: Corregidor, 1979.
*Poesía: Antología.* Prologue by Telma Luzzani Bystrowicz. Buenos Aires: Centro Editor de América Latina, 1982.
*Poemas.* Medellín, Colombia: Departamento de Bibliotecas, Universidad de Antioquia, 1984.
*Antología poética.* Madrid: Ediciones de Cultura Hispánica, 1985.
*Antología poética.* Buenos Aires: Fondo Nacional de las Artes, 1996.
*Eclipses y fulgores: Antología.* Prologue by Pere Gimferrer. Barcelona: Lumen, 1998.
*Relámpagos de lo invisible: Antología.* Selection and prologue by Horacio Zabaljuáregui. Mexico City: Fondo de Cultura Económica, 1998.
*Talismanes (27 poemas).* Selection by Ana Becciu. Barcelona: Plaza y Janés, 1998.

### Secondary Works

#### Critical and Biographical Studies

Colombo, Stella Maris. *Metáfora y cosmovisión en la poesía de Olga Orozco.* Rosario, Argentina: Cuadernos Aletheia, 1983.
Fernández Moreno, César. *La realidad y los papeles: Panorama y muestra de la poesía argentina contemporánea.* Madrid: Aguilar, 1967. (Chapter XIII, "La generación 'No corre,'" chronicles the generation of lyric poets to which Orozco belonged.)
Gómez Paz, Julieta. *Dos textos sobre la poesía de Olga Orozco.* Buenos Aires: Ediciones Tekné, 1980.

Kuhnheim, Jill S. "Cultural Affirmations: The Poetry of Olga Orozco and T. S. Eliot." *Confluencia: Revista Hispánica de Cultura y Literatura* 5, no. 1:39–50 (fall 1989).

———. *Gender, Politics and Poetry in Twentieth Century Argentina.* Gainesville: University Press of Florida, 1996. (This book focuses on the work of Olga Orozco and Alejandra Pizarnik. Kuhnheim's approach to Orozco is comparative, placing her within a modernist discourse framed by T. S. Eliot and Oliverio Girondo.)

Lindstrom, Naomi. "Olga Orozco: La voz poética que llama entre mundos." *Revista Iberoamericana* 132–133:765–775 (1985).

Liscano, Juan. "Olga Orozco y sus juegos peligrosos." In his *Descripciones.* Buenos Aires: Ediciones de la Flor, 1983. Pp. 73–101.

Molina, Enrique. [Untitled.] In *Páginas de Olga Orozco seleccionadas por la autora,* by Olga Orozco. Buenos Aires: Celtia, 1984. Pp. 297–299.

Nicholson, Melanie. "Darvantara Solaram, or the Rhetoric of Charm in the Poetry of Olga Orozco." *Letras Femeninas* 24, nos. 1–2:57–67 (spring–fall 1998).

———. "From Sibyl to Witch and Beyond: Feminine Archetype in the Poetry of Olga Orozco." *Chasqui* 27, no. 1:11–22 (May 1998).

———. "Olga Orozco and the Poetics of Gnosticism." *Revista de Estudios Hispánicos* 35, no. 1:73–90 (spring 2001).

Pellarolo, Silvia. "La imagen de la estatua de sal: Síntesis y clave en el pensamiento de Olga Orozco." *Mester* 18, no. 1:41–49 (1989).

Piña, Cristina. "Estudio preliminar." In *Páginas de Olga Orozco seleccionadas por la autora,* by Olga Orozco. Buenos Aires: Celtia, 1984.

Running, Thorpe. "Imagen y creación en la poesía de Olga Orozco." *Letras Femeninas* 13, no. 1–2:12–20 (1987).

Salvador, Nélida. "Olga Orozco." In *Enciclopedia de la literatura argentina.* Edited by Pedro Orgambide and Roberto Yahni. Buenos Aires: Editorial Sudamericana, 1970. Pp. 484–485.

Sefamí, Jacobo. "Olga Orozco." In his *De la imaginación poética: Conversaciones con Gonzalo Rojas, Olga Orozco, Alvaro Mutis y José Kozer.* Caracas: Monte Avila, 1996. Pp. 95–149.

Soler Cañas, Luis. *La generación poética del 40,* vol. 1. Buenos Aires, Ediciones Culturales Argentinas, 1981.

Tacconi, María del Carmen. "Para una lectura simbólica de Olga Orozco." *Sur* 348:115–123 (January–June 1981).

Torres de Peralta, Elba. *La poética de Olga Orozco: Desdoblamiento de Dios en máscara de todos.* Madrid: Playor, 1987. (The first book-length study of Orozco's work; highlights her fundamentally religious approach to poetry.)

Torres Fierro, Danubio. "Olga Orozco: Hacia el verbo primordial." In his *Memoria plural: Entrevistas a escritores latinoamericanos.* Buenos Aires: Editorial Sudamericana, 1986. Pp. 197–202.

# Octavio Paz

## (1914–1998)

---

### Enrico Mario Santí

I n his 1989 *Latin American Writers* article on Octavio Paz, Alberto Ruy-Sánchez offers a fascinating and comprehensive portrait of Paz's social, political, and literary development. This essay addresses the last eleven years of Octavio Paz's life, which saw the crowning of his lifelong career as a poet, diplomat, and an intellectual as well as one of the most prominent and polemical Latin American men of letters. The culminating event of this last period occurred in 1990, when he received the Nobel Prize for literature, the first ever given to a Mexican writer and the fourth to a Latin American author. In the late 1970s and the early 1980s, several compilations of Paz's works were published, notably *Poemas* (1979) and the multivolume *México en la obra de Octavio Paz* (1979 and 1987). Then came the 1988 editorial rescue of his earliest prose works, gathered together under the title *Primeras letras (1931–1943)* (First letters); the second Spanish edition of his complete poetry (1989); the monumental, illustrated edition of a portion of Paz's essays on art, *Los privilegios de la vista,* which appeared in Mexico City in 1990 under the imprint of the Cultural Center of Contemporary Art; and the 1990 Spanish-language video series for Mexico's Televisa network, *Mexico in the Work of Octavio Paz.* A Spanish edition of Paz's *Complete Works* (now calculated to run fifteen volumes) began to appear in 1991. In 1987 Paz completed his last book of verse, *Arbol adentro* (*A Tree Within,* 1988), though he continued to write, publish, and give public recitals until his death. With the best or at least most of his literary production behind him, these were Paz's years of consecration. In addition to the Nobel Prize, he received a number of international awards, more perhaps than any of his contemporaries; by the time he died, no less than twenty-five such accolades and ten honorary degrees had been bestowed upon him.

It was in fact in 1987 that Paz served as honorary president of the International Writers' Congress, which was held that year in Valencia, Spain. The congress was organized by the autonomous government of that Spanish province partly to commemorate the Second International Writers' Congress for the Defense of Culture that had met fifty years earlier in Valencia, Madrid, Barcelona, and Paris. Paz had attended the conference as a young man of twenty-three. "My deeper and more lasting impressions about that summer of 1937," he told his audience, "were born neither from my dealings with writers nor from discussions with my comrades about the literary and political themes that obsessed us. I was moved rather by the encounter with Spain and with its people. To see with my own eyes and touch with my own hands those landscapes, monuments and stones that, since childhood, I had heard about through my readings and my grandparents' tales."

Politics, specifically the role of intellectuals in national and international struggles, was of course very high on that congress's agenda. These were the last years of the Cold War, and the congress was being held amid discussions of a new climate of openness (glasnost) in the then Soviet Union. Paz's public career began in earnest in the early 1970s, his journal *Plural* (later *Vuelta*) serving as a forum for ideas that were as radical in art as they were critical in politics, particularly of one-party states (like Mexico) and authoritarian regimes. *Vuelta* became so prominent a journal that a South American version was launched late in 1988. Partly as a promotional tour, Paz visited Argentina, Uruguay, and Brazil that year. It was his first visit to South America, and it provided the occasion not only for lectures and poetry recitals but for personal meetings with other writers to whom he felt close, among them Jorge Luis Borges and Haroldo de Campos.

With the fall of the Berlin Wall and the consequent global discrediting of socialism, a revindication of Paz's public profile began to take place in the autumn of 1989. It had not yet been five years since he was burned in effigy in the streets of Mexico City for daring to criticize the antidemocratic tendencies of some of the parties in the Central American civil wars. An early sign of change came in June 1989 with the Alexis de Tocqueville Prize that was conferred upon him by the French Socialist President François Mitterrand. Paz responded with *Poesía, mito, revolución* (1989; "Poetry, Myth, Revolution," in *The Other Voice: Essays on Modern Poetry*, 1991): "What can the contribution of poetry be in the creation of a new political theory? Not new ideas, but something more precious and fragile: memory." This speech was the first of several he would deliver during his latter years on the crucial role of poetry in times of moral and political crisis. Also in 1989, separate collective homages in France (city of Aix-en-Provence) and Spain (Iberoamerican Institute in Madrid) were devoted to Paz, followed the next year by a weeklong academic seminar at Spain's El Escorial, the monastery, palace, and mausoleum built by Philip II. In this majestic setting Paz read his essay "La otra voz" (1989; "The Other Voice," in *The Other Voice: Essays on Modern Poetry*, 1991), arguably his clearest statement about the role of poetry in a troubled contemporary world: "Between revolution and religion,

poetry is the *other* voice. Its voice is *other* because it is the voice of the passions and of visions. It is otherwordly and this-worldly, of days long gone and of this very day, an antiquity without dates.... All poets in the moments, long or short, of poetry, if they are really poets, hear the *other* voice."

But by far the meeting that attracted the most attention at the time was the one that Paz and Mexican historian Enrique Krauze, coeditor of *Vuelta*, organized early in the fall of 1990. It was called "The Experience of Freedom," and it gathered in Mexico City over one hundred intellectuals from all over the world, particularly from the formerly Socialist countries. Discussion centered on "The Experience of Freedom" in the wake of the fall of the Berlin Wall, German reunification, and the demise of the Soviet Union. But because all the talks were held behind closed doors and broadcast via cable through Televisa, the Mexican TV network that cosponsored the event, some observers felt that the meeting had compromised free discussion, particularly since a few writers on the Left (notably novelists Carlos Fuentes and Gabriel García Márquez) were not invited. Yet, despite these critiques, the meeting became an unparalleled success, at least in Mexico, and it elevated Paz's stature as an international figure even further.

Many of the arguments that Paz would press at "The Experience of Freedom" had already been formulated in a small volume of essays that he published earlier that same year. *Pequeña crónica de grandes días* (1990; Small chronicle for great days) gathered some of the press articles from the previous year in which Paz had treated both the Berlin Wall crisis and the recent Mexican elections that showed a notable democratic turn. This was his third such book of politics (previously he had published *El ogro filantrópico* and *Tiempo nublado*), but it would certainly not be Paz's last shot at the subject.

That same fall came yet another event with which Paz was directly involved: the opening at New York City's Metropolitan Museum of "Art of Mexico: Splendors of Thirty Centuries," a traveling Mexican exhibition that Paz helped organize and for whose catalog he wrote the introductory essay. In its opening paragraph he remarks: "The Now wants to save itself, turned into stone or drawing, color, sound or word. This, it seems to me, is the theme that this Mexican art show displays before us: the persistence of the same will through an incredible variety of forms, manners and styles."

It was precisely during the week of the New York show's opening that the Swedish Academy announced that Paz was the recipient of the 1990 Nobel Prize for literature "because of his impassioned literary work, characterized by sensual intelligence and human integrity." Paz's Nobel lecture, "In Search of the Present," delivered in Stockholm later that year, returned once again to the theme of poetry's role in a troubled world, including its importance to a troubled self:

Only now have I understood that there was a secret relationship between what I have called my expulsion from the present and the writing of poetry. Poetry, in love with the instant, seeks to relive it in the poem, thus separating it from sequential time and turning it into a fixed present. But at that time I wrote without wondering why I was doing it. I was searching for the gateway to the present: I wanted to belong to my time and to my century. Later this desire became an obsession: I wanted to be a modern poet. My search for modernity had begun.

It is no exaggeration to say that the world, the Spanish-speaking world in particular, welcomed the news of Paz's Nobel Prize. In Mexico the news was overwhelmingly positive, despite malicious rumors to the effect that the prize had been given to Paz as a reward for services to then-President Carlos Salinas de Gortari, a Paz admirer who had been present at the opening of the New York art show. In Madrid numerous papers and journals dedicated special issues to the Mexican author. However, Paz himself saw the award as a mixed blessing: both a consecration and an additional public burden that left him even less time to write. And yet that same year he signed a contract with Barcelona's Círculo de Lectores (Reader's Club) to gather his complete works in fourteen volumes. Prior to his death, Paz reordered his works for this edition—which in 2001 was still being completed posthumously and reprinted by Mexico's Fondo de Cultura Económica—and penned a preface for each volume.

Thus, on the verge of his eightieth birthday Octavio Paz was busier than ever. Those of us who knew him personally then wondered how he ever had the energy to do so much, so well, and so quickly. Perhaps the most significant book he published immediately after receiving the Nobel Prize was *Itinerario* (1993; *Itinerary: An Intellectual Journey*, 1999), a volume of five essays (two of them long interviews) in which he addressed his own lifelong political trajectory or "itinerary."

Beginning in the late 1960s, Paz participated actively in Mexico's public life. He repeatedly turned down offers to run for office against the PRI or ruling party, of which he was a vocal critic. Paz even went so far as to toy with the idea of founding a new political party. But he preferred to voice his views independently and in writing, and as he himself often warned, "to keep my distance from the Prince." In *Itinerary*, Paz discusses the sense of alienation that always made him feel like a stranger or "pilgrim" in his own country. He identifies these feelings as the moral origin of his need to write about Mexican history and politics. At first the reasons were personal: as the child of a fair-haired Spanish woman he was mocked by other Mexican children for having blue eyes; later, he was scorned because of the apparent conflict between his poetry and his politics: "I felt that true literature, whatever its themes might be, was subversive by nature. My opinions were scandalous but, because I was so insignificant, they were largely ignored: they came from a nobody."

*Itinerary* also traces Paz's political evolution from a fanatical revolutionary to a skeptical liberal (with a good measure of surrealist moral faith, for which he was better known). It is also in this book (or rather, in his interview with journalist Julio Scherer, in its last section) that he outlines the political philosophy that he propounded to his death: the ideal intersection between liberal and Socialist political principles. This new philosophy, Paz argued further, "must also be conscious of the visions of man and woman held by the great poets, like the Greek tragedians[,] Dante, Shakespeare, Cervantes, and all modern poets. Man is a being made of passions and desires; he has a thirst for the infinite and he envies his neighbor. A new ethics and a new politics must be based on a real reality, not on abstractions."

It was in 1993, also, that Paz gave the first of several monumental poetry recitals in New York City, where he was joined at the Cathedral of St. John the Divine by fellow poets Joseph Brodsky, Derek Walcott, and Rita

Dove, along with an audience of more than three thousand. This record was topped the following year in yet another New York recital (this time at the Metropolitan Museum of Art), where, as part of the celebrations for his eightieth birthday, Paz and his English translator Eliot Weinberger were joined by poets Mark Strand, John Ashbery, Richard Howard, and Bei Dao. Similar recitals would be held the following years in New York City, Chicago, and Washington, D.C., and in 1996 in Miami Beach. Paz not only enjoyed reading his poetry in public but was very good at it. With a sense of true musicality and devoid of the flairs of drama or histrionics for which other poets are known, he was able to convey true emotion and, often, good humor.

Paz's eightieth birthday saw several celebrations both at home in Mexico and abroad. One of the first was the opening of an opera by Daniel Catán based on *Rappaccini's Daughter,* Paz's single play. Yet another was a commemorative reprint of *Blanco,* Paz's most ambitious poem, in its original long-strip format, along with a companion volume that gathered essays by various authors, correspondence with translators, and a facsimile edition of the poem's drafts. Yet the best birthday gift Paz gave himself: the publication of a book on love which he had been promising himself for the previous thirty years. Love, and particularly sexual love, is of course one of the most recurring and powerful themes in both Paz's prose and his poetry. *La llama doble* (1993; *The Double Flame: Love and Eroticism,* 1995) can be read as the discursive version of *Carta de creencia* (Letter of testimony), the long poem on the subject of love that appeared at the end of *A Tree Within.* As the lines "Words are uncertain / and they say uncertain things" had been the poem's thesis, so Paz set out in this prose book to restrict that uncertainty by analyzing concepts as slippery as love, eroticism, and sex.

As in *The Labyrinth of Solitude,* Paz's *Double Flame* is divided into nine chapters: two introductions, three on the history of love as represented in culture and particularly in literature, three more on its manifestations in the modern world (more often its crisis or absence), and a conclusion. Writing in the wake of the French novelist Stendhal (Marie-Henri Beyle), the Spanish philosopher and writer José Ortega y Gasset, and the French author Georges Bataille, Paz took a radically different approach. One of his aims was to address the demise of love in today's world as shown in its multiple crises, like the AIDS epidemic: "A vaccine for AIDS will be found someday, but if a new erotic ethics does not come into being, our lack of defense before nature and its immense powers of destruction will continue."

In *The Double Flame,* Paz explains that love, as opposed to sex or eroticism, has five components: (1) it is exclusive, (2) it results as much from the lovers' transgression as from (3) domination and submission, (4) "love is involuntary attraction towards a person and the voluntary acceptance of that attraction," that is, it shows the tension between fatality and freedom, and (5) love consists of "the indissoluble union of two contraries, the body and the soul." Sex, pure reproductive instinct, on the other hand, is not love, strictly speaking, though love does end up being sexual because "without physical attraction there can be no love." Eroticism, finally, "deviates or changes the sexual impulse and transforms it into pure representation," and it varies according to culture and individual taste. In short: "There can be no love without eroticism as there can be no eroticism without sex."

But perhaps the book's greatest contribution lies in its restatement of the relationship between love and ethics:

> The concept of person joins the concept of freedom since upon acknowledging the Other's freedom we acknowledge his singularity and his capacity to choose. To reconstruct our concept of person means, in turn, to become conscious of yet another concept, more metaphysical but at the same time more central, at least in the West: the concept of the soul, what in ancient theology marked individual singularity. Love is an attraction towards a unique person, a body and a soul.

For this reason, Paz argues, love presupposes respect toward the loved person, as sustained by a consciousness of the soul. And yet, modern ideologies are at fault for creating obstacles toward the fulfillment of the promise of love. "The crime of modern revolutionaries," Paz remarks, "has been to cut off the affective element from the revolutionary spirit. And the great moral and spiritual misery of liberal democracies has been its affective insensitivity. Money has confiscated eroticism because, earlier, souls and hearts had dried up."

Perhaps the least expected of Paz's contributions is the dialogue with science, and particularly cosmology, that appears at the end of *The Double Flame*. Analyzing several books by contemporary scientists (Alan Lightman and Roberta Brower, Francis Crick, and Gerald Edelman), Paz finds that "the questions that philosophy had stopped asking during the last two centuries—the questions about origin and finality are the ones that really count." Paz also notes, however, that in searching for a logical answer to such questions, science has ended up adopting dehumanizing models. "The analogy between the mind and the machine is but an analogy, useful perhaps from the point of view of science but which cannot be interpreted literally without the risk of terrible abuse."

In 1995, on the heels of *The Double Flame*, Paz published his last book of prose: *Vislumbres de la India* (1995; *In Light of India*, 1997). It is, at once, a memoir of his years living in India (during two separate periods: in 1952, for six months; and between 1962 and 1968) and an essay on the complexity of Indian civilization and history. Thus he remarks at the beginning of the book's second section, tracing the subject of the subcontinent's diversity:

> The first thing that surprised me about India, as it has surprised so many others, was the diversity created by extreme contrast: modernity and antiquity, luxury and poverty, sensuality and asceticism, carelessness and efficiency, gentleness and violence; a multiplicity of castes and languages, gods and rites, customs and ideas, rivers and deserts, plains and mountain, cities and villages, rural and industrial life, centuries apart in time and neighbors in space. But the most remarkable aspect of India, and the one that defines it, is neither political nor economic, but religious: the coexistence of Hinduism and Islam.

The book is divided into four sections: "The Antipodes of Coming and Going," a personal memoir; "Religion, Castes, Languages," on Indian history; "A Project of Nationhood," on Indian politics; and "The Full and the Empty," on Indian religion. It is one of Paz's most dazzling meditations in terms of breadth and depth.

The year 1995 was also the year when Paz's health began to decline. Problems began when he went through open heart surgery, which despite its success weakened him. Still, the following year he not only published a

new volume of translations of Indian poetry (*Kavya: 25 epigramas*, 1996) but also traveled both to Miami, where he participated in a recital with two other Nobel laureates (Czeslaw Milosz and Derek Walcott), and to Spain. It was in Madrid that summer, where Paz was invited to lecture on the Spanish poet Francisco de Quevedo, that he first read his last long poem, "Respuesta y reconciliación" (Response and reconciliation). As a young man, Paz had been an admirer of Quevedo's poetry, and modeled many of his own neo baroque sonnets after those of the seventeenth-century poet. In his lecture Paz traced what was in fact a lifelong admiration and punctuated his memoir with samples of his own poetry that over the years showed his dialogue with Quevedo. About the new long poem he remarked the following:

> I wrote it in December 1995 and I have revised it over and over during the last few months. It is divided into three parts. In the first I underscore the essential muteness of life and nature: we are the ones who speak on their behalf. In the second part, Time, cradle and grave of stars and man, makes its appearance. In the third part, I notice that within universal movement, even if a certain fate or finality should become visible, there is in fact a certain coherence or implicit rationality. Many scientists feel the same way. Through those windows that mathematics and the sciences, but also poetry, music and the arts, we can at times discover a universal reason: Time's other face. My poem is a response to a very ancient question and a reconciliation with our earthly fate.

Whatever physical weakness or deathly premonition the poet may have felt by then, it was compounded at the end of the year when a mysterious fire broke out in Paz and his wife's apartment in Mexico City. While the couple managed to escape safely, many precious antique books and art works were lost. (Mexican police determined that the fire had been caused by a short circuit in a TV set.) Because of the extensive damage to their apartment, Paz and his wife were forced to move to a Mexico City hotel, and although repair crews began work on restoring their place almost immediately, other health problems began to catch up with Paz. He would never return to live in that apartment. Indeed, while living in his temporary quarters he was stricken with intense pains that were diagnosed all too late as inoperable kidney cancer. Throughout 1997, even while battling the cancer, Paz lived to see the establishment of both an Octavio Paz Chair at the Autonomous University of Mexico and the Octavio Paz Foundation, a cultural institution financed with a mixture of government sponsorship and private endowment. Two testimonies of his lasting legacy became evident during his last month of life, when a volume gathering his correspondence with Mexican writer Alfonso Reyes appeared and a bibliography of his work (listing over seven thousand items) was published.

Paz died in Mexico City on 19 April 1998, barely three weeks after his eighty-fourth birthday. His body lay in state at Mexico's Palace of Fine Arts and the funeral was presided over by the president of Mexico, Ernesto Zedillo.

## SELECTED BIBLIOGRAPHY

### Primary Works Since 1986

#### Poetry

*Transblanco: Em torno a Blanco de Octavio Paz.* Edited by Haroldo de Campos. Rio de Janeiro: Editora Guanabara, 1986.

*Lo mejor de Octavio Paz: El fuego de cada día.* Selected with notes and prologue by Paz. Barcelona: Seix Barral, 1989.

*La llama doble: Amor y erotismo.* Barcelona: Seix Barral, 1993.

*Blanco/Archivo Blanco.* Edited by Enrico Mario Santí. Mexico City: Ediciones del Equilibrista, 1994.

*Delta de cinco brazos.* Barcelona: Galaxia Gutenberg, 1994.

*Reflejos, réplicas: Diálogos con Francisco de Quevedo.* Madrid: Ediciones La Palma, 1996.

*Figuras y figuraciones.* Illustrated by Marie-José Paz. Barcelona: Galaxia Gutenberg, 2000.

#### Prose

*Primeras letras (1931–1943).* Edited by Enrico Mario Santí. Barcelona: Seix Barral, 1988.

*Poesía, mito, revolución.* Mexico City: Editorial Vuelta, 1989.

*La otra voz: Poesía y fin de siglo.* Barcelona: Seix Barral, 1990.

*Pequeña crónica de grandes días.* Mexico City: Fondo de Cultura Económica, 1990.

*Convergencias.* Barcelona: Seix Barral, 1991.

*Al paso.* Barcelona: Seix Barral, 1992.

*Itinerario.* Mexico City: Fondo de Cultura Económica, 1993.

*Un más allá erótico: Sade.* Mexico City: Editorial Vuelta, 1994.

*Estrella de tres puntas: André Breton.* Mexico City: Editorial Vuelta, 1995.

*Vislumbres de la India.* Barcelona: Seix Barral, 1995.

*Correspondencia Alfonso Reyes/Octavio Paz (1939–1959).* Edited by Anthony Stanton. Mexico City: Fonda de Cultura Económica, 1998.

*Memorias y palabras: Cartas a Pere Gimferrer, 1966–1997.* Barcelona: Seix Barral, 1999.

### Translations by Paz

*Nineteen Ways of Looking at Wang Wei: How a Chinese Poem Is Translated.* With Eliot Weinberger. Mt. Kisco, N.Y.: Moyer Bell, 1987.

*Kavya: 25 epigramas.* Barcelona: Círculo de Lectores, 1996.

*Trazos. Chuang-Tzu y otros.* Mexico City: Ediciones del Equilibrista, 1997.

*Versiones y diversiones.* Barcelona: Galaxia Gutenberg, 2000.

### Collections

*The Collected Poems of Octavio Paz: 1957–1987.* Edited and trans. by Eliot Weinberger, with additional translations by Elizabeth Bishop and others. New York: New Directions, 1987.

*Obra poética: 1935–1988.* Barcelona: Seix Barral, 1990.

*Obras completas de Octavio Paz. Edición del autor.* Barcelona: Círculo de Lectores / Mexico City: Fondo de Cultura Económica, 1994– . 15 volumes.

*Los privilegios de la vista.* Mexico City: Centro Cultural de Arte Contemporáneo, 1990.

### Translations

*In the Middle of This Phrase and Other Poems.* Trans. by Eliot Weinberger. Helsinki: Eurographica, 1987.

*A Tree Within.* Trans. by Eliot Weinberger. New York: New Directions, 1988. (Translation of *Arbol adentro.*)

*In Search of the Present: Nobel Lecture, 1990.* Trans. by Anthony Stanton. San Diego, Calif.: Harcourt Brace Jovanovich, 1990.

*The Other Voice: Essays on Modern Poetry.* Trans. by Helen Lane. New York: Harcourt Brace Jovanovich, 1991. (Includes *Poetry, Myth, Revolution,* and a translation of *Poesía, mito, revolución.*)

*Sunstone.* Trans. by Eliot Weinberger. New York: New Directions, 1991. (Translation of *Piedra de sol.*)

*One Word to the Other.* Edited by Juan Hernández Asenter. Trans. by Amelia Simpson. Preface by J. Ortega. Mansfield, Tex.: Latitudes, 1992.

*Essays on Mexican Art.* Trans. by Helen Lane. New York: Harcourt Brace, 1993.

*Nostalgia for Death and Hieroglyphs of Desire.* Edited by Eliot Weinberger. Trans. by Weinberger and Esther Allen. Port Townsend, Wash.: Copper Canyon Press, 1993. (*Nostalgia for Death,* a collection of poetry by Xavier Villaurrutia, was originally published in Spanish as *Nostalgia de la muerte.* Paz's *Hieroglyphs of Desire* is a critical study of Villaurrutia.)

*The Double Flame: Love and Eroticism.* Trans. by Helen Lane. New York: Harcourt Brace, 1995.

*In Light of India.* Trans. by Eliot Weinberger. New York: Harcourt Brace, 1997.

*A Tale of Two Gardens: Poems from India, 1952–1995.* Edited and trans. by Eliot Weinberger, with additional translations by Elizabeth Bishop and others. New York: New Directions, 1997.

*Sade: An Erotic Beyond.* Trans. by Eliot Weinberger. New York: Harcourt Brace, 1998.

*Itinerary: An Intellectual Journey.* Trans. by Jason Wilson. New York: Harcourt, 1999.

## Secondary Works

### Critical and Biographical Studies

González, Javier. *El cuerpo y la letra: La cosmología poética de Octavio Paz.* Mexico City: Fondo de Cultura Económica, 1990.

Hozven, Roberto. *Octavio Paz: Viajero del presente.* Mexico City: Colegio Nacional, 1994.

Kim, Kwon Tae Jung. *El elemento oriental en la poesía de Octavio Paz.* Guadalajara: Editorial Universidad de Guadalajara, 1989.

"Leyendo a Paz." *Revista Canadiense de Estudios Hispánicos* 16, no. 3 (1992).

Littman, Robert, ed. *Octavio Paz: Los privilegios de la vista.* Mexico City: El Centro, 1990.

Mendiola, Víctor Manuel, ed. *Festejo: 80 años de Octavio Paz.* Mexico City: Ediciones El Tucán de Virginia, 1994.

*México en la obra de Octavio Paz.* 12 programs, 6 videotapes. Mexico City: Televisa, 1990.

Murillo Gonzalez, Margarita. *Polaridad-unidad: Caminos hacia Octavio Paz.* Mexico City: UNAM, 1987.

Poniatowska, Elena. *Octavio Paz: Las palabras del árbol.* Mexico City: Plaza y Janés, 1998.

Quiroga, José. *Understanding Octavio Paz.* Columbia, S.C.: University of South Carolina Press, 1999.

Rodríguez Ledesma, Xavier. *El pensamiento político de Octavio Paz: Las trampas de la ideología.* Mexico City: Plaza y Valdés Editores, 1996.

Ruy-Sánchez, Alberto. *Una introducción a Octavio Paz.* Mexico City: Editorial Joaquín Mortiz, 1990.

Santí, Enrico Mario. *El acto de las palabras: Estudios y diálogos con Octavio Paz.* Mexico City: Fondo de Cultura Económica, 1997.

Schärer-Nussberger, Maya. *Octavio Paz: Trayectorias y visiones.* Mexico City: Fondo de Cultura Económica, 1989.

*Siglo XX/20th Century: Critique and Cultural Discourse.* Special ed. Djelal Kadir. Vol. 10, nos.1–2 (1992).

*Travesías: Tres lecturas. Antología del autor.* Barcelona: Galaxia Gutenberg, 1996. (Cassette recording.)

Ulacia, Manuel. *El árbol milenario. Un recorrido por la obra de Octavio Paz.* Barcelona: Círculo de Lectores, 1999.

Underwood, Leticia Iliana. *Octavio Paz and the Language of Poetry: A Psycholinguistic Approach.* New York: Peter Lang, 1992.

Verani, Hugo J., ed. *Bibliografía crítica de Octavio Paz: 1931–1996.* Mexico City: Colegio Nacional, 1997. (Bibliography.)

Vizcaíno, Fernando. *Biografía política de Octavio Paz; o, La razón ardiente.* Málaga, Spain: Editorial Algazara, 1993.

### Interviews

*Pasión crítica.* Edited by Hugo J. Verani. Barcelona: Seix Barral, 1985.

*El poeta en su tierra. Diálogos con Octavio Paz.* Edited by Braulio Peralta. Mexico City: Editorial Grijalbo, 1996.

*Solo a dos voces.* Mexico City: Fonda Cultura Económica, 1999.

# Ricardo Piglia

## (1940–    )

## Daniel Balderston

One of Argentina's two most important living novelists (Juan José Saer is the other), Ricardo Piglia has seen his reputation grow steadily since the publication of his first book of stories, *La invasión* (The invasion), in 1967. *Nombre falso* (1975; *Assumed Name*, 1995), consisting of two parts, the novella *Homenaje a Roberto Arlt* and a story included as an appendix to it titled "Luba," and the novels *Respiración artificial* (1980, *Artifical Respiration*, 1994), *La ciudad ausente* (1992; *The Absent City*, 2000), and *Plata quemada* (1997; Burnt money) occupy central places in the Argentine narrative of the last twenty-five years of the twentieth century. Piglia also is known for his brilliant essays and lectures and for his film scripts and adaptations. To complete the picture, he has been an important editor of crime fiction in Argentina, bringing the "hard-boiled" tradition and its successors to the Argentine public. Piglia's work in various media (including the critical essay) can be characterized as an exploration of the possibilities of narrative, with an emphasis on chance, mystery, and ambiguity.

In a brief essay in *Formas breves* (1999; Short forms) titled "Tesis sobre el cuento" (Theses on the short story), Piglia argues:

*El cuento es un relato que encierra un relato secreto. No se trata de un sentido oculto que depende de la interpretación: el enigma no es otra cosa que una historia que se cuenta de un modo enigmático. La estrategia del relato está puesta al servicio de esa narración cifrada. ¿Cómo contar una historia mientras se está contando otra? Esa pregunta sintetiza los problemas técnicos del cuento.*

A short story is a tale that hides another secret story inside it. That is not because there is a hidden meaning that depends on interpretation: the enigma is nothing other than a story that is told in an enigmatic way. The strategy of the story hinges on that hidden narration. How to tell one story while another is being told? That question is a synthesis of the technical problems of the short story.

Piglia's views in this essay, which was originally published in the Buenos Aires newspaper *Clarín* (the largest daily newspaper in Argentina) in 1986, subsequently were extended in "Nuevas tesis sobre el cuento" (New theses on the short story), also included in *Formas breves*. It provides in a nutshell the essence of Piglia's approach to narrative; as we shall see, his reflections on these problems have illuminated his creative and critical works since the mid-1960s.

Piglia was born in Adrogué, in the province of Buenos Aires, on 24 November 1940. He came from a lower-middle class background, and his parents (Pedro Piglia, an insurance agent, and Aída Maggiori) were ardent Peronists (followers of Juan Domingo Péron, Argentina's president from 1946 to 1955 and from 1973 until his death the following year). Adrogué in the 1950s was a fading suburb of *quintas* (country houses) and vacation hotels, which had been favored by middle-class intellectuals of Buenos Aires, including the family of Jorge Luis Borges, in previous decades. In fact, it is the setting of Borges's story "La muerte y la brújula" (1942), in which the house Triste-le-Roy is based on Hotel Las Delicias, where Borges and others vacationed. It is also the setting of important films of the 1950s and 1960s, such as Argentine filmmaker Torre Nilsson's 1960 release *La mano en la trampa*. If Borges, who was at heart an urban writer born in the center of Buenos Aires, was interested in the edges of the city and wrote often of the suburbs and their inhabitants, Piglia, coming from one of those suburbs, looks toward the city center for the fundamental space of his fiction.

When Piglia was an adolescent, his family moved to Mar del Plata, which by then had evolved (thanks to Perón and the government policies of paid vacations and of union-owned vacation hotels and sports facilities) from an elite watering hotel on the Atlantic coast to the Argentine resort for the masses. (Many of the elites moved their own vacation houses to Punta del Este in Uruguay.) Mar del Plata's year was marked by an invasion of Buenos Aires tourists in the summer months and by a windy climate and rather empty atmosphere the rest of the year. In Piglia's semi-auto-biographical text "En otro país" (In another country), from in *Prisión perpetua* (1988; Life imprisonment), the discovery of his vocation as a writer came shortly after the 1955 overthrow of Perón, which greatly affected Piglia's family and other devoted Peronist families. In that text, however, his calling is attributed to an encounter between the young Piglia and an imaginary displaced New York writer named Steve Ratliff, after a character created by William Faulkner. In subsequent work, most notably in *Artificial Respiration*, Piglia was haunted by the figure of the failed writer, a writer whose projects and fantasies seem to matter more than the published work. For Piglia, the two great failed writers of Argentina—Macedonio Fernández (1874–1951) and Roberto Arlt (1900–1942)—interest him precisely for their unfinished projects. Among

these were Arlt's wild inventions (such as his 1929 novel *Los siete locos*) and Macedonio's novel composed mostly of prologues, *Museo de la novela de la Eterna*, which seem to embody the chaotic possibilities of the literary imagination, its struggle against limits and order, and its strivings toward an ideal absolute.

After studying history at the Universidad Nacional de La Plata, in the new planned city that was created in the late nineteenth century as capital of the province of Buenos Aires when the city of Buenos Aires became the federal capital, Piglia moved to Buenos Aires, where he became involved in various small leftist groups and literary magazines, most notably *Los libros* (from 1969 to 1974) and *Punto de vista* (from 1977 to 1983), and also worked for several publishers. His political and literary evolution brought him close to the testimonial novelist Rodolfo Walsh (who was kidnapped and killed in 1977 during the military dictatorship that led to the "disappearance" of some thirty thousand people), with whom he traveled to Cuba in 1967–1968. Piglia's activity in several small Maoist groups took him to China for three months in 1973. The leaders of one of those groups, to whom *Artificial Respiration* was dedicated—"A Elías y a Rubén que me ayudaron a conocer la verdad de la historia" (To Elías and Rubén, who helped me to know the truth of history)—would also number among the "disappeared." The importance of this political history cannot be overstated, though it is significant that Piglia's work turns on a political history that is implicit rather than explicit, making him a rather different kind of writer than many of the social realists who were important in the 1960s literary scene in Buenos Aires.

Piglia's first book of short fiction appeared in Cuba under the title *Jaulario* and in Argentina as *La invasión*. It consists of ten stories, ordered differently in the two editions. The best known of these is "Las actas del juicio" (The trial records), about the death of the nineteenth-century Argentine strongman and political figure Justo José de Urquiza (1801–1870), narrated by Urquiza's assassin (a former comrade-in-arms). This text brilliantly recreates the disillusionment that Urquiza's followers felt as his career evolved from the leader of the crusade against the dictator Juan Manuel de Rosas to petty tyrant. It suggests already that Piglia's take on historical fiction would focus more on collective hopes and individual failures than on the circumstantial details of the historical epoch being recreated (a tendency developed later in *Artificial Respiration*).

Stories of particular interest in *La invasión* include "Tarde de amor" (Evening of love), a story of homoerotic attraction and homosocial violence, and "La invasión," the first story in which Piglia's alter ego and sometimes narrator Emilio Renzi appears. This title story tells of Renzi's "invasion" of a prison cell where two prisoners have established a sexual relationship—when he is involuntarily placed in the same cell. Other stories relate different kinds of marginality. "La pared" (The wall) is a story of madness and isolation in a home for the elderly; "Una luz que se iba" (Dying light) tells of the rejection that the migrants—the "cabecitas negras" (the name of a migratory bird with a black head, used as a derogative term for mestizo immigrants to Buenos Aires from northern Argentina)—felt in Buenos Aires after the fall of Perón; and "Mata Hari 55" describes betrayals within the Peronist movement after the "Revolución Libertadora" of 1955.

In the prefatory note to "Mata Hari 55" Piglia writes:

*La mayor incomodidad de esta historia es ser cierta. Se equivocan los que piensan que es más fácil contar hechos verídicos que inventar una anécdota, sus relaciones y sus leyes. La realidad, es sabido, tiene una lógica esquiva; una lógica que parece, a ratos, imposible de narrar.*

The most uncomfortable thing about this story is that it is true. Those who think that it is easier to tell true stories than to make up an anecdote with all of its inner relationships and laws are wrong. Reality, we know, has a slant logic, a logic that seems, at times, impossible to narrate.

In this note, as later in "Tesis sobre el cuento," Piglia establishes a powerful but complex relationship between fiction and reality. The finest story of *La invasión*, "Las actas del juicio" (the story about the assassination of Urquiza), works out of the hallucinatory sense that history, although it seems a nightmare from which the subjects would like to wake up, remains a hallucination that is all-absorbing.

*La invasión* was followed by *Assumed Name*. This collection consists of five stories (one of which is a reprinting of "Las actas del juicio" from the previous

volume) and a famous novella, *Homenaje a Roberto Arlt* (Homage to Robert Arlt; so named in the first edition, though sometimes subsequently entitled *Nombre falso*, like the volume in which it appeared). The timing of the publication in 1975, in the chaotic period just before the military coup of March 1976 in Argentina, is recalled as singularly inauspicious at the beginning of *Artificial Respiration*.

In "El fin del viaje" (The end of the trip), the first story from *Assumed Name*, Emilio Renzi travels by bus to Mar del Plata after being told of his father's death. In the bus he encounters a strange woman who tells stories that Renzi gradually realizes are lies. "El Laucha Benítez" is the story of two boxers, Laucha Benítez and el Vikingo (the Viking), and of the violence and erotic attraction that are mixed in their relationship. Reminiscent of the great novella *Jacob y el otro* (1961) by the Uruguayan writer Juan Carlos Onetti, this story of Piglia's again underlines the importance of the homoerotic in the constitution of masculinity (an idea developed much later in *Plata quemada*).

*Homenaje a Roberto Arlt* represents a new direction in Piglia's fiction, explicitly mixing fictional narrative with literary criticism, somewhat in the way that Borges had done years earlier, but with a still greater attention to the reconstruction of a precise literary career and milieu. Concerned with the last year in the life of Roberto Arlt, the author of important fiction like *El juguete rabioso* (1926), *Los siete locos* (1929), and *Los lanzallamas* (1931) and of hundreds of journalistic pieces known as the "Aguafuertes porteñas," or Buenos Aires sketches, it is the tale of the narrator's attempt to locate and then to publish a lost original of Arlt's. The narrator here is not Emilio Renzi, but Piglia himself. In the novella Piglia is contacted by a friend of Arlt's, Saúl Kostia (a real person, mentioned in Onetti's memoir of Arlt), who tells him of an unpublished manuscript of Arlt's, "Luba," which corresponds to various notes of Arlt's that Piglia has been studying. Eventually Piglia buys the manuscript and is readying it for publication when Kostia publishes it—under his own name. This text is followed by that of "Luba," a story of a Buenos Aires prostitute and her world.

For many years critics did not know what to do with "Luba," with some (including Arlt's daughter, Mirta, who tried to collect royalties) thinking that it was indeed an Arlt original and others thinking that it was a brilliant imitation of Arlt by Piglia. It has been confirmed that neither hypothesis was correct: the text is actually an adaptation of a story by the Russian writer Leonid Andreev, whose Spanish title, "Las tinieblas," is mentioned a couple of times in *Homenaje a Roberto Arlt*. Indeed, a rereading today, in the knowledge that "Luba" was adapted by Piglia from Andreev, one of Arlt's literary models, rather than from Arlt himself, cannot but focus on the interesting use Piglia makes of the French journalist and socialist Pierre-Joseph Proudhon's phrase "property is theft" and of Borges' insights into the relations between literary creation and plagiarism. In one of the footnotes toward the end of *Homenaje a Roberto Arlt*, Piglia states that "Un crítico literario es siempre, de algún modo, un detective" (A literary critic is always, in some sense, a detective). This insight is crucial to Piglia's recasting of some of the conventions of crime fiction, which was anticipated by Borges in the 1940s but is developed in a masterly way here.

Unlike many writers of his generation and political leanings, Piglia spent much of the period of the military dictatorship (the "Proceso," or the Process of National Reorganization) in Buenos Aires, where he was lucky enough to survive, although on at least one occasion he narrowly escaped being detained. Not choosing exile would mark his subsequent writing, giving it an inward-looking, tormented quality. At the same time, though, he has stated in interviews that during the years of the Proceso he felt an estrangement from the city where he lived that was not unlike exile. *Artificial Respiration*, started before the Proceso but completed during it, expresses a constant sense of foreboding, of clear and present danger. It is a novel that takes great risks, not unlike those taken by its author in those years.

*Artificial Respiration* in many ways develops from *Homenaje a Roberto Arlt*. A brilliant synthesis of historical fiction, critical essay, crime fiction, and political writing, it stands as the central text of the literature written within the boundaries of Argentina during the military dictatorship of 1976 to 1983. (There is, of course, also an important body of exile literature, with which Piglia's novel provides an interesting dialogue.)

*Artificial Respiration*, like *Homenaje a Roberto Arlt*, also is haunted by the odd couple of Roberto Arlt and Jorge Luis Borges, as well as by some other odd couples (Adolf Hitler and Franz Kafka, Hitler and René Descartes, the Polish writer Witold Gombrowicz and Borges, to name a few). The novel begins with the publication (in April 1976, weeks after the military coup) of a novel by Emilio Renzi based on the life of an uncle, Marcelo Maggi, who vanished years earlier in a scandal that rocked the family. The novel reaches the uncle, who is living in Concordia, up the Paraná River toward Paraguay. The uncle and the nephew begin an exchange of letters that takes up most of the first half of the book. Also revealed is a series of documents relating to a project of historical research that Maggi is working on about an imaginary figure from nineteenth-century Argentine history, Enrique Ossorio. Ossorio, according to Maggi, was at work on a Utopian novel called *1979* at the time of his suicide in 1850. The fragments of the novel that are quoted are letters that very pointedly refer to the Argentine experience of the mid-1970s: torture, exile, and disappearance. When Renzi travels to Concordia to meet his uncle, the papers eventually are turned over to him by one of the uncle's friends. While awaiting Maggi's arrival, these two men engage in an astonishing all-night conversation about the relationship between reality and fiction, Argentina and Europe, history and philosophy. The uncle himself never appears; though it is never stated directly, he has become one of the "disappeared."

One of the Maggi's friends with whom Renzi has the all-night conversation is a Polish exile, Tardewski, loosely modeled on the Polish novelist Gombrowicz, who spent a quarter of a century in Argentina after landing there by chance in 1939. Tardewski has many interesting things to say about the relationship between Argentine to European culture. Another of Renzi's interlocutors that night, a local writer named Marconi, argues with Renzi about Borges and Arlt. In this section of the novel, Piglia clearly is using the two characters to debate the shape and values of the Argentine national literary tradition. The endless dialogue stands in, then, for polemical essays that Piglia sketches out here, and later develops in some of the interviews in *Crítica y ficción* (1986; expanded ed., 2000; Criticism and fiction) but never writes fully in essay form.

After the publication of *Artificial Respiration*—a difficult act to follow—a period of relative silence followed. Piglia's next book, *Prisión perpetua,* was a collection of short fiction and other prose, much of it republished. Essentially a new edition of *Assumed Name, Prisión perpetua* includes two new stories: one about an invented North American friend Piglia had in Mar del Plata, Steve Ratliff (based, as stated earlier, on a character from Faulkner), the other about the adventures of Friedrich Nietzsche's sister in South America.

Piglia's next major work, *The Absent City,* is a futurist fantasy based on certain aspects of the life and works of Macedonio Fernández. The story revolves around an imaginary museum in which the body of Fernández's wife, Elena de Obieta, has been preserved and turned into a speaking machine. An apocalyptic novel, it depicts Buenos Aires as a nightmare of ruins and ghosts. The protagonist of the novel, Junior, is a reporter and detective, and the intrigues he discovers by those who would destroy Fernández's speaking machine lead him into the future but also into the recent past: the speaking machine sees scenes of torture, disappearance, and madness. Part of the novel concerns James Joyce's tormented daughter Lucia, whose circular madness in the novel concerns the endless river of Joyce's *Finnegans Wake* (1939); other parts focus on Fernández's *Museo de la novela de la eterna,* an unfinished project that consists mostly of dozens of prologues.

One of the wonderful moments in *The Absent City* is the presence of Lazlo Malamüd, the Hungarian translator of the Argentine poet José Hernández's *El gaucho Martín Fierro,* who speaks a form of Spanish that consists almost entirely of lines from Hernández's great poem (1872; 1879). Those who remember him say: "Contar con palabras perdidas la historia de todos, narrar en una lengua extranjera" (He is telling in lost words the story of everyone, narrating in a foreign language). This is a perfect metaphor of Fernández's infernal machine, the central image of the novel, and, by extension, the quintessence of Argentine culture.

*The Absent City* was turned into an opera, *La ciudad ausente,* by the Argentine composer Gerardo Gandini, with a libretto by Piglia. It premiered at the Teatro Colón in Buenos Aires in 1995. The opera somewhat simplifies the structure of the book, turning the stories told by the speaking machine into a series of mini-operas. In 2000 there was also a brilliant adaptation of the novel as a comic book by Luis Scafati and Pablo de Sanctis.

Piglia's 1997 novel, *Plata quemada,* won that year's Premio Planeta, an award given by the Editorial Planeta for the best unpublished novel in Spanish. Piglia's receipt of the award gave rise to some controversy; apparently, the rules of the competition may have been side-stepped by the publisher, or perhaps by Piglia himself, which was regarded as damaging to his reputation for ethical behavior. In the note, Piglia (or Renzi) says that a first version of the novel was abandoned in 1970. That he took it up again after *Artificial Respiration, Assumed Name,* and *The Absent City* is testimony to his abiding interest in crime fiction and in true crime novels from Truman Capote to Rodolfo Walsh. It also testifies to a desire for a drastic change in register in his fiction after the three intensely bookish novels just mentioned. Many readers were surprised by the change in tone, in difficulty, in theme; *Plata quemada* is radically different from the novels that preceded it in publication, but connects thematically with earlier works, such as "Tarde de amor" and "La invasión."

The novel derives from a real-life crime story, a 1965 bank robbery in Buenos Aires that ended with some of the robbers fleeing to Montevideo, where they faced a bloody shoot-out. Narrated by Emilio Renzi, *Plata quemada* is based (according to the novel's epilogue) on press reports, interviews, and a chance conversation held on a Bolivia-bound train in 1966 with the girlfriend of one of the robbers. Tense and quick in pace, *Plata quemada* is also a novel of narrative experimentation, featuring subtle changes in point of view as the story unfolds.

Central to *Plata quemada* is the excruciatingly long showdown scene, which includes the burning of some of the stolen money and the tossing of it out into the street. The most intense moment of the shoot-out is the death of el Nene, one of the robbers, who bleeds to death in the arms of his lover, el Gaucho Rubio. The homoerotic charge of this scene grows out of the story of the lovers (told in the fourth chapter). It is one of the book's surprises that the hard-boiled world of the true crime novel yields to a scene of ravishing tenderness. The motion picture version of *Plata quemada,* directed by Marcelo Piñeyro with a script by Marcelo Figueras, was released in 2000, and the film script and other materials were published in the same year. The film emphasizes the homoerotic elements of the violent saga; it has had considerable popular success in Argentina and has been shown widely at film festivals around the world.

Piglia's treatment of masculinity is an issue of great interest in much of his work. Though distant from the radical critiques of machismo that one can find in the writings of Piglia's compatriots Manuel Puig and Néstor Perlongher, his work is haunted by a tense homosociality, or male bonding. In the early stories and in *Plata quemada* the sexual possibilities of male friendships are explored, but even in other works, where those possibilities are only implicit, the issue is important. Gabriel Giorgi, writing in an article for a volume published by the Instituto Internacional de Literatura Iberoamericana, argues for a queer reading of Piglia's work; though it is certainly a decentered vantage point (as have been various feminist approaches to Piglia), the project is important. Piglia's work, though usually heterosexual in content, is fraught with tension concerning the homoerotic, especially in relation to violent male bonding.

The corpus of Piglia's fiction, then, includes a number of excellent short stories, a brilliant novella, and three important novels. A significant portion of that work is characterized by a mixture of narrative and essay that grows out of Borges' experiments along those lines in the 1940s; indeed, like Borges, Piglia's fiction sometimes leans toward the essay of ideas, while his essays sometimes are marked by strong narrative characteristics. This is true, for instance, of the brief recastings of a story by Anton Chekhov in "Tesis sobre el cuento," where Piglia imagines how Chekhov's tale would turn out if told by Ernest Hemingway, Kafka, or Borges. There is a significant other body of work, however, that includes a number of the early stories and *Plata quemada*, where the affinities are more with the hard-boiled detective genre than with Borges. This is not to say that there is no contact between the two tendencies in Piglia's narrative: works like *Assumed Name* and *Artifical Respiration* also have underlying crime fiction plots, and their narrators function much like the hard-boiled detective created by Dashiell Hammett and Raymond Chandler.

Piglia was for many years the main champion of the hard-boiled tradition in Argentina. His first anthology along this line was called *Cuentos policiales de la Serie Negra* (1969; Hard-boiled crime stories), edited by Emilio Renzi, Piglia's alter ego. It was followed by a series of some thirty translations—a series interrrupted in 1976 by the military coup. The authors in the series included Chandler, Hammet, David Goodis, Horace McCoy, J. H. Chase, Charles Williams, and Cornell Woolrich; the translators included Rodolfo Walsh, Estela Canto, and Floreal Mazzia. The importance of the "Serie Negra" publications consisted partly in bringing to the attention of the Argentine reading public the writings of crime fiction authors who had been excluded from the anthologies and translation series edited by Borges and Adolfo Bioy Casares. Their *Los mejores cuentos policiales* (published in two volumes, 1943 an 1972) and dozens of titles for the "Séptimo Círculo," published by Emecé, had championed the armchair, or analytical, detective tradition. Piglia's editing efforts showed that the genre included other tendencies of great interest to younger generations of readers.

Piglia also participated in a fascinating rewriting of a series of major texts from Argentine literature, *La Argentina en pedazos* (1993; Argentina in pieces) in comic book form, with introductory texts by Piglia and comics by a series of avant-garde Argentine artists in the medium. In this work, Piglia delves once again into the relations between reality and fiction, into the construction of a social imaginary. As with the later adaptation of *The Absent City* to the comic book form, Piglia's collaboration with the illustrators of *La Argentina en pedazos* is evidence of his profound engagement with a great variety of media of popular culture. It is also one of the best places to see his skills as a literary essayist: his brief appreciations of Arlt, Borges, Julio Cortázar, Puig, and others are brilliant and suggestive.

A few of Piglia's essays, including two essays on the short story genre ("Tesis sobre el cuento" and "Nuevas tesis sobre el cuento") and one on Borges' last story ("El último cuento de Borges"), are included in *Formas breves*, but many of the author's essays on Puig, Borges, Arlt, the Argentine writer an critic David Viñas, and others remained uncollected at the end of the twentieth century. Additional works include collected and uncollected interviews with Piglia and book-length transcripts of conversations that took place at Princeton University. Piglia's conversations with Juan José Saer have been published in *Diálogos* (1995; Dialogues). The author also has published a few extracts from a diary he kept since adolescence, but the far greater part of that diary is unpublished.

Piglia is an exemplary independent intellectual. He intervenes in public debates but is not affiliated with any political party, which in the modern landscape of a debased and corrupt party politics in Argentina is something of a virtue. He often is interviewed for the media, and his role in recent years has been that of a public figure but not of a publicity hound. Piglia taught for many years at the University of Buenos Aires, where his classes on Argentine literature were the most popular courses offered. He resigned that post in late 2000 to take up a full-time teaching job in the United States, where he has lectured at Princeton and at the University of California at Davis. The author's work has been well known in Argentina for many years, but only in the late 1990s did it begin to circulate widely elsewhere in the Spanish-speaking world, thanks to new editions in Cuba, Mexico, Spain, and elsewhere. Translated into Portuguese and English, Piglia's works also have circulated to critical acclaim in Brazil and the United States.

One of the constants—even the commonplaces—of the criticism of Piglia's works is the search for a close correspondence with political and historical realities; this tendency is exemplified by my own writing on Piglia in the 1980s and by the recent work of Jorgelina Corbatta. Piglia protested—in a fascinating interview with Marina Kaplan published in the *New Orleans Review* in 1990—that that was a reductive reading of *Artificial Respiration* and other texts, but it is still common to read Piglia's work as primarily referential to the period of the "Dirty War" that devastated his generation.

The principal focus of criticism of Piglia's work has been a reflection on the relationship between literature and history, and between literature and politics. Although I am not averse to such readings, it seems to me that many of the readings resemble each other and do not serve to open new approaches and fresh interpretations. There have been a few new avenues of

critical research that are promising, however. First, there is Adriana Rodríguez Pérsico's introduction to *Cuentos morales* (Moral tales), the anthology of Piglia's short stories that Espasa Calpe published in 1995. Rodríguez Pérsico comments lucidly on various moments of Piglia's narrative and essayistic practice, and the connections between them, and concludes:

> Piglia thinks of literature as a private utopia. Literature provides a virgin territory of freedom; that is what provides its capacity for questioning and its potential for revealing external conflicts. In the fascinating exercise of its practice, the writer is bound necessarily to the present, forced to speak of the present moment in which he or she lives, even if that is not his or her immediate purpose. In turn, the reader is not immune when he or she finishes reading. Each time that this happens, the miracle of literature is renewed; in this sense, Piglia's narrative exemplifies a way of making literature that simultaneously prompts reflection and moves us. Perhaps the motive of this double calling is due to the fact that literature emerges from the heart of collective life.

Rodríguez Pérsico does not seem to discount the importance of the present moment, or rather of that double present: the moment of composition and also the moment of reception. Instead of that moment being something stable or fixed, literature's referentiality "prompts reflection" in an active sense: it destabilizes and surprises us. The reader inhabits for a moment what Gérard Genette, in his first essay on Borges in the 1960s, called a "literary utopia." What Rodríguez Pérsico calls a "virgin terrain of freedom" is that non-place that is utopia.

It is worth remembering the sensation of surprise and liberation that readers felt upon the publication of *Artificial Respiration*. That sensation of liberation does not depend entirely on the immediate situation of 1980. The fierce writing in *Artificial Respiration*—which takes us from an epigraph from T. S. Eliot's "The Dry Savages" ("We had the experience but missed the meaning, / and approach to the meaning restores the experience") to reflection on a famous phrase from the Austrian philosopher Ludwig Wittgenstein's *Tractatus Logico-Philosophicus* ("What we cannot speak about we must pass over in silence")—speaks of the conditions of possibility of the novel, and not in a purely negative sense. It is not silence but the fullness of reflection. What Rodríguez Pérsico deems a "private utopia" is this sensation, which does not depend solely on the moment of composition. It is a shared as well as a private experience, and as such is mobile and constantly renewable.

In the interview with Kaplan, Piglia commented:

I believe that coding is the work of fiction in any context. I don't believe that the ellipsis of political material performed by fiction depends on authoritarian situations. Perhaps the type of coding is different in the latter cases, and that would be interesting to research: whether there are different types of coding according to the different contexts within which the novelist works. I believe that fiction always codes and constructs hieroglyphs out of social reality. Literature is never direct. . . . What I do believe is that political contexts define ways of reading.

This formulation is similar to Piglia's notion in "Tesis sobre el cuento" that the fundamental problem of the short story is how to tell one story while seemingly telling another. It is also reminiscent of Piglia's reference in the preliminary note to "Mata Hari 55" that reality has a "slant logic," which makes it apparently impossible to narrate. "Slant logic" and "coded narration," constants in Piglia's work, are different ways of saying that literature is never direct.

From what vantage point are real events narrated in Piglia's works? Not from the interstices of everyday life, as the censor Arocena thinks in *Artificial Respiration*. Instead, the real is written from literature, as Jorge Fornet has stated eloquently in an article on *Homenaje a Roberto Arlt* for *Nueva Revista de Filología Hispánica*. The real, which according to Piglia in "Mata-Hari 55" "seems, at times, impossible to narrate," is narrated in an oblique way. Just as Borges states in "El Aleph" that the "central problem" of his tale "is impossible to resolve" because it is "the enumation, however partial, of an infinite set" so in Piglia the apparent impossibility is the point of departure.

José Javier Maristany notes in his recent book *Narraciones peligrosas*, at the close of one of the chapters on *Artificial Respiration*:

The text hides and makes visible at the same time: it is elliptical and explicit. Its apparent disarticulation as a collage of heterogeneous texts disconnected among themselves acquires meaning when we are able to perceive their functional interrelationships and their generic connections with those discursive practices that constitute the textual plot of society.

The key words here are "functional interrelationships," which are at once "elliptical and explicit." Although Maristany focuses on the theme of the political content of the novel, he does so more subtly than either Corbatta or I. Referentiality does not function in a simple way for Maristany. When he speaks of "interrelationships," and admits the heterogeneity and the elliptical nature of the text, he complicates their interpretation in a significant and interesting way.

I am not arguing that Piglia's works should not be read in relation to the tradition of the political novel. They can be read in those terms and also in other ways; the ways of reading their political content are not fixed or stable. Luckily, the period 1976–1983—atrocious years in the history of Argentina and its neighbors—are over, and these works (and those of some of Piglia's contemporaries) can be read with today's eyes, which are less passionate, perhaps, and more skeptical.

Piglia is one of the central figures in the Latin American novel of the "post-Boom" period, the literary and commercial phenomenon that took place in the 1960s. His intellectual rigor and honesty have given him great authority as a critic, while the fierce intelligence of his fiction has endowed it with a life of its own that does not depend anymore on the circumstances of its composition. Piglia's fiction from the early 1980s could be read today in Mexico, Cuba, and Spain as if just written, seeming to speak directly to contemporary dilemmas. The author's work in film and other media has given him access to an audience other than the somewhat reduced reading public for a literature that is often bookish and difficult. In some ways a continuation of the mixing of story and essay that characterized Borges' writing in the 1940s and 1950s, Piglia's work also is intensely involved with contemporary realities, making him an heir of Arlt and of certain moments in the writing of Cortázar. An independent intellectual of great authority, a brilliant writer, a renowned teacher and critic, Piglia is an essential voice of the turn of the millenium.

# SELECTED BIBLIOGRAPHY

## Primary Works

### Short Stories and Novels

*La invasión.* Buenos Aires: Jorge Alvarez, 1967. Published as *Jaulario* in Cuba. Havana: Casa de las Américas, 1967.
*Nombre falso.* Buenos Aires: Siglo XXI, 1975.
*Respiración artificial.* Buenos Aires: Pomaire, 1980.
*Prisión perpetua.* Buenos Aires: Sudamericana, 1988.
*La ciudad ausente.* Buenos Aires: Sudamericana, 1992.
*Cuentos morales.* Edited and with an introduction by Adriana Rodríguez Pérsico. Buenos Aires: Espasa Calpe, 1995.
*Plata quemada.* Buenos Aires: Planeta, 1997.

### Essays

"Clase media: Cuerpo y destino (Una lectura de *La traición de Rita Hayworth* de Manuel Puig)." In *Nueva novela Latinoamericana 2.* Edited by Jorge Lafforgue. Buenos Aires: Paidós, 1972. Pp. 350–362.
"Roberto Arlt: La ficción del dinero." *Hispamérica* 3, no. 7:25–28 (1974).
"Sarmiento's Vision." In *Sarmiento and His Argentina.* Edited by Joseph T. Criscenti. Boulder: Lynne Rienner, 1993. Pp. 71–76.
"Sarmiento the Writer." In *Sarmiento, Author of a Nation.* Edited by Tulio Halperín Donghi, Iván Jaksic, Gwen Kirkpatrick, and Francine Masiello. Berkeley: University of California Press, 1994. Pp. 127–144.
*Formas breves.* Buenos Aires: Temas Grupo, 1999.
*Crítica y ficción.* Santa Fe, Argentina: Universidad Nacional del Litoral, 1986. Expanded 2nd ed. Buenos Aires: Seix Barral, 2000.

### Anthologies

*Crónicas de Norteamérica.* Edited by Ricardo Piglia. Buenos Aires: Jorge Alvarez, 1967.
*Crónicas de Latinoamérica.* Edited by Ricardo Piglia. Buenos Aires: Jorge Alvarez, 1968.

*Yo: La autobiografía en la Argentina.* Selected and with an introduction by Ricardo Piglia. Buenos Aires: Tiempo Contemporáneo, 1968.
*Cuentos policiales de la Serie Negra.* Edited by Emilio Renzi (pseud. of Ricardo Piglia). Buenos Aires: Centro Editor de América Latina, 1969.
*Cuentos de la Serie Negra.* Edited by Ricardo Piglia. Buenos Aires: Centro Editor de América Latina, 1979.
*Las fieras: El género policial en la Argentina.* Edited by Ricardo Piglia. Buenos Aires: Alfaguara, 1989.
*Antología del crimen perfecto.* Edited by Ricardo Piglia. Buenos Aires: Planeta, 1999.

### Other Works

*El astillero.* Screenplay by Piglia. Based on novel by Juan Carlos Onetti. Directed by David Lipsyc. Produced by Rocca Producciones.
*Luba.* Screenplay by Ricardo Piglia. Directed by Alejandro Agresti. 1990.
*La Argentina en pedazos.* Illustrations by Enrique Breccia, Carlos Roume, Carlos Nine, Alberto Breccia, Crist, Solano López, Alfredo Flores, El Tomi, and José Muñoz. Buenos Aires: Ediciones de la Urraca, 1993. (Comic book.)
*La ciudad ausente.* Adapted for the stage by Gerardo Gandini with a libretto by Ricardo Piglia. Teatro Colón, Buenos Aires, 1995. (Opera.)
*Corazón iluminado.* Screenplay by Ricardo Piglia. Directed by Héctor Babenco. Produced by Productora HB Films. 1998.
*La sonámbula.* Screenplay by Ricardo Piglia. Directed by Fernando Spiner. Produced by Instituto Argentino de Cinematografía. 1998.
*La ciudad ausente.* Illustrations by Luis Scafati. Adaptation by Pablo de Sanctis. Buenos Aires: Océano, 2000. (Comic book.)
*Plata quemada.* Directed by Marcelo Piñeyro. Film script by Marcelo Figueras. Produced by Oscar Kramer. 2000. (Film script and diary published in Buenos Aires by Editorial Norma, 2000.)

### Translations

*Artificial Respiration.* Trans. by Daniel Balderston. Durham: Duke University Press, 1994. (Translation of *Respiración artificial.*)
*Assumed Name.* Trans. by Sergio Waisman. Pittsburgh: Latin American Literary Review Press, 1995. (Translation of *Nombre falso.*)

*The Absent City.* Trans. by Sergio Waisman. Durham: Duke University Press, 2000. (Translation of *La ciudad ausente.*)

## Secondary Works

### Critical and Biographical Studies

Avelar, Idelber. "Cómo respiran los ausentes: La narrativa de Ricardo Piglia." *MLN* 110, no. 2:416–432 (March 1995).

———. *The Untimely Present: Postdictatorial Latin American Fiction and the Task of Mourning.* Durham: Duke University Press, 1999. Pp. 86–135.

Balderston, Daniel. "El significado latente en *Respiración artificial* de Ricardo Piglia y *En el corazón de junio* de Luis Gusman." In *Ficción y política: La narrativa argentina durante el proceso militar,* by Daniel Balderston, David William Foster, Tulio Halperín Donghi, Francine Masiello, Marta Morello-Frosch, and Beatriz Sarlo. Buenos Aires: Alianza/University of Minnesota, 1987. Pp. 109–121.

———. "Latent Meanings in Ricardo Piglia's *Respiración artificial* and Luis Gusman's *En el corazón de junio.*" *Revista Canadiense de Estudios Hispánicos* 12, no. 2:207–219 (1988).

Barra, María Josefa. "*Respiración artificial:* Retórica y praxis." In *La novela argentina de los años 80.* Edited by Roland Spiller. Frankfurt am Main: Vervuert, 1991. Pp. 13–36.

Berg, Edgardo H. "La relación dialógica entre ficción e historia: *Respiración artificial* de Ricardo Piglia." *Cuadernos para Investigación de la Literatura Hispánica* 20:51–55 (1995).

———. "La conspiración literaria (sobre *La ciudad ausente* de Ricardo Piglia)." *Hispamérica* 25, no. 75:37–47 (December 1996).

Bratosevich, Nicolás, and Grupo de Estudio. *Ricardo Piglia y la cultura de la contravención.* Buenos Aires: Atuel, 1997.

Cittadini, Fernando. "Historia y ficción en *Respiración artificial.*" In *La novela argentina de los años 80.* Edited by Roland Spiller. Frankfurt am Main: Vervuert, 1991. Pp. 37–46.

Colás, Santiago. *Postmodernity in Latin America: The Argentine Paradigm.* Durham: Duke University Press, 1994. Pp. 121–149.

Corbatta, Jorgelina. *Narrativas de la Guerra Sucia en Argentina: Piglia, Saer, Valenzuela, Puig.* Buenos Aires: Corregidor, 1999. Pp. 45–64.

de Grandis, Rita. "La cita como estrategia narrativa en *Respiración artificial.*" *Revista Canadiense de Estudios Hispánicos* 17, no. 2:259–269 (1993).

———. *Polémica y estrategias narrativas en América Latina: José María Arguedas, Mario Vargas Llosa, Rodolfo Walsh, Ricardo Piglia.* Rosario: Beatriz Viterbo, 1993. Pp. 121–148.

Demaría, Laura. *Argentina-s: Ricardo Piglia dialoga con la generación del '37 en la discontinuidad.* Buenos Aires: Corregidor, 1999.

Echavarren, Roberto. "La literariedad: *Respiración artificial* de Ricardo Piglia." *Revista Iberoamericana* 49, no. 125:997–1008 (October–December 1983).

Fornet, Jorge. " 'Homenaje a Roberto Arlt' o la literatura como plagio." *Nueva Revista de Filología Hispánica* 42, no. 1:115–141 (1994).

———. "Un debate de poéticas: Las narraciones de Ricardo Piglia." In *Historia crítica de la literatura argentina.* Edited by Noé Jitrik. Vol. 11: *La narración gana la partida.* Edited by Elsa Drucaroff. Buenos Aires: Emecé, 2000. Pp. 345–360.

Gallo, Marta. "In-trascendencia textual en *Respiración artificial* de Ricardo Piglia." *Nueva Revista de Filología Hispánica* 35, no. 2:819–834 (1987).

Giorgi, Gabriel. "Mirar al monstruo: Homosexualidad y nación en los sesenta argentinos." In *Sexualidad y nación.* Edited by Daniel Balderston. Pittsburgh: Instituto Internacional de Literatura Iberoamericana, 2000. Pp. 243–260.

Gnutzmann, Rita. "Homenaje a Arlt, Borges y Onetti de Ricardo Piglia." *Revista Iberoamericana* 58, no. 159:437–438 (1992).

Grzegorczyk, Marzena. "Discursos desde el margen: Gombrowicz, Piglia y la estética del basurero." *Hispamérica* 26, no. 73:15–33 (April 1996).

Jagoe, Eva-Lynn Alicia. "The Disembodied Machine: Matter, Femininity, and Nation in Piglia's *La ciudad ausente.*" *Latin American Literary Review* 23, no. 45:5–17 (1995).

Levinson, Brett. "Trans(re)lations: Dictatorship, Disaster, and the 'Literary Politics' of Piglia's *Respiración artificial.*" *Latin American Literary Review* 25, no. 49:91–120 (1997).

Maristany, José Javier. *Narraciones peligrosas: Resistencia y adhesión en las novelas del Proceso.* Buenos Aires: Biblos, 1999. Pp. 55–105.

Morello-Frosch, Marta. "Ficción e historia en *Respiración artificial* de Ricardo Piglia." *Discurso Literario* 1, no. 2:243–255 (1984).

Newman, Kathleen. *La violencia del discurso: El estado autoritario y la novela política argentina.* Buenos Aires: Catálogos Editora, 1991. Pp. 95–114.

Pons, María Cristina. *Más allá de las fronteras del lenguaje: Un análisis crítico de "Respiración artificial" de Ricardo Piglia.* Mexico City: Universidad Nacional Autónoma de México, 1998.

Rodríguez Pérsico, Adriana. Introduction to *Cuentos morales*. Buenos Aires: Espasa Calpe, 1995. Pp. 9–34.

Romano Thuesen, Evelia A. "Marcelo: El presente sin presencia en *Respiración artificial* de Ricardo Piglia." *Nueva Revista de Filología Hispánica* 41, no. 1:279–291 (1993).

Solomianski, Alejandro. "El cuento de la patria: Una forma de su configuración en la cuentística de Ricardo Piglia." *Revista Iberoamericana* 63, no. 181:675–688 (1997).

*Interviews*

Kaplan, Marina. "Between Arlt and Borges: An Interview with Ricardo Piglia." *New Orleans Review* 16, no. 2:64–74 (summer 1989).

Díaz-Quiñones, Arcadio, Paul Firbas, Noel Luna, and José A. Rodríguez-Garrido, eds. *Conversación en Princeton*. Princeton: Program in Latin American Studies, Princeton University, 1998.

Piglia, Ricardo, and Juan José Saer. *Diálogos*. Santa Fe, Argentina: Universidad Nacional del Litoral, 1995.

# Nélida Piñón

## (1937–    )

---

## *Vera Regina Teixeira*

Nélida Piñón's literary career reached its apogee on 27 July 1989, when the writer was elected to the Brazilian Academy of Letters, after three decades of passionately performing the vital task of writing with strict, untiring, methodical and meticulous discipline, informed by brilliant creativity. Jorge Amado, the acclaimed creator of the unforgettable Gabriela (*Gabriela, Clove and Cinnamon*) and Dona Flor (*Dona Flor and Her Two Husbands*), had suggested, indeed insisted, that she submit her name for candidacy when a vacancy in the academy opened up. On the afternoon of her election, the daring that Piñón had shown in submitting her first attempt at a novel to the scrutiny of the intrepid grand dame of Brazilian letters, Raquel de Queiroz, when she was still an inexperienced youngster was only a distant memory. Courteously, de Queiroz had counseled the fledgling author that "if you want a destiny as a writer, learn at once to purge impurities from the text, even beloved phrases, to cross out the first outpourings, . . . talent becomes one's enemy if it is not well cared for." Piñón never forgot the hard lesson she learned during that early visit to de Queiroz, and the advice helped Piñón to persist in her inexorable vocation to weave dreams, make up stories, and preserve ancestral myths. She well knew that it was her mission to go beyond implacable daily reality and to transform it into the unexpected reality of fiction.

Nélida Piñón, the only child of Lino and Carmen Piñón, was born on 3 May 1937 in the city of Rio de Janeiro, then the capital of Brazil. She was heir to a family "of good breeding" who originally came from Galicia, just to the north of Portugal, on the northeastern coast of Spain, from where her maternal and paternal grandparents set off to settle in the New World. She acknowledges that she acquired her love of storytelling from her maternal grandfather, Daniel Cuiñas. For several years, Piñón devoted herself to creating significant and varied literary work, sometimes harshly criticized and misunderstood. By 1987, when her body of work had gained her a reputation as a first-rate author with unquestionable international stature and had earned her election into the Brazilian Academy of Letters, she had already published eight novels and three books of short stories. Election to the academy is the greatest honor to which a Brazilian intellectual can aspire in his or her own country. Piñón chose the day of her birthday, 3 May 1990, to take possession of Chair No. 30, succeeding Aurélio Buarque de Holanda Ferreira, the author of *Novo dicionário aurélio da língua portuguesa* (Aurélio's new dictionary of the Portuguese language), the first edition of which was published by Nova Fronteira publishers in 1974. As a curious coincidence, Master Aurélio also celebrated his birthday on that date. He and all of the previous occupants of this chair, "subdued by the magic of the Portuguese language," devoted themselves untiringly to cultivating the "last flower of Latium, both wild and beautiful." His predecessors included a philologist and a grammarian.

Noteworthy among the illustrious academics receiving Nélida Piñón on that solemn occasion were two women, pioneers of the venerable House that Machado de Assis founded in 1897: Raquel de Queiroz, elected to Chair No. 5 in 1977, and Lydia Fagundes Teles, elected to Chair No. 16 in 1985. From 1980 to 1983, Dinah Silveira de Queiroz had held Chair No. 7. Nélida Piñón thus became only the fourth woman to be invited to join the distinguished organization that had formerly been comprised solely of men for three quarters of a century. The Brazilian Academy of Letters, which was founded in 1897 along the lines of the *Académie Française,* was, like the latter, "the result of a pact between kindred spirits," according to a trustworthy witness. Many of its founding members shared affinities and feelings imbued with the abolitionist spirit prevalent among liberals in the late nineteenth century, with the abdication of Pedro II at the end of Brazil's Second Empire and the establishment of the Brazilian Republic.

In her acceptance speech, the new member of the academy admitted:

*Não sei que mestre, que mágico, que mãe misericordiosa, que amor desfeito no aluvião das montanhas me transmitiram a caprichosa convicção de que a palavra, espúria e nômade, tinha o dom de costurar todos os sentimentos. E que a palavra ainda, associada à história secreta das nações, e ao enredo indevassável do destino humano, se tornava a única chave com que forçar a porta do mundo, lacrada com cera e enigmas. Arrasto comigo seres arcaicos e memórias coercivas. A caravela que navega no meu imaginário, como herança, insiste em que levantemos as velas. O vento que assopra conduz-nos pelas grotas de geografia indômita, vistoria palavras e sentimentos cravados no peito alheio. Espinhos de uma roseira que pende sob o fardo de juras e queixumes solitários. O Brasil, saído desta fornalha, alimenta a fome verbal de seus filhos. . . . Aprendi, então, que para tal registro não se perder nas noites clandestinas, devíamos—tripulantes desta caravela—exceder-nos no próprio ofício de narrar. Sem reclamar contudo verdades ou certezas.*

I know not what master, what magician, what merciful mother, what love coming down in a torrent from the mountains conveyed to me the capricious conviction that words, being spurious and nomadic, have the gift of stitching up all feelings. And furthermore that words, being associated with the secret history of nations and with the impenetrable tangle of human destiny, become the only key with which to force open the door to the world, sealed with wax and enigmas. I drag along with me archaic beings and coercive memories. The caravel navigating in my imagination, like a legacy, insists that we raise the sails. The wind that blows guides us along the ravines of untamed geography, to inspect words and feelings set in another's breast. Brazil, which came out of this kiln, feeds the verbal hunger of its sons. . . . I learned, then, that in order for this record not to be lost in clandestine nights, we, the crew of this caravel, must outdo ourselves in our own craft of storytelling. Without, however, claiming any truths or certainties.

And it was thus that in the last decade of the twentieth century the horizons definitely opened up for this intellectual who was so passionate about her art and about her language, Portuguese, the ancient language of the *Cancioneiros* (Balladeers) and of *Os Lusíadas* (the Lusiads) of the old Iberian Peninsula. Five hundred years of coexistence in America, among Tupi Indian songs and African laments, had transformed that Portuguese into a "dark and coy, plaintive and excessive" language, where Piñón's art would find "a resting place and grace." During the 8th Annual International Authors' Festival, which took place in Toronto, Canada, from 16 to 24 October 1987, under the auspices of Toronto's Coach House Press, the author explained her intimate relationship with Brazilian Portuguese. "Brazilian Portuguese allows me to explore that richness, more so than the Portuguese spoken in Portugal. Ours is a vast language, steeped in reality, in the changing nature of reality. It recognizes that reality, while being in the present, also moves back into the past and forward into the future.[Brazilian Portuguese], therefore, makes great use of the gerund, that verbal form that seems to live in all three times at once" (Alberto Manguel, *A Series of Six Chapbooks*).

This was the time of the fruits, of harvesting the golden apples of her work, a time of awards, invitations, and international renown, although she had already enjoyed deep friendships with various Brazilian and foreign intellectuals and was well connected among the Latin American and European intellectual elites. Her stature was demonstrated by the invitation for her to be part of the jury in 1980 for the Neustadt Prize, the important international prize awarded by the literary review, *World Literature Today*, published in Norman, Oklahoma. Likewise attesting to her increasing renown is the fact that in a period of only twenty years, the author gave over twenty series of lectures and discussions at American and European universities. Finally, in 1991, in tight competition with over eighty foreign intellectuals, Piñón won the Henry King Stanford Chair in the Humanities at the University of Miami in Coral Gables, Florida, where she went on to teach postgraduate seminars in comparative literature.

Piñón's careers as novelist, short story writer, essayist, and university professor came together at a time when her humanity, her strength, and fragility were also coming to the fore. After a period of struggling with the difficult conquest of new natural frontiers, over and above those that traditionally arose to stand in the way of her dreams and ambitions, we see a combative, educated, and intellectual Brazilian woman predestined for deep and genuine originality and celebrating both the actualization of her dreams and the fulfillment of their promise:

> *Pleiteio a singularidade de participar de séculos pretéritos. De ser contemporânea de quem nasceu no albor do ano 1000. De trazer à minha imaginação sentimentos dispersos ao longo dos séculos e que enriquecem a magnífica solidão do homem. Ambiciono ser vizinha de uma matriz inaugural, e de impossível acesso, com a qual contudo sensibilizarei minha pluma de escritora.*
>
> *Recuso o incômodo compromisso de ser apenas mulher de minha triste época. Não aceito fabricar frases apressadas, falsamente concisas, a pretexto de agradar aquelas criaturas soltas nas ruas, nos salões, todas à cata do pão de cada dia, e já não dispõem de estrutura mental, sequer de minutos, para as frases subordinadas nascidas do engenho e da carência humana.*
>
> (O pão de cada dia, 1994)

I plead the singularity of taking part in centuries past. Of being a contemporary of those born at the dawn of the first millennium. Of carrying in my imagination feelings that spread out across the centuries and which enrich the magnificent solitude of man. I aspire to be a denizen of an inaugural matrix, and one where access is impossible, with which I will, nevertheless, make my writer's pen more sensitive.

I refuse the uncomfortable compromise of being merely a woman of my sorry times. I am not willing to fabricate hurried, falsely concise phrases, on the pretext of pleasing those creatures loosened on the streets, in the halls, all chasing after their daily bread, and who no longer have the mental structure, even for a few minutes, for subordinate sentences born of ingenuity and human need.

Nélida Piñón is a writer of great merit, and her intellectual career is among the most important in twentieth-century Brazilian and Latin American literature. Holding a degree in journalism from the Pontiffca Universidad Católica do Rio de Janeiro, she would early on realize her much longed-for dream of writing, nurtured since her childhood by the fascinating legends of her ancestral Galicia. She made her debut as a novelist with *Guia-mapa de Gabriel Arcanjo* (Gabriel Arcanjo's guidebook), which was published in 1961. At the time, Fausto Cunha, a literary critic for the Rio de Janeiro newspaper *Correio da Manhã*, described it as "the first attempt at a non-figurative novel that I know of in the Portuguese language, the first step toward the electronic novel." In another newspaper, *O estado de São Paulo*, her work was also praised: "the appearance of the book by Nélida Piñón as one of the possible starting points for the revival of the Brazilian novel." In 1962 the writer was invited to become a correspondent member of the Paris magazine *Nuevo mundo* by its editor, the Uruguayan intellectual, Emir Rodríguez Monegal.

In 1963 Piñón's second novel, *Madeira feita cruz* (Wood become cross) was published, and critic Walmir Ayala wrote a comment for the book jacket, hailing the young writer who "in a process going from the obscure toward elucidation, distributes chapters among the present and among remembrance in such a manner that you have, all of a sudden, an overall notion of a small community besieged by truth, by love, by the determination of those who have been predestined." With this second book, Ayala goes on to say, "we clearly see the next step, the flowering of a series of rich details already at the service of a moving story, together with the whole labyrinth of introspection which, in Nélida Piñón, is like a fever." The dense, symbolic, introspective, and disquieting text is molded into tough, asyntactic, and experimental language that narrates the present as well as the memories of Ana, Maria,

Pedro, and Francisco, archetypal characters in search of a truth that is forbidden to them.

This novel was followed by *Tempo das frutas* (1966; Time of fruition), her first collection of eighteen stories, all of them written in a minimalist style and devoted to penetrating the depths of the human condition in all its scatological bestiality, its debasing weakness, its eternal misery. The tales are true embroideries intermingling the sordid feelings and debasing emotions of humankind in a transitory and unfinished world. The story that lends its title to this collection of tales tells of a woman who discovers the unlikely pregnancy of a moribund old lady:

> *Teve nojo do seu cheiro como daquela velhice que era a aparência da morte. Esforçou-se em apreciá-la como se ainda pudesse conduzir a velha a seus anos iluminados. Mas, já a sua pele enrugara-se igual a terra mexida no uso, dissimulando sujeira nas suas trilhas mais secretas, através das quais perpetrou-se tanto crime, se acaso as seguíssemos haveríamos de descobrir.*

> [She] was nauseated by her smell, and by the old age that was the appearance of death. She attempted to see it as if it could return the old lady to her brighter years. But her skin was already wrinkled like land trampled by use, disguising the dirt in its most secret paths, along which so much crime was perpetrated, as we would discover if we were to follow them.

In "A moça e seu fruto" (The girl and her fruit) it is the man who is repelled by the castrating contact with his pregnant companion and he asks her, "Did you know that I killed a girl who also ate apples?" Only three years later, in 1969, and under the care of the same publisher, the novel *Fundador* (Founder) appeared. It received the Special Walmap Prize that same year.

In this, her third novel, Piñón takes up the narrative thread of her previous works and, in an obscure, almost cabalistic tale, records inaccessible worlds peopled by characters who multiply and blend together in absurd lives and fantastic adventures. Throughout it all, the natural and the apparently supernatural come together in an unusual and unexpected manner. What is most disconcerting is the author's use of a reverse ordering in time: the events of the novel are recorded and narrated from the standpoint of a future time that gradually calls forth a past that hovers between history, myth and the

subversion of myth, realism, and Latin American magical realism. Once again, the narrative voice seems to eschew communication, instead employing language that is as experimental as it is laborious, individualist, and metaphysical. The author's style discloses a desire to assume a stance that is distinctly innovative and daring.

At times, the text becomes a series of amazing plays on words, an arrangement of plots interwoven by extremely fine threads that are almost as difficult to trace as the tangled filaments of a spider's web, and the author builds her web with the same instinctive and voracious talent as that of the admirable spider. *Fundador* is a saga of the adventures (both past and future) of quasi-historical conquistadors and pioneers. Among these adventurers are Ptolemy, his friend Camilo, the invader of the Cordillera, and Johanus, the Founder for whom the novel is named. Johanus is the supreme authority, a "warrior of our lands," who struggles to win the sword of Sir Tristram and the map of Hispania that had been drawn by the great cartographer Theodore of Antioch but, curiously, signed by Ptolemy. These characters are followed by the Nun, who has left her convent and transformed herself into the eternal companion of all those who search for the promised land. The Nun appears throughout the tale, sometimes as a single woman, sometimes as several. In all her incarnations she is portrayed as busily praying or writing, but always devoted to the duty of populating the the new cities established by the Founder. "They sat one in front of the other. They did not move. The spiders worked around them so delicately. The tired webs were born, wrought the same by Founder and Nun. He showed her the books in which years ago their respective adventures were noted."

In the decade following the publication of *Fundador*, Nélida Piñón entered a phase of intense activity. Deeply emotional and disquietingly carnal novels and stories appeared, in which the author continued to employ the playfully experimental diction and acute introspection that characterized her previous work. In the 1960s, while she was preparing the short stories collected in *Tempo das frutas*, she had accepted an offer to become assistant editor of the review *Cadernos brasileiros*, a post she held for a two-year period from 1966 to 1967. In 1970 she began her teaching career, launching the program in Creative Writing Program at the School of Letters at the Federal University of Rio de Janeiro. This effort coincided with the darkest era in the political history of modern Brazil. In 1964 a military coup had put an end to the brief democracy led by President Juscelino Kubitschek de Oliveira, the creator of Brasilia. The new capital, a true pharaonic project carried out in the middle of nowhere on the continental plateau, revived the belief in miracles and a euphoric hope in the Brazilian mind, until cruel reality abruptly interrupted the utopian dream. On 14 December 1968, Rio de Janeiro's *Jornal do Brasil* published an unusual weather report on the front page: "Dark weather, suffocating temperatures. The air is stifling. The Country is being swept by strong winds. A high of 38° in Brasilia. A low of 5° in Laranjeiras." The weather appeared in the headlines because Marechal Costa e Silva, leader of the coup, had imposed official censorship by signing the proclamation of Institutional Act No. 5, indefinitely suspending the constitutional right of all Brazilian citizens to habeas corpus and initiating a state of terror in the nation. Like a slumbering giant, Brazil fell into a political coma from which it would not awaken for many years and which would leave an indelible mark on the national conscience.

Brazilians now lived with uncertainty about their own physical safety in the face of arbitrary laws and decrees that continually altered their civil and constitutional rights. Among those whom the government aimed its forces of repression most were the concerned and committed intellectuals, writers, musicians, composers, artists, university professors, and students who offered resistance and protested against the new regime. The youth-oriented songs of Caetano Veloso and Chico Buarque resonated among the combative idealists of these "rebel years," and the presence of Clarice Lispector became emblematic in the protest marches that took to the streets of Rio de Janeiro in 1966. Censorship, threats, and summary orders for imprisonment led, in many cases, to abuses, torture, exile, or even death on airplanes "headed for the high seas." It was not until 31 December 1978, that Brazilians reacquired the most basic human rights, when then-President Ernesto Geisel abolished Institutional Act No. 5 and proclaimed: "Brazilians will once again have the right to 'habeas corpus' in cases of political crimes,"

news that the *Jornal do Brasil* disseminated on the same page on which it printed the article, "Exilados Retornam."

In this political context, and perhaps because of it, Nélida Piñón was launched on the international market by Editora Emecé, a publishing house in Buenos Aires, with the Spanish-language edition of *Fundador* in 1973. Piñón herself had just published her fourth novel in 1972: *A casa da paixão* (The house of passion). This novel reconstructs the life of Marta, the only child in a household inhabited by her widowed and vulnerable father and Antonia, the housemaid who saw her come into the world and who zealously protects her from discovering her sensual nature. In intensely erotic and titillating prose that risks disclosing the most secret artifices of love, the text never crosses the line into pornography, due to the author's steadfast commitment to the use of creative and redeeming language. In this lyrically dreamlike narrative, the author outdoes herself in providing precious details about the metaphysical aspects of the pleasures of sex, wherein the body is transformed, turned generous by the exalted passion of the flesh. She places this transformation at the epicenter of the redemption of humankind, and sex becomes a mystical vehicle of revolt against original sin. Her poetic discourse brings together the real and the imaginary, treating copulation as regenerative and sacred in the ritual of sexual initiation carried out by Marta and Jerônimo, who has been chosen by Marta's father to teach her about men.

Literary critic Sônia Régis elucidates the writer's erotic discourse by placing it within a particular context:

> the body becomes an instrument of creation, a place where the process of consecrating the word by means of perfecting language takes place.... It is, however, an erotic discourse that is driven by the mystery of redemption that comes about in all creation—a linguistic advent that announces the unveiling of hidden or unnamed reality.
>
> ("Sarça Ardente," *A casa da paixão*, 1982)

Régis sees Marta as Piñón describes her, as the "lady of the house," whose body "is the sacrificial altar on which preference is given to the sensitivity of matter willing to transform itself by the fire (sun) of universal intelligence, devoted to the revelation of reality and the annunciation of the mystery" ("Sarça ardente" in *Casa da paixão*).

Another critic, Naomi Hoki Moniz, has concluded that the author has "reorganized and renewed the novel through densely symbolical and metaphorical language,"and insists that "although Piñón, like other Brazilian women authors, rejects the notion of a characteristically feminine literature, her works suggest that it is necessary to seek innovations in a world where language and meaning are controlled and defined by the male element" ("*A casa da paixão*: Ética, Estética e a Condição Feminina"). Where Regis seems to emphasize a *meta-determination* in Piñón's writing, Montiz appears to find in it "*an over-determination*: not only that of founding *another discourse* or of founding a discourse that gets to the essence, but also that of founding an *essentially feminine discourse*" (Horácio Costa, "A Margem de *A república dos sonhos* de Nélida Piñón"). Some years later the author provided her own explanation:

*Os sentidos humanos estão em todas as partes.Degustar, ouvir, sentir os músculos do coração, pensar, rir, amar são imposições e necessidades eróticas.*

*Uma vez que a terra está povoada pelos sentidos humanos, é natural que se impregne o texto da emoção que emana simultaneamente do corpo, do espírito e do mistério. E que passe a ser ato de vida e de rebeldia estética a apropriação do corpo físico e do corpo verbal.*

*Para representar os sentidos em seus textos, não carece o escritor de abordá-los com fome grosseira. Os feitos do desejo e a matriz dilacerante da paixão se captam às vezes com a palavra muda, o gesto severo, concebido em meio às sombras.*

*O mérito, então, de uma paisagem erótica repousa mais no tratamento literário que se dê a ela do que á exaustiva descrição. Não se limita, pois, a cortejar as superfícies cintilantes do corpo, fazendo-as por isso arder. É preciso o imaginário para engendrar o mundo dos sentidos.*

*O erotismo, assim, é a fruição de todas as manifestações do prazer que o homem, ao longo de interminável processo civilizatório, aprendeu a dispor através da prática diária da sua cultura.*

*Portanto, enquanto a moral fere freqüentemente o estético, a estética do erotismo não golpeia a moral.*

("Eros," *O pão de cada dia*)

Human senses are everywhere. Taste, hearing, feeling the muscles of the heart, thinking, laughing, loving are erotic impositions and needs.

Once the terrain is peopled by human senses, it is natural for the text to be impregnated by the emotion emanating simultaneously from the body, from the spirit and from mystery—and for the appropriation of the physical body and of the verbal body to become an act of life and of aesthetic rebellion.

To represent the senses in his texts, a writer does not need to approach them with crude hunger. The modes of desire and of the excruciating core of passion can be captured at times with a muted word, a stark gesture, conceived in the midst of shadows.

The merit, however, of an erotic passage lies more in the literary treatment given to it than in exhaustive description. It is thus not limited to courting the scintillating surfaces of the body, thus making them burn. The imaginary is necessary to engender the world of the senses.

Eroticism thus is the fruition of all the manifestations of pleasure which man, throughout the unending process of civilization, has learned to show through the daily practice of his culture.

Thus, although morality frequently offends the aesthetic, the aesthetics of eroticism do not clash with morality.

The novel *A casa da paixão* received the 1973 Mário de Andrade Prize from the São Paulo Art Critics Association for best fiction. It was followed that same year by *Sala de armas* (Hall of arms), a collection of sixteen stories woven out of the various intrigues and experiences of people "in search of the first word ever uttered by man." The stories gathered together in this volume derive from different points in the author's career, and many can be seen as embryos of other, later stories. Among them is the delicious "Ave de paraíso" ("Bird of Paradise"), where we learn about an extraordinary chocolate cake that can be used both as a secret weapon to snare a husband and as a man's fool-proof test of a woman's domestic ability. "Fronteira natural" (Natural boundary) is a fable, metaphor, or myth that, through the use of hyperrealism, portrays the experience of a village which is located a short distance from hell. Many adventurers are drawn there but few return. Of those who do return, we learn that

*muito embora não apresentem mutações físicas ou características de uma nova raça, regressam esquecidos da comunidade e nostálgicos de um mundo seguramente mais rico . . . emitindo sons de uma língua longínqua, . . . sem dúvida o esboço de uma*

*linguagem buscando expressão . . . linguagem estranha, apoiada
sobre matéria sonora independente e de rigorosa economia verbal.*

though they do not exhibit physical mutations or the
features of a new race, they come back having forgotten
their community and yearning for a world that is surely
more rich . . . emitting the sounds of a remote language,
without doubt the outlines of a language in search of
expression . . . a strange language, based on independent
sounds and employing a rigorous verbal economy.

One such adventurer, the most beautiful and the
most beloved, returns from hell enveloped in a mysterious air, like "one who has spent too much time around
miracles." When a number of the adventurers find that
they can no longer communicate, they all go en masse
to knock on the closed doors of hell, which was always a
natural boundary. In a later essay, "A esperança do
mito" (*O pão de cada dia*), the author sheds light on her
narrative goals regarding the use of myths:

*O mito é sempre mutável. Seu princípio obedece à carência que
nos habita e corrói as cordas dos nossos sonhos. O mito se
fortalece segundo as inúmeras versões que se fazem dele. Para
subsistir, inspira a mentira e a invenção. . . . A narrativa
mítica tem o mérito de devolver—nos ao epicentro do sagrado.
Àquele oco metafísico que existe resguardado em nossos corpos
e que para subsistir exige alimento, luz, fogo eterno.*

A myth can always be changed. It is born of a need that
inhabits us and it eats away at the chords of our dreams. A
myth grows stronger through the innumerable versions
that are made of it. To survive, it inspires lies and
invention. . . . A mythical narrative has the merit of
returning us to the heart of the sacred, that metaphysical
core that is safeguarded in our bodies and which demands
nourishment, light, eternal fire in order to live.

"Luz" (Light) is perhaps the most experimental text
in the collection. In addition to its fragmented syntax,
the text is arranged on the page in such a way as to
visually represent the subject matter. Thus the graphic
layout accentuates the descent along which the protagonist, described as a "sad smitten one" is dragged
during a journey, at the same time that it interrupts the
narrative flow. The story's mythical plot, registering
somewhere between the sacred and the profane, tells of
a woman who "goes proclaiming I am of bronze, as they

say, but I am of love for your love . . . the clearest light
belonging to the earth," who promises her mortal lover
eternal life through love, by means of a journey "into
the darkly darkish darkness." With her as his guide, he
allows himself to be led off, saying:

*Luz me prometera, descíamos cada degrau e não erafácil,
podíamos resvalar, ela me havia assegurado a existência de
precipícios por conviver com ardência, os dois , entre suor e
lágrimas, ela a Eurídice, ele  Orfeu sim eu me sabia atra-
vessava o paraíso dos mortos, esfinges, prantos pardais, e os
punha de lado, não admitíamos outros corpos que os nossos, e
sabendo Luz desta longa viagem, contava histórias, eu olvidando
esquecendo a aspereza do amor invencível.*

Luz promised me, we descended each step and it was not
easy, we could slip, she had assured me of the existence of
precipices from their coexisting with ardor. The two of
them proceeded in between sweat and tears, she being
Eurydice, he being Orpheus. Yes I myself knew going
through the paradise of the dead, the sphinxes, the gray
birds weeping, and pushed them aside, we did not allow
any other bodies other than ours, and Luz knowing of this
long journey, told stories, my unlearning forgetting the
harshness of invincible love.

These three stories in *Sala de armas* provide eloquent examples of the persistent dichotomous metaphors inherent in Piñón's literary project: hell/paradise,
perdition/redemption, possession/surrender, discovery/
mystery, shadow/light, future/past, and body/spirit, to
name but a few. They also illustrate the problem of the
transience of human life and the human penchant for
wandering. At the same time, they comprise an aesthetic Decalogue, according to which the author in-
vests herself in the task of transfiguring reality through
the regenerative and creative power of language, seeing
the word as both kernel and seed. It is on the basis of
this belief that she will manage to rescue her humanity
and immortalize it in myth.

For Piñón, the power contained in the word, as well
as in the gift of life that blossoms from it through the
invention of language, thus becomes primordial and
omnipotent. In patriarchal cultures, it has been traditionally accepted as an unquestioned notion that speech
and, therefore, the dominant role and power, belong to
man. This is challenged in "Colheita" (Harvest), which
at first seems to be a banal story about the return of a

man who ventured out into the world, abandoning home and wife as if he no longer harbored any memory of them. Surprisingly, however, something inconceivable occurs: the abandoned wife comes inexorably and gradually to usurp the man's storytelling instinct. Upon his return the husband, who presumes to reveal unknown worlds so that his wife, who had remained shut up within the four walls of her house, could enjoy the marvels that he had experienced, instead finds himself entangled in her tale of all that she has lived through. She had spent the years of his absence primarily waiting for his return; now, however, she remembers that "her richness was to enumerate with pleasure the daily chores to which she was confined." As the absolute mistress of enchanted words, "she took pleasure in gathering up the sound of her voice from her womb, like a tumor that grazes the innermost walls." As he listens, the husband begins to doubt the truth of his own experiences, feeling as if they are merely a false story, and as he sheds the last of his recollections he is able to insert himself wholly into her universe. The invention of reality would henceforth fall to the female voice:

ele foi arrumando a casa, passou pano molhado nos armários, fingindo ouvi-la ia esquecendo a terra no arrebato da limpeza. E quando a cozinha se apresentou imaculada, ele recomeçou tudo de novo, então descascando frutas para a compota enquanto ela fornecia histórias indispensáveis ao mundo que precisaria apreender uma vez que a ele pretendia dedicar-se para sempre.

he was straightening up the house, passing a moist cloth over the cupboards, pretending to hear her, he was forgetting the dirt in a fit of cleaning. And when the kitchen appeared immaculate, he began all over again, then peeling fruits for the compote, while she furnished stories indispensable to the world that he would need to understand now that he had decided to devote himself to it forever.

Thus "Colheita" imprints female discourse with legitimacy.

The publication of *Tebas do meu coração* (Thebes, so dear to my heart), her fifth novel and the one that solidified the author's ludic (playful) phase, followed in 1974, when the first edition in Portuguese appeared. (Only four years later, in 1978, the Spanish version by the Madrid publishing house, Editora Alfaguara, was released.) In this novel the author employs a continuous narrative thread and an intense manipulation of the vernacular. The plot is exorbitant and chaotic, an artistic performance that is as audacious as it is impenetrable. In this exhaustive and alienating text, the author seems to treat language itself as the beginning and end of the creative endeavor, insofar as the story she tells does not go beyond being a vehicle for enunciation.

The novel is set in a region that is divided up into Santíssimo and Assunção, two towns as primitive as they are mythical, separated by the Alvarado River. The cast of characters is large, their lineages entangled in a mixture of tragic and transcendental humor where reality belies reality.

*Naquele Primeiro de Julho, porém, Eucarístico começou a abater as árvores prometidas aos filhos como herança, logo que morresse. Avisada de que a família perdia as pompas mais nobres e pelas mãos de Eucarístico, Magnólia foi ao seu encontro. Pediu que se desse ao menos três dias para pensar. Não se destruía o patrimônio de uma vida inteira em poucas horas de machado. . . . Meses depois, ao derrubar as paredes da oficina com a maceta, sob os protestos ainda de Magnólia, até não sobrar um tijolo de pé, ninguém mais duvidou da espécie de trabalho que vinha executando com obsessão. Diante de todos expunha-se o bojo amplo e atrevido de um barco, a que faltavam leme, remos, as velas e o mastro.*

On that First of July, however, Eucaristo began to knock down the trees promised to his sons as an inheritance after he died. Notified that the family was losing its patrimony and this at the hands of Eucaristo, Magnólia went to find him. She asked that he give himself at least three days to think. You don't destroy the legacy of an entire life in just a few hours with an ax. . . . Months later, upon knocking down the walls of the workshop with a mallet until not one brick was left standing, again under the protests of Magnólia, there was no longer any doubt about what he was working on so obsessively. Before the eyes of all, the ample and daring bulge of a boat was revealed, lacking only a rudder, oars, sails and the mast.

The Spanish translation was accompanied by a comment by the Peruvian writer and critic Mario Vargas Llosa. In the following year, Vargas Llosa published his view of what he called "the experiment of

*Tebas de mi corazón.*" Calling it "radical . . . extreme . . . demented . . . a codeless obscurity, in that world there are no codes to decipher, no hidden logic . . . behind what takes place," he concluded that "as readers, we are faced only with the following choice: to accept this reality as it is, with a different logic than ours, a different rationality than ours, a different time and space than ours, or to reject it" ("Palabras de Vargas Llosa en la presentación de un libro de Nélida Piñón"). During this period, Umberto Eco's *Open Work*, published in 1962, had a revolutionary impact upon writing. It required the reader's involvement in the text, assuming that such involvement was integral to and constitutive of the creative process, and without which the narrative would remain unfinished. Piñón, however, adopted a different creative stance, offering an authoritative authorial discourse that subjects the reader to blind passivity and acceptance.

From Vargas Llosa, Piñón received both criticism and the beginnings of a mutual respect and sympathy that has intensified over the years. Testifying to this friendship is the dedication that appears in Vargas Llosa's 1981 novel, *The War of the End of the World*, which was based on the monumental 1902 historical novel *Os sertões*, by Euclides da Cunha. The dedication reads: "To Euclides da Cunha in the other world; and in this world, to Nélida Piñón." Similarly, in the piece "Mario," included in *O pão de cada dia*, Piñón reflects briefly on the presidential elections in Peru, examining the relationship between creation and the wielding of power:

> *Suspeito que se Mário fosse francês, jamais pleitearia a presidência. Mas sendo o Peru sua paixão e estigma, tema recorrente da sua magnífica obra, não é de estranhar que, em face do estraçalhamento da pátria, tenha provisoriamente trocado uma paixão pela outra.*

> I suspect that if Mario were French, he would never vie for the presidency. But given that Peru is his passion and his stigma, a recurrent theme in his magnificent opus, it is hardly strange that, faced with his country coming apart, he temporarily exchanged one passion for another.

Piñón had also expressed concern about her own country. In an interview long after the publication of *Tebas*, she said that she was troubled by:

> *uma visão de um Brasil fracionado, de um país de mil faces, onde o que importa . . . é a possibilidade de descobrir o passado e através dele, restaurar o futuro, restabelecer o debate, num processo que não é só do Brasil, mas de toda a América Latina.*

> a vision of a fragmented Brazil, of a country of a thousand faces, where what matters . . . is the possibility of discovering the past and through it, of restoring the future, reestablishing debate, in a process that is proper not only to Brazil, but to all of Latin America.

During the interview she also spoke of the imagination as "an inner resource . . . a great spark" that exalts the human being when it allows for crossing the boundaries of reality: "With imagination, he does not accept dogma, with imagination, he destroys convention. . . . Every time that the powers-that-be repress man, imagination is freed." Perhaps this belief comes from a desire to justify her creative processes, as well as justifying the obscurity with which she disguised a sensibility that was inopportune in the political climate of the time. In *The Buried Mirror: Reflections on Spain and the New World* (1992), Mexican writer Carlos Fuentes confirmed Piñón's stance when he wrote of the works of Cervantes and Velasquez:

> Cervantes teaches us to read anew, Velasquez teaches us to see anew. Certainly all great writers and artists do as much. But these two, working from within a closed society, were able to redefine reality in terms of the imagination. What we imagine is both possible and real.

How do those who, like Nélida Piñón, dare to give free rein to the imagination, manage to overcome the rigors and risks to which they are exposed? Artists like Piñón, who have devoted themselves for years to the task of weaving the quotidian with the fine threads of the imagination, create a new conceptual field for communication in their texts. Does an infinite process of invention come to bear within the text that would act on communication with all of the incantatory powers within its reach, even knowing that it is in the text that the author risks all criticism? Roland Barthes proposes that there is no way to impose limits and measurements upon a poetic text, for it does not need to lend itself to linguistic systematization. To reduce it to a logical and irreducible discourse would abort its ludic mission while stripping it of pleasure and obviating its attempt at subversion. One solution might be to separate the text from its context, to dislocate its link with the recipient, that is, the ideal reader, and to take the text as a primary object, a construct made of words that the artist orders and regenerates, creating with them his own language-object, negating the Barthesian concept that "one writes to be loved." Or one could even disagree with the Brazilian critic Leyla Perrone, for whom writing is a form of seduction "because it intends to act on the absent interlocutor, because it deals with all the vague, multiple desires that language is capable of putting into play and attaining on its own" (*Flores de Escrivaninha*).

It was during the late 1970s that the writer demonstrated her understanding of the peril in which Brazil's citizens lived. They had lost the right to make social and political claims and were in danger as well of losing the entire perspective of the past and any expectation of the future, to the extent that cultural censorship threatened to impoverish the national language. Piñón made it very clear, however, that over and beyond the desire to produce a best-seller, she was concerned with the quality of the text. This was her deepest commitment, the artistic manifestation of literary expression, and any other position would be tantamount to a disavowal of her responsibility as a writer. As a writer, she understood that her mission involved the production of texts. Furthermore, following the dynamic concept of "significance" put forth by semiotic theoretician Julia Kristeva (*Sémeiotikè: Recherches pour une sémanalyse*, 1969), she accepted that the text is precisely the space where discourse, in infinite permutations, achieves the rupture of the subject communicated, not being merely a simple mirror reflecting a reality. Perrone corroborates this notion: "The text is the place where the subject is produced with risk, where the subject is put into process and with it all of society, its logic, its morality, its economy" (*Texto, Critica, Escritura*). Whether as a coincidence or a revelation, we read in two pieces by Piñón that "Our daily bread was fantasy. That is how it came to be called world without end. Or simply, a poetic invention" ("O pão da fantasia," in *O pão de cada dia*). And, again:

*Simples coincidência ou as viagens são todas iguais? Para onde se siga, bate-se sempre à porta do inferno. . . . Neste inferno nasce o escritor. Leva ele à cintura a chave com que ambiciona desvendar estes espessos enigmas, sob a guarda de portas que se abrem e se fecham em surdina. . . . O óleo espectral da morte, contudo, lubrifica a fala narrativa do habitante do inferno. Sob o jugo do terror e dos presságios, este narrador examina ansioso o impacto e os imprevistos da história ao seu cargo. Não lhe falta, porém, apressar-se ou exagerar nas tintas. Tudo ali parece sereno, inexorável, imutável. Para sempre.*

("O discreto Hades," *O pão de cada dia*)

Is it mere coincidence or are all trips the same? Wherever you go, you always run up against the door to hell. . . . It is in this hell that a writer is born. At his waist, he bears the key which with he aims to uncover these thick enigmas, under the guard of doors that open and close stealthily. . . . The spectral oil of death nevertheless lubricates the narrative talk of the inhabitant of hell. Under the yoke of terror and of omens, this narrator anxiously examines the impact and the surprises in the story under his charge. Therefore he has no need to hurry or to exaggerate. Everything there seems serene, inexorable, immutable. Forever.

Another novel published in 1977, *A força do destino* (The force of destiny), also falls within the parameters of the ludic text. A decidedly intertextual exercise, the novel is constructed like a parody of Giuseppe Verdi's opera, *La forza del destino* (1869), whose librettos by Piave and Ghislanzoni were already a reworking of the Spanish melodrama, *Don Álvaro o la fuerza del sino*, written by the Duke of Rivas (1791–1836). Naomi Hoki Moniz has suggested that it is precisely in this book where Nélida Piñón achieves definition of herself as an artist through the aesthetic project. By means of a simultaneousness of linguistic registers, Piñón undertakes to turn the operatic text into a carnival, while simultaneously carrying out a deconstruction of the story and inserting herself into the text itself. The author's transformation into a fictional character could perhaps be a device to move from her closed space and place herself in the de-legitimizing space of the farce which, being an imaginary construct, was tolerated by the government censors.

The character of Nélida, a writer who is an accomplice in the flight of the tragic lovers, offers Verdi's Alvaro and Leonora a new existence: she reinvents them and sets them in the Portuguese-speaking world. She speaks to them in playful language during a series of events in which she futilely attempts to save the poor wretches.

*Padeço vendo Leonora ao chão, entregando a vida com raiva e inutilidade. Dói-lhe o corpo, e não posso ajudá-la. Provoca-me sua perda gretas no peito, eu sofro. . . . O que me terá Álvaro significado, até onde foi ele no meu coração. Não quero que ele morra, acreditem, por favor. . . . Ignoro os limites da minha vida, se me cabe perturbá-la com um afeto forte que ambas provamos, e eis o sal em nossas bocas. Esta porém é a simples história de uma história. E eu a sua discreta narradora.*

I suffer seeing Leonora on the ground, surrendering life with rage and futility. Her body aches, and I cannot help her. Her loss causes my chest to burst, I suffer. . . . I wonder what Alvaro meant to me, how deeply he went into my heart. I do not want him to die, please, believe me. . . . I do not know the limits of my life, it is up to me to perturb her with a strong affection that we both tried out, and here is the salt in our mouths. This is, however, the mere story of a story. And I am its discrete narrator.

In an interview with Beatriz Bonfim, Piñón was asked about the relationship of *A força do destino* to her previous books. The author responded thus:

*eu vejo em minha obra uma coerência diariamente violentada. Aparentemente o texto de hoje não perseguirá o texto de amanhã. Mas em que medida o texto de amanhã não é uma consequência inevitável do texto de hoje? Eu própria sou uma personagem protéica, de mil formas. Logo o meu texto, que lida basicamente e unicamente com o humano, é constituido de mil formas multiplicadas por todas as formas anteriores.*

I see in my works a coherence that is violated daily. Apparently, today's text will not follow tomorrow's text. But to what extent is tomorrow's text anything other than an inevitable consequence of today's text? I myself am a protean character with a thousand forms. Therefore, my text, which deals basically and only with the human, is comprised of a thousand forms multiplied by all of the previous forms.

Bonfim's question refers to the novelty of the discourse and narrative technique, as well as to the appearance of the author as a character, all of which were diametrically opposed to the creative approach that was followed in the preceding novel. And so that there will not be the least doubt about Piñón's intentions when she switches between the "narrated I" and the "narrative I," on more than one occasion we hear her shout:

*Unicamente por minhas mãos ingressariam ambos na língua portuguesa, que é, como expliquei a Álvaro, um feudo forte e lírico ao mesmo tempo. Um barco que até hoje singra generoso o Atlântico, ora consolando Portugal, ora perturbando o Brasil. . . . E porque ela se orgulha do que é humano, esta língua portuguesa, de rosto e sexo ardentes, é capaz de saber, apenas pelo apito do trem, se quarta-feira é dia dos amantes usarem-na quando se querem perder para sempre.*

*Daí esta língua precisar de que seus amantes se excedam, imaginem o coração incapaz de novo afeto. É nestas horas que a língua, sob tão grave ameaça, ganha dimensões impensadas.*

*Esta língua portuguesa, Álvaro, quer-se fazer ouvir para sempre. De cada palavra demanda uso e volúpias novas. Sem se importar com o pedaço do corpo de que abdicamos para preservá-la.*

It is only through my hands that both Álvaro and Leonora will enter the Portuguese language, which is, as I explained to Alvaro, a realm that is both strong and lyrical at the same time. A boat that till now generously straddles the Atlantic, now consoling Portugal, now perturbing Brazil. . . . It is because it is proud of what is human that this Portuguese language, of ardent face and sex, is capable of knowing from the whistle of a train if Wednesday is the day lovers use when they want to lose themselves forever.

Hence this language needs for its lovers to outdo themselves, to imagine a heart incapable of new affection. It is at these times that language, under such a serious threat, takes on unthought of dimensions.

This Portuguese language, Alvaro, wants to be heard forever. It demands new uses and pleasures for each word, without any concern for the body part that we abdicate to preserve it.

Bonfim asked Piñón why a writer writes. Is it a cathartic impulse, an ineluctable propensity for invention or even a need to communicate? Is it a feeling of irrevocable commitment vis-à-vis history or perhaps a desire to remake it? Is it a vocation for recording reality or the pleasure of imagining it? Is it a vocation for rebellion and transgression that leads the author to write? These questions had already been put to her beforehand, but no one response, however complex, can summarize all her reasons. Winner/Landers, the main character of the story "Romance Negro" (Black romance) by Brazilian writer Rubem Fonseca, asserts that "all literature, viewed from a given perspective, may be considered an escape. . . . Writers and readers, knowing that they are not eternal, escape in a Nietzchean manner from death. When we read fiction or poetry we flee the strict limits of the reality of the senses for another reality, one already said to be the only existing reality, the reality of the imagination."

Around this time, Piñón agreed to take part in the project of re-creating "Missa do galo" (Midnight mass), one of the most well-known stories by Machado de Assis. The project, ultimately published as *Missa do galo: Variações sobre o mesmo tema* (1977; Midnight mass: variations on a theme), featured original contributions by six authors, three women and three men, and was the brainchild of writer Osman Lins, who aimed to put into practice the anthropophagic principles of the modernists in a "highbrow" intellectual re-creation. In her volume *Texto, Critica, Escritura* (1978), Leyla Perrone has explained that literary anthropophagy exploits the "interrelatedness of the discourses of different time periods or of different linguistic areas . . . [and that it is] that task of continually absorbing and reworking other texts, wresting other meanings from them." The new *Missa do galo* texts thus maintain a dialogue with the original Machado discourse of imperial nineteenth-century Rio de Janeiro, while they introduce a discourse that is updated for the modern milieu of the height of the twentieth century. Lins notes the relentless originality of Piñón's version, which has a merely tangential relationship to the model, "freely expanding in unexpected directions . . . Nélida Piñón focuses on Menezes, probing his inner world and inventing for him a language that is as interesting as he is."

Only three years later, in 1980, the thirteen stories of *O calor das coisas* (The warmth of things) appeared, many of which are among the most well-received of the author's short works. "I Love My Husband," a satire on marital love and on the wife's role in marriage, is probably the story most often translated and included in both international as well as national collections. In 1980 Brazil was in the early days of its return to democracy and, over and above other concerns, Piñón was aware that national thinking was fragmented, diluted, and full of contradictions, and that the world

of language and literature was disintegrating as political censorship tried to silence it. In reviewing the book for *World Literature Today,* English critic John M. Parker observed, "The opening pages of the first story in Nélida Piñón's new collection seem to promise a form of direct commitment to contemporary Brazilian reality not previously found in this writer's work." Had contemporary Brazilian reality overcome the caution of self-censorship and captured the author's extremely sensitive imagination? Would this be the book where Piñón would confront history and craft her text in the context of the national political moment and where her voice would join the chorus of voices exposing the dictatorship? The narrator of the long opening tale, "O jardim das oliveiras" (The garden of olive trees), says, "Our death, Zé, belongs to whoever is present for it and to those who write about it. We are not our death. Rather we are the prolonged agony that lacks words with which to explain it to ourselves."

In this story, the obviously metaphorical title is loaded with references to the Gospels (Matt. 26:36–69; 27:1–44; 14:26–72; Luke 22:39). Within the transparent context of the narrative, the author weaves her lesson of passion and betrayal, as in the garden of Gethsemane, where a murder was sealed with a kiss. Piñón crafts her metatext within the context of ancient and modern records of individual experience, wrought with insistent echoes of the New Testament as the driving force of the creative process. In "O Jardim das Oliveiras" icons merge, heroes are demystified, and legends are invented in a new "version" of the sacred texts. Borrowing from well-known scatological lessons and even from the language of the Bible itself, Piñón invents an imaginary world in which to insert her tale, like so many others stored in the collective memory of that time and which, if not recorded, would fall into oblivion or would survive as merely some banal experience of daily unreality.

By portraying the protagonist as the hero of an anonymous episode and later framing it in a "biblical" context, the author robs the episode of its vile and inglorious reality. Transposing him to the legendary garden, she places him in a realm of fable, borrowing many voices and many roles from the drama of Gethsemane. She also gives her protagonist the dimensions of a tragic hero in whom all of the Christian icons can be glimpsed, although he does not manage to be any of them and contents himself with merely being a man who is free to love Luíza. She, like the reader, knows him to be "a mask without a past. Or a past with inventions, a biography to which changeable and false information is added." At a conference in 1995, the author observed that the sense of the miraculous and the persistence of wonder are a part of the Brazilian sensibility, where art exhibits "the aesthetic of want and magic. A disturbing alliance that transforms miracles, or hope in them, into an aesthetic variant. And which points up wonders as restorative facets of the American imagination."

Upon a careful reading, *O calor das coisas* presages the author's next great novel, already in gestation: *A república dos sonhos* (1984; *The Republic of Dreams*, 1989), the saga of a family of Galician immigrants who arrive in Brazil at the beginning of the twentieth century. Speaking of his fear of his own aging, that perhaps death will save him, the tortured man writes to Zé in "O Jardim das Oliveiras" and mentions the secret of his grandfather who "went on saving bread and money in order to be respected. . . . From his hands fell coins which rolled directly into his children's plates. Food came from him, just as dreams did. He had bought his grandchildren's dreams with his sweat." The author thus establishes a link between the new characters and those that preceded them, giving all of them legitimacy within the great tribe engendered by her creativity.

*The Republic of Dreams* was originally conceived as the history of patriarch and capitalist Madruga, who emigrated while young and penniless from Galicia to "make America" in Brazil in 1913. During the voyage by ship, paid for by an uncle, he strikes up a friendship with an onboard companion, the young Venâncio; their friendship will strengthen over time and will last to the end of both of their lives. One would have a life of success, wealth, and family; the other would lead a solitary and mediocre existence. The force that brings them together is Eulália, a rich, devoted, and discreet woman who agrees to marry Madruga and to found a Brazilian dynasty with him. The book itself is written by their granddaughter Breta, the family's writer, to whom Madruga has entrusted the task of recording his memories. In this undertaking, Breta includes her own recollections, along with those of other members of the clan,

having set herself the task of picking up all the threads with which to sew together the precious scraps of their lives. Using this warp and woof, Breta weaves the thick and carefully wrought cloth that will celebrate life and death in her family. Piñón hereby begins the first feminine discourse that attempts to crystallize the founding experiences of European immigrants in Brazil and to thereby sketch the reality of Brazil.

The narrative time period spans five generations and includes characters drawn from historical reality, along with others dreamed up or invented by the author and inserted into various historical or contemporary eras, in spaces that draw together the outskirts of the city of Rio de Janeiro and beyond it, Brazil and Europe.

> From when I was just a little girl, Madruga had clung to my very skin. He never left me, so that I wouldn't leave him. He made up his mind to prolong his life through me, inhabiting part of my soul as he added years to it. Reflected in him as though his senile presence would not let go of me, I had not had the strength to banish him in time. Because, my story having begun with him, he was still the one who was recounting it. In obedience to a dramatic instinct for succession, which obliged me to go into the question of who would take over my soul in the future. Whom to will it to, so that its owner would take it into his safekeeping at the appointed hour.

Although this novel may be eminently related to the rest of Piñón's vast fictional world, a new approach to the creative task can be observed. In this work, the author adopts a more communicative and less intransigent posture vis-à-vis the reader, particularly in her use of syntax and in the text's dependency on the nuances of symbolism. The poet Horácio Costa has asserted that, while *A casa da paixão* and *Tebas do meu coração* "capitalized on the deliberate utilization of the principle of ambiguity, placing an emphasis on the subjugation of the reader to a complex, ever changing text loaded with symbolism and metaphors, *A república dos sonhos* unfolds at a level of undisputable versimilitude, where the author's aims are clear and the story is punctuated by historical milestones." In this novel thus there is a greater emphasis on the "referential axis" that is more appropriate to a text that is a memoir and, albeit tenuously, autobiographical. Nevertheless, this novel contains the narrative originality, the flights of imagination, the dreamlike spaces, the finely wrought diction, and the structural agility worthy of the best memoir novels inside and outside of Brazil persist.

Piñón is the undisputed heir to the best storytelling tradition of family sagas that was founded at the end of the nineteenth century by Portuguese novelist Eça de Queiroz with *Os Maias* (1888) and, beginning in the 1930s, by Brazilian authors Érico Veríssimo with *O Tempo e o Vento,* Pedro Nava, with his voluminous memoirs, and Graciliano Ramos with *São Bernardo.* In addition to what the national masters taught her, Piñón learned from the great revivers of the narrative in the twentieth century, beginning with Thomas Mann, the ingenious German creator of *Buddenbrooks* (1902). Among these, her reading of William Faulkner is undeniably important, as is the interrelationship that her text in *The Republic of Dreams* has with *As I Lay Dying* (1930). She also has a profound knowledge of the issue of time, as set forth by Marcel Proust in his cycle running from *À la recherche du temps perdu* to *Les temps retrouvé* (1913–1927). On the other hand, the writer's vigorous literary undertaking never falls neatly within the realist canons of those authors. Rather, she remains faithful to the aesthetic principles that have guided her as an educated and modern woman and writer.

Faithful to the beautiful task of "inventing the real, transforming a false life into something real, or, even more relevantly, a real life into a false one" (in the words of Fonseca's Winner/Landers), Piñón embarked on another adventure, this time in the small city of Trindade, lost in time and in the geography of the interior of Brazil. This is the setting for *A doce canção de Caetana* (1987; *Caetana's Sweet Song,* 1992), where admirable or grotesque characters in the eternal human comedy are perpetually waiting for the progress and the art that would come to them with the return of a great diva named Caetana. Driven by the eternal love that Polidoro nourished for Caetana during an absence of twenty years, now reinvigorated by the diva's imminent return, the entire population goes to the train station, which has been renovated like the rest of the city, its hotel, and its theater, where one day the sweet song of Caetana will be heard.

The writing of *A doce canção de Caetana* was completed on 10 August 1987, and in the interview, "Nélida canta a Academia" (Nélida sings the Academy), granted to Geneton Moraes Neto on 5 December 1987, the author celebrated 26 years of literary activity. On that occasion, she discoursed about a writer's coexistence with the critics and the relative importance of a relationship between the author and the reader. To the critics, Piñón recommended an attitude of responsibility and seriousness in order for them to be effective. She admitted, however, that the reader is not the focus of her concern at the moment of creation, for if it were so, it would be, in the author's words, "a reader with a Ph.D., who is prosperous, extremely refined, and who loves me." Rather she hopes to reach many others in other time periods and spaces: "I want a riverside dweller to read me some day. Or his son. That is the reason why I write; also for a better country, in addition to my passions."

Her passions are precisely the cloth from which she wove the fragments that appear in *O pão de cada dia,* published in 1994. In this book, Piñón offers her readers a provocative and revealing testimony when she abandons her "fictional universe" and sets out on a pilgrimage toward her human, aesthetic, and ethical self. Through this text, the author affords critics a more judicious approach to her work. In it we also find copious references to her trips to the United States and to various European countries, trips that are part of her formative process. Piñón has always traveled. She studied in Galicia, resided in Europe, and became friends with a large number of intellectuals in various countries. More recently, the geographical moves accompany other trips of discovery and self-scrutiny that in turn result in the flowering of feelings, yearnings, and even vulnerabilities, hidden behind a multitude of masks protecting her face, her freedom, and her innermost nature.

The tales collected in *Até amanhã, outra vez* (Until tomorrow, once again), published in 1999, establish a level of communication between the author and the reader that results in a comfortable sense of trust, familiarity, and spiritual communion impossible in her previous work. The demands of the new millennium, characterized by the explosion of global communications and the blurring of geographical and intellectual borders, caused this writer, who is one of the most active both in Brazil as well as within the larger

American cultural landscape, to insert herself in her characters' world of magical realism and join them in inventing their own story. It was no longer enough for her to remain in the shadow of Breta. She felt confident enough to face the world without smokescreens, revealing herself to be a wise woman, a sorrowful daughter, and a faithful friend, as well as a conscientious, ambitious, and combative creator, and a citizen of a world where the complexity of life reaches metaphysical proportions:

*Sou quem nutre profunda nostalia por uma Galícia que conheci menina, mal sabendo que existia a geografia dos homens e que cada terra—dentro desta estranha noção de pátria—levava um nome. Um nome no mapa, um nome na geopolítica, um nome, sobretudo, na alma.*

I am she who nourishes a profound yearning for Galicia, which I knew when I was small, hardly knowing that the geography of man existed and that each land—within this strange notion of fatherland—bears a name. A name on a map, a name in geopolitics, a name, above all, in the soul.

Remaining indefatigable and active, with books of stories, novels, and tales translated into various languages and published in thirteen countries, Nélida Piñón holds a privileged position within the Brazilian intellectual class, the fruit of her long coexistence with the language, the letters, and the dilemmas of a Brazil that is as complex and moving as it is surprising and marvelous. Her national and international renown has been recognized with numerous honors, including the Juan Rulfo Prize for Latin American and Caribbean Literature for her overall work (Mexico, 1995), medals such as the Order of the Southern Cross (Brazil, 1990), the Ribbon of Dame Isabel the Catholic (Spain, 1992), the Castelão Medal (Galicia, Spain, 1992) and three Doctorate *Honoris Causa* degrees: from Florida Atlantic University at Boca Raton in 1996; from the University of Poiters, France, in 1997; and from Rutgers University in 1998.

Finally, on 5 December 1996, Nélida Piñón was elected president of the Brazilian Academy of Letters, becoming the first woman to hold this office, precisely in the year when the illustrious House of Machado de Assis was commemorating its hundredth anniversary.

In the speech she delivered upon taking office, the author defined herself:

Recently, in Mexico, I stated that Brazil was my dwelling and that I had the pleasure of serving literature with a woman's mind and body. And that I told stories because my memory is the collective memory of my feminine gender. A remote memory that was present throughout the painful pilgrimage of humanity on earth. A memory that was the caretaker of history, the protector of the myths that brought warmth to the living rooms and irrigated the imagination, the legends, the poetry. Of all, in short, that helped to soften the loneliness of man.

We must not be surprised, therefore, to hear her say:

I took part in various movements, was part of a number of projects, but I was never unbending in my position, I never allowed myself to be tied down. Because of this, I was able to evolve, to change. The only thing I do not allow is compromises with literature. I owe everything to literature, faithfulness, maturity. In it I find the ravine where I can safeguard my ethics. Literature helped me to polish my humanity. And I see literature with emotion, with tenderness, and with great humility.

*Translated from the Portuguese
by Elizabeth Welborn Cardinale*

# SELECTED BIBLIOGRAPHY

## Primary Works

### Novels

*Guia-mapa de Gabriel Arcanjo.* Rio de Janeiro, 1961.
*Madeira feita cruz.* Rio de Janeiro, 1963.
*Fundador.* Rio de Janeiro, 1969.
*A casa da paixão.* Rio de Janeiro, 1972.
*Tebas do meu coração.* Rio de Janeiro, 1974.
*A força do destino.* Rio de Janeiro, 1977.
*A república dos sonhos.* Rio de Janeiro, 1984; Lisbon, 1997.
*A doce canção de Caetana.* Rio de Janeiro, 1987.

### Short Story Collections

*Tempo das frutas.* Rio de Janeiro, 1966.

*Sala de armas.* Rio de Janeiro, 1973.

*O calor das coisas.* Rio de Janeiro, 1980.

*Cortejo do Divino e Outros Contos Escolhidos.* Porto Alegre, 1999.

### Other Works

"Missa do galo." In *Missa do Galo de Machado de Assis. Variações sobre o mesmo tema.* São Paulo, 1977. (An experimental exercise in creative writing with Antônio Callado, Autran Dourado, Julieta de Godoy Ladeira, Osman Lins, and Lygia Fagundes Telles.)

*O pão de cada dia: Fragmentos.* Rio de Janeiro, 1994.

*A Roda do Vento.* São Paulo, 1996. (Literature intended for younger readers.)

*Até amanhã, outra vez: Crônicas.* Rio de Janeiro, 1999.

### Translations

"Bird of Paradise." Trans. by Giovanni Pontiero. *Review* 76, no. 19:75–78 (winter 1976).

*The Republic of Dreams.* Trans. by Helen Lane. New York: Knopf, 1989. Austin, Tex.: University of Texas Press, 1991. London: Picador, 1994.

*Caetana's Sweet Song.* Trans. by Helen Lane. New York: Knopf, 1992.

### Secondary Works

### Critical and Biographical Studies

Academia Brasileira de Letras. "Nélida Piñón, Cadeira No. 30." *Anuário 1993–1997.* Rio de Janeiro, 1997. Pp. 200–211.

Areas, Vilma. "Do Adamastor Camoniano a *Sala de armas* de Nélida Piñón." *Coloquio,* 27:32–39 (1974).

Bianciotti, Hector. "L'arbre de Nelida Piñón." *Le Monde,* 8 February 1991, p. 27.

Brosnaban, John. "*The Republic of Dreams* by Nelida Piñón." *Booklist* 85, no. 19:1696 (1989).

Campos, Maria Consuelo Cunha. "O Romance da Nova República." *Minas Gerais, Suplemento Literário* 20, no. 962:5 (1985).

Coelho, Nelly Novaes. "*A casa da paixão* e as forças primordiais da natureza." *Convivium* 16, no. 3:216–228 (1973).

———. "Nelida Piñón, Prêmio 'Mário de Andrade.'" *Coloquio,* 15:74–77 (1973).

———. "*A república dos sonhos*: prêmio ficção/84 APCA: memória, historicidade, imaginário." *Convivium* 28, no. 3:257–265 (1985).

Costa, Horácio. "A Margem de *A república dos sonhos* de Nélida Piñón." *Luso-Brazilian Review* 24, no. 1:1–15 (1987).

Coutinho, Afrânio, and J. Galante de Sousa. *Enciclopédia da Literatura Brasileira.* Rio de Janeiro: OLAC/FAE/MEC, 1990.

Crespo, Angel, and Pilar Gómez Bedate. "Nélida Piñón de *Guia-mapa Tempo das frutas.*" *Revista de cultura brasileña* 24:5–27.

Cunha, Fausto. "Tebas de Todas as Portas." *Jornal do Brasil,* 7 September 1974.

Faria, Otávio. "Surge uma romancista." *Última Hora,* 15 September 1976.

———. "Nélida Piñón." *Última Hora,* 24 May 1978.

Fonta, Sérgio. "Nélida Piñón: O papo." *Jornal de Letras: Mensário de Letras, Artes e Ciências* 260, no. 2:6 (1972). (An interview with the author.)

Giudice, Vitor. "*Sala de armas.*" *Tribuna de Imprensa,* 13 June 1973.

———. "Tebas de Nélida Piñón." *Minas Gerais, Suplemento Literário,* 3 August 1974.

Gonzales Tosar, Luis. "Nélida Piñón ou a Paixon de Contar." *Grial: Revista Galega de Cultura* 28, no. 105:85–95 (1990).

Guimarães, Denise A. D. "Uma Poética de Autor: Leitura de um Texto de Nélida Piñón." *Estudos Brasileiros* 5, no. 9:39–55 (1980).

Gray, Rockwell. "On *The Republic of Dream* by Nélida Piñón." *Chicago Tribune,* 1989.

Hohlfeldt, Antônio. "Retrato de um Continente." *Minas Gerais, Suplemento Literário,* 4 January 1975, pp. 4–5. (A discussion of *Tebas do meu coração.*)

Issa, Farida. "Entrevista con Nélida Piñón." Trans. by Gregory Rabassa. *Nueva Narrativa Hispanoamericana* 3, no. 1:133–140 (1973).

Landers, Vlasda B. "Interview with Nélida Piñón." *Belles Lettres* 6:24–25 (1991).

Lara, Cecelia de. "O 'indevassável casulo': uma leitura de *A república dos sonhos* de Nélida Piñón." *Revista de Estudos Brasileiros* 27:27–36 (1987).

Lemon, Lee. "*The Republic of Dreams* by Nélida Piñón." *Prairie Schooner* 64, no. 2:131 (1990).

Maffre, Claude. "Les chemins du rêves dans *A república dos sonhos* de Nélida Piñón." *Quadrant,* 1988, pp. 165–182.

Martins, Wilson. "*A força do destino* by Nélida Piñón." *World Literature Today* 53, no. 1:95 (1979).

McNab, Gregory. "Abordando a História em *A república dos sonhos*: Brasil/Brazil." *Revista de Literatura Brasileira* 1, no. 1:41–53 (1988).

Medina, Cremilda. "Embarque no Sonho nesta República em Mutação." *Minas Gerais, Suplemento Literário* 20, no. 964:8 (1985).

Melillo Reali, Erilde. " 'Missa do Galo' e variazione sul tema: Sei riscritture di un racconto machadiano." *Annali Instituto Universitario Orientale* (Napoli, Sezione Romanza) 25, no. 1:69–124 (1983).

Milán, Eduardo. "Escribir en estado de alerta." *Revista de la Universidad de México* 36, no. 3:12–13 (1981).

Moniz, Naomi Hoki. "A casa da paixão: Ética, Estética e a Condição Feminina." *Revista Iberoamericana* 50, no. 126:129–140 (1984).

———. *As Viagens de Nélida, a escritora.* São Paulo, Campinas, UNICAMP, 1993.

Newman, Charles, and José Donoso, eds. *Contemporary Latin American Literature.* Evanston, Ill.: Northwestern University Press, 1969.

Nunez, Maria Luisa. "Review of *A força do destino* by Nélida Piñón." *Revista Iberoamericana* 45, nos. 108–109:712–716 (1979).

Ornelas, Joseph. "El mundo simbólico y filosófico de *Madeira feita cruz* de Nélida Piñón." *Nueva Narrativa Hispanoamericana*, 3, no. 1:95–102 (1973).

Page, Joseph A. "Saga of a Spanish Family and Its Fortunes in Brazil: *The Republic of Dreams* by Nélida Piñón." *Philadelphia Inquirer*, 20 August 1989.

Parker, John M. "Life in Limbo, Nélida Piñón: *Tebas do meu coração.*" *Times Literary Supplement*, 6 August 1976, p. 995.

———. "*O calor das coisas* by Nélida Piñón." *World Literature Today* 55, no. 4:650 (1981).

———. "*A república dos sonhos* by Nélida Piñón." *World Literature Today* 59, 4:578 (1985).

Paulino, Maria das Graças Rodrigues. "*Fundador*: A Subversão do Mito." *Cadernos de Linguística e Teoria da Literatura* 2:71–75 (1979).

Pereira, Teresinha Alves. "Sobre un cuento de Nélida Piñón: 'Sala de armas.' " *Revista de Cultura Brasileña* 49:118–120 (1979).

Pettorelli, Lapouge. "Ecrire dans la langue du Bresil, c'est reveler le Bresil tel qu'il est." *La Quinzaine Litteraire* 484:27–28 (1987).

Polk, James. "*The Republic of Dreams* by Nélida Piñón and Helen Lane." *New York Times Book Review*, 30 July 1989, p. 22.

Pólvora, Hélio. "A fisiologia da paixão." *Jornal do Brasil*, 11 July 1973.

Pontiero, Giovanni. "Notes on the Fiction of Nélida Piñón." *Review* 76, no. 19:67–71 (1976).

Regis, Sônia. "O calor das coisas." *O Estado de São Paulo*, 4 October 1981.

Ribeiro, Leo Gilson. "Nossa prece por Nélida." *O Estado de São Paulo*, 13 May 1978.

Riera, Carmen. "Entrevista con Nélida Piñón: la vida es la literatura." *Quimera: Revista de Literatura* 54–55: 44–49.

Ryan, Alan. "Chronicle of a Brazilian Family: *The Republic of Dreams* by Nélida Piñón." Trans. by Helen Lane. *Washington Post Book World* 19, 30 July 1989, p. 58.

Scholes, Robert. "Towards a Poetics of Fiction: An Approach through Genre." *Novel* 2:10–11 (1969).

Secco, Carmen Lucia Tindo. "A Metáfora da Traição em João Alphonsus e em Nélida Piñón." *Minas Gerais. Suplemento Literário* 14, no. 789:11 (14 November 1981).

———. *Além da Idade da Razão; Longevidade e Saber na Ficção Brasileira. Posfácio de Nélida Piñón.* Série Temas e Reflexões. Rio de Janeiro: Graphia, 1994.

Silverman, Malcolm. "*O calor das coisas* by Nélida Piñón." *Modern Language Journal* 65, no. 3:344–345 (1981).

Spielmann, Ellen. "Um Romance como Espaço Auto-Reflexao Literária: Nélida Piñón: A força do destino." *Revista de Crítica Literária Latinoamericana* 15, no. 30:209–219 (1989).

Steinberg, Sybil. "*The Republic of Dreams* by Nélida Piñón." *Publishers Weekly* 235, no. 17:59 (18 April 1989).

Stern, Irwin, ed. *Dictionary of Brazilian Literature.* New York: Greenwood Press, 1988.

Teixeira, Vera Regina. "Texto, Contexto e Pretexto na Obra de Nélida Piñón." *Letras de Hoje* (Porto Alegre), no. 1:109–117 (30 March 1995).

Vargas Llosa, Mario. "Palabras de Vargas Llosa en la presentación de un libro de Nélida Piñón." *Revista de Cultura Brasileña* 48:81–91 (1979).

Williams, Frederick G. "A Generational Schema and Luso-Brazilian Letters." *Luso-Brazilian Review* 7:57–82 (1970).

# Elena Poniatowska

## (1932–    )

## Sara Poot-Herrera

The work of Mexican writer Elena Poniatowska, already one of the most mature and prolific authors of the second half of the twentieth century, continues to expand and enrich itself into the millenium. Poniatowska is one of the most well-known contemporary authors in Latin America, primarily because of journalistic writings such as interviews, news articles, and chronicles. Increasingly, however, she is also gaining recognition for the novels and short stories she has created out of a mixture of fiction and nonfiction genres. Her work is distinguished by its consistently high quality, due not only to her untiring professionalism but also to the sheer joy she evidently takes in the act of writing. She possesses an unparalleled ability to express herself in both written and oral registers, while at the same time she selects and connects words to reveal the brilliance, rhythm, and poetry they contain. Her love affair with the word constantly renews her desire to listen to what others have to say and to record them accurately, incorporating them into a refined work of literature that artfully fuses orality and writing.

Poniatowska's keen ear for dialogue makes her a natural interviewer. For nearly half a century she has confronted her world with an insatiable curiosity that she converts into questions for her interviewees. In her hands, the interview has become a literary genre that passes from its original place of publication in newspapers and magazines into the permanence of collections or into an expanded form, such as the novel. Her first compilation of interviews, *Palabras cruzadas* (1961; Crosswords), is a kaleidoscope of cultural life in Mexico. The interviews can be read as both literature and journalism; taken together, these two modes of writing participate in the formation of another key genre in Poniatowska's work, the chronicle, which she perfected most famously in her classic text on the student movement of 1968, *La noche de Tlatelolco. Testimonios de historia oral* (1971; *Massacre in Mexico*, 1975).

That canonical work is the fruit of innumerable individual interviews. It showcases the perfection of a technique that allows Elena to seem absent or invisible in the process. Using the same innovative technique when gathering material and a similar use of real-life information, Elena has also demonstrated a new way of turning historical figures into fictional characters. The most important book of fiction to emerge from this strategy is Poniatowska's 1969 novel, *Hasta no verte Jesús mío* (*Here's to You, Jesusa*, 2001). Jesusa Palancares, protagonist of the novel, is one of Poniatowska's many fictional characters who serve to profile and protest a system that privileges only a few and oppresses its poor majority. Drawn from the marginalized lower classes, Poniatowska's characters speak in their own voices, telling about the injustices they have suffered. Poniatowska's novels thus become supplementary histories that register events and facts not to be found in official annals of her country; her fictional characters artistically voice a critical and morally committed posture that is shared by the silenced of the real world. This author's lifelong commitment to the poor of Mexico, and to the women of this historically sexist society, is all the more notable because she made this decision at a very tender age, despite being a daughter of the European nobility and member of the Mexican landed gentry.

Hélène Elizabeth Louise Amelie Paula Dolores Poniatowska Amor was born in Paris in 1932, as was her sister Sofía. Sofía, known as Kitzia, appears as Mariana's sister in the novel *La "Flor de Lis"* (1988; The "Fleur de Lis"). Mariana, the protagonist of that novel, comes to Mexico City as a child and, in her adolescent years, explores the city by walking around and taking buses with rural immigrants who had also come to claim the streets of the capital. She is thus a reflection of Poniatowska herself, who, while still a young woman, began to develop her lifelong moral commitment to the popular classes through her contact with the family's domestic servants.

Elena's father, Jean Evremont Poniatowski Sperry, was the son of Prince André Poniatowski and a descendent of the last king of Poland. Her mother, María Dolores Paula (Paulette) Amor Yturbe, was born of Mexican exiles who had remained in France until the beginning of the 1940s. During their years in Paris, the Poniatowska sisters grew up to the sound of gunshots during World War II; they painted their windows blue to make their house invisible to night bombers. The father served in the French forces and, for a time, the mother drove a support truck that doubled as an ambulance for Resistance fighters. It was ultimately decided, however, that Paulette would take both the girls to America. They left France on the ship *Marqués de Comillas*, docked in Havana, and from there traveled to Mexico City in 1942 on a two-engine plane. That same year, Italian photographer Tina Modotti died in Mexico. In *Tinísima* (1988), her most extensive novel, Poniatowska later paid homage to the photographer. In *Nomeolvides* (1996), a memoir that Poniatowska's mother wrote in French and English and which Elena later

translated into Spanish, Paulette reminds her daughters of their arrival in America: "México recibía a tres francesas, una de ellas de proveniencia mexicana, ustedes, francesa, americana, rusa y polaca. ¡Qué ensalada!" (Mexico was getting three French women, one of them of Mexican descent and the other two—you girls—of French, American, Russian, and Polish lineage. What a mixed salad!). Elena Poniatowska chose to be Mexican, and through her literature she made a serious, loving, and unswerving commitment to her adopted country.

In the nation's capital during the early 1940s, the family continued to speak French in their home on Berlin Street, not far from the Paseo de la Reforma, the famous thoroughfare whose name Poniatowska would later make the title of one of her books. The two sisters learned English in the Windsor School, and at home they learned Spanish from the women who took care of the household chores. At midyear in 1945 their father, who had visited the family a year earlier, came to stay for good; the war had ended and this nobleman, who had served as an officer, arrived in Mexico covered with honors and medals. Mexico City was by then the family's permanent home, and the youngest child, a boy named Jan, was born there in 1947. Elena and Kitzia joined the French Girl Scouts, and were later sent by their parents to study in the Sacred Heart Convent of Torresdale, Pennsylvania. Elena was a student in that boarding school from the end of the 1940s until the early 1950s. On her return to Mexico, while still quite young, she began her writing career by writing interviews and news stories; she has continued to practice journalism throughout her career.

With a 1953 assignment that involved asking the then U.S. ambassador to Mexico, Francis White, "a thousand questions," Poniatowska began devoting herself to an important aspect of her newswriting: the interview. Besides turning it into a major genre, she eventually used the interview as the basis for *Here's to You, Jesusa*. In 1953, however, she was writing for the newspaper *El Excélsior* under the pen name Hélène. She had originally chosen the pseudonym "Dumbo," but another female reporter was already writing as "Bambi" and the editor didn't want the entire Disney family on his staff. At about that time she called on Mexican writer Juan José Arreola, a master of literary narrative who, being no fan of journalism, encouraged her to publish her first work of fiction, *Lilus Kikus*, in 1954. By this time, Elena was working for the newspaper *Novedades* and had begun to publish in several Mexican magazines. Other dailies, besides *El Excélsior* and *Novedades*, also have accepted her pieces—*La Jornada* is among the most recent—and she has published widely in journals such as *Fem*, one of Mexico's most important feminist publications. As part of her commitment to *Fem* she wrote a retrospective piece on the journal's humanist mission and its writers; in the article she dramatized the critical issue of kidnapped and murdered political activists in Latin America with "*Fem* o el rostro desaparecido de Alaíde Foppa," a biographical homage to one of the magazine's female writers (*Fem, 10 años de periodismo feminista*).

The 1960s were fundamental for Elena Poniatowska: she honed her awareness of a corrupt political system's abuses and turned her attention to the downtrodden sectors of society. She began to produce a body of work dedicated to the victims who suffered from the deep inequities and injustices of her country. *Todo empezó el domingo* (1963), with illustrations by Alberto Beltrán, was the first testimonial effort to come out of this period. In 1968, a student protest movement embroiled Mexico in controversy and violence. On 2 October of that year, in the Plaza de las Tres Culturas, in a part of the capital called Tlatelolco, thousands of students gathered for a political demonstration, asking that the government satisfy a series of demands. The government responded, not with dialogue but with its army, whose soldiers fired on the civilian crowd. Hundreds of protesters and bystanders died in this attack. Some of the protesters sought asylum in nearby residences, others were hunted down, and hundreds were imprisoned, some of them remaining in custody without trial for years. The subsequent geovernment coverup and press censorship conferred upon *Massacre in Mexico* a great deal of importnace. To write the book, Poniatowska spent two years interviewing jailed dissidents after the massacre. This work, together with her most celebrated testimonial novel, *Here's to You, Jesusa*, has been translated into many languages and both are frequently reissued in new editions. They are classics for the study of Mexican history, culture, and literature.

Another tragedy in 1968 affected the Poniatowska family personally; Elena's brother Jan, who had participated in the student movement in October, was killed in December in an automobile accident. That same year, Elena married the scientist Guillermo Haro, who died in 1988, and about whom she would later write the award-winning novel *La piel del cielo* (2001). In 1969, after meeting Jesusa Palancares and witnessing the massacre at Tlatelolco, Elena became a Mexican citizen. Her father died in 1979, and the relationship between Poniatowska and her mother grew even closer.

In 2001 Paulette Poniatowska died. Her memoir, *Nomeolvides* engages in a dialogue with Elena's own *La "Flor de Lis."* The mother figure is fundamental to Elena Poniatowska's career and to her personal life as well. She is the mother of three children (Emmanuel, Felipe, and Paula, all of whom are married) and grandmother of six.

Poniatowska's literary career includes participation in and service to many organizations and programs associated with her art. She is co-founder of the Cineteca Nacional (National Film Archives), she helped found the publishing house Siglo XXI, and she is co-founder of several Mexican newspapers. Her ardent support and influence are a boon to the publishing world in Mexico. Among her innumerable activities, she participates in public forums, political protests, and in television and radio series; and she brings to the public a knowledge of important events and figures who would otherwise go unrecognized. In addition she supports social movements and causes, defends the rights of indigenous peoples, and visits jails and hospitals. She may be seen carrying her tape recorder as she walks about downtown or frequents the streets and bookstores near her house. Her work occasions frequent travel, perhaps to give a lecture or teach a class, often outside the capital or the country.

While paying homage to Nellie Campobello or Rosario Castellanos, it occurred to her that "La literatura de las mujeres es parte de la literatura de los oprimidos" (*Fem* 6 (1982): 21–27; Women's writing belongs to the literature of the oppressed); for this reason, she translates women writers from English and French into Spanish. An example of this work is her 1994 translation of *The House on Mango Street* (1983), a novel by chicana writer Sandra Cisneros. In addition she conducts a literary workshop, interviews a wide range of individuals and allows others to interview her, receives a constant flow of visitors to her home, joins in ceremonial book presentations, and generously acknowledges new writers, especially women: Silvia Molina, Ángeles Mastretta, Laura Esquivel, and Rosa Beltrán, among others.

Poniatowska saves and brings to public knowledge historical documents from important eras, denounces injustices, publishes in newspapers and magazines, and writes prologues for many genres of books; she also writes film scripts, cultivates her friendships, and treasures home and family. When asked, she willingly discusses her work. Despite such a heavy schedule, she also manages to do research, read, and somehow, miraculously and with passionate devotion, still reserves enough time for her own writing.

In recognition of her many accomplishments, Poniatowska has received numerous awards. In 1957 she received a scholarship from the Centro Mexicano de Escritores; in 1987 the Manuel Buendía Award for journalism; and in 1990 the Coatlicue Award, naming her "Woman of the Year." In 1993 she was given the Juchimán Award for Sciences and Communication and was invited to become a fellow of the Consejo Nacional para la Cultura y las Artes; in 1994 she won a Guggenheim Fellowship to write a manuscript that was provisionally entitled *T. Tauri* and was later published as *La piel del cielo*. In 1971 she wrote an open letter to refuse the Xavier Villaurrutia award for *Massacre in Mexico*, challenging Mexican president Luis Echeverría Álvarez by asking who was going to give an award to those killed in the 1968 massacre. She did accept the 1979 Premio Nacional de Periodismo; she was the first female journalist ever to be so honored. Her novels *Here's to You, Jesusa* and *Tinísima* received the Mazatlán Award in 1972 and 1992, respectively. Poniatowska has also received honorary doctorates from the Autonomous University of Sinaloa and the Autonomous University of the State of Mexico. She was named Doctor in Humanities and Letters by the New School for Social Research in New York and by Florida Atlantic University. In 2000 an homage to her was co-sponsored by the Asociación de Cronistas de Jalisco and the gay and lesbian community of Mexico. Her novel *La piel del cielo*

received the prestigious Editorial Alfaguara award in Madrid in 2001. The book was entered into the competition under the pen name "Dumbo," the name that she had wanted to use while writing for *El Excélsior* in the early 1950s.

Poniatowska's fame and far-reaching literary success derive from many factors: her exceptional use of language and its metaphors; her imaginative, lucid, flowing prose; and her humor, irony, and freshness of speech. She is renowned for giving voice to oppressed groups through her work, and for giving the marginalized their rightful place in Mexican history and culture. The sheer volume of her production over four decades has made the writer into the very often incendiary, living conscience of Mexico, and she has become one of her country's most published writers. Her works have been translated into English, French, Italian, German, Polish, Danish, and Dutch.

Elena Poniatowska's early texts reveal a variety of literary genres; in addition to interviews, chronicles, journalistic articles, and essays, she also wrote short stories, novels, and a play. As important as the volume and variety of her work is the way in which Poniatowska intertwines the genres of fiction and nonfiction. She has become known for using her work to express her surprise and admiration for people, events, and objects, as well as for practicing what might be understood as a demonstrated poetics of orality. The spoken word of the popular classes, whom she defends and individualizes in her writing, lend her the raw material for a linguistic latticework through which she interweaves diverse social registers and tonalities as she reworks the ephemeral orality of speech and turns it into the permanence of written art.

Poniatowska has discovered and cultivated of a written style that can internalize the poetry of oral expression. Her characters, real or imagined, embody the entire range of possible speech patterns, be they women, scientists, artists, politicians, laborers, craftsmen, domestic help, or foreigners, with adjustments made for the passage of time. She combines this stylistic variation with an attachment to the less privileged segments of society, in order to present a fully rounded narrative "history" of Mexico in the second half of the twentieth century. The realism of her fictionalized characters is heightened by having been created out of the myriad true-life individuals she has interviewed. In the midst of these stylistic innovations, she has maintained a critical vision, one that demands answers for all the questions she poses for modern Mexico, even as she presents answers of her own.

One may approach a characterization of Poniatowska's body of work from several angles. A study by genre could include an examination of the type of literature that emerges from the context of women's and other gender studies, while a cultural perspective would analyze her work from the standpoint of popular culture or from the perspective of the subordinate classes. Alternatively, one could approach the issue by examining the relationship of her literature to other art forms, including oral history. Still another approach, that of determining which rules of reading apply to given works, is more problematic; some scholars read *Lilus Kikus* as a short novel, others treat it as a book of short stories. *Here's to You, Jesusa*'s point of departure is an interview; it has been called a novel, a novelized interview, a documentary, and a testimonial novel, since this book devolves into a narrative innovation: the interviewer transforms her data into a testimonial spoken by the protagonist who was first the interviewee. The chronicle genre insinuates itself into books that are considered fiction; such is the case of *Tinísima*, for example. The essays *¡Ay vida, no me mereces!* (1985) and *Las soldaderas* (1999; The camp followers) are quite distinct despite belonging to the same genre. Poniatowska classifies *Luz y luna, las lunitas* (1994) as a chronicle, but it may also be read as a collection of essays. Other titles first appear as interviews and then, amplified and with narrative stance adjusted, are presented as essays. An example of this can be seen in the interview with Pita Amor, which was first published among other interviews in *Todo México*, then as one of the essays collected in *Las siete cabritas* (2000; The seven goats). The interview, the chronicle, and the essay are the genres that overlap and even contradict one other throughout the body of Poniatowska's work. It is simpler, therefore, to opt for a chronological analysis, starting in 1954 with the publication of *Lilus Kikus,* and ending in 2001 with *La piel del cielo* (The skin of the sky).

Poniatowska began her career as a writer of fiction with the publication of *Lilus Kikus,* in Juan José Arreola's *Los Presentes* collection. Poniatowska hand-painted the mushrooms that decorated the cover of the book, and five hundred copies were produced. The twelve short stories collected in this volume all feature the child, Lilus Kikus, as their main character. The child is seen in a variety of situations: Lilus and her superstitions; Lilus, curious and asking endless questions; Lilus interrupting her philosopher neighbor; Lilus and the women servants; Lilus believing that her nightmare, in which her doctor is the devil, is actually true; Lilus on vacation in Acapulco; Lilus and a tiny elevator in which God comes down to her soul. The third-person narrator who presents Lilus's actions and relations with the other characters appears to know the protagonist intimately, presenting the minute details of her games, her adventures, her happiness, her fears, and even her imaginary friend, Chiruelita. In sum, Lilus is a character drawn from literary realism, displaying the full range of human experience: she plays, questions, observes, loves, and fears, fully engaged with her surroundings. Everything she does is vouched for by the narrator's third-person consciousness. It is almost as if they are one and the same; at the very least, it seems that the narrator believes and takes note of all that Lilus invents.

Lilus has a magical childhood in which her mother encourages her fantasies, asking, "Lilus, niña mía, ¿cuándo aprenderás a encontrar tú sola la respuesta a esa infinidad de preguntas que te haces?" (Lilus, my daughter, when will you learn to find your own answers to the constant questions that you ask?) In a sense, Lilus's questions inhabit all of Poniatowska's works, for all of her writings ask questions and wonder about the world. Poniatowska posits these questions because, long ago, perhaps from the beginning, she began "creer en los signos, como Lilus creyó desde ese día" (to believe in signs, as did Lilus from that day forth). Poniatowska's work is filled with exclamation points and question marks, a truth she herself recognizes in her essay "A Question Mark Engraved on my Eyelids" (in *The Writer on her Work II*, 1991).

In 1956, two years after *Lilus Kikus* appeared, the magazine *Panoramas* published *Melés y Teleo* (*Apuntes para una comedia*), which is thus far the only drama Poniatowska has written. The title derives from the expression "me lees y te leo" (you read me and I read you), which suggests mutual, reciprocal readings. Besides the prologue and a forward, the work holds fifty-eight scenes, all parodies of Mexican intellectual and literary life in the 1950s. Although the author assures us it is not a *roman à clef*, it is easy to suppose that the reader can identify "the two antagonists, one short story writer who is realist, the other fantastic." The first is Terrón de Tepetate, who strongly resembles the Mexican short-story writer Juan Rulfo (Poniatowska interviewed him in "Terrón de Tepetate," which appears in *Palabras cruzadas*). The other character is the literary critic Garabito, called "Rusito," who is a representation of Juan José Arreola, the writer whose self-proclaimed greatest goal was to bring splendor to language ("más se preocupa por darle esplendor al lenguaje"). This use of fictionalized figures from real life is a continuing characteristic in Poniatowska's works.

*Melés y Teleo*, as with much of her writing, testifies about the historical time during which it was created. Thus it refers to Mexico's actual writers, but also comments upon the condition of women: "Y las mujeres literatas? Giran en otro planeta, en torno a sí mismas" (Women writers? They're from another planet, they spin around themselves). Characters representing Mexico's male authors conduct a dialogue about Mexico, which is, according to them, a sexist and surrealist country. They also talk about women, either to praise or attack them, and about literature. The point of the drama is to let each character have his say, and all the voices that argue and speak in critical tones parody the Mexican intellectual environment of the time.

It is also during the mid-1950s that Poniatowska began her lifelong career as an interviewer. In *Palabras cruzadas*, she tells us that by 1956 she had already put her questions to more than two hundred individuals. This 1961 book is divided in three parts of eight, five, and four interviews, respectively, constituting a sampling of the types of people, drawn from both the elite and popular cultures, whom she has interviewed throughout her career. Right from the start, while facing her subjects, she learned how to wait, to observe, to listen.

Poniatowska concentrates on her informant, to whom she inclines her ear and her ability to read. Instead of asking who she has interviewed, it might be easier to count those whom she did not interview. Her subjects include writers, politicians, painters, filmmakers, cartoonists, and other important national and international figures. In the first part of the book she presents her talks with the writer Alfonso Reyes ("Don Alfonso en su palomar"); former Mexican President Lázaro Cárdenas ("Mi general"; My general); painter Diego Rivera ("Añil y carne humana"); archaeologist Alfonso Caso ("El caso de la tumba siete"; The case of the seven tombs); poet Carlos Pellicer ("Aviador sin aeroplano"; Pilot without a plane); painter David Alfaro Siqueiros ("El coronelazo"); and writer Juan Rulfo ("El terrón de tepetate"). In the second part she includes musician Carlos Chávez ("Llave de sol"); French writer François Mauriac ("Invitación a la puerta" and "Nudo de víboras"); Spanish filmmaker Luis Buñuel ("Huesitos tiernos"); scriptwriter Cesare Zavattini ("Zavattini mío"; My Zavattini); writer Alejo Carpentier ("El hijo pródigo"; The prodigal son); and violinist Pablo Casals ("Casals en Jalapa"; Casals in Jalapa). In the third part there are interviews with Peruvian poet Alvaro Mutis ("Proust en Lecumberri"; Proust in Lecumberri) and muralist José Clemente Orozco ("La casa del pintor"; The house of the painter); she also writes "De las barbas de [Antonio] Vanegas Arroyo a las barbas de Fidel Castro" (From the beard of Vanegas Arroyo to the beard of Fidel Castro) and "Apuntes de La Habana." The section "Fechas y fechorías" (Dates and dastardly deeds) clearly presents a polling of the intellectuals of the moment—thinkers, politicians, painters, sculptors, and writers. Her reference to archives of the supplement *México en la Cultura* [*Novedades*] and from the magazines *Mañana* and *Política* explain where many of the interviews were first published between the years 1953 and 1961. As the title of the book indicates, the words cross each other, but they also cross cultural lines and traverse Poniatowska's own literary production. With these first interviews she reveals a hint of what she will go on to perfect: an "innocent move to checkmate" the person interviewed. Many of her early talks remain unpublished or appear only in the magazines and newspapers where she originally placed them, but many others have been included in her multi-volume collection *Todo México*.

Poniatowska's interviews have taken her to all parts of Mexico City and, in 1963, she published *Todo empezó el domingo*, seventy-eight Sunday chronicles with illustrations by Alberto Beltrán, each piece originally appearing in *Novedades* at the end of 1957. The book is dedicated to Ricardo Cortés Tamayo, the well-known master of Mexican popular culture and author of *Los mexicanos se pintan solos*. Poniatowska wrote the prologue for his book, which is also illustrated by Beltrán. For the 1998 edition of *Todo empezó el domingo*, Elena Poniatowska wrote a new chronicle, "¿De qué quiere su domingo?" (1997), a retrospective of the forty years that had passed since she began publishing her chronicles weekly in *Novedades*. In the introduction to the new edition, Poniatowska waxes nostalgic about the Mexico City she knew in the 1950s and of a contemporary Mexico that is much changed. In *Todo empezó el domingo* she immerses herself in the lifestyle of the poor, telling of nights in the Plaza Garibaldi, home of the mariachi bands, and of Sundays spent in Xochimilco, La Alameda, La Lagunilla, and also in the prison Lecumberri. She also writes of business and of daily jobs in the infinite corners of a city in infinite expansion that, even as it presses the poor to the margins of existence, has not entirely eradicated spaces where they can relax. Like those it represents, *Todo empezó el domingo* is entertaining, witty, and imaginative, because its discourse is intelligent enough not to take itself too seriously. Nonetheless, the author takes seriously the cultural phenomena she documents: traditions, handicrafts, and all that is born and lives on the streets of Mexico City and beyond. Her chronicles provide a detailed documentation of the capital's entertainment and work life.

In 1967 Poniatowska published her second book of short stories, *Los cuentos de Lilus Kikus*, which presents seven new narrations in addition to the original twelve of *Lilus Kikus*, as well as a cluster of five stories entitled "Herbolario." On the back cover, Juan Rulfo offers a synthesis of the most important characteristics of the child protagonist. Rulfo speaks of a Lilus who is both reflective and restless, a child who gives life to her fantasies and dreams. Above all, Rulfo insists on the magical qualities of both Lilus and the book. While the stories of *Lilus Kikus* overflow with a child's imagination, in the amplified edition the child has grown, and now is involved in issues of love and love lost in the life and times of a teenager, and of a woman. "La ruptura"

(The break-up), "La jornada" (The journey), "Canto quinto," "La felicidad" (The faithful), and "El recado" are stories of love, of love without a future, steeped in loneliness.

The transition from childhood to adolescence, from enchantment to disillusionment, is at the center of "La hija del filósofo" (The philosopher's daughter), in which a young girl is neglected by the men in her life and, as well, victimized by another man who, ostracized by the girl's father, avenges himself through her. The family forms the axis of other stories: family, home, and domestic objects that all, to some degree, share a relation with the author's own life in ways that are more fully developed in the later novel, *La "Flor de Lis." Los cuentos de Lilus Kikus* also tells about female servants and the ways they age in houses that do not belong to them ("Esperanza número equivocado"), while other stories narrate the invention of fantastic environments ("Canción de cuna" and "Cine Prado" [The Prado theater]). In the latter, the main character falls in love with an actress on the screen and finally stabs her out of jealousy. The fantastic completely takes over the story when the protagonist is jailed and the letter he writes from his cell is revealed to be the story itself.

One of the most important aspects of this collection of stories is the attention paid to words and names. In "La identidad" (The identity), for example, a character gives the only thing that he owns—his name—to another character; and in "La felicidad," a story of one paragraph, the female protagonist reflects upon the meaning of two words—*love* and *happiness*, and her reflections finally drive her to loneliness.

Near the end of the decade of the 1960s, *Here's to You, Jesusa* appeared, the first of Poniatowska's novels and one of her greatest. The sheer number of its readers and the volumes of critical studies it has inspired (and continues to inspire), as well as its publishing success (the constant new editions brought out), all justify the Mazatlán Award it won in 1972. The novel's protagonist is Jesusa Palancares, modeled upon the real-life character of Josefina Bórquez, an illiterate peasant woman who fought as a soldier in the Mexican Revolution. Palancares represents one of the strongest characters ever produced in Spanish literature, and she is the author's personal favorite. The fictional relationship between Poniatowska and Palancares begins when

Poniatowska visits a rooftop laundry on Revillagigedo Street in Mexico City and hears a distinctive voice that she recognizes. The impact of the woman's voice causes Poniatowska to seek an interview with Palancares, and she records their talks. Thus begins an adventure concerning two women from widely separated social classes who gradually redefine themselves through each other. With this book, Poniatowska inaugurated a new literary type: She turned a series of real-life interviews into a novel whose substance derives from Josefina Bórquez's voice, after it has passed through the filter of Poniatowska's creative and editorial judgement. The result is a work of fiction, published during the interviewee's lifetime, that is both spoken and written, and that is presented from the vantage of a shared vision about the social inequalities and injustices in Mexico. Poniatowska relied on her strengths as a writer throughout so that, while she respects Jesusa's voice (the only voice the reader hears from beginning to end of the novel), she simultaneously casts it into a fictional realm.

Jesusa Palancares's memory is long; it spans most of the twentieth century, from the 1910 Mexican Revolution to the mid-1980s, and she brings to life the times and places of her lifelong pilgrimage through severe misery and social marginalization: "Tengo el defecto de que todo lo que oigo se me queda en el pensamiento, todo" (One of my faults is that everything I hear sticks in my head, absolutely everything). As both witness to and participant in the Revolution, Jesusa develops a clearly defined posture: "Yo creo que fue una guerra mal entendida porque eso de que se mataran unos con otros, padres contra hijos, hermanos contra hermanos; carrancistas, villistas, zapatistas, pues eran puras tarugadas porque éramos los mismos pelados y muertos de hambre" (I think it was a poorly understood war because all that business of killing each other, fathers against sons, brothers against brothers; Carrancistas, Villistas, Zapatistas, well that was a bunch of nonsense because we were all the same, all of us were penniless peons dying of hunger).

It was also Jesusa's lot to live through the Cristero wars and other major events of the twentieth century. During her interview she relates all she has experienced and gives her strong opinions: "Así fue la revolución, que ahora soy de éstos, pero mañana seré de los otros, a chaquetazo limpio, el caso es estar con el más fuerte, el que tiene más parque. . . . También ahora es así" (That's the way the Revolution was: today I'm on this side but tomorrow I'll be on the other side, even to the point of treason, plain and simple; the idea was to be on the side of might, of the one with the most ammunition. . . . It's the same way now).

The daughter of a social revolution that failed to make Mexico's power structures more equitable, Jesusa nonetheless sees the war as a means to her own transformation: "La bendita revolución me ayudó a desenvolverme" (The blessed Revolution helped me develop), she tells her interlocutor, adding, "Si llegara a haber una revolución y se ofreciera, yo me iba a la guerra. Todavía tengo ganas de volver a las andadas" (If there was going to be a revolution, I was going to sign up for war. Even today, I still fight the temptation to take off for the open road). Her fighting spirit, which had defined her since childhood, grows stronger in wartime. Then, to that historic event there is added Mexico City's social space, which together with the Revolution constitute the foundational elements of Jesusa's life: "Desde que me vine a México se me quitó lo tarugo" (Since I came to Mexico City I have stopped being such a dolt).

The critical consciousness she acquires as a result of surviving in an arbitrary and unjust system is the window through which the novel reveals those injustices and the way Jesusa has decided to rebel against them. The author's representation of Jesusa's rebellion contributes to a denunciation against the historical and geographic marginalization of the disenfranchised poor. To the social oppression she has suffered, Jesusa opposes the freedom she claims as hers; to recover her own geography, she has created a stage on which to act out her life: "Un día de éstos me voy a ir sola para sentire la lluvia de nuevo, la de la montaña" (One of these days I'm going to go off by myself to feel again the freshness of a mountain rain).

Jesusa's memory was activated during her childhood when her father warned her not to forget her origins. Like the old and dignified race of native Indians who are her family's ancestors, Jesusa knows herself to be free, a pilgrim free to walk down many different roads: "Como a nadie le tengo que rendir cuentas, nomás me salgo y adiós. Me voy por allí sin rumbo o por un camino que yo sola discurro. Así soy, hija de la mala vida, acostumbrada a ir de un lugar a otro y a poner en cualquier parte los palos de mi sombrajo.... When I say I'm going, I go, and that's that" (Since I don't have to account for myself to anyone, all I do is say good-bye and take off. I leave with no destination in mind or along a route I travel alone. That's how I am, a daughter of misery, used to going here and there and sheltering where I may.... when I say I'm going, I go, and that's that).

Unlike people who cling to their roots, Jesusa demands wings so that when her time comes to die and someone comes to find her, "yo allá tan contenta volando en las tripas de los zopilotes" (there I'll be, happy as a clam, flying around in the belly of a buzzard). In her old age, Jesusa traces and retraces her past, recalling for her interviewer the memories of her life. Her character is like a photographic negative of all those traits of weakness and humility that so often typify a female personality in literature. At peace with herself, dignified and solitary, Jesusa demands a unique space with the words she utters at the close of the book: "Ahora ya no chingue. Váyase. Déjeme dormir" (That's enough. Stop bugging me. Go away and let me sleep). Jesusa Palancares's voice becomes the material with which Poniatowska transfers the reality of Josefina Bórquez's life into literature. The result is neither fiction nor poetry but a piece of social reality that does not end with the final pages of the book.

Jesusa Palancares has no ties on earth, not with people nor with any nationality. Instead, she identifies with economic circumstances:

*Al fin de cuentas, yo no tengo patria. Soy como los húngaros: de ninguna parte. No me siento mexicana, ni reconozco a los mexicanos. Aquí no existe más que pura conveniencia y puro interés. Si yo tuviera dinero y bienes, sería mexicana, pero como soy peor que la basura, pues no soy nada. Soy basura a la que el perro le echa una miada y sigue adelante. Viene el aire y se la lleva y se acabó todo.*

When all is said and done, I don't have a country. I'm like the Hungarian people: from nowhere. I don't feel Mexican, and I don't identify with them. In this country there is nothing but expediency and pure self-interest. If I were rich, I would be Mexican, but as I am lower than trash, well then, I'm nothing. I'm garbage that a dog will pee on before trotting on. Then the wind comes and carries it away and there's nothing left.

In that respect, Elena Poniatowska can identify with Jesusa Palancares. As the descendant of two families of exiles, the sense of "not belonging" permeated the earliest years of her life. Although Poniatowska decided to become a Mexican citizen, she could yet identify her attitudes with those of her character, Jesusa.

Shortly after giving Jesusa Palancares the last word in her first great novel, Poniatowska published *Massacre in Mexico*. Like *Here's to You, Jesusa*, this is a work that immediately claimed a permanent space in the canon of twentieth-century Mexican literature and is now considered the quintessential classic on the student movement in Mexico in the late 1960s. In this book, Poniatowska covers that signal phenomenon from the end of July 1968 until December of that same year. The author orchestrates a collective oral history that reports on the arrest of five hundred people who were in one or another way involved in the demand for a democratic dialogue with the government. The interwoven voices of hundreds individuals and groups compose a chorus of registers: the chants of the marchers and public demonstrators, the academics, the politicians, the officials, the ecclesiastic, the literati, the mothers, the people who were arrested and jailed, the workers, the soldiers, the artists and intellectuals, and the people in the streets. These interwoven voices result in a masterful oral chronicle that configures the collective memory of a bloody and unjust reality. The most tragic event covered in the book is the massacre of students and bystanders in the Three Cultures Plaza at the Nonoalco-Tlatelolco housing complex, at dusk on the evening of 2 October 1968. That shockingly violent government action against peacefully demonstrating citizens deeply affected public discourse for decades after.

The book is divided into three parts: "Ganar la calle," "La noche en Tlatelolco" ("The Night of Tlatelolco"), and "La crónica basada en los hechos a que se refieren los estudiantes en sus testimonios de historia oral" (The chronicle based upon the facts told by the students in their oral histories). About the second part, the author says:

*En su mayoría estos testimonios fueron recogidos en octubre y en noviembre de 1968. Los estudiantes presos dieron los suyos en el curso de los dos años siguientes. Este relato les pertenece. Está hecho con sus palabras, sus luchas, sus errores, su dolor y*

441

*su asombro. Aparecen también sus "aceleradas," su ingenuidad, su confianza. Sobre todo les agradezco a las madres, a los que perdieron al hijo, al hermano, el haber accedido a hablar. El dolor es un acto absolutamente solitario. Hablar de él resulta casi intolerable; indagar, horadar, tiene sabor de insolencia. . . .*

*Aquí está el eco del grito de los que murieron y el grito de los que quedaron. Aquí está su indignación y su protesta. Es el grito mudo que se atoró en miles de gargantas, en miles de ojos desorbitados por el espanto del 2 de octubre de 1968, en la noche de Tlatelolco.*

Most of these testimonies were gathered in October and November of 1968. The imprisoned students shared their stories with me over the course of the following two years. This story belongs to them. It is made with their words, their struggles, their mistakes, their pain, and their shock, without excluding their impatience, their ingenuity, their trust. Above all I am grateful to the mothers, to those who lost a child or a brother or sister, for having agreed to speak with me. Sorrow is something one must do absolutely alone. To speak of that pain is surely all but intolerable; to poke and prod about in it is an act of insolence. . . .

Here is the lingering echo of the screams of the dead and of those still living. Here is their indignation and their protest. It is the soundless cry that was choked off in thousands of throats, in thousands of eyes shocked wide open in fear on 2 October 1968, on the night of Tlatelolco.

Collective memory recalls and repeats Elena Poniatowska's words: "¿Por qué? Tlatelolco es incoherente, contradictorio. Pero la muerte no lo es. Ninguna crónica nos da una visión de conjunto" (Why? Tlatelolco is incoherent, contradictory. But death is not. No chronicle can give us a complete view). That the reader is able to hear the variety of voices in Poniatowska's writing is a testimony to the responsibility and moral faithfulness that she has exercised in this chronicle. *Massacre in Mexico* has become the classic testimonial about this scar on Mexico's recent social history.

Seven years after *Massacre in Mexico*, Poniatowska published *Querido Diego, te abraza Quiela* (1978; *Dear Diego*, 1986), a short novel created from imaginary letters that the painter Diego Rivera's first wife, Angelina Beloff (called Quiela in the novel) writes from Paris to her husband, who by the 1920s had returned to Mexico. This is a form of "truer-than-life" history, in part inspired by the novel *The Fabulous Life of Diego Rivera*, by Bertram Wolfe (1963). *Dear Diego* is composed of twelve letters: seven from 1921 (October to December) and five from 1922 (four from January and February, one dated July). In her loneliness and the cold of postwar Paris, Quiela—a painter and Russian exile—writes her letters and waits for her husband to return. Poniatowska had studied Angelina's life; she also Angelina's painting technique, an understanding of which was necessary in order to compose these letters. In order to write like Quiela, the author had to imagine herself as Quiela, to feel the loneliness of her sorrowful waiting and yet be able to distance herself from that persona in order to recreate the relationship that existed between Quiela and Diego Rivera. Silence and desolation are Quiela's companions; her son with Diego has died of meningitis, and her husband has returned to his homeland. These touching letters are written in a fluid style that resembles brush strokes on a canvas, and they reveal the hidden emotions of both the artist and the woman. With this refined, concise book, Poniatowska pays tribute to Quiela while preserving her dignity and stoicism. The short epilogue that closes the novel is the last touch of pain on the palette: years later when she is in Mexico, Diego passes next to his ex-wife without recognizing her. Many years have elapsed between the time of the letters and this incident, and Quiela has survived the silence, her strength of character and her art having saved her. *Dear Diego* is a portrait of the capacity of a woman who, even in abandonment, can love and grow.

Poniatowska's third book of short stories, *De noche vienes*, was published in 1979. Some of these pieces had been previously published in magazines and newspaper supplements, while five of the stories were taken from *Los cuentos de Lilus Kikus* (the stories in the "Herbolario" section). Other formerly published stories included in the collection include "La ruptura" (The rupture), "Cine Prado" "El inventario," "La hija del filósofo," "Canto quinto," "La felicidad," and "El recado." Nine new stories are added to these: "Estado de sitio," "El limbo" (Limbo), "Castillo en Francia," "Love story," "La casita de sololoi" (The house of celluloid), "Métase mi Prieta entre el durmiente y el silbatazo," "El rayo verde" (The green light), "De Gaulle en Minería" (De Gaulle in Minería), and "De noche vienes."

In "Estado de sitio," the female protagonist carries her heart in open hands as she walks the streets begging for love and attention, but knowing that she is neither seen nor heard as each day she seeks her death. "El limbo" is a family saga, related to the other stories in her collection and her later novel, *La "Flor de Lis."* In "El limbo" the privileged position of the young protagonist clashes with the pain of a servant woman who hides her dying newborn child. The vision and ideas of the well-to-do character and what the narrative voice tells us amount to a critical social commentary. In "Castillo en Francia," a woman narrates the last days of a famous architect whom she is visiting in his castle. A miniature movie theater in the castle excites the woman, who observes that: "vivir no es más que un acto de la imaginación" (living is no more than an act of the imagination), but the hope that this inspires is followed by a horrible "reality": in the theater a single film is shown over and over; the ailing architect presses his face into the breasts of the actress on the screen; and the text closes thus on the sordid fate of a past glory.

"Love story" narrates the power relationship between a servant and her mistress; the servant takes her revenge by defecating in the owner's bed when she is out of the house. "La casita de sololoi" ("sololoi" is the vernacular for the word "celluloid") narrates the fatigue and disillusionment of a married woman who searches her past for an escape from her tedious existence. That same night she returns to her "sweet home" (*dulce hogar*) to find that the only things awaiting her are her daily routine and eternal housework. "Métase mi prieta entre el durmiente y el silbatazo" is the story of a railway worker who, abandoned by his wife and unwilling to embrace modern machinery, flees on his old locomotive and disappears into the mountains.

"El rayo verde" is the story of a woman who, as a child, had been given the secret of happiness, then later abandoned. Later she acquired knowledge of men and discovered that "por cada mujer sobre la tierra hay un hombre dándole una orden" (for every woman on earth, there is a man to order her around). One day, the secret she had inherited helps her see a green light that appears from nowhere, a miracle made possible by the steadfast faith she had kept in the woman who had left her with the promise of happiness. "De Gaulle en Minería" is a fictionalized chronicle of the arrival of the

president of France in Mexico. The text is told in two voices and two times: memories of World War II are presented in the past tense and in the first person by a captain who attends De Gaulle's reception, and the reception itself is described in the present tense. The text is a simple homage to Elena's father, Captain Poniatowska, who participated in the war and, in the story, attends the reception with his wife and daughter.

"De noche vienes" tells of a young nurse, Esmeralda Loyden, who has five husbands whom she loves equally. She spends each night of the week with a different husband, reserving her weekends for the family home, caring for a father whom she is said to resemble. One of the husbands reports her bigamy to the police. In court, all who see her fall in love with her, They ask if she suffers and she answers "A veces, un poquito, cuando me aprietan los zapatos" (At times, when my shoes are too tight). For all her cheeky innocence, Esmeralda is convicted of bigamy and imprisoned in Santa Marta Acatitla. She is allowed conjugal visits from her five husbands, and sometimes they all arrive together on a Sunday, the same day that she is visited by employees of the Justice Department. The story's narration shifts at the end into the stiffness of legal jargon as her indictment and sentencing report are read. This document contradicts what she had told her accusers and records what has occurred during her time in jail. The story ends with the official slogan (coined in the revolutionary era) "Effective Suffrage, No Reelection," as if to seal an official report; in this case, the story's conclusion seals its report on a private life.

The same year also saw the publication of *Gaby Brimer*, a testimonial that documents the life of a handicapped person through her dialogue with Poniatowska. This book dismantles the stereotype of disabled people and reminds us, through Brimer's lucidity, that there are other worlds, and they are in this one.

*Fuerte es el silencio* (1980) contains five chronicles: "Ángeles de la ciudad" (Angels of the city), "El movimiento estudiantil de 1968" (The student movement of 1968), "Diario de una huelga de hambre," "Los desaparecidos" (The disappeared), and "La colonia Rubén Jaramillo." These well-written chronicles allow us to hear the "silence" of the poor in Mexico City; give voice to those who were murdered in 1968 and the oppressed workers who for years had "disappeared"; and tell the tale of the peasants called "parachutists" because of their way of dropping in out of nowhere during the night, who seized lands in the state of Morelos in 1973. These are the dispossessed of the city and countryside, the ones who speak of themselves as "no one," those who enjoy no privilege. Some were abandoned by society when they were born, others had their privileges and their freedom stripped away during the reign of an unjust government that traditionally victimized both the poor and those who fought to procure justice in their behalf. Because these problems remain unresolved, *Fuerte es el silencio* stands as a firm denunciation of repression—today, tomorrow, and for the history books.

Poniatowska's next published book was *Domingo 7* (1982), a collection of interviews with seven Mexican presidential candidates. The title plays with the date—the presidential election was held on the first Sunday of July in 1982—and with the number of candidates running for office. It also invokes the popular expression "Sunday the Seventh," which in Mexico means "to end up with a disagreeable surprise," a fact that for Mexican readers, at least, adds a layer of irony to the title. The candidates were Rosario Ibarra de Piedra for the Revolutionary Workers' Party; Manuel Moreno Sánchez for the Social Democrats; Arnoldo Martínez Verdugo for the Unified Socialist Party of Mexico; Miguel de la Madrid for the Institutional Revolutionary Party; Ignacio González Gollaz for the Mexican Democratic Party; Cándido Díaz Cerecedo for the Socialist Workers' Party; and Pablo Emilio Madero for the National Action Party. Poniatowska not only interviews the candidates, she also presents an overview of the personal and political development of each. She begins with Rosario Ibarra Piedra, an exemplary and unrelenting advocate for the "disappeared" (political and social protesters believed to be kidnapped and murdered by the government). Piedra's own son was snatched from her in 1975. This interview allows Poniatowska to challenge conventional beliefs about the rightful place of women in Mexico. "Pero ¿cuál es su lugar? En nuestro país, desde luego, su casa" (Just where do they belong? In our country, of course, in the home). She observes:

*si fueran contestatarias, innovadoras o verdaderamente rebeldes, estas borregas no hubieran llegado al poder. Rosario, en cambio, sí es una contestataria y una creadora de nuevas formas de lucha. Ha sabido renacer todos los días; convertir su sufrimiento personal en lucha política.*

if women had been less pliant, more innovative or outright rebellious, these [male] simpletons would have never gotten into power. Rosario, on the other hand, stands out because she does demand answers and creates new ways to fight. She has learned how to re-create herself daily, to turn her personal suffering into political activism.

While she is grateful to Rosario for her fight against repression in Mexico. Poniatowska, too, is an activist, a feminist, and firmly committed to the public good.

In one of the interviews, Poniatowska offers this digression:

*Después de tantas cuartillas escritas sobre cada uno de los candidatos a la presidencia, yo misma respongo (y supongo que también lo harán los lectores) cada vez que aparece la palabra "democracia" o la palabra "pueblo"; rechinan dentro de mis oídos como la aguja sobre el disco rayado, y es ya lo único que oigo: el sonsonete, la tonadita, para mí ya carecen de sentido. Podría yo hasta prescindir de ellas, encajonarlas bajo la etiqueta "Desechadas por uso y abuso."*

After so many pamphlets written about each of the candidates for president, I wince (as I suppose my readers do also) each time I hear the word "democracy" or the word "the people": they screech in my ears like the needle on a broken record, and now that's all I hear: meaningless sounds. I could actually dispense with them, and file them away under "Discarded because of overuse and abuse."

*Domingo 7* captures a moment in Mexican politics, registering each party's viewpoint and the personalities of the candidates, even as it permits readers to appreciate Poniatowska's own voice, vision, and literary style. With her notebook, pen, and tape recorder, the author adjusts her opinions and strengthens the impact of each interview. Poniatowska has said that this is her least favorite book, but readers may see it as a theoretical and practical manual of Mexican politics in the multi-party context of 1982.

Also published that year was *El último guajolote*, a book dedicated to the street vendors of Mexico. The author employs colloquial speech, and succeeds in turning the very streets, canals, and lagoons into a history. She combines prose with verse, song lyrics, and popular sayings, crafting poetry from the spoken language and constructing a chronicle of of the street vendors and their wares: poultry, fruits, and vegetables with their myriad colors and tastes; fruit juices, meals and snacks, clothes, housewares, things old and new, thousands of products for sale, to fix, or to exchange. Traditional crafts, the signs on the streets, vendors, and buyers all meet in this chronicle in which the streets of Mexico City, both real and fictional, are evoked through the skills of its artisans and its small merchants, and through the poetic prose of Elena Poniatowska.

In 1985 she published *¡Ay vida, no me mereces!*, a collection of essays that takes its title from Mexican author Juan Rulfo's classic novel *Pedro Páramo* (1955). The collection includes discussions of Mexican authors Carlos Fuentes, Rosario Castellanos, and Rulfo, as well as of the literary movement called the *Onda* (the Wave). In the introduction, Poniatowska proposes to typify her subjects with some formulaic phrases. For Fuentes, she writes "*¡Si tuviera cuatro vidas, cuatro vidas serían para ti!*" (If I had four lives to live, all four would be for you!); for Castellanos, "*¡Vida, nada te debo!*" (Life, I owe you nothing!); for Rulfo, "*¡Ay vida, qué mal me pagas!*" (Oh, Life, how ill you treat me!); for the *Onda*, "*¡Así como te has portado yo me retrato contigo, vida!*" (I will see myself in your image, Life, just as you have dealt with me!).

Poniatowska writes of Carlos Fuentes's passion for Mexico and for arts and letters and of his exuberant production, and says that his prolific work, all of it, is publishable. She analyzes his vitality, his intelligence, and his untiring creativity, as well as his "terrifying" tastes, his successes, and the prestige that he has brought to Mexican letters. She enumerates the titles of his books, and comments on them up to *Cambio de piel* (1987). Poniatowska writes of a Fuentes who has been successful in all of his endeavors and is liked by all. Inventing an adjective, she says she has been "Fuentes-fied," (bewitched by his charms): "I applaud from the corner with hands already aged, tired out from interviewing and applauding so many Mexican authors."

Of Rosario Castellanos, Poniatowska writes: "Fue, ante todo, una mujer de letras, vio claramente su vocación de escritora y ejerció siempre el oficio de escribir" (She was, above all, a woman of letters who clearly perceived herself as a writer and her work as a literary vocation). Poniatowska believes that Rosario Castellanos, precursor of the contemporary Mexican feminist movement, uses irony to teach that we should not to take ourselves too seriously. Nonetheless, her work is a very serious achievement: her writing evokes kindness and love, yet maintains a constant connection with death.

Poniatowskas's review of Castellanos's poetry, novels and short stories, dramas, essays, and news articles clearly reveals her admiration for the woman, her work, her accomplishments. Castellanos was an exemplary human being who happened to be a woman. She was an ambassador (to Israel) and Poniatowska's treasured friend. At one point in her own career, Poniatowska had asked Castellanos to contribute a poem for inclusion in *Massacre in Mexico*, and almost immediately received "Memorial de Tlatelolco." In a sense, Poniatowska follows in Castellanos's footsteps, for Rosario is said to have been a point of departure for twentieth-century women writers in Latin America.

Regarding Juan Rulfo, his brief, compact novel, *Pedro Páramo*, constitutes "trescientos veinticinco páginas (que) rayaron de una vez por todas la literatura mexicana" (three hundred twenty-five pages that forever changed the face of Mexican literature). Poniatowska remembers her first interview with Rulfo, in 1954; she spent half an hour waiting for an answer to her questions. Rulfo's silence, and the voices of the common folk who speak in his novel, are much the subject of her essay. She tells of the time someone asked Rulfo what he felt when he wrote and he answered: "remordimientos" (remorse). About Rulfo himself, a connoisseur of medieval, baroque, and renaissance music, she reports his complete lack of interest in anything modern. She informs us about Rulfo the hiker, the mountain climber, and a man comfortable in both the city and the country. She writes of Rulfo the orphan child, who grew up during the Cristero war (1926–1929) and experienced the character-forming traumas arising from the murder of male members of his family. We learn also that Rulfo was an avid reader and a photographer who worked at many jobs to support his family. She discusses his books and the time he spent in the Cologne Library, where she heard him read out loud with a voice so filled with the sadness that characterized his being.

She closes *¡Ay vida, no me mereces!* with a reflection on members of the *Onda* literary group, the *onderos*, who were writing a new kind of youth literature in Mexico during the 1960s and 1970s. She begins with a mention of the "indestructible, eternal" Jesusa Palancares and her "insolently youthful voice." Precisely because of this voice, Poniatowska joins Jesusa with the *onderos*: José Agustín, Parménides García Saldaña, and Gustavo Sainz being three of them. Poniatowska writes that the *onderos* chose a "generación norteamericana del lumpen, la de los beatniks, la de la protesta, el underground, el anti Vietnam, los contestatarios, los outsiders, los bums, los freaks" ([a] generation of U.S. proletarians misfits and rebels: beatnicks, the radical underground, Vietnam War protesters, outsiders and outcasts of every sort, bums and freaks) to serve as the inspiration and model for their literature. Poniatowska elaborates on the special language and attitudes of the *Onda* authors, noting that they are against solemnity and for rock and roll music, street culture, and a laid-back lifestyle. She identifies with them completely.

Poniatowska's next novel, *La "Flor de Lis,"* appeared in 1988. The title is taken from a famous tamale restaurant in Mexico City, while the flower itself (the fleur de lis) represents the French nobility. The phrase's multiple allusions suggests one of the author's constant themes: the fusion of high and low cultures, which characterized the author's own childhood and which will be this book's main concern. *La "Flor de Lis"* does have definite autobiographical elements. A part of the novel had been published previously, in the literary journal *Estaciones*, under the title of "El retiro" and with a comment describing the story as a fragment of a novel entitled *Naranja dulce, limón partido*. There are also connections between this novel and several of her short stories: "El inventario" (from *Los cuentos de Lilus Kikus*) and "El limbo" (from *De noche vienes*), for example.

In *La "Flor de Lis,"* the author's own family environment is fictionalized, and social and family transformations are presented from the point of view Poniatowska's alter ego, French-born Mariana. The landscapes of Mexico enter Mariana's consciousness through the eyes of her Mexican grandmother; her personal servant, on the other hand, teaches her Spanish and leads her through the streets of the city, where she absorbs Mexico's popular culture. Mariana visits the Villa of (the Virgin) Guadalupe and the Alameda, the city's central plaza; born to privilege, she nonetheless learns to wait at the corner for buses; and observes, by living through them, the changes that occur in her own household, within the elite social class to which she belongs, and throughout Mexico. The novel recreates an entire era by focusing on a sector of the population that is beginning to lose its historical privileges.

From the perspective of her childhood world of women—her grandmother, aunts, mother, sister, and servant girls—Mariana witnesses the transformation of her class and other changes that are generated within the household's family life. Mariana's mother, a venerated figure in the book, is presented as the quintessence of the submissive, passive, and dependent woman:

*Las mujeres estamos siempre a la espera, creo, dejamos que la vida nos viva, no nos acostumbran a tomar decisiones, giramos, nos damos vuelta, regresamos al punto de partida, nunca he querido nada para mí, no sé pedir, soy imprecisa y soy privilegiada*

We women are always left waiting, I think; we let life live us. We're not used to making decisions, we go around in circles, we meet ourselves coming and going, we go back to where we started from. I have never desired anything for myself. I don't know how to ask for anything. I'm helpless and privileged.

*La "Flor de Lis"* also addresses its protagonist's need for a homeland. The narrator, suspended between Europe and Mexico, finally opts for the second, as the following exchange takes place:

—*Pero tú no eres de México, ¿verdad?*
—*Sí soy.*
—*Es que no pareces mexicana.*
—*Ah sí, entonces ¿qué parezco?*
—*Gringa.*
—*Pues no soy gringa, soy mexicana.*
—*No se te ve.*
—*Soy mexicana porque mi madre es mexicana; si la nacionalidad de la madre se heredara como la del padre, sería mexicana.*

*—De todos modos, no eres de México.*

*—Soy de México porque quiero serlo, es mi país*

—But you're not from Mexico, are you?

—Yes, I am.

—But you don't look Mexican.

—I don't? Well, then, what do I look like?

—A *gringa*.

—Well, I'm not a *gringa*, I'm a Mexican.

—You don't look like it.

—I'm Mexican because my mother's Mexican; if the mother's nationality were inherited like the father's, I would be Mexican.

—Well, anyway, you weren't even born in Mexico.

—I'm from Mexico because I want to be. This is my country.

In *La "Flor de Lis"* Poniatowska recreates the past in order to reaffirm an identity. She turns herself into a fictional character who appropriates a new self by switching from a French identity to a Mexican one. Like the author herself, Mariana lives on the margins of society: she is an aristocrat who becomes a proletarian. And, like the author, Mariana chooses the center of the country to occupy the center of her being: the *zócalo* (central plaza), cradle and shroud of Mexico, a popular Mexico to which Poniatowska pays homage with her novel.

*Mi país es esta banca de piedra desde la cual miro el mediodía, mi país es esta lentitud al sol, mi país es la campana a la hora de la elevación, la fuente de las ranitas frente al Colegio de Niñas, mi país es la emoción violenta, mi pasís es el grito que ahogo al decir Luz [Mariana's mother], mi país es Luz, el amor de Luz. . . . Mi país es el tamal que ahora mismo voy a ir a traer a la calle de Huichapan número 17, a LA FLOR DE LIS.*

My country is this stone bench where I sit watching the day at noon, my country is this slow-moving sun, my country is the church bell that calls us to mass, the fountain with its little frogs in front of the Colegio de Niñas, my country is violent emotions, my country is the shout that I choke off when I say Luz, my country is Luz, my love for Luz. . . . My country is the tamale that right now I am going to bring home to 17 Huichapan Street, to LA FLOR DE LIS.

*Nada, nadie. Las voces del temblor* (*Nothing, Nobody: The Voices of the Mexico City Earthquake*, 1995), also

first published in 1988, offers an oral testimony of the earthquakes of 19–20 September 1985, in Mexico. Alongside the voices of the survivors of the disaster we hear the voices of the students, professionals, laborers, gang members, neighbors, and strangers who volunteered as rescuers. All these voices blend with the screams of happiness that greet the discovery of someone alive under the rubble, with the grave tone of the news headlines, and with the voices of the radio and television announcers, and with the voice of the government, which insisted on minimizing the importance of the tragedy in order to preserve its authoritarian status.

*Nothing, Nobody* takes its title from the way that the earthquake victims speak of themselves: "Yo ya no soy nadie" (I am nobody, now), "Who goes there?" "¿Quién anda ahí? —Nadie, soy yo. —Ya no tengo nada" (Who goes there? No one, it's only me. I don't have anything anymore). Poniatowska gathers voices that criticize the government, the construction companies who build the substandard buildings, and the businessmen who had profited from that shoddy construction, and presents these alongside representations of particular situations, such as the many sweatshop seamstresses who died because the factory in which they worked collapsed on them. The author's own voice can be heard here, denouncing owners who exploit rather than protect their workers. Poniatowska records the victims' voices in all their great variety, and in doing so she exposes an unjust social reality whose reprehensible inequities have been shaken into view by the earthquake. The victims we hear from in this book have lost their homes, their families, their everything. They turn out to be the same people who are always victimized. In her chronicles, Elena Poniatowska does not invent, but instead constructs a text from the basic materials given by her sources, especially those who speak as society's underdogs. These are the weakest, the silenced. These are the dispossessed who, just as in the chronicles of *Fuerte es el silencio*, are destined to become the strongest, the ones who cannot be accused of lying. The royalties earned by *Nothing, Nobody* were given to the victims of the earthquake—who were also victims of their society. Elena's moral commitment is undeniable: she surrendered the profits of her writing as an exemplary gesture.

Poniatowska's publications in the 1990s began with the first volume of an important series of collected interviews, *Todo México* (Mexico in its totality). This volume opens with a series of interviews from the 1950s, continues on into the 1970s (the majority of the interviews fall into this era), and concludes with one each from the 1960s and from 1990. In conducting the interviews and in writing them, Poniatowska has sought out full background information, including research, a procedure that she has followed throughout her career. The book is an exposition of the great names of literature (Jorge Luis Borges, Gabriel García Márquez), bullfighting (Manuel Benítez), architecture (Luis Barragán), film (Luis Buñuel, Maria Felíx, Yolanda Montes), boxing, and music (Lola Beltrán); for Poniatoswka, interviewing these figures presupposes that she become knowledgeable in the arts that each of them practiced. The resulting collection is a confrontation between popular and elite cultures, exactly what is implied in the title *Todo México*.

Part of the totality that is Mexico can be appreciated through photographs of its scenery, and Poniatowska has written about Mexico's photography. An example of this can be found in her book, *Manuel Álvarez Bravo: el artista, su obra, sus tiempos*, published by the Banco Nacional de México in 1991. For this book, Poniatowska worked with the images from one of Bravo's photography sessions. Poniatowska calls Bravo the only person who "has taken pictures of the invisible, of things that were not there, nor that ever were going to be there." She accompanied Bravo along the streets of Mexico City's downtown area (he is known as the photographer of the downtown) and studies, with him, its scenes and faces, subjects such as "Obrero en huelga, asesinado" (Striking worker, murdered), a brutal image that deeply impressed the French poet, André Breton, or his nude outdoor shots of models. In the course of these expeditions, Poniatowska expanded her knowledge of the history of photography and painting in Mexico, an expertise she reveals in her writing.

Poniatowska was also strongly impressed by a woman photographer named Tina Modotti. At the request of Gabriel Figueroa—a noted cinematographer about whom she wrote in the third volume of *Todo México*—Poniatowska first prepared a film script about Modotti that was never produced. Nonetheless, she continued with her research and the interviews that form the basis of the novel that took her ten years to write. In this novel, Modotti appears as the protagonist of *Tinísima* (1992). This book had been announced well in advance and was eagerly awaited by Poniatowska's readers. It covers the life of an Italian photographer who comes to Mexico in the first half of the twentieth century and dedicates herself to the cultural and political life there, to the point of becoming involved in the Communist Party.

Poniatowska comments on the process of writing this novel:

> *Tina Modotti pasó a formar parte de mi vida familiar de los últimos diez años. Siempre con ella a cuestas viajé, leí, estudié, comí, atribulé a los demás. . . . Al libro de Tina Modotti le debo no sólo diez años sino el haber investigado, leído, escrito, tirado, eliminado un sinfín de papeles. Asimismo pude conversar y entrevistar una y otra vez a hombres y mujeres que en México, en Italia, en España, en Francia, en Alemania, en Estados Unidos me contaron no sólo de Tina sino de su propia vida.*

Tina Modotti became a part of my family in those ten years. Everywhere I went I carried her with me, I read, studied, ate with her, I inflicted her on everyone else. . . . To this book on Tina Modotti I owe not only ten years but having researched, read, written, thrown away, and eliminated a million pieces of paper. At the same time I was able to talk to and interview over and over again, men and women who, in Mexico, Italy, Spain, France, Germany and the United States, not only told me about Tina but about their own lives.

Once again, a process of seeking and gathering precedes and accompanies the interview. The purpose of this book is to recreate the social, cultural, and literary history not only of Mexico (especially in the 1920s) but also of some of the most salient episodes of modern European history, particularly the Spanish Civil War. The thirteen years of chronological history covered in this narrative are amplified with a jump of nine years back in time to the year 1920. The twenty-two years thus covered are linked to significant events in Mexico, Germany, the Soviet Union, Spain, Cuba, the United States, Italy and France.

As she gathers information about Tina along this twisting geographical pilgrimage, Poniatowska understands the photographer's questions and makes them her own: "Cómo llegué aquí? ¿Qué era yo? La vida que llevo ahora ¿es verdaderamente mi vida?" (How did I get here? What was I? Is the life I'm leading now really mine?). Through Poniatowska, Modotti says: "México es de quien nace para conquistarlo. Yo nací para México. México es mío, yo soy de México" (Mexico belongs to whomever is born to conquer it. I was born for Mexico. Mexico is mine, and I am Mexico's). Modotti has fallen in love with popular Mexico, just as Poniatowska had, years before. That is why the author could understand Tina's initial contact with Mexico:

*La dulzura y el picor de los platillos mexicanos se estremecían en su paladar; el crujir de la tortilla tostada, el guacamole untuoso, el tequila descendiendo enardecido, el limón verde, más limón que en ningún otro país, templaban sus nervios; el mole le daba peso con sus especias achocolatadas y su caída, pero la espuma angelical de los merengues rosas, evanescentes, la subía al cielo.*

The sweetness and sharp bite of the typical dishes of Mexico trembled on her palate; the crunch of toasted tortilla, the oiliness of guacamole, tequila lighting a path of fire down the throat, and the bright green lime, more limey than in any other country, all calmed her nerves; the *mole* sauce put pounds on her with its chocolatey spices, a temptation she couldn't resist, but the angel-light foam of the evanescent pink meringue carried her straight up to heaven.

*Tinísima* begins with the assassination in January 1929 of Julio Antonio Mella, Tina's companion and the founder of the Cuban Communist Party; it ends with Tina's death in Mexico in January 1942, the year that Poniatowska herself first came to Mexico. With Mella's assassination, Tina's begins her pain-filled pilgrimage through Europe and then the United States. The novel continues on through Tina's first stay in Mexico, her wandering career as an interpreter in communist countries, her participation in the Spanish Civil War, and finally her return to Mexico, where she dies of a heart attack. Poniatowska accords a poetic death to Tina, but the novel is also a homage to a woman who sacrificed her art to the political cause for which she fought throughout her life.

Poniatowska followed Tinisima with the second volume of *Todo México* in 1993. The texts in this volume straddle the 1960s and 1970s, and concentrates mostly on artists. Among these are the actress Dolores del Río, photographer Lola Álvarez Bravo, diva Irma Serrano, painter Roberto Montenegro, movie legend Marlene Dietrich, painter María Izquierdo, popular actor Cantinflas, poet León Felipe and painter Jesús Reyes Ferreira. The only non-artist included in the volume is politician Barry Goldwater. These "full color" interviews depict a panorama of three decades in Mexico, seen from the point of view of those involved in the country's cultural production, whether as permanent residents or as visitors. Other important names, appear in the course of the interviews. For example, the interview with Marlene Dietrich, also contains references to the painter Antonio Peláez and the writer Elena Garro. Poniatowska is as impressed with Garro as she is with Dietrich. She also includes bibliographical information with each talk.

*Luz, y luna, las lunitas* was published in 1994; in it there appears a group of sixteen photographs titled "Los ojos de Graciela Iturbide" (The eyes of Graciela Iturbide). The images illustrate the "lights and moons" alluded to in the title and are occasionally accompanied by other photographs that have similar chiaroscuro qualities. Of the book's five chronicles, the first—a verbal "fiesta"—had been published earlier as *El último guajolote* (1982). The second piece, "Vida y muerte de Jesusa" (The life and death of Jesusa), is one of Poniatowska's most touching works. The text is tenderly dedicated to Josefina Bórquez, the marvelous human being and dignified woman of flesh and blood who served as inspiration for the character of Jesusa Palancares, one of the most powerful figures in Mexican literature of the twentieth century. This essay has its roots in "Hasta no verte Jesús mío" (Here's to you, Jesusa), an article that Poniatowska published in the journal *Vuelta* in 1978 that dealt with the writing of the novel of the same title. The essay that appears in *Luz, y luna, las lunitas* is divided into two parts, the first from 1978 and the second from 1987, the year Josefina Bórquez died. Bórquez's death inspired Poniatowska to write a long homage as a way of saying good-bye to one of Mexico's strongest critics of social injustice. In this piece, Poniatowska recalls Josefina's "capacity for indignation" and discusses the process of writing that led to the novel. In other words, Elena rereads herself and rediscovers the linguistic scaffolding that she relied on to construct *Here's to You, Jesusa*. This new text is thus the echo, mirror, synthesis, and enlargement of the first essay on the subject. It brings together the details of Jesusa's life that had shown the author the dark face of a Mexico that is both complex and long-suffering, a sad place illumined only by the dignity of people, like Jesusa Palancares, who never give up. Poniatowska acknowledges that although Jesusa has died, she has nonetheless inspired a most unforgettable fictional character.

Among the stories included in *Luz, y luna, las lunitas* is "Juchitán de las mujeres" (Juchitán made of women). As its title indicates, this tale is about a feminist territory in the Mexican state of Oaxaca. There it is the women who rule both day and night, it is they who select the men and take them to their beds. Juchitán is four hundred kilometers south of the city of Oaxaca, on the Isthmus of Tehuantepec. Photographs by Graciela Iturbide sweetly capture the town, while Poniatowska's words dance freely, like the Juchiteca women. The women of this town, like Jesusa Palancares, are wise enough to remain faithful and sensual for their men. Men and women alike possess a "nagual," an animal spirit that makes them strong and gives them a love for life, an existence that in the tropics is always full of hope and of naked skin.

Another tale included in this collection is "Se necesita muchacha," which focuses on the Mexico City that is known to the poor, particularly to women of the servant class. To write it, Poniatowska researched the world of female domestic servants in books and through direct personal observation. She also brings to the text childhood memories, recalling the times when she would sneak up to the rooftop room where her family's servants lived. One of the young women employed by the author's family was Magdalena Castillo, who devoted herself to the care of the two Poniatowska girls. From Magdalena and the other maids, young Elena learned not just the Spanish language, but also a class consciousness that she later reaffirmed as she walked the streets and crisscrossed the city in buses. The lessons she learned through close contact with the humble people in her life were strengthened in the first part of her writing career, especially during the 1960s.

In "Se necesita muchacha" the author holds a magnifying glass to the grime on Mexico's soul. Poniatowska gives voice to thousands of Indian women who work part- or full time, in a city distant from the communities in which they were born. They do the work of others, the chores that the mistress of the house pays them to do, receiving a meager wage for work that the mistress will not do herself. They are very young; they live at risk of being abused by their masters, are ordered around by their mistresses, and have no prospects for a better future. All they can do is keep their eyes on their work, an eternity of cleaning, cooking, ironing, and washing, for which they are eternally underpaid.

Poniatowska, venerates the working hands of women, and the characters in "Las señoritas de Huamantla" (The women of Huamantla) have their hands filled with embroidery, pious hands which work on a dress for the Virgin. In this story the author creates a tapestry of black and white signs, using the traditional embroidery of Huamantla, Tlaxcala, as an icon of historical symbolism. In the text, the women embroider a tapestry based on painted pictographs of Cortez traveling with doña Marina, providing the author with an opportunity to write about the Conquest of Mexico. The women embroider the tapestry during the night and offer the finished work, the virtuous product of their angelic hands, to the Virgin of Charity.

In 1996, following *Luz y luna, las lunitas*, Poniatowska next published the third volume of *Todo México*, which bears the subtitle *La mirada que limpia (Gabriel Figueroa)* [The purifying gaze (Gabriel Figueroa)]. Unlike the first two volumes, this book focuses its attention on the famous cinematographer (he made 224 films), but like the other books in the series it mentions numerous other important figures in, or visitors to, Mexico: José Clemente Orozco, María Félix, El Indio Fernández, Bruno Traven, Adolfo López Mateos, Alfonso Reyes, Luis Buñuel, Cantinflas, Diego Rivera, Frida Kahlo, John Ford, and Dolores del Río, to name but a few. In this interview and biography of one of the essential figures in twentieth-century filmmaking, Poniatowska presents Figueroa from the points of view of his various family members. The book covers several decades of politics, art, and cinematic production, especially within Mexico. In addition to the biography, this volume includes several of Poniatowska's earlier pieces, all of which revolve around the great filmmaker. The life and art of the cinematographer is illustrated by an exposition catalogue of one hundred photographs, first published in 1990.

*Paseo de la Reforma* appeared next, in 1996. This novel takes its title from one of the most historic streets in Mexico City, a street of elegant homes belonging to the wealthy. This grand avenue stretches from Chapultepec castle, past the Ángel de la Independencia and beyond, to the statue of the Spanish king, Carlos IV. The wealthy upper class form an exclusive neighborhood along its length, and it is lined by statues of the heroes of the nineteenth century. *Paseo de la Reforma* is a short novel in which an aristocrat, Ashby Egbert, is forever changed by an accident. While undergoing treatment in the hospital, he finds himself with patients from Mexico's lowest economic classes. After leaving the hospital he has another life-changing experience, falling in love with an intellectual named Amaya Chacel. Amaya becomes his mysterious lover; she is admired by men and women alike, passionate, manipulative, and committed to the cause of the landless farmworkers and to the student movement. At the end of the novel, by which time Amaya accompanies him only in memory, Egbert goes looking for his former impoverished friends from the hospital and becomes a teacher. Poniatowska portrays many historic figures, some with their real names, others thinly disguised; for instance, Amaya resembles the writer Elena Garro.

In 1998 Poniatowska produced *Cartas de Alvaro Mutis a Elena Poniatowska* (Letters from Alvaro Mutis to Elena Poniatowska), a compilation of twelve letters that the Colombian poet wrote to the author during his fifteen months in prison. The book opens with an extensive prologue of seven parts—"Pero sigo siendo el rey," "Las buñueladas de Buñuel," "La puerta," "El aislamiento," "El Cochambres," "El carcelazo," and "Yesterday"—and closes with a three-part epilogue in three parts—"Bitácora del Gaviero," "Premios y distinciones" and "Obras."

The first part of the prologue chronicles the history of the Black Palace of Lecumberri, its construction, its operation at the end of the 1950s, and the kindness of its director during those years. The prologue's second part tells of the people who came to visit Mutis while he was imprisoned. Among these visitors were Luis Buñuel, Alberto Beltrán, and Poniatowska herself.

In another part of the prologue the author reports on her attendance at the the presentation of a new play, "El Cochambres," written by Rolando Rueda de León, directed by Mutis, and staged at Lecumberri Prison. The performance provides Poniatowska with the occasion to meet the imprisoned leaders of a railway workers strike, among them Demetrio Vallejo. Poniatowska also mentions muralist David Alfaro Siqueiros and even Trotsky's assassin, both of whom were also in prison at the time. Elsewhere in the prologue she offers her observations of daily life in prison, which she witnessed during her Sunday visits to the poet. She also reproduces the letter that railway workers and political prisoners sent to Mutis to thank him for supporting them in prison, and another letter that several Mexican intellectuals wrote to the president of Mexico on behalf of the Colombian poet.

The heart of the text consists of Mutis's letters to Poniatowska. In one of these he offers this observation of *Lilus Kikus*, which Poniatowska had brought to him:

> *Me doy cuenta de la profundidad de tu mirada de escritora y de los tesoros que eres capaz de desenterrar de lo más escondido o de lo, aparentemente, más banal. . . . No sé cuál haya sido tu experiencia en el internado (es la segunda parte de Lilus Kikus que experamos mucho. . . . )*

> I am impressed by the depth of your vision as a writer and by the way you can bring forth the most deeply hidden values, and sometimes even those that seem to be trivial. . . . I don't know what your life was like in boarding school (that's the second part of *Lilus Kikus* and we are all awaiting a chance to read about it. . . . )

In the epilogue, Poniatowska briefly revisits the years of her friendship with Mutis during his imprisonment, and she accepts with generous understanding the silence that later grew between them:

> *Me di cuenta . . . que al volver sobre esos quince meses de encierro le significaban una tortura y que los rostros vistos en Lecumberri aunque sólo fuera los domingos, se bamboleaban frente a él como piñatas amenazantes*

I realized ... that to think again about those fifteen months of imprisonment was a torture for him and that the faces he saw in Lecumberri, even though only on Sundays, bobbed before him like threatening piñatas.

The epilogue concludes with information about Mutis's publications, his prizes, his life in the 1990s, his friends, and his poetry. Her book is both a remembrance of the writer and a chronicle of the decade of the 1950s.

The fourth volume of *Todo México* was also published in 1998. In this volume, Poniatowska groups together diverse figures of Mexican culture, drawn from interviews she conducted throughout her career, from 1953 to 1997. These interviews, many of them revised and updated for their new publication, include talks with the poets Renato Leduc and Rosario Sansores, the French writers François Mauriac and André Malroux, politician Fidel Velázquez, singer and arranger Francisco Gabilondo Soler ("Cri-Cri"), pianist José Iturbi, composer and singer Juan Gabriel, writer Max Aub, comic Jesús Martínez ("Palillo"), and photographer Walter Reuter. The subjects reflect Mexico as a home to artists, both domestic and visiting. This volume of *Todo México* is, in a sense, a big house with room for everything from the childhood of Cri-Cri, the singing cricket, to the different epochs of the famous sonnet by Renato Leduc, in which the word "time" is mentioned in every verse.

Also in 1998, Poniatowska published *Octavio Paz. Las palabras del árbol* (Octavio Paz: words of the tree). With this volume the author began a new project of literary friendship: she planned to give each of her friends the gift of a book exploring their life and works. This one harks back to the year 1953 when, at a party in the home of Carlos Fuentes, she first met Paz, the author of *Libertad bajo palabra*. Poniatowska goes on to tour the past, re-experiencing her memories of his poetry, family relations, and loves, including his relationship with his wife Marie-Jo. The book embraces every possible genre: interviews, letters, facts about his speeches and presentations, messages, anecdotes, trip itineraries, and memories. Elena admires Paz, the essayist of solitude, the young anti-fascist intellectual, the man who gave up his post as ambassador to India as a protest against the massacre at Tlatelolco. The work seals anew a pact of friendship that had grown distant for a time; just days before his death, Paz was able to read his friend's book.

*Juan Soriano. Niño de mil años* (Juan Soriano: the thousand-year-old child), also from 1998, is the second of Poniatowska's literary gifts to her friends. In this volume she writes about an artist from the Mexican state of Jalisco, and it is illustrated with Soriano's paintings. Within the text she includes notes written by the artist's friends and critics. A unique feature of the book is that Soriano's biography, from his birth in Guadalajara in 1920 to the present, is told in the artist's own words. Poniatowska puts her writing at the service of Soriano's voice, intervening only briefly. She closes the book with a series of interviews with the artist that she conducted over the years. These dialogues between Poniatowska and Soriano, who have been friends since 1953, form a second biography, one that is witty, sincere, and strong, like its subject, who is given to frank speech. More than just a tribute to one of Mexico's exceptional talents, this book is also a chronicle of the intellectual circles in which Soriano has moved for almost all his life.

The fifth volume of *Todo México* (1999) contains eleven interviews that were conducted between 1953 and 1997, including figures from both the national and global cultures: artists, architects, cartoonists, sculptors, historians, dancers, radio announcers, poets, and important female political figures, especially those from the left in recent years. This volume presents Poniatowska's interviews with Gloria Trevi, Mathías Goeritz, María Rojo, Gabriel Vargas, Henry Moore, Fernand Braudel, Pilar Rioja, Jacobo Zabludovsky, Benita Galeana, Salvador Novo, and Guadalupe Amor. The sum of these portraits paints a vision of a dynamic country engaged in change, and captures the varied tonalities and faces of Mexico's history and culture.

In 1999 the author also published *Las soldaderas*, about the participation of women in the Mexican Revolution. In writing this book Poniatowska relied heavily on what Jesusa Palancares had told her about her role in the Revolution and what Nellie Campobello wrote in her novel *Cartucho* (1988). In addition to these biographical testimonials, Poniatowska also searched the historical archives (the photographs accompanying the text, for example, are from the Archivo Casasola), and critical and historical studies. She cites authors, characters, and famous passages from *The Novel of the Revolution*, and illustrates statements with lyrics from *corridos* (popular songs composed about revolutionary heroes and events). After all this research, she concludes that "sin las soldaderas no hay Revolución Mexicana" (Without the *soldaderas* there would have been no Mexican Revolution).

Not only does Poniatowska discuss the literature and history of these camp followers, she also explains the origin of the term *soldadera*: "Durante todas las guerras e invasiones, los soldados utilizaban su "soldada" (palabra de origen aragonés) para emplear a una mujer como sirvienta. La mujer iba al cuartel a cobrar su sueldo o soldada. De ahí el nombre de soldadera" (During all wars and invasions, soldiers used their 'soldada' (word of Aragonese origin for salary) in order to pay a female servant. The woman would go to the base camp to collect her salary, or 'soldada.' That's where we get the word 'soldadera'). As part of this history lesson, Poniatowska also includes the names of real soldaderas, who were frequently photographed on trains, and she offers a history of their participation from precolumbian history through the wars of the nineteenth century. This book pays homage to the brave women who fought in the armed movement of 1910 in Mexico.

Poniatowska inaugurated the year 2000 with the sixth volume of *Todo México*, which contains ten interviews. In this book, the colors of painter Rufino Tamayo shine and we hear of the music of Carlos Chávez; actress Silvia Pinal appears amid the echoes of Buñuel's cinema, we listen to the Portuguese accents of Amalia Rodríguez, peruse Antonio Skármeta's writing, look out over Jean Louis-Barraut's stage, read about Prish Primish, marvel at the political commitment of José Revueltas's literature, savor Arthur Rubinstein's piano chords, and eavesdrop on a conversation with artist Víctor Manuel. In this volume, Poniatowska's artistry as an interviewer is once again displayed: she asks few questions, but many answers are given through her knowledge of her subjects.

Poniatowska's next book, *Las mil y una . . . (la herida de Paulina)*, also published in 2000, was written at the request of Marta Lamas and Isabel Vericat. It is about a thirteen-year-old girl in Mexicali who was raped by a drug addict who had burglarized her home. The daughter of a poor family from Oaxaca that had moved to Mexicali, in the state of Baja California, looking to improve their lives, Paulina, the victim of the rape, turns out to be pregnant. Although abortion is legal in Baja California, religious groups and doctors at the clinic where the procedure could have been performed blocked the child from terminating the pregnancy that had been forced upon her. Poniatowska places this tragedy in the context of Mexicali culture and politics. Neither the church, nor the federal government, nor local authorities made any attempt to protect the child, a situation that Poniatowska strongly denounces. The tragedy drew written protests from other women writers in Mexico City who supported Paulina's cause, and Poniatowska includes a sampling of these letters in her book. An indignant Poniatowska summarizes her career-long commitment to oppressed minorities in her epilogue, "Contener el mal del mundo" (To contain the evil of the world).

A third book published in 2000, *Las siete cabritas*, takes its title from a popular Spanish saying. Poniatowska has explained her choice of title thus: "Opté por *Las siete cabritas* porque a todas las tildaron de locas y porque más locas que una cabra centellean como las Siete Hermanas de la bóveda celeste" (I chose *Las siete cabritas* because they all [the women subjects of the book] were deemed crazy by their contemporaries; being "crazier than a goat," they sparkle like the Seven Sisters in the heavenly sphere). The women she refers to are stars of the Mexican cultural sphere: artist Frida Kahlo, poet Pita Amor, poet and painter Nahui Olin, painter María Izquierdo, and writers Elena Garro, Rosario Castellanos, and Nellie Campobello. In "Diego estoy sola, Diego ya no estoy sola: Frida Kahlo," Elena allows the painter to narrate her biography in first person. For Poniatowska, there are two Frida's, the one who has died and the one who "se queda para siempre entre ustedes, ella-yo la chingona, Frida Kahlo" (will always be among you, she-I, the 'chingona,' Frida Kahlo). "Pita Amor en los brazos de Dios," an essay based on the interview "Guadalupe Amor" from the fifth volume of *Todo México*, describes the talent and scandalous life of Pita Amor, a poet who is considered one of the most outrageous figures of the 1940s and 1950s. "Nahui Olin: la que hizo olas" is actually Carmen Mondragón, the poet and painter, a goddess whose eyes gleam with "a brutal eroticism that borders on violent," and about whom Adriana Malvido wrote *Nahui Olin, la mujer del sol*. "María Izquierdo, al derecho y al revés" is the painter from Jalisco whose merry-go-round ponies, the circus, horses, and still life pictures so impressed Antonin Artaud. "Elena Garro: la partícula revoltosa" deals with the seductive and contradictory nature of the fascinating writer of *Los recuerdos del porvenir*, champion of small farmers and their lands, an author with a bottomless trunk full of stories. "Rosario del 'Querido niño Guerra' al 'Caballitos de elote' " is based on letters that Rosario Castellanos wrote to her husband and son. The actual letters were published separately, under the title *Cartas a Ricardo* and with a prologue by Poniatowska. "Nellie Campobello, la que no tuvo muerte" is about the only female author to have written a novel about the Mexican Revolution. In presenting the stories of these seven unique women, Poniatowska does not neglect to speak of how each one lived with—or suffered from—love.

In addition to her novels and her interviews, Elena Poniatowska is noted for the texts she has written to accompany works by contemporary women artists. For example, she has written essays for several books of photographs by Mariana Yampolsky, including *La casa en la tierra* (1980), *La raíz y el camino* (1985), *Estancias del olvido* (1987), *Tlacotalpan* (1987), and *Mazahua* (1993). In January of 2001, Poniatowska published her own book on the artist: *Mariana Yampolsky y la buganvillia* (Mariana Yampolsky and the bougainvillea). The writer and the photographer have been friends for forty years, and their careers reflect their shared values. When she asks rhetorically to whom Yampolsky justifies her work, Poniatowska might be asking—and answering—for herself: "ante los oprimidos" (to the oppressed). The book covers Yampolsky's career and life from 1944, when she arrived in Mexico and was bewitched by its bougainvillea. Both Poniatowska and Yampolsky remain filled with the admiration of and astonishment by Mexico that each has felt since the 1940s, when they came to the country by their different paths.

Elena Poniatowska's works are all rooted in Mexican realities, and this is no less true for *La piel del cielo* (2001), which won the Alfaguara Prize in the year that it was published. In this novel the author combines literature and science; in addition, where before she had concentrated on the invention of women characters—Jesusa Palancares, Quiela, Tina—she now begins to imagine the masculine personality. The protagonist of *La piel del cielo* is the astronomer Lorenzo de Tena, alter ego of the real-life Guillermo Haro, Poniatowska's husband (she says she wrote this book in part as a keepsake for their children). Haro is fictionalized as a Mexican scientist whose gaze is literally and figuratively fixed on the night sky and its stars. Only Tena's dedication to his work and his discoveries tether him to Earth until he discovers love. Romance brings him joltingly into contact with reality and inspires him to lift his eyes again toward the heavens, where he discovers a new constellation of stars.

*La piel del cielo* provides Poniatowska yet another space in which to present her view of Mexican history. This time she focuses on the political situation of the 1940s, the bureaucracy of the scientific discipline and later changes in research. Important cultural figures also appear within a fictional world that here centers on Mexico's astronomical community. The novel begins when Lorenzo de Tena is a child, during the period of his first discoveries about the world. His mother is important influence in his life, constantly motivating him to scan the horizon for new possibilities. The narration develops around the inner workings of a family rejected by society: the father is from a "proper" rich family who has sired children with a poor country woman whom he has never married.

Upon the death of their mother, the children are accepted by the father's family and the novel then follows the development of a unique strength of character in the protagonist, who acts with a strict ethical conscience in his work and scientific vocation. Love will humanize him, for he discovers that its mysteries are as untouchable as "the skin of the sky," whose depths he can probe and catalog without ever being able to reach them. As in all of Poniatowska's work, love is a principal theme of *La piel del cielo*; she has said that "lo mejor es estar enamorada" (there is nothing better than to be in love). With love—for the word, for the other, for just causes, and for Mexico—Poniatowska has produced a body of work that is, fortunately for her readers, not yet complete and yet already indispensable to contemporary literature. *Here's to You Jesusa* and

*Massacre in Mexico* have been inscribed in the twentieth century's literary canon with indelible ink. In the course of her career, her writing has become richer and more complex, and by the 1990s the pace and volume of her production increases considerably. For example, from 2000 to April 2001, alone, she has published five books.

Quality accompanies the quantity of her works. Among the much-remarked linguistic merits of her writing is the rhythmic effect she achieves through precise word choice and composition. Her work is also noted for its use of diverse writing registers—the combination of history, interviews, and fictional elements in a text, for example—in which each transforms the others. This fusion of genres occurs frequently, and they constitute a kind of literary and cultural hybridity which is one of Poniatowska's grand contributions to contemporary literature.

Of paramount importance is the testimonial character of all her work, both fictional and nonfictional. Poniatowska's texts denounce the misery, want, and oppression suffered by marginalized groups. Her other great contribution to literature, is her capacity to combine the skill of listening with that of writing; a master of the art of verbal aesthetics, she is gifted with an acutely refined ear for the spoken work and a talent for turning it into literature.

An example of this is the short story "Tlapalería," published in *El cuento mexicano: Homenaje a Luis Leal.* In this story, a series of voices with distinctly varied tonalities and registers converge. Her use of visual imagery is another important recurring element in her works, particularly her focus upon the hands of the men and women who have created Mexico's arts, its crafts, the scientific discoveries, its manual labor and all manner of work. When this author writes, those other hands are present in hers.

Women are a powerful presence in Poniatowska's work. Whether as an invented character or a real-life figure turned into fiction, women workers, intellectuals, and artists are always featured in the foreground of her novels, stories, chronicles, and interviews. Although the male character is also important, with a strong presence in her chronicles and interviews, fiction, and in the biographies that she has written for the her

friends, the overwhelming majority of her situations and characters are taken from the world of women.

Beginning with her first book, *Lilus Kikus,* Elena has created a series of feminine personalities who inhabit both the popular and the privileged levels of society; whether Mexican or European, these women are frequently tied unbreakably to the figure of the mother. Her early young female protagonists, Lilus and Mariana, share a kinship with other literary figures, such as the little girl who narrates Nellie Campobello's novel, *Cartucho.* Campobello's character, who speaks of events she experienced or witnessed during the years of the Mexican Revolution, also has a close relationship with her mother. Similarly, Rosario Castellanos, with her novel *Balún Canán* (1957), creates another child character, one who speaks to us about oppression of the Mayan indigene in Chiapas. Poniatowska acknowledges her literary debt tto both of these authors, whose influences are reflected in her feminine characters.

Following the child of her first book, Poniatowska's next stories feature teenagers who in some way correspond to the author's own adolescent years. Like the author, these girls are aware that they are surrounded by young female servants and at the same time know themselves to be an integral part of the feminine segment of their families. The autobiographical character of these young protagonists is clarified even further in *La "Flor de Lis,"* a novel that pairs the European nobility—which corresponds to Poniatowska's own genealogy—and the popular classes in Mexico, with whom the author has always chosen to ally herself. Indeed, in this novel she recreates her own family life, at the center of which a character based upon her own mother. In the eyes of *Flor*'s adolescent girls, the world of their grandmothers, mothers, and aunts is seen to dissolve and recompose itself in tandem with the social environment in Mexico.

Overall, Poniatowska's work is deeply committed to the woman of Mexico, providing us with a series of memorable personalities created for the literary canon: the voice and vision of Jesusa Palancares, a combative and autonomous character, despite being victimized by economic, social and racist inequities in the twentieth-century Mexico; the fictionalized painter Angelina Beloff, the Russian emigré Quiela, whose art helps her cope with tragic circumstances; and the Italian photographer Tina Modotti, who sacrifices her personal life and her art for political causes. In recreating the lives of feminine figures, Poniatowska remakes the history of Mexico, where she lives and complies with obligations imposed on her by her writing. She also speaks of the years of poverty in Paris, where she was born, and the sufferings of other European countries in wartime; World War II was, after all, a decisive factor in her move to Mexico. But, if Europe is vividly present in her life and writing, the country that overshadows all others is Mexico; from her earliest youth, Poniatowska had distanced herself from the French colony and sought to know and identify with Mexico, with its streets and its people.

She accomplished this by learning the Spanish language from the women who lived in the servant quarters of her family home. These women, too, appear in her work, as much in her fiction as in nonfiction. As a group in society, women, especially if they are poor, were usually all but invisible; little was said about them in the nation's literature until Poniatowska and other women writers began to bring them out of their anonymity and, from within the domestic space where they live and work, set them to speaking in their own voices about themselves and the country that historically marginalized them.

Poniatowska's women love, hope, resign themselves, fail, and make sense of their lives; they are the woman who, with innocence and an angelical smile, conquers the very world she has mocked by having five husbands; they are the seamstresses who, victims of the earthquake of 1985, learn how to turn disaster to their advantage and organize the first-ever union of women workers; they are the strong women of Oaxaca; the embroiderers of Huamantla; the unskilled laborers; the girls hired into domestic service; the camp followers who were so integral to the Mexican Revolution; and the young women who suffer sexual abuse and about whom a deeply angry Poniatowska writes to denounce the rape of their dignity. They are also the artists whose talents uplift and broaden culture in Mexico: the painters, photographers, and writers.

This abundance of women is organized around two axes: the mother, Paula Amor Poniatowska, who is seen as the originator and the creator, and the invented character, the noble product of creativity. Jesusa Palancares. Through these, Poniatowska delineates the humanitarian origins of her vocation and her ethical commitment to it. In this sense, Poniatowska's characters are more than merely important in the kaleidoscope of her writing; they are the colors in a rainbow display of Mexico's entire culture, history, and literature in the twentieth century; their lives dramatize a gamut of events and social trends from before her time and contemporaneous with the trajectory of her own life. To read Poniatowska is to study the life of her country: the Mexican Revolution and its soldaderas of the 1920s; the nationalist politics of the 1920s, 1930s, and 1940s; the political oppression of the 1950s; the student movement of the 1960s; the social repression and political violence of the 1970s; and the Zapatista movement in Chiapas of the 1990s. Armed with her tape recorder, Poniatowska has captured the heart of Mexico, beating through the skin of its soil, and, like an angel whose wings are feathered with words, she has soared up to capture a glimpse of heaven's skin and harnass its power to terrify and strike down mortals with the passion of her creative will.

*Translated from the Spanish by Linda Egan and Timothy McGovern.*

## SELECTED BIBLIOGRAPHY

### Primary Works

*Lilus Kikus.* Mexico City: Los Presentes, 1954.

"Melés y Teleo (Apuntes para una comedia)." *Panoramas* 2:135–299 (1956).

*Palabras cruzadas.* Mexico City: Era, 1961.

*Todo empezó el domingo.* Text by Poniatowska; illustrations by Alberto Beltrán. Mexico City: Fondo de Cultura Económica, 1963.

*Los cuentos de Lilus Kikus.* Xalapa: Universidad Veracruzana, 1967.

*Hasta no verte Jesús mío.* Mexico City: Era, 1969.

*La noche de Tlatelolco. Testimonios de historia oral.* Mexico City: Era, 1971.

*Querido Diego, te abraza Quiela.* Mexico City: Era, 1978.

*De noche vienes.* Mexico City: Era, 1979.

*Gaby Brimmer.* Mexico City: Grijalbo, 1979.

*Fuerte es el silencio.* Mexico City: Era, 1980.

*Domingo 7.* Mexico City: Océano, 1987; 2nd ed., Mexico City: Cal y Arena, 1989.

*El último guajolote.* Mexico City: Martín Casillas-Secretaría de Educación Pública, 1982.

*¡Ay vida, no me mereces!* Mexico City: Joaquín Mortiz, 1985.

*La "Flor de Lis."* Mexico City: Era, 1988.

*Nada, nadie. Las voces del temblor.* Mexico City: Era, 1988.

*Todo México,* v. 1. Mexico City: Diana, 1990.

*Tinísima.* Mexico City: Era, 1992.

*Todo México,* v. 2. Mexico City: Diana, 1993.

*Luz y luna, las lunitas.* Mexico City: Era, 1994.

*Todo México,* v. 3: *La mirada que limpia [Gabriel Figueroa],* Mexico City: Diana, 1996.

*Paseo de la Reforma.* Mexico City: Plaza y Janés, 1996.

*Cartas de Alvaro Mutis a Elena Poniatowska.* Mexico City: Alfaguara, 1997.

*Todo México,* v. 4. Mexico City: Diana, 1998.

*Octavio Paz. Las palabras del árbol.* Mexico City: Plaza y Janés, 1998.

*Juan Soriano. Niño de mil años.* Mexico City: Plaza y Janés, 1998.

*Todo México,* v. 5. Mexico City: Diana, 1999.

*Las soldaderas.* Mexico City: Era-Consejo Nacional de la Cultura y las Artes-Instituto Nacional de Antropología e Historia, 1999.

*Todo México,* v. 6. Mexico City: Diana, 2000.

*Las mil y una. . .(la herida de Paulina).* Mexico City: Plaza y Janés, 2000.

*Mariana Yampolsky y la buganvillia.* Mexico City: Plaza y Janés, 2001.

*Las siete cabritas.* Mexico City: Era, 2000.

*La piel del cielo.* Madrid: Barcelona, 2001.

## Secondary Works

### Critical and Biographical Studies

Abreu Gómez, Ermilo. "Un libro mil veces admirable: *Hasta no verte Jesús mío.*" *La Cultura en México,* 4 February 1970, pp. 12–13.

Amar Sánchez, Ana María. "La ficción del testimonio." *Revista Iberoamericana* 56, no. 150:243–253 (1990).

———. "Las voces de los otros. El género de no-ficción en Elena Poniatowska." *Filología* 25, nos. 1–2:161–174 (1990).

Ascencio, Esteban. *Me lo dijo Elena Poniatowska. Su vida, obra y pasiones, contadas por ella misma.* Mexico City: Ediciones del Milenio, 1997.

Balboa Echeverría, Miriam. "Notas a una escritura testimonial: *Fuerte es el silencio* de Elena Poniatowska." *Discurso Literario* 5, no. 2:365–373 (1988).

Berry, John. "Invention, Convention, and Autobiography in Elena Poniatowska's *Querido Diego, te abraza Quiela.*" *Confluencia. Revista Hispánica de Cultura y Literatura* 3, no. 2:47–56 (1988).

Betanzos, Lourdes. "*La 'Flor de Lis':* El texto híbrido de Elena Poniatowska." *Romance Languages Annual* 9:410–413 (1998).

Blanco, José Joaquín. "Elena Poniatowska: píntame angelitos güeros." In *Crónica literaria: Un siglo de escritores mexicanos.* Mexico City: Cal y Arena, 1996. Pp. 373–376.

———. "Elena Poniatowska: la poderosa voz de los oprimidos." *Crónica literaria,* pp. 507–510.

———. "La bondad del padre Teufel." *La Jornada,* 1 April 1988. (A discussion of *La "Flor de Lis."*)

Bradu, Fabienne. "Pistas del tesoro." *Revista de la Universidad de México* 34, no. 8:41–42 (1980). (A discussion of *De noche vienes* and *Gaby Brimmer.*)

———. "Tina." *Vuelta* 193:43–45 (1992). (A discussion of *Tinísima.*)

Bungaard, Ana. "Identidad e historicidad. Los discursos del amor y la memoria en *Querido Diego, te abraza Quiela.*" *Sin imágenes falsas, sin falsos espejos: Narradoras mexicanas del siglo xx.* Edited by Aralia López González. Mexico City: El Colegio de México, 1995. Pp. 369–378.

Bruce-Novoa, Juan. "Elena Poniatowska: The Feminist Origins of Commitment." *Womens Studies International Forum* 6, no. 5:509–16 (1983).

———. "La búsqueda de la felicidad en *De noche vienes.*" In *Sin imágenes falsas, sin falsos espejos: Narradoras mexicanas del siglo xx.* Edited by Aralia López González. Mexico City: El Colegio de México, 1995. Pp. 379–392.

———. "Subverting the Dominant Text: Elena Poniatowska's *Querido Diego.*" In *Knives and Angels: Women Writers in Latin America.* Edited by Susan Bassnett. London: Zed Books, 1990. Pp. 115–131.

Camacho-Gingerich, Alina. "Elena Poniatowska." *Dictionary of Mexican Literature.* Edited by Eladio Cortés. Westport, Conn.: Greenwood Press. Pp. 533–336.

Capote Cruz, Zaida. "Biografía y ficción: el desafío de *Tinísima.*" In *Sin imágenes falsas, sin falsos espejos: Narradoras mexicanas del siglo xx.* Edited by Aralia López González. Mexico City: El Colegio de México, 1995. Pp. 405–412.

Carballo, Emmanuel. "*Lilus Kikus.*" *México en la Cultura,* 7 November 1954, p. 2.

———. "*Melés y Teleo.*" *México en la Cultura,* 15 July 1956, p. 2.

Castañón, Adolfo. "Elena Poniatowska: cultos de Antígona." In *Arbitrario de literatura mexicana*. Mexico City: Vuelta, 1993. Pp. 438–445.

Cella, Beatriz Susana. "Autobiografía e historia de vida en *Hasta no verte Jesús mío* de Elena Poniatowska." *Literatura Mexicana* 2, no. 1:149–156 (1991).

Chevigny, Bell Gale. "The Transformation of Privilege in the Work of Elena Poniatowska." *Latin American Literary Review* 13, no. 26:49–62 (1985).

Christ, Ronald. "Los cuentos de *Lilus Kikus*." *Recent Books in Mexico* 14, no. 5:5 (1967).

———. "The Author as Editor." *Review* 15:78–79 (1975). (A discussion of *Massacre in Mexico*.)

Cornejo Parriego, Rosalía. "Racialización colonial y diferencia femenina en *Love Story* de Poniatowska y *Cuando las mujeres quieren a los hombres* de Ferré." *Afro-Hispanic Review* 16, no. 2:10–18 (1997).

Davis, Lisa. "An Invitation to Understanding Among Poor Women of the Americas: *The Color Purple* and *Hasta no verte Jesús mío*." In *Reinventing the Americas: Comparative Studies of Literature of the United States and Spanish America*. Edited by Bell Gale Chevigny and Gari Laguardia. New York: Cambridge University Press, 1986. Pp. 224–241.

Dever, Susan. "Elena Poniatowska: la crítica de una mujer." In *Mujer y literatura mexicana y chicana: Culturas en contacto. 2*. Edited by A. López González, A. Malagamba and E. Urrutia. Mexico City: El Colegio de México; Tijuana: El Colegio de la Frontera Norte, 1990. Pp. 107–111.

Donoso Pareja, Miguel. "La caducidad del realismo." *La Vida Literaria*, April 1970, pp. 10–11. (A discussion of *Hasta no verte Jesús mío*.)

Earle, Peter G. "El tema del sacrificio en obras de Fernando del Paso, Elena Poniatowska y Ángeles Mastretta." In *Literatura Mexicana/Mexican Literature*. Edited by José Miguel Oviedo. Philadelphia: University of Pennsylvania Press, 1993. Pp. 34–43.

Espresate, Neus. "El otro Best-seller." *La Jornada* (anniversary issue) 11:9 (21 September 1995).

"La eterna impertinente." *La Jornada* (anniversary issue) 11:2 (21 September 1995).

Fernández Olmos, Margarita. "El género testimonial: aproximaciones feministas." *Revista Review Interamericana* 11, no. 1:69–75 (1981).

Flori, Mónica. "El mundo femenino de Marta Linch y Elena Poniatowska." *Letras Femeninas* 9, no. 2:23–30 (1983).

———. "Visions of Women: Symbolic Physical Portrayal as Social Commentary in the Short Fiction of Elena Poniatowska." *Third Woman* 2, no. 2:77–83 (1984).

Foppa, Alaíde. "*Querido Diego, te abraza Quiela* por Elena Poniatowska." *Fem* 2, no. 7:93 (1978).

Foster, David William. "Latin American Documentary Narrative." *Publications of the Modern Language Association of America* 99, no. 1:41–55 (1984).

Fox-Lockert, Lucía. "Elena Poniatowska: *Hasta no verte Jesús mío* (1969)." In *Women Novelists os Spain and Spanish America*. Metuchen, N.J.: Scarecrow Press, 1979. Pp. 260–277.

Franco, Jean. "Rewriting the Family: Contemporary Feminism's Revision of the Past." *Plotting Women: Gender and Representation in Mexico*. New York: Columbia University Press, 1989. Pp. 175–186, 225–227.

Friedman, Edward. "The Marginated Narrator: *Hasta no verte Jesús mío* and the Eloquence of Repression." In *The Antiheroine's Voice: Narrative Discourse and Transformations of the Picaresque*. Columbia: University of Missouri Press, 1987. Pp. 170–87.

Galindo, Carmen. "Vivir del milagro." *La Vida Literaria*, April 1970, pp. 8–9.

García, Gustavo. "A *Diego* desde el exilio del silencio." *Revista de la Universidad de México* 33, no. 1:42–43 (1978).

García Flores, Margarita. "Elena Poniatowska." In *Material de lectura 10*. Edited by Margarita García Flores. Mexico City: Universidad Nacional Autónoma de México, 1983.

García Hernández, Arturo. "Una bibliografía en el tiempo." *La Jornada* (anniversary issue) 11:18–19 (21 September 1995).

García Serrano, M. Victoria. "Apropiación y transgresión en *Querido Diego, te abraza Quiela* de Elena Poniatowska." *Letras Femeninas* 17, nos. 1–2:99–106 (1991).

Glantz, Margo. "De quién es el lenguaje." *La Jornada* (anniversary issue) 11:11 (21 September 1995).

Gnutzmann, Rita. "Tres ejemplos de escritura femenina en América Latina." *Letras de Deusto* 19, no. 44:91–104 (1989).

Gold, Janet M. "Elena Poniatowska: The Search for an Authentic Language." *Discurso Literario* 6, no. 1:181–91 (1988).

González Rubio, Javier. "Fuera de la mezquindad." *La Jornada* (anniversary issue) 11:8 (21 September 1995).

González Lee, Teresa. "Jesusa Palancares, curandera, espiritista o la patología de la pobreza." In *Mujer y literatura mexicana y chicana: Culturas en contacto 2*. Edited by A. López González, A. Malagamba, and E. Urrutia. Mexico City: El Colegio de México; Tijuana: El Colegio de la Frontera Norte, 1990. Pp. 93–97.

Gyurko, Lanin A. "The Literary Response to Nonoalco-Tlatelolco." In *Contemporary Latin American Culture:*

*Unity and Diversity*. Edited by C. Gail Gunterman. Tempe, Ariz: Center for Latin American Studies, 1984. Pp. 45–77.

Hinds, Harold E., Jr. "Review of *Masacre in Mexico* by Elena Poniatowska." Trans. by Helen R. Lane. *Latin America Literary Review* 4:94–96 (1976).

Hancock, Joel. "Elena Poniatowska's *Hasta no verte Jesús mío*: The Remaking of the Image of Woman." *Hispania* 66, no. 3:353–59 (1983).

———. "*Hasta no verte Jesús mío*: una heroína liberada." *El Universal*, 19 December 1981, p. 22.

Ibargüengoitia, Jorge. "La literatura de Tlatelolco." *Libro Abierto* 1:38–40 (1971).

Jaén, Didier T. "La neopicaresca en México: Elena Poniatowska y Luis Zapata." *Tinta* 1, no. 5:23–29 (1987).

Jörgensen, Beth E. "Elena Poniatowska." In *Spanish American Women Writers: A Bio-Bibliographical Source Book*. Edited by Diana E. Marting. Westport, Conn.: Greenwood Press, 1990. Pp. 472–482.

———. "Elena Poniatowska." In *Escritoras hispanoamericanas*. Edited by Diane Marting and Montserrat Ordóñez. Bogotá: Siglo XXI Editores, 1990. Pp. 500–512.

———. "La intertextualidad en *La noche de Tlatelolco* de Elena Poniatowska." *Hispanic Journal* 10, no. 2:81–93 (1989).

———. "Perspectivas femeninas en *Hasta no verte Jesús mío* y *La "Flor de Lis."*" *Texto Crítico* 14, no. 39:110–123 (1988).

———. "The Framing Questions: The Role of Editor in Elena Ponistowska's *La noche de Tlatelolco*." *Latin American Perspectives* 18, no. 3:80–90 (1990).

———. *The Writing of Elena Poniatowska: Engaging Dialogues*. Austin: University of Texas Press, 1994.

Kerr, Lucille. "Gestures of Authorship: Lying to Tell the Truth in Elena Poniatowska's *Hasta no verte Jesús mío*." *Modern Language Notes* 106, no. 2:370–394 (1991).

Krakusin, Margarita. "La ficción autobiográfica como fenómeno de identidad colectiva: Françoise de Graffigny y Elena Poniatowska." *Romance Languages Annual* 8:521–527 (1997).

Krauze, Ethel. "La flor de Elena." *Diorama de la Cultura. El Excélsior*, 21 April 21 1988, p. 3. (A discussion of *La "Flor de Lis."*)

Kuhnheim, Jill. "Redefining Marginality: Dis-identification in *Hasta no verte Jesús mío*." *Romance Quarterly* 42, no. 3:163–168 (1995).

Kushigian, Julia A. "Transgresión de la autobiografía y el *Bildungsroman* en *Hasta no verte Jesús mío*." *Revista Iberoamericana* 53, no. 140:667–677 (1987).

Lagos-Pope, María Inés. "El testimonio creativo de *Hasta no verte Jesús mío*." *Revista Iberoamericana* 56, no. 150:243–253 (1990).

Lamas, Marta. "Lo mejor es estar enamorada." *La Jornada* (anniversary issue) 11:10 (21 September 1995).

Lara Valdez, Josefina, and Russell M. Cluff, eds. "Poniatowska, Elena." In *Diccionario bibliográfico de escritores de México nacidos entre 1920 y 1970*. Mexico City: Instituto Nacional de Bellas Artes-Brigham Young University, 1993. Pp. 332–333.

Lazcano Araujo, Antonio. "La flor más bella, sus pétalos de hoja de tamal." *La Jornada de los Libros* 172:1, 7 (1988). (A discussion of *La "Flor de Lis."*)

Leal, Luis. "Tlatelolco, Tlatelolco." *Denver Quarterly* 14, no. 1:3–13 (1979).

———. "Jesusa Palancares, soldadera: del estereotipo al personaje." *Tinta* 2, no. 2:21–27 (1997).

Lemaître, Monique J. "Jesusa Palancares y la dialéctica de la emancipación femenina." *Hispamérica* 10, no. 30:131–135 (1981).

———. "La identidad asumida y el texto subversivo en *La 'Flor de Lis'* de Elena Poniatowska." *Explicación de Textos Literarios* 19, no. 1:27–37 (1990–1991).

López, Irma M. "Crónica de un desengaño: el México moderno en *Paseo de la Reforma* de Elena Poniatowska." *Chasqui* 28, no. 1:80–90 (1999).

———. "Tinísima: la (re)escritura de un mito." *Letras Femeninas* 23:149–161 (1997).

Lucas Dobrian, Susan. "*Querido Diego*: The Feminine Epistle in Writing and Art." *Revista Canadiense de Estudios Hispanos* 22, no. 1:33–44 (1997).

Manjarrez, Héctor. "La indiscreción de Elena Poniatowska." *Cuadernos Políticos* 30:102–114 (1981). (A discussion of *Fuerte es el silencio*.)

Martín Rodríguez, Manuel. "La posición de la narradora en *Hasta no verte Jesús mío*." *Tinta* 2, no. 2:38–48.

Marx, Joan F. "Palomas, parásitas y pecadoras: el eje femenino desde un punto de vista social en *La 'Flor de Lis'* de Elena Poniatowska." *Texto Crítico* 2, no. 3:115–124 (1996).

Mercado, Enrique. "Ya lo dijo el vate Velarde: empitona la camisa el mujerío." *La Jornada* 172:3, 6 (1988). (A discussion of *La "Flor de Lis."*)

Miller, Beth. "Elena Poniatowska." In *Mujeres en la literatura*. Mexico City: Fleisher, 1978. Pp. 89–91.

———. "Personas y personajes: Castellanos, Fuentes, Poniatowska y Sainz." *Latin American Literary Review* 4, no. 7:73–78 (1975).

Miller, Beth and Alfonso González, "Elena Poniatowska." In *26 autoras del México actual*. Mexico City: Costa Amic, 1978. Pp. 229–321.

Monsiváis, Carlos. "A veinte años de Tlatelolco." *La Jornada Semanal,* 13 October 1991, pp. 20–29.

———. "La abolición de la culpa." *La Jornada* (anniversary issue) 11:5–6 (21 September 1995).

———." 'Mira, para que no comas olvido . . .' las presiciones de Elena Poniatowska." *La Cultura en México,* 15 July 1981, pp. 2–5.

———. "Un cuarto de siglo." *Nexos* 192:71–72, 74–75 (1993).

Ochoa Sandy, Gerardo. "De *Lilus Kikus* a *Luz y luna, las lunitas.*" *Sábado* (supplement of *Unomásuno*), 11 February 1989, pp. 1, 3–4.

Otero, José. "Querido Diego, te abraza Quiela, destrucción y reconstrucción de la personalidad: lengua, estructura y símbolos del proceso." *Confluencia* 7, no. 2:75–83 (1992).

Pacheco, Jose Emilio Pacheco, "Elena Poniatowska aporta, en sus imcomparables cronicas, un espejo de la vida mexicana." *Mexico en la Cultura,* 30 October 1961, p. 3.

Paley Francescato, Martha. "Elena Poniatowska: convergencia en La 'Flor de Lis.'" *Hispamerica* 2, no. 62:127–132 (1992).

Peguero, Raquel. "Reportear para combatir el olvido." *La Jornada* (anniversary issue) 11:14–15 (21 September 1995).

Peralta, Braulio. "Un clásico vivo. Entrevista con Christopher Domínguez Michael." *La Jornada* (anniversary issue) 11:6 (21 September 1995).

———. "El pájaro de la literatura mexicana. Entrevista con Octavio Paz." *La Jornada* (anniversary issue) 11:7 (21 September 1995). (A discussion of "La eterna impertinente.")

Pérez Cruz, Emiliano. "La noche de un día difícil." *Revista de la Universidad de México* 33, nos. 44–45:43–54 (1978).

Pérez Pisonero, Arturo. "Jesusa Palancares, esperpento femenino." *Mujer y literatura mexicana y chicana: Culturas en contacto. 2.* Edited by A. López González, A. Malagamba, and E. Urrutia. Mexico City: El Colegio de México; Tijuana: El Colegio de la Frontera Norte, 1990. Pp. 223–229.

Pérez Robles, Xiúhnel. "*La noche de Tlatelolco.*" *Cuadernos Americanos* 177:79–82 (1971).

Pitol, Sergio. "La *Polonaise* brillante." *La Jornada* (anniversary issue) 11:8 (21 September 1995).

Poot-Herrera, Sara. "Del tornasol de *Lilus Kikus* al tornaviaje de *La 'Flor de Lis.*'" In *La infancia en narradoras mexicanas.* Edited by Nora Pasternac, A. R. Domenella, and L. E. Gutiérrez de Velasco. Mexico City: El Colegio de México, 1996. Pp. 386–405.

———."Elena (moramiento) de México: Poniatowska." *Si cuento lejos de ti (La ficción en México).* Edited by A.

Pavón. Mexico City: Universidad Autónoma de Tlaxcala, 1998. Pp. 115–133.

———. "*La 'Flor de Lis,'* códice y huella de Elena Poniatowska." In *Mujer y literatura mexicana y chicana: Culturas en contacto. 2.* Edited by A. López González, A. Malagamba, and E. Urrutia. Mexico City: El Colegio de México; Tijuana: El Colegio de la Frontera Norte, 1990.Pp. 99–105.

———. "*La 'Flor de Lis',* hojas de inventario." *Tinta* 2, no. 2:29–37.

———. "La voz de Jesusa Palancares, envoltura de su ser." In *Mujer y sociedad en América. VI Simposio Internacional.* Edited by J. Alcira Arancibia. Los Angeles: Cal State University, Northridge; Instituto Literario y Cultural Hispánico, 1990. Pp. 271–284.

———. "Las crónicas de Elena Poniatowska." *La Colmena. Revista de la Universidad Autónoma del Estado de México* 11:17–22 (1996).

———. "Una sillita al sol de Poniatowska para Octavio Paz." *Periplo, Revista Hispanoamericana de Literatura* 11:24–25 (2001).

Portal, Martha. "Elena Poniatowska." In *Proceso narrativo de la Revolución Mexicana.* Madrid: Espasa-Calpe, 1980. Pp. 285–292.

Price, Greg. "Elena Poniatowska." In *Latin America: The Writer's Journey.* London: Hamish Hamilton, 1990. Pp. 233–243.

Puga, María. "Elena Poniatowska, *La 'Flor de Lis'.*" In *Lo que le pasa al lector.* Mexico City: Grijalbo, 1991. 76–78.

Radnick, Laura. "Las memorias de Cronos en las manecillas de Dios." *Plural* 204:82–85 (1988).

Ramírez, Luis Enrique. "La memoria de México." *La Jornada* (anniversary issue) 11:3–4 (21 September 1995).

Reboreda, Aída. "Al terminar mi libro sobre Demetrio Vallejo haré una novela sobre mi mundo, la reacción: Poniatowska." *Unomásuno,* 5 October 1979, p. 17.

Resnick, Margery and Isabelle de Courtivron. *Women writers in Translation: An Annotated Bibliography 1945–1982.* New York: Garland Publishing, 1984.

Richards C. Katherine. "A Note on Constrasts in Elena Poniatowska's *De noche vienes.*" *Letras Femeninas* 12, nos. 1–2:107–111 (1991).

Robles, Martha. "Elena Poniatowska." In *La sombra fugitiva, escritoras en la cultura nacional,* vol. 1. Mexico City: Universidad Nacional Autónoma de México, 1985. Pp. 343–365.

Rodríguez, Ricardo. "Elena Poniatowska." *Hogar y vida* 8, no. 7:14–17 (1991).

Rulfo, Juan. "Los tiernos sueños de *Lilus Kikus.*" *La Jornada* (anniversary issue) 11:2 (21 September 1995)

Saborit, Antonio. "Las tentaciones de la solvencia." *Nexos* 128:45–47 (1988). (A discussion of *La "Flor de Lis."*)

Saltz, Joanne. "*Hasta no verte Jesús mío*: el testimonio de una mujer." In *Mujer y literatura mexicana y chicana: Culturas en contacto. 2.* Edited by A. López González, A. Malagamba, and E. Urrutia. Mexico City: El Colegio de México; Tijuana: El Colegio de la Frontera Norte, 1990. Pp. 231–38.

Schaefer, Claudia. "Updating the Epistolary Canon: Bodies and Letters, Bodies of Letters in Elena Poniatowska's *Querido Diego, te abraza Quiela* and *Gaby Brimmer*." In *Textured Lives: Women, Art, and Representation in Modern Mexico.* Tucson: University of Arizona Press, 1992. Pp. 61–87.

Scott, Nina. "The Fragmented Narrative Voice of Elena Poniatowska." *Discurso Literario* 7, no. 2 (1990): 411–20.

Shaw, Deborah. "Gender and Class Relations in *De noche vienes* by Elena Poniatowska." *Bulletin of Hispanic Studies* 72, no. 1:111–121 (1995).

———. "Jesusa Palancares as Individual Subject in Elena Poniatowska's *Hasta no verte Jesús mío*." *Bulletin of Hispanic Studies* 73, no. 2:191–204 (1996).

Shea, Maureen. "A Growing Awareness of Sexual Oppression in the Novels of Contemporary Latin American Women Writers." *Confluencia* 4, no. 1:53–59 (1988).

Smith, Richard Cándida. "¿Quién quiere usted que sea bueno?" *Oral History Review* 14:73–82 (1986).

Soler, Jordi. "La casa de las palabras." *La Jornada* (anniversary issue) 11:16 (21 September 1995).

Stabb, Martin S. "The New Essay of Mexico: Text and Context." *Hispania* 70:47–61 (1987).

Starčević, Elizabeth D. "Breaking the Silence: Elena Poniatowska, a Writer in Transition." In *Literatures in Transition: The Many Voices of the Caribbean Area. A Symposium.* Edited by Rose S. Minc. Gaithersburg: Hispamérica & Montclair State College, 1982. Pp. 63–68.

———. "Elena Poniatowska: Witness for the People." In *Contemporary Women Authors of Latin America: Introductory Essays.* Edited by Doris Meyes and Margarita Fernández Olmos. New York: Brooklyn College Press, 1983. Pp. 72–77.

Steele, Cynthia. "Gender, Genre, and Authority: *Hasta no verte Jesús mío* (1969) by Elena Poniatowska." In *Politics, Gender, and the Mexican Novel, 1968–1988: Beyond the Pyramid.* Austin: University of Texas Press, 1992. Pp. 28–65.

———. "La creatividad y el deseo en *Querido Diego, te abraza Quiela*, de Elena Poniatowska." *Hispamérica* 14, no. 41:17–28 (1985).

———. "La mediación en las obras documentales de Elena Poniatowska." *Mujer y literatura mexicana y chicana: Culturas en contacto. 2.* Edited by A. López González, A. Malagamba and E. Urrutia. Mexico City: El Colegio de México; Tijuana: El Colegio de la Frontera Norte, 1990. Pp. 211–219.

———. "Testimonio y autor/idad en *Hasta no verte, Jesús mío*, de Elena Poniatowska." *Revista de Crítica Literaria Latinoamericano* 18, no. 36:155–80 (1992).

Susti, Alejandro E. "Superposición discursiva en *Hasta no verte Jesús mío* de Elena Poniatowska: medios masivos y corridos revolucionarios." *Torre de Papel* 6, no. 3:68–89 (1996).

Tatum, Charles. "Elena Poniatowska's *Hasta no verte Jesús mío*." In *Latin American Women Writers: Yesterday and Today.* Edited by Yvette E. Miller and Charles M. Tatum. Pittsburgh: Latin American Literary Review Press, 1977. Pp. 49–58.

Taylor, Kathy. "Elena Poniatowska: Testimonial Tapestries." In *The New Narrative of Mexico: Sub-Versions of History in Mexican Fiction.* Lewisburgh, Penn.: Bucknell University Press; London and Cranbury, N.J.: Associate University Press, 1994. Pp. 30–58.

Turner, Frederick C. "Violencia and Social Change: The Cases of Mexico and Cura?ao." *Latin American Research Review* 14:251–255 (1979). (A discussion of *Massacre in Mexico*, by Elena Poniatowska, and *Social Movements, Violence and Change*, by W. A. Andersen and Russell R. Dynes.)

Urrutia, Elena. "La mujer en la guerrilla y dos libros de Elena Poniatowska." *Fem* 3, no. 12:99–102 (1980). (A discussion of *Tania, la guerrillera*, by Marta Rojas, and *The noche vienes*, by Elena Poniatowska.)

———. "La voz del silencio." *Fem* 5, no. 17:97–99 (1981). (A discussion of *Fuerte es el silencio*.)

———. "*Lilus Kikus*, por Elena Poniatowska." *Fem* 46:56 (1986).

Vargas, Margarita. "Power and Resistance in *De noche vienes* by Elena Poniatowska." *Hispanic Journal* 16, no. 2:285–296 (1995).

Vega, Patricia. "Tu retratito lo traigo en mi cartera." *La Jornada* (anniversary issue) 11:17 (21 September 1995).

Volek, Emil. "Las modalidades del testimonio y *Hasta no verte Jesús mío* de Elena Poniatowska." *Literatura mexicana/ Mexican Literature.* Edited by José Miguel Oviedo. Philadelphia: University of Pennsylvania Press, 1993. Pp. 44–67.

Volkow, Verónica. "Crónicas del silencio." *Revista de la Universidad de México* 36, no. 4:41–42 (1981). (A discussion of *Fuerte es el silencio*.)

Williams, Claudette. "Subtextuality in Elena Poniatowska's *Hasta no verte, Jesús mío.*" *Hispania* 77, no. 2:215–224 (1994).

Young, Dolly J. "Mexican Literary Reactions to Tlatelolco 1968." *Latin American Research Review* 20, no. 2:71–85 (1985).

Young, Dolly J., and William D. Young. "The New Journalism in Mexico: Two Women Writers." *Chasqui* 12, no. 2:72–80 (1983).

Zielina, María. "La falsa percepción de la realidad en 'Cine Prado'." *Mujer y literatura mexicana y chicana: Culturas en contacto,* vol. 2. Edited by A. López González, A. Malagamba, and E. Urrutia. Mexico City: El Colegio de México; Tijuana: El Colegio de la Frontera Norte, 1990. Pp. 87–91.

## Interviews

Banchik-Rothschild, Roberto. "An Interview with Elena Poniatowska." *Third World Forum,* 1 February 1988, pp. 8–9.

Beer, Gabriella de. "La revolución en la narrativa de Campobello, Castellanos y Poniatowska." *Semana de Bellas Artes,* 28 February 1981, pp. 2–5.

Belejack, Barbara. "An Enormously Exciting Time: Interview." *Mexico Journal,* 8 August 1988, pp. 3–4.

Berger, Beatriz. "Elena Poniatowska 'Rescato el México más humilde, más adolorido.'" In *Escritores de América: 31 entrevistas publicadas en Revistas de Libros de El Mercurio.* Santiago: Editorial Los Andes, 1993. Pp. 261–69.

Carmona, Krista Ratowski. "Entrevista a Elena Poniatowska." *Mester* 15, no. 2:37–42 (1986).

Collazo Mapa, Araceli. "Una entrevista con Elena Poniatowska." *La Voz,* 18 November 1999, p. 18.

Egan, Linda. "El papel de la mujer en la prensa mexicana: entrevista con Elena Poniatowska. Viernes, 12 de julio, 1991." *Tinta* 2, no. 2:6–20 (12 July 1991).

García Flores, Margarita. "Entrevista a Elena Poniatowska." *Revista de la Universidad de México* 30, no. 7:25–30 (1976).

García Pinto, Magdalena. "Entrevista con Elena Poniatowska, octubre de 1983, en su casa de Coyoacán." In *Historias íntimas: Conversaciones con diez escritoras latinoamericanas.* Hanover: Ediciones del Norte, 1988. Pp. 175–198.

Gazarian Gautier, Marie-Lise, ed. *Interviews with Latin American Writers.* Elmwood Park, Ill.: The Dalkey Archive Press, 1989. Pp. 201–216.

———. *Women Writers of Latin America: Intimate Histories.* Trans. by T. Balch and M. García Pinto. Austin: University of Texas Press. Pp. 163–181.

Kostakowsky, Lya. "La entrevistadora entrevistada." *México en la Cultura,* 26 May 1957, pp. 5, 11.

Leis Márquez, Amílcar. "La muchacha de la leña: Elena Poniatowska." *La Plaza,* September 1987, pp. 8–11.

López Negrete, Cecilia. "Con Elena Poniatowska." *Vida Literaria* 3:16–19 (1970).

Méndez Faith, Teresa. "Entrevista con Elena Poniatowska." *Inti* 15:55–60 (1982).

Miller, Beth. "Interview with Elena Poniatowska." *Latin American Literary Review* 4, no. 7:73–78 (1975).

Pacheco, Cristina. "A diez años de la noche triste de Tlatelolco: en charla con *Siempre!* Elena Poniatowska revive las horas más sombrías de México." *Siempre!,* 11 October 1978, pp. 30–31, 58–59.

Riggen, Patricia. "Entre un globo en el aire y un reloj desconchinflado." *Siglo 21,* 5 July 1992, pp. 8–9.

Romaní, Marta. "Los milagros de Elena Poniatowska." *La Jornada Semanal,* 6 December 1992, pp. 11–12. (A discussion of *Tinísima.*)

Roses, Lorraine. "Entrevista con Elena Poniatowska." *Plaza* 5–6:51–64 (1981–1982).

Salinas, Adela. "Los ojos que Elena Poniatowska tiene escondidos." *Revista de la Universidad Nacional Autónoma de México* 492:52–54 (1992).

Steele, Cynthia. "Entrevista con Elena Poniatowska." *Hispamérica* 18, nos. 53–54:89–105 (1989).

Venzor, Antonio. "'Ojalá se hagan más libros sobre mujeres como el de *Tinísima*,' dice Elena Poniatowska." *Siglo 21,* 4 February 1993, p. 5.

Zalce, Beatriz. "¿Mil miradas? Mil oídos y una sonrisa." *La Plaza,* September 1987, pp. 5–7.

# José Revueltas

## 1914–1976

*Jorge Ruffinelli*

José Revueltas was born in Durango, Mexico, on 20 November 1914. Three of his siblings are important figures in Mexican culture: Fermín as a painter, Silvestre as a musician, and Rosaura as an actress. José combined his literary vocation with political activism, and came to be known and admired for both. After his participation in the student movement of 1968 (despite his being neither a professor nor a student), and even more when he was imprisoned for that activity, he acquired greater prestige within the Mexican intelligentsia. When he died in Mexico City on 14 April 1976, he had the aura of sainthood among progressive intellectuals.

On the day of his burial in Mexico City, some government officials came to pay their respects, but they were shouted down by the students, writers, and family who were present. Revueltas was practically a cult figure who was strongly defended by his admirers and followers. By the beginning of the twenty-first century, that admiration has not diminished: his books are still being reprinted, and biographies and academic studies about him abound. Even though the Marxist philosophy that inspired him has more or less disappeared from national and international debates, his ideas are still put forth as the product of an authentic concern for human beings and not as political dogma. Moreover, his "Marxist" ideas were always sui generis, always mixed with strong Christian feelings.

From an early age Revueltas was convinced of the need for social struggle, and he tried to join the Mexican Communist Party (PCM) despite his extreme youth. The most tempestuous relations he experienced throughout his life were not amorous but political, and with his friends in political groups. More than once Revueltas was ousted from the PCM as well as from other political groups he helped found, such as the Spartacus Leninist League.

Being a political prisoner was also a central part of his life, from the age of fifteen, when he was convicted for "rebellion, sedition, and mutiny," until the end of the 1960s, when he was jailed in the sinister "Black Palace" of Lecumberri prison (now the Mexican National Archives). Revueltas was able to take literary advantage of every one of these instances. His early narratives, such as the short story "El quebranto" (1938; The surrender) and the novel *Los muros de agua* (1941; Walls of water), provide accounts of his early imprisonment. The 1941 novel re-creates his 1932 jailing in Islas Marías prison. Later, the time he spent in Lecumberri inspired one of his best novels, *El apando* (1969; Isolation cell). Nevertheless, Revueltas's work was not limited to "prison tales," and even *El apando*, which is about common, rather than political, prisoners, was conceived as an allegory about the human condition instead of testimony regarding personal circumstances.

During his first ten years as a writer, Revueltas had a clear idea about who were the "class enemies": the capitalist system and the bourgeoisie. The novels *Los muros de agua* and *El luto humano* (1943; *The Stone Knife*, 1947), as well as the stories in *Dios en la tierra* (1944; God on earth), offer a tumultuous portrayal of a Mexico still immersed in the violence of its Revolution (1910–1920) and unable to rid itself of the consequences. His most ambitious novels, however, from a literary and philosophical point of view, were written later and were of a radically problematic nature, being devoted to examining and criticizing his "comrades" in the PCM.

The publication of *Los días terrenales* (1949; Earthly days), perhaps one of Revuelta's two best-known novels, and the play *El quadrante de la soledad* (1950; Quadrant of solitude), opened an ideological debate and caused some of the most violent criticism ever seen in the Mexican cultural sphere. Between 1941 and 1944 his literature was inscribed in a personal and autobiographical frame of reference, but at the same time sought to relate itself to what was going on in the world. Its immediate antecedents were dramatic: the 1930s had witnessed the expansion of fascism: the pact between Germany and Japan against the Soviet Union, civil war in Spain and the triumph of the Francoist forces there. It also witnessed the start of World War II (1939) and Hitler's genocide of the Jews.

In his literary views of that period, Revueltas recognized and adopted nineteenth-century Russian realism, which still held sway in Spanish American culture due to the many translations available and the presence of an existential and metaphysical angst opposed to positivism. Between 1930 and 1950 Russian influence was felt in various parts of Latin America: Castelnuovo, Robert Arlt, and Ernesto Sábato in Argentina; Espínola and Juan Carlos Onetti in Uruguay; most indigenous writers in Ecuador; and Revueltas in Mexico. There was also a stylistic renewal in Mexican narrative: Agustín Yáñez, with *Al filo del agua* (1947; The edge of the storm) and Revueltas, with *El luto humano* (1943), his other best-known novel, became open to the new forms of European (Franz Kafka,

Marcel Proust, James Joyce) and American (William Faulkner, John Dos Passos) literature.

Revueltas was twenty when he was sentenced to a penitentiary at Islas Marías for the second time. Islas Marías meant a lot to Revueltas, as the insistence with which he referred to it made plain. During those initial imprisonments the writer as political militant was born. In the prologue to the 1961 edition he states:

> *Los muros de agua* collects some of my impressions during two forced instances that I had to spend in Islas Marías, the first in 1932 and the second in 1934. The clandestine activity to which the Communist Party was condemned in those years placed those of us who were militant Communists at daily risk of being jailed and being deported to that penal institution in the Pacific. I was not among the most persecuted: the jails never stopped having Communists within their walls around that time. There were stone walls in the penitentiary, in Belem prison (with which some comrades of the time became acquainted), and in Santiago Tlatelolco prison; and there were water walls in Isla María Madre of the Las Marías archipelago, in that vast and lonely Pacific that became for us an obsessive inmensity throughout the long months of imprisonment.

*Los muros de agua* narrates how five militant Communists were taken to live among true criminals—the human dregs of crime. The novel is written with a conventional structure and direct, crude language, in comparison with the much more sophisticated, suggestive, and ambiguous style that Revueltas developed later. The influence of Russian realism is obvious. The text mentions Leonid Andreyev and alludes to Nikolai Gogol, and in the prologue Revueltas does not forget Fyodor Dostoyevsky, and also considers the relation between reality and literature. It is also possible to compare *Los muros de agua* to *The House of the Dead*, in which Dostoyevsky re-created his dramatic experiences in a Siberian labor camp.

In the second edition of *Los muros de agua*, twenty years after the first, Revueltas added aesthetic reflections on realism to the prologue. He believed then that literature was not a "direct image" of reality because, as Dostoyevsky had pointed out, "reality always turns out a bit more fantastic than literature." What a well understood realism can accomplish—wrote Revueltas—is to "order, discriminate," and make reality harmonious "within a composition subjected to specific requirements." For the novelist those requirements implied following the "direction" (the tendency or movement) of reality, so as to make literature coincide with it. Although Revueltas did not express it that way, he tried to overcome traditional realism in order to convert it into a "materialist and dialectical" realism, which he defined as his own preference on many occasions.

*Los muros de agua* did not follow those theoretical postulates. As a consequence, it is only a partial "attempt." It was necessary, then, to find a Marxist aesthetic for his future works. For the moment, what had existed in his novel was the "intention, a try at what I consider realism." In the future one had to oppose the "realism" of those who submit themselves obsequiously to the facts as if they were something sacred, and also to the "realism full of vitamins, softened with talc, professionally enthusiastic, prudish, and run-of-the-mill, of those who consider themselves 'socialist realists.' " His search would consist of creating "a materialist and dialectical realism, that no one has tried in Mexico for the simple reason that there are no writers who are at the same time dialectical materialists." These notions and many akin to them were collected in the eighteenth volume of his complete works, *Cuestionamientos e intenciones* (1978; Questions and intentions).

Around 1941 Revueltas was a "party member," and his concept of militancy had not opened to the different facets of a contradictory prism. The main characters of *Los muros de agua*—Ernesto, Rosario, Marcos—are upright people, without deceptions or problems about their ideas. The conflicts, however, are developed within a careful exploration of the psychological theme of sexual desire. Given the ruling puritanical ideology, sexuality was a sinful and murky terrain, and Revueltas wanted to treat the topic more openly, in order to overcome it. What he achieved was the establishment of the foundation for a metaphor that would be very important at the end of his literary career: the metaphor of a "jail" expressed in existential and metaphysical terms. That is seen in the construction of the feminine character, Rosario, when the narrator finds parallels between the prison (physical and real), on the one hand, and family and religion, on

the other. When she was very young, Rosario experienced the religious cloister as a form of repression: "the nun's room, the familial jail, in which the choleric aunt enclosed her as an answer to her dubious sins."

Here sexual desire is seen as conflict, and later is mixed with other ethical conflicts when Rosario decides to seduce and give herself sexually to one of her jailers. Revueltas did not overcome the ideology of "purity" (with Christian roots) and became a spokesman for some of the novel's rhetorical questions as well as for the degraded imagining of the woman (from ethereal being in the connotation of her name, to "female" in heat):

> Why did she get ready to give herself in this way and to this man? Why not choose the clean, brotherly figure of Ernesto, or Marcos? Blood clouded her thoughts. It was an active and dirty blood, a decomposed blood, because when sin arrives, blood changes its mysterious composition: it picks up, like rivers during a storm, all the mud of its beds, all that the bitter and harsh trees of evil secrete. Her nose flapped like that of female animals in the forest, when spring appears. She was going to give herself.

From then on, conflictive sexuality appears in almost all of Revueltas's work as a problem without solution or satisfactory formulation. In *Los muros de agua* sexuality starts from a somber definition that is seldom seen in his later work: "The memory of sex—and even more, the memory of lost sex—is worse in what is lived and tangible, in the senses and the spirit, than sex itself. There aren't enough lamentations nor rage to feel completely in pain in that paradise of evil . . . in which remembrance is burning." *Los muros de agua* also contains another recurring motif of Revueltas's literature: eschatological representation in which grotesque images of bowel movements and feces abound—all the "low" and human that is traditionally opposed to the high and "spiritual." In his novel *Los días terrenales* Revueltas provides a gross and grotesque variant to René Descartes's famous proposition: "I defecate, therefore I am." Nevertheless, in his writing the presence of bodily detritus also has the function of pointing out a human "nature" that bourgeois and romantically inspired literature has generally hidden or denied.

Published two years after *Los muros de agua*, *El luto humano* was even more somber. Yet there is a remarkable difference: the intense use of allegory. *El luto humano* uses parable and a dense system of biblical references that had never before been seen in Mexican literature. It is loaded with national symbols (such as the eagle and the serpent), and mixes them into a didactic and political reflection—explaining agrarian reform, the irrigation system, and the Cristero rebellion of 1926–1929—and expresses them in a prophetic, dark, and radiant tone. The Uruguayan critic Alberto Zum Felde noted the essential merit of *El luto humano* from the point of view of literary history: "to have introduced into Mexican narrative a new internal dimension, which its solid objectivism is sorely lacking." There is hardly a narrative scheme in *El luto humano*. The characters wander around flooded lands, carrying a dead girl's body. This funereal exodus concludes with the characters' being stranded on a roof while the vultures circle, foretelling their death. The exodus makes the past come alive (a favorite Revueltas technique, employed in *Los muros de agua*), as well as the various stages of each character's life. This flashback technique, together with the "multiple perspective," recalls stylistic aspects of William Faulkner (*As I Lay Dying*), whom Revueltas had read to great advantage.

The most important aspect of the novel is its writing, which joins new levels of signification with metaphors and a smooth flow from the real to the symbolic. Thus, real water allows recollection of "the permanent shipwreck in which one lived," and the act of walking aimlessly is constructed as a metaphor for human existence. The presence of death is also permanent, for it is with death that the novel begins and ends. At the beginning: "La muerte estaba ahí, blanca, en la silla, con su rostro" (Death was there, white, in its chair, with its face). At the end the buzzards attack their victims: "Estos parecieron meditar por un instante, pero luego, sin vacilación alguna, arrojáronse encima de sus víctimas" (These [buzzards] seemed to ponder for an instant, but later, without any hesitation, they threw themselves on their victims).

The biblical fatalism is, and creates, a perspective, and it is from that point of view that reality is contemplated and played with. From that window reality is "ordered" into the coherent set of elements that forms the novel. Seen from that perspective, the world seems to be ruled by a terrible God who does not appear in the story, leaving earthly creatures in his place. At the level of Christian symbols, a constant presence is the Son Dead on Calvary, Christ, who represents the human and age-old suffering of every character. From that fatalism Mexico's "dark Genesis" is contemplated, as coming from the revolutionary blood and fire. In *El luto humano* the Revolution is as "savage" as it is in the work of Mariano Azuela (*Los de abajo*, 1915), or Martín Luis Guzmán (*El aguila y la serpiente*, 1928). Fifteen years after Guzmán's novel the historical revolution in *El luto humano* fascinated and repelled, presented as a barbarism both just and horrible. That was why Revueltas used "contradictory" adjectives: "The Revolution was all that is dear, dark, high, noble, and sinister."

After *El luto humano*, Revueltas published a book of short stories with a similar Christian anguish that is evident in the title: *Dios en la tierra* (1944). He was inspired by the Christian dogma of Christ the Redeemer, but he took away the mythic origin, the divine essence, and the evangelical blandness. His was a Christ created by men, a necessity converted into reality. The frame of the volume's fifteen stories is the Cristero rebellion of 1926–1929, in which priests and the faithful took up arms to defend freedom of religion and the economic interests that had been taken away by the Reforma in the middle of the nineteenth century, during the governments of Ignacio Comonfort and Benito Juárez. The violence during those years traced bloody paths in Mexico, but the Cristeros were marginalized from Mexican cultural memory, because the Revolution officially demonized the Church and its believers. Revueltas recovered that officially hidden story.

The book opens and closes with stories with Cristero themes. In the first, which gives the collection its title, the presence of a frightening and powerful God is announced in the facts and also in the narrator's prophetic voice, compounded by the harsh and violent tone chosen for the story: "The whole population was closed with hatred and stones," it starts, and the word "hate" is reiterated in overwhelming fashion in the story's twelve pages. All the stories describe and narrate scenes of unusual violence, belonging to the bellicose climate of the period represented. The last story ("¿Cuánta será la oscuridad?") takes up the survival and agony motif with a group of Protestants whom the Cristeros have ravaged and pillaged. In a style typical of the early Revueltas (the inclusion of questions with existential tone in the text or in the characters' consciences), the Pastor asks himself, while witnessing the savagery: "Why should things have to be this way? Why would there be nothing behind man, only fear?"

That violence is included in his conception of what is "Mexican," starting with "the eagle and the serpent" symbol, the country's national icon. Revueltas does not reject that violence but tries to understand it from the inside. For this reason the Marxist and simplified view that existed in his first books could no longer function here. According to the Marxist view, great evils would disappear once class differences disappeared. A more sophisticated, philosophical view guided Revueltas to end up with a philosophical pessimism exempt from religious consolation. For Revueltas, God is man's creation, God is "on Earth."

In 1976 Revueltas asserted: "I repeat what Auerbach says in his *Essence of Christianity*: God has not created man, rather it is men who have created God. God is a social and historical entity, and ideological. . . . Socially and historically, he rules relations among men, and therefore cannot do without that entity, whether one believes in it or not." A few years before he had said:

> The Virgin of Guadalupe exists as an objective fact in the conscience of Mexicans and as a moving factor in them. I am interested in the existence of Guadalupe devotees in Mexico because that contributes to the formation of an ethnic and psychological context, which as a writer I cannot ignore. For example, how do I treat the problem of God in *Dios en la tierra*? God exists here. Christ is a taciturn Christ, aggressive and furious in the Cristeros. Christ the King exists as a Cristero movement, as an objective entity, not as metaphysics, not as theological entity.

*Dios en la tierra* develops as a catalog of horrors. Beyond extreme situations—such as the jailer—all the characters in the collection are deformed beings, with deformities of body and soul, in accord with a grotesque aesthetic and narrative *tremendismo,* a miserable realism. There are feverish and delirious beings, brutalized and alienated by alcohol ("El abismo" [The abyss]; "La caída" [The fall]); a retarded child despised by his mother ("El hijo tonto" [The idiot]); a deformed person whose physical appearance arouses social fear and thus becomes "guilty" of all damnations ("La acusación" [The accusation]); the inscrutable Indian isolated from the civilized world, marginalized from life ("Barra de navidad"); the child who cries until he dies from hunger and becomes a symbol for all children ("Preferencias" [Preferences]); the man who infects his wife with syphilis, causing her to give birth to a blind son ("La soledad" [Solitude]); the miserable clerk to whom no one writes to assure him of his job ("Verde es el color de la esperanza" [Green is the color of hope]); the irrational and bloody violence of hunting ("La venadita" [The little doe]); and the presence of prostitution ("El corazón verde" [The green heart] and "Una mujer en la tierra" [A woman on earth]).

In the 1940s, while he was writing *Los días terrenales,* Revueltas poured into his "Notebooks" references to his writing as well as to his growing philosophical pessimism: "Fundamentally and essentially, I am a pessimist; deep within me there is a profound and incurable despair." He also wrote such terrible phrases as "Man was born for sainthood, for his own horrible suffering" and "People are horrible. And one is as horrible as they are." In 1949, the same year that his novel was published, he wrote: "How to get out of this darkness, from this terrible evil, from this suffering and uncertainty?" Revueltas tried to get out of the darkness by taking on the most difficult literary job possible, because in his novel, evil was going to be seen as coming not from social disorder, but from ideological dogmatism. The bourgeoisie stopped being the principal object of his analysis, and he devoted himself to the PCM. As a consequence, the novel provoked extensive polemics among his former companions in the struggle. Within this frame of reference Revueltas wrote two complex and ambitious novels, separated by fifteen years, *Los días terrenales* and *Los errores.* They were his personal response to the tragic question that came forth with the revelation of the Stalinist era crimes.

*Los días terrenales* presents its characters in dialectical opposition, a confrontation from which Revueltas extracted a different worldview. The novel is written against the "Catholic communism" of Fidel—the Communist leader in the novel—and, through him, against a dogmatic communism that believes in its doctrine and in its "inalterable principles," just as others believe in God, such as, the Cristeros in *Dios en la tierra*. His most brilliant arguments concern the pessimism/optimism dichotomy. What is to be the essence of political, party-based militancy and communism's objective? His answer is as simple as it is terrifying: it is not that man has to stop suffering, but that he stops suffering as an animal and begins to suffer as a man. The basic idea is that suffering does not end, because it is part of nature. Man is the only being with a tragic awareness of his finitude, and that condition allows him to deny himself, to lie, to look for false exit doors, to construct absolutes, mirages, and myths that will repress his free will. More and more clearly, for Revueltas literature had to return the capacity to suffer to human beings.

Thus, from that book on, terms such as "hope" and "despair," had to be redefined within a particular meaning, glossed from petit bourgeois anguish, and placed, for the better, within the theoretical framework of the "new man." These are basic notions for understanding Revueltas, his dialectic of "despair," his pessimism, and his idea of human "sickness." These notions were specially important during the years he wrote *Los días terrenales*, and not only because they were the philosophical marrow of his novel. In his "Notebooks" Revueltas wrote:

> Man makes himself a martyr by looking for absolute truths. But what is important is not that they exist but rather that Man have that propensity to look for them. What does that propensity mean? That Man needs something to hold on to in order to defend himself from Infinity. When he discovers those false absolute truths that are Love, Justice, Liberty, etc. . . . , he breathes calmly, and with the pleasure of a pig that has played around in mud. Why? Because he has hope and a reason for living; because he has stopped being a true man. Man should live without hope. He ought to know how to live without any hope, of no type whatsoever. Let us educate ourselves for that totally despairing life.

In his dialogues or thoughts these essayistic ideas acquire narrative character in the novel:

> What we try to create in the final analysis is a world of hopeless and solitary men. Of course not in the Wertherian and bourgeois sense of the word, not in the narrowly individualistic sense but rather, if one likes, in the biblical sense, as expressed in Ecclesiastes: a man heroically and happily desperate, inevitably alone, with no belief in absolutes. Screw any belief in absolutes! Men invent absolutes. God, Justice, Freedom, Love, etcetera, etcetera, because they are afraid of discovering man's intrinsic uselessness. Yes, what is amazing is not the nonexistence of absolute truths, but rather that man seeks them and invents them with the feverish and untempered eagerness of a cheating gambler, of a highly schooled thief. . . . One has to say it out loud: man has no purpose, no "reason" for living. He ought to live conscious of this in order to deserve being called a man. . . . Let us struggle for a classless society! Congratulations! But no, it is not to make men happy but to make them freely wretched, to take all hope away from them, to make them men!

The above quote is important because it clearly establishes the terms of a "Revueltasian" philosophy in the body of the novel and identifies the writer's concerns with those of some of his characters, especially with the ideas of Gregorio, who opposes Fidel. That hero/villain scheme is tempered and qualified by the characters' complexity, the situations, and the historical context. At the same time, Fidel the antagonist has been created as a dark character. From the time we meet him, circumstances serve to define him as a dehumanized being, cold, fanatical. His infant daughter has just died of hunger (a pathetic motif that Revueltas had used in a story from *Dios en la tierra*), but Fidel does not have time to shed a tear or have a memory while in front of the body, for he has to devote all his attention to the Party's activities, the newspaper, and militant organization. This thick and caricature-like design of the character's behavior is not very true to life, and at the same time reveals the hatred the writer felt toward a militant "type," for it also alludes indirectly to the lack of sensitivity of a greater symbol, the "Little Father" (Stalin).

A secondary character in *Los días terrenales* is the architect Ramos (chapter 7). Although his presence seems gratuitous, he functions as a spokesman for Revueltas's aesthetic ideas and defines the writer's position regarding the rules of Marxist aesthetics. A Communist and a dilettante, Ramos knows that the Party sticks to a determined line for "reasons of state." In the essay "Libertad del arte y estética mediatizada"

(1964), Revueltas characterizes those "reasons of state" as one of the greatest enemies of "the individual's freedom": "Art is, above all, the critique of reality: something more, then, than criticism in the hands of the citizenry; something more, it is worth saying, than politics."

Even in *Los días terrenales* Revueltas allows himself to feel pain when facing human beings' failure to overcome their social condition and the implicit weakness of ideological diversions. In *Los errores* (1964), he considered that there was no time for lamentations. Revueltas became determined about denouncing not only dogmatism but also the crimes committed because of it, and as a result of his philosophical "pessimism," he came to understand human beings as an "error" of nature. Between *Los días terrenales* and *Los errores* Revueltas published two short, complementary novels of less importance, *En algún valle de lágrimas* (1956; In some valley of tears) and *Los motivos de Caín* (1957; The motives of Cain), that nevertheless are interesting in the development of his writing and as an expression of his ideology. In them he seeks to elaborate on the portrayal of two conflicting social types whose existence reveals the deterioration of society. One is a petty usurer, the other a soldier (a Chicano) who has deserted from the Korean War. The former belongs to the national petit bourgeoisie through his rapacious habits; the other is part of imperialist wars started by "social and religious persecutions." Revueltas's personal concerns in these years had an increasingly political character. Between 1955 and 1956 his "Notebooks" record his attempt to rejoin the PCM after abandoning the Partido Popular. On "the day when Frida Kahlo's body was incinerated," he spoke with the painter David Alfaro Siqueiros about his attempt. Some months went by, and his friends predicted future conflicts and new ruptures for him ("They will not tolerate you for long . . . you will be back from that trip pretty soon.") In 1956 the PCM's Central Committee accepted his reentry. In 1957 Revueltas traveled to Europe, and upon his return wrote *México: Una democracia bárbara* (1968; Mexico: A barbarous democracy) as a result of a presidential report by Adolfo Ruiz Cortines; it was, however, really a hard attack on the political positions of Vicente Lombardo Toledano, head of the Partido Popular.

In 1957, still in Berlin, Revueltas wrote in his "Notebooks" that he visited the German writer Bodo Ushe:

> Bodo says, like Ludwig Renn, that our era is horrendous, even though it is also the era of the construction of socialism. True. But, the most horrendous of all eras? I doubt it very much. It is enough to remember that all writers and artists who lived in historical periods similar to ours, of radical transitions and spiritual crises, believed that theirs was the worst of the times lived by men before. Why should our era be the most horrendous of all? What is happening is that we writers have the ability to better perceive the horror, the desolation, the inhumanity of our time. One would need to study—and I am inclined to believe that it be so the problem of whether the artist ought to be the necessary nonconformist of any society, something that seems more and more inevitable in the contemporary era.

That was a good portrait of himself. With that "inhumanity of our time" as background, Revueltas wrote *Los errores* (Errors) and published the novel in 1964, provoking criticism even more virulent than for *Los días terrenales*.

The novel is set in Mexico in the 1930s, and Revueltas's analysis of the period is consistent with the opening line of *Los días terrenales*: denunciation and demythification of the PCM. He had lived in that period and experienced its consequences, so his analysis had a parallel in his personal life. His subjective point of view caused the most discomfort for his critics, who nevertheless recognized Revueltas's maturity as a writer, his literary vigor, and the stylistic excellence of his prose. Once the polemic lost historical validity, *Los errores* was recognized as the best novel that Revueltas had written until then.

What was easily criticized in *Los errores* was Revuelta's writing, in 1964, about the 1930s and not about the present; his association of the underworld with politics; and his referring only to Stalinism's crimes and not to the benefits of socialism. Critics also cited his apparent hostility to the PCM, which had expelled him once again in 1961. Nevertheless, no one could deny the truth of the ideological diversions or the brutal practices of Stalinism.

The plot of *Los errores* is original and is unfolded with expertise. The two plot lines relate crime to the activities of militant Communists, and they are parallel: the robbery and murder of a moneylender at the hands of El Enano, a dwarf, and Mario Cobián el Muñeco, on the one hand, and the ideological and political activities of leaders of the Mexican Communist Party. The final convergence, like the turn of a screw, is established when Cobián is made an agent of repression who uses the underworld to combat political agitation. (While he was a prisoner in Lecumberri years later, a similar story was denounced by Revueltas in a letter to Arthur Miller, then president of the PEN Club. According to that letter, the prison authorities had "let loose" common criminals among the political prisoners, with the purpose of punishing them.) The density of *Los errores* deserves extensive and complex analyses. It is organized into twenty-seven chapters and an epilogue, and each chapter introduces a new character or focuses on a particular episode of the plot. *Los errores* is not a "character novel," and although some characters acquire individuality, what matters most is the whole. In this novel Revueltas synthesizes various elements and motives that are quite distinguishable and characteristic of all his narrative.

The first motif is the disguise theory. In *Los errores* Revueltas takes up the theme of disguise that had appeared in the short novel *En algún valle de lágrimas*. Here Mario—carrying Elena in a suitcase—poses as a salesman to enter an old moneylender's shop without raising suspicion. As the novel opens, Mario looks at himself in the mirror and feels strange:

> *Le resultaba imposible decir qué era aquello: ese encontrarse con otra persona, esa metamorfosis en que apenas se reconocía. Pero sobre todo, no tanto por las alteraciones del disfraz (esto era lo de menos, como cuando se acude a una fiesta), sino por los actos a que el disfraz se destinaba. Una incertidumbre distante y vaga, algo todavía incrédulo respecto de la acción propuesta para el hombre en el espejo, que también, sin remedio, era Mario Cobián.*

It seemed impossible for him to say what that was: finding another person, that metamorphosis in which he hardly knew himself. But above all, it was not so much because of the disguise's alterations (that was the least of it, as when you go to a party) but because of the acts to which the disguise destined him. A distant and vague uncertainty, something still unbelievable regarding the act proposed by

the man in the mirror who, undoubtedly, was also Mario Cobián.

The disguise naturally has deep implications for the concepts of identity and change. Mario uses robbery as a door to a new life, one that will let him fit in, allowing him to be someone different from what he had been until then. His existential problems were so important to Revueltas that he devoted a substantial part of his essay "El autoanálisis literario" (1965; Literary self-analysis) to Mario and took that opportunity to illustrate his method of writing novels. In that essay he not only explains that character's personal failings but also uses him to explain his notion of "reality's movement": the literary work had to coincide with "reality's movement," it had to be achieved and be legitimate. "Mario lives off women, is a souteneur, an exploiter of prostitution, and his freedom from alienation regarding those circumstances can be understood only within their context, that is, as a slightly different form of being alienated." The character cannot sustain his dreams or illusions of a future free and independent life without exploiting prostitutes. His effort to free himself from alienation returns him to alienation, making him incapable of escaping the vicious circle.

With that example Revueltas wanted to show that his literary work was very different from "socialist realism" or bourgeois realism. In any of these two modalities writers believed in the "incessant perfection of the human being," and their novels reproduced that ideology rather than creating reality: "Their noble prostitutes with beautiful sentiments were ... condemned to redeem themselves, their thieves became reformed and the bad guys received the punishment they deserved." Life is not like that, Revueltas assures us, and therefore the literature that reproduces it is false.

The second motif is eschatology. The materialist vision of reality is a constant in Revueltas. In *Los días terrenales* almost a complete chapter is devoted to eschatological reflection when Gregorio steps in feces and complex reactions, memories, images, and thoughts are unleashed in his mind (chapter 9). This incident plays the same role that the madeleine does in Proust's *Remembrance of Things Past*. What was aristocratic exquisiteness in Proust is proletarian materialism in

Revueltas. In *Los errores* eschatalogy has contradictory functions. One is conventional, and consists of using it to represent the worst possible destiny for the characters. Thus, when Elena, in the locked suitcase, is thrown into the sewage canal, the latter represents the deserved punishment. On the other hand, excrement represents the material condition of every human being.

The motif appears more extensively and morosely in Mario's mind together with the conflictive memory of his mother urinating. That literary and mental image becomes a "caustic memory, full of silence, like in the movies of the time, an unbreathable noiseless act," that follows him all his life, harassing him with patricidal fantasies and oedipal love. The fluctuation between two mother figures and the son's two attitudes toward her—"Holy mother," "sacred mother," murdered mother, mother loved by the son with "dirty ardent desires"—makes the mother not only a character but also the stimulus for suffering without the possibility of solution. Although Revueltas does not explicitly extend the mother cult motif to Mexican society, it is possible to set it in that context. The debunking impulse of the maternal figure would be accomplished with greater force in *El apando*.

The third motif is avarice as agent. Don Victorino, the moneylender whom Mario and Elena are about to rob and finally kill, is almost a stereotype representative of petit bourgeois exploitation, and very similar to the renter in *En algún valle de lágrimas*. The petite bourgeoisie also represents the larger bourgeoisie and capitalism, in the way a microcosm obviously represents a larger reality: " 'Dinero, dinero,' suspiró don Victorino en tanto se encaminaba de nuevo hacia su escritorio. . . . Nada más vivo y palpitante que aquellas deudas reiteradas que el dinero encadenaba dentro del círculo hermetico, irrompible, de su movimiento, . . . ajena a los hombres y a su voluntad" ("Money, money," sighed don Victorino as he again walked toward his desk. . . . Nothing more alive and palpitating than those figures, than those repeated doubts that money linked to a hermetic and unbreakable circle of his movement, foreign to men and their will). The novel reserves the most severe descriptions and judgments for this character, and with his death, the novel seems to become an accomplice to the criminals who kill him.

The fourth motif is prison, one of Revueltas's most constant themes. In *Los errores* prison serves, among other things, to assert the possibility of deep knowledge between two characters, Olegario Chávez and Emilio Padilla. The following quote can be seen as extending the theme's importance to the entire narrative:

There you get to know one another deeply, there is no escape. That is why Olegario would know him more than anybody else. There life condenses its significance, and multiplies it to its most perfect nakedness, becomes openly barbaric, without amazement, identical to the confident nature with which one uses the toilet. The one who is a beast is there, without embarrassment, soulless, pleased to be able to do it, with the cigarettes that he smokes secretly so as to not share them with his buddies, with the special meal he is secretly served in the kitchens because of some bribe, the vileness with which he dissimulates—when there is something one ought to protest—the fear that comes through his pores, as if he were secreting excrement. You know who you are dealing with, what kind of guy, if you know his behavior in prison, and even better if he has been in prison next to you. You will certainly know if he is a scoundrel.

Prison is also a metaphysical concept that Revueltas develops to its limits in *El apando*.

The fifth motif is the political universe. This is the most important aspect of the novel. We have already seen the Mexican Communist Party's internal conflicts bloom in *Los días terrenales* but not become a crisis. In that novel the Party is represented by a sectarian and dogmatic individual, but the characterization is kept at an individual level. *Los errores* is different, since the deviation is not of a person but of the doctrine. Revueltas emptied his critical arsenal against Stalinism, something he had attempted in *Los días terrenales*. In the 1949 novel political dogma became "divine," the Party became God, and the militant became a fanatic, and in *Los errores* that image is picked up and treated more deeply. The Party becomes a church, and as in the Catholic and inquisitorial sixteenth-century Church, it becomes an executioner: its crimes are "priestly crimes by those who have made the Party a church and an inquisition."

Ironically, Marxism considered religion "the opium of the people," another way of alienating them. Revueltas turned this situation upside down, using "dialectical"

471

Marxism as a tool for analysis. At other times the procedures are simply rhetorical and demagogic, as when he asks himself, creating a false option, if "this century full of perplexities will be designated as the Century of Trials in Moscow or . . . the Century of the October Revolution." Here is a clue to Revueltas's work and thought. He did not write an anticommmunist literature from the outside, but from within. This made it even more difficult to define or catalog him as a writer or intellectual. Revueltas did not reject communism's ideas, and considered himself a "true" Communist until the end of his life. He therefore imposed on himself the mission of ending silences and getting the causes of a new ideological alienation into the open: "One has to reveal, in any way possible, the fact that power has entered into a process of decomposition that will end up poisoning and corrupting all of society."

That "mission," which Revueltas carried out with evangelical zeal, was that of a lone sniper, although he missed the quiet company of the "true Communists." In fact, they did not go along with him. Revueltas was a loner who looked for just causes and legitimate companions, such as the students in 1968. Revueltas's entries, expulsions, and reentries into the PCM were a solitary destiny and a truly personal struggle.

Had there not been the "impossibility" of belonging to any party—as was true of the character Jack Mendoza in *Los motivos de Caín*—Revueltas would have been just another Commmunist enthralled by doctrine turned into dogma, and not polemical. In 1960, in a volume titled *Dormir en tierra* (To sleep on earth), Revueltas published eight excellent stories, of which "La palabra sagrada" (The sacred word) and "Dormir en tierra" have practically become classics. Although he did not publish his third story collection, *Material de los sueños* (Dream matter), until 1974, the two books can be considered a continuous series. *Material de los sueños* includes a story from 1962 (the title story), three from 1965 ("Cama 11," "Sinfonía pastoral," and "Resurrección sin vida"), two from 1969 ("El reojo del yo" [Self-spying] and "Ezequiel o la matanza de los inocentes" [Ezekiel or the massacre of the innocents], and only one from the 1970s, "Hegel y yo" [1973; Hegel and I]).

The main theme of *Dormir en tierra* is the analysis of "appearance's other side," the struggle against the phenomenal, and the ironic view that occurs when that appearance corresponds to bourgeois society's convenience. The book gives two magnificent examples, "La palabra sagrada" and "La hermana enemiga" (The hostile sister), which examine the distorted values of the bourgeoisie and underline that social class's lack of scruples. In the second story he examines certain "abysses" of that class's soul. "La hermana enemiga" tells the story of a second marriage and a second daughter, facts that cause a grave identity conflict in the firstborn daughter and end in her suicide. Sibling conflicts are common in literature, but Revueltas takes the theme to extremes. It is not jealousy, but an extreme hatred, that causes a girl to do anything within her means to destroy her sister—behaving just like "savage capitalism." Hypocrisy, lying, and deliberate concealment prevent finding out the truth, which remains hidden within the folds of appearance. This appearance wants to replace reality, but it is only a "disguise," a lying reality full of darkness. To distinguish "clarity" in the darkness (a favorite Revueltas metaphor), it is necessary to destroy myths, false values, established notions, ideologies. This is the mechanism that rules Revueltas's conception of reality and determines his writing practice. The other stories help this adventure of the dialectical imagination, carrying the readers from darkness to clarity. In "El lenguaje de nadie" (The language of the dispossessed) language fails—not the story's language but the character's. A very poor Indian wants a small plot of miserable land, which could very well be given to him, since it is of no value. The woman who owns that land does not understand his "language," that is, she does not understand why someone would want a piece of useless land, and therefore suspects it may be worth something. How could a big landowner, who has devoted her whole life to exploiting the land, understand that the land could represent anything other than something exploitable? How could she understand a different language—which, as the story's title states directly, is "nobody's language"?

The story "Lo que sólo uno escucha" (What only one man hears) concerns the "other side" of reality, perhaps its authentic side, without the reader's knowing more about it than what a story can tell. Solitude, lack of communication, and the failure of a mediocre and frustrated artist (in this case, a violinist) happen in all walks of life, within the family, in art. Surprisingly, one day the musician's violin plays the purest notes and his hand acts like that of a master. That perfection foretells death. What destiny gives with one hand, it takes away with the other. Thus, the violinist's incommunicable happiness becomes solitude, then less communication, and finally total lack of communication: death.

The attempt to see within darkness and allow light into it is present in *Material de los sueños*, but the notion of reality becomes more and more abstract, almost without limits. Writing tries to capture ambiguous essences and phenomena, and the anecdote or "story" dissolves into pure verbal matter. Yet stories such as "Sinfonía pastoral," "Cama 11," and "Resurrección sin vida" (all from 1965) maintain the anecdotal level. The other stories tend to be introspective and abstract.

"Sinfonía pastoral" (Pastoral symphony) works, as "La hermana enemiga" and "La palabra sagrada" did in *Dormir en tierra*, from the axis of bourgeois hypocrisy, a hypocrisy based on corroded values whose false appearance must be preserved due to class interests. It is an intense story in which the reader knows what the characters hide. It tells how a man dies in a large freezer, while his lover does nothing to free him, in order to avoid revealing her marital infidelity. Her husband knows about her infidelity but does not reveal that knowledge, feigning ignorance and playing a sadistic waiting game. Both spouses prefer to let a man die rather than reveal deception (the woman) or being deceived (the man). At the end the couple returns home and decides to let the cook discover the man's frozen body, as if he were a "thief" accidentally trapped in the freezer.

In "Resurrección sin vida" (Resurrection without life) the political motif is inserted in a tale of guilt and expiation. This story of a man who has to kill a woman he loves for "reasons of state" presents the same challenging of Stalinist dogma found in *Los días terrenales* and in *Los errores*. As a whole the story is merely another example of a "premature death," a moral circumlocution for political assassination, which he had denounced in his novels. The motif of prison also appears in this story, as the metaphor of obedience transformed into a prison: "the appalling prison of obedience, an obedience so atrocious that it even becomes liberty."

In these stories Revueltas explores introspection and subjectivity, to the detriment of anecdotal aspects. More than stories there are sensations, more than narration there are images and thoughts. That is why the four vignettes that make up the piece titled "Material de los sueños" try to exhaust language and pursue inaccessible essences, presented as symbolic animal images, such as fish ("La multiplicación de los peces"; Multiplication of the fish), or scorpions ("El sino del escorpión"; The scorpion's fate), that seem more dreamlike than real. In the story "Cama 11" (Bed no. 11), which is subtitled "Un relato autobiográfico" (An autobiographical sketch), that tendency toward the subjective starts to alternate the character's thoughts with external events, then goes on to sensations produced by a tranquilizer while doctors perform an examination. From the sensations the story moves to end in an image of highly significant biblical resonance, when the character thinks: "Alguien me desciende de la cruz" (Someone brings me down from the cross). In those stories and in others, such as "El reojo del yo" and "Ezequiel o la matanza de los inocentes," exploration of language is not always successful. Literary language fails, Revueltas would say, because it belongs to the alienated human being, and thus language itself must be alienated. Language thus enters a vicious circle of attempt and failure, new attempt, new failure. The novel that took this adventure of the imagination and language to the limit is *El apando*.

In 1967, when he received the Premio Villarrutia from the hands of another writer—Agustín Yáñez, then secretary of education—Revueltas said gratefully: "Mister Secretary, I beg you to be the proper conduit to carry to the President my respectful greetings and my sincere thanks. What prizes of this type do is to reveal the humanistic character of the present regime."

The gratitude was not expressed with irony but with naive good faith. Irony would belong to history. Almost a year later, that same regime was responsible for the army's bloody repression of the protesters at the Plaza de las Tres Culturas, also known as Tlatelolco, and it jailed Revueltas on charges of inciting rebellion, sedition, conspiracy, homicide, and larceny. For two and a half years Revueltas was imprisoned with other political detainees. By that time the president must have forgotten the writer's gratitude, although he was receiving protests by letter or cable from all over the world about the jailing of Revueltas and dozens of his comrades. Among them was a letter from Arthur Miller, president of PEN International: "The student protests are nowadays in the social life of almost every country, and express underlying conflicts that can only be dealt with open dialog. . . . According to the communications I have received, the jailing of Mr. Revueltas seems to contradict and annul your government's manifested commitment to dialog and obtain a just resolution."

Imprisoned in the Castillo Negro de Lecumberri for months, experiencing difficulties that at times put his life in danger, Revueltas was one more political prisoner, but he aroused major international attention because he was a writer. Between February and March 1969 he wrote a long tale titled *El apando* (The isolation cell), and with it he seemed to meet the expectations that he would write the awaited "Lecumberri novel" or "the 68 novel." It was neither one nor the other, but both at once. *El apando* presents the story of three common prisoners, drug traffickers and addicts, and their attempts to bring drugs into the prison with the help of visitors. Thus, on the surface it appears to be an unpolitical tale.

Nevertheless, it was not Revueltas's style to write merely factual novels. When he raised his novel to symbolic levels, *El apando* acquired political and even philosophical significance. From the image of enclosure (an isolation cell is familiarly called an *apando*) Revueltas elaborated an increasingly alienated human being to the absolute level. His idea is that jail transcends the physical limits of a prison. The jailed and the jailer are prisoners, repressed society as well as the society that represses. In that context, besides being accidental, the notion of a jail is essential. That is why, even though *El apando* deals with common prisoners, social waste, for Revueltas their problems were greater and referred to every human being. He kept working with philosophical concerns of the type that asked whether there was some way out for human beings. The terms "exit" and "evasion" were borrowed from prison language, but in Revueltas's writing they also referred to the human

condition: "We are all prisoners, we are all guilty, we all want the way out, a lack of alienation."

*El apando* arose not only from a philosophical concern but also from an image that coincided with it and became concrete in the novel's verbal construction. Revueltas pointed it out: "They had put two guys from the *apando* in front of my cell, and they were then doing what I narrate at the start: they would stick their heads through the vent to ask for cigarettes." That this image, repeated several times in the text, was the nucleus of the work seems to be proved in an interview that Mercedes Padres conducted with Revueltas while he was in jail, before he finished writing *El apando*. She described the writer thus:

He smokes, he smokes a lot and writes, that is his sweet daily bread, the breath of his existence. That is how he finds the cell to be a scene where the most incredible things happen. Then people will think they are novels wrought in a boundless imagination and that they are crude realities, deep and heartbreaking realities. For example, the man who sticks his head out seems to be guillotined. That "head of the Baptist," as Revueltas says when my sight stops on that hirsute man who sometimes gazes absentmindedly at others with hate.

The most important themes and motives in Revueltas's literature converge in *El apando*, from the obsessive presence of the mother to the hermetic and repetitive image of the eyes. (Eyes are common in his writings as a hallucinating motif, but critics have not noticed or pointed out their presence and significance sufficiently.)

On the surface *El apando* is a tale from the crime page, "pulp fiction." The passages that make up its development—getting drugs into the prison, the continuous and humiliating disdain of two friends toward a third, the degrading sexual fantasies, the brutalization and "animalization" of the characters in a violent atmosphere—are presented as allegorical stages of a descent into hell. The feeling of being enclosed and asphyxiated is masterfully transposed to the text with a geometrical construction and a continuous verbal flux. The "geometry" is seen in the game of opposites and couples: Polonio-La Chata, Albino-Meche, and El Carajo and his mother (a monstrous couple). With that last "couple" Revueltas brought the Mexican Mother archetype to demythologizing limits and showed the mother-son relation as nourished by love and hate in similar doses, as well as the abuse and extortion between them that is a "normal" way of relating.

In *El apando* each character goes through multiple forms of literary description. Metaphors and epithets such as "El Carajo" (the prick) or "La vaca ordeñada" (the milked cow) degrade the characters they name even more. Invocation of the mother proves the text's obsessive insistence in adopting a degrading attitude: "The damned . . . bitch of [a] mother that had given birth to him"; "El Carajo's mother, amazingly as ugly as her son"; "God knows under what sordid and abject circumstances she may have mated, and with whom, to conceive him"; "He spoke like a child, said 'my Mom' when he had to say my fucking mother"; "But my mother the old mule was missing, the wretch was late."

Revueltas demystified such an important figure in Mexican life because demystification was part of the need to dialectically "illustrate" the dark areas of reality, which were symbols of alienation. But the symbol of absolute alienation was the expression "alienated geometry" that appears at the end of the book, which the author has explained thus:

> I take reality's extremes, its limits, then the critique [of reality] can become absolute criticism, not a halfway but rather a radical criticism, to the depths, where no character or situation is excluded. *El apando*, we can say, is a small limit novel because it brings all questionings to their limit. The jail itself is only a symbol because it is the city-jail, the society-jail. . . . The bars are nothing more than the invasion of space, and there I make a comparison: bars all over the place, bars in the city. Finally, when the characters go through the tubes, I say: "alienated geometry" and I finish up the image I had been working on. The problem is a bit philosophical, ontological. Geometry is one of the conquests of human thought, one of the highest in its development. Thus, to speak of alienated geometry is to speak of the supreme alienation of man's essence. Not the alienated being from the point of view of pure liberty but from thought and knowledge. That is the thesis, if there is one.

*El apando* is a thesis novel, the one that best expresses Revuelta's existential pessimism. It is also his last, a sort of ideological and philosophical literary legacy, as if he intuited that he did not have much time to live. Like his previous books, *El apando* corresponded to a stage in the development of his ideas and his sensibility regarding language. One could say that Revueltas's books mark the existence of his thought in the way vegetation shows the course of subterranean rivers in the desert. His skepticism, therefore, was an attitude and a consciousness-raising that corresponded to the final stage (characterized by alcoholism, sickness, and the proximity of death) in the development of his worldview.

The question nevertheless persists: Would there be some way out for human beings? Revueltas's radical skepticism seems to say no. But at the same time, did that negative answer respond to a deep analysis of reality that had reached objectivity? Or was it the product of taking a position in life, including the understandable fatigue resulting from a long political activism that had left him increasingly alone? Was his view of reality a consequence of historical changes, of the revelation of Stalinist abuse, and of the unstoppable predominance of dehumanizing capitalism?

These questions do not have unequivocal answers; readers can devise whatever answers they want. But Revueltas's important legacy to those readers—and to his own generation, to younger generations, and even to the future—is the example of a restless and questioning spirit. His legacy is also an integrity of thought that will not kneel to any doctrine, and the model of a writer who employed his talent not to write conformist or entertaining literature but to explore, questioning and demythologizing language to its utmost consequences.

## SELECTED BIBLIOGRAPHY

### Primary Works

#### Novels

*Los muros de agua*. Mexico City: Talleres de la Sociedad Cooperativa "Artes Gráficas Comerciales," 1941; 2d ed., 1961.

*El luto humano*. Mexico City: Editorial México, 1943.

*Los días terrenales*. Mexico City: Editorial Stylo, 1949; Madrid, CSIG; Nanterre, France, ALLCA XXe, 1991.

*En algún valle de lágrimas*. Mexico City: Fondo de Cultura Económica, 1956; Novaro, 1973; Era, 1979.

*Los motivos de Caín.* Mexico City: Fondo de Cultura Popular, 1957; Novaro, 1975.

*Los errores.* Mexico City: Fondo de Cultura Económica, 1964; Novaro, 1975; Era, 1979.

*El apando.* Mexico City: Era, 1969.

### Short Stories

*Dios en la tierra.* Mexico City: El Insurgente, 1944; Novaro, 1973.

*Dormir en tierra.* Mexico City: Universidad Veracruzana, 1960.

*Material de los sueños.* Mexico City: Era, 1974, 1979.

### Collected Works

*Obra literaria.* 2 vols. Mexico City: Empresas Editoriales, 1967.

*Antología personal.* Mexico City: Fondo de Cultura Económica, 1975.

*Obras completas.* Edited by Andrés Revueltas and Philippe Charon. Mexico City: Era, 1978–.

### Other Works

*Israel.* Mexico City: Sociedad General de Autores de México, 1948.

*Ensayo sobre un proletariado sin cabeza.* Mexico City: Logos, 1962.

*El conocimiento cinematográfico y sus problemas.* Mexico City: Universidad Nacional Autónoma de México, 1965.

*México: Una democracia bárbara.* Mexico City: Anteo, 1968; Era, 1983.

*Año nuevo en Lecumberri.* Mexico City: n.p., n.d. [1970].

*El cuadrante de la soledad.* Mexico City: Novaro, 1971.

*Diario en Cuba.* Puebla: UNAP, 1976.

*México 68: Juventud y revolución.* Compiled by Andrés Revueltas and Philippe Charon. Mexico City: Era, 1978.

*Cuestionamientos e intenciones.* Compiled by Andrés Revueltas and Philippe Charon. Mexico City: Era, 1978.

*Cartas a María Teresa.* Puebla: Premiá, 1979.

*Las cenizas: Obra literaria póstuma.* Compiled by Andrés Revueltas and Philippe Charon. Mexico City: Era, 1981.

*Tierra y libertad. Guión cinematográfico.* Mexico City: Era, 1981.

*Dialéctica de la conciencia.* Mexico City: Era, 1982.

*Los albañiles: Un guión rechazado.* Written with Vicente Lenero. Puebla: Premiá, 1983.

*Visión del Paricutín.* Mexico City: Era, 1983.

*Las evocaciones requeridas.* Compiled by Andrés Revueltas and Philippe Charon. Mexico City: Era, 1987.

*La palabra sagrada.* Edited by José Agustín. Mexico City: Era, 1999.

### Translations

*The Stone Knife.* Trans. by H. R. Hays. New York: Reynal & Hitchcock, 1947. (Translation of *El luto humano.*)

*The Youth Movement and the Alienation of Society.* New York: Merit, 1969.

*Human Mourning.* Minneapolis: University of Minnesota Press, 1990.

## Secondary Works

### Critical and Biographical Studies

Blanco, José Joaquín. *José Revueltas.* Mexico City: Terra Nova, 1985.

Carballo, Emmanuel, ed. *Revueltas en la mira.* Mexico City: Universidad Nacional Autónoma de México, 1984.

Escalante, Evodio. *José Revueltas: Una literatura "del lado moridor."* Mexico City: Era, 1979; 2d. ed., Zacatecas: Departamento Editorial, Universidad Autónoma de Zacatecas. 1990.

Irby, James E. "La influencia de William Faulkner en cuatro narradores hispanoamericanos." Master's thesis, Nacional Autónoma de México, 1956.

Melgoza Paralizábal, Arturo. *Modernizadores de la narrativa mexicana: Rulfo, Revueltas, Yáñez.* Mexico City: Instituto Nacional de Bellas Artes, 1984.

Negrín, Edith. *Entre la paradoja y la dialéctica: Una lectura de la narrativa de José Revueltas: Literatura y sociedad.* Mexico City: Colegio de México, 1995.

———, ed. *Nocturno en que todo se oye: José Revueltas ante la crítica.* Mexico City: Era/ Universidad Nacional Autónoma de México, 1999.

Peralta, Olivia. *Mi vida con José Revueltas.* Edited by Andrés Revueltas and Philippe Charon. Mexico City: Plaza y Valdés, 1997.

Rabadán, Antoine. *El luto humano de José Revueltas o la tragedia de un comunista.* Mexico City: Domés, 1985.

Ramírez Garrido, Jaime. *Dialéctica de lo terrenal: Ensayo sobre la obra de José Revueltas.* Mexico City: Consejo Nacional para la Cultura y las Artes, 1991.

Ruffinelli, Jorge. *José Revueltas: Ficción, política y verdad.* Veracruz: Universidad Veracruzana, 1977.

———. *Conversaciones con José Revueltas.* Veracruz: Centro

de Investigaciones Lingüístico-Literaria, Universidad Veracruzana, 1977.

Ruiz Abreu, Alvaro. *José Revueltas: Los muros de la utopía.* Mexico City: Cal y Arena, 1992.

Sheldon, Helia A. *Mito y desmitificación en dos novelas de José Revueltas.* Mexico City: Oasis, 1985.

Slick, Sam L. *José Revueltas.* Boston: Twayne, 1983.

Taylor, Marilyn R. Frankenthaler. *José Revueltas, el solitario solidario.* Miami: Ediciones Universal, 1979.

Torres M., Vicente Francisco. *Visión global de la obra literaria de José Revueltas.* Mexico City: Universidad Nacional Autónoma de México, 1985.

———. *José Revueltas, el de ayer.* Mexico City: Coordinación Nacional de Descentralización, 1996.

# Nelson Rodrigues

## (1912–1980)

## *David S. George*

Nelson Rodrigues is almost universally recognized today as Brazil's greatest playwright. The Brazilian press dubbed 2000 "The Year of Nelson Rodrigues." Many critics, both Brazilian and non-Brazilian, maintain that he is the most significant playwright of twentieth-century Latin America. This recognition has been posthumous. After experiencing early success in the theater, the author's reputation suffered badly during the second half of his life. Ruy Castro's authoritative 1992 biography takes its title, *O anjo pornográfico* (Pornographic angel), from a Nelson Rodrigues quote which serves as the book's epigraph: "I am a child looking at love through a keyhole. I've never been anything else. I was born a child and I'll die a child. The keyhole is, truly, my perspective as a writer of fiction. I am (and I always will be) a pornographic angel." The quote concisely sums up the sordid spectacle of life that Rodrigues observed as a child and an adult; it may also explain his meticulous and audacious transposition of that spectacle to page and stage, as well as the moralizing imperative underlying his literary dissection of aberration and obsession.

Nelson Rodrigues was born on 23 August 1912, the fifth of fourteen children. His birthplace was Recife, in the colonial center of northeastern Brazil. His father, Mário Rodrigues, was a fiery newspaperman who placed himself in the middle of the bitter and often violent political feuds of the day, both in Recife and later in Rio de Janeiro, where the family moved in 1916. Mário Rodrigues saw more than one of his Rio newspapers closed down and even trashed by mobs; he also landed in jail. His journalistic practices included prying into private lives, much like today's intrusive and sensationalist media; it proved fatal in 1929 when one of his newspapers accused Sylvia Seraphim, a member of Rio's elite, of adultery. Her response was to go to the paper's offices with a concealed handgun. Not finding Mario Rodrigues, she shot and killed Roberto Rodrigues, Mário's favorite son. The shooting was witnessed by Roberto's younger brother Nelson. The woman was acquitted by a jury when she based her defense on the honor code, ordinarily a male privilege. Mário, overwhelmed with grief, soon died of a stroke.

Nelson Rodrigues spent much of his childhood in a working-class neighborhood in Rio's North Zone, an environment that, with its distinct types and rituals, later became the stuff of his stories, newspaper columns, and plays: the relentless gossip which left no space for privacy and emphasized the melodramatic and the salacious, the embittered old maids, and widows who even before the official mourning period had ended, had begun new sexual relationships. There also were many deaths. There was one wailing mother in the neighborhood who seemed to lose a child every year. One of the dead children was Alaíde, a name Rodrigues used some years later for the dying protagonist of his play *Vestido de noiva* (1943; *The Wedding Dress*, 1980). (Another biographical source for *The Wedding Dress* was a diary written by a young woman, a previous tenant, that the Rodrigues children discovered in the attic of their home. It became a very effective plot device in the play.)

At age thirteen, Rodrigues became a crime reporter for one of his father's newspapers, the beginning of a long and illustrious career in journalism that would be his mainstay, even though his literary fame now rests more on his playwriting. His work as a crime reporter exposed him to the dark side of Carioca (Rio) life at a young age. The Rio of the 1920s, then the capital of Brazil, bore little resemblance to today's overcrowded megalopolis, its streets teeming with kidnappers and homicidal muggers, its drug traffickers shooting it out with the police. Back then, newsmen reported on crimes of passion and suicide pacts between young lovers whose parents had banned their union. Young Nelson Rodrigues specialized in the latter, displaying an admirable talent for inventing elaborate and melodramatic set pieces, including dialogue exchanged by the doomed sweethearts at the moment of death. Later in life he would lament—not entirely tongue-incheek—the decline in fabrication among reporters. Many of these pieces, though unsigned when they appeared in the newspaper, later found their way into his newspaper column "A vida como ela é" (Life as it is).

Mário Rodrigues's fortunes as a newspaper owner had declined in the wake of the 1930 political revolution led by populist-cum-Fascist Getúlio Vargas. (The Vargas dictatorship, modeled on Mussolini's, lasted until 1945.) The surviving members of the Rodrigues family began a life of extreme penury. Poverty meant poor nutrition, a factor contributing to Nelson's developing tuberculosis. He was institutionalized several times, and suffered associated health problems for the rest of his life.

Rodrigues performed a variety of newspaper tasks in his twenties, including opera critic. Because of the lackluster and backward state of Brazilian theater, it is often said that his drama came fully formed out of his own imagination. Although the assertion is partly true,

it also seems likely that he learned stagecraft through close observation of opera rehearsals and performances as a young critic, probably at Rio's Teatro Municipal. Touring European opera companies presented highly sophisticated productions, in contrast to most Brazilian staging. One factor propelling his playwriting does seem certain: after he married and fathered a child, he was desperate to augment the meager income provided by his newspaper work. He decided to write a play.

Rodrigues's first play was *A mulher sem pecado* (1941; Woman without sin). The play's production received relatively favorable notices, but the run was short and the hoped-for boost in income failed to materialize. Nevertheless, Rodrigues was encouraged enough to give playwriting another try. His next attempt shook the Brazilian theater to its foundations.

Rodrigues's second play, *The Wedding Dress,* placed the author definitively on Brazil's artistic map and changed the course of Brazilian theatrical history. It marked theater's entrance into the *modernista* movement that had begun in 1922 and revolutionized all the arts in Brazil. There was, however, one exception to this modernization: theater, which had stagnated, merely recycling outdated forms—melodrama, comedy of manners, vaudeville, and artificial thesis plays. *The Wedding Dress* represented a quantum leap both for Rodrigues's writing career and for the Brazilian stage, which through this play plunged into the world of the unconscious. The play's most important innovation is that it takes place almost entirely inside the mind of the protagonist, Alaíde, as she lies dying on an operating table after being hit by a car. The scenes flow from her memories, fantasies, and dreams. A few scenes correspond to external reality; for example, newspaper reports on the accident and the surgeon's raw, clinical descriptions of her fatal injuries. The final scene after Alaíde's death borders on the supernatural, as her ghost hands a wedding bouquet to her sister, who is marrying her widower.

The plot is a puzzle, the fragments of Alaíde's inner and outer life, which the dying woman attempts to put together. Ultimately, it is the reader/audience member who must assemble the pieces of the puzzle. The plot, set in modern times, deals with Alaíde's life. Before her marriage she lives in a large mansion with her parents. In the attic she discovers a diary written at the turn of the twentieth century. The author of the diary is a high-class, middle-aged prostitute, Madame Clessy, who was brutally murdered by her adolescent lover. Alaíde identifies increasingly with Clessy; her obsession represents an unconscious attempt to break from the stifling conventions of her social class and patriarchal Brazilian society. She carries her obsession into her marriage to Pedro, an unsatisfying and tempestuous union complicated by her sister Lúcia's love for Pedro and the suggestion that Alaíde had stolen him from Lúcia.

The scenes in the play include fantasies in which Alaíde interacts with Clessy, who died long before Alaíde's birth. Alaíde frequents Clessy's brothel, and the madam aids and abets her as she hallucinates murdering her husband. This story in part reflects the aesthetic of expressionism, with its inversion of internal and external worlds and its extremes of emotion. Whatever the sources of Rodrigues's inspiration, the Brazilian stage had never seen anything like this. A theatrical milieu dominated by nineteenth-century forms was suddenly thrust into the twentieth century.

The symbolism and the stagecraft of *The Wedding Dress* are as innovative as its central plot device (the view from Alaíde's unconscious). The play presents something unheard-of in its day: it mingles the levels of reality, memory, and hallucination while it projects mythical and archetypal symbols and suspends linear time, breaking with chronological plot organization. Following a circular path, the play continually turns back to the marriage ritual and its emblems: wedding gown, veil, flowers, music. The marital symbols are exhibited ironically; marriage itself is presented as a ritual which, instead of fulfilling its function of renewing life, represses desire and liberation. The playwright transforms the bridal gown, a sacred archetype of purity, into Alaíde's burial shroud, and the veil into a mask that hides the brutal social constrictions forced upon her in life. The ritual and archetypal features of the play determine its narrative structure and its scenic design, both revolutionary for their time. The problem in 1943, however, was this: Where would Nelson Rodrigues find a group of actors, a director, and a designer willing and able to take on his innovative project?

The group to stage *The Wedding Dress* was already in Rio. The company, Os Comediantes, was a group of amateurs impatient with the theater of the day, seeking a way to bring it into the modern age. The designer, Tomás Santa Rosa, was an illustrator and *modernista* painter interested in set design. The director, Zbigniew Ziembinski, was a Polish Jew fleeing the Nazi holocaust who had an extensive background in the new European theater, especially expressionist theater. Ziembinski, who arrived in Rio in 1941, soon became associated with Os Comediantes and Santa Rosa. They were looking for an inventive Brazilian text, and they found it in *The Wedding Dress*. Ziembinski took care of acting and lighting, while Santa Rosa designed the set, which followed the author's stage directions closely, with platforms and curtains correlating to the play's levels of consciousness. The flexible design allowed over a hundred scene changes, something unheard of at the time. Ziembinski's lighting directions also called for a large number of changes—over a hundred, according to contemporaneous reports. As stipulated in the playwright's stage directions, for the first time on the Brazilian stage there were microphones and loudspeakers which created something like a movie sound track. Rodrigues's novel plot structure and stage directions, along with Ziembinski's direction and Santa Rosa's design, created new possibilities for Brazilian theater in terms of dramatic structure and visual style.

The question still remains: How did Nelson Rodrigues conceive such a revolutionary project? A legend has sprung up according to which the author was a kind of primitive, untutored in theater arts. However, it is more likely that, as an opera reviewer, he had paid very close attention to the sophisticated staging of touring European companies. In addition, it is possible that the German expressionist cinema influenced him, as well as Orson Welles's *Citizen Kane*. Rodrigues also read the plays of Shakespeare, Eugene O'Neill, Henrik Ibsen, and Luigi Pirandello. But the basic hallucinatory conception of plot and character can probably be best explained in terms of his own experience. As he watched his beloved father, a sister, and brothers die, saw his family fortunes crushed, he must have felt he was living in a netherworld between life and death. During his long periods in the tuberculosis sanatorium, he experienced endless nights of feverish delirium at death's door. He later transposed them to *The Wedding Dress*'s basic structure flowing from Alaíde's dying, disintegrating consciousness.

*The Wedding Dress*'s stunning production opened on 28 December 1943 and ran well into 1944. It created a firestorm of controversy, with supporters hailing a new age for the Brazilian stage and the author as a genius, and detractors either scratching their heads in confusion or condemning the play's radical departure form staid tradition. Forward-looking critics of the time and contemporary scholars have agreed that the production modernized all aspects of Brazilian theater. Playwrights, directors, actors, designers, and theater companies would henceforth be able to utilize the full range of their creative potential. There were now new and younger theater audiences and a new criticism, immersed in the *modernista* aesthetic. The success of *The Wedding Dress*, in short, seemed to promise a brilliant career as a dramatist for Rodrigues. Fortune, however, dictated otherwise.

The year 1944 also brought Rodrigues a very different kind of success. He began writing pulp fiction for a newspaper in the *folhetim* (serial) format. The *folhetim*, written for a mainly female audience, was a kind of soap opera or romance novel, full of melodramatic twists and turns and overheated amorous intrigue. Rodrigues wrote under the pseudonym Suzana Flag. His first serialized piece, *Meu destino é pecar* (Sin is my destiny), was so successful that it was published as a book. Over his lifetime he wrote many *folhetim* pieces, as Suzana Flag and under other female pseudonyms.

In 1945 Rodrigues's theatrical successes continued, as new productions of both *The Wedding Dress* and his first play, *A mulher sem pecado*, brought him further acclaim. In 1946 he wrote a new play, *Álbum de família* (Family album), the first of his "mythic" plays. (Brazil's great theater scholar Sábato Magaldi has established the definitive three-part classification of Rodrigues's plays: psychological plays, mythic plays, and Carioca tragedies. *The Wedding Dress* belongs to the last category.) *Álbum de família* also initiated a phase that Rodrigues later called his "unpleasant theater"—and added, tongue in cheek, that audiences were in danger of catching typhoid from these plays. Incest, the central theme of *Álbum de família*, led the censors to protect the public from catching the "disease" by banning its

staging; although it was published in 1946, it was not produced theatrically until 1967. The prohibition was more than a little surprising, and quite controversial, because the fascist Vargas era had ended in 1945, and there was a widespread belief that Brazil had entered a new era of democracy. Although many of the country's most prominent writers weighed in on the side of Rodrigues, both defending the play's merits and condemning censorship, other critics deplored *Álbum de família* as a cesspool of immorality.

The fate of the play and of many that followed illustrates the great irony of Rodrigues's career. The early successes of *The Wedding Dress* and *Mulher sem pecado* led not to theatrical glory but to rejection and censorship. The standard-bearers of tradition and decency condemned his plays—and the playwright himself—as obscene and perverse. Governments banned his plays for years at a time. And the politicized, left-wing theater artists who appeared on the scene in the late 1950s and 1960s rejected the playwright and his work as reactionary.

In spite of the ostracism, Rodrigues never stopped writing for the stage. His plays continued to tear away the veil behind which lay the mysterious and hidden zones of the unconscious, and of taboo and forbidden desire. His attacks against patriarchal society and his unveiling of such forms of sexual violence as incest and rape led to charges of pornography and to censorship. Rodrigues's social critiques were non-Marxist, however; they were not based on notions of class struggle, anti-capitalism, or anti-imperialism. On the contrary, Rodrigues believed in the supremacy of the individual and abhorred anything that smacked of collectivism. The Brazilian left, weaned on the tenets of Marxism and ready-made ideological solutions for complex social ills, abhorred him.

In spite of his problems with the censors, Rodrigues did not give up on playwriting. *Anjo negro* (1947; Black angel) broke new ground by dealing with racial prejudice. Like *Álbum de família*, it was banned by the censors. Not only did it expose sexual taboos and infanticide, it portrayed the marriage of a black man and a white woman. Rodrigues's indefatigable efforts achieved a lifting of the ban, but the 1948 staging, over his protests, featured a white actor in blackface playing the black protagonist. There could be no clearer illustration of the author's argument that Brazil was not the color-blind society it imagined itself to be. The fact that the play had a satisfactory run of over two months was of little solace to the playwright.

In 1948 Rodrigues completed his next mythic play, *Senhora dos afogados* (Lady of the drowned). Based loosely on Aeschylus's *Oresteia* via Eugene O'Neill's *Mourning Becomes Electra*, *Senhora* tells the story of a family curse. Incest, as in so many of Rodrigues's plays, is the death force that annihilates the family. The play followed the now familiar pattern: it was banned by the censors. Thus, during 1948, two of Rodrigues's plays were prohibited by the censors: *Anjo negro* and *Senhora dos afogados*. Adding *Álbum de família* to the list, three of his "unpleasant" plays were banned over a two-year period. Although the prohibition was lifted on *Anjo negro* in 1948, *Senhora* was not staged until 1954.

In spite of having two plays censored, Rodrigues did not give up, however, and in 1949 he wrote *Dorotéia*, the last of the mythic plays (or, according to Rodrigues, an irresponsible farce). A lugubrious plot line is presented in a language akin to surrealism. It took directors several years to discover that the author meant what he said when he termed it an "irresponsible farce." Staged as a farce, and thus working against its tragic and mythical milieu, *Dorotéia* has had many successful productions in recent years. Indeed, most of Rodrigues's plays are now staples of both professional and amateur groups.

Rodrigues next turned to journalism, a move that would make him famous and sustain him financially until his death. He began his daily newspaper column, "A vida como ela é" (Life as it is). Each column took an event from everyday life, drawing in part on the author's experience as a crime reporter. Usually it pertained to passion or marriage or adultery, something tragic or sensational or salacious—or all of the above. In an age when marriage was considered Brazilian society's most perfect and sacred institution—although many couples openly lived out of wedlock—only Rodrigues spoke publicly about its inherent contradictions and its dark side, such as the fact that most men considered it their God-given right to have a mistress. As Ruy Castro writes on the flyleaf of *A vida como ela é*, the collection he edited in 1992, Rio in the 1950s was a city "where the neighbors kept a close watch on one another, where husbands and wives lived under the same roof with cousins and in-laws, in a veiled incestuous sensuality . . . and where the typical, and in a way perfect, marriage was comprised of husband, wife, and lover."

Rodrigues elaborated and poeticized the events he wrote about, creating a larger-than-life portrait by applying the power of psychological observation evident in his plays. The column became immensely popular; for years it was read and commented upon by all classes of people. Rodrigues published almost two thousand columns between 1951 and 1961. Though his theater was mostly scorned, censored, or ignored, *A vida como ela é* gave him a degree of popularity he never imagined. In recent years many collections of *A vida como ela é* have been published in book form. Some have been adapted to the cinema, and several were transposed to the stage, most notably by the director Luis Arthur Nunes in 1991.

Rodrigues composed his only monologue, *Valsa n° 6* (*Waltz #6*, 1998), in 1951. *Valsa* features an adolescent girl, Sônia, who has been stabbed in the back by her lover. As in *The Wedding Dress,* this play presents the thoughts of a dying protagonist, who reviews the events of her brief life. The title refers to a Chopin waltz that Sônia plays on the piano during her monologue. Rodrigues's inspiration was the overwhelming popularity of another theatrical monologue, Pedro Bloch's *As mãos de Eurídice* (Eurydice's hands). *Eurídice* is maudlin and overwrought, without any of Rodrigues's usual psychological depth, social criticism, or artistry. Ironically, Rodrigues's monologue was a box-office and critical disappointment.

*Valsa* was followed by *A falecida* (1953; The dead woman), which Rodrigues categorized as a "Carioca tragedy." (In reality it was a strange updating of the traditional comedy of manners.) The latter genre, popular in Brazil since the nineteenth century, was usually a light farce dealing with family foibles and featuring stock characters. Only Rodrigues's morbid imagination could turn such fare into tragedy. His Carioca tragedies are all set in Rio's Zona Norte (north zone), an area of working-class neighborhoods and slums on the city's outskirts where the author spent part of his childhood. In the Carioca tragedies Rodrigues descends from the flights of fancy of his mythic phase to the firm ground of life in the hardscrabble Zona Norte. The director José Alves Antunes Filho included *A falecida* in his ironically titled production *Paraíso zona norte* (1989; Paradise north zone). *A falecida* was made into a 1965 film by director Leon Hirszman, with acclaimed actress Fernanda Montenegro in the role of Zulmira.

One of Rodrigues's previously banned plays, *Senhora dos afogados* was finally produced in 1954, but it set off a storm of controversy. Audience members were divided during the performance, a minority shouting "genius" and the others booing and yelling that the author was a "degenerate." The author retorted with shouts of "idiots, idiots!" Something similar happened in 1957 when Rodrigues's *Perdoa-me por me traíres* (Forgive me for your betrayal), was staged after the censorship office had delayed its approval. In his book *O reacionário* (1977; The reactionary) Rodrigues recounts that during the performance a woman stood up in the audience and screamed that the author was a "pervert." After a local politician stood up, pulled out a pistol, and fired a warning shot, the play was banned. One of the scenes in *Perdoa-me* that so incensed audiences is the one in which a man begs his wife to forgive him after she has betrayed him in an adulterous affair—this in a society that even today frequently upholds the traditional honor code according to which the price of a woman's infidelity is death. *Perdoa-me por me traíres* was adapted for the cinema in 1983.

Rodrigues classified his next play, *Viúva, porém honesta* (1957; Widowed but proper), as an "irresponsible farce." In 1958 he returned to the Carioca tragedy, with the play *Os sete gatinhos* (The seven kittens). The play receiveed its most distinguished production in 1989 as part of Antunes Filho's production *Paraíso zona norte*. It was also adapted for the cinema in 1980. Rodrigues's next Carioca tragedy, *Boca de ouro* (1959; Gold mouth), like so many of his plays, had problems with censorship. It was made into a film in 1962 by the famed *cinema novo* director Nelson Pereira dos Santos. It was filmed again in 1990 by director Walter Avancini.

Rodrigues's next play was *Beijo no asfalto* (1960; Kiss on the pavement). It is the story of a man named Arandir, who happens upon the victim of a hit-and-run accident dying on the pavement. Arandir generously grants the dying man's last wish: a kiss. His gesture, a social taboo, unleashes a media feeding frenzy; Arandir's life is destroyed by accusations of homosexuality and even murder. The play is an indictment of both sensationalist media and homophobia. The work was first produced in 1961, and has since had several revivals. It was adapted for the cinema in 1980 under the direction of Bruno Barreto. (Barreto is best known for his *Dona Flor and Her Two Husbands* [1976], *Four Days in September* [1997], and *Bossa Nova* [1999], starring his wife, Amy Irving.)

In 1960 Rodrigues's life was again marked by tragedy. He left his wife, Elza, for another woman, with whom he had a daughter, Daniela. Born prematurely, the child suffered from the effects of cerebral palsy, including blindness and paralysis.

Rodrigues's next play, the Carioca tragegy *Otto Lara Resende ou Bonitinha mas ordinária* (Otto Lara Resende, or cute but vulgar), debuted in 1962. It was adapted for the cinema in 1963 and 1980. In 1963 Rodrigues was offered the position of writer for Brazil's first homegrown soap opera (*telenovela*), which he titled *A morta sem espelho* (The corpse without a mirror). A remarkable cast was assembled, including such acclaimed actors as Fernanda Montenegro and Sérgio Britto, with music by Antônio Carlos Jobim and lyrics by the poet Vinícius de Moraes (they had collaborated on "Garota de Ipanema [The girl from Ipanema]). Unfortunately, Rodrigues's name headed the morality guardians' blacklist, and a judge blocked the program's showing in prime time, consigning it to a late hour and thus ensuring its financial failure. The following year Rogrigues wrote two more soap operas; again, his reputation as an "immoral" dramatist proved to be an impediment.

Rodrigues continued his theatrical efforts with *Toda nudez será castigada* (1965; *All Nudity Shall Be Punished*, 1996). The play, directed by Ziembinski, was an immediate success, partly because the theatergoing public had become more broad-minded when it came to artistic treatments of taboos. After an initial six-month run in Rio, the production toured to several Brazilian cities over a three-year period. The play's definitive treatment came in the 1980s, in a production by Antunes Filho. The culmination of Rodrigues's Carioca tragedy series, *All Nudity Shall Be Punished* tells a tale of incestuous, deadly sibling rivalry. The play was adapted for the cinema by Arnaldo Jabor in 1973, and became one of the most widely viewed Brazilian films of that period. In Jabor's words, "Nelson's plays are made for the cinema, they're so visual and plot driven. He doesn't waste time on abstract concepts. His plays are about action, about facts, and his dialogue supports the action, all of which facilitates transposition to the screen" ("Parceiros e testemunhas").

Rodrigues suffered several personal tragedies in the 1960s: in 1966 his admired older brother Mário Filho died; Mario's wife committed suicide soon after; and Nelson's brother Paulinho and his entire family perished when their apartment building was swept away during a torrential rainstorm.

In 1966 Rodrigues published *O casamento* (The wedding), the only novel which did not first appear in the *folhetim* format. Published with an "adults only" warning label, it was temporarily banned but nevertheless became a runaway best-seller, rivaled only by Jorge Amado's *Dona Flor and Her Two Husbands*. Arnaldo Jabor's 1975 film version of *O casamento* was deemed "immoral" by critics from both the right and the left. Jabor later characterized the work on the flyleaf of the 1992 edition of *O casamento*: it "is a novel that clearly anticipates Rio's collapse as a city. In it are inscribed the invasion of the slums, the desperation of today's middle classes, hiding in fear behind barred windows."

Rodrigues began a new newspaper column, "Confissões" (Confessions), in the 1960s; it continued through the 1970s, nearly to the end of his life. It had an impact similar to that of "A vida como ela é" and shed considerable light on his relationship with the military dictatorship that began in 1964. Rodrigues openly defended the generals, believing they had saved the nation from Communist totalitarianism and refusing to give credence to reports of torture and disappearance. President Emílio Médici gave Rodrigues his personal "word of honor" that such reports were false and were meant to discredit the military's "redemption"—the generals' term for their coup—of Brazil. Though his enumerations of Soviet crimes against humanity—for example, the Stalin-led holocaust victimizing Russian citizens—are now widely accepted as historical fact, Rodrigues's naive faith in the military regime brought upon him the wrath not only of the activist left but also of much of the intellectual and artistic community.

The new theater companies of the 1960s, which protested military repression until they were forcibly closed in the 1970s, never staged a single play by Rodrigues. The new theatrical generation also avoided his drama because it seemed so out of touch with their concerns. (The leaders of that generation, Augusto Boal of Teatro de Arena and José Celso of Teatro Oficina, now swear allegiance to Rodrigues's dramaturgy. In fact, Celso staged *Boca de ouro* in 2000, in the rebuilt Teatro Oficina.) However, Rodrigues did put his military contacts to positive use, persuading the generals to free countless political prisoners, including Augusto Boal, whom he publicly defended in his column. When his own son Nelsinho was being hunted for subversive activities, Rodrigues persuaded the military authorities to allow him to leave the country. Nelsinho, however, refused to do so, and continued his resistance. When he was arrested and his father secured amnesty for him, he would not accept it and went on a hunger strike, becoming one of Brazil's few remaining political prisoners in 1979. Nelsinho finally left prison for the birth of his daughter (as fate would have it, shortly before his father's death).

Rodrigues's penultimate play, *Anti-Nelson Rodrigues* (1973), was staged in 1974. According to the critic Sábato Magaldi, the play, a return to the "psychological" phase, is a love story, cheerful and positive, as opposed to previous dramatic efforts; thus its "anti-Nelson Rodrigues" title. Rodrigues's last play, *A serpente* (1978; The serpent), which deals with a love triangle involving two sisters and leading to murder, represents a return to standard motifs. It received a noteworthy staging in a long-running repertory production (1994–2001) by Eduardo Tolentino and his company, Grupo Tapa.

Rodrigues's last book was a collection of newspaper columns titled *O reacionário* (1977; The reactionary). His health had declined precipitously in the 1970s. The tuberculosis and hunger he had experienced as a young man, as well as a lifelong addiction to tobacco, took their toll. In spite of surgery and hospitalization, his heart and lungs finally gave out, and he passed away on 21 December 1980.

Soon after his death, Nelson Rodrigues the dramatist began to be rediscovered. "Rediscovered" may seem a curious term to apply to someone whose seventeen plays were staged over a period of almost forty years, but the famous Nelson Rodrigues whose death was publicly mourned was the author of popular newspaper columns, films, and *folhetim* melodramas. The dramatist had been condemned in the 1940s and 1950s by self-proclaimed moralists and ignored by the protest generation of the 1960s and 1970s. Though his plays occasionally received successful productions in the latter years of his life, he was considered essentially a writer of updated comedies of manners, certainly not Brazil's greatest playwright. In 2000, however, according to Kato and Santos, "20 years after his death, [in] the year of Nelson Rodrigues, his genius is celebrated, his complete works are being republished, studied, staged, and filmed. . . . Nelson Rodrigues is resuming the place that was always his: that of the greatest playwright in Brazilian history." Though serious scholars may be skeptical about such effusive praise, it is worth noting that there were productions of nearly all of Rodrigues's dramatic works in 2000.

Three main factors set in motion the profound reassessment of Rodrigues's drama. First, theater critic and scholar Sábato Magaldi set out to demonstrate that Rodrigues was, indeed, a dramatist of towering stature. Magaldi dislodged his plays from the moral and political judgments in which they had been mired. He established a definitive typology of the plays as psychological, mythical, and Carioca tragedy. Magaldi's four-volume edition of Rodrigues's complete works, published between 1981 and 1989, included prefaces—lengthy meditations, really—which revealed the archetypal dimensions of the author's universe, the workings of his characters' unconscious, his laying bare of taboo subjects, the colloquial poetry of his dialogue, his innovative stage directions, and his rightful place as a consummate expressionist playwright.

Second, another writer who added to the growing Rodrigues mystique was the journalist Ruy Castro, whose biography *O anjo pornográfico* (1992) demonstrated the unbreakable links between the playwright's life and works. Castro has written an exhaustively documented, no-holds-barred account of Rodrigues's victories and failures in his professional and personal lives. It richly deserves an English translation, for it tells a story as compelling as any created by Rodrigues himself.

The third factor in the rehabilitation of Rodrigues's drama was the productions by Antunes Filho and his company, Grupo Macunaíma, in the 1980s. The first production, *Nelson Rodrigues o eterno retorno* (1981; Nelson Rodrigues the eternal return), was based on condensations of four of the dramatist's works: *Álbum de família*, *A falecida*, *All Nudity Shall Be Punished*, and *Boca de ouro*. Antunes Filho was especially interested in experimenting with the archetypal framework devised by Carl Jung and the mythical concepts of the philosopher-theologian Mircea Eliade.

Antunes saw the prism of archetype and myth as a means to change the stereotypical views attached to Rodrigues's drama. Antunes's project aroused the indignation of many critics and fellow directors, who resisted the idea of Rodrigues being anything other than a writer of comedies of manners, a dramatic formula which he had, ironically, superseded forty years earlier. He had gone far beyond the merely comedic, and Antunes Filho wanted to illustrate, through stagecraft, what Magaldi was in the process of demonstrating through scholarship. *Nelson Rodrigues o eterno retorno* had a long run in Brazil, went on national and international tours, received enthusiastic responses from audiences and critics all over the world, and won awards and prizes both in Brazil and abroad. This production was followed in 1984 by a shorter—and equally successful—version titled *Nelson 2 Rodrigues* and including only *All Nudity Shall Be Punished* and *Álbum de família*.

*Álbum de família* constitutes a hair-raising passage through a labyrinth of incest and murder. The family is headed by the rural patriarch Jonas. Ensnared in the incestuous web are his wife Senhorinha and their four children. Family photographs—the album of the title—mark the family members' rites of passage and furnish a respectable veneer for the incestuous relationships, murders, and apocalyptic outbursts of emotion. A parodic character called the Speaker provides a running commentary filled with insipid statements of hypocritical morality which gloss over the horrors taking place behind the pictures. *Álbum de família* does not belong to the realist canon; rather, it suspends the rules of cause and effect and replaces them with a mythical and archetypal cosmos. Like O'Neill's plays, *Álbum de família* can be seen in part as an updating of Greek tragedy; in the case of Rodrigues's play one thinks particularly of Sophocles' *Oedipus Rex* and *Electra*.

At the center of *All Nudity Shall Be Punished* is a case of deadly sibling rivalry. Patrício, the younger brother of the wealthy protagonist, Herculano, believes the latter failed to save him from financial ruin and sets out to destroy his older sibling. He sets up the straitlaced, widowed Herculaneo with the prostitute Geni and involves Herculano's son in his intrigue. The plot, as in *Álbum de família*, hinges on incest—indirect in this case—and fratricide/patricide/matricide. All the characters are afflicted, to some degree, with a pathological obsession with death and sexual repression, leading to a tragic denouement. Rodrigues's psychosocial criticism points, in the end, to a defense of moral and spiritual values, to the idea that the converse of the play's deadly chaos is eternal love, the fortress against life's woes, a healing balm rather than a death force.

Antunes Filho devised a unique style of stagecraft for his productions. Adapting the Polish theatrical pioneer Jerzy Grotowski's "poor theater" concepts, the Brazilian director utilized few elements for his set design. For example, a row of chairs in *All Nudity Shall Be Punished* suggested a brothel. Antunes Filho also created ritual-processional forms of movement to indicate the plays' mythical and archetypal dimensions.

Antunes Filho and Grupo Macunaíma staged another inventive production in 1989. Titled *Paraíso zona norte,* it included two Nelson Rodrigues plays, *Os sete gatinhos* (Seven kittens) and *A falecida* (The dead woman). The protagonist of *Os sete gatinhos* is Noronha, who feels humiliated by his menial position in the Chamber of Deputies. He is the father of five daughters, and his source of honor is that he upholds Brazilian society's ideal of feminine purity. Noronha is intent on ensuring that his youngest daughter will be a virgin when she marries. The four oldest daughters—who, unknown to their father, are prostitutes—donate the proceeds of their work to finance their younger sister's wedding. For them, their sister's virgin marriage will constitute a kind of redemption. Before the wedding, however, she stabs a pregnant cat, which gives birth to the seven kittens of the title. When her anxious parents take her to the doctor, an examination reveals her own pregnancy. The irony culminates when the father then turns his house into a brothel.

*A falecida* deals with the harsh conditions in Rio's Zona Norte. The protagonist, Zulmira, to compensate for the dissatisfactions of her life, embarks on a quest to prepare a luxurious funeral for herself, much to the consternation of her family. Life, however, plays tricks on the play's characters; Zulmira's quest goes unfulfilled, for she is buried in a cheap casket.

The "paradise" in the title of Antunes Filho's production is an allusion to Rio's designation as *cidade maravilhosa* (marvelous city)—with spectacular beaches, beautiful people, a pulsating samba beat, all making it a magnet for tourists from around the world. Rodrigues, however, had excavated deep beneath the surface in his journalism and Carioca tragedies, and uncovered the city's social ills, thus undoing the paradisiacal myth. He was decades ahead of his time in that undertaking, because Rio's myth-based facade was accepted almost universally in other quarters until the 1980s. In that decade street crime, kidnappings, abandoned children, and drug trafficking shattered the *cidade maravilhosa* chimera when the complex social realities of life in growing Latin American cities finally caught up with it.

*Paraíso zona norte* featured a set which provided a visual counterpoint to "paradise" by covering part of the stage with a plastic bubble containing a stairway by which the actors disappeared below the stage, a descent into hell. The semitransparent bubble suggested, simultaneously, a crystal palace in an amusement park, an old-fashioned sanatarium like the one where Rodrigues spent long periods convalescing from tuberculosis, and a train station where the daily tragedy of Rio's poor classes unfolds. (A similar idea was used by director Walter Salles, Jr., in his 1998 film *Central Station,* which received Academy Award nominations for best foreign film and best actress [Fernanda Montenegro in the role of Dora].) It is no small irony that Antunes's production included a sound track with music from

American epic biblical films, as a critique of Hollywood's maudlin mysticism. The production, a hit with audiences and critics, toured nationally and internationally, and received numerous awards.

With the success of Grupo Macunaíma's inventive productions, Rodrigues was truly becoming a star of the first magnitude in the Brazilian dramatic firmament. After Magaldi and Antunes Filho showed the way, scholars began to mine his oeuvre and produce increasing numbers of books and theses. Directors scrambled to stage his works, filmmakers came out with new adaptations, and publishers began the process of reediting his plays, newspaper columns, and novels.

A director who has followed Antunes Filho's lead is Luiz Arthur Nunes, also a prominent theater scholar. In 1993 he adapted several of Rodrigues's prose pieces for the stage (as several other directors did later). Nunes's production, A vida como ela é, was based on the newspaper columns which had brought Rodrigues such renown. The staging, at Brazil's national theater festival in the city of Curitiba, clarified the close ties between Rodrigues's journalism and his theater. The production was based on eleven of his stories featuring the usual exposure of taboos and critique of patriarchal society.

One of Brazil's most outstanding theater companies, Grupo Tapa, directed by Eduardo Tolentino, also followed the lead of Antunes Filho and Grupo Macunaíma. Tolentino said in 2000, "I think that any Brazilian company with . . . a vision has to stage one of Nelson's plays. He's Brazil's greatest playwright, without question" (Valéria). Tolentino's production shows the clear and conscious influence of Antunes Filho. In postmodernist fashion, Tolentino quotes or "recycles" such effects used by Antunes as ritual movement and staircases descending beneath the stage. Tolentino admits that the quotations are both affectionate and tongue-in-cheek. He also has developed his own visual style to indicate the levels of consciousness indicated in Rodrigues's stage directions. For example, his staging of The Wedding Dress features a large mirror upstage which can be tilted to reflect the action on various parts of the stage. Tolentino's production of The Wedding Dress has had a long run (1994–2001) in the company's repertory format. Tolentino and Tapa have also staged Rodrigues's A serpente. In addition, as an homage to the Polish émigré Zbigniev Ziembinski's 1943 production of The Wedding Dress, Tolentino has directed the work with Polish actors. The 2000 production, part of Brazil's quincentennial celebrations, received government sponsorship and played in the cities of Curitiba, Brasília, and Rio de Janeiro. The staging, presented in Polish, included electronic subtitles, like those utilized in opera. The production subsequently toured to Warsaw and other Polish cities.

In 2000 there were productions of nearly his entire oeuvre staged by many of Brazil's most distinguished directors. Teatro Oficina's José Celso, a member of the theatrical generation which had rejected Rodrigues out of hand, put on the Carioca tragedy Boca de ouro. He has this to say about his change of heart: "For many years I didn't have the courage to stage anything of his and I still haven't gone as far as I think I can with Nelson" (Kato and Santos).

In the "year of Nelson Rodrigues" Luiz Arthur Nunes staged A serpente and A mulher sem pecado. There were two productions of Bonitinha mas ordinária, one directed by Moacyr Goés, a protégé of Antunes Filho, and one by Marco Antônio Braz, who also directed Beijo no asfalto. Another production of Beijo was directed by Marcus Alvisi. There were also productions of All Nudity Shall Be Punished, by Cibele Forjaz, as well as of O sete gatinhos, Anjo negro, Perdoa-me por me traíres, and A falecida. The last, staged by Robert McCrea with the São Paulo company Teatro Fábrica, opened in London in 1998.

There were also numerous adaptations of Rodrigues's fiction and newspaper columns, such as A vida como ela é, directed by the author's son Nelson Rodrigues Filho in the new Teatro Nelson Rodrigues in Rio. (São Paulo opened a Teatro Nelson Rodrigues in 1999 with a stage version of the author's newspaper stories.) In 2000 Luiz Arthur Nunes directed Um menino de paixões de ópera (A boy with a passion for opera), based on Rodrigues's biographical sketches. The title refers to Rodrigues's love for opera as a young man. The Pia Fraus Teatro's production Flor da obsessão (Flower of obsession), which featured puppets in the place of actors, opened in 1996 and toured to the Miami Festival Fla/Bra in 2000. Caco Coelho adapted one of Rodrigues's folhetim novels, A mentira (The lie).

As we gaze across the last half of the twentieth century, we see many noteworthy playwrights crowded upon the Brazilian stage. A short list would include Jorge Andrade, Alfredo Dias Gomes, Ariano Vilar Suassuna, Plínio Marcos, Leilah Assunção, Oduvaldo Viana Filho, Consuelo de Castro, Naum Alves de Souza, Maria Adelaide Amaral. And yet one figure on that stage is being singled out. The works of Nelson Rodrigues, more than those of any other Brazilian playwright, not only have withstood the test of time but also are growing in stature at a vertiginous rate. His plays have withstood all approaches, whether directors treat his works cautiously, with traditional respect for dialogue and dramatic structure, or zoom in on them boldly, with avant-garde privileging of visual motifs. They have survived over half a century of artistic and ideological sea change. But the question remains: Will Nelson Rodrigues, as so many critics think he should, take his rightful place on the international stage? That is precisely what already seems to be happening in the Spanish-speaking countries of Latin America. Europe, with its openness to the cultural production of the emerging world, may yet welcome Rodrigues into its dramatic canon.

The case of the United States is more problematic because it is more introspective, insular, and provincial. Whatever the reason, the fact remains that few foreign authors are widely embraced, and outside of the occasional college production, the works of foreign playwrights are almost never staged. An article from the 17 December 2000 *New York Times*, however, presents an optimistic view of this issue. Reporting on Nelson Rodrigues's growing stature in Brazil, Larry Rohter writes that the New York-based director Terry O'Reilly of the Mabou Mines theater company is planning a production of *Dorotéia* in 2001. Furthermore, actress Amy Irving hopes to stage an Off Broadway production of *All Nudity Shall Be Punished*, also in 2001. Rohter quotes Irving on Nelson Rodrigues: "To me, he is the heterosexual Brazilian equivalent of Tennessee Williams, someone who writes about the lies and the hidden stories of the middle class, and I don't understand why he isn't huge." Compelling productions, stageworthy translations, and solid scholarship could yet make Nelson Rodrigues a force to be reckoned with in the United States.

## SELECTED BIBLIOGRAPHY

### Primary Works

#### Plays

*Álbum de família; Vestido de noiva.* Rio de Janeiro: Ediçoês do Povo, 1946.

*Anjo negro; Vestido de noiva; A mulher sem pecado.* Rio de Janeiro, 1948.

*Senhora dos afogados; A falecida.* Rio de Janeiro: Seção de Livros da Emprêsa Gráfica "O Cruzeiro," 1956.

*O beijo no asfalto.* Rio de Janeiro: J. Ozon, 1961.

*Bonitinha, mas ordinária.* Preface by Sábato Magaldi. São Paulo, 1965.

*Toda nudez será castigada.* Rio de Janeiro: Distribuidora Record, 1973.

*A serpente.* Rio de Janeiro: Editora Nova Fronteira, 1980.

*Os sete gatinhos.* Rio de Janeiro: Editora Nova Fronteira, 1980.

*Teatro completo.* 4 vols. Critical introduction by Sábato Magaldi. Rio de Janeiro: Editora Nova Fronteira, 1981–1989.

*Teatro completo.* Edited by Sábato Magaldi. Rio de Janeiro: Nova Aguilar, 1993. (Complete plays and selected critical essays.)

#### Fiction

*Escravas do amor.* Rio de Janeiro: Edições "O Cruzeiro," 1946. (As Suzana Flag.)

*Meu destino é pecar.* Rio de Janeiro: Edições "O Cruzeiro," 1946; 4th ed., 1998. (As Suzana Flag.)

*Minha vida.* Rio de Janeiro: Edições "O Cruzeiro," 1946. (As Suzana Flag.)

*A mulher que amou demais. Diário da Noite,* 1949. (As Myrna.)

*A mentira. Flan,* 1953. (As Suzana Flag.)

*O casamento.* Rio de Janeiro: Editora Guanabara, 1966; São Paulo: Companhia das Letras, 1992. (Notes by Arnaldo Jabor.)

*O homem proibido.* Rio de Janeiro: Editora Nova Fronteira, 1981. (As Suzana Flag.)

*Núpcias de fogo.* São Paulo: Companhia das Letras, 1997. (As Suzana Flag.)

#### Journalism

*A pátria em chuteiras: Novas crônicas de futebol.* Rio de Janeiro, 1955. Edited by Ruy Castro; São Paulo: Companhia das Letras, 1994.

*O remador de Ben-Hur: Confissões culturais.* Rio de Janeiro, 1957. Edited by Ruy Castro; São Paulo: Companhia das Letras, 1996.

*Asfalto selvagem.* 2 vols. 1959–1960. Rio de Janeiro: J. Ozon, 1960; São Paulo: Companhia das Letras, 1995.

*Cem contos escolhidos: A vida como ela é.* 2 vols. Rio de Janeiro: J. Ozon, 1961.

*O óbvio ululante: Primeiras confissões.* Edited by Ruy Castro. Rio de Janeiro: Liveria Eldorado, 1968; São Paulo: Companhia das Letras, 1993.

*A cabra vadia: Novas confissões.* Rio de Janeiro: Liveria Eldorado, 1970; São Paulo: Companhia das Letras, 1995.

*Elas gostam de apanhar.* Rio de Janeiro: Bloch, 1974.

*O reacionário: Memórias e confissões.* Rio de Janeiro: Editora Record, 1977; São Paulo: Companhia das Letras, 1995.

*A vida como ela é: O homem fiel e outros contos.* Edited by Ruy Castro. São Paulo: Companhia das Letras, 1992.

*A coroa de orquídeas e outros contos de A vida como ela é.* São Paulo: Companhia das Letras, 1993.

*A menina sem estrela: Memórias.* São Paulo: Companhia das Letras, 1993.

*Nelson Rodrigues: O melhor do romance, contos e crônicas.* Edited by Ruy Castro. São Paulo: Companhia das Letras, 1993.

*À sombra das chuteiras imortais: Crônicas de futebol.* São Paulo: Companhia das Letras, 1993.

*A dama do lotação e outros contos e crônicas.* Edited by Maura Sardinha. São Paulo: Editora S/A, 1996.

*Flor de obsessão: As 1000 melhores frases de Nelson Rodrigues.* Edited by Ruy Castro. São Paulo: Companhia das Letras, 1997.

### Translations

*The Wedding Gown: Tragedy in 3 Acts.* Trans. by José de Mara Nogueira. Washington, D.C.: Brazil-American Cultural Institute, 1978.

*The Wedding Dress.* Trans. and with an introduction by Fred M. Clark. Valencia: Albatros Hispanofila, 1980.

*The Wedding Dress; All Nudity Shall Be Punished; Lady of the Drowned; Waltz #6; The Deceased Woman.* Trans. by Joffre Rodrigues and Toby Coe; introduction by Sábato Magaldi. Rio de Janeiro: Funarte, 1998.

### Secondary Works

### Critical and Biographical Studies

Andrade, Ana Luiza. "In the Inter(t)sex(t) of Clarice Lispector and Nelson Rodrigues: From Drama to Language." In *Tropical Paths: Essays on Modern Brazilian Literature.* Edited by Randal Johnson. New York: Garland, 1993. Pp. 133–152.

Boff, Maria Luiza Ramos. "Nelson Rodrigues: A mulher em tres planos." *Travessia* (Florianópolis) 25:80–93 (1992).

Castro, Ruy. *O anjo pornográfico: A vida de Nelson Rodrigues.* São Paulo: Companhia das Letras, 1992.

Clark, Fred M. *Impermanent Structures: Semiotic Readings of Nelson Rodrigues' Vestido de Noiva, Álbum de Família, and Anjo Negro.* Chapel Hill: University of North Carolina Press, 1991.

———. "Relações impermanentes: Texto e espectador no teatro de Oswald de Andrade e Nelson Rodrigues." *Travessia* (Florianópolis) 28:105–123 (1994).

———. *Spectator, Character, Text: Semiotic Readings of Nelson Rodrigues' Theater.* Valencia: Albatros Ediciones, 1995.

Dennison, Stephanie. "Critical Responses to the Screening of Nelson Rodrigues." *Studies in Latin American Popular Culture* 19:129–144 (2000).

Fraga, Eudinyr. "Nelson Rodrigues e o expressionismo." *Travessia* (Florianópolis) 28:89–103 (1994).

———. *Nelson Rodrigues expressionista.* São Paulo: FAPESP, 1998.

George, David S. *Grupo Macunaíma: Carnavalização e mito.* São Paulo: Editora Perspectiva/Editora da Universidade de São Paulo, 1990.

———. *The Modern Brazilian Stage.* Austin: University of Texas Press, 1992.

———. "Encenador Gerald Thomas's Flash and Crash Days: Nelson Rodrigues Without Words." *Latin American Theatre Review* 30, no. 1:75–88 (fall 1996).

Guidarini, Mário. *Nelson Rodrigues: Flor de obsessão.* Florianópolis: Editora da UFSC, 1990.

Guinsburg, J. "Nelson Rodrigues: Um folhetim de melodramas." *Travessia* (Florianópolis) 28:7–10 (1994).

Johnson, Randal. "Nelson Rodrigues as Filmed by Arnaldo Jabor." *Latin American Theatre Review* 15–28 (fall 1982).

Kato, Gisele, and Renata Santos. "À sombra do Nelson imortal." *Bravo* 33: 44–49 (June 2000).

Lins, Ronaldo Lima. *O teatro de Nelson Rodrigues: Uma realidade em agonia.* Rio de Janeiro: Francisco Alves, 1979.

Lopes, Angela Leite. *Nelson Rodrigues: Trágico, então moderno.* Rio de Janeiro: Editora UFRJ/Tempo Brasileiro, 1993.

———. "Nelson Rodrigues: O trágico e a cena do esilhacamento." *Travessia* (Florianópolis) 28:67–87 (1994).

Magaldi, Sábato. *Nelson Rodrigues: Dramaturgia e encenações.* São Paulo: Perspectiva, 1987.

Martins, Maria Helena Pires. *Nelson Rodrigues: Seleção de textos, notas, estudos biográfico, histórico e crítico.* São Paulo: Abril Educação, 1981.

Martuscello, Carmine. *O teatro de Nelson Rodrigues: Uma leitura pscicanalítica.* São Paulo: Editora Siciliano, 1993.

Milaré, Sabastião. "Nelson Rodrigues e o melodrama brasileiro." *Travessia* (Florianópolis) 28:15–46 (1994).

Nunes, Luiz Arthur. "The Conflict Between the Real and the Ideal: A Study of the Elements of Naturalism and Melodrama in the Dramatic Works of Nelson Rodrigues." Ph.D. dissertation, University of Michigan, Ann Arbor, 1987.

———. "A poética do melodrama." *Bravo* 33:50–56 (June 2000).

Pereira, Victor Hugo Adler. "Nelson Rodrigues e a lógica da obscenidade." *Travessia* (Florianópolis) 28:195–218 (1994).

———. *Nelson Rodrigues e a obscena contemporánea.* Rio de Janeiro: Editora da UERJ, 1999.

Rodrigues, Stella. *Nelson Rodrigues, meu irmão.* Rio de Janeiro: J. O. Editora, 1986.

Rohter, Larry. "Reawakening the Giant of Brazilian Theater." *New York Times,* 17 December 2000.

Süssekind, Flora. *Nelson Rodrigues e o fundo falso.* Brasília: Ministério de Educação e Cultura, 1977.

Waldman, Berta. "A cena e o cio nacional: Uma leitura dos romances folhetins de Nelson Rodrigues." In *Toward Socio-Criticism: Selected Proceedings of the Conference "Luso-Brazilian Literatures, a Socio-Critical Approach."* Edited by Roberto Reis. Tempe: Center for Latin American Studies, Arizona State University, 1991.

Waldman, Berta, and Carlo Vogt. *Nelson Rodrigues: Flor de obsessão.* São Paulo: Brasiliense, 1985.

———. "Nelson Rodrigues en escena." Translated by Jorge Aguade. *Escritura: Revista de Teoria y Crítica Literárias* 14, no. 28:477–485 (July–December 1989).

## Interviews

Jabor, Arnaldo. "Parceiros e testemunhas." *Bravo* 33:52–53 (June 2000).

Valéria, Paula. "Eduardo Tolentino" (http://www.esfera.net/010/teatroetolentino.htm).

## Films Based on the Works of Nelson Rodrigues

*Meu destino é pecar.* Directed and written by Manuel Pelufo. Produced by Mario Civelli. 1952.

*Boca de ouro.* Directed and written by Nelson Pereira dos Santos. Produced by Jarbas Barbosa and Gilberto Perrone. 1962.

*Bonitinha, mas ordinária.* Screenplay by Jece Valadão. Directed by Billy Davis (pseudonym for J. P. de Carvalho). Produced by Jece Valadão and Joffre Rodrigues. 1963.

*Asfalto selvagem.* Screenplay by Clóvis de Castro. Directed by J. B. Tanko. 1964.

*O beijo.* Screenplay by F. Tambellini, Glauco Couto, and Geraldo Gabriel. Directed by Flávio Tambellini. Produced by Tambellini/Companhia Cinematográfica. 1965.

*A falecida.* Screenplay by Leon Hirszman and Eduardo Coutinho. Directed by Leon Hirszman. Produced by Joffre Rodrigues and Aluízio Leite Garcia. 1965.

*Engraçadinha depois dos trinta.* Written and directed by J. B. Tanko. Produced by J. B. Tanko Filmes. 1966.

*Toda nudez será castigada.* Written and directed by Arnaldo Jabor. Produced by R. F. Produções Cinematográficas/Ventania Produções/Ipanema Filmes. 1973.

*O casamento.* Written and directed by Arnaldo Jabor. Produced by Sagitário Filmes. 1975.

*A dama da lotação.* Screenplay by Neville d'Almeida and Nelson Rodrigues. Directed by Neville d'Almeida. Produced by Luiz Carlos Barreto and Nilton Rique. 1978.

*O beijo no asfalto.* Screenplay by Doc Comparato and Bruno Barreto. Directed by Bruno Barreto. Produced by Luiz Carlos Barreto. 1980.

*Bonitinha, mas ordinária.* Screenplay by Gilvan Pereira, Sindoval Aguiar, Jorge Laclette, and Doc Comparato. Directed by Braz Chediak. Produced by Luiz Carlos Barreto. 1980.

*Os sete gatinhos.* Written and directed by Neville d'Almeida. Produced by Terra Filmes/Cineville/Embrafilme. 1980.

*Álbum de família.* Screenplay by Nelson Rodrigues, Braz Chediak, Nelson Rodrigues Filho, Gilvan Pereira, and Sandoval Aguiar. Directed by Braz Chediak. Produced by BC Cinematográficas/Atlântida Cinematográfica/W. V. Filmes. 1981.

*Engraçadinha.* Written and directed by Haroldo Marinho Barbosa. Produced by Paulo Thiago. 1981.

*Perdoa-me por me traíres.* Screenplay by Gilvan Pereira, Joffre Rodrigues, Nelson Rodrigues Filho, and Braz Chediak. Directed by Braz Chediak. Produced by J. N. Filmes. 1983.

*Boca de ouro.* Written and directed by Walter Avancini. Produced by JN Filmes. 1990.

*Traição.* Screenplay by Patrícia Melo. Directed by Arthur Fontes, Claudio Torres, and José Henrique Fonseca. Produced by Produtora Conspiração. 1998.

*Gêmeas.* Screenplay by Elena Soárez. Directed by Andrucha Waddington. Produced by Riofilme/Columbia TriStar. 1999.

# Gonzalo Rojas

## (1917–    )

## Jacobo Sefamí

Gonzalo Rojas was born the seventh of eight children in Lebu, Chile, on 20 December 1917. His father, Juan Antonio Rojas Villalón, grew up in Chile's *norte chico*, a region north of Santiago in the province of Coquimbo, in the same valleys where Gabriela Mistral was also raised. Rojas believes that his grandfather, Jacinto Rojas Iglesias, was, in fact, a distant cousin of Mistral. Like Mistral, he also believes that he is a descendant of *conversos* (Jews who converted to Catholicism after the official decree of expulsion from Spain in 1492), thereby establishing his connection to Fernando de Rojas, the purported author of *La Celestina* (1499) who also shared a Jewish heritage. Rojas's father studied in a mining school, and by 1905, probably pushed by economic needs, relocated to Lebu, in southern Chile, where he found work in the underwater coal mines. In 1921, he met his death during a tragic gas explosion in the mines.

The family of Rojas's mother, Celia Pizarro, was originally from the province of Cadiz, Spain. After the death of her husband, and with many children to support, Rojas's mother moved in 1926 to Concepción, where she secured fellowships for several of her children to attend boarding schools. At his school's library, Rojas read Spanish writers from the Golden Age period and also learned Greek and Roman classics from his German teacher, Guillermo Jüneman. In order to keep his fellowships, Rojas had to excel in school.

At seventeen, Gonzalo traveled third class from Talcahuano (a port near Concepción) to Iquique (in the north of Chile, close to the border with Peru) on the ship *Fresia*. It was then that he began writing. Although most of his poems from this period remained unpublished (in *Cuaderno secreto* [Secret notebook]), Rojas included some of them in his later poetry collections. He also published some of his poems in *El Tarapacá*, a newspaper in Iquique, where his first work of prose, an essay on Ramón del Valle-Inclán, was also published. By 1936, after almost two years in the north, he returned to Concepción to finish his secondary education. From there he moved to Santiago to study law, there becoming acquainted with a variety of literary and cultural circles. In Santiago, he met the well-known poet Vicente Huidobro, who served as mentor of a newly founded surrealist journal, *Mandrágora* (of which seven issues were published between 1938 and 1943). Although Rojas did not appear as a founding member of the journal, he collaborated with Braulio Arenas, Teófilo Cid, and Enrique Gómez Correa (and later Jorge Cáceres) in practicing an avant-garde aesthetics. A few years later, however, Rojas separated from the group, dissatisfied with what he felt was its overly orthodox vision of surrealism and its desire for immediate fame and recognition.

In 1940 Rojas's mother died. He had transferred his studies to the School of Philosophy and Letters of the Instituto Pedagógico at the Universidad de Chile. In 1942, he met María Mackenzie, who, although recently married (at age eighteen), was about to break up with her husband. María accompanied Rojas to the northern Atacama Desert, where he spent several years teaching miners how to read and write, using works of Heraclitus as a pedagogical tool. Rodrigo Tomás, their first son, was born in 1943. They returned to Santiago in 1944, where Rojas worked in the Department of Communications and Culture at the Interior Ministry. A short while later, he was hired to teach at a German high school in Valparaíso. He adjusted his schedule in order to commute from Santiago to Valparaíso, spending half of the week in Santiago and half in Valparaíso. In 1946 he wrote *La miseria del hombre* (Man's misery), largely conceived during his trips by bus while commuting. He presented the volume for the poetry prize of the Sociedad de Escritores de Chile (Writers' Society of Chile). He won the contest, but the volume was not published as promised, and Rojas himself had to finance the printing of his first book in 1948.

In 1947 Rojas founded an institute of higher learning in philosophy and letters, which eventually became a school in the University of Chile at Valparaíso. Rojas called his administrative and teaching activities *poesía activa* (active poetry), since he believed that he had to be creative in finding new ways to promote institutions of higher learning, new teaching methodologies, literary workshops, and cultural exchanges and dialogues. In 1952 he was granted a chair in Chilean literature and literary theory at the Universidad de Concepción, returning to the place where he spent his childhood and adolescence.

In 1953 Rojas took his first trip to Europe, where he met the surrealists André Breton and Benjamin Peret. While at the Universidad de Concepción, he organized and led the summer school, which he initiated in 1955. He also organized three important gatherings of writers, first with a group of Chilean writers in 1958, then with writers from across Latin America in 1960, and finally with a group of internationally known scholars, writers, and artists in 1962. According to Carlos Fuentes,

it was during these meetings that the so-called Latin American "boom" generation was formed (see the list of participants in the chronology of *Obra selecta*, 1997). In 1958–1959 Rojas received the UNESCO fellowship for writers, which allowed him to live in Paris for a year. There he met not only European writers, but important Latin American intellectuals and poets who resided there, including Octavio Paz, Julio Cortázar, and others. During this stay, he was visited by Hilda Ortiz (later known as Hilda R. May), an ex-student of his from the Universidad de Concepción—and later a critic in her own right—whom he married in 1963. Also during this year, he toured ten cities in China.

In 1964 his second book, *Contra la muerte* (Against death), was published by Editorial Universitaria, in Chile. The same volume was published the following year, in an expanded and corrected edition, by Casa de las Américas, in Cuba. Due to the enormous impact of this journal and publishing house throughout Latin America at the time, Rojas's poetry received wider recognition. During these years, he met several of Cuba's most important poets, including José Lezama Lima, Fina García Marruz, Cintio Vitier, and Eliseo Diego. Also in 1964, Gonzalo, his second son, was born from his marriage to Hilda Ortiz.

In the wake of Salvador Allende's political victory in the 1970 general elections in Chile, Rojas was appointed cultural attaché of the Chilean embassy in China. After a year in China (1971–1972), he requested a transfer to Havana, where he had many good friends. He moved to Cuba in 1972; he was later ratified by the Chilean Congress as ambassador to that country, but he was not able to assume the post. On 11 September 1973, Rojas's diplomatic career, as well as his political and cultural future in Chile, was brusquely interrupted by Allende's defeat in a military coup led by Augusto Pinochet. Rojas was stripped of his diplomatic post and officially expelled from his university. Since his passport was no longer valid, he sought refuge in East Germany.

Rojas was offered a position at the University of Rostock, but was never allowed to teach because the administration refused to approve his syllabus. In 1975 he moved to Caracas, Venezuela, where he worked at the Universidad Simón Bolívar until 1979. While in Venezuela, he published *Oscuro* (1977; Darkness), a book that had a significant impact in the United States, Spain, and Latin America. In 1979 he was allowed to return to Chile. He and his wife built a house near Chillán, where he decided to reside permanently. Nonetheless, in the 1980s he accepted visiting positions at several U.S. universities, including Columbia, Pittsburgh, Chicago, and Texas at Austin. He then received a more permanent position at Brigham Young University in Provo, Utah, where he spent the late 1980s and most of the 1990s.

During these two decades he came to be recognized as one of Latin America's most important living poets. Several of his collections enjoyed wide circulation throughout Latin America and Spain, particularly *Del relámpago* (1981) and *Materia de testamento* (1988). The prizes, honors, and recognition of his work also multiplied in the 1990s. In 1992 he was awarded the Premio Reina Sofía de Poesía Latinoamericana, a prize instituted by the queen of Spain. That same year, he was honored with the National Prize for Literature in Chile. He was declared "Ciudadano Ilustre" (Illustrious Citizen) of Chillán and Concepción, and given the Medal of the University of Valparaíso. In 1998 he was awarded the Premio José Hernández, from Argentina, and the Premio Octavio Paz, from Mexico.

His wife, Hilda R. May, died in July 1995. Gonzalo Rojas currently resides in Chile, but travels frequently around the world to read his poetry and participate in numerous literary activities.

Since 1977, with the publication of *Oscuro*, Gonzalo Rojas has published his early poems in combination with new work (58 of the 126 poems in *Oscuro* come from his previous two volumes; 126 of the 177 poems in *Del relámpago* were initially published in *Oscuro*; and so on). Most of the books he published in the 1980s and 1990s reflect this procedure. Rojas has declared that the strategy is "*un ahondamiento creciente*" (a deepening growth) toward unity. That unity is comprehended and revealed in three divisions in *Oscuro* and *Del relámpago*. In the first of these, the emphasis is on rhythm, poetry, and writing; in the second, Rojas explores love and eroticism; in the third and last division, the main topics are human temporality, history, and society.

These three divisions or modes, according to Rojas, are the "registro del tres en uno del pensamiento poético" (the register of the three-in-one of poetic thought). In addition to its unquestionable Christian link (the Holy Trinity), the division follows the basic triad of surrealism (poetry-love-liberty), and the triple modernist ideal of José Martí and Rubén Darío (the search for harmony, the intuition of the origin, and the revelation of unity). However, Rojas does not limit himself to this division, arranging some of his other books in divisions of five, seven, or in none at all. At times, Rojas's critics have organized their studies around divisions of seven or ten; see, for example, the introductory study and the organization of the poetry selections by Marcelo Coddou in *Obra selecta* (1997), or the divisions in Sefamí (*El espejo trizado: La poesía de Gonzalo Rojas*, 1992) and May (*La poesía de Gonzalo Rojas*, 1991). In fact, the organization and order in which the texts appear conform more to a poetic order (through the association of certain images or metaphors) than a chronological one. Except for some articles dedicated exclusively to *La miseria del hombre* (see, especially, Coddou's critical edition) or the reviews of *Contra la muerte*, critics have tended to classify Rojas's poetry by theme. A detailed investigation of Rojas's work, however, could show clear differences between *La miseria del hombre* (chiefly influenced by expressionism), *Contra la muerte*, and the newer poems of *Oscuro*. One could even argue that the reissued poems are amended and transformed to stylistically resemble the later poems. Nevertheless, Rojas's finest poetry emerges with *Oscuro*. It is as this point that Rojas attained a unique voice within Latin American poetics, tightly linked to surrealist notions. His work is reviewed here based on the triad poetry-love-liberty, since this division makes it possible to understand the mechanisms with which Rojas adjusts his poetic vision to the circumstances of his life.

The foundation of Rojas's poetry lies in his childhood and place of birth. Rojas aptly describes Lebu in a footnote to one of his poems:

Leufü: *torrente hondo, en mapuche original. Después, en español, Lebu, capital del viejo Arauco invencible como dijera Ercilla en sus octavas majestuosas. Puerto marítimo y lluvial, maderero, carbonífero y espontáneo en su grisú, con mito y roquerrío suboceánico, de mineros y cráteres—mi padre duerme ahí—; de donde viene uno con el silencio aborigen.*

(*Del relámpago*)

*Leufü*: deep torrent, in Mapuche language. Later, in Spanish, *Lebu*, capital of the ancient and invincible Arauco, as Ercilla recounted in his wonderful octaves. A rainy seaport of wood and coal, spontaneous as the firedamp, with myth and underwater rocks, miners and craters—there my father sleeps—; where one originates from in the aboriginal silence.

Rojas uses this environment as the source of images for his poetry: the ocean, the river, the coal mine, and the mountains. In an interview with Sefamí, he comments: "The original trauma of nature is registered in me through the coal mine ... in this area of risk, of unending danger, of humidity, is where my poetry germinated." While the ocean and the river might suggest an infinite space, the coal mine is the depth in the dark that forces the speaker to look for clues to the mysteries of life.

It is understandable that Rojas has continually explored images of darkness and the darkness of the mines, since his father died there. In "Conjuro" (Conjuration), the speaker seeks to exorcise the temporal and spatial distances that separate him from Lebu, his childhood, his father, and his horse: "Espíritu del caballo que sangra es lo que oigo ahora entre el galope / del automóvil y el relincho" (The spirit of a bleeding horse is what I hear now among the galloping / of the car and the neigh. [*Del relámpago*]). Rojas explains in various interviews that he received a horse as the inheritance from his father after he passed away. A few months later, the horse was stolen, which taught him about the impact of loss. In combination with the loss of the father and the horse, Rojas also evokes the time when he learned how to read and discovered the magic of words:

*Voy corriendo en el viento de mi niñez en ese Lebu tormentoso, y oigo tan claro la palabra "relámpago.—Relámpago, relámpago." Y voy volando en ella, y hasta me enciendo en ella todavía. Las toco, las huelo, las beso a las palabras, las descubro y son mías desde los seis y los siete años; mías como esa veta de carbón que resplandece viva en el patio de mi casa. Tres meses veloces en el río del silabario. Pero las palabras arden: se me aparecen con un sonido más allá de todo sentido, con un fulgor y hasta con un peso especialísimo. ¿Me atreveré a pensar que en ese juego se me reveló, ya entonces, lo oscuro y germinante, el largo parentesco entre las cosas?*

(*Del relámpago*)

I go running in the wind of my childhood in that stormy Lebu, and I clearly hear the word "lightning.—Lightning, lightning." And I am flying with it, I even still shine with it now. I touch, smell, and kiss the words; I discover them and they are mine since I was six or seven years old; mine like that vein of coal that gleams living in the patio of my house. Three fleeting months in the river of the spelling-book. But words burn like fire: they appear to me with a sound beyond any sense, with a gleam and even with a special density. Do I dare to think that the obscure and the germinative, the deep similarity between things, was revealed to me in that play?

Thus Rojas is able to explore the intricacies of his life, using the aesthetic ideas of the surrealist movement. Words appear in the dark, like lightning.

Along with the materialization of language, Rojas attends to the sublime that conveys silence. Most of his critics, in fact, attribute considerable significance to Rojas's poem "Al silencio" (To silence), which was written in 1944 but first published in an anthology of Chilean poetry in 1957. This is a poem which, due to its bond with the sacred experience, serves as the "missing link" to a significant number of Rojas's poems:

*Oh voz, única voz: todo el hueco del mar,*
*todo el hueco del mar no bastaría,*
*todo el hueco del cielo,*
*toda la cavidad de la hermosura*
*no bastaría para contenerte,*
*y aunque el hombre callara y este mundo se hundiera*
*oh majestad, tú nunca,*
*tú nunca cesarías de estar en todas partes,*
*porque te sobra el tiempo y el ser, única voz,*
*porque estás y no estás, y casi eres mi Dios,*
*y casi eres mi padre cuando estoy más oscuro.*

Oh voice, unique voice: all the emptiness
    of the sea,
all the emptiness of the sea would not suffice,
all the emptiness of the heavens,
all the caverns of beauty
would be insufficient to hold you,
and even though mankind should fall silent and
    this world sink,
your majesty, you never,
you never would cease to fill all voids,
for you surpass time and being, oh singular voice,

for you are and you are not, and you are almost my
    Divinity,
and nearly paternal in my darker moments.

(Schizotext and Other Poems /<br>Esquizotexto y otros poemas, 1988)

The poem is commonly associated with the numinous, a philosophical category originated by Rudolf Otto in his book *Das Heilige* in 1917, translated into Spanish in 1925 as *Lo santo*, a book which Rojas himself read in his youth (translated into English as *The Idea of the Holy: An Inquiry into The Non-Rational Factor in the Idea of the Divine and Its Relation to the Rational*, 1957). The German philosopher derived the category's name from *numen* (god, divinity, divine inspiration, or majesty), to signify the essence of the sacred. The finest attribute of the numinous object is the *mysterium tremendum*; the indescribable (*mysterium*) product of an intense reaction, which stimulates a trembling in the presence of the phenomenon.

The numinous has many associations, including the sublime, the magical, silence, darkness, and emptiness. It is not accidental, assert Rojas's critics, that another of his most ostentatious poems is "Oscuridad hermosa" (Beautiful darkness). Beneath the realm of the sacred, silence, and darkness are signs that belong to the same unit. This idea of silence as the ultimate objective of poetry (with obvious parallels to mysticism) can be found in Baudelaire, and culminates in the works of Mallarmé. The plenitude of silence is an impossibility; attaining it signifies a complete mutual understanding where the subject would reach such a perfect unity with the object that words would be unnecessary; which is why, perhaps, one could insist on the word *casi* (almost), at the end of the poem ("you are almost my Divinity"). With this exploration of darkness and silence, the brilliance of the word "lightning" simultaneously appears, as the illumination that gives meaning to the discovery of the sacred. Invention is reached through the epiphanic circumstance that is created by silence. Thus, the word emerges like a revelation and, at the same time, like a demonstration of the failure of the sacred experience.

Rojas insists on images linked to respiratory difficulties: asthma, stuttering, gasping, stammering, suffocation, to indicate the frustration and the critical consciousness of the poetic act. In this he is probably influenced by the broken voice of César Vallejo, although Rojas never reaches the degree of impairing the syntax the way that Peruvian poet does. Nonetheless, José Emilio Pacheco has praised Rojas's rhythmic virtue: "Gonzalo Rojas's hearing is infallible. Every page of his honors the language in which it was written" ("*Oscuro*, de Gonzalo Rojas," *Vuelta*, July 1977). Curiously, this rhythm is attained by a combination of apparently contradictory rhythms: classical song and prosaic colloquial speech. Rojas asserts in a 1987 interview with Julio Ortega: "I have always liked the idea of [Ezra] Pound of seeing the double lineage of the poetic word in speech and song, in poetry. Now, my plan is to cross, to coerce the intersection of those two elements as far as I can achieve it." The "song" would mean many different rhythms: combinations of verses that vary from a single verse to poems composed of a single stanza of more than twenty verses. "Speech" not only gathers the colloquial expressions of the popular Chilean dialect, it also ministers, in specific cases, to a specialized vocabulary: words in Mapuche, usage of sixteenth-century Spanish by peasants from parts of southern Chile, psychiatric terms, parodical imitation of legal documents, language usage similar to the baroque of the seventeenth century, and so forth. Thus, by reuniting the sacred song with coarse prose, Rojas invents a unique rhythm that maintains a certain devotion to tradition, but playfully resists pomposity and the rhetoric of solemnity.

If the dialogue between the body and the word connotes the importance of the philosophical element in the articulation of language, the speaker in Rojas's poems emphasizes the spaces in which that body is situated and from which it speaks. Certain allusions have been made to Lebu as a place of origin that garners many of the geographical illustrations of Rojas's poetry. Later, to this place is added the site where he built his present house in Chillán. This house stands on mountain foothills, in a ravine through which the River Renegado flows. In his interview with Sefamí, Rojas asserts that "this space is very precious and it resembles my soul, without being maniacal. It is stony just like me, on the inside and the outside. It has the natural buzzing sound of a river the way I always wanted the poetic word to be. It even has the vibrations that could be characterized as one's physiological vibrations, these suffocations that create in me an imaginary space." In this way, the body is in a constant dialogue with the world.

The desire is to seek a connection of belonging and identity that permits the speaker a certain tranquillity. In other texts, Rojas searches for this projection in other elements of nature, such as stones, trees, rivers, or even certain animals. With stones, for example, he is able to conceive one of the essential circumstances for creation: idleness. "In idleness," says Rojas in his interview with Sefamí, "there is a magnificent enchantment: not doing anything, remaining satiated of the world's wonders . . . only from idleness you can find silence." Or, for another example, when he speaks of the trees, he binds them to the "old occupation of being quiet"; in other words, to silence. His dialogue with the world is thus transformed into an extension of his own poetic persona; at times, the dialogue is a fixated gaze that culminates with an epiphany or a revelation, as can be seen in the poem "Aletheia del faisán" (Aletheia of the pheasant), in *Materia de testamento*.

Although a good part of Rojas's poetry exhibits a fondness for placidity and harmony, there is always an equal number of texts that contradict or criticize that harmony. Some critics have read Rojas as if he is a poet of the unprotected outdoors. Julio Ortega points out to the poet himself that "unlike other poets who construct the home of language, or what one would call the place of the Logos, in your poetry what rather prevails is the vibration, the intonation of being unprotected in the same nomination. That is, an insufficiency and a power at the same time of this condition of being unprotected of the uttered word." The fact that Rojas was forced to live in exile already alludes to the circumstances that permeate his work. However, he industriously seeks to transform into positive that which is negative. For example, in "Transtierro," Rojas modifies (following the word invented by Spanish refugees in Mexico) *destierro*, banishment, to *transtierro*, implying that the banishment is alleviated by the fact that in the new place of residence the same language is spoken. The poem ends with the double connotation of the Spanish word *parto*, implying both to take a trip (from the verb *partir*), and to give birth (from the verb *parir*).

The questioning of the universal analogy could also be conceived by tedium and humor. See, for example,

"Daimon del Domingo" (Sunday's daemon), in which Rojas problematizes the traditional manner of understanding the world:

> *Entre la Biblia de Jerusalén y estas moscas que ahora*
> *andan ahí volando,*
> *Prefiero estas moscas. Por 3 razones las prefiero:*
> *1) porque son pútridas y blancas con los ojos azules y*
> *lo procrean todo en el aire como riendo, 2) por*
> *eso velocísimo de sus circunstancia que ya lo sabe todo*
> *desde mucho antes del Génesis, 3) por*
> *además leer el Mundo como hay que leerlo: de la*
> *putrefacción a la ilusión.*

> Between the Bible of Jerusalem and these flies
>     which presently circle about,
> I quite prefer the flies. I choose them for 3 reasons:
> 1) because they are vile and white with blue
>     eyes and as if laughing they breed in the
>     air, 2) also,
> they dart about their experience knowing all, long
>     before Genesis, 3) and
> they read the World as it must be read: from decay
>     to illusion.
>     (Russell M. Cluff and L. Howard Quackenbush)

To the poetry that establishes the dialogue with the world, one can also add the poetry that Rojas wrote about his parents. While in "Carbón" (Coal), a child's nostalgia and anxiety refer to the illusion of his father returning home, in "Celia" there is an attempt to sanctify the mother (see *Del relámpago*). But perhaps what is more prolific and obvious in Rojas's work is the dialogue that he establishes with writers and artists. A simple reading of the titles of his poems illustrates this tendency. (In 2000 Rojas published a book titled, precisely, *Diálogo con Ovidio* (Dialogue with Ovid, for example.) The list of writers with whom Rojas establishes such a dialogue is fairly long and includes numerous epochs: the classical Greeks and Romans, the Spanish Golden Age (with particular reference to Quevedo), writers from German Romanticism (Hölderlin, Novalis), French symbolism (Baudelaire, Rimbaud), and the avant-garde (Apollinaire, Tzara), as well as Rubén Darío, César Vallejo, Jorge Luis Borges, Julio Cortázar, Juan Rulfo, Octavio Paz, and a constant dialogue with the Chileans, Gabriela Mistral, Vicente Huidobro, Pablo Neruda, Pablo de Rokha,

Enrique Lihn, Jorge Teillier, and others. There is, in general, an emphasis on the tradition of visionary poetry. Common to many of his poems are words such as "illuminated," "hallucinator," "soothsayer," "lunatic," and "mad"; Rojas's work as a whole underlines the romantic notion of the poet who is capable of seeing "farther" than reality (through vision or epiphany) and understands like a privileged one the truths of the world.

Rojas's dialogues go beyond the realms of the literary: the paintings of Roberto Matta, the chords of Bach, the films of Luis Buñuel, the museum The Cloisters in New York, the music of John Lennon, and so forth. Rojas fully identifies with the categorization that Cortázar used to describe him: "poeta de rescate" (poet of recovery). In many interviews, he insists on citing the classics to demonstrate that there is nothing "new" (against the avant-garde emphasis on novelty). Rojas very frequently emphasizes certain aspects of the work (or life) of an artist to illustrate his relationship with that figure. Rojas is able to envision fragments of his own features in each of the artists and writers he portrays, referring to them as his spiritual family.

In his explanations about the world and men, Rojas puts special emphasis on eroticism as one of its fundamental regions, placing it at the center in *Oscuro* and *Del relámpago*. His wife Hilda R. May was also keenly interested in the topic of eroticism and edited a collection of ninety-three poems that deals with the topic exclusively: *Las hermosas* (1992). Rojas's approach to the topic adopts two antagonistic and complementary gestures: eroticism as an expression of mystic sacredness, and the intensity of the mundane and carnal joy. His attitude continues the surrealist notion of woman as the absolute, the representation of universal totality and the foundation of life.

It is based on this perspective that one should read Rojas's poem "Vocales para Hilda" (Vowels for Hilda), which was first published in *Oscuro*. The text uses short verses that reach a maximum point of brevity with the pronoun "you" (which often forms its own stanza). The text thus extends vertically on the page (109 verses) as if tracing out the svelte figure of a woman. The poem itself consists of a series of metaphors and nominations that characterize Hilda. The pronoun is repeated so frequently (twenty times) that the "you" becomes a totality that contains everything, including the poem

itself. Some of the metaphors in the text show a predilection for associating the terrestrial with the celestial. At the beginning, the poem departs from daily reality in order to find the transcendence of the feminine being through music:

> La que duerme ahí, la sagrada,
> la que me besa y me adivina,
> la translúcida, la vibrante,
> la loca
> de amor, la cítara
> alta:
> tú,
> nadie
> sino flexiblemente
> tú,
> la alta,
> en el aire alto

> She who sleeps there, my deity,
> who kisses me and reads my mind,
> translucent and vibrant,
> crazed
> with love, a slender
> zither:
> you,
> flexibly
> no one but
> you,
> so tall,
> in the airy heights
> (Russell M. Cluff and L. Howard Quackenbush)

Shortly thereafter, Rojas defines the "you" as "a string / vibrant in / the wind / over the astral / abyss," indicating how both the "you" and the music (in this case referring to a harp) serve as a safeguard against the anguish of the fall. Another metaphor also proposes the ascending line of the feminine being: the mountains, expressed in the poem through the volcano and the mountain range. It is not surprising that Rojas would associate woman with the geographical idiosyncrasy of his country. Juan Eduardo Cirlot, in his *Dictionary of Symbols* (1985), explains the typical symbolism of the mountain:

The mountain corresponds, because of its form that progressively widens when seen from above, to the inverted tree whose roots are facing the sky and whose top, now at the bottom, expresses the multiplicity, the expansion of the universe, the involution and the materialization. Based on this, [Mircea] Eliade can say that "the peak of the cosmic mountain is not only the highest point on earth but also the navel of the earth, the point at which creation begins (the root)." The mystic sense of the peak comes from the fact that it is the point of union between the earth and the sky, a center through which passes the axis of the world.

With this association, the notion of woman as the center and origin of the world is extremely clear. In Rojas's mystical aspirations, the poem is all-encompassing, to the degree of combining the all with the nothing, presence with absence. The repetition of "you" in the poem proposes woman as an absolute for the enunciating subject, with the gestation of these microcosms depending in its entirety on the feminine being. The culmination of the process is signaled in the final verses: "*tú,* // *que soplas/ al viento / estas vocales / oscuras, / estos / acordes / pausados / en el enigma / de lo terrestre: // tú:*" (you, // who voice / these dark / vowels / in the wind, / these / pulsating / strains / of the terrestrial / enigma: // you:). Although the title stresses the "Vowels for Hilda," it is Hilda herself who blows or generates these vowels. The air and the music, the Spirit and the Poetry, all combine in the expression of the original vowels. The vowel remits, in its turn, to the most elemental sound of the language and to the poetic creation. In this sense, love and poetry are intimately related; they are two forms of the sacred.

"Hilda" is not the only woman appearing in Rojas's poetry. In "*¿Qué se ama cuando se ama?*" (What do we love when we love?), the speaker expresses his sexual anxiety:

> *Me muero en esto, oh Dios, en esta guerra*
> *de ir y venir entre ellas por las calles, de no*
> > *poder amar*
> *trescientas a la vez, porque estoy condenado*
> > *siempre a una,*
> *a esa una, a esa única que me diste en el viejo paraíso.*

> I am consumed, oh Lord, by this war
> Of invasions and withdrawals, amongst them in the
> > streets, unable to love
> Three hundred at a time, being condemned
> > eternally to one,

> To that particular one, to the very one you gave
> > me in the paradise of old.
> > (Russell M. Cluff and L. Howard Quackenbush)

Imagined or not, many women appear as illuminations in occasional meetings or fortuitous circumstances. In his effort to sanctify women, Rojas places (in a dialogue with Baudelaire, in this case) special emphasis on a character both scorned and marginalized in society: the prostitute. Some poems, such as "Perdí mi juventud" (I lost my youth), "Cosmética" (Cosmetics), "Qedeshim qedeshot," and "Las adivinas" (Diviners), all of which are included in *Las hermosas,* present the brothel as a temple and the woman as priestess. According to the Chilean poet and critic Enrique Lihn, "Qedeshim qedeshot" illustrates the double movement that governs the poetry of Rojas: the sanctification of the profane and the profanation of the sacred. Hilda R. May indicates that Rojas was inspired to write this poem while on a trip to Cádiz (a city founded by the Phoenicians in the eighth century B.C.E.) shortly after having read about Phoenicia in the *Encyclopedia Britannica.* The Phoenician words "qedeshim" and "qedeshot" refer, in plural, to male (suffix "im") and female (suffix "ot") courtesans; Rojas does not use the grammatically correct term "qedeshah" (feminine singular). Regardless of this minor point, the reference to the sacred prostitute or "courtesan of the temple" is very eloquent for the purpose of trespassing the futility of the carnal act. The combination of the consonants K, D, SH (the Phoenician alphabet, which was the origin of the Semitic as well as the Greek and Latin alphabets, contains twenty-two consonants) refers back to words associated with the sacred (for example, *kadosh* in Hebrew means sacred). But Rojas's poem pokes fun at this intent to sanctify:

> *Pertenezco al Templo, me dijo: soy Templo. No hay*
> *puta, pensé, que no diga palabras*
> *del tamaño de esa complacencia. 50 dólares*
> *por ir al otro Mundo, le contesté riendo; o nada.*
> *50, o nada*

> I am a vessel of the Temple, said she: my body is a
> > Temple. There was never a
> whore, I surmised, who did not utter words
> of the magnitude of such pleasantries. 50 dollars

to pass into the other World, I answered laughing;
  or nothing.
50, or nothing.
        (Russell M. Cluff and L. Howard Quackenbush)

The poetic "I" never loses sight of the ambivalence of the encounter between the heavens and the earth; the speaker plays with the swaying motions of the sexual rite. If at the level of the language, Rojas attends simultaneously to the speech and the song, in this poem what is unusual is the combination of the old and the new world. With abrupt leaps, the text fluctuates between the sublime and the crude:

> . . . ahí mismo empezó a bailar en la alfombra el
> rito completo; primero puso en el aire un disco de
>     Babilonia y
> le dio cuerda al catre, apagó las velas: el catre
> sin duda era un gramófono milenario
> por el esplendor de la música; palomas, de
> repente aparecieron palomas.

> . . . at once began to dance the entire ritual
> upon the rug; first she put on a record from
>     Babylon, then
> wound up the cot, blew out the candles: in the
>     splendor
> of the music the cot undoubtedly became
> a millennial gramophone; doves,
> suddenly doves appeared.
>         (Russell M. Cluff and L. Howard Quackenbush)

If, according to Mircea Eliade, "Babylon was a Bâpîlanî, a 'door of the gods,' because this was where the gods came down to Earth," in the poem the record from Babylon represents the celestial music that descends from the high spheres (the harmony of this priestess who is preparing to execute her ritual) and is submerged to the maximum depth of chaos. The "terrestrial" and the rudimentary is the cot that, by its very mention, functions as a reminder that the scene takes place in a whorehouse.

Eroticism remains central even in Rojas's later poems, written when he was eighty years old. In the introductory text to *Tres poemas* (Three poems), the poet declares that "it is not true that love poems are written only at age 20. I keep on writing them and 'Río turbio' (Turbid river) came out a month ago. This was a truly seminal river, according to Cesare Pavese: 'poets are as rare as great lovers; it is not sufficient to have whims, furies, and dreams: one also should have hard testicles.' " "Río turbio" is a poem (divided in three parts) that refers to Rojas's relationship with Mafalda Villa, a thirty-six-year-old woman whom he met in February 1996 (summer, for South Americans), when he was almost eighty. The poem is fascinating for its open, direct, and uninhibited tone that attacks solemnity. The love affair is narrated with startles, thoroughly grasping both sensuality and elegance, emphasized by the unusual age difference and the magic of the moment. Another three poems are later introduced to complete the cycle surrounding Mafalda Villa, dealing with separation and disillusionment: "Pareja acostada en esa cama china largamente remota" (Couple lying in that Chinese bed longly remote), "Adiós a la concubina" (Farewell to the concubine), and "Alles nahe werde fern" (What is close is always far; see *Tres poemas* and *Diálogo con Ovidio*).

Besides casting poetry and love as means of accessing the absolute, the surrealists thought that art should pierce through its limits and have an effect on life. To achieve the goal of eliminating differences, the surrealists thought one must criticize social conventions, attacking the notions of nation, religion, and family. The ethical and social dimensions of surrealism continued the aspiration of Rimbaud to "change life." In an interview with Estrella Busto Ogden, Rojas said: "I believe that my adherence to surrealism was fundamentally for that, for defending the project of liberty, but a liberty like so, slightly anarchical if you like, utopian, but not a liberty that turns toward sectarian political parties" (Busto). Thus, although Rojas was a member of the diplomatic corps in China and in Cuba during the presidential term of Salvador Allende, he adopted a critical attitude toward the dogmatic socialism of the Communist Party.

An event that seems to have definitely marked his poetry was the military coup perpetrated in his country on 11 September 1973. As mentioned before, Rojas was in Cuba when the coup took place. As a consequence of the coup, he was officially divested of his administrative and academic duties at the Universidad de Concepción, and he found himself forced to remain in exile for many years. Hilda R. May said that the army entered his house in Concepción, destroying many of his personal files. His older son was taken to a concentration camp, where he remained for many months (May). In *Oscuro* (1977) and *Del relámpago* (1981) a number of poems are dedicated to the military coup: "Veneno con lágrimas" (Poison and tears), "Ningunos" (None), "Cifrado en octubre" (Coded in October), "Desde abajo" (From below), "Sebastián Acevedo," and many more. In "Veneno con lágrimas" Rojas sees in the Chilean coup a manipulation by the two superpowers, the United States and the former Soviet Union:

> Veneno con lágrimas es la fanfarria del país
> cuarteado, rajado
> metro a metro de su piel a hachazos,
> a balazos, por orden
> del aullido de las 4 cornetas, a contar
> de hoy martes once a las 3
> de este amanecer, veneno
> con lágrimas.

> Veneno con lágrimas y por lo menos dos
> manos sucias detrás de esto: la uña vieja
> de la baraja fría del mercader del
> Oeste, la enguantada y
> gélida del Este, hagan juego
> señores, el reparto
> de la misma túnica del
> hambriento sin réditos
> para nadie, clausurado
> el cielo para él. Veneno
> con lágrimas.

> Poison and tears is the fanfare of this land
> drawn and quartered, sliced up
> meter by meter, with its hide chopped up by
> gun fire, by the howling
> command of the 4 bugles, counting
> from today Tuesday the eleventh at 3
> at daybreak, poison
> and tears.

> Poison and tears and at least two
> soiled hands behind it all: the old light-fingered,
> double dealing, merchant from
> the West; the frigid, gloved
> hands from the East; place your bets,
> gentlemen, the dividing

> of the nonsubsistent robe of the
> starving man without profit
> for anyone, sealed
> heavens await him. Poison
> and tears.
>
> (Russell M. Cluff and L. Howard Quackenbush)

The poem details specific facts: the coup happened at 3:00 a.m. on Tuesday, 11 September. The coup comes as a consequence of the struggle for power. The irony is that the game is played by foreign interests, ignoring the poor, hungry people, from whom they want to take away that which they don't possess.

For many years, the Chilean military dictatorship upheld an oppressive regime that limited any expressions of protest. As is well known, many young people disappeared without a reason. Their desperate relatives looked for them, encouraged by the possibility that they might have escaped the country, perhaps by assuming a different identity. The uncertainty, however, created a horrible anxiety, because disappearances were generally associated with kidnapping by military personnel and subsequent torture and death. One of the first protests against the Chilean authorities' refusal to release any information about the missing took place in Concepción: Sebastián Acevedo, frustrated upon not receiving any information about his son, decided to burn himself in the public plaza as a demonstration of ultimate rebellion against censorship. Rojas wrote a poem based on this true story:

> Sólo veo al inmolado de Concepción que hizo humo
> de su carne y ardió por Chile entero en las gradas
> de la catedral frente a la tropa sin
> pestañear, sin llorar, encendido y
> estallado por un grisú que no es de este Mundo: sólo
> veo al inmolado.

> Sólo veo ahí llamear a Acevedo
> por nosotros con decisión de varón, estricto
> y justiciero, pino y
> adobe, alumbrando el vuelo
> de los desaparecidos a todo lo
> aullante de la costa: sólo veo al inmolado.

> All I see is his immolation in Concepción, his
> flesh made smoke and ablaze for all of Chile on
> the steps

of the cathedral in front of the troops without
flinching, without crying, in flames and
bursting from a firedamp not of this World: all
I see is his immolation.

All I see there is Acevedo burning
for us with the will of a true man, staunch
and just, pine and
adobe, lighting the flight
of the missing, all the
wailing up and down the coast: all I see is his
    immolation.
        (Russell M. Cluff and L. Howard Quackenbush)

The immolation (a sacrifice) implies giving a life, a
possession, for a cause. The death of Sebastián Acevedo
is a testimonial of his courage for all Chilean people.
The immutability of this man suggests an obstinacy
that shook out the fear and the terror of dying. Rojas,
interestingly, uses the verb *arder* (to light a fire) in the
positive sense: to vibrate with energy and passion. The
image of the man engulfed in flames also projects an
explosion of light that illuminates the situation of each
of the missing people all across Chile. The sacrifice of
this ordinary man is transformed in a lesson of history
and morality: his death acquires positive significance in
order to teach dignity, perseverance, fidelity, and love.
The message is clear, even the most authoritative
regime cannot repress the act. Inspired by this event,
other individuals in Chile have dared to protest the
abuses of the dictatorship.

The absence of freedom in Chile would soon find an
echo in Rojas's experience in the countries of the
Eastern European bloc. After the Chilean coup, the
government of Cuba helped Rojas obtain a position as a
professor at the University of Rostock, East Germany.
In 1974, the poet traveled to East Germany (without a
valid passport) and presented himself at the university
to offer a course on contemporary Spanish American
literature. However, after he announced that his course
would include Borges, the authorities canceled his
classes and left the professor without students. Rojas
was forced to spend a year at the university, unable to
travel (because of his passport situation) and confined
to an office that was somehow, very subtly, forbidden to
the students. This frustrating experience is expressed in
"Domicilio en el Báltico" (Residence on the Baltic):

*Tendré que dormir en alemán, aletear,*
*respirar si puedo en alemán entre*
*tranvía y tranvía, a diez kilómetros*
*de estridencia amarilla por hora, con esa pena*
*a las 5.03,*
        *ser exacto*
*y silencioso en mi número como un lisiado*
*más de la guerra, mimetizarme coleóptero*
*blanco.*
*Envejecer así, pasar aquí veinte años de cemento*
*previo al otro, en este nicho*
*prefabricado, barrer entonces*
*la escalera cada semana, tirar la libertad*
*a la basura de esos tarros*
*grandes bajo la nieve,*
        *agradecer,*
*sobre todo en alemán agradecer,*
*supongo, a Alguien.*

I must sleep in German, flutter,
breathe if possible in German between one
trolley and the next, a ten yellow blaring kilometers
per hour, burdened by this grief
at 5:03,
        to be exact
and numerically silent like one more
cripple from the war, mimeticize my coleopterus
whiteness.
Now to grow old, to spend twenty cemented years
Prior to that niche, in this prefabricated
crypt, and then sweep weekly
the staircase, pitching liberty
into those great
snow-covered dumpsters,
        gratitude,
above all give thanks in German,
I suppose, to Someone.
        (Russell M. Cluff and L. Howard Quackenbush)

The limitations on the speaker's liberty are defined
by the areas through which he must pass and by what
he must do. The first condition is a language that he
does not speak and that is established as an imperative
not only of communication but also of organic functioning: "sleep in German . . . breathe . . . in German."
In this precise machine, individual expression is not
allowed: the subject that had intended to rebel against
the rules of society is marginalized from others, condemned to silence, treated like a harmful insect. The

home of this human is a prison or a crypt. The odious routine and the tedium of the place are also paralleled by the construction of the prefabricated buildings that surround him. The subject is seen as a forgotten corpse. His routine of twenty years is seen immersed in an act that should be seen as ordinary: "tirar la libertad / a la basura" (throw out liberty / to the trash). All of the forces of the poem fall into this statement and into the final ironic conclusion: "agradecer, / sobre todo en alemán agradecer, / supongo, a Alguien" (gratitude, / above all give thanks in German, / I suppose, to Someone). That is, the help that this speaker has received (barely suggested in the text) is paid for at a high price: the loss of freedom.

The majority of the work of Gonzalo Rojas is a result of the poet's examination of his own persona. While the author situates his origins and responds to them, the constant search of self is one of the most frequent topics in the texts. Two obsessions dominate his later poetry: marginality with respect to fame, and a consciousness of being old while maintaining the stamina of a young person. If poetry, love, and social and political circumstances function as a triad that searches out a unity or an absolute, there is always the presumption that this unity is continually cracked. The fragmented unity can be symbolic of the persona that enunciates the poems. Perhaps one could encounter fragments of that persona in each one of the texts.

A series of poems refers to Rojas's place in the history of literature. In "Concierto" (Concert) he adopts the idea of the book as the execution of a vast and collective poem that supposes, in its turn, the creation of the world.

> Entre todos escribieron el Libro, Rimbaud
> pintó el zumbido de las vocales, ninguno
> supo lo que el Cristo
> dibujó esa vez en la arena, Lautréamont
> aulló largo, Kafka
> ardió como una pira con sus papeles
>
> . . . . . . . . . . . . .
> ¿qué
> hizo ahí Celan sangrando
> a esa hora
> contra los vidrios?

Together they wrote the Book, Rimbaud
painted the humming of the vowels, no one

knew what the Christ
traced in the sand on that occasion, Lautréamont
bayed eternally, Kafka
and his papers smoldered like a pyre

. . . . . . . . . . . . .
              what
was Celan doing there at that hour
bleeding
against the windowpane?
              (Russell M. Cluff and L. Howard Quackenbush)

The poem casts poetry as a choral exercise that goes far beyond the written word. The idea of a beginning and an end does not exist in the poem; there is no pre-established order that would indicate a specific chronological system to refer to the artists being mentioned, nor is there a type of sequence that leads to thinking in terms of a structured narrative. What there is in this concert is a great disparity of elements: writers of many eras and countries, divergent and contrasting actions. This chaotic enumeration is what consolidates, curiously, the unity and the totality of this universe. Perhaps the most disturbing image in the poem is that of Celan bleeding against the glass. In a text of the same period (see "Paul Celan," El alumbrado), Rojas identifies with Celan, whom he says he read very late in his life (in 1977), but with whose poetry he feels an intimate communication. Perhaps what attracts him the most is the theme of marginalization. In light of this parallel, it would be possible to see Celan functioning as the mask of Rojas himself. He is the outlawed (there are other poems that make similar references about this). The image—bleeding against the glass—gives the impression of someone who wants to jump to another orbit (to get either in or out). The glass can symbolize the separation between life and death or, as one could suppose in "Concert," between mortality and immortality.

But the paradox, finally, is that Rojas today figures among the best-known Latin American poets. His books circulate throughout Spanish-speaking countries and the number of his readers has grown considerably, as is evident in the variety and multiple editions of his poetry. Likewise, the critical bibliography of his work has increased greatly since the 1980s. Many younger writers, in particular, are his greatest fans.

The poetry of Gonzalo Rojas has reached its plenitude and its maximum vigor with the poet's old age. Rojas likes to identify himself as *viejoven* (a Spanish word that combines *viejo*, old, and *joven*, young). Young people arguably perceive the freshness and ease with which Rojas has been able to create a voice that is at once spontaneous and mature.

## SELECTED BIBLIOGRAPHY

### Primary Works

#### Poetry

*La miseria del hombre.* Valparaíso, Chile: Imprenta Roma, 1948. Reprinted in a critical edition, with notes, chronology, and bibliography by Marcelo Coddoe with the collaboration of Marcelo Pellegrini. Valparaíso, Chile: Puntángeles, Universidad de Playa Ancha Editorial, 1995.

*Contra la muerte.* Santiago, Chile: Editorial Universitaria, 1964. 2nd, exl. ed., Havana: Casa de las Américas, 1965.

*Oscuro.* Caracas: Monte Avila Editores, 1977.

*Transtierro.* Madrid: Ed. Taranto, 1979. (An anthology.)

*Antología breve.* Material de Lectura No. 66. Mexico City: Universidad Nacional Autónoma de México. 1980.

*Del relámpago.* Mexico City: Fondo de Cultura Económica, 1981. 2nd, exl. ed., 1984.

*50 poemas.* Illustrations by Roberto Matta. Santiago, Chile: Ediciones Ganymedes, 1982.

*El alumbrado.* Santiago, Chile: Ediciones Ganymedes, 1986.

*El alumbrado y otros poemas.* Madrid: Cátedra, 1987.

*Antología personal.* Mexico City: Universidad Nacional Autónoma de México, Universidad de Zacatecas, and Premiá Editora, 1988.

*Materia de testamento.* Illustrations by Roberto Matta. Madrid: Ediciones Hiperión, 1988.

*Schizotext and Other Poems / Esquizotexto y otros poemas.* Bilingual edition translated by Russell M. Cluff and L. Howard Quackenbush. New York: Peter Lang, 1988.

*Desocupado lector.* Illustrations by Michael Nerlich. Madrid: Ediciones Hiperión, 1990.

*Antología del aire.* Santiago, Chile: Fondo de Cultura Económica, 1991.

*Las hermosas. Poesías de amor.* Selections by Hilda R. May. Madrid: Ediciones Hiperión, 1992. Also published in Santiago, Chile: Editorial Los Andes, 1992.

*Cinco visiones.* Prologue by Carmen Ruiz Barrionuevo. Salamanca: Ediciones Universidad de Salamanca, 1992.

*Río turbio.* Valdivia, Chile: Editorial El Kultrún, Barba de Palo Ediciones, 1996. Also published in Mexico City: Editorial Vuelta, 1996; and in Madrid: Ediciones Hiperión, 1996.

*Obra selecta.* Selections, prologue, chronology, and bibliography by Marcelo Coddou. Caracas: Bibliotcea Ayacucho, Fondo de Cultura Económica, 1997. (Includes ten essays by Rojas.)

*América es la casa y otros poemas.* Edited and annotated by Alfredo Pérez Alencart. Salamanca: Centro de Estudios Ibéricos y Americanos de Salamanca, 1998.

*Tres poemas.* Prologue by Marcelo Coddou. Valparaíso, Chile: Puntángeles, Universidad de Playa Ancha Editorial, 1998.

*Diálogo con Ovidio.* Illustrations by Roberto Matta. Mexico City: Editorial Aldus, El Dorado Ediciones, 2000.

*Metamorfosis de lo mismo.* Madrid: Colección Visor de Poesía, 2000. (A collection of the all of Roja's poetry as of the date of publication.)

### Secondary Works

#### Articles and Reviews

Alonso, María Nieves. "Lo que es del fuego al fuego." *Acta Literaria* (Concepción) 15:17–33 (1990).

Araya, Juan Gabriel. "Una clave en el pensamiento poético de Gonzalo Rojas." In *Poesía y poética de Gonzalo Rojas.* Edited by Enrique Giordano. Santiago, Chile: Ediciones del Maitén, 1987. Pp. 143–153.

————. "Gonzalo Rojas: visión de un ir y volver." *Acta Literaria* (Concepción) 15:43–49 (1990).

Baeza Flores, Alberto. "Para leer a Gonzalo Rojas." *Revista Nacional de Cultura* 237:60–68 (July–August 1978).

Benedetti, Mario. "Gonzalo Rojas se opone a la muerte." In his *Letras del continente mestizo.* Montevideo: Arca, 1969. Pp. 120–124.

Busto Ogden, Estrella. "Gonzalo Rojas, juglar en la edad tecnológica." *La Juglaresca* 6:643–652 (1986).

————. "El motivo del rey en la poesía de Gonzalo Rojas." *Cuadernos Hispanoamericanos* 431:45–52 (May 1986).

————. "Del espíritu de postmodernidad en la poesía de Gonzalo Rojas." *Ibero-Amerikanisches Archiv* 15, no. 1:43–56 (1989).

*Chasqui. Revista de Literatura Latinoamericana* 22, no. 1 (May 1993).

Cluff, Russel M. "Crónica de una convivencia: Selección y traducción de *Esquizotexto y otros poemas* de Gonzalo

Rojas." *Ibero-Amerikanisches Archiv* 15, no. 1:117–130 (1989).

———. "El motivo del amor en la poesía de Gonzalo Rojas." *Chasqui. Revista de Literatura Latinoamericana* 22, no. 1:59–69 (May 1993).

Coddou, Marcelo. "Dimensión de lo erótico en la poesía de Gonzalo Rojas." *Texto Crítico* (Xalapa, Mexico: Universidad Veracruzana) 7, nos. 22–23:238–250 (July–December 1981).

———. "Presencia de Quevedo en la poesía de Gonzalo Rojas." In *Poesía y poética de Gonzalo Rojas.* Edited by Enrique Giordano. Santiago: Ediciones del Maitén, 1987. Pp. 177–184.

———. "Los poemas redivivos de Gonzalo Rojas o la vigilancia de la palabra." *Ibero-Amerikanisches Archiv* 15, no. 1:85–102 (1989).

———. "Proyección de Vallejo en la poesía de Gonzalo Rojas." *Revista Chilena de Literatura* 41:113–118 (1993).

———. "Conjunciones Octavio Paz / Gonzalo Rojas." *Revista Iberoamericana* 168–169:803–810 (July–December 1994).

Cortínez, Carlos. " 'La salvación' de Gonzalo Rojas." *Revista Iberoamericana* 106–107:359–367 (May–June 1979).

———. "En vez del parricidio: 'Carbón' de Gonzalo Rojas." *Enlace. Revista de Literatura en Lengua Española* 3–4:27–30 (March–June 1985).

Costa, René de. "Gonzalo Rojas: Between the Poem and the Anti-poem." *Latin American Literary Review* 6, no. 12:15–25 (spring–summer 1978).

Dapaz, Lilia. "Presencia de Huidobro en la poesía de Gonzalo Rojas." *Revista Iberoamericana* 106–107:351–358 (January–June 1979).

———. "*La miseria del hombre* como viaje de descubrimiento." *Revista Iberoamericana* 168–169:795–801 (July–December 1994).

Earle, Peter. "Breton y Rojas, hacia la plenitud." In *Poesía y poética de Gonzalo Rojas.* Edited by Enrique Giordano. Santiago: Ediciones del Maitén, 1987. Pp. 125–130.

Forster, Merlin H. "El concepto de 'ars poeetica' en la poesía de Gonzalo Rojas." *Chasqui. Revista de Literatura Latinoamericana* 22, no. 1:51–58 (May 1993).

Galaz-Vivar Welden, Alicia. "Gonzalo Rojas o la poesía del relámpago." In her *Altamarea. Introvisión crítica en ocho voces latinoamericanas: Belli, Fuentes, Lagos, Mistral, Neruda, Orrillo, Rojas, Villaurrutia.* Madrid: Ediciones Betania, 1988. Pp. 75–99.

Geissler, Eberhard. "Sobre la poesía de Gonzalo Rojas y su relación con Paul Celan." *Ibero-Amerikanisches Archiv* 15, no. 1:103–117 (1989).

Giordano, Enrique. "Gonzalo Rojas: Variaciones del exilio." In *Poesía y poética de Gonzalo Rojas.* Edited by Enrique

Giordano. Santiago: Ediciones del Maitén, 1987. Pp. 207–215.

Giordano, Jaime. "Gonzalo Rojas: Su diálogo con la poesía actual." In *Poesía y poética de Gonzalo Rojas.* Edited by Enrique Giordano. Santiago: Ediciones del Maitén, 1987. Pp. 199–206.

———. "Más allá de las palabras: Gonzalo Rojas." *Chasqui. Revista de Literatura Latinoamericana* 22, no. 1:31–37 (May 1993).

Gullón, Ricardo. "Gonzalo Rojas: Saludo a un gran poeta." *Insula* (Madrid) 380–381:5 (1978).

Hozven, Roberto. "Sobre el oficio mayor." In *Poesía y poética de Gonzalo Rojas.* Edited by Enrique Giordano. Santiago: Ediciones del Maitén, 1987. Pp. 161–176.

Janik, Dieter. "Epitafio y epitafios en la obra de Gonzalo Rojas." *Ibero-Amerikanisches Archiv* 15, no. 1:57–65 (1989).

Jiménez, José Olivio. "Una moral del canto: El pensamiento poético de Gonzalo Rojas." *Revista Iberoamericana* 106–107:369–376 (January–June 1979).

Lastra, Pedro. "Notas sobre cinco poetas chilenos." *Atenea* (Concepción) 380–381:148–154 (April–September 1958).

Lefebvre, Alfredo. "Descripción de la poesía de Gonzalo Rojas." *Atenea* (Concepción) 301–302:122–137 (January–February 1952).

———. "Análisis e interpretación de poemas: 'Al silencio.' " *Atenea* (Concepción) 380–381:148–154 (April–September 1958).

Lihn, Enrique. "Poetas fuera o dentro de Chile 77." *Vuelta* (Mexico City) 15:16–22 (February 1978).

López Adorno, Pedro. "Gnosis/lugar/ritmo: Notas en torno a la poética de Gonzalo Rojas." In *Poesía y poética de Gonzalo Rojas.* Edited by Enrique Giordano. Santiago: Ediciones del Maitén, 1987. Pp. 155–160.

Loveluck, Juan. "El espacio como abismo en la poesía de Gonzalo Rojas." *Ibero-Amerikanisches Archiv* 15, no. 1:79–84 (1989).

Loyola, Hernán. "Gonzalo Rojas o el respeto a la poesía." *Anales de la Universidad de Chile* 135:108–130 (July–September 1965).

Lyon, Ted. "Presentación de la generación chilena del 38: Una perspectiva de cincuenta años." *Ibero-Amerikanisches Archiv* 15, no. 1:19–32 (1989).

Mestre, Juan Carlos. "El discurso de la utopía en la poética de Gonzalo Rojas." *Chasqui. Revista de Literatura Latinoamericana* 22, no. 1:42–46 (May 1993).

Muñoz, Luis. "Visión con y contra la muerte de Gonzalo Rojas. Para una poética." *Acta Literaria* (Universidad de Concepción) 10–11:5–31 (1985–1986).

Nómez, Naín. "La permanencia en lo transitorio: Una constante estética y existencia en Gonzalo Rojas." In *Poesía y poética de Gonzalo Rojas*. Edited by Enrique Giordano. Santiago: Ediciones del Maitén, 1987. Pp. 135–141.

Ostria, Mauricio. "Aproximación a la poesía de Gonzalo Rojas." *Acta Literaria* (Universidad de Concepción) 18:9–23 (1993).

Pacheco, José Emilio. "*Oscuro,* de Gonzalo Rojas." *Vuelta* 8:41 (July 1977).

Pérez, Floridor. "Para una lectura de la poesía de Gonzalo Rojas." *Revista Chilena de Literatura* 13:117–142 (1979).

Pope, Randolph. "Gonzalo Rojas y la vida real." In *Poesía y poética de Gonzalo Rojas*. Edited by Enrique Giordano. Santiago: Ediciones del Maitén, 1987. Pp. 131–134.

Quackenbush, L. Howard. "La realidad detrás de la realidad: Gonzalo Rojas y lo numinoso." *Chasqui. Revista de Literatura Latinoamericana* 22, no. 1:23–30 (May 1993).

Rodríguez Padrón, Jorge. "Recado desde España. Encantamiento con desollamiento." Epilogue to *Antología del aire,* by Gonzalo Rojas (1991). Pp. 285–297.

Rojas, Nelson. "En torno a 'Almohada de Quevedo' de Gonzalo Rojas." *Chasqui. Revista de Literatura Latinoamericana* 16, no. 1:5–11 (February 1987).

———. "Física y metafísica en Gonzalo Rojas: 'La viruta.' " *Ibero-Amerikanisches Archiv* 15, no. 1:65–78 (1989).

———. "Gonzalo Rojas y la responsabilidad de la poesía." *INTI* 31:67–77 (spring 1990).

Sobejano, Gonzalo. "Gonzalo Rojas: Alumbramiento." In *Poesía y poética de Gonzalo Rojas*. Edited by Enrique Giordano. Santiago: Ediciones del Maitén, 1987. Pp. 63–67.

Sucre, Guillermo. "La metáfora del silencio." In his *La máscara, la transparencia*. Caracas: Monte Avila Editores, 1975. Pp. 340–342.

## Books and Monographs

Coddou, Marcelo. *Poética de la poesía activa*. Madrid: Ediciones LAR, 1984.

———. *Nuevos estudios sobre la poesía de Gonzalo Rojas*. Santiago: Ediciones del Maitén, 1986.

*Gaceta del Fondo de Cultura Económica* 347 (November 1999).

Giordano, Enrique, ed.. *Poesía y poética de Gonzalo Rojas*. Santiago: Ediciones del Maitén, 1987.

*Ibero-Amerikanisches Archiv* 15, no. 1 (1989).

May, Hilda R. *La poesía de Gonzalo Rojas*. Madrid: Ediciones Hiperión, 1991.

Rojas, Nelson. *Estudios sobre la poesía de Gonzalo Rojas*. Madrid: Playor, 1984.

Sefamí, Jacobo. *El espejo trizado: La poesía de Gonzalo Rojas*. Mexico City: Universidad Nacional Autónoma de México, 1992.

## Interviews

Araya, Juan Gabriel. "Conversaciones con Gonzalo Rojas." *Atenea* 465–466:269–280 (1992).

Benedetti, Mario. "Gonzalo Rojas y su poesía activa." In his *Los poetas comunicantes*. Montevideo: Biblioteca de Marcha, 1972. Pp. 145–171.

Busto Ogden, Estrella. "Una entrevista con Gonzalo Rojas." *Revista Iberoamericana* 135–136:677–685 (April–September 1986).

Jiménez, José Olivio. "Fidelidad a lo 'oscuro': Conversación con Gonzalo Rojas." *Insula* (Madrid) 20:380–381 (1978).

Maack, Ana María. "Gonzalo Rojas: Diálogo con la cordillera." In *Poesía y poética de Gonzalo Rojas*. Edited by Enrique Giordano. Santiago: Ediciones del Maitén, 1987. Pp. 113–120.

O'Hara, Edgar. "Gonzalo Rojas en el Torreón del Renegado." *Enlace. Revista de Literatura en Lengua Española* 3–4:34–37 (May–June 1985).

Ortiz, Hilda. "Conversando con Gonzalo Rojas." *Chasqui. Revista de Literatura Latinoamericana* 16, no. 1:13–18 (February 1987).

Ortega, Julio. "Gonzalo Rojas: Juicio de residencia." *Revista Chilena de Literatura,* 30 November 1987, pp. 89–114.

Piña, Juan Andrés. *Conversaciones con la poesía chilena*. Santiago: Ed. Pehuén, 1990. Pp. 85–125.

Sefamí, Jacobo. "Las visiones del alucinado." In his *De la imaginación poética. Conversaciones con Gonzalo Rojas, Olga Orozco, Álvaro Mutis y José Kozer*. Caracas: Monte Avila Editores Latinoamericana, 1996. Pp. 11–92.

Zapata, Miguel Ángel. "Gonzalo Rojas, entre el murmullo y el estallido de la palabra." *Inti* (Providence College) 26–27:313–323 (fall 1987–spring 1988).

# Jaime Sabines

## (1926–1999)

### Marco Antonio Campos

Jaime Sabines was born on 25 March 1926 in Tuxtla Gutiérrez, Chiapas, Mexico, in the same decade as four other poets who laid the foundation for modern Mexican poetry. Jorge Hernández Campos (b. 1921) is famous for his poem "El Presidente" (The president), which can be described as a bitter and disdainful portrait and at the same time honest and symbolic of the Mexican mandatories. Rubén Bonifaz Nuño (b. 1923) discovered new methods in writing the modern lyric by thoroughly exploring Greek and Roman poetry as well as pre-Hispanic poetry. Rosario Castellanos (b. 1925) is an icon in feminist mitography and the author of poems written with the sharpness of a knife and a cry from the heart. Eduardo Lizalde (b. 1929) continued the lineage of the British Romantic poet William Blake and the Argentine writer Jorge Luis Borges and has painted both the brightness and somberness of the tiger as a metaphor of multiplicity.

In a competition that took place in 1890, sponsored by the Republic of Mexico to elect the most popular poet, the people of Mexico City overwhelmingly crowned Guillermo Prieto. Prieto did not accept the victory and symbolically gave it to José Joaquín Fernández de Lizardi, Mexico's first great writer about the struggle for Mexican independence. If there were to be another, similar competition in present times, the majority of the votes no doubt would give the silver crown to Jaime Sabines. Why? Sabines, like José Martí, Pablo Neruda, and Iannis Ritsos, is a poet who belongs to that minority of poets admired not only by literary critics and university professors but also by the people. His poems appear to have been written by several hands and yet belong to everyone, including those who seem to put on antiseptic gloves before writing or those who aspire to have their poetry correspond with the ornaments and pomp of a high altar. The amazing fact is that Sabines scarcely contributed to his popularity. Like Juan Rulfo, another solitary poet, Sabines did not create a literary life for himself, nor did he possess the vanity of other poets and writers. To be concerned about whether he was praised for his work was a mindset that became unbearable to him. His public appearances were rare but always centered on the reading of his works. It was impressive how he could evoke an almost religious fervor from diverse groups of people, who would recite his verses and poems from memory. They muttered, they recited loudly, and they even sang his poems in unison. He never chose to give a conference or to become part of a roundtable discussion. His artistic public life was related only to poetry in general or, more precisely, to his own poetry. Like Rulfo, too, he simply published his books, and his huge readership deified them.

Sabines is appreciated and at times revered by readers with or without education because of his style of writing and the way he dealt with a variety of themes. His colloquial style, so disarmingly natural, makes the common reader believe in the wonderful illusion that poetry is simple, or at least accessible, and the more experienced readers are astonished by the difficult and mysterious accuracy of that simplicity. How could Sabines have discovered that special word or that small twist that gives new life to a verse and makes the verse appear to be shaped by him? Klaus Müller-Bergh has described this in a different manner: Sabines, he says, has "a personal language that expresses his impeccable analytical observation of everyday life" (*Poesía de vanguardia y contemporánea*). That is what makes Sabines distinctive. Just as when we read a poem by Borges, Neruda, or César Vallejo, we know that Sabines is in his own poems and in those of his imitators.

His subjects or, rather, the way in which he treats certain subjects makes the reader identify with them. In 1962 Sabines wrote in a lesser-known text that the poem "is the testimony of the time humankind has on earth. Singing or lamenting, complaining or protesting, crying or stammering, poetry has to reach the obscurity of mankind. Gloriously." Sabines talks about the ordinary events of daily life. Among these events might be walking along the beautiful or ugly streets of a city, observing people of all walks of life in public parks, going from bar to bar and drinking until senseless, finding and loving a woman, feeling ecstatic at the birth of a child, feeling irritated when ill, not understanding and feeling horror at the death of those close to us, and seeing in ordinary events the hatred, malice, or tenderness of other people like us. This is to carry on life "being aware only of the leg that hurts, the time to go to work, heartburn, the amount of money being spent, the time to go to bed." In short, it is to dazzle with flames in days of fire or to pick up the ashes of useless days. Sabines takes to the extreme the splendor of life and the destruction of things and people.

Starting in his youth, Sabines felt a mixture of disdain and mistrust for poets and artists. In *Tarumba* (1956), perhaps his best book, he asks blunt questions:

*¿Qué puedo hacer en este remolino*
*de imbéciles de buena voluntad?*
*¿Qué puedo con inteligentes podridos*

*y dulces niñas que no quieren hombre sino poesía?*
*¿Qué puedo entre los poetas uniformados*
*por la academia y por el comunismo?*

Where is my place among this whirlpool
of imbeciles with good intentions?
What can I do with wretched, intelligent people
and sweet girls who prefer poetry to men?
Where is my place among the poets shaped
in academies and by communism?

In another work, he complained of being a servant for both poetry and the devil.

This clever disdain becomes sharper and shifts from mockery and imitation in parts of *Yuria* (1967) and *Maltiempo* (1972) and in one of his last "poemas sueltos" (loose poems). The first, entitled "Un personaje" (A personage), relates the story of Jailai, a bearded man known for his poetry and intellect who had the fortune of publishing a book of poems twenty years earlier and whom young people sought for advice. His real importance becomes obvious when he eats and, more crudely, when he swallows. The second is a prose poem (he refers to it as a "journalistic article") in which he makes a distinction between those modern poets who are fascinated with creating verbal games and those who describe things in terms of the reality of everyday life. The first kind, the intellectual poets, belong to Olympus; they are praised in academia and in the sharp interpretations of critics. Only the second kind are true poets. The third piece is a mockery not only of himself but also of the categorizations formulated by critics and by well-informed readers, who both belong to the world of poets—as if anyone (perhaps Jaime Sabines) is a great, good, decent, or highly esteemed poet. Knowing this, the poet (perhaps Jaime Sabines) proudly goes out into the world, but no one recognizes him. He then decides that he is no longer a poet, but a pedestrian. And he is content with himself.

As with other notable poets born in the provinces, among them, Efraín Huerta from Guanajuato and Rubén Bonifaz Nuño from Veracruz, Sabines's work was felt in the body and soul of the inhabitants of Mexico City. The three books most representative of the last century are Huerta's *Los hombres del alba* (1944; Men of dawn), Bonifaz Nuño's *Los demonios y los días* (1956; Demons and days) and Sabines's *Diario semanario* y *poemas en prosa* (1961; Weekly diary and prose poetry). In *Diario semanario y poemas en prosa*, Sabines describes a reviving city, different from the cities described in the books by Huerta and Bonifaz in that his city becomes a revelation of sweetness and happiness. He describes in one passage that "es difícil sentirse perdido" (it is difficult to feel lost) in this city. As Sabines said in various interviews, he became attached to this book and wrote it like a song from his heart after the arduous years (1952–1959) spent in the city of Tuxtla Gutiérrez. José Casahonda Castillo says of those days in that city that Sabines spent them "in front of a chest of clothes in El Modelo," where he also sold "Spanish-styled piques, French embroideries, and Indian cloths" while he wrote *Tarumba*. *Diario semanario y poemas en prosa* is described as having been made of sunlight and water, of happiness and flight; it is a book where birds and leaves communicate with each other and where humans recognize themselves as tragic and heartbroken.

"After the tension and anguish of *Tarumba*," Sabines commented in an interview in 1983, "writing it [*Diario semanario y poemas en prosa*] was a relief and a game" (*De viva voz*). It was perhaps in his book *Adán y Eva* (1952; Adam and Eve), a more peaceful work, that he would even feel grateful. In the last section of the book, he mentions countless times the public walk of Santa María la Ribera, the neighborhood where he lived for many years. The Mexican poet Ramón López Velarde found this place so similar to Jerez that he thought he might even begin to hear recitals from the kiosk in Jerez of "Alejandra," "Fingida," "Blanca," "Poeta y campesino," and "Tu bién lo sabes." As he had done in *Horal* (1950; Hourly) and *La señal* (1951; The signal), in this book Sabines describes many streets and parks, movie houses and brothels, but we do not know exactly which ones. At the same time, we feel as though we are immersed in the central neighborhoods of the city.

Before *Diario semanario*, Sabines had described Mexico City in excerpts from "Qué alegre el día" (Joyous day) or "Los he visto en el cine" (I have seen them at the movies) as a "hidden" city. In his early work, the young Sabines tends to concentrate on his lonely room and the tavern or on the bar and cabaret he frequented in the evenings. Through numerous descriptions of the city and the actions of the people, he shows in these two poems an "open" city, where his poems from *Diario semanario* fit perfectly.

The style of writing Sabines uses in *Adán y Eva*, in passages from *Yuria*, and in *Maltiempo*, is prose poetry that has a rhythm he describes as being "the closest to the heart." Like very few poets, Sabines had the ease of expressing with perfect simplicity the workaday, or unpoetic, elements of our daily lives, even in complex and antagonistic situations. In the everyday events he encounters, even problems dealing with metaphysical questions—God, death, eternity, the passing of time and the soul—become terrestrial. For Sabines, God can have "la cara blanca y vacía" (a pale and empty face). Sabines can talk about God endlessly "con ternura y con odio, como de un hijo perdido" (with tenderness and hatred, like a misguided son), and death can appear at the time we are driving an automobile. In response to his friend Rubén Salazar Mallén, Sabines comments that eternity is "nothing more than a poor and diminished prolongation of our existence." At the same time, to affirm the beauty and depth of life, Sabines offered metaphors that approximate the sound of a headstone falling onto a grave: "Creer en la supervivencia del alma, es lo mismo que cargar su tabla mucho antes del naufragio" (To believe in the survival of the soul is the same as carrying one's own lifejacket before a shipwreck). It is about living as best we can, close to the earth and faithful to the earth. It is about listening to the sermons of the night, close to the discoveries that every day reveal themselves to our sight and far from the dreams that are only dreams. Sabines knows that the stars are of another world. He is a poet of the body and of the language of the body, like López Velarde or Neruda. Ramón Xirau describes Sabines's work as a contrast to that of the French poets Stéphane Mallarmé and Paul Valéry and the Spanish poet Jorge Guillén, where we find ourselves "facing a polished world, perfect as a stone eroded by water."

In the context of his daily and weekly experiences and those of others, Sabines relates to us what goes on around him so that we will come to know what goes on within him. He tells us about people gathering casually in groups around the movie theaters and bullfight arenas and about a funeral procession that passes through the streets. He describes the little girls who go to school, the old ladies who return from mass, the drunkards at the stadium, and the street vendors. He pictures the train station at Buenavista, where he bids farewell to a young lady named Rosa, who returns to Tuxtla because she has cancer and wants to die there. He describes the servant girls who parade around the town square of Santa María all dressed up, dreaming and waiting "mientras llegan a la prostitución o regresan al seno de la familia miserable" (while they sink to the level of prostitution or return in misery to the bosom of their families). This is not the lost world that such poets as Rabindranath Tagore and the ancient Japanese sang about; instead, it is the daily world "de las bombillas eléctricas, los automóviles, el grifo de agua, los aviones a propulsión a chorro" (of electric lights, automobiles, faucets, and planes). Instead of describing Tagore's girl who carries water, Sabines shows us the poor office typist who dreams about the lovers in Hollywood films.

Ramón López Velarde and Jaime Sabines are the two Mexican poets of the twentieth century best loved for their excellence in writing. López Velarde is known as the poet of desire, and Sabines is the poet of erotic realization. Born in Zacatecas, the conservative center of Mexico, at the end of the nineteenth century, López Velarde was opposed to Catholic education, which, he believed, repressed the wings of imagination. At the same time, he comforted himself with fleeting multitudes of young women. As Pablo Neruda writes, "the liquid eroticism of his poetry" arises in that environment and "circulates within the entire work as if it were buried, covered by the long summer, by the chastity directed to sin." Everything López Velarde aspires to or exhales has the aromatic air of women. He was even capable of returning to the Garden of Eden to invoke the primordial mother in one prose poem.

Love in Sabines's poetry is the happiness of the fire felt in the moment of lovemaking, which is felt by all lovers in the world and by those in love who search only to discover that they are alone and naked, beautifully lonely and naked on Earth. His most famous, though not his best, poem is, of course, "Los amorosos" (The lovers). Lovers are found in the obscurity of movie theaters, at quiet inner gates of houses, in furtive gardens, under the canopy of trees in the forest, along the sand of endless beaches, in rooms of broken-down motels and in rooms of the most expensive hotels. Whether they know it or not, in a sudden blaze of fire,

these lovers turn the places where they copulate into the ardent centers of the universe.

López Velarde's modern Adam is different, in that he searches for Eve from the beginning of time only to sin horribly. In Sabines's poetry, Adam and Eve live in the present time and in the present world without knowing about the consequences. Love is fully natural and pure. The slow discovery of bodies corresponds to the slow discovery of nature and the things of this world. It is like searching for the Garden of Eden having already committed the sin without being exiled by the Archangel.

Sabines's deceased relatives form a part of the literary iconography of Mexico. What Mexican poet or well-read person does not know aunt Chofi, Mayor Sabines or Doña Luz? Sofia, Chofi, a poor and lonely woman who is single and a virgin with a hunchback, nevertheless lives only to consecrate herself as a yielding sacrifice without reward, but in the end does nothing but become a bothersome thing that is always present. These unmarried aunts who are found in so many families are the subject of everyone's tenderness and endless pity:

> Tan miserable fuiste que te pasaste dando tu vida
> a todos. Pedías para dar, desvalida.
> Y no tenías el gesto agrio de las solteronas
> porque tu virginidad fue como una preñez de
>     muchos hijos.
> En el medio justo de dos o tres ideas que
>     llenaron tu vida
> te repetías incansablemente
> y eras la misma cosa siempre.

> You were so miserable that you gave your life
> to others. You asked to give, unprivileged one.
> You did not have the bitterness of those still
>     unmarried
> because your virginity was like an impregnation of
>     many children.
> Those two or three ideas which filled your life,
> changed you into many things tirelessly,
> yet you were always the same person.

For Sabines, the year 1961 ushered in a decade of terrible deaths in his family. The first death was that of his father. How was Sabines able to write an elegy so brilliant and unworldly in a publicly reserved manner during this family ordeal? How was he able to be so daring as to describe in certain passages, in such an honest yet fierce manner, his father's illness and his corporal decomposition at the time of death? In those passages of black and raging humor, there are also instances of sweetness coming straight from the heart, moments of gentleness and hope, and times when the weight of pain and sadness crushes us.

The only vivid lyrical passage that approaches the description of such a brutal death of a father is found in Octavio Paz's *Pasado en claro* (Clear past). Perhaps the most painful section in this work is the following:

> *Del vómito a la sed,*
> *atado al potro del alcohol,*
> *mi padre iba y venía entre las llamas.*
> *Por los durmientes y los rieles*
> *de una estación de moscas y de polvo*
> *una tarde juntamos sus pedazos.*
> *Yo nunca pude hablar con él.*
> *Lo encuentro ahora en sueños,*
> *esa borrosa patria de los muertos.*
> *Hablamos siempre de otras cosas.*

> From vomiting to thirst,
> tied to the torment of alcohol,
> my father came and went among the flames.
> Among the sleepers and the train tracks
> in a station of flies and dust
> we put together his remains one afternoon.
> I was never able to talk to him.
> Today, I find him in my dreams,
> in the dark world of the dead.
> We always talk about other things.

The alliance of the family, as it shines through in Paz's verses, is, sadly, an illusion. In Sabines's works, this alliance is alive, organic, as in Arabic clans. The affections of these self-enclosed family societies take such a form that a grievance against one member is understood to be directed toward the whole family. Sabines's love for his father was so deep that three years after his death in 1964, after having read the beginning of his elegy, the poet was harassed by his father's ghost and felt that he had not said everything he could have said. And so he pulled from his inner depths what was left to be said.

In an interview I conducted with Sabines in 1983, he reminisced about the conception and effect of the poem:

*Something about the Death of Mayor Sabines* came out like gushes of blood, completely outside every literary pretension. I say this clearly in a verse: "Damned the one who does not believe this is a poem!" I wrote it because it was necessary. It was there. It imposed itself on me. There is no major complicated theme: it is the process of the illness and death of my father. The old man had cancer. In May, after a trip to Chiapas, he began to bleed. We took him to a hospital, where it was discovered that one of his lungs had a tumor the size of a billiard ball. They operated on him like an animal. We believed that he had been saved. We then took him to Acapulco, hoping that he would live, but he felt bad again. It was obvious that he had become an invalid. In the poem "Of the Sea, Also from the Sea," the reference has a true reality. This was three and a half months after his death. It hurts me to remember. It is a poem that I cannot read, either alone or in public. I have read it twice in public, and I have cried. The theme was obsessive. I wrote and wrote. My father died on October 30, and his birthday was September 27. I continued to write sonnets until the first days of December, when I finished the first part. So what if I didn't think of elegies like those by Manrique or [Federico Garcia] Lorca? No, mine was about crying.

The poem is a superhuman protest against death. It is a poem that imprisons us from the first verse:

> *Déjame reposar,*
> *aflojar los músculos del corazón*
> *y poner a dormitar el alma,*
> *para poder hablar,*
> *para poder recordar estos día*
> *los más largos del tiempo.*

> Let me rest,
> loosen the muscles of the heart
> and let my soul sleep,
> in order to talk,
> to be able to remember these days
> the longest ones in time.

We are expecting what follows; we are already inside the poem. We then make the transition into the world of a sanatorium: white rooms and hallways, surgical tools, and barbed-wire fences. We wait tensely through nights of vigilance, the painful interrogations of doctors and nurses who come and go from the patient's room and who perhaps ignore more than anyone the dimension of tragedy. We hear the sharp cries and endless laments and enter into a sad resignation before the inevitable. The sight of the vigorous tree that is falling down piece by piece is fixed in the son's mind as he watches how death is prepared to cut down the tree with an ax. The father is like a Lebanese cedar or an oak from Chiapas. The poem has elements of angry complaint that interweave and explode, maledictions that resemble spitting in a person's face, secular prayers, and words of light and tenderness.

Three years later, after having written the second part of the elegy, Sabines seemed to assimilate this wounding of the soul and to be healed. The second part is written at a distance, but not too distant. There is a painful consciousness that he is standing before something that has been consumed, an atrocious piece of evidence that in the end "todo viene, todo pasa, todo se acaba" (things come and go, and everything ends). It is a realization that life is on loan to us, and we pass through earthly life like ghosts or shadows. We will never return. Sabines is more reflective in the second part, but in that reflection there are hair-raising descriptions and questions that make one shudder.

A few years later, his mother died, and the line of ancestors ended with her death. There was no other way of seeing things but laterally or forward. Sabines wanted to write a poem that would leave a trace of his mother that resembled a soft breeze and the germination of wheat, something quite different from the elegy written for his father. His mother wanted to live and insisted that everything was beautiful, but her blood "caía como un muro vencido" (fell like a defeated wall). In a fragment of compassionate farewell, he writes:

> *Lloverás en el tiempo de lluvia,*
> *harás calor en el verano,*
> *harás frío en el atardecer.*
> *Volverás a morir otras mil veces.*
>
> *Florecerás cuando todo florezca.*
> *No eres nada, nadie, madre.*

You will rain during the rainy season, you will be the summer heat, you will be the cool of the evening. You will die a thousand times more.

You will flower when the plants flower. You are nothing or anyone, mother.

It was his mother, Sabines said in an interview with Cristina Pacheco, who had taught them "simplemente el orgullo de ser hombres" (simply to be proud to be men).

After this, Sabines no longer wanted to write about dead relatives. It was an overwhelming burden. When his son Jaime died in 1969 at the age of twenty-two, Sabines composed a long poem but ended by shredding it and throwing the pieces into the street. "It is not possible to spend one's life talking about the dead," he said. "I am fed up with it. I am ashamed of it." His friend and fellow poet Efraín Huerta captured the moment in the following poem:

> *Jaime ya no puede con la Muerte:*
> *La de su padre el Mayor,*
> *La de Doña Luz*
> *("Me ha dejado triste*
> *tirado todo el día sobre mis sueños")*
> *Y ahora los veintidós años muertos*
> *De Jaimito*
>
> *Jaime ya no puede con la muerte*
>
> *Ahora Jaime-Tigre-Poeta*
> *Debe poder hasta la muerte con la Vida.*

Jaime can no longer deal with Death: The death of his father, the Mayor, The death of Doña Luz ("It left me feeling sad, spending the whole day with my dreams") And now, with Jaimito's twenty-two years finished

Jaime can no longer deal with death

And now, Jaime, the Tiger, and poet Has to deal with Life until death.

Jaime Sabines died of cancer in Mexico City on 19 March 1999. In the end, he said, "es inútil vivir / pero es más inútil morir" (it is useless to live / but it is more useless to die). With each step forward and backward through time, Sabines's poetry continues to grow. A great number of his lyrical pieces preserve their freshness and vitality today. They are so simple in design that they seem easy to understand, and yet they are so enigmatic that explaining or analyzing them is like untying a Gordian knot. We quickly forget whatever defects there may be in his work when we feel the telluric impetus of passages or stanzas that grow to acquire the strength of an earthquake or those impregnated with the deepest tenderness. W. S. Merwin, who translated the works of Sabines into English, has said, "His poetry is fleeting, elusive, and like no one else's" (*Pieces of Shadows*).

*Translated from the Spanish by Enrique Balladares-Castellón*

# SELECTED BIBLIOGRAPHY

## Primary Works

### Poetry

*Horal.* Tuxtla Gutiérrez, México: Departamento de Prensa y Turismo, 1950.

*La señal.* Mexico City, 1951.

*Adán y Eva,* 1952.

*Tarumba.* Mexico City: Colección Metáfora, 1956.

*Diario semanario y poemas en prosa.* Xalapa, México: Universidad Veracruzana, 1961.

*Recuento de poemas.* Mexico City: Universidad Nacional Autónoma de México, 1962.

*Yuria.* Mexico City: J. Mortiz, 1967.

*Maltiempo.* Mexico City: J. Mortiz, 1972.

*Algo sobre la muerte del mayor Sabines.* Mexico City: J. Mortiz, 1973.

*Nuevo recuento de poemas.* México: J. Mortiz, 1977. (Includes *Horal, La señal, Adán y Eva, Tarumba, Diario semanario y poemas en prosa, Yuria, Algo sobre la muerte del mayor Sabines,* and *Maltiempo.*)

*Poemas sueltos.* Mexico City: Ediciones Papeles Privados, 1981.

*Nuevo recuento de poemas.* Mexico City: SEP Cultura, 1986. (Compiled with *Otros poemas sueltos.*)

### Collected Works

*Uno es el hombre: Poemas seleccionadas.* Mexico City: Partido Revolucionario Institucional, 1989.

*Jaime Sabines de bolsillo.* Edited by Felipe Garrido. Guadalajara, México: Universidad de Guadalajara-Xalli, 1990.

*Antología poética.* Santiago: Fondo de Cultura Economica Chile, 1994.

*La luna.* Mexico City: CIDCLI, 1997.

*Los amorosos y otros poemas.* Edited by Mario Bojórquez. Tijuana, México: Consejo Nacional para la Cultura y las Artes, 1997.

*Sabines a la mano: Poesía escogida.* Mexico City: Casa Jaime Sabines, 1997.

*Al téquerreteque: Sabines para niños.* Mexico City, 1999.

*Un pedazo de hidra: Antología.* Edited by Mónica Plasencia Saavedra. Santa Cruz de Tenerife, Spain: La Página, 1999.

### Translations

*Tarumba: The Selected Poems of Jaime Sabines.* Trans. by Philip Levine and Ernesto Trejo. San Francisco, Calif.: Twin Peaks Press, 1979. (Bilingual edition.)

*Pieces of Shadow: Selected Poems of Jaime Sabines.* Trans. by W. S. Merwin. Mexico City: Ediciones Papeles Privados, 1995.

## Secondary Works

### Critical and Biographical Studies

Flores Liera, Guadalupe. *Lo sagrado en la poesía de Jaime Sabines.* Mexico City: Universidad Nacional Autónoma de México, 1996.

Hernández Palacios, Esther. *La poesía de Jaime Sabines: Análisis poético estrutural de "Algo sobre la muerte del mayor Sabines."* Xalapa, México: Centro de Investigaciones Linguístico-Literarias, 1984.

*Homenaje a Jaime Sabines.* Mexico City, 1997.

Mansour, Mónica. *Uno es el poeta: Jaime Sabines y sus críticos.* Mexico City: SEP Cultura, 1988.

*La poesía en el corazón del hombre: Jaime Sabines en sus sesenta años.* Mexico City: Universidad Nacional Autónoma de México, 1987.

Zarebska, Carla. *Jaime Sabines: Algo sobre su vida.* Mexico City, 1994.

*Discography*

*Jaime Sabines.* Presented by Ramón Xirau. Colección: Voz
viva de México. México, 1965.

*Jaime Sabines.* Selection and presentation by Sabines.
Colección: Y la poesía se hizo. México, 1988.

*Jaime Sabines.* Grabación del recital de homenaje en Bellas
Artes por sus setenta años. México, 1996.

# Juan José Saer

## (1937–    )

### Evelia Romano

Juan José Saer was born on 28 June 1937 in Serodino, in the Argentine province of Santa Fe, one of four children of José Saer and María Anoch. His parents were Syrian immigrants, born in Damascus; his father arrived in Serodino at the age of seventeen and his mother at the age of three. José Saer and María Anoch met and married in Serodino. The family moved to the capital of the province, the city of Santa Fe, in 1948. There Saer graduated from Colegio Nacional Simón de Iriondo (National High School Simón de Iriondo) in 1954. He began studying law but soon abandoned it to work as a journalist in the local newspaper *El Litoral* in 1956. Two years later, Saer enrolled in the Facultad de Filosofía y Letras, located in Rosario. There he took some courses until the mid-1960s, but he did not earn a university degree. After 1962 Saer taught courses on criticism, aesthetics, and history of cinema at the Instituto de Cinematografía de Santa Fe (Institute of Cinematography of Santa Fe), which was affiliated with the Universidad Nacional del Litoral (National University of the Littoral). During the late 1950s and early 1960s, in addition to his duties as journalist and teacher, Saer carried out a variety of other jobs that included selling books door-to-door in the cities of Rosario and Santa Fe, traveling as a salesman through the north of the province of Santa Fe and to the province of Chaco, and writing movie scripts in Buenos Aires. In 1968 Saer

obtained an official scholarship from the French government to study in France the relationship between the new trends in the cinema and the novel. In the following year he began working as a Latin American literature lecturer at the University of Rennes, where he was later appointed associate professor and *maître de conférences*. Saer was awarded tenure as *maître de conférences* at the same university in 1983. He lives in Paris and has two children from two different marriages.

If Saer's personal life story can be drawn in a few strokes, the course of his artistic and intellectual development should be considered in greater detail in terms of the configuration and comprehension of his original literary universe. Saer finds models in Felisberto Hernández, Jorge Luis Borges, Macedonio Fernández, and Antonio di Benedetto, whose works represent for him "the will to create a personal, unique discourse that is constantly reviewed, enriched, and sharpened in its style, to such a degree that the man behind the words becomes his own discourse and identifies with it completely" (*Una literatura sin atributos*, 1986).

During the 1950s, Saer's association with the writers of the Grupo Adverbio paralleled the publication of his first poems, short stories, and critical articles. Members of the initial Grupo Adverbio and other intellectuals, such as Hugo Gola, Hugo Mandón, Luis Vittori, Roberto Maurer, Jorge Conti, and Raúl Beceyro, formed the generation in which Saer is included. The group's interactions were informal, neither institutionalized nor programmatic. It is easy to recognize their meetings as the raw material for many scenes in Saer's narrative, in which a group of intellectuals and artists get together for the ritual of the Argentine barbecue (*asado*) and discuss theories and literary texts.

His formative years in this Argentine region, next to the Paraná River, confer on Saer's work one of its main characteristics: a physically and ideologically marginal position, outside the parameters imposed by the cultural hegemony of Buenos Aires. Saer's group was equally unaffected by the repercussions of the Latin American Boom and conceived their artistic work free from national and continental boundaries. The "Boom" was signaled by the emergence of novelists from various Latin American countries in the 1960s who engaged and transformed European and North American influences to renovate Latin American literary expression. Most of the works identified with this movement attempt to design a cultural utopia where aesthetic and political revolutions are synonymous. Magical realism, and the marvelous real, names coined by the Guatemalan Miguel Angel Asturias and the Cuban Alejo Carpentier, respectively, are characteristic of the "Boom" narrative. In his 1979 and 1980 critical essays "La selva espesa de lo real" (The thick jungle of reality) and "Una literatura sin atributos" (Literature without attributes), Saer warns against the danger of practicing a literature that can be defined a priori as Latin American (*Una literatura sin atributos*). Such praxis becomes an aesthetic program that dictates themes and styles, many of which tend to satisfy the categories held by the literary market and the expectations of a foreign audience that define Latin American culture based on stereotypes.

Saer's generation had intense exchanges with the Cinema School and the Institute of Cinematography of Santa Fe, both created in 1958. Through their relationship to the school, the group was in touch with innovative theories, particularly Italian neorealism. In Saer's early work, the preference for marginal characters, countrymen, and urban workers; a fascination with rendering their spoken language; and minute descriptions of their daily activities to reveal psychological processes are among the techniques that reflect a neorealist influence. The visual power of Saer's stories, with their suggestive use of light and shadows and their insistence on certain colors, shapes, and character's gestures, can be associated with the cinematographic language of the Italian filmmaker Michelangelo Antonioni. Above all, the application of such techniques stimulated the controversy around the conceptual implications of the realist school and its modes of representation.

In the Argentine artistic and intellectual circles of the 1950s and 1960s, there resurfaced a debate between art as form and art as compromise with social and political realities, exemplified by the works of Argentine writers Jorge Luis Borges and Roberto Arlt, respectively. Saer's adoption of the aforementioned techniques constituted a search for a position that proves wrong the dichotomy. According to Saer in his essay "Literatura y crisis argentina" (Literature and the Argentine crisis), the literary work consists of "a critical view of the world, which is not only conceived as a social structure but also, and perhaps foremost, as an object of human experience and knowledge" (*El concepto de ficción*, 1997). Saer's literature can be read as an allegory of the attempt to communicate with reality, departing from its resonance in the human consciousness, free from any ideological preconceptions.

The intellectual exchange of the initial years in Saer's career helped create a cosmos of readings formed by the personal preferences and aesthetic concerns of the group. These included Borges, Arlt, Felisberto Hernández, Juan Carlos Onetti, Macedonio Fernández, and di Benedetto within the River Plate literary panorama, and William Faulkner, Cesare Pavese, Alain Robbe-Grillet, Nathalie Sarraute, and Raymond Chandler among international authors. Juan L. Ortiz, a poet from the Argentine province of Entre Ríos, became a central figure of Saer's generation. Ortiz's spiritual and artistic guidance and the consistent reading of poets from Santa Fe, such as the Italian Giuseppe Ungaretti and the local Noemí Ulla and Aldo Oliva from Rosario, Santa Fe, nourished a conception of literature as an autonomous enterprise, ruled only by its own internal laws and unencumbered by political or aesthetic dogmas, literary trends, or market demands. Discipline in the work of forging the poetic word was both the road to follow and the goal to attain.

Saer published his first poems in the local newspaper of Santa Fe City, *El Litoral*, in 1954. Poetry was the point of departure for his literary project, not only chronologically but also formally. Saer was able to achieve the renovation and transformation of novel and short-story genres thanks to a constant reference and return to poetry. Saer declares in his dialogue with Ricardo Piglia (*Diálogo*, 1995) that his intention, in his whole oeuvre, has been to turn poetry into a work of distribution (typical of the narrative) and to make prose into a work of condensation (typical of poetic expression) through repetitions, rhythmic structure, and the insertion of poems in narrative texts. In this regard, Saer continues the transmutation of the genres that was characteristic of Ortiz, especially in his production of a poetry that was at the same time lyrical and narrative. The title itself of Saer's only book of poetry, *El arte de narrar* (The art of narrating), apparently paradoxical, marks precisely the confluence of both modalities, prose and verse. The first edition of 1977, dedicated to Ortiz and Oliva, consisted of poems composed between 1960 and 1975, organized into two sections: "El arte de narrar" y "Por escrito" (In writing). These sections reflect on the nature of language as a tool to express a blurry reality, and several poems pay homage to the masters of the poetic word: Dante, the Spanish poet Francisco de Quevedo, Dylan Thomas, Aldo Oliva, and James Joyce. The rhythm of the verses, the frequent syntactical overlapping between one line and the following line, and the re-creation of oral language through cadence and vocabulary contribute to making hazy the frontier between prose and poetry. The preference for long and free verses gives way to some poems in prose, or poems that consist of dialogues, a form to "stage" the poetic language (for example, "Diálogo bajo un carro" [Dialogue under a cart] and "Encuentro en la puerta del supermecado" [Encounter at the supermarket's door]).

*El arte de narrar* was published again in 2000 with two new sections: "Noticias secretas" (Secret news), poems dated between 1976 and 1982, and "La guitarra en el ropero" (The guitar in the closet), poems composed between 1981 and 1987. These additions continue the intense reflection of the poems from the first edition on the task of writing and constructing a world of memories and oblivion with the "leftovers" or "splinters" of an inherited language. They reaffirm the conception of poetry as a mode of engaging in a dialogue with the world, in a constant search and re-creation of language, the only native country of the poet. The power of the imagination transforms and equates memories, dreams, and experiences. In this way, these new poems also strengthen the essential thematic and formal connections among Saer's writings, which consolidate and progress with each poem, story, or novel without closure or exhaustion in any single text. In "Noticias secretas," Saer expresses the human desire of achieving luminous coincidence with the present moment in the taste of coffee and apples ("Café y manzanas") or in the erotic fullness of mythical loves.

In several of the poems in this section, the theme of the journey appears once again and brings back the traveler to an inner landscape of uncertainty. Here, "ya no se sabe / en qué mundo se está, y sobre todo si se está / en un mundo" ("Leche de la Underwood"); it's already impossible to know / in which world we are, and overall, if we are at all / in any world; Milk of the underwood). The poems from "La guitarra en el ropero" are briefer and have shorter lines. They embody the impossibility of apprehending reality and the acceptance of a chaotic world ruled by chance, which leads to silence as an answer, which is suggested by the title itself. The phrase "the guitar in the closet," extrapolated from a popular Argentine tango, "Mi noche triste" (My sorrowful night), refers to the hidden and silent presence of the singing instrument; we can sense its aura and its potential to regain voice in the future. Silence is nothing but the condition for the word to be heard, the necessary darkness for light to exist. The result is the imperative in the poem "El culto del cargo" (The cult of burden) to be born anew "from zero" and erase all separation between world and desire, dreams and reality.

As stated earlier, Saer believes in the necessity of being loyal to a singular discourse. This discourse unfolds in a particular region, the constant scenario of his stories, that becomes the sign and sum of his creative process. While his poetry refers to the impossibility of abandoning the native land because we take it with us wherever we go, his narrative universe—from the first short stories of *En la zona* (1960; In the zone) to his last novel, *Las nubes* (1997; The clouds)—shares the same setting in the Argentine littoral. This setting can be urban, as in *La vuelta completa* (1966; The complete turnaround), *Responso* (1964; Requiem), *Glosa* (1986; Gloss), and *Lo imborrable* (1993; Indelible); rural, as in *El limonero real* (1974; The real lemon tree); or primeval in the unbounded littoral plains, as in *El entenado* (1983; The Witness, 1990), *La ocasión* (1988; The Event, 1995), and *Las nubes*. The setting refuses a particular name, conforms to a constellation of spaces all linked by the confluence of rivers, and mirrors Saer's literature, where each work is separate but connected to the others.

This devotion to a particular geographic area could allow us to inscribe Saer's work within the realm of so-called regionalism. Following the footsteps of his mentor, Ortiz, however, Saer avoids altogether the folkloric element, which is also characteristic of regional literature. He prefers to concentrate on the gradual construction of the "zone" in each story and in each book. The persistent and expanding presence of Santa Fe and its surroundings functions as both the foundation for the invention of an imaginary space and as a reservoir of memories and experiences out of which the literary material is crafted.

At the same time, Saer's texts represent a physical and cultural space where national and international literary traditions intersect. In agreement with Borges's ideas in his essay "The Argentine Writer and Tradition," universal literature is interpreted and transformed according to local readings. Such an intersection generates tension within the texts between inner and external perspectives and between proximity and distance, which transforms the content of the geographic reference into a symbol of emptiness in the metaphysical sense and establishes the institution of a literary region. Much like other authors who have created an imaginary region in which to weave their fictions—Faulkner's Yoknapatawpha, Rulfo's Comala, and Onetti's Santa María—Saer inaugurates a space in his stories in which his literature can scheme its own reality.

The short stories of *En la zona* are a consideration of the plains as precisely a physical and cultural space. The stories written between 1957 and 1960 carry the original imprint of Saer's work with narration, and the author declares in the prologue that each conforms to a different method, ranging from pure invention to representation of everyday activities. The traditional and canonical form of the short story—with a calculated structure and a surprising or revealing ending—changes into a linguistic game that obliterates referent and plot. Events do not obey the order of cause and effect but the law of chance, which, in "Un caso de ignorancia" (A case of ignorance), becomes literary cause. The progression of the action is frozen in "Algo se aproxima" (Something is coming) to feel the nature of the imminence without giving it resolution. The reign of chance over rational explanations and the lack of movement in the plot reappear, heightened and intensified, in later novels, such as *The Event* and *Nadie nada nunca* (1980; *Nobody Nothing Never,* 1993).

*En la zona* also introduces us to some of the characters who reappear in later texts: Tomatis, Pichón y Gato Garay, Ángel Leto, Washington Noriega, César Rey, Soldi, Horacio Barco, and Pancho, among others. They form the background, or human landscape, against which all the stories are etched. Honoré de Balzac initiated this literary convention in the nineteenth century to increase verisimilitude. Saer applies it to criticize the realist mimesis and provoke the opposite effect: to negate the progression of the plot and to insert moments in any point of the space-time continuum to highlight the narrative structure. Continuity is fragmented, although fragments illuminate each other. With clear echoes from Macedonio Fernández's criticism of realist representation, the goal of the novel or the short story is not to imitate reality but to efface from the reader's perception all certainty about what is real.

*Palo y hueso* (1965; Stick and bone) opens with the story "Por la vuelta" (To the return), written in 1961, which establishes a clear link between this volume and *La vuelta completa*. The latter was Saer's first novel in terms of composition (1961–1963), although it was published in 1966, after the novella *Responso*. In both genres, short story and novel, the focus of the text is the conversation among a group of friends and their relationships. In the short story "Por la vuelta" we are told the reasons for the commitment of Pancho to a psychiatric institution, while in the novel, Pancho's problems are alluded to but never fully explained. Each text hints at the other, in a concentric movement that makes it difficult to establish with certainty if the short story continues the novel or vice versa. Long dialogues that portray the dynamic of the conversation and the mechanics of language per se, with literature as a frequent topic, also contribute to create a sense of self-referentiality, another key element in Saer's fiction. The narrator (Horacio Barco) of the story in "Por la vuelta," and an omniscient voice in the novel, exemplifies the two principal points of view employed by Saer: first-person and third-person narrators. The alternation formally illustrates the tension between narrating from inside and outside the story, multiplies the perspectives, and confirms the impossibility of crystallizing an event from either the confidential and subjective first person or the assumed omniscience of the third person.

*La vuelta completa* is a novel conceived in two stories apparently independent of each other, with two different protagonists, César Rey in "El rastro del águila" (The trace of the eagle) and Pancho in "Caminando alrededor" (Walking around), who come together, through their peripatetic courses, at a reunion that convokes all the characters in the final scenes. The novel, whose structure prefigures that of *Cicatrices* (1969; Scars), offers a subtle reflection on the limits of life and its relation to fiction. The abundant dialogues and the *mise-en-abîme* provoked by the stories within the stories (for example, "El pájaro profeta" [The prophet bird] and the stories of the monks) enact the difference between experience and knowledge, perception and reading. Paraphrasing the words of Tomatis in the book, all novels should respond to a structure as similar as possible to the structure of life. The proximity to life allows only the reproduction of fragments, so clear and recurrent, that exiles all the rest of reality. The closer we are to reality and sensation, the stranger they appear. The infinite repetition of the same details—clothing, colors, meeting places, the same routes for going and coming to places—gives unity to the novel, which is fragmentary and senseless but with an occult core of meaning that never emerges fully.

Departing from reality, the novel ends up detaching from it, in a complete turnaround toward the realm of consciousness. The actions of the characters succeed each other without intervals, to suggest that there is something behind the scenes that is never told. The denial of any transcendence and permanence becomes at the same time the possibility of asserting it through imagination and memory, pillars of Saer's universe:

*El no era nada, lo sabía. Pero haciendo un esfuerzo, evocando, resultaba indudable que era capaz de comprender y abarcar tantas cosas, cada una a su tiempo, como era debido, perfectamente clara, sin hacerse problemas sobre si eran un sueño o una realidad, ya que él podía reinar sobre ellas aunque su realidad fuese un mero sueño.*

He was nothing, he knew. But making an effort, remembering, it doubtless turned out to be that he was able to understand and encompass so many things, each one in its own time, as it was supposed to be, perfectly clear, without questioning if they were dreams or reality, since he could reign over them even if his reality was a mere dream.

The second story in *Palo y hueso* anticipates, on the one hand, the atmosphere and tone of the novel *El limonero real*, and, on the other, the intense play of light and shadows that distinguishes *Unidad de lugar* (1967; One place), his third collection of short stories. This volume is considered by critics as a turning point in Saer's fiction, owing to its further lessening of realistic elements, which signals an unwavering concentration on the praxis of writing and its power to illuminate that shadowy space of experience. The first short story, "Sombras sobre el vidrio esmerilado" (Shadows on the emery glass), depicts the birth of a poem through the memories and emotions of the poet Adelina Flores, to which the blurred vision of her brother-in-law through the glass bathroom door gives rise. The image of the polished glass symbolically signifies the impossibility of apprehending reality without filtering it through the processes of individual consciousness and remembered experiences. As in the novel *La vida breve* (1950), by Juan Carlos Onetti, where the creative process departs from the physical mutilation of a woman's breast, the scar on the chest of Adelina Flores is the sign of her past suffering, which acquires new and multiple meanings. The last story, "Fresco de mano" (Handmade fresco) can be read as the complement of the first, since it describes not the inner process but the physical place and material action of writing. The light is not thrown alternatively and symbolically over past and present feelings, as in the first story, but instead illuminates the text as it is being written, read, corrected, crossed out, and fragmented.

Saer wrote *Unidad de lugar* and *Cicatrices* around the time of his move to France. According to the critic Graciela Montaldo, these books mark three important developments in Saer's evolution: the solidification of his work as a cycle, the fulfillment of his intention to craft a discourse between prose and poetry, and the first steps toward a fusion of genres, where a concept of story or fiction prevails over other genre conventions. The novel *Cicatrices* consists of four stories that can be read independently and are narrated in the first person by four different characters: the young journalist Ángel Leto, the former lawyer and gambler Sergio Escalante, the judge Ernesto, and the millworker Luis Fiore. The event that connects all the stories is Luis Fiore's murder of his wife. Characters and story lines move in circles around the same space (the city and its surrounding area) and time (between February and June). The narration is punctuated by a leitmotif of light circles. They bring into focus different scenes, which only touch each other tangentially and by accident or else intersect briefly, without achieving transcendent signification. The repetitive wanderings of the characters and situations are conceived as "cones of light" that move or overlap, opening momentarily and closing again, to suggest the concentric nature of time and space.

The words of Tomatis in the novel offer a clue to its interpretation:

> *Hay tres cosas que tienen realidad en la literatura: la conciencia, el lenguaje y la forma. La literatura da forma, a través del lenguaje, a momentos particulares de la conciencia. . . . La única forma posible es la narración, porque la sustancia de la conciencia es el tiempo.*

> Only three things have reality in literature: consciousness, language, and form. Literature gives form to particular moments of consciousness through language. . . . The only possible form is narration, because the substance of consciousness is time.

The narrative processes initiated in *Cicatrices* mature in Saer's next novel, *El limonero real*. This novel portrays the last day of the year in the lives of a poor couple, Wenceslao and his wife, who live in the river islands of the Paraná delta. Their only son has died several years earlier in the city, and the woman, who is still mourning the loss of her son, rejects an invitation to an end-of-the-year party, despite the insistence of her husband and sisters that she attend. Wenceslao, on the contrary, goes to the party, held at the house of his sister-in-law; helps prepare the barbecue; and joins the celebration. The novel is divided into sections, each headed by the same sentence and describing the most banal of daily actions that combine recurrent memories of the deceased son, spoken words, and short journeys on the river. Each section resumes the previous account to narrate the same situations once again, adding details, changing the perspective, and creating a tidal rhythm in its constant advances and retreats. The fragmentary character of the novel and of each section imposes on the reader the task of reconstructing, more than the linear significance, what is happening as the story is being composed. The reading moves vertically instead of successively, deepening and multiplying the meanings of each object and action described time and again. In the center of the islander's backyard, and in the displaced and changing center of story, stands the image of the lemon tree. The tree is "real" because it symbolizes the concentration of space and time in one ever-present moment, eternal in its simultaneous production of flower and fruit that unites, like the art of writing, process and result, ubiquitous and always identical to itself, like each of Saer's stories.

*El limonero real* also emphasizes the role of perception in representation. This topic, which is pivotal in the novel *Nadie nada nunca*, also is advanced gradually in the brief and paradigmatic collection of short fiction *La mayor* (1976; "A" major). These stories represent a milestone in the transformation of the conventional short story and in the crafting of poetic prose. In addition, the stories "La mayor" and "A medio borrar" (Partly deleted) and the essay-type fiction that is included in the section "Argumentos" (Arguments) result from the application of themes and principles that are essential to Saer's writing style. In the first two short stories, the Proustian model of recovering experience through the senses is denied validity. Sensitive and intellectual perception is always distorting reality, because the language that expresses it is in permanent flux and leads us to interrogate the same things without achieving any certainity. The quality of memories as narrative material is explored in "Recuerdos" (Memories); the effects of traveling on human identity are examined in "Cambio de domicilio" (Change of address), "Manos y planetas" (Hands and planets), "En el extranjero" (In a foreign land), and "La dispersión" (Dispersion); and the intuition of a meaning that abides unreachable and sheltered from actual events is portrayed in "Al abrigo" (Sheltered).

*Nobody Nothing Never* also narrates such impossibility through a story that repeats the same scenes during a weekend in the life of Gato Garay in his house next to the river shore. As in *El limonero real*, the plot grows in circles from the initial phrase of each section: "No hay, al principio, nada. Nada" (There is, at the beginning, nothing. Nothing.) The killing of horses in the region constitutes the apparent driving enigma that is never resolved, because, as Beatriz Sarlo points out in her review of the novel, the real enigma is the negative response to the possibility of "writing" the movement, the perception of the passing moment. Repetition of actions, dreams, memories, and phrases, along with cuts and summaries of the story, freeze the temporal progression and annul the illusion of movement. The meaning is displaced from the superficial level of the action down to the more complex and ambiguous territory of perception. The Spanish title also can be translated as "Nobody ever swims," which refers to the character of the lifeguard on the river beach, who is a former swimming champion and is now limited to watching others move.

From *Unidad de lugar* to *Nobody Nothing Never*, Saer's style presents coincidences with objectivism, a movement initiated in France in the mid-1950s. Saer is attracted by the innovative proposals of this school, and some of them have had a strong impact on his work, particularly Michel Butor's conception of space, which concentrates on different places and times and real and minute physical description of locations with imaginary, routine, and surprising events. A translator of the works of Robbe-Grillet and an admirer of Nathalie Sarraute's fiction, Saer also is inspired by a local tradition represented by Alberto Vanasco and Antonio di Benedetto, both Argentine writers who practiced a type of objectivism *avant la lettre* in their inquiry into the epistemological and philosophical

scope of the narrative form. All the characteristics of objectivism—the condensing of the anecdote or plot, the disappearance or flattening of the character as such, the emphasis on gaze and perspective, and the estrangement of reality in morose and detailed descriptions—are used by Saer to dismantle the principles of authority for the faithful portrayal of reality in his own cultural context. The result, according to Alberto Giordano, is an "effect of unreality," which reveals that which is essential to reality while allowing it to remain hidden or denied. Literature is able to show such a covert side of reality without explaining it and to reaffirm its uncertain nature.

The narrative insistence on the uncertain character of reality, and of our knowledge of it, gives lyrical overtones to several passages of *The Witness*, perhaps the most widely read novel by Saer. This work inaugurates a third period in Saer's artistic evolution, distinguished by a more linear organization of the story and a noticeable reduction in the repetition of scenes and narrative sequences. The novel exemplifies, however, the themes and style identified throughout Saer's production: the setting of the action in the littoral zone that serves as the stage for all his stories, the thinning out of the plot and the consequent descriptive concentration and poetic density of the language, and the reference and representation of the process of narrating in the act of narrating itself.

In *The Witness* the reference to history, already present to a lesser degree in previous short stories, such as "Paramnesia," "El viajero" (The traveler), and "El interprete" (The interpreter), appears stronger than before. The stories are set in different moments of the conquest and colonization of America. Francisco del Puerto, an obscure historical figure, is the protagonist and narrator. He was the only survivor of the 1515–1516 expedition of Juan Díaz de Solís to the River Plate, which was defeated by the natives. The young Spaniard lives ten years with the Indians and witnesses their cannibalistic ritual, celebrated once every year. After returning to Spain, the character relearns his native language and devotes his time to the "invention" of his memories to rescue through them people and events. The narrator reflects constantly on the act of writing while engaged in writing, allowing the author and the reader to disembowel the creative process of the novel itself. The authority of the account is deconstructed by the character's constant doubts about the cognition and interpretation of reality in his experience between cultures, signaled by his life with the Indians and his readjustment to the European world. The narrator recognizes in the cannibalism of the Indians not the essential human impulse to devour an external entity, nonexistent to the extent that is not cognizable, but the most ancient and intimate desire to devour ourselves. The novel allegorizes a universal and eternal human concern: the encounter with the "other" leads the narrator to question his own self in the tension between seeing and being seen, narrating and being narrated, eating and being eaten.

The Event also has a historical setting, the time of economic materialism at the end of the nineteenth century. In contrast to the faith in knowledge and science that characterizes those times stands the protagonist, Bianco, who seeks to demonstrate the superiority of the spirit over matter, while he is tormented by the suspicion of an adulterous relationship between his wife and his friend that is never clarified. The story takes place in the year 1871, in the midst of political and cultural developments that shaped the following decades. The plot unfolds during the emergence of a nationalist epic discourse that led to the publication of *Martín Fierro* by José Hernández in 1872, which came to be considered the national poem of Argentina. The historical and literary contexts are clearly established, but the peripeteia of Bianco's story ignores or contradicts such contexts. The discrepancy effects a tension between history and story that implies a criticism of realism and truthful representation, even in the case of historical accounts and of the novel as epic genre. In *The Event*, similarly to *The Witness*, Saer incarnates a conception of historical facts as fictional, which he explains in his 1973 essay on *Zama* by Antonio di Benedetto (*El concepto de ficción*), an exemplary novel in its treatment of history:

> No hay, en rigor de verdad, novelas históricas.... Toda narración transcurre en el presente, aunque hable a su modo, del pasado. El pasado no es más que el rodeo lógico, e incluso ontológico, que la narración debe dar para asir, a traves de lo que ya ha perimido la incertidumbre frágil de la experiencia narrativa, que tiene lugar, del mismo modo que su lectura, en el presente.

In fact, the historical novel does not exist.... Every account occurs in the present time, even if it portrays in its own way the past time. The past is nothing but the logical or even ontological roundabout that the narration needs to follow in order to grasp, through already perished moments, the fragile uncertainty of the narrative experience, which, like the act of reading, happens always in the present.

*The Event* arises in the ubiquitous space of the "plains," also the omnipresent setting in *Las nubes*, whose time frame is also the nineteenth century as well, though in the early decades. Saer's book-essay *El río sin orillas* (1991; The river with no shores) provides the exegesis of that legendary space of the "pampas," crucial to the development of Argentina since colonial times. This "imaginary treatise," as Saer subtitles his essay, details the challenges that the narrator faces when attempting to depict, and therefore define, the nature of such space and the inhabitants. Saer states in this treatise that "nada de lo que nos interesa verdaderamente nos es directamente accessible" (nothing that is truly interesting to us is accesible in a straight line). To apprehend that silent and empty landscape, there is always the need to detour through previous textual representations and evocations: the travel journals of such foreign naturalists as Charles Darwin, the Spaniard Felix de Azara, and the Frenchman Alcides D'Orbigny; the descriptions of missionaries such as the Italian Father Cayetano Cattaneo; and historical sources such as the American James R. Scobie's. Their reports of the region are stronger than any direct experience of the plains and stimulate other representations of a region that is at the same time identical and constantly changing. Saer concludes that the abstract character of this physical space is a "mirage," as qualified in *The Event*, shaped according to our own chimerical projections. In particular, the foreigner's perspective, with the freedom of the outsider's interpretation—both the protagonists of *The Witness* and *The Event* are "foreigners" in their contexts—rediscovers the landscape and enriches it with his or her own cultural and imaginary schemes. Saer finds in the historical evolution of the River Plate area the same dissolution of all truthful or monolithic renditions of its origins and development. He equates time (the nineteenth century in particular) and space (specifically the plains) as categories emptied of all a priori or fixed interpretations, and therefore perfect material for literary elaboration.

If history is the "logical and ontological roundabout" in *The Witness* and *The Event*, politics appears as the roundabout in *Glosa* and *Lo imborrable*. References to Argentine political history were present in previous works: the period after the 1955 coup d'etat that overthrew Juan Domingo Perón in *Responso* and *Cicatrices*, the allusion to leftist movements in *La vuelta completa*, and the violent repression during the 1976–1983 dictatorship allegorized in the arbitrary killing of horses in *Nobody Nothing Never*. In *Glosa* and *Lo imborrable*, the reference to state terrorism during the period of dictatorship is more direct, but it continues to function as a contingent detail in the accumulation of individual memories of living experiences.

*Glosa* narrates the stroll of Ángel Leto and the character named simply the "Mathematician" in three parts of seven blocks each. While walking, they are trying to reconstruct the birthday party of Washington Noriega, which neither of them attended, according to versions heard from other people. They gloss the oral indirect discourse of others at the same time that the story "glosses" the political repression as it intersects with the individual experiences of the characters. The story is projected into the future, from 1961 to 1979, when the reader learns that Leto will kill himself, cornered in a clandestine apartment by the repressive forces. Past and future stories combine and are always triggered by a written or oral text; language itself becomes the concave mirror of that other distorting mirror of memory, which blends words, dreams, and reality. The equating of read or heard versions of events with actual situations does not aim to minimize the violence and injustice of real events, but rather to emphasize their potential meaning and to escape the crystallization of any official discourse. As in *Nobody Nothing Never*, the story itself denies the possibility of progression, overlapping evoked images and present emotions, different times and places in the same space.

The epigraph is a poem by Tomatis whose lines are repeated and commented upon throughout the novel. This trait resembles the rigid structure of the medieval poetic form "gloss," in which the lines of the initial stanza are repeated and elaborated in each consecutive strophe. The exact arrangement of the poetic form is embodied in the geometric design of the streets that the characters walk. The infinity of the poetic word fits within the set limits of the prose accounts and provokes its implosions. Saer believes that *Glosa* is the work closest to his project of composing a novel in verse and portraying the universe of actions and emotions of a narrative within the conceptual organization of a poem.

It is not a surprise that the text of *Lo imborrable*, which glosses another text (the novel *La brisa en el trigo*, written by the character Walter Bueno), and the life of Tomatis also lead the protagonist to create poetry. Tomatis responds to the desire of reconstructing his own fragmented self through the power of poetry:

> La medida, el verso, la rima, la estrofa, la idea pescada en alguna parte de la negrura y que hace surgir, ondular, plegarse el vocabulario, acumulado misteriosamente en los pliegues orgánicos, se vuelven rastro en la página, . . . que, por haber puesto un freno a la dispersión, a causa del prestigio heroico de toda medida, ya imborrable, me apacigua.

> Measure, verse, rhyme, strophe, the idea grasped in some dark inner place and made to emerge, wave, fold the words accumulated in the creases of the body, all became traces on the page, . . . that restrain dispersion, thanks to the heroic prestige of all measure, and, already indelible, appease myself.

Writing and its simulation of the empirical world rescue reality, which is in constant dissolution, and turn imaginary and lived experiences into indelible "scars," "traces," or "clusters."

The transmutation of genre conventions was started in Saer's praxis of narrative poetry and lyrical prose, and continued in all his narrative production through the transcendence of both the short story's and the novel's traditional parameters. The deconstruction of these literary categories also is achieved by the incorporation of other genres or subgenres within his novels: children's stories and the folk tale in *El limonero real*, essay in *Cicatrices*, theatrical allegory in *The Event*, and the poetic form of gloss in the novel *Glosa*. In his last two novels, *La pesquisa* (1994; *The Investigation*, 1999) and *Las nubes*, the police fiction and the travel journal are the respective genres whose parameters are used and transformed. In *The Investigation* the central topic of the doppelganger, inaugurated by the American writer Edgar Allan Poe's detective stories, multiplies at different levels throughout the novel. There are the inspector-criminal as protagonist, the two locations of Paris and Santa Fe, the combined search for the perpetrator of the crimes and the author of a manuscript found in Santa Fe, the double reading of the French police news and the unpublished novel, and the two distinct possible endings that hinder the resolution of the mystery and remind us of Borges's "Garden of Forking Paths." Pichón Garay brings to his friends in Santa Fe the story of the crimes committed in Paris. Although *Las nubes* is set in the nineteenth century and takes the form of a travel journal, it reverses the process. The journey of Doctor Real through the infinite "pampas" to transport five patients from Santa Fe to Doctor Weiss's house in Buenos Aires is read by Pichón Garay on his computer screen in Paris. Pichón Garay and Doctor Real are both returning to their homeland after European stays, as Saer himself has returned periodically to Santa Fe since his self-exile in 1968. They realize that their memories and perceptions of the region are warped by their foreign experiences. The stories, traveling through them, also are dislocated and read between "here" and "there," in the frontier between the regional and the universal, exterior objects and the inner self.

*Lugar* (Place), published in 2000, signals a return to short fiction that resembles the short stories in *La mayor*, owing to the difficulty of cataloging them within a specific genre. The rhythm of the prose has become less interrupted by commas and the syntax less altered by the normal word order. The stories repeat the traces of Saer's former books, affirming once again his entire production as a cycle, which makes it unnecessary to insist on the "unity" of his literary work, as in the 1967 collection of short stories. The most striking difference is that the setting is not the littoral anymore. The stories, which once again combine places and times, real and imaginary situations, quotidian and unusual events, take place in Vienna's market, an airport in Dakar, a Greek tavern, Paris, or Santa Fe. The enigma of the universe and the inscrutable nature of human consciousness are the same in all places. In the context of global societies ruled by consumerism and materialism, Saer once again finds in language the possibility of reminding us of our contingency and of resisting the mirage of reality through literature that is an alternative way of existing in the world.

Forged at the margins of literary conventions and trends, from a region founded on the autonomy of creation and an exclusive compromise with language, the work of Saer occupies a central place in Argentine literature today and makes him one of the most accomplished authors of contemporary literature. Several films based on Saer's fiction, the Spanish Nadal Award (1987), the French Roger Callois Prize (1999), and the translation of his work into several languages are testimonies to his talent. His creative universe exists independent of reality and indelible in our memory. The reader of that universe receives a gift similar to the one that Barco gets from reading Petrarch's work in one story from *Lugar*: moments of intense lucidity in which we can glimpse who we think we are or, perhaps, who we really are.

## SELECTED BIBLIOGRAPHY

### Primary Works

#### Novels

Responso. Buenos Aires: Jorge Alvarez, 1964.
La vuelta completa. Rosario, Argentina: Biblioteca Popular Constancio C. Vigil, 1966.
Cicatrices. Buenos Aires: Sudamericana, 1969.
El limonero real. Barcelona: Planeta, 1974.
Nadie nada nunca. Mexico City: Siglo XXI, 1980.
El entenado. Buenos Aires: Folio Ediciones, 1983.
Glosa. Buenos Aires: Alianza, 1986.
La ocasión. Barcelona: Destino, 1988.
Lo imborrable. Buenos Aires: Alianza, 1993.
La pesquisa. Buenos Aires: Seix Barral, 1994.
Las nubes. Buenos Aires: Seix Barral, 1997.

#### Short Stories

En la zona. Santa Fe, Argentina: Castelví, 1960.
Palo y hueso. Buenos Aires: Camarda Junior, 1965.
Unidad de lugar. Buenos Aires: Galerna, 1967.
La mayor. Barcelona: Planeta, 1976.
Lugar. Buenos Aires: Seix Barral, 2000.

## Nonfiction

*Una literatura sin atributos.* Santa Fe, Argentina: Universidad Nacional del Litoral, 1986. (Essays 1979–1981.)

*El río sin orillas: Tratado imaginario.* Madrid: Alianza, 1991.

*El concepto de ficción.* Buenos Aires: Ariel, 1997.

*La narración-objeto.* Buenos Aires: Seix Barral, 1999.

## Poetry

*El arte de narrar: Poemas, 1960–1975.* Caracas: Fundación para la Cultura y las Artes del Distrito Federal, 1977.

*El arte de narrar: Poemas 1960–1987.* Buenos Aires: Seix Barral, 2000.

## Other Works

*Por un relato futuro: Diálogo/Ricardo Piglia, Juan José Saer.* Santa Fe, Argentina: Centro de Publicaciones, Universidad Nacional del Litoral, 1990.

*Diálogo/Ricardo Piglia, Juan José Saer.* Edited by Sergio Delgado. Santa Fe, Argentina: Centro de Publicaciones, Universidad Nacional del Litoral, 1995.

## Collected Works

*Narraciones.* 2 vols. Buenos Aires: Centro Editor de América Latina, 1983.

*Juan José Saer por Juan José Saer.* Buenos Aires: Editorial Celtia, 1986.

## Translations

*The Witness.* Trans. by Margaret Jull Costa. London: Serpent's Tail, 1990.

*Nobody Nothing Never.* Trans. by Helen Lane. London: Serpent's Tail, 1993.

*The Event.* Trans. by Helen Lane. London: Serpent's Tail, 1995.

*The Investigation.* Trans. by Helen Lane. London: Serpent's Tail, 1999.

## Secondary Works

### Critical and Biographical Studies

Cariello, Graciela. *Un viaje por el río de Saer.* Rosario, Argentina: Artemisa, 1995.

Dalmaroni, Miguel, ed. *Literatura argentina y nacionalismo: Gálvez, Fogwill, Saer, Aira.* Serie Estudios e Investigaciones 24. La Plata, Argentina: Universidad Nacional de La Plata, 1995.

Dalmaroni, Miguel, and Margarita Merbilhaá. " 'Un azar convertido en don': Juan José Saer y el relato de la percepción." In *La narración gana la partida.* Edited by Elsa Drucaroff. Vol. 11 of *Historia crítica de la literatura argentina.* Buenos Aires: Emecé, 2000. Pp. 321–344.

Fernández, Nancy. *Narraciones viajeras: César Aira y Juan José Saer.* Buenos Aires: Biblos, 2000.

Foffani, Enrique, and Adriana Mancini. "Más allá del regionalismo: La transformación del paisaje." In *La narración gana la partida.* Edited by Elsa Drucaroff. Vol. 11 of *Historia crítica de la literatura argentina.* Buenos Aires: Emecé, 2000. Pp. 261–289.

Giordano, Alberto. *La experiencia narrativa: Juan José Saer, Felisberto Hernández, Manuel Puig.* Rosario, Argentina: B. Viterbo, 1992.

Gramuglio, María Teresa. "Juan José Saer: El arte de narrar." *Punto de Vista* 6:3–8 (July 1979).

———. "La filosofía en el relato." *Punto de Vista* 20:35–36 (May 1984).

———. "El lugar de Saer." In *Juan José Saer por Juan José Saer.* Buenos Aires: Celtia, 1986. Pp. 261–299.

Grandis, Rita de. "The First Colonial Encounter in *El entenado* by Juan José Saer: Paratextuality and History in Postmodern Fiction." *Latin American Literary Review* 21, no. 41:30–38 (June 1993).

Jitrik, Noé. "Lo vivido, lo teórico, la coincidencia." *Cuadernos Americanos* 2:89–99 (March–April 1984).

———. "Entre el corte y la continuidad. Juan José Saer: Una escritura crítica." In *La vibración del presente.* Mexico City: Fondo de Cultura Económica, 1987. Pp. 169–181.

Montaldo, Graciela. *Juan José Saer: El limonero real.* Buenos Aires: Hachette, 1986.

Néstor, Ponce, Sergio Pastormelo, and Dardo F. Scarvino. *Literatura policial en la Argentina: Waleis, Borges, Saer.* Serie Estudios e Investigaciones 32. Buenos Aires: Comité Editorial, Facultad de Humanidades y Ciencias de la Educación, Universidad Nacional de La Plata, 1997.

Premat, Julio. "El cataclismo de los orígenes: La pampa histórica de Juan José Saer." *Río de la Plata* 17–18:689–700 (July 1997).

———. *La dicha de Saturno: Escritura y melancolia en la obra de Juan Jose Saer.* Amsterdam: Portada Hispanica, 2001.

Pons, María Cristina. *Memorias del olvido: Del Paso, García Márquez, Saer y la novela histórica de fines del siglo XX.* Mexico City: Siglo XXI, 1996.

Prada, M., and Ana Rebeca. *"Nadie, nada, nunca" de Juan José Saer: Cifra de la violencia.* La Paz, Bolivia: Facultad de

Humanidades y Ciencias de la Educación, Universidad Mayor de San Andrés, 1998.

Riera, Gabriel. "La ficción de Saer: ¿Una 'antropología especulativa'? (Una lectura de *El entenado*)." *MLN* 111, no. 2:368–390 (March 1996).

Romano, Evelia. "La ocasión para narrar: Historia, alegoría y realidad en un texto de Juan José Saer." *Nueva Revista de Filología Hispánica* 47, no. 2:99–119 (1999).

Sarlo, Beatriz. "Narrar la percepción." *Punto de Vista* 10:34–37 (November 1980).

Stern, Mirta. "El espacio intertextual en la narrativa de Juan José Saer: Instancia productiva, referente y campo de teorización de la escritura." *Revista Iberoamericana* 49:965–981 (October–December 1983).

———. "Juan José Saer: Construcción y teoría de la ficción narrativa." *Hispamérica: Revista de Literatura* 13:15–30 (April 1984).

*Films Based on the Works of Juan José Saer*

*Palo y hueso*. Directed by Nicolas Sarquís. Argentina, 1968.

*Les trottoirs de Saturne (Las veredas de Saturno)*. Screenplay by Juan José Saer, Hugo Santiago, and Jorge Semprún. Directed by Hugo Santiago. Produced by Hubert Niogret. France, 1986.

*Nadie nada nunca*. Directed by Raúl Beceyro. Instituto Nacional de Cinematografía Argentina (INCAA), 1988.

*Cicatrices*. Directed by Patricio Coll. Argentina, 2001.

# Antonio Skármeta

## (1940–      )

## Randolph D. Pope

Antonio Skármeta was born 7 November 1940 in Antofagasta, Chile. A port city, situated in the midst of one of the most arid zones in the world and at a great distance from Santiago, Chile's capital, Antofagasta experienced a boom in the nineteenth century due to nitrate and silver mines, and continued to see a relative prosperity as an active port for copper mines in the twentieth century. It attracted immigrants from Eastern Europe, among whom were the families of Skármeta's parents, Antonio Skármeta Simunovic and Magdalena Catalina Vranicic. While they both were born in Chile, their parents came from the island of Brač, today in Croatia, and which, at the time, belonged to the Austro-Hungarian Empire. The fascination that the child felt for the stories his grandparents told about their country of origin would result decades later in *La boda del poeta* (1999; The poet's wedding).

Skármeta's texts are characterized by a wide range of references to high and low culture, but at their root there is a fascination with the pleasure of telling a good story, a pleasure he remembers first experiencing when listening to radio plays at home in Antofagasta. Some days, when the electricity was down (a not infrequent occurrence during Skármeta's childhood), he used to make up possible continuations of the stories for his family. He recalls one day when the electricity was working, but his grandmother nevertheless turned off the radio and asked him to tell the story instead. He knew then he wanted to become a writer. His narrators often show this pleasure of storytelling, a histrionic flair, a tendency to curl up sentences and jump to surprising flights of poetry. This makes any classification of his writing as "realist" too limited, even though his topics are usually drawn from the lives of ordinary people leading relatively modest lives. The author's admiration for the sea, apparent in several of his stories, may also stem from his early years in Antofagasta, a region with extended beachfronts and mild weather that encourages outdoor activities.

In 1947 his family moved to Santiago in search of better economic opportunity, but two years later they emigrated to Buenos Aires. At the time, Argentina's capital was a vibrant and prosperous city, and in his three years there Skármeta got to know the city well. He worked as an errand boy, riding his bicycle before school started each morning to deliver fruit for an Italian shop owner to houses of the upper bourgeoisie in Belgrano. On his return to Chile he found literary life dominated by a series of great poets, including Gabriela Mistral, Pablo Neruda, and Vicente Huidobro. Mistral had already received the Nobel Prize in 1945, while Neruda would accept the same honor in 1971. Both of them appear frequently as characters in Skármeta's texts, and he has edited an anthology of Neruda's poems, *Neruda: Una herencia de alegría* (Santiago: Televisa, 1998), for which he also wrote an admiring introduction. At the same time, the Chilean novelists he could look up to, such as Eduardo Barrios and Manuel Rojas, were definitely more local, and their works were characterized by realism, so he chose instead to emulate the Russian and North American masters, such as Fyodor Dostoyevsky and Ernest Hemingway.

Skármeta attended the Instituto Nacional High School, where Ricardo Lagos, who became president of Chile in January 2000, was one of his fellow students. The Instituto Nacional is a remarkable public school in a city dominated by private institutions, and many other distinguished writers have studied there, among them Ariel Dorfman, Skármeta's contemporary, and Luis Sepúlveda, a distinguished voice of the younger generation. Skármeta's favorite authors at the time included Baudelaire, for whom he organized an homage in 1953. Among his activities in high school he worked as a puppeteer, thus beginning his long association with the stage.

In 1959 Skármeta entered the University of Chile, where he studied philosophy. His first two short stories, "El Señor Ávila" (published in *Cuentistas de la Universidad*) and "El joven con el cuento" (published in *Boletín del Instituto Nacional*) also appeared that year. In the second of these stories a young university student is given the opportunity to take care of a small cabin and a dilapidated caboose oddly stranded in the desert, next to the sea. There are here many constants that will reappear in Skármeta's later work. The young man is learned, but disillusioned with dry scholarly work. His return to nature, silence, and solitude is restorative. Nevertheless, leaving Santiago also means losing the support of society, and in the course of the narrative a Hitchcock-like tension develops, first by the fact that before he is left alone, he is given a gun to defend himself against intruders (an ominous sign), and this is followed by the noises of marauders in the night. The story concludes with festive solidarity; the marauders turn out to be a father and son who are looking for shelter for the night, and they join the young man in searching for clams and then eating them with plenty of wine. This swing between rejection of social contact and the celebration of fellowship exemplifies a grounding polarity in Skármeta's writing.

In 1962 Skármeta worked aboard a ship that took him to California. The experience of his brief stay there was incorporated into one of his finest short stories, "La Cenicienta en San Francisco," which won a second prize in a respected contest organized by the Compañía Refinería de Azúcar de Viña del Mar, a sugar refining company. "La Cenicienta en San Francisco" tells a straightforward story: a young Chilean man who is visiting San Francisco leaves a noisy party, retiring to an attic with a woman he has just met, Abby. She speaks only English, a language the traveler hardly understands. Drinking beer, resorting to mime and rudimentary vocabulary, they grow closer and make love. The morning after, they separate, she to play the role of Cinderella in a play and he knowing he must return to his country, never to see Abby again. For a Latin American writer of those years, a time in which sex was hushed and connected in novels either with the sublime or the sordid, there is a startling novelty in the intensity of the masculine character's desire, in his almost hungry need to make love with a woman he hardly knows. As in much of Skármeta's later work, the result seems so natural that the important accomplishment of this story could easily pass undetected today. Alcohol, pleasure, and sex are presented free from moral considerations that would condemn them or give them symbolic greatness. They are beyond good and evil, as natural as thirst, appetite, or sleep. Clearly, though, this narrative aggressively subverts the moral and social codes of Chile, a country in which the Catholic Church still has so much power that even today there is no legal access to divorce or abortion. Cinderella, of course, is not only the role Abby plays, but also a reference to how the young man feels, free for one night of bohemian life abroad before he must return to a home where this sort of freedom is only found in books, movies, and fantasy. In an article published in the journal *Mensaje* in May 1983, Skármeta explained his project when writing "La Cenicienta en San Francisco":

> me pareció que la sociedad estaba envuelta en un espeso lenguaje retórico a través del cual se imponía a ella la visión que una desprestigiada burguesía tenía de la existencia y la comunidad. Insensible en aquellos años al movimiento de

*renovación política que se venía gestando, muy dificultoso y muy complejo para quien no estuviera en la pomada, operé una violenta retirada hacia lo más elemental en el ser humano y hacia los narcisistas impulsos de una ansiosa intimidad. La espantosa rutina de una sociedad joven, tempranamente convencionalizada y burocratizada, me provocó a alentar las fuerzas más naturales en mi actitud. Me parecía pavoroso que se hubiera perdido el sentido de percibir la existencia como algo repleto de misterio, de futuro, de mareadora sensualidad.*

It seemed to me that society was enveloped by a thick rhetorical language that was used to impose upon it the discredited bourgeoisie's vision of existence and community. In those years I was not tuned in to the movement of political renovation that was then being born, very difficult and very complex for someone who was not in the know, so I proceeded to recoil violently toward the most basic essence of the human being and towards the narcissistic drives of an anxious private life. The horrible routine of a young society that had become conventional and bureaucratic far too soon drove me to cultivate in my behavior the energies that were closest to Nature. It seemed terrible to me that we had lost the capacity to perceive existence as full of mystery, of future, of dizzying sensuousness.

In 1963 Skármeta married Cecilia Boisier, a painter, with whom he had two sons, Beltrán in 1966 and Gabriel in 1968. He collaborated with his wife in several translations from French and English into Spanish. After Skármeta graduated from the University of Chile in Santiago with a degree in philosophy, he returned to the United States, this time with a Fulbright Scholarship to study philosophy at Columbia University. While there he read Julio Cortázar's *Rayuela* (1963), and the impact of this novel was so great that he transferred to the study of literature in the department of Spanish and Portuguese. He subsequently obtained an M.A. in Spanish with a thesis on Cortázar.

There are numerous similarities between Skármeta and Cortázar: they both excel at writing short stories that manage to transform the quotidian into a memorable event; they both employ a playful language, partly irreverent and partly extremely learned, even artificial; they both celebrate jazz and bohemianism; and both are deeply engaged in social causes. Their differences are also instructive: where Cortázar introduces surprising elements that are frequently fantastic and magical,

Skármeta prefers to create an epiphany that comes more from the characters' feelings and language than from the events themselves. Both authors could be connected with the tradition of Ionesco and Beckett, in which absurd situations convey an existential despair. Situations that frequently border on the grotesque are saved from hopelessness by compassion and solidarity, the joy of creative language, and a mischievous delight in creating havoc for a well-ordered society.

In general, Skármeta has distanced himself from the authors of the Latin American "Boom," such as Fuentes, Vargas Llosa, and Cortázar, claiming that they were more involved in creating a higher literary reality and experimenting with language, while he and his generation were initially more interested in being the narrators of an emergent Latin American reality. This position is most clearly elaborated in an interview with Monika Walter, in which Skármeta claims that the oppositional value of most of the experimental prose of the Boom writers was accessible mostly to just an elite few, and that they employed for their criticism precisely those elements of high culture that the Latin American bourgeoisie admired. In his book *The Post-Boom in Spanish American Literature* (1998), Donald Shaw has used the term "post-Boom" to describe the group of writers with which he associates Skármeta, among them Luisa Valenzuela and Elena Poniatowska, providing a general and insightful description of the period.

In 1966 Skármeta started teaching contemporary philosophy at the University of Chile in Santiago, with particular emphasis on the work of Heidegger, Sartre, and Ortega, to whom he added Camus and the pre-Socratics. His academic background is surprisingly muted in his creative work, in which he prefers to avoid the ponderousness and erudition that often afflict scholarly writing. He has nonetheless written several important critical essays, however, dealing with such subjects as Cortázar, Vargas Llosa, and the new Latin American narrative.

In his short story of 1967, "Entre todas las cosas lo primero es el mar" (Among all things, the sea comes first), Skármeta revisits his conflicted relationship with the academic establishment. In this story the narrator's cousin claims that the most important thing for him is the sea, so he repairs a car in order to spend a day at the beach. This talented mechanic wants to drop out of the university; he wants instead to write, to understand the world freshly. The trip to the coast, the cleansing swim, the soothing effect of the sunny chatter with his cousin and a girlfriend, all are wonderfully described, so that when the rebel returns to hit his books, readers know this encounter with the sea has at least temporarily reconciled him with his studies.

By this time Skármeta was contributing essays to Chile's better-known magazines, *Ercilla* and *Ahora* (weeklies modeled after *Time* magazine), and *La Quinta Rueda*, an innovative literary publication. Unfortunately his pieces that have been published in periodical literature have not yet been collected. His essays, many of them published as a biweekly column in *Caras*, cover a multitude of topics, from football to Marlon Brando, are finely attuned to a young, contemporary, and even trendy audience, and are spiced with humor. His journalism, as in the case of García Márquez or Vargas Llosa, is characterized by his capacity to tell a good story engagingly and his ability to always keep his readers in mind.

It is not simply coincidence that he began his career with a remarkable series of impeccable short stories, before he ventured into the novel. In fact, in 1967 he won first prize in a short story contest sponsored by the Chilean newspaper *La Nación*, with "Mira donde va el lobo" (Watch out for the wolf). This first-person narrative tells the story of a lowly conquistador during the Spanish colonization of Chile. When a group of soldiers attempts to return to Spain, the governor tricks them and steals their accumulated wealth. It is a story of the thieves being robbed, so a picaresque atmosphere prevails, in spite of the pain and treason described in the story. The narrator's mannerisms. his nostalgia for the past, the weight of his traumatic memories, the unforgettable vision of the ships awaiting in the port of Valparaíso, supposedly to take them to home and family, and the final reversal of fortune are perfectly and tightly woven into a desolate yet proud narrative: "I was abused, but I was there," the narrator seems to affirm; "I was one of them, and that belonging is what is left for me to treasure."

Skármeta's first book is *El entusiasmo* (Enthusiasm), published in 1967 by the venerable Chilean publishing house of Zig-Zag, in Santiago, where the masters of the previous generation, Manuel Rojas and José Donoso, had published their early masterpieces (*Hijo de ladrón*, 1951, and *Coronación*, 1957, respectively). In the back cover blurb for *El entusiasmo*, readers are told that these stories "participan de una noción del mundo que no quiere tener nada que ver con el orden del pasado" (partake of an image of the world that does not want anything to do with the old order), and the author is rightly associated with the North American writers J. D. Salinger and Jack Kerouac. This book contains "La Cenicienta en San Francisco" (Cinderella in San Francisco), "El joven con el cuento" (Young man with a story), "Al trote" (Trotting), "Entre todas las cosas lo primero es el mar" (Among all things, the sea comes first), "Días azules para un ancla" (Blue days for an anchor), "Nupcias" (Wedding), "Relaciones públicas" (Public relations), and "Mira donde va el lobo" (Look out for the wolf). Of those stories, "Nupcias" and "Relaciones públicas" are notable for different reasons. "Nupcias" is a disturbing, brief narration of an event that takes place in a subway, where a man steals (or imagines he does) an unknown woman's shoe as a way to express his admiration for her. The story flickers between what appears to be a tone of endearing farce and the point of view of the woman, for whom this clowning is obviously a horrifying experience. Is this a breach of urban protocol, of the necessary distance that allows strangers to travel packed together in a subway car? Is it a heroic gesture of rebellion precipitated by loneliness, or merely an exercise in sophomoric aggression? Does the woman agree to be kissed, or is this development only a figment of the imagination of the shoe thief, who is a Hispanic immigrant? The story remains ambiguous, and this is where its anxious charm resides. As an expression of the loneliness and lack of communication fostered by the big city, and of the fantasy life of an urban commuter, the story is good-humored. As a portrait of the possible violence that a woman can encounter when she becomes a sexual object of desire in a random encounter, however, this is a disturbing story.

Also notable is "Relaciones públicas," a story that is based upon Skármeta's experiences in Buenos Aires. Here a Chilean has beaten a young Argentine boy, and the victim's brother comes to exact revenge. After a prolonged fight the Chilean and the Argentines become friends. These rituals of initiation into a community are certainly part of male mythology, and they recur in Skármeta's work, even up to his most recent novel.

The year 1969 saw the publication of several of Skármeta's translations from English into Spanish. While he took this work on in response to economic necessity, he has chosen his texts according to his own literary preferences. Among the works he has translated are *An American Dream* by Normal Mailer, *The Pyramid* by William Golding, *Typee* by Herman Melville, *Visions of Gerard* by Jack Kerouac, and *The Last Tycoon* by F. Scott Fitzgerald. More important, in 1969 he received the Casa de las Américas Prize, at the time arguably the most prestigious honor for short story collections in the Spanish-speaking world, for *Desnudo en el tejado* (Naked on the roof). This collection includes one of his most successful stories, "El ciclista del San Cristóbal" (The cyclist of Saint Christopher's hill). Again, the story line is relatively simple. An adolescent has two worries on his birthday: his mother, who is seriously sick, and a bicycle race in which he will participate the next day. Together with his father he watches over his mother's restless sleep, and they talk about their fear that she may soon die. Curiously, he discovers he has some sort of special power this day, for fire does not hurt him when he plays with the flames of the burner on the gas stove. Early in the morning he leaves for the race, a steep climb up a hill, on top of which a large image of the Virgin Mary overlooks the city. After his victory he returns home, fearing his mother will be dead, but instead she has recovered. Did his effort in the race have some sort of magical connection with his mother's improvement? It is up to the reader to decide. The epic struggle of the race is muted and left to glow quietly, as the story is framed by the cyclist's concern for his mother's health.

There is a sentimental audacity in this piece, and it is characteristic of Skármeta's appreciation of affectionate family interactions. For all the rebelliousness of many of his youthful characters, they are not cut off from other family members. The choice of a modest topic is also characteristic of Skármeta's work; great events do find a place in his writing—the Allende government and the putsch that ended it in 1973

appear frequently, as do events related to the poet Pablo Neruda—but they are never the narration's focus, only its background. There is no anxious need to load the text with greatness or historical transcendence. Instead, the stories keep insisting on the interest of daily life, preferring the bicyclist to the car driver, the poorly paid city policeman to the general, the mailman to the politician, the girlfriend of the guerrilla hero to the hero himself. There is here something unusual, because in spite of their modest lives these characters are not devoured by hate or boredom, nor are they terminally frustrated or bitter. On the other hand, they are not altogether happy, successful, exemplary, or flagwavers. They are amazingly normal, without ever being boring, something as difficult to attain in literature as the easy grace of a slow movement in Mozart (a composer frequently invoked by Skármeta), or the shoes painted by Van Gogh—perfectly ordinary, well worn, and miraculous.

In Skármeta's work there is a sympathetic contemplation of daily life, without an attempt to elevate it through allegory and baroque language (as one can see in Severo Sarduy, for example), or to incorporate it through supercilious irony (as in Manuel Puig). If one were to find precursors of this approach in other Chilean authors, one would have to consider Manuel Rojas (1896–1973), a master portraitist of menial and migrant workers who are always close to poverty and failure, but also full of life and determination, or Fernando Alegría's notable first novel about Chilean immigrants to California, *Caballo de copas* (1957; *My Horse González*, 1964). The difference with Rojas and Alegría is clear, though, a few lines into "El ciclista del San Cristóbal," where the reader finds a mention of the Russian satellite Sputnik, which the cyclist sees from his house's balcony. This detail, and the fact that the young man has also read about Sputnik in the newspaper, shows a world that is international and multicultural in scope, a world that the more provincial characters of Rojas and Alegría could not have suspected. As he leaves home, the young cyclist hums a Beatles tune; after the race, he drinks a Coca-Cola; the names of the other cyclists in the race and of his schoolmates reflect the immigration that has made of Chile, Argentina, and Uruguay such complexly textured countries with multiple roots extending back to all the nations of

Europe. The cyclist is part of a family, a team, a country, and an international culture. In his first works, Skármeta presents his characters as effortlessly connected with a wide and borderless culture. One could add here that life and literature coincide, for Skármeta has moved easily to other cities and cultures, from New York to Berlin. His outlook has never been that of a tourist or a melancholy expatriate.

In "El ciclista de San Cristóbal" one can observe another notable characteristic of Skármeta's writing. The narrator uses a surprising register of Chilean Spanish, mixing high and low language forms freely, creating unusual turns of phrase, and ending with a private mix and melody that is all his own. This quality may easily be lost in translation or missed by readers who assume he is simply recording colloquial Chilean speech. In an interview published in the *Revista de Libros* of *El Mercurio*, Skármeta affirmed:

> *Me interesa lo popular hasta el punto de armar con ello mis mundos, pero, por favor, no me interesa lo folclórico, ni sus acotamientos sentimentales en torno a cierta tradición. Tampoco me interesa una captación naturalista del lenguaje chileno o del lenguaje de cada país, sino lo popular, sometido a una tensión culta.*

> (Escritores de América)

I am interested in the popular to the point that I use it to build my worlds but, please, I am not interested in folklore, nor in the accompanying sentimentality that is fixed on one tradition. Nor am I interested in a precise reproduction of Chilean language or of each country [where my characters live], but in the popular submitted to the tension of high culture.

This tension between popular and high culture is found in almost every sentence of the story. For example, in the following line one word stands out as singularly learned and ponderous for an adolescent narrator: "Desde el balcón de la Alameda vi cruzar parsimoniosamente el cielo ese Sputnik ruso" (From the balcony overlooking Alameda Avenue, I saw that Russian Sputnik cross the sky parsimoniously). But the sentence continues, switching to a more colloquial and youthful vocabulary: "y no tomé ni así tanto porque al día siguiente era la primera prueba de ascensión de la temporada" (and I didn't drink even a sip because the first uphill race of the season would be on the next day).

This tension between cultural levels is similar to another defining trait of Skármeta's prose, his sudden shifts from a hip prose interspersed with slang and even a few vulgar expressions, to flights of inspired lyricism, often "cooled down" by a trivial detail that brings the text down to earth. This story, "El ciclista del San Cristóbal," later became the title of an anthological collection of Skármeta's short stories published in 1973 by Editorial Quimantú with great success, selling over thirty thousand copies at a time of great economic crisis in Chile.

*Desnudo en el tejado* contains other notable short stories. In "A las arenas" (To the sands), the narrator, stranded in New York, sells his blood at a hospital and then spends the money in an evening of partying, jazz, and sex. Music and affection shared among those down on their luck and short of money has a cleansing and redeeming value. If poverty reduces the main character to a victim of capitalist vampirism, the music of Ella Fitzgerald and a night spent with a young woman allow him to recover his joy and dignity. "Basketball," another story in this collection, is a whimsical tale about the sport, in which the main character's primary concern is to make love for the first time. The numerous connections between sport and sex are thinly veiled, and some readers may find the adolescent's obsession with scoring amusing, while others may consider it a prime example of male aggression.

Skármeta's next short-story collections are *Tiro libre* (Free kick), published in 1973, and *Novios y solitarios* (Grooms and lonely people), published in 1975. The first book contains "Pescado" (Fish), "El último tren" (The last train), "Uno a uno" (One to one), "Primera preparatoria" (First grade), "Enroque" (Castling), "Balada para un gordo" (Ballad for a fat man), "El cigarrillo" (The cigarette), "París," and "Profesionales" (The professionals). "Uno a uno" is perhaps the most elaborate of these stories, and Skármeta uses it as the first story in a book misleadingly (for it contains only a few stories) entitled *Cuentos completos* by the publishing house Sudamericana. In the story, a man and a woman check into the elegant Hotel Carrera in Santiago to celebrate their winnings after a day at the races. As usual in Skármeta's stories, money is not invested or otherwise sensibly administered, but used instead to buy a moment of freedom. The first part of the story is presented in italics to express the emotions the man feels during the race, and these few pages are among the most inventive and poetically successful of the author's entire body of work. In contrast, the subsequent behavior of the couple appears boorish, and their drunken departure to the coast is only too predictable.

The second volume of stories, *Novios y solitarios*, contains several previously published tales, along with a new story "De la sangre al petróleo" (From blood to oil), a remarkable and vivid dramatization of the sudden violence that can erupt anywhere in contemporary society. This is one of Skármeta's most matter-of-fact stories, fast-moving and effective. This story may have such vividness because it is based on a terrorist attack that Skármeta witnessed in Rome's Fiumicino Airport on 17 December 1973. Palestinian terrorists bombed the Pan Am office at the airport, killing thirty-two people and injuring fifty, before taking seven Italian policemen hostage and hijacking a plane to Athens. In Skármeta's fictional treatment of the incident, the contrast between the blood of the dead and the concerns of the surviving travelers, intent on continuing their business—symbolized by oil—is presented in an almost melancholic manner, since the narrator believes solidarity and compassion are becoming virtues of the past.

Also included in this volume is one of Skármeta's best stories, "La llamada" (The telephone call). In it, a former student who now is a member of the police approaches a high-school teacher. The conversation appears to be friendly, but the teacher, who already has been detained and released, fears he will be again taken for interrogation. The teacher's tension and fear are artfully conveyed by his attempt to recall the number of cigarettes left in his pocket, knowing that if he is arrested he will not be allowed to buy more. While nothing appears to have happened, once the teacher is left alone, he forsakes a telephone call he was about to make. Clearly, his former student has effectively delivered a message of intimidation. Skármeta's decision to provide a glimpse of the devastating effect of a dictatorship by focusing on an almost trivial encounter—the story never affirms that there is more, except in the teacher's mind—reveals again his predilection to avoid the grand statement and to give instead a close description of daily life.

The year 1970 was an important year in the history of Chile. Salvador Allende, the candidate of a united leftist front, was elected president with only a plurality of the votes. Skármeta, along with many other intellectuals, actively participated in the Allende campaign and in related programs aimed at making culture a national activity and not merely the privilege of a few. Using funds from a grant provided by the Goethe Institute, he offered the first of his writers' workshops, beginning with a seminar named after Heinrich Böll. Fifteen writers attended Skármeta's workshop each year for the next three years, among them many of the younger writers who are famous today, such as Alberto Fuguet and Andrea Maturana. These seminars were part of a very active and important cultural development in Chile that created structures where writers could meet, learn, and be read seriously. Enrique Lafourcade and José Donoso, among the older generation, and Diamela Eltit, among the new, offered other well-known writing workshops. Skármeta has described in an interview the importance of the Allende years:

> *Mi evolución ha estado muy ligada a mi biografía personal y a mi biografía colectiva. Es decir, el intento de mi literatura es siempre tratar de hacer latir al unísono mi historia privada, íntima, con la historia colectiva, a ver si logro, en algunos momentos, algunos acordes juntos. De modo que mi literatura cambia según grandes hitos. En una primera etapa es un intento de responder con fantasía al enigma que el mundo nos propone. Una solución plena de la riqueza fantástica del universo, un asumir del propio cuerpo, casi un deber moral de ser fantástico, de ser rebelde, el deber de sentir, como jóvenes, que la poesía es el deber del hombre en el mundo. . . . La segunda etapa me viene impuesta desde fuera, de una manera muy violenta, con el golpe. Yo creo que ahí, en vista de la extrema brutalidad de este acontecimiento, se relativiza mi fe en el ser humano. . . . Tengo una mirada más dedicada a ver el drama, a reconocer el dolor en la gente, lo que Isabel [Allende] llamaba esa sensación de solidaridad, de sentirme afectado comunitariamente.*
>
> (*Revista Chilena de Literatura* 32, 1988)

My evolution has been deeply intertwined with my personal biography and with my collective biography. What I mean is that what I try to do in my literature is always to make my private history, my intimate one, beat with the same pulse as collective history, hoping to strike in a few instances a common chord. Therefore, my literature changes according to large milestones. In a first stage it attempts to respond with fantasy to the enigma the world poses to us. This solution is infused by the fantastic richness of the universe, by coming to terms with my own body; there was almost a moral duty to be fantastic, rebellious, a duty to feel, as the young people we were, that poetry is the duty the human being has in this world. . . . The second stage came to me imposed from the outside, in a very violent manner, by the putsch. I believe that there, when I saw the extreme brutality of this event, my faith in the human being became relative. . . . My view now is dedicated more to noticing the drama, to recognizing the suffering of people, what Isabel [Allende] called a feeling of solidarity, of being affected as a whole community.

Skármeta's first novel, *Soñé que la nieve ardía* (1975; *I Dreamt the Snow Was Burning*, 1985), was written when the author was already in exile, after the military putsch of General Augusto Pinochet on 11 September 1973 ended Salvador Allende's democratically elected experiment in a socialist government. A few months later, Skármeta, who had been a militant in the Movimiento de Acción Popular Unitaria (MAPU), a leftist splinter party, was already in Buenos Aires, where he remained until 1975, when he went to Berlin. There he lived the rest of his exile years, before returning to Chile in 1989. Among the personal costs of his exile was his divorce from Cecilia Boisier in 1981. Later in Berlin he met Nora Preperski, a German, whom he married in 1989, the same year in which their son, Fabián Cristóbal, was born. While he was in Berlin, Skármeta took several brief visiting professorships in the United States, at Colorado College and at Washington University in St. Louis, Missouri, where he was appointed distinguished visiting professor. He returned to Missouri to teach for one semester every other year from 1988 to 1998.

In his essential book, *Antonio Skármeta and the Post Boom*, Donald Shaw writes that "Skármeta's whole work is dominated by a desire to find a new compromise between observed and created reality, one which would represent neither a return to old-style realism nor a prolongation of the Boom." Therefore, when attempting to tell the epic story of the Allende government and its downfall, Skármeta avoids the wide historical focus that has been favored, for example, by Carlos Fuentes, or the complex mix of realist observation with a refined

manipulation of narrative time that Mario Vargas Llosa has made famous, or even the baroque and learned tone of an Alejo Carpentier or Augusto Roa Bastos. Instead, in *Soñé que la nieve ardía* there are three intertwined stories that are easily followed. Arturo, a young soccer player, arrives in Santiago from the provinces, hoping to triumph in this sport, where he excels, but he does not attain this goal. He does, at least, achieve his second dream, which is to make love to a woman for the first time. Several of the people who live in the boardinghouse on Antofagasta Street, where Arturo is staying, work in unions and political parties, some of them becoming victims of the putsch's violence. Their story is one of collective projects and political action. A third story line deals with two modest entertainers, Señor Pequeño (The Small Man) and his partner, an angelic giant, who together look for work and for a way to escape the brutal men who pursue them because Señor Pequeño has stolen a fighting cock.

Arturo's story, as Grínor Rojo has shown, is the reversal of a canonical Chilean novel of the nineteenth century, Alberto Blest Gana's *Martín Rivas* (1862), in which a young man comes from the provinces and successfully moves up the social ladder by helping out a family of the upper bourgeoisie and then marrying into it. The relation among the three story lines in *Soñé que la nieve ardía* is fragile. In particular, the episodes involving Señor Pequeño seem disconnected from the rest of the novel, although they show another ability Skármeta frequently displays in his narratives: dramatic flair. The relation between Señor Pequeño, his awkward companion, and their quest, on the one hand, and the characters of Beckett's *Waiting for Godot*, on the other, has been observed often, but what matters most is Skármeta's decision to bring theatricality into the novel and tinge it with an absurdity that is frequently compassionate and humorous. In a 1987 interview with Andrew Bush, Skármeta explained:

*Solamente tengo un libro que es mi gran amor: se llama Guillermo Shakespeare. . . . Mi proyecto estético es utilizar el lenguaje de una manera dramática. Mis grandes amores no son narrativos; me interesan la poesía, el teatro y el cine. Cada vez más me estoy inclinando por un tipo de prosa histriónica, por decirlo así, que tiene guiños conversacionales y también vericuetos más complejos. Este es mi proyecto: buscar imágenes que hagan avanzar el relato pero que al mismo tiempo brillen en sí mismas.*

(*Revista de Estudios Hispánicos* 21, no. 2)

I have only one book that is my great love: it is called William Shakespeare. My aesthetic project is to use language dramatically. My great loves are not narrative; I am interested in poetry, theater, and film. More and more I tend to a type of histrionic prose, so to say, that brings the reader into a conversation and also into a more complex labyrinth. That is my project: to look for images that make the story move along but at the same time are resplendent on their own.

This method of blending drama and novel is confirmed in a 1993 interview with García-Corales, in which he reasserts that Shakespeare is the author who has influenced him the most, because his own conception of narrative is connected to theater and film: "A mí me interesa la literatura con drama" (I am interested in a literature that has drama), he says, and adds, "Mi literatura tiene una puesta en escena igual a la del cine" (My literature is staged, just as film is; *Chasqui* 22, no. 2). In West Berlin he taught screenwriting at the German Academy of Film and Television from 1978 to 1981. There is no doubt that the connection of his narrative with the stage and the screen is profound and most knowledgeable. Perhaps the Señor Pequeño episodes can be read as a dramatization of many Chileans' hopes, their expectations of a socialist utopia that proved to be illusory and disastrous when confronted with the reality of a dependent economy and a powerful bourgeoisie. They also serve as a counterpoint to the other stories told in this novel about the last months before the military uprising, stories that could become too sentimental, since the *compañeros* and *compañeras*, as the supporters of the government call themselves, are mostly generous, hardworking, and good-humored, while Arturo, who does not join the left, is exemplarily punished with the failure of his egotistical ambitions.

Señor Pequeño brings to the text the world of the circus and neighborhood birthdays, rented costumes, and the momentary splendor of makeshift stages. This sideshow also introduces a different sort of violence, one that is unrelated to politics and derives from the conventions of film noir and hard-boiled detective

novels. Skármeta thus avoids closing his world around an ideology by always leaving an opening for surprises, creative disorder, and humor that is more conducive to the compassionate smile than to the belly laugh. As he explained in his interview with Andrew Bush, for him "lo esencial de la realidad es ser impenetrable" (what is essential about reality is to be impenetrable). In *Soñé que la nieve ardía*, a writer called Antonio appears briefly and speaks about literature's task in a revolutionary society:

*ahora todos los escritores vamos a ir por todas partes para que no quede una palabra sin escribirse, pero que no se hiciera ella la ilusión (le habla a una muchacha, Susana) de que la cosa fuera tan chancaca, de que escribir un poema era pura cosa de irle sacando punta al lápiz y ahí estamos, de que il cuore va bene y que la cosita romántica y ya, pero que hay que liberar la expresión, que es una especie de picardía.*

now all writers are going to go everywhere so that not even one word remains without being written, but she should not be of the illusion (he tells a young woman, Susana) that it would be nice and easy, that to write a poem was just a matter of sharpening your pencil and we are ready, with *il cuore va bene* and the cute romantic stuff and so on, but we must liberate our capacity to express ourselves, and this will need some cunning.

This liberated style takes the form of a rebellion against "literature" as an elitist pursuit, concerned mostly about itself. Skármeta has a story to tell—the coming of age of young men and the social upheaval of Chilean democracy—and he uses for this purpose a language that can be heard on the radio, in the streets, or in a corner bar. Yet that language is transmuted, its creativity teased out by a gentle irony and freed from the quotation marks or italics that would have accompanied it in most other novels.

In 1980 Skármeta published *No pasó nada* (also published as *Nopasónada* and translated into English as *Chileno*), a novella that must be considered among the best of his narrative works. As he explains in the prologue of the Plaza y Janés edition, this novel grew from his observation of Chilean and other Latin American exiles in Europe. On the one hand are the grownups, "despojados de su ámbito natural, desprovistos de sus utopías" (stripped away from their natural surroundings, impoverished without their utopias), living in melancholy ghettos and unable to blend into the countries where they now lived. On the other hand, their children easily learn the new language, become streetwise, learn the international pop culture, and fall in love, creating for themselves a new life that is free of nostalgia and that enables them to navigate the double code of two cultures. The story itself is told in the first person, with the sort of hip but also denuded international language that a sixteen-year-old boy, Lucho, taken from his mother-tongue country, would naturally have.

Lucho plays a rough soccer game, and when reprimanded for his fouls, he just exclaims, "No pasó nada," ("nothing has happened," or "no problem"), an expression that becomes his nickname. The story is partly about growing up, partly about male friendship and bonding. Lucho is walking his girlfriend home when he is accosted by some beer-drinking adolescents. Defending himself, he kicks one of them, Hans, knocking him to the ground in great pain and eventually causing Hans to go to the hospital. Hans's brother calls Lucho on the telephone and arranges a meeting to seek revenge. After a prolonged fight, they become friends. By the end of the story Lucho also has found a new girlfriend. These relatively small events acquire a modest epic dimension, as Lucho's success in overcoming of loneliness, threats, and challenges appears as an undiluted triumph.

Skármeta spent a month in Nicaragua, invited there by Peter Lilienthal to write a script for a movie that eventually was filmed but that also became his next novel, *La insurrección* (1982; The insurrection). It tells the story of the successful Sandinista uprising against the Somoza dictatorship, which culminated on 19 July 1979 with the defeat of the dictator. Ricardo Gutiérrez Mouat has characterized this novel as a national romance without irony, because the novel unhesitatingly celebrates the victory of the people of the town of León over the military and the dictator. But Gutiérrez Mouat and Monique Lemaître have also indicated that this novel presents a portrait of women that questions the traditional Latin American machismo, from which the left and the guerrillas are not exempt. Donald Shaw has called *La insurrección* not only a revolutionary novel but also a feminist one (*Nueva narrativa latinoamericana*).

There are many unforgettable characters here: the mailman Agustín, who instead of delivering letters, which mostly bring bad news, throws them into his chicken coop; Vicky Menor, who overcomes prison and rape with her integrity and love intact; the oldest woman in town, who participates actively in the uprising; and, above all, the whole town, as it falls into step to battle the oppressor. The novel incorporates not only the entire town of León, but also is hospitable to texts of other writers, among them a "sampling" and reframing of stories by Ariel Dorfman (in chapter VI, "En familia," which is drawn from from *Cría cuervos*), García Márquez (*La mala hora*, for the episode in which the military strongman visits the barber), plus a whole chapter, XXV, that transcribes Pablo Neruda's "Oda al fuego." The long monologue of a mother who lost her son in battle (which appears in chapter XXVIII) is a modified version of the transcript of an actual interview with a Nicaraguan woman. In this, Skármeta is reaching back to an important tradition of Latin American testimony, of which some of the most famous examples are Miguel Barnet's *Biografía de un cimarrón* (1966; *Biography of a Runaway Slave*, 1994) and Rigoberta Menchú's *Me llamo Rigoberta Menchú* (1983; *I, Rigoberta Menchu: An Indian Woman in Guatemala*, 1984). *La insurrección*, as a collective work, re-creates in the text the experience of solidarity that is described within it. And, as Borges famously demonstrated in his story "Pierre Menard, autor del *Quijote*," a text even if reproduced identically, but in a different context and time, can be new and original.

In the early 1980s, while in Berlin, Skármeta was planning to write a long novel that would encompass the whole of Chilean history. From this project, a small section of the text acquired a life of its own, when the possibility arose of writing and directing a new movie. Skármeta proposed the subject of a postman in a small coastal town, Isla Negra, where the most famous inhabitant and the only one to receive much mail was the poet Pablo Neruda. First, Skármeta wrote a play in two acts, and this was performed in a theater in East Berlin, directed by Alejandro Quintana. It was also produced as a radio drama by the Sudwestfunk and published in German. Skármeta later produced the movie in Portugal with German funds, with a faithful portrait of Neruda provided by Roberto Parada and an excellent actress, Marcela Osorio, as Beatriz González. It obtained several prizes, among them the Premio del Jurado y del Público of the Huelva Festival, in Spain, in 1983. It also won a prize in Biarritz and Burdeos, and the Adolf Grimme Preis in Germany, as well as the Georges Sadoul prize for the best foreign film of the year in France.

In 1985, two years after the production of the movie, the novel, which had already been translated and published in four other languages, was published in the United States, in Spanish, by Ediciones del Norte. In 1989 the Italian publisher Garzanti suggested changing the name of the novel to *Il postino di Neruda,* and Skármeta approved. His second film, based on *Ardiente paciencia,* was directed by Michael Radford in 1994, and starred the Italian actor Massimo Troisi as Mario and Philippe Noiret as Neruda. For this joint French, Italian, and Belgian production, the producer used the new title, and subsequent Spanish editions of the novel have been called *El cartero de Neruda.* The movie was nominated for five Oscars and obtained one for best music. The haphazard and multinational story of this masterpiece, its lack of a clear original, its existence in several versions and in different genres, tells not only the story of exile but also of myth. Ultimately the story does not depend on a single representation, but has become by now a cumulative interpretation of the encounter of an adolescent with poetry, love, and politics.

In 1969, when the novel begins, Mario Jiménez delivers letters to Neruda and starts asking questions about poetry that amuse the great poet. After buying Neruda's *Odas elementales,* Mario discovers that words can be used as metaphors, and he seeks to learn from the poet. The postman has a practical reason to be interested in the power his customer has with words, since Mario is in love with a young woman, Beatriz (the echo of Dante is unavoidable), but does not know how to approach her. Metaphors will allow him to lose his inhibitions and conquer Beatriz, under the distrustful eyes of her mother, who suspects metaphors are thinly veiled realities. The novel has its epiphanies: Neruda receives the Nobel Prize, and Mario and Beatriz make love. It has its moments of sadness: the poet must go away to serve as an ambassador in Paris, and ends up missing his coastal home, inspiring Mario to capture

some of the sound of the sea in a cassette recorder. Finally, it has its tragic conclusion: the end of democracy, the death of the poet, and Mario's apprehension by the secret police. While the novel ends with the word *amargo* (bitter), the overarching feeling is one of melancholic celebration, of solidarity, love, friendship, poetry, and nature. Elemental forces, such as the sea and fire, are powerfully invoked with texts sampled from Neruda himself, and they have a permanence that the dictatorship could not claim. Ultimately, poetry is the provider of life, and endures. The novel has been translated into over twenty-five languages.

Skármeta's involvement in the filming of *Ardiente paciencia* was part of a long series of activities in the area of cinematography. As scriptwriter, he wrote *La victoria* (1973), a film directed by Peter Lilienthal; *Es herrscht Ruhe im Lande* (The whole country is at peace), also directed by Lilienthal (1975); *Aus der Ferne sehe ich dieses Land* (I see this country from a distance), based on *No pasó nada* and directed by Christian Ziewer (1977); *La insurrección,* directed by Lilienthal (1979); *Die Spur der Vermißten* (The trail of the missing), directed by Joachim Kunert (1980); *Si viviéramos juntos* (1982; If we all lived together), a documentary about Chilean artists residing in Europe; and his own film version of *Ardiente paciencia,* which he directed in 1983. In 1998 he had a new script ready for production, entitled *Dry Manhattan.* He has also written numerous radio plays, among them versions of *Ardiente paciencia* and *Match Ball.* He has recently finished a film adaptation of Isabel Allende's *Eva Luna.* Skármeta's radio play *Die Suche* (The search) received the European Broadcasting Union Prize in 1977.

Skármeta's next novel, *Match Ball* (1989), is unusual when compared to his earlier work. The main character is Raymond Pabst, in his early fifties, a Harvard graduate and successful medical doctor who, married to an aristocratic German woman, lives in Berlin. He falls in love with a pubescent and upcoming German tennis star named Sophie Mass, following her on the road and abandoning his patients and family. A rival emerges in a young Spanish admirer of Sophie, but she strings both suitors along and shares her affection and sexuality with both of them, to the great irritation of her lovers. The novel is clearly reminiscent of Nabokov's *Lolita,* but this echo is only one of the many intertextual allusions of which this metaliterary novel is chock-full. In an interview with Marcelo Coddou, published in the *Revista Iberoamericana*, Skármeta has said that he wrote this book to prove his versatility and to write a novel that would not be immediately read in Europe and the United States as a Latin American exotic product ("Sobre *Match Ball*: Entrevista a Antonio Skármeta").

When Pabst is finally brought to jail for seducing a minor, his lawyer tries to present a defense based exclusively on examples garnered from literature in which the heroes are mature men who fall in love with adolescent women. Yet in Pabst's case there is more going on than simply a reiteration of some previous case, since Sophie remains somewhat of a mystery. In a very well-done study, Carlos Schwalb has succeeded in showing that Sophie belongs to a new reality, one that books up to now could not have described (" 'Fagocitos' postmodernos: El poder asimilador de las imagenes en la novela *Match Ball* de Antonio Skármeta," *Revista Chilena de Literatura* 53, 1998). Pabst, just like Alonso Quijano, also a man in his fifties who has been seduced by literature, turns out to be an anachronism, and Gordana Yovanovich has rightly compared him to an aged *pícaro* (*Play and the Picaresque*, 1999). Therefore, Pabst, in his Faustian enterprise of becoming younger to conquer a young woman and the pleasures of youth—to live fully, a pursuit most characters in Skármeta's narrative share—ends in jail and failure, reduced to a pale reiteration of literary models that have the devouring power of a Platonic ideal. He is a shadow of the great tragic and canonical heroes, but at least he has the consolation of having attempted to live his passion to the hilt.

For its international and upper-class setting, its lack of social concerns, and its amusing if not especially creative language, this novel appears eccentric to Skármeta's narrative. And yet there are numerous points of contact, continued obsessions at work: the powerful drive of sex, the pleasure of sports, the delight in poetry, and a jaundiced look at the upper class and its frivolity. The title has been subsequently changed for the Spanish edition to *La velocidad del amor* and in English to *Love-Fifteen*.

His return to Chile allowed Skármeta to write three more novels, of which two have been published, *La boda del poeta* (1999; The poet's wedding) and *La chica del trombón* (2001; The girl of the trombone). The first one tells the story of a 1913 wedding on the island of Gema, off the coast of Malicia, places that are transpositions of the island of Brač, from whence Skármeta's grandparents emigrated to Chile. From the first sentence readers know they are in the terrain of the fabulous, of understandings that have been filtered through many tellings and imaginations: "Érase una vez un tiempo pleno en una lejana isla de Costas de Malicia" (Once upon a time life was whole and perfect in a faraway island of the Malice Coast). The novel starts out with the planning of one wedding that is briefly told and that ends tragically, followed twenty years later by a second wedding, this time of Alia Emar and Jerónimo Frank, a rich store owner. This second wedding is thrown into confusion by the intervention of Esteban Coppeta, who is in love with Alia, and by the announced arrival of an Austrian punitive expedition, coming to quell the island's independent youth. The transition into modernity is marked by the arrival of films and powerful electric lights, while the miraculous belfry of the island's church connects the town to a mythical past. The defending forces murder eleven soldiers from the Austro-Hungarian army, bringing about a savage reprisal against the island, including the rape of Alia Emar. Esteban and other companions escape to Italy and then to Chile.

Donald Shaw sees in this novel a darkened view of the world for Skármeta, since here the revolutionary spirit is not redemptive and love is not a solution. He finds in *La boda del poeta* a parody of romantic motifs and disenchantment with politics, since the rebellion of the islanders and the Austrian repression are presented as aimless violence, without glory and ultimately disastrous. Yet the novel also expresses a heartfelt nostalgia for a lost paradisiacal world, where everything was simultaneously smaller, more accessible, and familiar, and larger, magnified by gossip and credulity. This novel received the Altazor Prize in Chile for the best novel of the year, and in Italy it was awarded the Grinzane Cavour Prize 2001, given to the best novel published in Italian translation.

*La chica del trombón* is loosely connected to *La boda del poeta*. Esteban Coppeta and many other of his countrymen now live in Antofagasta. There a jazz trombonist brings a baby to Esteban, supposedly the granddaughter of Alia Emar. This girl, named Magdalena, soon shows that she is not only strong—she will later ride a motorcycle—but also independent, obsessed with leaving Antofagasta for New York. Her attempt to escape, and Esteban's wild swim to the ship where she is a stowaway, provide a memorable first and emblematic scene of the strong bond that unites them, and also of Magdalena's conflicted relations with her country of adoption. After the family goes to Santiago, Esteban dies, and his wife strikes a friendship with one of Magdalena's teachers, Sepúlveda, a socialist who will connect them with Allende and the socialist campaigns. Magdalena changes her name to Alia Emar, just as her best friend, Palacios, changes his to York New.

As the country is not content with its subordinate and mediocre economy and the prevalence of social injustice, the children in their games play that they are elsewhere, where they can be someone else, creating a gap between expectations and reality that each day becomes more painful, but also more powerful. The relationship of Magdalena/Alia and Palacios develops into love, while in a parallel action, in the background, Allende finally mounts a successful campaign. The novel playfully introduces several related stories, one of an aging boxer, another about a car that will come to represent the years of Allende's campaign. Gabriela Mistral and Pablo Neruda each have cameo roles, serving as examples of how the international dimension that Alia and Palacios desire is not necessarily opposed to a deeply rooted Chilean existence.

Palacios becomes an actor and is invited to go to the Actors' Studio in New York, the culmination of all his dreams. Yet, in a moving decision, he decides to stay with Alia, who is about to have his baby. The novel closes with a joyous celebration of Allende's victory, which readers know will turn into a nightmare three years later. This is the great adventure that Palacios and Alia had dreamed of, with its jubilation and its pain. Most of the novel is told from the point of view of Alia, presenting once more one of the strong and resourceful women that appear so often in Skármeta's writing.

"La composición" (The composition), a short story first published in 1978, in which a schoolchild realizes the representatives of the dictatorship want to obtain information by having the class write about what their families do each evening, and therefore modifies reality to protect his parents, was published in the year 2000 with illustrations by the Spanish artist Alfonso Ruano. It received several honors, among them the best illustrated book by the Catalan Publishers Association.

In Chile, Skármeta has been the director and principal animator for *El show de los libros* (The book show), a program that has been on the air since 1992 and quickly became extremely popular, in spite of its late hour, for its entertaining mix of brief segments containing interviews, dramatizations, readings, and every other aspect relating to books. The jazzy and offbeat rhythm; the unconventional, even irreverent tone; and, above all, the presentation of the world of books as both joyful and meaningful brought the program lasting success. It received Spain's Ondas Prize in 1996 for the best Latin American cultural program, as well as the 1997 Midia Prize, awarded to the best program on Latin American television. It was still being produced in 2001. In 1999 Skármeta began producing *La torre de papel*, a cultural program styled after *El show de los libros*. This new show is broadcast by People and Arts in the United States, Spain, Portugal, and Latin America, including Brazil. Since April 2000, Skármeta has served as the Chilean ambassador to Germany and lives in Berlin.

## SELECTED BIBLIOGRAPHY

### Primary Works

#### Novels and Short Stories

*El entusiasmo.* Santiago de Chile: Zig-Zag, 1967. (Contains "La Cenicienta en San Francisco," "El joven con el cuento," "Al trote," "Entre todas las cosas lo primero es el mar," "Días azules para un ancla," "Nupcias," "Relaciones públicas," and "Mira donde va el lobo.")

*Desnudo en el tejado.* Havana: Casa de las Américas, 1969. (Contains "El ciclista del San Cristóbal," "A las arenas," "Una vuelta en el aire," "Final del tango," "Pajarraco," "Basketball," and "Desnudo en el tejado.")

*Tiro libre.* Buenos Aires: Siglo Veintiuno Argentina Editores, 1973. (Contains "Pescado," "El último tren," "Uno a uno," "Primera preparatoria," "Enroque," "Balada para un gordo," "El cigarrillo," "París," and "Profesionales.")

*El ciclista del San Cristóbal.* Santiago: Quimantú, 1973. (Contains "Basketball," "Mira donde va el lobo," "El ciclista del San Cristóbal," "Relaciones públicas," "Nupcias," "La Cenicienta en San Francisco," "A las arenas," and "El cigarrillo.")

*Novios y solitarios.* Buenos Aires: Losada, 1975. (Contains "De la sangre al petróleo," "Relaciones públicas," "La Cenicienta en San Francisco," "Nupcias," "Mira donde va el lobo," "El ciclista del San Cristóbal," "A las arenas," "Una vuelta en el aire," "Final de tango," "Pajarraco," "Basketball," "Desnudo en el tejado," "La pareja," "La llamada," and "Hombre con el clavel en la boca.")

*Soñé que la nieve ardía.* Barcelona: Planeta, 1975.

*No pasó nada.* Barcelona: Pomaire, 1980. Also *No pasó nada y otros relatos.* Santiago: Pehuén, 1980. (Contains "No pasó nada," "De la sangre al petróleo," "La llamada," and "Hombre con el clavel en la boca." The prologue of the edition in Barcelona: Plaza y Janés, 1996, pp. 7–19, is notable. There is a student edition geared to the English-speaking market in Grínor Rojo and Cynthia Steele's *Ritos de iniciación.* New York: Houghton Mifflin, 1985.)

*La insurrección.* Hanover, N.H.: Ediciones del Norte, 1982.

*Ardiente paciencia.* Hanover, N.H.: Ediciones del Norte, 1985. (Published in later editions by Plaza y Janés as *El cartero de Neruda.*)

*Match Ball.* Buenos Aires: Sudamericana, 1989.

*La Cenicienta en San Francisco y otros cuentos.* Santiago: Editorial Andrés Bello, 1990.

*Uno a uno. Cuentos completos.* Buenos Aires: Editorial Sudamericana, 1996. (Contrary to the title, it includes only "Uno a uno," "La Cenicienta en San Francisco," "París," "Profesionales," "El último tren," "Nupcias," and "La llamada.")

*La boda del poeta.* Madrid: Editorial Debate, 1999.

*La composición.* Illustrations by Alfonso Ruano. Caracas: Ediciones Ecaré, 2000.

*La chica del trombón.* Madrid: Editorial Debate, 2001.

## Edited Books

*Joven narrativa chilena después del golpe.* Clear Creek, Ind.: American Hispanist, 1976.

*Poesía joven de Chile.* Munich: Federlese, 1985.

*Santiago, pena capital: Narraciones.* Santiago: Documentas, 1991.

*Música ligera/Obertura de Antonio Skármeta.* Santiago: Grijalbo, 1994.

## Essays

"El motivo de la oposición campo-ciudad en dos dramas chilenos: *La canción rota,* de Antonio Acevedo Hernández y *Pueblecito,* de Armando Moock." *Revista Chilena de Literatura* 1:31–41 (1970).

"Trampas al perseguidor: La narrativa de Cortázar." *Mapocho* 20:33–44 (1970).

"La burguesía invadida: Egon Wolff." *Revista Chilena de Literatura* 4:91–102 (1971).

"Vargas Llosa, el último realista." In *Asedios a Vargas Llosa.* Edited by Luis Díez. Santiago: Editorial Universitaria, 1971. Pp. 204–208.

"Carlos Droguett: Toda esa sangre." In *La novela hispanoamericana.* Edited by Cedomil Goic. Valparaíso: Ediciones Universitarias, 1973. Pp. 161–175.

"La novísima generación: Varias características y un límite." *The American Hispanist* 1, no. 3:4–6 (1975).

"Tendencias en la más nueva narrativa hispanoamericana." In *Enciclopedia Labor.* Barcelona: Planeta, 1975. Pp. 751–771.

"Nueva narrativa chilena después del golpe." *Casa de las Américas* 112:83–94 (1979).

"Narrativa chilena después del golpe." In *Primer coloquio sobre literatura chilena (de la resistencia y el exilio).* Edited by Poli Délano. Mexico City: UNAM, 1980. Pp. 53–74.

"Al fin y al cabo, es su propia vida la cosa más cercana que cada escritor tiene para echar mano." In *Más allá del Boom.* Edited by David Viñas. Buenos Aires: Folios, 1981. Pp. 263–85. (Also in *Texto Crítico* 7:72–89 [1981], and in *Del cuerpo a las palabras: La narrativa de Antonio Skármeta.* Edited by Raúl Silva Cáceres. Madrid: LAR, 1983. Pp. 131–147. Also published as "Una generación en el camino." *Nueva Sociedad* [Caracas] 56–57:133–46 [1981].)

"*La insurrección:* Gambito nicaragüense de film y novela." *Texto Crítico* 7, no. 22–23:90–95 (1981).

"Perspectiva de los novísimos." *Hispamérica* 10, no. 28:49–64 (1981).

"Words Are My Home." *Review* 27:8–10 (1981).

"IV: La Generación de 1940–1969; VII: La Generación de 1939 en adelante: Bolivia, Chile, Perú." In *Narrativa hispanoamericana 1816–1981: Historia y antología.* Edited by Angel Flores. Mexico City: Siglo XXI, 1982. Pp. 9–12, 11–19.

"Suprarrealidad e irrealidad en los cuentos de Juan Rulfo." In *Spanien und Lateinamerika.* Edited by Carlos Segoviano and José M. Navarro. Nuremberg: Deutscher Spanischlehrer Verband, 1984. Pp. 779–792.

"La nueva condición del escritor en el exilio." *Araucaria de Chile* 19:133–141 (1988).

*Heimkehr auf Widerruf: Chile im Umbruch? Politische Reflexionen.* Munich: Piper, 1989. (Contains essays written originally in German, and others translated from Spanish.)

"Chile 1989: Bretón en el hipódromo." *Hispamérica* 55:107–112 (1990).

"Europe: An Indispensable Link in the Production and Circulation of Latin American Cinema." In *New Latin American Cinema.* Edited by Michael T. Martin. Detroit, Mich.: Wayne State University Press, 1997. Pp. 263–269.

"*Lobos y ovejas*: 20 años de un clásico de los años sesenta." *Revista Chilena de Literatura* 51:117–119 (1997).

## Translations

*Chileno.* Trans. by Hortense Carpentier. New York: Morrow, 1979.

*The Insurrection.* Trans. by Paula Sharp. Hanover, N.H.: Ediciones del Norte, 1983.

*I Dreamt the Snow was Burning.* Trans. by Malcolm Coad. London: Readers International, 1985.

*Watch Where the Wolf Is Going.* Trans. by Donald L. Schmidt and Federico Cordovez. Columbia, La: Readers International, 1991.

*Burning Patience.* Trans. by Katherine Silver. St. Paul, Minn.: Graywolf Press, 1987. Also published as *The Postman.* New York: Miramax Books, 1995.

*Love-Fifteen.* Trans. by Jonathan Tittler. Pittsburgh: Latin American Literary Review Press, 1996.

*The Composition.* Trans. by Elisa Amado. Illustrated by Alfonso Ruano. Toronto: Groundwood Books, 2000.

## Movies and Documentaries

*La victoria.* Script by Skármeta; directed by Peter Lilienthal. 1973.

*Es herrscht Ruhe im Lande.* Script by Skármeta; directed by Peter Lilienthal. 1975.

*Aus der Ferne sehe ich dieses Land.* Based on Skármeta's *No pasó nada*; directed by Christian Ziewer. 1977.

*La insurrección.* Script by Skármeta; directed by Peter Lilienthal. 1979.

*Die Spur der Vermißten.* Script by Skármeta; directed by Joachim Kunert. 1980.

*Si viviéramos juntos.* Script by Skármeta. 1982.

*Ardiente paciencia.* Script and direction by Skármeta. 1983.

*Abschied in Berlin/Despedida en Berlín.* Directed by Skármeta; based on his short story "Pescado." 1984.

*Pequeña revancha.* Based on Skármeta's short story "La composición"; directed by Olegario Barrera. 1985.

*In der Wüste.* Based on Skármeta's short story "A las arenas"; directed by Rafael Fuster Pardo. 1986.

*Il Postino.* Script by Skármeta; directed by Michael Radford. 1994.

*Dry Manhattan.* Script by Skármeta; based on his short story "A las arenas." Not yet filmed.

*Eva Luna.* Script by Skármeta. Not yet filmed.

## Secondary Works

### Critical and Biographical Studies

Bumas, Ethan. "Metaphor's Exile: The Poets and Postmen of Antonio Skármeta." *Latin American Literary Review* 21, no. 41:9–20 (1993).

Dorfman, Ariel. "¿Volar? Un estudio en la narrativa de Skármeta y Edwards." *Revista Chilena de Literatura* 1:59–78 (1971).

Flores, David. " 'Nupcias': Sentido y forma en su contexto literario." *Revista Chilena de Literatura* 50:5–19 (1997).

Lemaître, Monique. *Skármeta: Una narrativa de la liberación.* Santiago: Pehuén, 1991.

Mickett, Carol. "Alternative Image: An Interview with Antonio Skármeta." *New Letters* 65, no. 2:70–84 (1999).

Rojo, Grínor. "Una novela del proceso chileno: *Soñé que la nieve ardía,* de Antonio Skármeta." *Cuadernos Americanos* 212:238–261 (1977).

———. "Notas sobre *Chileno!* de Antonio Skármeta." *Texto Crítico* 7, no. 22–23:96–108 (1981).

———. "Explicación de Antonio Skármeta." *Hispamérica* 13, no. 37:65–72 (1984).

Schwalb, Carlos. " 'Fagocitos' posmodernos: El poder asimilador de las imágenes en la novela *Match Ball* de Antonio Skármeta." *Revista Chilena de Literatura* 53:117–123 (1998).

Shaw Donald. *Antonio Skármeta and the Post Boom.* Hanover, N.H.: Ediciones del Norte, 1994.

———. "Skármeta: Contexto e ideas literarias." *Revista Iberoamericana* 60, nos. 168–169:1051–1061 (1994).

———. "Antonio Skármeta." In *Modern Latin-American Fiction Writers, Second Series.* Edited by William Luis. Detroit, Mich.: Bruccoli Clarck Layman, 1994. Pp. 299–306.

———. *The Post-Boom in Spanish American Literature.* Albany: State University of New York Press, 1998.

———. *Nueva narrativa latinoamericana: Boom, Posboom, Posmodernismo,* 6th ed. Madrid: Cátedra, 1999.

Silva Cáceres, Raúl, ed. *Del cuerpo a las palabras: La narrativa de Antonio Skármeta.* Madrid: LAR, 1983.

Sklodowska, Elzbieta. "*Ardiente paciencia* y *La casa de los espíritus:* Traición y tradición en el discurso del post-boom." *Discurso* 9, no. 1:33–40 (1991).

Yovanovich, Gordana. "La unificación de lo personal y lo social en una novela postmoderna de Antonio Skármeta." *Alba de América* 12, nos. 22–23:227–233 (1994).

Yovanovich, Gordana. *Play and the Picaresque: Lazarillo de Tormes, Libro de Manuel, and Match Ball.* Toronto: University of Toronto Press, 1999.

*Interviews*

Blanc, Mario. "Antonio Skármeta: Cuentos y novelas." *Chasqui* 18, no. 2:64–78 (1990).

Bush, Andrew. " 'Señalar las discrepancias': Rosario Ferré y Antonio Skármeta hablan de Cortázar." *Revista de Estudios Hispánicos* 21, no. 2:73–87 (1987).

Coddou, Marcelo. "Sobre *Match Ball:* Entrevista a Antonio Skármeta." *Revista Iberoamericana* 56, no. 151:579–582 (1990).

Colvile, Georgiana M. "An Interview with Antonio Skármeta." *Latin American Literary Review* 20, no. 39:27–36 (1992).

Cortínez, Verónica. "Polifonía: Entrevista a Isabel Allende y Antonio Skármeta." *Revista Chilena de Literatura* 32:79–89 (1988).

García-Corales, Guillermo. "Entrevista con Antonio Skármeta: De *El entusiasmo* a *Match Ball.*" *Chasqui* 22, no. 2:114–119 (1993).

Gras Balaguer, Menene. "Entrevista con Antonio Skármeta." *Insula* 41, no. 478:1, 14 (1986).

Larraín, Ana María. "Escribo con una vibración ondulatoria." In *Escritores de América: 31 entrevistas publicadas en "Revista de Libros" de El Mercurio.* Edited by María Elena Aguirre. Santiago: Editorial Los Antes, 1993. Pp. 185–193.

Pagni, Andrea. "Entrevista con Antonio Skármeta." *Discurso Literario* 5, no. 1:59–73 (1987).

"The Book Show." In *The Writer in Politics.* Edited by William H. Gass and Lorin Cuoco. Carbondale: Southern Illinois University Press, 1996. Pp. 35–59.

Xaubet, Horacio. "Antonio Skármeta y la generación hiperrealista: Entrevista." *Revista de Estudios Hispánicos* 23, no. 2:75–99 (1989).

Walter, Monika. "Interview with Antonio Skármeta." *Weimarer Beiträge: Zeitschrift für Literaturwissenschaft, Ästhetik und Kulturtheorie* 24, no. 12:72–87 (1978).

# Mario Vargas Llosa

## (1936– )

### Sara Castro-Klaren

Before the publication of *La ciudad y los perros*, (1963; *The Time of the Hero*, 1966), the realm of Peruvian letters was dominated by the towering twentieth-century figures of José Carlos Mariátegui, César Vallejo, and José María Arguedas. Mariátegui had laid the foundation for a debate about the constitution of Peru as a modern national state. In doing so, he established the idea that Peru's indigenous masses were the crucial factor for understanding not only Peru's history but also the possibility of a future national literature. Both of these notions, the constitution of the nation's citizens and the character of its literature, will, with varying emphasis, remain a point of contention for Vargas Llosa through out his literary and political writing.

Mariátegui achieved a position of great influence among Peruvian and Latin American intellectuals during his lifetime, with the publication of his review, *Amauta* (the Inca poets and court intellectuals), and his watershed book, *Siete ensayos de interpretacion de la ralidad peruana* (1928; *Seven Interpretative essays on Peruvian Reality*, 1971). Vallejo, a contemporary of Mariátegui, did not achieve a similarly influential role during his lifetime. Considered one of the greatest poets of the Spanish language, Vallejo's importance grew in intensity and prestige only after his premature and dramatic death in 1938. His poetry, prose, and theater were fundamentally iconoclastic and deeply innovative. In his writing and with his actions, Vallejo achieved an unprecedented degree of aesthetic and political commitment to an inviolable human solidarity. His poetry constitutes a devastatingly original critique of the limits of language and the possibility of meaning itself that is only comparable to Jorge Luis Borges's later work with philosophy and textuality. Vallejo's work became an unavoidable point of reference, a beacon for all future writing in Peru and throughout Latin America.

In less overtly reflexive and self-asserting ways, Arguedas continued, philosophically and politically, in the footsteps of the two great men who preceded him. His best novel, *Los rios profundos* (1958; *Deep Rivers*, 1985), established Arguedas as the major Peruvian novelist just at the time when Mario Vargas Llosa was seriously beginning his career as writer. Arguedas's fictional world expanded considerably after the publication of this autobiographical novel. He departed from incisive recollections of life in Andean villages and moved on to a portrayal of the contradictions of the large urban centers in coastal Peru. Arguedas rendered, in a tender and moving realism, the vision of the world of the Quechua people, whether they remained in their ancestral communities as heirs to the process of destructuration and resistance that the

Spanish conquest inaugurated, or they migrated into the various enclaves of modernization and waves of disarticulation that the history of Peru has entailed.

It is within this context of national literature that Mario Vargas Llosa began his literary career as an adolescent in 1952, with the staging of his play *La huída del inca* (The flight of the Inca) in Piura. He resided in this small northern Peruvian town during his high school years, in the household of his maternal grandfather. Vargas Llosa was born on 28 March 1936 in Arequipa, in Southern Peru. His mother, Dora Llosa, belonged to a relatively well-to-do family of old aristocratic name and connections that included a former president of the republic, José Luis Bustamante y Rivero, as well as a former embassador to the League of Nations, Victor Andres Belaunde. His father, Ernesto J. Vargas, came from a less well-established provincial family, which at the time had entered the ranks of Lima's middle class. His mother and father separated before the time of his birth. His young mother rejoined the benevolent, patriarchal household of her father in Arequipa, and soon after Mario's birth the whole Llosa clan moved to Cochabamba, Bolivia, where the head of the family had secured a position as the administrator of a cotton plantation near Santa Cruz. There Mario spent his entire childhood. To this day Vargas Llosa regards this period in his family's history as a paradise. In his recent memoirs, *El Pez en el Agua* (1993; *A Fish in the Water,* 1994), Vargas Llosa recounts his experiences during that time: "In that house I was pampered and spoiled to extremes that made a little monster out of me." The whole Llosa clan doted on Marito, as the young man was affectionately called, and the little pet grew up reading the best of children's literature. The family told him that his dad was dead, and little Mario's nightly bedtime ritual included saying a prayer for his deceased dad and planting a kiss on his father's photograph. Consequently, the most important day of Vargas Llosa's life was established beforehand; it would be the day, many years later, when the future author was already attending school in Piura, when his mother took him to meet his father. Mario quickly discovered how very much alive his authoritarian father was, indeed.

To say that in 1950 Vargas Llosa's parents reconciled is both an under- and an overstatement. In *A Fish in the Water,* Vargas Llosa vividly recollects the traumatic experience of being kidnapped by his own parents. At the age of twelve, the young adolescent was abruptly and forcibly removed from the warmth of the grandfather's house, from his school, and from his friends when his parents tricked him into an ice cream date that evolved into a drive to the beach and ended in a dreary, tiny house in Lima. The terror of this experience is fictionalized in a similar episode in the life of one of the cadets in *The Time of the Hero.* Forced to live practically as a prisoner in the house of his jealous, strict, and abusive father, Vargas Llosa's life turned into a nightmare. The years spent under his father's vigilance were surely formative ones that gave rise to a rebel, a man who came to believe that reading and writing books were acts of revenge, a sort of insurgency, an act of infinite defiance, for reading quietly in his room was one of few forbidden activities that the adolescent could "get away with."

Dissatisfied with his son's attachment to his mother and his mother's family, and with the boy's passion for reading, the father decided to send the fourteen-year-old to the Leoncio Prado Military Academy. This period marks Vargas Llosa's second great encounter with pain and violence. The young man who was to become the author of brutal tales discovered, in these troubled years, the relentless physical, verbal, and psychological abuse that was woven into the routines of the Academy's daily life. Doubtless, he suffered a profound alienation, but he also decided to survive, to move beyond the negative influence of his father and the limitations imposed by institutions such as the military academy. As he would put it, he found the courage to search for freedom, and in that search he sustained himself through myriad acts of self affirmation.

Like Mariátegui and many other Latin American writers, the young man, aspiring to be an intellectual, began to feel an acute need to leave the confines of his native country and search for wider horizons in Europe. Even before finishing his college degree (he majored in literature at the University of San Marcos, in Lima), he began looking for a fellowship that would permit him to travel to Paris, and to live there for some time.

Partly because his father refused to support his literary studies, and also because it is common for Latin American university students to take part-time work,

Vargas Llosa had to find jobs in order to support himself during his days as an undergraduate student. He worked for Panamerica Television as a newscaster, and he was a local reporter for several Lima newspapers. His writing ability was recognized almost everywhere, from the advertising copy he wrote for magazines, to the news bulletins he composed for radio and print media. His most productive and intellectually significant association of this period, however, was his employment as research assistant with the well-known and well-connected Peruvian historian, Raul Porras Barrenechea. The young man and the senior professor found that they had a great deal in common, from their interest in history as a tale of human action and adventure to their style of doing things. To this day Mario Vargas Llosa continues to express, in essays and interviews, his admiration for Porras's understanding of history and his gratitude for Porras's intellectual tutelage on questions of history and literature.

The aristocratic Porras had become practically an institution in Lima, and under his sponsorship Mario Vargas Llosa gained access to fellowships. Porras also may have actually saved Vargas Llosa's life. When the young man was only nineteen years old and still in college, he married his own aunt, Julia Urquidi, a divorcée who was thirteen years his senior. His father was outraged, and it was Porras who convinced Vargas Llosas's father not to kill his son for this offense.

As soon as he got his degree from San Marcos, Vargas Llosa secured a grant to pursue doctoral studies in Spain. According to his accounts and those of his first wife (*Lo que Varguitas no dijo*, 1983; *What Varguitas Didn't Say*, 1983), he spent most of his time reading as well as writing and rewriting the manuscript of what was to become his first novel, *The Time of the Hero*. The novel attempted to capture his recollections of his two years spent as an adolescent in the Leoncio Prado Military Academy in Lima. When the scholarship ended, he did not feel ready to return to Peru. His desire to spend an extended period of time in Paris was only greater now that he was in Spain and so, without much money, he and Julia moved to Paris in 1959.

Vargas Llosa's journalistic experience, earned during his college years in Lima, served him well in Paris. Despite his limited command of the French language, he was able to find work as a radio journalist at the Radio Television Française, which aired a program in Spanish. Parallel to, and often closely interwoven with his fictional writing, Vargas Llosa has produced an enormous body of journalism. He has written and continues to write for major newspapers and magazines in Latin America, the United States, and Europe, covering both current political and cultural events. The contribution of this journalistic output cannot be underestimated when considering Vargas Llosa's early achievement of international stature.

His early experience with the military as an overtly ideological institution, together with his initiation into the arresting show of the world that his involvement in journalism and broadcasting offered him can, in retrospect, be seen as major influences on the fictional world that Vargas Llosa depicts: the spectacular clash between strict, opposing codes and the tragi-comic theater that breaking such codes produces. Soap-opera plots, war, organized violence, and wanton, dysfunctional families, fanaticism of all sorts, infanticide, incest, murder, prostitution, and sexual aberrations, appear and reappear in all of his novels and plays. Life is presented as a sordid carnival in his many novels, from his first, *The Time of the Hero*, through his most recent, including *La fiesta del chivo* (2000).

The cafe life that Vargas Llosa had so thoroughly enjoyed in Lima was, of course, an even greater temptation in Paris. However, he was not about to loose sight of his goal—writing novels—and so he exerted great self-discipline and avoided the dissipation that was the common fate of third world intellectuals in Paris at the time. Instead, he devoured the French classics and read French erotic literature. He also wrote, cut, reorganized, and polished the manuscript of his first novel, which was provisionally entitled *Los impostores* (*The impostors*). Though he was still a young and unknown writer, he had already received minor awards. In 1958 he had won a short trip to Paris as the first-place prize for one of his short stories in a contest sponsored in Peru by the *Revue française*. A year later he had won the Leopoldo Alas Prize, one of Spain's many literary awards, for his first collection of short stories, entitled *Los jefes* (1959; *The Cubs and other Stories*, 1979).

The young writer struggled with a manuscript that grew ever larger and, as it grew, become more technically demanding. Aware of the technical complexity as well as the scandalous potential of the novel's pornographic contents, Vargas Llosa nonetheless set out to find a publisher. A chance meeting with Carlos Barral, one of the owners of the influential Catalan publishing house Seix Barral, decided the fate of the manuscript. The book was retitled *La morada del héroe* (The home of the hero). Soon after submission it was not only accepted for publication, but it also won, by a rare unanimous vote, the annual Spanish Biblioteca Breve Prize, administered by Seix Barral. This prize had never before been awarded to a Spanish American writer, and it was the first of many major international prizes to be won by Vargas Llosa in his long career as novelist.

The novel was once again retitled and was published in 1963 as *La ciudad y los perros,* and it first appeared in English translation in 1966. It quickly rose to the crest of the "new" wave of Latin American novels that were gaining international prominence. Vargas Llosa was the youngest of a handful of writers to be associated with the international critical and marketing success of Latin American literature during this period, which has been called the "Boom." The early 1960s also saw the publication in Spanish and translations of Julio Cortazar Rayuela (*Hopscotch*, 1963), Carlos Fuentes (*The Death of Artemio Cruz*, 1962), and Gabriel García Márquez (*One Hundred Years of Solitude*, 1967).

When the novel was read in Lima, few were unmoved by its artistic and political reach. The impact of the tale and the details of political and sexual violence and corruption catapulted Vargas Llosa into instant fame. The author's open and fully fleshed adoption of the Sartrian concept of "literature as fire," as a kind of permanent state of insurrection against the established order, was not lost on the military, however. They ordered that all available copies of the book be burned in the main quad of the Leoncio Prado Military Academy.

The novel was now a scandal. It had clearly achieved a political and very public reading, thus confirming Vargas Llosa's thesis, also derived from Sartre, about the political power of writing. The wealth of technical innovations that it incorporated made it a dazzling text and established it as a challenge to any reader. The story it told was gripping. It appealed to a very basic motive for reading literature: the desire to experience, in the realm of the imagination, a human drama in which we can become deeply involved for philosophical, political, emotional and aesthetic reasons and pleasures.

In retrospect, it is evident that this novel constitutes the thematic as well as rhetorical touchstone of Vargas Llosa's narrative oeuvre. In his later novels he would repeat, change, enhance, add, and drop aspects of the narrative structure of this novel; but the skeleton of this first book would always be visible as the basic structure of his narrative and political imagination. While one can clearly see changes in Vargas Llosa's novelistic trajectory, through tragedy, satire, humor, history, and autobiography, each and every text is anchored on the same narrative, political, and rhetorical assumptions, convictions, and practices. In contrast to the established literary tradition, which employed a realism respectful of the categories of linear time, a consistent and continuous point of view, identifiable omniscient or first-person narrators, and narrative unity, *The Time of the Hero* can be seen as an exploration, even a flaunting, of a variety of avant-garde narrative rhetorical devices associated with the trail-blazing work of James Joyce and especially the William Faulkner of *Light in August* (1947). Most of these techniques affect the nature of the point of view, the identity of the narrator, and the tone and register of the language created for each of the many stories buried within the main frame of the narrative.

In *The Time of the Hero,* as well as in Vargas Llosa's later novels and plays, the novelist mixes at will, and without warning, interior monologue, omniscient narration, individual memories recounted in conversation, flashback, straight reporting, and the quick give-and-take of two or three speakers in conversations that actually take place in overplayed sequences. Sudden shifts in point of view and the withholding of the identity of the narrator combine to produce a first impression of narrative chaos. Not only are the identities of many narrators withheld until later in the novel, but information about plot elements is also denied to the reader, who thus finds the task of linear reading transformed into an exercise in puzzle solving. The reader is no longer the passive recipient of the solution to a mystery that the author has worked out beforehand. Instead, the reader must be willing to search for the key to a murder or to some other secretly held fact that is buried deep within the entrails of the novel, just as many of the characters in the story must do.

Storytelling by Vargas Llosa is not centered on the question "What happened?" or even "Why did it happen?" but rather on "How did it happen?" for it is not always possible to know why things happen, especially when it comes to violence. Nonetheless, the novel always rewards the reader with the pleasure of seeing a pattern emerge out of chaos, and in the end all the plot elements can be tied together. However, wanton, senseless violence, as both the motivation of the story and as its concluding mechanism, looms greater and greater as the author's ouevre develops over the span of fifty years. It becomes particularly disturbing in *Lituma en los Andes* (1993; *Death in the Andes*, 1996), where no explanation, other than human nature, is offered for horrific and almost gratuitous acts of violence.

The story line of *The Time of the Hero*, as it will be with most of his novels, is actually very simple. At the command of Jaguar, the leader of a school gang, a cadet in a military academy, a young man named Cava, steals the questions for an examination. Though it is witnessed by another cadet (El Esclavo), Cava's crime is not discovered by school officials until much later. The honor code operating among the cadets keeps them silent. Finally, under siege from a number of contradictory desires, El Esclavo reports the theft, and an investigation follows. The investigation uncovers much more than just the theft of an examination. It shows that many things are rotten to the core in an institution that has become far removed from its educational goals and has dedicated itself to initiating its cadets into the most cynical *machismo* (an exaggerated code of masculinity in honor-bound societies). Later, while on maneuvers, Jaguar kills the informer. Although the murderer is fingered by another cadet (Alberto, who writes pornographic tracts), the military authorities decide that, in view of what has been uncovered, the best thing is to pretend that nothing irregular has happened. This declaration has an indelible and irreversible effect on the understanding of life gained by the cadets, who are thus, after their last year of "education," returned to society.

The combination of a simple story line with a complex narrative rhetoric may appear paradoxical.

However, the narrative dwells exhaustively on the portrayal of a violent society, which is mirrored in both the military academy and Jaguar's gang. The boys' fears, when faced with the saturating violence of the academy, are portrayed from several perspectives and from differing distances. Their violent and cynical responses are revealed by a juxtaposition of scenes, the effect of which is reminiscent of the speed and illusion of authenticity found in cinéma vérité. In an orgiastic scene involving the rape of a hen, for example, the statements of different voices succeed each other with such speed and detailed precision that the reader is forced to forget the need to know who is narrating or who is doing what to whom, for he feels himself assaulted and overwhelmed by the "facts" that compose the repulsive scene in which the boys engage. The complications in the novelistic form as it is embedded in this narrative are constantly bulldozed under by relentless action. In *The Time of the Hero*, as well as in Vargas Llosa's other novels, something urgent and insufficiently portrayed is always happening, either in the inner world of a character or in the social world.

*The Time of the Hero* tells the story of six adolescent boys, sent by their parents to finish high school in a military academy named for a young hero in Peruvian history: Leoncio Prado. The parents' choice of a military academy is predicated on their need to have their sons become educated men. Drawn from different geographical, class, and racial sectors of Peru's society, the boys suddenly find themselves thrown together. While they seem ready to interact across the barriers that separate them and to accept the leveling the comes from their shared membership in a military organization, they nevertheless remain apart, each trapped in the identities that have been assigned to them by the society outside the walls of the academy. Only in the social phenomenon of Vargas Llosa's later historical novel, *La guerra del fin del munda* (1981; *The War of the End of the World*, 1984), will it be possible to see people breaking beyond the barriers of their former lives and identities and coming together to form a new community. Only in that later novel's depiction of the historic rebellion in Canudos do the oppressed overcome the internalized barriers, imposed by the dominant class, that serve to keep them apart. In *The Time of the Hero*, alienation grows in the light of day, in the halls and patios of the military academy. At night, it assumes fantastic guises.

Because of Vargas Llosa's own professed admiration for Jean-Paul Sartre's existentialism, this novel has often been read as an existentialist account of young men acting in rebellion against the corrupt established order, in order to gain their freedom and dignity. Within this reading, it has also been necessary to accept that none of the boys, not even the "poet," Alberto, gain any freedom, for they all succumb to the rules of organized violence and fratricidal war and learn to exploit them as an essential part of survival.

The social organization at the military academy, which serves as a mirror image of family life in the city, is based on the assumption that the hierarchical authority embodied in the rules of machismo prevails even if it requires a denial of concrete reality. In this world there is only one rule: the strong dominate. All members of society take their place in the pecking order, with Jaguar, allegorically, at the top and El Esclavo at the bottom. An individual must accept, endure, or return the violence that envelops him. When ordered, he must steal an examination, drink urine, rape or be raped, lick another boy's boots. He must, in turn, exert equal violence upon those below him in order to keep his place in the hierarchy, or he risks falling further down. This behavior ensures that the individual is "protected" by the system that thus allows his survival, just like any fascist organization.

If the system's justification is survival, murder would seem to be an intolerable transgression of its rules. Yet the epilogue of the novel shows that despite Alberto's hypocritically heroic stance in identifying Jaguar as the killer of El Esclavo and in revealing many other ghastly deeds, the system will use any means at its disposal to uphold the illusion that the order it sustains resembles justice or education. Therefore, for the convenience of those who are invested in the status quo, and this includes Alberto's "good" family, all parties agree to pretend that nothing has happened to violate the rules of justice or truth. Lieutenant Gamboa, the only person who insists on acknowledging the truth, is banished. Thus the breached circle closes, having made "impostors" of all the cadets, having certified to the inauthenticity of everyone involved. The character of Gamboa is the prototype for a later Vargas Llosa

character, Lituma, who is sent to investigate a crime in *Death in the Andes*.

The brutal and numbing reality that Vargas Llosa depicts in *The Time of the Hero* is physically organized around two socio-spatial centers: the city and the academy. Between these two poles, the past and present of the lives and needs of the novel's adolescent characters become articulated. In *La casa verde* (1966; *The Green House*, 1968), his second novel, Vargas Llosa attempts to bridge even wider spatial, temporal, and social gaps. The action of the novel takes place in a distant part of the sparsely populated Peruvian jungle and in the desert coastal town of Piura. The web of the plot spans three generations and includes more than thirty-four characters.

Just as his experience at home under the arbitrary rule of his father and his years in the military academy became an unforgettable memory for Vargas Llosa, his early adolescence in Piura also serves as a wellspring of actors and events that emerge in the ever-present autobiographical slant of his novels. His youthful firsthand discovery of the Peruvian jungle enables him to introduce yet another sort of ecosystem into his novelistic world. According to *La historia secreta de una novela*, (1971; A novel's secret story), when he began working on *The Green House* he was attempting to fashion into narrative form his obsessive memories of a legendary whorehouse on the outskirts of Piura. As his imagination elaborated this site of the forbidden, however, the memories of stories he had heard about a Japanese bandit and rubber trader in the Amazon jungle kept disturbing his narrative of the desert. The need to write about the jungle became pressing, but Vargas Llosa was aware that his firsthand acquaintance with the jungle was brief and that Latin American letters already boasted a long and rich tradition of works set in the Amazonian basin. He thus set out to read everything he could find that was set in the South American tropics, including decidedly third-rate stories and novels, in order to both improve the mimetic capacity of his language and to avoid the pitfalls into which many of his predecessors had fallen, particularly their overuse of descriptive detail. He also understood the need to rewrite the story of one of his characters, a Japanese outlaw named Fushia, in light of insights gained from his reading of Joseph Conrad's *The Heart of Darkness*.

The result was a composite of five major stories, bridged at most times by the lives of two characters: Sergeant Lituma and Bonifacia. These two characters move in inverse directions, traveling between Piura in the desert to Santa Maria de Nieva in the Amazon jungle. The narrative begins at a river near Santa Maria de Nieva. A group of Spanish nuns, supported by a detachment of soldiers, are attempting to kidnap native girls in order to "save them" by forcibly separating them from their families and culture and enrolling them in a Catholic boarding school. From this point on, the narrative begins to move backward, chronicling a tale of violence, misery, and sexual serfdom. The novel tells of the rape of a blind girl, Antonia, by old Anselmo, a musician in Piura; the sale of the adolescent Lalita into concubinage with the Japanese outlaw Fushia, who operates somewhere along the border between Peru and Brazil; the flight of Bonifacia from the nuns' convent into matrimonial servitude with Sergeant Lituna; Fushia's death in a leprosarium; and Bonifacia's final descent into the Piura whorehouse known as La Casa Verde.

In this novel Vargas Llosa attempts the seemingly impossible: to bring together many disparate fragments of the lives of people who move in a territory cartographically conceived as Peru. Four institutions—the army, the church, the family, and the whorehouse—become the vehicles by which the lives of these characters establish relations of mutual exploitation and violence. Life is depicted as an ever-changing adventure in pain, humiliation, and general abjection that people can never hope to understand, much less to change.

In *The Green House* Vargas Llosa exercises his passion for the telling of the adventure, a legacy of his early reading of the works of Alexander Dumas. Bonifacia and Sergeant Lituna hold the novel together inasmuch as they, directly or indirectly, maintain relations with all the other characters, but the adventures of Fushía and Anselmo have proven more captivating to some readers. However, it is Lituma and Bonifacia who reappear in later works by the author. Both are key protagonists in the play *La chunga*, (l986), and Lituma plays a role in both *Quién mató a Palomino Molero?* (1986; *Who Killed Palomino Molero?*, 1989) and *Lituma en los Andes* (1993; Death in the Andes, 1996).

No matter what the ambitions or desires of the characters, they all end their lives miserably. The women, who in Vargas Llosa's novels are modeled on the stereotypical roles of women in patriarchal societies, hope only to attach themselves to men who will not be too cruel, offering in exchange all the services a female (body) can provide within or outside the household. For the men, the higher their ambition, whether for money or for power, the greater their fall.

Even simplified, the story is not easy to summarize. At the outset, Bonifacia has already been kidnapped by the nuns and raised in their school. When a fresh group of captured girls arrives, Bonifacia, now a young woman, can no longer collaborate in their imprisonment and lets the girls go, against the commands of the nuns. For this she is berated and expelled from the convent. Having nowhere to go, she finds asylum in the home of Lalita, Fushia's former sex slave, who takes Bonifacia in as a sort of servant. Lalita is now living with Nieves, the sergeant who originally helped the nuns kidnap the Aguaruna girls and who polices the Amazonian rivers on behalf of the Peruvian army.

When Lalita was an adolescent, her mother practically sold her to the rubber king, Fushia. The ambitious Japanese outlaw took the pubescent girl to his river island, and bedded her there. In those days, Fushia controlled a pirate army with which he raided the native villages to steal rubber and women. Lalita escaped from Fushia's orgies and sadism and now lives in contentment with Nieves. Lalita introduces Bonifacia to Nieves's friend, Sergeant Lituma. They marry. Upon his discharge from the army, Lituma returns to Piura, where his new wife, Bonifacia, is found to be exotic, and Lituma's buddies begin to call her Selvática (Wildflower). She soon has to support them all by working at La Casa Verde, where she meets Chunga, the current owner of the whorehouse and daughter of the mysterious Anselmo and the orphan girl Antonia. The story ends with the revelation that Fushia had contracted leprosy while living on his island and has subsequently lost control over his army of pirates. He is finally seen floating down the river in the kind company of Aquilino, who is taking him to a leprosarium.

To narrate this complex group of stories, each replete with adventures of its own, Vargas Llosa uses the plethora of narrative devices he so innovatively deployed in his first novel, and comes up with additional innovations as well. He once again exploits the device of starting to tell the story after the critical event has already taken place. From this position his narrator can move forward with a present-tense narrative or backward through reminiscence, in order to recall the events that led up to the point when the narrative began. In *The Green House,* Vargas Llosa introduces a narrative device he calls "telescopic conversations," which place two characters in conversation about past events. However, each time a person speaks, the statement he or she makes is picked up by a character participating in yet another conversational situation, this one occurring within the story being narrated by the original conversationalists. The result is a double-helical narrative structure in which the author superimposes one distant set of events over another, and sets both of them to rest upon yet another, distant set of events, achieving something reminiscent of the rabbit-hole effect of Lewis Carroll's *Alice in Wonderland.*

Vargas Llosa also superimposes one point of view over another, one temporal sequence over another, one social or geographical space over another. The reader is presented with a series of fragments or puzzle pieces that must be fitted together in order to gain a sense of the linear sequence or spatial correspondence by which all the events can acquire meaning. The characters are almost never presented in solitary introspection. It is in conversation, in relation to another person, that they attempt, in the telling of "what happened," to understand, though without much success, the sequence of events that have come to constitute their lives. This is a daring strategy, but necessary for dealing with the diversity of historical elements included in *The Green House.*

*The Green House* stands as an important achievement precisely because Vargas Llosa has succeeded in interweaving all these disparate, and at times competing, narrative traditions and realities. He creates something new that stands above the sum of its fragments. In the speed of the shifts, similar to the speed of film, the distances and limits separating the parts become imperceptible. The reader learns to adjust and readjust his focus in order to see or rather to establish a pattern of meaning, and the narrative pace, like an avalanche, overwhelms the reader's resistance, enticing him to

read on even though he has yet to secure key pieces of information. The reader learns to enjoy the sheer speed of the narrative, the cuts, the shifts, the surprises, and the joy of discovery.

In spite of the sense of fragmentation and the torrential movement of the story, a close scrutiny of the novel shows that the author has taken care to organize his material with scrupulous rigor. The novel is divided into four books and an epilogue. Each book in turn contains a prologue and three or four chapters, and each chapter is further divided into sequences, five in the first two books and four in the last two. In contrast to the arrangement in *The Time of the Hero,* the length of the chapters and number of sequences in *The Green House* are carefully regulated, as they will be almost all of the author's subsequent novels and plays.

The critical reception of this novel was characterized by almost universal acclaim. Vargas Llosa was celebrated as one of the group on Latin American intellectuals who believed in the coming of a liberating and progressive socialism for Latin America. The hope was to overthrow Peru's dependence on (foreign) capital and to challenge the negative, clientelist (imperialist) influence of the United States. By this time Vargas Llosa had visited revolutionary Cuba and participated as judge in several of the prizes awarded by Casa de las Américas, Cuba's premier publishing house. *The Green House* was quickly translated into some twenty European languages, and in 1967 it was selected for the Rómulo Gallegos Prize.

While working on his next novel, Vargas Llosa refurbished an older manuscript, *Los cachorros* (1967; *The Cubs and Other Stories,* 1979). With this truculent story about a young man who loses his sexual organ when bitten by a dog, Vargas Llosa returns to the theme of adolescents growing up in a society dominated by the principles of machismo. Any possible heroic stance is wasted in the rituals of initiation into manhood that are required of the upper-class boys who do not have to attend the brutal military academy.

With *Conversacion en la Catedral* (1969; *Conversation in the Cathedral,* 1974), originally published in two volumes, Vargas Llosa returns to Lima, the part of Peru that he knows best, and to his own experiences in that city during the time of Manuel Odría's dictatorship (1948–1956). As the author makes abundantly clear in his memoir, this novel is indeed autobiographical. Once again we see the portrayal of a young man facing choices that will define his life irreversibly. Vargas Llosa returns to the problem of authenticity, to the Sartrean problems of commitment and freedom. He describes the places and social groups that he knows intimately—places that he frequented during his university years when plotting against the dictator and participating in several communist and Trotskyite groups. Such activism was a way in which Vargas Llosa and his friends could engage their awakening to history, and the novel depicts the asphyxiating and corrupt political atmosphere of the period. The authenticity of Vargas Llosa's portrayal is not so much based on research as it is on his enormous capacity for recall of detail, names, and meetings, and on his evocation of the personal quirks and styles of each of the characters who, almost without exception, are based on the lives of the author's own friends and acquaintances. This can be clearly seen by reading the novel side by side with *El pez en el agua*.

*Conversation in the Cathedral* takes place, on one narrative level, during a four-hour conversation between Santiago Zavala and his father's former servant, Ambrosio. The conversation takes place in a miserable and fetid little bar in Lima, and it serves as an enveloping structure within which many other conversations between other characters take place. The days of the Odría regime are evoked from many points of view and points in time, in an effort to identify how and why Santiago Zavala has become Zavalita, a failed rebel, a failed writer, and a stillborn hero.

Once again Vargas Llosa minimizes the presence of the omniscient narrator to almost imperceptible level. The narrative task is given instead to the characters, who often narrate without properly identifying themselves, creating many opportunities for the reader to become confused. It is often difficult to tell, for example, when Ambrosio is talking to Santiago, whom he addresses as Niño, or when he is talking to his master and homosexual partner, Don Fermin. The conversational structure in *Conversation in the Cathedral* works in the manner of stacked Russian dolls or Chinese boxes, for the outer casing of the conversation between Santiago and Ambrosio at times contains as many as six other simultaneous conversations. These conversations within conversations, located at different times and involving different people, unite in a polyphonic performance. Each time a character speaks, often not in response to the statements made by the person he or she is physically addressing, a bit more of the "how" of the story becomes clear to the reader.

Santiago accidentally runs into Ambrosio, his father's former chauffeur. While drinking at the bar called The Cathedral, Santiago probes Ambrosio's recollections in order to confirm his suspicion that Ambrosio is, in fact, the murderer of La Musa, a well-known whore. As the past is evoked, the voices of the other participants in the plot begin to tell their part in the story. Don Fermin Zavala, a well-to-do aristocratic industrialist, has become a senator in the parliament of the dictator. Though as an aristocrat despises the lower-class military and its front man, Odría, he nonetheless collaborates with them in order to maintain certain very important privileges for his business enterprises and for the well-being of his family.

Santiago, his favorite son, has been growing uncomfortable with the political and socioeconomic structure of the country, and especially with the compromising role his family and class play in the sociopolitical process. In the subsequent rejection of his class and especially his father, Santiago decides to attend San Marcos, a public university attended by members of the rebellious lower classes, who hope that education will help them to gain political power. There he considers the idea of joining the "revolutionary" critics of the status quo, whose dissatisfaction he fully shares. These young men and women see no alternative to the political process but to become active Marxists and communists. This is a step that Santiago can never take, according to him, for he lacks faith in any ideology.

Nevertheless, Santiago plays along as a member of a clandestine cell. The cell's existence is discovered by the dictator's secret police, for they have placed Santiago's father's own home and telephone under surveillance. Santiago is detained along with all the other members of the clandestine cell, but because of his father's connections with the regime, he is freed in less than twenty-four hours. The other students are processed and punished. Santiago once again feels that his father has robbed him of an opportunity for heroism. Instead of gratitude he feels rage and resentment. He moves out of the paternal household and finds a job as a reporter for the criminal page of a local newspaper, *La Crónica*. In this occupation he learns firsthand about the life of degradation and violence common to many Peruvians. Santiago gets ever more anxious and pessimistic about his future, which he begins to understand as inescapable failure.

Through Ambrosio's narrative we, along with Santiago, learn that Cayo Bermúdez, the minister of the interior, is the man who ordered the tap on Santiago's father's telephone, because of his political alliance with Don Fermín. Much like Vladimiro Montesinos, head of the Secret Police during Alberto Fujimori's presidency (1990–2000), Cayo Bermúdez maintains the illusion of a normal home, in which he keeps two whores, La Musa and Queta, for his own amusement and for the amusement (and later blackmail) of the upper-class men who support or benefit from the dictator's regime.

The two whores have a lesbian liaison, which Cayo Bermúdez enjoys as a voyeur. This theme will eventually achieve full development in *Elogio de la Madrastra* (1988; *In Praise of the Stepmother*, 1990) and *Los cuadernos de don Rigoberto* (1997; *The Notebooks of Don Rigoberto*, 1998). Don Fermín not only accepts invitations to Don Cayo's parties but one day rides off with Don Cayo's childhood friend and now chauffeur, Ambrosio. This huge and humble black man becomes, despite of his own heterosexuality, Don Fermín's homosexual partner. The fact that Don Fermín's homosexuality is publicaly known in the world of pimps and whores is discovered by Santiago when he investigates the truth about La Musa's murder. He overhears Queta tell his editor at *La Crónica* that Ambrosio killed La Musa in order to protect Don Fermín from blackmail.

Once again Vargas Llosa brings together a veritable human multitude to populate his novel. As in *The Green House*, most of the characters, and therefore most of the flavor, tenor, and vision of the world that marks their speech, come from the urban lower classes. The linguistic practices that mark this type of discourse had thus far been represented in literature only sporadically, and had almost never been treated as a source of literary language. While it is true that Vargas Llosa is not a linguistic innovator, as Vallejo was in both prose and poetry, he has nevertheless made a new and important contribution by employing popular linguistic practices in his novels as a way to empower the mimetic quality of his creations.

This novel tells its sordid and scatological tale at a galloping rhythm. One shocking discovery follows another equally pornographic or violent scene. It is difficult to say in which of Vargas Llosa's novels the reader's revulsion, and curiosity, are most intensely and deftly engaged. In *Conversation in the Cathedral*, however, the central character, Santiago Zavala, is someone with whose needs and goals the reader can comfortably identify. Unlike the boys in *The Time of the Hero*, and unlike the revolting and pathetic Fushía, Santiago is clean, educated, handsome, seductive, and perhaps sincere. His enterprise is presented in a positive light. Santiago's character is positioned at the crux of the most important questions facing Latin American nations, then and now: Is freedom possible? What are the interconnections of individual freedom and economic well being? Can economic democracy be achieved with or without a political (socialist?) revolution? These questions were particularly pressing at the time when the novel was published, for it was already apparent that the Cuban revolution was not providing the answers that so many had hoped for.

This novel remains the only text by Vargas Llosa in which the possibility of a heroic character is provided. The novel openly presents itself, formally and historically, as an autobiography. For these and other reasons that have to do with the fact that we indeed recognize the fictional world as Peru itself, the failed search of Santiago Zavala and his transformation into the gray Zavalita (who turns out to be a very unsympathetic character) the story touches the reader's sense of empathy more intensely than the stories of other, equally alienated characters in Vargas Llosa's fiction.

In *Conversations in the Cathedral* the characters are immersed in evil. Everything contributes to the infernal atmosphere. Nothing, not even love, such as Ana's for Santiago, mitigates the fallen state. Quite to the contrary, everything is divisive, everyone is suspicious. Race separates, politics divide, kinship disconnects, money keeps people apart, social position isolates. The relation of victim to oppressor is the only one possible, and this relation, as in *The Time of the Hero,* is mediated by violence. *Conversation* is perhaps Vargas Llosa's most bitterly pessimistic novel before he turned to literary criticism and the cultivation of parody, and this shift coincides with his break with the Cuban revolution over the case of the dissident writer Heberto Padilla.

Between 1969 and 1975, Vargas Llosa published a number of critical texts. Most of these and the many others, including political pieces, that he has published since, were later collected in three volumes entitled *Contra viento y marea* (1986, 1986, 1990; Against wind and tide). Aside from numerous interviews and essays in which he speaks of his narrative art, Vargas Llosa's first influential piece of literary criticism appeared in 1969 as a prologue to the first modern Spanish edition of the Catalan chivalric novel *Tirant lo Blanc* (first Spanish edition, 1511), by Joanot Martorell. One of the curious effects of Vargas Llosa's criticism has been to provide other critics with concepts and suggestions for interpreting his own fiction. In earlier essays and interviews he had made the point that Martorell's novel, like his own work, attempts to capture reality on more than one plane. He is impressed by Martorell's stress on storytelling and adventure as the essential ingredients of the novel, in opposition to moral disquisitions and political concerns. Although Vargas Llosa lived and breathed the development of the French *nouveau roman* (new novel) in Lima and Paris, he never found himself in tune with this literary experiment, whose stated goal was to write novels that lacked characters or action, or both. In his later book on Gustave Flaubert, *The Perpetual Orgy: Flaubert and "Madame Bovary"* (1975; English translation published in 1986), Vargas Llosa refers to practitioners of the *nouveau roman*: "Even though almost all of them [Alain Robbe-Grillet, Michel Butor, and Claude Simon] bored me, with the exception of Beckett . . . who also bored me but somehow I felt the boredom justified, I always liked them because they openly proclaimed the importance of Flaubert for the modern novel."

Vargas Llosa's literary criticism has been amazingly consistent. He focuses on writers whose work he admires, among whom he numbers such authors as Gustave Flaubert, George Bataille, Joseph Conrad, Jorge Luis Borges, Jean Paul Sarte, Albert Camus, Gabriel García Márquez, César Moro, the Marquis de Sade, José María Arguedas, Isaiah Berlin, Leon Tolstoy, and even anthropologists such as Bronislaw Malinowski, Levi-Brulh, Claude Levi-Straus, and James G. Frazer. Reading them has had a profound influence on his own writings. Ernest Hemingway and William Faulkner belong in the category of strong misreadings. Their novelistic strategies gravitate heavily on Vargas Llosa's own possiblities and desire for innovation. In addition to his prolific output as novelist, journalist, and critic, Vargas Llosa has also co-authored books: one with Oscar Collazos and Julio Cortázar, another with Martín de Riquer, and a third, with Angel Rama, in which he discusses García Márquez and the problematics of the Latin American novel.

A close reading of his literary criticism demands that it be taken in conjunction with what he has said in numerous interviews about his own work, because these texts are cut of the same cloth. In interviews given to enthusiastic and friendly critics such as Elena Poniatowska, José Miguel Oviedo, and Cano Gaviria, to mention just three early instances, there appears a tight coincidence of interest and critical concepts between what Vargas Llosa says of his own novelistic practice and his critical appreciation of the work of the writers he admires passionately, even when he has misread them. For Vargas Llosa the novel, as the narrative form capable of integrating all possible other discursive modalities, achieves its maximum and essential expression in the work of Flaubert. For the author of serious and parodic novels, historical, pornographic, and political narratives, the novel is the supreme genre that feeds on the rotting flesh of the past or individual experience, "cannibalizing" all objects and experiences, and in doing so feeds the imagination while it opens up unforeseen possibilities for freedom and subversion.

For Vargas Llosa the novel, and literature itself, is inextricably linked to the "system of freedom that is the greatest contribution the West has made to all of humanity" (*Contra viento y marea,* vol. III). Vargas Llosa here understands freedom as the individual's capacity to rebel against all manner of things: familial, institutional, or state oppression; the literary system; established novelistic forms; intellectual establishments; and moral prohibitions. He also believes in the capacity of the novel to represent reality in the fullest sense. He calls this the "totalizing vocation" of the novel and sees Flaubert's *Madame Bovary* (1857) and García Márquez's *One Hundred Years of Solitude* (1967) as prime examples of this idea.

Although he does not acknowledge having read Henry James's prologues to his novels, a systematic study of Vargas Llosa's critical approach, shows that his ideas owe much to James's theory of the novel and to the systematization of James's thought developed by the American school of New Criticism in the 1960s, the same period when Vargas Llosa was studying for his doctorate in literature in Spain. Michael's Bakhtin's theory of the novel, especially his ideas on the novel's dialogic structure and its capacity to reinscribe and recirculate all manner of discourses, would appear to be central in Vargas Llosa's own sense of the novel as a "cannibalistic" and "totalizing" genre. Bakhtin was popularized in France in the 1960s by Julia Kristeva, but Vargas Llosa does not reference Bakhtin's work. With respect to ideological or propagandist ends, Vargas Llosa feels that the novel is, or ought to be, truly ideologically disinterested, representing all aspects of life with equal passion and verisimilitude. This view, however, seems to be at odds with the Sartrean notion that "literature is fire," which, given the political thrust of Vargas Llosa's more recent novels, *Historia de Mayta* (1984; *The Real Life of Alejandro Mayta*, 1986) and *Death in the Andes*, he does not seem to have quite left behind.

With his book on Flaubert, Vargas Llosa modifies his outlook on the relation of literature to society. He repudiates his understanding of Sartre and begins to think that Camus, of the two existentialist writers, better represents his own thinking. The emphasis is no longer on insurgency. Revenge now appears paramount. Writing as revenge is a view that he continues to espouse even today: "For Flaubert, who throughout his life repeated that he wrote in order to take revenge on reality, it was his negative experiences that in the end proved to be more stimulating artistically" (*The Perpetual Orgy*).

Vargas Llosa's book on García Márquez is basically the doctoral thesis that he presented in Madrid. In this book he develops the concept of the novelist's personal obsession, or demons, as the creative source of the form and content of the text. In this view, all novels would be keenly and demonically autobiographical. Vargas

Llosa carefully traces the relation of materials in the novelistic text to psychological, physical, or intellectual events in the writer's life, plainly breaking with two of the chief tenets of New Criticism: the autobiographical fallacy and the "autonomy" of the text.

For biographical material, Vargas Llosa draws heavily on his (then) close friendship with García Márquez. In the case of Flaubert, he quotes amply from the thirteen volumes of Flaubert's correspondence and relies on Sartre's book on Flaubert, *L'idiot de la famille* (1971–1972). Vargas Llosa's critical analysis of Flaubert retains a number of the concepts he had advanced for the reading of García Márquez, including the idea of the "total" novel, narrated by means of "mutations in the narrator," consisting of interwoven stories organized as "communicating vessels," all deployed within a combination of "planes of reality," and "times." These concepts, along with the notion that the modern novelist, that is, the true heir to Flaubert, sets himself up as a sort of god within the fictional text, have their source in Flaubert's own works.

In a certain way, Vargas Llosa's critical work clears the air and opens up the possibility of a new departure for his fictional work. After pondering and learning from the work of the two masters of revenge, wondrous imagination, and humor (García Márquez and Flaubert), Vargas Llosa published his own first parodic work. In *Pantaleón y las visitadoras* (1973; *Captain Pantoja and the Special Service*, 1978) he returns to three themes from his previous work: the military, the whorehouse, and the Peruvian jungle. The reality depicted in this new novel is as scatological as in his other books. This time, however, the humor that he so carefully analyzed in García Márquez is clearly evident, for example in Pantaleón Pantoja's efforts to determine the number of orgasms necessary to satisfy the army troops stationed in the Amazon basin. The humor is definitely raunchy, and it relies on two principles: exaggeration and the exploitation of the perception of class and cultural differences.

Much of what Pantaleón does is funny because he is a *cholo* (a lower class mestizo) and a *huachafo* (a person of the lower class who erroneously imitates the lifestyle of the upper, Europeanized classes) who misreads the instructions given to him by his social and cultural "superiors." If he were more aware, as an upper-class person would have been, he would not have accepted the mission he is given. He would realize instead that it is a cynical assignment, set up for failure. Pantaleón is the grotesque counterpart of Lieutenant Gamboa, who also falls prey the army's fraudulent self-representation as a serious institution bound by an honor code. Within the context of the internalized post-colonial imagination Pantaleon is funny because, through his failed attempts to imitate his social "betters," he exposes their own lack of authenticity. Laughter ensues because he enables us to perceive the gap between the authentic and its imitation, on the one hand, and from his failed attempts at imitation, which reveal the inauthenticity of the original that is being imitated.

As the story unfolds, the reader becomes aware of the fact that the author has marshaled many kinds of narrative modes, some of which are more closely linked with the social sciences than with fiction. Dialogues, letters, radio and print journalism, commentaries, official memoranda, and scientific and statistical studies chronicle the adventures of Pantaleón as he tries to accomplish his mission: to provide a satisfactory sexual service for the troops stationed in the jungle. Although happily married to Pochita, Pantaleón is promoted to captain and receives his orders for a most unusual assignment: he must pose as a civilian but think as a military man and organize the delivery of prostitutes to the barracks in the jungle. Having calculated the number of prostitutes required, the number of soldiers to be serviced, and the number of "lendings" that each man requires to satisfy his sexual needs, he proceeds to organize his service. Pantaleón and his crew arrive at each army post by boat or plane, secretly but punctually. There he has the men line up, so that each may receive equal benefit from the "lending" service.

Eventually Pantaleón, in his statistical and experimental zeal, decides that he ought to try out his own product. He falls prey to the jungle aphrodisiacs and the charms of "La Brasileña," one of his coveted prostitutes. His determination to succeed by literally following instructions keeps him going despite his growing doubts about his task. Eventually the secret of his work is revealed, and the neighboring villages demand his services for themselves or denounce those same services. At the same time, a strange cult, given to

infanticide and other excesses, begins to gather momentum in the jungle and Pantaleón becomes involved with it. His final undoing comes when a radio broadcaster named Sinchi (a name that means "warrior" in Quechua) denounces the prostitution service to his outraged and hypocritical middle-class audience. The army disowns Pantaleón. He is demoted and sent to remote part of the highlands where, in another story (Death in the Andes) and many years later, Lituma and Gamboa will live out yet another harrowing tale of violence.

With Captain Pantoja and the Special Service, Vargas Llosa blazes new trails, both in literary technique and in tone and tenor, and he prepares the parodic background for his subsequent novel, La tia Julia y el escribidor (1977; Aunt Julia and the Script Writer, 1982). A critical controversy arose over Pantaleon and Vargas Llosa's perceived reversal of his earlier view of literature as criticism and subversion against oppression. He responded to this controversy by arguing that through the parodic mode he continued to criticize an obviously distorted and unjust society.

Both of Vargas Llosa's parodic novels unabashedly embrace the huachafo and the corny linguistic and social modalities of the Peruvian middle and lower classes as seen from above, from the security of aesthetic authority. Pocha's letters, Sinchi's radio communiques, the preaching of the cult's leader, the army communiques—all are parodic imitations of some invisible but "correct" model of letter writing or news broadcasting, as the case may be. Yet we know, of course, that Pocha's letter and La Brasileña's obituary are indeed Vargas Llosa's own writing, his devilishly clever stylizing of the huachafo.

With Aunt Julia Vargas Llosa returns to autobiography, but with comic, distancing twists. Here he tells the story of nineteen-year-old Marito who, while working as a newscaster in a radio station, falls in love with and marries his thirty-two-year old aunt. This story of incestuous love is told in chapters that alternate with the story of Pedro Camacho, a Bolivian soap-opera writer whose intertwined plots of excess and madness has the entire listening population mesmerized. Camacho is a veritable writing machine, as is Marito, who holds down seven writing jobs. Marito marvels at Camacho's capacity for invention, for keeping straight the several plots of the soaps that he writes simultaneously, and for sheer physical stamina. As if alluding to Borges's writing theory, he suggests that Camacho may actually be just dictating from some invisible master text. Marito, in contrast, has not yet found his voice. He tears apart his failed short stories and manages to earn a living by recasting the writing of others into his news bulletins.

In the end Camacho goes mad because he cannot keep the plots of his nine soap operas separate. As in Vargas Llosa's own fiction, Camacho's characters die in one story only to reappear in another, eliciting public outrage. Marito is asked to come in as the scriptwriter's replacement, for the radio station owner sees no difference between the fiction written by Camacho and the news bulletins written by Marito. The books ends with a scene in which Marito, now transformed into the famous writer Vargas Llosa, triumphantly returns to Lima from Paris, acclaimed as a celebrity.

The novel plays on a counterpoint between the comic autobiography and the soap opera as two types of fiction that imitate one another. Vargas Llosa's first wife, Julia Lerquide, recognizes this mimesis and thinks that their love affair could easily fit in Camacho's serials. Though we read the autobiographical chapters under the illusion that they are part of the novel and we read Camacho's tales of infanticide, incest, castration, patricide, prostitution, and genocide as the product of an imagination bordering on madness, we cannot fail to realize that the two narrative modes belong to the same author. Marito and Pedro Camacho are, of course, the products of one man's imagination. What is more, the themes that Camacho touches upon and the characters that he creates are not far removed from what Vargas Llosa has explored in his previous work, for example, nymphets, sexual perverts preaching under the aegis of newly minted religions, and the myth of the giant black penis. These are all icons that will continue to appear in Vargas Llosa's future novels.

This novel marks the first, but not the last, time that Vargas Llosa deals with historical characters, friends, and family, and uses their real names. This willingness to mix fiction with personal memories will be radicalized in *A Fish in the Water*, which was written after the author lost the race for the presidency of Peru. In *A Fish in the Water* he alternates autobiography with a very personal account of the political struggle of his own

presidential bid. Precisely because Vargas Llosa deals with his family in this journalistic style, Julia Urquidi (the author's first wife) was outraged by the publication of the novel. Feeling used and unfairly portrayed, she published her own memoirs, giving a very different account of how their marriage took place and how it foundered in Paris, soon after the success of *The Time of the Hero*, due to unforeseen affective and sexual pressures.

In many of his interviews and through the activities of characters such as Ambrosio, Amalia, Aunt Julia, Ana, and Marito, Vargas Llosa has revealed that he is addicted to movies of all kinds. In fact, some ten years after the book's publication, he was intimately involved in the making of a movie version of *Pantaleon*, although the project was not critically successful. In 1973 he was asked by the Brazilian cinematographer Rui Guerra to adapt for the screen the great Brazilian historical account of the destruction of the rebels in Canudos by the Brazilian army. In his masterpiece *Os Sertões* (1902; *Rebellion in the Backlands*, 1944), Euclides da Cunha unforgettably described the rebellion of Antonio Conselheiro and the people of Brazil's northeastern backlands. To prepare for the project, Vargas Llosa went to Brazil and traveled to the backlands of Bahia to familiarize himself with the territory. The movie, however, was not made.

After having invested an enormous amount of time in researching the events and historical context of Canudos, Vargas Llosa decided to write a historical novel which turned out be very close to the text that da Cunha had authored almost a hundred years earlier. Vargas Llosa wrote a gripping adventure tale in *The War of the End of the World*, perhaps his greatest novel to date. Set in the style of high realism bordering on naturalism, Vargas Llosa bores into the problem of religious and political fanaticism, no doubt stirred by both the rising tide of liberation theology and the activities of the Shining Path guerrillas in Peru. In this novel, corrupt and misguided politicians, faltering and inadequate ideological systems, ridiculous yellow journalism, sexual excesses of various sorts, mutilation, murder, starvation, and a blundering military make for a potent mix that leads to the annihilation of a large group of Brazilian peasants. The forty or so lives that the author develops within the novel are cut short in the inexorable historical apocalypse of the last days of the siege of Canudos by the Brazilian army.

While Vargas Llosa has added a good number of characters to da Cunha's original account, the thrust of the story remains faithful to that of the Brazilian original. As usual, Vargas Llosa develops the story in a pair of locales, with two sets of characters and stories. As he deploys them, they begin to intersect. The events in the *sertão* (backlands), chronicled by da Cunha, have been balanced in *The War of the End of the World* with another set of events in Bahia, the capital city of the Brazilian state. Galileo Gall, a European phrenologist, is the most completely fictional character, and yet according to Vargas Llosa this figure is based a Spanish scientist. The Barão (Baron) may be based on the true-life character of the Barão de Gerembão. Gonçalvez Viana, who appears as a character in Vargas Llosa's novel, was indeed a local politician. The myopic journalist seems to be a parodic version of Euclides da Cunha himself.

Although modeled on the double helix of Bahia and the backlands, this is, narratively speaking, one of the most traditional novels that Vargas Llosa has ever written. Each character's antecedents are carefully and sequentially given until the point when he or she meets the religious mystic António Conselheiro and decides to follow him. As in da Cunha's account, Conselheiro is followed by all sorts of outcasts, from the innocent faithful to former bandits. The central figure of Conselheiro remains, as in da Cunha's version, shrouded in mystery. There is a patent absence of interiority in the presentation of Conselheiro, which would introduce some degree of rationality to the obstinacy of his goals and methods.

António Conselheiro is a lay brother who travels around the miserable villages and towns of the backlands of Bahia, repairing abandoned cemeteries and churches. He lives exclusively on alms. As time goes on, he begins to preach repentance, announcing that the end of the world is near. In the backlands and in Conselheiro's conception of the world, this means that the end of suffering is approaching and that the chance for a peaceful rest in the embrace of sweet Jesus is a real possibility. Others, uprooted men and women, also wander in the backlands. As they meet, they begin to gather together into a group. Some pious women join the traveling band as do several former outlaws. As the group grows, Conselheiro's preaching becomes more frequent. One thing leads to another and suddenly the authorities realize that the group poses a challenge to society. Many now heed Conselheiro rather than following common law. Conselheiro challenges the new laws on civil marriage passed by the recently inaugurated Brazilian republic, and he claims the right to preach in the established churches. Some priests see no harm in this, for at least he attracts the unfaithful parishioners. Other priests, however, perceive Conselheiro as a dangerous challenge to their authority and resentfully oppose him. Slowly, hostilities between the Church and Conselheiro grow. The civil authorities respond similarly, and a detachment of soldiers is sent to apprehend him. His followers decide to surprise the soldiers by taking the initiative. The first battle between Conselheiro and the army takes place, and although they suffer many losses, Conselheiro's people win.

The news spreads like wildfire in Bahia. Conselheiro's ragged "army" is said to be enormous and well supplied with English riffles. Time passes, and Conselheiro, together with an ever-swelling number of followers, settles in the abandoned lands of Canudos, by the banks of the Vassa Barris, one of the few permanent streams in the parched backlands. In Canudos his lieutenants—former merchants, bandits, carpenters, and midwives—build a miserable but orderly and cohesive society. It is at this point that the Brazilian army lays siege to Canudos. It takes more than a year and a half of vicious war, and four separate, butchering assaults by thousands of Brazilian soldiers to defeat the settlement at Canudos. In the end, however, Canudos and the people who had assembled there are totally destroyed, in one of the many genocides that have occurred in the history of Latin America.

The account of the war of Canudos relies on the full display of Vargas Llosa's powerful narrative talent and techniques. This gripping tale is comparable in excitement to the feats of *The Three Musketeers*, by Alexandre Dumas, Leon Tolstoy's *War and Peace*, or *The Sound and the Fury* by William Faulkner. Even readers familiar with da Cunha's *Rebellion in the Backlands* find themselves hoping, for example, that Pajeú, the one-eyed bandit, will return safely from his mission, or that a catastrophe will befall the Brazilian army, so that the adventure and survival of Canudos will last just a little longer.

With this novel Vargas Llosa opens yet another field for himself: the historical novel. He returns to it with equal success in *La fiesta del Chivo* (2000), an account of the last days of the dictatorship of Rafael Leonidas Trujillo (1930–1961) in the Dominican Republic. Vargas Llosa's passion for revolt and revolution seems insatiable. He has repeatedly taken up the subject as a journalist, writing for the *New York Times Magazine* and other newspapers on both the Nicaraguan Sandinista revolution and the Maoist guerrilla group, Sendero Luminoso (Shining Path). *The Real life of Alejandro Mayta* deals entirely with the making of yet another possibility of revolution in Peru.

In two plays, *La señorita de Tacna* (1981) and *Kathie y el hipopotamo* (1983), Vargas Llosa centers part of the action on characters who are either writers or would-be writers. (The plays were later translated and published in *Three Plays: The Young Lady from Tacna, Kathie and the Hippopotamus, La Chunga*, 1990.) In *The Young Lady from Tacna*, the character Belisario holds the conviction that writing is the only tool capable of rescuing the past from the debris of oblivion. The narrator of this play takes every opportunity to experiment with and meditate on the possible ways of telling his story, dramatization being only one of them. The opposite is true in *Kathie and the Hippopotamus*. Kathie Kennedy, the idle wife of a rich man, has nothing that can save her life from the doldrums of mediocrity. She does, however, have a desire to fantasize. Kathie cannot write, so she hires Santiago Zavala, from *Conversation in the Cathedral*, to write her "memoirs" of an imaginary trip to Africa. Not unlike the story of Marito and Aunt Julia or *The Real life of Alejandro Mayta*, this fabricated autobiography has more in common with soap operas and various elements of plot production than with any deep experimentation into the nature of the linguistic sign or dissemination.

In *The Real Life of Alejandro Mayta* Vargas Llosa pushes further some experiments he had already started in his plays and novels. This work is an almost essayistic inquiry into the relation between writing (a means of representation) and reality itself. In this novel the question of writing and its complex, paradoxical relation to fiction and history becomes paramount. It is within the framework of this larger topic, writing, that the novel's preoccupation with ideology, be it Christianity or Marxism, must be considered. In chapter four the writer in the novel asserts his desire to learn "what is the connection . . . the secret thread that ties together. . . the Catholic Church . . . and the obscure revolutionary," while the authorial voice keeps reassuring the reader that his only goal is to write a novel that draws its "power of suggestion and invention, its color and dramatic force," from the "veracity of many testimonies" but that it "would nevertheless be an unrecognizable version of what happened."

These problematic relations between happenings and elaborated "facts," between testimony and reporting, between reporting and elaborating history or fiction, between the truth and a version of the events, are posited by the story itself. Mayta's story, the story of a strange, sad, caring, and searching person—hardly a revolutionary—is reconstituted by a character presented as the author of the novel. This character, the "writer," speaks directly to the reader, thus breaking one of the most cherished conventions of Flaubertian realism and the indirect narrative mode in which the bulk of the story is told. This writer also meets directly and speaks with most of the other characters in the novel.

Presumably this writer is Vargas Llosa himself, for, like him, the fictional character is a famous and respected writer who lives in Lima, runs every day on the Barranco beach, is influential enough to be received by anyone he needs to interview, and speaks to the reader with the understanding that he is indeed a writer of novels concerned with fundamental historical questions. The novel is clearly the story of a generation in the same way that *Conversation in the Cathedral* defines the path of Vargas Llosa's generation. In the course of the novel, the writer does create a story about Mayta, along with a meditation on the chances, wisdom, possibilities, and ideologies of revolutionary change in Peru.

With the 1987 publication of *Who Killed Palomino Molero?* Vargas Llosa returns to the coastal setting of *The Green House*. Lituma reappears in this detective novel, which is strewn with false clues and which ends with a problematic closure. The Dr. Watson in the investigation of the brutal murder of an innocent young man is Palomino Molero. The novel begins after the murder has already occurred. The first scene conveys, in conversation, the details of the murder. The rest of the narrative moves both forward and backward in search of motive and the identity of the murderers. Vargas Llosa's dazzling narrative techniques are almost too consciously displayed in the service of superfluous suspense, for the fate of the characters fails to engage the sympathy of the reader. In *La fiesta del Chivo* Vargas similarly blends the thrust of the murder mystery with great historical depth, thus producing another gripping tale which rivals *War of the End of the World*.

As if needing a respite from so much fanaticism and failed revolutionaries, in the decade of the 1990s, before and after his run from Peru's presidency, Vargas Llosa turned to the full exploration of sexual pleasure. The *New York Times Magazine* review of *The Notebooks of Don Rigoberto* (1998) states that "Vargas Llosa's latest work of fiction is a pornographic novel; at least it would be if it weren't so artistic." This novel revels in highly detailed and charged sex scenes. It explores the entire sexual spectrum, ranging from the conventional, to all sorts of fetishism and into the bizarre. Fonchito, in his early adolescence, seduces his stepmother, Don Rigoberto's estranged wife, through his enticing and voyeuristic discussions and writing on art, especially the paintings of Egon Schiele. The characters in this novel have migrated from the earlier *In Praise of the Stepmother* (1990). In this "happy family" Fonchito gets his material from art school, writes anonymous erotic letters to Don Rigoberto and Doña Lucrecia, and oversees the amorous rituals between Doña Lucrecia and her servant, Justiniana. The story is set among the wealthy in Lima. This is not an attempt to depict the utopia of the poor and forgotten, as in *The War of the End of the World*, nor is it the general dystopia of many of Vargas Llosa's other novels, such as *El hablador* (1987; *The Storyteller*, 1989) or *The Time of the Hero*. Instead, Fonchito's family inhabits a sort of "pornotopia," a place where the only important desire is arousal, where the erotic commingling of art and sex erase the line between fiction and reality, lies and truth, art and life, dream and desire. In addition, *The Notebooks* constitutes an extended appropriation of the work of Egon Schiele. The novel is a supreme example of *ekphrasis*, in which the verbal description of the painting overtakes the original. Critics have pointed out

how entire scenes in the novel, which includes reproductions of Schiele's paintings, constitute narrative renditions of Schiele's abundant erotic work. The narrator's emphasis on color, light, form, framing, and composition of the amorous scenes alludes openly to compositional elements in the visual image. Lucrecia and Justiniana imitate the poses of the verbal descriptions that Foncho, the aspiring painter, makes of the drawings by Schiele. As in most pornographic art, women are displayed as sexual objects. Lucrecia, seduced by Foncho's desire to be a painter of eros, is induced, with Justiniana, to imitate the poses and desires of Shiele as mediated by the adolescent Fonchito and in relation with don Rigoberto's own fantasies.

Critics have pointed out that Vargas Llosa and Schiele coincide in believing in the redeeming power of art, in seeing art as a refuge and challenge to the established order as well as a trigger for the imagination. These are ideas that Vargas Llosa has espoused continuously and which he repeated in his inaugural speech in accepting the chair in Ibero-American studies at Georgetown University on 25 April 2001. In these two explicitly erotic novels as well as in much of his previous work, Vargas Llosa constructs a world in which pleasure is closely linked to transgression and in which the father-son relationship is at once displaced and fused.

Vargas Llosa's fictional world has been surprisingly constant in the face of continuous exploration of the further limits of his ideas and narrative techniques. One book always dovetails into the other, even when they seem to strike in novel directions. *The Storyteller* gains in fullness when discussed within the context of Vargas Llosa's polemical relation to anthropology and *indigenismo* in Peru. In fact this polemic can be traced right back to his earliest writings, for the autobiographical references to his membership and later falling out with the San Marcos University Marxist club, Cahuide, are openly confirmed in his memoirs of the period. The mutual dependence between the author as anthropologist—his science and the object of his science (the primitive)—are subjected to a merciless and at times sarcastic cutting in *The Storyteller*. The fact that Vargas Llosa's construction of the Machigenga in this novel has much to do with his reading of Malinowski and Levi-Brulh is yet another aspect of Vargas Llosa's dispute with the *indigenistas* over the object of their mutual desire: to understand the Indian in Peru, and by way of such understanding to discover the meaning of Peru's history and its possible future.

This lifelong polemic takes on more open and bitter tones after Vargas Llosa's participation in the investigation of the murders of Uchuraccay. On 26 January 26 1983, eight journalists were massacred at Uchuraccay, a small village in the high Andes near Ayacucho, the stronghold of the Shining Path guerillas. As with other killings, it proved impossible to determine whether villagers, in self defense, or guerillas, who appeared to be villagers, had killed the journalists with or without provocation. Vargas Llosa agreed to head a presidential investigative committee, which found it difficult to reach consensus on its findings. The role of the military and its questionable human rights record came under keen scrutiny in the press. The report rendered proved highly controversial and some believed that it helped fuel the resentment and antagonism already imbedded in the guerilla uprising. Vargas Llosa's public and painful break with the Cuban revolution, his attacks on the Shining Path guerrillas in Peru, his personal break with many leftist intellectuals in Peru and abroad, his subsequent warm embrace of neoliberalism and his defeat in his bid for the presidency of Peru firmly established Vargas Llosa in the ranks of the Right in Peru. Such positioning pitted him in an open ideological struggle with any and all ideas bearing any semblance to Marxism, socialism, and neo-Marxism. Because several prominent indigenista intellectuals of the first half of the century had been Marxists or socialists also, Vargas Llosa often blankets indigenismo with Marxism, forgetting the fact that although both political programs clamor for a system in which Indians can exercise their citizenship more fully, they have different intellectual and social histories in Peru. His collection of essays on Peruvian writers and especially on indigenismo in Peru and Mexico, *La utopía arcaica: José María Arguedas y las ficciones del indigenismo* (1996) can only be understood within the broad reaches of this polemic, in the very long history of Peruvian cultural and political life. Vargas Llosa recognizes the breadth and complexity of debate when he attempts to trace it to the founding pages on the subject of indigenismo, authored by Garcilaso de la Vega, an Inca, and Guaman

Poma. However, such short, journalistic essays on exceedingly complex and rich subjects and topics contribute less to clearing the ground that to laying a shaky foundation.

Vargas Llosa does not sufficiently appreciate the fact that these two colonial intellectuals were already grappling with the central conundrum not only to Peruvian history but to the Americas and the world itself, for the question has much to do with the West's colonial expansion across the globe, of which recent "globalization" trends are but a later stage. Vargas Llosa does not connect the questions asked by indigenismo to the colonial history of the West and to the history of the peoples that the West defines as "others." Quite to the contrary, he deals with it as part of a local, exotic, and capricious dispute between two kinds of idealized Peruvians: those who think from the perspective of the Coast, a more or less Eurocentric perspective, and whose who think from the perspective of the Andes, a more or less nativist perspective. By polarizing the question of the Indian into a contrast between civilization and barbarism, just like colonial discourse already has done, Vargas Llosa is able to set up a series of exclusionary oppositions which in the end allow him to say that Arguedas did not really understand Andean culture any better than any one else, that he always passed himself of as a victim, that he wanted to preserve an archaic time that never really existed, and most importantly, that indigenismo really stands in the way of progress. For Vargas Llosa all indigenismo has to offer is a misguided notion of an archaic (primitive) utopia.

In order to construct this argument, Vargas Llosa ignores a great deal of ethnohistory, cultural criticism, and anthropology. In his reading of Arguedas's work he brings in his Christian concept of the demonic origins of artistic creation. The artist, possessed by demons, is compelled to speak the truth. His reading of Arguedas' work is more than merely a strong misreading, for it borders on the capricious. It does not take into consideration the many well-grounded arguments that have been raised in opposition to his own position. *La utopía arcáica* is, nonetheless, an excellent example of fearlessly polemical writing. It stands as a supreme example of Vargas Llosa's ability to write with great passion and conviction. He does argue from a postmodern disillusion and a concern with the truth, but he destabilizes the beliefs he attributes to his opponents by pitting universals and essentializing concepts against relative "truths" and contextual considerations. *La utopía arcáica* is less about Indian civilizations and indigenismo than it is about Vargas Llosa's way of constructing arguments, his political and aesthetic preferences, and his own utopian hopes for neoliberalism, for at the root of the argument stands the fact that the indigenistas identify with Indian ways and values, and Vargas Llosa rejects them roundly for both aesthetic and ideological reasons, or in response to demons of his own. Despite his rejection of Sartre, and precisely because of his embrace of neoliberalism, in *La utopía* Vargas Llosa reminds us that he remains a passionately committed artist. It is perhaps fitting that this essay should end with a reference to the author's own preoccupation with the status of the "truth" in these postmodern times, for in his praise of "lies," as in *La verdad de las mentiras* (1990; The truth about lies), the reader faces a prolific writer of formidable talent, an indefatigable will to craft an indelible and unforgettable image of the world made possible only by the power of his writing and its reference to the real world, a world crafted by the power of language in us all, but not necessarily anchored in the power of lies. Somehow his fiction is linked to truths that readers recognize and long to understand.

# SELECTED BIBLIOGRAPHY

## Primary Works

### Fiction and Journalism

*Los jefes.* Barcelona, 1959.
*La ciudad y los perros.* Barcelona, 1963.
*La casa verde.* Barcelona, 1966.
*Los cachorros.* Barcelona, 1967.
*Conversacion en la Catedral.* 2 vols. Barcelona, 1969.
*Garcias Márquez: Historia de un deicidio.* Barcelona, 1971.
*La historia secreta de una novela.* Barcelona, 1971.
*Pantaleón y las visitadoras.* Barcelona, 1973.
*La orgía perpetua: Flaubert y Madame Bovary.* Barcelona, 1975.

*La tia Julia y el escribidor.* Barcelona, 1977.
*Entre Sartre y Camus.* Barcelona, 1981.
*La guerra del fin del mundo.* Barcelona, 1981.
*La señorita de Tacna.* Barcelona, 1981.
*Kathie y el hipopotamo.* Barcelona, 1983.
*Historia de Mayta.* Barcelona, 1984.
*La Chunga.* Barcelona, 1986.
*Contra viento y marea.* Volume I (1962–1972). Barcelona, 1986.
*Contra viento y marea.* Volume II (1972–1983). Barcelona, 1986.
*Quien mato a Palomino Molero?* Barcelona, 1986.
*El hablador.* Barcelona, 1987.
*Elogio de la Madrastra.* Barcelona, 1988.
*Carta de batalla por Tirant lo Blanc.* Barcelona, 1990.
*Contra viento y marea.* Volume III (1964–1988). Barcelona, 1990.
*La verdad de las mentiras.* Barcelona, 1990.
*Lituma en los Andes.* Barcelona, 1993.
*El loco de los balcones.* Barcelona, 1993.
*El pez en el agua.* Barcelona, 1993.
*Desagfisoa la libertad.* Madrid, 1994.
*La utopía arcáica: Jose Maria Arguedas y las ficciones del indigenismo.* Mexico City, 1996.
*Los cuadernos de don Rigoberto.* Barcelona, 1997.
*La fiesta del Chivo.* Barcelona, 2000.

## Translations

*The Time of the Hero.* Trans. by Lysander Kemp. New York: Harper and Row, 1966.
*The Green House.* Trans. by Gregory Rabassa. New York: Harper and Row, 1968.
*Conversation in the Cathedral.* Trans. by Gregory Rabassa. New York: Harper and Row, 1974.
*Captain Pantoja and the Spcial Service.* Trans. by Gregory Kolovakos and Ronald Christ. New York: Harper and Row, 1978.
*The Cubs and Other Stories.* Published in Spanish as *Los Cachorros,* trans. by Greghory Kolovakos and Ronald Christ. New York: Harper and Row, 1979.
*Aunt Julia and the Scripwriter.* Trans. by Helen R. Lane. New York: Farrar, Straus, and Giroux, 1982.
*The War of the End of the World.* Trans. by Helen R. Lane. New York, 1984.
*The Perpetual Orgy: Flaubert and "Madame Bovary."* Trans. by Helen Lane. New York: Farrar, Straus, and Giroux, 1986.

*The Real Life of Alejandro Mayta.* Trans. by Alfred MacAdam. New York, 1986.

*Who Killed Palomino Molero?* Trans. by Alfred MacAdam. New York, 1987.

*In Praise of the Stepmother.* Trans. by Helen Lane. New York: Farrar, Straus & Giroux, 1990.

*The Storyteller.* Trans. by Helen Lane. New York: Farrar, Straus & Giroux, 1990.

*Three Plays: The Young Lady from Tacna; Kathie and the Hipopotamus; La Chunga.* Trans. by David Graham-Young. London: Fabar and Fabar Ltd., 1990.

*A Writer's Reality.* Edited and with an introduction by Myron I. Lichtblau. Syracuse, 1991.

*Fiction: The Power of Lies.* Trans. by Victoria Bundoora. Australia: La Trobe University, 1993.

*A Fish in the Water: A Memoir.* Trans. by Helen Lane. New York: Farrar, Straus & Giroux, 1994.

*Literature and Freedom.* Australia: Center for Independent Studies, Occasional Papers, 1994.

*Death in the Andes.* Trans. by Edith Grossman. New York: Farrar, Straus & Giroux, 1996.

*Making Waves.* Edited and trans. by John King. New York: Farrar, Straus & Giroux, 1996.

*The Notebooks of Don Rigoberto.* Trans. by Edith Grossman. New York Farrar, Straus, & Giroux, 1998.

## Secondary Works

### Biographical and Critical Studies

Alonso, Carlos. *La tia julia y el escribidor: The Writing Subject's Fantasy of Empowerment."* PMLA 106 (January, 1991): 46–59.

Benedetti, Mario. "Vargas Llosa y su fértil escándalo." In *Homenaje a Mario Vargas Llosa,* edited by Helmy F. Giacoman and José Miguel Oviedo. Madrid, 1972. Pp. 245–262.

———. "Ni cínicos ni oportunistas." In *El desexilio y otras conjeturas.* Buenos Aires, 1985. Pp. 173–177.

Bernucci, Leopoldo. *Historia de un malentendido: Un estudio transtextual de* La guerra del fin del mundo *de Mario Vargas Llosa.* New York: Peter Lang, 1989.

Boland, Roy. "Demonios y lectores: Génesis y reescritura de *Quien mató a Palomino Molero?" Antípodas* 1:160–182. (December 1988). (Special issue on Mario Vargas Llosa, edited by Roy Boland.)

———. *Mario Vargas Llosa. Oedpus and the "Papa" State. A Study of Individual and Social Psychology in Mario Vargas Llosa's Novels of Peruvian Reality.* Madrid: Editorial Voz, 1988.

Boldori de Baldusi, Rosa. *Vargas Llosa: Un narrasor y sus demonios.* Buenos Aires: Garcia Cambeiro, 1947.

Brotherston, Gordon. "Social Structure: Mario Vargas Llosa." In *The Emergence of the Latin American Novel.* Cambridge, England: 1977. Pp. 110–121.

Castro-Klarén, Sara. "Fragmentation and Alienation in *La casa verde." Modern Language Notes,* February, 1972, pp. 286–299.

———. "Humor and Class in *Pantaleón y las visitadoras." Latin American Literary Review,* 7, no. 13: 64–79 (1978).

———. "Locura y dolor: La elaboración de la historia en *Os Sertões y La guerra del find del mundo." Revista de Critica literaria Latinoamericana,* 10, no. 20: 207–230 (1984).

———. "Santos and Cangaceiros: Inscription without Discourse in *Os Sertões* and *La guerra del fin del mundo." Modern Language Notes,* 101, no. 2: 366–388 (1986).

———. *Understanding Mario Vargas Llosa.* Columbia, S.C.: University of South Carolina Press, 1992.

———. "Monuments and Scribes: *El hablador* Addresses Ethnography." In *Structures of Power: Essays on Twentieth-Century Spanish-American Fiction.* Edited by Terry J. Peavler and Peter Standish. Albany: State University of New York Press, 1996. Pp. 39–59.

Christ, Ronald. "Talk With Mario Vargas Llosa." *The New York Times Book Review,* 9 April 1978, pp. 11, 32–33.

Cornejo Polar, Antonio. "La historia como apocalipsis." *Qué hacer* 33:15–21 (1985).

Davis, Mary E. "Dress Gray *y La ciudad y los perros:* El laberinto del honor." *Revista Iberoamericana* 47, nos. 116–117: 117–126 (1981).

Gerdes, Dick. *Mario Vargas Llosa.* Boston, 1985.

Geisdorfman-Feal, Rosemary. *Novel Lives: The Fictional Autobiographies of Guillermo Cabrera Infante and Mario Vargas Llosa.* Chapel Hill: University of North Carolina Press, 1986.

Harss, Luis, and Barbara Dohmann. *Into the Main Stream.* New York, 1967.

Hernandez de López, Ana Maria. *Mario Vargas Llosa: Operia Omnia.* Madrid: Pliegos, 1994.

Johnson, Dane. "Chased by Life, Politics, Demons: Flying to Fiction". *Review of Contemporary Fiction,* 17, 1: 9–13 (1997).

Kendrick, Walter. "Erotomania." *The New York Times Book Review,* 28 June 1998, p. 10.

Kerr, Lucille. *Reclaiming the Author: Figures and Fictions from Spanish America.* Durham: Duke University Press, 1992.

Klarén, Peter Flindell. *Peru: Society and Nationhood in the Andes.* Oxford: Oxford University Press, 2000.

Kristal, Efrain. *Temptation of the Word: The Novels of Mario Vargas Llosa.* Nashville: Vanderbilt University Press, 1998.

Lauer, Mirko. *El sitio de la literatura: Escritores y politica en el Peru del siglo XX.* Lima: Mosca Azul, 1989.

Lewis, Marvin. *From Lima to Leticia.* New York: University Press of America, 1983.

Machen, Stephen M. " 'Pornoviolence' and Point of View in Mario Vargas Llosa's *La tia Julia y el escribidor. Latin American Literary Review* 9, no. 17: 9–16 (1980).

Marti-Peña, Guadalupe. "Egon Schiele y *Los cuadernos de don Rigoberto de Mario Vargas Llosa*: Iconotextualidad intermedialidad." *Revista Iberoamericana* LXVI, no. 190: 93–111. (January–March 2000).

Moody, Michael. "Paisajes de los condenados: El escenario natural de *La casa verde.*" *Revista Iberoamericana* 47, nos. 116–117: 127–136 (1981).

Morello-Frosch, Marta. "Of Heroes and Martyrs: The Grotesque in *Pantaleón y las visitadoras.*" *Latin American Literary Review* 7, no. 14: 40–44 (1979).

Muñoz, Braulio. *A Storyteller: Mario Vargas Llosa Between Civilization and Barbarism.* New York: Rowman and Littlefield, 2000.

Ortega, Julio. *La contemplación y la fiesta.* Lima, 1968. Pp. 123–133.

Oviedo, Jose Miguel. *Mario Vargas Llosa: La invencion de una realidad.* Barcelona, 1970.

———, ed. *Mario Vargas Llosa: El escritor y la crítica.* Madrid, 1981.

Oviedo, Jose Miguel, et al. "Focus: *Conversation in the Cathedral.*" *Review of the Center for Inter-American Relations* 75: 5–37 (spring 1975).

Rama, Angel, and Mario Vargas Llosa. *García Márquez y la problemática de la novela.* Buenos Aires, 1974.

Rebaza-Soraluz, Luis. "Demons and Lies: Motivation and Form in Mario Vargas Llosa." *Review of Contemporary Fiction,* 17. no.1: 15–25 (Spring, 1977).

Rodríguez Rea, Miguel Angel. *Tras las huellas de un crítico: Mario Vargas Llosa.* Lima: Universidad Católica, 1996.

Roscoe, Ada, ed. *Mario Vargas Llosa: Un indefatigable narrador.* Madrid, 1997. (Special issue of *Explicación de Textos.*)

Rossman, Charles, and Alan Friedman, eds. *Mario Vargas Llosa: A Collection of Critical Essays.* Austin and London, 1978.

Sommers, Joseph. "Literatura e ideología: La evaluación novelística del militarismo en Vargas Liosa." *Hispamerica* 4, no. 1: 83–117 (1975).

Standish, Peter. *Vargas Llosa: La ciudad y los perros.* London, 1982.

Urquidi Illanez, Julia. *Lo que Varguitas no dijo.* La Paz: Khana Cruz, 1983.

Williams, Raymond Leslie. *Mario Vargas Llosa.* New York: Ungar, 1986.

*World Literature Today.* Mario Vargas Llosa Issue 52, no. 1 (1978).

# Ida Vitale

## (1923–    )

## *Hugo J. Verani*

Ida Vitale D'Amico was born in Montevideo, Uruguay, on 2 November 1923. By her own account, she had a solitary childhood: without brothers or sisters, isolated from other children of her age, and raised among eccentrics, Masons, atheists, and austere puritans—an odd combination of cultured people who kept her out of school until the third grade. She found an escape in reading and in the use of her imagination. In spite of her unusual upbringing, or possibly because of it, Vitale is the least autobiographical of modern Uruguayan poets. She does not chronicle her private life in interviews or articles, nor does she use the facts and circumstances of her biography as poetic material. As a result, her poetry is neither a means of describing concrete experiences nor a vehicle for self-expression, but a search in the domain of feelings and thought processes, more suggestive than representative.

Vitale entered the Law School of the University of the Republic in Montevideo in 1942, and later its School of Humanities, but she did not complete her degree. From March 1947 to October 1948, she was coeditor of a literary review, *Clinamen,* in which many of her early poems and book reviews were published. Her principal mentor was the prominent Spanish writer José Bergamín, who lived in exile in Montevideo from 1947 to 1954; she also gained the notice of the Nobel Prize winner Juan Ramón Jiménez, who in 1948 included her work in a reading called "Presentation of Young Spanish American poetry" in Buenos Aires, a recognition that went largely unnoticed at the time. Vitale married the eminent critic Ángel Rama in 1950, and since 1964 has been married to the noted poet Enrique Fierro.

Although the writing of poetry is the central focus of Vitale's professional efforts, she actively participates in public life and other cultural activities. She was a professor of literature in Montevideo from 1956 until 1973, when the military dictatorship in Uruguay forced massive numbers of intellectuals into exile. She also became a regular translator from four languages (French, Italian, Portuguese, English) for major publishers in Argentina and Mexico; a perceptive critic whose numerous articles remain uncollected; a regular participant in symposia and colloquia in Europe and the Americas; a member of the editorial board of renowned Mexican journals such as *Vuelta* and its successor, *Letras libres;* a prolific contributor to cultural journals; and a knowledgeable connoisseur of modern art who also has a discerning and flawless ear for classical music. Vitale's wit, irony, irrepressible disposition, as well as her extraordinary agile mind (and sharp tongue) make an indelible impression on those she meets. An example of her quick wit was displayed when Mariano

Arana, mayor of Montevideo, greeted her in public as "eximia poeta" (illustrious poet). She fired back, perhaps in jest: "In Mexico I am an *eximia poeta*, but here I am just an *ex-simia* [an ex-monkey]," no doubt alluding to the great recognition and following her poetry has in Mexico, in contrast to the puzzling critical reticence in Uruguay. However, it may also be an ironic response, sharp with sarcasm, from a writer who rejects the notion of mimesis, of literature as simian imitation or representation of the concrete world.

Vitale lived in Mexico from 1974 to 1984, a beneficial exile that gave her an opportunity to meet and to develop affinities and friendships with such like-minded writers as Octavio Paz, Álvaro Mutis, and Alejandro Rossi, who provided her with the impetus to excel. Since 1990 she has divided her time between Montevideo and Austin, Texas, also spending long periods in Mexico, where her poetry has been issued by leading publishers.

Vitale began writing at a time of unparalleled creative production in Uruguay. The presence of the formidable fiction writers Felisberto Hernández and Juan Carlos Onetti, and her contemporaries' impatience with and intolerance toward the literary establishment, resulted in an increasingly manifest rebellion against convention. Uruguayan writers, and poets in particular, sought a renewed conciseness for their work, rejecting sentimentality, eloquence, embellishment, and willful obscurity. Reacting against the overly esthetic stance of their immediate predecessors, the poets of Vitale's generation were determined to expand the sphere of literature. Some opted to liberate the imagination while others chose to regard literature as a social activity. Vitale was part of a community of writers and artists (the painter Joaquín Torres García [1874–1949] was a mentor for decades) in which competition was intense and friendship—although crucial in earlier years—did not always prevail. Ángel Rama referred to this group of intellectuals as the "critical generation," for their propensity to bring all aspects of Uruguayan and Latin American cultural and literary life under serious scrutiny. In addition to Rama, this group included Mario Benedetti, distinguished for his ability to write in many genres; José Pedro Díaz; Carlos Real de Azúa; and Emir Rodríguez Monegal.

With the exception of such major figures as Vicente Huidobro, Pablo Neruda, and Octavio Paz, poetry has historically played a marginal role in Latin American culture. In addition, its already peripheral position was further displaced during the second half of the twentieth century by the extraordinary success of Latin American narrative. In Uruguay, a number of poets born in the early 1920s highlighted the predicament of modern poetry through the production of an impressive corpus of writing over the course of more than fifty years. Four individuals are at the forefront of this change: Mario Benedetti (b. 1920), Idea Vilariño (b. 1920), Amanda Berenguer (b. 1921), and Ida Vitale (b. 1923).

Benedetti is the group's dominant personality, overshadowing the others in the public eye. Widely known and celebrated, albeit grudgingly recognized by many, Benedetti is able to write casual, conversational, and spontaneous poetry as few others have done. He is a popular favorite who reaches a wide audience of readers (and listeners, since many of his poems have become songs). Since his early *Poemas de la oficina* (1956; Office poems), an important book in the development of the modern colloquial idiom and unconventional subject matter, Benedetti has exemplified the idea of a socially committed writer striving to communicate directly and without ambiguities.

Although the other three poets—Vilariño, Vitale, and Berenguer—lack the wide popularity of Benedetti, they figure prominently on any list of modern poets, and their works reveal the richness and diversity of the different voices of this generation. All three are just beginning to receive wider and more comprehensive critical attention outside Uruguay. This delayed recognition is due in part to their books being published mainly in inadequately distributed small editions, and in part to the fact all three believe the poetic act is "a performance in words"—as Robert Frost once put it—without concessions to facility and superficiality.

Vilariño's poetry is dominated by a dramatic intensity, by a heightening of emotional tension. She assumes a tone of anguished desolation and abandonment, as if stating feelings of an eternally dispossessed soul. Her work is transparently confessional, particularly in *Poemas de amor* (1957; Love poems), her most acclaimed book, written with a seemingly casual disregard for language and poetic rhetoric that nonetheless produces a powerful and uncommon fusion of sensibility and craftmanship. Berenguer, on the other hand, is more daring in her use of innovative methods of composition, taking risks the others do not; for instance, in *Composición de lugar* (1976; Space composition), each poem is assembled in three dazzling versions. The experimental character of much of her poetry and, primarily, her high capacity to integrate the physical world with the most intimate and personal realms have resulted in memorable poems.

Vitale is an isolated and exceptional figure among the poets of her generation in Uruguay. Although her poetry resists general statements, I would argue that it is the most significant example of the modern concern with language, a tendency that represents the culmination of a self-conscious and fundamental movement in literature, especially prominent during the twentieth century. Its distinctive character lies in Vitale's subtle awareness of the power of language to suggest hidden states of mind without expressing them directly and, more important, in her ability to attain the greatest intensity of expression. Building upon the hermetic tradition of the French symbolists, particularly Stéphane Mallarmé and Paul Valéry, she is also a legitimate heir of two great Spanish masters, Juan Ramón Jiménez and Jorge Guillén. Vitale belongs to a lyric tradition of lucidity and self-containment, seeking forms of expression to evoke her subject matter as precisely as possible, to find the most exact terms to convey emotions or thoughts, emphasizing a poetry of the intellect, at times cryptic and hermetic, particularly in her later writings. As a thoroughly conscious artist who deliberately condenses the poem to an absolute essentiality, she eliminates or reduces to a minimum unnecessary connectives and adjectival modifiers, and uses figurative and metaphorical language sparingly, extracting rhetorical devices that are frequently considered poetic. The suggestive indeterminacy of her poems makes them rarely denotative but richly connotative. This, combined with the enigmatic resonance of the spoken cadences of her verses and their simultaneous disclosure and concealment, make Vitale's poetic voice unlike any other.

Vitale uses language in a very special way. "Lucidity" and "subtlety" are terms applied to her poetry, and she pursues them without compromise. Her language may be logical and precise, but the multiple meanings intertwined in poems rich with elusive interpretations are not. For the most part, the language of her poems is deceptively straightforward, without sentimentality or eloquence, but it is also an idiom very different from the language normally used to depict the inner world. The austerity of her poems and the transparency of her images, always at the verge of revealing a secret but never quite doing so, aim to achieve a precise impact. There is an element of mystery in what Vitale says, something she alludes to but keeps to herself. Again, Vitale is not deliberately obscure, for the reader can understand her poetry perfectly well on a superficial level. Complex themes are presented in a condensed form, masterfully captured in both their materiality and their mystery, their directness and their abstraction. Critics have often praised the "rigor" of Vitale's poetry without developing the notion further. I would agree, if "rigor" is used to mean the pursuit of clear language and clear ideas. However, it is not rigor that she aspires to in her poetry, but expressiveness, concision, and reflexive synthesis.

The distinctive character of Vitale's poetics is her preference for precise language, for an absolute discourse detached from the person speaking and, in a sense, depersonalized, as if language itself were speaking. This tendency toward the impersonality of art is recognized as a Valerian ideal. In his discussion of William Butler Yeats, T. S. Eliot explains this model as one that from an "intense and personal experience, is able to express a general truth; retaining all the particularity of his experience, to make of it a general symbol" (*On Poetry and Poets*, 1961). Such wisdom is more evident in Vitale's later writings, where a "general truth" comes through, achieving a rare freedom of expression that allows her poems to be universal. These poems express a perspective that transcends her personal universe to embrace widely shared emotions.

Vitale wrote her first poem, a sonnet, as a teenager; it was published in September 1942 in *Hyperión* but has never been collected. Nonetheless, her beginnings were inauspicious: too few poems published too far apart. Perhaps developing as a writer in the shadow of her famous husband (Rama) damaged her self-confidence. Or maybe she was just too busy raising a family. Vitale's well-known disdain for publicity also likely inhibited her early progress among intellectual friends bent on being public figures. Certainly, her perfectionism precluded the possibility of an outpouring of poems. Be that as it may, three slim collections with a total of only fifty-two poems, published over three decades and attracting little critical attention, would not have earned her a distinctive place in Latin American poetry; that has been done by her work since the 1970s. Not even her early recognition by Aldo Pellegrini, who included her in his celebrated *Antología de la poesía viva latinoamericana* (1966) alongside such major poets as Octavio Paz, José Lezama Lima, Gonzalo Rojas, Nicanor Parra, and Enrique Molina, hastened the acceptance of her poetic work. She did not begin to cement a reputation until the publication of *Oidor andante:* (1972; Errant listener).

Nevertheless, Vitale's early poems were quite distinctive and skillful, and the unity of her first three books is remarkable. *La luz de esta memoria* (1949; The light of this memory), *Palabra dada* (1953; The given word), and *Cada uno en su noche* (1960; Each one in his night) properly suggest a continuity of thought, vision, and language. In fact, Vitale herself highlights the unity of composition by including eight poems from the first two books in *Cada uno en su noche*, adding only eighteen new ones. Each title includes one of the main concepts of her poetry during this period—"light," "night," and "word"—providing a unity of tone that harmonizes with the author's vision. In a 1963 article Mario Benedetti states that Vitale's work can be considered as a single poem that rescues images associated with her vision of the day—images of despair, discontent, and the passing of time—to reorganize and expand them in search of a definitive voice. While the early books may be read this way, I would rather highlight Vitale's attitude toward poetry during these formative decades: first, she converts poetry from personal expression into an impersonal composition; second, she creates a self-conscious persona, aware of a self-imposed necessity for verbal precision; and third, she develops a way of writing poetry about human feelings not as an abstract proposition, but rather as images (apparently) without depth, as an encounter

with the everyday or universal elements of the world, evoking in the reader a compelling view of indeterminacy, an artistic product that radiates nuances and ambiguities reminiscent of a painting by René Magritte. In other words, Vitale underlines the uncertainty of the perception of reality. She names objects precisely, but their arrangement on the page and their interrelation imply more than they say, mean more than they represent.

*La luz de esta memoria* was composed by hand and printed on a press operated in the home of Vitale's friends Amanda Berenguer and José Pedro Díaz. It has been reprinted in a facsimile edition to celebrate its half-century of existence. When Vitale included the book in two subsequent collections of her work, she eliminated only "Epístola" (Epistle) and reworked a few pieces (but refrained from rewriting them, a common practice among modern poets). The book, consisting of fifteen poems, has surprisingly fresh emotional intensity and suggests subtle shades of feelings while subordinating the essential matter of the poem. Few writers achieve the maturity of voice in their first book that Vitale does—she avoids descriptions, incidents, circumstantial sketches, and reflections of the world of appearances. The powerful and compelling images of darkness and of a recurring inner void, intertwined with a search for light and air, demonstrate this point very well.

The title of the book is taken from a line of poetry by the seventeenth-century Spanish poet Lope de Vega, in which a contrast with the dark night is established in the next line, which is used as the epigraph of *La luz de esta memoria*. Two striking lines of the first poem, "La noche, esta morada" (The night, this dwelling), brilliantly present the conflict that is central to Vitale's work. They display a contrast, a duality of vision and poetic attitude, prevalent throughout this early period: "Despacio la esperanza / viste su piel de olvido" (Slowly hope / puts on its skin of forgetfulness). This is a haunting image of futility. On the one hand, the speaker names diverse manifestations of the apparent surface of reality; on the other hand, the concentration of expressive nouns, and the emotions they provoke, multiplies allusions to states of mind and feelings of despair. Life is seen as loss and dispossession ("el cielo vuelto un hueco sin voz y sin orillas" [the sky turned into a hollow without voice and without limits]) by a poetic persona who favors a desolate tone to which she consistently returns. In a climax of emotional intensity in the final verses, the figure of the poet is savior of the ruins, where everything "viene a salvarse en mí" (comes to be saved in me).

Nostalgia for what is lost, for the fleeting nature of pleasure and time, underlines each poem in *La luz de esta memoria*. This is evident in the poem that closes the book:

> Así se va la tierra que pisamos,
> así de pronto todo, amor o hiedra,
> es un vano pretexto del deseo,
> forma huidiza, nube.
> Sólo el recuerdo,
> quebrado en piedras falsas,
> finge la luz,
> rescata la hermosura.

> The earth we step on slips away,
> suddenly everything, love or ivy,
> is a vain pretext of desire,
> elusive shape, cloud.
> Only memory,
> broken into false stones,
> imitates light,
> rescues beauty.

These lines may be taken to illustrate the emotional effect generated by the arrangement of familiar words and concepts into original combinations, avoiding clichés of language and stylized presentations of human feelings and experiences. Helena Corbellini (1997) perceptively noticed the significance of the poems that open and close *La luz de esta memoria*, remarking that they constitute Vitale's *ars poetica*, perhaps without realizing the fullest implication of this insight. As will later become apparent, Vitale places programmatic poems—perhaps even the most significant ones—at the beginning and the end of each book, as if to indicate a direction for the reader to follow.

Unfulfilled dreams and the memory of them occur repeatedly and obsessively in these poems. For example, in "Para quién, dime al fin para quién" (For whom, tell me at last for whom), the sense of loss of love, of silence, and of desolation is delicately advanced by the image of light slowly descending toward the sea, an intensely lyrical vision full of cryptic suggestions, and by the reappearance of one of Vitale's preferred images, "un cielo sin orillas" (a sky without limits), suggesting a life without center and a sense of exclusion from any kind of community. These images remain mysteriously interwoven, retaining their freshness and impact:

> pero ya no hay memoria,
> en cuentro sólo un cielo sin orillas,
> una pena celeste donde la noche
> recomienza el sueño.

> There is not even memory left,
> I find only a sky without limits,
> a celestial sadness where the night
> begins to dream again.

If the emphasis in *La luz de esta memoria* is on the skillful expression of subtle but impersonal states of mind, the next book, *Palabra dada*, intensifies the experience of solitude and even anguish, placing a sensitive, civilized, and passionate speaker in a world in which "the given word" means very little. The meditation on life and death, and the recurring identification of time and night are of great significance. Fears and dreams, encounters and losses are depicted in a subdued lyricism: "Sólo un polvo de sueño / importuno en mis manos" (Only a dust of dreams / imprudent in my hands). The perfectly transparent language does not contain any enigmas or ambiguities. Vitale finds the precise words to reveal a desolate situation without conventional emotionality. Clarity, concision, ellipsis, and synthesis are developed to perfection to convey the feel of human experience with lyrical intensity.

The instability of meaning and the fear that the traditional usage of language is unable to communicate shades of feeling and thought are ever present in modern literature. In "Canon," Vitale's first poem of *Palabra dada*, the poetic voice laments the failure of language to reflect meaning. Even everyday activities and simple objects, let alone traditional poetic motifs (night, love, friendship, death), become challenges for the self-conscious poet: "Ya todo ha sido dicho / y un resplandor de siglos / lo defiende del eco" (Everything has been said / and a glare of centuries / protects it from the echo). As a means of expression, language has been overused over the centuries, becoming an element to be questioned and doubted, heightening its inability to convey meaning. Poetry therefore objectifies a mood of questioning language and reality itself, of stressing the uncertainty of the perception of reality.

*Cada uno en su noche* has only eighteen new pieces, but it may well be Vitale's most important contribution during her formative years. In a way, it is an anthology of her early work, for it includes selections from the two previous books. Primarily, from one poem to the next, Vitale achieves what she has been seeking, a consummate abstraction of intense feelings. From the beginning, her work is marked by a progressive avoidance of literary estheticism, by a search for the essential word, as Clara Silva (1972) noted. Her poetry, elegiac in nature, is haunted by the emptiness and misery of life: the absence of love, solitude, an inner void, and the fleeting nature of time are expressed in a direct yet elusive language, discarding pure stylization in favor of clear and straightforward statements. Yet at the same time it is a language that asserts the indeterminacy of meaning, transparent yet full of obscure connotations. However, as Rafael Courtoisie (1991) observes: "It does not deal with an obscure and inextricable profundity, but rather with a profundity more difficult to achieve, that of the simple formulation, of precision, and of synthesis."

Poetry is concerned with the external world as well as with the inner world. An excellent example is "Este mundo" (This world), the first poem of *Cada uno en su noche*, one of Vitale's most representative and anthologized works. The lucid but agonizing acceptance of the world we live in, within self-imposed necessities, is the apparent motif of the poem:

> *Sólo acepto este mundo iluminado*
> *cierto, inconstante, mío.*
> *Sólo exalto su eterno laberinto*
> *y su segura luz, aunque se esconda.*
> *Despierta o entre sueños,*
> *su grave tierra piso*
> *y es su paciencia en mí*
> *la que florece.*

> I accept only this illuminated world
> certain, inconstant, my own.
> I exalt only its eternal labyrinth
> and its unwavering light, even though it may hide.
> Awake or dreaming,

> I walk on its solemn earth
> and its patience in me
> blossoms.

The impact of the successive contrasts between water and fire, heaven andhell; the conflict between the temporary and the eternal, between certainties and inconstancies lead Vitale to inquire into the value of life, to undertake a conventional metaphysical search. Yet in "Este mundo," though the world may be the object under scrutiny, the emphasis is on the wonder of being alive. The calm and restrained acceptance of the world with its never fulfilled "promises," and the subtle juxtaposition of two contrasting verbs in the subjunctive mood representing universal antinomies, enable Vitale to end the poem reflexively. She accepts the world as it is, with a lucid understanding of its limitations and withholding any existential exasperation:

> *Yo sólo en él habito,*
> *de él espero,*
> *y hay suficiente asombro.*
> *En él estoy,*
> *me quede,*
> *renaciera.*

> I only live in it,
> from it I expect,
> and there is enough wonder.
> I am in it,
> were I to remain,
> to be reborn.

In "Todo es víspera" (Everything awaits), the last poem in *Cada uno en su noche*, Vitale turns to a simple object, a shiny new pitcher, as an impersonal correlative of the speaker's emotion. But the speaker also superimposes on the pitcher emotional and moving images related to the fundamental theme of the piece, the dream of a rebirth into a less negative place. Images of air and light are juxtaposed against darkness and stagnation, serving to reveal the meaning of the title of the collection:

> *Cada uno en su noche*
> *esperanzado pide*
> *el despertar, el aire,*

*una luz seminaria*
*algo donde no muera.*

Each in his night
hopefully asks for
dawn, air
a seminal light
something where it does not die.

The poems gain their distinctive texture from the tendency to objectify a mood on everyday objects, such as the pitcher above (and many others, such as doors, bridges, walls), usually used as signs of alienation, or to transform elements of nature (earth, wind, night, shadows, rain, fire) into symbols of futility, in order to mask the revelation of a "verdad mortal" (mortal truth), unnamed but intimated "en su precisa exactitud" (in its precise exactitude), as we read in "Cercado ajeno." Nothing more precise, for instance, than the response to the onerous demands imposed upon a housewife in "Obligaciones diarias" (Daily obligations). After detailing them, the poet adds, with an ironic twist:

> *Pero no pienses,*
> > *no procures,*
> > > *teje.*

> But do not think,
> > do not try,
> > > knit.

But the simplicity of Vitale's poetry is deceptive. As Enrique Fierro has indicated, she writes "poems of deceptive transparency, of difficult access, that reaffirm the poet's trust in words as the only means to express poetic experience, however much this might appear unyielding to them." In its emphasis on such methods, her depiction of the "real world" may appear abstract to the average reader; the avoidance of description and observation, and the exclusion of historical referents in favor of direct statements, constitute a form of silence and concealment. Yet, the external world functions as an objectified setting for inner conflicts. The profound personal feelings that Vitale finds within herself are transformed into human feelings, impersonal but certainly individualized.

An even longer silence (twelve years) preceded the publication of *Oidor andante:* (1972), an intricate title that most likely refers to the errant (*andante*) movement of the poems toward their listener (*oidor*), toward the type of reader for whom they are destined. Vitale's poetry is more ambitious in this collection, most notably in regard to her awareness of the precarious nature of language, of the inability of language to convey her intentions. The book is an intellectually rigorous exercise in concentrated expression and elliptical composition, which renders her poetry ambiguous and provides the basis for multiple readings. In her first three books Vitale's main concern was to find a form in which she could present the turmoil of her soul. From *Oidor* on, she writes a more self-conscious verse, widening her interests and progressively adding new subjects, nourished perhaps by philosophical skepticism and certainly by an increased reflexivity and ironic intent.

Since *Oidor andante:* Vitale's poetic credo has included the distinctive traits of her mature poetry: new and more complex themes, increased use of cultural references, and the effects of the passing of time. Although Vitale continues many of the tendencies of her early work, the indeterminacy of her poetic practice, the calculated vagueness of her references, and the elusiveness of meaning merge to form highly complex and intellectualized creations. In these later works she adds a heightened awareness of the power of language in her attempt to find the most exact equivalence between the words used and the effects she wishes to communicate, taking the process of understatement ever farther.

The book opens with "La palabra" (The word), a poem about the power of language—or, rather, about the fusion of the poet, the word, and the world, emblematic of Vitale's search for the precise word among so many possibilities available:

> *Expectantes palabras,*
> *fabulosas en sí,*
> *promesas de sentidos posibles,*
> *airosas,*
> > *aéreas,*
> > > *airadas,*
> > > > *ariadnas.*

> *Un breve error*
> *las vuelve ornamentales.*

*Su indescriptible exactitud*
*nos borra.*

Expectant words,
fabulous in themselves,
promises of possible meanings,
graceful,
> aerial,
>> angry,
>>> Ariadnean.

A small error
makes them ornamental.
Their indescribable exactness
erases us.

The alliteration, the melodious rhythm, the myriad connotations, the sustained mystery of the implications, the blank spaces on the page, and the unifying images awaken emotional and intellectual associations in the reader's mind. It is certainly a masterpiece of poetic creation. The language used is neither ornamental nor ostentatious, but exact and precise. Yet for all its exactness, meaning remains elusive, though the enjoyment of the poem is not diminished; on the contrary, its enigmatic nature is augmented by its indeterminacy. The multiple alliterations and meanings (*airosas,* / *aéreas,* / *airadas,* / *ariadnas*), an instance of untranslatable verse, are much more than the display of an artful mastery of language and idea. They are a means of releasing the creative power of language; a search for wisdom and objectivity, and primarily for transparency, under the semblance of obscurity, a notion indispensable in the poetry of Pierre Reverdy, Juan Ramón Jiménez, and Octavio Paz. "La transparencia es todo lo que queda" (Transparency is all that remains) appears at the end of Paz's *Blanco,* a poetic exploration of the capability of language to create an analogical vision of the world. Similarly, Vitale strives to make words transparent and impersonal, to approximate thoughts and feelings as closely as language permits, eliminating verbal imprecision and, for the most part, the use of rhetorical devices. This is the daily battle of the poet, as the poem "La batalla" (The battle) implies, a notion that reaches its full significance in her most recent books.

Reflections on language permeate *Oidor andante:,* but these reflections never become the exclusive subject matter of the poem, as is the case in much of contemporary writing, where poetry becomes a tributary of literary theory. There is a poem, "Del miedo como denominador" (Fear as a denominator), about the impotence of language to reject fear as a common factor of life, about the simulacrum of dialogues and the dread of ending in silence, with all communication remote. The presence of silence—or, rather, the desire for silence—among "un bosque de palabras" (a forest of words) characterizes "Reunión" (Meeting). In another poem, ("Cuadro" [Picture]), the image of an illusory ordered world, as Antonio Melis (1983) indicates, disintegrates as a result of the destructive nature of human beings. Poetry for Vitale is a profound experience that gives life its meaning, as she reminds us in "Seguro de muerte" (Death insurance), where the speaker "fía en la salvación por la palabra" (trusts in salvation by the word), in a world without the safe dependence on traditional ideals.

*Oidor andante:* is perhaps the book least distanced from Vitale's personal experiences. She seldom writes poems about particular events, but here we find a few ("Ciudad vieja" [Old town], "Sala de profesores" [Professors' lounge], "Reunión"), which reflect circumstances of her life in Montevideo. However, the composition and specific character of the poems are essentially the same as all others. Incidental effects do not circumstantially identify any physical setting as one alluded to in the poems named, nor there is any social intent. They become abstract experiences, depersonalized moments of observation by a persona that is implicitly involved yet consciously breaks away from the representation of a particular situation, emphasizing the effect of the episode on the speaker's mind.

Most important, as the result of an increasingly jaded vision about the overuse of poetry to solve the shortcomings of life and society, Vitale incorporates irony into her poetry. Nowhere is this more directly portrayed than in "Capítulo" (Chapter), a playful yet serious criticism of some contemporary literary practices. Without preamble a voice announces, in twelve capitalized lines, the discovery of "LA FÓRMULA IRISADA / QUE CLARAMENTE / NOS EXPLICA

EL MUNDO" (the iridescent formula / that clearly / explains the world to us). History, the future of the self, the mysteries of the world, "EL LUGAR DEL TESORO" (the hiding place of the treasure)—everything is simplified or solved. In two final lines, in lowercase, a voice simply states: "Pero luego el capítulo / no llegó a ser escrito" (But then the chapter / was never written), revealing by the use of irony the utopian nature of such an enterprise. Discovering the true meaning of everything also provokes, as Carlos Pereda (1998) argues convincingly, a reflection on the arrogance and "conceited self-deception" of those searching for a simplification of the complexities of the human condition.

"Calco por transparencia" (Tracing by transparency) opens Vitale's next book, *Jardín de sílice* (1980; Garden of silica), as if to continue the reflection on the notion of transparency introduced in *Oidor andante*:

> Por transparencia
> se ve el fuego
> devorar
> las más altas cortezas
> en los jardines escalados.
> Sobrevive un gorjeo,
> brújula tersa.

> By transparency
> we see fire
> devouring
> the highest barks
> in the terraced gardens
> A chirp survives
> polished compass.

Here, the idea of transparency implies a metaphysical attempt to grasp in words a primordial unity. Vitale develops this notion further in "Contra el tiempo" (Against time), a poem in which the rhythm of being, the melody of the celestial spheres, "aún toca a transparencias, / arriba, contra el tiempo, / entre las luces" (still playing transparencies, / above, against time, / within the lights). Silence, music, time, and light assume a quality of transparency, with implications both vast and obscure. Transparency thus becomes a synonym of the indescribable essence of the universe.

*Jardín de sílice* is divided into three parts. In the first, "Calco por transparencia," the ability of language to

capture reality is repeatedly questioned. The increased use of phonemic plays ("jirones de Girondo"); wordplay, such as paronomasia ("El otoño presagia traslados / traslada los presagios" [Autumn foretells copies / it copies omens]); rhetorical questions; antithesis; hypothetical resolutions; learned expressions—as if to suggest the irreducible unintelligibility of the world—become more commonplace. The second part, "Íconos" (Icons), is an intertextual exercise based on the works of other writers and of painters, converting culture into the subject matter of poetry: Quevedo's diabolical visions, Magritte's dreams and clouds, Escher's endless staircases, Brauner's monsters. And the last section, "Jardín de sílice," elaborates on the image of a garden of silica, a desolate landscape, where "hay que pagar la consumición del tiempo" (one has to pay for the wasting away of time), at the edge of silence and death, where only the "fertilidad de la desdicha" (fertility of misery) grows incessantly.

Since the 1980s, Vitale has published three collections of poems, several anthologies, and two books of prose. An increased interest in her writings is, of course, related to these more recent volumes and their availability.

*Sueños de la constancia* (1988; Dreams of perseverance) is Vitale's most important publication to date. It includes all her earlier volumes, as well as a previously unpublished book, which lends the collection its title. In Spanish *constancia* means perseverance, but also proof and written evidence. The dreams of the poet are finally realized; the struggle is over; the proof is now available for anyone to enjoy and judge, published in an edition widely available to the reading public. Once again the opening poem, untitled and in five parts, is an exploration of language by a poet conscious of the power of words to create their own reality, and for the need to awaken them to fulfill their mission. It is a poem about the nature of poetry itself, a poem that interrogates language and our assumptions about it. The first and shortest of the five parts reads:

> Palabras:
> palacios vacíos,
> ciudad adormilada.
> ¿Antes de qué cuchillo
> llegará el trueno

*—la inundación después—*
*que las despierte?*

Words:
                    empty palaces,
drowsy city.
Before what knife
will come the thunder
—later the flood—
that awakens them?

Cultural references and intertextual relations, traced to *Oidor andante:*, increase noticeably in this book. They suggest that literature is a continuum of languages and cultures. I am not referring to the homage rendered to other artists—including Quevedo, Baudelaire, and Magritte—prevalent since *Jardín de sílice*. The emphasis now is more deliberate, as the series "Acto de conciliación" (Act of conciliation) exemplifies. It includes thirteen poems, in all of which a line is taken from another poet, duly credited in notes. The specific viewpoint that informs the poems, derived alphabetically from Guillaume Apollinaire to Ramón Xirau, provides an interplay of intellects and subtle correspondences for an appropriately attuned reader. It shows, as Jorge Luis Borges taught us, that universality is one of the distinguishing features of Latin American literature. Naturally this type of poetry presents difficulties, but reading these works is rewarding even without knowledge of the writings evoked. Vitale's poems are not a mere commentary on other writers' works, but examples of her critical ability to build upon the experience of others, reconciling their interests with her own production. For instance, "No dicen, hablan, hablan" (They do not say, they speak, they speak), a line taken from a poem by Octavio Paz, deals with a passion shared by both poets that is present in all their writings: the concern with language as an object of reflection and the elusiveness of meaning, the distance that separates the "word" from the "real object."

The poetic is certainly not limited to one form, the lyric. In recent years, Vitale appears not to be satisfied with the assumption that poetry must be restricted to verse. Two singular books in her production are *Léxico de afinidades* (1994; Lexicon of affinities) and *Donde vuela el camaleón* (1996; Where the chameleon flies).

*Léxico de afinidades* includes short texts primarily in prose, ordered alphabetically in a sort of personal dictionary, from abracadabra to zuibitzu. Though written in prose, the texts have quite different tonalities, oscillating from extended poetic images to reflections on words, including narrative tales and a few poems in verse. The chaos of the world offers her an opportunity to classify it and organize it, but the world is endless and arbitrary, and in a manner reminiscent of Borges she questions her own classification: "Su vastedad puede parecerse al caos que busca sustituir" (Its vastness can resemble the chaos it is trying to replace). The book includes whimsical and ludic texts alongside serious cultural preoccupations, a format suggestive of a diary or a notebook. There are portraits, childhood memories, melancholic evocations of family members, introspective reflections, aphorisms, humorous texts, travel accounts, brief narrations, remarks on art and literature, homages to writers and artists (Borges, Rubén Darío, Felisberto Hernández, Paul Klee). The selection of entries is arbitrary, conforming to no arrangement other than the curiosity and selective affinities of the author. Literature benefits from change, innovation, and new ways to defy staleness. Under P, Vitale states a definition of poetry: "Las palabras son nómadas; la mala poesía las vuelve sedentarias" (Words are nomadic; bad poetry makes them sedentary). She may continue writing these kinds of books, as she stated in an interview with Daniel González Dueñas and Alejando Toledo: "Lo que importa más que nada es la libertad con la que pude escribir el libro. Así querría seguir escribiendo" (What matters most is the freedom I had to write the book. I would like to continue writing this way). *Léxico de afinidades* is a noteworthy collection of unpredictable and fragmentary texts, independent from one another, displaying a freedom and a pleasure of writing not found in any other book by Vitale.

The Mexican edition of *Donde vuela el camaleón* (2000) contains twenty-seven texts, ranging from one paragraph to five or six pages. The title, taken from the writings of Leonardo da Vinci, is a reference to the chameleon, which changes colors without losing its identity, no doubt an allusion to the author herself, who is now writing prose without undergoing significant changes. The writing points in multiple directions:

toward the prose poem or the poetic short story, vignettes or allegorical tales. What maintains the poetic character of the work is the artifice, the fantastic incarnations, the mythological figures, and an enchanting anachronism of texts that draw on the imagination without adhering to any rules. For the most part, there is no description or narration, but a sustained metaphor as a story line. For instance, "characters" are named after colors; a gray sparrow dreams of being blue; a cloud is born of tears; a "regulation," able to fly, longs for the possibility of becoming a "precept" or a "dogma"; a story, "Un monumento para Eva" (A monument for Eve) tells the life of a woman who collects words. "Los poderes del blanco" (The powers of white), in which there is a story line, is a splendid allegory about the infinite ramifications of writing, about "las ilimitadas posibilidades de un cuaderno en blanco . . . espejo inagotable del inagotable mundo" (the possibilities of a blank notebook . . . inexhaustible mirror of the inexhaustible world). The texts of *Donde vuela el camaleón* are playful and liberating fantasies by a writer in complete control of her creative faculties.

*Procura de lo imposible* (1998; Search for the impossible), Vitale's most recent book of poetry, is also her longest: it includes ninety pieces. Throughout her poetic works, as we have seen, concise expression contrasts with the elusiveness of meaning, formal precision with the enigmatic character of her writing. This is even more true of *Procura de lo imposible*. How can this search for the impossible be read? Alfredo Fressia (1999) has stated that this is a poetic discourse reaching out toward an "absolute song," and it certainly can be read as a daring venture toward pure singing. The book opens with a series of six pieces, grouped under the heading "Soltar el mirlo" (Releasing the blackbird), and ends with a group of fifteen prose poems, "La voz cantante" (The singing voice). The emphasis moves from pieces in which we read about birds singing in the open, from a celebration of free and pure singing in communion with nature, to those where the natural element of singing is transformed into words set to a delightful rhythmic prose, so sonorous that in effect they imitate music, stressing writing as play. "Song is existence," says the third of Rilke's *Sonnets to Orpheus*. And existence is a synonym of presence and being.

The great variety of poems in *Procura de lo imposible* is gathered in eight series. Reminiscences of cities, poems about particular sites, elegies for lost friends, dialogues with other poets, meditations on nature and on life, landscapes of dreams, and, as she calls them, "images of a floating word" represent the variety and vitality of Vitale's poetry. Nonetheless, perhaps the most engaging poems are those dealing with the evanescent nature of the literary moment. This experience is magnificently represented in "Mariposa, poema" (Butterfly, poem), in which the interwoven images of night and movement represent the fluttering of a nocturnal butterfly while a poet searches for inspiration, and in the instant of incantation and wonder caused by the extraordinary fluidity of a bird's chirping in "Colibrí" (Hummingbird). The closing lines of this poem are filled with emotional as well as with intellectual intensity: "y entonces por un segundo / sentir cómo late el mundo" (and then for a second / to feel the world's heartbeat).

A series of fourteen poems, published in the Mexican periodical *Fractal* in 1999 and to be included in the forthcoming *Reducción del infinito*, reveals Vitale's interest in a literature based on intertextuality. Written for a circle of initiates, Vitale's poems establish a dialogue with the work of Julio Herrera y Reissig, Uruguay's foremost modern poet. The title, "Solo lunático, desolación legítima" (Lunatic solo, legitimate desolation), alludes to two groups of poems by Herrera: "Tertulia lunática (1909; Lunatic gathering) and "Desolación absurda" (1903; Absurd desolation). Like Herrera y Reissig, Vitale structures her verses in the conventional model of the *décima* (a ten-line poem, with eight-syllable verses). Both poets use internal and consonant rhymes, a form that allows for very little freedom. In addition, Vitale skillfully appropriates the unusual rhyme favored by her predecessor: the first verse and the fourth end with the same word. Here are two examples, the first by Herrera and the following by Vitale:

> *Oh mariposa nocturna*
> *de mi lámpara suicida,*
> *alma caduca y torcida,*
> *evanescencia nocturna;*
> *linfática taciturna*

de mi Nirvana opioso,
en tu mirar sigiloso
me espeluzna tu erotismo
que es la pasión del abismo
por el Ángel Tenebroso

Oh, noctural butterfly
suicidal victim of my lamp,
faded and twisted soul,
nocturnal evanescence;
taciturn lymphatic
of my hypnotic Nirvana,
in your stealthy look
your eroticism frightens me
like the passion of the abyss
by the Dark Angel.

El cielo cuando aparace
a una loma retrepado
y tras árboles brotado
como más cielo aparece
¿Quién entonces lo merece
sino el que a diario se asombra
de vivir más, casi sombra,
que lo que una mariposa?
Mirándolo se reposa
y vuelve a amar lo que nombra.

The sky when it appears
reclined on a hill
rising behind trees,
appears to be a larger sky.
Who then deserves it
but one astonished daily
by living more, almost a shadow,
as a butterfly?
Watching it one rests
and loves again what is named.

Vitale's poem reiterates a form, but she is not engaged merely in the imitation of a procedure. Her series pays homage to the musicality inherent in words, and her selection of an Uruguayan poet is undoubtedly also an act of recuperation. Nonetheless, the mood, emotions, and temperament are quite different. Gone is the spirit of anguished decadence of a tortured soul, the atmosphere of death, and the morbid eroticism so prevalent in Herrera's nocturnal poems. Vitale illuminates nature, restoring to poetry the power to convey the

wonder of everyday life and a sense of cosmic love. Once again, Vitale's capacity to capture the ecstasy of the world and her talent to express it confirm her as one of the greatest living Latin American poets.

## SELECTED BIBLIOGRAPHY

### Primary Works

#### Poetry

La luz de esta memoria. Montevideo: La Galatea, 1949. Second facsimile ed., Montevideo: Vintén, 1999.

Palabra dada. Montevideo: La Galatea, 1953.

Cada uno en su noche. Montevideo: Editorial Alfa, 1960. Second ed., Montevideo: Arca, 1964.

Oidor andante:. Montevideo: Arca, 1972. Second ed., Mexico City: Premia, 1982.

Jardín de sílice. Caracas: Monte Ávila, 1980.

Fieles. Mexico City: El Mendrugo, 1976. Second ed., enl., Mexico City: UNAM, 1982. Third ed., Montevideo: Ediciones de la Banda Oriental, 2000. (Anthology and prologue by Pablo Rocca.)

Entresaca. Mexico City: Oasis, 1984. (Anthology.)

Sueños de la constancia. Mexico City: Fondo de Cultura Económica, 1988. (Includes La luz de esta memoria, Palabra dada, Cada uno en su noche, Oidor andante:, Jardín de sílice, and Sueños de la constancia.)

Obra poética I. Montevideo: Arca, 1992. (Includes La luz de esta memoria, Palabra dada, Cada uno en su noche, Oidor andante:.)

Jardines imaginarios. [Mexico City]: Ditoria, 1996. (Included in Procura de lo imposible.)

Material de lectura. Selections by Ida Vitale, with an introductory note by Víctor Sosa. Mexico City: UNAM, 1998. (Anthology.)

De varia empresa. Caracas: Pequeña Venecia, 1998. (Included in Procura de lo imposible.)

Procura de lo imposible. Mexico City: Fondo de Cultura Económica, 1998.

Reducción del infinito. Barcelona: Tusquets, in press.

#### Prose

Léxico de afinidades. Mexico City: Vuelta, 1994.

Donde vuela el camaleón. Montevideo: Vintén, 1996. Second ed., Mexico City: Ediciones Sin Nombre/Casa Juan Pablos, 2000.

*Un invierno equivocado.* Illustrations by Isabel Pin. Mexico City: CIDCLI, 1999. (Short book for children.)

*Libro natural.* Mexico City: Paidós, in press.

### Critical Studies

Diego, Eliseo. *Divertimentos y versiones.* Prologue by Ida Vitale. Montevideo: Arca, 1967.

*Juana de Ibarbourou: Vida y obra.* Capítulo Oriental, no. 20. Montevideo: Centro Editorial de América Latina, 1968.

*La poesía de los años veinte.* Selected by Ida Vitale. Capítulo Oriental, no. 21. Montevideo: Centro Editorial de América Latina, 1968.

*Los poetas del veinte.* Montevideo: Centro Editorial de América Latina, 1968.

"José Santos Vega o el humor serenísimo." *Sin Nombre* (San Juan) 5, no. 2:15–20 (1974).

"Octavio Paz: Hacia el blanco." *Eco* (Bogotá) 163:98–106 (May 1974). Reprinted in *Acerca de Octavio Paz.* Montevideo: Fundación de Cultura Universitaria, 1974. Pp. 41–54.

"Alberto Girri, poeta de lo real." *Sin Nombre* 5, no. 3:65–69 (1975).

"Lavanda y un nuevo símbolo onettiano." *Texto Crítico* (Mexico City) 6, no. 18–19:70–72 (1980).

"Poesía y crítica: La dispersión y el límite." In *Los escritores hispanoamericanos frente a sus críticos.* Toulouse: Université Toulouse-Le Mirail, Service des Publications, 1983. Pp. 149–152.

"Las partituras secretas de un poeta: Enrique Casaravilla Lemos." *Studi di Letteratura Ispano-americana* (Milan) 13–14:7–13 (1983).

Casaravilla Lemos, Enrique. *Material de lectura.* Selections and notes by Ida Vitale. Poesía, no. 106. Mexico City: UNAM, 1984.

Hernández, Felisberto. *Material de lectura.* Selections and note by Ida Vitale. Cuento Contemporáneo, 20. Mexico City: UNAM, 1984.

Supervielle, Jules. *Amigos desconocidos.* Selections and prologue by Ida Vitale. Mexico City: Vuelta, 1994.

## Secondary Works

### Critical and Biographical Studies

Benedetti, Mario. "Ida Vitale y su obra de un solo poema." In *Literatura Uruguaya Siglo XX.* Montevideo: Arca, 1988. Pp. 329–331.

Corbellini, Helena. "Ida Vitale: La revelación exacta." In *Historia de la literatura uruguaya contemporánea,* vol. 2. Edited by Heber Raviolo and Pablo Rocca. Montevideo: Ediciones de la Banda Oriental, 1997. Pp. 143–163.

Courtoisie, Rafael. "*Cada uno en su noche* de Ida Vitale." In *Diccionario de literatura uruguaya,* vol. 3. Edited by Alberto Oreggioni et al. Montevideo: Arca, 1991. Pp. 61–62.

Fierro, Enrique. *Los poetas del 45.* Montevideo: CEDAL, 1968. Pp. 497–512.

Fressia, Alfredo. "El encuentro del canto." *El País* (Montevideo) 490:13 (26 March 1999). (Review of *Procura de lo imposible.*)

García Pinto, Magdalena. "Ida Vitale." In her *Historias íntimas.* Hanover, N.H.: Ediciones del Norte, 1988. Pp. 251–281. Translated by Trudy Balch and Magdalena García Pinto in *Women Writers of Latin America,* by García Pinto. Austin: University of Texas Press, 1991. Pp. 223–246. (Interview.)

González Dueñas, Daniel, and Alejandro Toledo. "Ida Vitale y Enrique Fierro: Léxico de afinidades mexicanas." *Periódico de Poesía* (Mexico City) 8:32–39 (1994). (Interview.)

Melis, Antonio. "Uruguay: I poeti nel tempo della povertá. Ida Vitale." *Studi di Letteratura Ispano-americana* (Milan) 13–14:243–258 (1983).

Ortega, Julio. "Ida Vitale: *Jardín de sílice.*" *Vuelta* 4, no. 48:42–43 (November 1980). (Review.)

Pereda, Carlos. *Crítica de la razón arrogante.* Mexico City: Taurus, 1998. Pp. 85–87.

Ramond, Michele. "La nuit alchimique de Ida Vitale." *Río de la Plata* (Paris) 7:49–61 (1988). In Spanish, "La noche alquímica de Ida Vitale." *Cuadernos Americanos* (Mexico City) 4, no. 1:178–189 (1990); also in *Nuevo Texto Crítico* (Stanford) 3, no. 1:143–152 (1990).

Sefamí, Jacobo. "Ida Vitale." In *Contemporary Spanish American Poets.* Westport, Conn.: Greenwood Press, 1992. Pp. 196–197. (Bibliography.)

Silva, Clara. "Misterio de la palabra." *El País* (Montevideo), 27 February 1972, p. 2. (Review of *Oidor andante:*)

Velázquez, Jaime G. "La consumición del tiempo." *Revista de la Universidad de México* 36, no. 2:38–40 (June 1981). (Review of *Jardín de sílice.*)

# INDEX

# INDEX

## A

*Abdul Bashur, Dreamer of Ships* (Mutis), **Supp. I,** 375–376

Abolitionism, *see* Blacks

*The Absent City* (Piglia), **Supp. I,** 407

Acevedo Díaz, Eduardo, **299–302**
  association with Batalle y Ordóñez, 300
  comparison with Margarinos Cervantes, 302

"Acomodador, El" (Hernández, F.), **Supp. I,** 310

Acosta, Joseph de, **47–50**
  comparison with Las Casas, 50
  critical assessment, 50

*Adán Buenosayres* (Marechal), 891–892

*Adán y Eva* (Sabines), **Supp. I,** 511

*A Descoberta da América pelos Turcos* (Amado), **Supp. I,** 25–26

*Adioses, Los* (Onetti), 1092, 1093

"A él" (Gómez de Avellaneda), 178

*Affonso Arinos* (Amoroso Lima), 782, 787

African-Americans, *see* Blacks; Negritude Movement

Afro-Antillean movement, 948, 949, 1385

Afro-Cuban avant-garde movement, 1021, 1168

Afro-Cuban ethnology, **Supp. I,** 120–128

Afro-Cuban Poetry
  Ballagas, 1082, 1083, 1385
  Guillén, 1084, 1385

*Agrestes* (Cabral), 1251, **Supp. I,** 115

*Agriculture in the Torrid Zone (La agricultura de la zona torrida)* (Bello), 131

*Água Viva* (Lispector), 1306

"Aguas de recuerdo" (Cabrera Infante), 1385, **Supp. I,** 135–136

Agustini, Delmira, **649–653**
  erotic poetry's relationship with mysticism, 651–653
  *modernismo* duality, 649, 650, 651, 653
  themes, 651, 653

"Ainda uma Vez—Adeus" (Gonçalves Dias), 188

*A la estátua del Libertador* (Caro), 280

"A la estrella de Venus" (Heredia), 137

*Alamos en la azotea* (Wolff), 1313

"A la plata" (Carrasquilla), 343, 348

*A la vacuna* (Bello), 130

Alberdi, Juan Bautista, 153–157
  biography of Wheelright, 156
  creator of *La Moda*, 154
  critical assessment, 157
  influence on Gallegos, 605
  influences on, 153, 154, 155

*Alborto y motín de los indios de México del 8 de junio de 1692* (Sigüenza y Góngora), 73–74

*Album de familia* (Castellanos), 1299

*Álbum de família* (Rodrigues), **Supp. I,** 482, 486–487

Alegría, Ciro, **1099–1102**
  awards and honors, 1099
  critical assessment, 1102
  imprisoned for political activity, 1099
  interest in plight and culture of Indians, 1100, 1101–1102
  interflow of temporal dimensions, 1101
  member of Alianza Popular Revolucionaria Americana, 1099
  political activity, 1099
  use of amalgamation, 1100, 1101

"Além do passaporte" (Ivo), **Supp. I,** 324

Alencar, Jose de, **195–201**, 1119
  critical assessment, 196, 201
  influence on Machodo de Assis, 201, 254, 256
  influences on, 196, 198
  narratives set in Rio de Janiero, 199
  rural social narratives, 199, 336, 746
  serial publications, 200

*Aleph, El* (Borges), 851, 852, 1337

*Alfarrábios: Crônicas dos tempos coloniaes* (Alencar), 197, 198, 199

"Alfrombra como lírica" (Girri), **Supp. I,** 300–301

*Alguma Poesia* (Drummond), 957, 958, 959–961, 962, 963, 967

"Alguns toureiros" (Cabral), **Supp. I,** 108, 110

"A lição de poesia" (Cabral), **Supp. I,** 106

Allende, Isabel, **Supp. I,** 1–13
  compared to García Márquez, **Supp. I,** 6
  journalism, **Supp. I,** 3–4

Allende, Salvador, 1006, 1284, 1396

*All Green Shall Perish (Todo verdor percerá)* (Mallea), 981, 983–984

*All Nudity Shall Be Punished (Toda nudez será castigada)* (Rodrigues), **Supp. I,** 484–485, 486, 487

*Allocution to Poetry (La alocución a la poesía)* (Bello), 131

"Almada, O" (Machado de Assis), 261

Almagro, Diego de, 44

*Alma America* (Chocano), 544–548

Alonso, Amado, influence on Bomal, 113

"Al partir" (Gómez de Avellaneda), 175, 178

"Al rescoldo" (Güiraldes), 622

"Al silencio" (Rojas), **Supp. I,** 496–497

*Alsino* (Prado), 644–645, 646

*Al sol y bajo la luna* (Tablada), 443

*Altazor; o, El viaje paracaídas* (Huidobro), 759–760, 923

*Aluno relapso, O* (Ivo), **Supp. I,** 317, 328

Alvares de Azevedo, Manuel Antônio, influence on Machado de Assis, 256

Amado, Jorge, **1153–1160, Supp. I,** 15–30
  attitude toward bourgeoisie, 1156
  awards and honors, 1155, **Supp. I,** 26
  best-selling books, 1157, 1160
  Brazilian Communist party membership, 1153–1154, **Supp. I,** 18
  Brazilian popular culture as theme, 1154
  compared with Steinbeck and Dos Passos, 1156

critical assessment, 463
critical judgement by, 462
description of Mexico City's slums, 461
experimental novels, 460
influence on other Latin American
    writers, 463
influences on, 458
Mexican Revolution, 655, 657, 658
*Azul . . .* (Darío), 398–399

## B

"Baby H. P." (Arreola), 1231
Bacon, Francis, influence on Montalvo, 215
"Bailarina, La" (Ferré), **Supp. I,** 217–218
"Balada de plomo y yerro" (Cabrera
    Infante), **Supp. I,** 137
Balbuena, Bernardo de, **53–56**
influences on, 54
"Balcón, El" (Hernández, F.), **Supp. I,** 310
Ballagas, Emilio, **1081–1086**
Afro-Cuban poetry, 1082, 1083
avante-garde elements, 1082
awards and honors, 1085
compared with Unamuno, 1083
critical assessment, 1082
influences on, 1085, 1086
neoromantic poetic mode, 1084, 1085
themes, 1082, 1083
Balmes, Jaime Luciano, 279
*Baltasar* (Goméz de Avellaneda), 177
"Balthazar's Marvelous Afternoon" ("La
    prodigiosa tarde de Baltazar")
    (García Márquez), 1334
Balzac, Honoré de
influence on Alencar, 196
influence on Blest Gana, 206, 211
Bandeira, Manuel, **629–637**
awards and honors, 629, 630
Brazilian *modernismo*, 629, 632, 958
critical assessment, 637
essays and columns, 631, 633
fear of death, 630
influences on, 630
poetic experimentation and rhetoric,
    633–637
poetry, 631–633
wordplay, 635, 636
*Banquete de Severo Arcángelo, El* (Marechal),
    888, 892–893
"Barba metafísica, La" (Hernández, F.),
    **Supp. I,** 306
*Barrabás y otros relatos* (Uslar Pietri), 1057,
    1059

*Barranca abajo* (Sánchez), 534
*Barren Lives (Vidas secas)* (Ramos), 746,
    747, 749–750, 751
Barrett, Rafael, influence on Roa Bastos,
    1210
Barrios, Eduardo, **611–617**
awards and honors, 612, 613
critical assessment, 617
influenced by Schopenhauer and Nie-
    tzsche, 614
*Barro de la sierra* (Icaza), 1064, 1065
*Bases y puntos de partida para la organizacíon
    política de la República Argentina*
    (Alberdi), 155
*Batalla de José Luna, La* (Marechal), 894
Batista, Fulgencio, 832–833, 1386
Batlle y Ordóñez, José
relationship with Acevedo Díaz, 300
relationship with Sánchez, 536
Baudelaire, Charles
influence on Cambaceres, 271
influence on Cruz e Sousa, 360
influence on Eguren, 514
influence on López Velarde, 665
influence on Lugones, 495
influence on Tablada, 442
influence on Valencia, 480
translation into Spanish by Casal, 368
*Bay of Silence, The (La bahía de silencio)*
    (Mallea), 982, 983, 984
*Beatriz Cenci* (Gonçalves Dias), 186
Beauvior, Simone de, influence on
    Castellanos, 1296, 1297
Beckett, Samuel, Mexican poetry anthology
    translation by, 1171
*Before Night Falls* (Arenas), **Supp. I,** 65–66
*Beijo no asfalto* (Rodrigues), **Supp. I,** 484
*Bejeweled Boy, The (El alhajadito)*
    (Asturias), 866, 871
*Belerofonte matemático, El* (Sigüenza de
    Góngora), 72
Bello, Andrés, **129–133**
influences on, 130
publisher of *El Araucano,* 132
relationship with Blanco White, 131
relationship with Gallardo, 131
relationship with Irisarri, 130
*silvas americanas,* 131, 683
stay in England, 130–132
Benedetti, Mario, **1255–1260, Supp.
    I,** 568
critical assessment, 1260
Cuban Revolution, 1258
depiction of middle class, 1257
exile, 1255, 1260

influences on, 1256
leader of "Movement of the Indepen-
    dents of 26 March," 1259
themes, 1256
writings on Uruguayan experience,
    1255–1259
*Benevolent Masters (Los amos benévolos)*
    (Laguerre) 1049, 1051, 1053
Béquer, Gustavo Adolfo, influence on
    Silva, 378
"Berceuse Blanca" (Herrera y Reissig), 528
Bergson, Henri, influence on Amoroso
    Lima, 782–783, 786
Berlanga, Thomas de, 2
*Bernardo, o Victoria de Roncesvalles, La*
    (Balbuena), 53–54, 56
*Bestiario* (Cortázar), 1177, 1179–1180
Betancur, Belisario, 1329
*Betrayed by Rita Hayworth (La traición
    de Rita Hayworth)* (Puig), 1406,
    1407–1408
Bierce, Ambrose
Fuentes' characterization, 1372
influence on Rulfo, 1222
*Bígardos del ron, Los* (Marín Cañas),
    991–993
*Big Mama's Funeral (Los funerales de la
    Mamá Grande)* (García Márquez),
    1331, 1333–1335, 1338
*Biografía para uso de los pájaros* (Carrera
    Andrade), **Supp. I,** 173–174
Bioy Casares, Adolfo, **1201–1207**
humor, 1206
influenced by Dunne, 1204, 1205
influenced by Galton, 1204
member of group of *Sur,* 1202
relationship with Borges, 1201, 1202,
    1203, 1207
relationship with Ocampo, 1202
themes, 1203, 1204, 1205, 1206
use of framed narrative, 1204–1205
*Birds Without a Nest (Aves sin nido)* (Matto
    de Turner), 306–307, 1100
*Black Messengers, The (Los heraldos negros)*
    (Vallejo), 728, 729
*The Black Sheep and Other Fables*
    (Monterroso), **Supp. I,** 351–354
Blacks
Afro-Cuban poetry, 1082–1083, 1084,
    1385
Castro Alves' antislavery poems,
    292–296
Cruz e Sousa on situation in Brazil,
    360–362

influence on Mármol, 182

# C

"Caballo imaginado a Dios" (Monterroso),
**Supp. I,** 353

Cabeza de Vaca, Alvar Núñez, influence
on Garcilaso, 43

Cabot Prize, Arcinegas, 800

Cabral de Melo Neto, João, **1247–1252,**
**Supp. I, 103–118**
awards and honors, 1248, **Supp. I,** 116
comparison with Wittgenstein, **Supp.**
**I,** 108
concretist elements, 1248, 1319
*cordel* poems, 1247
critical assessment, 1251
early influences, **Supp. I,** 105
Generation of '45 in Brzail, 1247
influenced by Moore, 1251
influence on, 1248
metaphorical transformations, **Supp. I,**
109–110
poetic techniques, 1249, **Supp. I,**
108–109
poetry as construction, 1248, 1250
poetry of reflective concentration, **Supp.**
**I,** 111
storytelling poetry, **Supp. I,** 115
view of words, **Supp. I,** 112–113

Cabrera, Lydia, **Supp. I, 119–131**
Afro-Cuban culture, **Supp. I,** 120–121
critical assessment, **Supp. I,** 124
ethnological works, **Supp. I,** 125–126,
127–128
methodology in preserving narratives,
**Supp. I,** 125
short stories, **Supp. I,** 126–127, 128

Cabrera Infante, Guillermo, **1383–1390,**
**Supp. I, 133–148**
awards and honors, 1386, 1388, **Supp.**
**I,** 136
betrayal as theme, **Supp. I,** 142–143
compared with Mallarmé, **Supp. I,**
133–134
critical interest in Cuban music, **Supp. I,**
146–147
Cuban Revolution, 1383, 1387, 1388,
1389, **Supp. I,** 139–140
film criticism, 1384, 1387, 1390, **Supp.**
**I,** 138
imprisoned by Batista regime, 1386
influenced by Borges, **Supp. I,** 134–135,
138–139, 141–142

influenced by Eliot, **Supp. I,** 134–135
influenced by Hemingway, 1386, **Supp.**
**I,** 138
influenced by Petronius, **Supp. I,** 135
influences on, 1384
literary essays, **Supp. I,** 141
relationship with and denunciation of
Castro, 1387, 1388, 1389
social criticism, 1385, 1389

*Cacau,* Amado, 1153, 1154, 1157

*Cachoeira de Paulo Alfonso, A* (Castro
Alves), 291, 295–296

*Cacique* (political boss), Rulfo's writings on,
1220–1221, 1222

Cadalso y Vazquez, José de, influence on
Fernández de Lizardi, 125

*Cada uno en su noche* (Vitale), **Supp. I,**
572–573

*Caetés* (Ramos), 747, 748

Cain, G., *see* Cabrera Infante, Guillermo

"Calco por transparencia" (Vitale), **Supp.**
**I,** 575

Calderón de la Barca, Fanny, diaries of,
1297

Calderón de la Barca, Pedro, influence on
Juana Inés de la Cruz, 93

*Calendario manual y gufa universal de
forasteros de Venezuela, El*
(Bello), 130

Callado, Antônio, 783

*Calor das coisas, O* (Piñón), **Supp. I,**
426–427

Câmara, Eugênia, 290–291

Cambaceres, Eugenio, **269–276**
admiration for Zola, 269
development of Spanish-American
novel, 269, 274
Generation of 1880, 269
naturalism, 269, 271, 273–273, 275

*Camino de las horas* (Prado), 644

Camoes, Luiz Vaz de, influence on
Mattos, 66

*Camp, The (El Campo)* (Gambaro), 1323,
1324–1325

*The Campaign (La campaña)* (Fuentes),
**Supp. I,** 238–242

"Campana de San Blas" (Carrera
Andrade), **Supp. I,** 170

*Campesinos,* Rulfo's depiction of, 1218

Campo, Estanislao del, **229–233**
critical assessment, 232–233
*gaucho* poetry, 230–233
influenced by Ascasubi, 230
influenced by Hidalgo, 230

Campoamor, Ramón de, 543

Camus, Albert, influence of, 1280

*Canaíma* (Gallegos), 607–607

"Cançao do Exílio" (Gonçlaves Dias), 186

"Cançao do Tamoio, A" (Gonçlaves Dias),
187, 190

*Cancionero del amor infeliz* (Blanco
Fombona), 507–508

*Canillitia* (Sánchez), 532–533, 534

Cansinos-Asséns, Rafael, influences on
Borges, 847

*Cantaclaro* (Gallegos), 607

*Cántaro fresco, El* (Ibarbourou), 804

*Canto a la primavera y ostro poemas*
(Villaurrutia), 977

*Canto errante, El* (Darío), 406–407

*Canto General* (Neruda), 688, 1004, 1005,
1009–1010, 1012, 1347

*Canto nacional* (Cardenal), **Supp. I,**
157–158

*Cantos,* Gonçlaves Dias, 188

*Cantos a Berenice* (Orozco), **Supp. I,** 385

*Cantos de la prisión y del destierro* (Blanco
Fombona), 505

*Cantos del Pacífico, Los* (Chocano),
543–544

*Cantos del peregrino* (Mármol), 182–183

*Cantos de vida y esperanza* (Darío),
402–405, 541

Canudos, War of the, *see* War of Canudos

*Cão sem plumas, O* (Cabral), **Supp. I,**
107, 111

*Captain Pantoja and the Special Serv-
ice (Pantaleón y las vistadoras)*
(Vargas Llosa), 1422, 1430, **Supp. I,**
556–557

*Captain's Verses, The (Los versos del capitán)*
(Neruda), 1005

Carballido, Emilio, **1289–1292**
depiction of nineteenth-century Mexican
history, 1292
fantastical realism, 1290–1291
influences on, 1292
one-act plays, 1292
portrayal of large provincial families,
1290
revitalization of Mexican national theater, 1289–1290
themes and subjects, 1290, 1292
traditional comedies, 1291

Cardenal, Ernesto, **Supp. I, 149–166**
critical assessment, **Supp. I,**
154–155, 163
culture and plight of indigenous peoples,
**Supp. I,** 152–153, 161–162
epigrams, **Supp. I,** 150

# E

*Eccentric Neighborhoods* (Ferré), **Supp. I,** 221–222

Ecuador

Carrera Andrade, Jorge, **Supp. I, 167–185**

Ecuadorian *modernismo*, **Supp. 1,** 168

*Educação pela pedra, A* (Cabral), **Supp. I,** 113–114

Eichelbaum, Samuel, **797–800**

awards and honors, 800

critical assessment, 798–799, 800

departure from *gaucho* tradition, 797, 798, 798, 799, 800

development of *crillo* (creole) characters, 799

dramatic characterization, 799

influences on, 797, 798, 799

portrayal of strong female characters, 799–800

themes, 798

"Elegía de María Belén Chacón" (Ballagas), 1083

"Elegía sin nombre" (Ballagas), 1085

"Elena" (Isaacs), 248

Eliot, T.S.

compared with Cabrera Infante, **Supp. I,** 134

influence on Paz, 1166

Elís Levis, José, influenced by Zeno Gandía, 325

Elmere, Edwin, 546

El Salvador

Salazar Arrué, Salavdor (Salarrué), **875–878**

*Elvira: o, La novia del Plata* (Echeverría), 141–142

*Empeños de una casa, Los* (Juana Inés de la Cruz), 88, 99

*Encanto, El, tendajó mixto* (Garro), **Supp. I,** 273–274

*Encomienda* system, Roa Bastos, 1209

*End of the Game* (Cortázar), 1177

"En el final era el verbo" (Orozco), **Supp. I,** 387

*En el revés del cielo* (Orozco), **Supp. I,** 386–387

"En el teocalli de Cholula" (Heredia), 138–139

*Enemigos del alma, Los* (Mallea), 984–985

*Engenheiro, O* (Cabral), 1248, 1249, **Supp. I,** 106–107

"En la diestra de Dios Padre" (Carrasquilla), 348–349

*En la luna* (Huidobro), 762

"En la palabra, a tientas" (Girri), **Supp. I,** 298

*En la sangre* (Cambaceres), 270, 274–275

"En las cumbres de Chisacá" (Isaacs), 249

*En la zona* (Saer), **Supp. I,** 520

"En mi cumpleaños" (Heredia), 136

*Ensayo* genre, Vasconcelos, 575–576, 580–583

*Entertaining Advetures of the Grandson of Juan Moreira (Divertidas aventuras del nieto de Juan Moreira)* (Payró), 414, 416

*Entrañas de niño* (Carrasquilla), 345–346

"Entre todas las cosas lo primero es el mar" (Skármeta), **Supp. I,** 531–532

*Entusiasmo, El* (Skármeta), **Supp. I,** 532–533

"En una tempestad" (Heredia), 136

Environmentalism, Parra, 1199

*Epicédio* (Costa), 114

Epic poetry

Borges, 847–848

Ercilla, 23–31

Lugones' theories, 500

Oña 59, 60–62

Epictetus, influence on Hernández, 237

*Epílogo wagneriano a la "politica de fusión"* (Herrera y Reissig), 520–521

"Epistle to José Coronel Urtecho" (Cardenal), **Supp. I,** 160

"Epistle to Monsignor Casáldiga" (Cardenal), **Supp. I,** 159–160

*Epistolario* (Heredia), 139

"Epitáfo" (Andrade), **Supp. I,** 44–45

*Epitah of a Small Winner (Memórias Póstumas de Bras Cubas)* (Machado de Assis), 254, 255, 261, 262, 263, 336

*Epopeya de Artigas, La* (Zorrilla), 328

*Epopeya nacional: Porfirio Díaz, La* (Tablada), 443

Ercilla y Zúñiga, Don Alonso de, 23–31

critical assessment, 30–31

influence on Oña, 59, 61

influences on, 26, 28, 29

*Eros relacionable* (Lezama Lima), 1127

*Errores, Los* (Revueltas), **Supp. I,** 469–472

*Errores del corazón* (Goméz de Avellaneda), 177

*Esa sangre* (Azuela), 461–462

*Esau and Jacob (Esaú e Jacó)* (Machado de Assis), 255

*Escena comtemporánea, La* (Mariátegui), 794

*Escena social, Una* (Blest Gana), 205–206

*Escola das facas, A* (Cabral), **Supp. I,** 114

*Eso y más,* (Salarrué), 878

*Espatolino* (Goméz de Avellaneda), 178

*Espectador, El* (newspaper), **Supp. I,** 251–252

*Espetón de oro, El* (Villaverde), 170

*Espíritu de Martí, El* (Mañach Robato), 823

*Espumas Flutuantes* (Castro Alves), 290, 291, 292, 293

"Esquecer e Lembrar" (Amorosa Lima), 786

*Estação central* (Ivo), **Supp. I,** 320, 323, 325–326

*Estadolibrismo* ("Unitedstatesim") (Marqués), 1240

*Estampas de la Biblia* (Ibarbourou), 805–806

*Ésta mañana* (Benedetti), 1256

*Estanque inefable, El* (Carrera Andrade), **Supp. I,** 169

"Este mundo" (Vitale), **Supp. I,** 572

Estrada Cabrera, manuel, 546, 865, 866, 867

*Estrela da Vida Inteira* (Bandeira), 629, 630

*Estrêla de absinto, A* (Andrade), **Supp. I,** 39

*Estrimentismo* (stridentism), Gorostiza's opposition to, 925

*Estudio sobre el utiltarismo* (Caro), 279

*Enternal Curse on the Reader of These Pages (Maldición eterna a quien lea estas páginas)* (Puig), 1407, 1410

*Eternal Feminine, The (El eterno femenino)* (Castellanos), 1299

Euclides da Cunha, *see* Cunha, Euclides da

"Europa curvou-se ante o Brasil, A" (Andrade), **Supp. I,** 44

*Eva Luna* (Allende), **Supp. I,** 7–8

*The Event* (Saer), **Supp. I,** 524–525

*Evolución política y social de Hispanoaméricana, La* (Blanco Fombona), 505–506

*Examen del quijotismo* (Mañach Robato), 832, 834

*Excursión a los indios ranqueles* (Mansilla), 240

*Excursión a Vuelta Abajo* (Villaverde), 170

*Exiles, The (Los desterrados)* (Quiroga), 553, 554

*Exorcismos de esti(l)o* (Cabrera Infante), 1388–1389, **Supp. I,** 141–142

*Exóticas* (González Prada), 284

*Expedientes, Los* (Denevi), 1265

*The Experience of Freedom,* **Supp. I,** 396

"Explicación falsa de mis cuentos" (Hernández, F.), **Supp. I,** 312–313

"Explosión" (Agustini), 65

*Great Zoo, The (El gran zoo)* (Guillén), 952, 953

*Green House, The (La casa verde)* (Vargas Llosa), 1422, 14224–1426, 1428, 1429, **Supp. I,** 550–552

"Greenpraise" (Brull), **Supp. I,** 77–78

*Gregório de Mattos e Guerra: Uma Revisao Biográfica* (Rocha Peres), 65

"Grimorio, El" (Anderson Imbert), 1106, 1108–1109

*Gringa, La* (Sánchez), 533, 534

*Grito de gloria* (Acevedo Díaz), 299, 301

Group of *Sur, see Sur*

Grupo Adverbio, **Supp. I,** 517–518

Grupo Tapa, **Supp. I,** 488

*Guajiro, El* (Villaverde), 170

*Guanabara* (journal), 187

*Guapo del 900, Un* (Eichelbaum), 798, 799

*Guarani, O* (Alencar), 196, 197, 198, 336, 746

Guatemala
   Asturias, Miguel Ángel, **865–872**

Gómez Carrillo, Enrique, **465–468**

*Guerra dos Macates, A* (Alencar), 197, 198, 199

*Guerra gaucho, La* (Lugones), 498–499

Guevera, Ernesto (Che), 1379

*Guia-mapa de Gabriel Arcanjo* (Piñón), **Supp. I,** 417

*Guía triste de París* (Bryce), **Supp. I,** 99

Guillén, Nicholás, **947–954**
   Afro-Antillean movement, 948, 949, 1385
   Afro-Cuban poetry, 1084, 1385
   awards and honors, 947, 952
   influenced by Spengler, 948
   Marxism, 947
   reaction to Negritude movement, 947–948
   *son*-poems, 948

Guimaráes Roas João, **1069–1079**
   awards and honors, 1069, 1070
   Brazilian *modermiso*, 1070, 1072
   conception of art, 1078–1079
   critical assessment, 1073
   departure from traditional regionalism, 1071, 1073, 1319
   depiction of *jagunço*, 1075, 1076
   fusion of prose and poetic elements, 1075
   linguistic innovations, 1070–1071, 1072, 1075, 1078
   synthesis of opposites, 1072–1073, 1078–1079
   themes, 1076, 1077

use of myth and fantasy, 1072

Güiraldes, Ricardo, **619–626,** 1111
   association with Arlt, 882
   critical assessment, 625–626
   *gaucho* literature, 473, 560, 883, 888

*Guirnalda del silencio, La* (Carrera Andrade), **Supp. I,** 169–170

Generation of 1922, 620, 810
   influence on Laguerre, 1050
   poetry, 624–625

*Guitara, La* (Echeverría), 143–144

Gutiérrez, Joaquín Posada, 280

Gutiérrez Nájera, Manuel, **351–355**
   critical assessment, 352–353
   *crónicas*, 352, 354
   French influence, 351, 354
   influence on Rojas, 594
   pen names, 352
   poetry, 352–353, 354–355
   short stories, 353

Guzmán, Martín Luis, **655–661**
   Mexican Revolution novels, 655
   relationship with Villa, 655–659

Gúzman, Ruy Díaz de, 1209, 1210

# H

*Hacedor, El* (Cabrera Infante), **Supp. I,** 141–142

Haiku form, Tablada's use of, 444, 445

*Hand and the Glove, The (A Máo e a Luva)* (Machado de Assis), 254, 262

"Hay hombres blancos, pardos y negros" (Cabrera), **Supp. I,** 123

*Heartbreak Tango (Boquitas pintadas)* (Puig), 1407, 1408–1409

"Heights of Maccho Picchu" ("Alturas de Macchu Picchu") (Neruda), 1001, 1004, 1010

Heiremans, Luis Alberto, **1347–1351**
   Christian conception of world, 1349, 1350, 1351
   critical assessment, 1351
   discrepancy between reality and dreams, 1348
   dramatic works, 1348–1351
   Generation of '50, 1347
   influences on, 1349, 1350
   themes, 1348

*Hell Has no Limits* (Donoso), **Supp. I,** 207

Hemingway, Ernest
   influence on Bryce Echenique, **Supp. I,** 90

influence on Cabrera Infante, 1386, **Supp. I,** 138

influence on García Márquez, 1329, 1332, 1333, 1334, **Supp. I,** 254

Henríquez Ureña, Pedro, **597–600**
   influence on Gorostiza, 930
   philosophical influences, 598–599

*Heptamerón* (Marechal), 890

Herculano, Alexandre, influence on Alencar, 198

Heredia, José María, **135–139**
   aesthetic theory, 139
   critical assessment, 138–139
   Hispanic romanticism, 135–136
   historical works, 139
   influence on Gómez de Avellaneda, 175, 176
   influences on, 136
   literary essays, 139

*Here's to You, Jesusa* (Poniatowska), **Supp. I,** 439–441, 450

"Hermana agua, La" (Nervo), 427

Hernández, Felisberto, **Supp. I, 303–316**
   critical assessment, **Supp. I,** 306, 309–310
   early fiction, **Supp. I,** 306–307
   fantastic tales, **Supp. I,** 309–310
   relationship with Clemente Colling, **Supp. I,** 305
   theme of remembrance, **Supp. I,** 308

Hernández, José, 150, 160, 235–244
   biography of Gálvez, 588
   critical assessment, 236, 242–244
   director of *El Rio de la Plata*, 239
   Lugones' lectures on *Martín Fierro*, 494, 500
   Martínez Estrada's interpretation of *Martín Fierro*, 812
   *Martín Fierro* compared with other gauchesque works, 230, 233, 241
   philosophical influences, 237

Hernández Girón, Francis, 24

*Hernán Cortés: Creador de la nacionalidad* (Vasconcelos), 579–580

*Heroínas mexicanas* (Fernández de Lizardi), 125

Herrán-Hay Treaty, 279–280

Herrera y Ressig, Julio, **519–528,** 547
   critical assessment, 525, 528
   friendship with Carreras, 520, 521
   *modernismo*, 520, 522, 523

Hesse, Herman, 1304

Hidalgo, Alberto, 484, 488

Hidalgo, Bartolomé, 147, 150, 230

influence on García Márquez, 1329, 1330

influence on Martínez Estrada, 810, 811

Kant, Immanuel, influence on Henríquez Ureña, 599

*Kindergarten* (Wolff), 1313

*Kingdom of theis World, The (El reino de este mundo)* (Carpentier), 1022, 1023–1024, 1025, 1027

Kinoe, Eusebio Francisco, 72

Kipling, Rudyard, influence on Quiroga, 556

Kircher, Athanasius

correspondence with Sigüenza y Góngora, 73

influence on Juana Inés de la Cruz, 96

*Kiss of the Spider Woman, The (El beso de la mujer araña)* (Puig), 1407, 1409, 1410

## L

*Laberinto de amor* (Marechal), 889–890

"Laboratório da noite, O" (Ivo), **Supp. I,** 319–320

*Labyrinth of Solitude, The (El laberinto* de la soledad) (Paz), 1168, 1169, 1171, 1362

*Labyrinths* (Borges), 843, 853, 854, 957, 858

Laforgue, Jules, influence on López Velarde, 665

*Lagar* (Mistral) 680, 682–683

*Lâgrima de Mulher, Uma* (Azevedo), 337

Laguerre, Enrique A., **1049–1053**

awards and honors, 1050

compared with Zeno Gandía, 1050

depiction of coffee plantations, 1052

depiction of Puerto Rican personality, 1050

focus on urban social problems, 1051

Generation of 1930 member, 1050

influences on, 1050

magical realism, 1051

social and political aspects, 1050, 1051

themes, 1052–1053

*Laguna sagrada de San Joaquín, La* (Cabrera), **Supp. I,** 127

Lamartine, Alphonse de

influence on Echeverría, 143

influence on Heredia, 136

*Lanchas en la bahía* (Rojas), 816, 818

*Lanzallamas, Los* (Arlt), 881, 883

*Lanza y sable* (Acevedo Díaz), 299, 301–302

Larra, Mariano de, influence on Alberdi, 154

Larreta, Enrique, **471–475**

dramatic works, 474

*modernismo*, 471–473

portrayal of *gaucho* life, 473–474

Las Casas, Bartolomé de, **1–7,** 19, 50, 1100

critical assessment, 6–7

Latin American new novel, *see* New novel

*Lattitudes* (Carrera Andrade), **Supp. I,** 172

*Laucha's Marriage (El casamiento de Laucha)* (Payró), 414–415

Lavalle, Juan, 148

Lawrence, D.H., influence of, 936, 1280

*Lazarillo: A Guide for Inexperienced Travelers Between Buenos Aires and Lima, El (El larazillo de ciegos caminantes desde Buenos Aires a Lima)* (Carrío de la Vandera), 107

*Larazillo de ciegos* (Bueno), 109

*Larazillo de Tormes* (anonymous), 109

*Leaf Storm (La hojarasca)* (García Márquez), 1330, 1331–1332, 1343, **Supp. I,** 251

*Lean Lands, The (las tierras flacas)* (Yáñez), 996, 997

*Lenguas de diamante, Las* (Ibarbourou), 803–804

*Leoncia* (Goméz de Avellaneda), 176

*Leonor de Mendonça* (Gonçalves Dias), 186

Leopardi, Giacomo

influence on Heredia, 136

influence on Machado de Assis, 256

Lévi-Strauss, Claude, influence on Donoso, 1280

*Léxico de afinidades* (Vitale), **Supp. I,** 576

*Leyendas de Guatemala* (Asturias), 866

*Leyes de la versificación castellana* (JaimesFreye), 419

Lezama Lima, José, **1125–1129,** 1279

concept of poetry, 1127–1128

critical assessment, 1127, 1129

"difficult writer," 1125

image theory, 1128

"imaginery eras," 1128

Lezamic manner, 1128

*origeneists*, 1125, 1126

use of *Eros relacionable*, 1127

*Libertad baja palabra* (Paz), 1188

*Libertad de imprenta* (Caro), 280

*Libertinagem* (Bandiera), 630, 632, 633, 634

"Library of Babel, The" ("La biblioteca de Babel") (Borges), 857

*Libra astronómica y filosófica* (Kino), 72

*Licao de Coisas* (Drummond de Andrade), 970

"Lição de poesia, A" (Cabral), **Supp. I,** 106

*Life and Death of M.J. Gonzaga de Sá, The (Vida e Morte de M.J. Gonzaga de Sá)* (Lima Barreto), 565, 566, 567, 569

*Life in the Argentine Republic in the Dyas of the Tyrants (Facundo)* (Sarmiento), 148, 155, 160, 161, 162, 163–164, 241, 415, 471, 604, 961

*Ligera excursión ideológica* (Caro), 279

Lihn, Enrique, influenced by Mistral, 688

*Lilus Kikus* (Poniatowska), **Supp. I,** 437

Lima, Jorge de, **765–769**

awards and honors, 767

critical assessment, 769

influence on, 769

surrealism, 766

Lima Barreto, Alfonso Henriqus de, **565–572**

alcoholism, 571

posthumous publications, 566, 567, 568

themes, 570

*Limonero real, El* (Saer), **Supp. I,** 522–523

*Linda 67* (Del Paso), **Supp. I,** 196–197

*Linguagem* (Ivo), **Supp. I,** 323

Lins do Rego, José, **909–912**

awards and honors, 909

critical assessment, 912

depiction of plantation society's decay, 910, 911

influences on, 909

preface to Lima's poems, 766

regionalist movement, 909

Sugar Cane Cycle, 909–911

*Li-Po otros poemas* (Tablada), 444

*Lira Paulistana* (Andrade), 772

Lispector, Clarice, 1303–1307

awards and honors, 1304

critical assessment, 1304–1305, 1307

influenced by Mansfield, 1304

introspective fiction, 1303, 1304

manipulation of time, 1305, 1306

short stories, 1305–1306

sociopolitical subject matter, 1307

themes, 1303

*Literary Currents in Hispanic America* (Henríquez Ureña), 598

*Literary Experience, The (La Experiencia literaria)* (Reyes), 697, 698

*Literature aregentina, La* (Rojas), 592

*Livre-objets*, Sarduy book publishing technique, 1439

Psychoanalytic method, Sábato's use of, 1140

*Pubis Angelical (Pubis angelical)* (Puig), 1407, 1409, 1410

*Puerta de salida* (Heiremans), 1348

Puerto Rican national identity, **Supp. I,** 223–224

Puerto Rico
  Ferré, Rosario, **Supp. I, 217–231**
  Laguerre, Enrique A., **1049–1053**
  Marqués, René, **1237–1244**
  Páles Matos, Luis, **821–829**
  Zeno Gandía, Manuel, **321–325**

Puig, Manuel, **1405–1411**
  alienation as theme, 1408
  characters' psychosexual conflicts, 1406
  critical assessment, 1411
  film scripts, 1411
  influences on, 1407
  novels, 1407–1410
  opposition to Perón government, 1407
  theater, 1410–1411
  themes, 1408, 1410

*Pursued, The (Los perseguidos)* (Quiroga), 553

## Q

*Quaderna* (Cabral), **Supp. I,** 111–113

*Quadro Sintético de Literatura Brasileira* (Amoroso Lima), 784, 787

"Quatzalcóatl" (Cardenal), **Supp. I,** 161–162

Quecha Indians, 1131–1135

*Queen of Rapa Nui, The (La reina de Rapa Nui)* (Prado), 645–646

Queiroz, José Maria Eca de, influence on Ramos, 748

Queiroz, Rachel de, **1119–1122**
  critical assessment, 1121, 1122
  *crônicas*, 1120, 1120–1122
  dramatic works, 1121–1122
  first woman elected to the Brazilian Academy of Letters, 1119
  influence on Ramos, 748
  leftist politics, 1120
  "novel of the 1930's in the Northeast," 1119, 1122
  oral language technique, 1120
  São Paulo *modernismo*, 1119
  social justice theme, 1119, 1120
  use of omniscient narrator, 1120

Quevedo y Villegas, Francisco Gomez de
  influence on Juana Inés de la Cruz, 90, 93
  influence on Valle y Caviedas, 79, 80

*Quijotita y su prima, La* (Fernández de Lizardi), 121, 124–125

Quintana, Manuel José
  influence on Chocano, 543
  influence on Goméz de Avellaneda, 175

"Quinze, O" (Queiroz), 1119–1120

Quiroga, Horacio, 519, **551–557**
  critical assessment, 557
  influences on, 554–556
  short story genre, 551, 553–557
  themes, 554, 556–557

Quiroga, Juan Facundo, 148, 155, 160, 161, 551, *see also Life in the Argentine Republic in the Days of the Tyrants [Facundo]*

## R

*Ráiz del hombre* (Paz), 1165

*Ráiz salvaje*, Ibarbourou, 804–805

Ral, Adelaide, *see* Martí, José

"Raleigh" (Cardenal), **Supp. I,** 150

Ramos, Graciliano, **745–752**
  comparison of *Anguish* with Sarte's *Nausea*, 749
  comparison of *Barren Lives* with Steinbeck's *Grapes of Wrath*, 750
  critical assessment, 752
  influenced by Queiroz and Flaubert, 748
  social protest as theme, 750–752
  use of interior monologues, 749

Ramos, Samuel, influence on Paz, 1164

*Raros, Los* (Darío), 400

*Rasgos biográficas del general Angel V. Peñaloza* (Hernández), 235

*Ratos entretenidos* (Fernández de Lizardi), 121

*Raucho: Momentos de una juventud contemporánea* (Güiraldes), 622

*Reacionário, O* (Rodrigues), **Supp. I,** 485–486

*Realidade Americana, A* (Amoroso Lima), 787

Realism
  Azuela, 458–459
  Gálvez, 585, 587–588
  Machado de Assis, 256–257, 263
  *see also* Fantastical realism; Magical realism; Naturalism; Symbolic realism

*Real Life of Alejandro Mayta (Historia de Mayta)* (Vargas Llosa), 1422, 1433, **Supp. I,** 560

*Real maravillosa, see* Magical realism

*Reason of State (El recurso del método),* (Carpentier), 1028–1029

*Rebellion in the Backlands (Os Sertoes)* (Cunha), 387, 389, 390–393

"Recados" (messages) (Mistral), 682

"Recado terreste" (Mistral), 686–687

*Recollections of Things to Come* (Garro), **Supp. I,** 276–279

*Recordaçoes do Escriva Isías Caminha* (Lima Barreto), 565, 567, 568

*Red* (Uslar Pietri), 1058, 1060

*Redentores* (Zeno Gandía), 322, 324–325

*Red Lances, The (Las lanzas coloradas)* (Uslar Pietri), 1058, 1059

*Reduccíon del infinito* (Vitale), **Supp. I,** 577–578

*Reencuentro de personajes* (Garro), **Supp. I,** 281–283

*Reflections (Reflejos)* (Villaurrutia), 976, 977

*Reflejos* (Villaurrutia), 976, 977

Regionalist movement, Lins do Rego, 909

*Reglas de congo* (Cabrera), **Supp. I,** 127–128

*Regreso de tres mundos* (Picón Salas), 904, 906

*Reina de Rapa Nui, La*, Prado, 645–646

*Reinaldo Solar* (Gallegos), 604–605

*Relación de lo sucedido a la Armada de Barlovento* (Sigüenza y Góngora), 73

"Relaciones públicas" (Skármeta), **Supp. I,** 532–533

*Religión y las escuelas, La* (Caro), 279

*Remotando el Uluán* (Salarrué), 876, 877

Renard, Jules, 1106

*Reo de nocturnidad* (Bryce), **Supp. I,** 98

*The Republic of Dreams* (Piñón), **Supp. I,** 427–428

"Resaca" (Cabrera Infante), 1385–1386, **Supp. I,** 136–137

*Resaca, La* (Laguerre), 1049, 1052–1053

*Rescados contando a Chile* (Mistral), 680, 687

*Reseña de los Hospitales de Ultramar* (Mutis), **Supp. I,** 370–371

*Residence on Earth (Redsidencia en la tierra)* (Neruda), 923, 1003, 1004, 1007–1009, 1012

"Respuesta y reconciliación" (Paz), **Supp. I,** 399

*Ressurreiçao* (Machado de Assis), 254–255, 262

# LIST OF SUBJECTS BY COUNTRY

The following list indicates the native countries of Latin American writers treated in this supplement.

## ARGENTINA

Alberto Girri (1919–1991)
Tomás Eloy Martínez (1934– )
Olga Orozco (1920–1999)
Ricardo Piglia (1940– )
Juan José Saer (1937– )

## BRAZIL

Jorge Amado (1912–2001)
Oswald de Andrade (1890–1954)
João Cabral de Melo Neto (1920–1999)
Lêdo Ivo (1924– )
Nélida Piñón (1937– )
Nelson Rodrigues (1912–1980)

## CHILE

Isabel Allende (1942– )
José Donoso (1924–1996)
Gonzalo Rojas (1917– )
Antonio Skármeta (1940– )

## COLOMBIA

Gabriel García Márquez (1927– )
Alvaro Mutis (1923– )

## CUBA

Reinaldo Arenas (1943–1990)
Mariano Brull (1891–1956)
Lydia Cabrera (1899–1991)

Guillermo Cabrera Infante (1929– )

## ECUADOR

Jorge Carrera Andrade (1902–1978)

## GUATEMALA

Augusto Monterroso (1921– )

## MEXICO

Fernando del Paso (1935–)
Carlos Fuentes (1928–)
Elena Garro (1920–1998)
Octavio Paz (1914–1998)
Elena Poniatowska (1932– )
José Revueltas (1914–1976)
Jaime Sabines (1926–1999)

## NICARAGUA

Alfredo Bryce Echenique (1939– )
Ernesto Cardenal (1925– )

## PERU

Mario Vargas Llosa (l936–)

## PUERTO RICO

Rosario Ferré (1938– )

## URUGUAY

Felisberto Hernández (1902–1964)
Ida Vitale (1923– )

# A SELECTION OF
# INTERNATONAL LITERARY PRIZES

## LATIN AMERICAN LAUREATES

### NOBEL PRIZE IN LITERATURE (Sweden)

Conferred annually since 1901 by an international jury of the Nobel Prize Commission to writers worldwide.

1945   Gabriela Mistral (Chile)
1971   Pablo Neruda (Chile)
1967   Miguel Ángel Asturias (Guatemala)
1982   Gabriel García Márquez (Colombia)
1990   Octavio Paz (Mexico)

### PREMIO LITERARIO CASA DE LAS AMÉRICAS (Cuba)

Established in 1959 by the government of Cuba, this prize has been conferred annually since 1960 by the Casa de las Américas (initially under the name of Concurso Literario Hispanoamericano) to Spanish American writers for a specific literary contribution in various genres, including poetry, short story, novel, theater, and essay. Since 1964 its official name has been Premio Literario Casa de las Américas, and the competition was opened to Brazilian writers. After 1970 new literary categories were added, and the competition was extended to writers of other languages of Latin America, such as French, Creole, English, chicano, and in 1994, to writers of indigenous literatures. The following list of laureates includes only the names of those writers treated in the *Latin American Writers* series.

1960   Ezequiel Martínez Estrada (Argentina), for the essay *Analisis funcional de la cultura.*
1962   Emilio Carballido (Mexico), for the play *Un pequeño día de ira.*
1963   Osvaldo Dragún (Argentina), for the play *Milagro del mercado viejo.*
1965   José Triana (Cuba), for the play *La noche delos asesinos.*
1966   Osvaldo Dragún (Argentina), for the play *Heroica de Buenos Aires.*
1969   Antonio Skármeta (Chile), for the short story "Desnudo en el tejado."
1982   Ana Lydia Vega (Puerto Rico), for the short-story "En cara nublado y otros cuentos de naufragios."

## PREMIO INTERNACIONAL DE NOVELA RÓMULO GALLEGOS (Venezuela)

Conferred since 1967 by the government of Venezuela to an author from Spanish America or Spain for the best novel written in Spanish. Originally conferred every five years, since l987 it has been a biennial award.

1967   Mario Vargas Llosa (Peru), for his novel *La casa verde*.
1972   Gabriel García Márquez (Colombia), for his novel *Cien años de soledad*.
1977   Carlos Fuentes (Mexico), for his novel *Terra nostra*.
1982   Fernando del Paso (Mexico), for his novel *Palinuro de México*.
1987   Abel Posse (Argentina), for his novel *Los perros del paraíso*.
1989   Manuel Mejía Vallejo (Colombia), for his novel *La casa de las dos palmas*.
1991   Arturo Uslar Pietri (Venezuela), for his novel *La visita en el tiempo*.
1993   Mempo Giardinelli (Argentina), for his novel *Santo oficiio de la memoria*.
1997   Ángeles Mastretta (Mexico), for her novel *Mal de amores*.
1999   Roberto Bolaño (Chile), for his novel *Los detectives salvajes*.

## THE NEUSTADT INTERNATIONAL PRIZE FOR LITERATURE
### (United States)

A biennial award conferred since 1970 by the University of Oklahoma and the journal *World Literature Today*.

1972   Gabriel García Márquez (Colombia)
1982   Octavio Paz (Mexico)
1992   João Cabral de Melo Neto (Brazil)

## PREMIO CERVANTES DE LITERATURA (Spain)

Conferred annually since 1975 by the government of Spain to Spanish-language writers from Spain or Spanish America.

1976   Alejo Carpentier (Cuba)
1978   Jorge Luis Borges (Argentina)
1980   Juan Carlos Onetti (Uruguay)
1981   Octavio Paz (Mexico)
1984   Ernesto Sábato (Argentina)
1987   Carlos Fuentes (Mexico)
1989   Augusto Roa Bastos (Paraguay)
1990   Adolfo Bioy Casares (Argentina)
1992   Dulce María Loynaz (Cuba)
1994   Mario Vargas Llosa (Peru)
1997   Guillermo Cabrera Infante (Cuba)
1999   Jorge Edwards (Chile)

## PREMIO PRÍNCIPE DE ASTURIAS, LETRAS (Spain)

Conferred annually since 1981 by the Fundación Príncipe de Asturias to Spanish-language writers from Spain or Spanish America.

1983   Juan Rulfo (Mexico)
1986   Mario Vargas Llosa (Peru)
1990   Arturo Uslar Pietri (Venezuela)
1993   Claudio Rodríguez (Spain)
1994   Carlos Fuentes (Mexico)
1997   Alvaro Mutis (Colombia)
2000   Augusto Monterroso (Guatemala)


## T. S. ELIOT AWARD (United States)

Conferred annually since 1983 by the Ingersoll Foundation of Chicago to writers worldwide.

1983   Jorge Luis Borges (Argentina)
1987   Octavio Paz (Mexico)
1991   Mario Vargas Llosa (Peru)


## PREMIO DE LITERATURA LATINOAMERICANA Y DEL CARIBE JUAN RULFO (Mexico)

Conferred annually since 1991 at the Feria Internacional del Libro, Guadalajara, Mexico, to Spanish-language writers and to writers of other regional languages of the Americas, such as Portuguese, French, and English.

1991   Nicanor Parra (Chile)
1992   Juan José Arreola (Mexico)
1993   Eliseo Diego (Cuba)
1994   Juan Ramón Ribeyro (Peru)
1995   Nélida Piñón (Brazil)
1996   Augusto Monterroso (Guatemala)
1998   Olga Orozco (Argentina)
1999   Sergio Pitol (Mexico)
2000   Juan Gelman (Argentina)


## PREMIO DE POESIA IBEROAMERICANA REINA SOFIA

Conferred annually since 1992 by the Universidad de Salamanca and the Patrimonio Nacional de España to writers from Spain, Portugal, Spanish America, and Brazil for poetry written in the Spanish or Portuguese language.

1992   Gonzalo Rojas (Chile)

1994   João Cabral de Melo Neto (Brazil)
1997   Alvaro Mutis (Colombia)
1999   Mario Benedetti (Uruguay)
2001   Nicanor Parra (Chile)


PREMIO IBEROAMERICANO DE NARRATIVA JORGE ISAACS (Colombia)

Conferred biennially since 1997 at the Festival Internacional de Arte de Colombia by the Instituto Proartes de Cali to Spanish- and Portuguese-language writers of Spanish America, Brazil, and Portugal.

1999   Mario Vargas Losa (Peru)
2001   Nélida Piñón (Brazil)

# LIST OF CONTRIBUTORS

Daniel Balderston
University of Iowa
RICARDO PIGLIA (1940– )

Vittoria Borsó
Heinrich Heine Universität,
Düsseldorf
FERNANDO DEL PASO (1935–)

Marco Antonio Campos
Universidad Nacional Autónoma
de México
JAIME SABINES (1926–1999)

Sara Castro-Klaren
Johns Hopkins University
MARIO VARGAS LLOSA (l936–)

Verónica Cortínez
University of California,
Los Angeles
ISABEL ALLENDE (1942– )

César Ferreira
University of Oklahoma
ALFREDO BRYCE ECHENIQUE (1939– )

David S. George
Lake Forest College
NELSON RODRIGUES (1912–1980)

Cedomil Goic
The University of Michigan and
Universidad Católica de Chile
JOSÉ DONOSO (1924–1996)

Lanin A. Gyurko
University of Arizona
CARLOS FUENTES (1928–)

Mercedes López-Baralt
University of Puerto Rico
ROSARIO FERRÉ (1938– )

Alfred Mac Adam
Barnard College
GUILLERMO CABRERA INFANTE (1929– )

Adriana Méndez Rodenas
University of Iowa
ELENA GARRO (1920–1998)

Nivia Montenegro
University of Kentucky
LYDIA CABRERA (1899–1991)

Klaus Müller-Bergh
University of Illinois at Chicago
MARIANO BRULL (1891–1956)

Melanie Nicholson
Bard College
OLGA OROZCO (1920–1999)

J. Enrique Ojeda
Boston College
JORGE CARRERA ANDRADE
(1902–1978)

Michael Palencia-Roth
University of Illinois at Urbana/
Champaign
GABRIEL GARCÍA MÁRQUEZ (1927– )
ALVARO MUTIS (1923– )

Sara Poot-Herrera
University of California at
Santa Barbara
ELENA PONIATOWSKA (1932– )

Randolph D. Pope
Washington University
ANTONIO SKÁRMETA (1940– )

Pablo Rocca
Montevideo, Uruguay
FELISBERTO HERNÁNDEZ (1902–1964)

Evelia Romano
The Evergreen State College
JUAN JOSÉ SAER (1937– )

Jorge Ruffinelli
Stanford University
AUGUSTO MONTERROSO (1921– )
JOSÉ REVUELTAS (1914–1976)

César A. Salgado
University of Texas at Austin
REINALDO ARENAS (1943–1990)

Enrico Mario Santí
University of Kentucky
OCTAVIO PAZ (1914–1998)

Jacobo Sefamí
University of California at Irvine
GONZALO ROJAS (1917– )

Nicolas Shumway
University of Texas at Austin
TOMÁS ELOY MARTÍNEZ (1934– )

Vera Regina Teixeira
Northwestern University
NÉLIDA PIÑÓN (1937– )

Gilberto Mendonça Teles
Pontifícia Universidade Católica
do Rio de Janeiro
OSWALD DE ANDRADE (1890–1954)
LÊDO IVO (1924– )

Hugo J. Verani
Director, Centro de Estudios
en Mexico
IDA VITALE (1923– )

Nelson H. Vieira
Brown University
JORGE AMADO (1912–2001)

Alan West-Durán
Northeastern University
Ernesto Cardenal (1925– )

Saul Yurkievich
Paris, France
Alberto Girri (1919–1991)

Richard Zenith
Lisbon, Portugal
João Cabral de Melo Neto
(1920–1999)